**Foreign Relations of the
United States, 1964–1968**

Volume VIII

International Monetary and Trade Policy

Editor	Evan Duncan
	David S. Patterson
	Carolyn Yee
General Editor	David S. Patterson

United States Government Printing Office
Washington
1998

DEPARTMENT OF STATE PUBLICATION 10526

OFFICE OF THE HISTORIAN

BUREAU OF PUBLIC AFFAIRS

For sale by the U.S. Government Printing Office
Superintendent of Documents, Mail Stop: SSOP, Washington, DC 20402-9328
ISBN 0-16-048203-8

Preface

The *Foreign Relations of the United States* series presents the official documentary historical record of major foreign policy decisions and significant diplomatic activity of the United States Government. The series documents the facts and events that contributed to the formulation of policies and includes evidence of supporting and alternative views to the policy positions ultimately adopted.

The Historian of the Department of State is charged with the responsibility for the preparation of the *Foreign Relations* series. The staff of the Office of the Historian, Bureau of Public Affairs, plans, researches, compiles, and edits the volumes in the series. This documentary editing proceeds in full accord with the generally accepted standards of historical scholarship. Official regulations codifying specific standards for the selection and editing of documents for the series were first promulgated by Secretary of State Frank B. Kellogg on March 26, 1925. These regulations, with minor modifications, guided the series through 1991.

A new statutory charter for the preparation of the series was established by Public Law 102–138, the Foreign Relations Authorization Act, Fiscal Years 1992 and 1993, which was signed by President George Bush on October 28, 1991. Section 198 of P.L. 102–138 added a new Title IV to the Department of State's Basic Authorities Act of 1956 (22 USC 4351, *et seq.*).

The statute requires that the *Foreign Relations* series be a thorough, accurate, and reliable record of major United States foreign policy decisions and significant United States diplomatic activity. The volumes of the series should include all records needed to provide comprehensive documentation of major foreign policy decisions and actions of the United States Government. The statute also confirms the editing principles established by Secretary Kellogg: the *Foreign Relations* series is guided by the principles of historical objectivity and accuracy; records should not be altered or deletions made without indicating in the published text that a deletion has been made; the published record should omit no facts that were of major importance in reaching a decision; and nothing should be omitted for the purposes of concealing a defect in policy. The statute also requires that the *Foreign Relations* series be published not more than 30 years after the events recorded. The editors are convinced that this volume, which was compiled in 1993, meets all regulatory, statutory, and scholarly standards of selection and editing.

Structure and Scope of the Foreign Relations Series

This volume is part of a subseries of volumes of the *Foreign Relations* series that documents the most important issues in the foreign policy of the 5 years (1964–1968) of the administration of Lyndon B. Johnson. The subseries presents in 34 volumes a documentary record of major foreign policy decisions and actions of President Johnson's administration. This volume presents the record of general foreign economic policy, financial and monetary policy, and trade and commercial policy. Volume IX, International Development and Economic Defense Policy; Commodities, documents the Johnson administration's foreign assistance and international development policies, East-West trade policies, the management of the U.S. stockpile of strategic materials, and commodities.

Principles of Document Selection for the Foreign Relations Series

In preparing each volume of the *Foreign Relations* series, the editors are guided by some general principles for the selection of documents. Each editor, in consultation with the General Editor and other senior editors, determines the particular issues and topics to be documented either in detail, in brief, or in summary.

The following general selection criteria are used in preparing volumes in the *Foreign Relations* series. Individual compiler-editors vary these criteria in accordance with the particular issues and the available documentation. The editors also tend to apply these selection criteria in accordance with their own interpretation of the generally accepted standards of scholarship. In selecting documentation for publication, the editors gave priority to unpublished classified records, rather than previously published records (which are accounted for in appropriate bibliographical notes).

Selection Criteria (in general order of priority):

1. Major foreign affairs commitments made on behalf of the United States to other governments, including those that define or identify the principal foreign affairs interests of the United States;

2. Major foreign affairs issues, commitments, negotiations, and activities, whether or not major decisions were made, and including dissenting or alternative opinions to the process ultimately adopted;

3. The decisions, discussions, actions, and considerations of the President, as the official constitutionally responsible for the direction of foreign policy;

4. The discussions and actions of the National Security Council, the Cabinet, and special Presidential policy groups, including the policy options brought before these bodies or their individual members;

5. The policy options adopted by or considered by the Secretary of State and the most important actions taken to implement Presidential decisions or policies;

6. Diplomatic negotiations and conferences, official correspondence, and other exchanges between U.S. representatives and those of

other governments that demonstrate the main lines of policy implementation on major issues;

7. Important elements of information that attended Presidential decisions and policy recommendations of the Secretary of State;

8. Major foreign affairs decisions, negotiations, and commitments undertaken on behalf of the United States by government officials and representatives in other agencies in the foreign affairs community or other branches of government made without the involvement (or even knowledge) of the White House or the Department of State;

9. The main policy lines of intelligence activities if they constituted major aspects of U.S. foreign policy toward a nation or region or if they provided key information in the formulation of major U.S. policies, including relevant National Intelligence Estimates and Special National Intelligence Estimates as may be declassified;

10. The role of the Congress in the preparation and execution of particular foreign policies or foreign affairs actions;

11. Economic aspects of foreign policy;

12. The main policy lines of U.S. military and economic assistance as well as other types of assistance;

13. The political-military recommendations, decisions, and activities of the military establishment and major regional military commands as they bear upon the formulation or execution of major U.S. foreign policies;

14. Diplomatic appointments that reflect major policies or affect policy changes.

Sources for the Foreign Relations Series

The *Foreign Relations* statute requires that the published record in the *Foreign Relations* series include all records needed to provide comprehensive documentation on major U.S. foreign policy decisions and significant U.S. diplomatic activity. It further requires that government agencies, departments, and other entities of the U.S. Government engaged in foreign policy formulation, execution, or support cooperate with the Department of State Historian by providing full and complete access to records pertinent to foreign policy decisions and actions and by providing copies of selected records. Most but not all of the sources consulted in the preparation of this volume have been declassified and are available for review at the National Archives and Records Administration. The declassification review and opening for public review of all Department of State records no later than 30 years after the events is mandated by the *Foreign Relations* statute. The Department of State and other record sources used in the volume are described in detail in the section on Sources below.

Focus of Research and Principles of Selection for Foreign Relations, 1964–1968, Volume VIII

On the basis of a review of already published documentation, such as the *American Foreign Policy* series, Department of State *Bulletin*, and the annual reports of the Department of the Treasury, as well as research in government repositories, the editors decided to focus mainly on the following subjects for the research and selection of documents for inclusion in this volume: 1) balance-of-payments matters; 2) international financial matters, including decisions by the International Monetary Fund and the central bank governors; 3) a series of international monetary crises involving sterling, gold, and the French franc; and 4) trade and commercial subjects.

In response to the persistent and even worsening U.S. balance of payments, the Johnson administration developed several initiatives to attempt to ameliorate the situation. Because some of the bilateral and multilateral financial and monetary negotiations with foreign countries became intertwined with balance-of-payments matters, documentation on general balance-of-payments policy and international financial and monetary policy was combined in a single compilation. The other compilation in the volume, trade and commerce, covers export promotion programs and bilateral tariff issues but focuses particularly on the complicated multilateral Kennedy Round negotiations within the context of the General Agreement on Tariffs and Trade.

Editorial Methodology

The documents are presented chronologically according to Washington time or, in the case of conferences, in the order of individual meetings. Memoranda of conversation are placed according to the time and date of the conversation, rather than the date the memorandum was drafted.

Editorial treatment of the documents published in the *Foreign Relations* series follows Office style guidelines, supplemented by guidance from the General Editor and the chief technical editor. The source text is reproduced as exactly as possible, including marginalia or other notations, which are described in the footnotes. Texts are transcribed and printed according to accepted conventions for the publication of historical documents in the limitations of modern typography. A heading has been supplied by the editors for each document included in the volume. Spelling, capitalization, and punctuation are retained as found in the source text, except that obvious typographical errors are silently corrected. Other mistakes and omissions in the source text are corrected by bracketed insertions: a correction is set in italic type; an addition in roman type. Words or phrases underlined in the source text are printed in italics. Abbreviations and contractions are preserved as found in the source text, and a list of abbreviations is included in the front matter of each volume.

Bracketed insertions are also used to indicate omitted text that deals with an unrelated subject (in roman type) or that remains classified after declassification review (in italic type). The amount of material not declassified has been noted by indicating the number of lines or pages of source text that were omitted. Entire documents withheld for declassification purposes have been accounted for and are listed by headings, source notes, and number of pages not declassified in their chronological place. The amount of material omitted from this volume because it was unrelated to the subject of the volume, however, has not been delineated. All brackets that appear in the source text are so identified by footnotes.

The first footnote to each document includes the document's source, original classification, distribution, and drafting information. This note also provides the background of important documents and policies and indicates whether the President or his major policy advisers read the document. Every effort has been made to determine if a document has been previously published, and, if so, this information has been included in the source footnote.

Editorial notes and additional annotation summarize pertinent material not printed in the volume, indicate the location of additional documentary sources, provide references to important related documents printed in other volumes, describe key events, and provide summaries of and citations to public statements that supplement and elucidate the printed documents. Information derived from memoirs and other firsthand accounts has been used when appropriate to supplement or explicate the official record.

Advisory Committee on Historical Diplomatic Documentation

The Advisory Committee on Historical Diplomatic Documentation, established under the *Foreign Relations* statute, reviews records, advises, and makes recommendations concerning the *Foreign Relations* series. The Advisory Committee monitors the overall compilation and editorial process of the series and advises on all aspects of the preparation and declassification of the series. Although the Advisory Committee does not attempt to review the contents of individual volumes in the series, it does monitor the overall process and makes recommendations on particular problems that come to its attention.

The Advisory Committee has reviewed this volume.

Declassification Review

The final declassification review of this volume, which was completed in 1997, resulted in the decision to withhold about three-quarters of one percent of the documentation selected. Five documents were denied in full. The remaining documentation provides an accurate account of U.S. international monetary and trade policies during this period.

The Information Response Branch of the Office of IRM Programs and Services, Bureau of Administration, Department of State, conducted the declassification review of the documents published in this volume. The review was conducted in accordance with the standards set forth in Executive Order 12356 on National Security Information and applicable laws, which was superseded by Executive Order 12958 on April 20, 1995.

Under Executive Order 12356, information that concerns one or more of the following categories, and the disclosure of which reasonably could be expected to cause damage to the national security, requires classification:

1) military plans, weapons, or operations;
2) the vulnerabilities or capabilities of systems, installations, projects, or plans relating to the national security;
3) foreign government information;
4) intelligence activities (including special activities), or intelligence sources or methods;
5) foreign relations or foreign activities of the United States;
6) scientific, technological, or economic matters relating to national security;
7) U.S. Government programs for safeguarding nuclear materials or facilities;
8) cryptology; or
9) a confidential source.

The principle guiding declassification review is to release all information, subject only to the current requirements of national security as embodied in law and regulation. Declassification decisions entailed concurrence of the appropriate geographic and functional bureaus in the Department of State, other concerned agencies of the U.S. Government, and the appropriate foreign governments regarding specific documents of those governments.

Acknowledgments

The editors wish to acknowledge the assistance of officials at the Lyndon B. Johnson Library of the National Archives and Records Administration, especially David Humphrey and Regina Greenwell, and other officials of specialized repositories who assisted in the collection of documents for this volume.

David S. Patterson, Carolyn Yee, and Evan Duncan collected, selected, and edited the volume, under the general supervision of former General Editor Glenn W. LaFantasie. Bruce F. Duncombe performed additional research and review under the guidance of Patterson. The editors acknowledge the assistance of Francis M. Bator, President Johnson's Deputy Special Assistant for National Security Affairs, who reviewed this volume before publication. Rita M. Baker, Vicki E. Futscher, and Deb Godfrey did the copy and technical editing, and Breffni Whelan prepared the index.

William Z. Slany
The Historian
Bureau of Public Affairs

April 1998

Johnson Administration Volumes

Following is a list of the volumes in the *Foreign Relations* series for the administration of President Lyndon B. Johnson. The titles of individual volumes may change. The year of publication is in parentheses after the title.

Print Volumes

Contents

Sources

The editors of the *Foreign Relations* series have complete access to all the retired records and papers of the Department of State: the central files of the Department; the special decentralized files ("lot files") of the Department at the bureau, office, and division levels; the files of the Department's Executive Secretariat, which contain the records of international conferences and high-level official visits, correspondence with foreign leaders by the President and Secretary of State, and memoranda of conversations between the President and Secretary of State and foreign officials; and the files of overseas diplomatic posts.

When this volume was being compiled, all Department of State records consulted were still under the custody of the Department, and the footnotes citing Department of State files suggest that the Department is the repository. By the time of publication, however, all the Department's indexed central (or decimal) files for these years were permanently transferred to the National Archives and Records Administration (Archives II) at College Park, Maryland. Many of the Department's decentralized office (or lot) files covering this period, which the National Archives deems worthy of permanent retention, will also be transferred from the Department's custody to Archives II over the next several years.

The editors of the *Foreign Relations* series also have full access to the papers of President Johnson and other White House foreign policy records. Presidential papers maintained and preserved at the Presidential libraries include some of the most significant foreign affairs-related documentation from the Department of State and other Federal agencies including the National Security Council, the Central Intelligence Agency, the Department of Defense, and the Joint Chiefs of Staff.

The Department of State arranged for access to the many audiotapes of President Johnson's telephone conversations that are held at the Johnson Library. The first audiotapes became available to the editors in late 1994 with most audiotapes following during 1995, 1996, and 1997. Although compilation of this volume had already been completed, the editors added references to and summaries of selected transcripts of the President's relevant telephone conversations to this volume in the final stages of review. The summaries, including quoted extracts from the audiotapes, were prepared in the Office of the Historian specifically for this volume.

In preparing this specific volume documenting U.S. international monetary and trade policies during the Johnson administration, the editors concluded that the records of the Department of State would constitute the core of the published record. An invaluable reference work was *Current Economic Developments*, a bi-weekly classified publication compiled by the Bureau of Economic Affairs in the Department of State. Derived from Department of State contemporary cable traffic and internal memoranda, *Current Economic Developments* provided timely narrative summaries of a wide range of foreign economic topics for policy-makers. The issues of the periodical were useful in providing important background information to the editors, and a few of the articles were selected for inclusion in the volume. The editors also made extensive use of Presidential papers and other White House files at the John F. Kennedy Library and the Lyndon B. Johnson Library, which included significant documentation from the Department of the Treasury and the Office of the Special Representative for Trade Negotiations on foreign economic policy. Documents in the records of the Department of Commerce at the Washington National Records Center supplemented the Department of State and Presidential files.

All this documentation has been made available for use in the *Foreign Relations* series thanks to the consent of the foregoing agencies, the assistance of their staffs, and especially the cooperation and support of the National Archives and Records Administration.

The following list identifies the particular files and collections used in the preparation of this volume. The declassification and transfer to the National Archives of these records are in process. Many of the records are already available for public review at the National Archives. The declassification review of other records is going forward in accordance with the provisions of Executive Order 12958, under which all records over 25 years old, except for file series exemptions requested by agencies and approved by the President, should be reviewed for declassification by 2000.

Unpublished Sources

Department of State

Central Files. See National Archives and Records Administration below.

Lot Files. These files have either been transferred or are in the process of being transferred to the National Archives and Records Administration at College Park, Maryland, Record Group 59.

Ball Files: Lot 74 D 272

Files of Under Secretary of State George Ball, 1961–1967.

Conference Files: Lot 66 D 110

Collection of documentation on international conferences abroad attended by the President, the Secretary of State, and other U.S. officials, May 1961–December 1964.

EB/ICD/FTD Files: Lot 73 D 105

Files of the Fibers and Textiles Division, Office of International Commodities, Bureau of Economic Affairs, 1966–1969.

EB/ICD/FTD Files: Lot 73 D 183

Files of the Fibers and Textiles Division, Office of International Commodities, Bureau of Economic Affairs, pertaining to cotton and textiles, 1964–1972.

EB/ICD/TRP Files: Lot 75 D 413

Files of the Tropical Products Division, Office of International Commodities, Bureau of Economic Affairs, pertaining to coffee, sugar, and other tropical products, 1962–1969.

EB/ICD/TRP Files: Lot 75 D 462

Files of the Tropical Products Division, Office of International Commodities, Bureau of Economic Affairs, pertaining to sugar, 1961–1964.

EB/ICD/TRP Files: Lot 78 D 52

Files of the Tropical Products Division, Office of International Commodities, Bureau of Economic Affairs, pertaining to cocoa, 1958–1974.

EB/ICD/TRP Files: Lot 79 D 354

Files of the Tropical Products Division, Office of International Commodities, Bureau of Economic Affairs, pertaining to coffee, 1959–1975.

EB/IFD/OMA Files: Lot 73 D 19

Files of the Office of Monetary Affairs, Office of International Finance and Development, Bureau of Economic Affairs, pertaining to balance of payments, 1963–1971.

EB/IFD/OMA Files: Lot 73 D 185

Files of the Office of Monetary Affairs, Office of International Finance and Development, Bureau of Economic Affairs, pertaining to balance of payments, 1965–1971.

S/P Files: Lot 70 D 199

Files of the Policy Planning Council, 1963–1964.

National Archives and Records Administration, College Park, Maryland

Record Group 59, General Records of the Department of State

Subject-Numeric Indexed Central Files

AGR: Agriculture (general)
AGR 1: General policy, plans
AGR 1 US: General U.S. policy, plans
AGR 1 EEC: General EEC policy, plans
AGR 3: Organizations and conferences
AGR 3 GATT: Organizations and conferences, GATT
AGR 5: Laws and regulations
AGR 12 US: Crop production and consumption
AGR 15: Food supply
E 1 JAPAN–US: General economic policy & plans between Japan and the U.S.
E 1 NATO: General NATO economic policy and plans
E 1 US: General U.S. economic policy and plans
E 2–2 US; U.S. economic review
ECIN 3 EEC: Economic integration of the EEC
EEC 3: General matters pertaining to the EEC

FN 1 US: General U.S. financial policy and plans
FN 9: Foreign investment
FN 9 US: U.S. foreign investment
FN 10: Foreign exchange
FN 10 IMF: Foreign exchange, IMF
FN 12 JAPAN: Balance of payments, Japan
FN 12 UK: Balance of payments, U.K.
FN 12 US: Balance of payments, U.S.
FN 13: Capital movements
FN 16 US: U.S. revenue and taxation
FT CAN–US: Foreign trade between Canada and the U.S.
· FT JAPAN–US: General foreign trade policy and plans between Japan and the U.S.
FT 3 GATT: Foreign trade, GATT
FT 4 CAN–US: Trade agreements between Canada and the U.S.
FT 4 GATT: Foreign trade, GATT
ET 4 JAPAN–US: Trade agreements between Japan and the U.S.
FT 4 US/TEA: U.S. trade agreements, Trade Expansion Act
FT 7: Tariff negotiations
FT 7 EEC–US: tariff negotiations between the EEC and the U.S.
FT 7 GATT: Tariff negotiations, GATT
FT 7 JAPAN–US: Tariff negotiations between Japan and the U.S.
ET 11 JAPAN–US: Quantitative trade restrictions and controls between Japan and the U.S.
FT 11 UK–US: Quantitative trade restrictions and controls between Japan and the U.S.
FT 12 JAPAN: Trade liberalization, Japan
FT 12 UK: Trade liberalization, U.K.
FT 13 UK: Duties, U.K.
FT 13–2 JAPAN–US: Tariffs between Japan and the U.S.
FT 13–2 US: U.S. tariffs
FT 14 US–Japan: Dumping of goods between the U.S. and Japan
FT 25–5; Illegal dumping of goods
FT (EN) US: U.S. export
INCO–COTTON: Cotton industry and commodities
INCO–COTTON EEC: EEC cotton industry and commodities
INCO–GRAINS EEC: EEC grains industry and commodities
INCO–GRAINS GATT: GATT grains industry and commodities
INCO–GRAINS UK: U.K. grains industry and commodities
INCO–GRAINS UK–US: Grains industry and commodities between the U.K. and the U.S.
INCO–GRAINS 4 UK: UK. grains agreements
INCO–GRAINS 4 UK–US: Grains agreements between the U.K. and the U.S.
INCO–GRAINS 17 UK–US: Trade of grains between the U.K. and the U.S.
INCO–POULTRY: Poultry industry and commodities
INCO–POULTRY US: U.S. poultry industry and commodities
INCO–POULTRY EEC: EEC poultry industry and commodities
INCO–POULTRY GATT: GATT poultry industry and commodities
INCO–POULTRY 17 EEC: EEC poultry trade
INCO–WOOL: Wool industry and commodities
INCO–WOOL IT: Wool industry and commodities of Italy
INCO–WOOL UK: Wool industry and commodities of the U.K.
INCO–WOOL US: Wool industry and commodities of the U.S.
INCO–WOOL 4 GATT: Wool GATT agreements
INCO–WOOL 4: Wool trade agreements
INCO–WOOL 17: Wool trade
INCO–WOOL 17 US: U.S. wool trade
INCO–WOOL 17 US–IT: Wool trade between the U.S. and Italy

INCO–WOOL 17 US–JAPAN: Wool trade between the U.S. and Japan
POL FR–US: Political affairs and relations between France and the U.S.
POL JAPAN–US: Political affairs and relations between Japan and the U.S.
POL UK–US: Political affairs and relations between the U.K. and the U.S.
POL 1 JAPAN: General political policy toward Japan
POL 1 UK–US: general policy between the U.K. and the U.S.
POL 3: Political affairs and relations
POL 7 GER W: Visits and meetings to West Germany
STR 1: General strategic trade control policy
STR 5: Export control regulations and procedures
STR 7: Shipments of U.S. goods
STR 7–1: Transaction checks
STR 7–2: Technical data controls
TP: Trade promotion and assistance
TP 7–1: Visits by U.S. citizens
TP 7–3 IA: International tourism agreements
TP 7–3 OECD: OECD tourism
TP 7–3 US: U.S. tourism

Washington National Records Center, Suitland, Maryland

Record Group 59, Records of the Department of State

E/CBA/REP Files: FRC 72 A 6248

Lot 70 D 467: Master set of the Department of State classified internal publication *Current Economic Developments* for the years 1945–1969, as maintained in the Bureau of Economic Affairs.

Record Group 40, Records of the Department of Commerce

Office of the Under Secretary of Commerce Files: FRC 68 A 5947

Executive Secretariat Files, 1963–June 1965.

Office of the Secretary of Commerce Files: FRC 69 A 6828

Executive Secretariat files, 1962–1964.

Office of the Assistant to the Secretary of Commerce Files: FRC 70 A 7017

Files of the Assistant to the Secretary of Commerce (Fred Simpich), 1965–1968.

Office of the Secretary of Commerce Files: FRC 71 A 6617

Executive Secretariat Files, 1965–1966.

Office of the Secretaries of Commerce Files: FRC 74 A 20

Files of C. R. Smith and Alexander Trowbridge, 1967–1968.

Office of the Secretary of Commerce Files: FRC 74 A 30

Subject files of the Executive Secretariat, 1967–1968.

Office of the Secretary of Commerce Files: FRC 74 A 31

Files of the Executive Secretariat, 1967–1968.

Record Group 56, Records of the Department of the Treasury

Office of the Assistant Secretary for International Affairs: FRC 75 A 101

Files of the Deming Group, Advisory Committee on International Monetary Affairs (Dillon Committee), Ossola Group, and Cabinet Committee on the Balance of Payments.

Office of the Assistant Secretary for International Affairs: FRC 83 A 26,

  Files of the Deputy to the Assistant Secretary, and Secretary of the International Monetary Group Files, 1947–1977.

Office of the Assistant Secretary for International Affairs: FRC 76 A 108

  Files pertaining to the balance of payments, 1966–1971.

Office of the Under Secretary for Monetary Affairs: FRC 79 A 14

  Files of Frederick L. Deming and Paul A. Volcker, 1963–1969.

Lyndon B. Johnson Library, Austin, Texas

Papers of Lyndon B. Johnson

National Security File
  Committee File
  Country File
  McGeorge Bundy Files
  Memos to the President
  Name File
  National Security Action Memoranda
  National Security Council Histories
  National Security Council Meetings
  Subject File
  Walt W. Rostow Files

Office Files of the White House Aides
  Edward R. Fried
  Ernest Goldstein

Special Files
  Administrative Histories
  Cabinet Papers
  President's Daily Diary
  Recordings and Transcripts of Telephone Conversations and Meetings
  Task Force Reports

White House Central Files
  Confidential File
  Subject File

Other Personal Papers
  Francis M. Bator Papers
  Henry H. Fowler Papers
  William M. Roth Papers
  Dean Rusk Papers, Personal Appointment Books
  Anthony M. Solomon Papers

John F. Kennedy Library, Boston, Massachusetts

Papers of C. Douglas Dillon, 1964–1965

Papers of Christian A. Herter, 1964–1966

Published Sources

Cairncross, Alec. *The Wilson Years: A Treasury Diary, 1964–1969.* (London: The Historians' Press, 1997)

De Vries, Margaret G. *The International Monetary Fund, 1966–1971: The System Under Stress,* Vols. I and II (Washington: International Monetary Fund, 1976)

De Vries, Margaret G., and J. Keith Horsefield. *The International Monetary Fund, 1945–1965; Twenty Years of International Monetary Cooperation,* Vols. I, II, and III (Washington: International Monetary Fund, 1969)

Evans, John W. *The Kennedy Round in American Trade Policy: The Twilight of the GATT?* (Cambridge, MA: Harvard University Press, 1971)

General Agreement on Tariffs and Trade. *Basic Instruments and Selected Documents, Twelfth Supplement: Decisions, Reports, etc. of the Twenty-first Session* (Geneva: The Contracting Parties to the General Agreement on Tariffs and Trade, 1964)

Johnson, Lyndon B. *Vantage Point: Perspectives of the Presidency, 1963–1969* (New York: Holt, Rinehart and Winston, 1971)

Office of the Special Representative for Trade Negotiations. *General Agreement on Tariffs and Trade 1964–1967 Trade Conference: Report on United States Negotiations,* 2 Vols. (Washington: Office of the Special Representative for Trade Negotiations, 1967–1968)

Rostow, W.W. *The Diffusion of Power: An Essay in Recent History* (New York: The Macmillan Company, 1972)

U.S. Congress. *The Foreign Policy Aspects of the Kennedy Round: Hearings Before the Subcommittee on Foreign Economic Policy of the Committee on Foreign Affairs, House of Representatives, Eighty–ninth Congress, Second Session* (Washington: U.S. Government Printing Office, 1966)

———. *Foreign Trade and Tariff Proposals: Hearings Before the Committee on Ways and Means, House of Representatives, Ninetieth Congress, Second Session, on Trade Proposals,* Parts I and II (Washington: U.S. Government Printing Office, 1969)

U.S. Department of State. *American Foreign Policy: Current Documents, 1964, 1965, 1966, 1967* (Washington: U.S. Government Printing Office)

———. *Department of State Bulletin, 1964, 1965, 1966, 1967, 1968* (Washington: U.S. Government Printing Office)

U.S. Department of the Treasury. *Annual Report of the Secretary of the Treasury on the State of the Finances for the Fiscal Year Ended June 30, 1964, 1965, 1966, 1967, 1968* (Washington: U.S. Government Printing Office)

U.S. National Archives and Records Administration. *Public Papers of the Presidents of the United States: Lyndon B. Johnson, 1963–64, 1965, 1966, 1967, 1968–69* (Washington: U.S. Government Printing Office)

Abbreviations

A, airgram
AID, Agency for International Development
AL, Aviation Liaison Division, Office of Aviation, Bureau of Economic Affairs, Department or State
ASP, American Selling Price
AUTEC, Atlantic Underwater Test and Evaluation Center
AVE, ad valorem equivalent

B, Office of the Under Secretary of State for Economic Affairs
BAOR, British military aircraft
BBC, British Broadcasting Company
BIC, Bureau of International Commerce, Department of Commerce
BIS, Bank for International Settlements
BNA, Office of British Commonwealth and Northern European Affairs, Bureau of European Affairs, Department of State
BOB, Bureau of the Budget
BOP, balance of payments
B/P, balance of payments
BST, British Standard Time
BUSEC, series indicator for telegrams to the U.S. Mission to European Regional Organizations

CA, circular airgram
CAB, Civil Aeronautics Board
CAN, Office of Canadian Affairs, Bureau of European Affairs, Department of State
CAP, Common Agricultural Policy, refers to agricultural policies of the Common Market; series indicator for White House telegrams
CCC, Commodity Credit Corporation, Department of Agriculture
C/D, certificate of deposit
CDT, Central Daylight Time
CDU/CSU, Christian Democratic Union/Christian Socialist Union
CEA, Council of Economic Advisers
CET, Common External Tariff
CIA, Central Intelligence Agency
COB, close of business
CP, Contracting Party (Parties); Cabinet Paper
CRU, Collective Reserve Unit
CST, Central Standard Time
CU, Office of the Assistant Secretary of State for Educational and Cultural Affairs
CXT, common external tariff
CY, calendar year

D, Office of the Deputy Administrator, Agency for International Development
DA, Discover America, Inc.
DAC, Development Assistance Committee
DAG, Development Assistance Group
DC, developing country
DEF, Department of Defense
DOD, Department of Defense

E, Bureau of Economic Affairs, Department of State
EA, Office of East Asian Affairs, Bureau of Far Eastern Affairs, Department of State
EC, European Community
ECE, Economic Commission for Europe (UN)
EEC, European Economic Community
EFTA, European Free Trade Association
EMA, European Monetary Agreement
ENI, Ente Nazional Idrocarburi
EUR, Bureau of European Affairs, Department of State
EXIM, Exim Bank, Eximbank, Export-Import Bank

FAC, Office of the Deputy Coordinator for Foreign Assistance, Office of the Under Secretary of State for Economic Affairs
FCIA, Foreign Credit Insurance Association
FDIP, Foreign Direct Investment Program
FE, Bureau of Far Eastern Affairs, Department of State
FN, International Finance Division, Office of International Financial and Development Affairs, Bureau of Economic Affairs, Department of State
FonMin, Foreign Minister
FonOff, Foreign Office
FRB, Federal Reserve Board
FRC, Federal Records Center (Washington National Records Center)
FRG, Federal Republic of Germany
FY, fiscal year
FYI, for your information

G, Office of the Deputy Under Secretary of State for Political Affairs
GA, U.N. General Assembly
GAB, General Agreements to Borrow
GARIOA, Government Assistance and Relief in Occupied Areas
GATT, General Agreement on Tariffs and Trade
GER, Office of German Affairs, Bureau of European Affairs, Department of State
GNP, Gross National Product
GOF, Government of France
GOJ, Government of Japan
G/PM, Office of the Deputy Assistant Secretary of State for Politico-Military Affairs

H.R., House of Representatives Resolution
H. Rept., House of Representatives Report

IATA, International Air Transport Association
IBM, International Business Machines, Inc.
IBRD, International Bank for Reconstruction and Development
ICFEP, Interdepartmental Committee of Under Secretaries on Foreign Economic Policy
IDA, International Development Association
IDB, Inter-American Development Bank
IET, Interest Equalization Tax
ILO, International Labor Organization
IMA, International Monetary Affairs, Bureau of Economic Affairs, Department of State
IMF, International Monetary Fund
INR, Bureau of Intelligence and Research, Department of State
IP, International Payments Division, Office of International Monetary Affairs, Bureau of Economic Affairs, Department of State
ITA, Independent Television Authority

J, Japan Desk, Bureau of East Asian and Pacific Affairs, Department of State
JEA, Joint Export Association, Department of Commerce

KR, Kennedy Round

LDA, lesser developed area
LDC, less developed country

M, Office of the Under Secretary of State for Political Affairs
MAP, Military Assistance Program
MDS, Moutant de Soutien
MFN, most favored nation
MITI, Ministry of International Trade and Industry (Japan)

NAC, National Advisory Council on International Monetary and Financial Problems
NASA, National Aeronautics and Space Administration
NATO, North Atlantic Treaty Organization
NEEC, National Export Expansion Council
NSC, National Security Council
NTB, national tariff barrier

OA, Office of Aviation, Bureau of Economic Affairs, Department of State
OECD, Organization for Economic Cooperation and Development
OEEC, Organization for European Economic Cooperation
OEP, Office of Emergency Planning
OFDI, Office of Foreign Direct Investment, Department of Commerce
OFE, Office of International Finance and Economic Analysis, Bureau of Economic Affairs, Department of State
OIA, Office of International Affairs, Department of the Treasury
OIF, Office of International Finance, Department of the Treasury
OIN, Office of Industrial Nations, Department of the Treasury
OMA, Office of International Monetary Affairs, Bureau of Economic Affairs, Department of State
OR, Office of International Resources, Bureau of Economic Affairs, Department of State
OS, Office of the Secretary, Department of the Treasury
OT, Office of International Trade, Bureau of Economic Affairs, Department of State
OTC, Organization for Trade Cooperation

P.L., Public Law
POL, petroleum, oil, lubricants

QR, quantitative restriction

RG, Record Group
RPE, Office of Atlantic Political and Economic Affairs, Bureau of European Affairs, Department of State
RTS, revised tariff schedule

S, Office of the Secretary of State
S. Rept., Senate Report
S. Res., Senate Resolution
SDR, Special Drawing Rights
septel, separate telegram
SIC, standard industrial classification
SIG, Special Interdepartmental Group

S/P, Policy Planning Council, Department of State
S/S, Executive Secretariat, Department of State
STR, Office of the Special Representative for Trade Negotiations

TA, Trade Agreements Division, Office of International Trade, Bureau of Economic Affairs, Department of State; trade agreements
TAC, Interdepartmental Committee on Trade Agreements
TEA, Trade Expansion Act of 1962
TEACC, Trade Expansion Act Advisory Committee
TEC, Trade Executive Committee
tel, telegram
TNC, Trade Negotiations Committee
TSC, Trade Staff Committee
TSUS, Tariff Schedules of the United States
TT, Office of Transportation and Telecommunications, Bureau of Economic Affairs, Department of State
TUC, Trade Union Congress
TVA, Tennessee Valley Authority
TWA, Trans World Airlines

U, Office of the Under Secretary of State
UK, United Kingdom
UN, United Nations
UNCTAD, United Nations Conference on Trade and Development
USC, United States Code
USDA, United States Department of Agriculture
USDel, United States delegation
USEC, United States Mission to the European Community
USG, United States Government
USRO, United States Mission to European Regional Organizations
UST, United States Treaties and Other International Agreements
USTR, United States Trade Representative
USTS, United States Travel Service

VCP, Voluntary Commerce Program

WP, working party

Persons

Ackley, Gardner H., Chairman, Council of Economic Advisers, from 1964

Auchincloss, Kenneth, Executive Assistant to the Special Representative for Trade Negotiations until 1965

Ball, George W., Under Secretary of State until September 30, 1966; Representative to the United Nations, June 26–September 25, 1968

Barr, Joseph W., Under Secretary of the Treasury from April 29, 1965

Bator, Francis M., Senior Economic Adviser, Agency for International Development, until April 1964; Staff Member, National Security Council, April 1964–1965; Deputy Special Assistant to the President for National Security Affairs, 1965–September 1, 1967

Bell, David E., Administrator, Agency for International Development, until July 31, 1966

Black, John W., Deputy Director, U.S. Travel Service, to 1964; Director, 1965–May 20, 1968

Blumenthal, W. Michael, Deputy Special Representative for Trade Negotiations

Brandt, Willy, Vice Chancellor of the Federal Republic of Germany and Foreign Minister after December 1, 1966

Brimmer, Andrew F., Deputy Assistant Secretary of Commerce for Economic Affairs until 1965; thereafter Member, Board of Governors of the Federal Reserve System

Bundy, McGeorge, Special Assistant to the President for National Security Affairs until February 28, 1966

Bundy, William P., Assistant Secretary of State for East Asian and Pacific Affairs

Califano, Joseph A., Jr., Special Assistant to the Secretary and Deputy Secretary of Defense, 1964–1965; thereafter Special Assistant to the President

Callaghan, James, British Chancellor of the Exchequer, October 16, 1964–November 29, 1967; thereafter Home Secretary

Carswell, Robert, Special Assistant to the Secretary of the Treasury until 1965

Clifford, Clark M., Secretary of Defense from March 1, 1968

Colombo, Emilio, Italian Minister of the Treasury

Connor, John T., Secretary of Commerce, December 16, 1964–January 7, 1967

Couve de Murville, Maurice, French Foreign Minister until May 31, 1968; thereafter Finance and Economic Affairs Minister

Daane, J. Dewey, Governor of the Federal Reserve Bank

De Gaulle, Charles, President of France

Debré, Michel, French Finance and Economic Affairs Minister, January 9, 1966–May 31, 1968; thereafter Foreign Minister

Deming, Frederick L., Under Secretary of the Treasury for Monetary Affairs from February 1, 1965

Dillon, C. Douglas, Secretary of the Treasury until April 1, 1965.

Eckstein, Otto, Member, Council of Economic Advisers, until 1966

Eminger, Otmar, Chairman of the Deputies of the Group of Ten from October 1964

Erhard, Ludwig, Chancellor of the Federal Republic of Germany until December 1, 1966

Fowler, Henry H., Under Secretary of the Treasury until April 1, 1965; thereafter Secretary of the Treasury

Fried, Edward R., Member, Policy Planning Council, Department of State, until October 24, 1965; Deputy Assistant Secretary of State for International Resources, Bureau of Economic Affairs, October 24, 1965–August 15, 1967; thereafter, Staff Member, National Security Council

Gordon, Kermit, Director, Bureau of the Budget, until 1965

Hedges, Irwin R., Agricultural Trade Representative, Office of the Special Representative for Trade Negotiations, to June 1967; Deputy Assistant Administrator, Office of the War on Hunger, Agency for International Development, from July 1967

Herter, Christian A., Special Representative for Trade Negotiations until December 30, 1966

Hodges, Luther H., Secretary of Commerce until December 1964

Holt, Harold E., Prime Minister of Australia from January 26, 1966

Hughes, Philip S., Assistant Director for Legislative Reference, Bureau of the Budget, until 1966; thereafter Deputy Director, Bureau of the Budget

Humphrey, Hubert H., Democratic Senator from Minnesota until December 29, 1964; Vice President of the United States from January 20, 1965

Jenkins, Roy, British Home Secretary, December 22, 1965–November 29, 1967; thereafter Chancellor of the Exchequer

Johnson, G. Griffith, Assistant Secretary of State for Economic Affairs until May 1, 1965

Johnson, Lyndon Baines, President of the United States

Johnson, U. Alexis, Deputy Under Secretary of State for Political Affairs until July 12, 1964; Deputy Ambassador to Vietnam, July 1964–September 1965; Deputy Under Secretary of State for Political Affairs, November 1, 1965–October 9, 1966; Ambassador to Japan from November 8, 1966

Katzenbach, Nicholas deB., Deputy Attorney General, Department of Justice, until February 13, 1965–October 3, 1966; thereafter Under Secretary of State

Kaysen, Carl, Deputy Special Assistant to the President for National Security Affairs

Kiesinger, Kurt Georg, Chancellor of the Federal Republic of Germany from December 1, 1966

Kitchen, Jeffrey C., Deputy Assistant Secretary of State for Political-Military Affairs until February 1967

Knowlton, Winthrop, Deputy Assistant Secretary of the Treasury for International Monetary Affairs until August 2, 1966; Assistant Secretary, August 2, 1966–January 31, 1968

Leddy, John M., Representative to the Organization for Economic Cooperation and Development until June 15, 1965; thereafter Assistant Secretary of State for European Affairs

Linder, Harold F., President and Chairman, Export-Import Bank

Love, James S., Deputy to the Secretary of Commerce for Textile Programs until 1966

Mann, Thomas C., Under Secretary of State for Economic Affairs, March 18, 1965–May 31, 1966

Martin, William McChesney, Jr., Chairman of the Board of Governors, Federal Reserve System

McCloy, John J., Chairman, Chase Manhattan Bank, and consultant to President Johnson

McGhee, George C., Ambassador to Germany until May 21, 1968

McNamara, Robert S., Secretary of Defense until February 29, 1968

McQuade, Lawrence C., Assistant to the Secretary of Commerce 1965–1967; thereafter Assistant Secretary of Commerce for Domestic and International Business

Menzies, Sir Robert, Prime Minister of Australia until January 26, 1964

Miki, Takeo, Japanese Foreign Secretary, December 23, 1966–October 29, 1968

Mills, Wilbur D., Democratic Representative from Arkansas; Chairman of the House Ways and Means Committee

Moro, Aldo, Prime Minister of Italy until June 19, 1968

Nitze, Paul H., Secretary of the Navy until June 30, 1967; thereafter Deputy Secretary of Defense

Okun, Arthur M., Member, Council of Economic Advisers

Pearson, Lester, Prime Minister of Canada until April 20, 1968
Percival, LeRoy F., Jr., Deputy Director, Office of Atlantic Political-Economic Affairs, Bureau of European Affairs, Department of State, July 1964–July 1967
Petty, John R., Deputy Assistant Secretary of the Treasury for International Monetary Affairs, August 1966–May 15, 1968; thereafter Assistant Secretary

Reischauer, Edwin O., Ambassador to Japan until August 19, 1966
Rey, Jean, Member of the Commission of the European Economic Community in charge of External Relations until July 1, 1967; thereafter President of the Commission of the European Communities
Robertson, James L., Member, Board of Governors of the Federal Reserve System; Vice Chairman from 1966
Rostow, Eugene V., Under Secretary of State for Political Affairs from October 14, 1966
Roosevelt, Franklin D., Under Secretary of Commerce until June 1965
Rostow, Walt Whitman, Counselor and Chairman of the Policy Planning Council, Department of State, until March 31, 1966; Special Assistant to the President from April 1, 1966
Roth, William M., Deputy Special Representative for Trade Negotiations until March 24, 1967; thereafter Special Representative
Rusk, Dean, Secretary of State

Sato, Eisako, Prime Minister of Japan from November 9, 1964
Schiller, Karl, West German Economic Minister from December 1, 1966
Schnittker, John A., Under Secretary of Agriculture from 1965
Schultze, Charles L., Assistant Director, Bureau of the Budget, until June 1, 1965; thereafter Director until January 29, 1968
Schweitzer, Pierre-Paul, Managing Director of the International Monetary Fund
Shaw, William H., Assistant Secretary of Commerce for Economic Affairs, 1967–1968
Smith, Bromley, Executive Secretary, National Security Council
Smith, Cyrus R., Secretary of Commerce from March 6, 1968
Solomon, Anthony E., Assistant Secretary of State for Economic Affairs from June 1, 1965
Southard, Frank A., Jr., Deputy Managing Director of the International Monetary Fund
Staats, Elmer B., Deputy Director, Bureau of the Budget, until 1966
Stevenson, Adlai E., Representative to the United Nations until July 14, 1965
Strauss, Franz Josef, West German Finance Minister from December 1, 1966

Takeuchi, Ryuji, Japanese Vice Minister of Foreign Affairs
Trezise, Philip H., Deputy Assistant Secretary of State for Economic Affairs until October 1965; Representative to the Organization for European Economic Cooperation from October 26, 1965
Trowbridge, Alexander S., Assistant Secretary of Commerce for Domestic and International Business until May 1967; Acting Secretary of Commerce, February 1, 1967–June 14, 1967; Secretary, June 14, 1967–February 28, 1968
Trued, Merlyn N., Acting Assistant Secretary of the Treasury for International Affairs, 1964–April 29, 1965; thereafter Assistant Secretary until June 10, 1966
Tuthill, John W., Ambassador to the European Economic Community until June 7, 1966; thereafter Ambassador to Brazil

Volcker, Paul A., Deputy Under Secretary of the Treasury for Monetary Affairs until November 23, 1965

Willis, George, II, Deputy to the Assistant Secretary of the Treasury for International Monetary Affairs

Widman, F. Lisle, Director, Office of Industrial Nations, Department of the Treasury

Wilson, James Harold, Prime Minister of the United Kingdom from October 16, 1964

Wyman, Thomas G., Assistant Secretary of Commerce for Domestic and International Business until December 1965

Wyndham White, Eric, Director-General, General Agreement on Tariffs and Trade

General and Financial and Monetary Policy

1. **Memorandum From Secretary of the Treasury Dillon to President Johnson**[1]

Washington, January 31, 1964.

SUBJECT

New Authorization of the Exchange Stabilization Fund

The British Government has decided to sell approximately $300 million of the American stocks which they originally expropriated from their own citizens during the early days of World War II. They are doing this because they wish to have the proceeds in more readily available form should they be needed to bolster their international reserves.

Sales have already commenced and should be completed some time in April or May. Under ordinary circumstances this action would show up as an equivalent increase in the United States balance of payments deficit.

We have, however, been able to work out with the British a special procedure which will avoid this unfortunate contingency. The British will invest the proceeds in securities of agencies of the U.S. Government, for example, the Home Loan Bank. Such securities are treated in our balance of payments statistics as the equivalent of long term investments. In other words, as far as balance of payments statistics go, they are no different from the common stocks which the British own at present.

On the other hand, if the proceeds had gone into U.S. Government bonds, they would have been treated as liabilities by the Department of Commerce and would have increased our payments deficit.

The proceeds of the sales which are being made from day to day in the market will be accumulated and invested in these agency bonds just before the end of each quarter. In order to avoid an impact on our balance of payments in the period between the sale of the common stocks and the investment of the proceeds in government agency bonds, we have arranged with the British to deposit the dollar proceeds in the Exchange

---

[1] Source: Johnson Library, White House Central Files, Confidential File, FI 9, Monetary Systems. Secret. Dillon transmitted this memorandum to Bill Moyers, the President's Special Assistant, on February 3 under cover of a memorandum that stressed the importance of confidentiality in this matter: "Any leak from here would go far to destroy the spirit of confidence with which the British Treasury now deals with us and which we find very valuable."

Stabilization Fund.[2] We will pay them interest on these deposits at the same rate as if they had invested the funds in 90 day Treasury bills.

The acceptance of deposits in dollars or foreign currencies by the Exchange Stabilization Fund would be a new procedure, and accordingly, Presidential authorization is required under the Gold Reserve Act of 1934. Therefore, I am transmitting herewith a formal request for your approval of the acceptance of foreign government deposits by the Exchange Stabilization Fund either in dollars or in foreign currency.[3] If you approve, would you please return the original for the Treasury files.

This operation by the British is extremely confidential, and they are very insistent that there be no leak until after it has been completed, when they intend to make an appropriate announcement which they will coordinate with us. It is also in our own interest that this be kept confidential until properly released in order to avoid rumors that the British are selling because of a possible lack in confidence in the dollar. Only two or three individuals in the Treasury are aware of this transaction and I am not informing anyone outside of the Treasury for the present.

Douglas Dillon

---

[2] For provisions of the Exchange Stabilization Fund, see section 10 to the Gold Reserve Act of 1934, P.L. 73–86 (68 Stat. 337).

[3] Not printed.

---

2.   Editorial Note

On March 30, 1964, John C. Bullitt, Assistant Secretary of the Treasury for International Affairs, distributed to the members of the Executive Committee of the Cabinet Committee on the Balance of Payments for their comment and review an early draft report to the President from the Cabinet Committee on the Balance of Payments. (Johnson Library, National Security File, Balance of Payments, Volume I, November 27, 1963 thru October 31, 1964, Box 1, Confidential) The March 30 memorandum was sent to Assistant Secretary of State Johnson, Assistant Secretary of Defense Hitch, Assistant Secretary of Commerce Holton, Deputy Special Representative for Trade Negotiations Roth, Assistant Budget Director Schultze, Dr. Chenery at AID, and Ackley at the Council of Economic Advisers.

On April 13, Bullitt sent the Executive Committee a revised draft report to the President on the balance of payments incorporating "most of the comments which were received on the March 30 draft." The transmittal memorandum indicated the Executive Committee would meet on April 21 "for the purpose of agreeing on a final text for submission to the President." (US/3/106; Washington National Records Center, RG 56, OASIA Files: FRC 75 A 101, Cabinet Committee on the Balance of Payments) The April 13 draft amended very little the March 30 draft.

On April 24, Bullitt sent the Secretaries of the Treasury, Defense, and Commerce, the Under Secretary of State, the AID Administrator, the Special Representative for Trade Negotiations, the Director of the Bureau of the Budget, the Chairman of the Council of Economic Advisers, and McGeorge Bundy at the White House, all of whom were the members of the Cabinet Committee on the Balance of Payments, the proposed memorandum to the President from the Cabinet Committee, which had been revised following discussion of an earlier draft by the Executive Committee, for their consideration at the Cabinet Committee meeting on April 28. (US/3/113; ibid.) The draft version of the report to the President distributed on April 24 and classified Secret, included a significant restructuring of the last half of the April 13 draft and was quite close to what finally went to the President on May 1.

Under cover of a May 1 memorandum to the Cabinet Committee, Secretary Dillon sent its members copies of "the Report to the President from the Cabinet Committee on Balance of Payments as delivered to the President today. The attached report has been revised in accordance with the discussion at the April 28 meeting of the Cabinet Committee." Dillon continued: "The language classified 'Secret' on page 4 of the Summary and Recommendations, paragraph numbered 9, third sentence, has been deleted from all copies of the Report except those delivered to the President and to each member of the Committee." (Ibid.) For the May 1 report, see Document 5. A separate, May 1 memorandum from Dillon also went to members of the Committee with the less sensitive version of the report. (US/3/13; Washington National Records Center, RG 56, OASIA Files: FRC 75 A 101, Cabinet Committee on the Balance of Payments)

3.   Memorandum From Secretary of the Treasury Dillon to President Johnson[1]

Washington, April 24, 1964.

SUBJECT

First Quarter Balance of Payments Results

We now have preliminary overall balance of payments figures for March which are reasonably complete and reliable. When added to the more complete figures for January and February they show an overall unadjusted surplus of just over $200 million for the first quarter.

Quarterly balance of payments figures are subject to strong seasonal influences of various kinds: a prime example is the heavy outflow for tourist travel abroad during the third quarter of each year. As a result quarterly figures are only used after adjustments for seasonal variations which are calculated by technicians in the Department of Commerce. These seasonal adjustments serve to reduce our surplus or increase our deficit in every quarter except the third when they work in the opposite direction. Last year the seasonal adjustment for the first quarter increased the deficit by $180 million. This calculation has not yet been made for the first quarter of this year. Should the adjustment be the same this year as last we would have an overall seasonally adjusted surplus of $25 million in the first quarter or $100 million at an annual rate.

However, the chief of the technical staff at the Department of Commerce, who is responsible for these figures, is extremely conservative. Therefore, I would not be surprised if the seasonal adjustment this year turned out to be somewhat larger so as to eliminate any overall surplus.

These first quarter figures will be published by the Department of Commerce as *preliminary* estimates some time the latter part of May. Your earlier statement that we might be in approximate overall balance should be borne out of that time. However, these quarterly figures are subject to further revisions on the basis of more complete information which will become available early in June, and which will be the basis of the *official* Commerce Department figures for the first quarter to be published in late June. This revision could easily run as high as $50 million, which it did in the most recent case when the deficit for the fourth quarter of 1963 was increased by $50 million between the publication of preliminary figures in February and final figures in March. Such a change could easily wipe out the small overall surplus that seems likely to be reported in the preliminary figures.

---

[1] Source: Johnson Library, White House Central Files, Confidential File, FO 4–1, Balance of Payments, 1963–1965. Confidential.

Another important element to bear in mind is the fact that the most popular figure for portrayal of balance of payments results is our balance on "regular transactions", which excludes all special arrangements, such as advance repayments of debts and advance payments on military orders. While we do not have good figures yet and will not have them until about the first of June, it seems likely that progress payments received from Germany on military purchases during the first quarter were somewhat larger than actual deliveries. This excess will be classified by the Department of Commerce as a special transaction. Therefore, it is likely that our balance on "regular transactions" during the first quarter will turn out to be in deficit by anywhere from $50 to $100 million, or $200–$400 million at an annual rate. The fact that we may have a small surplus on an overall basis and a deficit on regular transactions will undoubtedly cause some public confusion but the press is likely to put most weight on the regular transactions figure.

All of the above indicates the complexities involved in our balance of payments statistics and the dangers in making any public use of early and preliminary estimates. The preliminary figures we now have for the first quarter are $150 to $200 million less favorable than the result that would have been calculated on the basis of the flash weekly figures which were all we had at the time of your original press comment. Such a shift in figures is not at all unusual. I took this probability into account in telling Chairman Heller, at your request, that we might well break even in our balance of payments during the first quarter. It was because of this sort of uncertainty that I also asked him to caution you against any public use of such preliminary horseback estimates.

Finally our weekly figures show us once more running a fairly substantial deficit in April. We see no reason to expect a continuation of the exceptionally favorable first quarter results, although we do expect that 1964 will, for the first time, show really substantial progress toward our goal of eliminating the deficit.

Douglas Dillon

4.   Memorandum From Secretary of the Treasury Dillon to President Johnson[1]

Washington, May 1, 1964.

SUBJECT

Your Meeting with the Cabinet Committee on Balance of Payments, May 4, 1964

Purpose

To receive the latest report of the Cabinet Committee and discuss its recommendations and related developments.

Background

This will be your first formal meeting with the Cabinet Committee on Balance of Payments. The Committee meets from time to time to consider broad policy questions and serves to coordinate our Government efforts in the balance of payments field necessary "to the defense of the strength and stability of the dollar". It has in the past reported to the President at about this time of the year—when final results for the previous year have become available—and has recommended any new policies that the circumstances required. In December, I informed the members of the Committee of your wish for it to continue as in the past.

The Cabinet Committee's Report to you is attached.[2] The Report has been substantially agreed to by all members of the Committee, although some may wish to comment on matters of emphasis. The principal elements of our present program, together with recommendations for the future, are contained in the summary at the beginning.

We hope to obtain your approval for continuing with the over-all program and of the recommendations for new action—subject to whatever modifications you may find desirable.

Members of the Cabinet Committee, in addition to myself as Chairman, are the Secretary of Defense; the Secretary of Commerce; Under Secretary of State Ball; the Administrator of AID; the Director of the Bureau of the Budget; the Special Representative for Trade Negotiations; the Chairman of the Council of Economic Advisers; and Special Assistant Bundy. Governor Herter will be out of the country.

Suggested Procedure

The meeting could be informal. You might call on me, as Chairman of the Committee, to lead off with a summary of the latest developments

---

[1] Source: Johnson Library, National Security File, Balance of Payments, Vol. 1, November 27, 1963 thru October 31, 1964, Box 1. Limited Official Use.

[2] Not attached; see Document 5.

in our balance of payments and gold and with the highlights of the Report. You may also wish to call on others to comment on particular aspects of our program.

It would be most helpful if you would reaffirm to the group the need for continued vigorous action to carry out the balance of payments program, pointing out particularly that we cannot relax our efforts now just because of the unusually favorable results during the first quarter. We should not count on the first quarter's improvement to continue—in fact, developments in April show that our substantial favorable balance in March was largely fictitious and has already been offset. A more accurate assessment of first quarter results, in the context of expected results for the year as a whole, is a deficit on the order of $1–$1-1/4 billion at annual rates. This clearly shows the difficult road we have ahead if we are to continue progress towards elimination of the deficit and achievement of sustainable equilibrium. Furthermore, any signs of relaxation by us could shake European confidence and thereby affect their willingness to hold dollars rather than demand gold.

Douglas Dillon[3]

---

[3] Printed from a copy that indicates Dillon signed the original.

---

5.   Report From the Cabinet Committee on Balance of Payments to President Johnson[1]

Washington, undated.

SUMMARY AND RECOMMENDATIONS

Attached to this summary is a comprehensive report from the Cabinet Committee on the Balance of Payments, including a review of the 1963 results, an evaluation of performance under existing programs to reduce the deficit, and the outlook for the period ahead.[2]

---

[1] Source: Johnson Library, National Security File, Balance of Payments, Vol. 1, November 27, 1963 thru October 31, 1964, Box 1. Secret (With Limited Official Use Sections). The report was submitted under a cover sheet dated May 1.

[2] Not printed.

During 1963, the deficit on regular transactions—excluding special inter-government financing—decreased from 1962's $3.6 billion to $3.3 billion. However, results in the second half of 1963 differed sharply from the first half: the deficit on regular transactions dropped from a $4.6 billion annual rate to a $2.0 billion rate.

This sharp improvement was largely due to reduced capital outflows—owing in good measure to announcement on July 18, 1963, of the proposed Interest Equalization Tax and the Federal Reserve's increase in its discount rate.[3] There was also an increase in exports. The improvement in both of these areas may prove to be somewhat greater than can be sustained through 1964.

The improved performance in 1963 was a major factor in cutting our net gold loss to foreigners to $392 million. Overall gold losses totaled $461 million, because of domestic sales of $69 million. The lower gold loss also reflects the effects of enlarged Russian gold sales and the success of our efforts over the past three years to strengthen our capacity for financing the deficit.

But even if present favorable conditions continue, the deficit on regular transactions for 1964 is projected to run between $1.5–$2 billion. This would show substantial improvement over 1963—and be the lowest deficit since 1957—but it would still be on the high side of the safe margin of tolerance. It is *essential that we continue to show steady and substantial progress in eliminating the deficit.*

President Kennedy's July 18 Balance-of-Payments Message set specific targets for savings totaling $2 billion, which consist of:

—reduction of $300 million in the annual rate of gross outlays for defense by January 1, 1965 compared to 1962;
—reduction of over $200 million in 1965—as compared with 1962—in cost of strategic materials acquired from foreign sources;
—continuation of AID policies tying commitments to U.S. exports, resulting in a decline of AID expenditures entering our balance of payments in fiscal year 1965 to not over $500 million;
—savings by other agencies, together with those expected from revisions of programs under the Agricultural Trade Development and Assistance Act, of $100 million a year; and
—$1 billion annual savings from the combined effect of the increase in short-term interest rates and the Interest Equalization Tax.

---

[3] On July 18, 1963, President Kennedy delivered a special message to Congress on the balance-of-payments problem. See *Public Papers of the Presidents: John F. Kennedy, 1963*, pp. 574–584. In his message, President Kennedy recommended the enactment of an "interest equalization tax," which "would stem the flood of foreign security sales in our markets and still be consistent with both economic growth and free capital movements." The interest equalization tax was signed into law on September 2, 1964; see Document 12. The Federal Reserve Board approved on July 16, 1963, a rise in the rediscount rate, i.e. bank rate, from 3 to 3-1/2 percent, effective July 17. The Board said that its action was designed to aid U.S. efforts to combat the international balance-of-payments problem.

It now appears that, with continued effort, these targets can be attained. Further progress will require us to:

1. *Maintain wage-price stability.* It appears that at last our trade balance may be benefiting from our relatively stable prices over the last few years. In the face of the increasing determination of the Western European countries to curtail inflation, it is absolutely vital that we maintain the stability of our own prices over the period ahead if we are to achieve balance of payments equilibrium and stem the gold outflow.

2. *Reinforce efforts to increase our exports,* including efforts to provide adequate commercial personnel abroad as well as favorable credit facilities. In this connection, give maximum support to the National Export Expansion Coordinator, who is also Executive Director to the Cabinet Committee on Export Expansion.[4] The Coordinator is giving particular attention to the expansion of exports of consumer goods to the developed countries and to further improvements in government policies and operations so as to facilitate exports. Based on past experience, direct Presidential intervention will be needed to obtain the modest appropriations required to mount an adequate export program.

3. Press the Congress to appropriate the funds requested by the U.S. Travel Service to promote foreign travel in the United States. (The Congress cut them for FY 1964.)[5]

4.[6] Give prompt and effective encouragement, by means of a Presidential statement and widespread publicity, to the "See America" program, including support for earliest practicable Senate action. In view of the delay in this program, it should be extended to include 1965.[7]

---

[4] The Interagency or Cabinet Committee on Export Expansion was established by President Johnson when he signed Executive Order 11132 on December 12, 1963. This committee served in an advisory capacity to the Secretary of Commerce and had as members: Secretary of Commerce, Chairman; Secretary of the Treasury; Secretary of Agriculture; Secretary of State; Secretary of Defense; President of the Export-Import Bank of Washington; Administrator of the Small Business Administration; and Administrator of the Agency for International Development. (28 *Federal Register,* p. 13533; see also Department of State *Bulletin,* January 6, 1964, pp. 25–26)

[5] A handwritten notation by Bundy in the margin next to this paragraph reads: "$19 million."

[6] A handwritten notation by Bundy in the margin to this paragraph reads: "See Lohil Public Committee."

[7] On August 15, 1964, President Johnson announced at a news conference that he had signed a joint resolution, P.L. 88–416 (78 State. 388), and issued a proclamation (Proclamation 3607, "See the United States in 1964 and 1965," August 15 (29 *Federal Register,* p. 11883, 3 CFR 1964 Supp.) calling on American citizens to "see more of our country, to visit and to enjoy our historic shrines and our scenic wonders." See *Public Papers of the Presidents of the United States: Lyndon B. Johnson, 1963–64,* Book II, pp. 964–965, for the complete text of President Johnson's announcement.

5. *Assure enactment of the Interest Equalization Tax without crippling amendments.*

6. Continue efforts to secure freer and more efficient European capital markets, so as to meet their own needs, as well as increased participation in meeting the capital needs of the less developed countries.

7. Review promptly the recommendations of the Presidential Task Force on "Promoting Increased Foreign Investment in United States Corporate Securities and Increased Foreign Financing for United States Corporations Operating Abroad," delivered to you on April 27, 1964.[8] The Secretary of the Treasury will present recommendations to you based on this review.

8. Actively discourage further interest rate increases abroad, particularly in Canada.

Begin Secret

9. *Achieve additional savings in military expenditures.* Secretary McNamara, at President Kennedy's request, proposed a further program of $375 million of reductions over and above the $300 million announced in July. A part of this program was approved in September which is estimated to result in gross savings of approximately $125 million. Among other actions proposed by Secretary McNamara, State and Defense are to prepare a political-military plan of action for review by you for the withdrawal of 10 tactical air squadrons from Europe;[9] Defense has under study a possible reduction of an additional 30,000 Army logistical support personnel in Europe; and State and Defense are keeping under informal review the political-military factors related to a withdrawal of one or both U.S. divisions from Korea. Defense will continue to make every effort to find additional savings, consistent with our basic political-military requirements. (End Secret)

10. *Continue to press vigorous government-industry efforts in military export sales* so that cash receipts may be maintained at least at $1 billion annually.[10]

11. *Urge all agencies and regulatory commissions to take the balance of payments fully into consideration in their policies and decisions.* In its recent report on the balance of payments, the members of the Joint Economic Committee unanimously recommended, "that the Government inten-

---

[8] President Kennedy appointed a Task Force on Promoting Increased Foreign Investment and Increased Foreign Financing on October 2, 1963. The Task Force, chaired by Under Secretary of the Treasury Henry H. Fowler, submitted its report to President Johnson on April 27, 1964; for extracts, see *American Foreign Policy: Current Documents, 1964,* pp. 1182–1190. See also Document 24.

[9] A handwritten notation by Bundy in the margin next to this paragraph reads: "England & France."

[10] A handwritten notation by Bundy in the margin next to this paragraph reads: "Germany Offset."

sify its efforts not only with respect to the balance-of-payments effects of its own expenditures, but also with regard to its regulatory and other activities."[11] Accordingly, we recommend that you send letters to this effect to the heads of all governmental agencies and regulatory commissions appointed by the President.

12. Continue active implementation of the so-called gold budget procedure, whereby the Bureau of the Budget reviews estimates of Government agencies' international transactions and recommends savings. However, it should be recognized that, while a tight rein must be kept on increases in overseas expenditures, significant further savings below those already projected cannot be expected without basic program changes.

CONCLUSION

Having recorded a dramatic improvement in our external payments position since last July, any slackening of our efforts now, in the absence of assurance that this improvement will continue, would seriously weaken confidence in the dollar. So, we must continue to push all parts of our over-all program to eliminate the deficit. This is the only way we can make good on:

—President Kennedy's pledge of February 6, 1961, to achieve overall equilibrium in our international payments and thus halt gold losses,
—your pledge that the dollar will remain fully interchangeable with gold at the present fixed price of $35 an ounce.[12]

---

[11] This report has not been further identified.

[12] On February 6, 1961, President Kennedy delivered a special message to Congress on the gold crisis. In this message, he proposed several initiatives to lower the deficit in the nation's balance of payments and to stem the outflow of gold. For text, see *Public Papers of the Presidents of the United States: John F. Kennedy, 1963*, pp. 57–66.

In his annual message to Congress on the State of the Union, January 8, President Johnson said, "This administration must and will preserve the present gold value of the dollar." See *Public Papers of the Presidents of the United States: Lyndon B. Johnson, 1963–64*, Book I, pp. 112–118, for the complete text of his message.

6.   **Memorandum From the President's Special Assistant for National Security Affairs (Bundy) to Secretary of State Rusk, Secretary of the Treasury Fowler, and Secretary of Defense McNamara[1]**

Washington, May 8, 1964.

SUBJECT

German Offset Purchases and Troop Strength

Following a discussion by the Cabinet Committee on Balance of Payments of German offset purchases as related to U.S. troop deployments in Germany, the President summarized the United States position as follows:[2]

1.   The U.S. supports the existing arrangements for its six-division force in Germany.

2.   These existing arrangements, however, have two components: offset purchases in the previously agreed amounts and U.S. force levels.

3.   If the Germans unilaterally alter the status quo by not living up to their offset commitments to us, we shall be forced to reconsider the question of U.S. force levels.

4.   During his next visit to Germany, Defense Secretary McNamara is to make certain that there is no misunderstanding on the part of the German Government with respect to the above.[3]

McGeorge Bundy[4]

---

[1] Source: Johnson Library, National Security File, Subject File, Balance of Payments, Vol. 1, November 27, 1963 thru October 31, 1964, Box 1. Confidential.

[2] The President met with the Cabinet Committee on Balance of Payments on May 4. No minutes of this meeting have been found, but for Secretary Dillon's memorandum to the President in preparation for the meeting, see Document 4. For the Cabinet Committee report that was discussed at the meeting, see Document 5.

[3] Secretary of Defense McNamara visited Bonn May 9–11 to discuss free world defense policies with German Defense Minister Von Hassel.

[4] Printed from a copy that indicates Bundy signed the original.

7.   Memorandum From Secretary of the Treasury Dillon to
      President Johnson[1]

Washington, May 13, 1964.

SUBJECT

First Quarter Balance of Payments Results

The Department of Commerce has just compiled the preliminary official balance of payments results for the first quarter. As I indicated to you in my memorandum of April 24, 1964,[2] they have included a seasonal adjustment of $250 million which is substantially higher than has been seen in the past for the first quarter. As a result, on a seasonally adjusted basis, our overall deficit for the quarter amounted to $41 million or $165 million at an annual rate. The deficit on regular transactions amounted to $139 million, the difference being accounted for by advance progress payments on military sales. At an annual rate this deficit would be approximately $555 million.

These figures substantially bear out our earlier expectations but they should be heavily qualified when used because of the artificial and temporary nature of the improvement during March. As you will recall, we received an inflow of $250 million in short-term funds from Canada during March, all of which was reversed during the first three weeks of April. We now have the pre-preliminary, "flash" report on the April results which shows a substantial overall deficit, and points to a deficit on regular transactions of at least $395 million for April. Apparently, some of this represented temporary adverse flows that have come back to us early in May. Nevertheless, on an overall basis, the data indicate that so far this year our deficit on regular transactions has been running at an annual rate somewhere between $1.5 and $2 billion. This is right in line with the prognostication of the staff experts of the Cabinet Committee on the Balance of Payments. It underlines the importance of continued governmental efforts in this area, and particularly the crucial importance of favorable Senate action on the interest equalization tax.

Douglas Dillon

---

[1] Source: Johnson Library, White House Central Files, Confidential File, FO 4–1, Balance of Payments (1963–1965), Box 32–39. Confidential.

[2] Document 3.

8.   Letter From President Johnson to Secretary of State Rusk[1]

Washington, May 14, 1964.

Dear Mr. Secretary:

On July 18, 1963, President Kennedy, in a Special Message to Congress on Balance of Payments, outlined a comprehensive program to eliminate the deficit in our balance of payments, and stated that this nation will maintain the dollar as good as gold, freely interchangeable with gold at $35 an ounce.[2] I have reaffirmed the July 18 Message as the policy of this Administration.

The Cabinet Committee on Balance of Payments has reported to me[3] that substantial progress has been made since last July in our program to eliminate the balance-of-payments deficit and that, with continued effort, the targets set in the July 18 Message can be attained. I am gratified by this report and wish to commend you for the contribution that your Agency has made in this effort.

While we can take justified pleasure in our progress, the deficit is still with us and much remains to be done before the job is finished. It remains imperative that we continue to push all parts of our program to achieve equilibrium in our international accounts. Only in this way can we assure that confidence in the dollar will be maintained and that the United States will continue to meet its national objectives, both at home and abroad.

I count on you to continue your efforts.

Sincerely,

Lyndon B. Johnson

---

[1] Source: Department of State, Central Files, FN 12 US. No classification marking.
[2] See footnote 3, Document 5.
[3] Document 5.

9.   Telegram From the Embassy in France to the Department of
      State[1]

Paris, June 16, 1964, 7 p.m.

6157. From Secretary Dillon for Dillon, Ball, Heller, McGeorge
Bundy, William McChesney Martin, Dale and Harley.
      Subject: Group of Ten Ministerial meeting, morning session, June
15.[2]
      1. Ministers and Governors of Group of Ten held full day meeting
at French Finance Ministry June 15 under chairmanship Giscard d'Estaing, to discuss report prepared by their Deputies on outlook for functioning of international monetary system and future liquidity needs.[3]
Secretary Dillon and Governor Daane represented US.
      2. Speaking as Chairman of Deputies, Roosa presented Deputies'
report to Ministers. Underlined that experience of working closely
together for extended period of months had enabled Deputies learn
much about one another's views and had developed spirit of cooperation. Pointed out that in effort sort out differences for Ministers, report
may seem fail put adequate weight on satisfactory functioning of system. Reviewed briefly genesis major recommendations in report—study
of adjustment process, multilateral surveillance, and study group on
reserve assets—pointing out in particular that term "multilateral surveillance" decided upon because it could be used without change in
virtually all of the languages into which report would be translated. On
IMF, Deputies had in mind that after meeting for nearly whole year and
representing substantial share Fund resources, group should appropriately try reach general view, but certainly not get into details properly
left to IMF Executive Directors. Since Deputies had been unable arrive at
agreed position, analysis in report on IMF quotas formulated in terms of
alternatives, with choice left for Ministers. Finally Roosa flagged continuing need for secrecy until Ministerial statement ready for publication
around the time of publication of IMF Annual Report in early August.
Since no general comments on report, discussion moved to specific
agenda topics.

Adjustment Process.

      3. Roosa acknowledged important contribution of German delega-
tion to work of Deputies under this heading. Stressed WP–3 would draw

---

[1] Source: Department of State, Central Files, FN 10. Confidential; Exdis.
[2] The Group of Ten Ministers met in Paris June 15–16 to discuss the international
monetary system.
[3] This report has not been further identified.

upon its examination of current problems as sort of case book for study, and in that way avoid being drawn away from problems of real world into purely theoretical exercise. Kristensen (OECD) said OECD felt WP–3 well qualified undertake this work and that Secretariat would cooperate fully. Schmuecker (Germany) expressed satisfaction of German Govt that its proposals had been recommended by Deputies and reserved right at appropriate time to suggest a final date for report by WP–3. Schweitzer (IMF) stated his understanding IMF would be associated with work of WP–3 in studying adjustment process. Giscard pointed out Group of Ten could not settle this question, which lay within province of OECD, although he personally hoped for satisfactory solution. Kristensen said he supported Schweitzer's point, particularly since terms of reference of WP–3 provide for establishing necessary liaison with other international organizations. Said would present matter of IMF association with WP–3 work on adjustment process to upcoming meeting of EEC as parent body of WP–3. Group then adopted mandate on adjustment process, with Chairman noting German intention to request agreement on date for conclusion, at an appropriate time.

Multilateral Surveillance.

4. Roosa stressed evolutionary nature of concept of multilateral surveillance, which is intensification of process of cooperation and group appraisal that has already been taking place in bodies like Basle meetings of Central Bank Governors and WP–3. A second aspect of this concept is to complete and systematize exchange of information on means of financing B/P deficits and surpluses with appropriate safeguards to protect sensitive data. Since BIS has already been playing important role in this field, Deputies have recommended that it be requested act as center for collection of data and for transmission to WP–3, which will make appraisal. Ferras (BIS) and Holtrop (Netherlands), speaking in his capacity as chairman of BIS Board, confirmed BIS would accept this assignment. Holtrop added that he and fellow Central Bank Governors accepted with understanding it would in no way inhibit Central Banks from discharging their responsibilities for market conditions.

5. Dillon said US feels agreement on multilateral surveillance is point of substantial significance which we strongly support. Said we thought objective fine and were prepared go as far as necessary to achieve it. At same time, recognize that need for prompt action and for confidentiality in market operations will ordinarily preclude prior consultations at time when established bilateral and other assured credit facilities actually used. But do envisage full discussion of uses made of such facilities and of scope for altering or enlarging them. Must also keep constantly and fully in mind need to insure secrecy in order protect market. Feel this whole exercise will strengthen WP–3 and make its work

more effective, particularly work on adjustment process. Cannot yet spell out exactly how all aspects of work should be conducted. Must allow it evolve with experience, in same way as US efforts in past three years.

6. There then followed lengthy discussion of meaning and import of "multilateral surveillance," provoked by question from Maudling (UK) as to how much freedom of action members of group would have under these arrangements both to utilize existing bilateral facilities in case of need, and to work out new or enlarged facilities. Roosa said Deputies had not felt it either feasible or wise to make precise formulation of process involved. Thought it better to have process evolve over time. Everyone recognized need for prompt and decisive action in face of payments emergency. Clear agreement that no obligation consultation prior to use of existing facilities. Only obligation would be let all participants know at least total volume of operation. Then there would follow process of mutual discussion and appraisal, from which all would try to benefit and others to be as helpful as possible to participant in difficulty. Colombo (Italy) and Witteveen (Netherlands) supported this line of agument. Giscard, speaking as French representative, recalled agreed formula for multilateral surveillance much less organized and much less concrete than French had originally proposed and would have liked to see adopted. Said France feels this is most important element to emerge from Deputies' work. Said would like to see this process operate along same lines as formulation of incomes policy in domestic economy: look at consequences of individual actions and decisions on whole and try to reach consensus about general lines to follow. Moreover, felt need for role for Ministers in process, for it often involves decisions with political implications, for which Ministers must take responsibility.

7. Maudling said he was still confused; in the future, would there be any barrier to his entering into bilateral discussions with view to enlarging UK swap with US, for example? Roosa pointed out there would be no such barrier, but in spirit of multilateral surveillance, would be useful discuss with other members of group. Result might be participation of others, better overall arrangement meet problem. Holtrop recalled Central Banks would still be free act in crisis situation, but that multilateral surveillance called for exchange of views on proposed future arrangements, with honest attempt reach mutual understanding. Giscard, Van Lennep (Netherlands) and Colombo all echoed this theme. Blessing said Deputies' report had been wise in leaving discretion to Central Bank Governors re sensitive areas, while at same time putting more discipline into system.

8. Dillon said that since neither WP–3 nor BIS Governors were in continuous session, any arrangement necessary to protect international monetary system could always be put into effect promptly and immedi-

ately and on bilateral basis. But in case of establishment new or enlarged arrangement and in absence of crisis, proposal should be discussed with other Governors in BIS framework. After listening to discussion, participant would be under neither legal nor moral obligation to be bound by discussion. Each party could do what he wanted. However, it was expected all would gain by discussion.

9. Maudling said that despite all of foregoing assurances he was still somewhat unhappy about this proposal, which went rather further than he had thought. Asked his colleagues for time to reflect somewhat further. Accordingly, final decision on multilateral surveillance temporarily passed over.

Study Group on Reserve Assets.[4]

10. Roosa, speaking as Chairman of Deputies, said under Deputies' proposal, this study group would not be concerned with question of whether or not there is need for another kind of reserve asset, but only with detailed descriptions of various types that might be used if such need should develop. Deputies believed this work could proceed without endangering present system and casting doubts on existing reserve assets provided there was careful presentation to outside world. Could say this represented careful forward planning in financial sphere, just as in military sphere governments prepare for contingencies they hope will never materialize. Next spring suggested as target date for completion of work of study group. Group would not be expected reach conclusions, but rather assemble elements for appraisal prior to IMF annual meeting.

11. Dillon said that for the record, while supporting creation of study group, he wanted to outline strong US feelings in this matter. Draft mandate makes clear study should take full account of implications for present international monetary system of various proposals studied. To US this means any new type reserve asset, if found necessary, would be used to add to, supplement and strengthen present reserve assets and not to replace them. In other words, there should be nothing suggested that would in any way impair or inhibit use of present reserve assets and credit facilities. He felt there was clear understanding of this within

---

[4] The Study Group on the Creation of Reserve Assets was known as the Ossola Group after its Chairman, Rinaldo Ossola, Vice Chairman of the Bank of Italy. The May 31, 1965, Report of this Study Group to the Deputies of the G–10 and the July 1964 Report of the June 1964 G–10 Deputies Meeting that established the Study Group are in the Washington National Records Center, RG 56, OASIA Files: FRC 75 A 101, World/1/545, Study Group on Creation of Reserve Assets (Ossola Group), World/1/545, Report to the Deputies of the G–10. This Record Group also contains papers submitted to the Study Group by G–10 members and the IMF during 1964 and 1965; handwritten notes from Study Group meetings taken by George H. Willis, Deputy to the Assistant Secretary of the Treasury for International Affairs; minutes of Study Group meetings; earlier drafts of the May 31, 1965, Report; and a scattering of related items until early 1967.

group, but public presentation must leave no doubts on this score. No Minister challenged or commented on this statement.

12. After adopting draft mandate for study group, morning session concluded.

Bohlen

10.   Telegram From the Embassy in France to the Department of State[1]

Paris, June 16, 1964, 7 p.m.

6156. From Secretary Dillon for Dillon, Ball, Heller, McGeorge Bundy, William McChesney Martin, Dale and Harley.

Subject: Group of Ten Ministerial meeting, afternoon session, June 15.[2]

1. Most of afternoon session of Group of Ten devoted to discussion of IMF quotas. Roosa, speaking as Chairman of Deputies, opened with résumé of this section of Deputies report. Said Deputies had recognized not appropriate attempt reach detailed discussion on IMF quotas in Group of Ten but that they did note central position of IMF in monetary system. Thus saw our study would be incomplete if did not devote considerable attention to this matter. Outlined various points to be considered: (A) selective increases; (B) general increase, where Deputies report presents three alternatives; (C) special arrangements involving Fund: (I) GAB, where no particular recommendation, only that Deputies be asked study in 1965 in light decision on quotas; (II) differing views on size of gold payment. Deputies all hoped Ministers could reach common ground on Fund, before public learned of differences of view within group, and press followed its customary practice of trying to exploit such differences for manufacture of sensational news. Schweitzer (IMF) followed with argument in favor of substantial quota increases. Said relationship between quotas and criteria used to set original quotas (national income, foreign trade, etc.) had fallen from 100 to 35 for all Fund mem-

---

[1] Source: Department of State, Central Files, FN 10. Confidential; Exdis.

[2] For a report of the morning session, see Document 9.

bers in intervening period, to 31 for Ten and 45 for all others. Stressed that meeting of minds among Ten on issue of quota increase would be very helpful in quinquennial review.

2.   Dillon pointed to improvement in US B/P DG 12 months ending next June 30: deficit down to about $1.8 billion on regular transactions, with every expectation improvement will continue; over-all deficit to be financed only $1.25 billion or less because of debt prepayments and advance payments for military equipment. Moreover, private foreign dollar holdings up $1.9 billion in last 18 months, and conversely official holdngs back to level at beginning 1963, down $700 million since first of year. Indication is that private demand for dollars will continue absorb official holdings. This indicates need for expanded IMF quotas.

3.   Dillon said Ten, as countries with greatest responsibility for international monetary system should provide leadership on quota issue, which will arise in quinquennial review in any case. It not conceivable Ten could study monetary system for a whole year and pass over Fund. While it not necessary reach agreement now, or even prior to Tokyo, it should be done before Executive Directors begin their discussions and before world begins to think we cannot find an agreement among ourselves on this subject. At same time must be careful not create impression Ten have arrogated to themselves decision that properly belongs to Fund.

4.   On substance, Dillon described US views as follows:

(A) Favor selective increases, particularly for certain countries that supply usable resources to Fund. These increases would be designed give members in question position within Fund more nearly commensurate with their present economic strength and would replenish Fund's supply of usable currencies. Would also be reply to reports that circulate from time to time about disproportionate US influence in Fund. Recognize actual voting strength has never played important role in Fund's operations, but for our part, would welcome adjustments making combined EEC quotas equal to US quota. Of course, this matter for EEC countries themselves to decide.

(B) On general increase, US favored 50 percent but realized this not supported by others around table whose views we value. Therefore in interest reaching agreement willing suggest range 30 to 35 percent. Believe this reduces difference among us to point where should be possible reach agreement. Would also be prepared agree to spacing of such an increase over time, say five years.

(C) Think it important in connection with quota increase to avoid gold drain from reserve centers into Fund. There are several ways achieve this, but we would suggest limiting gold payments to 5 percent of increase with limiting of gold [garble] drawing rights to amounts actually paid in gold.

(D) Should note that spreading out of actual payment of quotas over time would not solve gold drain problem. But it would moderate pace of LDC drawing on Fund. US believes IMF should remain purely monetary institution. Without quota increase more and more countries will inevitably move into upper credit tranches, and it will become increasingly difficult maintain proper discipline on such drawings.

5. Witteveen (Netherlands), taking familiar Dutch line, questioned that future liquidity needs were justification for quota increase, arguing that question of what these needs were had been referred to study group on reserve assets. In meantime IMF should be satisfied with increase of modest proportions. Dollar holdings in last five years had been too great and had caused inflation in Europe. Fact such holdings now being reduced to manageable proportions not argument for quota increase. Dillon pointed out requirements would increase over next five years and that expansion credit facilities to meet such requirements would not create inflation. Maudling (UK) commented that study group concerned with owned reserves only. Giscard d'Estaing (France) confirmed.

6. In following discussion all delegations indicated support for some kind of action on IMF quotas. Gordon (Canada), Maudling (UK), Wickman (Sweden) and Ishino (Japan) all spoke in favor of substantial general increase, as well as selective increases, using arguments similar to those put forward by Dillon. Colombo (Italy), Blessing (Germany) and Witteveen (Netherlands) supported "modest" or "moderate" general increase, which some of them quantified as 15–20 percent, plus selective increases. Dequae (Belgium) argued no need for general increase but could see justification for selective increases in order realign quota structure in conformity with present economic strength of various members. In subsequent intervention, said would not make oppositign to general increase matter of principle. Giscard made statement in which he suggested over-all increase of 15 percent plus selective increases, or perhaps in monetary terms only slightly more than $2 billion, with total all increases perhaps reaching 20 percent.

7. Germany, Canada and Japan were only countries to indicate they they would be interested in selective increase in their own quota. (In subsequent Deputies' meeting Emminger indicated for planning purposes Germany would not want see own quota increased beyond $1.2 billion as combined result selective and general increase.) Colombo (Italy) made statement that Italy could not envisage selective increase at this time because of unfavorable B/P position. Such increase would be misunderstood by public opinion in Italy.

8. On problem of size of gold payment, Belgium, France, Italy, Netherlands and Germany all spoke in favor maintaining 25 percent requirement, using familiar argument that this necessary keep lid on LDC's and that in any event basic rules of IMF should not be changed

prior to completion Ossola study. Dillon and Maudling argued necessity find method keep gold payments from creating drain on reserve centers. Dillon underlined particular US interest in this point, emphasizing dollar is only currency fully and legally convertible into gold; moreover, in view key position dollar in monetary system, we believe this concerns not only US but all countries. Schweitzer said this very complex and technical problem with many possible variations, which should appropriately be left for study and decision in IMF Board.

9. Holtrop (Netherlands) noted two main tendencies within group, one which said general quota increase should be no higher than 20 percent and another which said it should be no lower than 30 percent. Noted that percentage decided on for general increase would affect countries' attitudes about selective increases. Suggested Deputies should be asked prepare some figures that Ministers could look at in June 16 meeting. This suggestion adopted and further discussion quota problem put over until next day.

Institutional Problems.

10. Giscard explained he must excuse himself for other business. Asked Dillon chair discussion institutional problems.

11. Taking up renewal of GAB first, Dillon said no need discuss now. Deputies should be asked take up after Tokyo, working closely with IMF management. This agreed.

12. Agreement was rapidly reached that Ministers should have continuing roles in studying over-all monetary system including functioning adjustment process and multilateral surveillance. Such role strongly urged by France as of key importance and readily accepted by all others.

13. Once this established, Dillon pointed out that role of group significantly changed from original concept of supervision of GAB. Would seem necessary to keep strict limit on size of group and to assure that membership of Ministerial group and WP–3 be identical. Agreement readily reached on this point.

Kristensen pointed out this meant Japanese entry into WP–3, which would [could?] not be further enlarged. Expressed view this could readily be accomplished. Van Lennep as Chairman of WP–3, said essential in interest effective work limit WP–3 to membership of Group of Ten. De Lattre and Kristensen said Deputies could develop some role for EMA, which would be used to satisfy Austrians and others who would be denied entry into Group of Ten and WP–3.

14. Thus as by-product of meeting, US achieved without argument long sought twin objectives of Japanese membership in WP–3 and agreement on Ministerial level meetings for WP–3, which now identical to Group of Ten but which it understood will take place more frequently in

future and will review work of WP–3. After close of meeting Japanese effusively thanked Dillon for decision on WP–3.

15. Next meeting of Ministers set for Tokyo on Monday,[3] following opening speeches and preceding call on Emperor. Japanese to give working luncheon for Group of Ten Ministers.

16. As to chairmanship, it decided that alphabetical rotation should commence at Tokyo using French language and starting with Italy, which follows France. Italians then suggested they cede Tokyo chairmanship to Japanese, which agreed on understanding Italy would chair December meeting. Meeting then adjourned.

17. Informal agreement reached with France, UK and Germany on US suggestion that next year's chairman of Deputies be Emminger with Plumptre as Deputy. Formal decision left for Tokyo meeting.

Bohlen

---

[3] June 22; no documentation on this meeting has been found.

---

11.   Memorandum From Secretary of the Treasury Dillon to President Johnson[1]

Washington, June 17, 1964.

SUBJECT

   Paris Meeting of Finance Ministers of the Group of Ten on the International Monetary System

The two-day meeting in Paris, June 15 and 16, on the international monetary system went as well as could be expected. Full and acceptable agreements were reached on all phases of the past year's work, except for the exact size of the quota increase to be supported next year in the International Monetary Fund. Ground was laid for an acceptable compromise on this issue within the next month.

A number of institutional changes were approved to further regularize and strengthen cooperation among our governments on interna-

---

[1] Source: Johnson Library, National Security File, Subject File, Trade–General, Vol. 1 [1of 2], Box 47. Official Use Only. Copies were sent to Ball, Heller, Martin, and Bundy.

tional monetary problems. As an important by-product, we obtained, without even trying, two objectives which we have sought in vain over the past two years. One was Japanese entry into Working Party III of the OECD, the restricted group which considers balance of payments and international monetary problems. Second, was an agreement to hold regular ministerial meetings of Finance Ministers to oversee the work of Working Party III. This has seemed particularly important to us because it institutionalizes in solid form the less formal arrangements we have had to date on international monetary cooperation.

Another plus out of the year's work and the decisions of the Ministers was the satisfaction expressed in the present workings of the international monetary system and the agreement that any changes in the future should be evolutionary in nature and not revolutionary. The more extreme suggestions of some, and in particular the main thrust of the French attack on the dollar, have been permanently sidetracked.

Certain possible improvements in the system, of a less radical nature, have been assigned to a working level group for about nine months further study designed not to reach conclusions, but to clearly specify how the various alternatives would work, and what the advantages and disadvantages of each would be, including their effect on the present working of the international monetary system. This will enable the Ministers' Deputies to consider these questions substantively next spring and summer and report to the Ministers prior to the 1966 meeting of the International Monetary Fund.

The major discussion centered around the size and form of the increase in the International Monetary Fund which the representatives of the Ten would support next year when a regular five-year review of IMF operations is scheduled to take place. The United States, supported by the United Kingdom, had originally felt that quotas in the Fund should be increased by as much as 50% with some additional increases for certain countries, in particular Germany, whose quotas do not adequately reflect their present economic strength. We realized from the first that this position was somewhat extreme and would probably have to be compromised. On the other side, the French, the Dutch and the Belgians started out believing that there should be no increase at all in the quotas of the Monetary Fund. The Deputies, during their ten months' work, were unable to make any progress in compromising these extreme positions.

During the meeting we proposed as a compromise an increase of somewhere between 30 and 35% *plus* further selected increases for certain countries, such as Germany. The Common Market countries, on the other hand, for the first time all accepted the principle of an increase. They presented a united front which stopped at a total of 20%, *including* special increases for certain countries.

After a clear impasse was reached, the French Finance Minister adjourned the conference briefly for private talks with a few leading Ministers. At that time I told him that as a rock bottom we would accept a 25% increase *plus* selected increases for Germany and certain other members. I said that if this was not acceptable, we would be forced to carry the argument to the International Monetary Fund Executive Board during their regularly scheduled review next year, and at that time we would naturally return to our original 50% position and all others would be free to do likewise. The Common Market Ministers were extremely agitated by this thought, since it would be far more difficult for them to maintain their extreme position in the IMF forum where the underdeveloped countries, all of whom want large increases, are represented. The Managing Director of the Fund, Mr. Schweitzer, a Frenchman, who was present at our meetings, was very helpful since he stated that a 25% general increase was the smallest that he could in good conscience recommend.

Accordingly, the matter was put over for further consideration next month after the Common Market Ministers have another chance to meet together in one of their regularly scheduled meetings. It was clear that all of them will recommend acceptance of our proposal rather than risk moving the argument into the IMF forum. Our final proposal is also acceptable to the U.K.

It was obvious that at this meeting the EEC Ministers were operating under strict directives from higher authority, de Gaulle in the case of the French, which did not permit them to agree to any compromise that went beyond their proposal. Since the further increase we are asking of them is not really very great, and since they are extremely anxious to avoid the consequences of a public split within the IMF, I am reasonably confident that they will accede to our compromise in the course of the next month. Such a compromise would represent achievement of the minimum position which had been agreed upon here on an inter-agency basis before the Paris meeting.

Douglas Dillon[2]

---

[2] Printed from a copy that indicates Dillon signed the original.

12.   Editorial Note

On September 2, 1964, President Johnson signed into law P.L. 88–563, formally known as the Interest Equalization Tax. (H.R. 8000, 88th Congress; 78 Stat. 809) This tax was designed to increase the cost to foreigners of obtaining long-term capital in the United States. It was intended to reduce a heavy outflow of dollars resulting from borrowing and stock issues of foreign governments and businesses in the United States, which was a major factor in the balance-of-payments deficit.

President Kennedy first introduced the idea of an Interest Equalization Tax in a special message he delivered to Congress on July 18, 1963. For text, see *Public Papers of the Presidents of the United States: John F. Kennedy, 1963*, pages 574–584.

The tax was designed to increase the cost of foreign borrowing in this manner: Americans would pay a tax (at rates provided in the bill) when they acquired a foreign security (primarily stocks or bonds). It was expected that the American purchasers would pass on the extra cost of the tax to the foreigner either through charging a higher interest rate on a loan or by demanding a discount on the purchase of stock. The tax rates provided in this law were designed to increase the cost of borrowing in the United States by about 1 percent. With that increase, the cost of obtaining capital in the United States was expected to be at a level comparable with European markets and, the administration hoped, make the American markets less attractive to foreigners. Less foreign borrowing would cut the outflow of dollars from the United States and improve the nation's balance of payments. (*Congressional Quarterly Almanac*, volume XX, pages 545–550)

On the same day, September 2, 1964, President Johnson issued Executive Order 11175 (29 *Federal Register*, page 12605) exempting the application of the Interest Equalization Tax to the acquisition by a U.S. citizen of stock or debt obligation of Canada. The exemption had been discussed with Canadian representatives in July 1963. (For text of a joint U.S.–Canadian statement on the proposed Interest Equalization Tax, dated July 21, 1963, see Department of State *Bulletin*, August 12, 1963, page 256.) On September 3, President Johnson issued Executive Order 11176, which allowed for the inspection of certain Interest Equalization Tax information returns by the Board of Governors of the Federal Reserve System and the Federal Reserve Banks. (Circular telegram 437, September 4; Department of State, Central Files, FN 16 US)

13.   Telegram From Prime Minister Wilson to President Johnson[1]

London, October 24, 1964.

T57W/64. Following is message from Prime Minister to President.

My first task on forming my administration has been to undertake with my senior colleagues a thorough review of our present financial and economic situation.

We knew, while in opposition, that the position was deteriorating: but we deliberately refrained from turning it into a major election issue in order not to undermine confidence.

Now that we have examined all the facts I find the situation is even worse than we had supposed. In brief, we are faced with a probable deficit on external account for this year which may be as high as 800 million: and a suspected deficit, for next year, if we do nothing about it, which, while much less, would still be quite unacceptable.

My colleagues and I have therefore determined to take firm remedial measures. In deciding on our programme of action we have been guided by two main purposes. First, to avoid a repetition of the stop and go policies which have plagued the steady growth of the British economy since the end of the war. Secondly, to ensure that the short term measures which are necessary to meet the immediate situation should not hamper our action to get the balance of the economy right for the longer term.

We have considered and rejected two alternative courses of action: the first, with all its repercussions on the international exchanges, will be obvious to you, and this we have rejected now, and for all time: the second, an increase in interest rates, I am against in principle both because of its restrictive effect on the economy and because of its impact on your own problems, especially at this time. Our immediate situation has to be dealt with by means which we would, of course, have preferred to avoid both for the sake of the British public at home and our friends overseas.

On Monday, the government will be telling the nation what the situation is and announcing an eight point programme to set the economy moving on the right lines.[2]

The programme in brief is as follows:

---

[1] Source: Department of State, Central Files, FN 12 UK. Top Secret; Exdis. The times of transmission and receipt are illegible.

[2] On October 26, the British Government announced a plan to correct the United Kingdom's balance-of-payments deficit, estimated between £700,000 and £800,000 for 1964. The plan's principal measures comprised a 15 percent surcharge on all manufactured or semi-manufactured imports and a system of export rebates averaging 1-1/2 percent.

1. Steps to reduce imports from all sources by imposing a system of temporary charges on all imports, with the exception of foodstuffs, unmanufactured tobacco and basic raw materials.

2. Plans to increase exports, including a scheme for relieving exporters of some part of the burden of indirect taxation which enters into the cost of production of exports, unimproved export credit facilities, the establishment of a Commonwealth exports council, cooperative selling arrangements for small firms.

3. Consultation with both sides of industry on plans to increase productivity and to evolve an incomes policy related to productivity: A price review body to be established.

4. A policy to make it easier for workers to change their jobs in accordance with the needs of technological progress.

5. A policy to foster more rapid development in the underemployed areas of the country.

6. A strict review of all government expenditures. The object will be to relieve the strain on the balance of payments and to release resources for more productive purposes by cutting out expenditure on items of low economic priority, such as prestige projects. The government are communicating to the French Government their wish to re-examine urgently the prestige project.[3]

7. The social programmes of the government to be unfolded in the Queen's speech.

8. Consultation with the International Monetary Fund on the use by the United Kingdom of its drawing rights.

I have thought it right to let you know what we propose in advance of any public statement, first because I set great store by close and continuing co-operation with the American administration over the whole international field, economic and commercial as well as political and military, and also because my colleagues and I are most grateful for the co-operation we are receiving in these difficult times from the United States authorities. Some of the measures we shall have to take will hurt, but I can give you my assurance that not only are they temporary and not intended to be protectionist, but we consider them essential if we are to have a strong economy as a basis for playing our proper part in international affairs.

We have sent Sir Eric Roll[4] to explain these measures in more detail to members of your administration.

---

[3] Reference is to the Concorde airplane, a joint French-British Government effort, which was considered a "prestige project." Prime Minister Wilson's wish to re-examine the Concorde project aroused deep concern in France, and Roy Jenkins, U.K. Minister of Aviation, visited Paris October 29–30 for talks with several French Ministers.

[4] U.K. Permanent Under Secretary, Minister of Economic Affairs.

The Foreign Secretary will be in Washington this coming weekend and will be able to put our action in the economic [illegible source text] into the perspective of our general approach to international problems.

---

14.   Telegram From President Johnson to Prime Minister Wilson[1]

Washington, October 24, 1964, 2326Z.

CAP 64270. For the Prime Minister from the President. For morning delivery.

Thank you for your message giving me the outlines of your new economic program and for the further details given us today by Eric Roll.[2]

While we always regret the recourse to restrictive measures I fully recognize the need for strong action in defense of sterling. I welcome your assurance the import surcharges are temporary in nature and will be removed as soon as your balance of payments permits.

I am also most pleased at your desire to avoid recourse to higher interest rates.

I wish you every success in your effort to protect the pound. Success in this effort will reinforce the position of the whole free world.

---

[1] Source: Department of State, Central Files, FN 12 UK. Confidential; Exdis.

[2] See Document 13. No record of Roll's meeting with U.S. officials on this occasion has been found.

15.   Circular Telegram From the Department of State to Certain Posts[1]

Washington, October 26, 1964, 6:10 p.m.

739. For policy guidance and background information texts are reproduced below of statement by State and press release by Treasury Department concerning new balance-of-payments program announced today by United Kingdom government.[2]

In discussions of new British program, US reps should indicate some reservation and caution as to acceptability of British line of action, in spite of fact that public statements by USG necessarily somewhat optimistic since faced by fait accompli. US of course recognizes need for remedial measures by UK. At same time problems will be created for international economic policies and multilateral arrangements such as GATT and IMF. Much will depend on implementing measures adopted by UK and on duration of program. Further guidance will follow as appropriate, and reporting of effects and reactions to British program is requested.

Begin Unclassified

Statement by State Department to press, October 26:

US Comments on British Moves to Deal with Balance of Payments Problems

The United States Government welcomes the speed and vigor with which the British Government has moved to deal with the problems relating to its balance of payments and to the underlying economic situation of the United Kingdom. While we naturally regret that the situation has led the British Government to deem it necessary to resort to emergency import charges, we are gratified that these charges are to be nondiscriminatory, and by the categorical assurance that the charges are strictly temporary and will be reduced and eliminated as soon as possible. The United States Government is confident that the wholehearted cooperation of the British Government in the Kennedy Round will in no way be impaired. The United States Government stands ready to cooperate in any way that it appropriately can with the British Government in dealing with these problems.

For release at 9 A.M., Eastern Standard Time, Monday, October 26, 1964

---

[1] Source: Department of State, Central Files, FN 12 UK. Limited Official Use; Priority; VerbatimText. Drafted by Leocade Leighton (E/OFE) on October 26; cleared by Frank M. Tucker (EUR/BNA), Joseph A. Greenwald (E/OT), Thomas E. Summers (EUR/RPE), and Widman (Treasury); and cleared by Benjamin Caplan (E/OFE). The telegram was sent to 56 posts.

[2] Regarding the October 26 British announcement, see Document 13.

The United States Treasury today issued the following statement:

The new British Government has acted promptly and effectively to maintain the strength and stability of the pound sterling. Its temporary measures strike at the inflated imports which have been the principal source of immediate pressure on the pound. Its longer-run measures affecting productivity, incomes and prices can provide the improvement that is needed in the competitive position of the United Kingdom in world markets.

It is gratifying that the action taken is nondiscriminatory in form and avoids any damaging repercussions upon the functioning of the international monetary system. The import charges will for a time have a moderately adverse effect upon our trade as well as upon that of other countries but there is no painless corrective, either for the United Kingdom or for the rest of the world. The United States welcomes the British determination to reduce and remove these import charges at the earliest opportunity.

Existing arrangements for international financial cooperation have proved their effectiveness in recent years and are again demonstrating their capacity to maintain the smooth functioning of the international monetary system.

Rusk

---

16.   Telegram From Prime Minister Wilson to President Johnson[1]

London, October 27, 1964, 1980Z.

T75W/64. Very many thanks for your prompt and helpful reply to my message about our economic situation.[2]

Our plan has now been launched, and it has, on the whole, been very well received both at home and abroad. People seem to think it a sensible start to a vigorous attack on our problems. As a result, sterling is already strengthening and the stock market is more than steady. There have, of course, been some squeals from overseas, but these are mostly for the record.

---

[1] Source: Department of State, Central Files, FN 12 UK. Confidential.

[2] See Documents 13 and 14.

Without your sympathetic understanding and the co-operative attitude of your administration as demonstrated in Mr. Dillon's statement,[3] we should have had a much more difficult task ahead of us. Naturally this makes us all the more determined that the dislocations caused by our policies should be removed as soon as possible. Once again may I say how much I appreciate what you said and I at least realise that this was not easy in the middle of an exhausting election. Thank you very much.

---

[3] Presumably a reference to the Treasury's October 26 statement; see Document 15.

---

17.   Letter From the Chairman of the Cabinet Committee on Balance of Payments (Dillon) to President Johnson[1]

Washington, October 30, 1964.

Dear Mr. President:

I have completed a review of our balance of payments position at this time, a review based on complete data for the first half of this year and partial data for the third quarter. This review shows that our national balance of payments program has produced striking results.

Our payments deficit on regular transactions through September of this year has been running at an annual rate of about $2 billion, against $3.9 billion in 1960 and $3.3 billion in 1963.

Our performance in selling goods abroad has made an important contribution to this improved position. Our exports this year have continued to run at record levels. They are 12 percent above a year ago and 27 percent above the 1960 level. Much of this improvement reflects the stable price level we have achieved domestically over these years, making our goods increasingly competitive in markets abroad.

Our imports have also risen as would be expected with the improved performance of our domestic economy—but at a slower rate than exports. As a result, our surplus on commodity trade is running close to $6-1/2 billion, as compared with about $4-1/2 billion in 1960 and $5 billion in 1963.

---

[1] Source: Johnson Library, National Security File, Subject File, Balance of Payments, Vol. 1, November 27, 1963 thru October 31, 1964, Box 1. No classification marking.

A very significant part of the improvement in our balance of payments results from the actions we have taken to cut the outflow of dollars for Government spending abroad. In that regard, we are well on our way toward reaching the target of a $1 billion reduction in Government spending from 1962 levels which was set in President Kennedy's Balance of Payments Message of July 18, 1963.[2] During the fiscal year ended last June 30, we achieved more than one-half of that target. The impact of our aid expenditures abroad during that year was $340 million less than in 1962, while military expenditures and procurement of strategic goods were down by $180 million. And this was accomplished in the face of substantially rising costs abroad.

We must, of course, to protect our balance of payments position, carry forward and realize full success in achieving the $1 billion target—which will then have virtually its entire impact on our balance of payments in 1965.

On capital account, the flow of our savings into securities dropped to about $400 million, compared with $1.7 billion in the previous twelve months. While performance on our other capital accounts has been less satisfactory, expanding investment opportunities here at home have improved the attractiveness of investment in the United States—both for American and foreign investors.

This over-all improvement in our balance of payments has been the key factor inspiring new confidence in the dollar in markets throughout the world. This improvement has been crucial

—in bringing our gold losses to a halt—indeed, our total gold holdings so far this year have shown an increase for the first time in seven years; and
—in sustaining the close international financial relationships which have been developed to provide an effective answer to any speculative outburst against our currency in world markets.

The job is not yet complete—a gap still remains. That gap must be closed. But we have taken a long step forward. With the combined effort of Government and private sectors, we can reach that goal.

Douglas Dillon

---

[2] See footnote 3, Document 2.

18.   Letter From the Chairman of the Task Force on Foreign Economic Policy (Kaysen) to President Johnson[1]

Washington, November 25, 1964.

Dear Mr. President:

Attached is the report of your Task Force on Foreign Economic Policy. It is the product of earnest thought and discussion carried on over a period of several months. It represents a genuine consensus on the nature of our goals in foreign economic policy, their relative importance in our foreign policy as a whole, and the principal means to achieve them.

The Task Force included consultants from outside the Government, all of whom have had intimate experience with the problems of foreign economic policy in both Government and non-Government activity, and experienced and responsible officers of your Administration, charged with the formulation and execution of polices in this sphere. The report accordingly embodies not only our judgment of what is desirable, but the fruit of hard experience in assessing what is necessary and possible.

You instructed all your Task Forces to disregard narrow problems of feasibility in terms of domestic political tactics. We have followed that instruction; but we are aware that some of our recommendations do not fit the going assumptions about domestic politics that currently condition foreign economic policy. We recognize that this poses a vital question for you of assessing what kind of new political consensus can be developed and what policies it should be used to support.

May I express the thanks of the whole committee for the opportunity to be of service to you in your vital tasks.

Respectfully yours,

Carl Kaysen

Attachment[2]

REPORT OF THE PRESIDENT'S TASK FORCE ON FOREIGN ECONOMIC POLICY

Introduction and Summary

A. Foreign Policy in the Coming Decade—The Economic Challenge

Since the end of the Second World War, the dominant theme of United States foreign policy has been the confrontation with the Soviet

---

[1] Source: Department of State, S/P Files: Lot 70 D 199, Economic Policy—1964. Secret.

[2] Secret. The Appendixes are not printed.

Union, the leader of the Communist world. The main content of policy was military or quasi-military. No similar single overriding concern will dominate foreign policy in the years ahead. One central theme will be our relations with the two-thirds of the world's people who live in the poor countries. In part as a consequence of this shift of focus from East-West relations to North-South relations, the instruments of policy will be increasingly economic. But, even within the developed world, economic concerns will grow in importance not only in our relations with the other advanced countries of the Free World but in our relations with the Communist bloc.

In the immediate aftermath of the War, American policy addressed itself to relief and reorganization of shattered nations. When the Soviet threat emerged in north Iran, Greece and Berlin, emphasis shifted to military and quasi-military responses. We deployed the weapons of economic policy essentially as an adjunct to the political-military effort to contain the Soviet thrust. Even in the Marshall Plan the element of confrontation with Communism, internal and external, was of decisive importance. Aid to the economies of Western Europe became an aspect of the development of the North Atlantic Alliance.

This emphasis on the military features of policy intensified after the outbreak of the Korean War. The bulk of United States foreign assistance went to support weak states on the periphery of the Soviet Bloc with whom we were in military alliance. In Europe our economic policies were organized around the drive toward a united Western Europe seen as a counterweight to the Soviets.

Developments of the last few years have changed the elements of this post-War policy. The Soviet Union has apparently accepted the present facts of military power in an age of nuclear missiles. So long as we maintain our own defenses at an appropriate level of effectiveness, we can anticipate that the Soviets will continue to accept these facts. Further, while we hope for progress in arms control and disarmament that will institutionalize the stability of East-West military relations, the Task Force's recommendations do not depend on this.

Change has affected the coalitions as well as their leaders. The other countries of the Communist world are increasingly pursuing their own national interests. They are less willing to accept a unilateral Soviet definition of what their course should be. In Europe itself, which was both the main arena and the main prize of the post-War struggle, the nations of the West have renewed their economic strength and demonstrated their political stability. China, it is true, continues to be a military threat to its neighbors as well as a trouble maker all over the underdeveloped world. But, in terms of demands upon our policies and our resources, the Chinese threat is of a different order of magnitude from that posed by Soviet policy in the 40's and 50's. For all these reasons, the military confrontation that has dominated the recent past can be expected to assume a lesser position in the future.

In these circumstances, relations with the underdeveloped world will come to occupy an increasingly critical place in United States foreign policy. Eighty-five poor nations contain two-thirds of the world's people. For the most part these nations are new, their governments are inexperienced and unstable, and they are in the grip of rapid change. In the pre-War period, most of these peoples were organized and governed under the colonial system. The disappearance of the system has made them visible and audible to the whole world. Despite their weaknesses they are a real factor in world politics. The sheer weight of numbers would make them important. Their significance is magnified by the UN system, by political and economic competition between and within the two great coalitions, and by the fact that the population of the southern hemisphere is mostly colored. For these reasons we have come increasingly to recognize that a view of the world centered on the North Atlantic is a parochial one.

All in all, the less developed world looks to be both the greatest challenge to our creative powers and the largest source of cumulating instability in the years ahead. The United States, the leading power and the richest country in the world, has an immense stake in a process of change in these countries which, though it cannot be smooth and painless, leads toward stable, open societies. That alone is sufficient to focus our attention and effort. Beyond this interest is our deeper, humanitarian concern in improving standards of life in the poorer two-thirds of the world. It is proper to argue a course of policy on grounds of interest but it would be both unwise and untrue to American tradition to deny its humane foundations. Since material progress is a necessary condition for the kind of change we seek in the less developed countries, economic questions will form the main substance of our relations with them.

Our relations with Western Europe, Canada, Japan, Australia, and New Zealand will likewise increasingly reflect economic concerns. The United States no longer occupies the dominant position it did in the first post-War decade. Their renewed strength and the military stalemate have permitted these countries to take independent and often irritating political positions. The Western Alliance, like the Communist coalition, has become looser. Nevertheless, the basic domestic political aims of governments in the Western coalition are increasingly similar and our national economies are more and more interdependent.

In the past two decades, we have made progress towards a working system of economic relations within this developed world, a system that permits all countries to pursue their common economic goals—prosperity, growing output and expanding trade. Economic welfare in all these countries, as well as our own, depends heavily on the effectiveness of this machinery and on further advance towards a unified economy for the whole area. Moreover, in the present circumstances, continued elaboration of common economic institutions may provide the best available approach to the goal of North Atlantic unity.

In the last analysis, developed and underdeveloped worlds are linked within the context of economic policy, even more than we sometimes thought they were in the context of military alliances. The prosperity and growth of the developed world affects the prospects of the underdeveloped world directly through the flow of trade. Equally important is the impact of prosperity in the advanced countries on their willingness to give aid. At the same time, prosperity and progress in the developed world cannot long remain secure in the face of misery and violence in the poor countries.

This picture, with its strong emphasis on economic, rather than military, problems, is drawn in the broadest strokes. The concrete everyday world of foreign policy will doubtless continue to be filled with alarms and uncertainties, whether in the familiar terrain of Berlin, the Taiwan Straits, the Congo and Indonesia or in new arenas. Yet even these will alter because they are less likely to trigger a Soviet-American clash.

Economic policies by their nature operate over the long term. Thus there is ordinarily some leeway in the timing of decision and the execution of policy. But this should not blind us to the need to initiate action well before crises develop, and to persevere even when results are not immediately visible.

Our effectiveness in achieving the goals toward which the recommendations of the Task Force are directed will bulk large in the historical appraisal of America's performance in these years.

The subsequent sections of this summary contain the most important recommendations of the Task Force and the reasoning supporting them. A more detailed analysis of the basis of these recommendations and further proposals for action are contained in chapters on Aid (I), Trade (II), and Money (III).

[Here follow the rest of the Introduction and Summary; Chapter One, "Aid;" and Chapter Two, "Trade." Chapter One and pages 19–26 of Chapter Two are printed in volume IX, Document 20.]

Chapter Three

Money

Three important tasks remain on the agenda of international financial policy for the new Administration. These are (I) Ending the deficit in the U.S. balance of payments. (II) Protecting U.S. gold reserves against conversion of outstanding dollars. (II) Reforming the international monetary system.

Solid progress toward all three goals has been made in the past 3-1/2 years. But we are not yet out of the woods. As the leader of the Free World, the U.S. continues to bear heavy commitments overseas for defense. Elsewhere in this report the Task Force stresses the critical need for increasing development assistance and for liberalizing trade flows especially from developing countries. Another task force urges the importance of full prosperity and rapid economic growth at home. International financial difficulties can seriously jeopardize both U.S. leadership abroad and U.S. prosperity at home. It is the job of international financial policy to facilitate the basic objectives of foreign and domestic policy.

I. Ending the payments deficit

Table I indicates the progress that has been made in reducing the deficit since 1960. The reduction of the officially financed deficit, col. (3), is especially encouraging. This is the part which we must finance either from our reserves of gold or its equivalent or by adding to the potential claims on our reserves held by foreign central banks and governments. It must be our objective to reduce this figure to zero, or even to convert it to a surplus for two or three years. The remainder of the total deficit represents accumulation of short term dollar claims by private individuals, businesses, and banks abroad, and by nonmonetary international and regional organizations. Since expansion of world trade and the world economy increases their needs for dollar balances, a moderate deficit in column (2) is normal and poses a distinctly lesser threat to U.S. reserves.

TABLE 1

U.S. Balance of Payments Deficits 1960-64 (billions of dollars)

| | (1) | (2) | Officially Financed | | | | |
| | | | (3) | (4) | (5) | (6) | (7) |
Calendar Year	Regular Deficit	Privately Financed[1]	Total	By Gold	By Short Term Claims	By IMF	Other-wise[2]
1960	3.9	0.3	3.6	1.7	1.1	0.4	0.4
1961	3.1	1.1	2.0	0.9	0.6	0.1	0.6
1962	3.6	0.2	3.4	0.9	0.7	0.6	1.2
1963	3.3	0.6	2.7	0.5	1.6	0.0	0.6
1964 (est.)	2.5	1.2	1.3	0.2	0.5	0.3	0.3

[1] Includes nonmonetary international and regional organizations.
[2] Advance repayment of long term debt to U. S., advances on U. S. military exports.

Further progress depends mainly on a continuation of current policies. There are no new measures that deserve serious consideration unless the situation deteriorates or unless improvement is disappointingly slow. Some measures currently in force are expedients counter to basic U.S. policy and should be abandoned when the situation permits.

Capital movements. The Interest Equalization Tax, effective retroactively as of July 1963, has helped the balance of payments by cutting the outflow of portfolio capital by $1 billion a year. It is scheduled to expire December 31, 1965; hence a decision is required fairly soon whether to ask for extension.

As of now, an extension appears necessary. However, the measure is not desirable as a permanent fixture and it will become less effective the longer it is used. Some issues now postponed because the tax is expected to be temporary will be floated when it is extended. Ways of evading the tax will be found. Funds will flow out through channels not now taxed or controlled, such as direct investment by U. S. corporations. Meanwhile we may hope that the development of European capital markets and the decline of profit opportunities in Europe relative to those at home will reduce the investment outflow. In this connection, it is important to maintain strong incentives for domestic investment, especially an expanding domestic economy operating close to its capacity. It is also important to maintain diplomatic pressure, in OECD and elsewhere, for the improvement, liberalization, and internationalization of European capital markets.

If, contrary to present indications, the balance of payments deterio-rates, further measures to limit capital outflows would be the first line of defense. Under existing legislation, the President can extend the Interest Equalization Tax to bank loans beyond one year—a step which could have substantial results. The present exemption of Canadian issues from the tax can be terminated. Additional steps would include further meas-ures to tax or control all bank lending to foreign borrowers. In the event of a serious deterioration, corporate direct investment in developed countries could be temporarily limited. Although capital controls are not desirable and are difficult to administer, they are used by almost all other countries and it is the view of the Task Force that they are preferable to restrictions on trade or tourism.

European governments have kept the U.S. under considerable dip-lomatic and economic pressure to tighten monetary policy and to raise interest rates. Anti-inflationary monetary policies in several European countries have recently raised interest rates there.

In the U. S. during the past 3-1/2 years, the policies of the Federal Reserve and the Treasury have partially reconciled and partially com-promised the conflicting claims upon them—external pressures for higher rates and the needs of the domestic economy for monetary expan-sion. The Task Force does not believe that these policies have assigned too low a priority to external balance. As the balance of payments stands now, we would not recommend tighter monetary policy until and unless it is appropriate for the U. S. economy. We cannot in the long run solve our persistent payments problem by attracting funds at rates which are out of line with domestic profit opportunities. Of course the Federal Reserve must be ready to engineer sharp temporary increases in short term rates in case of a speculative flight from the dollar.

Government outlays abroad. Federal overseas programs already bear a large share of the burden of adjustment to the payments deficit. Government outlays abroad must pass a more severe test than other budget expenditures. To save foreign exchange, preference in procurement is given to U.S. suppliers even when their costs are higher, and foreign aid is tied to purchases in the U.S. These programs must be continued, at least for the immediate future; indeed, the expansion in aid the Task Force recommends will have to be so far as possible an expansion of tied aid. But the Task Force does not believe we should otherwise extend measures of this kind. Over the long run, indeed, as the balance of payments improves, we should try to return to the principle that all government expenditures, whether in dollars or foreign currency, should be judged by the same criteria, balancing their benefits against their dollar costs. Of course, economies justified on their own merits should always be sought. In the next few years, considerable savings may be possible in military outlays overseas.

Goods and Services. The U.S. has a large and growing export surplus. Although the steady expansion of business activity has increased our imports, our exports have advanced even faster. U.S. exports have been helped by the continued expansion of the European and Japanese economies and by an improved competitive position. American labor costs and prices have been stable while our major competitors have been experiencing moderate inflation. Price and cost stability continues to be important for the U.S. We do not yet know what upward pressures on wages and prices will result from further reduction in unemployment and excess capacity. Lacking direct powers, the Administration has no choice but to continue the policy of "moral suasion" exemplified by the wage-price guideposts, choosing carefully the strategic occasions when the influence of the President and of public opinion can be effective.

The government can do very little else in this field. Campaigns for promoting U.S. exports and attracting tourists to our shores can be continued and improved. We have rightly avoided both export subsidies and the imposition of import duties or quotas for balance of payments reasons. In the Kennedy Round and other commercial policy negotiations, we must of course protect the balance of payments. But it is doubtful that these negotiations can improve our position. U.S. travel abroad is a large and growing deficit item. But restrictions on such travel would be difficult to enforce, politically unpopular, and contrary to the larger interests of U.S. foreign policy.

II. Managing Existing Dollar Holdings

The $12-1/2 billion of official short term dollar obligations held by foreign central banks remain a serious problem to the United States. By ingenuity, innovation, and tireless negotiation, U.S. officials have managed over the past 3-1/2 years to increase this figure by about $2 billion while losing only $2.2 billion of gold. Nevertheless, it is clear that some countries would prefer more gold and fewer dollars than they now hold. Solution of the U.S.'s chronic balance of payments difficulties would undoubtedly increase foreign willingness to hold dollars. Even then, however, gold withdrawals might be triggered by temporary U.S. deficits or by political events; and they can always be used as a diplomatic weapon against the U.S.

The present situation reflects a delicate balance of interests. The parties have some interests in conflict, and some in common. The U.S. wishes to protect its gold reserve while maintaining the convertibility of gold and dollars at the established rate. Therefore, the U.S. is led to take measures, sometimes in serious conflict with basic objectives of foreign and domestic policy, to maintain the confidence of its short term creditors. While their potential claims on gold give these creditors considerable power, they cannot press the U.S. too hard. Large withdrawals of gold from the U.S. might force the U.S. off gold, impairing the gold value of the creditors' dollars and damaging the whole international monetary system. Moreover, while these countries push the U.S. to solve its balance of payments problem, not all solutions are palatable to them. They do not welcome the prospect of an increased U.S. export surplus, a solution which would subject them to increased competition at home and abroad. Neither do they welcome reduction of U.S. military outlays in Europe. They prefer U.S. measures to limit public and private flows of capital.

Thus the U.S., though superficially in the suppliant position of a debtor dependent on the goodwill and forebearance of its creditors, holds some strong cards. It is not easy to play them, or even to make credible threats to play them. The cards must remain implicit in the background of the dialogue. But it is important that neither side forget they are there. All countries have a common stake in the effective functioning of the payments system. We should use these realities, so far as possible, to obtain understandings that our existing obligations will not be converted into gold.

This is one important objective of U.S. international monetary negotiations in the next few years. A second and broader objective is permanent general improvement in the world monetary system, for which studies and negotiations are already under way. (See Part III.) These two goals of negotiation are interrelated. The extent to which existing dollar obligations need to be consolidated and the time when this should be done depend in part on the course and the success of the wider negotiations. A general strengthening of the system will diminish its potential instability and increase confidence in the gold-dollar parity. What the U.S. must guard against, however, is the danger that our share of the benefits of general monetary reform might be dissipated in paying off old short term debts. Any general monetary improvement, whether in the IMF or elsewhere, will make additional reserve assets or additional international credit available to the participants, including the U.S. The purposes are to smooth the adjustment to future imbalances, not to alter the financing of past deficits, and to add to the stock of world reserves, not to replace the dollars now in use. These purposes would not be accomplished if, as the French proposal originally contemplated, the U.S. were forced to use the new international reserve and credit facilities to repay old debts. If this were the only benefit to the U.S., the game would not be worth the candle.

We need have no apologies for providing the world with dollar reserves in the past. We must insist that bygones be bygones, and that the improvements in the monetary system are built on the assumption that existing dollar debts continue to be held in one form or another.

Long-Run Borrowing in Foreign Currency. The most promising method of consolidating debts is probably to convert them into long term debts carrying an exchange guarantee.

Over the past three years, we have introduced a new type of instrument into the world's payments system in the form of U.S. securities denominated in foreign currencies. At present we have outstanding to four European countries a total of $1 billion in obligations denominated in their currencies, with maturities ranging up to two years. For the creditors, these securities provide an exchange guarantee in terms of their own currency and their issuance thus removes one important reason for reluctance to hold U.S. obligations. Our issuance of such securities has provided a means for dealing with new dollars coming into official reserves abroad from current transactions and for converting existing dollar holdings into longer term debt.

We should seek much longer maturities for these obligations. The U.S. is certainly a prime credit risk and the precedent of the Marshall Plan should have some weight. The Task Force believes that the U.S. could over time contemplate gaining $5–7 billion of such longer term loans with maturities of, say, ten to fifteen years. In some cases, central banks may be convinced that the extension of long-term credit is a feasible use of their reserves. In other cases, the foreign governments themselves must be convinced of the desirability of budgeting for such investment funds received from taxes or domestic borrowing. Either result will take time to accomplish but the objective of longer term credit should remain.

To some extent countries will be reluctant to tie up their international reserves in longer term loans for fear that their own payments positions will deteriorate meanwhile. This fear can be allayed by bilateral or multilateral arrangements which would insure that in such contingency the U.S. will either repay the loan early, or transfer it to another country in a strong reserve position, or to the International Monetary Fund. The development of such techniques will introduce a new degree of transferability for these longer term obligations and may thus provide additional flexibility for the U.S. in dealing with its international payments position.

The Gold Cover Requirement. One unilateral action which could help to defend U.S. gold reserves is to repeal or modify the 25-percent gold reserve requirements now imposed on the Federal Reserve Banks. At present approximately $13 billion of our total gold stock is impounded as reserves against the deposit and note obligations of the Federal Reserve Systems. These liabilities are the base of our domestic monetary system. They will grow as the economy grows, and the required gold cover will increase along with them.

The United States and Belgium are the only major countries still retaining a domestic monetary reserve requirement in the form of gold. Most other industrial countries suspended or abandoned their legal reserve requirements during the War or post-War periods and have not reinstated them.

Actually, U.S. law permits the Board of Governors of the Federal Reserve to waive the 25-percent requirement for an initial 30-day period and to renew such waiver for successive intervals of 15 days. No limit is placed on the number of successive renewals which the Board may make. There are other provisions of law, however, which impose progressively increasing charges upon those Federal Reserve Banks for whom the Board has issued waivers. These charges would be nominal until the gold stock had fallen to about $6.5 billion.

The present law clearly contemplates the possible use of the required gold in the event of a crisis. President Kennedy stated at the outset of his Administration that the entire gold stock is available for monetary use in defense of the dollar. Chairman Martin has subsequently made public statements to Congressional committees and elsewhere, which make clear the Board's understanding of its present authority. Nevertheless, there remains some nagging doubt around the world concerning the ready availability of the "impounded $13 billion" for use in meeting United States external obligations. The risk remains that any crisis which led to the outflow of a substantial part of our present "surplus gold" (the excess over the required gold) would cause a rush to purchase on the part of other central banks and monetary authorities. As the actual level of our gold reserves approached 25 percent, concern would mount that the United States might in practice impose a gold embargo.

The best defense of our existing gold stocks against this eventuality would be to eliminate or greatly to reduce the present gold cover requirement. However, serious questions of psychology and confidence are involved, and the proposal will have to be carefully timed and explained.

The public case for change should not be related to the possibility of gold losses. It should instead be focused on the restraint implied for our own domestic economic growth by the existence of the 25-percent requirement.

An expansion of basic bank reserves and of currency in circulation is necessary to service our expanding economy, even at stable prices. Such expansion has already brought the effective gold ratio for the Federal Reserve below 30 percent. In prudence, it can be suggested, the United States must economize further on the use of its underlying base of gold reserves, before the 25-percent limit is reached. The comparable requirements until 1945 were 40 percent against Federal Reserve currency and 35 percent against the deposits kept in Federal Reserve Banks by commercial banks. Those ratios were combined and lowered to 25 percent at the end of World War II when Congress saw that they would otherwise impose an unnecessary brake upon the expansion of the money supply and of the national economy. On the same grounds, a clear need will soon appear for further reducing or removing the requirement.

A choice will have to be made, when the right time arrives, between full removal or some modification of the requirement. Full removal is preferable but may not be politically possible. As a fall-back position, one possible modification would be to remove the requirement for gold against deposits in Federal Reserve banks, while keeping the requirement only against the issuance of Federal Reserve notes (currency). Another might be to lower both the deposit and note requirements to 15 percent, or 10 percent. If any requirement is kept, the Federal Reserve should be permitted to count not only gold but holdings of convertible foreign currencies and other international reserve assets.

As to the timing of legislative action by the United States, it would be desirable to propose the change when the dollar is reasonably strong and exchange markets are calm, and when there are good prospects of Congressional approval without lengthy debate. A new Administration with a strong popular mandate and a large Congressional majority should seize the opportunity to take action early in 1965. Obviously it is essential to succeed in Congress with whatever recommendation the Administration makes. Failure to secure fairly prompt Congressional approval could trigger a gold flight.

III. Improvement of the International Monetary System

The Needs. Since the Second World War the nations of the free world have used gold and dollars as the principal means of settling the net balances in their transactions with one another. Broadly speaking, countries in surplus have added to their official monetary reserves in gold and dollars, and countries have financed deficits by drawing down their reserves of gold and dollars. The United States has played a unique role in this system, a role which has carried with it both advantageous privileges and burdensome responsibilities. The use of the dollar as a reserve currency has permitted the U.S. to run chronic deficits, since they could be financed simply by incurring further short term dollar liabilities to foreign central banks and governments. At the same time, the U.S. has committed itself to maintain the convertibility of these dollars into gold at a fixed price on demand. Consequently, at the discretion of foreign governments, the U.S. can be called upon not only to finance its current deficit in gold instead of dollars but to sell gold for the dollars they have previously accumulated.

The gold-dollar reserve system has worked well. Its success has been due in part to the availability of supplementary means of financing payment deficits. The International Monetary Fund has, from its beginning in 1945, been an important source of financing for underdeveloped countries. In recent years it has become increasingly important for industrial countries, including the U.S.[3] Consequently, drawing rights in the International Monetary Fund are increasingly recognized as supplementary reserves which countries in deficit can count on.

The past few years have been rich in other financial innovations, thanks especially to the imaginative leadership of the U.S. The major governments and central banks have developed a number of lending techniques which make it possible for countries to finance short term deficits without use of dollars and gold. From the beginning of the swap arrangements in mid-1962 through last August, total drawings by all central bank partners amounted to $1.9 billion—thus providing that amount of liquidity at key points of strain. Developments during 1964 have given ample evidence of the great potential for meeting liquidity needs that exists in the execution of currency swaps with other countries, the orderly handling of forward operations in other currencies, and, as discussed earlier, the issuance of United States Government obligations denominated in foreign currencies. In addition to these government obligations, it should be possible to aim at increasing the outstanding lines of currency swaps, that now amount to $2 billion. Over the long run, continuing efforts should be devoted to enlarging them, and in the next few years it might be possible to double the outstanding amount.

Nevertheless it is generally agreed that further and more systematic innovations in international monetary arrangements need to be made in the next few years. At the official level, recognition of this need led both the "Group of Ten"[4] and the IMF to study improvements which might be adopted by multilateral agreement. These international studies, begun in 1963, are still under way, although interim reports were made this year and discussed at the annual meeting of the IMF in Tokyo in September.

---

[3] The fear that use of the Fund would be an admission of weakness which would impair confidence has been overcome. Under a $500 million standby arranged with the Fund in 1963, the U.S. has drawn $300 million. This "broke the ice" and, because it was skillfully timed and explained, it has caused no difficulties for the dollar in foreign exchange markets. [Footnote in the source text.]

[4] The major monetary powers—technically the members of the IMF who participate in the IMF's General Arrangements to Borrow: Belgium, Canada, France, Germany, Italy, Japan, Netherlands, Sweden, the United Kingdom, and the United States. With Switzerland, the Ten become Eleven. [Footnote in the source text.]

As the studies continue, they assume more and more the character of a negotiation which will shape the final outcome. Therefore, it is important for the U.S. Government to have a clear position regarding its objectives and its bargaining strategy.

Why is it that the gold-dollar system needs further modification? There are two main reasons:

(1) First, it is doubtful that the world supply of reserves in the form of gold and dollars can match the world's need for reserves. To provide a desirable margin of safety in assessing probable reserve needs, we should anticipate that imbalances in international payments will grow at least as fast as the world economy and world trade. But the stock of gold and dollar reserves cannot in the long run be counted on to grow so fast. At the same time, year-to-year increases in the supply are likely to be erratic and unreliable, and may bear little relation to the needs of the world economy.

The major sources of new gold are South Africa and the Soviet Union. These supplies depend on technological and economic developments affecting the profitability of gold mining. They are also vulnerable to political developments. Some new gold disappears into private hoards, in amounts that vary with tastes and speculative whims. Purchases of new gold by monetary authorities have been increasing total reserves by an average of only one percent per year since 1960.

The long run growth in dollar reserves will cease altogether as soon as U.S. payments are, on the average over a period of years, in balance. It is indeed the reluctance of foreign countries to accept increases in reserves *in this form* which makes it necessary to end chronic U.S. deficits. Their reluctance stems in part from fears that the U.S. will not be able to maintain covertibility of dollars into gold. But it also stems in part from a feeling that no one country should have the privilege of "printing money" to run unlimited deficits—a privilege the U.S. would possess if its currency were automatically accepted by other governments without limit. In the financial field, as elsewhere, we are confronted by demands from our allies that international arrangement should be more symmetrical and multilateral than in the past.

But when the U.S. is in balance on average over a number of years, its payments position will no doubt fluctuate. Deficits in some years will provide dollars for international reserves, and surpluses in other years will withdraw them. But the timing of these deficits and surpluses may not coincide with overall needs for changes in the supplies of reserves.

(2) Second, the gold-dollar system contains some danger of instability. Large scale conversions of dollars into gold are always possible. Such conversions would not only diminish the gold reserves of the U.S.; they would also reduce the total world stock of reserves, since the converted dollars would simply disappear from international use. The opposite is also conceivable. The world supply of reserves could be suddenly

inflated if other countries wearied of gold and decided to convert some of their gold reserves into dollars.

There is now considerable international agreement on this diagnosis. There is also agreement on the obvious implication—new international reserves of some kind must be created.

One possibility is the use of other national currencies. The U.S. has already acquired other convertible currencies in token amounts. Future U.S. surpluses would not extinguish reserves if the U.S. accumulated the currencies of countries then in deficit rather than repaying its own short term debts. This possibility has merit, but its usefulness is limited by the reluctance of countries other than the U.S. and the U.K. to assume the responsibilities of reserve currency status. Consequently there is agreement that major reliance must be placed on multilateral creation of reserves.

Here is where agreement ceases. The main issues were made clear in discussion at Tokyo. The French and Dutch favored the creation outside the Fund of a new reserve asset, the Collective Reserve Unit, to replace national currencies in the reserves of the members of the Group. The U.S., supported by Canada and the U.K., emphasized improvement and expansion of the International Monetary Fund. The technical details of these proposals are discussed in an Appendix.

As originally designed, the CRU proposal does not meet the world's monetary needs, and it is particularly disadvantageous to the U.S. It restricts rather than facilitates expansion in the supply of reserves. It links the total supply rigidly to gold. To the outside world it might appear as a premium gold price and thus stimulate private speculation. It takes no account of the monetary needs of countries outside the group. It diminishes the importance and usefulness of the International Monetary Fund by vesting crucial monetary functions in a rival agency. For the U.S. it may well mean an initial loss of gold reserves, with no commensurate quid pro quo.

These defects are not inherent in the notion of a composite reserve unit, and no doubt the plan could be revised to eliminate them. But reserve creation can be achieved within the IMF, which already provides a reserve asset based on a mixture of national currencies in agreed proportions. Therefore—and especially in view of the restrictive spirit in which the present CRU proposal has been advanced—it seems better for the U.S. not to try to recast the CRU proposal but to work toward the alternative of improving the IMF. Indeed, developments since Tokyo indicate that the French proposal has very little support even within the Six. The studies of the Group of Ten will apparently focus on the IMF, although at least one major country, Germany, is not at present particularly receptive to either approach.

One feature of the CRU, but not unique to the CRU proposal, is the idea that all countries should move toward a uniform ratio between their gold holdings and their other primary reserves. This suggestion has some merit for the long run. The U.S. has experienced gold losses in the past simply because dollars moved from a central bank with a low customary gold ratio into a central bank with a high gold preference. But the U.S. must certainly resist proposals which would increase the average gold ratio and require the U.S. to pay out gold either to conform to a common ratio itself or to enable European countries that now have large dollar holdings to reach a high gold ratio.

The Task Force believes that, now that the issue has been joined, the U.S. should support the Fund vigorously in the coming negotiations. There are strong political reasons for this approach. The Fund is a worldwide organization. U.S. leadership should seek to strengthen worldwide organizations such as the Fund rather than building up competing organizations of narrower membership. Underdeveloped countries will, in one way or another, share the deliberations and the benefits associated with reserve creation in the Fund. They will be excluded from the decisions of a rich country's club and from their fruits. The U.S. obviously has a strong interest in avoiding suspicions and tensions between have and have-not countries.

Once the idea of acting outside the Fund is abandoned, European pressure is likely to take the form of proposals to set up with the Fund special monetary arrangements and decision procedures for the Group of Ten.

The idea of a club within the Fund continues and enlarges the precedent established by the General Arrangements to Borrow. The U.S. should seek to avoid this so far as possible and to build changes in the Fund into its normal procedures of operation and government. This does not mean that all advantages of membership of the Fund must be available to all members at all times. But eligibility must be defined by universalistic rules, applicable to all members, rather than by arbitrary distinctions between members. And Fund decisions should be made in its Board, where the Ten have in any case a preponderance of the weighted votes.

It is true that since 1960 the pressure of events has necessarily limited the number of countries involved in major international monetary consultations, negotiations, and actions. Bilateral ties between central banks and other financial officials have become closer. The U.S. Federal Reserve System has participated actively and regularly in discussions among major central banks at the B.I.S. in Basle. In the OECD, the international financial situation is regularly reviewed by Working Party 3, in which only the Eleven are represented. In their recent report the Group of Ten agreed to a "multilateral surveillance" of credits granted and received, to be carried out in the consultations at the B.I.S. and OECD.

The development of monetary institutions in which only rich countries participate has already aroused some suspicion and resentment on the part of the other 92 members of the Fund. One reason is that the underdeveloped countries correctly understand that it is in part European reluctance to grant them larger credits which lies behind European preference to work outside the Fund. From the viewpoint of the U.S., the major aid-giving country, any multilateral assistance to underdeveloped countries which may be a by-product of international monetary expansion is pure gain.

The open disclosure at Tokyo of differences of view regarding the role of the IMF was probably a good thing. Previously, the success of our day-to-day and month-to-month negotiations to defend the dollar seemed to depend on blurring and postponing this issue. Now that the Ten have agreed to disagree on that point, at least temporarily, the U.S. is free to take leadership in pushing for monetary improvements within the Fund.

Until now, we have acquiesced in the view that no changes in the Fund can be seriously proposed without unanimous support of the Ten. If the French and the Dutch persist in their current attitudes, the time will soon be at hand for us to try a new strategy. At some point we must make clear that we will press for certain changes in the Fund whether or not France and Holland agree. It would be fortunate if our balance of payments and reserve positions were strong at the time, but the issue may not wait that long. We should try to split the Six, especially to obtain the support of Italy and Germany, countries which are more disposed to sympathize with the U.S. position. We can probably count on the support of the U.K., Canada, the Scandinavian countries, Japan, and most of the rest of the world. If a large majority of the IMF, both in weighted votes and in number, agrees to important change in the Fund, it is doubtful that France will refuse to participate in new arrangements.

Technically, the IMF can be easily adapted to meet new monetary needs. A variety of procedures are available, and it is no exaggeration to say that anything which might be done outside the IMF can be done inside the IMF. Use of the IMF has the advantage of building on familiar procedures and utilizing an experienced organization. The IMF is already recognized as a supplementary source of reserves for financing payments deficits. Its use in this role can be greatly increased without abruptly overturning present arrangements, in particular the continued use of dollars as international reserves.

The IMF provides its members both unconditional and conditional liquidity for meeting balance of payments deficits. Both kinds can be increased, in whatever proportions desired. The major techniques for increasing the contribution of the Fund to international liquidity are listed below. But the choice of techniques is a less important matter than agreeing, both within our own government and with other governments, on our objectives. In the opinion of the Task Force, the U.S. should aim high. Along with new monetary gold, the Fund will be the major source of new unconditional reserves. Its contribution should be sufficient to enable total reserves to grow roughly at the same rate as the world economy. The availability and use of other Fund credit should grow at a similar pace. The U.S. will want to be strongly on the side of frequent and adequate expansion of the Fund.

The major techniques available, discussed in further detail in an Appendix, are as follows:

(1) *Increasing quotas.* General agreement to a 25-percent increase in quotas has already been reached. However, the customary requirement that one quarter of new quotas be paid in gold threatens the U.S. with a gold loss of $650 million, of which $400 million would be the gold subscriptions of other members. Consequently, we must press, even over the opposition of the French and others, for ways to increase quotas without gold payments. If this problem is solved, we should seek a further general increase in quotas and perhaps a system of regular annual increases. Meanwhile, it is also important that additional special increases in quotas be arranged for European countries whose weight in the Fund is now too small.

(2) *Increased automaticity.* The U.S. should seek to make a larger part of the quota (50 percent instead of 25 percent) available to members on a virtually automatic basis.

(3) *General Arrangements to Borrow.* The U.S. should support a renewal of the agreement under which the Ten will lend their currencies to the Fund in case of need. But our aim in the long run should be to give the Fund sufficient command over resources that it does not need to borrow currencies in circumstances which give the lenders special powers of decision over Fund operations.

(4) *Fund investments and deposits.* There are a variety of possible transactions by which the Fund could provide members with international reserve assets in exchange for other assets. Essentially through these transactions the Fund would create international reserves by acquiring member currencies, or World Bank bonds, or long term obligations of member governments. The U.S. should support the evolution of the Fund in this direction.

New arrangements of this kind can achieve within the Fund whatever positive results could be accomplished by creation of a new reserve asset, like the CRU, either outside the Fund or in a club nominally inside the Fund. But they would have none of the disadvantages of the CRU proposal. The reserve asset within the Fund would be one whose value and usefulness to members is already established by experience. Its supply and use need not be tightly linked to gold. Nor does it need to supplant the holding of reserve currencies outside the Fund, encourage private speculation in gold, or promote a general move toward less economy in the use of gold by central banks.

---

19.   Briefing Paper Prepared by the Department of State and the Department of the Treasury[1]

PMW/B–15   Washington, December 4, 1964.

VISIT OF PRIME MINISTER HAROLD WILSON
December 7–8, 1964[2]

International Economic Situation

The Prime Minister has asked that the "International Economic Situation" be put on the agenda for his talks with the President. We have no details as to what aspects of this wide-ranging topic Wilson wishes to discuss, but we believe that he will merely present some of his ideas on various topics in general terms for US consideration. No deep or detailed discussion is envisaged.

He will almost certainly talk about the world trade and payments situation because of its bearing on the UK balance of payments position. He may also wish to touch on the need for new imaginative action to help the low income countries; an "international new deal" for the LDCs was the phrase used by the head of the newly created Ministry of Overseas Development at the recent Colombo Plan meeting.[3]

I. World Trade and Payments Situation

    1. *International Liquidity:* Prime Minister Wilson is known to be concerned about the "international liquidity problem," i.e., the sufficiency of

---

[1] Source: Department of State, Conference Files: Lot 66 D 110, Visits and Conferences, 1964. Limited Official Use. Drafted by Jerome Jacobson (E), William K. Miller (OFE), Selma G. Kallis (OT), Ruth A. Gold (OR), George H. Willis (Treasury), Harold J. Shullaw (BNA), Frank M. Tucker (BNA), and Robert C. Creel (EUR), and cleared by Ammon O. Bartley (S/S–S).

[2] British Prime Minister Harold Wilson visited Washington December 7–8 to discuss with President Johnson the international economic situation. For remarks upon Prime Minister Wilson's arrival in Washington on December 7, together with the text of the joint communiqué released at the close of their talks on December 8, see *Public Papers of the Presidents of the United States: Lyndon B. Johnson, 1963–64*, Book II, pp. 1643–1650.

[3] The Consultative Committee of the Colombo Plan for Cooperative Economic Development in South and Southeast Asia held its 16th annual meeting in London November 17–20, 1964.

the international money supply (monetary reserves and credits) to finance expanding international trade. His general thesis is that if world trade is to expand, major and reasonably automatic expansion of international credit is also needed. In addition, because of its severe recurrent balance of payments difficulties, the UK has a very strong interest in longer-term sources of finance.

There is general recognition that world reserves and money supply will probably require expansion as the volume of world trade increases. European central bankers favor some expansion of credits but place heavy emphasis on the avoidance of inflationary monetary expansion. They are not sympathetic to the idea of extending more credit to chronic debtor countries and consider that the United Kingdom and the United States should take steps to correct their balance of payments deficits.

The US favors measures to provide adequate international liquidity but does not consider that this is the time for any major new initiative. For the present we are concentrating on carrying through the recently agreed increase in quotas in the International Monetary Fund so as to put them into effect next year. This should handle the international credits issue at least for the immediate future.

We do not yet know enough about Wilson's ideas to make any substantive response appropriate if he should make specific suggestions, and it would be best, therefore, if he should put forward any specific proposals, to say we would need to consider them before taking any position.

(A fuller discussion of this subject is appended at page 5.)

2. *Kennedy Round:* The Prime Minister may refer to the urgent interest of the UK in the success of the Kennedy Round and express gratification at the recent US decision to table our non-agricultural exceptions list despite the lack of progress on treatment of agriculture in the negotiations. The Prime Minister may caution, however, that because of the complexities and the entrenched positions of farmers in all countries, agriculture may lag behind industry in the Kennedy Round. He may go further and suggest that at some point it may be necessary to divorce industry and agriculture. The UK is interested in industrial exports only. However, it is in our trade interest to obtain the reduction of trade barriers on both industrial and agricultural products, and we are convinced that a combined package will include more benefits for industry as well as for agriculture. It thus is important to keep the pressure on in agriculture in order to get the best over-all deal not only for the US but also for other countries, including the UK.

II. Helping the Less Developed Countries (LDCs)

Because so many Commonwealth members are LDCs, the UK would like to play a larger role in helping them, but in ways that do not further burden the UK balance of payments. After reaffirming the intention of the UK—strapped as she is—to continue to provide financial aid on favorable terms, the Prime Minister may propose a series of measures to help the LDCs in the trade and payments field, measures that would be less costly, and perhaps even helpful, to the British economy. He may propose:

1. *Commodity Agreements:* More commodity agreements to provide stability in the prices and production of primary commodities important to the trade of the LDCs, such as cocoa, tea, sisal, and jute.

2. *Favored Treatment for LDC Manufactures:* Increased imports by the advanced countries of LDC-manufactured goods, by imposing lower duties on goods coming from LDCs than on those from advanced countries.

The UK grants duty-free entry to imports from the Commonwealth. As a result, it imports relatively more LDC-manufactured goods than does the US and substantially more than does the EEC. At the UN Conference on Trade and Development last Spring,[4] the then British Government proposed a system of generalized tariff preferences from all advanced countries to all LDCs, a measure warmly supported by the LDCs and warmly opposed by the US.

3. *International Credit for LDCs:* Substantial expansion of international credit availabilities for the LDCs (presumably through new IMF techniques), such credits to be directed to spending in debtor countries, e.g., UK and US.

4. *World Food Aid:* International action to channel food surpluses from advanced countries to meet the needs of hungry nations. (The UK is not a food-exporting country. What contribution would the UK make in support of world food aid?)

U.S. Position

With respect to these proposals, we might respond as follows:

The US recognizes that the low-income countries need stable and growing earnings from trade as well as increased aid on favorable terms.

1. *Commodity Agreements:* We are prepared to help develop and support commodity agreements to stabilize markets and arrest price erosion in those cases where workable arrangements can be devised. We are, however, aware of the great technical difficulties in putting together and executing such agreements.

2. *Favored Treatment for LDC Manufactures:* We believe there are two effective ways to help the LDCs increase their exports of manufactured

---

[4] The U.N. Conference on Trade and Development was held in Geneva March 23–June 16, 1964. For developments at this conference, see *Yearbook of the United Nations, 1964,* pp. 195–207.

goods: (a) by reducing tariff and non-tariff barriers in world trade, and (b) by helping them produce and market more effectively, for example, by offering technical assistance in export promotion and quality control, by encouraging regional groupings of LDCs to widen the internal market so as to develop industries of efficient size.

We hope to see significant reductions in trade barriers to LDC exports on a multilateral basis within the Kennedy Round. We are opposed to preferential treatment for LDC exports, believing such arrangements would prove to be unworkably complex and divisive, would benefit only a few LDCs at best, would lead to quantitative restrictions to protect injured industries in the advanced countries, and give the LDCs a vested interest in high tariffs among advanced countries to assure a significant margin of preference for LDCs.

3. *International Credit for LDCs:* We should go no further than indicate our willingness to study any specific proposals in this matter the Prime Minister may put forward.

4. *World Food Aid:* We are making our food surpluses available to feed the hungry not only through our PL 480 program but also multilaterally through the pilot World Food Program to whose modest resources the US is now contributing in excess of 50%. We would hope to see others increase their contributions to such programs, making available cash as well as surplus foods. We also need a more concerted and systematic effort to increase agricultural productivity in the LDCs so that they can over time feed themselves.

International Economic Situation—Appendix

International Liquidity

Prime Minister Wilson has at times expressed concern about the "international liquidity problem", that is, the adequacy of the supply of international monetary reserves and international credit in relation to expanding international trade. In Washington last year, as leader of the Opposition, he called for an expansion of credits from the IMF to developing countries that could be spent only in "debtor countries" such as the US and the UK. In London recently he has commented in general terms on the need for steps to increase and strengthen world liquidity.

In his conversations scheduled for December 7 and 8, he is expected to mention the importance he attaches to progress in the field of international liquidity, rather than to bring up specific proposals or suggestions. The British have encountered severe balance of payments difficulties on several occasions in the past ten years. The recent financial assistance of $3 billion is short-term and the United Kingdom now has a very strong interest in alternative and longer-term sources of credit, in addition to the earlier feeling that more reserves would give them greater leeway in internal policies.

Apart from the United Kingdom case, there is a general feeling that reserves are adequate for the world as a whole in the immediate future, allowing for the 25 percent increase in the resources of the International Monetary Fund (IMF) that is now in process of negotiation in the IMF. There is general recognition that in the longer run, there is likely to be a need for more international liquidity, with the continuing growth of world trade and payments. However, European central bankers and governments place heavy emphasis on the avoidance of inflationary monetary expansion. They are also not sympathetic to extending more credit to chronic debtor countries, especially those in a less developed stage. They consider that the United Kingdom and the United States should correct their balance of payments deficits, and that the less developed countries do not need liquidity but rather aid and capital investment.

The United States places particular emphasis on the importance of improved credit facilities, and regards the immediate need as met by an expansion in the resources of the IMF and further development of our bilateral credit arrangements. Looking ahead to a longer-term future, we feel that the Europeans, especially the French and the Dutch, are too restrictive in their attitude towards the further development of the international monetary system. The French particularly favor control of future reserve creation by a small group of major financial powers, with an important role for the central banks of Europe, acting through the Bank for International Settlements. Although other European countries are not so restrictive in their approach, the leading Continental powers lean in the direction of a conservative approach through a limited group. The United States, the United Kingdom, and the other members of the Group of Ten favor the use of the IMF for assuring an orderly growth of international liquidity for a wider group of countries. (The Group of Ten is composed of Western European countries plus the US, Canada, and Japan.) The entire subject of the long-run problem of liquidity is closely related to the need for effective policies to correct balance of payments deficits and surpluses. Detailed examination of both questions is being actively pursued through special study groups established last year by the Group of Ten.

U.S. Position

The United States' view is that this is not a time for any major new initiative in the field of international liquidity. The monetary system is now weathering quite well the shock occasioned by the recent British difficulties, and it would be unsettling to consider any new approach. Our objective at present should be:

1. We should concentrate on carrying through the 25 percent increase in quotas now in process in the International Monetary Fund so as to put it into effect next year. This should handle the international credit problem at least for the immediate future.

2. We should press forward on the studies now under way on ways to supplement the present reserve system of gold and reserve currencies, if that should be needed in the longer run.

3. We should also press forward with the study of the proper way to minimize and correct balance of payments deficits and surpluses and with the program of international financial cooperation and consultation that has done so much to facilitate the handling of our own deficit and to meet the problems of other countries such as the United Kingdom.

It should probably be sufficient at the December 7 and 8 meetings to agree with the British Prime Minister on the importance of the liquidity question, and of our proceeding with the current program of attacking it. We should also indicate our satisfaction with the close working relations with the British technical people that have been in effect for the past two years and which currently are being intensified. If, contrary to our expectations, the Prime Minister were to make any specific proposals, they should not be given any encouragement until we have had the necessary time to give them appropriate consideration. At the present time we have no knowledge of any new specific ideas that he might have in mind.

---

20.   **Paper Prepared for the Cabinet Committee on Balance of Payments[1]**

Washington, December 9, 1964.

BALANCE OF PAYMENTS PROSPECTS AND POLICIES

1.   Progress to Date

Our deficit on regular transactions now looks to be between $2-1/4 and $2-1/2 billion for 1964.

—That will be well below $3.3 billion 1963 deficit, *but progress has fallen short of widely shared earlier expectations of decline to $2 billion or less.*

---

[1] Source: Kennedy Library, Herter Papers, Balance of Payments (January 29, 1963 thru April 24, 1965), Box 6. Limited Official Use. The source text bears no drafting information. A copy of the paper, without the handwritten notations, is in the Johnson Library, National Security File, Subject File, Balance of Payments, vol. 2 [2 of 2], Box 2. A December 9 covering memorandum from Dillon to the members of the Cabinet Committee on Balance of Payments is ibid. The Cabinet Committee comprised Secretaries McNamara and Hodges; Under Secretary Ball; David Bell; Christian Herter; Kermit Gordon; Gardner Ackley, Council of Economic Advisers; McGeorge Bundy; and William McChesney Martin, Board of Governors of the Federal Reserve System. The paper was distributed in preparation for an afternoon meeting with Secretary Dillon on December 9 and for a meeting with President Johnson on December 10.

—Deficit has widened to about $3 billion rate for second half, perhaps reflecting in some part side effects of U.K. crisis.

With the deficit smaller and good first half results contributing to confidence, the net gold outflow subsided, but large December losses now expected to bring gold drain for year to estimated $175–$200 million.

—The earlier stability was partly fortuitous—reflecting first large Russian sales early in year and then some backwash of U.K. difficulties in form of gold sales to us.

2.   *Looking Ahead*

Our technical experts foresee further limited gains in 1965, bringing the deficit on regular transactions slightly under $2 billion. If realized, that would be the smallest deficit since the balance of payments became a problem in 1958—but little if any better than what had been hoped for this year. Thus, *the outlook is for the eighth straight year of large deficits.*

3.   *Elements in the Problem*

Our commercial trade surplus should reach a record $3.4 billion in 1964—a better-than-expected gain of $1.1 billion. Strong markets abroad helped, *but in addition, our own price stability is beginning to pay off in strengthening our world-wide competitive position.*

—However, on present reading, we cannot count on so large a commercial trade surplus in 1965; our experts now foresee a decline of about $750 million. The U.K. import surcharges and slower growth in Canada and some other markets will tend to restrain export growth, while an inventory buildup in steel and elsewhere is expected to swell imports.

On Government overseas account, President Kennedy scheduled a $1 billion reduction from the 1962 level by the end of this year—with full effect in 1965. This included savings of $500 million through tying of aid, $300 million from lower defense spending, and $200 million from reduced purchases by AEC abroad. That target, on present schedules, should be closely approached.

—AID has virtually reached its target.
—Defense is about $35 million behind schedule, partly reflecting pay increases. Moreover, plans for certain additional military reductions have been set aside, largely for political reasons, and $125 million of approved further reductions are not scheduled to be effective until 1966.
—Purchases by AEC are being reduced on schedule.

Clear slippage is apparent in private capital outflows, despite the restraining influence of the Interest Equalization Tax on purchases of foreign securities.

—Bank loans—only partly related to exports and special Japanese needs—ran at a record $2.2 million annual rate in first three quarters, despite declines in short-term lending over the summer.

—Direct investment is reaching a new peak of over $2 billion.

—Some liquid funds have moved abroad, despite effort to maintain short-term interest rates at competitive levels.

—New Canadian securities—exempt from IET—turned out to be larger than expected, particularly in recent months.

The travel account is another important drag on progress. Tourist spending abroad continues to rise rapidly, reaching $2.9 billion, $1.7 billion more than foreigners spend here.

4.   *Evaluation*

Continuing, visible progress toward reducing our deficit is essential to assure adequate financing for our deficit and to maintain confidence— already affected by side effects of the U.K. crisis.

—In this context, the technicians' current forecast would be judged disconcertingly high by European creditors—too high to be fully certain of orderly financing.

—*Present policies must be continued and reinforced—and "emergency backstops" prepared—to assure that forecast can be bettered and the ground laid for further significant progress in CY 1966. The "safety margin" today is not adequate.*

5.   *Indicated Program*

A.   *Basic to all else is continued price and cost stability*— the key both to export expansion and continued confidence in our longer-run prospects.

—This suggests reiteration of "guideposts", close attention to key wage and price decisions, and continued emphasis on measures to spur productivity and cost-cutting.

B.   On that foundation, *our export effort should be further strengthened* through:

1.   Increased emphasis by Commerce on locating foreign markets, contacting potential new exporters, and promotion of cash sales which are more immediately productive than credit sales on extra liberal terms. Strong Presidential backing will be needed for adequate appropriations to carry out this program.

2.   More flexible policies by Maritime Administration to (a) permit shipment of Government-financed exports in foreign ships where necessary to make sale, and (b) correct shipping cost differentials that discriminate against U.S. exports.

3.   Exploration by affected agencies of opportunities for developing Iron Curtain markets, including judicious use of credit where this leads to accompanying cash sales.

C.   *Re-examination of targets for reductions in AID and Defense spending abroad is required to prevent slippage and to seek out further areas for savings.* Necessary actions should be taken to assure: (1) Germany meets commitment for military orders and payments to U.S. which fully offset U.S. defense spending in Germany during 1965 and 1966, and (2) the $125 million additional DOD reductions approved in October 1963 for implementation in calendar 1966 are carried out.

D. To restrain the losses on travel account, it is essential to:[2]

1. Extend legislation limiting duty-free tourist imports, possibly with a reduction in present $100 per trip limit.[3]

2. Invigorate the "See America Now" program with adequate appropriations, centralized responsibility, and top level support.

3. Assure that fare decisions by the CAB take into account balance of payments implications of foreign travel.[4]

4. *As a major "backstop" for our effort, we should devise a workable tax on overseas U.S. tourists for possible implementation well before heavy summer tourist season.*[5]

E. *Reductions in the heavy net capital outflow are essential* to achieve the needed reduction in the balance of payments.[6]

1. *Renewal of the basic Interest Equalization Tax legislation* will be required.[7]

2. *Implementation of tax changes and other measures required to improve climate for foreign purchases of U.S. securities should be expedited.*

3. We must be prepared to close Canadian exemption if anything like present borrowing rate is maintained ($380 million in fourth quarter). However, the Canadians have indicated clear recognition of need for lower rate next year.

4. Increasing domestic loan demands may slow rise in foreign bank lending. If not, the IET will need to be extended to bank term loans.

5. Monetary policy is doing what it can at the moment to minimize outflows of short-term funds while supporting domestic growth. Its flexibility in meeting future contingencies must not be impaired. Monetary policy will also need continued support from Treasury debt opera-

---

[2] A handwritten notation in the left margin reads: "too strong."

[3] A handwritten notation at the end of this sentence reads: "study on effect now underway."

[4] A handwritten notation in the left margin reads: "Unclear what BP effect would be. Study needed."

[5] A handwritten notation in the left margin reads: "Ball strongly disagrees. Capital outflows more important. Distorted social values. Tourism has helped our internat'l position."

[6] Two handwritten notations appear below this paragraph. One reads: "Balance with something on private capital outflow." The second reads: "Include OECD study of border tax policies."

[7] President Johnson recommended an extension of the Interest Equalization Tax for 2 years beyond December 31, 1965, in a speech to Congress on February 10, 1965; see *Public Papers of the Presidents of the United States: Lyndon B. Johnson, 1965,* Book I, pp. 170–177.

tions and from intervention in foreign exchange markets to meet objective of avoiding incentives to shift liquid funds abroad.

F. In the best of circumstances, we must be prepared for further gold losses. Declining ratio of gold to Fed note and deposit liabilities (now near 28 per cent) underscores need for relaxing 25 per cent gold cover requirement, making gold unambiguously available in defense of dollar. (The primary public justification for this move lies in coming need to provide for the long-run expansion in the monetary base required by domestic growth.)[8]

6.   Recommendation

A tentative decision should be taken to send a special balance of payments message to the Congress on or about March 15, when detailed figures on 1964 results first become available. This message could reiterate Presidential determination to substantially improve our payments and to take all needed measures to that end.

It could report results of effort to reduce Government expenditures overseas, request extension of Interest Equalization Tax, emphasize need for action on other items in legislative program and announce any further steps which may be necessary.

---

[8] A handwritten notation in the left margin reads: "Move fast. State of Union."

---

21.   Memorandum From the Chairman of the Council of Economic Advisers (Ackley) to President Johnson[1]

Washington, December 10, 1964.

SUBJECT

The Balance of Payments

1. *The facts about our progress in correcting the balance-of-payments deficit*—which you used so effectively during the campaign—*have not appreciably changed.*

The *regular-transactions deficit* for 1964 is now conservatively estimated at $2.4 billion

—down 28% from 1963's $3.3 billion;
—down 39% from the 1958–60 average of $3.9 billion.

---

[1] Source: Johnson Library, National Security File, Subject File, Balance of Payments, Vol. 2 [2 of 2], Box 2. No classification marking.

This will be the *best year-to-year gain since 1957.*

If the December results are as good as December last year, *the 1964 deficit will be even less than the expected $2.4 billion.*

If we measured our deficit the way most European countries do, our deficit this year would be about $1 billion, down from about $2.4 billion last year (measured the same way).

2.   We are expected to lose some gold in December. Even so, *our gold losses for the year* (now estimated at $175–200 million) *will be the lowest since 1957*

—down about 60% from last year
—down almost 90% from the average of 1958–60.

And our gold losses this year will be less than half the $0.5 billion loss forecast at the beginning of the year.

3.   To be sure, *the 1964 deficit is now estimated as somewhat higher than the $2 billion hoped for at the beginning of the year.*

But most foreigners took our earlier estimate with a few grains of salt.

Foreigners (e.g., the OECD last week)[2] continue to compliment us for the very substantial improvement we have made.

A prominent American banker who specializes in international finance and is in very close touch with European bankers told me yesterday he thinks our problem is so nearly solved that he wants us to relax some of our present measures. I think this is premature, but indicates there is also optimism in financial circles.

4.   It is remarkable that *this year's deficit has apparently been financed with little increase of our "official liabilities" abroad* (to governments and central banks).

And our official liabilities to Europe will have been substantially *reduced* this year.

This is partly a tribute to continued brilliant Treasury management, and partly to the improved position of the LDC's.

But *foreign private businesses* have also been happy to hold a large part of the dollar balances created by our deficit

—because they *need* larger balances to finance their trade and payments;
—because they *have renewed confidence* in the soundness of the dollar.

5.   *The conservative estimate of the technical experts is for a further $600 million (about 25%) improvement of our deficit next year.*

If it began to appear next year that we were not going to get this improvement, *we would want to consider further measures.*

---

[2] The Ministerial Council of the OECD met in Paris December 2–3, 1964. For text of the communiqué issued at the conclusion of this meeting, see *American Foreign Policy: Current Documents, 1964,* pp. 497–499.

We should have some *further stand-by measures in preparation.*

But we can't decide now on the specific measures we would need to use. For example, we might wish to use our authority to apply the Interest Equalization Tax to bank loans, but only if the volume of such loans stays high.

6.   Some people seem frightened by *an alleged parallel to the British case. But the situations are in no sense similar.*

Our export surplus is large and steadily improving—they have had a steadily worsening *trade deficit.*

Our costs have been stable for 7 years; theirs have risen about 16%.

Our reserve position is infinitely stronger. Our deficit this year will be about 15% of our reserves; their deficit will exceed 2/3 of their reserves.

Their official liabilities are 2-1/2 times their reserves; ours are less than our reserves.

We have much more room for maneuver than they—our imports are less than 3% of GNP; theirs 17%.

7.   *This doesn't mean that we could never have a run on the dollar.* We could (and we did in 1960 when our deficit was considerably worse).

But—unless the British should devalue—there *seems much less risk of a run now than in a long time.*

There is *no way we could reduce that risk to zero*—especially so long as we remain a reserve currency, which we must, short of a whole new international monetary system.

We have *many defenses against a run:* our still massive gold stock; a flexible discount rate with no ceiling; our network of swaps; the IMF; a massive "package" of emergency support such as we put together for the U.K.

8.   Certainly, we are not yet out of the woods on the balance of payments.

We need to keep on doing everything we are doing now, and there may be some things we can do better.

We should *continue to underline to the world our determination to protect the dollar* at all costs. Amending our "gold cover" requirement will make even clearer that our gold will be used to defend the dollar.

There is surely *no reason for panic. A hastily conceived program* of added measures that promised only minor gains or that involved high costs to our other objectives *could be taken as a sign of our own loss of confidence.*

Gardner Ackley[3]

---

[3] Printed from a copy that bears this typed signature.

22. Memorandum From Secretary of the Treasury Dillon, the Under Secretary of State (Ball), and the President's Special Assistant for National Security Affairs (Bundy) to President Johnson[1]

Washington, December 11, 1964.

SUBJECT

Task Force Report on Foreign Economic Policy

We have analyzed the Task Force Report on Foreign Economic Policy, which covers aid, trade, and money.[2] Our analysis of the sections on trade and money follows. A separate report on the aid section will be submitted by David Bell.

I. Recommendations of the Task Force

The Task Force Report makes the following important recommendations—and we concur in them, except as noted:

1. The United States should continue its present efforts to reduce tariffs as quickly as possible, and to hold strongly to the most-favored-nation principle.

2. The United States should, as a matter of basic policy, resist all attempts to impose non-tariff restrictions on imports.

3. The United States should encourage easy access to our markets for imports from the less-developed countries. In particular, the United States should offer freer access for their less sophisticated manufactures.

4. To avoid serious domestic repercussions from rising imports, the United States needs not only fiscal and monetary measures to maintain full employment, but also a comprehensive program of mobility assistance to facilitate the adjustment of labor and capital to economic change, whether caused by import competition, technological advance, changes in consumers tastes, government policies, or other factors.

5. The United States should encourage trade with the Soviet Union and Eastern European countries. Competitive but not concessional credit arrangements should be extended to these countries and the United States should negotiate with them bilateral agreements that would provide, among other things, for most-favored-nation tariff treatment on an individual country basis.

6. The United States should continue our present policies for dealing with our balance of payments problems. If additional measures are

---

[1] Source: Department of State, Central Files, E 1 US. Secret.
[2] Document 18.

required, first priority should be given to further restrictions on private capital movements. The Report suggests the following sequence of measures: Extending the interest equalization tax to bank loans over one year; further measures to tax or control bank lending to foreign borrowers; temporarily limiting direct corporate investment in developed countries. (We are unanimous in the view that widening the application of the IET should have first priority if additional measures are required, and that no decision on the priority or nature of other steps need be taken at this time.)

7.   The United States must seek two essential improvements in the international monetary system: first, a more orderly process of reserve creation; and second, a more automatic mechanism for making international credit available to countries in balance of payments difficulties, on terms that correspond to the realities of the adjustment process. (The Treasury would emphasize the need to continue to proceed in an evolutionary way, over a period of time, and to relate these improvements to the realities of international financial relations and the need for effective adjustment policies. There is a difference of view between the Treasury and the Task Force on the nature of these realities, and in particular on the strength of the United States bargaining position.)

8.   During the interim period, while the improvements described in paragraph 7 are being put into effect, the United States should try to fund that portion of the United States short-term debt that is held by official holders through long-term loans from countries in a surplus position. The United States should also encourage European long-term lending to the United Kingdom, even if it somewhat reduces the amounts available to the United States. (We are unanimous in giving first priority to exploring longer-term loans to the United Kingdom by countries in a surplus position; but this should not be pushed and is not likely to be accomplished until the United Kingdom has demonstrated a willingness to adopt policies that will achieve fundamental improvement in its balance of payments position. We are also agreed that funding of an appropriate portion of our existing short-term obligations at some point would be useful. We see great practical difficulties, however, in achieving such funding in the near future. Therefore, we believe that it is important to press countries in a surplus position to accept more of the special securities of longer maturity that the United States has introduced into the monetary system.)

(The Task Force Report emphasizes that recommendations 7 and 8 are inter-related in the sense that early achievement of either diminishes somewhat the urgency of the other, but it emphasizes that there is no time to lose in pursuing the general objectives that underlie recommendations 7 and 8.)

II. *Proposed Presidential Statements*

We do not, at this stage, recommend a separate Presidential Message to Congress concerning foreign economic policy. We do, however, recommend that you include in your Inaugural Address, and more fully in your State of the Union Message the following points from the Task Force Report:

1. A reaffirmation of our general commitment and determination to expand world trade and of our specific undertakings: to lower tariff barriers through the Kennedy Round negotiations and other measures; to resist domestic pressures to increase tariffs and impose other protectionist restrictions on free trade; to insure less developed countries increased opportunities for exports to the United States; to cooperate in measures to stabilize prices of selected international commodities; and to carry out your instructions for developing further contacts with Eastern European countries.

2. Strong support for "economic mobility" assistance for those sectors of our economy that must adjust to increasing imports, base closings or other changes in the economic environment. This could be an important part of your general remarks about meeting human needs in the quest for the Great Society.

3. A reaffirmation of your intention to bring our balance of payments into equilibrium, and at the same time to achieve agreement with our friends on further substantial improvements in the international monetary system.

At an appropriate time, it may also be advisable for you to send a Special Message to the Congress concerning the balance of payments.

III. *Proposed Legislation*

We recommend the following legislative proposals to give effect to the Task Force proposals:

1. A general program to facilitate "economic mobility." As noted above, this would not be peculiarly related to foreign economic policy. It would replace, or at least supplement, the existing adjustment assistance provisions of the Trade Expansion Act.[3]

2. Legislation to eliminate the 25 percent gold reserve requirement; or if, as the Treasury feels, this is not feasible, legislation to limit the applicability of this requirement to Federal Reserve note liabilities. (See Annex A)[4]

---

[3] The Trade Expansion Act of 1962 was approved on October 11, 1962. (76 Stat. 872) For excerpts, see *American Foreign Policy: Current Documents, 1962,* pp. 1383–1396.

[4] Not printed.

3. An "East-West Trade Act" authorizing you to negotiate with Communist countries for trade agreements that would include most-favored-nation treatment, whenever you find such agreements to be in the public interest.

4. Enabling legislation under the International Coffee Agreement,[5] legislation to correct the revised tariff schedule, and the repeal of the Saylor Amendment to the Mass Transportation Bill.[6]

Douglas Dillon
George W. Ball
McGeorge Bundy[7]

---

[5] For a summary of the provisions of the International Coffee Agreement, 1962, signed at U.N. Headquarters in New York on September 28, 1962, and entered into force provisionally on July 1, definitively on December 27, 1963, see *American Foreign Policy: Current Documents, 1962*, pp. 1140–1142. For complete text of Agreement, see 14 UST 1911.

[6] Not further identified.

[7] Printed from a copy that bears these typed signatures.

---

23. Memorandum From Secretary of the Treasury Dillon to President Johnson[1]

Washington, December 29, 1964.

By letter dated April 29, 1964,[2] you directed me to follow up on the Governmental action required to implement the Report of the Task Force on Promoting Increased Foreign Investment and Increased Foreign Financing, headed by the then Under Secretary of the Treasury, Henry H. Fowler, which was delivered to you on April 27, 1964.[3]

This follow-up has now been completed, and the attached report is being submitted in compliance with your directive.[4] By far the most important recommendations deal with changes in our tax laws to

---

[1] Source: Johnson Library, National Security File, Subject File, Balance of Payments, Vol. 2 [2 of 2], Box 2. No classification marking.

[2] Not found.

[3] For excerpts of this report, see *American Foreign Policy: Current Documents, 1964*, pp. 1182–1190.

[4] See Document 24.

improve the climate for foreign portfolio investment in the United States. The Treasury, after consultation on technical detail with the staff of the Joint Committee on Internal Revenue Taxation, is in general accord with the recommendations of the Task Force in this area, as more fully described in the attached report.

In view of the importance of this subject to the business community and to our balance of payments, I recommend an early White House Press Release or a statement by you at your next press conference along the lines of the attached draft.[5]

A fuller description of the details of our tax recommendations could be included in the balance of payments message which we are recommending that you send to the Congress in February or March, depending on how the international payments situation evolves during the coming weeks.[6]

Douglas Dillon[7]

---

[5] Not printed.

[6] President Johnson delivered a special message to Congress proposing measures to correct the balance-of-payments deficit on February 10, 1965. See *Public Papers of the Presidents of the United States: Lyndon B. Johnson, 1965*, Book I, pp. 170–177.

[7] Printed from a copy that indicates that Dillon signed the original.

---

24.   Memorandum From Secretary of the Treasury Dillon to President Johnson[1]

Washington, December 29, 1964.

STATUS OF RECOMMENDATIONS OF THE FOWLER TASK FORCE

Introduction

The report of the Task Force on Promoting Increased Foreign Investment and Increased Foreign Financing, headed by the then Under Secretary of the Treasury, Henry H. Fowler, contains 39 recommendations

---

[1] Source: Johnson Library, National Security File, Subject File, Balance of Payments, Vol. 2 [2 of 2], Box 2. No classification marking.

designed to help the United States reduce its balance of payments deficit and defend its gold reserves.[2] Of these, 22 are directed to the private sector of our economy and 17 recommend Governmental action. All of the recommendations requiring action by the Government and not involving legislation have already been implemented by the appropriate Departments or Agencies. The recommendations requiring Governmental action which are expected to have the most immediate impact in increasing the inflow of foreign capital are those dealing with a revision of the United States system for taxing foreigners investing in the United States. The Treasury Department, after consultation with the staff of the Joint Committee on Internal Revenue Taxation as to technical aspects, has developed a series of legislative proposals for revisions in our current system of taxing nonresident alien individuals and foreign corporations. These proposals cover all the items discussed by the Task Force and generally follow the recommendations of the Task Force in liberalizing our present system.

The Treasury Department recommends that your program include the implementation of these tax proposals and in furtherance of this, the Treasury Department has suggested that a sentence on this subject be included in your State of the Union message. An outline of these proposals has been presented to the Bureau of the Budget and a legislative draft is being prepared. It is estimated that adoption of these proposals will cause a negligible revenue loss. It is extremely difficult to measure the precise impact of the adoption of these proposals on our balance of payments because of the various factors affecting the level of foreign investment in the United States. However, the effect of these recommendations will undoubtedly be favorable from a balance of payments viewpoint and, when combined with an expanding U.S. economy, may result in a significant increase in foreign investment.

Task Force Recommendations Relating to Tax Matters

The Task Force intended its recommendations to be implemented unilaterally through legislative change rather than bilateral tax treaty negotiations. The Treasury Department agrees that this is the proper course of action to follow. However, in order to protect the United States position in bilateral treaty negotiations, the Treasury Department recommends that you be given flexible authority to eliminate the liberalizing changes with respect to citizens of any foreign country which, when requested by the United States, refuses to provide reciprocal advantages for United States citizens.

The Treasury Department makes the following recommendations in the principal tax areas discussed in the Task Force report:

---

[2] See footnote 3, Document 23. Regarding the establishment of the Fowler Task Force, see footnote 4, Document 5.

1. *Estate Tax* (Recommendation 29). The Task Force recommends that our estate tax on intangible property owned by nonresident aliens be unilaterally eliminated. The Treasury Department agrees in principle that the rate of estate tax should be substantially reduced but in lieu of the Task Force recommendation of total elimination of tax on some property and maintenance of the present rates on all other property, it proposes a reduction of the rate of tax on all property. Under the Treasury Department proposals, the personal exemption would be substantially increased from $2,000 to around $30,000 and the top rate would be reduced from the present 77 percent to 15 percent. This will bring U.S. effective estate tax rates substantially below those prevailing in the United Kingdom, Canada and Italy, although they would still be higher than those of Switzerland, Germany, France, and the Netherlands. Under present law foreigners, on the average, have been paying substantially heavier estate taxes on their portfolio investments in the United States than have United States citizens. The Treasury Department proposal will bring the effective rates for foreigners down to the level of those generally applicable to U.S. citizens.

2. *Income Tax, Capital Gains, and Related Proposals* (Recommendations 30–34). In general, the Treasury Department proposes that the recommandations of the Task Force regarding taxation of the income and capital gains of nonresident aliens be implemented by legislation. The principal exception is in connection with the taxation of real estate income (Recommendation 34 (ii)). The Task Force proposes that in certain instances a nonresident alien should not be regarded as engaged in trade or business here because of activities related to real estate. However, such a rule might deprive the alien of substantial benefits under the provisions of present law. The Treasury Department therefore proposes that a nonresident alien be permitted to elect to be taxed on income from real estate (and mineral royalties) as though engaged in trade or business here.

3. *Deduction of Expenses of Placing Stock Overseas* (Recommendation 21). The Internal Revenue Service has indicated that in specified instances it will rule that the expenses of placing a corporation's stock overseas would be deductible by it for tax purposes. It is accordingly believed that no legislation is required to implement this recommendation.

Additional Tax Changes Proposed

To achieve a comprehensive and integrated revision of our system of taxing nonresident aliens, a number of changes, some of which are liberalizing in nature, beyond those proposed by the Task Force need to be made. Of these changes, the only one which is a significant deviation from present law will continue to tax for a ten-year period the U.S. income and estates of those citizens who choose to abandon their United

States citizenship. This will discourage a citizen from giving up his citizenship to take advantage of the favorable tax treatment to be provided for nonresident aliens.

The Treasury Department also proposes that banks and others withholding on the U.S. source income of nonresident aliens be required to remit withholding taxes on a quarterly basis rather than annually as at present. This change will bring withholding procedures in this area more closely into line with those prevailing in the case of withholding on domestic wages and employee F.I.C.A. taxes.

Task Force Recommendations Relating to Non-Tax Matters

1. *Recommendations directed to the Securities and Exchange Commission.* Task Force Recommendations 4 and 5 have been implemented through the publication by the SEC on July 9, 1964, of Securities Act Release No. 4708,[3] outlining the Commission's interpretation of certain portions of the statutes regulating public offerings of U.S. securities to foreign purchasers outside the United States. It is believed that this release has, generally speaking, accomplished the objectives of these Recommendations. The Commission is also taking steps to implement Recommendation 9 under which the SEC would serve as a center for information on requirements and practices in selling securities abroad.

2. *Recommendations Directed to the Federal Reserve Board of Governors.* The Federal Reserve Board of Governors has advised the Chairman of the Senate Banking and Currency Committee[4] that it would favor legislation implementing Recommendation 16 permitting greater administrative flexibility in setting maximum interest rates. With respect to Recommendation 17, the Board has undertaken to keep its regulation of time and savings deposit interest rates reasonably related to market rates. In accordance with this principle, the Federal Reserve Board recently raised the ceiling on time deposits from 4 to 4–1/2 percent and increased the ceiling on savings deposits to a flat 4 percent on all deposits.

3. *Recommendations Directed to the Department of State and the Treasury Department.* Recommendations 35–39 suggest that the Department of State and the Treasury Department take an active role in a number of related areas, principally through the Organization for Economic Cooperation and Development (OECD), to urge actions designed to increase the breadth and effectiveness of free world capital markets and to ease restrictions on the free international flow of capital. As a result of efforts initiated by the United States, the Council of Ministers of the OECD has

---

[3] Not found.
[4] Senator A. Willis Robertson (D.–Virginia).

recently requested that the Committee for Invisible Transactions seek means of improving the capital markets of member countries.

Douglas Dillon[5]

---

[5] Printed from a copy that indicates Dillon signed the original.

---

25.   Memorandum From Secretary of the Treasury Dillon to President Johnson[1]

Washington, January 4, 1965.

SUBJECT

The Current Gold Situation and Future Prospects

For the year 1964 total U.S. gold losses amounted to $125 million. Of this, $36 million was lost in transactions with foreigners and $89 million went to meet domestic industrial and artistic needs. This compares with a total loss in 1963 of $461 million, of which $392 million went to foreigners and $69 million was required to meet domestic needs. The fourth quarter showed an overall loss of $172 million, of which $95 million occurred during the month of December. The sterling crisis increased our losses since some of the funds flowing out of London went to countries which traditionally hold their assets primarily in gold, and they thereupon converted these extra dollars into gold. For instance, during the fourth quarter we sold $40 million to Belgium, $60 million to the Netherlands, and $51 million to Switzerland.

The $36 million overall loss to foreigners in 1964 was the net result of very much larger purchases and sales. Total sales amounted to approximately $943 million, which was largely offset by purchases of $907 million.

The immediate prospect for early 1965 is for a substantial acceleration in the gold outflow. This is due to a number of factors, the most

---

[1] Source: Johnson Library, Bator Papers, Balance of Payments Message, February 10, 1965, Memos [2 of 2], Box 16. Confidential.

important of which relates to decisions about to be taken by the French Government. We have had a number of informal exchanges with the French in which they have indicated that it is their intention to convert their excess dollars into gold by purchase from us. They have told us that they consider their excess dollars to be those above the amount required for a comfortable working balance plus enough to cover their post-war debts to the U.S. and Canada. On this basis they have told us that they would continue to hold about $1,100 million in dollars.

The French now hold about $1,400 million in dollars so we can look forward to conversion of about $300 million. They apparently have not yet decided on the timing of this conversion. They have mentioned a number of possible alternatives, one of the latest of which involves the conversion of $150 million during January.

An AP story from official French sources today indicates that the possibility of some advance debt repayment remains open. However, we cannot count on this. The whole matter has evidently been the subject of controversy within the French Government over the past few weeks. We should know the definite answer this week or next.

In addition to this conversion of existing balances, the French tell us they will convert any 1965 balance of payments surplus to gold on a monthly basis. If their surplus continues next year at the same rate as 1964, their monthly takings would be nearer $50 million than this year's $34 million.[2]

In addition to the French purchase, the Spaniards have stated their desire to purchase $210 million of gold over a seven month period. The first $30 million was sold to them during December. This program is designed to restore their gold ratio by July 1 to its former level of approximately 50% from its present 40% level. The Spaniards ran a surplus of over $300 million during 1964 and took no gold at all so that their gold ratio substantially declined. They expect some further surplus during the first part of this year and their purchase program is designed to offset both last year's accumulations and their expectations for the first part of 1965.

The third unfavorable factor in the situation is the prospect that Soviet sales of gold during 1965 will drop back to their normal annual level of between $200 million and $250 million. Last year their sales totalled approximately $435 million, all during the early months of the year. The year before they ran over $500 million. These extra sales were used to finance the purchase of wheat from Canada and the U.S., and are no longer required. Lower Soviet gold sales will reduce the flow of gold

---

[2] Beginning here and extending down the next two paragraphs are several marginal handwritten numbers and arithmetical calculations.

into the London market and hence reduce the gold we might otherwise expect to receive as our share of the operations of the London gold pool.

During 1964 we received $393 million from the operations of the London gold pool, all of it during the first three quarters of the year. During the fourth quarter the U.K. crisis unsettled the gold market, and the entire supply was taken by private sources with nothing available for Central Banks. In fact, there was a deficit of somewhat over $50 million in the operations of the gold pool which was met by reducing the jointly owned "kitty" from $40 million to under $10 million, as well as by some unilateral support from the U.K.

The net of all this is that our likely losses of gold to foreigners will be at least $500 million during 1965. Most of the loss should occur during the early part of the year when the French are expected to convert their excess dollars. This is a conservative estimate. Without substantial improvement in our balance of payments, losses to foreigners could easily reach or exceed the roughly $800 million levels of 1961 and 1962.

Douglas Dillon[3]

---

[3] Printed from a copy that indicates Dillon signed the original.

---

26.   Memorandum From Secretary of the Treasury Dillon to President Johnson[1]

Washington, January 5, 1965.

SUBJECT

The U.S. Balance of Payments Situation

The improvement since 1960:

Last year's deficit on regular transactions is now estimated at about $2.8 billion—$500 million below the 1963 level and about $1 billion below 1960 but well above the $2 billion target we had established earlier. The improvement over 1960 was the net result of

—A commercial trade surplus up by $500 million.
—Investment income up over $1.5 billion.

---

[1] Source: Johnson Library, Bator Papers, Balance of Payments Message, February 10, 1965, Memos [2 of 2], Box 16. Confidential.

—Effect of Government expenditures overseas down over $1 billion.

—Net losses on tourist account up $500 million.[2]

—U.S. purchases of foreign securities unchanged (but only because of the announcement of interest equalization tax in July 1963).

—Longer term bank lending to foreigners up sharply by over $500 million.[3]

—Short-term capital outflows up by $400 million.

—Direct investment higher by $500 million.[4]

In brief, improvement has been substantial in those areas which our previous programs targeted—but this improvement has been offset by sharply increased bank lending and continually heavier tourist spending abroad.

Current problems:

The fourth quarter 1964 deficit was particularly large, running at an annual rate of over $4 billion. The sterling crisis has impaired confidence in the dollar. Losses of gold have resumed, $172 million being lost in the fourth quarter with still larger losses expected in the coming months. Details regarding the gold situation are covered in a separate memorandum.[5]

Foreign exchange markets continue extremely uneasy both because of the sterling crisis and a general cautionary attitude toward *both* sterling and *the dollar.* The gold price in London stands at the highest level since the Cuban crisis *despite substantial official intervention.* Gold losses of about $250 million are foreseen for January and perhaps $600 million for the January–July period.

To sustain confidence in the dollar and avoid further substantial gold losses, it is essential to take steps to insure a reduction in the 1965 deficit to well under $2 billion.

The suggested program:

A special balance of payments message to the Congress reviewing developments since 1960, reaffirming that a change in the price of gold is out of the question and pinpointing the measures required to achieve further improvement. These steps will include:

—Announcement that the Gore amendment to the Interest Equalization Tax has been imposed by the President so that the tax falls on

---

[2] A handwritten notation presumably by Bator in the left margin reads: "no real objection."

[3] A handwritten notation presumably by Bator in the left margin reads: "no real objection."

[4] A handwritten notation presumably by Bator in the left margin reads: "no control proposed."

[5] Not found, but see Document 25.

bank loans with maturities of one year or more to foreigners (other than loans directly associated with the financing of U.S. exports).[6] Imposition of the tax would affect bank lending now running at about $1 billion annually, cutting the outflow by up to perhaps $300 million.

—Recommend a two-year extension of the Interest Equalization Tax, thus continuing to curb foreign security sales in the United States capital market by developed countries abroad.

(To minimize the possibility of heavier bank lending of less than one year, the Federal Reserve should be encouraged to amend Regulation A affecting commercial bank access to the Federal Reserve's discount window, to deter short-term lending to foreigners.)

—Recommend imposition of a travel tax of $100 per person per trip, applicable to trips outside the United States in excess of an appropriate minimum time period (or, alternatively, exclusive of travel to Canada, Mexico, and the Caribbean Islands). The tax would be designed to effect savings of around $250 million. In the absence of this measure U.S. travel expenditures can be expected to increase again by some $300 million in 1965. (This proposal has not been discussed with other Government agencies but, initially at least, will be opposed by the State Department. The proposal is nevertheless essential to provide a rounded attack on the serious balance of payments problem.)[7]

—Recommend extension for two years of legislation limiting tourist exemption to $100 which otherwise would expire on June 30.[8]

—Recommend legislation to improve the tax treatment of foreign portfolio investment in the United States and further encourage other efforts to make foreign long term investment here more attractive.[9]

—Some further reductions, beyond those already planned, in Government expenditures abroad, particularly military. This will involve difficult political decisions but is an essential element in any meaningful balance of payments program.[10]

—Reemphasis of need for price stability and improved exports.[11]

---

[6] The Gore Amendment to the Interest Equalization Tax (see Document 12), gave the President standby authority to apply the tax to the acquisition of foreign debt obligations by commercial banks, which had been exempted by the IET law.

[7] A handwritten notation presumably by Bator in the left margin reads: "Will be violently opposed by traveling public."

[8] A handwritten notation presumably by Bator in the left margin reads: "OK."

[9] A handwritten notation presumably by Bator in the left margin reads: "OK."

[10] A handwritten notation presumably by Bator in the left margin reads: "Strongly disagree."

[11] A handwritten notation presumably by Bator in the left margin reads: "Where is control over internal investment?"

The measures respecting tourism and Government expenditures abroad will require policy decisions by you before the message to the Congress can be fully developed. In addition, Commerce may recommend legislation to undertake an expanded guaranty program on export credits to be administered by the Export-Import Bank (the Eximbank will oppose this) and consideration of some incentive to U.S. exports along the lines announced recently by the British Government (this latter aspect is aimed primarily at bargaining with European governments regarding competitive equality of treatment for exports rather than a balance of payments measure).

From previous experience I am reasonably certain that it will be impossible to obtain agreement of interested Departments and agencies on the elements of a useful program. Final decisions will have to be taken by you in a number of instances. This may well require several meetings with you, which should be undertaken in the near future. These meetings must be kept in complete confidence since advance leaks regarding the program could have seriously adverse repercussions. If you desire, I can hold a preliminary meeting of the Cabinet Committee on the Balance of Payments to clarify the issues.

We have so far made real progress against a background of a stable price level. But the improvement remains inadequate—if, as must be the case, a dollar of unquestioned integrity at home and abroad is to go hand-in-hand with progress in establishing the Great Society.

Douglas Dillon[12]

---

[12] Printed from a copy that indicates Dillon signed the original.

27.   Memorandum by the Chairman of the Council of Economic Advisers (Ackley)[1]

Washington, January 11, 1965.

MEMORANDUM FOR

Cabinet Committee on Balance of Payments:
Secretary of the Treasury
Secretary of Defense
Secretary of Commerce
Under Secretary of State
Administrator of AID
Special Representative for Trade Negotiations
Director, Bureau of the Budget
Mr. Bundy, the White House

SUBJECT

Balance-of-Payments Program

Secretary Dillon's memorandum of January 8 calls for further steps to improve our balance of payments.[2] The program recommendations contained in his memorandum, however, do not appear to exhaust the possibilities. Set out briefly below are additional or alternative steps that should be considered before decisions are reached.

Many of these possibilities involve the area of direct investment, one of the largest and most steadily expanding drains on our balance of payments. Governments of most of the developed countries would be happier if this flow were reduced; indeed the current magnitude of such investment (at a time when the U.S. is running large deficits and asking surplus countries to hold enlarged low-yielding liquid claims against us) appears to be impairing their willingness to cooperate with us in other areas. Since at least a temporary reduction in this flow is also in the U.S. interest, it would seem that this is a promising area in which to move.

1. *The IET could be extended, in some form, to direct investment,* with or without an exemption for that portion of direct investment associated with the export of machinery and equipment from the United States. A somewhat higher tax rate might be needed, given the higher return from direct than from portfolio investment. As a minimum, the definition of direct investment in the IET could be changed so that the tax would apply to all purchase of stock in (or other means of taking over) *existing* foreign enterprises.

2. *Moral suasion could be tried in the field of direct investment.* This could be done by a strong general Presidential appeal, or directly with

---

[1] Source: Johnson Library, National Security File, Subject File, Balance of Payments, Vol. 2 [2 of 2], Box 2. Confidential. A copy was sent to the Chairman of the Board of Governors, Federal Reserve System.

[2] Not printed. (Ibid.)

key firms. Or one or more business groups could be encouraged to set up a voluntary self-policing effort.

3. *Taxation of income from private foreign investment could be strengthened.* In the new climate of opinion, tax measures such as those proposed but not enacted in 1962 might be reintroduced with perhaps greater chance of enactment. In any case, a renewal of these proposals might cause prospective investors to hesitate.

4. Additionally or alternatively, the *Europeans could be quietly encouraged to use their existing controls on investment* to cut back on American direct investment in their jurisdictions. In fact, our official posture has been just the opposite.

5. *In the area of bank loans, moral suasion might be even more effective than extension of the IET,* particularly because it could be applied to loans of any term. But any effort to use *either* moral suasion or the IET runs into both political difficulties and possible ineffectiveness unless the Canadian loophole is closed. Canadian authorities should be willing—as a part of the price for their continued IET exemption—to close this loophole themselves if we move to reduce the foreign lending of our own banks.

6. If the IET is extended to banks, the definition of a loan of over one year should be altered to include renewals of shorter-term loans, and an increase in the tax rate should be considered.

7. If American travel is to be taxed (and I am not convinced it should), some effort should be made to reduce its highly regressive character. Regressivity would be lessened if the tax were applied to the sale (or purchase) of international ship and airline tickets, with perhaps a higher rate on more expensive accommodations. (The Treasury suggestion for an exemption on short trips would appear to make the tax more regressive.) We should certainly consider reducing the customs exemption to $50, and eliminating the liquor allowance.

8. On the price stability front, a request that Congress enact a concurrent resolution affirming the principles of the price-wage guideposts might be considered, in order to give greater moral sanction to these principles. Perhaps there is an alternative and less difficult way to strengthen the authority of the guideposts.

Gardner Ackley[3]

---

[3] Printed from a copy that bears this typed signature.

28. Memorandum From Secretary of the Treasury Dillon to President Johnson[1]

Washington, January 15, 1965.

SUBJECT

Balance of Payments Problems with Canada

We have one balance of payments problem with Canada which it would be important for you to mention to Prime Minister Pearson.[2] This is the necessity for continued reasonable restraint by the Canadians in the sale of new security issues in the American market, under the exemption which you have given them from the provisions of the Interest Equalization Tax.[3]

In 1963, when the principle of the exemption was agreed with the Canadians,[4] they indicated that they could and would control the volume of their borrowings in the United States by lowering their long-term interest rates so that Canadian sales of new issues in our markets would not lead to any increase in overall Canadian monetary reserves. Measuring from the introduction of the Interest Equalization Tax in July 1963, Canada has generally fulfilled this obligation with the exception of a $180 million repayment of their debt to the International Monetary Fund. They have claimed that this did not add to their reserves while we felt that it should be included. However, an honest misunderstanding was certainly possible on this item, and in any event it is now water over the dam. We now have a clear agreement with the Canadians that any further transactions with the IMF will count as additions to their reserves.

When we look at the year 1964, however, the situation is different. Overall Canadian reserves did rise by $81 million during the calendar year, without counting the IMF repayment of $180 million which served to hold down the rise in published reserves. During this period the outflow of dollars into new Canadian issues amounted to $676 million which is much too high for a permanent level. This situation became particularly acute in the fourth quarter when the new issue outflow to Canada rose sharply to $359 million or an annual rate of over $1.4 billion. The

---

[1] Source: Johnson Library, National Security File, Subject File, Balance of Payments, Vol. 2 [2 of 2], Box 2. Limited Official Use.

[2] Canadian Prime Minister Lester B. Pearson met with President Johnson at the LBJ Ranch January 15–16. For an exchange of remarks between the President and the Prime Minister on January 16 prior to their signing of a U.S.-Canadian agreement on trade in automotive products, together with the text of the agreement, see Department of State *Bulletin*, February 2, 1965, pp. 191–194.

[3] A handwritten notation in the left margin reads: "See also p. 3."

[4] See *Foreign Relations*, 1961–1963, vol. IX, p. 180, footnote 2.

reason for this sudden burst was that some Canadian borrowers had held up their borrowings pending final approval of the Interest Equalization Tax and assurance by the President of a Canadian exemption. The Canadians now assure us that they expect a sharp decrease in new issues in the coming months. This is in accord with our own best information.

I raised this matter with Finance Minister Gordon in Tokyo in early September,[5] and we stressed its importance to the Canadians during November and early December when the Governor of the Bank of Canada, Mr. Rasminsky, who negotiated the original exemption, came to Washington to talk with me.

As a result of these conversations, Finance Minister Gordon informally suggested to the Canadian Provincial authorities that it would be helpful, in the coming months, if they maximized their use of the Canadian market for new borrowings and avoided the New York market. At the same time, and for the first time since July 1963, the Bank of Canada by its operations in Canadian government bonds lowered the interest rate differential between long-term Canadian bonds and U.S. government bonds to approximately .80 percent from the 1 percent differential which had long been customary. Early in January, in accord with this policy, the Ontario Hydroelectric Commission successfully sold a $79 million new issue in Canada which under other circumstances would undoubtedly have been done in New York.

While the Canadians are now cooperating reasonably well, one reason for their cooperation is their knowledge that the Interest Equalization Tax will probably have to be extended later this year. They wish to build a record in the coming months that will give assurance to our Congress that the Canadian exemption can be safely maintained. There is a danger that renewal of the Act will again be followed by a burst of Canadian borrowing in New York.

It is important for you to indicate to Prime Minister Pearson your awareness of this problem, and its importance to our over-all balance of payments situation. It would help if you could stress the need for Canada to reduce her dependence on the New York market to the maximum extent possible not only prior to Congressional action on the extension of the Interest Equalization Tax but also thereafter. You could tell Prime Minister Pearson that any new bulge in Canadian sales in the New York market after the extension of the tax would put great pressure on you to set a ceiling on Canadian borrowings under the terms of the law.

Prime Minister Pearson may reply that Canada will make every attempt to carry out her agreement, but that the prospects are for a deteri-

---

[5] Secretary Dillon was in Tokyo for the joint annual meeting of the IMF and the IBRD September 5–11, 1964. His meeting with the Canadian Finance Minister has not been identified.

oration in the Canadian current account balance during 1965 which will have to be made up by borrowing abroad. The Canadians have a habit of being unduly pessimistic about their trade prospects. They expected their 1964 trade balance to be worse than the 1963 results. In fact, it turned out better. If Pearson should answer in this vein you might tell him that we are more optimistic than they regarding Canadian balance of payments prospects, and that, in any event, borrowing in our market should be held down until actual results in other areas of their payments clearly indicate a necessity for some increase in order to maintain the level of their overall monetary reserves.

Douglas Dillon

29.   Memorandum of Conversation

Washington, January 19, 1965.

[Source: Department of State, Central Files, FN 16 US. Limited Official Use. 2 pages of source text not declassified.]

30.   Memorandum From the Acting Director of the U.S. Travel Service (Black) to Secretary of Commerce Connor[1]

Washington, January 21, 1965.

SUBJECT

U.S. Travel Service—Priority Items

There are only two matters affecting USTS which require your immediate attention:

---

[1] Source: Washington National Records Center, RG 40, Records of the Office of Fred Simpich, Assistant to Secretary of Commerce, 1965–1968: FRC 70 A 7017, Secretary's Staff Meetings, 1965. No classification marking.

1. *Proposed Travel Tax.* We discussed this briefly at Tuesday's staff meeting.[2] In summary, Treasury has proposed the imposition of a $100 tax per person on travel abroad by U. S. citizens as a means of cutting down our balance-of-payments losses in the travel sector. This has been considered at the Cabinet level and a final decision should be made within the next week or so. If approved, this tax would be announced in a special balance-of-payments message to Congress by the President early next month. Assistant Secretary Holton has the action on this problem and can give you more details.

USTS is strongly opposed to the tax on outbound travel, as we believe it would have repercussions on our own program to attract more foreign visitors here. We think the timing is bad, inasmuch as our "travel deficit" has not increased during the past year. However, if savings on our travel account are required, we propose instead that the duty-free allowance for returning U.S. residents be cut and that the Government officially promote the use of U.S.-flag carriers by U.S. citizens. These measures, we believe, would effect the savings required by Treasury and would be far more acceptable politically here at home.

I have discussed this problem in detail with Under Secretary Roosevelt, and he has a memo from us outlining our position at length.[3]

2. *Travel Advisory Committee.* At our staff meeting, you mentioned the need for close consultation with industry in shaping the Commerce Department's policies. In the travel field we have a formal advisory group—the Travel Advisory Committee—composed of 36 representatives of carriers, hotels, travel agents and other business interests concerned with international travel. The Committee meets quarterly in Washington, and our first meeting of this year should be held early next month, if possible.

I would like to set a meeting date rather soon—but would like to fix a day when you could join with us and at least say "hello" to the group. Secretary Hodges customarily attended at least the first meeting of the TAC every year.

Attached is the press release listing the TAC members, including those newly appointed.[4]

[2] The minutes of the Secretary of Commerce's staff meeting on Tuesday, January 19, refer only briefly to the Tourist Tax. (Ibid.)

[3] Not further identified.

[4] This Department of Commerce press release, G 65–7, January 15, is not printed. Secretary Connor announced the appointment of 36 members to the 1965 Travel Advisory Committee, of whom 16 were members of the 1964 Travel Advisory Committee. All members served without compensation for a 1 or 2-year term.

31.   Memorandum From the President's Special Assistant for National Security Affairs (Bundy) to President Johnson[1]

Washington, January 22, 1965.

SUBJECT

Balance of Payments Committee Work

This morning we had the best meeting yet of the Cabinet Committee on the Balance of Payments, but there is still several days' work before we will be in shape to talk with you.

There is now a pretty general agreement on a number of specific items. The most important are:

a. The Gore Amendment to tax bank lending of *one year or more,* imposed at the present rate basis (a large item).

b. Encouragement of foreign investment in the U.S. (a small but useful item).

c. Limitations on free imports by U.S. tourists (also small but useful).

d. Increases in the interest equalization tax on capital outflow (middle-sized).

e. A quite general effort in partnership with the Fed and perhaps with an additional tax to control both bank and non-bank short-term capital movements. (This may be a quite substantial item, since there appears to be a large pool of short-term funds of U. S. corporations which is held abroad for very small interest advantages.)

f. A further intensification of savings on the military dollar account. This is more for show than for use, and it has important budgetary costs because U.S. oil is more than twice as expensive as Middle East oil for some of our forces, but we all agree that it is worth including for appearances sake.

g. Finally, there is agreement, at least for the moment, that we should open an attack on overseas investment in the developed countries, but not by proposing legislation this year. The idea is that with John Connor as your Chief of Staff you should mount a major campaign of personal leadership with the top business leaders whose firms do most of this investing. Connor and McNamara believe that this would have a very substantial effect for a year or so, and that then we could ease up if conditions improve or move to legislation with less business opposition than we would be sure to get now.

The ways and means of some of the more complex parts of this program—notably the limitations on short-term capital movement—are being examined over the week end. We are also trying to get harder figures on projected savings, though there is inevitably a lot of guess work in all this. We should have a further report for you then.

---

[1] Source: Johnson Library, National Security File, Subject File, Balance of Payments, Vol. 2 [2 of 2], Box 2. Personal and Confidential.

The one item which is losing ground in the Cabinet Committee is the tax on tourist travel. An interesting coalition led by Rusk, Ball, Connor and Herter is strongly opposed. Their arguments turn on the damage to our own citizens of a regressive tax, the bad political impact abroad, the damage to our own tourist program, and effects on the Kennedy Round.

All of this will culminate in recommendations next week for a Presidential message. In addition, it looks as if you would be asked to take on three particular tasks:

1. The work with the business leadership on overseas investment already explained.

2. A message to Mike Pearson to emphasize to the Canadians the importance of limiting their very heavy borrowing in our market. (This would then be followed up hard by Treasury and State.)

3. A personal word from you to Bill Martin which would have two components:

a. You care even more about confidence in the dollar than he does, and this program is designed to prove it.
b. You expect to hold him to the promise he gave in the Committee today—that if confidence can be sustained, U.S. domestic credit will be kept easy. This is regarded by Gordon, McNamara and Ackley as very important in the light of the strong possibility that we may need even easier credit before the end of this year.

The clearly dominant judgment of your Committee now is that we must have a strong widely based program. We don't have it yet, but we are getting there.

McG. B.

---

32.   **Memorandum of Conversation**

Washington, January 22, 1965.

[Source: Department of State, Central Files, FN 16 US. Confidential. 2 pages of source text not declassified.]

33. Report From the Cabinet Committee on Balance of Payments to President Johnson[1]

Washington, undated.

REPORT TO THE PRESIDENT ON BALANCE OF PAYMENTS

I. Situation and Program

Fourth Quarter Results.

Preliminary data for the fourth quarter show a sudden and substantial worsening of our payments position. As compared with a November projection of about $900 million, the actual fourth quarter deficit is now estimated to have been almost $1.6 billion. Most of the $700 million difference is apparently accounted for by larger than projected outflows of short-term funds and long-term bank loans and by a failure to receive the British debt repayment of $138 million.

Factors contributing to the fourth quarter deterioration appear, in part, to have been temporary, but

—the sudden change for the worse, plus
—the failure to achieve a more rapid reduction in our stubbornly large deficit that has persisted for seven years, plus
—the resumption of large gold outflows

have revived serious concern about the strength of the dollar.

Prompt action is needed to deal with the situation. This can best be announced by a special balance-of-payments message in early February. This message should contain a strong reaffirmation of your determination to defend the dollar and a description of actions which you have ordered or are requesting from Congress to improve the situation.

Trend in the Deficit.

Some improvement has been made in our balance of payments since 1960, our worst year.

—Our commercial exports in 1964 were $4.4 billion above the 1960 level, thanks to an exceptionally large increase ($2.8 billion) last year, partly due to unusual agricultural exports to the Soviet zone.

---

[1] Source: Washington National Records Center, RG 40, Records from the Office of Franklin D. Roosevelt, Jr., Under Secretary of Commerce, 1963–June 1965: FRC 68 A 5947, Correspondence: The President, 1965. Confidential. The source text is attached to a February 1 memorandum from Secretary Dillon to the Cabinet Committee on Balance of Payments in wich he requested "final comments, if any, to Acting Assistant Secretary Trued by noon on Tuesday, February 2, 1965, so that we may transmit the report to the White House on Tuesday afternoon." A copy was also sent to Martin, Chairman of the Board of Governors, Federal Reserve System.

—Our imports were only $3.8 billion above the 1960 level, showing a percentage increase lower than the growth of our national income.

—Private investment income was $1.9 billion higher in 1964 than in 1960, with an exceptionally large increase during 1964 due to several special transactions.

—Government expenditures abroad last year had a $1 billion lower net balance of payments impact than in 1960. Included in the decline was about $675 million of net military expenditures.

—The adverse balance on travel on the other hand, was almost $400 million larger in 1964 than in 1960, although it showed no deterioration from the 1963 level.

—Long-term bank credits to foreigners were some $850 million higher in 1964 than in 1960 and direct investment abroad was almost $500 million higher.

—Short-term capital outflows (presently estimated at about $2.2 billion) were also about $850 million higher than in 1960, but this outflow is highly variable, having been as low as $550 million in 1962 and as high as $1,550 million in 1961.

—Net purchases of foreign securities in 1964 were at about the 1960 level, but would have risen by a substantial amount in the absence of the Interest Equalization Tax. As it was, the tax discouraged all U.S. security flotations by the advanced countries at which it was directed.

These various changes were reflected in the regular transactions deficit which showed the following trend:

Years	$Billion
1960	3.9
1961	3.1
1962	3.6
1963	3.3
1964 (est.)	3.1

The $500 million reduction in the last two years combined is much too slow a rate of improvement to ensure the avoidance of a serious crisis of confidence in the dollar. A reduction in the 1965 deficit significantly below $2 billion, with clear prospects for further substantial improvements in 1966, must be our objective.

Outlook for 1965.

Table 1 shows the composition of our estimated $3.1 billion deficit on regular transactions for 1964—final figures of this breakdown will not be available until early March—and a projected range of $2.5 billion to $3.2 billion for 1965.[2] (The upper limit of the range would have been

---

[2] Table 1 is not printed.

raised by several hundred million dollars by one agency representative and the lower limit would have been lowered by several hundred million dollars by another agency representative, but the majority favored the range shown.)

This range is to be interpreted as follows:

—The upper limit of $3.2 billion indicates that under our present program the deficit could well be greater than the 1964 deficit, even in the absence of a crisis of confidence in the dollar.

—The lower limit of $2.5 billion indicates that the deficit, under the most favorable circumstances, will probably not show more than a moderate decline from the 1964 level.

—The mid-point of $2.85 billion indicates that, in the absence of a crisis of confidence, the deficit will *most* probably show only very slight improvement from the 1964 level.

But in absence of marked improvement from the 1964 position *there is no assurance against a crisis of confidence,* particularly in view of resumption of gold losses. To get assurance, we must adopt measures which can be expected to reduce the deficit by more than $1 billion in 1965 (bringing our probable deficit well below $2 billion), and by an additional amount in 1966.

Program and Possible Savings.

Table 2 shows nine agreed measures and potential savings for 1965.[3]

These measures do not offer equally firm prospects for savings. (There is not sufficient experience with moral suasion to afford confidence in estimating results. There is also no sound basis for checking individual banker's judgments as to how much in additional exports would be achieved in 1965 by expanded export financing facilities.)

They also differ in respect to the time-pattern of the expected savings. (In case of moral suasion, for example, effect is likely to be rather quickly achieved but could be short lived.)

Finally, indirect effects of measures—particularly in stimulating possible evasions—vary greatly. A tax on one form of capital will lead to some increase in outflow through untaxed channels. Allowance was made for this in estimated savings by keeping them on conservative side, rather than by showing more optimistic amounts accompanied by partially offsetting increases in other forms of outflow.

II. Agreed Program of Immediate Measures

The agreed measures provide total estimated savings of $1,470 million in 1965. These measures, however, as noted above, are not of equal

---

[3] Table 2 is not printed. The nine measures are discussed in detail in Section II below.

firmness as far as savings anticipations are concerned. The first six measures in Table 2 which are the firmest in this respect total only $630 million. Each of the measures is commented on in the following paragraphs.

If the measures finally adopted should not constitute an effective program, the only alternative would be a considerable tightening in bank credit availability, with inevitable repercussions on our domestic economy.

Apply and Broaden Gore Amendment.

Gore Amendment. Application of the Gore Amendment by Executive Order on the data of your message to the Congress is expected to reduce the $1,300 million of projected disbursements under long-term bank loans to advanced countries to about $1 billion. Net disbursements (after estimated repayments) to *advanced* countries would then be about $300 million.

Despite the tax Japan will probably want to borrow $200–$300 million in view of its high domestic rates and customary recourse to the U.S. for financial capital. At the present schedule of tax rates, a number of other advanced countries will also want to continue borrowing here. Their residents even now are reportedly committing themselves to reimburse the lending U.S. bank for the tax, if it is applied.

Higher IET Rates. If Congress were to raise the schedule of tax rates and make it applicable to all U.S. long-term bank loans made after the date of the message—measure number 3 of Table 2—some of these borrowers would drop out of the U.S. market and an additional $200 million of savings for the balance of payments would probably be achieved.

Non-Bank Long-Term Lending. The above savings estimates make an allowance for some leakage through other channels, although as noted below such leakage might be somewhat restricted through a strong moral suasion effort. One of these channels of leakage which it seems appropriate to restrict by application of the tax is non-bank long-term lending to foreigners—measure number 2 in Table 2. Such lending has not been sizable (apart from a special transaction last year in connection with the British Columbia Hydroelectric Project); but it could grow as an escape channel from the tax on long-term bank lending unless it also were subject to the tax. A modest saving of $20 million is projected in 1965 from applying the tax to long-term non-bank loans—for example, loans by insurance companies, trust funds, etc. The export and less developed country exemptions to bank loans would also apply to non-bank loans.

Military Expenditures Abroad.

In view of the previous actions taken by Defense, further substantial reductions in expenditures could be effected only through a major realignment of our forces overseas. Possible additional actions by Defense include cutting purchases of petroleum abroad with substantial increases in budgetary costs (increases range from 25% for returning Av Gas to approximately 100% for jet fuels and roughly 200% for Navy special fuel oil), holding Army strength overseas generally below authorized levels, thinning out of personnel in certain selected countries and other economies which are also likely to increase budgetary costs. Further savings in 1966 are possible through similar actions. No withdrawal of combat units per se is contemplated under these strength restrictions. Balance of payments savings are estimated at $50 million in 1965 and $100 million in 1966, excluding contingencies which may arise in Southeast Asia.

State notes that in light of our existing situation abroad, particularly in the Far East, these proposals would require careful consideration in detail to assure that our political military interests abroad are not undercut.

Tourist Duty-Free Imports.

Request Congress in extending tourist duty-free exemption for two years to reduce amount of exemption from $100 to $50 and confine it to items accompanying tourist; also remove the special exemption for liquor.

Possible savings: approximately $40 million in 1965 if put into effect by May 1; $50 million to $60 million in 1966. The combined savings from these actions have been estimated conservatively to allow for possibility that reduced expenditures for foreign goods may be offset to some extent by increased expenditures for services within the foreign country.

Such action would leave U.S. policy still as liberal or more liberal than that of other advanced countries. Some increase in administrative cost would be necessary to make reductions effective but most, if not all, would be offset by additional revenue earned.

Encourage Foreign Portfolio Investment in U.S.

This measure would involve new legislation permitting easier tax treatment of foreign portfolio investment in the United States. Modest savings are projected for 1965 since the bulk of the effect would be expected to accrue only with a lag. Effects in later years could be substantial.

Moral Suasion.

After extensive discussion, there was unanimous agreement that, under present circumstances and at the present time, a strong across-the-board campaign of moral suasion over all forms of direct investment and bank and non-bank lending will produce as favorable results as tax action and would avoid the very real dangers of attempting to secure legislation in this area.

As Applied to Non-Banking Business Community. The business community strongly believes that direct investment abroad benefits the balance of payments in the long run because of the repatriated profits and because of the exports which many direct investment projects generate. Large balance of payments savings could result if firms were consciously to consider the impact of their total operations on our immediate balance of payments problems. They should be urged

—to reduce over the coming months their holdings of short-term investments abroad;
—to exercise restraint in financing their direct investments abroad with U.S. funds;
—to avoid or postpone direct investments in projects which do not promise clearly to be profitable, i.e., marginal projects should be avoided;
—to increase the repatriation of income earned abroad;
—to increase their exports to and through their manufacturing and sales affiliates abroad; and
—to open up new export markets in countries where they are not now active.

A special White House meeting of the operating heads of the two or three hundred non-banking corporations most involved in direct investments and in exporting would be arranged, at which you could give a frank statement on our balance of payments situation.

—You would appeal to them to assess carefully the impact of their decisions on the balance of payments.

—To measure the degree to which such cooperation was forthcoming, you would request that each corporation send to the Secretary of Commerce a quarterly report on changes in their short-term investments abroad, changes in their direct investments, their repatriated earnings and their exports, and a report on actions taken to reduce the outflow of funds from the United States or increase the inflow of funds to the United States.

Large outflows of direct investment, particularly to Western Europe, as Table 3 shows, suggest the possibility of large balance of payments savings by some form of restraint, without serious short-run reduction in net income from accumulated direct investment abroad.[4]

In addition to their direct investment in foreign subsidiaries, many large U.S. companies make investments in liquid assets abroad (bank deposits, foreign Treasury bills, etc.) *directly out of the U.S. head office.* Also, firms that do not have subsidiaries frequently keep deposits or

---

[4] Table 3, entitled "U.S. Direct Investments, 1963 and 1964," is not printed.

holdings of money market instruments abroad as a form of short-term investment.

—Such liquid funds held in advanced countries as of the end of last September amounted to over $2 billion of which over $1.5 billion was in Canada, $300 million in the U.K. and about $125 million in Japan.

—A small part of these holdings represent working balances for operations abroad; the great bulk of them represents short-term investment.

It is recommended that in your address to business leaders you also exert moral suasion for a reduction in these short-term foreign investments in the interests of helping our balance-of-payments position.

—The small number of companies which hold a large portion of these funds abroad may be even more receptive to reducing these holdings than to cutting back their plans for direct investment abroad over the next few years.

—The short-term investments yield only slightly higher interest earnings than what they could earn in the U.S., whereas direct investments generally offer much wider profit differentials over a period of time.

A fairly substantial response to moral suasion on this item might, therefore, be expected from the large corporations.

Substantial withdrawal of funds on their part may well exert some upward pressure on interest rates in foreign money markets which would tempt other U.S. firms or individuals to add to their holdings abroad. Hence, we have estimated a net saving of only about $200 million from this moral suasion effort.

Care would have to be exercised in this effort to avoid disrupting the money and exchange markets in countries from which funds might be withdrawn by U.S. corporations.

—If large amounts were actually transferred back to the United States, repercussions would undoubtedly be felt on both the London and Japanese markets; there would, in fact, be a substantial risk of aggravating the sterling crisis and of creating difficulties for Japan.

(U.S. funds held in Canada are either reinvested back in the U.S. or in London, so that no serious repercussion on the Canadian domestic money market is foreseen although the banks there would lose some profitable middleman business. To the extent Canadian banks respond by reducing their own American investments, our balance of payments as presently calculated would be improved, but the change would not affect the net flow of dollars into official hands abroad or pressure on our gold stock.)

—Since we do not want to aggravate the weakness of sterling or create a crisis atmosphere in the Japanese money market, an abrupt "across-the-board" withdrawal of funds from abroad would be dangerous, and this must be considered in implementing this measure.

As Applied to Banking Community. In addition to the application of the IET to long-term bank loans, moral suasion on banks to reduce their loans to foreigners would be exercised through the Federal Reserve, the Comptroller of the Currency, and the FDIC. This moral suasion would be accompanied in the case of banks by some reduction in credit availabilities (lower level of net free reserves) so as to reinforce the moral suasion effort.

The Federal Reserve could also be encouraged to consider amending Regulation A so that extension of rediscount facilities to a member bank could be based in part on whether or not that bank is expanding its total foreign lending activity.

Savings from this operation are estimated at $100 million.

Moral suasion would be particularly effective if it also involved a Federal Reserve request to banks to limit the increase in loans to foreigners, both short- and long-term, to 5 percent a year. (It was 36 percent in 1964.) An additional $100 million of savings, or more, could be achieved.

Note: With taxation of long-term bank loans to foreigners—intensified if the schedule of tax rates is raised by Congress, at our request, as recommended above—and with application of moral suasion on both long-term and short-term bank lending to foreigners, we will want to give particular attention to any resulting problems affecting Japan because of both political and economic considerations. Any recommendations in this area will be forwarded in a separate memorandum to you.

As Applied to Canadian New Issues. Canadian security issues in this country have for nearly a decade fluctuated between $200 million and $700 million a year. Before 1963, the annual totals of such issues did not exceed about $450 million; only in 1963 and 1964 were the record totals of about $700 million reached. Canadian issues promise again this year to reach a large volume unless restraint is exercised.

It is essential that the volume of new issues of Canadian securities sold in the U.S. during 1965 be significantly reduced from the 1964 level. This will require, at the least, strong representations to the Canadians, including a further conversation on your part with the Prime Minister, or, as an alternative, the exercise of your authority to set an over-all limit on Canadian borrowing here. (Savings in either event should total at least $100 million.)

Export Measures

Long-range health of our payments balance depends in large measure on our success in this area. A one per cent increase in our commercial exports over the 1965 forecast would reduce the deficit by about $225 million.

The most basic requirement is for maximum emphasis on, and success in, the maintenance of continued cost and price stability in our domestic economy.

Combined with this, reinforcement of our export promotion program is needed. Here relatively *inexpensive* measures can pay off in a substantial way. The export expansion program, with a fiscal year *1965* budget of less than $10 million, clearly earns many times this amount in additional foreign exchange.

—The Administration should press Congress vigorously to grant the full fiscal year *1966* export expansion budget request of somewhat over $12 million. If the export promotion measures made possible by the expanded budget combined with the trade development proposals in the Magnuson Bill (establishing trade development corps of private businessmen, use of local currencies for trade promotion and establishment of sales and service centers abroad) were put into effect, the estimated gain in exports during 1965 would be $20 million and much more in later years.

—Support Federal Maritime Commission's efforts to investigate and eliminate apparent discrimination against U.S. exports in shipping rates. (Requires no legislation.) No savings are estimated from this action during 1965.

Commerce Department consulted with a group of major banks involved in export financing. Each bank gave its estimate of the minimum total figure per year in export financing business that, in its judgment, is lost to that bank because of the inflexibility of the present export financing program and the lack of a program of the kind contemplated by the Magnuson bill. Each bank has also given what it thinks is a *minimum* estimate of the total business being lost each year by all the banks on short and medium-term credit. The consensus of the banks with whom this was discussed was that a minimum of $300 million of desirable export business on short and medium terms is not now being done because of present Exim Bank limitations. With a 20 per cent down payment by foreigners on $300 million of additional purchases in the U.S. and a $40 million installment payment by foreigners later in the year, the gain in balance of payments receipts during 1965 is estimated at $100 million. In view of the above

—current Export-Import Bank procedures should be eased to assure fully competitive risk-taking in financing of U.S. products and services and in extension of export guarantees.

"See the U.S.A."

Vigorous implementation of a program to persuade Americans to travel more at home and less abroad would achieve some savings for the balance of payments during 1965. The savings would be small, however, due to the fact that many spring and summer travel plans are made in January and February. A promotional program may divert to domestic attractions some of the travel which otherwise would go to Mexico and Canada. But it seems unlikely that the bulk of the contemplated trips to Europe would be affected during 1965. A substantial travel tax would be required for this purpose, as discussed below.

—You should appoint an administrator of the "See the U.S.A." program who would launch measures designed to reduce American overseas travel in 1965 and 1966. (Estimated savings in 1965—$20 million; in 1966—$100 million.)

III. Other Measures

Travel Tax.

—Legislation establishing for 2 years a travel tax to all foreign countries outside the Western Hemisphere, with an exemption for students and teachers (including those covered by Government programs—e.g., Fulbright scholars) departing the U. S. for at least a nine months' period of study abroad, and for Government personnel on official business.

(Estimated 1965 savings @ $100 per trip—$140 million.)

(Estimated 1965 savings @ $200 per trip—$275 million.)

Arguments for:

Travel outlays by Americans, including fares, are one of the largest outflow items in the balance of payments and are expected to total over $3 billion in 1965 in absence of any action. While U. S. receipts from foreign tourists began to rise in past two years and our net tourist deficit in 1964 appears to have remained constant, further large increases in American travel abroad are expected.

The tax would be directed at an expenditure item which for the most part is in luxury category, and can be postponed with relatively little hardship. At same time, reduction in this category, perhaps more than in any other, will be at the expense of the countries of continental Western Europe in the best position to absorb the reduction.

Reduction in expenditures contemplated would still leave total payments for tourists for 1965 and 1966 at about the same level as in 1964, thus would not be significant reduction in earnings of activities dependent on tourist industry such as U. S. or foreign airlines and shipping lines. In addition, no significant effect on U. S. aircraft sales to foreign countries seems likely since (a) the tax is for only 2 years, (b) the bulk of the savings will not come from reduction of the number of travelers (but from shorter stays and less spending per trip) and (c) the effects which are expected on the number of travelers will largely be limited to potential *increases*.

Tax on this item would broaden balance-of-payments program

—by having a favorable psychological effect on the million U. S. military personnel and their dependents serving overseas who are well aware that previous programs have omitted any actions relating to tourism, and feel very strongly that they have had to bear a major burden of previous action programs.

—and tending to lessen opposition and adverse reaction of financial community to variety of measures restraining investments, which, in contrast to tourist expenditures, offer eventual large return.

It would bring sizeable needed savings in a way that cannot easily be affected by leakages.

Arguments against:

Many countries look on all current account transactions as basically same in nature and would argue that restriction on tourism contradicts U. S. stand on liberalizing international trade. Some feel could compromise our position in current Kennedy Round negotiations under GATT.

The tax would be regressive. Lower income travelers, who spend relatively small amounts on their trips abroad, would not be able to afford the tax. The big spenders would; and would spend as much abroad as before.

Less developed countries outside the Western Hemisphere might make protest since many of them trying to build up their tourism business.

In longer range context, there is also the question of the merit of curtailing international travel and contacts with foreigners. Private travel may have important long run benefits to our international relations, and U. S. citizens may feel that freedom of movement is being challenged.

Some retaliation by foreign countries may occur. This could both reduce net effect of tax by reducing our tourist receipts, and raise problems involving our political relations abroad. Some believe there is a possibility of repercussions on the trade account—e.g. aircraft sales. The increase in costs to American tourists from the tax could bring added pressures by air and shipping lines to reduce fares.

Taxes on Direct Investment and Short-Term Investments.

The Cabinet Committee on Balance of Payments unanimously agrees that present circumstances do not require action in these areas. Vigorous efforts at moral suasion offer the best hope of gain in the immediate future and run far less risk of triggering widespread anticipation of comprehensive controls which, by inciting heavy outflows of funds, could defeat the entire program. The State Department and Council of Economic Advisers however believe that consideration should be given to a tax in these areas if a tax on tourist travel is to be adopted.

As regards direct investment, some suggest that it be limited to so-called "takeover" transactions; this would involve serious technical problems of definition and administration. Application of the tax would also raise difficult technical questions of how to exempt exports, associated with direct investments abroad, without either virtually losing deterrent effect of tax, on the one hand, or taxing many direct investment operations which possibly would create additional U. S. exports, on the other hand. The Department of Commerce feels that the business community would strongly resent such action and would continue their projects despite the tax.

---

34.   Memorandum From the President's Special Assistant for National Security Affairs (Bundy) to President Johnson[1]

Washington, February 1, 1965.

SUBJECT

Cabinet Committee Meeting on Tuesday[2]

1.   Douglas Dillon now agrees to a balance of payments meeting on Tuesday, and I enclose the almost final draft of an agreed paper from the Cabinet Committee to you, for your reading this evening.[3]

2.   As you will see the principal divided issue that remains is the travel tax.

3.   In the background there are also latent differences about the effectiveness that "moral suasion" has on those who control short-term capital controls and overseas equity investments, but I myself see no way around a trial period on this, in the light of Jack Connor's determination to make them work. If he fails, your position in going for legislation will be that much stronger. If he succeeds, even for a year or so, we have done something important.

4.   Still one major aspect of the "moral suasion" problem is whether we are really ready to act if it fails. You may remember that Don Cook[4]

---

[1] Source: Johnson Library, National Security File, Subject File, Balance of Payments, Vol. 2 [1 of 2], Box 2. No classification marking.

[2] February 2.

[3] Document 33.

[4] Don Cook, President of the American Electric Power Company, was nominated to succeed Secretary Dillon as Secretary of the Treasury but did not accept the nomination.

emphasized this point to me very hard. It may be worth your while to press Connor and Dillon on this point. They will assure you of their readiness to recommend stronger measures if, against their expectations, moral suasion does not work. It may be important for you to have those assurances in hand.

5.   Douglas Dillon wants you to know that he talked to Don Cook for 45 minutes this afternoon, and he thinks that Cook is on board on this program. He admits that Cook does not like the travel tax but says that Cook emphasized the necessity of doing "enough." Douglas thinks that this constitutes a tacit acceptance of the travel tax. I myself doubt this very much in the light of my own talks with Cook, so I plan to have an informal chat with him tomorrow morning and will pass the results on to you.

6.   The overall descriptive tone of this memorandum is gloomier than your Economic Advisers and your Budget Bureau would wish, but we have agreed not to fight over the mood music. I have not yet heard final January figures (and one thing certain is that monthly figures do not prove much), but it remains interesting that the heavy December outflow was overbalanced by the inflow of the first three weeks of January.

7.   Let me offer one final, more general point: the immediate balance-of-payments problem is troublesome and can even become dangerous, but the underlying position of the dollar is as strong as the economy of the United States. It is only in the world of central bankers that the U. S. monetary position is "weak." It is much better to defend the dollar, as we are now doing, than to have to show the bankers who is boss, but it is always worth remembering that Franklin Roosevelt did not weaken his eventual place in history by his refusal to let gold be his master.

8.   I believe Don Cook shares the basic conviction in the paragraph last above. That is one reason I was so greatly impressed by him.

McG. B.[5]

---

[5] Printed from a copy that bears these typed initials.

35.   Memorandum From the Chairman of the Council of Economic Advisers (Ackley) to President Johnson[1]

Washington, February 1, 1965.

SUBJECT

The New Program for the Balance of Payments

1.   You will be receiving a report tomorrow from Secretary Dillon, containing the Cabinet Balance of Payments Committee's recommended program.[2] This memorandum is *by way of background for your consideration* of this program.

2.   *The fourth quarter worsening of our payments is a definite source of concern.* But it may not be quite as bad as it looks on the surface. *Several temporary factors were at work* (in addition to British non-payment):

—some of the increase in bank lending was done to beat the application of the Gore amendment (one top N.Y. banker admits to me that this was a *big factor*);
—new Canadian security issues were bunched up to follow passage of the interest equalization tax;
—some U.S. corporations apparently delayed bringing back their foreign earnings in order to take advantage of the 2 point cut in the corporate tax rate for 1965;
—some of the outflow of short-term bank credit was related to year-end "window dressing," as suggested by the fact that we had a big surplus in the first two weeks of January.

3.   The public knows that the fourth quarter wasn't good, but not just how bad it was. There could be an *adverse business and public reaction, here and abroad, when the official figures become public in the middle of February. That alone is good reason for prompt and decisive action.*

4.   There is danger in too small and too weak a program. But *there is also danger in too strong and restrictive a program.*

It can cause dislocations here and abroad that would be worse than our deficit—for example, this is no time to be pulling funds out of the U.K.
It can look as though we are desperate or panicky, and thereby cause loss of confidence.

5.   The list of *measures on which everyone agrees seems about right* as a program. We can't be sure that additional measures won't be needed in

---

[1] Source: Johnson Library, National Security File, Subject File, Balance of Payments, Vol. 2 [1 of 2], Box 2. No classification marking. The source text was attachment 1 of 2 to a February 2 note from Francis Bator to McGeorge Bundy. Attachment 2, telegram 204 from the Embassy in Luxembourg, February 1, is not printed.
[2] Document 33.

the future, but the odds are good that this package will do the trick, both in its effects on confidence and its direct effects on payments and receipts.

6. However, if you think the agreed-on package is not enough, *there are 3 major possibilities for more*:

A tax on tourists;
A tax on "take-over" investments (where an American company buys out an existing business abroad—which is the kind most resented and which does the least to help our exports);
A tax on short-term business "investments" abroad (where corporate treasurers deposit temporarily idle funds in foreign banks, or buy short-term paper overseas to make an extra 1/4 to 1/2% more than they can get here).

We would oppose the tourist tax as a means of enlarging the package unless it is combined with one or both of the other two. However, these are complicated actions which would take some time to prepare.

7. If the Fed works at it seriously, *"moral suasion" on bank lending could save us much more than the $200 million estimated by the Treasury.* Last year, bank loans to foreigners increased 36% or nearly $2 billion; that should not be permitted to happen again. Most of this business is done by a handful of banks. The Fed can set a quantitative guideline for each bank, backed up by its various controls (including especially the discount privilege), and by its detailed and frequent reports on every foreign loan.

8. Confidential conversations with the New York Federal Reserve Bank convince us that they know how to run a "moral suasion" policy. But Bill Martin must take the lead. *I think it is important for you to talk to him about his role in making moral suasion on the banks really effective.*

9. *The Fed plans to tighten money a little as part of the balance of payments program.* Monetary conditions have been kept easier in the last couple of months than we could have expected. I can't object to a *modest* tightening, even though it will certainly do the domestic economy no good.

10. But it's important for our prosperity that the tightening be *modest. This is another matter for discussion between you and Bill Martin.* (In the past, such discussions have involved the "quadriad"—which would mean Martin, Dillon, Gordon and Ackley meeting with you. But, if you prefer, a private meeting with Martin could provide the opportunity. In either case, I'll be happy to supply briefing material.)

11. Secretary Connor will be in charge of the "moral suasion" on businesses other than banks to restrain direct investment and short-term lending. *This can be quite effective if it's handled right. We should make sure, though, that we have some clear rules of the game.* Most businesses will coop-

erate if they know exactly *what* we want them to do, and know that *all* other firms are being asked to do the same thing.

Gardner Ackley[3]

---

[3] Printed from a copy that bears this typed signature.

---

36.   Editorial Note

On February 4, 1965, in response to a question at a press conference, French President Charles de Gaulle called for a gradual return of the world monetary system to the gold standard. De Gaulle called for nations having international financial responsibilities to consider paying off their balance-of-payments debts solely in gold. Gold, he said, was the only "unquestionable monetary basis which did not bear the mark of any individual country," and therefore the most equitable standard upon which to conduct international financial transactions. For text of his statement, see *American Foreign Policy: Current Documents, 1965*, pages 219–221.

A February 4 Treasury Department statement objected to President de Gaulle's proposal to revert to the full gold standard, arguing that such a monetary system had "collapsed" in 1931 and was "incapable of financing the huge increase of world trade" that marked the 20th century. For text, see ibid., page 221. Secretary Dillon sent a copy of the press release under cover of a February 4 memorandum to President Johnson. (Johnson Library, Bator Papers, Balance of Payments Message, February 10, 1965, Memos [1 of 2], Box 16)

37.   Notes of Telephone Conversation[1]

Washington, February 5, 1965, 10:30 a.m.

The President
Robert Carswell

The President said he was calling because he was very upset about leaks out of the Treasury about the balance of payments. It has hurt us and more than that it has hurt my pride. Anybody over there who can't be loyal to us ought to leave. I took over a lot of people and thought they were loyal. I don't know whether we have any Harry Dexter Whites over there or not, but I have direct evidence that it is coming out of Treasury. Both Treasury and State are leaking and I want it stopped. You tell the Secretary I want it stopped. Mr. Carswell said we would see there were no leaks. The President said that if the Normandy plans were handled the way this balance of payments message was handled, Eisenhower would have never crossed the channel. And what's worse, some of these leaks are mischievous. Check your doors and see who is coming in to see these people. They tell me they don't have time to say anything about de Gaulle and then they turn around and simultaneously issue a statement and talk to reporters. The reporters tell me they are quite busy at Treasury and have a lot of speculative stories coming out of there, but always from people who won't let themselves be quoted. Mr. Carswell said we would see there are no leaks. The President said Mr. Carswell should make it his personal assignment. The President said he wanted that balance of payments message out as soon as he can get it. If you have to work round the clock to get it out, we are going to get it out. The President said he did not want to read about this conversation in the press the way he had read about a conversation he had with the Budget Bureau last week. Mr. Carswell said that would not happen.

---

[1] Source: Kennedy Library, Dillon Papers, History File 1965, 1/65–3/65, Box 44. No classification marking. Drafted by Robert Carswell, Dillon's Special Assistant.

38.   Memorandum From Francis M. Bator of the National Security Council Staff to President Johnson[1]

Washington, February 7, 1965.

Mr. President:

Bill Moyers suggested that, despite the hour, I send in the attached draft of the Balance of Payments Message this evening.[2] Gardner, Walter and I finished it this afternoon, and I have gone over it with Secretary Dillon.[3] He liked it, and made only minor suggestions, all incorporated in the draft.

The only issues on which your Government is still divided are:

1.   *The rate schedule under the Interest Equalization Tax (page 10).*

Ackley, as you know, wants us to ask for an increase in the tax rate. He feels that without an increase the whole package lacks punch. Dillon and Martin want to keep the rate where it is. They are worried about making the bankers angry just when we are asking their help.

2.   *What you say in the Message about tightening money.*

The draft contains two alternative paragraphs on monetary policy, on pages 12 and 13.

—Alternative A is Ackley's preference, but according to Dillon it will be unacceptable to Martin and, if for no other reason, Dillon himself is opposed.
—Alternative B is acceptable to Dillon and, he thinks, probably to Martin. Ackley feels it represents a retreat from your position in your Economic Report.[4]

There is a chance for a sensible compromise which will make it clear that you are against a general tightening of credit, such as would hurt us at home, yet leave Martin satisfied that he has enough flexibility. At any rate, Ackley, Dillon and Gordon will try to work something out tomorrow, before the issue is brought to you for a decision.

Apart from the above, there is one more important and new issue. Martin, Connor and Dillon believe that to insure the effective coopera-

---

[1] Source: Johnson Library, National Security File, Subject File, Balance of Payments, Vol 2. [1 of 2], Box 2. No classification marking.

[2] Presumably a draft of the President's message on the balance-of-payments problem. No drafts have been found. For text of the February 10 message, see *Public Papers of the Presidents of the United States: Lyndon B. Johnson, 1965*, Book I, pp. 170–177.

[3] Dillon does not know about Heller. [Handwritten footnote in the source text.]

[4] The Annual Message to the Congress: The Economic Report of the President was delivered on January 28. For text, see *Public Papers of the Presidents of the United States: Lyndon B. Johnson, 1965*, Book I, pp. 103–117.

tion of Connor's businessmen and Martin's bankers they will have to be assured of some protection from the anti-trust laws. This would require legislation. Katzenbach is uncomfortable but willing, and pending your decision, is drafting some language for insertion in the Message on pages 4 and 12.

One last point concerns the Canadians. Dillon recommends that you call Pearson to get him to agree that they will sharply cut down on their borrowing. A memorandum on this will be over first thing in the morning.[5]

Also first thing tomorrow I will get copies of the draft Message (on an eyes-only basis) to Gordon, Connor, Ball, McNamara and—he just walked in—Bundy, none of whom have yet seen it. We should be ready to present to you all outstanding issues and to ask for your final decision on the entire package by mid-afternoon.

I apologize that this is so late and that the draft is not in perfect order, I did not finish with Dillon and then Katzenbach until 9:30 p.m. and then had to make changes in the draft.

Francis M. Bator[6]

---

[5] Presumably a reference to Document 41.
[6] Printed from a copy that bears this typed signature.

---

39.   Memorandum From Francis M. Bator of the National Security Council Staff to the President's Special Assistant for National Security Affairs (Bundy)[1]

Washington, February 8, 1965.

Mac,

We settled both outstanding issues—see the attached memorandum[2]—at a session this morning with Dillon, Gordon and Ackley.

On the Canadian business (see p. 2 of the memo) I am holding Dillon's much too long memorandum,[3] and will ask him to raise the matter

---

[1] Source: Johnson Library, National Security File, Subject File, Balance of Payments, Vol. 2 [1 of 2], Box 2. No classification marking.
[2] Not attached and not found.
[3] Tab A to Document 41.

with the President at the meeting. If the President agrees to call Pearson, we can do the necessary staff work. All the President will have to do is to read Pearson what he proposes to say about Canadian borrowings in the Message[4] (p. 3, para. 4) and tell Pearson that if he is not agreeable, there will be enormous pressure on the W.H. unilaterally to impose a quantitative limit on Canadian flotations, which the President can do under the Act,[5] or, as a second step, to lift the Canadian exemption.

A clean copy is being typed now for the President's use this afternoon. If you agree, I will attach a note that there is agreement among the principals, both on the monetary policy language (see p. 13) and against raising the tax rate. (On the latter, Gardner is reluctant but will go along.)

I have asked Nick Katzenbach to the meeting in case the President has any questions about the antitrust provisions (see last para., p. 1, of my memorandum to the President,[6] and point *Six* on p. 4, and p. 12 of the draft).

In your absence I am afraid I have had to move in hard during the past three days to make all this come off. I don't think I brought dishonor to your office—and the Message is in pretty good shape, both in substance and in terms of interdepartmental politics. Incidentally, I have O.K.s on the Message from Dillon, Ackley, Connor (with one minor quibble which I settled with marginal assistance from Dillon), McNamara, Gordon and Bell. I am expecting calls momentarily from Ball—who will be happy—and, most important, Bill Martin, with their reactions. I told Martin that if he has any serious objections, we shall call off the meeting with the President and have it out with the principals.[7] With Dillon in accord, I expect that Bill will fall in line.

Don't forget that, for the record, the draft was written by Ackley and myself, with suggestions by Moyers.

FMB[8]

---

[4] Reference is to the balance-of-payments message.

[5] Reference is to the IET.

[6] Document 38.

[7] This meeting with the President was held on February 8 at 6:26 p.m. (Johnson Library, President's Daily Diary) to discuss the final draft of his message on balance of payments which was delivered on February 10. No record of this meeting has been found. Francis Bator, in a separate note to Secretary of Commerce Connor and the other principals of the Cabinet Committee on Balance of Payments, requested that he receive comments either in writing or by telephone on the draft balance-of-payments message by 3:30 p.m. on February 8, since President Johnson was to meet with them later that afternoon "to review all outstanding issues, as well as the draft." (Ibid., Bator Papers, Balance of Payments Message, February 10, 1965, Memos [2 of 2], Box 16) See also Document 40.

[8] Printed from a copy that bears these typed initials.

40.   Memorandum From the President's Special Assistant for National Security Affairs (Bundy) to President Johnson[1]

Washington, February 8, 1965.

SUBJECT

Balance of Payments meeting

1. As I understand it, all outstanding issues have been brought within range of agreement, except for the issue of domestic monetary policy, which is highly controversial (see para. 3 below).

2. Dillon will handle the presentation and will discuss, among other things: (1) a possible call from you to Pearson; (2) the question of need for legislation freeing the bankers and businessmen from anti-trust fears.

3. Dillon will specifically exclude from the discussion in this meeting reference to domestic interest rates on page 13 of the message.[2] This is to avoid a wrangle in the meeting and a possible question of Martin's prerogatives. He and Martin and Gordon and Ackley will try to settle this question of language and substance out of court and only if there is a continuing argument will the matter come to you directly. Your interest in maintaining easy credit will of course be defended throughout by your people.

McG. B.

[1] Source: Johnson Library, National Security File, Subject File, Balance of Payments, Vol. 2. [1 of 2], Box 2. Secret.
[2] Reference is to a draft of the balance-of-payments message.

41.   Memorandum From the President's Special Assistant for National Security Affairs (Bundy) to President Johnson[1]

Washington, February 9, 1965.

SUBJECT

Your call to Prime Minister Pearson on Balance of Payments

1.   The object of this call is to get Pearson's consent to a reaffirmation of the existing Canadian commitment to avoid excessive borrowing from the U.S. What Dillon would like is for you to read to Pearson the paragraph which we want to put into the message on this subject.[2] It reads as follows:

"To stop the excessive flow of funds to Canada under its special exemption from the Equalization Tax, I have sought and received firm assurance that *the Canadian government will take the steps needed to hold these outflows to levels consistent with that special exemption.*"

2.   You can point out to Pearson that this language merely reaffirms existing clear Canadian undertakings, and that it is of great importance to be able to use it in your message if you are to avoid heavy pressure from many quarters to set a strict dollar limit for Canadian borrowings.

3.   The fact is that we will have to impose such a limit

—if Canadian reserves continue to grow
—if Canadian interest rates rise sharply
—or, if Canadian banks start pulling back to Canada money which they now hold in the United States.

4.   You will probably also want to tell Pearson that you are about to invoke the Gore amendment and impose the Interest Equalization Tax on bank loans of one year or longer, with no exemption for Canada. Pearson is probably expecting this news, but he is entitled to hear it from you. The Canadians will not be very much hurt by it because they have been raising their money by selling bonds instead of by borrowing from our banks.

---

[1] Source: Johnson Library, National Security File, Subject File, Balance of Payments, Vol. 2 [1 of 2], Box 2. No classification marking. Attached to the source text are two notes from McGeorge Bundy, both dated February 9. The first to Juanita Roberts, Personal Secretary to the President, reads: "The President should make the call as early as possible this afternoon." A handwritten notation on the upper left corner of this note reads: "3 pm Feb. 9, 1965." The second note informed the President: "This is the scenario for your call with Pearson. He may need time to consult, and you can give him a few hours—but not more—because the message has to go to bed tonight." The President telephoned Pearson at 4 p.m. on February 9 (ibid., President's Daily Diary), but no record of their conversation has been found.

[2] Reference is to President Johnson's balance-of-payments message.

5.   Pearson may argue that the Canadians are already doing all they can to limit their long-term borrowing in New York. You will probably not want to get into the details of the long argument in Douglas' memorandum (Tab A). You can simply say that your experts (Dillon and Martin) strongly disagree—and that in any case you have no real alternative but to ask for performance on the existing Canadian undertaking.

6.   On a separate subject, Dillon tells me that if the Canadians agree to this language, the Japanese would like a sentence or two about what has been happily agreed with them. No one sees any objection to these sentences, but Douglas wants to be sure that you were informed of their existence.

McG. B.

P.S. On the Canadian air agreement,[3] you probably will not wish to raise the subject yourself, but if Pearson mentions it, it would be worthwhile to say that you have been reviewing it yourself and that the plan which you have now approved (very slightly different in language from the last Canadian proposal) goes just as far as we can possibly go. This may help him get past any lingering doubts in his Cabinet over a bargain which is clearly better for Canada than what now exists.

Tab A[4]

Washington, February 8, 1965.

MEMORANDUM FOR THE PRESIDENT

I.   Canada has become a special problem for the United States balance of payments position.

A. Net capital flows from the United States to Canada have always been large but have become appreciably larger in the past three years.

1.   Final figures for 1964 are not yet available in detail but we can identify the following flows:

a.   Sales of new Canadian issues in the United States through our capital markets in 1964 totalled $687 million. These were exempt from

---

[3] Canadian and U.S. representatives held two rounds of meetings, concluding on May 1 and July 23, 1964, concerning the renegotiation of the Air Transport Agreement of 1949 (10 UST 773). It was decided to report to their governments on the results achieved and to meet again following further study with a view to concluding the negotiations. See Department of State *Bulletin,* May 25, 1964, pp. 884–885, and ibid., August 10, 1964, p. 188.

[4] No classification marking.

the Interest Equalization Tax. (There are regular repayments and redemptions of outstanding securities each year. In 1964 these are estimated at about $100 million. The net new issue figure thus would be smaller than the gross figure of $687 million.)

b. Other transactions which affect our balance of payments and which are exempt from the Interest Equalization Tax—mainly purchases of Canadian securities in Canadian markets and buying of Canadian mortgages in Canada by U. S. residents totalled gross about $300 million.

c. At the end of September, 1964, reported short-term claims of U.S. nonbanking corporations and individuals were $285 million larger than on the comparable date in 1963. On the other hand U. S. banking claims on Canadian banks at the close of November, 1964, were just equal to their year earlier level.

d. Direct investment by U. S. corporations in Canada in 1964 was much smaller than usual—perhaps no more than $50 million.

B. All of these flows added to our balance of payments problem.

1. But it is important to note that Canada buys far more goods and services from the United States than she sells to us—about $1.4 billion more.

a. The Canadians assert that they have to get capital inflow from abroad to balance their trade and service (current account) deficit. Since their deficit with the United States is so large and since they are neighbors they look to us for most of that capital inflow.

1. In 1964 they estimate that net capital inflow was about $550 million on long term and about $300 million on short term. Most of this was from the United States.
2. Gross long term inflow to Canada from the United States was about $950 million. Gross flowback to the United States was about $400 million and includes redemptions and repayments. (The British Columbia hydroelectric power transaction inflated both gross inflow and outflow figures in 1964. About $250 million of the long term inflow to Canada was accounted for by this transaction; about $200 million of the reflow from Canada to the United States was also due to this transaction.)

b. If shut off from United States capital flows in any great degree, Canada asserts she would have to cut back on imports from the United States. This is certainly correct.

II. Mr. Deming met on last Wednesday and Thursday with Mr. Plumptre, Canadian Deputy Minister of Finance, to explore possibilities of reducing United States capital outflow to Canada.

A. A key point in the discussions was the size of the prospective 1965 current account deficit for Canada.

1. This figure is critical because it represents the amount that has to be financed largely through capital flows from the United States.

a. In 1964 the current account deficit was about *$515* million.

b. Long and short term capital inflow was about *$850* million net.

c. The Canadian increase in reserves was thus about *$335* million, although about half of this *$166* million represented a repayment of their borrowing from the International Monetary Fund. Their published reserve figure rose only about *$81* million.

2. The official Canadian estimate of their 1965 current account deficit is $825 to $925 million, some $300 to $400 million more than in 1964.

a. The prospective increase, they say, reflects mainly a return to no more than normal grain sales to the USSR (the special 1964 sales added $300 million to their receipts) and an expected growth in imports as their GNP expands.

b. We believe the 1965 deficit estimate is too high; in fact, in December Canadian career officials told us privately that they expected the deficit to be no more than $600 or $650 million—about $100 million more than in 1964. [2 *lines of source text not declassified*]

3. The importance of the figure is that if Canada operates on the basis of a $900 million current account deficit and continues to receive the exemption from the Interest Equalization Tax on the basis that she will borrow no more than to keep her reserves constant, she will borrow in the United States in 1965 at least as much as in 1964.

4. If the current account deficit is no more than $600 million, the amount of Canadian borrowing in the United States in 1965 might be *$200 million less than in 1964—a real saving in capital outflow and a real reduction in our overall deficit.*

B. Mr. Deming, however, could get nowhere with Mr. Plumptre on a smaller figure for the 1965 Canadian current account deficit and consequently could get no assurance of any lessening of Canadian borrowing in the United States.

1. The major form of such a reduction in new borrowing probably would be in a smaller volume of new Canadian issues in our capital markets.

2. Mr. Plumptre did express the opinion that such borrowing probably would not be larger than in 1964 and might be a shade less.

3. He also offered to explore the possibility of retiring about $100 million in Government of Canada bonds now held mostly in the United States by selling an offsetting issue in Canada. This would have the same effect as a reduction in new issues in our markets.

4. The Canadians also promised to do what they could on interest rates as to keep them in their present rough balance with U. S. rates and thus moderate the flow of short term U. S. capital to Canada. They also offered to explore their entire rate structure to see whether something more might be done in this field. (Further action to reduce Canadian

interest rates is clearly possible if the Canadians so desire and probably would actually help the Canadian economy.)

C. But, in essence we have no *positive* assurance of any lessened drain on our capital account by Canada.

III. We need to come to some sort of working agreement with Canada for 1965. You already have discussed the problem with Mr. Pearson. Ideally we would like agreement along the following lines:

A. Some reasonably firm assurance that new Canadian issues in our markets would be held to no more than $500 million in 1965 ($200 million less than in 1964) or that any excess over that figure be offset by the retirement of Government of Canada debt held in the United States. (Canada may be unable to give this reasonably firm assurance. There is no constitutional power possessed by the Dominion Government to control the form or level of provincial borrowing.)

B. Some reasonably firm assurance that Canada will attempt to encourage an interest rate structure which will decrease short term flows from the United States. (Canada can give this assurance if it so desires.)

C. Reasonably firm assurance that Canadian banks will not actively seek to attract additional U.S. dollar balances. Such action would tend to negate our efforts to cut our bank lending abroad.

D. Reasonably firm assurance that Canadian banks and their U.S. branches would *not* pull back to Canada funds now held in the United States. A very large share of present balances owned by U.S. residents but deposited in Canadian banks is used in our money markets. Should these be withdrawn in order to make loans in Europe, it would adversely affect our balance of payments and also would hurt our U.S. banks competitively—which would make it difficult to carry out our moral suasion efforts to reduce U.S. bank foreign lending.

The Bank of Canada can certainly be helpful in both Items C and D.

I suggest that you call Prime Minister Pearson and read him the text of what you would like to say in the Balance of Payments Message regarding Canada and seek his agreement. You might point out to him that unless you can make such a statement the pressures to fix a dollar limit for Canadian borrowings might prove irresistible. You might also point out that the same would be true if Canadian reserves continued to grow or if Canadian banks did not cooperate in the efforts which we will be making in the bank field. Such a conversation may well produce the results we desire. If not, it will certainly pave the way for any future action we may feel compelled to take.

Douglas Dillon

42.   Telegram From the Embassy in Japan to the Department of State[1]

Tokyo, February 10, 1965, 9 p.m.

2508. Pass Treasury. Subject: IET talks.

1. Understanding reached with GOJ, subject Washington approval, as follows:

(A) U.S. will give exemption on $100 million per annum of GOJ and GOJ guaranteed securities.
(B) IET will be paid on all other securities and loans.
(C) On private issues, GOJ will permit payment of IET. However, will limit issues within overall limit of Japanese borrowing existing in December 1964.
(D) GOJ will control term loans within December 1964 limit.
(E) On short-term and other capital flows, where GOJ has no direct controls, U.S. and Japan will consult closely, especially if any untoward flows occur, and GOJ will cooperate through indirect controls.
(F) Ad hoc task force will provide basis for reconciling divergencies in B/P data and for continuing consultation looking to cooperation in U.S.–Japan financial relationship.

2. Discussions conducted in friendly, relaxed atmosphere. GOJ officials obviously greatly relieved, pleased at U.S. willingness consider Japanese problem in sympathetic light. Proposed MOF publicity release (separate Embtel)[2] stresses U.S.–Japan friendship, close U.S.G.–GOJ consultative relationship, GOJ understanding of importance U.S. achieving B/P equilibrium.

3. Ambassador wishes express appreciation to Treasury for despatch Ass't Secretary Trued to Tokyo at this critical point, with helpful U.S. position.[3] Believe outcome these talks will be positive contribution to U.S.–Japan partnership and to stability Sato government. Instead of being severe liability it seemed at first, this necessarily unpopular action because of wise handling, has strengthened Japanese confidence in partnership and value of U.S.–Japan consultative arrangements.

Reischauer

---

[1] Source: Department of State, Central Files, FN 16 US. Confidential.

[2] Neither this Ministry of Finance press release nor the telegram has been found.

[3] Acting Assistant Secretary of the Treasury Merlyn Trued and Deputy Assistant Secretary of State for Economic Affairs Philip Trezise traveled to Tokyo February 6–7 to meet with economic leaders in Japan to discuss the Interest Equalization Tax. No documentation on their discussions has been found.

43.   Memorandum From Acting Secretary of the Treasury Deming to President Johnson[1]

Washington, February 12, 1965.

SUBJECT

Reaction to Your Balance-of-Payments Message[2]

Domestic Reaction

1. Although the balance-of-payments message was overshadowed by the news from Viet Nam, first reports indicate a calm and generally favorable reaction in this country. A number of leading businessmen and bankers made public statements welcoming the call for voluntary restraint and promising their support. Critical comments were confined mainly to a few questions as to the adequacy of the program, and the desire among bankers for a more positive statement on monetary policy. An undertone of reluctance was evident, however, in reports of private comments by industrialists.

2. Some of the bankers' comments were:

David Rockefeller (Chase Manhattan) said he was "pleased with the voluntary approach" to private capital movements. The business and banking communities would certainly respond. He expressed "disappointment at the President's silence on monetary policy" but conceded that this was "basically a Federal Reserve responsibility." He hoped the Federal Reserve "would take action on its own in line with the President's program."

George S. Moore (First National City) said, "We approve of the basic decision to seek the voluntary cooperation of bankers and businessmen instead of resorting to exchange controls as some had feared", but added, "We would have been happier if the President's message had been more positive on monetary policy".

Gabriel Hauge (Manufacturers Hanover) said, "The emphasis on voluntary cooperation in many areas is as wise as it is welcome as an alternative to controls. Certainly bankers will be glad to intensify their cooperation with the Federal Reserve in every possible way. Coupled with supporting action in the field of credit policy by the Federal Reserve, the group of measures outlined in the President's message can have a decidedly favorable impact on our overseas deficit."

Thomas S. Gates (Morgan Guaranty) said, "We stand ready to cooperate in any program that helps the balance of payments", but added that

---

[1] Source: Johnson Library, National Security File, Subject File, Balance of Payments, Vol 2 [1 of 2], Box 2. No classification marking.

[2] Reference is to the President's February 10 message; see footnote 2, Document 38.

"the traditional instrument" of monetary policy "should not be over-looked."

3. Roger Blough issued a helpful statement, saying:

"The persistence of the balance of payments problem requires defi-nite action and the President's message proposes a number of construc-tive measures. The voluntary actions provided are especially welcome."

However, nationwide surveys by the financial press suggest that industrial corporations have some questions concerning cutbacks in direct investment overseas. Many firms were obviously concerned that their competitors, especially foreign companies, might gain an advan-tage by continuing to expand abroad. Several industrialists said that their companies were already helping the balance of payments. But despite remarks such as these, it was also evident that the Presidential appeal carried great weight.

4. No effects on domestic financial markets could be attributed to the message. The bad news from Viet Nam was the dominant influence. U.S. Government securities were off one or two thirty-seconds upon receipt of the Viet Nam news but remained virtually unchanged thereaf-ter. Quotations on the New York Stock Exchange fell sharply both yester-day and Wednesday.

Foreign Reaction

3. The first reaction in Europe was to approve the emphasis on reducing capital outflows, but some worries were expressed as to whether the methods chosen would be completely effective. Almost everywhere on the Continent there were questions about achievement of the objectives without a positive contribution by our monetary policy. British officials were sympathetic but were concerned about the possible withdrawal of short-term funds which could adversely affect their own external position.

6. Some of the comments reported by our Embassies were:

The President of the German central bank (Blessing) called it a "good program" but stressed that it was absolutely essential that the U.S. achieve balance of payments equilibrium within 18 months. He very much hoped that the availability of credit would be reduced.

A high official of the German Economics Ministry said the program embarked the U.S. on the road to exchange controls when the problem was simply excess liquidity. He also cautioned that a solution was "extremely urgent".

Common Market Vice-Chairman (Marjolin) regretted that the interest equalization tax was being extended. But given the unwillingness to even try raising long-term interest rates, the present package might well be the best feasible.

The Governor of the Italian central bank (Carli) expressed support.

A director of the Belgium National Bank concluded that the measures should eliminate a major part of the capital outflow.

French officials had no comment.

7. The Japanese and Canadian governments appeared to be well satisfied with the way we handled their special situations.

In an official statement, the *Government of Japan* expressed "understanding and sympathy", although "there might be varied views with regard to the appropriateness of individual measures" and "their impact on the Japanese economy should be carefully studied." The $100 million exemption for Japan was termed "most encouraging and would serve to maintain the stability of the Japanese balance of payments."[3]

An official statement by *Canadian Finance Minister* Gordon found the message "reassuring", and added that "it is clear that . . . they have taken account of our situation here." The U.S. measures would probably not leave Canada "entirely untouched" but there did not appear to be anything which would cause Canada "serious difficulty." The statement went on to renew "the assurance of the Canadian Government that our (Canadian) policies will continue to be directed towards general stability in our (Canadian) foreign exchange reserves."

8. Foreign exchange markets were calm with the dollar slightly stronger. Although the London gold market reacted unfavorably, this seems to have resulted primarily from the events in Viet Nam.

Frederick L. Deming[4]

---

[3] In his message, President Johnson exempted from the Interest Equalization Tax purchases by U.S. residents of new securities issued or guaranteed by the Government of Japan, up to an aggregate amount of $100 million each year, because an "application of the Tax to bank loans of over one year will, in my judgment, create a sufficient threat to the international monetary system."

[4] Printed from a copy that indicates Deming signed the original.

---

44.   Editorial Note

On February 18, 1965, President Johnson met with U.S. leaders in international business and banking to discuss their voluntary cooperation in a program to reduce the balance-of-payments deficit. The President addressed the leaders in the East Room of the White House at 1:40 p.m. For text of his remarks, see *Public Papers of the Presidents of the United States: Lyndon B. Johnson, 1965*, Book I, pages 206–208.

Beginning at 5:45 p.m. on February 18, Secretary of Commerce John T. Connor held a press conference to answer questions concerning President Johnson's meeting with business and banking leaders. At this press conference, Secretary Connor announced his intention to establish a balance-of-payments advisory committee of the Department of Commerce whose membership would consist primarily of leading business and banking leaders. In addition, Secretary Connor discussed the Department of Commerce's 1965 Voluntary Cooperation Program (see Document 45). A transcript of the press conference is in the Washington National Records Center, RG 40, Records of the Office of Franklin D. Roosevelt, Jr., Under Secretary of Commerce, 1963–June 1965: FRC 68 A 5947, Correspondence: The President, 1965.

On February 24, Secretary Connor issued a press release naming nine prominent business executives to advise him on the voluntary cooperation program to reduce the U.S. balance-of-payments deficit. The Balance of Payments Advisory Committee of the Department of Commerce was composed of the following: Albert L. Nickerson, Chairman of the Board, Socony Mobil Oil Company (Chair); Carter L. Burgess, Chairman of the Board, American Machine & Foundry Company; Fred J. Borch, President, General Electric Company; Carl J. Gilbert, Chairman, The Gillette Company; Elisha Gray, II, Chairman, Whirlpool Corporation; J. Ward Keener, President, B.F. Goodrich Company; George S. Moore, President, First National City Bank; Stuart T. Saunders, Chairman, Pennsylvania Railroad Company; and Sidney J. Weinberg, General Partner, Goldman, Sachs & Company. (Department of Commerce Press Release G 65–29; Department of State, Central Files, FN 12 US)

45.   Paper Prepared in the Department of Commerce[1]

Washington, February 18, 1965.

PROGRAM OF VOLUNTARY COOPERATION WITH THE BUSINESS COMMUNITY TO IMPROVE THE U.S. BALANCE OF PAYMENTS

I.   Program Objective

The program is designed to encourage business executives to achieve improvements in the balance of payments on certain international transactions of their firms. The balance can be improved either by increasing credits, i.e., exports, earnings from foreign investments, repatriations of capital, or by reductions in debits, chiefly new investments. The methods by which these improvements can be achieved will be left to the decisions of each company participating in the program.

Most companies now have an excess of credits over debits in their international transactions, i.e., their net transactions tend to be a favorable factor in the balance of payments. Only a few corporations pay more to foreigners through capital investments than they receive from them through investment incomes and exports.

—*But it is necessary to ask the business community to expand substantially their contribution toward balancing our foreign accounts.*

Voluntary cooperation is sought only with respect to selected transactions with developed countries. Investments in less developed countries continue to be encouraged. Exports to both developed and less developed countries will also be encouraged.

II.   Which Firms will be Asked to Participate

Firms with investments in developed countries of $10 million or more at the end of 1964 or exports of $10 million or more during 1964 will be asked to participate in the program. These criteria will produce a roster of 400–500 companies.

III.   Periodic Reports will be Requested

1.   The firms will be requested to fill in a quarterly questionnaire containing data on their past transactions and quarterly projections for the following year. The first questionnaire will also cover 1964 as a whole.

---

[1] Source: Washington National Records Center, RG 40, Records from the Office of Franklin D. Roosevelt, Jr., Under Secretary of Commerce, 1963–June 1965: FRC 68 A 5947, Correspondence: The President, 1965. No classification marking. The source text bears no drafting information.

2. The chief executives of each firm will be asked to return with each questionnaire a commentary describing the steps they have taken to achieve the improvement indicated and the reasons for short-falls, if any.

3. Each participating firm will be requested to notify the Secretary of Commerce of new investment projects of $10 million or more to be undertaken in developed foreign countries. The notification should include a general outline of the proposed financing arrangements.

IV. Alternative Means of Achieving Improvements

Business firms will be encouraged to pursue a number of policies to improve the balance in 1965:

1. Expansion of exports through independent channels and to or through foreign affiliates.

2. Development of new export markets in countries in which they are not now active.

3. Acceleration in the repatriation of income earned in developed countries.

4. Avoidance or postponement of direct investment in marginal projects and in projects which do not quickly result in higher exports or investment incomes in developed countries.

5. Restraint in financing new direct investments in developed countries with funds raised in the United States or earned abroad and which would ordinarily be repatriated.

6. Greater use of funds raised in developed countries to finance direct investments in those countries, although the financing charges are higher than in the United States.

7. Sale of equities in foreign subsidiaries to residents of the host countries.

8. Increased use of American flag vessels and airlines.

9. In the short run major improvements in the balance of payments can be achieved by minimizing the outflow of short-term financial funds and by orderly repatriation of such funds previously invested abroad.

V. Guidelines for Improvement in 1965

The program does not require that the Commerce Department *set* specific and detailed goals for individual businesses. But it does appear desirable to *suggest* the type of improvement toward which individual enterprises should aim:

1. *Short-term Foreign Financial Assets.* These foreign assets (mainly interest-bearing deposits and short-term commercial and government obligations) held by United States nonfinancial corporations amounted to about $2.0 billion at the end of last year, having increased by at least $0.5 billion during the year.

—These holdings (except for small balances required for working capital) should not be increased above the volume outstanding on December 31, 1964.

—Wherever possible, these holdings should be reduced in an orderly fashion, during the course of 1965, to a level roughly equal to the amount outstanding at the end of 1963.

2. *Exports, Earnings on Investments and Other Capital Transactions.* Corporations should review all of their opportunities to make a greater contribution to the improvement in the Nation's balance of payments.

Improvements could result from:

—An increase in exports.
—An increase in earnings on investments and income from royalties, fees, etc.
—A reduction in capital outflows for direct investment.

Each of these should be examined separately, but which of these means (taken alone or in combination with others) the corporation adopts is a matter to be decided by the chief executive of each firm.

—However, the general aim should be an improvement during 1965 amounting to about 15–20 per cent of the performance in 1964.

—Moreover, firms enjoying favorable markets abroad are expected to contribute relatively more to the improvement in the balance of payments than those firms whose markets are growing more slowly.

—Appropriate contributions are also expected of those firms whose new investments in 1964 were substantially financed by foreign receipts.

VI.   *Administration of the Program*

1. The questionnaires, commentaries and advance notifications are to be returned to the Office of the Secretary of Commerce. The Secretary has assigned the Assistant Secretary for Economic Affairs the responsibility for operation of the statistical and analytical part of the program within the Department.

2. A staff responsible to the Assistant Secretary for Economic Affairs will examine the returned questionnaires and commentaries and evaluate them to determine whether the improvements set by the firms conform to the recommended goal, and whether the actual performance conforms to the previously set targets.

3. In those cases where the questionnaires and commentaries indicate a less than desirable performance, they will be brought to the attention of the Secretary of Commerce who will designate one of his Secretarial Officers to discuss with the responsible executives means to improve the performance of their firms. If these discussions are not successful, the Secretary of Commerce himself will contact the firm.

4. In the conduct of the program, the Secretary will have the assistance of an Advisory Committee of prominent business executives.

46.   Minutes of Meeting of the Balance of Payments Advisory Committee[1]

Washington, February 26, 1965.

The Balance of Payments Advisory Committee of the Department of Commerce met at 2:30 p.m. on February 26, 1965 in Room 5855 of the Department of Commerce.

The Secretary of Commerce opened the meeting by outlining briefly the legal basis of such advisory committees and by making some general comments about the balance of payments voluntary program for the business community.[2] He suggested that Mr. McQuade act as the Secretary of the Advisory Committee and then asked Mr. Nickerson, who had been designated as Chairman of the Advisory Committee, to preside.

There was considerable discussion of how to get maximum business cooperation and of what kind of a reporting system would meet the needs of the Government without unduly burdening participants in the voluntary program. The consensus arising out of the discussion favored a program which would ask the chief executive officer to make a personal commitment to achieve a net gain in the balance of payments performance of his company. He would be asked (a) to set up a balance of payments ledger for his company, (b) establish a dollar figure for improvement in 1965 over its 1964 performance and, (c) thereafter, be free to achieve that target by such means as the company might choose for itself out of the various available techniques. It became clear that the Advisory Committee felt the key to success lies (1) in obtaining a personal commitment from the chief executive officer of each participating company to achieve a target of improvement in its balance of payments performance and (2) in getting them to set satisfactory targets and achieve them.

It was pointed out that prospects for getting cooperation in the voluntary program would be improved by minimizing formalities and by asking for as little technical information as might be reasonably needed. There was considerable discussion of the amount of detail which busi-

---

[1] Source: Washington National Records Center, RG 40, Records of the Executive Secretariat, Office of the Secretary, 1965–1966: FRC 71 A 6617, Balance of Payments Committee for the Department of Commerce, January–June. No classification marking. An attached list of participants is not printed; however, all members of the Balance of Payments Advisory Committee (listed in Document 44) except Moore attended. Others in attendance included: Secretary Connor, Assistant Secretary (EA) Andrew Brimmer, Assistant Secretary (DIB) Thomas G. Wyman, National Export Expansion Coordinator Daniel Goldy, Assistant to the Secretary Lawrence C. McQuade, and George F. James of the Socony Mobil Oil Company, Inc.

[2] See Documents 44 and 45.

nesses should be asked to supply in any questionnaire or other government form.

The Committee then considered the merits of a system of prior notification and consultation with the Department of Commerce on larger direct investment transactions. The system of asking for an overall result did not make it essential to review separately any one element (including direct investment) of a company's overall accounts. Therefore, it was recommended that there be no organized system of notification and consultation but that companies be asked to scrutinize direct investment transactions and seek to minimize the balance of payments effects of any such investments.

There followed discussion of certain specialized factors, such as the less developed countries, Canada, Japan, and the United Kingdom. Thereafter, the Secretary briefly reviewed the consultation held to date between the Department and companies contemplating significant overseas investment projects.

The Committee then adjourned.

Lawrence C. McQuade
Secretary

---

47.   **Action Memorandum From the Deputy Assistant Secretary of State for Economic Affairs (Trezise) to the Under Secretary of State (Ball)**[1]

Washington, undated.

SUBJECT

> Department of State Comments on Proposed Letter from Secretary Connor to U.S. Business Executives Implementing the Moral Suasion Program on Direct Investment

Problem

Secretary Connor has sent you a copy of the letter (Tab B)[2] he proposes to send to about 500 top corporate executives, to implement the moral suasion program on direct investment. He has requested your comments and suggested changes.

---

[1] Source: Department of State, Central Files, FN 12 US. No classification marking. Drafted by Benjamin Caplan (E/OFE) and C. Fred Bergsten (E/OFE) on March 4.

[2] The letter and Secretary Connor's transmittal note to Ball are attached but not printed. The letter is a draft of the one printed as Document 52.

Summary

The program outlined in the letter has been considerably watered down from its original concept at the request of the Advisory Committee. Items dropped are: (1) Advance notification of any foreign investment of $10 million or over; (2) Virtual elimination of the 15–20% proposed guidelines for cutbacks in foreign investment; and (3) A watered down reporting system.

The program spelled out in this letter is probably inadequate to assure meaningful compliance by the corporations. Its proposed guidelines, reporting requirements, and instructions are so vague and generalized that it would be difficult for corporations to comply with them, even acting in the best of faith. There are also significant omissions in the list of items to be reported. The best that we can probably do at this time, however, is to give support to the approach and note that the program may have to be tightened in the future. We should at least recommend some specific changes in both the letter itself and the reporting form, to close some of the loopholes.

Discussion

Secretary Connor had originally planned to send out a quite comprehensive set of instructions and reporting forms. After meeting with his Advisory Committee of businessmen last Friday, however, he decided not to require any reports.[3] The present draft represents a compromise between those two positions, although it leans more toward the latter.

The trouble with the proposed letter is that it sets no firm guidelines for standards for the companies to meet. Even the idea that companies should report large transactions before undertaking them has been dropped. This approach increases the likelihood that companies, even acting in the best of faith, will not make maximum contributions because of the fear that their competition will take advantage of the program's flexibility. Under this program, the burden of proof will be largely on the Government to tell the companies where they should have done better—not, as it should be, on the companies to justify their not having adhered to guidelines. The program which Commerce originally developed would have satisfied these criteria, although it may have required too much paperwork.

Several specific problems are listed in the Annex of the proposed letter from you to Secretary Connor, with proposed changes in the letter to take care of them without changing the tenor of the overall approach.

1. The most important is the problem of Canada. Secretary Dillon had committed himself to special treatment for Canada in the field of

---

[3] For minutes of this meeting, see Document 46.

direct investment and your letter makes this problem clear. Secretary Dillon took a different view on investment of corporate liquid funds in Canada. Your letter takes a different view of this problem because of the special relationship between Canada and Euro-dollar loans to the U.K. At a meeting yesterday, the Canadians stated that loans to the U.K., largely with U.S. dollars, had been very heavy in the last quarter.[4] Since the U.K. problem is so delicate, it is important to urge caution with respect to withdrawals from Canada as well as with respect to direct U.S. investment there.

3. [sic] Although investment in LDC's is not to be discouraged, companies should be required to report on their activities there to preclude evasion conducted through LDC affiliates. Such evasion could be particularly important for holding companies in Panama, Liberia, etc.

4. The proposed reporting form does not make it clear that unremitted earnings are to be reported, although we understand that it intends to do so. Since this area is of vital importance in assessing the overall performance of a company, it should be clearly included.

5. The proposed reporting form does not require information on imports by the companies although there is a textual reference to them. This is another important area, and should be included for all reporting forms.

Recommendation

That you sign the attached letter, with annex (Tab A).

Tab A

Letter From the Under Secretary of State (Ball) to Secretary of Commerce Connor[5]

Washington, March 4, 1965.

Dear Jack:

Thank you for the opportunity to comment on your proposed letter asking for the cooperation of the industrial executives in reducing our

---

[4] This meeting has not been further identified.

[5] No classification marking. Drafted by Benjamin Caplan (E/OFE) on March 4 and cleared by Sharon E. Erdkamp (BNA).

balance of payments deficit. I do have some major comments which relate to Canada and the United Kingdom.

As you know, we have a special arrangement with Canada under the IET. We are greatly concerned that, as the letter now stands, corporations will be encouraged to reduce investment projects in Canada. To that extent, it would force the Canadians to float more securities in the New York market to maintain their level of reserves. There would thus be no net benefit to our balance of payments. The psychological effect, moreover, of the suggestion of a cutback in investment in Canada could be serious since the markets there are already quite nervous. You will recall that Secretary Dillon discussed this point at your meeting on February 18 and stated that the program should not affect any direct investment project in Canada. I would strongly urge that special mention be made of Canada in your letter. I am attaching suggested language to this effect.

One other problem affects both Canada and the United Kingdom in connection with the investment of corporate liquid funds. I agree that U.S. corporate liquid funds that are invested in Canada and loaned to continental Europe should be withdrawn in an orderly manner. However, as you know, a large part of these funds are loaned by Canadian banks to the United Kingdom. Since your letter stresses caution in such withdrawals when invested directly in the United Kingdom, I believe that similar caution is needed in the case of Canada. Suggested language is attached.

A few additional specific comments are annexed. Most of them would serve to clarify somewhat the guidelines for business reporting.[6]

Sincerely,

George W. Ball[7]

---

[6] The annex is not printed.

[7] Printed from a copy that indicates Ball signed the original.

48.   Memorandum From Secretary of the Treasury Dillon to President Johnson[1]

Washington, March 5, 1965.

Efforts on your balance of payments program are now concentrated on developing and publicizing more detailed guidelines for financial institutions and industrial firms. As expected, many problems of detail have come to the surface with respect to assuring appropriate priorities for export credits and developing countries and making allowance for the special problems of Japan, Canada, and the U.K. Both the Federal Reserve and Commerce have worked with technical people from finance and industry to help resolve these problems, and remaining issues are now being settled among the interested agencies. The Treasury has continued to serve as a coordinating focal point.

I believe we have now found ways to implement the guidelines fully consistent with our separate special commitments negotiated with Canada and Japan, assuring them of continuing access to our capital markets for limited amounts of funds. Most importantly, no limitations are being suggested for purchases of longer-term foreign bonds by American long-term investors beyond the restraints inherent in the Interest Equalization Tax, which has proved effective in that area. This permits the basic Canadian and Japanese exemptions from the Interest Equalization Tax to remain fully effective.

At the same time, we do not plan to ask for a reduction in direct investment in Canada since, under our understanding with the Canadians, a reduction in direct investment would permit them to sell more bonds in the U.S. market, thus merely shifting the U.S. capital outflow from the more profitable direct investment area into the less attractive long-term loan area. The problems in this area were discussed with a Canadian financial delegation in Washington again this week, and I believe they are satisfied with our approach.

As Secretary Connor will be reviewing for you in more detail, the program with industrial firms will be made more informal than planned earlier, with less emphasis on detailed reporting and general guidelines, but with a concentrated effort to enlist the personal cooperation of the top executives of international companies on a continuing basis. This approach, which was warmly supported by the business advisory

---

[1] Source: Johnson Library, Bator Papers, Balance of Payments Message, February 10, 1965, Memos [2 of 2], Box 16. No classification marking. Submitted under cover of a March 5 note to Francis Bator from Robert Carswell in which he wrote: "The original of the attached memorandum has gone to Mr. Busby who requested it on behalf of the President and said it should be sent directly to him."

group, will be incorporated in a letter from Secretary Connor to the chief executive officers of affected firms next week. The Federal Reserve this afternoon released their detailed guidelines for the banks, for publication in Monday papers.

There has been some loose talk and press stories that outflows of funds in the current quarter are far exceeding the adverse fourth quarter results. On the basis of all the information we have, that impression is totally false. However, it is not yet clear, amid the cross currents affecting the exchange markets, what sort of improvement we can expect this quarter over the previous three months. As I indicated to you earlier, visible results in terms of balance of payments data from the current program cannot be anticipated before the second quarter, and it could be even longer before its *full* effects are apparent.

Already, however, there are scattered indications in the foreign exchange and money markets that the program is beginning to bite. For instance, rates in the "Euro-dollar" market, where U. S. dollars are borrowed and lent by European banks, have risen by as much as 1/4% since your Message,[2] probably as a result of some curtailment in the supply from this country. The flow of U. S. funds into Canadian finance company paper, upon which we receive partial reports, has been minimal since February 10, after a heavy volume earlier in the year. In addition, the dollar has been somewhat stronger in the exchange markets, and the latest weekly balance of payments data show a sizable surplus, following a small surplus a week earlier—certainly encouraging even though these data are subject to erratic swings.

The response from business and financial leaders who have been personally exposed to the program remains encouraging.

Douglas Dillon[3]

---

[2] Reference is to President Johnson's February 10 message to Congress; see footnote 2, Document 38.

[3] Printed from a copy that indicates Dillon signed the original.

49.   Action Memorandum From the Assistant Secretary of State for Economic Affairs (Johnson) to Secretary of State Rusk[1]

Washington, March 11, 1965.

SUBJECT

Special Report of the NAC on IMF Quota Increases

The Treasury Department, supported by State and other U.S. agencies, has taken the lead in working out arrangements for a 25 percent increase in IMF quotas. These arrangements contain measures designed to reduce the impact of the quota increases on the U.S. gold stock.

The attached Special Report (Tab B)[2] explains these arrangements. It emanates from the National Advisory Council on International Monetary and Financial Problems (the NAC) which was set up in 1946 under the Bretton Woods Agreement. The NAC coordinates the United States position on international financial matters, including the IMF. You are a statutory member.

The NAC almost never meets. Its work is handled by a staff committee where E assures State representation on IMF matters. We have examined the Special Report and have no objection to it.

Recommendation

That you sign the transmittal letter (Tab A) to the President and the Congress.

Tab A[3]

Washington, March 12, 1965.

To the President and to the Congress:

The National Advisory Council on International Monetary and Financial Problems transmits herewith its Special Report on Proposed Increases in Quotas of the International Monetary Fund.

---

[1] Source: Department of State, Central Files, FN 10. No classification marking. Drafted by Michael E. Ely (E/OFE) on March 11 and cleared by Benjamin Caplan (E/OFE).

[2] Not printed.

[3] No classification marking. Tab A was sent under cover of a March 11 note from Alexander Rattray (S/S–S) to Edward S. Little (S) informing him that "Treasury hand carried this package to the Department this afternoon and is anxious to obtain the Secretary's signature on the transmittal letter to the President and to the Congress at the earliest possible moment. The letter has been signed by Secretaries Dillon and Connor and by FRB Chairman Martin."

The Council recommends the enactment of legislation to authorize an increase in the quota of the United States in the International Monetary Fund by $1,035 million, from $4,125 million to $5,160 million, as part of a general 25 percent increase in Fund quotas under the conditions set forth in the Report.

Douglas Dillon
Secretary of the Treasury
Chairman, National Advisory
Council on International
Monetary and Financial Problems

Dean Rusk
Secretary of State

John T. Connor
Secretary of Commerce

William McC. Martin, Jr.
Chairman, Board of Governors
of the Federal Reserve System

Harold F. Linder
President and Chairman
Export-Import Bank of Washington

50.   Personal Message From Prime Minister Menzies to President Johnson[1]

Canberra, March 12, 1965.

Mr. President,

This note is designed to be direct and clear, as it should be in a communication to one whose friendship I value, and whose sympathetic understanding of Australia and her problems we have great reason to appreciate.

Since you informed Congress on 11th February, 1965, of the measures you proposed to take to improve the external payments position of the United States I have been studying, with my colleagues in the Australian Government, the likely effects of those measures upon our situation, abroad and at home.[2]

So far as we can see, Australia does not come within the several reservations stated by you and designed to lessen the impact of your measures upon various countries such as Canada, Japan, the United Kingdom and others more generally described as developing countries.

I feel I should say to you that while we fully and warmly understand the reasons for the action your Administration is taking to deal with its balance of payments problem, we fear that this action as it now stands could have adverse effects on Australia which we imagine it would be no part of the United States intention to inflict.

When the Interest Equalisation Tax was first announced, we pointed out to the United States Administration our interests in the matter but did not seek exemption from it. Amongst other reasons, we wanted to avoid the embarrassment this might have caused your Administration in its negotiations with certain other countries on this matter.

We do not seek exemption from the tax now, but we do wish to bring to your notice the facts of our economic situation which will be relevant to the Administration of the system of voluntary restraint to which United States investors are being asked to conform in making decisions about investments abroad.

---

[1] Source: Johnson Library, National Security File, Subject File, Balance of Payments, Vol. 2, December 8, 1964 [1 of 2], Box 2. No classification marking. Sent under cover of a memorandum from Australian Ambassador Waller to the President on March 12. In this memorandum, Waller wrote: "I have been directed by the Prime Minister of Australia, Sir Robert Menzies, to transmit to you as a matter of urgency, the attached message dealing with proposed measures on the external payments position of the United States and their likely effects on Australia. As you will see, the message points out the serious effect on Australia which these measures could have."

[2] Presumably a reference to President Johnson's February 10 message to Congress; see footnote 2, Document 38.

Australia is not a "developed" country in this sense that the mature, capital-exporting and highly-industrialised countries of Europe are developed.

On the contrary, we have an immense task of developing a relatively under-populated continent which, while rich in some resources, presents in other respects most formidable difficulties of climate, terrain and distance. As yet we have a population of little more than 11,000,000 people. Like the United States in earlier years, we are endeavouring to build our numbers up by large-scale immigration. But this effort necessarily adds to our capital needs.

Although by now we have achieved a large and varied production of goods, and in fact generate from our own savings more than four-fifths of the capital we require, we must perforce rely heavily on export earnings and on capital inflow to obtain abroad additional resources for growth.

Australia is a free enterprise economy that has welcomed private overseas investment and treated it with exactly the same consideration that it gives to private investment of Australian origin. Moreover, Australia has joined with other free world countries in measures to promote freer international trade and payments and, to this end, maintains an "open" economy with practically no quantitative restrictions on imports and no restrictions on current payments. Although subject to formal control, repatriation of capital invested in Australia is not, in practice, refused.

Being predominantly an exporter of primary products, Australia experiences large fluctuations in the amount of her export receipts and, being in a phase of rapid development, normally has a deficit in her current balance of payments. Though this varies from one year to another, it has to be covered by net capital inflow. By far the greater part of this has comprised private overseas investment in Australia. In the eight years from 1956–57 and 1963–64 the accumulated deficit on current account amounted to $2,417 million. During that period, the annual inflow of private overseas investment (including undistributed income) in companies in Australia totalled $3,022 million, of which $1,147 million came from the United States and Canada—most of it from the United States.

Ordinarily Australia has a large current account deficit with the United States. In 1962–63 Australia's exports to the United States totalled $297 million while her imports from the United States amounted to $478 million. Her net invisible payments to the United States in that year were $181.2 million giving a deficit on current account of $362.2 million. In 1963–64, with exports of $312.9 million, imports of $559.9 million and net invisible payments of $194.7 million, her current account deficit with the United States rose to $441.7 million. In the half year to December, 1964, Australia's recorded exports to the United States were $153.2 million compared with $180.3 million for the same period of 1963, a decline of 15% whereas Australia's recorded imports from the United States increased as between these two periods from $273.7 million to $392 million, a rise of 43%.

In this connection, we feel constrained to point to the contrast between the rapid expansion of United States exports to Australia— Australia now being the fastest-growing of the United States major commercial markets—and the manner in which United States policies impede Australian efforts to expand exports to the United States of some major Australian export commodities.

The United States, alone among major trading countries, maintains a very high tariff on raw wool, despite many representations and negotiations aimed at reduction or elimination of Duty: quotas imposed on lead and zinc in 1958 remain unchanged despite a greatly improved world market situation: United States domestic legislation imposes limitations on, and creates uncertainties for, the Australian export trade in meat: the continuance of access for Australian sugar is uncertain and the size of the present Australian quota is not commensurate with Australia's position as the world's second-largest sugar exporter.

In 1963–64 these commodities accounted for 81% of total Australian exports to the United States. They are the products of which Australia must chiefly depend if a significant expansion of exports to the United States is to be achieved and if the progressive deterioration in our trade and payments balances with the United States is to be arrested and redressed. Yet, with respect to each of them, United States restrictions of one kind or another prevent or impede expansion.

This current account deficit with the United States has been offset in part by capital inflow from the United States, most of it on private account. In 1962–63 the annual inflow from the United States and Canada (by far the greater part being from the United States) of private overseas investment (including undistributed income) in companies in Australia was $201.6 million, and this increased to $220.2 million in 1963–64. In the latter year, the inflow from the United States and Canada was not far short of half of the total of $481.6 million of private overseas investment in companies in Australia.

To turn now to our immediate situation, it is a fact that in 1963–64 Australia's export production was high and for most exports reasonably good prices were received. Capital inflow was strong and our external reserves were strengthened.

For the present financial year, however, the prospects are much less favourable. Export prices have fallen, local demand for imports has been strong and, although capital inflow has been fairly well sustained, it is certain that substantial drawings will be made on our external reserves.

These seem certain to decline over the year as a whole by appreciably more that £A100 million ($224 million).

For the financial year ahead, the signs point to a continued drain on our external reserves. We have greatly enlarged our defence programmes and this will entail substantial additions to oversea payments for defence equipment and supplies. Oversea expenditure in 1965–66 and latter years arising from existing defence commitments and the new three-year defence programme is estimated at about £A400 million or the equivalent of about $880 million, of which about £A250 million or some $550 million will relate to procurement in the United States.

Although recent arrangements reached with you to phase payments for some major items over a longer period will ease the burden to some extent, it will still be considerable. At the time we undertook these commitments we had no reason to anticipate that our payments' position vis-à-vis the United States would be altered for the worse by action of the kind you have since announced.

An additional consideration is that the Australian Government has commitments of nearly $200 million in the United States over the next five years in respect of debt maturities and sinking fund commitments. This figure is exclusive of instalment repayments of approximately $130 million due to the International Bank over that period.

Although a relatively large-scale importer of capital, Australia is nevertheless a donor and not a recipient of international aid. Australia has, in fact, played her full part in various international aid arrangements and also provides a considerable amount of aid, both civil and military, on a bilateral basis to less-developed countries. The development of Papua and New Guinea is a prime Australian responsibility and one that is making large and increasing calls on Australia's resources. Requests for additional aid are being received from other developing countries as well and in most cases are met to the best of our ability. Our recent gift of wheat to India worth nearly $9 million is a case in point. These all add to the pressures on our external resources.

In what at present appears to be a deteriorating balance of payments situation, any substantial falling off in capital inflow would be a matter of serious concern to the Australian Government. Furthermore, since we hold the bulk of our external reserves in sterling, any drawings we have to make on our reserves will tend to increase Britain's balance of payments difficulties which are, of course, a matter of international concern.

In drawing attention to these facts, the Australian Government hopes that, in setting oversea investment targets for United States Banks and other businesses, the Administration will take full account of the Australian situation and will not take action likely to result in any substantial reduction in the flow of private American capital to this country.

This is not to say that we would oppose the issue by United States investors of some equity capital in their subsidiaries here to finance new investment in this country: indeed it would accord with an attitude we have frequently expressed. We have made it clear on many occasions in the past that we think it desirable for oversea investors to take in Australian investors as partners in businesses established in Australia.

On the other hand, however, we would be troubled and embarrassed if United States investors were to begin repatriating capital, substantially increasing the proportion of profits remitted or adding largely to their fixed-interest borrowings or other forms of capital-raising in Australia which would give Australian investors no equity share in the businesses in question. Developments such as these could very well force upon us the need to reconsider the policies we have hitherto followed in these areas. This we should regard as regrettable in the extreme, especially if it resulted in a conflict of policies, with subsequent confusion in, and disruption of, established and greatly valued financial and commercial relationships between our two countries.

Our own policies in these important fields have, we believe, had the encouragement and approval of successive United States Administrations. We should like to think that it will be possible to continue them without detriment to ourselves and without impairing the effect of the policies you find necessary to strengthen your own balance of payments and uphold the world standing of the dollar.

I am, Mr. President, and with warm personal regards,

Yours sincerely,

R. G. Menzies[3]

---

[3] Printed from a copy that indicates Menzies signed the original.

51.   Letter From President Johnson to Prime Minister Menzies[1]

Washington, undated.

Dear Mr. Prime Minister:

I have read with great care your letter of this morning concerning the effects on Australia of our balance of payments program.[2] I have asked the Secretary of State, the Secretary of the Treasury, and the Secretary of Commerce to give the problems you raise the careful and understanding attention which is traditional in our relations as close allies and good friends. I expect to receive their report during the course of next week and shall write you further about these difficult matters at that time.

Sincerely,

lbj[3]

---

[1] Source: Johnson Library, National Security File, Subject File, Balance of Payments, Vol. 2 [1 of 2], December 8, 1964, Box 2. No classification marking. Drafted by President Johnson and Francis Bator on March 12.

[2] Document 50.

[3] Printed from a copy with these handwritten initials, indicating the President signed the original.

---

52.   Letter From Secretary of Commerce Connor to Certain U.S. Business Leaders[1]

Washington, undated.

The President has asked me to handle the voluntary cooperation program with American industry which is a key part of our overall effort to improve our Nation's balance of payments situation. Since the success of this program depends entirely on full cooperation and help from the heads of the U.S. corporations doing a significant amount of business internationally, I am writing to you to enlist your personal support.

---

[1] Source: Department of State, Central Files, FN 12 US. No classification marking. The source text is enclosure 1 to CA–9786 to all diplomatic posts, March 19. The text of the airgram indicates that the letter was sent to over 600 heads of U.S. business enterprises. Regarding the drafting of and suggested revisions to this letter, see Document 47.

As you can see from the enclosed press release,[2] the Advisory Committee for this industry program, chaired by Mr. Albert L. Nickerson, Chairman of the Board of Socony Mobil Oil Company, is composed of outstanding leaders from the business community who have been active in direct overseas investments and international trade. That Advisory Committee met with me on February 26, and strongly urged that our program be set up on as informal and personal a basis as possible, with a minimum of formal reporting requirements and other "red tape." All members of the Advisory Committee have given me their judgment that the leaders of American industry will respond quickly and favorably to that kind of approach and that, as a result of such leaders taking personal responsibility for this effort, our voluntary program will produce significant reductions in the balance of payments deficit. The Advisory Committee is particularly in favor of a flexible approach that enables each company head to work out his own program, based on the operating facts of his own business, rather than limit the means of meeting each company's objective by having the government prescribe some formula of general application.

That advice makes sense to me, and the form of the program that we had been planning has been modified along the lines suggested.

Consequently, I ask for your help specifically as follows:

1. Please set up for your company a balance of payments "ledger" for the year 1964 which shows the selected debits and credits. I enclose a summary work sheet to indicate the needed figures, and some instructions to help your technical people in preparing it for you.[3]

2. After looking at your 1964 results—and we realize in most cases a significant favorable balance will be shown—please consider how that 1964 result can be improved for the years 1965 and 1966. We have been thinking in terms of an average improvement in balance of payments terms, in 1965 of 15–20 per cent over the 1964 results. We realize, however, that any such target will be inappropriate for many corporations—either on the low or high side—but the important thing is to make an extraordinary effort. Therefore, we have concluded that only you are in a position to set up a reasonable but meaningful objective for your own company, in light of your operating facts and problems. The nine suggestions listed on the enclosed press release do not exhaust the list of possibilities that you and your associates can put together in devising an approach meeting the national purpose, yet tailored to your particular circumstances. In short, I am asking you to establish, *and then let me know,*

---

[2] The Commerce press release, February 24, announcing the establishment of the Balance of Payments Advisory Committee of the Department of Commerce is enclosure 2 to CA–9786. It is not printed, but see Document 44.

[3] The work sheet is enclosure 3 to CA–9786. It is not printed.

your best *personal* estimate of how much of an improvement in terms of net dollars you think your company can make overall in 1965, compared with 1964 by taking all feasible steps to help the Nation deal with this serious problem.

3. It would also be helpful for us to have a few of your summary figures for the year 1964 showing credit and debit items separately. The work sheet referred to in paragraph 1 would be appropriate for your 1964 report and should be returned to us. It may also be helpful in calculating your 1965 target. We understand that for many firms or industries, such as petroleum operations or contract construction, there may be a need to include in their "ledger" other information on foreign transactions in order to show a realistic balance of payments performance. In such situations, we would welcome any supplementary figures you wish to supply, and will take them into consideration in reviewing your results.

4. Because of the unique opportunity to shift short-term assets and make an early improvement in the balance of payments, I would also like to have your figures at the end of 1963 and 1964 for short-term assets held abroad either directly or through U.S. banking or other financial institutions. In addition, we would like to have figures on such assets held in developed countries by your subsidiaries and branches.

5. I would like to receive your first set of figures by April 15, if this is possible, and I hope it is.

6. Thereafter, I am asking you to send me quarterly reports through the years 1965 and 1966 showing the data in paragraphs 2, 3 and 4 above and revisions, if any, in your overall goal for the year. You should also give your personal evaluation of points or problems you consider to be of particular significance.

7. While prior notification regarding substantial new investments or expansions abroad, including information indicating how they would be financed, would be helpful, we have decided against a formalized program asking for such information. It is our hope that the overall estimates and reports that I am requesting will prove to be adequate, and that the results will be clear enough to obviate the need for prior notification of new investments. We, of course, expect that care will be taken to minimize the balance of payments effects of large investments and either we, or the appropriate Federal Reserve officials when their program is involved, would be glad to discuss such situations should you so desire.

8. We shall be very glad to talk on the telephone or meet with you to discuss this or any other aspect of this voluntary program of interest or concern to you as it moves along.

Your company's report and estimates will be treated by us as strictly "Confidential" and shown only to those few government officials who are working with us directly in this program. We do plan to put together a periodic summary of the reports in aggregate terms for consideration with the Advisory Committee and for reports to the President, the Cabinet, and the public.

There are a few special problems which I would like to call to your particular attention.

First, we regard the national objective of increasing the contribution by private enterprise to growth in less developed countries of such importance that we do not wish this program to inhibit the flow of these investments.

Second, while relatively rapid progress in repatriating short-term financial funds invested abroad, wherever appropriate, would be helpful, we request that this be done with caution in the case of balances in countries subject to balance of payments problems. We are naturally concerned not to cause difficulties on the exchanges and it would be desirable for companies with large balances to consider consulting with the appropriate Federal Reserve Bank on this problem.

Third, we do not anticipate cutbacks in Canadian direct investments, but firms should take particular care to assure that short-term funds put at the disposal of your subsidiaries in Canada serve only to meet operating needs in Canada. Opportunities should be explored for obtaining at least a portion of working capital requirements from the Canadian market. In this process, we hope that short-term investments in Canada by parents or subsidiaries clearly in excess of working requirements will not be increased. No doubt opportunities will arise to reduce these balances, particularly those denominated in U.S. dollars, but this should be done only in a gradual and orderly way.

I am sure you are aware of the vital importance of improving the U.S. balance of payments position. Such improvement is essential to international monetary stability, to this Nation's economy, and to continued business progress. The capability of this nation to manage its international fiscal affairs is being carefully watched around the world.

President Johnson is confident, as am I, that you will cooperate with us in this extremely important program of serious concern to you and to our country. We urgently need your help.

Sincerely yours,

John T. Connor[4]

---

[4] Printed from a copy that bears this typed signature.

53.   Memorandum From Secretary of the Treasury Dillon to President Johnson[1]

Washington, March 17, 1965.

SUBJECT

Gold Transactions

The Treasury gold stock will show a decline of $250 million this week. This decline will be announced tomorrow afternoon at the weekly press conference of the Federal Reserve Bank of New York and will be reported in the press Friday morning.[2]

This decline will provide for sales of $232 million to France. $150 million is being sold this week, which will complete the French program of reducing their dollar balances of $300 million. In addition, there will be a sale next week of $82 million to cover the French balance of payments surplus in February. France has publicly stated that it intends to take enough gold each month to cover the preceding month's surplus. Future French gold purchases will therefore depend on developments in the French balance of payments. Surpluses are not expected to continue at anywhere near the February level.

We have backgrounded the financial press thoroughly so that the drop in the gold stock should be attributed to France. The stories should also indicate that this transaction completes the French program of reducing the dollar balances, as announced by them in January.

Including this week's transaction, the decline in the Treasury gold stock so far this year will amount to $825 million, nearly as large as the total loss in each of the years 1961 and 1962. During the coming quarter, the gold stock is expected to continue to decline but at a reduced rate. Even with full success in our balance of payments program we could easily lose up to $250 million during the second quarter. Thereafter losses, if any, should be much smaller. With success in our balance of payments program, it would not be surprising if the U.S. actually began to gain gold during the second half of the year. These projections are necessarily very tenuous and should not under any circumstances be used in public discussions.

Douglas Dillon[3]

---

[1] Source: Johnson Library, Bator Papers, Balance of Payments, 1965 [1 of 4], Box 14. Limited Official Use.

[2] March 19.

[3] Printed from a copy that indicates Dillon signed the original.

54.   Letter From President Johnson to Prime Minister Menzies[1]

Washington, March 24, 1965.

Dear Mr. Prime Minister:

We have now had a chance to give careful study to your letter of March 12 concerning the effect on Australia of our balance of payments program.[2] We fully understand the importance that your Government attaches to this matter, and appreciate the frankness with which you expressed your concern.

I am grateful, too, for your sympathetic understanding of the reasons which impelled us to take forceful action. We think it fair to claim that because of the special role of the dollar in international monetary arrangements, early and substantial improvement in the United States' balance of payments is in the interest not only of the United States, but also of the entire Free World. We are determined to eliminate the United States' international deficit, and I am happy to be able to say that the February 10 program already appears to be taking hold.

We understand, of course, that external capital is of great importance to Australia. In terms of the high standard of living of the Australian people, and the remarkable pace of advance during the past decade, Australia must be counted one of the advanced countries of the world. But as you point out, yours is a country with a great potential for further development. As an old friend and ally, we have watched with admiration your record of achievement, and we know the importance of continued Australian success. We attach high value to the good economic relations between Australia and the United States.

In the present instance, we believe after careful review that our balance of payments program is not likely to have a serious adverse effect on the Australian economy. The part of the program supervised by the Secretary of Commerce is designed to avoid any undue disruption in the growth of sound business relationships. Indeed, I understand that certain large direct investments in the production of iron ore in Australia are planned for the near future. And in the case of loans by our banks and financial corporations, we intend to emphasize primarily the need to curb the outflow of such funds to industrialized countries already rich in reserves.

We believe, therefore, that this program will not impose undue strain on Australia. But it is always possible that specific actions under a

---

[1] Source: Johnson Library, National Security File, Subject File, Balance of Payments, Vol. 2 [1 of 2], December 8, 1964, Box 2. No classification marking.

[2] Document 50.

program of this sort can have consequences for a friend that outweigh their value to the general program. I have asked the Secretary of the Treasury and the Secretary of Commerce to give a careful hearing to Australia's view in any particular case which might be of this sort.

On our general commercial relations, I can assure you again that a reduction in trade barriers, in agriculture as well as in industry, is a prime objective of United States policy. As I wrote you last August,[3] our negotiators in the Kennedy Round will bend every effort to help bring the Geneva negotiations to a successful conclusion.

Again, let me thank you for your letter and for your forthright statement of views.

Sincerely,

Lyndon B. Johnson

---

[3] Not further identified.

---

55.   **Memorandum From the Deputy Assistant Secretary of State for Politico-Military Affairs (Kitchen) to Secretary of State Rusk**[1]

Washington, March 24, 1965.

SUBJECT

Probable Shortfall in German Military Offsets of DOD Balance of Payments Expenditures: Possible Redeployment of US Forces in Germany

1.   On March 3, we described results of two days of discussions between concerned US officials in Bonn on the German offsets problem (Tab A).[2]

---

[1] Source: Department of State, Central Files, DEF 12–5 (GER W). Secret. Drafted by Howard Meyers (G/PM) on March 23, concurred in by Assistant Secretary for European Affairs William R. Tyler, and sent through George Ball. Copies were sent to Ambassador Thompson and Mann.
[2] Tab A, a March 3 confidential memorandum from Kitchen to Ball on the German offset discussions, is not printed.

2.   The difficulties anticipated in achieving full offset of US defense expenditures of $1.35 billion for CY 1965–1966 now appear even greater than earlier anticipated. On February 26, FRG officials told the DOD "arms salesmen" that they were only willing to show a potential procurement of $542 million for these two calendar years. Of this sum, $192 million would involve a carryover of purchases from previous years plus some orders already placed in the first two months of 1965. The Germans said they could not anticipate meeting the $1.35 billion goal through military purchases and that the US should accept as offsets German purchases in other fields (e.g., Boeing aircraft sales to Lufthansa). Further, the MOD officials said they had been unsuccessful in persuading the Ministry of Finance to agree to substantial advance payments on orders prior to delivery, an important US objective in terms of relieving our balance of payments problems. Attached at Tab B are pertinent tables indicating the procurement problem, in terms of the items accepted by the Germans as a potential and those which US negotiators would consider possible.[3]

3.   I call these matters to your attention now because we have been informed that Mr. McNamara, on March 22, asked his negotiators why they should not simplify their negotiations by telling the Germans that, if the FRG cannot meet the US balance of payments costs in Germany, then the US would pull out US Divisions. The implication is, of course, that our force levels will be determined primarily, if not wholly, by the amounts of German purchases of US military goods and services, and not by other considerations of a political or military nature.

4.   I think it would be a grave error to use now tactics of the kind described above, which Mr. McNamara may be considering. Negotiations on the offsets are in an early stage; the picture may not be as bad as the German tactics would indicate. Even if the offsets will not be adequate, the US should very carefully consider what then needs to be done, rather than, as a low-level negotiating tactic, making a threat which is bound to have the most serious meaning for our relations with Europe, and particularly with Germany. Apart from the issues of common defense, I would think that too direct a link between our balance of payments problems and our own level of forces would tend to undermine precisely that confidence in the US economic position which bears directly on our balance of payments position. Finally, we have stated publicly a number of times that we will maintain our present level of combat forces in Germany as long as they are needed. The President, in fact, most recently made this point when CDU/CSU majority leader Rainer Barzel saw him on February 24.[4]

---

[3] Tab B, "Tables on Procurement" is not printed.

[4] The meeting included the President, Barzel, German Ambassador Knappstein, and the Country Director for German Affairs Alfred Puhan, and lasted from 12:01–12:30 p.m. No other record of this meeting has been found. (Johnson Library, President's Daily Diary)

5. I recommend that:

A. You find an appropriate occasion to speak to Secretary McNamara and to Secretary Fowler along the lines of the argument in paragraph 4 above.
B. Alternatively that you sign the letter attached (at Tab C) to Secretary McNamara, copies of which would be sent to Secretary Fowler and McGeorge Bundy.

Tab C

Letter From Secretary of State Rusk to Secretary of Defense McNamara[5]

Washington, April 4, 1965.[6]

Dear Bob:

I have been informed there is presently a considerable question whether the Federal Republic of Germany will, through the purchase of US military goods and services, wholly offset for CY '65–'66 US defense expenditures in Germany entering the international balance of payments. I gather that this is a question of both German ability and willingness to achieve this goal, as well as the FRG view that German purchases of items other than US military goods and services should be considered as offsets.

I have been greatly impressed by the skill and determination demonstrated by DOD officials in working with German officials and American business organizations to develop agreed areas for German offset purchases. In addition to the various balance of payments benefits, these activities have helped draw the Germans closer to the US in standardization of equipment and understanding our politico-military thinking.

I hope that, as I understand has occurred in the past, your negotiators will successfully demonstrate to the German side that there are available items for mutually desirable offsets. In achieving this end, however, I trust that we will not use tactics which imply that failure to meet fully US defense expenditures through these offsets will involve a consequential reduction of US military forces in Germany. I believe it

---

[5] Secret. Drafted by Howard Meyers (G/PM) on March 25. Copies were sent to McGeorge Bundy and Fowler.

[6] The April date is stamped on the source text, presumably indicating the date of signature.

would be very undesirable to convey, even by implication, that the level of US forces would be determined primarily, if not wholly, by the amount of German purchases of US military goods and services, rather than by other considerations of both a political and military nature.

I know you are aware that the German elections will take place this fall and that this fact alone may well affect the offsets negotiations. You may also recall that Ambassador Knappstein told the President on February 9 that the situation could arise in which German military purchases under the offset agreement would in fact constitute partial financing of our balance of payments deficit derived from massive US business investment in Germany.[7] This capital outflow, of course, has been moderate but I mention the matter to note that the German Government is itself under a variety of pressures related to the relationship between our balance of payments and German military offset purchases. Moreover, we could not threaten to reduce the level of our forces in Germany without examining carefully the effect this might have on our relations with and commitments to our other NATO partners.

May I assure you that the State Department whole-heartedly supports this effort to achieve these offset goals, and that we will cooperate fully in these negotiations. In view of their interest in this subject, I am sending copies of this letter to McGeorge Bundy and Joe Fowler.

Sincerely,

Dean[8]

---

[7] President Johnson met with German Ambassador Knappstein on February 9 at the White House. For President Johnson's remarks at the conclusion of his meeting, see *Public Papers of the Presidents of the United States: Lyndon B. Johnson, 1965*, Book I, p. 169.

[8] Printed from a copy that indicates Rusk signed the original.

---

56.   Memorandum From Secretary of the Treasury Dillon to President Johnson[1]

Washington, March 27, 1965.

SUBJECT

Final Report on the Balance of Payments

The week ending Wednesday[2] showed another surplus, the fifth in a row in the rough weekly data we receive from the Federal Reserve Bank

---

[1] Source: Johnson Library, White House Central Files, Confidential Files, FO 4–1, Balance of Payments (1963–1965), Box 32–39. Confidential.

[2] March 24.

in New York. The latest surplus was considerably larger than earlier ones. These reports for the three weeks since March 3d now show a cumulative surplus of $250 million. In addition, the week ending March 3d showed an exceptionally large surplus of $270 million. However, since this week covered a portion of February there is no way of knowing, until we get the monthly figures for March later in April, how much of that surplus is attributable to March and how much may have already been included in the monthly figures for February. Since the final figures for February show a deficit of $475 million, somewhat larger than I had expected, my guess is that a good portion of the $270 million surplus for the week ending March 3d will turn out to be March transactions and will add to the size of the surplus we seem to be running this month. While these weekly figures are crude and represent only a sample of the total, they are useful in projecting the general trend. In view of the steady nature of the surplus over the past five weeks, it is likely that banks not covered in the weekly sample survey are also recording surpluses. Therefore, the monthly figure for March could well turn out to be even more favorable than our weekly totals indicate.

These favorable weekly figures, the general strength of the dollar in foreign exchange markets and the rise in rates in the Eurodollar market all are clear evidence that our voluntary program is working as well or better than we could possibly have hoped. This is now generally recognized in financial circles both here and abroad.

This improvement may, however, have come just in the nick of time. Sterling has been weak over the past couple of weeks as the impression has grown that the United Kingdom budget, which is now due to be presented on April 6, will turn out to be inadequate. This impression has been reinforced by the speech given last week by the official British representative at the International Monetary Conference of the American Bankers Association at Princeton. Should this prove to be the case, it is highly possible that, prior to the first of June, the European countries will join in forcing the British Government to choose between substantial further restrictive action, such as increased sales taxes on consumer items, or a devaluation of sterling. They have the capacity to do this simply by refusing to agree to renew the support which they gave sterling last November and which runs out in May. It had been expected that the United Kingdom would make another drawing from the Monetary Fund in May for the purpose of paying off the bilateral support remaining from last winter's exercise. With an inadequate budget it is doubtful if the International Monetary Fund would, or could, agree to an additional drawing by the United Kingdom.

While it is impossible to render any final judgment on the above until the British budget has been submitted and reactions to it are available, a strong speculative attack was launched against sterling yesterday

(Friday) by the French. Rumors that sterling would be devalued over the weekend were spread through Paris accompanied by substantial sales of sterling by French banks some of which may have been short sales. This attack forced the price of sterling below $2.79 for the first time since last November. The fear soon spread to other centers on the continent of Europe as well as to New York. The British were forced to support sterling heavily. I do not have the final figure for this support but apparently it amounted to about $75 million. The British tell us that they are prepared to continue such support at least until after their budget has been published and the reaction to it is available.

It is hard to understand the reasons for the French attack on sterling unless they figure that in this way they can indirectly attack the dollar. A devaluation of sterling would throw the foreign exchange markets of the world into a turmoil at least for a period. However, provided the devaluation is not too extreme, I feel confident that the dollar is now in a position to ride out the storm without too much difficulty. Prior to the immediate present, this would not have been the case and a sterling devaluation would have posed the gravest of difficulties for the dollar.

Should it appear in the coming weeks that a devaluation is inevitable, it is highly important for us and others that it not be too drastic. It is always a severe temptation to a devaluing country to go very far once the basic decision to devalue has been made. The general feeling in continental European circles is that an appropriate figure for a devalued pound sterling would be $2.50, as compared to the present rate of $2.80. This would be a devaluation of 10.7 percent. We agree that, if devaluation occurs, and we hope it won't, it should not go beyond the $2.50 level. Any greater devaluation would put heavy and possibly unbearable strains on the entire international monetary system. Should it appear that the British are seriously considering devaluation, it is important that we concert closely with them and, if necessary, intercede at the highest levels, including conversations between yourself and the Prime Minister, in order to hold any devaluation to the $2.50 level.

I am attaching a clipping from the *Commercial and Financial Chronicle* which is interesting in connection with this whole matter. It was written prior to Friday's attack on sterling. I do not know the author.[3]

In the Cabinet meeting I said that, even if our balance of payments program was successful, we could look forward to the loss of $300 to $350 million more gold in the second quarter.[4] $175 to $200 million of this can be expected in April. This is largely due to a one-time $80 million purchase by Italy. When the Italians were in trouble last year they were

---

[3] Not attached.

[4] The President held a Cabinet meeting on Thursday, March 25, in the White House. (Jonson Library, President's Daily Diary)

forced to sell $200 million of their gold. Beginning last summer they have been doing very well in their balance of payments and have built back their dollar holdings. They now feel it necessary to reconstitute their gold holdings to the total owned prior to last spring's sale. The Bank of Italy has apparently been able to find in their own commercial banking system all but $80 million of the amount needed to reconstitute their holdings.

The annual report of the Bank of Italy will be published in May and they wish to show their gold holdings up at that time. They intend to explain in this report that they have simply reconstituted their stock and will expressly disassociate themselves from French policy and express their faith and confidence in the dollar. Italy now holds about $1.7 billion of their reserves in dollars. Their gold ratio is about 55 percent, the lowest of any of the major European powers. The Italians have been very cooperative and cannot be criticized in any way for their forthcoming gold purchase.

I have warned my colleagues here in the Treasury of the possibility that the French may well decide that their current working balances of $400 to $450 million are larger than they need and may therefore decide to purchase another $150 million in gold at any time. The present figure was given to me orally by the French Finance Minister with no one else present. Although the French have since publicly indicated that their objective was to limit their dollar holdings to the area of $1,050 million to $1,100 million, the working balance included in this figure is considerably larger than required and could easily be reduced by $150 million.

You should also be aware of an ominous development that took place in the French Finance Ministry last week. As part of an extensive international reorganization, much of which may have been useful, the office which has handled external financial affairs was abolished and its duties transferred to the domestic office. The chief result was to leave Andre de Lattre, the capable civil servant who has headed the office for some time, out of a job. He was away on a week's vacation and first learned of the change through the press. De Lattre is one of the two or three ablest men in Europe in the international field and has always been close and friendly to the United States even when loyally supporting French policies in which he did not believe. [3 lines of source text not declassified]

While it looks like we may be heading into a stormy period for the international monetary system in view of possible devaluation in the United Kingdom and the current French attitude, I feel confident that your program has given the dollar all the strength needed to weather the storm and more besides. However, should there be a British devaluation, there would undoubtedly be at least temporary repercussions on the dollar. In such circumstances and in order to indicate their determination to defend the dollar, I would not be at all surprised if the Federal Reserve Board were to increase their discount rate to 4-1/2 percent from the present 4 percent level. The wisdom or necessity for such action would depend on the force of the international reaction to a sterling devaluation. However, should a discount rate increase be necessary it would be better to have it come soon rather than late as was clearly indicated by the British experience last fall.

In the event such an increase in the discount rate were to take place, it would be my feeling that it should be rescinded in a few months, once the exchange markets had settled down. I am not aware of any intention of the Federal Reserve Board in this connection, and I do not even know if they have discussed the matter. However, this would be such an obvious reaction to a sterling devaluation that I felt I should bring it to your attention before leaving.

I am attaching a table showing the breakdown of our first quarter gold losses.[5] The Austrian purchases are the first portion of an eight month $100 million program. The Belgium purchases are in accord with their long-standing policy of keeping all their reserves in gold except for minimal working balances. The same applies to the Dutch and Swiss purchases, although the Swiss have allowed their dollar balances to increase considerably above what had previously been their normal practice. The Spanish purchase is the 2d, 3d and 4th installment of a $210 million program that will be completed in June. The United Kingdom purchases are to cover our share of the recent *losses* in the London gold pool. The Turkish purchase is partly the reversal of a temporary sale to us, but they have purchased about $10 million for reasons that are unexplained. The other small purchases, expect for Salvador, were to make payments due to the International Monetary Fund. Except for the French figure, the general dimensions of which are public knowledge, these individual figures should be held in great confidence until their publication in June.

In view of the extreme sensitivity of the contents of this memorandum, no copies are being circulated outside the Treasury.

Douglas Dillon

---

[5] Not attached.

57.   Memorandum From Secretary of the Treasury Fowler to President Johnson[1]

Washington, April 13, 1965.

SUBJECT

An Early Preliminary Look at First Quarter Balance-of-Payments Results

The *preliminary* results for the first quarter are encouraging in view of the sizeable deficits in January and February.

The preliminary *over-all* deficit figure is $161 million which, on a seasonally adjusted basis, amounts to almost $500 million—or an annual rate of $2 billion as compared with $2.8 billion last year. (We do not yet have the data to compute the *regular transactions* deficit which *excludes* special receipts from debt prepayments, advance payments on military exports and net sales of non-marketable, medium-term securities to foreign governments. These receipts last year averaged $167 million per quarter. Last year's *regular transactions* deficit was $3.1 billion.)

The encouraging thing about the first quarter data is that we began to run weekly surpluses in the latter part of February which have continued to date. The March surplus was $518 million. This situation undoubtedly reflects the operation of your February 10 program. It also may reflect to a considerable extent an improvement in the merchandise trade surplus which deteriorated badly during January and February due to the dock strike.

The decline in our gold stock during the first quarter ($833 million) greatly exceeded the unadjusted deficit ($161 million) with the result of substantial decline in foreign dollar holdings ($732 million) and minor changes in other reserve assets.

Cabinet Committee on Balance of Payments

The Committee will meet on Monday, April 19, to discuss the operation of the February 10 program. I will send a memorandum on the discussion.[2]

Publication and Use of Data

We do not publish these figures for the *overall* deficit at this time. The Commerce Department publishes sometime in mid-May the figures for

---

[1] Source: Johnson Library, Bator Papers, Balance of Payments, 1965 [3 of 4], Box 14. Limited Official Use. Fowler became Secretary of the Treasury on April 1. For text of President's Johnson's letter accepting Dillon's resignation, see *Public Papers of the Presidents of the United States: Lyndon B. Johnson, 1965,* Book I, pp. 347–348.

[2] Not found.

the *regular transactions* deficit. The figures in this memorandum should not be released for two reasons:

(a) the figures published in May that are of key importance are a different computation (the *regular transactions deficit*);
(b) the new material figures themselves often change *substantially* because at this stage they are preliminary returns.

I would therefore recommend that you *not* use figures if you wish to comment now on this subject. You are safe in stating generally that there has been a substantial recent improvement in our balance of payments, commencing about the time your new program was announced. That will be true, no matter what revisions in the figures are made to convert them to a *regular transactions* deficit and to eliminate errors in the preliminary returns.

Henry H. Fowler[3]

---

[3] Printed from a copy that indicates Fowler signed the original.

---

58.   Minutes of Meeting of the Balance of Payments Advisory Committee[1]

Washington, April 28, 1965, 2:30 p.m.

The Balance of Payments Advisory Committee of the Department of Commerce met at 2:30 p.m. on April 28, 1965 in Room 5855 of the Department of Commerce.

Mr. Nickerson called the meeting to order, and asked Mr. Morton to report on the progress of the public education campaign about the balance of payments voluntary program for the business community. Mr. Morton described the campaign with examples from all of the major

---

[1] Source: Washington National Records Center, RG 40, Records of the Executive Secretariat, Office of the Secretary, 1965–1966: FRC 71 A 6617, Balance of Payments Committee for the Department of Commerce, July–December. No classification marking. A list of participants is not printed; all members of the Balance of Payments Advisory Committee of the Department of Commerce (see Document 44) attended except Fred J. Borch, Carl J. Gilbert, and Elisha Gray II. Also attending from the Commerce Department were: Secretary Connor, Andrew Brimmer, Alexander Trowbridge, Lawrence C. McQuade, and James G. Morton. George F. James, Socony Mobil Oil Company, attended as a technical alternate.

media. He also suggested a meeting in the reasonably near future at which each member of the Advisory Committee might send the public relations representative of his firm to consider better use of this resource in support of the voluntary program. The proposal was accepted.

Mr. Nickerson then called upon Secretary Connor and Dr. Brimmer for a review of the voluntary program to date. This covered the following:

1. A report and discussion on the unofficial balance of payments figures for the first quarter.
2. Consideration of the effects which our balance of payments program appear to be having on Western European capital markets.
3. A review of the incomplete data compiled on the basis of the 344 companies which had submitted summary work sheets as of April 23, and a discussion in tentative terms of some of the issues indicated by the data.
4. A review and discussion of the progress report which the Secretary would present to the President at a meeting later in the afternoon.
5. A consideration of the merits of making available to the public the list of participants in the voluntary program. The consensus on this point was that it would be unwise to publish such a list at this stage, but the question should be reconsidered after the results are all in.

Dr. Brimmer pointed out that the form for the quarterly reports will follow the format for the summary work sheets sent out with the Secretary's initial letter.[2] Only historical data will be requested.

He then asked for views on the merits of establishing guidelines for the treatment of short term financial assets held abroad. After considerable discussion, it was agreed that issuance of such a guideline would be desirable and that it should ask companies to bring their overseas balances of short term financial assets down to the level of December 31, 1964 and, if possible, down to the level of December 31, 1963.

A draft of a proposed letter from Secretary Connor to United States affiliates of foreign corporations was presented, discussed and agreed to be appropriate.

The Committee considered briefly a suggestion that the United States tax laws be amended to permit a U.S. base corporation to enjoy deferral of its earnings from foreign operations similar to that already enjoyed by U.S.-owned foreign corporations. The Committee recommended that the Commerce Department consider the merits and demerits of this suggestion with other departments of the Government to see what action might be appropriate.

Discussion also took place on (1) the desirability of greater attention to the Export expansion effort, (2) liberalization of the Export-Import Bank financing and (3) the effect of the Federal Reserve Board's 105%

---

[2] See Document 52 and footnote 3 thereto.

rule on the financing of exports and of transactions in less developed countries.

Monday, July 12 was selected as the tentative date for the next meeting of the Advisory Committee, subject to confirmation. It was agreed that the technical committee should meet at least one week earlier.

Mr. Nickerson then adjourned the meeting.

Lawrence C. McQuade
Secretary

59.   Letter From Secretary of Commerce Connor to President Johnson[1]

Washington, April 28, 1965.

Dear Mr. President:

I am pleased to report to you that the business community, in response to your appeal for voluntary cooperation, will substantially increase its contribution to the balance of payments during 1965. The preliminary evidence suggests that this improvement will probably exceed $1.2 billion. This amount would represent an increase of about 14 per cent compared with the companies' performance in 1964.

Before I comment further on the voluntary cooperation program with the business community, let me stress the necessity to view the performance as part of your overall effort to reduce the nagging deficit in our balance of payments. You undoubtedly are getting reports on that part of your program being conducted by the Treasury Department, Federal Reserve System and other agencies of the Federal government. Moreover, I know you are also following the "See the USA" effort which private industry is making under the leadership of the Vice President.

If you would permit me, I would like to make a cautionary comment which might be helpful in appraising the following account of progress which is indicated under the voluntary program with industry. First of all, the expected improvement of around $1.2 billion does not mean that

---

[1] Source: Washington National Records Center, RG 40, Records of the Executive Secretariat, Office of the Secretary, 1965–1966: FRC 71 A 6617, Balance of Payments Committee for the Department of Commerce, Meeting April 28, 1965. No classification marking.

we can count on reducing the deficit by that amount—independently of other factors affecting the balance of payments. Because of rising production and incomes in the United States, we should expect an increase in the level of imports, and this will partly off-set the improvement anticipated. Moreover, we may also expect a further rise in travel expenditures by Americans going abroad which probably will be matched by the increase in expenditures of foreigners coming to our shores. The reports in hand reflect the companies' first estimate of the improvement they believe they can achieve in 1965. During the course of the year many of them may find it necessary to make modifications.

On the other hand, the increase of $1.2 billion expected for the business community does not by any means include the substantial contribution which the commercial banks will undoubtedly make toward improving the balance of payments in 1965. In addition, nonbank financial institutions will also register gains.

These cautionary comments aside, I think the anticipated improvement does reflect an extra effort, and the business community should be commended for the contribution they are making.

I thought it was vital that we give you an early report of the progress that is being made under the voluntary program. You may recall that I asked the chief executives of the companies cooperating with us to give me by April 15 their estimate of the expanded contribution they think they can make to the balance of payments in 1965. By the end of last week, we were able to tabulate replies from 344 companies. Responses are still coming in, and we expect to receive estimates from over 500 companies. The general comments have been highly favorable and they strongly endorse the voluntary approach to the program. About one half of the companies have made some form of explicit endorsement—either of the program or of the method of carrying it out. About two-thirds of the replies include some explanation as to how the 1965 improvement will come about.

While most of the improvement during 1965 will reflect export expansion, indications are that restraint will also be exercised on direct investment. In most cases where companies feel that for orderly business development they must proceed with direct investment projects, they propose to rely on foreign borrowing to finance a large proportion of the planned capital outlay. While a few companies, especially some of the newcomers to international business, may encounter difficulties in raising money, it appears that most companies who plan to borrow abroad will be able to do so.

The business community has made a vigorous response to your call for their assistance in improving the balance of payments. Nevertheless, we are faced with a deficit of considerable magnitude, and its reduction to manageable size will also require a sustained effort on the part of all of us throughout the rest of this year. We must be constantly on guard against a hasty acceptance of signs of improvement as evidence that the basic problem has been solved.

Finally, I would like to acknowledge the valuable assistance I have received from the Department of Commerce's Advisory Committee on the Balance of Payments under the Chairmanship of Mr. Albert L. Nickerson, Chairman of the Board of Socony Mobil Oil Company. I am confident that the members of that Committee, along with the rest of the business community, are prepared to continue making a concerted effort to improve the balance of payments.[2]

I am sure you will agree with me that the response so far to your voluntary balance of payments program demonstrates the willingness and ability of American business to join with the government in a combined effort to cope with a critical national problem.

Respectfully yours,

John T. Connor

---

[2] For a complete list of members, see Document 44.

---

60.   **Report From the Voluntary Cooperation Program Coordinating Group to the Cabinet Committee on Balance of Payments[1]**

Washington, May 26, 1965.

SUBJECT

Operating Problems under the Voluntary Cooperation Program

Since the announcement of the President's balance-of-payments program, a small informal group has been meeting periodically in the

---

[1] Source: Johnson Library, National Security File, Balance of Payments, Vol. 2 [1 of 2], December 8, 1964, Box 2. Limited Official Use. The report was sent under cover of a May 26 memorandum from Merlyn N. Trued to the Cabinet Committee on Balance of Payments. A copy was also sent to Martin, Chairman of the Board of Governors, Federal Reserve System.

Treasury Department to discuss operating problems arising under the voluntary cooperation program. In particular, the group has endeavored, through consultation, among the agencies directly concerned, to insure a coordinated interpretation of the Commerce Department and Federal Reserve guidelines in specific cases. These cases fall into several general categories which are discussed below.

1. LDC's

The Federal Reserve 105% guideline for commercial banks includes credits to LDC's as well as to borrowers in developed countries. Concern arose on the part of State and AID that banks would tend to lend to borrowers in advanced countries rather than meet the credit requirements of LDC's. A situation involving bank reluctance to make an $80 million credit to Brazil indicated the need for a more definitive guideline regarding bank credits to LDC's. After thorough inter-agency consultation, a Federal Reserve guideline was established giving bank credits to LDC's a priority next only to U.S. export credits. The Brazilian case and a number of other smaller credit transactions have undoubtedly been facilitated by this encouragement to the banks to accommodate LDC credit requests.

The Treasury is periodically providing to the agencies directly concerned a detailed list of U.S. bank long-term loan commitments to LDC borrowers as well as data on the net outflow of bank funds, short and medium term, to LDC's. The data show that LDC's have received about $440 million of long-term bank commitments so far this year (thru mid-May)—$218 million since February 10. Last year's commitments amounted to $926 million.

Another aspect of bank financing for LDC's arose with respect to U.S. exports of military equipment to these countries. DOD will probably not have sufficient MAP funds available during the remainder of this fiscal year to provide credits for military equipment sales to a number of less-developed countries, including $8–10 million for Venezuela, $2 million for Malaysia and varying amounts for other LDC's. The banks have not been generally receptive to the extension of such credits because they are generally considered to be less remunerative than other foreign credits, and have suggested that such credits be exempted from the 105% ceiling in cases where they know that DOD favors the transaction. In this situation the possibility of Export-Import Bank financing was explored. The Bank agreed to extend a military equipment export credit to India but is not eager to extend credits directly to the other countries, even with a DOD guarantee. The Bank is willing to purchase paper from DOD's credit portfolio, but DOD's legal authority to make such sales is questionable. It now appears that DOD may be able to delay extension of the credits mentioned above until its MAP funds are restored by the FY 1966 appropriation. If this should not turn out to be the case for particular credits, the matter of Export-Import Bank financing will be re-examined.

Another aspect of bank credits to LDC's involves financing of AID's extended risk guarantee programs (for example, Latin American housing). Some banks have indicated that they would not be disposed to lend for such programs within the 105% ceiling for the reason noted in the paragraph above. This situation will require continuing attention to determine whether the programs are being affected. In the case of the housing programs, a large part is being financed by non-bank financial institutions which are not subject to any guidelines in the case of loans of over 5 years' maturity.

A special situation arose with regard to U.S. bank credits to Mexican customers by banks along the Mexican border. For many of these banks, the base date of December 31, 1964, under the Federal Reserve 105% guideline, was a seasonally low date for credits to Mexico. After the situation was reviewed, the Federal Reserve advised that where a bank could not absorb a seasonal variation within its total foreign business under the guideline, it might base its 105% ceiling figure on the monthly average of outstanding credits during 1964 or use some other appropriate seasonal adjustment.

2.   Export Credits

Despite the likelihood that the turnover of outstanding commercial bank credits to foreigners enables the banking system as a whole to take care of any necessary increases in export financing during the year, there has been considerable pressure to have export credits removed from the 105% ceiling. The Federal Reserve has resisted this pressure on the grounds that this would greatly weaken the effectiveness of the guidelines in view of the difficulty of assuring that so-called "export credits" actually were essential to the accomplishment of exports in each particular case. The Federal Reserve has indicated to banks that they may exceed their 105% ceiling on a temporary basis to make bona fide export credits as long as they work towards a return to their ceiling amounts within a reasonable length of time.

The Co-ordinating Group discussed a number of cases involving reported reluctance of banks to engage in export financing and where appropriate the agencies concerned have discussed the situation with the banks themselves.

The Export-Import Bank requested and received a decision from the Federal Reserve that commercial bank loans which are participated in or guaranteed by the Export-Import Bank are exempt from the 105% ceiling. It was recognized that this exemption posed the danger of a great increase in requests for Export-Import Bank (and FCIA) guarantees. Review of the situation is being coordinated through the NAC to insure that such a patent abuse of the Export-Import Bank exemption privilege is not allowed to develop. The Federal Reserve informed the Coordinating Group that it feels free to tell commercial banks, if necessary, that the Export-Import Bank guideline is subject to change.

3.   Japan

Application of the program to Japan has given rise to a special situation in view of the agreement worked out by Assistant Secretary of the Treasury Trued and Deputy Assistant Secretary of State Trezise for a $100 million exemption from the IET of obligations issued or guaranteed by the Government of Japan and an understanding that the guidelines would not interfere with an increase in U.S. export financing for Japan, expected to be proportional to the estimated ten per cent increase in U.S. exports to Japan in 1965.[2]

With regard to the $100 million exemption, it was necessary to provide that underwriters or institutional lenders would not be deterred by the Federal Reserve guidelines from purchasing Japanese Government or government guaranteed obligations. It was also necessary to arrange for maintaining a record of such issues in order that the $100 million tax-free limit would not be exceeded. In the latter connection, it was agreed that only issues purchased by U.S. persons at the time of issue or within 90 days thereafter should be counted against the $100 million exemption amount. A special Treasury form was devised for use by underwriters or other U.S. lenders to obtain tax exemption for purchases within the $100 million exemption.

With regard to export credit financing for Japan, it was necessary to develop statistics which showed the amount of such financing in the past as a base for the expected increase during 1965. Progress has been made in reconciling Japanese and American data, and an approach is currently being made to Japanese officials for agreement that an approximately $70 million increase during 1965 in outstanding acceptances and collections (plus identifiable short- and long-term export credits) would fulfill the understanding.

A third problem that has arisen involving Japan relates to application of the Federal Reserve guidelines to Japanese agency banks in the U.S. The Japanese claimed that to put their U.S. agency banks under the 105% ceiling imposed a double restraint on them since the greater part of their dollars was furnished by their head offices which, in turn, obtained most of these funds from American banks operating under the 105% ceiling. The agency banks make the bulk of their loans to Japanese trading companies situated in the U.S. and to foreign borrowers outside of Japan.

---

[2] See Document 42.

It was tentatively decided not to ask foreign agency banks in the U.S. to report to the Fed on conformance with the 105% ceiling. U.S. bank loans to Japanese agency banks in the U.S., however, would fall within the Fed's guideline No. 13 (revised) dealing with loans to U.S. residents. A watch will also be kept over the activities of Japanese agency banks to see if they are accepting bills and then selling them in the U.S. market as a means of raising additional funds to lend abroad. The Japanese trading companies' foreign transactions fall under the guidelines issued by the Commerce Department to American affiliates of foreign companies.

4.   Australia

In March the Prime Minister of Australia in a letter to the President expressed his concern about the effect on Australia of the U.S. balance-of-payments program.[3] The President's reply indicated that, in the judgment of the U.S. Government, the U.S. balance-of-payments program was not likely to have a serious adverse effect on the Australian economy.[4] The President indicated he was asking the Secretaries of the Treasury and of Commerce to give a careful hearing to any particular problems that the Australians might wish to discuss in connection with the program's operation. Following this exchange of letters, various letters arguing the Australian case have been received by Commerce, Federal Reserve and Treasury. In early May Mr. Harold Holt, the Federal Treasurer of Australia, visited Washington and met individually with Secretaries Fowler, Rusk and Connor and Vice Chairman Balderston and Governor Robertson.

The coordinating group discussed the Australian approach and proposed agency replies in order to insure that a consistent position would be presented. In particular, it seemed important to avoid any appearance of concession to Mr. Holt's request that Australia be exempt from the IET.

5.   Canada

The Co-ordinating Group has discussed on several occasions the operation of the arrangement with Canada whereby its special status under the IET would not be taken advantage of to obtain funds in the U.S. and pass them along to borrowers in other developed countries. It seemed that an appropriate guideline from the Canadian Government to Canadian banks would be for the latter, at most, not to draw down their assets in the U.S. by an amount larger than that needed to pay off U.S. firms' withdrawing deposits from Canadian banks. By adhering to this guideline, Canadian banks would not be shifting funds from New York to the Euro-dollar market at a time when Canadian residents had special

---

[3] Document 50.
[4] See Documents 51 and 54.

privileges regarding borrowing in the U.S. (from other than banks). Such a guideline was given by the Canadian Minister of Finance to the chartered banks and reports to date suggest that Canadian banks have not been acting as a "pass-through" for U.S. funds.

6.   U.S. Affiliates of Foreign Companies

The status of U.S. affiliates of foreign companies has required special consideration by the Co-ordinating Group to minimize the possibility that any threat of an exchange control procedure under the voluntary guidelines might induce the foreign parents to repatriate existing investment in the U.S.

Under the Federal Reserve guidelines, a U.S. affiliate of foreign banks is not subject to the 105% ceiling on foreign credits; but otherwise is treated in the same way as a U.S. owned bank. Also under its revised guideline 13, the Federal Reserve has noted that loans to U.S. affiliates of foreign business firms could interfere with the program if such loans represented an attempt to evade the limitation on direct loans by the U.S. bank to the foreign parents, or if such loans were to finance operations of the U.S. affiliates which would normally have been financed from abroad.

The Federal Reserve guideline to *non-bank financial institutions* is also applicable to American affiliates of foreign companies.

The Co-ordinating Group discussed Commerce Department guidelines for the U.S. affiliates of foreign business firms and a letter inviting their cooperation was issued along with a request for the filing of a special report on their assets and liabilities by U.S. affiliates of foreign firms. It was made clear that participation in the program by U.S. affiliates of foreign companies was not to be construed as a restraint on the remittance of earnings or the repatriation of capital.

Several specific cases involving the operations of foreign affiliates have been considered by the Co-ordinating Group. In one case the U.S. affiliate of a foreign firm was borrowing in the U.S. to make funds available for other subsidiaries in less-developed countries. To minimize the immediate impact on the U.S. balance of payments, the foreign parent company arranged to transfer to the U.S. for investment in long-term certificates of deposit an amount equal to what its U.S. affiliate was borrowing in the U.S. for transfer abroad.

7.   Relation of Program to U.S. Imports and Exports

The President of the British Board of Trade expressed his concern to the Secretary of Commerce that the voluntary program induced American firms to reduce their imports from the U.K. He was particularly worried about the possible effect of the program on the decision of U.S. airlines to purchase U.S. rather than British aircraft. After discussion within the Co-ordinating Group, it was agreed that a clear statement should be made to the effect that limitations on imports have no place in the U.S. voluntary cooperation program.

The question was raised of whether the program requires that investment in LDC's by U.S. firms be tied to the export of U.S. goods and services. The Co-ordinating Group agreed that the program does not involve any such restraints on private investment in the developing countries, although it is hoped that emphasis on increased exports under the program may lead American firms investing anywhere abroad to use a larger amount of U.S. equipment than might otherwise be the case.

8.   Foreign Request for U.S. Government Guarantees

A number of situations have arisen in which foreigners have sought some kind of a U.S. Government guarantee in connection with the completion of credit transactions under the hypothetical situation of institution of U.S. exchange controls before the transactions were completed. In one case foreign commercial banks requested a potential U.S. borrower to obtain a statement from the U.S. Government to the effect that in the event of exchange controls the borrower would be permitted to honor a guarantee of repayment. In another situation American banks wanted an assurance from the U.S. Government that if exchange controls were imposed they would not be made retroactive to existing commitments by American banks to foreign borrowers.

A statement was prepared for use, as appropriate, to the effect that no expression by the U.S. Government was called for on such a hypothetical matter.

9.   Classification of Firms under Guidelines

Several cases arose in which it was not clear whether a particular U.S. firm should fall under the Federal Reserve guidelines or the Commerce Department guidelines. For example, the General Motors Acceptance Corporation, as a wholly owned subsidiary of General Motors, might have been reasonably made subject to either set of guidelines; but it was decided in view of the predominantly financial nature of its business to make it subject to the Federal Reserve guidelines for non-bank financial institutions. It was also decided that a leasing corporation involved in financing a new foreign subsidiary should come under the Federal Reserve non-bank financial guidelines.

10.   Revision of Fed Guideline to Non-Bank Financial Institutions

The Fed has asked the Co-ordinating Group to consider a revision of this guideline on the following points: (1) raise from 5 years' to 10 years' maturity the claims on foreigners subject to the 105% ceiling and include within the 10 year maturities, the portion of claims in the form of serial notes falling due within ten years; (2) include under the 105% ceiling both dollar and foreign-denominated deposits regardless of maturity; and (3) make all forms of direct investment in foreign branches and subsidiaries subject to the 10 year cut-off mentioned above.

11. U.S. Taxes

Several cases were discussed by the Co-ordinating Group in which a company had stated that it would take certain action in compliance with the program if it received some form of special tax consideration from the U.S. Government. It was noted that the Treasury had already adopted certain policies designed to facilitate compliance with the program; viz., the announcement of a procedure whereby current dividend distributions could be reclassified and excluded from gross income if the Internal Revenue Service subsequently adjusted the income realized from transactions between U.S. corporations and their foreign affiliates. Furthermore, the Treasury had adopted policies which allowed taxpayers to make repatriations tax free under certain circumstances.

Several of the cases which had been presented to the Group involved requests that the Treasury treat certain amounts advanced by U.S. corporations to their foreign affiliates as debt whereas under existing laws such advances would be treated as contributions to capital. The Treasury is considering this problem which is complex because taxpayers similarly situated seek different results and any solution may well have significant domestic tax implications.

---

61. Report From the Cabinet Committee on Balance of Payments to President Johnson[1]

Washington, June 7, 1965.

Over-all Balance of Payments to Date

It is still much too early to reach any firm conclusion about the effects of the new program. The figures so far look good—but certainly in part they reflect only temporary factors.

---

[1] Source: Johnson Library, National Security File, Subject File, Balance of Payments, Vol. 2 [1 of 2], December 8, 1964, Box 2. Confidential. The report was sent under cover of a memorandum from Secretary of the Treasury Fowler to the members of the Cabinet Committee on Balance of Payments on June 7. A copy was also sent to the Chairman of the Board of Governors, Federal Reserve System.

March and April showed over-all surpluses of $483 million and $153 million—a substantial turnabout from the $707 million deficit for January–February, and $102 million deficit for March and April 1964. But,

—a good part of this improvement reflected simply the rebound of exports after the termination of the dock strike,
—one-shot reflows of corporate funds back to the United States,
—and, a cessation of the very large capital outflows undertaken in January and early February in anticipation of the February 10 Message.

Data on Program Still Sketchy

We do not yet have much data on the detailed accounts. Nevertheless, it is clear that bank lending fell sharply after the February 10 Message. The increase in net claims on foreigners reported by banks amounted to about $400 million in January and February; was only $140 million in March; and, in April loan repayments actually exceeded new lending, bringing about a reflow of bank funds of $190 million.

The only other statistical evidence we have of the results of the program is the large pull-back of U.S. corporate funds from Canada in March—thus,

—a real assessment of the program will not be possible for several more months.

Reduction in 1965 Deficit If Program Successful

The program has the potential of bringing about a sizeable cut in the deficit this year. *If the measures in fact live up to their potential*—and assuming no big leaks in other parts of the balance of payments—we see the

—possibility of the 1965 deficit being reduced to the range of $0.7–$1.5 billion,

compared to $3.1 billion for 1964.

This would be better than the forecast for the program as originally recommended in January.

Major reason: banks were given a ceiling of a 5 percent increase for short and long-term lending instead of mere exhortation to hold down the former and leaving the latter entirely to the IET. We now hope for a $1.8 billion cut in bank lending, but

—it will only be realized if the other parts of the program are also carried out.

Other major savings in capital outflows projected for this year: direct investments—$200 million; short-term holdings and long-term investments by U.S. corporations abroad (other than direct investments and foreign securities)—$800 million.

These savings in capital outflows will be partially offset by a probable increase in U.S. purchases of new foreign securities of $340 million, giving a net saving in all private capital outflows of $2.5 billion for the year.

Exports should increase by $0.6 to $1.4 billion or 2.5 to 5.5 percent. Agricultural exports are expected to fall $400 million from last year (when our grain shipments were unusually high) while other exports should rise by $1.0 to $1.8 billion.

But these export gains are expected to be offset by an equivalent increase in imports. On balance, *we see no improvement in the trade surplus this year and maybe a worsening.*

Net military expenditures could decrease by $150 million, depending on needs to meet developments in Southeast Asia and in the Dominican Republic that cannot be offset by increased savings elsewhere.

The travel deficit will probably worsen by $250 million.

The dollar outflows from our foreign assistance program are continuing to decline. Other government capital outflows will probably increase due largely to a draw-down by the U.K. of last November's $250 million Export-Import loan.

Gold Outflows Continuing

While current developments suggest some improvement in our position, our continued heavy gold losses urge caution. The *gold outflow* in March and April totaled $512 million, and the total outflow for 1965 to date is $1.1 billion—half of which was to France. This was a serious deterioration, only partly owing to the low level of losses last year.

The large gold sales, along with the U.S. surpluses in March and April, brought about a reduction of some $1.2 billion in dollar holdings of foreign central banks. Dollar holdings of private foreigners rose by $590 million in January and February (following the trend of the last half of 1964) but declined in March and April by $380 million.

Even if we get a big improvement in the deficit *we must expect further gold losses this year* (offset, of course, by a reduction in dollar liabilities to foreign official institutions). If we do not get the large improvement our loss could prove intolerable, and make our bargaining position very weak. This signals the fact that no weakening of the program—in any of its points—must be permitted.

Problem Areas

Apart from the question of whether the program meets its objectives, some frictions and pressures have become apparent. Some of the major ones are:

—a number of bank officials and some corporate officials are pressing for a relaxation of the ceiling;
—some banks feel they are carrying a disproportionate part of the burden;

—some corporations which plan to borrow abroad more of the funds needed for investment are finding it difficult to locate loans;

—there is some concern about the difference in treatment of export financing and less-developed countries under the Fed and Commerce programs;

—the recent wage settlement and subsequent price increases in the aluminum industry are a disturbing indication that the guideposts are not being taken seriously enough either by labor or industry. Procedures throughout the government need to be reviewed to assure that the implications of the guideposts are fully recognized by both labor and industry in order to better promote our objective of price stability.

We are working jointly to see that the above do not develop into real problems. At present, the situation does not indicate any need for changing the program. Indeed, success in realizing our projection for 1965 depends on how vigorously we push *all your February 10 measures.* All parts of the program are inter-related and slackening off or failure in one part will inevitably lead to challenges of other parts. In summary, we must

—guard against premature optimism,

—ensure that no one sector is or appears to be carrying the brunt of the program alone,

—and, impress on all sectors, including the Congress and the public at large, the necessity to follow through on *all parts of the program.*

Looking Beyond the Program

Whatever the success of the program we must continually bear in mind the fact that these are temporary measures.

Permanent equilibrium will depend on our success in the more basic measures such as further improving our competitive position, making our economy a more rapid absorber of investment funds, and getting the other major countries to carry more of their and the world's financing needs.

In the next report, we will give a projection of the U.S. payments position for some time ahead and consider its implications for policy. When the temporary measures we have taken are either no longer effective or are inappropriate, it will remain of key importance that we sustain a strong U.S. dollar as an underpinning to an over-all strong U.S. position.

Report on Individual Measures of Program

Following is a report on each of the ten points of your February 10 Message:

1–3. Interest Equalization Tax.

The requested legislation—to extend the tax through 1967 and broaden the coverage to all borrowing over one year maturity instead of three year maturities as at present—is expected to come before the House

Ways and Means Committee probably in July. We do not have any indications of serious problems in the House or Senate but attempts will be made to weaken the IET or even let it expire, on the grounds it has been made unnecessary by the voluntary cooperation program.

In the meantime, the IET continues to be very effective. The amount of taxable new security issues purchased by U.S. residents is negligible and Americans continue to *reduce* their holdings of outstanding foreign securities.

Canadian new issues—which are exempt—amounted to about $150 million during January–April (they were $693 million for all last year). But since Canadian reserves have not increased this year it appears that they are in conformity with our agreement that the exemption will not be used to increase their reserves.

Japan—which has an exemption up to $100 million a year—successfully floated its first issue ($22.5 million) here since early 1963. Their next issue in the U.S.—amounting to $20 million—is expected this summer.

Bank loans with maturities of one year or more came under the IET by your Executive Order of February 10.[2] This coincided with the introduction of the Fed's voluntary cooperation program and the two working together have sharply curtailed bank long-term lending. In the period January 1–February 10 such lending to advanced countries was $570 million, but from February 10 to date it has amounted to less than $70 million, one-half of which was to Japan.

4. Voluntary Cooperation Program for Banks.

Banks seem to be cooperating fully with the program but continued cooperation will depend on evidence that all parts of the balance-of-payments program are effectively contributing to improvement.

The target established by the Fed was that banks should limit the net increase in their claims outstanding on foreigners (i.e., new loans minus loan repayments) to five percent of the amount outstanding at the end of 1964. This would allow a net outflow of $470 million in 1965 for banks under the program (some bank lending, such as loans guaranteed by the Export-Import Bank, is exempt from the 105 percent ceiling).

By the end of February, $370 million of the $470 million had already been used—the bulk of it before February 10—and in March there was a further net increase of $40 million, leaving $60 million for the rest of the year (this is the net result of some of the banks being already over their target by $270 million while the remaining banks are under their ceilings by $330 million).

---

[2] Executive Order 11198, "Imposition of Interest Equalization Tax on Certain Commercial Bank Loans" (30 *Federal Register* 1929), authorized President Johnson to impose the tax on bank loans abroad with maturities of one year or more, with appropriate exemption for borrowers in developing countries.

Since some major banks over the ceiling at the end of March are reducing their claims, the outflow for the remainder of 1965 could well be lower than the March rate, giving an outflow for the year of $600 million or less. All in all, it might be reasonable to expect an improvement for the banks under the program of $1–$1.5 billion.[3]

Indications are that banks are giving priority to export credits and to loans to the less-developed countries. We feel that there is ample room to accommodate a reasonable outflow for these priority areas while still keeping under the 105 percent ceiling.

5. *Antitrust Exemption for Banks.*

This legislation—to enable banks and other financial institutions to work together on the voluntary cooperation program without running afoul of the antitrust laws—has been reported by the House Judiciary Committee with amendments.

6. *Voluntary Cooperation Program for Corporations.*

The cooperation of the business community in this program has been firmly established and the replies received from the companies indicate that they will collectively make an important contribution to the solution of the balance-of-payments problem.

The Secretary of Commerce has asked 585 companies to supply data on their foreign transactions for 1964 and to indicate what improvement in the net total for these transactions they expect for 1965.[4] As of May 21, 543 companies had replied and data for 438 firms could be tabulated, giving figures for their earnings from all their exports, and on investments and other current transactions, along with their capital outflows to developed countries.

The net balance for all these transactions in 1964 was a credit of $10.9 billion and the reporting firms estimated that this would be increased to $12.2 billion in 1965, an improvement of $1.3 billion.

It should be noted however that this $1.3 billion improvement cannot be interpreted as a potential reduction in our balance-of-payments deficit. A good part of the improvement anticipated is in the form of increased exports (the reporting firms account for over 40 percent of total U.S. exports), and a substantial improvement in our exports was already anticipated even in the absence of the program and is included in our current projection. The same cautionary comment applies to dividends and interest earned by these companies.

Virtually all of the companies submitting comments on direct investment clearly understand the basis of the request that they exercise

---

[3] Differs from $1.8 figure on page 2 because Federal Reserve program excludes credit guaranteed by Ex-Im Bank, bank claims for account of customers and bank claims by U.S. affiliates of foreign banks. [Footnote in the source text.]

[4] See Document 52.

restraint and indicated their determination to cooperate to the maximum extent feasible. A number of companies, although not specifically asked, volunteered the information that they have deferred or canceled investment projects in developed countries which they had originally planned to make in 1965. Some companies reported that the launching of the program caught them with investment commitments which were well along toward completion and could not be stopped without abandoning sizeable investments.

In response to the request that they raise more of their funds in developed countries, about 20 percent reported that they have borrowed or are planning to borrow abroad to finance investment projects (and, in many cases, in spite of added cost).

Several firms reported that they will try to raise funds by selling shares abroad in their foreign subsidiaries. In three or four cases the company stated that it had changed its plans to buy up minority interests in its affiliates abroad.

Over half of the 438 companies reported that they held no short-term financial assets abroad at the end of 1964. The remaining firms reported they held $1.5 billion—$1.0 billion in Canada—at the end of 1964, an increase of $437 million during the year. The companies appear to be cooperating in a significant way in reducing these holdings.

In order to strengthen the program, Secretary Connor has decided to send letters to some 3,000 firms not previously contacted. This letter will briefly describe the program and ask for cooperative efforts similar to those now self-imposed by the current participants, except that quarterly reports will not be requested.

7. Government Expenditures Abroad.

In conformance with your desire to reduce military expenditures abroad, the Defense Department has undertaken a program to reduce expenditures by an additional $50 million this year and $100 million in 1966, excluding expenditures related to increased activity in Southeast Asia. However, the increased operations relating to Southeast Asia currently are expected to cost $100 million in 1965, more than offsetting the projected additional savings for this year. Nevertheless, other savings, primarily reduced procurement of uranium, may reduce total military expenditures this year by $60 million from the 1964 level, depending on developments in Southeast Asia and the Dominican Republic.

Receipts from deliveries of military equipment are expected to increase by $90 million in 1965, giving an improvement up to $150 million in net military expenditures.

AID continues to seek further balance-of-payments savings, but possibilities for further major reductions are now limited if the U.S. is to continue to meet its foreign policy objectives. In addition to continuing to tie over 85 percent of its commitments to U.S. goods and services, AID has taken several measures which will lead to increased substitution of our foreign currency holdings for dollar expenditures. The dollar outflow in 1964 from AID operations was cut to well under $500 million and it is anticipated that this will fall to $400 million or less in 1965.

The remainder of the Federal agencies currently estimate little if any change in their payments from calendar year 1964 to 1965. Gradual increases in such items as pensions and annuities are offset by savings in other agencies. There was, however, a one-time saving of about $105 million in 1964 which is not expected to reappear in 1965. This was the result of drawing down the funded balances of previously reserved foreign currencies which will not be freed for other uses.

In total, Federal agencies continue to make a substantial contribution to reducing the balance-of-payments deficit. The latest gold budget data shows that on a fiscal year basis, the Federal excess of payments on regular transactions declined more than 23 percent ($630 million) from 1963 to 1965, and are expected to decline another 13 percent ($290 million) from 1965 to 1967. Gross payments, that is before deducting receipts, declined 15 percent ($725 million) from 1963 to 1965, but are expected to rise by 4 percent ($175 million) from 1965 to 1967. The Budget Director is sending you separately a summary report on the gold budget status.[5]

8. Tourism.

The legislation to reduce the duty exemption allowed returning U.S. residents has been reported by the House Ways and Means Committee. However, the Committee did not eliminate the to-follow privilege as we had proposed, which reduces our projected savings of $75–$125 million. On the other hand, the Committee added a provision reducing the amount of alcoholic beverages allowed free from duty from one gallon to one quart and limited the privilege to persons over twenty-one.[6]

There is little to indicate that the "See the U.S.A." program has yet taken effect.[7] Passport applications in the first four months of this year were up substantially over last year and current indications are that our foreign travel expenditures in 1965 will be $450 million over 1964.

On the other hand, expenditures here by foreign tourists are expected to rise by 10 to 15 percent, continuing the encouraging trend

---

[5] See Document 62.

[6] President Johnson signed H.R. 8147 on June 30. P.L. 89–62 (79 Stat. 208) made permanent the existing temporary law that goods with a value of up to $100 could be brought into the United States duty-free by U.S. residents returning from abroad after an absence of not less than 48 hours once every 30 days, but stipulated that the $100 valuation would apply to the retail value of the goods, rather than wholesale value as under the existing law. For President Johnson's statement after signing the bill, see *Public Papers of the Presidents of the United States: Lyndon B. Johnson, 1965,* Book II, pp. 712–713.

[7] Regarding this program, see footnote 7, Document 5.

which began last year when the increase was 17 percent. The net result of these increased expenditures and receipts is expected to raise the travel deficit by about $250 million this year to a level of $1,850 million.

9. *Export Promotion.*

The Commerce Department has conducted a vigorous cooperative business-government program to further stimulate U.S. exports. Since the first of the year Commerce has:

—initiated a new export promotion device abroad (sample display centers), introducing products of almost 400 U.S. firms new to the export markets;

—opened an additional trade center, and sponsored U.S. trade shows and engaged in other commercial show activities yielding estimated sales of more than $22 million thus far this year and 100 new agency relationships.

In the year ending March, 1965, manufacturing unit-labor costs in the United States dropped about 1 percent, despite an increase of 3.6 percent in average hourly wages. In foreign countries, these costs were generally stable, so that the U.S. improved its international competitive position. U.S. wholesale prices in March were up 0.9 percent from a year earlier, but this was less of an increase than in the other major countries except Japan.

The typical collective bargaining outcome thus far in 1965 has been reasonably close to the guideposts. But the most recent settlement in aluminum was close to 4 percent. It is not clear how much influence this will have on later settlements in steel and other industries. In general, however, the outlook is for maintenance and possibly some further improvement in the U.S. international competitive position this year.

The outlook is uncertain for a favorable settlement of the contract dispute in the shipping industry, and a strike on both the East and West Coasts may occur. This would seriously disrupt exports. On the other hand, a settlement purchased at the expense of an inflationary wage settlement may also have seriously adverse effects on the balance of payments.

The effort to expand U.S. exports is supported by the Federal Maritime Commission, which feels that the present ocean freight rate structure appears to be discriminatory and this may be an impediment to the U.S. export expansion effort.

The F.M.C. program includes (i) a greater effort to assist shippers in obtaining more equitable rates from the steamship conferences; (ii) recommendations for negotiations with foreign governments on production of information and to urge their acceptance of our efforts to eliminate discrimination against U.S. exports; (iii) increased pace of regulation of activities and rate practices of ocean carriers and, if necessary, disapproval of conference agreements.

10. Removal of Tax Barriers to Foreign Investment in the United States.

Hearings on the legislation to accomplish this purpose are scheduled to begin in the House Ways and Means Committee in late June or early July.

---

62.   Memorandum From the Director of the Bureau of the Budget (Schultze) to President Johnson[1]

Washington, June 8, 1965.

SUBJECT

"Gold Budget"

Attached is a *summary of our latest "gold budget"* report on the international transactions of Federal agencies.

Secretaries Fowler and Connor have informed me that *many businessmen and bankers,* involved in the voluntary balance of payments cooperation program, *have wanted to know what the Federal Government is doing about its own dollar outflow.*

The Secretaries and I believe that *we have a good story to tell.* The Federal Government's own outflow of funds abroad has been sharply reduced—as shown in the attached gold budget report.

The gold budget summary itself is *not suitable* for release.

However, I have drafted the attached statement which you may wish to use with the press on the first appropriate occasion.[2] It has been checked with Secretaries Fowler and Connor.

Charles L. Schultze[3]

---

[1] Source: Department of State, Central Files, FN 12 US. No classification marking. The memorandum was sent from Secretary of the Treasury Fowler to the members of the Cabinet Committee on Balance of Payments on June 16. A copy was also sent to the Chairman of the Board of Governors, Federal Reserve System.

[2] Not printed.

[3] Printed from a copy that indicates Schultze signed the original.

Attachment[4]

Washington, June 8, 1965.

MEMORANDUM FOR THE PRESIDENT

SUBJECT

The "Gold Budget"—International Transactions of Federal Agencies

Highlights

The latest gold budget data which we have just reviewed and compiled shows:

The *net dollar outflow* abroad from the Federal Government's regular activities will have *fallen by 23%—$635 million between fiscal year 1963 and 1965.*

The net outflow is programmed to *fall by another 13%—$290 million between 1965 and 1967.*

Between 1963 and 1965 the major improvements occurred through *reductions in payments.* In the *next two years* the forecasted improvements result from an *increase in receipts*—payments actually rise slightly during this period.

We have found that in the past agencies tend to be *overoptimistic in their receipts estimates.* Since most of the projected improvement in the next two years comes from an increase in receipts, agencies will have to redouble their efforts to meet their goals.

The improvements have been obtained (1) *without sacrificing essential U.S. commitments abroad,* and (2) *in the face of rising price and wage levels in most overseas areas where we spend our dollars.* A more detailed summary is attached.[5]

Charles L. Schultze

---

[4] No classification marking.

[5] Not printed.

63.   Memorandum From the President's Special Assistant for National Security Affairs (Bundy) to President Johnson[1]

Washington, June 12, 1965, 9:30 a.m.

The attached paper from Joe Fowler represents a real achievement by Joe and Francis Bator. What Joe is now asking is that you should instruct him to do what everyone really wants him to do—namely, take the lead in an important, quiet study of the next steps on the monetary front. A Presidential instruction is needed simply because while everyone agrees in principle that the Treasury should do this job, they will not pitch in energetically except with a Presidential summons. The paper is carefully drawn so as to commit you to nothing and yet to force a broad-gauged study of the problem as a whole. As Joe Fowler points out in his covering memorandum, this plan has so far been held between his office and mine. Before we ask for your final signature, we would like your permission to talk about it with Gardner Ackley and George Ball. Bator assures me that they would be favorable, but we would not wish to go outside the immediate White House–Treasury circle unless this is something which you think well of, at least in principle.

McG. B.

OK to check with Ball and Ackley
OK for Joe Fowler to check with the panel of consultants proposed on page 4 of the memorandum[2]

Attachment[3]

Washington, June 11, 1965.

MEMORANDUM FOR THE PRESIDENT

SUBJECT

Forward Planning in International Finance

Attached is a proposed draft memorandum from you to me which has been worked out by Under Secretary for Monetary Affairs, Fred Deming, and Francis Bator of your staff.[4]

---

[1] Source: Johnson Library, Bator Papers, International Monetary Reform, President's Instructions—June 1965, Box 7. No classification marking.
[2] Both of these options are checked. A handwritten notation next to the options reads: "OK—good. L."
[3] Secret.
[4] The draft is identical to the June 16 memorandum to Secretary Fowler, Document 64.

I would like to discuss the last paragraph on page 4 with you at some appropriate point so that the panel of outside consultants which you spoke to me about some weeks ago could be constituted officially and have the constituency and complexion that would accomplish the purposes you and I have in mind. I have some additional names to suggest in addition to those obvious ones listed and have approached only one of them that you mentioned to me when we discussed this before. With your permission, I would like to approach the remaining ones so that an appropriate announcement could be made well in advance of the visit of the Chancellor here at the end of this month.

It goes without saying that no one will have seen the attached memorandum but the two of us and Messrs. Deming and Bator. However, I would think that before transmitting it, if you approve, you would want to have Bator clear this with George Ball who, I understand, continues to be in charge of this area in State by agreement with Tom Mann and the Secretary.

Henry H. Fowler

64. Memorandum From President Johnson to Secretary of the Treasury Fowler[1]

Washington, June 16, 1965.

SUBJECT

Forward Planning in International Finance

It has become clear to me that we must develop policies, covering a considerable period in the future, with respect to the development of the international monetary and payments system and the role of the United States in the system. The actions we have taken to bring our payments

---

[1] Source: Johnson Library, Bator Papers, International Monetary Reform, President's Instructions—June 1965, Box 12. Secret. The memorandum was sent under cover of a June 16 note from Francis Bator to Secretary Fowler in which he wrote in part: "Will you send copies to Messrs. Ball, Ackley and Martin? You might wish to call their attention to the President's caution on page 3 about secrecy and need-to-know." A copy of the note and memorandum were sent to McGeorge Bundy. This memorandum is also printed in Lyndon B. Johnson, *The Vantage Point: Perspectives of the Presidency, 1963–1969,* pp. 597–598.

into balance will, over time, put substantial pressure on reserves abroad and hence on international trade and the growth of the world economy. The Free World will need some way of systematically producing the additional liquidity which has been supplied by the payments deficits of the United States. This will require international agreements among the nations which are the primary sources of liquidity. I recognize that considerable study has been devoted to these issues by the Long-Range International Payments Committee, chaired by the Treasury.[2] However, I believe that it would now be desirable to push forward with more intensive effort, so as to be fully prepared for full scale negotiations when the time is ripe and right.

In the light of your leading responsibility within the Government for forward planning on international monetary problems, I should like you to organize a small high-level study group to develop and recommend to me—through you, and the other principals directly concerned—a comprehensive U.S. position and negotiating strategy designed to achieve substantial improvement in international monetary arrangements.[3] The Study Group should consist of appropriate senior officials from the Treasury, the State Department, the Council of Economic Advisers, the Board of Governors of the Federal Reserve System,

---

[2] Not further identified.

[3] In November 1965, George H. Willis, Deputy to the Assistant Secretary of the Treaury for International Affairs, assumed responsibility for coordinating the activities of this Study Group, which became known as the Deming Group. During Willis' tenure, until the end of the Johnson administration in January 1969, numerous documents were distributed to the members of the Group. A record of these documents is in the Washington National Records Center, RG 56, OASIA Files: FRC 75 A 101, Deming Group. Approximately 50 percent of the documents distributed to the Deming Group were IMF papers and reports. Others were public statements by U.S. and foreign government officials related to international monetary matters, and some of the papers originated in the business and academic communities. The Deming Group papers include transcripts of G–10 Deputies meetings, many of which took place at the OECD Chateau de la Muette in Paris, and which were prepared by the Treasury Attaché at the Embassy in Paris, Donald J. McGrew, and forwarded by McGrew to Willis for distribution in Washington. When the G–10 Deputies met in other locations, Willis sometimes drafted the minutes, but McGrew also occasionally attended. Other Deming Group papers are memoranda and letters from the U.S. Executive Director of the International Monetary Fund, William B. Dale, reporting on such matters as IMF Executive Committee meetings and his conversations with IMF Managing Director Pierre-Paul Schweitzer and others at the IMF. According to a January 17, 1966, distribution list for Deming Group papers, the members were William B. Dale (IMF), Francis Bator (NSC), Richard N. Cooper (Department of State), J. Dewey Daane (Federal Reserve Board), Arthur M. Okun (Council of Economic Advisers), Robert Solomon (Federal Reserve Board), and at Treasury Deming, Trued, and Willis. Bradfield at Treasury and McGrew in Paris were not members of the Group but were on the distribution list for the papers. (Ibid.) Willis attended many Deming Group and other meetings related to international monetary affairs, including G–10 Deputies Meetings and annual meetings of the IMF, and took often voluminous notes on their deliberations. Spiral notebooks containing Willis' handwritten notes are ibid., RG 56, Assistant Secretary for International Affairs, Deputy to the Assistant Secretary and Secretary of the International Monetary Group: FRC 83 A 26, Willis' Notes 66–69.

and the White House. I understand that you would have in mind that it would be chaired by the Under Secretary of the Treasury for Monetary Affairs.

Without attempting to lay down rigid terms of reference, the following are some of the questions I have in mind:

1. What are the possible means of reducing the United States' vulnerability to political and economic pressure through the threatened conversion into gold of any overhang of official dollar balances?

2. What are the possible and feasible means of assuring that credit will be available to deficit countries in amounts and on terms—maturity, interest, and automaticity—consistent with the realities of the adjustment process in a world of fixed parities where sharp deflation is not an acceptable alternative?

3. How can we assure that the amount of reserve assets will expand at a rate which will facilitate maintenance of full employment, reasonably stable prices, and expansion of world trade? Any revised or new system for creating reserves should insure against the instability inherent in a two-reserve asset or multiple-asset arrangement in which one asset is judged to be absolutely safe in terms of convertibility into the other(s), whereas convertibility the other way is unavoidably judged more uncertain.

The Study Group should explore which of the elements in the various proposed schemes of reform would be acceptable to the United States, which entirely unacceptable, and which might well be appropriate for negotiation.

In considering these questions, I would like the Study Group to take full account of the interrelations between our monetary and economic objectives, and our more general foreign policy objectives. It should explore the entire range of actions open to the United States which would bring to bear our economic strength, and our political strength, to secure reforms which would be desirable in terms of the full range of our objectives. It should take into account a variety of contingencies with regard to the cooperation of other governments and explore what unilateral steps the United States might take to achieve progress. It should spell out alternatives with respect to timing.

In addition to the above general questions, the Study Group should give urgent and thorough consideration to the special situation of the United Kingdom, which is of major foreign policy concern. Specifically, it should consider what steps the United States could take to arrange for a relief of pressure on sterling, so as to give the United Kingdom the four- or five-year breathing space it needs to get its economy into shape, and thereby sharply reduce the danger of sterling devaluation or exchange controls or British military disengagement East of Suez or on the Rhine.

The Study Group should be small and it should work in the strictest secrecy, with knowledge of its existence and access to its work available on a strict need-to-know basis. Its work would not be a substitute for the continuing work, under your chairmanship, of the Cabinet Committee on the Balance of Payments (and the Executive Committee), the National Advisory Council on International and Financial Problems, and the Long-Range International Payments Committee. It is my desire that these committees continue their valuable work.

I believe it would be useful for you also to establish a panel of consultants, consisting of people outside of Government with broad knowledge in this field, who would be available to you for counsel. This consultant group might also be relatively small and include people from the academic, banking, and business communities. It would be appropriate to include people formerly with the Government, such as Douglas Dillon, Robert Roosa, and Kermit Gordon.[4]

I should like to receive a progress report on the work of the Study Group by August 2, 1965, and from time to time as appropriate. In addition, I shall expect periodically to meet with you and the other officials concerned to discuss the problems and prospects.

Lyndon B. Johnson

[4] On July 16, 1965, Secretary Fowler, in conformity with Executive Order 11007 of February 26, 1962, formed the Advisory Committee on International Monetary Arrangements. Fowler's July 16 announcement named the following Committee members: Douglas Dillon, Robert V. Roosa, Kermit Gordon, Edward Bernstein, Andre Meyer, David Rockefeller, and Charles Kindleberger. Walter W. Heller and Frazer B. Wilde were soon added to the Committee. Francis M. Bator joined in September 1967, replacing Kindleberger who had resigned in 1966. The Advisory Committee, which became known as the Dillon Committee after its Chairman, met 33 times between July 16, 1965, and December 4, 1968. Summaries of meetings, minutes of meetings, and sets of papers distributed for meetings of the Dillon group are in the Washington National Records Center, RG 56, OASIA Files: FRC 75 A 101, World/1/540, Dillon Committee Records. A photocopy of Fowler's July 16 announcement of the Advisory Committee on International Monetary Arrangements, including a brief statement of its terms of reference, is ibid., WOR/1/540 Advisory Committee on International Monetary Arrangements–General–Vol. I.

65. Memorandum From the Under Secretary of State (Ball) to Secretary of the Treasury Fowler[1]

Washington, July 28, 1965.

SUBJECT

Some Thoughts on the British Crisis

Tony Solomon and John Leddy have been keeping me informed of the talks in Treasury on the UK situation. My own thinking is running along the following lines:

1. If the new program fails to convince and a massive run on sterling threatens or develops, we should then tell HMG that we will do everything possible to round up maximum multilateral support, provided they take the further internal measures we deem necessary. We should be very tough in our demands, even though we cannot expect full performance—including a freeze—or partial freeze—on wages and prices, stiff down payments on hire purchase, use of the so-called "regulator" to increase the purchase tax. By "maximum multilateral support," I mean something like $3–4 billion, of which we would have to provide 50% or maybe 75%. This would be a short-term arrangement—say 6 months—to give everyone a chance to assess the longer-term situation.

I understand this is substantially the proposed line of action shaping up in the Treasury talks.

2. The *procedure* for carrying out 1, above, will probably require telephonic exchanges with the other members of the Group of Ten. (We talked about this yesterday.)[2] I can't see any other practical way of raising the money. If the UK were to ask for a meeting of the Group of Ten in Paris, the visibility of a conclave of Finance Ministers and Central Bankers would probably touch off a further run. The French would be given a golden opportunity to wreck the operation if that is what de Gaulle decides he wants. And the representatives at Paris would be out of touch with their heads of state and other officials whose support for the operation is essential.

I would concur, therefore, in what I understand to be Fred Deming's view—that we try to round up short-term funds over the wire. This would begin with the most willing (the Germans) and wind up with the least (the French). The Group of Ten should meet *afterwards* and *quickly* to sort out the longer-run problem.

---

[1] Source: Department of State, Ball Papers: Lot 74 D 272, Fowler Memorandum. Secret; Personal.

[2] This exchange has not been further identified.

I believe that this procedural point is also in accord with the consensus of the talks at Treasury.

3. But I am frankly appalled at the thought, put forward during the Treasury talks, that we should suggest to the British, at any point, that we would tolerate the devaluation of sterling. I think we should let them know in no uncertain terms that *any* change in the sterling rate is out of the question.

I know the technical arguments for a mild devaluation of, say 10% to 15%, for which everyone else, or nearly everyone, would be expected to stand still. But I think it is politically unrealistic to expect any British Government to take a half-measure of this kind—particularly since it would have to take some further internal steps to give it credibility. I believe the British will either take their political medicine internally or make a big move externally and hope to muddle through in the scramble to pick up the pieces.

If they should make a big external move they would wreck much more than the monetary system. Our foreign political and defense policies would be badly mangled. The United States, as the leading Western power, could not engage in economic and financial warfare with other major trading nations of the world and still maintain functioning military alliances—or, in fact, effective cooperation of any kind. The devaluation of sterling would set in train forces that could complicate the crises in both the Far East and Europe.

4. Ever since 1961 I have been beating the drums for reform of the international monetary system. But we must avoid *at all costs* achieving reform through the process of chaos. A *substantial* devaluation of sterling—in my judgment the only kind of devaluation politically possible for the UK—would result in just that. Monetary infighting through floating rates, threats of countervailing duties, the suspension of gold purchases and sales, and the ensuing collapse of the IMF and Kennedy Round would not only louse up world trade but would shatter the free world political and defense system that is already seriously strained by Viet-Nam, the stresses in Anglo-German relations, the hardening of the Soviet line, the crisis in the Common Market, and the vagaries and intransigence of the Master of the Elysée. A "monetary conference" under these circumstances would—by comparison—make the World Monetary Conference of 1933 look orderly and constructive.

5. I conclude, therefore, that

(a) We should insist that sterling be held at $2.80—and use all necessary instruments of persuasion to back up that insistence.
(b) We should be prepared to offer necessary financial assistance ourselves, and necessary help in rounding up funds from Europe.
(c) We should insist that in order to accomplish (a) and (b) the British finally face up to the need for adequate internal measures.

(d) We should insist that they maintain their political and defense commitments in Europe and East of Suez.

(e) We should tell them that failure on their part to proceed along these lines could entail a collapse of the existing monetary, political and defense structure of the Free World and put an intolerable strain on our relations.

George W. Ball[3]

---

[3] Printed from a copy that bears this typed signature.

---

66.   Memorandum From the President's Special Assistant for National Security Affairs (Bundy) to President Johnson[1]

Washington, August 5, 1965, 9:30 p.m.

SUBJECT

The Sterling Crisis Deepens

1. The British have been into us on three wires today reporting their growing concern for the very near future of Sterling—and we think they are right to be worried. Cromer at the Bank of England has called Martin repeatedly, Callaghan at the Exchequer has called Fowler, and Derek Mitchell in the Prime Minister's office has just talked to me for a half-hour on the secure direct line.[2]

2. In essence, the situation is this. There is heavy pressure against Sterling from a variety of sources. They lost $80,000,000 yesterday and $180,000,000 today. Estimates of possible losses tomorrow run between $300,000,000 and $500,000,000. If it goes on at this rate into next week, they would literally run out of reserves and be forced into devaluation in a very few days.

3. This situation has triggered intense trans-Atlantic discussion of the basic proposal discussed with you by Joe Fowler a week ago.[3] The essentials of this emergency deal are three: first, that the British take

---

[1] Source: Johnson Library, National Security File, Country File, United Kingdom, Trendex (Burke Trend), 4/65–8/65, Box 215. Secret.

[2] For a British Treasury official's view of the crisis, which was not alleviated until the central banks in the Group of Ten (except France) provided credit to the United Kingdom on September 10, see Alec Cairncross, *The Wilson Years*, pp. 65-77.

[3] No record of this conversation has been found.

action which we can responsibly report to central bankers as proof of their readiness to make an effective defense of Sterling over time: second; the U.S. takes the lead in organizing a central bankers' defense; third, the Europeans—especially the Germans—agree to go with us in a big way so that we are not left with an essentially U.S. defense of Sterling. It remains the flat opinion of all your advisers that it would be better to let Sterling go than for us to take on its defense without a major foreign contribution.[4]

4.   The British know that this is our position. Their difficulty is in finding the right proof of their continued determination. Of the available measures, only one meets their double requirement: that it pleases the bankers and also makes sense economically; that one is a wage-price freeze. Such a freeze requires legislation, and Parliament rose today! Still more serious, from the Prime Minister's point of view, is the fact that, in his judgment, he simply cannot unilaterally announce a wage-price freeze in the first week of August without losing an intolerable amount of his union support. The unions will feel betrayed, because the Trades Union Congress meets in September, and this issue should be settled between the government and the congress there, democratically, not now, by fiat. Mitchell *says* that the Prime Minister would rather devalue and go to the country than try to impose a wage freeze now.

5.   The best the British seem prepared to do is to give us private assurances now that they will get a wage-price freeze in September—either by agreement with the TUC or by legislation obtained in spite of union resistance. (It seems clear to me that Wilson believes that he can get union support in September and then put it through Parliament in a special session. This is what he is prepared to promise, with ifs, ands, and buts still undefined.)

6.   We have not yet focused sharply as a government on the question whether such assurances would give us enough to take to the European central banks. Francis Bator's first guess is that it could be done this way if the assurance is strong enough for Bill Martin to believe in it. We will know more on this tomorrow when Deming gets back from London tonight and Callaghan gives more details to Fowler.

7.   Meanwhile there are two special problems:

First, tomorrow itself may produce a deadly hemorrhage of Sterling. The best we can do to guard against this is for the Fed to act on its

---

[4] Strategies for dealing with a Sterling crisis were under active consideration in the Deming Group. Papers for the Group by George H. Willis include "Emergency Financial Assistance for the United Kingdom," July 27, and "Contingency Planning for Emergency Phase of Sterling Problem," August 20. (Washington National Records Center, RG 56, Assistant Secretary for International Affairs, Deputy to the Assistant Secretary and Secretary of the International Monetary Group: FRC 83 A 26, Contingency Planning 1965–1974, Cotingency Planning for Emergency Phase of Sterling Problem 8/20/65)

own in local defense measures of a straight short-term sort. This Martin has already undertaken to do.

Second, Mitchell made it very clear in his talk with me that if the Prime Minister is faced with imminent devaluation, he will try to come over here and dump the problem in your lap, no matter what stage of agreement or disagreement the two governments may be at. I have told Mitchell in the strongest possible terms that there should be no such visit unless we agree to it, and that I do not myself see what the virtue of it is. I told him that if we had an understanding the visit was unnecessary, and that if we did not have one, I would think it very dangerous indeed. I am sure the Prime Minister will not come without further consultation (he is in fact on a train to the Scilly Isles, because if he changed his plans and stayed behind it might deepen the panic for tomorrow). But we may have to make our point with them again tomorrow.

8.   Francis Bator is watching this problem through the night. In particular he will meet Deming's plane at midnight and arouse us all if there is a need for nighttime action. Otherwise, we will be on deck early to watch the London market. Then we will meet with Fowler at 10:00 a.m. and be ready to report to you at 11:00 a.m, when Fowler already has an appointment with you.[5]

McG. B.

---

[5] The President met with Fowler, Ball, Deming, Gardner Ackley, McGeorge Bundy, and Bator on Friday, August 6, from 11:10 to 11:35 a.m. (Johnson Library, President's Daily Diary)

---

67.   Minutes of Meeting of the Cabinet Committee on Balance of Payments[1]

Washington, August 18, 1965.

Balance of Payments Considerations.

Secretary Fowler called attention to several factors that might put the third quarter balance of payments into deficit even after seasonal

---

[1] Source: Johnson Library, Fowler Papers, International Balance of Payments—Classified Material: Cabinet Committee on Balance of Payments, 8/65–12/66, Box 52. Confidential. Drafted by Philip P. Schaffner (Treasury) on August 20. Another record of this meeting, sent under cover of an August 25 memorandum from Acting Assistant Secretary of the Treasury for International Affairs Knowlton to the Cabinet Committee on Balance of Payments, was sent to President Johnson. (Department of State, Central Files, FN 12 US)

adjustment. These were the possible further decline in the trade balance, a more than normal increase in tourist expenditures abroad, and the probable increase in bank loans since banks have now about $400 million of leeway under the Federal Reserve 105% ceiling. He pointed out that these factors warn against an over-optimistic attitude. Secretary Connor said he was concerned about the appearance of price increases throughout the economy and the fact that a number of recent wage settlements appeared to exceed the guidelines established by the Council of Economic Advisers. He referred specifically to the Aerospace Corporation settlement.

Mr. Okun said that 4% was tending to become the normal rise in recent wage settlements. He said the developments concerning the minimum wage bill are disquieting and that, if approved, the bill would have two unfortunate results. It would hinder a balanced regional growth of the U.S. economy, and it would raise prices of such items as apparel, shoes, and lumber. In this connection he mentioned that the proposed pay increase for Government employees set a very bad precedent for wage and price stability in private industry. He said that the rises in prices were to a considerable extent concentrated in food items, and these may be temporary rises; but hides, leather and certain other goods, including some industrial goods, were also showing some increases. Director Schultze remarked that the President had said he would not be the chief wrecker of the wage-price guidelines in referring to the proposed Government pay increase. Senator Monroney will hold hearings of his Committee on the proposed pay increase on Monday. Director Schultze thought that the Senate would produce a more responsible bill than the House had approved but that it would still be excessive—probably a two-year bill with average increases of from 9 to 9-1/2%. The Administration, on the other hand, hoped for a one-year bill with an average increase of 3%. There was some possibility that this session of Congress might end without final action on any bill. Secretary Fowler remarked that these two pieces of legislation are extremely important for the success of our entire balance-of-payments program. He asked Secretary Connor about the status of the marine workers' strike. Secretary Connor said that the marine engineers, one of the three groups on strike, had agreed to accept a new contract and that at least for the next six months no inflationary effects resulting from the settlement would be felt.

Director Schultze said that the Budget Bureau is considering the possibility of more sales out of Government stockpiles as a substitute for imports. He thought that the Symington bill would probably not be approved this session of Congress but added that there was some authority to sell additional amounts from stockpile even without passage of the bill. Secretary Fowler indicated that the Mint was using stockpile nonferrous metals for its purposes. Secretary Connor said the Douglas Committee was still working on the problem of discrimination in ocean freight rates. In response to a question from Secretary Fowler, Assistant Secretary Brimmer indicated that Commerce had estimated that the probable effect on the U.S. balance of payments of ocean freight rate discrimination against U.S. exports was about $60 million a year.

Mr. Okun reported on the extent to which the recent excise tax cut had been passed on to consumers. He said that on an over-all basis, 75% of the cut had been passed along, with a complete adjustment in prices by automobile companies and dealers and a few other industries, but with little or no reduction by manufacturers of automatic pens and pencils, phonograph records, and sporting goods. Under Secretary Ball said that we were losing an opportunity to make substantial wheat sales to Russia because of our policy that 50% of the shipments be made on U.S. ships with their high freight rates. Secretary Fowler indicated that we still got some indirect benefit from the Russian wheat purchases. The Canadians presumably will not have to borrow as much in our market because of their large receipts from wheat sales to Russia. Also, the Russians will have to sell gold to pay for such purchases and we will share in the pool purchases of their gold. He asked what were the problems in getting some of the Russian wheat purchases for the U.S., since such sales would help to get our exports back towards last year's level which did include some extraordinary shipments to Russia. Secretary Connor said as far as private U.S. sales were concerned there was no obstacle except the opposition of the longshoremen. Under Secretary Ball said that in addition to labor opposition there was an Administrative order issued under the previous Secretary of Commerce that raised a problem although the legal basis for the order was somewhat doubtful in his view. He said the Administration could make a new decision which would waive the 50% shipping requirement, and he thought that we could muster Congressional support for such a position. This would be fruitless, however, if the longshoremen continued their refusal to load ships with wheat going to Russia.

The Secretary indicated that there was no evidence of adverse effect on U.S. exports from the Federal Reserve voluntary program for banks. He asked Mr. Hitch[2] about the outlook for Defense expenditures in the Vietnam area. Mr. Hitch said it was very difficult to estimate what the additional expenditures would eventually be. Secretary Fowler referred to the joint work of Treasury and Defense in setting up a program involving the use of Military Payments Certificates for preventing the leakage of dollars through military personnel into the black market.

---

[2] Charles J. Hitch, Assistant Secretary of Defense (Comptroller).

Balance-of-Payments Projection for 1968.

The Secretary referred to the projection that had been requested from the Executive Committee for a U.S. balance-of-payments position in 1968 on the assumption that the voluntary program would have been ended by that time. He said the Executive Committee was undertaking a critical evaluation of the projection that had been made by a technical group and that the Executive Committee would formulate policy implications of the projection for discussion by the Cabinet Committee at its next meeting, probably in November. He asked that the existence of this projection be kept closely guarded. He referred briefly to the results of the projection, and he pointed out that there was a large element of judgment about the magnitude of the items in the projection.

Balance-of-Payments Concept.

Mr. Capron of the Budget Bureau reported on the results of the Evaluation Committee's consideration of the Bernstein report on U.S. balance-of-payments statistics.[3] He said there was unanimity in recommending that both the present concept and the official settlements concept be published in the regular balance-of-payments articles of the Commerce Department. The following procedure would be adopted. An exchange of letters between Director Schultze and Secretary Connor agreeing on the recommendation would be made public by means of a letter to Senator Proxmire, whose Committee had actively introduced the use of the official settlements concept for measuring the balance-of-payments deficit. It was hoped that this procedure might have some value in getting Congressional support for a $260,000 supplemental appropriation which the Office of Business Economics in Commerce would need in order to put into effect the statistical improvements recommended in the Bernstein report. Both he and Mr. Capron expressed their appreciation for the cooperation of Walter Lederer, Chief, Balance of Payments Division, Office of Business Economics, Department of Commerce, in the Evaluation Committee's formulation of recommendations for improving the statistics. Assistant Secretary Brimmer said that it would probably be December before the two deficit concepts could be shown in the *Survey.* Assistant Secretary Solomon indicated that it might

---

[3] Published as Review Committee for Balance of Payments Statistics, *The Balance of Payments Statistics of the United States, A Review and Appraisal; Report to the Bureau of the Budget* (Washington, D.C., U.S. Government Printing Office, 1965). The Review Committee for Balance of Payments Statistics was appointed in April 1963 by the Bureau of the Budget to study the adequacy of U.S. balance-of-payments statistics and to make recommendations for their improvement. It was headed by Edward M. Bernstein, former research director of the IMF, whose principal recommendation was to shift the method of defining balance-of-payments surplus or deficit from the "liquidity" concept to an "official settlements" concept. (*Current Economic Developments,* No. 727, May 11, 1965, pp. 11–13; Washington National Records Center, E/CBA/REP Files: FRC 72 A 6248, *Current Economic Developments*)

be useful if the IMF were to do some work in standardizing the official settlements concept for use by the advanced countries. Assistant Secretary Trued remarked that the Fund had been doing work in this field for the last two years and that he would ask the U.S. Executive Director if anything further could be done. Secretary Fowler called attention to the fact that the National Bureau of Economic Research was not going to be able to continue its research on the development of a better export price index and that it was necessary to decide whether the U.S. Government should pick up and continue the Bureau's work. Director Schultze indicated that the Labor Department was considering this possibility. Secretary Fowler referred to a speech made by Senator Symington on August 3 in which the Senator made some comments about the effect of U.S. aid to Latin America on our exports to that area. He said he would appreciate it if Mr. Bell would look into this matter and review the draft letter from the Secretary to Senator Symington.[4]

Mr. Roth indicated that there would probably be no progress in the Kennedy tariff negotiation round until after the German and possibly the French elections. He suggested that the Secretary of Agriculture might be added to the membership of the Cabinet Committee on Balance of Payments and Secretary Connor believed that the Secretary of Labor should also be added to the membership. Secretary Fowler thought these were both appropriate additions and indicated that he would check this matter with the President.

Philip P. Schaffner[5]

---

[4]Secretary Rusk's draft letter to Senator Symington has not been further identified.
[5] Printed from a copy that bears this typed signature.

68.   Memorandum for the Record[1]

Washington, September 20, 1965.

RECORD OF MEETING WITH THE PRESIDENT AND BALANCE OF PAYMENTS CABINET COMMITTEE, 11:30 AM–1 PM, MONDAY, SEPTEMBER 20, 1965

ATTENDING

Fowler, Deming, Volcker; McNamara; Ball, Mann; Martin; Ackley, Okun; Bell; Staats; Brimmer; Califano, Bator

Fowler opened with a brief report on the progress of the balance of payments program, results during the first half of the year, and prospects for the rest of this year and 1966. Essentially, he summarized the September 10 Cabinet Committee Report to the President (at Tab A), especially pages 1–2.[2] His central conclusions were that:

—the Federal Reserve's program for banks and financial institutions is working exceedingly well;
—the results of the corporate program was much less clear, with a sharp rise in direct investment during the first half and a danger of still further increases by next year.

There followed a discussion organized around the various major components of the balance of payments:

1.   Direct Investment

It was agreed that we would have to give serious thought, *on a contingency basis*, to possible tightening of the corporate program and perhaps even eventual imposition of mandatory controls. The President asked for estimates of the fraction of direct foreign investment accounted for by 25–50–75 firms, *and instructed Commerce to make recommendations to him about a possible White House meeting with up to 75 of the key business people, before October 3. Brimmer promised a report from Commerce by COB Tuesday, September 21.*[3] Ball suggested that the Treasury explore possible

---

[1] Source: Johnson Library, National Security File, Subject File, Balance of Payments, Vol. 2 [1 of 2], December 8, 1964, Box 2. No classification marking. Drafted by Bator on September 21. The memorandum was sent under cover of a September 22 memorandum from Bator to President Johnson, in which he wrote: "I understand from Joe Califano that you wish to have an informal record of the balance of payments meeting on Monday. Here it is."

[2] Presumably a reference to Report from the Cabinet Committee on Balance of Payments to the President, September 10, not attached but ibid., in which an appraisal of the balance-of-payments situation was summarized in great detail. This report was sent under cover of a September 10 memorandum from Acting Secretary of the Treasury Joseph W. Barr to members of the Cabinet Committee on Balance of Payments. (Ibid.)

[3] See Document 69.

tax incentive devices which would make investment in the U.S. more attractive than investment abroad, and encourage financing from foreign sources.

2.   Exports

After some discussion of export performance during the first half of '65 and the prospects for the rest of '65 and '66, *the President instructed Commerce, in consultation with the Council of Economic Advisers to report on further steps to encourage exports.* (Fowler and Bill Martin reported that there was no hard evidence that the Bank program was cutting into exports by tightening export credit. A survey of exporters now underway will provide a surer basis for judgment by mid-November.)

3.   Military Spending

McNamara reported Defense Department progress on reducing net dollar expenditures abroad (expenditures less offsets). In 1961, the net figure was $2.7 billion; the current estimate for 1965 is $1.6 billion, of which about $.5 billion is accounted for by Southeast Asia. ($400 million in Europe; $500 million in Southeast Asia; $250 million in Japan; $200 million in Canada; $250 million in the oil countries.[4] Spending in Germany is fully offset.[5] (The Canadians offset only hardware and not stationing costs.) *The President instructed Ball to take charge of a State–Defense exercise to recommend steps we might take to reduce the drain in Japan and Canada. Ball promised a report by COB Friday, September 24.[6]* (Bator suggested to McNamara that an estimate be made of the *real* drain into European reserves via Japan and Canada, given their high rate of spending, at the margin, in the U.S.)

4.   A.I.D.

The President asked for views on Senator Douglas' suggestion that we cut aid to French overseas territories. Bell pointed out that the amounts involved ($10–$20 million) were much smaller than Senator Douglas had indicated, but agreed that the question should be looked at. Bell reported that A.I.D. and the Federal Reserve were jointly reexamining the effectiveness of aid tying, and that the Council and Treasury would also be involved. (Following previous Presidential instruction, Komer and I will watch this carefully, and will referee any dispute.)

Bell listed three major categories of outright dollar expenditure:

(1) Public and private money funnelled through the multilateral institutions, IBRD, IDA, IDB, etc. We have made some progress here by

---

[4] I rechecked this: $150 million is POL; $100 million is other (Latin America, etc.). [Handwritten footnote in the source text.]

[5] The next sentence was crossed out; it reads: "In Japan, spending exceeds the offset by about $250 million; in Canada by more than $200 million."

[6] This report has not been identified.

eliminating advance payments, but there is no way really to change the system.

(2) That portion of the salaries of A.I.D.-financed people living overseas which is spent for local goods and services. A.I.D. has encouraged savings in U.S. banks and purchases of U.S. goods through commissaries and PXs, and will continue these efforts. Bell estimated that about one-third of the salaries of overseas employees is not directly returned to the U.S.

(3) Dollar expenditures in Southeast Asia and Jordan. The drain here is very tough to stop without program cutbacks. The local administrative machinery is simply incapable of operating on a tied-aid basis.

5.   *Use of Local Currencies in Lieu of Dollars*

Bell reported that there are eight countries where our local currency balances are in excess of foreseeable needs, principally India, Pakistan, the UAR, and Yugoslavia. (The Polish balance is being converted and repaid in dollars.) He indicated that we would keep looking for constructive ways to use these currencies, but that it is most unlikely that we will achieve major dollar savings.

The President asked whether our local currency balances weren't evidence that PL 480, Title I[7] programs are, in effect, large-scale giveaways. It was agreed that this is true of such programs in the excess currency countries.

There followed a discussion of the justification for further PL 480, and indeed for further aid, to India and Pakistan while they are using their foreign exchange and other resources to buy and produce weapons to fight each other.

It was agreed, and the President so instructed, that as a general rule, PL 480 agreements should be on a year-by-year basis. (Bell remarked that the *three-year UAR agreement was clearly a mistake.*)

6.   *Over-all Balance of Payments Prospects*

The President asked how our February 1965 forecast will look in retrospect in January 1966. We replied that, during the first half of 1965 the voluntary program, taken as a whole, worked better than we expected and that we will probably better our projection for the entire year.

The President asked whether a $1.5 billion deficit for CY 1965 would justify shifting to a mandatory program. The discussion on this did not reach a conclusion. *It was agreed that Fowler would put the Executive Committee to work on an estimate for the rest of 1965 and 1966, as well as on recommendations for a contingency program to be ready in case the 1965 results turn*

---

[7] P.L. 480, the Agricultural Trade Development and Assistance Act of 1954, enacted July 10, 1954 (68 Stat. 454).

out to be unsatisfactory. (When the President asked Fowler whether we know what we would do if the voluntary program clearly failed, the Secretary answered: Yes, Sir. We will have to shift to a mandatory program.)

The President instructed the Cabinet Committee to report to him in two weeks on our progress in contingency planning.

7. *Other Topics*

The President instructed Defense to report on where the Indians and Pakistanis get their oil, and whether anything could be done by the international oil companies to "regulate" the flow. Defense is expected to produce a report by the end of this week.

---

69. Memorandum From Secretary of Commerce Connor to the President's Special Assistant for National Security Affairs (Bundy)[1]

Washington, September 21, 1965.

SUBJECT

Report on the Voluntary Program to Improve the Balance of Payments

Enclosed is a report on the voluntary program to improve the balance of payments which I sent to the President today. I also want to call it to your *personal* attention.

I think it is vital that we continue to remind ourselves of the strategy underlying the cooperative effort by the business community, and I think we should also keep in mind our anticipations about the expected timing of the basic results from the voluntary restraint of direct investment.

It may be recalled that when we launched the program last winter—and as we have stressed on a number of occasions since then—we said that we do not expect the benefits of voluntary restraint on long-term direct investment to show up until the closing months of the year. The main reason was the substantial backlog of projects which the companies already had underway when the program was begun. Moreover, the

---

[1] Source: Johnson Library, Bator Papers, Balance of Payments, 1965 [3 of 4], Box 14. No classification marking.

time lag between the start and completion of such projects is consider-able, and it will take a number of months for the companies to work through the backlog. Consequently, although the companies might have taken immediate steps last February and March to restrain the direct investment outflow, it would be late this year or early next year before we began to see the detailed evidence in the balance of payments statistics.

On the other hand, the companies could repatriate quickly short-term financial assets held abroad in excess of their normal requirements. This they have done. In the first six months of this year, they reduced such holdings by $575 million compared with a net increase of $588 million in the first half of 1964. More detailed comments on the progress of the voluntary program are given in the enclosed report.

Jack

Enclosure[2]

Washington, September 21, 1965.

REPORT ON THE VOLUNTARY PROGRAM TO
IMPROVE THE BALANCE OF PAYMENTS

The evidence available after six months operations under the volun-tary program indicated that:

—Business corporations are making serious efforts to meet the requirements of the program.
—The balance of payments has benefited from measures recom-mended by the Department of Commerce and effected by the participat-ing companies.
—Circumstances not subject to control of business leaders, includ-ing strikes and adverse economic developments abroad, have made it more difficult for some of the corporations to increase their balance of payments contributions. But the over-all results may still be in the neigh-borhood of the improvement projected earlier.

Short-term Financial Assets

We asked the companies to reduce their foreign holdings of short-term assets during the course of 1965 so that at year end they would be no

---

[2] No classification marking.

higher than the level held on December 31, 1963. The companies have reduced these funds faster than anticipated; by the end of June they had already nearly reached the goal we recommended for December 31, 1965.

The pattern of change is as follows:

	Participating Companies Reported		Shown in U.S. Balance of Payments
	Outstanding	Net Changes from prior date shown	Net Changes from prior date shown
		(millions of dollars)	
12/31/63	927		
12/31/64	1,426	+499	+588
3/31/65	1,202	−224	−265
6/30/65	985	−217	−310
6 months 1965		−441	−575

These data indicate that the participating companies are adhering to our guideline on short-term financial assets, and they have accounted for the bulk of the reductions in corporate holdings of such funds.

Exports

Exports are the largest category of transactions upon which cooperating companies are relying to effect improvements in their balance of payments contributions. In 1964, exports accounted for two-thirds of the range of alternative transactions used in calculating improvements.

Tabulations for 507 companies show an estimated total improvement of $1.3 billion for 1965, or an increase of 10 per cent in their net contributions compared with 1964. Early in the year exports were adversely affected by strikes, and many companies have reported that some of these losses are irretrievable. The companies indicated only a slight improvement in the first half of 1965 rate compared to their 1964 total exports (3 per cent on an unadjusted basis). But the general outlook for exports during the second half of the year does appear somewhat better, and the statistics are expected to show a much better rate of gain. First half results are shown in the following figures:

Non-Agricultural Exports

	380 Participating Companies	All U.S. Companies (Bureau of Census figures)
	(millions of dollars)	
1964	11,277	19,740
Jan–June 1965	11,586	20,377
Per cent increase (unadjusted annual rate)	+3 per cent	+3 per cent

Transmittal of Income

In addition to the repatriation of foreign short-term funds, the companies show a healthy increase in transmittal of foreign earnings. The following seasonally adjusted data are from the over-all balance of payments statistics.

Direct Investment Income

Period	Millions of dollars seasonally adjusted 1964	1965	Percentage Increase from year ago
1st Quarter	968	1,061	9.6
2nd Quarter	955	1,148	20.2
6 month Total	1,923	2,209	14.9

The increases in both of the quarters of 1965 were impressive. The first quarter flow in 1964 and 1965 may have been influenced by reductions in tax rates. However, the further increase from the first to the second quarter of this year appears to reflect efforts of the companies under the program.

Direct Investment

When the voluntary program was announced, many companies had projects in such advanced stages of development that they could not be cut back, postponed, or eliminated. The large build-up in the outflow of investment funds in the last quarter of 1964 and the first quarter of this year was still evident in the second quarter. These levels are excessive, and we expect substantial reductions in the second half.

Under the program we asked only for restraints on private direct investment in developed countries other than Canada. Balance of payments data and reports of the companies indicate that they are following these guidelines.

Direct Investment Outflows
(millions of dollars seasonally unadjusted)

	All Areas	Europe	Other Developed Countries*	Reported by 380 Companies**
1964, Year	-2,376	-1,342	-206	-2,288
1st Half	-1,026	-670	-100	n.a.
Qtr. I	-420	-288	-61	n.a.
II	-606	-382	-39	n.a.
1965				
1st Half	-2,066	-903	-152	-1,306
Qtr. I	-1,115	-536	-82	-765
II	-951	-367	-70	-541

---

*Except Canada

**Including re-invested earnings of foreign affiliates

The program of restraint on capital outflows is concentrated on Western Europe. From the first to the second quarter of 1965, the direct investment outflow to Europe declined by $169 million and dropped below the level in the second quarter of 1964. The outflow to other developed countries includes Japan, Australia, New Zealand, and South Africa. The increases there reflect large investments in iron ore ventures in Australia that were underway when the program was initiated.

The data from the participating companies (including reinvested earnings) show a decline of $224 million from the first to the second quarter reflecting the restraints on outflows to Western Europe.

We did not ask for restraint on direct investment outflows to Canada or to less developed countries. The evidence indicates that the companies have shown restraint on capital outflows to the areas specified in the program. Because of the backlog of projects underway, we expected that it would take some time to get reductions of any significance in investment outflows.

Significant new foreign borrowings will permit additional offsets to the capital outflows. The companies have volunteered information on new foreign borrowing which add up to about $400 million. Among these are a number of large flotations of bond issues, between $20 and $30 million each, to be marketed mainly in Western Europe. As these funds become available to their foreign affiliates, it will be possible to cut back on flows of funds from the U.S.

Summary

The results to date clearly indicate that the companies are seriously trying to carry out the program as we have defined it. The degree of success will be determined not only by the efforts of the companies and our exhortations, but also by external circumstances which are not amenable to alteration on our part or the part of the companies. The most serious obstacle to overcome is the poor export performance which hampered progress in the first six months of 1965. It will require serious efforts to obtain improvements elsewhere to offset the potential short-falls on exports. But if all the companies, including those with large improvements on exports, make every effort to increase other foreign earnings and limit the outflow of funds, the over-all results may still be in the neighborhood of the improvement projected earlier.

70.   **Memorandum From the President's Deputy Special Assistant for National Security Affairs (Bator) to Secretary of the Treasury Fowler**[1]

Washington, September 30, 1965.

SUBJECT

Some thoughts for the Balance of Payments Meeting this Afternoon

I have now had time to go over the report of the Balance of Payments Information Committee on the 65–66 prospects, and to give some thought to where we go from here.[2] The following more or less random suggestions are for your consideration only: (I'll give Mac a copy if and when he gets involved in this).

1.   I think the most immediate problem is one of third and fourth quarter cosmetics. There is not much we can do about the third quarter now, but there are a number of quick-fix operations we could mount which would substantially reduce the 4th quarter deficit. We could push DOD payments from December to January, talk to the British about the use of their remaining EX-IM money and the handling of the portfolio, etc. Needless to say, these things would have to be kept even more quiet than budget finagling in June, but it seems to me worth the effort and risk.

2.   From a longer-term standpoint, I think that the situation does warrant a substantial tightening of the Commerce program as soon as possible. I do not mean a shift to anything like a mandatory operation with sanctions. Rather, I have in mind a tightening which is entirely consistent with the spirit of the February 10 voluntary operation: (a) a sharpening of the criteria (Jack Connor, I understand, will have suggestions for us on this today); and (b) changes in the reporting system designed to give us more information much earlier on what is happening. (We might wish also to consider urging Jack to institute a system of advanced warning on major investments.)

3.   It seems to me that the above steps are warranted even if one believes that our '65 performance is likely to be pretty good relative to what we expected. Except for the help we gave the U.K., we have done a good deal better than expected over-all, and only the direct investment component has been really troublesome. Thus, there seems no reason for us to recommend to the President at this stage a qualitative change in the

---

[1] Source: Johnson Library, Bator Papers, Balance of Payments, 1965 [3 of 4], Box 14. Secret; Eyes Only.

[2] This report has not been found.

over-all program in the direction of mandatory restraints. But I don't believe we should simply sit tight.

4. Obviously, we cannot ignore the possibility that our present forecasts are still too optimistic. In terms of your bargaining position on international money, we simply cannot afford a serious deterioration during the next year and a half. Hence I would think it important that the third element in the present package (on top of quick-fixes and a tightening of the Commerce operation) should be preparation of a full blown contingency package to keep in the safe, following the model of the Deming Committee.[3] November 1 seems an appropriate target date—(I have not checked this with Stan Surrey).[4]

5. In connection with security, it would seem to me useful for you and the Cabinet Committee to instruct that all matters pertaining to the work of the Cabinet Committee be formally classified SECRET and handled on a strictly need-to-know basis. You might wish to consider taking some specific steps in connection with the Slevin problem.

Let me say again that, whereas my own judgment about the present situation is based in part on extended conversations with Art Okun, as well as Fred, Merlin, and Stan, this is a memorandum for you alone (and Mac, if and when he gets involved). The only copy is in my safe.

Francis M. Bator[5]

---

[3] Reference is to the Deming Group; see footnote 3, Document 64.
[4] Stanley S. Surrey, Assistant Secretary of the Treasury for Tax Policy.
[5] Printed from a copy that bears this typed signature.

71.   **Minutes of Meeting of the Cabinet Committee on Balance of Payments**[1]

Washington, September 30, 1965.

Secretary Fowler said that he envisaged several meetings culminating in a report to the President around the end of October. It was agreed that the next meeting of the Cabinet Committee would be on Monday, October 18, at 4:30.

The Secretary turned to the balance-of-payments projections which had just been made by the Lederer Committee[2] and said that he had had a very violent reaction to it. He said that three things arose in his mind as a result. One, he would talk to the British about their borrowing $250 million from the Ex-Im Bank, in the hopes of discouraging them. Secondly, it will be necessary for the Fed to announce very soon that the 1966 base would be based on the end of 1964 claims as now. Third, that some changes might be necessary in the Commerce program and he would want to hear from Secretary Connor on that.

He also suggested that it might be necessary to raise the IET rate above the current one percent for next year. He also suggested that we might want to limit all non-bank loans, that is more than ten years as well as less than ten years, to the 105 percent ceiling.

Secretary McNamara said that he shared Secretary Fowler's concern and that we would need additions to the program and this should be the purpose of the next meeting. He said that he was not impressed by the actions that we had taken over the last several years to help our trade balance. He said that he had heard that U.S. businessmen do not know how to sell and that he didn't know whether this was true or not but that we needed more information on costs and prices. He said that he was very impressed with the recent moves which the British had been making to help their basic trade position. He felt that Secretary Fowler might want to appoint some subcommittee chaired by the CEA to look into these basic factors.

Secretary Connor said that they had been doing something on exports, that the National Export Expansion Council had been reorganized (headed by Mr. Foy)[3] and that they would have some specific rec-

---

[1] Source: Johnson Library, Fowler Papers, International Balance of Payments Committee—Classified Material: Cabinet Committee on Balance of Payments, 8/65–12/66, Box 52. Secret. The source text bears no drafting information.

[2] Presumably a reference to a committee headed by Walter Lederer, Chief, Balance of Payments Division, Office of Business Economics, Department of Commerce. The committee and its projections have not been further identified.

[3] Fred C. Foy, Chief Executive Officer, Koppers Company, Pittsburgh, served as Chairman of this Council, which was enlarged and revitalized. For President Johnson's August 20 statement on the role of this Council, see *Public Papers of the Presidents of the United States: Lyndon B. Johnson, 1965*, Book II, pp. 951–952.

ommendations. He said that he had been visiting around himself. It was true that we had neglected the import side but he understood that we would not want to undertake such things as surcharges or voluntary restraints on imports as the Japanese had done.

Secretary McNamara asked if we could have brought in proposals on this for October 18 and Secretary Fowler agreed that the Executive Committee would handle this.

Secretary Connor reported that he was meeting with his advisory committee on October 11 and that they would have some suggestions in other areas as well as their own. He said that the voluntary program was working and gave the following specifics:

He said that the program had first been explained to the businessmen on February 18 and that some had not gotten under the program until as late as April, therefore the second quarter should be the test. He said that he had given them latitude to make the method of their own improvements to their own situations. There had been no stress on the capital investment part of the program and that they had not been asked to cancel plans which were underway. He noted for example an Australian iron ore refinancing project.

He said that where he had asked for the businesses to give priority they had come through. $575 million had been repatriated in short-term funds and this cost the corporations money. Also remittances were up from $1061 million in the first quarter to $1148 million in the second quarter and that this was against the trend and that this cost money.

He had suggested guidelines only for the developed countries and investment in Western Europe in the second quarter was down. Direct investment outflows of 380 firms decreased by $220 million in the second quarter compared to the first quarter. He said that foreign borrowing had amounted to $480 million and that this was unprecedented although we had no bench mark with which to compare it.

Capital outflow in the first half of $2041 million is a problem but net income of the corporations after taking account of remittances was a plus $260 million in the second quarter compared to a minus $98 million in the first quarter. He said he was looking carefully at the capital flows and the advisory committee was thinking of alternatives.

Exports in the second quarter had increased and this was a result of the ending of the dock strike but it still reflected some effort by the firms. They would need a big increase in exports to meet the $1.3 billion improvement that they had set for themselves in 1965. He said it looks like we will get an increase in exports but we don't know if it will be enough for this. The advisory council program will be public information in the next few weeks.

On imports he said that they were not in the program but that he had asked particular companies to report on anticipated imports and to encourage them to export components of their products to their foreign subs.

Secretary Connor said that the tourist gap was still a real problem. He said that it looked like we would get more receipts from abroad next year and this was good but the U.S. tourist should not be neglected, should we limit their expenditures? He closed by saying that we should not blame the corporations at this point.

Secretary Fowler emphasized the necessity for secrecy on these deliberations, that all documents should be classified secret and limited to a need to know basis in distribution.

Secretary Fowler said that on the projected deficit of $2 billion for this year a good part of this was due to the U.K. situation—there were the liquidations of securities, the Ex-Im credit of $250 million and the failure of the British to make their debt repayment at the end of this year. He said that as they improve there would be less drain on the U.S.

Under Secretary Ball said that the State Department would circulate proposals well before the next meeting. He felt that overall we had done pretty well when we look back at what we expected to do before February 10.

Secretary Fowler said that this was true if we compared it to our pre-February 10 projections but it was not so good when we look at our June 7 report which forecast a deficit of between $.7 and $1.5 billion.[4]

There was further discussion of the necessity for strict secrecy. Secretary Fowler said that he got the impression that the delegates to the IMF meeting had come here with the impression that we were doing quite well but after being here now have the impression that we are doing very poorly. He said that there are all sorts of rumors circulating at the Sheraton Park Hotel.

Mr. Bator said that we should make a distinction between doing something for the immediate future and doing something for the longer-run, that is 1966. He felt that we should first turn our attention to some quick-fix, the cosmetic approach to the fourth quarter. He said that the deficit for the second half of this year in the projection of $1.34 billion works out to an annual rate of $2.68 billion and that the newspapers will be quick to make this calculation and point out that we were doing poorly. So we must get this second half figure down.

Mr. Ackley felt that on the whole the program had been successful. He said that we should now look for major savings, that we should not be diverted with numerous minor things. Direct investment was the biggest disappointment in the program and this is where we should look.

Mr. Martin said that he agreed with Mr. Ackley. He also agreed that foreigners had come here optimistic and now as Secretary Fowler noted

---

[4] Document 61.

they appeared to be pessimistic about our balance of payments. He then asked Mr. Robertson to report.

Mr. Robertson said that he agreed that we must indicate that the base for 1966 would be the end of 1964. He said that he was going shortly to inform the banks how they had done overall in July and August and that this could be the occasion for announcing this. He said that only 45 banks were over the 105 percent ceiling—by a total of $75 million—but that banks as a whole were under the ceiling by $575 million as of the end of August. There had been a further decline in claims outstanding of $200 million in July and August.

Mr. Trued asked whether or not Mr. Robertson would mention what the percentage ceiling would be to the banks when he announced to them we would keep the 1964 base. Mr. Robertson said that he had not planned to indicate that now, that maybe the results of the fourth quarter would be better than it looks at this point. He said that at the next meeting he would have some suggestions on the non-bank part of the program. He noted that while their outflow had been $1 billion last year it was only $146 million this year thus far. He said that here there was a problem of putting Canada in jeopardy.

Secretary Fowler said that he would discuss with Governor Robertson and Mr. Martin later the problem of the non-bank program and the Canadian banks. It was then agreed by all that the Fed should go ahead and announce the 1966 base would be the end of 1964 claims outstanding.

Mr. Trued again raised the question of whether the percentage ceiling would be indicated. Secretary Connor said that when the Fed announces what its base for 1966 would be that this would naturally raise the question of the base for the corporations, and that if he should be asked this question he would say that the base for the corporations would also be 1964. This was agreed to by all.

Secretary Fowler said that we would have to look at the issue of Canadian securities. He said that he would want to ask the Canadians to resume their efforts of last year of restraining municipal borrowing.

Secretary Fowler then said in regard to the Commerce program for the fourth quarter, could we urge more corporations to bring more liquid funds back and he then noted that as of the end of June they still held almost a billion dollars in liquid investments.

Secretary Connor said that we must be careful to avoid making firms afraid of mandatory measures. He said that he had not recommended anything of a mandatory nature in his paper.

Secretary Fowler said in regard to rumors on mandatory controls perhaps it was best simply to take the advisory committee of Secretary Connor into confidence and to let them know the kinds of things we are thinking about and by that they will know we are not contemplating mandatory measures.

Secretary Connor said that there would be no problem of talking with them and assuring them that we were not contemplating mandatory controls.

Mr. Bator raised the question of whether we should have agreed some safe language for the press and the public in regard to the kinds of measures that we are contemplating.

There was then an extended discussion of the posture that the Government should assume in this interim period while we are considering the new measures to avoid a repetition of the speculation which was rampant prior to the February 10 program. While the group felt that we wanted to assure the banks and businesses that they need not fear mandatory controls, on the other hand some expressed fear that this might involve locking us in and that we should avoid making any commitments which would bind us in this respect. Mr. Roth expressed the hope that we should not lock ourselves in and then possibly be in the position where we would have to take a quick look and make a quick decision on measures necessarily avoiding mandatory controls. He hoped that we would not have to take quick action for example on export subsidies, import surcharges and tourist restrictions.

Mr. Gaud said he had little to add to the discussion. AID was down to an irreducible minimum but they would do their best to see what more they could do.

Mr. Schultze noted that the gold budget was due in September 15 but most of the agencies had not yet reported so he encouraged them to hurry up and get their reports in.

There was further discussion of the problem of public posture during this interim period and Secretary Fowler suggested that we might look at what we did and did not do in this period prior to February 10 and learn from that.

It was pointed out that one basic difference between then and now was that the public realizes that we have less latitude or leeway now before imposing controls than we had then.

It was generally agreed that rather than to try some scheme to assure the public about the mandatory controls it would be better for Secretary Connor to simply act naturally.

Secretary Fowler wondered if there wasn't some way to avoid banks and firms rushing money overseas in an attempt to get under the wire by letting them know either directly or indirectly that whatever they did between now and then would be held against them, that whatever we did the base would be set at a period early enough not to allow them to profit by moving money out before some new program was announced.

The fear was expressed, however, that this might accentuate the fears of the banks and businesses.

---

72.   Memorandum From the President's Deputy Special Assistant for National Security Affairs (Bator) to President Johnson[1]

Washington, October 1, 1965, 7:25 p.m.

SUBJECT

Interim Report on Balance of Payments Contingency Planning

The Cabinet Committee met yesterday afternoon to discuss the latest projections for the rest of '65 and for '66, and the proposals of the various departments for possible tightening of your program.[2] Joe Fowler's report will be over shortly, but you might wish to have a preliminary indication of where we are.

We have not yet come to any final conclusions—work is still going on—but it was generally agreed that:

1.   The best evidence suggests that our 1965 performance, *taken as a whole*, and *excluding* money transferred to the British, is likely to be much better than we forecast in January–February. The only really disturbing component has been direct business investment. (None of the British transfer reflects the recent support package. It consists mostly of a drawdown of last year's swap and Ex-Im loan, and a partial cashing in of their portfolio of U.S. securities.)

2.   However, even in the absence of another scare like the one last January, we cannot afford to sit on our hands. If we take no action, the deficit during the second half of 1965 is likely to be appreciably larger than during the first six months. We are working on three fronts:

(i)   *Quick-fix operations* to reduce the 4th quarter deficit. Charlie Schultze, working with Defense, will be doing the sort of job on the December outflow that he does on the June budget figure. (Needless to say this largely cosmetic operation is even more sensitive than the rest.) Also, Joe Fowler will start talking with the British tomorrow about limiting their drawings and transfers during the rest of the year. We'll have a

---

[1] Source: Johnson Library, National Security File, Balance of Payments, Vol. 3 [2 of 2], Box 2. Secret; Sensitive.

[2] See Document 71.

go at the Canadians about their borrowing in New York after their elections.

(ii) *A serious tightening especially of the Commerce Program.*[3] Even on a pessimistic view, the evidence does not *now* justify a shift to a mandatory program with sanctions. But we do need much sharper criteria, and much fuller reporting by the companies of what they are doing. Jack Connor and his people are hard at work on this, and will consult with his advisory committee. Jack is perfectly clear that he has got to move.

(iii) *Contingency planning.* The current forecast may still be too optimistic—we have to hedge our bets. Joe Fowler and all your other principals and experts know and share your view that we cannot afford another serious deterioration in the balance of payments. Thus on an absolutely top secret basis, we are preparing a full-blown contingency package in case we run into real trouble.

Timing. On most of the fourth quarter quick-fix operations, we should be ready in a week or two. (Those which involve negotiations with the British and Canadians will take longer.) None will require Presidential involvement.

Recommendations for tightening Connor's program will be on your desk during the last week in October at the latest. I agree with Fowler and Connor, and so do Ackley and Schultze, that this is not too leisurely a schedule. Getting a revised program in shape and working it out with the key business people takes time. The risks of too hasty and therefore faulty action outweigh the risks of a 3–4 week delay. Nothing is more likely to produce a hot-money crisis than an emergency atmosphere generated by the government.

In the meanwhile, we'll be taking two preliminary steps early next week. On Monday,[4] the Fed will announce that the *base* for calculating the banks' 1966 target will remain what it has been: the volume of credit outstanding on December 31, 1964. (There has been speculation that we will shift to a higher base which would tend to penalize the most cooperative banks and might suggest that we are in a mood to relax the bank program for 1966. The proposed Fed announcement is at Tab A.)[5]

In his Tuesday speech to the American Bankers Association, Joe Fowler will try (i) to reassure the business community that we are not about to impose mandatory controls (this to minimize the threat of a panicky shift of corporate money to Europe, without really tying our hands) and (ii) to, nevertheless, warn them that the voluntary program needs beefing up (something they already expect). His proposed language is at Tab B;[6] we'll be working on it over the weekend.

---

[3] Reference is to the voluntary program.

[4] October 4.

[5] Not found.

[6] The draft of Fowler's October 5 speech was not attached.

Security. All internal papers having to do with balance of payments policy will be classified *secret* and handled on a strict need-to-know basis. This is not likely to stop Slevin, Bartlett, et al. but it should make things somewhat more difficult for them.

Francis M. Bator[7]

---

[7] Printed from a copy that bears this typed signature.

---

73. Letter From the Assistant Secretary of State for Economic Affairs (Solomon) to Secretary of Commerce Connor[1]

Washington, October 7, 1965.

Dear Mr. Secretary:

At the balance-of-payments meeting on September 30, you surprised me a bit when you said that European countries were restricting tourism, and indicated that a change in such practices might be of significant help to the United States balance of payments.[2] Upon checking again we have verified that all the major European countries have already liberalized restrictions over tourist expenditures. They either exercise no exchange restrictions and formalities at all—that is they are de jure liberalized—or they exercise formalities only to establish the bona fides of transactions (to prevent evasion of regulations over capital outflows)—that is they are de facto liberalized. The only exceptions in Europe are among the smaller countries including several in the less-developed category: Finland, Norway, Iceland, Greece, Turkey, and Yugoslavia.

Outside Europe, the only developed Free World countries still restricting tourism are Japan, New Zealand, and South Africa. I agree, of course, that efforts should continue to be made to obtain liberalization in these countries. Work in this direction is going on in the OECD and the IMF.[3]

---

[1] Source: Department of State, Central Files, FN 12 US. No classification marking. Drafted by Leocade Leighton (E/OMA) and R.N. Cooper (E/IMA).

[2] See Document 71.

[3] The source text identifies an enclosure, "Status of Liberalization of Tourism Among OECD Countries," which has not been found.

With respect to less-developed countries, I believe that a more selective approach is desirable. Many of these countries are short of foreign exchange and allocate such exchange as they have to high priority items, such as essential imports. We may well not wish to urge them to allocate their scarce foreign exchange instead for tourist travel by those of their residents with a high enough income to permit travel. Relaxation of restrictions in such instances would benefit the United States balance of payments very little in any case.

The big gains from liberalization have already been made.

With best regards,

Sincerely yours,

Anthony M. Solomon[4]

---

[4] Printed from a copy that bears this typed signature.

---

74.   Memorandum From Secretary of the Treasury Fowler to President Johnson[1]

Washington, October 12, 1965.

Your Cabinet Committee on Balance of Payments met on September 30 in the first step toward an intensified and comprehensive review of our present position and the outlook for 1965 and 1966.[2] Two or three more meetings will be held during October in order to complete this detailed study. The next one is scheduled for Monday, October 18. Specific recommendations with respect to the balance of payments program will then be forwarded to you. This is an interim report.

Although a firm evaluation and appropriate recommendations must await further detailed analyses and assessment, some broad conclusions seem warranted, as follows:

—We are reasonably on target with your balance of payments program; results for the entire year 1965 promise to be close to those we

---

[1] Source: Johnson Library, Fowler Papers, International Balance of Payments—Classified Material: Cabinet Committee on Balance of Payments, 8/65–12/66, Box 52. Secret. Drafted by Merlyn N. Trued on October 11.

[2] See Document 71.

anticipated at the beginning of the year. The specific balance of payments items contributing to this performance vary significantly from those we expected *but the total result indicates a successful over-all program thus far.*

—Some immediate actions are necessary to guard against a sharp worsening of the payments situation during the *fourth* quarter of 1965. The actions required are outlined below.

—The preliminary outlook for 1966, *on the basis of the present program,* is for modest improvement; reinforcement particularly of the Commerce Department program is essential if satisfactory progress toward equilibrium is to be assured.

The *Federal Reserve program* with respect to banks and nonbanking financial institutions is paying off handsomely, far in excess of our expectations, and promises effectiveness at least through next year. Banks have more than done their job: they are now $600 million below their permitted ceiling on credits to foreigners. This very success, however, poses a threat to the fourth quarter results if banks move vigorously toward the ceiling during the rest of 1965. To help guard against such a sudden outflow, the Federal Reserve has

—advised the institutions concerned that the ceiling for 1966 will employ the same end-of-1964 credit base. Banks therefore need not rush out to make loans to bring them up to their current ceiling in fear that a new base will be established which would penalize their failure to be at maximum lending capacity to foreigners. Even with this precautionary step, some adverse effect in the fourth quarter remains a clear possibility.

Substantial reinforcement of the *program administered by the Department of Commerce* is clearly in order in view of the very heavy increase in direct investment abroad this year and the indications that this will continue. A reinforcement of that program is now in the making. It essentially will involve

—the establishment of firm guideposts for corporate behavior in investing abroad, sharp tightening of performance standards and improvement in the Department of Commerce's ability to analyze performance results and undertake frequent discussions with the laggards. We believe such tightening could bring about substantial improvement, yet retain the essentially voluntary nature of the program.

Improved performance in this corporate sector is essential in the very practical sense of balance of payments results—but also to insure that other parts of the over-all program remain acceptable as being fairly imposed.

More immediately, Commerce will

—re-emphasize to the corporations the need to continue to repatriate earnings, to borrow abroad and bring back all dollars held abroad not absolutely needed for working purposes.

This should help to minimize strains even while the new measures are being developed and issued.

Also, I took advantage of the presence here during the Bank and Fund meeting of Lord Cromer, head of the Bank of England, to urge the deferral by the United Kingdom of any further action on their part this year (such as a drawdown of their long standing Export-Import Bank Credit) that might adversely affect the 4th quarter picture.[3] I believe they will be in a position to cooperate and are willing to do so.

Other measures are also now under critical review to determine those further gains that can be recorded with the application of feasible measures to exports, tourism, military and economic aid—particularly important over the longer-run.

The above observations suggest that your present program, suitably reinforced but basically voluntary, can bring the improvement needed in our balance of payments this year and a further stride toward equilibrium in 1966. We must, however, continue to be constantly alert to any indication that the program is faltering since the balance of payments results remain critical to world wide confidence in the dollar and to our ability to gain any meaningful step toward substantial improvement of the international payments system. *We do not foresee at this time any need for more drastic measures.* Indeed, these could be sharply counterproductive. Nevertheless, contingency planning within a small interagency group will continue at the top of the working agenda. Your Committee is fully aware that this phase of interagency planning must be strictly guarded since rumor of it could bring about substantial speculative or anticipatory outflows of funds.

Our final report will also look further ahead to the U.S. balance of payments position at the end of our current temporary program and set forth the alternative courses of action which might be taken to assure sustained equilibrium in our balance of payments beyond the immediate period ahead.

Henry H. Fowler[4]

---

[3] Presumably a reference to the annual meeting of the IMF and IBRD in Washington September 27–October 1. Fowler's reference to his efforts vis-à-vis the United Kingdom on that occasion have not been identified.

[4] Printed from a copy that indicates Fowler signed the original.

75.   Memorandum of Conversation[1]

Washington, October 20, 1965, 4:30–6:45 p.m.

PARTICIPANTS

Treasury—Secretary Fowler and Mr. Knowlton
CEA—Mr. Arthur M. Okun and Otto Eckstein
White House—Mr. Francis Bator
AID—Mr. William S. Gaud, Deputy Administrator
Federal Reserve—Governor James Louis Robertson
Commerce—Secretary Connor
Defense—Secretary McNamara
State—Under Secretary Ball
Agriculture—Under Secretary John A. Schnittker
BOB—Charles Schultze, Director
BOB—Mr. Roth, Deputy Special Representative for Trade Negotiations

SUBJECT

Cabinet Committee (Principals Only) Meeting

Secretary Fowler opened by referring to excerpts from his October 15, 1965, Hot Springs speech, which explained the *nature and setting* of the present balance of payments problem.

Secretary Fowler then outlined the steps that had been proposed to date to help the fourth-quarter results (United Kingdom deferment of Export-Import Bank loan; no further U.K. liquidation of securities; and payment of their year-end debt service charges). He then asked Mr. Gaud if AID could help. Mr. Gaud said no—in fact, there would be a $20 million outflow to the Dominican Republic (through the OAS).

Secretary Fowler asked Secretary McNamara whether DOD could do more, and he replied he "didn't believe so." Biggest expense personnel, and nothing could be done there. Ludwig Erhard's personal agreement to meet offset commitments must be obtained. Secretary Fowler asked Mr. Bator to "crank this in" to the White House meeting. Secretary McNamara then stated that the 1965 balance of payments consideration was not the central consideration, that the *over-all* 1965, 1966, and 1967 offset picture must be examined and clarified. Erhard would arrive late in the year (December) and there would be little he could do to help our balance of payments picture at that stage, and other issues were of more basic importance. *Getting orders* was crucial.

Secretary Fowler then asked Governor Robertson whether more could be done to discourage bank outflows in the fourth quarter. Gover-

---

[1] Source: Johnson Library, Fowler Papers, International Balance of Payments Committee—Classified Material: Cabinet Committee Meeting, 10/20/65, Box 53. Secret. Drafted by Knowlton on October 25. The meeting was held in Secretary Fowler's Conference Room.

nor Robertson said no—the banks will hold back if they possibly can. Secretary Fowler asked whether it would be productive for Governor Robertson to make a few key calls on important banks at the end of the year to avoid any unnecessary loan payments late in 1965, and the Governor again stated that he did not believe this would be helpful. There was then a discussion of the advisability of extending the Fed guidelines to loans of more than 10-year maturity from non-bank financial institutions and of the possibility of cutting off the flow of these funds to Canada. Governor Robertson pointed out that 90 per cent of the outstanding loans and investments made by this kind of institution had maturities of more than ten years and 70 per cent of these were held in Canada. This year there has been an inflow of this type of money from all *areas (in the aggregate)* other than Canada. Secretary Connor, like Secretary Fowler, had the feeling that there were leakages to Canada through his program as well as through the Fed program. It was agreed that Under Secretary Deming and Mr. Knowlton would meet with Governor Robertson to discuss extension of the guidelines to Canada at 2:30 p.m. the following afternoon. Secretary McNamara stated that we should get from his people the latest description of Canadian offset agreements. He said Canada simply was not carrying its share of the free world defense. Undersecretary Ball said we could and should be tough with the Canadians.

Secretary Fowler asked Secretary Connor what had been done since his letter, dated October 14, 1965, to corporations.[2] Had there been any organized telephone calls to make sure that businessmen were making every effort to cooperate? Secretary Connor replied that telegrams had been sent to delinquents and that his group was awaiting replies and putting together other information in an effort to improve the program. Secretary Fowler asked whether it would be appropriate to have corporations sign "purpose statements" and to make it a requirement that these be filed with banks before corporations could borrow money. The "purpose statement" would be signed by the chief executive of the corporation in question; it would state how much of the loan would go abroad; and it would indicate that the corporation believed its activities were consistent with the Commerce voluntary program. Governor Robertson said the banks would object strenuously, that the Fed's program (under guideline 13) already stipulates that loans must be within the spirit of the Commerce program.

There was then some additional conversation about Canada and the fact that it had become what it was hoped it would not become in June 1963, i.e., an important loophole in the program.

---

[2] Not found.

After discussion of whether exports should not be separated out of the Commerce Department's overall targets, Secretary Connor stated that he was inclined to agree with Secretary Fowler that they should.

There was then conversation about whether corporations were giving up a greater return by restricting overseas direct investment the banks had been forced to forego. Governor Robertson objected strongly to this inference, stating that bank returns were "surer and quicker".

Secretary McNamara got up to go, mentioning that he had some ideas about savings in his area but they were importantly contingent upon coming up with steps to limit tourist spending.

Secretary Fowler asked Mr. Schultze what progress was being made on the work necessary to bring out balance of payments figures on an official settlements basis. Mr. Schultze said he knew of no bottleneck here but would check into it immediately.

The conversation then turned to agricultural matters, and the meeting gradually began to break up. It was agreed that Messrs. Bator and Schultze would prepare a memorandum on the 50 percent agricultural bottoms problem. It was generally felt that "an appeal to all reasonable men" was a more sensible approach than any efforts to make a "deal" with the longshoremen.

At the very end of the meeting Secretary Fowler made reference to a Symington–Fowler Plan on P.L. 480 loans. Mr. Schultze said that he had a plan designed to increase overseas military savings by providing investments in Export-Import Bank participations. He agreed to talk to Paul Volcker about this matter the following day.

Winthrop Knowlton

76.   Memorandum From Secretary of the Treasury Fowler to President Johnson[1]

Washington, October 22, 1965.

SUBJECT

Balance of Payments—Fourth Quarter Bolt and Nut Tightening

In view of our immediate concern with making the maximum progress in moving our international payments for 1965 towards balance, given the program in your February 10 Message, this memorandum will deal mainly with the actions we have taken or have pending dealing with the fourth quarter of 1965. However, a few brief comments on *1966* programming follow.

I. Programming for 1966

Your Cabinet Committee on Balance of Payments is heavily engaged in preparing a program for 1966. It will formulate the various options you will wish to consider in tightening and making more effective any lagging elements in the existing program and defining the best mix of additional measures *that should produce a balance or slight surplus in 1966. That will be our objective.* On present evidence, we believe we can achieve that objective with a beefed-up version of your voluntary program. There is no evidence now to suggest that we will need a mandatory program. (Needless to say, we are doing some very quiet contingency planning in case our expectations are badly disappointed.)

Since the full dress meeting of the Cabinet Committee on September 30, which was the subject of a separate memorandum to you dated October 12 (see Attachment A)[2] the Executive Committee, headed by Assistant Secretary of the Treasury Trued and composed of similarly positioned personnel in the various participating departments and agencies, has been working on a day-to-day basis on various aspects of the program. On Monday, October 18, there was another meeting of the Cabinet Committee attended by both principals and assistants.[3]

Because of the number of people involved, the need for a high degree of confidentiality in this important phase of programming, and the need to consider frankly a number of disagreeable alternatives, I decided that the best procedure would be to have a series of quiet meet-

---

[1] Source: Johnson Library, National Security File, Subject File, Balance of Payments, vol. 3 [2 of 2], Box 2. Secret. A handwritten notation on the first page reads: "M—to Texas. L."

[2] Document 74.

[3] No record of this meeting has been found.

ings with the Cabinet Committee principals alone absent any staff. This reduces the number in the room to about ten or eleven who are in every case the head or deputy head of the department or agency. Mr. Bator is participating in these meetings.

We had the first of these restricted meetings on Wednesday, October 20,[4] and have another scheduled for next Wednesday, October 27. So that you may be aware of the type and range of questions we will be discussing in this series of meetings for principals only, I am attaching a folder containing the agenda, some tables which provide the statistical background for our programming, and an initial list of questions we are asking each other in hammering out the individual program options for 1966 (see Attachment B).[5]

It does not seem useful to burden you with the review of the dialogue going on at this time. I only want to make you aware of the fact that it is going on and the type of questions we are considering. We are driving to have conclusions and recommendations which will be framed in alternative options for you to consider some time between the first and fifteenth of November.

So much for 1966 programming.

II. Dealing With Fourth Quarter

Now to return to what we are doing to minimize additional outflows in the fourth quarter. The following will summarize actions taken and contemplated:

1. Holding Back Bank Loans

The Federal Reserve Board (Governor Robertson) reports that the banks are approximately $575 million below their permitted ceiling on credits to foreigners under the Federal Reserve Board voluntary program. Because this success in this program through the third quarter posed a threat to fourth quarter results if the banks felt 1966 ceilings might be related to 1965 loan totals, the Federal Reserve Board on October 1 advised banks and nonbank institutions cooperating in its program that the ceiling for 1966 would employ the same end of 1964 credit base. Therefore, the banks need not rush out to make loans to bring them up to their current ceiling in fear that a new base will be established which would penalize their failure to be at maximum lending capacity to foreigners. A copy of the Federal Reserve Board press release is attached (see Attachment C). I have asked Governor Robertson to give immediate consideration to the desirability of personal requests to the heads of the biggest participating banks and nonbank institutions to hold back in any further outlays in 1965 that would affect the 1965 results.

---

[4] See Document 75.
[5] Not attached.

2.   *Holding Back Direct Investment Flows and Maximizing Repatriation of Profits and of Short Term Corporate Funds*

The task here has been to walk a tight rope in the light of the disturbing statistics on the levels of direct corporate investment abroad in the first six months of 1965 which became public knowledge in mid-September. We have had to avoid arousing fears that mandatory controls were in the offing which would prompt many companies to repeat the pattern of the last quarter of 1964 when it seems that large amounts were sent out of the country in order to escape anticipated mandatory controls. On the other hand, we had to avoid any appearance either of being willing to accept an ineffective voluntary program in the Department of Commerce or adjudging it to be ineffective until sufficient evidence was accumulated.

For my own part, I have tried to accomplish this by the background press conference I held at your request on Friday, October 1, and public statements in both the American Bankers Association speech on October 5 and the Business Council speech on October 15. In both speeches I indicated we were in the process of re-examining that program to determine what, if any, additional measures "of a voluntary character" should be taken, including "a guidelines program to achieve further improvement in the year ahead." These two speeches with pertinent excerpts dealing with the Department of Commerce voluntary program marked are attached (see Attachment D).[6]

In the meantime Secretary Connor has specifically disavowed any intention of proposing a program of mandatory controls. He has had several full-day meetings with his Advisory Committee to appraise the situation and determine what the facts are and what conclusions can be drawn.

As a result, I believe the stimulation of outflows in the last quarter of 1965 out of fears that mandatory controls might be imposed early in 1966 has been minimized if not completely avoided. At the same time, I believe *my* statements have put industry somewhat on notice that we are not going to be content with a second-best effort. To get the flavor of general talk and opinion, you will want to read an article in *The New York Times* for October 20 by Mr. Rossant. (See Attachment E).[7]

As a second string to our bow in dealing with the fourth quarter, Secretary Connor wrote a letter on October 13 to the Chief Executive Officers of the 567 participating companies in the voluntary program specifically urging three actions designed to produce the best results in the fourth quarter on the corporate side. He said in the letter:

---

[6] Not attached.
[7] Not printed.

"In addition to the plans you may already have in mind, I would like to suggest the following special steps:

"1. A review of current foreign payments plans to stretch out or reprogram expenditures and dollar outflows to minimize the impact in the final quarter of 1965.

"2. Further reductions, where possible in light of business needs, of short-term assets held for parent company account in foreign countries. Our May 13 guideline on handling of short-term assets asked for reductions to a level not exceeding the amount outstanding on December 31, 1963. Our statistics indicate that non-financial corporations still hold substantial amounts of excess liquid funds abroad. Many firms have not yet reached the 1963 level, and I urge them to accelerate their repatriations.

"3. Where possible and appropriate, the drawing down and return to the United States of excess amounts of liquid funds held by your foreign affiliates. A close review of all your foreign affiliates may indicate ways of achieving a more efficient use of funds held abroad by different units."

I have asked Secretary Connor and spoken personally to several key members of his Advisory Committee urging them to carry on and support a "word of mouth" campaign by telephone calls, etc., to back up and support the Secretary's letter appeal. Secretary Connor has also asked the Chief Executives of the 567 participating companies in the Commerce voluntary program to speed up the submission of their third quarter reports and to give their personal estimate "of what you think will be the level of your company's foreign transactions, during the fourth quarter and for 1965 as a whole, for the items listed in the work sheet." This may help restrain last quarter excesses. A copy of Secretary Connor's letter and the covering press release are attached (see Attachment F).[8]

3.   *Minimizing Military Expenditure Impact on the 1965 Balance of Payments*

I have asked Secretary McNamara to ascertain whether there are any Defense Department out-payments abroad which affect 1965 balance of payments results that could be stretched over into 1966. I have also asked him to work through his Mr. Kuss[9] and Treasury Assistant to the Secretary Charles Sullivan in obtaining any additional advance payments from the Federal Republic of Germany on our military offset agreement in 1965. Messrs. Kuss and Sullivan are having a conference with the Germans on November 4 on this and related matters. If they are unsuccessful, you may wish to bring this up when Chancellor Erhard visits here. It is Secretary McNamara's clear preference to give first priority in that discussion of the military offset agreement to the longer range

---

[8] This letter and press release were not attached and have not been found.

[9] Henry J. Kuss, Jr., Deputy Assistant Secretary of Defense (International Logistics Negotiations).

necessity for West German action to take the budget action and place the orders that will avoid a shortfall in their commitment to a full offset. He thinks emphasis on advance payments in 1965 might detract from the larger long-range objective. You may wish to do both depending on the situation at the time. Attached is a memorandum from Treasury Assistant Sullivan dealing with the only two possibilities of maximizing offset payments in 1965 (see Attachment G)[10]

4.   *Minimizing Aid Outflows in the Fourth Quarter*

I have hammered hard at Director Bell, Deputy Director Gaud, and Budget Director Schultze on locating possibilities of deferring aid outflows in the last quarter of 1965. The results have been negative. Unless they can come up with some new leads in this area, I do not see any real possibilities for concrete savings in this area.

5.   *Minimizing United Kingdom Fund Withdrawals*

As I indicated to you earlier, I took advantage of the presence here during the Bank and Fund meeting of Lord Cromer, head of the Bank of England, to urge the deferral by the United Kingdom of any further action on their part this year that might adversely affect our fourth quarter picture. He encouraged me to believe, and *subsequent probes* with Bank of England authorities have confirmed our hope, that they will be in a position to defer a drawing-down of their long-standing Export-Import Bank credit for $250 million which they had contemplated utilizing in the fourth quarter. I also hope that they will minimize any further liquidation of their government-owned corporate securities in the United States which they have been selling off during the past year in order to liquify their assets for use in meeting their problems. For your information, these liquidations have adversely affected our balance of payments by $492 million through the third quarter of this year. The deferment of these items would be an extra dividend in our September 10 operation.

6.   *Holding Back Canadian Outflows to Canada*

In 1963, when the Interest Equalization Tax was announced, there was a large kickback from Canada which, as you know, depends upon U.S. capital outflows to make up for its chronic trade deficit. It was agreed by Secretary Dillon and Canadian Minister of Finance, Walter Gordon, that Canadian issues in the New York market would be exempt from the IET with the side understanding that Canadian financing would not be used to push Canadian reserves beyond their level at that time which was approximately $2.8 billion. This involves an undertaking by the Canadian Government to do something to restrain their pri-

---

[10] Tab G, a memorandum from Sullivan to Secretary Fowler, October 21, on "Maximizing Military Offset Payments in CY 1965: Germany and Italy," is not printed.

vate and public borrowers in the New York market if it should appear that this exempt excess is resulting in fattening Canadian reserves.

When Minister Gordon was here for the Bank and Fund meeting we arranged a joint United States-Canadian Treasury meeting on or about November 15 (following the Canadian election on November 9) to review the workings of our arrangements in the light of the intervening voluntary program for the banks. My reason for requesting this meeting is that I have been accumulating some information that leads me to believe Canadian private institutions might become a large loophole in both of our voluntary programs. This is a long term problem and November 15 will be adequate time to discuss it. However, I am calling Gordon next week concerning a study now in process to ask him to take steps with certain private and public Canadian borrowers, who are scheduled in the New York market between now and the first of the year to raise approximately $222 million, to hold off or defer these financings if it appears that they would result in pushing Canadian reserves beyond the level stipulated in his understanding with Secretary Dillon.

Whether I can obtain any results will depend upon (a) the Canadian appraisal of their own reserve outlook for the turn of the year, and (b) Gordon's willingness to approach private or public borrowers in the middle of a campaign to postpone their borrowing arrangements in the New York market until after the first of the year.

7. *What Will Be the Result of All This?*

You know my disinclination to make forecasts, so let's look at the record.

Last January in Secretary Dillon's "Report to the President on the Balance of Payments"[11] it was estimated that an agreed program of immediate measures which was incorporated in your February 10 Message would provide total estimated savings of $1,400–$1,500 million in 1965 but it was also pointed out that some of the measures "are not of equal firmness as far as savings anticipation are concerned."[12] Applying this January estimate to the $3.1 billion 1964 deficit on a regular transactions basis would have produced a deficit of $1.6 to $1.7 billion. A re-estimate of the situation was made in the "Report to the President from the Cabinet Committee on the Balance of Payments" dated June 7.[13] It was said in that report that:

"The program has a potential of bringing about a sizeable cut in the deficit this year. If the measures in savings live up to their potential—and assuming no big leaks in other parts of the balance of payments—we see

---

[11] Document 33.

[12] This quotation appears in Document 33.

[13] Document 61.

the possibility of the 1965 deficit being reduced in the range of $0.7–$1.5 billion, compared to $3.1 billion for 1964."

In the next quarterly report to you, dated September 10,[14] the Cabinet Committee stated:

"The 1965 deficit now seems likely to fall in the *upper* end of the range of $0.7–$1.5 billion we projected in our June report."

Two major factors have combined to move our current estimates of the deficit to a range of $1.5 to 2.0 billion—matching the original February forecast for the program and falling short of the optimistic expectation of last June. They are:

(1) The decline in exports in the first six months due to the dock strike and the lack of any repeat orders for Soviet wheat shipments such as in 1964. These factors and expanding steel imports, presumably as a hedge against the strike, resulted in a drop in our trade balance for the first six months compared to 1964 levels of approximately $1,700 million.

(2) Impact on balance of payments due to sales by the United Kingdom Government from its portfolio of United States stocks in order to fortify its reserve position. These sales have had approximately $500 million of impact on our balance of payments this year.

The last quarter will probably tell the tale between a very real success and a modest and reassuring improvement. I am shooting for a net deficit on a regular transactions basis of $1.5 billion for 1965 as compared to $3.1 billion in 1964. I would not be too surprised if the final figure is in excess of that up to $2 billion. I should be very disappointed if it goes beyond that. The most likely cause of such a bad outcome would be another scare like last winter that we were about to impose mandatory controls.

Henry H. Fowler

Attachment C

Federal Reserve Press Release[15]

Washington, October 1, 1965.

U.S. commercial banks, cooperating in the Federal Reserve-administered program for voluntary restraint of foreign credits, reduced their

[14] See footnote 2, Document 68.
[15] No classification marking. A typed note at the top of the page reads: "Advance for release in morning newspapers, Monday, October 4, 1965."

foreign loans and investments by another $200 million in July and August, it was announced today.

J. L. Robertson, who is conducting the program for the Board of Governors of the Federal Reserve System, praised the cooperation of the banks and other financial institutions for making the program even more successful than might have been anticipated in its objective of helping to achieve the improvement the President has called for in the U.S. balance of international payments.

Governor Robertson said that the July–August developments, coming on top of a $300 million reduction in the second quarter that already had offset most of the $400 million increase in this year's first quarter, leave the banks with a leeway of $575 million, as of August 31, under the suggested target level.

Of the banks reporting in August, he added, there were only 45 whose foreign claims were in excess of the target—which is set at 105 per cent of the amount of each bank's foreign credits outstanding on December 31, 1964—and then only by a total of $75 million. Every bank is expected to bring its total foreign credits within its target figure not later than March, 1966.

Respecting the future of the Voluntary Foreign Credit Restraint Program, Governor Robertson said that despite the progress which has been made, we must persevere in the program of restraint until equilibrium is attained in our balance of payments.

He said that the program presently administered by the Federal Reserve would need to be extended through 1966. While it is too early to determine what might be an appropriate objective for next year, or what changes in detail might be desirable, he said that any target for next year will continue to have as its base the December 31, 1964, outstandings of each financial institution—bank or non-bank. Any other approach would penalize those who have been the "best performers" of 1965.

77.   Memorandum of Conversation[1]

Washington, October 27, 1965, 4:30 p.m.

PARTICIPANTS

> Treasury—Secretary Fowler and Mr. Knowlton
> CEA—Mr. Otto Eckstein
> White House—Mr. Francis Bator
> AID—David Bell, Administrator
> Federal Reserve—Governor James Louis Robertson
> Commerce—Secretary Connor
> Defense—Secretary McNamara
> State—Under Secretary Ball
> Agriculture—Under Secretary John A. Schnittker
> BOB—Mr. Charles Schultze, Director
> BOB—Mr. Roth, Deputy Special Representative for Trade Negotiations

SUBJECT

> Cabinet Committee (Principals Only) Meeting

At the start of the meeting Mr. Knowlton passed out a refined version of the balance of payments forecast distributed the previous week.[2]

Secretary Fowler began by stating that he thought it was time for the group to come up with constructive suggestions for Secretary Connor's voluntary program. He said Treasury had tentative proposals which he would introduce in a moment but first he wanted to go around the table to see what others had to say.

Mr. Schultze said he would stick his neck out by recommending that:

(1) Exports be removed from the calculation of a target for corporations;
(2) The period 1962–1964 be used as a base for each capital flow;
(3) Targets be established for each of these items;
(4) Credit be given for increments of capital equipment exports; and
(5) Some incentive be given to improve over-all exports.

He said he realized that this was complicated but the best he could do.

Governor Robertson said that he would use 1962–1964 as a base, that he would set a target designed to reduce direct investment by one-third (presumably from the 1965 level), and that he would have a prescribed level for overseas working capital.

---

[1] Source: Johnson Library, Fowler Papers, International Balance of Payments—Classified Material: Cabinet Committee Meeting, 10/27/65, Box 53. Secret. Drafted by Knowlton. The meeting was held in Secretary Fowler's Conference Room.

[2] Not found.

Mr. Roth said he, too, would take exports out and that he would establish guidelines for the remaining items. He expressed uncertainty about what figure was really necessary as an objective, indicating a preference for coming up with different programs designed to meet different overall balance of payments objectives.

Mr. Eckstein said that he, too, would take exports out and that he preferred a system that utilized corporations' foreign net assets as a base.

Mr. Bell said that he had nothing to add but wanted to be sure that the distinction between developed and less developed countries continued to be a feature of the program. Secretary Connor indicated that this might be a problem but did not stress the point. He then read figures that showed an increase in U.S. direct investment in the less developed countries from $275 million in the first quarter (1965) to $367 million in the second, coupled with a decline in such investment in developed countries from $840 million to $584 million.

Secretary McNamara said that we should make a good clear distinction between direct investment and exports. The program should have "good, clear" targets. He raised the question of whether we had an able financial analyst working full time gathering and analyzing statistical background data for the program. He then stated that the President believed that the program had failed and that he (Secretary McNamara) for one didn't understand what the program was really all about.

Secretary Connor said that new information was being obtained. He believed that we should leave the 1965 program alone, he expected to have a new program approved in January 1966. It would have a strong direct investment emphasis.

Secretary McNamara then asked how many companies accounted for various percents of total investment. Secretary Connor replied that 100 companies accounted for about 80 percent of the direct investment involved in the program.

Secretary Fowler then circulated the Treasury memorandum entitled "Comments on the Commerce Voluntary Program," dated October 27, along with a list of recommendations.[3] The group read the material. Secretary Fowler then made a pitch for using the net asset base.

Secretary McNamara said why didn't we select 25 companies and get good information. Secretary Fowler asked how long it would take a corporation to fill out Table II (Treasury memo attachment).[4] Secretary McNamara said that any corporation of the sort in the Commerce Department program could do it in 20 minutes.

---

[3] Entitled "Comments on the Commerce Voluntary Program," not printed. (Johnson Library, Fowler Papers, International Balance of Payments—Classified Material: Cabinet Committee Meeting, 11/3/65, Box 53)

[4] Not attached, but a copy is ibid., 10/27/65, Box 53.

Secretary Connor then stated that he, Larry McQuade, and Dr. Brimmer were consulting with corporations every day. He said that while the suggestions he had just received at the meeting were interesting and would be considered, they were not new. He said that based on consultation with his advisory committee (which was a strong one, including men like Sidney Weinberg and George Moore) and the corporations and based on receipt of additional information on the fourth quarter results, he would be prepared with a specific program in the near future.

Secretary Fowler then made the point that the bank program could not be jelled until the Commerce program was set. He said he thought that the Commerce program would be more effective and better received by the business community if it were more specific.

Secretary McNamara returned to his suggestion that we get key information from a group of 25 companies. He said that if we couldn't get a feel for our objectives in this manner, he just didn't know how we *would* come up with a program that could be rationally explained. He for one was not going to sign any recommendations to the President unless he understood the statistical framework in which objectives and guidelines had been selected. For all he knew, a decline of $1 billion in direct investment might create chaos for certain companies. Did we really know what we were doing?

Secretary Connor replied that he believed the net improvement in direct investment and repatriated earnings in 1966 should and would be about $1 billion. His preliminary thinking was that we should set a target for direct investment of 110 percent of the 1964 flow. This would create a figure of $2.6 billion. He said we should set a target of repatriated earnings of 20 percent above 1964 figure. This would create an inflow of $4.5 billion. The difference between these two flows would be $1.9 billion, compared with $900 million estimated for 1965. He said emphatically these guidelines should apply to all countries.

Mr. Bator then asked Secretary Connor whether, in view of the feelings expressed at the meeting, he didn't think it would be helpful if a small technical advisory group were established represented by Treasury, Budget, CEA, and perhaps an outside expert to inform the various principals about the statistical frame of reference in which Commerce was making decisions. Secretary Connor said he thought this "might be a good idea".

The discussion turned to the matter of the mid-November press conference, what should be said before it, what should be said at it, and when we should have a new program ready for the President. Mr. Bator said that he was deeply concerned that he and others had told the President that everything was under control and that we were moving ahead satisfactorily. Secretary Connor interjected that what people had been telling the President and what everyone in fact had been trying to make clear for months to the public was that the second quarter was abnormal and that the third quarter would show a deficit.

Secretary Fowler said that there should be a press conference in mid-November comparable to the one in June with good strong statements from Chairman Martin, Secretary Connor and himself. The idea of conditioning the public to the third quarter deficit beforehand was dismissed. The point was made by one member of the group that we should state at the press conference that the third quarter deficit was actually somewhat lower than we anticipated.

Secretary Fowler then said that "he was more worried about what people said after the press conference than before." Returning to the subject of when we should have a program for the President, he said that he had to have a *report* for the President in early November presenting him with various options, if not a concrete program in detail.

Secretary McNamara returned to the subject of the technical advisory group. He asked specifically for deadlines. Secretary Connor said he would have recommendations with respect to a new program for the Cabinet Committee (principals only) meeting the following week. Secretary McNamara asked then whether it was the general understanding that the advisory group would by then have looked at the statistical back-up for the Commerce recommendations so that it could decide what more would be needed and so that all necessary statistical information would be obtained by no later than the first of the year. Secretary Fowler indicated that this was the understanding.

Secretary Fowler then asked Secretary McNamara to comment on possible savings in the military area. The latter distributed several tables. Talking first about Table 53: U.S. Defense Expenditures and Receipts Entering the International Balance of Payments (dated October 19, 1965),[5] he pointed out that the net adverse balance of military expenditures would have been $1,218 million in calendar year 1966 had Southeast Asian expenditures remained at the calendar year 1960 level. In view of increases there, he said the figure now looked as though it would be $1,812 million, up from $1,472 million in calendar year 1965. He said that it was possible that the figure might be $125 million higher than this if proposals to increase military strength in Southeast Asia by another 125,000 troops went forward. In discussing another table (Possible Actions to Reduce Department of Defense Foreign Exchange Costs), he mentioned that additional savings looked pretty limited. Two big possibilities on the receipt side—$25 million from Canada and $50 million from Japan—would be "very hard to do soon". The Japanese problem was pretty difficult. Henry Kuss had been on a selling mission to Canada but nothing major could be expected soon.

---

[5] None of the tables cited is printed. (Ibid., 9/30/65, Box 53)

There was then a brief flurry of conversation about Canada, with Mr. Ball stating that he thought we were in a position to put pressure on Canadians. Secretary Fowler mentioned that a Canadian delegation would be down the next morning (October 28), and Treasury was going to discuss with them the possibility of curtailing Canadian securities issues in the fourth quarter. Mr. Ball said that in the past we had given way too easily with the Canadians.

Secretary McNamara then turned to the possibility of compulsory savings programs for overseas troops. He said he thought he could relate it to the pay increase and produce a savings of $80 million. In the ensuing conversation, it was agreed other governmental employees overseas would also have to be included in the program. Mr. Schultze said he would look into the problems of such a program in a little more detail.

Secretary Fowler then asked Mr. Schnittker whether Agriculture would head up a task force to examine the whole outlook for food and agricultural exports, examining the balance of payments implications of the over-all picture, the picture vis-à-vis the USSR and the Soviet Bloc, and PL 480. The task force would be chaired by Agriculture and include representatives from Treasury, AID, Budget and possibly State. Mr. Schnittker said that Secretary of Agriculture was away but that he would begin immediately to draw up a memorandum, as Secretary Fowler suggested, giving the task force its terms of reference.

The meeting then returned to a discussion of military matters, with reference first to Japan. Mr. Ball said that he would be sending Secretary Fowler a memorandum on the Japanese situation soon but warned that "it would be discouraging." Secretary McNamara said the Japanese problem required five years of intensive psycho-analysis. Secretary Fowler asked what the effect would be if we withdrew certain of our troops. Secretary McNamara said that unfortunately the Japanese would welcome this.

Secretary Fowler then asked Secretary McNamara about military prospects in the Netherlands and the Netherlands Antilles. He was tired of Holtrop lecturing him on lack of American financial discipline. Couldn't we give him a shove? Secretary McNamara said a sales program was under way but it was minor. The trouble with the Netherlands was that she wanted a nuclear submarine and we wouldn't give her one. Secretary Fowler asked about the Philippines. Secretary McNamara said there was very little potential here. They had a $22 million military assistance program. We hoped they would send troops to Vietnam but if they did so, we would have to pay for them. The Philippines, he said, was "a real trouble spot."

In discussing the exchange problem in South Vietnam, it was agreed to wait 60 days and look at the effectiveness of the present exchange control system there shortly after the beginning of the year. Secretary McNamara described this as a "very serious problem."

Secretary Fowler then asked Mr. Ball for his comments on tourism. Mr. Ball stated that there were three approaches: (1) restriction on dollar transfer; (2) taxes; and (3) a voluntary approach. He ruled out the first and third. The first [would] involve, black market dollars, was messy, futile, etc.; the third would not be effective. He then went through the list of possible taxes and described the pros and cons of each (mostly cons). The four types of taxes were: (a) head tax; (b) fare tax; (c) reported expenditure tax; and (d) a "presumptive" travel expenditure tax based on the number of days spent abroad and the level of the traveler's domestic income tax. Mr. Bator said that the presumptive travel expenditures tax was "ingenious". The rest of the group expressed more amusement than interest.

Secretary Fowler then read a letter that he had recently received recommending differential passport charges. The charges would differ for three groups: tourists, businessmen, and students and scholars. There would be a scale of graduated charges based on frequency of departures from the U.S. Funds gathered would be used to subsidize Commerce's U.S. Travel Service.

Mr. Schultze suggested that the gap between 17-day fares and regular fares had had the effect of limiting the average expenditures of travelers abroad, and he wondered whether more work shouldn't be done to see whether changes in pricing techniques couldn't further reduce the average per capita expenditures abroad. Mr. Ball seemed to think that this might be worth pursuing, but there was very little reaction from the rest of the group.

Secretary McNamara stated that he felt that the group was not being sufficiently optimistic about the possibility of steps in the tourist area. He said that we would have a different environment in 1966. There was the Vietnam crisis; the domestic budget would be "fantastic"; and if there were a compulsory savings plan for Government employees abroad, it would make tourist restrictions considerably easier to sell.

Mr. Bator commented that there was a double pay-off from tourist measures: (1) the effect it had on our ability to make all the other programs tougher; and (2) the direct savings from the tourist measures themselves.

At this point, the subject of the Interest Equalization Tax came up. Secretary Fowler mentioned to Governor Robertson that he would not be replying to his memorandum of the previous day (October 26)[6] because he didn't want any more put down on paper on this particular subject

---

[6] Not found.

than was absolutely necessary. He hoped that others who had received the memorandum would not respond either. Mr. Bator expressed the view that a broader and more flexible IET was probably the ultimate solution to our basic problem. Secretary Fowler said that if we were to go the IET approach in 1966 we would be "taking advantage of a short-term crisis to get a long-term tool". Mr. Eckstein said that he really didn't think that we were in sufficiently dire straits to pull this particular stop.

Secretary Fowler said that he would blame Mr. Bator for bringing up this subject at this time. In closing the meeting, Secretary Fowler said that he would be in touch with the group about reconvening the following Wednesday or Thursday (November 3 or November 4) at the same time.

Winthrop Knowlton

---

78.   **Memorandum From Secretary of the Treasury Fowler to President Johnson**[1]

Washington, November 16, 1965.

SUBJECT

    Progress Report on Balance of Payments—Bolt and Nut Tightening—*Supplement to October 22 Memo*[2]

I want to bring you up-to-date on balance of payments developments—both our work on preparing a program for 1966 and our most recent efforts to "tighten bolts and nuts" in the fourth quarter.

I.   *Programming for 1966*

The Cabinet Committee continues to work hard on this. Since my memorandum to you on October 22, we have had two more meetings of the small, principals only, Cabinet Committee group—on October 27th[3] and November 3rd[4]—at which a variety of proposals was discussed. Secretary Connor is actively engaged in the formulation of a new voluntary

---

[1] Source: Johnson Library, National Security File, Subject File, Balance of Payments, Vol. 3 [2 of 2], Box 2. Secret.

[2] Document 76.

[3] See Document 77.

[4] No record of this meeting has been found.

Commerce Department program, which he has presented for consideration to the full Cabinet Committee today, Tuesday, November 16. Governor Robertson also presented the Federal Reserve program for 1966.

Governor Robertson, Secretary Connor, and I will hold a joint press conference on Wednesday, November 17—to announce the third quarter balance of payments results. It is presently believed that the third quarter deficit seasonally adjusted came to $615 million on a regular transactions basis, a $485 million deficit on an overall basis, but will show a surplus of $260 million on an official settlements basis. Public release of the third quarter figures is bound to have some adverse effects since it is unexpectedly large, but we shall have to minimize the impact.

It is my objective to present to you during the week of November 21 specific proposed changes in our voluntary programs for banks, nonbank financial institutions, and for corporations. (It may be possible to announce the general outlines of the Commerce program at the Wednesday press conference in a way that does not commit us to specific *quantitative* results but which nevertheless helps restrain outflow for the rest of the year; we might simply say, for example, that the new guidelines will depend on *combined* 1965–1966 corporate performance, so that any outflow this year will count against the corporation in question next year.)

To the extent that changes in the voluntary program fall short of bringing us into balance next year (and this is a matter of deciding to what degree these programs can *prudently* be tightened), our efforts are also directed toward presenting you in the near future with preliminary recommendations on *new* measures—including possible legislation—to be publicly unveiled if and when necessary in 1966.

On Friday, November 19, a bilateral U.S.-Canadian meeting on balance of payments will take place in Ottawa.[5] This is the second meeting that has been held to discuss joint problems in this area. (The first took place on July 26, 1965.)[6] Assistant Secretary Merlyn Trued will head the U.S. delegation, and it is our intention to negotiate an arrangement (in all likelihood involving a tightening of the Federal Reserve voluntary program for non-bank financial institutions) that will result in a lower level of Canadian borrowing in U.S. capital markets next year.

On Saturday, November 20, Secretary Freeman will submit to me the recommendations of a special task force on agricultural exports.

The principals of the Cabinet Committee during the course of their three meetings also have been addressing themselves in depth to other aspects of the 1966 program—government expenditures abroad (mili-

---

[5] No record of this meeting has been found.

[6] For an account of this meeting, see the Department of Treasury press release, July 26, in the *Annual Report of the Secretary of the Treasury on the State of the Finances, 1966* (Washington, 1967), p. 497.

tary, aid and civilian), tourism, factors affecting our trade balance, foreign investment in the United States, etc. A full program incorporating decisions on the entire range of 1966 plans can be put together by December 1.

II.   Dealing with the Fourth Quarter

In my memorandum of October 22, I listed a number of steps we *had taken or planned to take* to minimize additional outflows in the fourth quarter. Generally speaking, I believe we have been successful in this respect. Without going into detail, let me just cite a few specific instances where special efforts are paying off:

1. Through a cooperative effort with the Canadians (launched on Tuesday, November 9) we are meeting with good success in persuading Canadian borrowers to defer deliveries of U.S. dollars until 1966.[7] These deferments already exceed $100 million and may reach $150 million in the remaining weeks of the year.

2. The World Bank has agreed to offset an $18 million IDA encashment by purchase of a like amount of 13-month certificates of deposits. The Inter-American Development Bank is making arrangements to hold drawings until 1966 on a $75 million non-interest bearing demand note of ours which it holds, while operating on short-term certificates. We are carefully screening all of the loans of the various U.S. lending agencies to make sure that 1965 *disbursements* are minimized.

3. Arrangements are being made to limit the 1965 balance of payments impact of aid to the Dominican Republic.

4. The military is well along in its analysis of possible year-end savings, and Secretary McNamara will be discussing this matter with me next week.

5. The United Kingdom has formally agreed with Under Secretary Deming not to take down the $250 million Export-Import Bank loan this year; and they have stated that they will handle further liquidations—if any—of their U.S. securities portfolio in a manner that does not hurt our payments picture.

6. The visit to Bonn of Treasury and Department of Defense officials early in November developed fairly firm prospects for an additional $80 million of advance payments on military offset arrangements being made before December 31, 1965.

As to "what will be the result of all this," I continue to believe, as I expressed to you in my memorandum of October 22, that we will end up the year with a deficit in the range of $1.5–$2.0 billion. Quite clearly some of the things we are doing to help the last quarter will come back to hurt

---

[7] Regarding the postponement of Canadian securities issues, see the Department of the Treasury press release, November 9; ibid., pp. 499–500.

us in 1966. But this simply means that, in developing a stronger overall 1966 program, recognition must be given to a less encouraging outlook. I intend to take full account of this in presenting the program to you.

Henry H. Fowler

79.   Memorandum From the President's Deputy Special Assistant for National Security Affairs (Bator) to President Johnson[1]

Washington, November 16, 1965, 2:40 p.m.

SUBJECT

Your meeting this afternoon with Joe Fowler[2]

Fowler will be asking for your preliminary approval of the broad outlines of the 1966 balance of payments program. We have worked out two alternative packages. One of these would leave us with a small but appreciable deficit of about $500–$700 million; the other would take us to zero or into surplus. Fowler will recommend, and I would agree, that you approve the more ambitious option. He will also tell you that to sell that option to Connor's clients and the banks, it would be necessary for the government to dramatize the balance of payments program *as part of the total effort connected with the Viet Nam war.* What he would like to say— for the first time tomorrow at the press conference announcing the third quarter deficit—that the world is no longer the same as it was a year ago, that we are in a serious shooting war, and that our voluntary program to bring the balance of payments under control reflects the kind of national effort that is required from all parties.

I thought it might be useful for you to have a prior private indication of the kind of basic change of approach that Fowler will suggest. Connor wants to take a similar tack. However, Rusk, McNamara and Bundy have

---

[1] Source: Johnson Library, Bator Papers, Balance of Payments, 1965 [1 of 4], Box 14. Eyes Only.

[2] The President met with Fowler and Bator in the Oval Office beginning at 3:25 p.m. to discuss the balance of payments and other economic issues. (Ibid., President's Daily Diary) No record of the meeting has been found. Presumably Fowler presented his memorandum, Document 78.

not been involved in this discussion and hence have not yet had their say. (My own prejudice, for what it is worth, is that your policy of the past year of being very careful not to over-dramatize the Viet Nam war is still right. It will be difficult enough over time to maintain room for Presidential maneuver and hold off pressure from those who still believe in the notion of a simple, clear-cut military victory.)

Francis M. Bator[3]

---

[3] Printed from a copy that bears this typed signature.

---

80.   Minutes of Meeting of the Cabinet Committee on Balance of Payments[1]

Washington, November 24, 1965.

The following attended the meeting for principals only of the Cabinet Committee on Balance of Payments on Wednesday, November 24, 1965:

Secretary Fowler, Chairman
Secretary McNamara, Defense
Secretary Connor, Commerce
Under Secretary Ball, State
Under Secretary Schnittker, Agriculture
Mr. Ackley, CEA
Mr. Bell, AID
Ambassador Roth, Trade Negotiations
Mr. Bator, White House
Governor Robertson, Federal Reserve
Assistant Secretary Trued, Treasury

A draft of the proposed Memorandum for the President was distributed to the members attending the meeting prior to Secretary Fowler's joining the group. A copy of the draft is attached.[2] A number of minor errors in the text and some inconsistencies in figures were pointed out and corrected.

---

[1] Source: Johnson Library, Fowler Papers, International Balance of Payments—Classified Material: Cabinet Committee Meeting, 11/24/65, Box 53. Secret. The meeting was held in Secretary Fowler's office.

[2] Not attached, but a copy is ibid.

When he joined the group, Secretary Fowler said that he proposed to send the Memorandum for the President forward as promptly as possible but that any member disagreeing with the program as outlined in the draft could submit his own views which would go along with the Report to the President.[3] Secretary Fowler noted that substantial strengthening of the program was required in the light of the balance of payments results in 1965 and the outlook for next year, particularly as it involved prospective increases in outlays owing to the war in Vietnam.

Secretary Connor emphasized the need to get the program out quickly since businessmen were becoming very critical at the delay in finding out what was being proposed; he hoped that it could be gotten out certainly by December 1. He also felt it important that the President should be in some way linked into an announcement of the program since direct Presidential support for the measures would be necessary. Secretary Connor said that the program for industry as set forth in the draft Memorandum was acceptable to him but wished to add, for purposes of proper perspective, a reference to the fact that the projected outflow of direct investments next year would not be more than in 1964, since it was noted that the outlays would be well above the average of the 1962–1964 period. Secretary Connor emphasized that the program would be a tough one to sell and would occasion many and varied complaints, but he was willing to sell it and thought that the business community would find it tolerable, although unwelcome.

Secretary Fowler said that he did not see, with respect to the Federal Reserve program, that the outlook for 1966 justified any increase in the ceiling for banks lending to foreigners and referred to his previous comment that this should be left aside with an intent to look at this area again next summer when the balance of payments trends for the year were more evident. That would be the time when some increase in the ceiling might be appropriate. Governor Robertson said that he would, of course, seek to administer as best he could whatever program the Cabinet Committee decided upon. He wanted to emphasize, however, that it was important in his view to keep the program voluntary since an involuntary program would never do the job while at the same time creating grave difficulties. He noted that the banks had done an admirable job in the past year. He did not think it appropriate to hold to the 105 percent ceiling since the banks would view this as demonstrating that cooperation would not pay off and they would therefore be likely to move right up against the 105 percent ceiling, rather than remain comfortably below. He felt that continuation of the 105 percent ceiling might lead banks to go well over the guideline and there was a good possibility that we would then have a greater outflow than if the ceiling were raised. The program

---

[3] A copy of the report, November 26, is ibid.

would be resented and we would run a real danger of testing too severely its voluntary nature. Governor Robertson said he had previously suggested a new ceiling of 110 percent but he had given further thought to the question and would now suggest that the ceiling be raised by one percentage point a quarter, thus setting a ceiling for the last quarter of 1966 at 109 percent of the base. This would help smooth out any outflow for the year, give banks the satisfaction of having outstanding performance rewarded, and insure even more fully that our exports would find adequate financing.

Governor Robertson emphasized that we simply could not permit lack of financing to endanger our exports since an increase in exports was essential to longer run balance of payments equilibrium. Governor Robertson estimated that the additional outflow of bank funds to foreigners would be only some $100 million higher than it was with the retention of the 105 percent ceiling, with another roughly $70 million or so also in view if the Cabinet Committee agreed that, on grounds of equity, smaller banks ought to be given some lending capacity.

The Cabinet Committee discussed the points raised by Governor Robertson and promptly reached general agreement on a program along the lines he proposed.

Secretary McNamara was asked whether he wished to have an increase in expenditures for military spending in Vietnam wound into the forecast for 1966 but said that he would prefer to leave the reference to those increased expenditures in a footnote. Mr. Bell suggested language with respect to that part of the Report dealing with further possible savings in the AID program and the language was incorporated into the Report.

Secretary Fowler raised a question as to whether something more should be said on tourism expenditures but Mr. Bell suggested that there was danger in talking about this area at a time when there was no concrete proposal to deal with it effectively. Mr. Bell felt that as a general rule it was better not to mention the subjects if we were not prepared to act promptly.

Secretary McNamara said that he thought very strong reference to the desirability of selling wheat to the Soviet bloc should be incorporated in the draft, and this should be vigorously pushed. Secretary Fowler and others agreed this was an area in which we were losing sales needlessly and hoped that the Administration would succeed in eliminating obstacles to such sales.

Secretary Fowler said that we would be in touch as to a specific time for release of the Report, he wished to send it along to the President at the

Ranch by Friday,[4] and would also then receive some indication as to how it would be announced. Secretary McNamara requested that the table attached to the Memorandum be expanded to show our balance of payments position since 1960, and Secretary Fowler requested that charts be prepared to show major changes in balance of payments items.

Secretary Fowler asked that the principals quickly convey their comments or approval of the revised Memorandum for the President that would be circulated on Friday. Secretary McNamara said that he would be out of the country but that he knew that the program now was all agreed to and he would give Secretary Fowler his proxy. Under Secretary Ball and Ambassador Roth also said that Secretary Fowler had their approval in hand.

Merlyn N. Trued[5]
Secretary to the Cabinet Committee
on Balance of Payments

---

[4] November 26.
[5] Printed from a copy that indicates Trued signed the original.

---

81.   Memorandum From Secretary of the Treasury Fowler to President Johnson[1]

Washington, November 26, 1965.

I attach a memorandum to you from the Cabinet Committee on Balance of Payments containing an appraisal of the balance of payments outlook for 1966 and recommending measures that should go far toward bringing an end to the deficits.[2] The program recommended was approved by the following members of the Cabinet Committee on Balance of Payments, or their representatives, at a meeting on Wednesday, November 24:[3]

---

[1] Source: Johnson Library, Bator Papers, Balance of Payments 1965 [3 of 4], Box 14. Secret. Three handwritten notations appear on the source text. The first in the upper left corner reads: "Recd Ranch 11–27–65 9:30 a." The second in the bottom left corner reads: "fr bedroom 11–30–65 10:20a." The third at the top reads: "L," in presumably the President's handwriting.
[2] Not attached; apparent reference to Document 82.
[3] See Document 80.

Defense: Secretary McNamara
Commerce: Secretary Connor
State: Under Secretary Ball
Agriculture: Under Secretary Schnittker
AID: Mr. Bell
Special Representative for Trade Negotiations: Mr. Roth
CEA: Mr. Ackley
White House: Mr. Bator
Federal Reserve: Governor Robertson

Upon receiving your approval, we are prepared to move promptly to make the nature of the program known publicly and to follow through to assure its effectiveness.

Henry H. Fowler

---

82.   **Report From the Cabinet Committee on Balance of Payments to the President**[1]

Washington, November 26, 1965.

SUBJECT

1966 Balance of Payments Program

The Cabinet Committee has completed its appraisal of the balance of payments outlook for 1965 and 1966. Table I, attached, shows the U.S. balance of payments since 1960, including an estimate of our deficit this year and a projection for 1966, with and without a reinforced program.[2] The results of this appraisal and the recommendations for action to bring our accounts close to balance next year are set forth in this memorandum.[3]

1.   Estimated 1965 Results

We have taken a number of steps in attempting to guard against serious fourth quarter deterioration in our balance of payments. Neverthe-

---

[1] Source: Johnson Library, National Security File, Balance of Payments, Vol. 3 [2 of 2], Box 2. Secret.

[2] Table I, "U.S. Balance of Payments 1960–1966," is not printed.

[3] A graph, "Dollar Outflows from Selected Accounts in U.S. Balance of Payments, " covering 1960 to 1965, is not printed.

less, certain substantial outflows during October—which may still prove to be window dressing by Canadian banks prior to the end of their fiscal year on October 31, 1965 and reversible during the fourth quarter—may prove to be more than temporary. If these flows are reversed, the over-all deficit this year could, *at best*, total $1.3 billion; if not reversed, the over-all deficit could well run to $1.5 billion. On a regular transactions basis, the deficit would run between $1.7 billion and $1.9 billion. *Table I shows the optimum results that can be expected.*

The deficit on official transactions this year is difficult to predict in view of the possibility of a large fourth quarter shift between foreign private and foreign official dollar holdings.

2.   The Outlook for 1966

With a simple continuation of our present program, we would expect the 1966 over-all deficit to be $1.4 billion, and the regular transactions deficit $1.6 billion. These projections, shown in Table I, allow for an increase in total Department of Defense overseas expenditures of $290 million, attributable entirely to our intensified effort in Southeast Asia. These expenditures will be only partially offset by increased military receipts. A further $200 million increase in expenditures may occur next year and worsen the projected deficit by that amount (see footnote b of Table I).

3.   Immediate Decisions: The Voluntary Programs

The Cabinet Committee believes that the lion's share of our 1966 improvement must come from a reinforced Commerce Department program.

The program recommended by Commerce calls for

—the continuation of a *voluntary* approach
—use of an over-all target for corporations similar to that of 1965 but importantly buttressed by

(1) a new target designed specifically to limit direct investment, and
(2) a formula which will give each company and the government a basis for judging individual company performance.

—improved reporting and forecasting procedures, with coverage expanded to include 900 companies as against 500 at present.

The Cabinet Committee asks your approval of this proposed program, which will more specifically provide that

—direct investment (including reinvested earnings) during the two-year period 1965–1966 be limited to 90 percent of such outflows during the three-year period 1962–1964. (This formula would allow average annual investment during 1965–1966 at a rate equal to 135 percent of the 1962–1964 annual average.)

—the direct investment target apply not only to all developed countries (including Canada) but also to the following oil-producing countries (traditionally classified as less-developed countries):

Abu Dhabi	Libya
Bahrein	Neutral Zone
Iran	Qatar
Iraq	Saudi Arabia
	Indonesia

The importance of the petroleum industry in the over-all direct investment picture and the size of its activities in these countries are such that the program cannot achieve results of the desired magnitude unless these additional geographical restraints are imposed. This effort should be reinforced by

—extending the Interest Equalization Tax to these areas as well.

Application of this new Commerce Department target on the expanded geographical basis proposed is expected to bring balance of payments savings of $1.1 billion in direct investment and related capital flows. This is a substantial drop from the $3.4 billion level of outflow now estimated for 1965, but it should be noted that the level of direct investment permitted is still substantially higher than the annual average outflow during the 1962–1964 period, although it is no higher than the outflow in 1964 alone.

The Commerce program calls also for continued repatriation of corporate overseas cash balances. If these repatriations amount, as expected, to $200 million, the over-all contribution of the new Commerce program next year would be $1.3 billion.

As regards the program administered by the Federal Reserve, the Cabinet Committee asks your approval of the Federal Reserve's program for 1966 on a voluntary basis with the modifications noted below.

There can only be deep satisfaction regarding the results of the bank program during 1965—bank lending to foreigners dropped from the exceptionally high $2.5 billion levels in 1964 to an estimated $260 million in 1965.

The Cabinet Committee is keenly aware of this contribution and the need to sustain broad support of the program. It believes it highly desirable—indeed, essential—in the face of this performance not to appear to apply even harsher measures. It is also desirable now to provide some margin of lending capacity to banks now effectively precluded from foreign lending because they had little or no such lending on their books as of the base date of December 31, 1964. The Committee therefore recommends that

—the ceiling for bank lending to foreigners be raised from 105 percent of the December 31, 1964 base by 1 percent per quarter, thus setting a new ceiling of 109 percent for end of 1966; and

—small banks be permitted to lend up to $450,000 each, provided such lending by each bank covers U.S. exports being financed for its regular customers or provides credit to a developing country.

These revisions should materially assist in assuring that financing of U.S. exports remains adequate.

It is estimated that, under these revisions, net bank lending will rise in 1966 to $400 million, from $260 million in 1965. Of the $140 million increase, $70 million will result from lending allowed by the special provision for small banks. This modest increase in lending under the higher ceiling assumes the same high degree of bank cooperation that has characterized the past year.

As regards the program for nonbank financial institutions (insurance companies, pension funds, etc.), the Cabinet Committee recommends that

—the tax exemption for new issues for Canada be continued without limitation as to amount (see discussion below) and that the exemption for up to $100 million of Japanese issues also be continued;
—the Interest Equalization Tax be applied to the nine countries listed earlier in the memorandum;
—net purchases of securities of developed countries other than Japan and Canada be limited under the Federal Reserve program during the period ending December 31, 1966, to 105 percent of the amount of such securities held by one of these institutions on September 30, 1965.

It is estimated that application of these measures, including the Canadian arrangement discussed below, will bring net balance of payments savings of at least $200 million.

3. *New Canadian Agreement*

Extensive discussions with Canadian officials have been held to determine how a cutback in net Canadian long-term borrowing in the U.S. can be best accomplished. We have now agreed that a cutback is in order and that this can be accomplished by Canadian action to use some $300–$400 million of its reserves (which now stand at $2.9 billion, or about $200 million above the June 1963 base used in connection with the exemption from the Interest Equalization Tax given to Canada in July 1963)[4] to cover its over-all current account deficit.

The Canadians strongly and persuasively urge that we not approach the objective by setting any quota for Canada, since the establishment of such a quota runs serious risk of triggering chaos in the market and bringing about heavy losses to Canadian reserves.

As an alternative, the Canadians have agreed to

—use some $300–$400 million of Canada's own reserves to finance part of its 1966 deficit;

---

[4] See Document 12.

—purchase from Americans an amount of outstanding Canadian securities, thus providing an inflow of long-term capital to the U.S. and offsetting the balance of payments impact of that amount of new security issues so as to limit the net flow of capital into Canada to the amount of its over-all current account deficit *less* the use of $300–$400 million of Canada's reserves;

—sell us $200 million of gold to provide help on that front.

Most importantly, we believe continued cooperation is assured and that Canada will fully honor its commitments and assist us in stopping any leakages through Canada.

4.   *Other Measures*

Barring a deterioration in the underlying fundamentals, the above measures should bring us within $35 million of balance on an over-all basis, and within $220 million on a regular transactions basis, next year. The proposals relating to the voluntary programs can be announced and implemented quickly.

At the same time, the Cabinet Committee believes it important to make clear to the public that these changes by no means comprise the entire program. To reinforce the efforts described above, the following additional steps should also be taken:

—all government agencies must intensify their efforts to hold down the balance of payments costs of their programs. AID has proposed certain additional steps which should assure some further reduction in its offshore expenditures, despite larger anticipated economic aid costs in Vietnam and Southeast Asia; against a background of climbing expenditures, the military must ensure—through cost reductions, military offset arrangements, etc.—that the deterioration in its payments is no worse than it need be; the Director of the Budget must continue to examine our many miscellaneous civilian programs for possible Gold Budget savings.

—legislation to encourage foreign investment in the United States (the so-called Fowler Task Force bill) should be passed by the Congress as soon as possible.[5]

—in the travel area, an interagency Task Force is now preparing a report to the Cabinet Committee setting forth possible measures to dampen our net losses on this account, including the possibility of cutting expenditures by government personnel abroad through an involuntary savings program. Pending completion of this study, the *Discover America* program must be continued and every effort made by government officials—by letter and public statement—to encourage the activities of the private sector in this field; the Commerce Department should seek additional appropriations for the U.S. Travel Service, currently operating at a marked competitive disadvantage in relation to its foreign counterparts; and the Administration should publicly endorse the efforts of the Civil Aeronautics Board to encourage all-inclusive charter tours of the United States.

---

[5] See Document 24.

—in the field of non-agricultural exports, attention should focus on taking all appropriate measures that would intensify U.S. export efforts during 1966; in this connection, the export survey—results of which are expected to become available in February—should be carefully studied to determine what new measures in the area of export promotion would be of assistance.

—in the field of agricultural exports, changes in the commodity export credit program, in pricing of export certificates, and further tightening of P. L. 480 programs will help produce gains, in the view of the inter-agency task force on agriculture, of up to $60 million in 1966. Easing of trade restrictions with Communist nations through removal of cargo preferences and relaxation of licensing requirements could yield another $100–$500 million in exports in 1966, and the Cabinet Committee believes efforts to encourage these sales should be made in the coming year, with particular emphasis on sales of wheat to the Soviet Union. A special Task Force now has under preparation a detailed study of this entire area for submission to the Cabinet Committee.

Potential 1966 savings from these various activities could amount to $150–$300 million.

---

83.   Memorandum From the President's Deputy Special Assistant for National Security Affairs (Bator) to President Johnson[1]

Washington, November 29, 1965, 9:05 p.m.

SUBJECT

Announcement of Balance of Payments Program

1. I understand that you have spoken to Joe Fowler about the Cabinet Committee report which he sent you last Friday,[2] and that you are

---

[1] Source: Johnson Library, Bator Papers, Balance of Payments, 1965 [1 of 4], Box 14. Secret. The source text was accompanied by two typewritten notes. The first, from Francis Bator to Jake Jacobson, has the following handwritten notation: "Recd Ranch 11–30–65 4:00 p." The note reads: "We need Presidential approval on this by Wednesday [December 1] noon at the latest, if we are to go ahead Thursday [December 2] 9 a.m. (the only time Fowler, Connor, etc. can make it). Will you call me as soon as you have an answer? Many thanks." A handwritten circle appears around the words: "Wednesday noon." The second, from President Johnson, November 30, 8:55 p.m., reads: "What I would do is to have Bill Moyers preside at the press conference—call it at the White House. I would probably try to do it early Thursday [December 2] morning, so it won't conflict with what we are doing down here that afternoon."

[2] Document 82.

agreeable to an early announcement of the revised program. *If you agree, we will plan to go ahead with an announcement on Thursday.*[3] (Connor is scheduled to soften-up the Business Council on Thursday, and they are a leaky lot. Also, quite apart from leaks, the sooner we give the corporations the new ground rules the better. They generally make their capital-budgeting decisions for the year during the early part of December.)

2. To make it clear that the new program is your program, I would recommend that:

(i) There be a Fowler–Connor–Martin–McNamara–Bell press conference *at the White House.* Fowler and Connor are agreeable.
(ii) We release a letter from you to Fowler approving the recommendations of the Cabinet Committee and instructing him to put them into effect. *A draft of such a letter is at Tab A.* (I read it to Joe on the telephone. He likes the idea, and had no problems with the draft.)[4]
(iii) As an alternative to (i), we could skip the press conference and simply release a Presidential letter, and a sanitized, spruced-up version of the Cabinet Committee's memorandum to the President.[5] The appropriate Assistant Secretaries and I would background the press on the technical details. (Fowler's man Donnelly will be in touch with Bill Moyers about your preference as between (i) and (iii).)

3. On the substance of the program, let me just say that, in my judgment, the Cabinet Committee proposal represents our best move *for now.* I think it a fair three-to-one bet that most of Connor's clients will play ball—for awhile. (For the first time, each company will be given a formula by which both the company itself and we will be able to judge whether it is doing its share. We are doing for the corporations *now* what we did for the banks last February.) In the end, I suspect that we will have to go further and impose a tax on virtually all capital outflow. But there is a good case for moving one step at a time. If Connor's people do not play ball, we will be in a stronger position to impose a tax, after having given the voluntary route a real try. If they do go along for awhile—as I think likely—you have more time to consider asking Congress for a standby

---

[3] December 2. The press conference to announce the 1966 Balance of Payments program was held on December 3.

[4] Tab A was not attached. For the version of the letter, December 2, from President Johnson to Secretary Fowler, released on December 5, see *American Foreign Policy: Current Documents, 1965,* pp. 1074–1075.

[5] A summary of the recommendations submitted to President Johnson by the Cabinet Committee on the Balance of Payments, December 3, was released on December 5; see ibid., pp. 1075–1076.

tax, with a variable rate, which is what we will need for the long pull. (I'll do a longer separate memo for you on this if you wish.)

FMB

A public letter from President to Fowler (as at Tab A)

Announce program on Thursday, Dec. 2, but no press conference

White House press conference (Fowler, et al) on Thursday, Dec. 2[6]

---

[6] This option is checked. A handwritten note, presumably by the President, reads "with Moyers."

---

84. Memorandum From the President's Deputy Special Assistant for National Security Affairs (Bator) to Secretary of Defense McNamara[1]

Washington, November 30, 1965.

As a way of getting a Presidential seal of approval on the revised balance of payments program, I proposed to the President (with Joe Fowler's approval) that he authorize the release of a letter from himself to Fowler, as Chairman of Cabinet Committee, approving the recommendations of the Committee and instructing that we put them into effect. A copy of a draft which I sent to the Ranch this morning is attached.[2] If you have any comments or suggestions, please have someone in your office call me.[3]

The tentative plan is either to have a press conference led by Joe Fowler at the White House on Thursday morning, or simply to release the President's letter[4] and a sanitized version of the Cabinet Committee report,[5] with no press conference but backgrounding by appropriate

---

[1] Source: Johnson Library, Bator Papers, Balance of Payments, 1965 [1 of 4], Box 14. Confidential. Copies were sent to Secretary Connor, Charles Schultze, David Bell, Gardner Ackley, and Robertson.

[2] Not attached; a copy of a draft on the same subject, November 29, by Bator, is ibid., National Security File, Subject File, Balance of Payments, Vol. 3 [1 of 2], Box 2. This draft letter is identical to the version dated December 2 and released on December 5; see footnote 4, Document 83.

[3] See page 2—(on McNamara's Memo). [Handwritten footnote in the source text. The memorandum has not been identified.]

[4] See footnotes 3 and 4, Document 83.

[5] See footnote 5, Document 83.

members of the Executive Committee. We'll know the President's preference on this by Wednesday morning.

Francis M. Bator[6]

---

[6] Printed from a copy that bears this typed signature.

**85.   Memorandum From Secretary of the Treasury Fowler to
President Johnson[1]**

Washington, January 27, 1966.

SUBJECT

1965 Balance of Payments Figures

Following the State of the Union Message we received from the
reporting banks flash figures on the balance of payments, which showed
a surplus of $87 million for the month of December and an over-all deficit
of $1,207 million for the year. (Attachment A)[2]

On January 26, 1966, I received the "wire" figure (based on reports
from more banks than can be included in the early "flash" figure). It
showed a December *deficit* of $16 million (as compared with the *surplus*
of $87 million in the "flash") and an over-all deficit for the year 1965 of
$1,310 million. (Attachment B)[3]

It will be another three weeks or so before the final balance of payments figures are in, compiled as they are from a more detailed breakdown of components than can be had for the "flash" and "wire" figures.
More often than not, the final total is somewhat worse than the "wire"
figure—usually within a range of $30 million.

I will report to you as soon as I have complete information in hand.

Henry H. Fowler

---

[1] Source: Johnson Library, National Security File, Subject File, Balance of Payments,
Vol. 3 [1 of 2], Box 2. Secret. Sent under cover of a January 27 note to President Johnson from
Fowler that reads: "I would advise that under no circumstances should any information on
the figures in the attached memorandum be given out. As you know, we take the utmost
care to give out no figures until the final ones become available although, as you know, their
necessary distribution for working purposes within the government has, in the past,
resulted in leaks."
[2] Attachment A, dated January 20, is not printed.
[3] Not found.

86.   Circular Telegram From the Department of State to Certain Posts[1]

Washington, February 14, 1966, 7:50 p.m.

1544. Treasury Secretary Fowler, Commerce Secretary Connor, FRB Chairman Martin and Governor Robertson held press conference February 14 on 1965 balance of payments. Text of statements being airmailed. Key points follow: Secretary Fowler reported that liquidity deficit 1965 $1.3 billion, improvement of $1.5 billion over 1964 in very large part attributable to effectiveness of voluntary cooperation program.

1965 record plus tightening of program for 1966 give reason to believe will be continuing improvement in private capital areas. Prospect of legislation to encourage foreign portfolio investment in U.S., increase in investment income, moderation of direct investment outflows, and expanding trade surplus offer most promising areas for improvement in 1966. Main imponderables are rising balance of payments costs in Southeast Asia and direct and indirect impact of Viet Nam on domestic economy and trade. Not possible to say how these factors will affect 1966 figures. Equilibrium (balance on liquidity concept plus or minus $250 million) remains 1966 goal. U.S. cannot be certain that "present measures as they currently operate will lead us to that goal if foreign exchange costs of Viet Nam rise sharply over increases presently projected." As of now program believed effective and see no reason to change its character.

Deficit on official settlements somewhat less than $1.4 billion. Failure private dollar holdings to grow ascribed to large increase in 1964, dollar repatriation by American firms, tightening of domestic credit in several countries, and improvement in outlook for sterling.

Adverse factors in 1965 included trade surplus which declined from $6.7 billion to $4.8 billion, tourist deficit which rose from $1.6 billion to $1.8 billion, direct investment abroad which larger although fourth quarter figure not yet available, and $500 million conversion of long-term assets into liquid assets by U.K. Government.

Favorable factors included shift in bank credit from $2.5 billion outflow to slight inflow, shift in non-bank claims on foreigners, excluding U.S. purchases of foreign securities from outflow of $900 million to inflow of around $300 million.

Secretary Connor explained deterioration in trade account by slower pace of economic activity in major foreign markets and accelera-

---

[1] Source: Department of State, Central Files, FN 12 US. Unclassified. Drafted by F.L. Widman (Treasury) on February 14; cleared by Trued and approved by Richard N. Cooper. Sent to Bern, Bonn, Brussels, The Hague, London, Paris, Ottawa, Rome, Stockholm, Tokyo, and Zurich.

tion in domestic economic activity. Also emphasized sharp turnabout in direct investment outflow after mid-1965, with annual rate at first half at $4.1 billion and total figure expected be well below $3.4 billion. Connor noted also borrowing by American companies in fourth quarter of about $175 million through sale of securities to foreign investors, which will be recorded in U.S. statistics. Additional sum of about same amount raised through sale of securities by subsidiaries abroad which does not affect U.S. balance of payments data. Amount borrowed by firms incorporated in U.S. can be considered partial offset to direct investment outflow.

Governor Robertson reported that foreign loans and investments of banks reporting under voluntary program showed increase for 1965 of only $155 million. Thus banking system was $320 million below target suggested by 1965 guidelines. With this margin plus additional expansion consistent with 1966 guidelines, banks expected to have more than ample leeway to accommodate all priority credit needs in 1966.

In response to question re impact direct investment guidelines on Canada, Connor said expected impact be small but planned watch situation carefully.

Rusk

---

87.   Department of the Treasury Memorandum[1]

Washington, March 18, 1966.

TAX ON TOURIST TRAVEL

If it is found necessary to institute a tax for the purpose of reducing tourist travel and expenditures abroad, the following would appear to be a suitable tax for this purpose.

---

[1] Source: Department of State, Ball Papers: Lot 74 D 272, Balance of Payments. Confidential. The source text bears no drafting information, but when Fowler later forwarded the memorandum to the President, he identified the memorandum as a Department of the Treasury paper (see Document 90). Sent under cover of an April 26 letter from Acting Secretary of the Treasury Barr to Under Secretary of State Ball. In this cover letter, Barr wrote in part: "At the President's request, I am recirculating the attached memorandum entitled 'Tax on Tourist Travel'; so that you may give it further careful consideration. Would you please prepare any comments you may have in time for a meeting Secretary Fowler will convene on the subject next week."

Over-all Objectives of Tax

To achieve its maximum impact on reducing tourist expenditures abroad, the tax should combine the following two features:

(1) The tax should be of such a nature as to deter a substantial group of people from making trips abroad that they would have otherwise taken; and
(2) In the case of tourists who do decide to make their trips regardless of the tax, the tax should be designed to minimize the period for which they stay abroad.

The first objective can best be obtained by requiring people to pay out a substantial sum of money before being permitted to leave the country. The second objective can best be obtained from a tax based on the number of days the person stays abroad.

A flat tax for each trip, computed without regard to the length of the trip, would deter some people from making trips but would have relatively little effect on reducing the length of stay of those people who decide to make the trip regardless of the tax. In fact, such a tax could have the effect of encouraging some longer trips than would otherwise have been taken on the theory that once the tax is paid, the tourist may take the attitude that he might as well get the maximum benefit out of his trip.

A tax graduated on the basis of the number of days abroad without requiring an initial outlay would minimize the length of trips but might not have a substantial impact on reducing the number of people making trips. Therefore, a tax which combines these two features would appear to be the most desirable type of tax.

It is also important in designing this type of tax that it be readily understandable by the public, for if people do not understand their liability, its deterrent effect may be substantially reduced. This objective requires simplicity. Moreover, as with any tax, ease of administration and compliance is a desirable objective.

General Outline of Tax

Basically, the proposal would impose a tax of a specified amount per day of travel abroad, with a requirement that a substantial amount of the tax be deposited before the individual leaves the United States. The following is a more detailed description of the proposal, utilizing a rate structure that would reduce foreign exchange expenditures by at least $585 million per year. If a different balance of payments effect is desired, the rates would have to be adjusted accordingly. A discussion of the impact of this proposal on expenditures is included at the end of this memorandum.

(a) *Rate of tax and amount of deposit.* The tax would be at a rate of $6 per individual for each day spent abroad, with a requirement that $100 of the tax be deposited by each individual before he leaves the United States.

Under this approach, if a husband and wife travel together, each would pay the basic $6.00 per day tax and a total deposit of $200 would be required. Taking into account the 5-day exemption described below, this $100 deposit would be equivalent to the tax due on a trip of about three weeks which would appear to be about the minimum length of a vacation trip to Europe. In recognition of the fact that vacation trips to Canada, Mexico, and the Caribbean may be of shorter duration, the deposit would be reduced to $50 for individuals leaving on trips to these areas.

If it is desired to make this tax progressive, one way of accomplishing this would be to impose the tax at a daily rate of 1/10 of 1 percent of the individual's adjusted gross income for tax purposes, with a minimum of $6 per day and a maximum of $50 per day. The amount of the deposit should probably remain at $100 for simplicity's sake.

(b) *Maximum tax.* In order not to impose too heavy a burden on people who go abroad for extended stays, such as for visits to relatives, the tax would apply to a maximum of 90 days of a trip. Utilizing the flat $6.00 per day rate, this would mean a maximum tax of $540 per trip for each individual.

(c) *Exemptions.*

(1) *Trips of five days or less.* In order to exempt short trips to Mexico and Canada and short business trips abroad, the first five days of a trip would be exempt. Moreover, individuals who certify that their trip will be five days or less would be exempt from the deposit requirement.

(2) *Students.* An exemption from the tax and deposit requirement would be granted to individuals going abroad to enroll full-time in a foreign school. In order to keep this exemption administrable, it would not be extended to students whose educational pursuits abroad are in the nature of travel or informal instruction from an individual.

(3) *Businessmen transferred abroad.* An exemption from both the tax and deposit requirement would be granted to employees (and their families) who are being transferred abroad for an extended period, such as six months to a year. A similar exemption would be granted to self-employed people who are going to operate their business abroad for such an extended period.

(c) *Procedures for paying tax.* The tax would be administered by the Internal Revenue Service. The airlines, shipping companies, and customs officials (in the case of automobile travel to Canada and Mexico) would be required to collect the deposit required of individuals before they can leave the United States. Any additional tax due, or a refund of part of the deposit, would be paid or claimed by the tourist on his return to the United States. The mechanics of the system would work as follows:

(1) A return form would be developed and distributed to the carriers, and to the customs officials on the Canadian and Mexican borders. Prior to his departure from the United States, each individual would be

given a return form on which is stamped the date of his departure. The individual would, at that time, fill in his name, address, and social security number and give a copy of the form and his $100 deposit ($50 in the case of trips to Mexico, Canada and the Caribbean) to the carrier (or customs official). The carrier (or customs official) would indicate on the original retained by the individual that the deposit had been made. If the individual falls within one of the exempt categories listed above, he would so certify on the form and would not have to deposit any money. The carrier (or customs official) would then forward the copy of the form it received with the deposit, if any, to the Internal Revenue Service. The individual would retain the original of the form to serve as his tax return.

(2) On his return to the United States, the individual would present his copy of the return form to the incoming carrier (or customs official) to have the date of his reentry stamped thereon. The individual would then compute the actual amount of tax due for the trip on this return form and remit any balance due to the Internal Revenue Service within a specified period after his return. Immediate payment could be required if desired although this may present a problem for an individual who is short of funds on his return. The form would serve as a refund claim if the deposit exceeded his tax. An individual qualifying for an exemption would, nevertheless, file his return with the Internal Revenue Service although no tax would be remitted.

If an individual loses his copy of the return form before coming back to the United States, he would obtain a new form from the incoming carrier (or customs official), on which is stamped his date of reentry. He would then complete the return, including information as to his date of exit and the amount of his deposit, and file it with the Internal Revenue Service with any tax due. Since the Internal Revenue Service will have already received a copy of the form filled out when the individual departed, which indicates the date of his departuure and whether he made a deposit, it will have information from which to verify the final return.

(3) In order not to impede daily commuter traffic into Canada and Mexico, some procedure will have to be worked out for identifying a commuter so that it is not necessary to stop him each time and go through the formal reporting requirements. Possibly the border card system used for Mexico could be extended to Canada.

Effect on Foreign Exchange Expenditures

On the basis of the travel estimates for 1966, it is estimated that the above described tax would save from $585 million to $1,170 million in foreign exchange per year. This includes savings from individuals who forego trips on account of the tax as well as savings attributable to reduced expenditures by those who do make trips despite the tax. The lower figure would result, if on an over-all basis, foreign expenditures were reduced dollar for dollar by the amount of tax or potential tax. The higher figure would result if the reduction in foreign expenditures was twice the amount of tax or potential tax. There is no definitive answer as to how travelers would react to such a tax. About the best that can be said is that it seems quite likely that the foreign exchange savings would be between the two extremes.

Any estimate of savings in foreign exchange should be adjusted downward for possible exemptions. An exemption for students taking at least a full semester abroad could be ignored as it might involve less than .3 of 1 percent of the total of travelers abroad for over five days. An exemption for students taking summer trips could represent 10 percent of the base. (In 1963, 12.6 percent of the passports were issued to persons who listed their occupation as "student".) Military personnel and their dependents are excluded from the basic figures. Business personnel going abroad for extended tours of duty also probably are of minor consequence. An exemption for ordinary business trips (over five days) might represent as much as 10 percent of the travel.

---

88.   **Minutes of Meeting of the Cabinet Committee on Balance of Payments**[1]

Washington, March 25, 1966.

The following persons were present:

Treasury Dept.—Secretary Fowler, Under Secretaries Barr and Deming, Assistant Secretary Trued and Mr. Schaffner
Defense Dept.—Secretary McNamara and Mr. Robert Kovarik
Commerce Dept.—Secretary Connor, Mr. Gerald Pollack, and Mr. Lawrence McQuade
State Dept.—Under Secretary Mann, Mr. A. Solomon, and Mr. Cooper
Agriculture Dept.—Under Secretary Schnittker and Mr. Koffsky
AID—Mr. Gaud, Mr. Gustav Ranis, and Mr. Gordon Chase
Trade Negotiations—Governor Herter and Mr. Malmgren
Budget—Assistant Director Zwick, Mr. R. Richardson
CEA—Chairman Ackley, Mr. Arthur Okun, and Mr. Frank Schiff

---

[1] Source: Johnson Library, Fowler Papers, International Balance of Payments Committee—Classified Material: Cabinet Committee Meeting, 3/25/66, Box 53. Secret.

White House—Mr. F. Bator
Federal Reserve—Chairman Martin, Governor Daane, and Governor Brimmer

The Secretary said that major changes since last November's forecast of the 1966 situation resulted from the Vietnam situation and the trade outlook; that it was prudent to plan for a lower trade surplus than had been forecast. He wanted to present additional steps involving $1-1/2 billion of balance-of-payments savings this year for the President's consideration about a month from now.

Secretary McNamara said that DOD expenditures abroad were now estimated at about $350 million higher for 1966 than contemplated last November. (The $350 million includes the "up to $200 million" which was footnoted in last November's projection.) The Secretary said that there was no possibility of reducing deployment of troops abroad, but there were possibilities of increasing procurement of U.S. goods. Petroleum purchases could be shifted back to the United States, although at a 125% increase in price. Altogether, he felt that it might be possible to save $125 million of expenditure in Southeast Asia during calendar year 1966 by returning to the U.S. procurement of P.O.L., various types of equipment and supplies. He concluded by saying that Defense would try to pare $350 million off the CY 1966 projected net military expenditure abroad of $2,152.8 million, thus bringing it down to $1,800 million.

The Secretary asked whether most of the DOD increase in expenditure outside of Vietnam was due to rising prices, and Secretary McNamara assured him that it was. The Secretary then asked whether the projected $350 million balance-of-payments saving would be made despite rising prices abroad, and Secretary McNamara indicated that that was what he contemplated. The savings would include a number of measures in addition to returning procurement to the U.S.—for example, it would include any increase in voluntary savings of military personnel abroad that might be induced by higher interest rates on their savings.

The Secretary next asked about the possibilities of diverting part of the increased reserves accruing to Vietnam, Thailand, Taiwan, Korea, and the Philippines (from our military expenditures) into U.S. agency bonds. He said that State Department help in this matter would be needed and wondered whether a discreet circular to the Embassies in these countries would be useful to get the negotiations started.

Mr. Solomon said that the State Department was already trying to get the Vietnamese Government to invest in U.S. bonds (presumably agency bonds). He pointed out that DOD expenditures in Southeast Asia were over a billion dollars higher than in 1961. He and Mr. Trued would work together in developing an approach to the Governments of the countries involved.

The Secretary asked if anything more could be done to press offset negotiations with Japan and Spain. Secretary McNamara replied that there was no prospect for accomplishing anything with these countries this year but that he thought this should be pushed hard in the future. The Secretary then referred to the importance of obtaining maximum payments during CY 1966 from Germany under the offset agreement. Secretary McNamara said that, as far as he was concerned, the Germans would be faced in this negotiation with the prospect of "no money—no troops."

Mr. Gaud then described recent AID efforts to achieve balance-of-payments benefits by encouraging more LDC expenditures in the U.S. He indicated they had been educating the missions to give this subject much more attention. He proposed that a committee be set up to analyze four types of countries: one group where we do well in exporting on a commercial basis and where we have a significant aid program; another where we do well but have no aid program; third group where we do poorly even though we have an aid program; and a fourth type where we do poorly and have no program.

Secretary Connor said that he would set up a meeting of the appropriate agencies to see what could be done to improve U.S. commercial markets in the LCD's. The Secretary indicated that Mr. Herter's office might be interested as well as State, AID, and Agriculture.

Mr. Gaud then went on to discuss dollar financing of local currency costs in AID-recipient countries. He said this problem had been reduced to a magnitude of "ten's of million's of dollars" and that where it was done at all, it was done under a letter of credit procedure. There was a question of how effective this tied procedure actually was, and this matter was being studied by Mr. Zwick's committee.

The Secretary inquired whether AID could draw up a budget of maximum local cost financing for this year leaving the distribution of the total amount among various recipient countries on a flexible basis. He felt that with such a budget, it would be possible to trip individual country programs more effectively. Mr. Gaud promised to provide an estimated range for these expenditures, the countries in which they would be made, and the reasons for doing it.

With regard to expediting deliveries of U.S. goods rather than procuring offshore, Mr. Gaud said that as of March 15, AID was buying offshore only for Vietnam and Laos; and that offshore procurement for these two countries would be made only in countries where we have special AID interest and a tied letter of credit arrangement—for example, in Taiwan, Korea, Thailand, etc. Furthermore, he said that in most cases offshore procurement was limited to items of which the U.S. is a net importer. He said that the current procedure will mean more procurement in the U.S. He indicated that some items, however, would be very expensive if procured from the U.S. rather than offshore and in some cases transportation costs effectively ruled it out—e.g., cement.

Mr. Gaud said that he thought AID recipients could be encouraged to hold some of their reserves here and specifically referred to Tunisia as a possibility. The Secretary noted that that would make these countries realize that we had a balance-of-payments problem.

The next subject discussed was the operation of the gold budget procedure. Mr. Zwick said that the March 15 submission was the latest and that this submission had been accompanied by a Presidential reminder to each agency to take a hard look at its overseas expenditures. He said that submissions had not yet been received from State, DOD, Interior, Peace Corps, HEW, and that the submission from AID, as yet, was only an informal one. He also said that submissions by NSF, NASA, AEC, and Treasury were not complete in various respects. The Secretary indicated that he had gone over the Treasury submission and that Mr. Zwick may have not seen the most recent version.

Mr. Zwick indicated that the gold budget procedure had degenerated. Budget intended to have oral hearings on the basis of the March 15 submission with some of the agencies and to ask for hard explanations of deviations of expenditures from earlier projections. Budget would then send a report through the Cabinet Committee on Balance of Payments to the President. He felt that the State Department would have to build a "gold budget" procedure into its Embassy administrative system. He also emphasized that to get any real savings from the "gold budget" procedure required program changes. He thought that unless agencies were prepared to face up to this fact, a great deal of time and effort would be spent with no appreciable results in the form of balance-of-payments savings.

Mr. Solomon indicated that State Department was trying to have more international conferences held in Washington as a balance-of-payments measure. Under Secretary Mann indicated that there were possibilities for additional savings abroad by reducing the number of military attachés, reducing the number of administrative personnel in the Embassies, and by restricting services to American tourists. Mr. Bator said he would like to know what portion of expenditures abroad are for administrative overhead. Under Secretary Mann referred to the fact that the Veterans Administration maintains a staff in Mexico to service the handling of paychecks to U.S. retired persons there.

Mr. Zwick went on to indicate that if you take out DOD and AID expenditures abroad plus uncontrollable items, such as interest payments to foreigners, there remained about $486 million of disbursements abroad per year, of which State and USIA make $300 million. This leaves about $180 million for other agency expenditures. In answer to a question about research expenditures abroad, he said that project research expenditures, other than DOD, were about $30 million. Under Secretary Barr indicated that any failure to make all possible savings exposed the Government to criticism from the business community as well as the Congress.

The Secretary asked when the Budget Bureau could formulate some alternative programs designed to achieve balance-of-payments savings through some priority rating among the various overseas programs. Mr. Zwick thought this would be possible by the 15th or 20th of April. The Secretary indicated that the Committee would look for BOB suggestions at that time to consider as possible recommendations to the President.

Discussion then turned to possibilities of debt prepayments. Mr. Solomon indicated that State Department would give the Committee its estimate next week of the negotiating possibilities. The Secretary asked Messrs. Deming and Trued to work on this subject from the Treasury side. He then asked about the possibilities of increased savings from overseas personnel. He pointed out the President's great interest in the voluntary savings promotion plan and that pressure on the military abroad to do more savings would not be discriminatory, since more pressure is going to be put on civilian personnel here at home. Mr. Mann thought that the salaries of junior State Department officers abroad were too low to offer much possibility for increased savings; but he suggested we might ask Government people here and abroad to buy U.S. automobiles instead of foreign cars.

Mr. Kovarik said that he thought with a 6% or 7% interest rate on savings, DOD could get something additional from military personnel. Mr. Kovarik and Secretary Connor emphasized that anything involuntary in the Government personnel field should be tied to some type of tourist restriction.

On the latter subject, the Secretary indicated that he understood estimated departures of U.S. tourists for Europe were up 11.6% above the first quarter of last year. He had talked about the tourist problem with the Vice President, and he thought a great number of steps could be taken to earn more foreign tourist dollars in the U.S. He thought that a centralized management within the Government was a good step in this direction. The other alternative would be to place a tax on U.S. tourism abroad or adopt a program of strong moral suasion. Under Secretary Mann inquired about what would happen to the U.S. tourist industry in Canada and Mexico if we did any such thing. He pointed out that Mexico earns $500 million a year net from its U.S. tourist trade and that any reduction of this would hurt them. The Secretary said he would welcome any comments on this subject—whether along the lines of continuing as we are, or centralizing management responsibility for promoting foreign tourism in the U.S.—something he would regard as a minimum step—or imposing a tax or strong moral suasion on U.S. tourists. He said we must ask Congress to cut the $100 duty-free gift limit. Secretary Connor said he would prefer a vigorous moral suasion effort to a tax. He thought such an effort would get enough citizens to thinking about balance-of-payments savings that some could actually be achieved. The Secretary asked what agency had responsibility for encouraging the holding of conventions in the U.S. Secretary Connor said that his agency did and that they had been working on this.

Discussion then turned to the subject of increased wheat exports. Mr. Koffsky said that the Soviet-bloc may not be in the market for U.S. wheat this year at all but that at any event, we will not know for a few months. If they were to come in, they might buy as much as $100 million on an annual basis. He pointed out, however, that the U.S.S.R. does not like the discrimination in cargo preference and, therefore, might try to avoid buying here at all. In the long run, he thought the solution depended on the Labor and Justice Departments. The Secretary inquired whether a long-run package involving some short-term subsidy of transport cost might be the best solution and Mr. Koffsky agreed that it would.

With regard to raising prices on U.S. wheat export, Mr. Koffsky said that they had moved the price up about 2/3rds of the $.10 a bushel that had earlier been mentioned. When the 1966 crop outlook is more clear—around the middle of the year—they would hope to be able to move up the other 1/3rd. With prices $.10 per bushel higher, the annual savings for the balance of payments would amount to about $45 million a year. He said that the over-all outlook for agricultural exports in 1966 suggested a $300 million increase over the 1965 level.

The Secretary referred to the Douglas Task Force recommendations on liberalizing export credit and guarantees and providing a special rediscount facility. Secretary Connor said there were three Task Force reports and that he felt that the chairmen should be given a chance to discuss their reports and their recommendations at an early meeting of the Cabinet Committee on Balance of Payments.[2] Mr. Daane indicated that this would be satisfactory with the Federal Reserve, although they had not studied these reports. Mr. Trued suggested that it might be better to have the meeting with a smaller group of agencies having a direct interest, and Governor Brimmer suggested that, in view of the highly technical nature of many of the Task Force recommendations, the Executive Committee should take a close look first. The Secretary then suggested the following procedure. The Executive Committee should prepare a concise summary and evaluation of the issues in each report. This would be followed by a preliminary meeting of five or six appropriate agencies to get familiar with the issues. Then there could be a meeting of the Cabinet Committee on Balance of Payments with the Task Force chairmen, as

---

[2] These reports have not been further identified.

guests, or of a smaller group of department heads. With regard to establishment of individual firm export targets, Secretary Connor said that he did not think this made much sense in connection with Commerce's present program in view of the many problems involved in setting up export quotas. He indicated that his Advisory Committee was meeting with him on Monday, March 28, and that this subject might be further considered there.

The Secretary then mentioned the subject of stockpile disposals which he said combined price stabilization, budgetary, and balance-of-payments objectives. The Secretary asked about the feasibility of Government industry working groups to improve U.S. competitiveness from both an export and import viewpoint. Secretary Connor thought such a procedure would not be worthwhile now while the Commerce program was going on and that in fact it could lead to a lot of mischief. Secretary Connor then gave a progress report on the Commerce voluntary program. He said that small companies were having trouble with the report form that was due in mid-February under the tightened program. The data for about 500 companies, however, show that the 1965 program was a success; and that a $1.3 billion target was reached by the 500 firms. They also repatriated about $400 million of liquid assets from abroad. With regard to the 1966 program, the reports of 541 companies show figures which do not reconcile with the latest OBE figures on projected plant and equipment expenditures abroad. The latter which will be announced shortly will show a 24% higher level for 1966 than the actual for 1965; and this implies that a great deal of foreign borrowing will be necessary to meet the two-year target. The companies did show a much better performance in the last half of 1965—better than had been anticipated—so that the 1966 savings will be somewhat less than had been anticipated.

Mr. Bator asked Secretary Connor whether he thought that the OBE estimates of plant and equipment expenditures were overly pessimistic, in view of the decline in last year's actual expenditures below the projected level. Secretary Connor thought the OBE figures might be a good indicator in a stable period but not in one of rapid change. He thought the estimate for 1966, however, might be closer to the truth than last year's projection proved to be in view of the fact that some companies had carried over expenditures from 1965 into 1966.

Governor Daane reported that as of the end of February, 1966, banks were more than $800 million below their permissible ceiling and $255 million below the December 31, 1964, base.

Philip P. Schaffner[3]

---

[3] Printed from a copy that bears this typed signature.

89.   **Memorandum From the Executive Committee of the Cabinet Committee on Balance of Payments to the Committee**[1]

Washington, undated.

SUBJECT

A program of measures to reduce the 1966 potential deficit

Your Executive Committee has undertaken a thorough review of all the balance of payments accounts, seeking to develop a program which could be used to reinforce existing measures and assure a reduction in whatever deficit may be in prospect. The Executive Committee does not have a new forecast of the balance of payments for this year and believes that it is impossible, at this time, to bring forward any precise estimates. However, there seems to be a strong probability that the likely deficit will need sharp trimming. We are seeking to devise a program of additional measures that might gain savings in the order of $1.5 billion this year. The results are set forth below.

Measures to be acted upon immediately

(1) *As regards Government expenditures:*

(a) AID should explore the most feasible means of reducing the impact of expenditures on the balance of payments below the forecast made in last December's program. (*Background Information:* AID has undertaken a review of its activities to determine the implications of securing a $100 million reduction in the balance of payments impact of its program. Mr. Bell may wish to comment on this item.)

(b) Military expenditures (net) should be brought back to the $1.8 billion level forecast in the December program (a reduction of $350 million from the January forecast). (*Background Information:* The January forecast showed net military expenditures abroad rising to $2.15 billion. Secretary McNamara may wish to comment on this item and the implications of the $350 million cut in anticipated net spending. A significant part will involve purchases in the United States of petroleum and petroleum products; action is underway to confer with Secretary Udall to discuss domestic production allowables.)

---

[1] Source: Department of State, Ball Papers: Lot 74 D 272, Balance of Payments. Secret. The memorandum was sent under cover of an April 18 memorandum from Assistant Secretary of the Treasury Trued to the Cabinet Committee on Balance of Payments. Trued informed the Committee members: "Secretary Fowler has asked me to send you the attached material which will form the basis for discussion at tomorrow's Principals only meeting of the Cabinet Committee on Balance of Payments. The meeting will take place at 10:30 a.m. in the Secretary's conference room." Minutes of this meeting have not been found, but see Document 90. Copies of this memorandum were sent to Vice President Humphrey and Chairman Martin of the Federal Reserve System.

(c) Negotiations looking to offset agreements should be undertaken with Spain and Japan as quickly as possible. (*Background Information:* A full offset with Spain over a 5-year period is now in effect so that there is no occasion to negotiate further on an offset. However, Spanish military requirements are substantial and there is expectation that additional sales of military equipment will in fact take place. As regards Japan, it is proposed to send a group to Tokyo to initiate discussions looking toward an offset arrangement in conjunction with discussions seeking to obtain some debt prepayment or investment of Japanese reserves in non-liquid liabilities of the United States, or both. For this purpose, a Treasury, State and Federal Reserve Mission visiting the Far East, under 2 (b) below, will be joined in Tokyo by DOD representatives. Negotiating instructions have been prepared—copy attached.)[2]

(d) Every effort should be made to gain maximum advance payments during 1966 under the German offset agreement. (*Background Information:* The German offset provides $1,350 million for FY 1966–FY 1967 combined. Arrangements are close to completion that will assure receipt by the United States of $721 million in CY 1966. This requires a special arrangement with the Central Bank of Germany since German budget availabilities would not cover these payments. It is contemplated that, at an appropriate time, we will explore with German officials the possibility of some debt prepayment, taking advantage of the same type of arrangement.)

(e) Gold budget controls should be made effective to assure over-all expenditure ceilings held to absolutely essential levels, with effective review procedures. (*Background Information:* Budget Director Schultze may wish to comment on the status of the gold budget review.)

(2) *As regards foreign debt to the U.S. and foreign central bank reserve portfolios:*

(a) Negotiations should be promptly undertaken to obtain as much further World War II debt prepayments as possible. (It does not seem realistic to expect to obtain more than $300 million.) (*Background Information:* Debt outstanding includes Austria, $47 million; Belgium, $73 million; Britain, $4 billion; France, $392 million; West Germany, $225 million; Italy, $144 million; Japan, $786 million, of which $409 of GARIOA account; Netherlands, $66 million; Spain, $412 million. It is anticipated these negotiations will be undertaken very shortly after the meeting of the Group of Ten Deputies in Washington on April 19.)

(b) Negotiations be undertaken immediately with other countries, including Taiwan, Philippines, Korea, Japan, Thailand and Vietnam—all recipients of increased military expenditures in Southeast Asia—as well

---

[2] Circular telegram 2034, April 16, is attached but not printed. A copy is also in Department of State, Central Files, FN 12 US.

as Mexico and Venezuela, to gain investment of as much as possible of their official reserves in non-liquid liabilities of the U.S. ($200 million). (*Background Information:* Information on recent changes in reserves holdings of the five Southeast Asian countries—excluding Vietnam—is contained in the attached cable of instructions (Circular 2034, April 16, 1966). Defense expenditures in the five countries are expected to increase $150 million from calendar 1965 to calendar 1966. A special task force has been established in connection with financial problems in Vietnam and measures, if feasible, to handle its reserves will be dealt with as part of the over-all problem.)

(3) *As regards travel expenditures:*

(a) Centralized program management be promptly adopted under the U.S. Travel Service to coordinate the Government travel program, perform liaison with States and the private sector and administer all funds directed toward promoting tourism in the U.S.; to this end, all agencies should support the request for a larger budget for USTS before the Congress. (*Background Information:* Correspondence between Secretary Fowler and the Vice President regarding this matter is attached.[3] Commerce has prepared a memorandum describing how the efforts of USTS would be made more effective with annual budgets of $4.7 million, $10 million, and $15 million and, in the case of the $15 million budget, an expanded mission involving *both* the promotion of international and domestic travel. Secretary Connor may wish to comment on these alternatives.)

(b) In conjunction with a possible travel tax, renewed consideration should be given to obtaining powers for contingent use of a higher interest equalization tax (savings could amount to $50–$100 million) and also for broadening its coverage to direct investment (in which case savings could be much higher).

(c) Renewed consideration should be given to a tax on travel abroad. (*Background Information:* A technique for imposing a tax has been developed which would impose a per diem tax on travel abroad—$6 per individual per day—with the requirement that $100 be deposited before departure from the United States. Foreign exchange savings could amount to roughly $600–$1,100 million. For the Caribbean, Canada and Mexico, the deposit would be $50 per individual. The maximum would be set at $540 per trip per individual. The tax could be made progressive by imposing the tax at a daily rate of 1/10 of 1% of the individual's adjusted gross income for tax purposes with a minimum of $6 per day and a maximum of $50 per day. A lower tax rate would of course bring less savings. Consideration would need to be given to measures that

---

[3] The correspondence consists of two memoranda, both from Vice President Humphrey to Secretary Fowler, one dated April 13 and the other dated March 25, which includes a draft letter from Fowler to Vice President Humphrey. These memoranda are not printed.

would ease the very sharp impact on the travel industry in the United States.)

(d) A proposal to cut the customs duty-free allowance from $100 to $10 should be submitted to the Congress ($20–$30 million in 1966; up to $100 million in 1967).

(4) *As regards private capital:*

(a) Direct investment outflows should be held to the $2.4 billion level or lower (to be sought through individual consultations rather than a public change in the program).

(5) *As regards exports and imports:*

(a) The Export-Import Bank has developed a number of steps, including a limited rediscount facility, to reinsure the availability of export financing. The proposed steps should be introduced promptly.

(b) Emphasis should be given to the need for U.S. businesses to remain export conscious and to insure that an appropriate part of output continues to be sold abroad—over the longer run, this is essential to maintaining markets.

(c) Export consciousness should be reinforced throughout our missions abroad, including aggressive effort in aid recipient countries, to reinsure the effectiveness of "tying" and to help gain additional markets. (*Background Information:* AID has prepared a memorandum on this subject, and Mr. Bell may wish to comment on it.)

(d) The United States must be in a position to respond if the Soviet Bloc offers to make further purchases of wheat in the free world. In the immediate case, a method of subsidized transport costs to overcome the 50–50 shipping requirement must be available.

(e) Consideration should be given to raising the export price of wheat further upward if the 1966 crop outlook makes it feasible.

(f) Maximize sales from stockpile. (*Background Information:* Items which we import and which are in stockpile surplus include: aluminum, $700 million; bauxite, $85 million; lead, $400 million; nickel, $225 million; rubber, $475 million; tin, $325 million; and zinc, $380 million.)

Further Studies

The following studies are underway and should be agressively pursued over the next few months:

(1) A four-country study relating U.S. exports to aid status.

(2) Review of the NEEC Task Force reports for possible further measures to enhance export potential.

(3) Study of industries to determine export potential and means of enhancing likelihood of realizing the full potential.

(4) Analysis and evaluation of the interrelationship between exports and private direct investment.

90.   Memorandum From Secretary of the Treasury Fowler to
President Johnson[1]

Washington, April 23, 1966.

SUBJECT

Balance of Payments Reprogramming on Tuesday, April 19

On last Tuesday we had a three-hour closed unofficial meeting for
Principals only of the Cabinet Committee on Balance of Payments.[2] The
purpose of the meeting was to consider what additional measures might
be programmed to gain additional savings in the order of at least $1.5 bil-
lion this year. This is desirable in view of the facts that (a) our trade balance is deteriorating both due to high activity here and the indirect costs
of Vietnam and (b) the direct foreign exchange costs of Vietnam are rising. The first quarter will show a deficit at an annual rate of $2 billion plus
in contrast to the $1.3 billion deficit in 1965—both figures on the "over-
all" basis we use. The outlook for the remainder of the year is for a substantial deficit that might well exceed last year's.

I am attaching for your information the memorandum which was
the basis of our discussion.[3] Those in attendance include the following:

The Vice President
Treasury: Secretary Fowler
                                   Assistant Secretary Trued
Defense: Assistant Secretary
                                      Robert N. Anthony
State: Under Secretary Ball
Commerce: Secretary Connor
Agriculture: Under Secretary Schnittker
AID: David Bell
Trade Negotiations: Governor Herter
Budget: Director Schultze
CEA: Mr. Ackley
White House: Mr. Bator
Federal Reserve: Governor Robertson

(Secretary McNamara was unable to attend at the last moment
because of hearings on the Hill.)

---

[1] Source: Johnson Library, Bator Papers, Balance of Payments, 1966 [2 of 2], Box 15.
Secret. The memorandum was sent under cover of a handwritten note to Bator, April 23, in
which Fowler wrote: "The President reviewed these Saturday afternoon—April 23 in our
conference. I am transmitting them for his additional reference or for his files."
[2] No other minutes of this meeting, summarized in the memorandum printed here,
have been found.
[3] Not attached, but presumably it is Document 89.

The most significant aspect of the meeting was general opposition to any proposal for a tax on travel abroad as outlined in Item 3c of the attached memorandum on page 4, except for Treasury and Defense, who are keeping an open mind on the question. I think it would be fair to say that everyone else is definitely opposed.

However, even those opposed to a tax program on travel were in general agreement that the present situation was unsatisfactory and that something in the nature of a voluntary program to appeal to the American tourists to stay at home for the duration of the Vietnamese hostilities was well worth considering. This would put the treatment of travel on an equivalent basis to the voluntary programs for financial institutions and corporations.

Without some effective affirmative move to cut back substantially on the travel deficit, I can see in the attached program of possible measures additional savings in the order of magnitude of only $750 million.

We shall have to face up to decisions as to the announcement of the additional measures recited in the memorandum including whatever we decide on travel between now and the 20th of May when the official first quarter figures are announced.

Therefore, upon my return from the Inter-American Development Bank meeting in Mexico City next Thursday,[4] I would like to sit down with you and some of your advisors and discuss this situation informally. Unless you have some preference to the contrary I believe these informal discussions of new programming are preferable to official meetings of the Cabinet Committee on Balance of Payments.

For your further information on the travel problem I am attaching a memorandum worked out here in the Treasury Department entitled "Tax on Tourist Travel".[5] This has not been put forward as a concrete proposal by Treasury but as a contingency measure describing the most suitable tax for that purpose if a tax restraint should ever be determined to be necessary.

Henry H. Fowler

---

[4] April 28.
[5] See Document 87.

91.   Report From the Voluntary Cooperation Program
       Coordinating Group to the Cabinet Committee on Balance of
       Payments[1]

Washington, April 26, 1966.

SUBJECT

Operating Problems under the Voluntary Cooperation Program

Since the announcement of the President's balance-of-payments program, a small informal group has been meeting periodically in the Treasury Department to discuss operating problems arising under the voluntary cooperation program. In particular, the group has endeavored, through consultation among the agencies directly concerned, to insure a coordinated interpretation of the Commerce Department and Federal Reserve guidelines in specific cases. Following are the major issues considered since the date of the last report of the Group, November 16, 1965:[2]

1.   Convertible Bonds Issued by U.S. Corporations in Europe

Some of the bond issues abroad by U.S. subsidiaries to replace outflows of U.S. capital carry the privilege of conversion at a later date into the stock of the parent corporation in the U.S. This convertibility privilege tends to lessen the U.S. balance-of-payments gain from U.S. subsidiaries' issues abroad for several reasons. First, it makes such issues an attractive alternative for European investors who would otherwise have purchased U.S. corporate stocks without any new incentive. Secondly, when the conversion takes place the stock in the U.S. parent may be sold to Americans without the latter having to pay the IET.

In order to minimize these disadvantages, U.S. underwriters for these European issues were urged by Treasury to make the right-of-conversion date as late as possible, and no sooner than the scheduled expiration date of the IET, July 31, 1967. Also, the Group supported the Commerce Department's guideline instruction that the U.S. parent company take a debit in the calculation of its program progress for the amount of any conversions when they occur.

---

[1] Source: Department of State, Ball Papers: Lot 74 D 272, Balance of Payments. Limited Official Use. In a May 2 covering memorandum to the Cabinet Committee on Balance of Payments, Assistant Secretary of the Treasury for International Affairs Trued identified the report as the third report of this interagency coordinating group. A copy was also sent to Martin, Chairman of the Federal Reserve System.

[2] A copy of the undated report was transmitted under cover of a November 16 memorandum from Trued to the Cabinet Committee on Balance of Payments. (Johnson Library, National Security File, Subject File, Balance of Payments, Vol. 3 [2 of 2], Box 2.

2. *Problems Relating to the Balance-of-Payments Program As Applied to Canada*

A considerable amount of time was spent on problems related to Canada. The large amounts of Canadian new bond issues being floated in the U.S. market in the fall of 1965 were accompanied by a build-up in Canadian reserves. Consideration was given by the Group to the extension of the guidelines on purchases of long-term securities by nonbanking financial institutions to cover securities of ten years or more maturity. Since these institutions are the primary buyers of long-term Canadian securities this would have put Canadian issues under control.

The Canadian response to this proposed action was an agreement early in December, 1965 whereby Canada would in 1966 reduce its reserves to a level slightly below that of July, 1963 ($2.7 billion). The Canadian Government would be prepared to buy its own outstanding obligations owned in the United States in order to meet its reserve target. (Such purchases were made in the amount of $44 million in January.) The U.S., in turn, was to continue to permit unlimited access in the U.S. market to new Canadian long-term security issues. The Canadian authorities also agreed to sell $200 million of gold to the U.S. in 1966.

Purchases by Canadian insurance companies, either directly or through their U.S. branches, of U.S. "Delaware subsidiary" issues designed to be sold abroad was another problem. Canadian companies were financing these purchases in part by selling off some existing holdings of U.S. securities, thereby negating the favorable balance-of-payments impact for which the offshore securities were designed. Also, there was that much less for purchase by European investors who would furnish a desirable market for such issues from a U.S. balance-of-payments viewpoint. The U.S. informally requested the Canadian authorities to urge their insurance companies to refrain from further purchases of these securities.

The Canadian response, after discussions early in March, was a guideline issued by the Canadian Government to all Canadian investors asking them not to acquire securities denominated in Canadian or U.S. dollars which are issued by U.S. corporations or their non-Canadian subsidiaries and which are "subject to the U.S. interest equalization tax if purchased by U.S. residents."

Long-term security issues in Canada by foreigners other than Americans were considered to have a negative impact on the U.S. balance of payments since such borrowings in effect constitute a "pass through" of U.S. funds through Canada to third countries.

The Bank of Canada and the Government have been discouraging such third-country issues in Canada. The Canadian Minister of Finance has stated such issues will continue to be discouraged since they increase pressure on the Canadian capital market and lead to increased borrowing in the United States by Canadians.

The Canadian Government conferred with the U.S. Government on a draft of some guiding principles for good corporate behavior for Canadian subsidiaries of foreign companies. This draft was reviewed from the viewpoint of possible conflict with the VCP and appropriate comments were forwarded to the Canadian Government which released the guiding principles under a statement by the Minister of Trade and Commerce on March 31, 1966.[3]

3. *Question of Borrowing in United States by Developed Countries for Reinvestment in U.S. or in Less Developed Countries*

The Group considered several proposed borrowings in the U.S. as regards their consistency with the VCP guidelines. One type involves borrowing in the U.S. *for investment in the LDC* by an "LDC corporation" which is a *subsidiary* of a corporation in a developed country. The other involves borrowing in the U.S. *for investment in the U.S.* by such a subsidiary.

The first type of borrowing qualifies for the LDC exemption under the IET unless the borrowing firm was availed of primarily for making a transaction which the U.S. lender could not have made directly without paying the IET.

The second type of borrowing is, as a rule, subject to the IET.

As regards the Federal Reserve guidelines for nonbank institutions which are the major investors in such cases, they do not place any ceiling on credits of *over ten years maturity* extended to less developed countries. Credits to developed countries other than Canada and Japan are subject to a percentage ceiling (zero in the case of Europe) under the nonbank guidelines, without reference as to whether the proceeds are to be used abroad or in the U.S. The guidelines also ask institutions to refrain from making loans to U.S.-based subsidiaries and branches of foreign companies which would substitute for funds normally obtained from foreign sources.

The Coordinating Group considered a specific case of a proposed borrowing by an LDC subsidiary last year. The borrowing by an LDC subsidiary of ENI, the Italian oil company, was to be guaranteed by ENI, with the proceeds being used in the LDC. After discussion by the Group, the Italian Government was informed that such a borrowing, with a parent guarantee, would be inconsistent with our program.

A case of the second type of borrowing arose in the Fund of Funds case. The Fund of Funds wanted an exemption in the IET legislation for borrowing in the U.S. where the proceeds were to be reinvested in the

---

[3] This statement has not been found.

U.S. This was opposed on the grounds that such an exemption would have to apply to any borrowing in the U.S., where the stated purpose was for reinvestment in the U.S. It would not be feasible to assure that such investment did not merely replace investment of foreign funds in the U.S., or that an equivalent amount of foreign capital already invested here might not later be withdrawn.

The latest case involved a borrowing in the U.S. by an "LDC subsidiary" of a U.K. corporation, with the subsidiary transferring the entire proceeds of the borrowing to a U.S.-based British subsidiary. The latter, in turn, was to invest the proceeds in a printing firm in the U.S. While this particular borrowing arrangement would probably have been exempt from the IET only by virtue of a special exemption which was written into the IET legislation for another purpose, a restructuring of the transaction clearly would have made it possible to avoid the tax.

The prospective U.S. lender, an insurance company, requested a ruling that the Federal Reserve guidelines did not apply, on the grounds that the loan was essentially a domestic loan. It was claimed that U.K. exchange controls and the high premium which the U.S. parent corporation would have had to pay to acquire investment dollars in the U.K. effectively precluded the possibility of an inflow of U.K. funds into the U.S.

Treasury opposed a ruling that this was not a foreign loan, whereas the Federal Reserve had so ruled and had informed the underwriters.

The following points were made:

The Fed maintained that if there is good reason to believe that the investment in the U.S. would not or could not be made from foreign capital, there was no reason to interfere with the use of U.S. capital.

Also, the Fed believed it would not be consistent or fair for the U.S. to discourage or deny European borrowings in the U.S. for investment in the U.S. when we were encouraging U.S. firms to borrow abroad for financing foreign investment.

Finally, the Fed pointed out that, unlike previous cases considered, the loan agreement in this case made it impossible for the invested funds to be repatriated for at least five years.

Treasury maintained that while there might be a strong presumption of no balance-of-payments loss in a particular case, a precedent would be set for cases where the question was more debatable. Also, there was no assurance that an equivalent amount of existing U.K. investment in the U.S. would not be liquidated.

With regard to encouraging our firms to borrow in Europe, Treasury pointed out that such borrowings are allowed by only a few of the European countries (not including the U.K.). Furthermore, such U.S. borrowing abroad is generally accompanied by large inflows of U.S. capital, whereas foreign borrowing here for investment in the U.S. is rarely accompanied by much inflow of foreign capital. Finally, to allow borrowing in the U.S. for investment here by corporations of developed countries, thus possibly releasing their other sources of funds for use elsewhere, at a time when we are restricting foreign investment by U.S. corporations, would tend to undermine cooperation under the voluntary program.

4. Proposed Exemption from IET for Foreign Branch Dollar Loans

When the IET was made applicable to the banks on February 10, 1965 it was felt that to exempt the loans of foreign branches would leave the possibility of evasion of the IET by the parent banks, either through a direct transfer of funds from the parent to the branch for lending to foreigners or by the parent steering its depositors away from itself to its branches abroad. However, in recognition of the facts that foreign branches had to compete with foreign-owned banks which are not subject to the IET and that non-U.S. residents were the main source of foreign currency deposits of the branches, foreign currency loans by branches were exempted from the IET.

The banks have requested similar treatment for dollar term loans by their branches abroad. They make this case primarily on the basis that there has been a change in conditions both as they affect the branch banks' competitive position and the U.S. balance of payments.

As a result of the voluntary cooperation program, corporations are now financing more of their foreign operations from foreign sources. To a great extent they are raising these funds through bond issues in Europe. However, they cannot meet their financing needs entirely through this source since the capacity of the European bond markets is limited and because bond issues are not an appropriate method for all types of financing. The other changed condition is the Federal Reserve guideline for commercial banks which applies to the latters' loans to their foreign branches as well as to other foreigners.

The banks argue that because of the increased demand for dollar term loans by U.S. subsidiaries abroad, foreign branches of U.S. banks are finding the tax a competitive handicap. Rather than pay the tax, U.S. subs may seek loans from foreign-owned banks or look to the U.S. for funds, thus tending to increase dollar outflows from the U.S. To cope with this situation, some U.S. branch banks abroad have made loans to the U.S. parent manufacturing company which then transfers the funds to its foreign subsidiary.

The banks maintain that to the extent loans can be made by their branches abroad, the pressure on the head office for foreign loans is reduced. They contend that the ability to make long-term loans would be an important incentive to their branches to induce depositors to lengthen the maturities of their deposits, thus tending to reduce the flow of dollars into central banks and their possible conversion into gold. Finally, they believe that their branches' ability to make tax free dollar term loans would not attract a private capital outflow from the U.S. Several banks stated it was their policy not to have their overseas branches accept transfers of deposits from U.S. residents.

The Coordinating Group concluded that the banks' position was reasonable and the Treasury will request legislation to exempt from the IET dollar term loans by foreign branches of U.S. banks.

In case such exemption should have the effect of attracting dollar deposits from the U.S., a legislative provision will be requested giving the President the authority to reimpose the IET on dollar loans if necessary.

5.   *Exemption of Bank Loans to Canada from IET*

When the Executive Order was issued September 5, 1964, exempting new issues of stock or debt obligations by Canadians from the Interest Equalization Tax, bank loans were not subject to the Tax.[4]

In February, 1965, when medium- and long-term bank loans were made subject to the IET, we did not recommend an exemption for such loans to Canada. They had historically been relatively unimportant and it seemed advisable to keep exemptions to the minimum.

In recent months, however, some U.S. banks have emphasized that there is no logical justification for a difference in the treatment under the IET of loans with maturities of one year or more made by banks compared with those of nonbank lenders.

Given the financial understanding we have with the Canadians and the fact that bank loans to Canada would be counted against the Fed ceiling, action along these lines did not seem likely to have any serious balance-of-payments effects. Any increase in bank lending to Canada—not likely to be large in any case—could lessen Canadian demands on our capital market in other forms.

For reasons of equity, therefore, the Group agreed to recommend to the President that he issue an Executive Order amending the Canadian exemption to the Interest Equalization Tax to provide for inclusion of bank loans with maturity of one year or more within the terms of the exemption.

---

[4] Regarding Executive Order 11175, see Document 12.

92.   Memorandum From Vice President Humphrey to Secretary of the Treasury Fowler[1]

Washington, April 29, 1966.

Following are my comments on the memorandum entitled "Tax on Tourist Travel."[2]

1. If the tax would save from $585 million to $1.17 billion in foreign exchange per year, as estimated, it certainly should be given serious consideration.

2. It should be considered, however, in context of our overall travel program, its effect on other components of it, and of our long-standing policies favoring freedom of movement and exchange.

A. When press reports of such a contemplated tax appeared last year, an immediate increase resulted in purchase of tickets to foreign destinations and of passport renewals—reportedly by people trying to get in under the wire before imposition of any such tax. We might be prepared for a repetition of this, which would, for a short time at least, result in a greater outflow than previously.

B. A good share of the support we now enjoy from the travel industry, from other parts of the private sector, and from the communications media for our positive, voluntary Discover America program is due to the fact that the program has not entailed restrictive measures.[3] I have no doubt there would be an immediate loss of support—and, in fact, active opposition—among large parts of these groups were restrictive policies now introduced.

C. It would seem that only the most desperate of situations should compel us to take steps toward reversal of our traditional policies encouraging freedom of movement and exchange. Not only would adverse public reaction ensue, but we might well expect general retaliation from foreign governments.

3. In summary, I would support such a travel tax only as a "last resort" in closing the travel gap. I would recommend, before taking any such step, that we first adopt other measures as outlined in my memo to you of April 19.[4] That is:

A. United States Travel Service budget increase and expansion.

B. Reduction in the present duty-free tourist exemption.

---

[1] Source: Johnson Library, Fowler Papers, International Balance of Payments Committee—Classified Material: B/P Travel Expenditures Restraints [1 of 2], Box 46. Confidential.

[2] Document 87.

[3] Regarding this program, see footnote 7, Document 5.

[4] Not found.

C. Increase of the present passport fee.
D. Intensification and reorientation of our voluntary Discover America Program.

93.   Minutes of Meeting[1]

Washington, May 4, 1966, 11:30 a.m.

MINUTES OF THE MEETING ON TRAVEL TAX

PARTICIPANTS

The Vice President
Treasury—Secretary Fowler and Messrs. Trued and Knowlton
State—Under Secretary Ball
Defense—Mr. Robert Kovarik
Federal Reserve—Chairman Martin
White House—Mr. Francis Bator
Agriculture—Under Secretary Schnittker
Trade Negotiations—Governor Herter
Budget—Director Schultze
CEA—Chairman Ackley
AID—Administrator Bell
Vice President's Office—Mr. Van Dyk

Secretary Fowler said the sole purpose of the meeting was to review, at the President's request, the proposed travel tax. As background, he said he would like first to discuss the first quarter balance of payments results. He described the different figures revealed by the weekly, flash and wire reports, indicating that the wire showed a seasonally adjusted first quarter deficit of $513 million. He said that this figure was not complete—we would have to wait for Commerce's tabulations later this month—but that usually there was not a great deal of variation between the wire and final results. The Secretary said the April results, as meas-

---

[1] Source: Johnson Library, Fowler Papers, International Balance of Payments Committee—Classified Material: 1968 Balance of Payments Travel Expenditures Restraints [1 of 2], Box 46. Secret. Drafted by Knowlton on May 5. Sent under cover of a May 5 memorandum from Deputy Assistant Secretary of the Treasury for International Affairs Knowlton to Secretary Fowler in which Knowlton wrote: "Attached are minutes of yesterday's meeting on travel tax. Mr. Trued has *not* seen the attached because he is out of town today." The meeting was held in Secretary Fowler's Conference Room.

ured by the weekly figures, were "no better" than those for the first quarter. He then compared first quarter 1966 figures with those of the fourth quarter 1965. In response to a question from Mr. Bell, he compared first quarter 1966 results with those of a year ago. In the latter connection, he pointed out that January and February were terrible a year ago and much better in 1966. However, March 1966 was worse than March 1965. In concluding his summary the Secretary pointed out that on the official settlements basis, we showed a surplus in the first quarter of 1966.

Secretary Fowler then read a Memorandum from Secretary Connor (dated May 2, 1966, attached) who could not be present at the meeting.[2] He then asked the Vice President for his views. The Vice President read from a memorandum previously sent to the Secretary (dated April 29, 1966, attached).[3] After finishing, he pointed out that the travel tax violated an American tradition that extended back to the beginning of the Republic: namely, the tradition of not interfering with the movement of people. He said that the proposed tax would have a tremendously hard time on the Hill and that it would have to be coupled with mandatory controls over direct investment. If we were going to continue with our voluntary programs for financial institutions and corporations, people would expect a similar, voluntary program for tourists. If we were going to have a tax on tourism, we must expect demand for mandatory controls on capital flows. We must expect retaliation from other countries. This would certainly affect the efforts of our travel people abroad, which admittedly were not as good as they should be to begin with. Airlines would feel the pinch, too.

Secretary Fowler then mentioned that Treasury now had a more refined estimate of possible savings from the tax, and while he intended to come back to this subject later he would mention in passing that we were now thinking in terms of a $300–$500 million saving. More could be obtained, of course, if the per diem tax rate were increased.

The Vice President then interjected that in his view a progressive tax, linked to levels of income, would be impossible to administer. Messrs. Schultze and Bell disagreed.

Mr. Bell then asked whether moral suasion wasn't one of the alternatives open to the President. The Vice President responded that there was a limit on the amount of "admonishing" the President could do. You could only tell people so much. We were already telling farmers what they could plant. We were telling businessmen that profits were too high. If the problem was as it seemed to be, we had to come to grips with it as a matter of public policy. Furthermore, there was a real difference between a voluntary approach with banks, where we were dealing with hundreds

---

[2] Not found.
[3] Not attached, but printed as Document 92.

of institutions, and a voluntary approach for hundreds of thousands of tourists.

Secretary Fowler then asked for Chairman Martin's views on the tax. Chairman Martin stated that four members of the Board had studied the proposal carefully and unanimously agreed that the tax was a mistake. He tended to the view that domestic income tax increases and monetary measures were required to help solve the problem.

Under Secretary Ball then attacked the tax on a number of different grounds:

1. State Department figures indicated that the savings would be only $200–$250 million this year.
2. The Supreme Court, "which takes the Fifth Amendment seriously," would question the constitutionality of the proposal. If the "Governmental interest" amounted to a mere $250 million, this would certainly cause enough doubt on this score to result in litigation.
3. There would be unfavorable repercussions from Britain, Canada and other places.

Secretary Fowler asked if the five-day exemption were not adequate to take care of this in the case of Canada and Mexico. Under Secretary Ball stated that it would not. He said David Bell would have to make up any loss of tourist revenues in less developed countries and in places like Greece. He went on to describe the tax as "socially undesirable" and "unbecoming to the leading power with responsibilities in the four corners of the world." He said that he would give this tax very low priority indeed and that under any circumstances it would have to be accompanied by an interest equalization tax applying to capital flows across the board. The tax would certainly have to be progressive; we could not have the "jet set" lolling on the Riviera while school teachers stayed home. He for one believed that exhortation efforts were futile. They penalized the good people. The rascals would pay no attention.

Secretary Fowler then asked whether the Vice President, Chairman Martin and Under Secretary Ball would hold such strong views if the travel tax were coupled with a substantial income tax in June. The Vice President said that he would feel less strongly about it. (He mentioned in passing that we must not forget the tax would have an adverse impact on aircraft exports.) Chairman Martin and Under Secretary Ball said that they both felt just as strongly, even if the tax were part of a broader tax package.

The Vice President said we must realize that we would be "faced square" with demands for a tax on direct investment. Since he was under the impression that our voluntary program was working well, he was inclined not to fool with it.

Mr. Bator said that he had very little to add to the comments that had already been made. He said that he could conceive of a travel tax as part of a broad program that would include both higher income taxes and a broadened IET but he might have trouble with it even on this basis if the savings amounted to only $250 million. He suspected that Secretary McNamara would disagree with him on this.

Under Secretary Schnittker said he agreed with the negative comments that had already been made.

Mr. Schultze said that he, too, felt negative toward the proposal but was deeply concerned by the lack of alternatives. He said he would be willing to look at the tax later along with other tough measures.

Secretary Fowler then asked Chairman Martin and Governor Herter how the tax would be viewed abroad if placed in the context of a tough over-all program. Both Chairman Martin and Governor Herter agreed that the reception would be unfavorable—not viewed as U.S. determination but U. S. desperation. Governor Herter went on to say that basically he agreed with Under Secretary Ball's position. The tax was bad psychologically, even as a part of the broader package. He was afraid that he was old fashioned enough to believe that more domestic income taxes and tighter monetary policy were the medicine required. (The Vice President said there was no need to feel ashamed of this position.)

Chairman Okun said that he agreed on the lower estimates of savings from the tax. The Council's estimate was $360–$400 million without retaliation. He said that he, too, took a dim view of the proposal but since the alternatives for achieving, say, savings of $1 billion in the second half were so limited we might have to consider it as part of a package. On the other hand, he was afraid that in view of all the Administration's talk about using simple and flexible tools to manage the economy, a travel tax might complicate the problem of selling a straight income-tax increase.

Mr. Bell said that the impact of the proposed travel tax on less developed countries was surprisingly large. He believed they would have to be given an IET-type exemption. He shared Mr. Schultze's concern about the lack of alternatives but if the amounts saved were as small as everyone said, should we really consider this proposal as part of a package?

Mr. Schultze said that we could, of course, scale up the tax and wouldn't that help rebut Under Secretary Ball's argument about its constitutionality? Under Secretary Ball said that he didn't think it would.

Mr. Kovarik said that it was important to consider the relationship of this tax to the position of our troops overseas and what we were asking them to do. He said that even taking this factor into account he could visualize the tax *only* as part of a package. (He said he had not had a chance to obtain Secretary McNamara's latest thinking on the proposal.)

Mr. Schultze then asked if Secretary Fowler could spend five minutes or so explaining the importance of the $1 billion saving they were all groping for.

The Vice President asked, "Why is it that people are spending more money on travel anyway?". The Secretary said that the answer was easy: they had more money to spend. The Vice President then said, "Let's hit the money with the type of measures that Chairman Martin has been recommending." We would have to devise some equitable pattern. We might have to encourage savings. Perhaps there was some way to put taxes in escrow. He had been giving a lot of thought to these matters.

Secretary Fowler said we were really getting the equivalent of tax increase already as people moved into higher brackets by earning more money. He was afraid Congress would spend any tax increase. If he could find a safe place down in Kentucky where he could go with the extra revenues and hide, he would agree that a tax increase might make sense.

The Vice President said we could not escape the fact that "the deficit is there." He had been told that the deficit itself was inflationary. Couldn't we have a tax in the form of a Vietnamese surcharge?

Secretary Fowler said that we must have a two-pronged approach: if we have higher taxes we must hold to the President's budget. Both were necessary.

The Vice President said that Congress hadn't finished with all the appropriations yet. He thought there would be reductions in NASA and AID programs. He said the Vice President would get medicare before he got his new house.

In summing up the meeting, Secretary Fowler said that the views of the group were as follows:

1. It was overwhelmingly against a travel tax by itself.
2. A minority believed that it might be possible and desirable to pass a travel tax as part of a broader, tougher package of measures (presumably including increased income taxes and a stronger IET).
3. But the majority probably wouldn't buy the travel tax on this basis either.

He said he would convey these views to the President. He wanted to caution the group that this consensus did not necessarily represent the final resolution of the issue.

As the group departed the Vice President mentioned that he still favored going ahead with the other travel measures that had been discussed at earlier meetings; namely, beefing up the U. S. Travel Service.

Winthrop Knowlton

94.   Memorandum From Secretary of the Treasury Fowler to President Johnson[1]

Washington, May 10, 1966.

SUBJECT

Balance of Payments—1966

I. Appraisal of the 1966 Outlook

The balance of payments picture continues to be disturbing. The first quarter deficit, which will be revealed publicly *on May 18* for the first time and in some detail—in the regular quarterly Department of Commerce Report—will total about $600 million, seasonally adjusted, on an over-all (liquidity) basis. This is an annual rate of $2.4 billion, compared to a $2.8 billion deficit in 1964 and a $1.3 billion deficit last year.

On an official settlements basis, the first quarter deficit, seasonally adjusted, amounted to about $300 million which annualizes at $1.2 billion, compared with $1.3 billion last year. As you recall, we began publishing this deficit along with the over-all deficit starting in the final quarter of 1965, as a result of the recommendations of the Bernstein Committee.[2]

The Cabinet Committee on Balance of Payments is in unanimous agreement on additional measures that would, if successfully implemented, yield savings of about $800 million. Such savings would bring the 1966 deficit back to $1.6 billion, *assuming no underlying deterioration from the deficit rate in the first quarter.* Unfortunately, there is reason to believe such deterioration may be taking place. If this proves to be the case, the measures on which the Cabinet Committee has reached agreement will not only fail to achieve, by a substantial margin, our goal of equilibrium, but the year could end with a deficit *substantially* worse than in 1965. The fundamental problem can be summarized as follows: our *trade* surplus is shrinking; growth of our *services* surplus is being held back by the growing tourist deficit; together, our surplus on *goods and services* combined will not be sufficiently large to compensate for

—the governmental dollar outflows now increasing substantially because of the superimposition of new Southeast Asia costs on the costs of our other commitments throughout the world; and

—private capital outflows, despite the fact these have been reduced by our two voluntary restraint programs instituted in February 1965 and tightened in December and by the operation of the Interest Equalization Tax enacted earlier.

---

[1] Source: Johnson Library, National Security File, Subject File, Balance of Payments, Vol. 3 [1 of 2], Box 2. Secret.

[2] See footnote 3, Document 67.

What we *do* about this situation and what we *say* about it involve decisions as important as any your Administration will have to make.

This memorandum is designed to shape the issues.

II. *What We Have Been Doing About It*

When the 1966 program was announced on December 3,[3] the following assumption was publicly presented as one of the reasons for the belief we could reach equilibrium this year.

—our trade surplus will widen from the annual rate of $5.0 billion generated in the first nine months of 1965 but is likely to remain somewhat below the high level of $6.7 billion in 1964. In 1964, our trade position benefited from an unusual convergence of events including strong industrial demand abroad, large agricultural sales, and shipments in anticipation of a dock strike. In 1965, events have been less favorable, including unusually strong domestic demand, less strong demand from key nations abroad, a dock strike, and a high level of steel imports in anticipation of a strike in that industry.

This seemed reasonable at the time in view of the fact that the preliminary figures for the third quarter and October indicated a favorable upturn from the lower levels in the first two quarters.

However, when the figures for the fourth quarter become available in January,[4] the possibility of a less favorable trade surplus began to emerge.

Moreover, there had been a significant change in the 1966 gross national product estimates from the $710 billion level which characterized the mid-November period when the 1966 balance-of-payments program was determined. The Economic Report in January estimated $722 million, giving rise to the probability of a substantially increased volume of imports.[5]

Also there were indications from the Department of Defense in late January that the balance-of-payments costs in Southeast Asia were running at or beyond the high end of the range forecast in November exercise.

When these developments became observable in January, we adopted the policy of hoping for the best but preparing for the worst.

Accordingly, Treasury instituted a quiet "nuts and bolts" tightening exercise of the type used in the fourth quarter. *For a description of the steps taken see Attachment A.*

---

[3] See footnote 3, Document 83.

[4] See Document 85.

[5] For text of report, January 27, see *Public Papers of the Presidents of the United States: Lyndon B. Johnson, 1966,* Book I, pp. 96–109.

More significantly, we began to forge additional measures and to explore others which could compensate for the deterioration which might develop from these or other sources.

Treasury Assistant Secretary Trued and Deputy Assistant Secretary Knowlton conducted a penetrating review which developed the issues described in a memorandum dated March 3, 1966 ("Summary of Balance of Payments Review")[6] which Mr. Bator and I discussed with you early in March.

During the first few weeks in March, I held a series of bilateral discussions with

—the Vice President and Secretary Connor on the tourist problem;
—Secretary McNamara on military expenditures;
—Administrator Bell on the aid program; and
—Budget Director Schultze on the gold budget.

By the end of March it had become clear that an additional $1.5 billion of savings would be required this year to bring us into equilibrium (cf. my memorandum to you dated March 30). (Attachment B)

The full Cabinet Committee on Balance of Payments met on March 25 to discuss a wide range of possible new measures;[7] it has continued to meet, on an informal basis, throughout April and early May.

On May 3, it reconsidered, at your request, the proposed tourist tax.[8] The Committee still finds itself overwhelmingly opposed to such a tax—providing it is submitted to Congress as an isolated proposal. An important new factor in our most recent negative appraisal was the belief, based on additional statistical analyses done by Treasury, State, and CEA, that the measure was not likely to generate net annual savings of more than $300 million with the per diem rate set at $6. By doubling or tripling the per diem rate, of course, we might achieve higher returns but it seemed exceedingly doubtful to the group that these would amount to more than $600–$800 million. In 1966, with nearly five months gone, the savings would be much smaller. A minority of the Committee believes the tax would deserve more serious consideration if it were proposed as part of a broader tax package that would include higher income taxes and a strengthened Interest Equalization Tax covering direct investment outflows.

As a result of these deliberations (covering a period of nearly three months), the Cabinet Committee, as noted at the beginning of this memorandum, has reached agreement on additional measures which could provide savings of $800 million in 1966. A list of these recommendations,

[6] Not printed. (Johnson Library, National Security File, Subject File, Balance of Payments, Vol. 3 [1 of 2], Box 2)

[7] See Document 88.

[8] An apparent reference to the meeting on May 4; see Document 93.

which we have already begun to implement, is attached. (See Attachment C) The bulk of savings would come, essentially, from further cutbacks in the balance of payments costs of the military program, from prepayment of debt owed the U.S. by other countries, and by diversion of a portion of official foreign holdings of dollars into long-term investments in the U.S.

III. Fundamental Decisions That Face Us Now

It is clear that we have reached the stage where we must make new and fundamental decisions about the nature of our whole program. The actions upon which we are agreed will not bring us into equilibrium in 1966, or even close to it. A number of them, quite frankly, are designed to "buy time"; they will help us, as in the case of debt prepayments, in 1966 but will not constitute recurring factors of strength.

We are faced with the following basic alternatives. (Alternatives (2) and (3) are not mutually exclusive but can be used together, in varying combinations):

Alternative (1)

Live with a substantial deficit—in the range of $1.5–$2.5 billion—for the duration of the Vietnam conflict, avoiding major changes in foreign policy and any major additional restrictions on imports, private capital outflows, and tourism, other than those incorporated in the present program.

We would state publicly that our goal was still that of reaching equilibrium but acknowledge that because of Vietnam it would be more difficult and take more time to achieve than previously anticipated.

We would pledge to continue to make every possible effort to minimize the balance of payments impact of present government programs. We would continue the voluntary restraints on capital outflows, and we would intensify efforts to stimulate exports looking to the long run improvement of the trade balance. But we would not fundamentally change the nature of our present program.

Alternative (2)

Reduce the deficit by cutting back U.S. commitments overseas.

This alternative would call for major changes in our foreign policy. It would require important reductions in our foreign economic assistance and military programs.

Alternative (3)

Reduce the deficit by introducing new economic and balance of payments measures at home.

This approach would require consideration of an income tax increase and a basic change in the character of our voluntary restraint program for capital outflows.

An income tax increase is not likely to have an important effect on the size of the deficit in 1966. It could not be passed until later this summer, and, unless it were substantially larger than anything we have recently been contemplating, it could not take more than a small bite out of gross national product until next year. However, it would have a constructive impact on psychology abroad; it would be construed as evidence of the seriousness of our intent in coping with our payments problem. This, in turn, could help to limit conversions of dollars into gold. And by gradually moderating the rate of increase in domestic demand, an income tax increase would, over time, help to reduce the pressure of imports and provide a margin of excess manufacturing capacity for exports.

In conjunction with our consideration of a domestic income tax increase, we would take another look at the impact of monetary policy on our payments position to see whether any further tightening would help *and* whether it could be tolerated here.

Private capital outflows could be further restricted by converting the Interest Equalization Tax into a broad, flexible instrument that would, in addition to capital outflows presently covered, apply to direct investment. This would not only change the character of our present program—subjecting corporations to law instead of appeals for voluntary compliance—but would involve for the first time a drastic cutback, instead of a moderation, in the rate of direct investment. If necessary, the Federal Reserve's voluntary restraint program for financial institutions would be tightened at the same time.

Regardless of your decision on the above alternatives, we will want to make suitable attempts to minimize gold conversions or other disruptive impacts on foreign exchange markets. (See discussion in Part V below.)

IV. What We Say About It

What we say at the time of the Department of Commerce Report in the first quarter and what we do thereafter are matters of considerable significance.

So that you may know what we have said in the past, let me review the highlights from public statements starting last September at the IBRD and IMF meeting.

From your address to the World Bank and International Monetary Fund last September:

"The U. S. has taken firm action to arrest the dollar drain. Should further action be necessary in the future, such action will be taken.

"I want to be very clear about this. We must in our own interest and in the interest of those who rely on the dollar as a reserve currency, maintain our payments in equilibrium. This we will do."[9]

From your public letter to me of December 2, 1965:

"We have done well, but we must do even better. The deficit has been much smaller since February 10 than for several years past. At its peak, in 1960, it reached $3.9 billion, three times the rate so far this year. But the present deficit is still too large. To assure that the dollar will remain as good as gold, we have to show the world that we can bring our accounts into sustainable balance, and keep them in balance."

From my statement at the White House press conference on December 3:

"Against this background, and after an analysis of the other relevant balance of payments accounts, we concluded that new measures were necessary to reach our goal of equilibrium—by which for next year we mean a quarter of a billion dollars or so either side of exact balance on an overall basis. With these new measures we are confident, barring unforeseen circumstances, that we will reach that goal."[10]

From your Economic Report to the Congress in January, 1966:

"Decisive progress was made in 1965 toward reducing our balance of payments deficit. Though the results for 1965 are gratifying, we cannot afford to relax. We have not yet balanced our external accounts.
"For 1966, external balance is our goal."

In view of developments in January and early February, I took advantage of the February 14 press conference on the fourth quarter Department of Commerce report to lay the groundwork for an unfavorable turn, should it later develop.[11]

I said, after analyzing the 1965 performance and discussing the key items on which we were counting for improvement in 1966:

"Now I would like to go over with you some of the main components of this 1965 record as they bear upon the future. There are both favorable and unfavorable elements.

"The $1.5 billion net reduction in the payments deficit on an overall basis occurred despite heavy outflows on private capital account during the early months and despite setbacks for the year as a whole in trade and other accounts. The improvement is in very large part attributable to the

---

[9] Johnson made these remarks on October 1, 1965, at the annual meeting of the World Bank and the International Monetary Fund in Washington. For full text, see *Public Papers of the Presidents of the United States: Lyndon B. Johnson, 1965*, Book II, pp. 1030–1034.

[10] Regarding this statement, see footnote 3, Document 83.

[11] No transcript of this press conference has been found, but most of Fowler's statement on that occasion is quoted below.

effectiveness of the program of voluntary cooperation which President Johnson called for in his balance of payments message of February 10, 1965.

"This 1965 record, and the tightening and sharpening of this phase of the President's balance of payments program for 1966, give reason to believe that there will be continuing improvement in the private capital area.

"I would hope particularly that the Foreign Tax Investors Act, now in the House Ways and Means Committee, could become law this year, providing the basis for a long term expansion of the scale of private foreign portfolio investment in the United States.

"This prospect, the increase in investment income, a moderation of direct investment outflows, and a movement toward an expanding trade surplus, interrupted in 1965 by special circumstances, offer the most promising areas for our march toward equilibrium in 1966.

"*Of course the two main imponderables are the rising balance of payments costs in Southeast Asia in both the military and the aid programs which are the result of Vietnam and the direct and indirect impact of Vietnam on the domestic economy and the balance of trade.*

"With this in mind, we must certainly make every effort—we must not fail in our continuing efforts, both in and out of government—to find and to make every reasonable and practicable offset to the impact of Vietnam on our balance of payments.

"*But, it should be kept in mind that the balance of payments costs of the Vietnam conflict are not permanent or ordinary costs, and that, although we have made provision for an increase in these costs in our outlook for 1966, it is simply not possible to say at this time how greatly, in fact, they will affect our balance of payments in 1966.*

"What I can tell you now is that we still have equilibrium, as we have defined it, as our goal for 1966, *but we cannot be certain that present measures as they currently operate will lead us to that goal if the foreign exchange costs of Vietnam rise sharply over the increases presently projected.* Let me add and emphasize that as of now the program we have is an effective program, and we see no reason to change its character." (Underlining ours.)[12]

It has been the custom for Secretary Connor, Chairman Martin, Governor Robertson and I to hold a press conference concurrently with the release of the Department of Commerce quarterly reports. To fail to have the customary press conference on this occasion and attempt by a nontechnical statement and question-and-answer period to deal with the

---

[12] Printed here as italics.

problem would be undesirable. Accordingly, unless you advise me otherwise, I intend to go through with it.

A text of what I should say is of the first order of importance and is Item 1 on the agenda for discussion.

Attachment D describes, in a preliminary way, the major changes that appear to account for the difference in first quarter results from our original forecast in November.

V. What We Do To Prevent A Crisis

We may have difficulty in the weeks immediately ahead in persuading other countries—particularly the important surplus countries of Western Europe—that we are still serious when we say we mean to solve our balance of payments problem. What we say on May 18th will, of course, have an important bearing on this, but no matter how effectively we rationalize the first quarter deficit, there is a possibility that our determination to move toward equilibrium will be questioned. And if so, we could be faced with a further deterioration of the deficit; acceleration of dollar conversions into gold; and a speculative run on the London Gold Market.

I hope this will not come to pass but we should clearly prepare for the contingency. Treasury and the Federal Reserve will work together, utilizing the tools at hand, to minimize the dangers of this kind of chain reaction and to place us in the strongest possible technical position should it arise.

If we are not confronted with an *immediate* crisis, there is still the real possibility that we will have one later in the year. Instead of coping with these threats on an ad hoc quarterly basis, I wonder if the time has not come for the U.S. to try to make informal arrangements with the major dollar holding nations of the world that would preclude such a crisis for the duration of Vietnam conflict.

Under Secretary of the Treasury Deming is leaving for Rome on Thursday, May 12, for the next round of negotiations with the Group of Ten; Chairman Martin leaves for Europe on Monday, May 16, for talks with a number of central bankers; and later this month I am scheduled to attend an American Bankers Association meeting in Madrid and Granada, where I may see a number of my European counterparts.

I propose that we give serious consideration to asking the key dollar-holding nations, during these visits, to pledge *not to convert dollars they presently hold* and *not to convert any additional dollars* that may accrue to them as long as the Vietnam struggle continues. To accomplish this, we will have to state in the strongest possible terms that:

1. We most emphatically *do* intend to bring our balance of payments into equilibrium.

2. The Vietnam conflict, with its attendant direct and indirect balance of payments costs, has made it difficult for us to do this as soon as we had hoped. But we will do it.

3. We are bearing virtually the entire burden of the Vietnam conflict. We view this as a commitment on behalf of all free nations. We do not ask others to see it this way, but we do ask that they not act in a manner that will prevent us from meeting our commitments and/or destroy the international financial institutions that are such a vital part of the world we are attempting to defend.

4. We believe that the major dollar-holding nations of the world have a choice: they can exercise patience and restraint, minimizing pressure on the dollar; or by making abnormal, new demands on our gold supply, they can risk serious disruption to the international monetary system—to the detriment of us all.

Henry H. Fowler

Attachment A[13]

STEPS TAKEN DURING 1ST QUARTER TO IMPROVE OUR BALANCE-OF-PAYMENTS POSITION

1. We persuaded the IBRD to invest $71 million of its liquid dollars in long-term certificates of deposit.

2. We successfully negotiated a Brazilian investment of $50 million in long-term certificates of deposit and a prepayment of a $29 million gold loan.

3. We arranged for the Bank of Italy to purchase $40 million of non-negotiable, non-convertible, medium-term U.S. government bonds against military orders to be placed in the U.S.

The above provided $190 million of first quarter savings. At an annual rate—excluding the one-time repayment of the gold loan by Brazil—this amounts to $644 million.

---

[13] Secret.

Attachment (B)[14]

Washington, March 30, 1966.

MEMORANDUM FOR THE PRESIDENT

SUBJECT

Cabinet Committee on Balance of Payments meeting of March 25

Your Cabinet Committee on Balance of Payments met Friday, March 25, to review current balance of payments prospects on the basis of the latest information. This review showed that our target of equilibrium this year—or even a deficit short of that goal by any reasonable amount—is unlikely to be achieved without further action.

We do not have at this point any detailed forecast of the balance of payments this year. Nevertheless, some key changes in the assumptions we used last November indicate the clear likelihood of a short-fall. The principal change lies in the trade surplus forecast which may fall $1.5 billion below the November forecast of $6 billion. This anticipated change results from the modification of the $710 billion GNP assumption used last November to something in excess of the $722 billion used in your January Economic Report. As a rule of thumb, for every $5 billion of additional GNP on top of an already burgeoning economy one might expect a drop in the trade balance of three to four hundred million dollars. In addition, outflows related to our commitment in Vietnam have moved up by $341 million.

Under these circumstances, your Cabinet Committee on Balance of Payments believes it only prudent to make a further intensive review of our payments program with the view toward finding steps to cut $1.5 billion off whatever deficit now seems in prospect.

In fact, I had already initiated the development of some proposals for additional steps along the lines of the attached "Summary of Balance of Payments Review", dated March 3, which I handed you on March 4 when you, Francis Bator and I had a brief meeting on this subject.

---

[14] Secret.

Attachment C[15]

Additional Measures For Balance-of-Payments Savings in 1966 Agreed Upon Unanimously By the Cabinet Committee on Balance of Payments.

The Cabinet Committee on Balance of Payments agrees unanimously that the following measures should be taken as promptly as possible. Potential savings are estimated at $800 million.

1. The Department of Defense and AID must again intensify their efforts to reduce the balance of payments costs of their programs. Secretary McNamara believes that he can cut the adverse 1966 impact of military activities by about $300 million from $2,150 million to $1,850 million—which would bring the military deficit within $50 million of our original forecast of last December. AID, however, believes that only nominal further cuts in the balance of payments costs of its program are possible (see attachment).[16]

2. Under Secretary of the Treasury Deming will begin negotiating immediately with a number of major European countries to obtain prepayment of debt owed the U.S. The potentials of this exercise depend importantly on the willingness of the French and Italians to prepay. Our present judgment is that we have a reasonably good chance of obtaining $200–$300 million.

3. Assistant Secretary of Treasury Trued has left for the Far East on Tuesday, May 10th, to obtain agreement from Japan, Korea, Taiwan, and the Philippines to invest as much of their official dollar reserves as possible in the United States in forms that help our payments statistics. The reserves of these countries are higher than they otherwise would be because of U.S. expenditures for the Vietnam war. At the same time, the U.S. economic task force in Vietnam will urge the Vietnamese authorities to place a portion of their dollar reserves in long-term instruments in the U.S.A. Thailand is already cooperating with us in this matter. All told, the possible returns from these six countries could come to $200 million.

Mr. Trued will also explore the possibility of a Japanese debt prepayment. If deemed necessary to obtain meaningful help from the Japanese, we will send a team to Tokyo to negotiate a military offset agreement.

4. We will also attempt to persuade key Latin American and Middle Eastern countries with strong reserve positions to place a portion of *their* reserves in long-term instruments here. These countries are not necessarily beneficiaries of the Vietnam war but they have, in a number of

---

[15] Secret.

[16] An attachment identified as "Memo to Secretary Fowler from Administrator Bell (AID), 5/3/66," was not attached and has not been found.

instances, benefited from U.S. economic assistance and investment, and they can be made to understand that failure of the U.S. to solve its balance of payments problem will pose serious difficulties for them as well as for us. There may be another $150 million potential from such countries as Mexico (where negotiations began during my recent visit), Venezuela, Saudi Arabia, and Kuwait.

The Cabinet Committee also believes the following measures—the savings from which are more difficult to quantify but probably do not exceed $100–$200 million—should be promptly implemented (agreement is not unanimous in all cases):

1. Better review procedures should be developed to assure effective functioning of gold budget controls.

2. Every effort should be made to gain maximum advance payments during 1966 under the German offset agreements (negotiations are presently in progress).

3. In its management of its voluntary program, the Commerce Department must make every effort to see that companies that are over their direct investment targets are brought back to the target level. If no companies are over the target and some are under, we should be able to reduce direct investment below the $2.4 billion forecast.

4. The U.S. Travel Service should assume centralized management of the Government travel program, performing liaison with States and the private sector and administering all funds directed toward promoting tourism in the U. S. To this end, all agencies should support a request for a substantially larger budget for USTS before the Congress.

5. A proposal to cut the customs duty-free allowance from $100 to $10 should be considered along with other tax measures for possible submission to the Congress. (Savings could amount to $20–$30 million in 1966; up to $100 million in 1967.)

6. The Export-Import Bank is considering the advisability of establishing a limited rediscount facility to reinsure the availability of export financing. The facility should be introduced as soon as possible.

7. Emphasis should be given to the need for U.S. businesses to remain export conscious and to insure that an appropriate part of output continues to be sold abroad—over the longer run, this is essential to maintaining markets.

8. Export consciousness should be reinforced throughout our missions abroad, including aggressive effort in aid recipient countries, to reinsure the effectiveness of "tying" and to help gain additional markets.

9. The United States must be in a position to respond if the Soviet Bloc offers to make further purchases of wheat in the free world. In the immediate case, a method of subsidized transport costs to overcome the 50–50 shipping requirement must be available.

10. Consideration should be given to raising the export price of wheat further upward if the 1966 crop outlook makes it feasible.

11. We should maximize sales from stockpile. (Items which we import and which are in stockpile surplus include: aluminum, $700 million; bauxite, $85 million; lead, $400 million; nickel, $225 million; rubber, $475 million; tin, $325 million; and zinc, $380 million.)

Attachment (D)[17]

FIRST QUARTER 1966 BALANCE-OF-PAYMENTS ANALYSIS

The following paragraphs show how first quarter performance for certain major items in our balance of payments—some of them still estimated—differed from that visualized in the projection sent to you on November 26, 1965. We will not have firm data for certain items for some weeks.

Trade. In our November projection, we looked forward to a $6 billion trade surplus in 1966. During the first quarter, the trade surplus ran at a $4.5 billion annual rate, compared with $4.8 billion for the year 1965 and $5.1 billion (annual rate) in the fourth quarter.

Exports in 1966 were expected to amount to $28.7 billion. They ran at an annual rate of $28.4 billion in the first quarter, about $300 million higher than the fourth quarter 1965 annual rate.

Imports in 1966 were projected at $22.7 billion. In the first quarter, they ran at an annual rate of $23.9 billion, about $900 million higher than the fourth quarter annual rate.

Military. Firm figures are not yet available for the first quarter, but it is possible that the net military balance-of-payments deficit has been running at an annual rate several hundred million dollars higher than the $1.8–$2.0 billion forecast in November.

Government Grants and Capital (AID, etc.). So far as we know, there has been no significant change from forecast.

Direct Investment Income and Outflow. Firm figures are not yet available but it is likely that direct investment outflows are running above the $2.4 billion rate forecast for the year as a whole, and that investment income also may be lower than expected. These first quarter shortfalls could conceivably amount to $1 billion at *an annual rate.*

New Foreign Security Offerings. We were hurt here in the first quarter, primarily because of $150 million of Canadian offerings postponed from

----

[17] Secret.

late 1965. (The Canadians partially offset this by buying back $45 million of their own securities from U.S. holders.) In our November forecast, we expected foreign security offerings in 1966 to total $1.1 billion. In the first three months, excluding the $150 million of postponed Canadian issues, they are estimated to have totaled $300 million, equivalent to an annual rate of $1.2 billion.

Bank Claims. In the November forecast, we anticipated an *outflow* of $400 million from the bank sector in 1966. Instead, there was a first quarter *inflow* of $260 million which consisted of inflows in January and February offset by about a $100 million outflow in March. Annual rate of inflow in the first quarter was $1 billion.

---

95.   Memorandum From the President's Deputy Special Assistant for National Security Affairs (Bator) to President Johnson[1]

Washington, May 11, 1966, 5:45 p.m.

SUBJECT

Balance of Payments

1. The first quarter results are poor: an overall deficit running at $2.4 billion per year. (The 1965 rate was $1.3; 1964, $2.8.)

2. Unless we take drastic action, the rest of 1966 is not likely to improve much:

—The Cabinet Committee is agreed on nut-and-bolt tightening which will gain $600–$800 million at most;
—But that will only offset the deterioration which would otherwise be likely.

3. There are two reasons for this dismal picture:

(a) The rise in dollar spending *in* Vietnam.
(b) The rapid expansion of the domestic economy. Since November the GNP forecast for '66 has gone up by $20 billion—from $712 billion to $732 billion. This will probably produce about $1–$1.2 billion in extra imports.

---

[1] Source: Johnson Library, National Security File, Subject File, Balance of Payments, Vol. 3 [1 of 2], Box 2. Secret; Sensitive.

4. To get the calendar '66 deficit much under $2 billion would take *drastic* action. Direct investment and tourists would be the most likely targets. In both cases, a big improvement would require a tax (or a moratorium) almost immediately—further "voluntary" measures will not do the job.

5. Any other direct action on components of our payments would involve enormous costs:

—Import controls would lead to retaliation. With a still large export surplus, we would be the loser. Also, 30 years of trade policy would be in shambles.

—Foreign aid provides no way out. To make a real savings of $100 million, we would have to cut the aid program by about $500 million or more. To get anywhere on this front, we would have to gut the program.

6. *The most powerful medicine would be a large general tax increase.* This would begin to help by the 4th quarter of '66, and make a very large difference by 1967. (It could and perhaps should be supplemented by a tax on direct investment.)

7. Without a tax increase, we are likely to be in balance of payments trouble well into 1967. And the likely sharp rise in prices during 1967 would cast a balance of payments shadow well beyond 1967.

8. Whatever we do—short of drastic and immediate action on tourists and direct investment—there will be a substantial deficit in calendar 1966. Dollars will accumulate in the hands of foreign central and private bank and individuals. *This does not necessarily mean massive conversion of these dollars into U.S. gold.*

9. Stopping such conversions will take some effort—Joe Fowler will have suggestions for you this afternoon.[2] *I think his program will almost certainly prevent a real run on gold during the rest of this year.* The French will pose special problems, but we can probably hold the other Europeans in line.

10. Even at worst—contrary to what some bankers will tell you—*a run on gold which would force us to declare a moratorium on sales is not the end of the world.* Far from it. The present rules of the international money game place an excessive burden on the U.S. By moving with speed and skill following stoppage of U.S. gold sales, we could within a few months negotiate new rules which would make far more sense all around. Because of our economic strength, trading position, and competitive [text missing], our negotiating leverage would be enormous.

FMB

---

[2] The President met with Secretary Fowler and others on balance-of-payments issues from 6:57 to 8:10 p.m. (Johnson Library, President's Daily Diary)

96.   Circular Telegram From the Department of State to Certain Posts[1]

Washington, May 13, 1966, 10:04 p.m.

2237. Direct and indirect US expenditures associated with Viet Nam military operation and support thereof are exerting adverse impact on US balance of payments. Cabinet Committee on Balance of Payments is seriously concerned with these developments and US Government at highest level desires mitigate this impact to utmost feasible extent.

US assumption of worldwide military and political responsibilities provides major benefits, economic and financial as well as political, to nations of Western Europe. Europeans should not expect US to continue carrying financial burden these responsibilities with Viet Nam costs as they now appear and simultaneously to fulfill demands of finance ministers and central bank governors with respect to balance of payments equilibrium without resort to measures which are not in interest either of Europe or US. We believe time has come when European nations should demonstrate intention to cooperate more fully with US in financial field.

US will be making financial approaches to most industrial nations of Europe which have long-term debt to US seeking prepayment of all or part of outstanding obligations. In some cases there will also be discussions concerning reserve policies of monetary authorities. Since extreme care must be taken to avoid misinterpretation of US action and loss of confidence in the US dollar, approaches will be conducted quietly under cover provided by scheduled multilateral meetings and with approaches tailored to specific country situations. In some cases active support of Ambassador and political elements of Embassy may not be necessary, but where requested and likely to contribute to success of endeavor such support should be provided.

Separate messages to individual posts follow.

Rusk

---

[1] Source: Department of State, Central Files, FN 12 US. Secret; Limdis. Drafted by F. L. Widman (Treasury) on May 13; cleared by Winthrop Knowlton (Treasury) (in draft), Ralph E. Lindstrom (E/OMA), Francis M. Bator, Marvin W. Humphreys (S/S), Walter J. Stoessel (EUR) (in draft), and George S. Springsteen (U); and approved by Anthony M. Solomon (E). Sent to Bonn, Brussels, The Hague, Madrid, Rome, Vienna, and Paris.

97.   Circular Telegram From the Department of State to Certain Posts[1]

Washington, May 18, 1966, 7:52 p.m.

2270. Balance of payments data for first quarter revealed today at joint press conference held by Secretaries Fowler and Connor and Vice Chairman Robertson of Federal Reserve Board. Data show deficit on liquidity basis (all figures in millions of dollars) of 582 seasonally adjusted (80 unadjusted). On official settlements basis seasonally adjusted deficit 262. Main elements include exports of 7,113 and imports of 6,007; new security issues 454 with inflow of 132 from redemptions and transactions in outstandings; banks report net inflows of 120 on long-term and 135 on short-term. Foreign purchases of U.S. securities showed net of 151 and foreign long-term claims on U.S. banks provided inflow of 36.

In prepared statement Secretary Fowler said that in terms of over-all results U.S. had "been little more than holding our own" since mid-1965 beginning with large buildup in direct and indirect costs of military and aid operations in SE Asia. In reaching this conclusion Fowler took into account shifting of 150 of Canadian security issues from fourth quarter 1965 to first quarter 1966 and fluctuations in flow of receipts from military offset arrangements with Germany. Adjusting for these factors over-all deficit becomes 377 in third quarter 1965, 341 in fourth quarter and 382 in first quarter 1966.

Fowler referred to: (a) rising balance of payments costs in SE Asia of military and aid programs and (b) direct and indirect trade impact of Viet Nam on domestic economy. Said both direct and indirect effects substantial, noting trade surplus had dropped to annual rate of 4,400. Exports increased at annual rate of 350 over fourth quarter while imports up 1,000. Concluded U.S. might have moved substantially closer to equilibrium during these quarters absent Viet Nam buildup.

Fowler then listed actions being taken including: (a) President on March 8 instructed Government Departments to reduce dollar outflows to absolute minimum;[2] (b) DOD began in March to consider new measures to reduce foreign exchange costs of its activities; (c) AID continues efforts to minimize aid in form of financial resources rather than real resources; (d) Foreign Tax Investors Act "should become law as soon as

---

[1] Source: Department of State, Central Files, FN 12 US. Unclassified. Drafted by F.L. Widman (Treasury) on May 18, cleared by Winthrop Knowlton (Treasury), and approved by Matilda Milne (E/OMA). Sent to 14 European posts and Tokyo, and pouched to Mexico City, Rio de Janeiro, Buenos Aires, and New Delhi.

[2] President Johnson's March 8 memorandum to Cabinet officers and heads of major agencies is printed in *American Foreign Policy: Current Documents, 1966*, pp. 975–976.

possible" to help expand private foreign portfolio investment in U.S.; (e) Government studying ways of increasing effectiveness of present program designed to stimulate travel in U.S.; (f) Commerce attempting make clear that exports are matter of critical concern. The Export-Import Bank has announced adjustments in its policies and other recommendations in reports of National Export Expansion Council under study.

Concluding statement Fowler said "our goal is still the achievement of equilibrium—sustained equilibrium. The multiple costs of Viet Nam have made the task more difficult to be sure, and it may be that we will have to settle for an interim objective of equilibrium exclusive of the costs of Viet Nam . . . we will reach an appropriate degree of equilibrium and we will do so in ways consistent with our obligations, as we see them, to our own citizenry and to the remainder of the Free World."

Secretary Connor in supplementary statement drew attention to fact that data on voluntary balance of payments program of corporate community released last week reflected only projections of 618 companies and not entire business community. Said he expected meet with Commerce Department's Advisory Committee and assess expectations for future. Government not in position to specify arbitrary goals since program voluntary, but would identify realistically obtainable objectives. Connor said he felt that in absence of program capital outflows in 1966 would have exceeded 1965 level by one billion or more. Connor also pointed out that companies were not cutting back on investments in LDCs. He also said he thought it likely the over-all tabulations had a conservative bias and that actual performance might be better than projections reported by companies. "At this juncture we should perhaps agree simply that evidence so far indicates that the companies are well within the direct investment target and will make a healthy improvement in other accounts as well."

Robertson characterized performance of financial institutions as "remarkable" but denied that success scored at expense of other important national objectives. Said that although was no statistical evidence on effect of program on exports, fact that banking system was over 800 below ceilings suggested by guidelines indicated that program "has afforded and still affords ample room for all bankable export credits."

Questions by reporters concentrated heavily on estimate costs Viet Nam conflict and on possibilities of restrictions on U.S. tourist expenditures abroad. There was also noteworthy question on whether Germany falling behind in meeting offset. On Viet Nam costs Fowler stated $700 million figure used last fall still constitutes fair estimate minimum figure for Viet Nam costs, but indicated very difficult predict size of effort necessary and therefore what actual cost might turn out to be. Fowler said tourist balance prospects have recently been carefully examined and it was decided not to take any restrictive measures, such as tourist tax. In answer question whether U.S. citizens should have any qualms about traveling abroad Fowler replied "Each should decide for himself." On German offset Fowler's reply was that arrangement with Germans did not contemplate any quarter-to-quarter schedule but he had every confidence Germans will meet offset target for period as a whole. When asked why U.S. with $700 billion economy should be concerned with deficit of say $2 billion a year, Fowler answered simply "Because other people are concerned."

Rusk

---

98.   **Memorandum From Secretary of the Treasury Fowler to President Johnson**[1]

Washington, June 7, 1966.

SUBJECT

    Action to cut balance of payments deficit in 1966

This memorandum summarizes the results of action taken since the decision was made on May 11 to make every effort to gain prepayment of official debt owed to the United States and to gain foreign official cooperation in converting dollars held in liquid form into longer term investments.[2] Both of these actions cut our potential balance of payments deficit. The outlook on this front for assistance this year is quite promising—as shown in the attached schedule.[3]

As you know, we had anticipated this broader effort when the first quarter results deteriorated. To cut the first quarter deficit, Treasury officials contacted officials of the World Bank and gained the conversion of $71 million held in liquid form to longer term investments. In addition, Deputy Assistant Secretary Knowlton approached Brazilian officials en route to Buenos Aires and gained a $50 million long term investment. Finally, Treasury discussions with the Italians gained a $40 million advance military payment during the first quarter. As a result, the first quarter deficit on the liquidity basis was reduced by $161 million.

---

[1] Source: Johnson Library, White House Central Files, Confidential File, FO 4–1, Balance of Payments (1966), Box 32–39. Confidential.

[2] No record of this meeting has been found. See footnote 2, Document 95.

[3] Not printed.

Immediately after our May 11 meeting, our Embassies abroad were informed of possible approaches, and we requested their evaluations.[4] The immediate result was action by financial officials of Thailand to convert $47 million of liquid holdings into longer term deposits.

Assistant Secretary Trued held discussions immediately with financial officials in Japan, Korea, Taiwan and the Philippines—countries which benefit particularly from our expenditures in Southeast Asia. These discussions led to Japanese agreement for assistance to us of $300 million as an absolute minimum, with a potential further gain—assuming Japanese balance of payments does not reverse in highly unexpected fashion—of at least $200 million. Cooperation was promised by the other three countries within the capacity of their limited reserves and potential reserve gains this year, and we estimate at least $100 million assistance from those three combined.

Discussions have been held with officials of Mexico and Venezuela. Mexican officials have agreed to $80 million of these operations and $50 million is likely from Venezuela.

Discussions with World Bank and IDB officials have resulted in $270 million thus far in the second quarter. (Long term investments by the World Bank have been designed to offset its prospective $175 millon bond issue.)

On the occasion of his trip to Western Europe for meetings of the Deputies of the Group of Ten, Under Secretary Deming took occasion to discuss debt prepayment potential. As a result, Italy is prepaying $123 million of Export-Import Bank loans either this quarter or next. Belgian, French, Netherlands, German and Austrian officials are giving sympathetic consideration now. Realistic prospects for prepayment action would suggest perhaps no more than $200 million total from these countries this year.

These European prospects will be followed up in further conversations by Under Secretary Deming as he attends meetings of the Deputies of the Group of Ten and the Economic Policy Committee of the OECD in late June and early July, and I expect to visit with the Finance Ministers of France and the Netherlands when I attend the meeting of the Ministers and Governors of the Group of Ten in late July.

We now anticipate contacting certain other countries in the Middle East. A Treasury official will visit those countries where significant amounts might be obtained. At this point, we propose to limit ourselves to countries where significant amounts are involved since it is desirable to avoid widespread discussions that could trigger counter-productive concern over our position without the promise of substantial benefit to

---

[4] See Document 96.

us. However, approaches to some less promising countries can be held in reserve until later this year and, if necessary, action taken then to obtain further gains.

The attached schedule summarizes results thus far and prospects for the remainder of the year.

I should make it clear that even with the success we have had to date in this exercise, it does not appear as though the second quarter deficit will be lower than the first ($582 million on the liquidity basis). Furthermore, even if we are successful in obtaining debt prepayments and long term investments in the second half of the year, as indicated in the attached schedule, we will still be a considerable distance from equilibrium for the year as a whole. However, these efforts should help keep the deficit within reasonable bounds—from the standpoint of impact on public confidence and the foreign exchange markets—while we formulate fundamental new measures to cope with the basic problem.

Henry H. Fowler

99.   Memorandum From Secretary of the Treasury Fowler to President Johnson[1]

Washington, June 21, 1966.

SUBJECT

French Gold Purchases

I have just authorized another $100 million drop in the Treasury gold stock, which will bring the reduction for the first six months to $300 million.

Our sales of gold to France in the first half will total $324 million. In other words, exclusive of French purchases, our gold supply during the first six months would have increased—even after allowing for domestic industrial purchases. A $150 million sale by Canada has been most helpful. (The Canadians intend to sell an additional $50 million later this year.)

As you know, the French policy is to convert all dollar accruals into gold. Even with no accruals, however, they adhere to a policy of convert-

---

[1] Source: Johnson Library, Bator Papers, Balance of Payments, 1966 [2 of 2], Box 15. Confidential. A copy was sent to Bator.

ing a minimum of $34 million per month. Monthly conversions during the first half have averaged $54 million. However, French reserves have increased by over $100 million in the first two weeks of June, and conversions in July (which are based on June accruals) could run very substantially in excess of the monthly average to date.

Even though our gold losses are much smaller than last year, I am disturbed about the French attitude and by the implications of a continuation of their present gold-buying policy.[2] I would like to discuss the situation with you privately.

I plan to meet for the first time with Michel Debre, the new French Minister of Economy and Finance, at the Hague on July 25–26. The occasion will be the meeting of the Ministers of the Group of Ten, convened to consider the G–10 Deputies' report on international monetary reform.

Henry H. Fowler[3]

---

[2] Reflecting the concern with French gold purchases, Assistant Secretaries of State Solomon and Stoessel, on July 19, sent a memorandum to Under Secretary Ball entitled "A Proposal to Isolate France in the Field of International Finance." (Washington National Records Center, RG 56, Assistant Secretary for International Affairs, Deputy to the Assistant Secretary and Secretary of the International Monetary Group: FRC 83 A 26, Contingency Planning, 1965–1973, Contingency Planning 1966 Dale and Solomon Material) Solomon and Stoessel discussed the U.S. Government's decision to unilaterally cease selling gold to France, a policy of "selective non-convertibility." They noted that "an attempt to isolate France via selective non-convertibility would involve two major changes in U.S. policy. The first change would be to broaden the NATO crisis to encompass economic issues. Cessation of gold sales to France might appear to be the opening round of bilateral economic warfare. The second change would be to risk starting down the path of non-convertibility of the dollar into gold." In fact, this latter policy was under active consideration in the mid-1960s; a number of papers on breaking the dollar's link to gold, including a March 5, 1966, memorandum entitled "Breaking the Link to Gold," probably drafted by William B. Dale, U.S. Executive Director to the IMF, are ibid.

[3] Printed from a copy that indicates Fowler signed the original.

100. Memorandum From the President's Deputy Special Assistant for National Security Affairs (Bator) to President Johnson[1]

Washington, July 6, 1966.

SUJBECT

Balance of Payments

At Tab A is a complicated memorandum from the Secretary of the Treasury reporting on actions to limit the 1966 payments deficit.[2] We have been unexpectedly successful in arranging for about $1.5 billion of debt prepayments and long-term investment by foreign governments. About $600 million of this took place during the first half of '66. $900 million will be the gain during the 2nd half.

There are a number of points you should note:

1. The so-called "long-term investment"—accounting for $1.35 of the $1.5 billion—involves a switch by foreign central banks from holdings of liquid dollars to longer-term dollar securities. This is useful cosmetics; increases in foreign holdings of long-term securities do not count as part of our deficit. But it is a one-time gain. We cannot count on another $1 plus billion next year.

2. I do not believe that the $1.5 billion gain is likely to reduce our 1966 deficit, on a liquidity basis, much below $1.5–$2 billion (the 1965 rate was $1.3 billion; 1964 was $2.8 billion). Dollar spending in Vietnam, and, more important, the deterioration in our trade account (due to the still rapid expansion in the economy), will more than offset the gain.

However, we will be able to give you a much clearer picture of the prospects when we get preliminary results for the second quarter in mid-July.

3. I do not believe—and Fowler and your other economic advisers agree—that the situation calls for further drastic action. (It *would* take drastic steps sharply to reduce the deficit.) A serious run on gold during the rest of this year is *most* unlikely. And even if it should happen—*after November*—we would come out of it in better shape than we are in now. The truth is, that the present rules of the international money game are stacked against us. If the Europeans force a crisis, our economic strength and real bargaining leverage would soon become very clear to all concerned.

---

[1] Source: Johnson Library, National Security File, Subject File, Balance of Payments, Vol. 3 [1 of 2], Box 2. Secret; Very Sensitive. Handwritten at the top of the source text is the initial "L".

[2] Tab A, not printed, is a June 30 memorandum from Fowler to President Johnson entitled "Action to cut balance of payments deficit in 1966." It is very similar to Document 98.

4. The only pre-November danger is a run on sterling. With a strong UK reserve position, and the strike settled, I think it an even money bet that there will be no massive run during the summer. But it is certainly no better than an even bet. After a couple of good weeks, they are now beginning to lose money again.

5. If they can hold out until the autumn, their tough tax increase—which goes into effect in September—will take some of the pressure off the economy, holding down imports and releasing resources for export. But meanwhile, they are having a terrible time holding down wage rates and prices. This is not surprising, with unemployment at less than 1.5%.

6. Wilson's calculation is that, as long as total demand keeps pulling on capacity, business investment will keep expanding. If they can get investment up from 18% of GNP to about 25%, they will be able to increase productivity (and potential output) much faster than during the past fifteen years. (They are working hard to get investment into industries with the greatest technological and export potential.)

7. The risk Wilson takes is that the pressure of demand on capacity—which is needed to encourage the high rate of investment—will cause prices to get even more out of line. If so, devaluation will become increasingly hard to avoid.

8. Some of your advisers would consider a British devaluation a near disaster. I, myself, am increasingly convinced that—if it comes after November—it might offer us a unique chance to force a change in the rules of the game on gold. But these are preliminary as well as heretical thoughts. In the meanwhile, Deming, Okun, Solomon and I are working to bring our contingency plans of last summer up to date. We will be in good shape to spell out for you the choices, well before any real trouble.

FMB

101. Minutes of Meeting of the Cabinet Committee on Balance of Payments[1]

Washington, July 14, 1966.

Second Quarter Results and Outlook.

Secretary Fowler opened the meeting with a discussion of the current balance-of-payments situation and outlook. The preliminary second quarter "liquidity" deficit was down by several hundred million dollars from the $554 million deficit in the first quarter. The "official settlements" deficit may be roughly the same as in the first quarter.

The trade surplus which amounted to $4.5 billion in the first quarter on an annual rate basis was about a billion dollars less in the second quarter and averaged about $4 billion for the first half. First half exports were only about 2-1/2 percent above the first half 1965 level while imports were up about eight percent.

Gross military expenditures had risen in the second quarter and probably private capital outflows were somewhat higher.

A series of special transactions, however, netted us about $300 million to $400 million on the favorable side in the second quarter. These included: Canadian security repurchases; sizable investments in U.S. long-term assets by several international institutions; and long-term investments in C/D's by several countries benefiting directly from our expenditures in connection with Vietnam.

While the preliminary "liquidity" deficit for the first half was somewhat under $1 billion, the projection for the second half is somewhat over $1 billion based on a trade balance at about the level of the first half; a rise in military expenditures more than offset, however, by increased German military offset payments; some rise in direct investment; a small outflow of bank funds; and a considerable inflow of special receipts of the types that occurred in the second quarter. Without such receipts the deficit for the year would be nearer to $3 billion than to $2 billion.

Secretary Fowler then called on various agencies to discuss progress in meeting their targets.

Secretary McNamara indicated that their current projection of net expenditures was $1,980 million dollars—over $150 million above the $1,812 million goal they had set themselves last November, if one excludes the $200 million allowance for possible contingencies that had

---

[1] Source: Johnson Library, Fowler Papers, International Balance of Payments Committee: Cabinet Committee on Balance of Payments, 8/65–12/66, Box 52. Confidential. Drafted by Philip P. Schaffner (Treasury) on July 19. The meeting was held at the Treasury Department.

been made at that time. They expect to hold this year's net expenditures at the $2 billion level. This assumes receipts under the German military offset agreement of $575 million in the second half. It also assumes a savings of $20 million to $40 million through a partial shift of petroleum procurement to the United States. He anticipated no force reductions this year in Europe. In fact, there would be a build-up by the end of the year of 15,000 troops to reinstate the level in Germany that had existed at the beginning of 1966.

Secretary Fowler asked about the possibilities of recouping something from U.S. military property in France.

Secretary McNamara thought nothing was likely to come of this in the near future. He mentioned that we have several kinds of rights that should be negotiated as a package at the appropriate time. These rights cover about $1 billion of grant military aid deliveries in operable condition and with a current value of possibly $200 million to $400 million, as well as about a billion dollars in investment in bases.

Secretary Fowler pointed out that if it were not for French purchases of gold here, we would actually have a net accumulation of gold so far this year.

Under Secretary Ball said that we needed to maintain our "over-fly" rights in France, a factor that had to be considered in considering a negotiation for a financial settlement on our property there. We have reversionary rights for some of our expenditures in connection with bases for which the French acknowledge some settlement responsibility. We also have a theoretical right to compensation for moving costs on the grounds that the French breached an agreement, but there is almost no chance of obtaining anything on this basis. Finally, we have recapture rights to MAP grant military aid deliveries where there may be some possibility of a financial settlement, but any immediate prospect for such a settlement is very dim.

Secretary Fowler said he planned to talk to the French at The Hague meeting of the Group of Ten Ministers on the subject of another French debt prepayment; but he also wanted another "string to his bow." He would talk further with Secretary McNamara and Under Secretary Ball about developing some bargaining approach on a financial settlement.

Secretary Fowler asked Secretary McNamara whether expenditures abroad other than in the Southeast Asia area could be trimmed.

Secretary McNamara indicated that 50 percent of the 1966 budgeted amounts outside the Southeast Asia area is already being deferred.

AID Director Bell indicated that his agency in November had projected savings of $90 million for 1966. However, due to greater than contemplated draw-downs of U.S. subscriptions by international organizations, the net savings will only be about $45 million. Gross expenditures will be around $427 million in 1966 rather than the $382 million that had been hoped for.

Secretary Fowler asked about the various studies that were being made to promote our commercial exports to AID-recipient countries and to improve the letter of credit procedure for tying our aid dollars. He pointed out that a number of countries showed a very poor record of commercial imports from the U.S. between 1957 and 1964 when their aid imports from the U.S. were increasing. He thought that a study of this situation deserved high priority.

Mr. Bell referred to the Commerce–AID study on this subject. He also said that in order to guard against aid-financing of U.S. products that aid-recipient countries would otherwise purchase on commercial terms, AID was reviewing its eligible list of commodities.

Mr. Bator reported that there would be something ready by the end of the month regarding improvement of the letter of credit procedure.

The Secretary questioned Mr. Bell about his position that assignment of AID export specialists to each field mission for the purpose of promoting U.S. exports would seem inappropriate within the context of AID's functions and responsibilities. He thought that the commercial attachés could work more effectively if there were one person in each AID mission to whom they could turn for cooperation in promotion of exports.

Mr. Bell replied that they would be glad to cooperate with the commercial attachés but that they were not in the business of export promotion. He asked to be informed of any cases of non-cooperation.

Under Secretary Ball indicated that State was considering a merger of its economic and commercial sections in each embassy to make commercial trade promotion more effective.

Secretary Connor said that there was little chance of approval of an increase in the number of commercial attachés by Representative Rooney's subcommittee.[2] He thought we were losing out on exports to Japan, for example, because of price reasons, due in part to Japan's proximity to markets like Korea.

Gold Budget.

Budget Director Schultze said that they had just finished their "gold budget" report based on the March submissions and that the combined net outflow on a "regular transaction" basis had declined from $2.8 billion in FY 1963 to $2.4 billion in FY 1964 to $2.2 billion in FY 1965. In FY 1966, however, they rose to $2.6 billion and the prospective figure for FY 1967 was $2.9 billion. It would drop again to $1.8 billion in FY 1968 on the

---

[2] Representative John J. Rooney (D.–N.Y.), Chairman of the Subcommittee on Appropriations for State, Justice, Commerce, the Judiciary, and Related Agencies.

assumption of no war after July 1, 1967. The rise between FY 1965 and FY 1967 was more than accounted for by DOD and AID expenditures in connection with Vietnam. The expenditures of other agencies were about level in FY 1966 and 1967 but their receipts were accelerating so that their net expenditures showed a decline of about $167 million.

BOB has sent letters to six major agencies with research operations abroad asking for a submission of their budgeted costs and personnel requirements for such operations by August 6. (Combined research expenditures abroad amounted to around $35 million per year.) Budget was also looking into the possibilities of acquiring for government use abroad blocked foreign currencies held by private U.S. firms, of selling more savings bonds to civilian personnel abroad, and of using our excess currency holdings in certain countries more intensively. BOB was studying U.S. dollar outflows to international organizations to determine what portion returned for expenditures in this country. Finally, they were talking to the Agriculture Department about the latter's expansion of agricultural sales promotion activities under the Agriculture Marketing Act.[3]

With regard to a point raised by Under Secretary Barr, he said that he would take a look at payments under the Philippine veterans' claims settlements.

Commerce Programs.

Secretary Connor said that the first quarter special VCP reports showed no discrepancies from the regular OBE reports filed by companies under the program. He pointed out that the majority of companies would better their targets and would complete their projected schedules for borrowing abroad. He had talked or written to about half of the 49 companies which were failing to meet their targets by $5 million or more.

Secretary McNamara asked about the reason for the large increase in U.S. imports.

Secretary Connor replied that all types of imports were increasing. He thought production shortages were accounting for both the large increase in imports and for the relatively small increase in exports.

Secretary McNamara did not think that shortages played an important role. He feared we are freezing ourselves in at a high level of imports that would be difficult to reverse. He did not believe that the rise in DOD expenditures due to the Vietnam conflict had an important adverse effect on our trade balance. He pointed out that Defense expenditures were a smaller percentage of GNP than in the previous four or five years.

---

[3] Agricultural Marketing Act of 1946, 7 USC 1621–1627 (60 Stat. 1087) amended and approved on September 7, 1966, P.L. 89–556 (80 Stat. 694).

He asked whether somebody might see if the Brookings people had made a revision of their projection of the U.S. trade balance in 1968.

Secretary Fowler asked Mr. Knowlton to inquire about this matter. He then asked Secretary Connor why projected direct investment income was down.

Secretary Connor replied that he was not sure of all the reasons, but that according to his Business Advisory Committee, profits of U.S. subsidiaries abroad were lower due to growing competition. He would look further into the matter.

With regard to getting railroads to reduce their freight rates on coal hauled for export, Secretary Connor said that the companies claim the U.S. can sell all coal available for export at present prices. He did not think, therefore, that there was any possibility of getting the railroads to reduce rates, particularly in view of the fact that they had to provide more service in connection with coal for export.

Secretary Fowler referred to a letter from a firm which indicated it had greatly increased its use of American ships. He wondered whether more could be done on this score.

Secretary Connor replied that there was a shortage of U.S. commercial ships due to DOD use in connection with the Vietnam war.

Secretary McNamara said he could pull ships out of moth balls, man them with Navy crews, and release the ships he was now using for commercial transport.

Budget Director Schultze thought that such an operation would involve a high budget cost relative to the prospective balance-of-payments savings.

Secretary Fowler pointed out that the transportation business we are losing under the present arrangement might be lost to us forever.

It was agreed that Commerce and Labor would prepare a plan on this matter for DOD consideration. Budget Director Schultze asked that Budget be allowed to review the plan.

Federal Reserve Program.

Governor Robertson said that banks were about $119 million under their December 31, 1964, level of claims on foreigners and almost $800 million under their target ceiling. He thought there might be a very small outflow in the last half of their year, but not as much as $1 million.

Secretary Fowler asked if the Federal Reserve knew whether a disproportionate share of our import financing were being done by American institutions rather than by the foreign exporters and their financing institutions.

Governor Robertson said he would look into the matter.

Possible Announcements For Mid-August Press Conference.

Secretary Fowler then turned to the list of possible items for announcement in connection with the mid-August press conference on the second quarter balance-of-payments results. He requested that Commerce and AID in connection with BOB and others work on the plan for a high level trade mission to AID-recipient countries to promote U.S. exports. He promised to send some Treasury material on this subject to Commerce and AID.

With regard to the opening of the Exim rediscount facility the Secretary said that he hoped it could be announced at the mid-August press conference.

With regard to announcement of the clarified IRS guidelines for intra-company pricing, the Secretary expressed a wish to review this matter with Secretary Connor.

The possibility of announcing an expansion of the U.S. Travel Service depended on a BOB study which would be completed within a few weeks.

With regard to requesting Congress to further reduce exemptions for U.S. tourists, the Secretary indicated his staff had estimated possible savings of $100 million per year. He had not yet made up his mind about an approach to Congress.

P.S.

102. Memorandum of Conversation Between U.S. and British Officials[1]

Washington, July 29, 1966, 12:15 p.m.

SUBJECT

International Monetary Situation

PARTICIPANTS

See attachment[2]

The Prime Minister said there had been general agreement in recent years about the need to increase liquidity. This was required by the rapid increase in world trade; moreover, the successful completion of the Kennedy Round would require greater liquidity.

The Prime Minister spoke briefly on the meetings of the Group of Ten, saying that Secretary Fowler gained an important procedural victory at The Hague but there is still a danger of being sabotaged by divisions among some of the members of the group as well as by the outright obstruction of France. Nevertheless, he hoped that the Group of Ten could agree and that this agreement could be expanded "from the 10 to the 100 countries".

The Prime Minister said that one problem the British have, as well as the United States, is that of the balance of payments; we must correct this. Otherwise, the two great reserve currencies of the world will be driven into a corner by the self-righteous members of the Group of Ten who do not have any responsibilities for world development, banking or military assistance.

The Prime Minister noted it would be useful if we could start to do some thinking in the event that we fail to make progress in the Group of

---

[1] Source: Department of State, Central Files, POL 7 UK. Confidential; Exdis. Drafted by Walter J. Stoessel, Jr. (EUR) and approved by S and U on August 4, Bator on August 15, and Widman (Treasury) on August 24. The meeting was held in the Cabinet Room of the White House. The source text is labeled "Part 5 of 6." Prime Minister Wilson visited Washington July 28–29. In preparation for President Johnson's meeting with Wilson, Secretary Rusk, on the morning of July 29, discussed over the telephone with the President several subjects for discussion. Concerning Wilson's financial program, the President observed that "he's biting some bullets and has some tough days ahead and so have we." He said that he would listen to the Prime Minister and if any U.S. financial involvement or public commitments were required, he would suggest talks on a multilateral basis and with "our financial people." The Secretary agreed. (Johnson Library, Recordings and Transcripts, Recording of Telephone Conversation between President Johnson and Secretary Rusk, July 29, 1966, 10:40 a.m., Tape F66.18, Side B, PNO 1)

[2] The attached list is not printed. The President; Secretaries Rusk, Fowler, and McNamara; and Under Secretaries Ball and Deming participated for the United States. Prime Minister Wilson, Denis A. Greenhill of the British Foreign Office, and British Ambassador Sir Patrick Dean participated for the United Kingdom.

Ten. He knew that we had our Dillon Committee and the British have a counterpart of this committee. They should get together and the staffs should talk purposefully about their problems.

The Prime Minister stressed that the British intend to solve their balance of payments problem. They are some 200,000,000 pounds short and it should be possible to overcome this gap.

Secretary Fowler commented that we should concert on the timetable in connection with our efforts concerning the liquidity problem. He was satisfied by the report of the Deputies, which will be made public August 25; he felt that the public would be gratified at the measure of agreement reached by the Deputies. Even the technicians of the Bank of France had found a substantial measure of agreement. Secretary Fowler thought there had been sufficient agreement at The Hague meeting to enable us to move into the IMF. This can be a very significant step, since the question of liquidity must be resolved in a broader context rather than in the secret deliberations of the Group of Ten.

Secretary Fowler continued that there is agreement among the Group of 9 on the need for machinery for achieving liquidity. A decision to activate the machinery is a different matter—much will depend on the U.S. and the UK bringing their balances of payments into order. Early activation is very important to help finance expanding world trade, to make reserves available for orderly balance of payments adjustment, particularly since sharp deflation is not an acceptable method of adjustment. Another, and very basic reason for moving in this direction is that it will provide a means of reducing the vulnerabilities of the UK and U.S. currencies. We should press hard with the idea of establishing machinery for handling the liquidity problem in time for the IMF meeting in September 1967.

The Prime Minister said that it was good to move on procedural matters but that it was important to agree between ourselves on the problem before September 1967. Our currencies are vulnerable and can be affected adversely by political and by economic speculation. The French have acted in this sense by selling sterling at the time of the bombing near Hanoi and Haiphong; in doing this they were really aiming at the United States.

Secretary Fowler said that the only rationale for French policy on gold is a political one. The events at The Hague meeting indicated that we have to keep the pressure on the Dutch, Italians, Germans and Belgians to hold them firm in connection with the French.

The Prime Minister said that the French policy in economics was the policy of Rueff, which is outdated and, in fact, was outdated before 1931.

The Prime Minister said that he would proceed firmly to defend sterling.[3] He was grateful for the help of the Federal Reserve System and the superb operations they had mounted. The more the world understands that the dollar and sterling are linked together the better it will be. But if necessary, the British will stay up on their own. They are not going to bring the dollar down with them.

Secretary Fowler stated that the other seven countries—Germany, Italy, Holland, Belgium, Japan, Canada and Sweden—must share in the multilateral defense of sterling. They cannot go their own way since their whole position would be threatened if sterling were endangered.

---

[3] The Prime Minister's assurances notwithstanding, the Treasury Department, presumably in collaboration with other interested agencies, was giving considerable thought to what might be done if sterling were devalued. In a July 18 paper entitled "Contingency Plans for Use in the Event of a Sterling Devaluation," four options were summarized. Subsequent papers fleshed out these options, went into an analysis of their economic implications, and set out operational plans, including lists of key contacts in 20 countries and the IMF and draft messages to Embassies and guidance for Ambassadors. (Washington National Records Center, RG 56, Assistant Secretary for International Affairs, Deputy to the Assistant Secretary and Secretary of the International Monetary Group: FRC 83 A 26, Secret–Contingency Planning, 1966–67) The dated papers range from July 18 to August 14, 1966. The papers are not addressed to any particular individual and do not contain drafting information. They are arranged in their folder under cover of an index headed "Contingency Planning."

---

103.   Telegram From the White House Situation Room to President Johnson, in Texas[1]

Washington, August 29, 1966, 12:08 a.m.

CAP 66596. Mr. Rostow has asked this message to be sent to you. Arrangements have been made to inform Secretaries Rusk and McNamara.

From Prime Minister to the President.

Like you, I am sure we must keep in being the essential arrangements which have deterred aggression in the Atlantic area. I should be

---

[1] Source: Johnson Library, Bator Papers, Trilaterals, Box 19. Secret. A stamped notation at the top of the first page reads: "Sent WHCA 1966 AUG 29 00 08." The original date of the message from Prime Minister Wilson is not legible on the source text. President Johnson was at the LBJ Ranch August 26–30.

the last to want to break down the framework within which the United States has sustained the defence of Europe and a German contribution has been made possible under satisfactory safeguards. Whether the balance of deterrence in Europe need be maintained at its present level is something which we must study urgently together. Indeed, we already have studies in hand: A prime concern must certainly be to work for matching reductions on the Soviet side. You may recall that I told you when we met that Kosygin showed considerable interest in matched reductions.[2]

Against this background I am very ready to agree to the tripartite talks which you propose. On my return to London I shall give urgent consideration to these with my colleagues. I feel bound to say, however, that we should be most reluctant to enter into such talks without bilateral discussions with you first. Obviously the well-being of NATO depends very largely on agreement between its three leading countries, and I realise that you do not want to give any impression of ganging-up with us against the Germans. But since we both keep troops in Germany at a heavy cost in foreign exchange, we share a special interest in these talks: and it seems to me essential that we should first consider our position together. I will arrange for a Minister or Ministers to be ready to go to Washington this week. Unless we concert our position, there is the risk of the Germans playing us off against each other.

As I emphasized to you when we met at the end of July,[3] my major concern at present is to take effective action to safeguard sterling, both in its own right and as the first line of defence for the dollar. We have taken drastic measures to cut down spending power at home. We are also determined to deal directly with the drain of foreign exchange abroad. A major and urgent part of this is the need to stop the haemorrhage of foreign exchange flowing from the stationing of our forces in Germany, and what is at stake for us is the success of our programme of economic measures in defence of the currency. If what we are doing is going to result in a lasting cure, we must move fast and I am glad to see that you accept that some of the decisions with which we are now faced cannot await the outcome of tripartite talks.

For this reason I am sure you will understand that we cannot afford to hold up the talks in NATO, on which we have already embarked and of which the next round indeed begins on Monday.[4] I hope that your representatives will be authorised to make a substantive contribution to these talks.

---

[2] This meeting has not been further identified.

[3] See Document 102.

[4] Presumably August 29.

Similarly, the Anglo-German Mixed Commission already has an agreed timetable and programme of work and in view of the need to secure the highest possible German financial contribution we could not contemplate any interruption of the Commission's work.

Let us then advance on all these fronts at once. When you have heard from Erhard, we must consult again about a time and place for our talks. We shall be ready at any time.

104. Editorial Note

West German Chancellor Ludwig Erhard visited Washington September 24–27, 1966. In a telephone conversation on September 24, most of which focused on a possible cut or suspension of government spending along with a tax bill to balance expenditures and revenue and to bring about an easing of interest rates, President Johnson and Secretary of the Treasury Fowler also discussed what the President might say personally to Erhard on the question of U.S.-West German "offset" payments for the support of U.S. forces in Germany. Fowler emphasized that the Germans should "pay up in advance . . . their money obligations to us . . . between now and next June 30." They had "paid up to date only 20 percent of their 2-year commitment," he continued, and "we ought to be awfully firm on Erhard to pay up," especially since the German economy was in good financial condition.(Johnson Library, Recordings and Transcripts, Recording of Telephone Conversation between President Johnson and Secretary Fowler, September 24, 1966, 4:15 p.m., Tape F66.26, Side A, PNO 1) For a memorandum of President Johnson's conversation with Erhard on September 26 on this and other defense issues, see *Foreign Relations, 1964–1968*, volume XIII, pages 471–478.

In a telephone conversation with President Johnson later the same day, Secretary of Defense McNamara reported on his just concluded meeting with German Defense Minister Kai-Uwe von Hassel. On the question of offset payments, McNamara said that the German position was complicated, and he concluded from his conversation with von Hassel that the Germans "would fulfill the present offset agreement, but it would lag along a while." McNamara argued that "one of our objectives must be to put ourselves in a position so that we can say to Mansfield that they did fulfill it, even though it's by hocus pocus." He concluded that the result would be "satisfactory to me, and I think Joe [Fowler] would probably accept it grudgingly ultimately." (Johnson Library, Recordings and Transcripts, Recording of Telephone Conversation between President Johnson and Secretary McNamara, September 24, 1966, 7:40 p.m., Tape F66.26, Side B, PNO 1)

---

105. Memorandum From Secretary of the Treasury Fowler to President Johnson[1]

Washington, November 8, 1966.

SUBJECT

Balance of Payments Planning for 1967

The Cabinet Committee on Balance of Payments has had two recent meetings and is deeply engaged in planning for next year.[2] We have covered the waterfront in our discussions, giving attention to both the *overall outlook* and *the major components* of our balance of payments statement (emphasizing trade, tourism, government expenditures, and capital outflows covered by our voluntary programs).

These meetings have made it clear that there are unusual uncertainties ahead:

—the fate of the German offset (Will we receive the $1,000 million owed us between now and June 30th?)
—the cost of Vietnam
—the domestic economic program for 1967.

It is clear that the decisions we make on the domestic front with respect to fiscal and monetary policies will have an important impact on our trade surplus and our capital flows next year.

The Cabinet Committee believes that *our overall objective in 1967 should be to "continue to move toward balance of payments equilibrium as fast as the continued financial costs of Vietnam permit".*

Even if those uncertainties described above are resolved on the favorable side, our forecasts suggest an unacceptable deficit in 1967—in

---

[1] Source: Johnson Library, Bator Papers, Balance of Payments, 1966 [2 of 2], Box 15. Secret. Drafted by J.R. Petty (OS).

[2] These meetings have not been further identified.

relation to this objective—*if we do not continue an active restraint program.* With this starting point we have been considering a program basically voluntary in character.

—Industry has cooperated under the Commerce program so far. Can we tighten the program without having it come apart at the seams?

—The Federal Reserve guidelines have a large leeway, due to tight money conditions. Can we tighten this program while providing adequate financing for lesser developed countries and exports?

—Governmental outflows have been reduced by improved procedures and other than more efficient management of these procedures in 1967 it is difficult to find other significant savings.

—The Interest Equalization Tax expires June 30 and its extension should be planned.

—The tourism outflow continues to mount.

—in view of the Vietnam emergency would the people respond to an appeal to moderate foreign travel?
—would such an appeal help sell stiffer programs to banks and corporations?

—Foreign travel in the U.S. still lacks active stimulus. Can we get appropriations for an enlarged U.S. Travel Service?

Timing of announcement could be done in two phases:

—Outline by early December the voluntary character and highlights of the corporate and bank programs, in time for industry's forward planning.

—Detail the *full* program at the time of your Budget Message, waiting until then because of the major influence the Government's 1967 economic program has on our balance of payments picture.

If you agree, I could indicate at my November 14th press conference (on third quarter balance of payments results) the nature of this proposed timetable in order to dispel any uncertainties.

Henry H. Fowler[3]

---

[3] Printed from a copy that indicates Fowler signed the original.

106.   Minutes of Meeting of the Cabinet Committee on the Balance of Payments[1]

Washington, December 5, 1966, 3 p.m.

Secretary Fowler reviewed briefly the most recent forecast we have for 1967 which, as of now, includes a trade surplus of $4.9 billion, a GNP of $790 billion and a 6.8 percent growth (of which four percent is real). Without a balance of payments program this adds up to deficit in the neighborhood of $3 billion on a liquidity basis. Secretary Fowler read to the Committee much of his November 8 Memorandum to the President[2] including the time schedule which recommends the possible announcement of the first stage of the 1967 program, particularly the corporate and bank program early in December with the rest of the program to be tied into the Economic Message in January.

Mr. Knowlton advised the group that the Executive Committee felt that the Federal Reserve program was generally satisfactory and while there were minor wording changes, particularly regarding Canada and Japan, they have been resolved and there is no need to trouble the Cabinet Committee. Chairman Martin said that the Federal Reserve is ready to release their program.

Mr. Knowlton, reporting on the Executive Committee's attitude about the Commerce Department's proposal, said there was a strong feeling that the program should be tightened further, specifically that Commerce should shoot for the level on an O.B.E. basis of $2.4 billion (less Delaware subs) compared with projected net direct investment outflows for next year of $2.75 billion. The Executive Committee explored several methods by which Commerce might tighten the program believing that Commerce should decide how to employ these techniques.

Secretary Fowler asked can the Commerce Department program be tightened without losing the success or the character of the program. Mr. Connor feels, Secretary Fowler said, that if we introduce a net direct investment target below $2.75 billion we will be risking having the program come apart at the seams. The past formula would allow corporations to have a goal of 135% and Commerce has already tightened the program to 125%. The Secretary reviewed the net direct investment fig-

---

[1] Source: Johnson Library, Fowler Papers, Voluntary Program, Box 16. Confidential. Drafted by John R. Petty (Treasury) on December 10. The meeting was held in Secretary Fowler's Conference Room. A list of participants is not printed; the following attended the meeting: Gaud (AID), Schnittker (Agriculture), Schultze (BOB), Ackley (CEA), Secretary Connor, Secretary McNamara, Martin (Federal Reserve), Rostow (State), Roth (Trade Negotiations), Fowler, Knowlton, and Petty (Treasury), and Bator. Copies were sent to Secretary Fowler and Knowlton, Petty, and Schaffner.

[2] Document 105.

ures for 1964–1967 and referred to the attitude of the Executive Committee where it was felt that lower figures were justified. He added that it was the conclusion of the IMF consultants that there be further tightening in the corporate program, but their recommendation was not quantified. The Secretary said he recognized that Secretary Connor and his Advisory Committee can not stretch their program too far, nevertheless a further reduction in the over-all target is desirable. If we measure what happened on the direct investment account in 1966 against estimates, we realize that there is some slippage. Secretary Fowler also said that government is working under a handicap in outlining the balance of payments program before the Administration's Economic Message is ready. This problem of planning could be even worse next year and it would be preferable to decide on the program after the President had prepared his Economic Message. This would argue for extending the termination date of next year's program until March 31, 1968. The figures could be adjusted; for example to averaging net direct investments of $3 billion over five quarters, rather than $2.4 billion over the year. This stretch-out could be accompanied by a request to industries to moderate their expansion overseas and it would assist forecasting. Finally he said that the export target set for industries next year could be a little more strenuous than that anticipated in the proposed program.

Secretary Connor said he wanted to clarify certain misconceptions which the Committee seemed to harbor. The Commerce program was not aimed exclusively at reducing capital outflows, there are other selected transactions which indicated increased exports and a high repatriation of foreign earnings. He mentioned that the reporting companies contributed $1.4 billion in 1965, $1 billion in 1966, and $2 billion is forecast in 1967 of which $1.6 billion of this latter figure comes from an increase of exports. Secretary Connor said that he felt that the $4.9 billion trade surplus forecast for 1967 was perhaps optimistic, and that in general in planning a program we are just playing with numbers, none of which we can be sure of; therefore, if we are going to keep the program on a voluntary basis we must wait until industry tells us what they can do before we decide if the program can be tightened any further. The Secretary said that the program objective in 1967 is designed to maintain the same level of outflow as that achieved in 1966. He argued that it was not reasonable to tighten the program further during a period of growth in gross plant and equipment expenditures. Furthermore he did not feel that the activities of the 722 reporting companies could be related in a meaningful way to the O.B.E. figure, because of the several items involved in the latter compilation over which the Commerce Department has no control. With respect to the idea of putting the program on a five quarter basis the Secretary argued that this would create a great inconvenience to companies, an inconvenience which is not justified.

Mr. Knowlton emphasized that the trade estimate was put together by an interagency group chaired by the Commerce Department. He added that exports grew by more than 12 percent in 1966 and Commerce was asking their companies to achieve less in export expansion in 1967 than they did in 1966. Secretary Connor questioned how meaningful an export target was, since it was in the interest of corporations to push these as much as possible anyway. Secretary Fowler thought a higher target might encourage them to work a little harder. Secretary McNamara said that more exports are not equivalent to an improvement in net direct investments, which is the objective. He went on to raise the broader question that he feared the U.S. was cutting its foreign policy too close because of balance of payments considerations. If this results in cutting back on our objectives we would be paying a very serious price indeed. Nevertheless he recognized that balance of payments considerations are a fact of life—a concern shared by all. It is all mythology, but it is a myth in which people believe and therefore we must contend with it.

In conclusion, Secretary McNamara agreed that the total projected deficit for 1967, after applying the proposed program, was still too large and further efforts would be required. Secretary Connor suggested that there might be a cutback in Vietnam. Secretary McNamara felt that this suggestion identified the issue: We are being asked to cut back in our basic foreign policy objectives in order that U.S. corporations may continue their investing overseas. In dealing with this entire balance of payments problem, we are running too close to the line, always being ready to cut back in our effort to achieve our basic objectives in order that we may satisfy the balance of payments standard.

Secretary Fowler, referring to the projections, said that even on the most optimistic estimates, he felt that there was a need to bring direct investments down further and, in addition, industry must be asked to stretch out its foreign expansion—just as all aspects of the United States Government and private alike are asked to moderate expenditures: no one is asking that they be stopped. Secretary McNamara felt that the balance of payments program, that is, the Federal Reserve and Commerce programs were too thin to recommend to the President, and standing alone they were unsatisfactory. Secretary Rostow commenting on his recent trip observed that while the myth of equilibrium was being preached, a deficit of around $1.5 billion was bringing home to the Europeans what the true implications were to everybody of the United States reaching equilibrium. Moreover, he felt that increasingly we were getting support for what we were trying to achieve in Vietnam. Secretary Fowler, in referring to Secretary McNamara's statement, stated that we are all in the business of cutting things fine these days; we are seeking to proceed with a great society, foreign aid, Vietnam, and free capital flows, all in the framework of a free economy. This can only be achieved by cutting things very fine and he suggested that the Commerce program was not cut fine enough. Secretary Connor believed that his program was as far as he could go; that to tighten it further might cause it to come apart at the seams. If the program is to maintain its voluntary character, the Secretary said there was strong recommendation to continue it at the 125 percent level. If the objectives are not met in the future those who change it will say that industry has failed.

Mr. Bator said he felt that the key to the problem rests in the continued expansion of gross plant and of equipment expenditures overseas. Using this continued growth as a justification for the higher direct investment figure was not appropriate. On the contrary, he concluded that this growth figure had to be pared down. Secretary Connor said that he did not think this was possible on a voluntary basis, although he intended to include in his announcement a plea for moderated expenditures in the year ahead. Ambassador Roth inquired if it was possible to establish a 120 percent target and adjust it upward if the reports to be received in February indicated that this was necessary. Mr. Knowlton inquired if substantial foreign investments (less Delaware subs) were $2.9 billion, and if the reporting companies accounted for $1.9 billion, then after allowing for less developed countries and certain financial transactions from Canada, there remained a hole that might be plugged. He inquired if a group might not be set up to examine this area and suggest methods to close these holes. Secretary Connor explained that there were signs that the nature of the gross plant and equipment expenditures was changing. It appeared that there was evidence of few *new* ventures and increasingly more money was being spent on expanding existing operations.

Secretary Fowler said the issue is, is it reasonable to reduce direct net investments from $2.75 billion to $2.4 billion? "No," said Secretary Connor, not in the face of growing expenditures. Mr. Bator said that the risk of trying to save $300 million more in the Commerce program was less than the other risks that are involved. Secretary McNamara argued that we must not push too fast to achieve our burden sharing objective. Secretary Fowler said that if $300 or $400 million were saved in the Commerce program, severe efforts for further improvement are still required in other areas. Secretary Connor felt that it would not be possible to tighten the Commerce program further without losing the voluntary character of the program. He thought that the Federal Reserve program had in fact been loosened.

Secretary Fowler distributed the proposed letter from the President to the Chairman of the Balance of Payments Committee. The general comments on this letter were favorable but final comments were reserved.[3] Secretary McNamara said that the confidential memorandum

---

[3] An apparent reference to the letter cited in footnote 5, Document 107.

to the President should reflect the attitude that the members were not satisfied with just a bank and corporate program, and that additional measures were required in the travel and export stimulation areas, to mention a few.[4]

Secretary Fowler said he did not want to bring a divided issue before the President, and asked if he could not say it was the sense of the Committee that the Commerce program should be marginally tighter. Administrator Gaud inquired if the Committee was ruling out the possibility of efforts in the area of tourism. The tourist flow gives no benefit to the balance of payments in either the long or short run. Should we not do something here? Secretary Connor argued for an appeal by the President that the tourists moderate their foreign travel, referring to the sacrifices being made in Vietnam. Secretary Fowler referred to the notes of the last meeting, where there was a suggestion (1) that the President make an appeal to the public on tourism, (2) that passport fees should be increased with the proceeds going to support the U.S. Travel Agency, and (3) reduction in the customs exemption.[5] Secretary McNamara called the overall program limited and asked for another program which would cut the tourist outflow and build the foundations for the future when we would not be plagued by this problem. Secretary Fowler agreed with the need for a long-term program, but emphasized the importance of announcing in the very near future the continuation of the voluntary cooperation program on the balance of payments, in order that industry may be given time to plan and comply. Secretary Rostow said that he was impressed with the argument that some restraint on tourism would help the private business community respond to the appeal and meet their target. Secretary McNamara felt that a passport fee increase was not restrictive. It would support the President's appeal and it would provide the revenue needed for the travel service. It was agreed that his recommendation could be included in the confidential letter to the President, although legislation may be required to obtain the increased fee. Director Schultze dissented on the budgetary grounds that earmarked funds were undesirable. Secretary Fowler emphasized that while only the short range programs are being discussed today, long-term measures will be actively pursued, such as encouraging the inflow of capital; developing foreign capital markets; mechanics to put the restraint program on a standby basis but ready to be reinvoked; encouragement of tourism in the United States; export promotion and possible tax incentives; realigning the balance of payments costs of military commitments; sharing the burden of assistance to the LDCs; and IMF reform. Chairman Ackley reserved judgment on whether an increased passport fee on tour-

---

[4] Presumably a reference to Document 108.
[5] This meeting has not been further identified.

ism was enough, or whether we should not examine a tax on foreign travel. Mr. Knowlton urged that the timing of any action on tourism be postponed until January and not to have it coincide with the forthcoming announcement on the bank and corporate program. Secretary Fowler concurred, stating that he had to discuss this with Vice President Humphrey. He added that Treasury was prepared to reduce the customs exemption to $10. Mr. Bator felt that tightening the tourist program could only be achieved if the corporate program was tighter. Secretary Fowler added that extension of the IET would be required, and that the possibility of a change in the economic policy mix underscored the need for the tax extension. Under Secretary Schnittker said that in our forthcoming examination of long-term measures, we should re-examine the issue of cargo preference as well as switching soy beans from a restricted to a general license. Secretary Connor agreed that this was timely.

JR Petty

---

107. Memorandum From Secretary of the Treasury Fowler to President Johnson[1]

Washington, December 6, 1966.

Enclosed is my report of the Cabinet Committee on the Balance of Payments covering the first stage of the program we recommend for 1967.[2] You will recall in my previous memorandum of November 8,[3] I suggested that this program be announced in two stages. The first announcement would come in early December and it would pertain to the Federal Reserve and Commerce Department programs. We feel that it is necessary to get this announcement out in order that industry may incorporate the guidelines in their own forward planning, as well as to remove any apprehension about the nature of next year's balance of payments program, apprehension which may cause speculative capital outflows in the final weeks of the year. The second stage of the 1967 program

---

[1] Source: Johnson Library, National Security File, Subject File, Balance of Payments, Vol. 3 [1 of 2] Box 2. Confidential.

[2] Not enclosed, but presumably a reference to Document 108.

[3] Document 105.

should be detailed at the time of your Economic Message. I suggested waiting until then because of the major influence the Government's 1967 economic program has on our balance of payments picture. When we discussed this at the Ranch, you indicated that this timing made sense.

On the first phase of our 1967 program I had hoped to be able to forward a unanimous recommendation from your Cabinet Committee. However, after nearly three hours of discussion on Monday,[4] involving the principals only, preceded by previous Cabinet Committee meetings and a number of contacts at the staff level we have been unable to reconcile one difference in judgment on the issue, described in the attached report, of the appropriate degree of tightness in the Commerce program. We must submit this issue to you for resolution.

If you can see your way clear to approve the proposed programs, and decide the unreconciled issue, we would hope to be able to announce these measures this Friday, at a joint press conference held by Secretary Connor, Chairman Martin (or Governor Robertson), and myself. I will be abroad in Athens next week, at the King's Prayer Breakfast, and then at the NATO Ministerial Meetings. Therefore, if it is not possible to make the announcement by Friday, we would not hold a joint press conference but simply release the various documents to the press when you approve the Federal Reserve program and the proposals for the Commerce program or some modification thereof. Secretary Connor and Governor Robertson would deal with press inquiries as they consider appropriate.

Assuming you approve the continuation of the program, the material to be released to the public would include (1) a letter from you to me as Chairman of the Balance of Payments Committee giving your approval (Tab A);[5] (2) the Department of Commerce release describing their program (Tab B);[6] and (3) the Federal Reserve release describing their program (Tab C).[7]

Henry H. Fowler[8]

---

[4] December 5. See Document 106.

[5] The tabs were not attached. The approved version of the letter was released to the public on December 12 at a White House press conference; for text, see *American Foreign Policy: Current Documents, 1966*, pp. 981–982.

[6] The approved version of the press release was released to the public on December 13 at a Department of Commerce press conference; for text, see ibid., pp. 982–985.

[7] Regarding Secretary Fowler's statement, December 13, announcing the 1967 Balance of Payments Program, see Document 110.

[8] Printed from a copy that bears this typed signature.

108. Memorandum From the Cabinet Committee on Balance of Payments to President Johnson[1]

Washington, December 6, 1966.

SUBJECT

Continuation of the Voluntary Cooperation Program in 1967

Your Cabinet Committee on the Balance of Payments has been engaged in an intensive appraisal of the balance-of-payments outlook for 1966 and 1967. Completion of this appraisal and formulation of an over-all program for next year must await decisions on next year's budget and other aspects of domestic economic policy.

However, one *major* element of the program requires an immediate decision, with a view to public announcement as soon as possible— hopefully by the end of this week. This concerns the continuation of the voluntary cooperation program for *business corporations, banks, and other financial institutions* administered by the Commerce Department and the Federal Reserve Board.

1. *Estimated 1966 Results*

With one month to go, we believe that our 1966 liquidity deficit could range between $1.3–$1.8 billion. The wide range, at this late date, is attributable, among other things, to uncertainty about the timing of off-set payments and debt prepayment by Germany between now and year-end. These inflows could range from $200 million to $450 million.

Our official settlements deficit in 1966 will clearly be very substantially below last year's figure of $1.3 billion.

You are, of course, familiar with the reasons why our 1966 liquidity deficit will, at best, be no lower than last year and—as indicated above— conceivably could be somewhat higher:

—the increased military expenditures and other costs due to Vietnam,

—plus a further worsening of our trade account due to the rapid expansion of our domestic economy,

—offset, in large part, by gains on private capital transactions, including in particular large inflows of foreign capital associated with recent high interest rates.

The improvement in the 1966 official settlements deficit is importantly a result of tight money and high interest rates here. U.S. banks

---

[1] Source: Johnson Library, National Security File, Subject File, Balance of Payments, Vol. 3 [1 of 2], Box 2. Confidential. Secretary Fowler sent the memorandum to President Johnson under cover of Document 107. A handwritten note at the top of the source text reads: "$7 billion."

have not only curtailed lending abroad, but have borrowed money from their foreign branches. Such inflows have sucked dollars out of foreign official holdings—helping us on the official settlements basis.

2. The 1967 Outlook

The Cabinet Committee believes that even if everything breaks reasonably well next year on the trade front, on the German offset, on the level of Vietnam expenditures, and on the size of capital outflows, we still will be confronted—*in the absence of continued voluntary programs*—with a liquidity deficit very substantially in excess of this year's figure. The Cabinet Committee believes that our over-all objective in 1967 should be to continue to move toward balance-of-payments equilibrium as fast as the continuing foreign exchange costs of Vietnam permit.

Continuation of the voluntary programs could bring the deficit back down to a level of $1.5 billion, although the judgment of many of the Cabinet Committee members (based on past painful experience) is that there is likely to be slippage in elements of this forecast, and the deficit could easily run higher. These views underlie the Committee's conviction that not only should

—the voluntary programs be continued,
—but that they be tightened to the greatest extent possible compatible with their voluntary nature,
—and additional measures both for 1967 and for the longer term should be undertaken.

3. The Commerce Voluntary Program

The Cabinet Committee believes that continuation of the Commerce Voluntary Program to restrain direct-investment outflows of business firms and to limit retention of overseas earnings in 1967 is essential. Secretary Connor has recommended a 1967 program calling for business corporations:

—to increase their global exports $1.6 billion,
—to increase repatriation of earnings $300 million,
—to reduce the combination of direct investment outflows and overseas retained earnings by $100 million from the 1966 level,
—to stretch out or cut back on marginal gross plant and equipment outlays by overseas subsidiaries.

The proposed 1967 program makes the same distinction between developed and less developed nations as in 1966 (its purpose is to restrain capital flows only to the former).

The program has been examined and approved by the Commerce Department's Advisory Committee on the Balance of Payments, which considers it tough but feasible. Secretary Connor believes the program as formulated pushes the voluntary approach as far as it can go.

The Cabinet Committee approves the general outline of Commerce's proposed program and is in agreement with all specifics *except one*—and it is an important one. The Committee believes that the additional $100 million savings in direct investment outflows and overseas retained earnings (over and above the 1966 program savings) under the proposed 1967 program is inadequate, and *additional savings of $300 million should be sought by further tightening of the guideline. This, it is hoped, would have the effect of bringing direct investment outlays in 1967 back to the 1964 level. Secretary Connor dissents from this recommendation on the ground that it is an unreasonable expectation. The Committee, on the other hand, believes these additional savings should be sought because the remaining options for gains of this magnitude are extremely limited.*

A draft press release and letter from Secretary Connor to the participating corporations spelling out the 1967 program are attached as Tab B.[2]

4. The Federal Reserve Voluntary Program

The Cabinet Committee also recommends a continuation, and tightening, of the Federal Reserve voluntary program for banks and other financial institutions.

The Federal Reserve Board has recommended a program under which banks

—will receive no increase in their present guideline ceiling (109 percent of the December 1964 base)

—but will be permitted to move only gradually up to that ceiling by the end of 1967

—providing that *90 percent of the allowable increase in credits must be used either for loans to less developed countries or for export financing, leaving only 10 percent for non-export loans to developed countries.*

The banks are approximately $1.2 billion below the 109 percent ceiling now, so they will have plenty of leeway under the extended 109 percent ceiling. On the other hand, there is a sharpened focus under the recommended program on loans to less developed countries and on export credits. This is consistent with our other balance-of-payments efforts (e.g., the establishment of the Ex-Im rediscount facility).

The permissible increase in non-export credits to developed countries in 1967 would be only $120 million.

The proposed program for the non-bank, financial institutions for 1967 will replace three different guidelines used in the 1966 program with a single guideline permitting an increase of 5 percent in outstanding foreign assets covered under the program over the 15 months from October 1, 1966, through December 31, 1967. This guideline will permit

---

[2] See footnote 6, Document 107.

increases in these assets between October 1, 1966, and December 31, 1967, of about $100 million.

The Cabinet Committee concurs in the Federal Reserve Board's recommended program, the proposed release of which is attached as Tab C.[3]

5. *Other Measures under Consideration*

We are very much aware of the difficulty of reaching a decision on the Federal Reserve and Corporate Programs for 1967 without a complete picture of the other measures that the Committee may later recommend depending somewhat on the outlook for the economy in January and the fiscal and monetary policy mix still to be determined.

Additional measures we are recommending now for inclusion in your Economic Message include

—extension of the Interest Equalization Tax, which expires July 31, 1967. This has proven effective in limiting the accessibility of our capital market to foreigners. The recommendation for extension may include provisions for tightening the IET and making it more flexible (these features have not yet been discussed by the Committee).

—measures to reduce the travel deficit (increase in passport fees to provide funds for encouraging travel to the United States, cut in customs exemptions, and a voluntary appeal to U.S. citizens to restrain travel plans outside the hemisphere for the duration of the Viet Nam conflict).

—follow-up actions to exploit passage of Foreign Investors Tax Act.[4]

—continuation and possible tightening of our balance-of-payments arrangements with Canada.

The Committee views with concern the continuing and increasing tourist gap which this year places a net deficit burden on our balance of payments of approximately $1.8–$1.9 billion, having increased from $1.2 billion in 1961. In view of the request Government has made of industry and financial institutions, not to mention the sacrifices of our men in the field, it is both appropriate and timely to introduce modest measures to call the public's attention to the large dollar drain from tourism, seeking their cooperation in moderating this outflow.

The Vice President wants to see the final tourism program before it is submitted to you formally. I am, therefore, giving him a copy of this memorandum.

While there is still not unanimity, the Cabinet Committee is preponderantly in agreement that, as a minimum, the new measures listed above are required in the travel area, both because of their impact on the travel deficit itself and the reinforcing influence they may have on the

---

[3] Tab C was not found; see footnote 7, Document 107.

[4] President Johnson signed the Foreign Investors Tax Act of 1966 on November 13, 1966; P.L. 89–909 (80 Stat. 1539).

efforts of businessmen and bankers called upon to make greater sacrifices in 1967 than before. (See Tab D for dissenting views.)[5]

Decisions Required at This Time

The Cabinet Committee recommends:[6]

(1) That you approve continuation of the Federal Reserve voluntary program on the basis outlined above.

(2) That you approve a continuation of the Commerce voluntary program.

(3) If (2) above is approved, that you approve the recommendation of your Committee that the program recommended by Commerce be tightened to provide additional balance-of-payments savings of $300 million,

or, you approve the level recommended by Commerce, whose judgment is that further tightening is unrealistic on a voluntary basis.

(4) The Committee requests that you indicate your over-all approval of this proposed continuation of the Commerce and Federal Reserve voluntary programs in the form of a letter, attached as Tab A,[7] to be released in connection with public announcement of the two programs for 1967.

(5) The Committee further recommends that such public announcement be made by Secretaries Fowler and Connor and [Chairman Martin] [Governor Robertson][8] at a press conference to be scheduled for Friday, December 9.

---

[5] Tab D was not found and has not been further identified.
[6] There is no indication on the source text if the recommendations were approved or disapproved.
[7] Tab A was not attached; see footnote 5, Document 107.
[8] Brackets in the source text.

109. Memorandum From the President's Deputy Special Assistant for National Security Affairs (Bator) to President Johnson[1]

Washington, December 7, 1966.

SUBJECT

1967 Balance of Payments Program

The attached memorandum from Secretary Fowler contains the recommendations of your Cabinet Committee concerning the balance of payments program for 1967.[2] Specifically, the recommendations are that:

1. We continue the Federal Reserve Voluntary Program to restrain bank lending to foreigners. The Cabinet Committee is unanimous on this.

2. We continue the voluntary Commerce program on direct investment abroad. There is no argument about the need for the program, but there is an important division between Jack Connor and the rest of us on how tight the Commerce guidelines should be:

—Connor proposes guidelines which would reduce the target for direct investment outflow and overseas retained earnings only by $100 million or so below the 1966 target.

—Joe Fowler and the rest of the Committee recommend that we tighten the guidelines by some $400 million, thereby trying to reduce direct investment outflows in '67 to their 1964 level.

This is a tough decision. On the merits, my vote is strongly with Fowler and the rest of the Committee. There is a powerful case, given our situation, for putting more of a squeeze on direct investment abroad. However, this goes directly counter to the judgment of the Cabinet officer responsible for operating the program. Jack is worried that any such tightening will cause a quiet revolution among his clients—that an increasing number will begin to welch on the program, and that this could become contagious.

I do not want to hold up the Fowler memo for a full-dress exposition on our balance of payments prospects. On the above decision, I would urge that—before making up your mind—you have a talk on the telephone with Fowler and, especially if you are leaning toward a decision against him, with Connor. If you then wish to have further views from me, I will be standing by.

Francis M. Bator

---

[1] Source: Johnson Library, National Security File, Subject File, Balance of Payments, Vol. 3 [1 of 2], Box 2. Confidential.

[2] Not attached, but presumably Document 108.

110. Editorial Note

On December 13, 1966, Secretary Fowler held a press conference to announce the administration's 1967 Balance of Payments Program. This program, in large part, included the continuation of the Department of Commerce's Voluntary Cooperation Program for U.S. business corporations and financial institutions. The Commerce program, Fowler announced, would remain voluntary, but would "call upon the participating corporations to increase their 1967 contributions on the major selected transactions by at least $2 billion above the 1966 level." (*Annual Report of the Secretary of the Treasury on the State of the Finances for the Fiscal Year Ended June 30, 1967,* pages 326–327)

During the press conference, Secretary Fowler supplemented his briefing by liberally quoting from President Johnson's December 12, 1966, letter to him in which the President approved the recommendations of the Cabinet Committee on Balance of Payments to continue the Voluntary Cooperation Program. This letter is printed in *American Foreign Policy: Current Documents, 1966,* pages 981–982.

111. Minutes of Meeting of the Cabinet Committee on Balance of Payments[1]

Washington, January 4, 1967, 3 p.m.

The Secretary opened the meeting with a brief review of the expected 1966 balance-of-payments results. He thought the "liquidity" deficit would be at the upper end of the $1.3 billion–$1.8 billion range which had been mentioned in the December 6 Memorandum to the President.[2] He thought the "reserve transactions" balance would show a marked improvement over last year's $1.3 billion deficit. The trade

[1] Source: Johnson Library, Fowler Papers, International Balance of Payments—Classified Material: Cabinet Committee on Balance of Payments, 1967–68 [2 of 2], Box 52. Confidential. Drafted by Philip P. Schaffner on January 10. The meeting was held at the Treasury Department. A list of participants is not printed; the following attended: Secretary Fowler, Deming, Knowlton, Petty, and Schaffner (Treasury), Secretary McNamara and Robert N. Anthony (DOD), Secretary Connor, Rostow and Solomon (State), Winn Finner (Agriculture), Administrator Gaud and Gustav Ranis (AID), Roth (STR), Director Schultze and Charles J. Zwick (BOB), Okun (CEA), Bator, Governors Robertson, Daane, and Brimmer (Federal Reserve), and T. Van Dyk (Vice President's Office).
[2] Document 108.

account would be off by $1 billion or more, with exports up over $3 billion and imports up over $4 billion. Direct military expenditures abroad, mostly due to Vietnam, would be about $800 million higher than in 1965. Offsetting the approximately $1.8 billion deterioration in the trade and military expenditure items were

(1) large inflows of long-term capital from foreign official agencies and international organizations (up $940 million);
(2) large debt prepayments by foreign governments (up $240 million); and
(3) nonrepetition of the large adverse impact of about $660 million in 1965 resulting from U.K. liquidation of its portfolio of private U.S. securities and postponement of its service on the postwar loan.

The Secretary pointed out that the "reserve transactions" balance also benefited from an inflow of around $3 billion of short-term private funds particularly through the foreign branches of U.S. banks. Part of these came out of official reserves abroad. He thought next year's "reserve transactions" balance would be closer to the "liquidity" balance than it had been in 1966. He then asked Secretary Connor whether there had been any reaction to the announcement of the new Commerce program. Secretary Connor said that the reaction was one of understanding and promise of continued cooperation. He had received only about ten company complaints. Forms for the revised program were now being mailed, but it would be mid-February before any data would be available. The Secretary indicated the President's interest as well as his own in doing anything that might be helpful to the successful operation of both the Commerce and the Federal Reserve voluntary programs.

Governor Robertson said that some of the banks think they are being penalized for having done a good job but that he fully expected continued cooperation from the banking community.

The Secretary referred to page 5 of the Memorandum to the President in which reference was made to other measures that the Committee may later recommend depending partly on the outlook for the economy in January and on the fiscal and monetary policy mix still to be determined. The Secretary said that while some aspects of the program are long term in nature, we must give them some impetus at this time. He has, therefore, asked his staff and the Executive Committee to intensify their operations particularly with regard to two sectors.

First, the private financial community must be energized to spread the message about benefits accruing to foreign investors under the Foreign Investors Tax Act. Part of the objective of the Fowler Task Force (namely, the stimulation of capital markets in Western Europe) has been achieved but the second objective—stimulation of foreign interest in U.S. securities—has not yet progressed very much and we must actively encourage this development.

Secondly, our trade surplus is too low. We must do more to strengthen interest in penetrating foreign markets. Export credit facilities have been improved for this purpose, but we may also need export incentives of some kind consistent with our role as a leading trading nation.

In the Government field, expenditures under the military and aid programs are long-term problems on which we must continue to work. Secretary Connor said that two other action groups of the National Export Council were preparing reports on the export outlook. One deals with aid to LDC's and the other with the export outlook in general. The Secretary expressed interest in seeing these reports when they were completed. He then asked Mr. Knowlton to discuss the Executive Committee views on strengthening of the IET.

Mr. Knowlton said that while an ironclad case could not be made for going to a 2% annual burden now, we could point to the fact that the spread between some longer term U.S. and foreign rates is in excess of 1%. A further easing of U.S. rates would probably make a rise in the tax rate necessary. It was also important to move to the 2% rate effective as of the date of requesting new authority from Congress so as to forestall anticipatory outflows of U.S. capital. With regard to application of the tax to maturities of less than one year, he said the Executive Committee had decided that further study was desirable.

Governor Robertson thought there would be a real need to apply the IET to the shorter range maturities, although it would be unwise at this time to do so. He also thought the margin within which the IET could be moved ought to be large enough to cover the possible interest differential. He would, therefore, suggest asking for Congressional authorization to move up to a 3% annual rate equivalent. Mr. Knowlton remarked that the Executive Committee had concluded this was a matter for Treasury's judgment in light of the situation in Congress and other factors. Mr. Deming said that he saw no objection in principle to applying the tax to shorter maturities but that operative problems might be very difficult. Mr. Knowlton pointed out that if it became publicly known that the tax might be applied to maturities of under one year, speculative outflows might be stimulated. Secretary Connor said he thought there was no case for requesting as much as 3% from Congress or for applying the tax to maturities of less than one year. He felt the latter request would meet strong Congressional opposition. Governor Robertson remarked that the IET should be strong enough to carry the whole load of controlling capital outflows when the voluntary cooperation program ended.

The Secretary remarked that it appeared to be an open question of whether the Executive Committee proposal went far enough. He said that perhaps by the time the Ways and Means Committee gets to this item, further study within the Government will have produced a definite recommendation particularly with regard to the application of the tax to shorter maturities. Mr. Okun remarked that we may want standby authority to apply the tax to under one year maturities even though we do not intend to use it immediately. Mr. Solomon remarked the more flexibility you request from Congress the more guarantee you must give about how you intend to use the flexibility. Mr. Knowlton pointed out that the Japanese would be quite worried about the application of the tax to maturities under one year and that this might lead them to activate their large existing credit liens with U.S. banks. He also thought that firms making U.S. direct investment abroad would be tempted to put short-term funds abroad through this or other channels in anticipation of direct investment controls.

The Secretary said that while there are different views in some respects, there apparently is agreement that the tax should be extended for three years and that flexible authority to change the burden of the tax from zero to 2% should be sought. He next turned to the recommendations regarding tourism and said that the Government must emphasize the balance-of-payments impact of foreign travel, not with the idea of stopping the outflow of tourist dollars but with the idea of leveling it off. He asked Mr. Knowlton for a summary of the Executive Committee views on this subject.

Mr. Knowlton said the majority of the Committee believed some closer alignment of tourist guidelines with business and bank guidelines is necessary, although there were some individual agency objections to doing anything in the field of tourism. With regard to passport fees, there was almost unanimous disapproval of tying the proceeds to the USTS budget. Such tying would not avoid Congressional difficulties, and it might represent more funds than USTS could use effectively.

As an alternative, the Executive Committee was suggesting a high-level Task Force including representation from the travel industry. This Task Force would suggest how the Government might wisely spend funds to attract foreign tourists to U.S., how states and cities might cooperate in the effort to attract foreign visitors, etc. The President would announce he intends to request funds from Congress to implement feasible recommendations of the new Task Force.

Mr. Knowlton said that this approach would have several advantages, including receipt of the travel industry's support of whatever program was finally adopted.

Mr. Van Dyk thought that the foreign travel gap in 1967 would be no larger than in 1966 despite the fact that travel by Americans is increasing at the rate of 10% a year. He thought this indicated that the situation was not so serious. Any program regarding travel abroad, therefore, should be voluntary and completely positive. He discussed the "Discover America" program and said that the private travel industry's efforts had been enlisted on the basis of no government restrictions on travel. The Vice President felt that support of the travel industry would be lost under any other condition.

Mr. Van Dyk said that $350 million was the extent of our travel deficit with Europe. It was hardly worth endangering the President's prestige by having him make an appeal to the public with the object of reducing this gap. With regard to increased funds for the USTS, he said that Representative Rooney objected to the USTS per se. With regard to the proposed Task Force, he thought it would proliferate bureaucracy. He said that a new travel bill is being prepared in Congress which would formalize the USTS coordinating function, enable USTS to encourage travel by Americans within the U.S., and raise the budget request to $10 million. Representative Ullman would sponsor the new bill in the House; Senators Javits and Magnuson in the Senate.

Secretary McNamara said he thought a moderate appeal by the President to the public would help. He favored an increase in the passport fee to $25 and earmarking of an appropriate amount of the proceeds for USTS.

He thought that in general we must act more firmly on the balance-of-payments program. Continuation of the deficit was adversely affecting our foreign policy and our military policy abroad. The deficit problem must be solved. He said that the voluntary cooperation programs were not so voluntary. He, therefore, saw no reason why tourism could not be treated on a stricter basis. He ended by saying that he did not ask for any exemption from tightening of the duty-free privilege or the gift privilege for military personnel abroad except those in combat zones.

Mr. Schultze said with regard to tying passport fee proceeds to the USTS budget, there was no easy Congressional approach. He thought the Task Force proposal would be helpful in supporting the request to Congress for more funds for USTS which he said he personally approved. He did not approve the higher passport fee which he felt was a regressive tax. If something had to be done in this area, he would prefer to go back to some of the proposals which were discussed earlier in the year and which took income differences into account. With regard to a public appeal by the President, he disapproved a strong approach but did not feel strongly about a mild approach. The Secretary asked him to read Tab E which contained draft language for such an approach.[3] Mr. Van Dyk said that he thought one paragraph (first full paragraph on page 3) was all right if the last phrase about asking Congress to tighten further our customs exemptions was changed to a positive note about interna-

---

[3] No tabs have been found.

tional travel year. Mr. Gaud said he approved the Tab E draft and preferred the Task Force approach to the passport fee. Mr. Roth did not think
a Presidential appeal would be effective; it would possibly be embarrassing to the President if not effective. He though the Tab E material was
possibly too detailed. He agreed with Mr. Van Dyk about losing support
of the travel industry if they suspected Government restrictive measures
would be taken. He preferred the Task Force approach to the passport
fee.

Secretary Connor did not think that Government steps in the tourist
field would reduce cooperation from the travel industry. He liked the Tab
E draft although he would delete the reference to economic controls on
page 3 of the draft. He said that it was important to keep the spotlight on
the travel deficit which he said would continue to grow worse as the
large jets begin to operate. Mr. Solomon said that a CAB analysis indicated the reduction of fares to between $200 and $250 per round trip
would stimulate an increment of foreign travel to the U.S. equal to the
increment of U.S. travel to Europe. The big new jets would bring fares
down close to this level. The Secretary referred to analyses that the travel
gap would be $4 billion to $5 billion by 1974 or 1975. With this huge deficit facing us, the private sector in the Government would have to do
much more to attract foreign tourists here. He thought that there were
two questions:

(1) How to achieve a tapering off in the outflow of U.S. tourist dollars?
(2) How to promote foreign tourism to the U.S. as a long-term measure?

He wondered whether encouraging Americans to travel in the U.S.
did not reduce the emphasis on promotion of foreign travel to the U.S.
Secretary Connor remarked that the "Discover America" program really
did not have much to do with bringing foreigners to the U.S. and that the
proposed new Task Force would be helpful in this area. He also favored
raising the passport fee to $25 but without earmarking the proceeds for
USTS. Mr. Rostow thought that the travel problem might be mentioned
in some general Presidential message. He did not think the travel gap
reflected relative income levels only. There were other obstacles in the
U.S. to the flow of foreign visitors here. He thought it was all right if a
Presidential message would ask for a moderating of travel and spending
abroad by U.S. tourists. He referred to the fact that he had taken the same
position in an earlier Cabinet Committee meeting. He thought a higher
passport fee would be all right but not with the proceeds earmarked for
the USTS. He opposed a reduction in the U.S. tourist exemption. He
recalled that $50 had been proposed by the OECD as a norm for the
amount of tourist exemption, but reducing the tourist exemption would
cause very difficult problems in the Western Hemisphere. The Mexicans

and Caribbean Islands counted on tourist trade heavily and the Canadians are having an international fair in 1967. The Secretary asked why the U.S. should have a higher exemption than major European countries, and Mr. Rostow replied that he supposed because we were a richer country. The Secretary remarked we were not richer in balance-of-payments terms. Mr. Rostow said that the reductions in the tourist exemption would not produce much in balance-of-payments savings. Mr. Solomon supplemented this by estimating that gross savings would be from $10 million to $30 million and net savings from $5 million to $15 million at the most. He pointed out that Mexico allows $80 duty free to its returning tourists. Mr. Knowlton said we estimated $50 million gross savings from the tourist package being proposed. Mr. Solomon added that Mexico was very sensitive about the border traffic situation and that the Caribbean Islands need tourist money badly. Mr. Rostow said that irritating some countries like Greece might not be worth the benefits we get from the tourist exemption. He also thought that travelers would be induced to falsify their returns if there were any further reduction in the exemption.

Mr. Bator thought the Task Force proposal was a good idea. He thought the passport fee was a miserable sort of regressive tax. With regard to the Presidential appeal, he thought that if an appeal were to be made—and he was not sure of its desirability—it should have a moderate approach. He thought that it was a mistake to talk about a travel gap any more than one might talk about a banana or machinery gap. He did not think the proposed tourist measures would have much balance-of-payments savings effect. The Secretary said that the period of time for which we should try to moderate travel by Americans might be debatable, but the draft Presidential appeal was a short-term one. Mr. Okun thought the Task Force approach was all right and said he had changed his mind about a possible Presidential appeal in reading the draft language in Tab E. He did not know how much good it would do, but he did not think the appeal as drafted would stir up any strong feelings. With regard to a passport fee, he said he agreed with Mr. Schultze. With regard to reducing tourist exemptions, he said he admired the Secretary's willingness to tackle Congress on this matter in view of last year's bad experience. He wondered, since the approach might fail, whether it was desirable to have it on the record. On the other hand, if the Secretary felt that he could get it, he should try. He mentioned that Mr. Ackley was worried about the adverse effect of tourism measures on confidence in the dollar. Governor Robertson agreed that tourism was an important item in our balance of payments but that he thought any measure in this field should be limited to encouragement of foreign tourists to visit the U.S. Anything else would be ineffective, embarrassing to the President, harmful to our market for jet planes abroad, and trivial as a balance-of-

326 Foreign Relations, 1964–1968, Volume VIII

payments measure. A Presidential appeal would be construed as a desperation step that would hurt the dollar. He thought the reduction of the exemption from $100 to $50 would create a political storm, but that it was the least undesirable of the measures proposed. He did approve of the reduction of the number of times a year that the tourist exemption might be used. He claimed that applying the duty to the total value of purchases would cause more spending abroad rather than less spending. He said there would be no psychological value for the Federal Reserve program by launching a tourist program. Mr. Finner of Agriculture said that the only gain he saw in the tourist program would be to give the balance-of-payments program a more well rounded appearance. He thought the Task Force proposal was all right. Mr. Connor added to his previous endorsement of the proposals by saying that he would also favor the $100 to $50 reduction. He did not think that the Bahamas would have any problem this year if the tourist duty-free exemption were lowered. Any problem would be confined to the Virgin Islands. Mr. Van Dyk said that the Vice President thought the reduction of the customs exemption was not necessarily bad if it were designed to reduce spending rather than travel. The Virgin Islands would be the only area where there might be a problem.

Mr. Okun remarked that there had also been talk of a $5 processing fee on returning tourists in addition to the proposed new base for assessing duty. He did not think this was equitable. Mr. Deming remarked that he thought it was like the Paris airport tax. The Secretary then turned to the subject of the Latin American housing authority problem and said he understood that there was agreement in the Committee on the proposed allocation of funds, as between fiscal year 1968 and fiscal year 1969.

P. Schaffner[4]

---

[4] Winthrop Knowlton initialed below Schaffner's signature, presumably indicating his approval of the minutes.

112. Memorandum From the Under Secretary of State for Political Affairs (Rostow) to President Johnson[1]

Washington, January 10, 1967.

SUBJECT

Proposal to Reduce the U.S. Customs Exemption

The Department of State is strongly opposed to the Cabinet Committee on Balance of Payments' recommendation that the customs exemption for returning travelers be reduced from $100 to $50. All members of the Committee agree that the savings from such a reduction would be very small. The $25–50 million (on a gross basis) suggested by Treasury is high, and, of course, the net or real balance of payments saving would be much less.

This small measure would not generate important psychological gains. The similar reduction in the allowance in 1965 certainly did not. In fact, the psychological effect might be negative since we would have to portray the travel gap as a serious problem but would be proposing only a de minimis measure in response. Chairman Martin and other Federal Reserve Governors think that the proposal could hurt confidence in the dollar by arousing expectations of possible future restrictions on other types of current account expenditures.[2]

The proposal would create serious political problems. The economies of many of our Caribbean neighbors are dependent upon expenditures by U.S. tourists and many other less developed countries would also be affected seriously. It would hurt our efforts to expand U.S.-Mexican trade, which you discussed recently with President Diaz Ordaz[3] and would provoke a Mexican protest. The measure would run counter to programs to increase inter-American travel undertaken in the context of the Alliance for Progress and would provide an unfortunate backdrop for the Inter-American Summit Meeting. It would cause concern in Canada because of Expo 67.

We do not believe the minor savings are worth these costs, and recommend that the exemption not be reduced. If you decide to approve a reduction, we urge that it be applied only outside the Western Hemisphere. An alternative, but distinctly less preferable arrangement,

---

[1] Source: Johnson Library, National Security File, Subject File, Balance of Payments, Vol. IV, January 1967 [1 of 2], Box 3. Confidential.

[2] Reference is to an undated statement from Martin, attached to Document 107, but not printed.

[3] President Johnson met with Mexican President Diaz Ordaz at Amistad Dam on the Rio Grande on December 3, 1966.

would be to exempt countries contiguous to the United States and neighboring islands.

Eugene V. Rostow

---

113.   Editorial Note

On December 20, 1966, Secretary of the Treasury Fowler telephoned President Johnson to report on his recent meetings in Paris with Debré and Callaghan. (Later in the conversation, Fowler read a detailed memorandum of his conversation with Debré.) At these meetings, Fowler believed the three expressed a common concern over "worldwide tight money and high interest rates." Rather than leave the situation "to the mercies of the Central Bank Governors and whatever they may decide, particularly with reference to international capital flows," Callaghan wanted to convene an early meeting of the big four Finance Ministers in London to "work together toward a general easing of monetary conditions and reversal in this interest rate escalation in the Western world." Specifically, Fowler hoped the meeting would "give the Fed no balance of payments reasons for holding back on monetary ease, which I fear the New York bank will constantly throw in the picture." If the four could get a "general understanding," they might extend it to the Italians and Dutch. When interest rates in the United States moved down, "they will then try to move down with us," and thus there would not be a "balance of payments hurdle in our going forward with the right kind of monetary policy for our domestic problems." Germany, Fowler added, would be a key player in this process.

In the ensuing discussion, President Johnson agreed among other things that the proposed meeting was "a helluva good initiative." He wanted Ambassador McGhee to know that the Germans had "to help and play ball here." He also said that Federal Reserve Board Chairman Martin should "help us by easing money, and I think you ought to tell him just as cold and hard and tough as you know how that you and your people and many other people really think that they ought to let the banks know by letter . . . that they are going to ease this situation." He emphasized that the "white elephant, ivory tower crowd at the Federal Reserve" needed to loosen up some by buying Fannie Mae paper, for example, before tight money plunged the nation into a depression.

Fowler replied, "I couldn't agree with everything you've said more." He thought some monetary ease would occur, "but it's a question of how much and how fast and how far it goes." He thought that declining interest rates were all right domestically, but they had to counter the argument that the loosening would "cause capital outflows and our balance of payments will be ruined." When Fowler remarked that the administration had to rely on its legislative program and international negotiations "to make other people come along so we won't be hurt," President Johnson agreed. The President reemphasized that the Federal Reserve should buy Fannie Mae paper and that Fowler should talk to Martin about these matters. (Johnson Library, Recordings and Transcripts, Recording of Telephone Conversation between President Johnson and Secretary Fowler, December 20, 1966, 11:47 a.m., Tape F6612.02, Side A, PNO 4)

In a January 4, 1967, memorandum to President Johnson, Francis Bator noted that he knew Fowler had already mentioned the upcoming meeting to the President. He explained that its purpose "is to try to stop the international tight-money competition of the past year, with governments driving up interest rates to protect their balance of payments," and he requested permission to accompany Fowler and Deming there. The President wrote on the approval line of this memorandum: "Heartily. This is very important & you can make an excellent contribution as you always do. L." (Ibid., Bator Papers, Chequers Trip, Box 8)

On January 12, James Callaghan, British Chancellor of the Exchequer, sent a message to the Group of 10 Finance Ministers informing them of the upcoming four-power monetary conference. Callaghan's message recalled that at the NATO Ministerial Meeting in Paris in December 1966 he had talked separately with Debré and Fowler about fiscal and monetary policy, "and in particular the implications of this for world interest rates." Although Schiller was not in Paris, Callaghan had had a similar conversation on that occasion with Willy Brandt. Callaghan summarized these conversations as follows: "We were all inclined to think that interest rates were too high and could, with advantage, be brought down." Although unable to pursue the subject in Paris, he had since arranged with Debré, Fowler, and Schiller to meet in London January 21–22 "to try and see whether we can make some progress. For public purposes we shall announce the subject for discussion in general terms such as monetary policy and international co-operation." (Telegram 5499 from London, January 12; Department of State, Central Files, FN 10 IMF) The text of a slightly expanded version of this message from Callaghan, January 12, is in the Johnson Library, Bator Papers, Chequers Meeting, January 21, 1967, Box 8.

On January 16, the Department of the Treasury issued a press release announcing that the upcoming meeting of the four Finance Ministers would be held at Chequers, the Prime Minister's country residence, January 21–22. "The meeting," the press release indicated, "will focus mainly on interest rates and possibilities for further relaxation of monetary stringency." The Treasury release said that Secretary Fowler "welcomed the meeting and the opportunity it presented for a cooperative exploration of the ways and means of achieving a rational and timely easing of monetary conditions." It also noted that there might be speculation that other matters such as the price of gold or the reevaluation of sterling might be discussed at the Chequers meeting, but it was expected that the discussion would be limited "'to discuss international interaction of monetary and credit policies,'" as outlined in Callaghan's public announcement calling the meeting. The press release added that Fowler had already made it explicit (in circular telegram 115957, January 10; Department of State, Central Files, FN 19) that the raising of the price of gold was unacceptable to the U.S. Government. Text of the press release is in circular telegram 119071, January 16. (Ibid., POL 7 UK)

Circular telegram 119071 also informed U.S. posts privately that "Major attention expected center on international effects of German monetary policy."

A January 17 Department of the Treasury paper summarized the U.S. objectives at the upcoming meeting. (Johnson Library, Bator Papers, Chequers Meeting, January 21, 1967, Box 8)

For documentation on the Chequers meeting, see Documents 115 and 116.

---

114.   Memorandum From the President's Deputy Special Assistant for National Security Affairs (Bator) to President Johnson[1]

Washington, January 13, 1967.

SUBJECT

Supplementary Balance of Payments Measures

At Tab I is a memorandum from your Cabinet Committee on the Balance of Payments recommending measures to supplement the Com-

---

[1] Source: Johnson Library, National Security File, Subject File, Balance of Payments, Vol. IV, January 1967 [2 of 2], Box 3. Confidential. Attached to the source text is a note from Bator to the President, January 17, saying that he understood that the original of this memorandum, forwarded to the President on Saturday morning, January 14, may have been lost and that "I am afraid we need decisions almost right away if the Economic Report is to get out on time."

merce and Federal Reserve programs you approved last month.[2] The
major points and issues are as follows:

1. The Committee unanimously recommends that we ask the Congress for a three-year extension of the Interest Equalization Tax
(IET)—which expires on July 1—together with new authority to vary the
tax *rate* from 0 to 2% (instead of the present flat rate of 1%). This tax is our
strongest current restraint on foreign borrowers. The variable rate will
allow us to increase the restraint if easier money at home leads to a
greater incentive for foreigners to borrow in our markets. (The detailed
argument on this is on page 1–3 of the Fowler memorandum, Tab I.)

O.K.[3]

No

2. The Committee unanimously recommends an expanded travel
program, but is divided on some of the details.

(i) *Travel Task Force.* Everybody agrees that you should appoint a
high-level Task Force to recommend ways to expand travel to the U.S.
from abroad. It should be chaired by a senior businessman, and have
members from both industry and government. The Committee is also
agreed that, in announcing this Task Force, you should pledge your willingness to approach the Congress for much more money for the U.S.
Travel Service—up to perhaps $25 million instead of the current $3 million—to carry out any recommendations you approve. (Fowler thought
it might be appropriate for the Vice President to act as your agent in this.
Thus, he suggests that the Task Force report to the Vice President.)

(Details are on pages 3–5 of the Fowler memorandum, Tab I.)

O.K.[3]

No

(ii) *Raise the Passport Fee From $10 to $20–$25.* Your advisers are
divided:

—The Vice President and McNamara favor it and would earmark
the proceeds for the U.S. Travel Service.
—Connor, Gene Rostow, and Freeman would raise fees, but *not* earmark the receipts.
—Fowler would prefer to fund the Travel Service through a larger
regular appropriation, but would favor raising passport fees and earmarking them if that is the only way to get more money for USTS.

---

[2] Tab I is a memorandum to the President, dated January 12 and signed by Fowler, not
printed. The Department of Commerce program refers presumably to its voluntary program with the business community for 1967. The text of a Commerce undated draft
announcement of this program is attached to a memorandum from Fowler to President
Johnson, December 12, 1966. (Ibid., Vol. 3 [1 of 2], Box 2) An undated draft press release prepared by the Board of Governors of the Federal Reserve System outlining new guidelines
for financial institutions cooperating with the President's voluntary program is ibid.
[3] This option is checked.

—Ackley, Schultze, Gaud, Bill Martin, Bill Roth, and I are for higher appropriations for the Travel Service, but *against* a higher passport fee on grounds that: it will not deter travel; it won't really allow us to get around Mr. Rooney's opposition to a higher USTS budget; and, last, it is a very regressive form of taxation which will only hurt our poorest travelers. In addition, Schultze strongly objects to the precedent of earmarking. (Details are on pages 5–7 of Fowler's memorandum, Tab I.)

Raise the fees

Earmark them for USTS

Don't raise fees[4]

(iii) *Presidential Appeal to U.S. Travellers.* A majority of the Committee—including Fowler and Connor—believes that equity requires that we make some pitch to the traveller to balance what we have said to the corporations and the banks. The rest of us feel that such an appeal would not save much money, that it would squander your prestige in a futile cause, and would create an undesirable impression that every traveller is violating the explicit wishes of his President. My own strong vote is against such an appeal. (Details are on pages 8–10 of the Fowler memorandum, Tab I. At Tab I–B, is a draft Presidential Message on travel prepared by Fowler. The proposed appeal is on page 4, at Tab "Appeal".)[5]

I will make the appeal

No[6]

(iv) *Reduce Customs Exemption for Returning Travellers from $100 to $50.* Fowler favors this reduction, particularly because of its psychological effects. State and the Fed argue that the expected savings of $25–$50 million are not worth the substantial political and economic problems this would cause us abroad, particularly in Latin America. Gene Rostow's memorandum, at Tab I–C,[7] gives a full exposition of the State view. State has my vote.

O.K.

No[6]

(v) *Legislation Imposing a $2 Handling Charge on Tariff-Exempt Gift Packages.* The Committee is unanimously in favor.

O.K.[8]

No.

---

[4] This option is checked, and the President wrote in the margin: "See me."
[5] The draft Presidential message and the proposed appeal are not printed.
[6] This option is checked.
[7] See Document 112.
[8] This option is checked. Below this paragraph are listed the options: "O.K." or "No." The former is checked.

Bator Comment.

The extension of the IET is a serious and important part of the balance of payments program. I strongly favor the Committee's recommendation. If you approve, Fowler will approach Mills and Long to pave the way.

A serious effort to get foreigners to travel in the U.S. could be of long-term importance. Thus, the Task Force is a good idea. The other proposals are much more marginal. I have given you my views on each; none is of great significance.

Fowler proposes to announce all of these steps in your Economic Message on January 26.[9] Thus, it would be very helpful if we had your decisions by Monday or Tuesday—in time for Ackley to have prepared a printed draft for your review toward the end of the week.

Francis

Speak to me on all unchecked items[10]

---

[9] For text, see *Public Papers of the Presidents of the United States: Lyndon B. Johnson, 1967,* Book I, pp. 72–89.

[10] This option is not checked. Just above it is an indecipherable word followed by "L[yndon]."

115. Record of Meeting[1]

Chequers, England, January 21, 1967.

RECORD OF MEETING AT CHEQUERS ON SATURDAY, 21ST JANUARY, 1967

PRESENT

Chancellor of the Exchequer
Mr. Secretary Fowler
Mr. Deming
Mr. Bator
Sir William Armstrong
Sir Denis Rickett
Mr. Ryrie (Secretary)

Meeting of Finance Ministers on Monetary Policies

Mr. Secretary Fowler said that in his view the object of the meeting should be to make it easier for those responsible for monetary policies in the leading countries to understand how their policies affected others. It was important to press the Germans to take more fiscal action so as to enable them to adopt easier monetary policies. He did not think that it would be possible for those present to commit themselves to specific courses of action, but an effort should be made to reach a consensus on the general direction which policy should take.

The Chancellor of the Exchequer saw the object of the meeting as being to put some pressure behind Central Banks where necessary to take action to lower interest rates and Governments where appropriate to take action which would make it easier for Central Banks to lower interest rates.

An American draft communiqué was considered.[2] The Chancellor of the Exchequer thanked Mr. Fowler for providing this draft and said that he and his officials would consider it further.

[Here follows discussion of the Common Market; see *Foreign Relations, 1964–1968*, volume XIII, pages 529–530.]

International Liquidity

The Chancellor feared that a failure to reach agreement in the discussions on international liquidity was a real possibility and a question

---

[1] Source: Johnson Library, Bator Papers, Chequers Trip, Box 8. Secret. No drafting information appears on the source text. Copies were sent to 10 British officials and Bator. An attached note from Bator to Eugene Rostow, February 1, indicates that the "attached is for your personal information. Please do *not* circulate." Bator added that he was also sending copies of this record to Walt Rostow, John Leddy, Tony Solomon, Bob Bowie, Nick Katzenbach, and John McNaughton.

[2] The undated draft communiqué is ibid., Bator Papers, Chequers Meeting, January 21, 1967, Box 8.

might arise whether all the other Continental countries would be willing to enter an agreement without France. He thought that the French Government would go on using international monetary questions for political purposes against the United States. He interpreted their recent moves on gold as motivated partly by fear that agreement would be reached without them on a new form of international reserve asset.

Mr. Secretary Fowler expressed his agreement and said it remained to be seen how far the French would go to obstruct progress. From a certain point obstruction could be counterproductive from their point of view. He was firm of the opinion himself that the only course was to press ahead with the negotiations and not allow ourselves to be diverted by the French tactics.

It was the opinion of both sides that the recent Belgian proposal,[3] purporting to be a possible basis for a compromise between the French and the "Anglo Saxon" points of view, could not be taken seriously.

---

[3] Presumably reference is to a December 27 paper distributed by National Bank of Belgium Governor Ansiaux to Governor O'Brien of the Bank of England and Charles Coombs at the Federal Reserve Bank of New York following a recent meeting of the three in Basle at the Bank for International Settlements. A copy of the paper, with its "compromise formula," was sent to Under Secretary of the Treasury Deming by C. de Strycker of the National Bank of Belgium under cover of a letter dated January 4, 1967. The de Strycker letter and Ansiaux paper were distributed to members of the Deming Group as DG/67/9 by George H. Willis on January 9, 1967. (Washington National Records Center, RG 56, OASIA Files: FRC 75 A 101, Deming Group) In the closing paragraph of his letter, de Strycker looks forward to discussing the compromise formula with Deming when they planned to meet in London in about 3 weeks, presumably a reference to the G–10 Deputies Meeting on January 24 at Lancaster House, following the January 21–22 meeting of Finance Ministers at Chequers (see Document 116). The G-10 Secretariat report, DG/67/63, indicates that both Deming and de Strycker were at the Lancaster House meeting. (Washington National Records Center, RG 56, OASIA Files: FRC 75 A 101, Deming Group) The U.S. Delegation's minutes of the Lancaster House G–10 Deputies meeting are papers DG/67/31 and DG/67/31, Supp. 1, distributed to members of the Deming Group by Willis on January 30 and February 2, 1967, respectively. These reports of the Deputies meeting refer to a forthcoming French proposal that would first be discussed in the Monetary Committee of the EEC; see footnote 4, Document 116.

116.   Memorandum From Secretary of the Treasury Fowler to President Johnson[1]

Washington, January 23, 1967.

SUBJECT

Meeting at Chequers

Attached you will find a copy of the communiqué on the meeting of the Finance Ministers this past weekend.

It was a very useful meeting and accomplished as much as we could reasonably hope.

I believe all present have a sincere conviction that further easing of monetary stringency in the major industrial countries and capital markets "would be helpful in the context of the development of their own economies and of the world economy as a whole". Whether or not they will be able to assure that the monetary policies of their respective countries "should have regard to the effect on other countries" which is particularly applicable to the Germans, the Italians and, to a lesser degree, the French, remains to be seen.

As you can see, the last sentence in paragraph three amounts to a "best efforts" agreement to cooperate in such a way as to "enable interest rates in their respective countries to be lower than they otherwise would be". The telling part of the paragraph is, of course, the qualifying words "within the limits of their respective responsibilities" which spells out that the central bankers have considerable to say in this area and, of course, Parliaments or the Congress insofar as taxing and fiscal policy is concerned.

At the very least, the meeting set a very good tone on this subject and focused attention on the need for cooperation by the Common Market countries if we and the U.K. are to keep our rates on a downward path without causing substantial balance of payments outflows.

The Germans moved down their bank rate a half point last week but need to do a great deal more for their own good (because their economy looks relatively stagnant) and to reduce the gap in rates as pictured in the attached chart entitled "Central Government Bond Yields",[2] which has been expanding over the last three years.

---

[1] Source: Johnson Library, Bator Papers, Chequers Trip, Box 8. No classification marking. A covering memorandum from Walt Rostow to President Johnson, January 23, briefly summarizes Fowler's "preliminary report," adding that Bator, who accompanied Fowler to the United Kingdom, will upon his return "give you his impressions of the Chequers meeting as well."

[2] Not found.

The situation in the money market rates (see attached chart on money market rates)[3] does not particularly point to Germany. There we must watch the Eurodollar rate which, happily, has been coming down with our short-term money rate.

I had a brief side exchange with Mr. Debré, the French Minister, concerning his recent antics in connection with gold and the liquidity negotiations.[4] Also, I had several side conversations with Chancellor Callaghan who expects to be here next month for a series of bilateral meetings with us. I would like to fill you in sometime on these side meetings since they were highly relevant not only to our financial but to our overall political situation vis-à-vis Western Europe and the U.K.

Henry H. Fowler

Attachment[5]

COMMUNIQUÉ

1. Ministers of France, Germany, Italy, United Kingdom and United States met at Chequers on January 21st and 22nd 1967 for informal discussions about the international interaction of their respective countries' economic and monetary policies. The Ministers taking part were M. Michel Debré, Minister of the Economy and Finances of France; Professor Karl Schiller, Minister of Economics of the Federal Republic of Germany; Signor Emilio Colombo, Minister of the Treasury of Italy; Mr. Henry Fowler, Secretary of the Treasury of the United States; and Mr. James Callaghan, Chancellor of the Exchequer of the United Kingdom. The meeting was arranged at the invitation of Mr. Callaghan.

2. The Ministers welcomed recent steps taken by some of the countries represented to ease credit and monetary stringency which in the past had played a useful part in moderating their domestic inflationary pressures. They agreed that in some countries some further easing

---

[3] Not found.

[4] A memorandum of Fowler's conversation with Finance Minister Debré on January 22 is in the Johnson Library, Fowler Papers, International Classified Material: International Monetary Conference, 1967–1968, Box 58. The Deming Group Papers contain DG/67/58, a January 10 Press Release to which is attached a translation of Debré's interview on gold and international monetary reform that appeared in *Le Monde* on January 8–9. DG/67/57 is a February 15 paper from Willis to Deming on "First Reaction to French Proposals for Reform of IMF," an assessment of the French proposal that was to be presented to the EEC Monetary Committee February 15–16. (Washington National Records Center, RG 56, OASIA Files: FRC 75 A 101, Deming Group)

[5] No classification marking.

would be helpful in the context of the development of their own economies and of the world economy as a whole.

3. The monetary policies called for in the present situation should be adapted to the different conditions obtaining in their respective countries and should have regard to their effect on other countries. The Ministers agreed that they would all make it their objective within the limits of their respective responsibilities to co-operate in such a way as to enable interest rates in their respective countries to be lower than they otherwise would be.

4. No other question was dealt with at the meeting.

117.   Current Economic Developments[1]

Issue No. 772   Washington, January 31, 1967.

[Here follow articles on unrelated subjects.]

CONGRESS ASKED TO CONTINUE INTEREST EQUALIZATION TAX

Secretary Fowler announced on January 25 that Treasury is sending to Congress a bill: a) to extend the Interest Equalization Tax for another two years, b) to give the President authority to vary the effective annual rate of the tax between zero and two percent per year, and c) to raise the effective rate to two percent retroactive to the date of submission.[2] Unless extended, the IET would expire July 31, 1967.

The Interest Equalization Tax is an essential part of the US balance-of-payments program. As it now stands, it seeks to abate the outflow of dollars from the US by adding approximately one percentage point to the annual interest costs to foreigners from developed countries (excluding Canada from all new issues and with a limited exemption for Japan) who borrow in the US for periods of one year or longer. Similar provisions apply to the purchase of foreign equities by US residents. The tax has been useful in holding down our balance-of-payments deficit by limiting

---

[1] Source: Washington National Records Center, E/CBA/REP Files: FRC 72 A 6248, *Current Economic Developments*. Unclassified. The source text comprises page 16 of the issue.

[2] For an excerpt from the January 25 Treasury announcement, see *American Foreign Policy: Current Documents, 1967*, pp. 1080–1081.

new foreign borrowing in US capital markets, in limiting purchases by US residents of outstanding foreign issues, and in reinforcing the Federal Reserve voluntary restraints program on capital outflows by financial institutions. The extension is necessary while pressure continues on our balance of payments, while capital markets abroad continue to be insufficiently responsive to domestic and international needs, and as a reinforcement to the continuing voluntary program administered by the Federal Reserve Board.

Rates of Tax

The maximum effective rate of 2 percent per year would be double the rate under the present law. To achieve this objective, the tax on the acquisition by a US person of a debt obligation of a foreign obligor would be increased in accordance with a table on the basis of the period remaining to maturity, to achieve such an effective rate. Debt obligations with a period remaining to maturity of less than one year will continue to be exempt from the tax. The tax on an acquisition by a US person of stock of a foreign issuer covered by the tax would be increased from 15 percent to 30 percent.

Flexibility

The bill would give the President authority to increase or decrease, by Executive Order, the rates of tax if he finds that the rates currently in effect (whether such rates are those set forth in the statute or a prior Executive Order) are lower or higher than those necessary to limit the total acquisition by US persons of stock of foreign issuers and debt obligations of foreign obligors within a range consistent with the balance-of-payments objectives of the US. The proposed flexibility would thus facilitate the lowering of interest rates in the US, providing protection in the case of a possible emergence of a wider difference in the yield on investments in this country and elsewhere, and providing a tool that could be used sensitively to affect yields on the foreign investment of US funds in response to changing needs and comparative costs of money here and abroad.

To ensure that the proposed flexibility does not induce accelerated purchase by US residents of foreign debt obligations or foreign equities prior to enactment of the legislation, the bill sent to the Congress would make the new rates effective January 26, 1967.

Exemptions

Loans connected with exports continue to be exempt from the IET so as to assist the American business community in keeping US exports—a major favorable element in our balance-of-payments accounts—at a high level. There is no change in the exemption afforded direct investments. Moreover, loans to and investments in less-developed countries are exempt from the tax, as before. The existing exemption for new Canadian security issues is continued, as is the limited exemption for loans to Japan.

[Here follow articles on unrelated subjects.]

---

118.   Memorandum From the President's Special Assistant (Rostow) to President Johnson[1]

Washington, March 29, 1967, 7 p.m.

SUBJECT

Two Steps to Help the Balance of Payments

In the attached, Secretary Fowler asks you to approve two ways of using his Exchange Stabilization Fund to help the balance of payments. He proposes to use the Fund:

—to guarantee payment of a German offset obligation we would sell to the U.K. in a complicated, 3-cornered deal designed to *shift $100 million in receipts into the first quarter.* (If we do this, *we must do it before midnight, Friday, March 31.*)

—to buy U.S. Government agency securities and sell them, usually at a discount, to foreign central banks and other official holders.

Fowler has blanket authority to use the Exchange Stabilization Fund for any purpose which will strengthen the dollar. But the law requires that he have the President's approval.

3-Cornered Arrangement

Fowler, Ackley, and the rest of us are very worried that a very large first-quarter payments deficit would produce serious pressure for tight money—which is just what we don't need. Fowler's proposal would take advantage of an opportunity to sift $100 million in inflow from the second quarter to the first. This would not solve the problem, but it would help. Basically, Fowler suggests the following:

---

[1] Source: Johnson Library, National Security File, Subject File, Balance of Payments, Vol. IV, January 1967 [2 of 2], Box 3. Confidential. An attached undated note from "A." (presumably Alice M. Caubet) to Lois Nivens, indicates, among other things, that regarding authority for the Secretary of the Treasury to use Exchange Stabilization Funds "Mr. Smith has asked Mr. Hamilton to do a memo to Sec. of Treas., by tonight for Mr. Rostow's signature." That memorandum is presumably the one printed here.

—we would transfer to the British $100 million in German offset obligations which will be paid in the second quarter.

—in return, the U.K. would immediately pay us the $100 million, *less* the interest we would normally pay on a similar amount in Treasury bills.

—through the Exchange Stabilization Fund, we would guarantee payment of the German obligation.

Obviously, *we would have to forego $100 million in anticipated second-quarter receipts,* but your advisers are agreed that the first-quarter problem is serious enough to be worth it.

This transaction would *not* be made public. If it leaked, we could be charged with gimmickry, but Fowler believes he has an effective defense: we are simply trying to keep our balance of payments difficulties from being exaggerated through uneven receipts under the US-FRG offset deal.

Purchases of Securities

This proposal is aimed at the longer term. The market is now so structured that there are relatively few sales of U.S. agency securities to foreign governments and central banks. Fowler's proposal is that the Exchange Stabilization Fund buy these securities at the going rate and sell them to official foreign holders, usually at a slight discount (1/8–3/8 of a point). The Exchange Stabilization Fund would take the small losses involved.

Fowler is confident this operation would not cause any trouble on the Hill if it were noticed at all. (The Exchange Stabilization Fund is not audited outside the Treasury and does not require appropriations.) If criticism did develop, he believes we could show that the benefits to the balance of payments far outweigh the cost to the Fund.

Recommendation

I recommend that you approve both proposals. The CEA concurs.

Walt

Approve guarantee of German note in 3-cornered deal[2]

Disapprove

Speak to me

Approve Fund purchases of agency securities[3]

Disapprove

Speak to me

---

[2] This option is checked.

[3] This option is checked. A handwritten note by Alice Caubet next to these approvals reads: "notified Hamilton's ofc. 3/30/67 3:10. amc. Dene said E. Hamilton will take care of notifying as nec." Dene is unidentified.

Attachment

Letter From Secretary of the Treasury Fowler to President Johnson[4]

Washington, March 29, 1967.

Dear Mr. President:

As you know, the Government of the Federal Republic of Germany has agreed to make deposits in the U.S. Treasury at agreed intervals for the purchase of military equipment in the United States. We propose to transfer to the Government of the United Kingdom before the end of this calendar quarter all U.S. rights to receive from the Government of the Federal Republic of Germany during the second calendar quarter a deposit of $100 million, receiving therefor $100 million discounted to yield the current bill rate. We also propose to have the Exchange Stabilization Fund guarantee to the Government of the United Kingdom payment on the deposit.

The proposed transaction would prevent an adverse impact on the balance-of-payments position of the United States which results from deposits being made by the Government of the Federal Republic of Germany at a rate slower than approximately even quarterly amounts. Purchase of this asset by the Government of the United Kingdom during the first calendar quarter would be reflected as a long-term inflow of dollars during the first calendar quarter. The Government of the United Kingdom has dollars available to make the proposed purchase and it may be willing to enter into the transaction provided its own investment is guaranteed by the Exchange Stabilization Fund.

I believe it would also be desirable for the Exchange Stabilization Fund to have the authority to purchase U.S. agency obligations and to sell them to foreign governments, central banks, and monetary institutions, making such sales at discount whenever this would be appropriate. Not more than a reasonable percentage of the assets of the Fund would be applied to this program.

Authority for the Exchange Stabilization Fund to make such purchases and sales would be helpful in our effort to sell medium- and long-term U.S. agency obligations to foreign official holders. Such sales are reported as long-term inflows of dollars in our balance-of-payments statistics.

The Secretary of the Treasury, with the approval of the President, has the authority to use the Exchange Stabilization Fund for the issuance of

---

[4] No classification marking.

the proposed guarantee and for the proposed purchases and sales of U.S. agency obligations under Section 10 of the Gold Reserve Act of 1934 (32 U.S.C. 822a). This section authorizes the Secretary of the Treasury, with the approval of the President, ". . . to deal in gold and foreign exchange and such other instruments of credit and securities as he may deem necessary to carry out the purpose of . . ." the Exchange Stabilization Fund. The section also provides that "The Fund shall be available for expenditure, under the direction of the Secretary of the Treasury and in his discretion, for any purpose in connection with carrying out the provisions of this section, ..." On September 4, 1934, the President granted his approval for the Secretary of the Treasury to purchase or sell foreign exchange for the account of the Fund for present or future delivery. On June 5, 1962, the President approved a recommendation that the Exchange Stabilization Fund be authorized to receive and hold deposits of currencies drawn pursuant to exchange stabilization agreements, which the Treasury enters into from time to time with foreign governments and central banks, and to pay interest on such deposits. On February 10, 1964, you authorized an extension of this authority to include the acceptance from foreign governments, central banks, and official monetary institutions of deposits of dollars and foreign currencies unrelated to exchange stabilization agreements and to pay interest on such deposits.

I recommend that you authorize me to use the Exchange Stabilization Fund to guarantee payment to the Government of the United Kingdom under the proposed transaction described above and to purchase U.S. agency obligations and to sell them at market price or at discount to foreign official holders. If you approve my recommendations, will you please so confirm in writing in the space provided below.[5]

Faithfully yours,

Henry H. Fowler

---

[5] An approval line at the end of Fowler's memorandum bears the President's signature.

119.   Letter From Secretary of the Treasury Fowler to the German Minister of Finance (Schiller)[1]

Washington, April 6, 1967.

Dear Mr. Minister:

Ever since our meeting in England in January,[2] I have been looking forward to an opportunity to have some conversation with you on various subjects that could not be considered during our limited time at Chequers. I had hoped that an occasion would present itself when you might visit Washington and we could have adequate time for such discussion. I still look forward to that possibility, hopefully in the near future, but meanwhile I feel it desirable to write you briefly about the state of negotiations on new international liquidity.

We are now entering a critical phase in these negotiations on a plan for reserve creation. The Finance Ministers of the European Economic Community will shortly be meeting on this matter. On April 24–26 in Washington the third Joint Meeting of the Executive Directors and the Deputies will be a crucial negotiating session.

Professor Walter Heller will be seeing you on April 11, in Germany. I know he will be discussing this subject with you then and I want to set down briefly some of my thoughts. Professor Heller, as a member of our Advisory Committee on International Monetary Arrangements, is, of course, conversant with our views on these matters.

As you know, it is our very earnest desire to see the Governors of the International Monetary Fund, at their Annual Meeting in September 1967, approve the structure and major provisions of a plan for reserve creation in a form that will really meet the reserve needs of the world in the future. To do this, it will be necessary that the negotiations of the next few months be pressed forward by all parties, so that an adequate consensus on a plan can be achieved by the summer months.

It would be most unfortunate if the thorough and intensive work done on this matter since the Fall of 1963 by the Deputies of the Group of Ten, and in the International Monetary Fund, should fail to provide us with an acceptable plan. I am concerned that this result would lead to grave consequences in the future evolution of the monetary system and in the financial relationships of Europe and America. This I most urgently wish to avoid. The attitudes taken by the Governments of the

---

[1] Source: Johnson Library, Bator Papers, McCloy Trip, June 1967, Box 8. Confidential; Personal. Attached to Document 124. Copies of this letter were distributed to members of the Deming Group as DG/67/91 on April 6. (Washington National Records Center, RG 56, OASIA Files: FRC 75 A 101, Deming Group)
[2] See Documents 113, 115, and 116.

EEC countries, and especially that taken by your Government, will play a central role in determining the outcome.

As I see it, the world needs to be assured that a plan exists which can provide for an adequate supplement to existing reserves over the years ahead. In this way we can avoid the uncertainties that promote instability in gold and exchange markets, and we can provide an essential sustaining element to the forward march of economic growth and world trade.

In my judgment, the best way to accomplish this purpose is through a proposal for a reserve unit. The Outline of an Illustrative Reserve Unit Scheme circulated in the Fund under date of February 23, 1967,[3] has many of the characteristics I believe necessary for a convincing plan, although I do not subscribe to every specific aspect of that scheme. That is, I feel the Fund is on the right track in providing an unconditional asset that is directly and independently transferable and not tied to gold or other assets, and with fully segregated accounting and resources. I believe I would favor using somewhat modified procedures on holding and use of the asset, and I certainly would eliminate the compulsory use of new assets to repay in advance outstanding drawings from the Fund. But, in broad outline the Illustrative Scheme seems to me to be a good one. The Fund's plan was discussed at the Deputies meeting of March 30–April 1, 1967 at The Hague, and some changes were suggested at that time. It will come in for further detailed discussion at the April 24–26 Joint Meeting.

There have recently been suggestions that a drawing rights plan might be developed having the same essential characteristics as the reserve unit plan described above, including unconditionality, non-repayability (to ensure its status as a permanent reserve asset), adequate provisions for acceptance, segregated accounting and resources, and reasonable convenience and visibility in use through direct transferability. The Fund itself, in its alternative illustrative plan for drawing rights, attempted to design a drawing rights scheme that would be fully equivalent to its reserve unit scheme. I believe that many of the Deputies share the view that this attempt fell short of a really effective plan for reserve creation.

I am told that the EEC Ministers may be seeking agreement on a plan for new reserve creation at their April 17 meeting. My great concern is that proposals might be put forward that fall far short of what is needed. Should that be the case, there would be little prospect of reaching the goal

---

[3] Text in Margaret Garritsen de Vries, ed., *The International Monetary Fund, 1966–1971: The System Under Stress* (Washington: International Monetary Fund, 1976), vol. II, pp. 15–23. The IMF paper was distributed to members of the Deming Group as DG/67/62 on February 24. (Washington National Records Center, RG 56, OASIA Files: FRC 75 A 101, Deming Group)

which is of such high importance for both our countries and for the world as a whole.

As you know, the President has indicated the importance we attach to these negotiations in his recent letter to the Chancellor.[4] Vice President Humphrey is also stressing their importance in his conversations in Europe.[5]

Should you feel that it would be useful to pursue this subject further, in addition to your forthcoming conversations with Professor Heller, Under Secretary Deming could undertake to come to Germany. As you know, he has the primary responsibility for this subject in the Treasury and is our principal spokesman in the meetings of the Deputies of the Group of Ten.

I should appreciate having your own assessment of these important forthcoming negotiations.

Sincerely yours,

Henry H. Fowler

---

[4] Reference may be to President Johnson's March 11 letter to Chancellor Kiesinger; see *Foreign Relations*, 1964–1968, vol. XIII, pp. 546–549.

[5] Vice President Humphrey visited several European countries March 28–April 8.

---

120.   Memorandum From Secretary of the Treasury Fowler to President Johnson[1]

Washington, April 22, 1967.

SUBJECT

Meeting with Chancellor Kiesinger [2]

Since I did not want to interrupt your hectic schedule to talk about the matter covered in the attached papers, I thought at least I should let you know:

---

[1] Source: Johnson Library, White House Confidential Files, CF, TA 1 (1967–1969). Confidential.

[2] On April 23, George E. Christian announced that President Johnson would go to Germany to attend the funeral of Konrad Adenauer and that he would call on Chancellor Kiesinger.

1. I have indicated to Secretary Rusk in Attachment A the negotiatory background which makes highly important some mention by you to Kiesinger of our disappointment in the German role at the Munich meeting of the EEC Finance Ministers last week.

In my judgment, if you do not so indicate to Kiesinger, the Germans will read your omission to mention it as a signal that you personally are not unhappy with their performance; and they will take any sign of unhappiness from other U.S. sources as a mere reflection of technical Treasury discomfiture which is not to be given any great weight.

2. I heartily subscribe to the Bator memorandum to you, a copy of which is Attachment B.

Henry H. Fowler

Attachment A

Memorandum From Secretary of the Treasury Fowler to Secretary of State Rusk[3]

Washington, April 22, 1967.

SUBJECT

International Monetary Reform

You are familiar with the fact that the President's letter to Chancellor Kiesinger stated his hope that the German Government would support agreement on a contingency plan for the creation of new reserves at the September meeting of the International Monetary Fund.[4] The Chancellor's reply stated that the German Government would "contribute to the best of its ability."[5]

I wrote two letters to Economics Minister Schiller, outlining the American position and strongly expressing our opinion that a meaningful plan for reserve creation should be agreed upon by September.[6] I said

---

[3] Confidential.

[4] See footnote 4, Document 119.

[5] Not further identified.

[6] For the first of these letters, see Document 119. In the second letter, dated April 14, Fowler expressed, among other things, his "great concern" that at the forthcoming meeting of the EEC Finance Ministers in Munich "proposals might be endorsed, and possibly put forward publicly, by the EEC Ministers in very general terms (based upon unspecified and perhaps very limited common ground)—proposals which would not provide a basis for an adequate drawing rights scheme, but would appear to rule out, so far as the EEC is concerned, the alternative of reserve units." (Johnson Library, Fowler Papers, International Countries: Schiller Meeting of June 19, 1967, Box 39) Copies of the April 14 letter from Fowler to Schiller were distributed to members of the Deming Group as DG/67/131. (Washington National Records Center, RG 56, OASIA Files: FRC 75 A 101, Deming Group)

equally strongly that I hoped the Common Market Ministers would not agree on a weak plan for international monetary reform just in order to accommodate the French.

Walter Heller followed up my first letter to Schiller with a three-hour visit, in which he made these same points and told Schiller that a German position half-way between the United States and France was not a useful position. I also wrote a letter to Minister of the Treasury Colombo, of Italy,[7] making the same points I made to Minister Schiller, and we had conversations with van Lennep of the Netherlands to this same end.[8]

At the Common Market Ministers meeting on April 17, Italy and the Netherlands stood up for a good plan, while Germany moved to a position closer to the French.[9] Schiller and Debre had had a meeting prior to April 17 and apparently had agreed on a German-French position, which was supported by Belgium.

With the negotiations now moving into their critical phase, it is a matter of high importance that the President make known to the Chancellor that we regard the German position at Munich as counter-productive. It produced a Common Market attitude on reserve creation which is far short of what the world wants and needs. Failure on the President's part to make this point strongly probably would convince the Germans that what they did had American approval and could result in an impasse in the negotiations.

The attached memorandum from Francis Bator to the President makes the points clearly and succinctly, and I cannot improve on it. I hope you will do your best to get the President to say to the Chancellor what Francis has outlined.

Henry H. Fowler[10]

---

[7] Not found.

[8] No record of these conversations has been found.

[9] F. Lisle Widman, Director, Office of Industrial Nations, Department of the Treasury, sent memoranda to Under Secretary Deming reporting on the April 17 meeting, based on information he received by telephone from Treasury Attaché McGrew in Paris. (Papers DG/67/102 and DG/67/104, dated April 18 and April 19; Washington National Records Center, RG 56, OASIA Files: FRC 75 A 101, Deming Group)

[10] Printed from a copy that indicates Fowler signed the original.

Attachment B

Memorandum From the President's Deputy Special Assistant for National Security Affairs (Bator) to President Johnson[11]

Washington, April 22, 1967, 11:30 p.m.

SUBJECT

Important points for Kiesinger, Wilson and Moro

I know that you don't want to talk business on the trip. However, if you do *not* make a few key points on the hot issues,—particularly Kennedy Round and international money—we could suffer at the bargaining table right in the middle of the crunch.

I. Economic Negotiations: Kennedy Round and International Money.

Kiesinger and Moro are key figures on both fronts. Both are for success in the Kennedy Round, but don't realize what a disaster failure would be in terms of US-European *political* relations. On international money, the Italians took our side in the recent caucus of EEC Finance Ministers, and should be thanked. The Germans ganged up with the French. If we can't bring them back, the negotiations will fail and the balance of payments will become a much more serious political constraint on your domestic and foreign policies—we might even face a gold crisis.

Points to be made (Kiesinger and Moro):

—Worried about two great economic negotiations coming to head soon. (Kennedy Round in next two weeks, international money in next 3–4 months.)

—Don't wish to talk specifics on sad occasion; Bill Roth and Joe Fowler representing my position very precisely;

—But, failure of either would be *major political trauma* in US-European relations.

—Don't want to sound gloomy, but U.S. must have major movement from present positions on both fronts if President is to withstand domestic political pressures threatening to bring on new wave of protectionism and isolationism:

—Vital to have EEC movement on agriculture in *Kennedy Round.* Need further loosening on grains and tariff items. (U.S. pleased by EEC decision to put up 3 million tons for food aid, but needs much greater.)

—On *international money*, must have agreement on some kind new money that can be counted as part of reserves. *New credit won't do.* (Ger-

---

[11] No classification marking.

mans sided with French for new *credit* rather than new *money*. Italians resisted and should be thanked.)

—Hope Kiesinger and Moro will keep personal track of both negotiations. Can't overstress danger of angry, divisive, isolationist political reaction in U.S. if either fails. Would damage political cohesion of Atlantic Community.[12]

---

[12] Following the meeting in Bonn between President Johnson and Kiesinger on April 26, the two made public remarks indicating that they had talked about a wide range of issues of mutual concern, including international monetary matters. See *Public Papers of the Presidents of the United States: Lyndon B. Johnson, 1967*, Book I, pp. 462–463. No record of their private conversations has been found.

---

121. Memorandum of Conversation[1]

Bonn, April 27, 1967.

PARTICIPANTS

> Karl Schiller, Economic Minister, Germany
> W. W. Rostow

The following is designed to supplement the account in Bonn's 12850 of the April 27, 1967,[2] exchange between Schiller and myself on the Munich money agreement.

1. The reporting cable suggests accurately the line of Schiller's justification. It was basically political. He had brought the French along some distance. He felt the non-repayability provision would not apply to the U.S. The transferability provision might not be wholly satisfactory, nor clear; but it was a move in the right direction. On the other points of interest to us, there was evidently more work for them to do. The Munich agreement was incomplete.

2. He suggested strongly that this was a negotiating position in which we should bear in mind two factors:

---

[1] Source: Johnson Library, National Security File, Name File, Rostow Memos, Boxes 7 and 8. Secret. Drafted in Washington on May 1.

[2] Telegram 12850 is dated April 26, not April 27. A copy is in Department of State, S/S–I Files: Lot 79 D 247, Secretary's Memoranda of Conversation, Reel 1.

—the substance of what emerged from Europe would depend on what could be negotiated for Europe by way of a larger voice in the IMF;

—in the minutes of the meeting it was agreed that the Six would have to reconvene if no agreement with the Americans was reached.

He claimed they had set in motion a process of movement in Europe towards the U.S. position. The movement was incomplete. But he felt there was time in hand because the German agreement on gold provided the U.S. security and the state of the U.S. balance of payments provided the world liquidity. We could continue to run a balance of payments deficit for some time without fear of a U.S. crisis or a world liquidity crisis. He was strongly urging us, in effect, to negotiate a drawing-rights scheme which met our requirements (non-repayment, transferability, etc.) rather than make a rigid stance on a new medium of payment at this time.

My reply to him was that, while we respected the diplomatic achievement of bringing the French along and getting the beginnings of a European position that was not in total confrontation with our interests, we did not face a diplomatic problem but a technical problem; namely, that if we did not solve this question properly, we might have "a traumatic event" in the field of international money which could have grave consequences. I recalled the inter-war years. Whatever solution we reached had to meet certain technical criteria or the problem would not be solved, however elegant the diplomacy. He knew as well as I the difference between finding a supplement to gold as a reserve instrument and enlarging, on a conditional basis, IMF credit facilities.

Afterwards, on the lawn, when the President and Chancellor Kiesinger were briefing the press on their private exchanges, Schiller sought me out and said: "I know where we have to end up in this monetary matter. Please tell your people not to be too rigid: We must do this by stages. We know you are not going to change the price of gold. We are supporting the dollar with our commitment on gold in the tripartite negotiations. We can make much further progress beyond Munich on a drawing-rights basis." Then he repeated his hope we would not be excessively rigid. I indicated no concessions whatever in our present proposal.

We exchanged sentiments of satisfaction at being able to discuss this matter so directly, as old friends, given our common work in 1962–64 on Berlin viability.

Walt

122.   Current Economic Developments[1]

Issue No. 779   Washington, May 9, 1967.

[Here follow articles on unrelated subjects.]

PLANS FOR CREATION OF SUPPLEMENTAL RESERVES DISCUSSED AT RECENT MEETINGS

At a recent joint meeting in Washington, the IMF Directors and the Group of Ten Deputies confirmed an agreement to proceed with work toward the establishment of a contingency plan for creation of supplementary reserves.[2] The Germans and other EEC countries joined the French in endorsing expanded drawing rights in the Fund but not on some of the important questions which would determine whether the rights would be more like money or more like credit. Although the US favors a reserve unit scheme, it did not rule out the possibility of compromising on a drawing rights arrangement that would constitute a new and meaningful supplementary reserve asset. We continue to hope for approval of a contingency plan at the annual IMF meeting in September.

Need for Reserves

On the need for reserves, Treasury Under Secretary Deming made two main points at the joint meeting. First, under the present situation, countries have to gain reserves at the expense of other countries. This could lead to a series of restrictive actions as one country after another tries to avoid loss of reserves by restrictions on aid, trade, and capital movements. Secondly, Mr. Deming said, the traditional sources of reserves have dried up in recent years. The gold supply increased only about $250 million in 1965 and was negative in 1966. Additions of dollars to monetary reserves all but disappeared last year as a result of a small US deficit and substantial gold conversions. In the past two years, the US balance of payments has provided rather limited amounts.

The participants discussed the possible qualitative and quantitative criteria to assess the need for additional reserves and its urgency. They talked about various symptoms which could one day lead to the conclusion that the creation of reserves was needed and also the various quantitative criteria which could guide future judgment. The result of the

---

[1] Source: Washington National Records Center, E/CBA/REP Files: FRC 72 A 6248, *Current Economic Developments*. Limited Official Use. The source text comprises pages 20–22 of the issue.

[2] This meeting convened in Washington April 24–26. Background on the major issues and U.S. preparations for the meeting is in *Current Economic Developments*, Issue No. 777, April 11, 1967, pp. 3–4. (Ibid.)

discussion was that all criteria had to be appreciated or measured together and that, finally, it was to a large extent a matter of collective judgment.

Plans for Reserve Creation

Two categories of plans for creating supplemental reserves were discussed. One would involve the creation of reserve units, probably in an affiliate of the IMF. The other would involve the creation of a new category of drawing rights, i.e., automatic drawing rights, in the Fund or in an affiliate of the Fund. No decision was taken as to the choice between these two main approaches. Both, however, would amount to the creation or some kind of new unconditional reserve asset.

Under Secretary Deming said that there was a pressing need for a plan and that there were serious risks if a plan were not agreed upon by September. The US would not, however, be satisfied with an ineffective and excessively restrictive plan. The need was for international money, not improved credit facilities, and the best way to do this was through a reserve unit. Such a true international reserve asset is unconditional in use, readily convertible into intervention currency, has adequate provisions for holding and use, is directly transferable, and is held in segregated accounts, preferably in an affiliate of the IMF. The burden of proof is on those who would advocate that reserve creation could take a form other than units to show that such an asset could meet the requirements of being fully accepted as a third form of international money.

In the discussion that followed, the Executive Directors of the non-Ten and the Deputies from non-EEC countries emphasized the urgency of reaching agreement on a contingency plan and the need for creating a money-like asset. Almost all said that they favored units over drawing rights. They also stressed that the asset must be unconditional, non-repayable, directly transferable, and segregated from regular IMF accounts. The non-Ten Executive Directors made clear that, if in the past they had no preference for units over drawing rights, this was because drawing rights had certain institutional advantages in being closely associated with the Fund. The EEC proposals for making restrictive changes in the regular Fund operations, however, had resulted in a loss of this advantage of institutional simplicity and, as a result, they now had a preference for reserve units.

In this discussion and in subsequent discussions, clear differences of views emerged among the EEC countries on the issues left open in the communiqué on the EEC Finance Ministers' meeting in Munich.[3] Some of the EEC Deputies actually seemed to chaff under the restrictions that

---

[3] The Munich communiqué has not been found. Regarding its general contents, see footnote 7, Document 124.

they could not take a position until a common position had been agreed among the Six.

Under Secretary Deming concluded the discussion of the illustrative schemes by reiterating the US preference for a reserve unit and US opposition to a decision making formula that would give one country or a small group of closely associated countries a veto. Mr. Deming also suggested that in order to give the plan reality for the public in general and to define for parliaments the approximate extent of their obligations, the plan should mention the general scope of the amount of reserve creation that is contemplated. This amount could be expressed in various ways: a) as a specific amount for each year of the first five years, b) as a range for this period, or c) as a total amount with the time period not specified. Inclusion of such a provision would not prejudice the collective decision on the timing of reserve creation. He suggested that this matter be discussed at the next meeting.

After the joint meeting, Mr. Deming said in a press backgrounder that a figure of $2 billion a year for the growth in reserves of all types was being talked about more and more. The need for reserves can be related to a number of different factors but the results tend to center around $2–2-1/2 billion a year as a good quantitative judgment, though one cannot make a calculation with absolute precision, Mr. Deming said.

Remaining Problems

The first main questions which have to be decided in any kind of scheme are those related to the scheme's entry into force and the way decisions will be taken, especially decisions concerning the activation of the scheme, i.e. the actual creation of new reserve assets. The second main questions are the use, transfer, and acceptability of these new assets—how they can be issued, how they are transferred, directly or indirectly, what the obligations are to accept and to hold them; and so on. A third question is the nature of the resource backing for these schemes and, in the case of the drawing rights scheme, whether the resources would be merged with other resources of the Monetary Fund or whether the resources provided for that scheme would be segregated. A fourth question is whether there should be any reconstitution or repurchase provision linked with prolonged or extensive use of the new assets.

Future Meetings

The Deputies and Executive Directors agreed to meet again in Paris June 19–21. In preparation for these meetings, the Fund staff will prepare papers on transferability and on separability, a revision of its illustrative units scheme, and substantially revised drawing rights proposal. The French and Dutch representatives, with some other support, urged that a working party of the Deputies be organized, after the meeting of the

Deputies of the Group of Ten, and meet in Paris on May 18–19 to prepare an agreed plan.

[Here follow articles on unrelated subjects.]

123. Memorandum From Acting Secretary of Commerce Trowbridge to the Chairman of the Cabinet Committee on Balance of Payments (Fowler)[1]

Washington, May 15, 1967.

SUBJECT

Export Expansion Program

As you suggested, I have developed a rather substantial increase in our program for expanding our commercial exports. In order to get the program rolling, I am suggesting that the Balance of Payments Committee endorse our approach and that the President be asked to approve. The President could announce the program on May 23 in connection with granting "E" awards for excellence in exporting to ten companies at the White House.[2] On this occasion he will indicate that he is authorizing the Department of Commerce to request additional funds from Congress in the form of a supplemental appropriation.

This supplemental appropriation for F.Y. 1968 would roughly double the on-going F.Y. 1967 level—from $14.4 million to $27.7 million. We are projecting a F.Y. 1969 appropriation request of $39.7 million. The Bureau of the Budget would review these requests in the normal way, of course, and all I am asking at this time is the approval in principle by the Balance of Payments Committee of this program of increased export promotion.

Our program for F.Y. 1968, including the supplemental appropriation, is self-contained, in the sense that no additional manpower would be expected to be provided by the Foreign Service. The F.Y. 1969 request

---

[1] Source: Washington National Records Center, RG 40, Executive Secretariat Files: FRC 74 A 30, Balance of Payments Cabinet Committee. No classification marking. Drafted by Lawrence A. Fox, Director of the Bureau of International Commerce, on May 12.

[2] For this announcement by President Johnson on May 23, see *Public Papers of the Presidents of the United States: Lyndon B. Johnson, 1967*, pp. 558–560.

will be coordinated with the Department of State to make certain that necessary Foreign Service support is included in State's budget.

The expanded export promotion program is premised on (a) the need for larger surpluses in our trade account to help achieve a fundamental improvement in our current account earnings, and (b) sustained improvement in the trade account being achievable if U.S. industry is stimulated to make a greater continuing commitment to export. Expansion of Department of Commerce trade promotion services can assist materially, but other measures in export finance and the tax area are required if the goal of a substantial increase in exports is to be achieved.

The supplemental appropriation for F.Y. 1968 essentially calls for an increase in our existing types of export promotion activities. We would:

1. Expand our trade and industrial exhibitions overseas.
2. Open new trade centers overseas.
3. Undertake new trade missions and mobile trade fairs.
4. Expand our automated commercial information program, including new and intensified export trade development programs.
5. Expand our promotional programs in the United States to make U.S. industry more export-minded.

Additionally, in F.Y. 1968 we would make a start toward some newer techniques and programs which would become operative in F.Y. 1969. Most of the F.Y. 1968 program would be built on existing programs in the industrialized countries. In F.Y. 1969 we would continue to expand our efforts in hard-currency markets but would begin a more comprehensive and longer-range program in certain of the developing countries.

Our program is based, in part, on the April 3, 1967 recommendations of the National Export Expansion Council[3] and can be expected to have widespread industry support.

The attachment provides a summary of the program and estimated costs.[4] Multi-year funding is proposed for those aspects of the program requiring advance commitment authority.

A.B. Trowbridge[5]

---

[3] These recommendations have not been found.

[4] Not found.

[5] Printed from a copy that bears this stamped signature.

124. Memorandum From the Under Secretary of the Treasury for Monetary Affairs (Deming) to John J. McCloy[1]

Washington, May 17, 1967.

SUBJECT

Further Developments in International Monetary Negotiations

This memorandum summarizes major developments in international monetary negotiations since my memorandum of April 22, 1967,[2] with particular reference to the German role in these negotiations. It also indicates why we have not been satisfied with the German posture in these negotiations, and presents some arguments as to why we think it is in the German interest to take a more vigorous and constructive position, even to the extent of breaking with the French on this issue if the French remain too negative and dilatory in their tactics.

Prior to the meeting of the EEC Finance Ministers on April 17, Secretary Fowler wrote two letters to Economics Minister Schiller and on April 21 the Minister replied. (Copies of this correspondence attached at Tab A.)[3] Walter Heller visited Schiller on April 11 and Vice President Humphrey discussed the liquidity question with Chancellor Kiesinger and Vice Chancellor Brandt during his visit to Bonn. As you know, President Johnson mentioned this topic in his letter to the Chancellor and subsequently discussed it with him personally.[4] (Points made by the President summarized at Tab B.)[5] Despite all of this the Germans moved much closer to the French and Belgians and away from the Italians and Dutch toward a "weak" form of new liquidity.

Following the meeting of the Finance Ministers of the EEC, the Group of Ten met with the Executive Directors of the IMF in a Joint Meet-

---

[1] Source: Johnson Library, Bator Papers, McCloy Trip, June 1967, Box 8. Confidential. McCloy was the U.S. representative to the trilateral offset negotiations.

[2] Deming's memorandum has not been found.

[3] Only Fowler's first letter to Schiller is attached; it is printed as Document 119. Regarding his second letter, see footnote 6, Document 120. The purported text of Schiller's April 21 response was distributed to members of the Deming Group as DG/67/129 on May 10. The memorandum from George H. Willis reads "Attached as DG/67/129 is Minister Schiller's reply to Secretary Fowler," but the attached document, in English, is not on a letterhead and presumably is a U.S. Government translation of a letter in German. In the English text, Schiller mistakenly thanks Fowler for his letters of April 6 and 13 (not 14). Secretary Fowler's reply to Schiller's April 21 letter had an extended gestation period with drafts on May 10 (DG/67/126) and May 29 (DG/67/145) before actually going out on June 1 (DG/67/150). Fowler also wrote Italian Treasury Minister Colombo on June 1. (DG/67/149; Washington National Records Center, RG 56, OASIA Files: FRC 75 A 101, Deming Group) For text of the letter, see Document 126.

[4] See footnote 4, Document 119, and Attachment B to Document 120.

[5] Neither this summary nor any of the other tabs has been found.

ing on April 24 and 25, 1967, in Washington. The position taken in the EEC Communiqué (Tab C)[6] was defended strongly by the French and Belgian spokesmen, and, under the "solidarity" principle, by the Dutch spokesman (although he was in fundamental disagreement with it). Chairman Emminger of Germany, who also disagreed with the EEC position, defended it but gave it a somewhat more flexible interpretation than the others. The Italian representative obviously chafed under the restraint imposed by the French attempt to stifle individual national positions and present only a common EEC position. Largely because of the aggressive suggestions for a much stronger control of EEC nations over the regular operations of the IMF, and the critical tone of the Monetary Committee's Report on the operations of the IMF,[7] the developing nations expressed a preference for a reserve unit as against the drawing right principle endorsed by the EEC. In the past the developing nations had not shown much interest in the form of the asset. They also strongly objected to some aspects of the voting procedure proposed by the EEC for activation of a reserve creation plan, which they considered discriminatory.

I made the U.S. position clear in the following terms:

"Perhaps some of the characteristics of money could be provided through a drawing right scheme, if its characteristics included unconditionality, ready convertibility, non-repayment, adequate provisions for acceptance, holding and use, transferability and segregation of accounts in an affiliate. With all these characteristics, a new reserve asset would constitute a credible, convincing and generally accepted supplement to gold and reserve currencies . . . a unit would be better, but I was willing to be convinced that a drawing right could have these characteristics, though I remained somewhat skeptical. For a scheme to be credible, the world must be convinced that there was a solid and substantial decision-making apparatus, which assured that decisions would be taken in a

---

[6] See footnote 7 below.

[7] This report of the Monetary Committee of the EEC has not been found, but according to the official IMF history, the EEC Finance Ministers at Munich on April 17 approved that committee's recommendations:

"That committee had proposed that there be opened in the Fund new automatic drawing rights, with both accounting and financing separated from other drawing rights in the Fund, which would be usable in accordance with well-defined rules drawn up in advance and directly transferable between the monetary authorities of the member countries. Furthermore, when the Fund's Articles of Agreement were amended to include such new drawing rights, other amendments should be made. Many of these amendments were drawn along the lines of the earlier French suggestions. Conditions attached to drawing rights in the credit tranches should be tightened. The definition of par values and of the Fund's unit of account should be simplified by retaining only the reference to a weight of fine gold. An 85 per cent voting majority should be required for various decisions in the Fund, particularly those for general changes in quotas and for the creation of additional reserves, and this majority ought to include at least half the major creditor countries." (Margaret Garritsen de Vries, ed., The International Monetary Fund, 1966–1971: The System Under Stress, vol. I, pp. 132–133)

sober and conservative fashion. Also, however, one had to know that the decision-making apparatus was a viable one and that the decisions, however sober and conservative, could in fact be taken. One needed a very high, qualified vote and some sort of apparatus to prevent a veto by one country or a small group of countries."

I also suggested that to give the plan reality and precision for legislatures and for the general public, the agreement should specify the amount of reserves to be created each year for the initial 5-year activation period. The timing of the initial activation would be governed by the decision-making procedure. I mentioned a figure of $10 billion, or of $2 billion each year for five years, as had been suggested in one of the IMF plans.

At the close of the Joint Meeting, Mr. Schweitzer held a press conference (Tab D) in which he gave a cautiously optimistic forecast of the possibility of reaching an agreement to take some action at the September Annual Meeting of the IMF in Rio de Janeiro. However, there was one disturbing feature during the meetings. In order to expedite the negotiations, the United States suggested that the International Monetary Fund revise its two draft plans—one providing for a reserve unit and one providing for a drawing right[8]—in the light of the discussion at the meetings, so that these drafts would be available to the Deputies meeting in Paris on May 17 to 19, 1967. The EEC members took exception to this, and the Fund has now delayed this revision, so that there will not be available to the Deputies a "good" drawing right scheme as prepared by the Fund. In order to have an effective basis for discussion at the Deputies meeting May 18–19, the United States has therefore developed two schematic plans, so as to avoid being faced with a single alternative prepared by the EEC. These two plans represent the type of reserve unit or drawing right scheme that the United States would consider meaningful and constructive, and will probably be introduced informally by the United States at the meeting of the Deputies on May 18 and 19 (Tab E and Tab F).

The introduction of the U.S. plan to the Deputies meeting should enable us to determine whether the French approach is one of serious willingness to negotiate or pure delay. It should also make this clear to the Germans and other Europeans. If the French do not strongly object to the U.S. drawing right plan (Tab F), then the major negotiating problem will be the postponement of the controversial suggestions in the EEC Monetary Committee's Report for tightening up the policies and voting procedures in the regular operations of the IMF—a very serious matter. In this event, we will need to seek the help of the Germans in separating

[8] Reference is to the IMF's "Outline of an Illustrative Reserve Unit Scheme," February 23, and "Outline of an Illustrative Scheme for a Special Reserve Facility Based on Drawing Rights in the Fund," February 28, which are reproduced ibid., vol. II, pp. 15–23 and 24–29, respectively.

this highly explosive issue from progress on a plan for reserve creation, in order to make any progress at the September meeting.

If, on the other hand, the French strongly object to the "good" characteristics of a drawing right scheme that have been introduced into the U.S. plan, then there will be intensive negotiation on these points. They may object to the non-repayment feature, although this plan adopts a suggestion thrown out by Dr. Emminger. They may also object to the clear segregation of the new reserve asset from the regular credit facilities of the Fund, through the establishment of an affiliate. They may find difficulty with the relatively easy system of transferring drawing rights from the using country to the recipient country. Or it may become clear that a basic objection is to the size of the obligation to accept the new asset.

In other words, this U.S. draft plan brings out rather clearly the issues that we had hoped the Germans would have brought home to the French and Belgians at the time of the April 17 meeting in Munich. (See Tab G) At that time the Germans went very far in accepting the French insistence on the principle of repayment, barely kept the door open for some vague form of segregation of the newly created assets, and did little more than hint at the possibility of some more liberal form of transfer that would distinguish the new asset from the older credit facilities. Up until the time of the April 22 meeting, the German Bundesbank representative and Chairman of the Deputies had been a strong and helpful advocate of a reserve unit plan, that was quite clearly a form of money rather than credit facilities, although it is true that the German Ministry of Economics had earlier expressed some interest in a drawing rights scheme.

Another major issue that concerns the United States is the question of a veto on the activation of the plan by the EEC countries, acting under a unit rule, and possibly against the convictions of some of the other countries. While it is true that the Europeans in general are more cautious regarding the need for new reserves than is the United States, the experts of Germany and Italy could be expected to be much quicker to recognize the need for activating the plan than the French, in future years. The French never agree to EEC solidarity in areas that, like the international monetary sphere, are not covered by the Treaty of Rome, unless it suits their interest. It would be tragic if we should establish a plan and then find that nothing came of it because the French were able to dictate an EEC veto.

It is increasingly clear that the German posture during the next three months will be of the greatest significance in determining the outcome of the negotiations. Despite our desire for an agreement in September, it would not be in the interest of the world to bind ourselves to a weak and unpromising plan of reserve creation, which would make it more difficult to proceed to develop bilateral monetary defenses of the dollar and the gold exchange standard. We might thus have the worst of both worlds—an ineffective multilateral system and a general resistance on the part of European countries to constructive bilateral arrangements to economize gold and avoid strain on gold and exchange markets. Thus the Germans should not assume that we will be prepared to agree to a feeble and weak plan of the type the French might most easily be persuaded to join.

Nevertheless, we recognize that there are serious risks in a breakdown of these negotiations, both of a short-term and longer-term character. These risks should be brought home to the Germans. Tab H suggests some of these risks.

One other point deserves comment. General deGaulle in his press conference and the French on numerous occasions have charged that the United States interest in reserve creation results from a desire to continue financing our balance of payments deficit. This is *not* the case. We are genuinely interested in providing what we consider an essential prerequisite for the continued development of the world's monetary and trading system without lapsing into cumulative restrictions on capital movements and on trade itself. (See Tab I) In a world in which all economic indices have a clear secular uptrend, we simply cannot expect the level of world reserves to remain stagnant without constraining international transactions. No country maintains a constant level of domestic money but in all countries the trend is steadily upward in the domestic money supply.

At the same time, our ideas as to the magnitude of new reserve creation are quite conservative. We would not expect reserve growth to exceed 2 or 3% per annum, whereas much higher figures are steadily recorded for the growth of domestic money supplies. In terms of our balance of payments deficit, the amount of new reserves that would become available to the United States would hardly be as much as $500 million a year at the most. Most Europeans would not regard this sum, even if it were used to finance a U.S. deficit, as in any way significantly affecting the U.S. desire to reach equilibrium as soon as the Vietnam situation permits.

Frederick L. Deming[9]

---

[9] Printed from a copy that bears this typed signature.

125. Memorandum of Conversation[1]

Washington, May 26, 1967, 4:15 p.m.

PARTICIPANTS

IMF:
Mr. Schweitzer
Mr. Southard
Mr. Polak

U.S.:
Secretary Fowler
Under Secretary Deming
Mr. Willis
Mr. Dale

SUBJECT

International Monetary Negotiations

Secretary Fowler first raised the subject of recent developments in the gold market.

Mr. Schweitzer said that they did not know all the details as to what was happening in the gold market. His view was that, despite unusual demands, in the present circumstances we should continue to support the market. Mr. Schweitzer thought that the French would be prepared to participate in an additional rallonge to support the market.

Under Secretary Deming reported that one participant (a professor) at a recent meeting of academics and financial officials of the Ten at Bellagio suggested establishing a pool of $10 billion instead of continuing to provide bits and pieces. While $10 billion was excessive, what about establishing a pool of $500 million to $1 billion?

Mr. Schweitzer thought that would be wonderful. Would the U.S. be willing to provide 50% of the amount? He was not sure that the public, in general, knows much about the size of the gold pool and its possible supplementary resources.

Under Secretary Deming pointed out that over time the pool has acquired $1 billion in gold. It was pointed out that it is not strictly speaking a pure pool operation, because South Africa supplies gold to the pool, and on the other hand the contributors to the pool may replenish their gold reserves by converting dollars into gold.

Continuing, Mr. Schweitzer said that his personal guess was that we should proceed as if nothing had happened in the Middle East, and it would be dangerous to let the price move above $35.20. He was not sure it would be a good idea to make a startling announcement that a large amount was being set aside for the pool. This would have the disadvan-

---

[1] Source: Johnson Library, Bator Papers, Letters and Memoranda of Conversation, Box 9. Limited Official Use. Drafted by George H. Willis on June 2 and approved by Deming. The meeting was held in Secretary Fowler's Conference Room.

tage of appearing to fix a limit for support of the pool and would also be taken as official recognition that we expect a severe crisis. He preferred to avoid the impression of official panic.

Under Secretary Deming asked whether it would be useful to make some announcement by the pool or by the Group of Ten countries and Mr. Schweitzer repeated that he would rather play it down. He mentioned that Mr. Parsons[2] of the Bank of England had not appeared to be much concerned. He thought the Bank of France would be very unhappy to see the price of gold rise in London. Whatever Mr. deGaulle wants to achieve, this should not be done through the London Gold Market.

Secretary Fowler then took up the subject of the negotiations on reserve creation. He mentioned that Minister Schiller will be in Washington on June 16 and that Minister Colombo will be here sometime between June 5 and June 15. The EEC Finance Ministers meet in Rome on June 5, in their capacity as Governors of the European Investment Bank. The Secretary wanted to discuss some of the technical elements in the U.S. proposals to determine whether they present problems to the IMF. He also wanted their evaluation of the "parliamentary" situation in Rio, and particularly whether it would be desirable to make a proposal on reserve creation even though there were some substantial objections from EEC countries.

Mr. Schweitzer found it very difficult to make an assessment of the current negotiating position. He was worried about two things. First, the EEC now appears to seek a common position. This could mean that the negotiations would drag out a long time because they have differences of opinion and they are in no hurry. Second, there is a danger that the EEC will take a common position at the lowest common denominator and the deGaulle press conference was rather forbidding. On the other hand, for the foreseeable future it is not likely that there will be a break in the EEC. Both Kiesinger and deGaulle are afraid of a break. DeGaulle feared a break if he remained too negative, and Mr. Schweitzer does not think any pressure on Germany will produce a break. It is too late now for that during the next year or two. The other EEC countries do not want an open break with France.

Continuing, Mr. Schweitzer said there is room for dragging the French along under pressure from the Germans and Italians. The French will resist and it will be like dragging a mule, but deGaulle will be open to some limited pressure.

It would probably help if the U.S. would consider a drawing right plan. If we are to have agreement this year, it would probably have to be in the form of a drawing right that is somewhere beyond the French conception and somewhat less than the U.S. preference. The French have

---

[2] Sir Maurice Parsons, Deputy Governor of the Bank of England.

been surprisingly yielding on the issue of separation. Mr. Schweitzer interpreted Mr. Larre's[3] position in the IMF to mean that drawings on the new drawing right would not make use of regular Fund resources.

Mr. Schweitzer thought that a completely negative result in Rio would be a very unhappy result. The blame could easily fall on the most innocent country. The attitude of the countries outside of the Group of Ten was a bit complex and their views differ. They don't care much about the distinction between the drawing right and the reserve unit. They are jockeying for position, and since Munich they have preferred reserve units, but they won't make a basic issue on this. On decision-making, they feel strongly on the "diplomatic" issue of a special unit vote for creditors, but they could accept an 85% majority, including plus votes for creditors. What they oppose is a self-appointed inner group like the U.N. Security Council.

Concerning changes in the IMF itself, anything that would change the present voting rights in the IMF is wholly unacceptable. This is like playing with fire with one qualification. Thinking in terms of legal provisions as the French do, it is now possible by a simple majority to make access to the credit tranches automatic. We will probably have to find some language to prevent that, as the Europeans have a good case there. Mr. Schweitzer would strongly oppose any other change in existing voting procedure, as a political disaster and not needed. He would try to convince the Six that this was against their interest.

Mr. Schweitzer said that if he were a member of the Deputies Group, he would be concerned because the Group appeared to prefer long discussions to getting down to the business of agreeing on specific language. He had hoped that we had left that point, since general discussions could go on for years. His suggestion of IMF outlines had been designed to bring the joint meeting to bear on specific language. The U.S. illustrative plans were useful, and the IMF would try to come up with specific language.

Mr. Schweitzer felt that the Ministers would not be able to deal with the complex questions of holding, use and transfer, and this probably meant that a wide discretion for guidance would have to be left to the agent in the future unless the Deputies could reach agreement on some specific principles.

Mr. Polak[4] hoped that it would not be necessary to explain to Ministers more than the issues of repayment and decision-making.

Mr. Willis pointed out that it is now realized by the Deputies that the provisions on holding and use are really at the heart of the whole scheme,

---

[3] René Larre, French representative on the Board of Executive Directors of the International Monetary Fund.

[4] J.J. Polak, Economic Counselor, International Monetary Fund.

are tied up with the other issues, and there is some reluctance to delegate full discretion to the agent.

Mr. Polak noted that it might be possible to agree on roughly three quarters of the U.S. principles on transfer and use.

Summing up his remarks, Mr. Schweitzer said: (1) do all we can to drag the French along, (2) don't expect a split in the EEC, and (3) try to agree on specific language. The Fund would try to present some specific language that would not be the same as the U.S. scheme. Although the French had opposed the Fund initiative in providing language, it was essential that the Ministers have specific language before them.

Secretary Fowler stressed that at least one element, paragraph 11 of the Monetary Committee Report, applying high qualified majorities to basic policy decisions, would have to be given up and brushed out of the way. Mr. Southard agreed that the paragraph is anathema to the non-Ten countries, and that the unit vote of creditors is also unacceptable.

Under Secretary Deming thought that the EEC would give up the unit vote for creditors.

Concerning the 85% weighted vote, Mr. Schweitzer said that the non-Ten countries realize they could not have activation if there is no EEC participation, and they do not oppose 85%, including bonus votes for creditors.

Secretary Fowler thought it made an important difference whether the qualified majority was 75% or 85%. An 85% majority is a very attractive incentive for the EEC to stick together. Mr. Dale reported that Mr. Kafka[5] thought the Europeans might stick together on constitutional provisions, but might be easier on actual operations.

Secretary Fowler was worried whether the plane would ever be able to fly with an 85% majority. Mr. Southard suggested that the non-Ten do not believe the EEC will really resist the pressure to create reserves when a plan is in effect.

Secretary Fowler made clear that he was fearful that 85% would permit an effective veto by one country, and stated that he would not want to be a party to it. He read a copy of his statement at The Hague[6] on this point. He mentioned that the Dillon Advisory Committee did not agree with Mr. Schweitzer and thought there was a possibility of splitting the EEC this year.

---

[5] Alexandre Kafka, Brazilian representative on the Board of Executive Directors of the International Monetary Fund.

[6] Reference is to Fowler's statement to the meeting of the Finance Ministers and Central Bank Governors of the Group of Ten at The Hague on July 26, 1966. A copy of this statement is Attachment B to the Summary of Meetings of the Ministers and Deputies of the Group of Ten at The Hague, Netherlands, July 25–26, 1966, dated August 15, 1966. (Department of State, Ball Papers: Lot 74 D 272, Balance of Payments)

Mr. Schweitzer said that he had welcomed the Secretary's statement at The Hague which had killed the earlier European idea of a two-tier vote. However, it would be futile to try to prevent, through a voting arrangement, a common position on the part of a few countries. If we were to proceed by amending the IMF Articles, this required 80% of the weighted votes and 60% of the individual member votes.

The Secretary raised the possibility that the French might require a private understanding with the Germans and Italians that if any one of them was opposed to activation, the others, regardless of their views on the merits, would not vote for it. Was this a danger and should we worry about it? Mr. Schweitzer agreed this was a danger but there was not much that could be done about it.

Mr. Willis referred to Mr. Larre's position that a precondition for activation was a change in IMF voting procedures. Mr. Southard reported that the alternates of the EEC Monetary Committee were to meet on reform of the IMF on June 5–6.

Mr. Schweitzer said he had no reason to believe that the Monetary Committee proposal of a highly qualified vote to establish major Fund policies was important to the French with the one exception that he had mentioned earlier concerning a vote to liberalize credit tranches.

Under Secretary Deming thought that if the non-Ten countries did take a strong position, the voting majority could be negotiated at 80%. The EEC could reach this level by increasing its quotas, thus accepting responsibilities commensurate with its growing importance.

Secretary Fowler said he would accept Mr. Schweitzer's technical judgment that it is not worth proceeding if the EEC won't play, but it troubled him to give up in advance the right to try. If the rest of the world had the power to proceed without the EEC, this would mean that there was a better chance to obtain EEC participation. The Secretary would hate to give the EEC a legal blocking power in addition to its practical veto.

Mr. Schweitzer said the French were worried that it would be difficult to resist activation once the scheme was established, and he thought they had a point if a slowdown develops in world trade. He did not think $2 billion a year would be created but something like $1 billion a year.

Secretary Fowler inquired as to why, if 75 percent of the votes wanted to go ahead and 15 percent could opt out, the 15 percent should exercise a veto on the power of the 75 percent to proceed.

Mr. Schweitzer was not sure that 75 percent participation would mean anything more than the Anglo-Saxon countries extending credit to the developing countries, and there would be no real reciprocation in such a system.

Turning to reconstitution, Under Secretary Deming said that France will apparently insist on very specific terms so as to make the asset both ostensibly and really a credit facility. Was it better to have this or nothing?

Mr. Schweitzer thought that the French wanted to have it ostensibly credit but perhaps not really credit. Mr. Polak said that the IMF proposal on reconstitution would not do for the French. They must have a precise repayment obligation. Mr. Schweitzer suggested the gold tranche provisions on repayment, and Mr. Polak said the French want something tougher than the present gold tranche repayment arrangements.

Mr. Schweitzer thought we should resist compulsory provisions in the charter, and rely on representations by the Agent. We would be over the hump if we could sell this to the French. Mr. Polak said that Minister Debre will not buy this. Mr. Southard thought this was the toughest issue.

Under Secretary Deming thought that if the French are not honest and are merely delaying, the EEC might split. Mr. Willis reported an Italian comment to the effect that the French regard reform of the IMF as a prerequisite for activation of the reserve creation plan. They also wanted an advance definition of an excessive drawing and a numerical statement of a repayment obligation.

Returning to the question of voting, Secretary Fowler suggested tying the opting out provision to the initial vote in the U.S. band proposal, with a provision that those opting out would not block a second vote. Mr. Schweitzer said there was nothing to prevent any group of countries from setting up a glorified multilateral swap. Without the EEC countries, the burden would fall on the U.S. and it would not be a truly reciprocal arrangement.

Secretary Fowler said he would be prepared to argue with Congress that the U.S. should not retain a veto if the rest of the world wanted to go ahead but should merely opt out. The Secretary was not sure that he could make the case and win it at the Ministers' meeting. Perhaps he would try to do so at Rio.

Mr. Schweitzer called attention to the problem of the Belgian Congo, and urged that the U.S. consider giving help to the Congo. They have worked out an arrangement with the copper company. The amount is small but it has an important political aspect. Mr. Southard said that he had been told that the Treasury was lukewarm on this.

George H. Willis

126. Telegram From the Department of State to the Embassy in Italy[1]

Washington, June 1, 1967, 12:48 p.m.

205832. For Korp. From Treasury. Secretary Fowler requests that following letter be given to Minister Colombo:

Begin verbatim text

"Dear Mr. Minister:

"I appreciate the opportunity to respond to your message of May 23[2] and to comment on international monetary negotiations in the light of the recent meeting of Deputies of the Group of Ten, the forthcoming informal gathering of EEC Finance Ministers in Rome on June 5, and the Joint G–10–IMF meetings to be held in Paris June 19–21.

"I want you to know also that I deeply appreciate the fact that Italian representatives in intra-EEC discussions have consistently maintained the constructive position that new reserve assets should embody qualities of international money even if in the form of drawing rights and that the EEC common position should be one that is a reasonable basis for further negotiation with the rest of Group of Ten and other members of IMF. The United States representatives have felt that the Italian representatives in the Deputies meetings and the Joint meetings have made most valuable and constructive contributions. I believe the fact that the EEC position has been kept open on a number of important points with respect to the characteristics of the asset has been a crucial factor in keeping alive the possibility of achieving some satisfactory agreement in September, 1967. I am very glad to hear that the Italian delegation at the EEC Monetary Committee meeting on May 26 was instructed to maintain this position.

"Concerning your suggestion that the time is approaching when a common position of the EEC will have to be taken, I would like to share with you my conception as to the most desirable course of further negotiations. It now appears that five major issues require some solution in order to permit agreement in September on a satisfactory plan. These issues are: (a) segregation of accounts, resources and administration from IMF regular resources, (b) satisfactory provisions for use, transfer and holding, (c) provisions relative to reconstitution, (d) process for reaching decisions on creation of reserves and (e) treatment of EEC pro-

---

[1] Source: Department of State, Central Files, FN 10. Confidential; Immediate; Limdis. Drafted by Willis; cleared by Bator, Deming and Fowler (Treasury), and John C. Colman (E/OMA); and approved by Colman. A similar letter from Fowler to Schiller on negotiations regarding international reserves was transmitted in telegram 206501 to Bonn, June 1. (Ibid.) See footnote 3, Document 124.

[2] Not found.

posals to change voting procedures and certain administrative procedures in the IMF itself.

"It is possible that none of these issues can be resolved by the Deputies and that all of them will have to go to the Ministers for resolution in July. However, it is our hope that the Deputies and Executive Directors can make sufficient progress so that (a) and (b) can be resolved at the Joint meeting, permitting agreed versions to go to the Ministers.

"Our substantive views on these points have been set forth in two plans distributed at the last Deputies meeting. As you know, with respect to (a), we strongly prefer an IMF affiliate, which we think logic fully justifies, both on conceptual and operational grounds. I understand why you may prefer not to support such an affiliate. We believe it would be helpful if the EEC position at the least favors substantive separation of accounting and resources.

"With respect to (b), we consider it important that all use of the asset be subject to the basic rule that other reserves should not be increased when the asset is spent—a form of the balance of payments need test. We also believe that both voluntary and guided transfers should comply with this basic principle. The U.S. plan would not distinguish between allocated and acquired reserve assets. If we understand correctly, the EEC Monetary Committee document submitted at the last Deputies meeting would exempt some acquired reserve assets from this rule. The approach in this document seems to permit voluntary unguided transfers only for reconstitution by a debtor (in the system) when such transfers reduce creditor holdings.[3] The U.S. plan envisages a wider scope for unguided transfers, generally at the initiative of the debtor, but not when this would reduce holdings of the new asset by a surplus country. That is, there would be no waiving of the reserve loss test for either debtors or creditors. One reason for our position is the desire to avoid massive and destabilizing shifts between holdings of dollars and new reserve assets which could result from unguided transfers in the absence of such a rule. Another reason is that we do not think it would be helpful if a new reserve creation scheme seemed to divide the world into a dollar bloc and a new reserve asset bloc. Furthermore, it would be unfortunate if acceptance or holding limits were used up in the course of financing shifts in reserve composition instead of payments imbalances. Over the longer term, more freedom could be permitted. We hope the EEC position would maintain this basic rule developed by the Ossola Working Group.[4] The U.S. plan also gives members the right to convert balances of

---

[3] Regarding this EEC Monetary Committee document, see footnote 7, Document 124.

[4] Reference is to the Working Party on Provisions to Ensure Acceptability of a New Reserve Asset created by the Group of Ten in late November 1966. It was commonly referred to as the Ossola Working Group after its chairman, Rinaldo Ossola of the Bank of Italy. (*The International Monetary Fund, 1966–1971*, vol. I, p. 115)

their own currency into the new asset, subject to both the basic reserve test and acceptance limits. I hope it will be possible to have no differences or minor differences on these provisions between two alternative plans to go to Ministers.

"Issues (c) and (d) seem highly likely to go to the Ministers for resolution. With respect to (c), virtually everyone in the Deputies group and among the Executive Directors is in agreement that the new asset should be money-like in character and hence should have no reconstitution provisions beyond those necessary to assure the liquidity of the plan and the natural desire of any nation to restore its reserve position. Nevertheless, the problem of reconstitution seems difficult in view of French insistence on a numerical formula for forced reconstitution and pressure for advance description of 'persistent users.' Since this view is particularly difficult to reconcile with the concept of money, rather than credit, and we sense considerable nuances among the EEC, I hope this matter can be kept open, even within the EEC, with at least some alternatives put forward as unresolved EEC views for further discussion at the Joint meeting and the G–10 Ministerial meeting. The U.S. is not disposed to go beyond the position outlined in the U.S. draft plans. It seems to us that an asset which central banks might not count as part of their reserves, would simply not provide the kind of stability we need for the international monetary system.

"With respect to (d), we assume that the issue is clearly one for the Ministers, even should there be close agreement among the Deputies and Executive Directors. Three basic formulae have been set forth: (1) one based on the present IMF procedure for quota increases—80 percent of the weighted votes (plus possible additional weight for creditors in the system); (2) the tentative EEC proposal of an 85 percent weighted vote (plus possible additional weight for creditors) and plus a unit voting supplement; and (3) the U.S. band proposal developed fully in the two plans referred to above.

"All three proposals recognize the principle that a successful plan must include most, if not all, of the countries of the Free World and particularly the major industrial, trading and financial nations. All recognize the principle that a successful plan must have at its base a wide consensus and, therefore, widespread support. It is our judgment that no unit vote proposal can be negotiated. It has been strongly opposed by the Executive Directors of all countries except the EEC. We feel further that an abnormally high weighted vote, which permits a veto by a very small number of countries, cannot really be justified.

"With respect to (e), we very much hope that this issue will not be made a part of the liquidity exercise and, consequently, will not need resolution either by the Deputies, the IMF, or G–10 Ministers at the July meeting.

"We are disturbed at the possibility implied, but not clearly expressed, that the French government will ask for some indeterminate degree of parallel action in changing voting procedures in regular IMF operations before approving a reserve creation plan in September. We would be bound strongly to resist this. Such a controversial proposal should be treated separately from reserve creation and examined on its merits. There simply is not enough time to do both jobs this summer. I hope and believe that other members of EEC will not wish to see agreement on reserve creation founder on this new and a separate idea that has just been brought forward in recent weeks.

"In conclusion, I want to reiterate my strong conviction that the basic need is creation of a new international reserve asset that will have unquestioned characteristics of money rather than merely credit. I gain great reassurance in knowing that you share this conviction.

"Recent events in the exchange and gold markets have again demonstrated the importance of proceeding rapidly to establish a plan for reserve creation. They also underline our and your basic view that the new asset should have characteristics that will make it convincing as a supplement to gold and reserve currencies and, thus, be helpful in meeting any renewed agitation concerning a gold shortage. I strongly concur in your point that it is quite important to avoid disaccord in international monetary negotiations, provided agreement can be reached on a good, meaningful plan for deliberate reserve creation. We cannot, however, afford to produce a plan which will not do the job.

"I look forward with pleasure to your visit to Washington and to discussing with you these matters in greater detail, either during the periods June 7 to 9 or June 13–14. Would it be possible for you to take time out from your busy schedule? These dates would work very well in terms of the negotiating calendar.

Sincerely yours, Henry H. Fowler"

End verbatim text.

Please deliver above verbatim text to Minister Colombo.

Rusk

127.   Memorandum From the Director of the U.S. Travel Service, Department of Commerce (Black) to Acting Secretary of Commerce Trowbridge[1]

Washington, June 5, 1967.

SUBJECT

"Discover America, Inc."

REF

My Memo of May 24th[2]

I was a little disturbed by Bob Short's[3] call on you on the 26th—particularly since I understand that USTS' "lack of cooperation" with Discover America was the main topic of conversation. Neither Ted Van Dyk nor anyone on Short's staff advised me of the visit in advance. I also think that, before coming to you with his grievances, Short should have had a chat with Barnet[4] or me. A large part of our "communications problem" with DA stems from Short's long-evident reluctance to deal directly with us on problem areas.

In our business we work with scores of organizations in the travel industry. I believe our record of cooperation with all of them has generally been a good one—with the notable exception of DA. Quite frankly there has been a great deal of totally unnecessary friction between us—beginning over one year ago. I had been most reluctant to burden either you or Secretary Connor with this problem, but Short's visit to you plus his pretensions to the vice-chairmanship of the President's foreign travel task force makes it necessary that you know the whole story.

I am attaching some back-up material, including a detailed chronology of USTS/DA relations (attachment C)[5] and a list of specific projects in which we have assisted DA (attachment D). Hopefully you may have a chance to glance at some of this before I see you.

The Issue

Briefly stated, our differences with DA are an offshoot of a larger issue: Who is in charge of the foreign travel program of the Federal Gov-

---

[1] Source: Washington National Records Center, RG 40, Department of Commerce Files: FRC 74 A 20, U.S. Travel Service, 1967–1968. No classification marking. Although the memorandum is addressed to the Secretary of Commerce, Trowbridge was still serving as Acting Secretary until June 14, when he was sworn in as Secretary.
[2] Not found.
[3] Robert E. Short, Chairman of Discover America, Inc.
[4] Sylvan M. Barnet, Jr., Deputy Director of the U.S. Travel Service.
[5] None of the attachments is printed.

General and Financial and Monetary Policy   373

ernment, the Vice President or the Secretary of Commerce? I will have more to say about *this* problem in my memo on Commerce's role vis-à-vis the upcoming foreign travel task force.

The specific issue with DA is their insistence that they are the President's "official" agency for coordinating private industry efforts to promote travel both *to* and within the United States. We support DA's role as a catalyst for the promotion of domestic travel by Americans, but cannot accept that they have any official role overseas. Our position is grounded in both law and logic.

Legal Position of "Discover America"

DA does not now and never has had any "mandate" to promote foreign travel to this country. Bob Short was appointed by the President on May 1, 1965, as "national chairman" to coordinate private industry programs for promoting *domestic travel*—under authority of Section 3 of H.J. Res. 658, PL 88–416 (Ullman Resolution).[6] Section 2 of this Resolution makes clear that the promotion of travel *to* the U.S. is the responsibility of "appropriate Federal agencies." Admittedly, this original Ullman Resolution (attachment E) could have been more carefully drafted, but its legislative history makes clear that the "nation wide effort" was intended to be a strictly domestic undertaking.

This Resolution expired on December 31, 1965. A second "See the USA" resolution (S.J. Res. 98, PL 89–235) was passed on October 2, 1965,[7] expiring at the end of last year. Section 3 of this Resolution (attachment F) authorized the President to extend the appointment of the "national chairman". Whether deliberately or by oversight, Short's appointment was not extended.

In other words, Short (and consequently DA) never had more than a domestic "mandate" and even that expired a year and a half ago.

Finally, both the Certificate of Incorporation (Article 2(a)) and the By-Laws (Article I, Section 4) of DA, dated June, 1965, state that the purpose of the corporation is "to promote, in cooperation with officials and agencies of the Federal Government, tourism and travel *within* the borders of the United States, ..." Short not only has no Federal "mandate", but lacks even a corporate basis for his overseas ambitions.

Practical Arguments Against Two Competing Tourist Agencies Abroad

In their recent report on USTS, the Budget Bureau/Commerce survey team discussed the role of DA overseas and, in one of their few judgments with which we agree, concluded (p. VIII–8):

---

[6] Approved August 11, 1964; 78 Stat. 388.

[7] 79 Stat. 910.

"... USTS feels, and the team agrees completely, that institutional promotion of travel *to* the United States (singularly or in cooperation with private enterprise) should be left to the Travel Service; duplication abroad would be as confusing as it would be wasteful."[8]

When it first became apparent—in the spring of 1966—that DA intended to enter the foreign arena, I wrote a long, friendly letter to Short outlining in detail all of the reasons why this was a bad idea from a practical point of view (attachment B). To be on the safe side I gave an advance copy to Ted Van Dyk—who advised against sending it on the grounds that "it might make Short mad." This letter, dated May 10, 1966, was thus never sent, but it is still as valid today as it was then.

Recommendation

I believe a review of all the attachments will indicate that if USTS has erred in its dealings with DA it has been on the side of diplomacy and over-compromise. We have reluctantly come to the conclusion that Short understands and respects the mailed fist more than the velvet glove.

All that is keeping USTS and DA from enjoying a fine, fruitful relationship is the "mandate" or "to and within" problem. I propose that we clear this up, for once and all, by forwarding the enclosed letter (attachment A) to Bob Short.

---

[8] This report has not been found.

---

128.   Memorandum of Telephone Conversation[1]

Washington, June 12, 1967, 9:30 a.m.

PARTICIPANTS

John J. McCloy
Frederick L. Deming
Francis Bator

SUBJECT

Mr. McCloy's Trip to Germany

---

[1] Source: Johnson Library, Bator Papers, McCloy Trip, June 1967, Box 8. Confidential. Drafted by Deming.

Jack McCloy called up on Monday morning to give a brief telephonic report of his visits to Francis Bator and me. He expects to get something down in writing in more detail.

He spent all evening (dinner) with Abs,[2] having a three or four hour conversation. He talked with him about personalities and what the state of thinking is with respect to international liquidity. Abs seemed to be quite knowledgeable and up to date. He seemed to be convinced that new reserves were needed and said that there was a good deal of such sentiment in France in the private banking community. He also said that Emminger is a close friend of Chancellor Kiesinger and they exchange views frequently (Emminger has never mentioned this to me). Abs commented that Minister Schiller was quite sensitive about our interpretation of his performance in Munich. He was hurt that general U.S. opinion was that he had failed at Munich. His own position is that he had brought France a long way. Abs advised against McCloy talking to Strauss or Kiesinger on this visit. In any event, Strauss was away in Bavaria, so it would have been difficult to have seen him. McCloy had had previous word that Strauss had wanted to see him, but he did not press.

McCloy had lunch with Blessing[3] and Emminger. Emminger did most of the talking, and Blessing seemed content to let Emminger carry the ball. In McCloy's words, Blessing seems to be coasting. Blessing seemed to be quite antagonistic to the French approach to the whole liquidity exercise.

Emminger was quite optimistic that an agreement could be worked out by the time of the Rio meetings. He thought the only real issue was the repayment issue, and he thought France might go considerably further than present indications. In any event, he thought that, in order to get France isolated, it was necessary to give others (EEC) the impression that they have used all possibilities to bring France along. He thought the final agreement would work out somewhere between the Munich Communiqué and the U.S. position.

Emminger noted that, in his own judgment, it was a losing game to talk in terms of units. At the same time, he said the unit case was really not entirely lost, and there was a possibility that the plan might end up as a unit plan (it is not clear whether he was talking about a plan to be approved at the Rio meeting or something that might evolve in the future).

Emminger made two strong points. He said that he wished the U.S. would concentrate more closely on what we mean by "reconstitution."

---

[2] Hermann J. Abs, President of Deutsche Bundesbank.
[3] Karl Blessing, Central Bank Governor of the International Monetary Fund for West Germany.

The language we have used so far is too general. What actual terms of reconstitution could we live with? Schiller repeated this point to McCloy.

Second, is there anything more that the United States can do to stress the fact that its concern about international liquidity is not rooted in its feeling that this would be relief for its balance of payments position. He said there needed to be more "propaganda" on this, that he had mentioned this point to me on several times (which is true). One positive suggestion he made was that it would be useful to get an article published in the *Neue Zuricher Zeitung* (Franz Aschinger is the economic writer for this paper). He thought the paper would do a good job and that this would be quite useful.

Emminger stressed the point that he hoped I realized that he, Emminger, is trying to exhaust all possibilities with France before isolating them. He also noted that the Belgians were more on the U.S. side than the U.S. thinks. They are beginning to talk in terms of an *asset* and seem to be moving more in the direction of flexibility. Finally, Emminger noted that the Middle Eastern crisis had operated in favor of contingency planning.

McCloy saw Schiller only briefly as he came off the Bundestag floor to talk to him for a few minutes. An unexpected budget hearing had been scheduled and Schiller was very much on the defensive with the budget—he was being attacked both by his own party members (SPD) and by some of the Free Democrats.

The only point McCloy concentrated on with Schiller, given the short time, was to stress the fact that we wanted Germany to be objective—that we weren't asking them to follow slavishly a U.S. line. We were convinced, and Schiller seemed to be, that we needed agreement at Rio.

McCloy confirmed that Schiller was very defensive and hurt about our evaluation of Munich. He was bringing an expert with him to Washington to sit in on the meetings on Monday, June 19. He mentioned Secretary Fowler's recent letter,[4] although not substantively.

Schiller insisted that he was very close to Debre and thought he could have some influence on him.

McCloy spent quite a lot of time with Schiller's personal assistant, Fritz Fischer. Fischer took a lot of notes and promised to get them to Schiller. McCloy followed the general talking paper line with Fischer.

McGhee did not accompany McCloy to see Schiller since he was away. McCloy talked to McGhee only on the phone, and McGhee stressed the point he has made on many occasions—that we were putting more pressure than was desirable on the Germans.

---

[4] See footnote 1, Document 126.

McCloy mentioned, in conclusion, that he had stressed with Abs, Blessing, and with Fischer that, in the general political situation, we needed more symbols of unity in the alliance. He bore down hard on the problems we faced in the future and the necessity for getting a good arrangement on international liquidity as part of the financial wall for the alliance. He thinks he got these points across most strongly to Abs and Fischer. He also stressed with all of them that the IMF reform proposals, if taken precedent or parallel with the liquidity exercise, would slow down the whole process. Emminger was in agreement on this point but responded that, as long as we tell them that we are willing to talk about this letter, he thinks it will be alright. He thinks it may be necessary to permit France to take a reservation on this point with respect to contingency planning, by which I take it to mean that he thinks France might still use this as a lever with respect to activation. Emminger thoroughly agreed that it would complicate things to talk about this now.

Frederick L. Deming[5]

---

[5] Printed from a copy that bears this typed signature.

---

129.   Memorandum of Conversation[1]

Washington, June 19, 1967, 2:30 p.m.

PARTICIPANTS

United States
Secretary Fowler
Honorable Francis Bator, White House
Honorable Arthur Okun, CEA
Assistant Secretary Knowlton

Germany
Minister Karl Schiller
Mr. Ernst Jirka, First Secretary
Baron Herbert A. van Stackelberg
Mr. Johann Schoellhorn, State Secretary Ministry of Economics

SUBJECT

International Liquidity

The Secretary opened the meeting by stating that the liquidity exercise was not related to the United States balance of payments deficit. He

---

[1] Source: Johnson Library, Bator Papers, Liquidity Negotiations, Box 9. Limited Official Use. Drafted by Knowlton and approved by Fowler. Another copy with a few handwritten changes and additions is ibid., Letters and Memoranda of Conversation, Box 9. The meeting was held in Secretary Fowler's Conference Room.

knew there had been talk in Europe to that effect. Nothing could be far-
ther from the truth, as any simple analysis of the arithmetic proved. He
gave Mr. Schiller charts showing the trend of the U.S. payments position
in recent years.[2]

Mr. Schiller said he had a message from Debre, who was "angry".
Schiller considered it vital to review the "eight Munich points". He said
that the French had a much harder paper and that the Munich points did
not represent a "second Munich with an umbrella."

As Mr. Schiller began to go through the points, Secretary Fowler
stated that he did not want to turn the meeting into a drafting exercise.
Instead, he wanted to make several key issues clear. Mr. Schiller persisted in proceeding down the list.

On Point 1, Secretary Fowler said that recognition of an actual shortage of liquidity was neither a necessary nor desirable prerequisite to
agreement on the need for additional liquidity. He said that reserves had
grown in the post-war period and must continue to grow. He showed Mr.
Schiller a table that summarized post-war reserve growth.[3] He said there
must be a regular accretion, determined in a orderly manner. If we
waited for a visible shortage, the emergency would be upon us. There
would not be much debate then about the need for additional liquidity.
We would already have fallen into a pattern of restrictionism akin to that
of the 30's.

Dr. Schoellhorn said that Point 1 could be read as consistent with
Secretary Fowler's views. Secretary Fowler said that, in fact, Point 1 did
not read that way and he took exception to it. Dr. Schoellhorn expressed
agreement with Secretary Fowler's view in substance on Point 1.

On Point 2 Mr. Schiller laid stress on the reference to "alternative
solutions" (alternative to the creation of additional reserves) and said
that the French had capitulated on the issue of an increase in the price of
gold. The Secretary said his interpretation of the French position on gold
was a bit different but that he could agree with the last sentence of Point
2, which was similar in substance to the Hague Communiqué.[4]

Secretary Fowler said he could live with Point 3. He did not believe
that reserves should be created with "Milton Friedman automaticity"
but that there should be secular growth.

There then ensued a lengthy discussion of Point 4 (voting procedures). Mr. Schiller said the EEC was strongly united on this matter and
insisted on 85 percent approval to activate a plan.

---

[2] These charts have not been found.

[3] This table has not been found.

[4] Reference apparently is to the communiqué issued at The Hague by the Ministers
and Governors of the Group of Ten on July 26, 1966; for text, see *American Foreign Policy:
Current Documents, 1966*, pp. 185–186.

Secretary Fowler said that he had a way out of this difficulty. It was his own personal view. He would prefer that the suggestion come from a country other than the U.S. before presenting his proposal, he said that he wanted to make it clear that the United States welcomed a larger role for individual countries in the EEC. It had favored larger quotas for Germany in the past and would do so again. It would welcome a larger role for France, Belgium, Italy—in fact for any country that wanted and was entitled to it. As he read the Treaty of Rome, however, the Secretary said that he saw no binding commitment for these countries to operate as a bloc, especially on a world problem and in a world organization like the International Monetary Fund. He pointed to the difference in EEC behavior in the case of NATO matters (in which an individual country had gone its own way) and international monetary matters (in which the bloc seemed compelled to work together). If the EEC acted as a bloc, it would inevitably end up with the lowest common denominator as a plan. The United States simply would not go along with this. And this was not really the sentiment of the United States alone but that of the Free World. In fact, within the EEC, he sensed that the Italians, Germans, and others found themselves reluctantly engaged in the painful process of dragging a single delinquent along.

Turning to his specific thoughts on voting procedures (which he made clear did not represent a formal United States position), the Secretary suggested that the contingency plan be activated initially for five years. A 75 percent weighted vote could activate an agreed *minimum* annual amount for this five year period. Any activation in excess of the minimum amount in any given year would require an 85 percent weighted vote. At the end of five years, future activations and amounts would be controlled by the normal IMF 80 percent weighted vote procedure. There would, of course, be a normal determination of quota levels during this period—or possibly a special re-determination of quotas. He foresaw that the EEC would have at least a 20 percent weighted vote during the second five-year period, which would give those countries their "proper influence." This approach had the advantage of not frightening the world with an outcome at Rio that included an explicit EEC veto. To be perfectly frank about it, the world looked at the EEC as "hard-nosed central bankers preoccupied with gold." While he did not personally share this view, it was widely held.

In the ensuing conversation, Mr. Schiller stressed again that the EEC was united on this issue. Dr. Schoellhorn said that in fact there had been an amendment to the Mandate of the Monetary Committee calling for the group to act together on international monetary matters. Secretary Fowler said this confirmed his fears on the matter. Dr. Schoellhorn disputed the lowest common denominator theory and said that in fact the French had been brought quite far along.

Mr. Bator said that we should not worry too much too soon about accommodating the French. The critical point was to persuade France that the rest of the EEC would join the rest of the world even if France would not go along. Once this became credible to the French, they would join. That was the historical pattern.

Mr. Schiller said that the French had been extremely irked by the formal German policy statement on dollars and gold. The Secretary asked why France would be critical of a country that was clearly attempting to support the international monetary system in a constructive way. Dr. Schoellhorn said they were irked because it was a bilateral agreement without consultation.

Mr. Schiller then said that while Chancellor Erhard had often been willing to agree with conflicting propositions made by the United States and France, thus putting himself in an awkward and helpless position, Chancellor Kiesinger wanted to "win the French to a common solution with you (the United States)." The present German regime did in fact want to revive the Franco-German Treaty.[5] He said that Germany was taking a "loyal Triangular position." There might be another way—to let the French go to Rio alone in splendid isolation but the German people would not understand this. They would view it as a failure of government policy.

The Secretary asked if there were any alternatives. Messrs. Schiller and Schoellhorn stated "the common way," in which (presumably) Germany acted as an honest broker narrowing differences between France and the United States.

The Secretary said that the United States would be willing to give up its veto. It was not taking a parochial position. As for the "common way," he said that he had tried that approach—his first port-of-call in the summer of 1965 had been France.

The Secretary then read excerpts from his Granada speech,[6] emphasizing that unanimity was not necessary in international cooperation but that "the preponderant majority must not be immobilized." He could deal with Point 4 in that spirit. He could meet the German concern with inflation but he could *not* in international financial matters give credibility to a world of blocs.

Mr. Schiller said that the EEC had been a U.S. "baby", with George Ball one of the fathers. Secretary Fowler said it had been designed as an "outward looking" baby.

---

[5] For text of the Franco-German Treaty on Organization and Principles of Cooperation, signed at Paris on January 22, 1963, see *Documents on Germany, 1944–1985,* pp. 834–838.

[6] Reference is to Fowler's speech to the Thirteenth Annual Monetary Conference of the American Bankers Association at Granada, Spain, on May 27, 1966; for text, see *Annual Report of the Secretary of the Treasury on the State of the Finances for the Fiscal Year Ended June 30, 1966* (Washington, 1967), pp. 438–447.

Dr. Schoellhorn said that Point 4 made reference to EEC voting rights not only in connection with new liquidity but regular IMF operations. The Secretary said he "understood this perfectly and rejected it completely." Mr. Bator pointed out that this provision immeasurably complicated the negotiating job between now and September.

Mr. Schiller reiterated that the minority must be protected; otherwise, there would be a wave of public protest. The Secretary said that the Bretton-Woods negotiators thought that an 80 percent weighted vote provided that protection. At the time of Bretton-Woods, western Europe was a "wrecked battle ground." United States blood and treasure had helped revitalize it. Was it asking too much of western European nations now to play by the rules of the game?

Mr. Schiller said "we will reach a solution."

Mr. Bator said the wrong kind of compromise would do the world no good. Many French officials don't want the price of gold to go up in any event. The others must be made to realize that gold won't go up. "The game won't be played that way."

Secretary Fowler said that if the world divided into two blocs—a gold bloc and a dollar bloc—Germany would be isolated with the French in the former.

Dr. Schoellhorn said it was wrong to say the EEC wasn't expansionary; even France was basically expansionary.

Secretary Fowler asked whether politics or economics was more important to de Gaulle. Mr. Jirka replied that "economics are the basis of de Gaulle's politics." Mr. Schiller said de Gaulle had learned something from the election. Debre was basically an expansionist. Secretary Fowler agreed. He said he believed he was fundamentally more expansionist than Giscard d'Estaing. He said nevertheless he did not want political solutions superimposed on the international financial system.

Mr. Schiller made a long speech on German loyalty to the U.S.A.

Secretary Fowler said he had no doubts on this score but what we must focus on is making the first step—and it must be on the right path and a big enough step to convince the world that the price of gold would not go up. Otherwise, we would have crisis after crisis. The French may have abandoned the direct approach in the increase of the price of gold but could be seeking the same result by their efforts to abort the liquidity exercise.

The conversation then turned to Points 7 and 8 of the Munich Communiqué. Mr. Okun said that we were not seeking a simple quota increase or conventional drawing rights but something new: a first-class asset. It must be as good as gold. If people couldn't transfer it, how highly would it be held in their esteem? Why do we work so hard to restrict the asset? Why not lean over backwards to make it attractive?

Mr. Schiller dismissed this as "semantics."

Mr. Bator said there was one clear test: would central bankers count the new asset in their reserves freely and willingly? If not, we would have "the Gresham problem." Would people consider that they owned the asset or they owed it?

Dr. Schoellhorn said that asset must be under some kind of control; there could be too large a volume created. Secretary Fowler said that Dr. Schoellhorn had confused the problem of the amount of the asset with the quality of the asset. Mr. Okun said that the present "basket" approach to an IMF drawing would not be satisfactory in the case of the new asset.

Mr. Bator pointed out that there was a strong bias in the international financial system toward the running of surpluses. This was a question of political reality and conservative bookkeeping. It was all very well to talk about letting the new asset "evolve" but there was a short-term problem too: the gold pool. The President was acutely conscious of this problem.

Secretary Fowler expressed displeasure at the recent French failure to replenish the gold pool.

Secretary Fowler said that Germany has the primary responsibility for the outcome of the liquidity negotiations—both success or failure; the world sees it that way. Dr. Schoellhorn said he accepted this but liquidity alone was not enough. Countries must pursue the right economic policies as well.

Secretary Fowler said the U.S. understood this perfectly. It was fully behind the adjustment process report. We must protect existing liquidity. With the formation of blocs, the value of gold as a reserve asset would be endangered. The international financial system must stand on a tripod: (1) present holdings of gold and foreign exchange must be preserved as reserves; (2) the dollar must be kept as good as gold and the United States must thus solve its balance of payments problem; (3) new forms of liquidity must be devised.

Mr. Bator said that we could not labor for three years and produce a "mouse." Dr. Schoellhorn asked whether the drawing rights described in the communiqué were a "mouse." Mr. Bator asked whether Germany would treat them as owned assets. Mr. Schiller did not respond to the question but instead disputed Mr. Bator's earlier point on the bias in the system toward surpluses. He said that Germany was attempting to reduce its surplus. Dr. Schoellhorn said that Germany had a current account surplus and an overall balance as its objective. Mr. Bator said this proved his point; if Germany were willing to run down its reserves $2 to $3 billion, and if other countries would do the same from time to time, gold would be enough. But they would not do this.

Mr. Schiller asked whether a second Chequers meeting either in Paris or Bonn would be helpful. Secretary Fowler said he would go anywhere anytime to expedite progress, but he would leave to Mr. Schiller the question of who would be invited and where and when. There was a brief discussion on whether Debre could operate more flexibly in or out of Paris. There was an inconclusive discussion of the timing of the ministerial meeting. There was some feeling that another Chequers meeting would be better after the next ministerial meeting than before.

Mr. Schiller and Secretary Fowler outlined the public and Congressional pressures that confronted them as the negotiations proceeded. Mr. Bator and Secretary Fowler emphasized the increasing "linkage" between the liquidity negotiations, the balance of payments problem, and United States military expenditures abroad including western Germany.

Schiller said that if liquidity and the offset arrangements got "mixed up," great damage would be done. He took credit for proposing the purchase of long-term bonds by the Bundesbank.

The Secretary said that modern military and political alliances must have a financial wall. We have bought time in the case of the German offset—thanks to Schiller. We want to go as far as we can in the liquidity negotiations not to disrupt relationships with France, but France was really not the first order of priority. The problem transcended France. We have expressed willingness to talk of drawing rights instead of units. We wanted a plan to evolve with many nations responsible for its creation.

Mr. Schiller said the plan would have "many fathers."

In closing, Mr. Schiller said that the German Government was taking a very quiet line on U.S.-Vietnam policy despite growing public feeling in Germany that the U.S. was increasingly immobilized by this difficult situation.

In closing, Secretary Fowler and Mr. Bator stressed the constant attention being paid to the liquidity negotiations by the President, Vice President, the Secretary of State, and the Under Secretaries of State, Mr. Deming, Mr. Okun, and Mr. Bator. In the aftermath of the Kennedy Round, it was clearly the "big item on the agenda."

Winthrop Knowlton

130.   Memorandum for the Record[1]

Washington, June 21, 1967.

SECRET

Telephone Call from John McCloy (Wednesday, June 21, 1967 at 10:23 a.m.)

McCloy telephoned in to report that, at Kiesinger's request, he called the Chancellor on Monday (?). They talked about:

1.   Money

—Kiesinger knew the French had backed away from Munich. (I had told McCloy this when he telephoned from Germany on Sunday to tell me about Kiesinger's invitation.)

—McCloy argued the case for a plan by September, for real money rather than credit, etc. He also urged Kiesinger to make up his mind on the merits, and not give in to French blackmail.

—Kiesinger said that the German decision would definitely reflect their judgment about the economic need. Further, he, Kiesinger, will be strongly influenced by Emminger, a schoolmate and an old friend.

—Kiesinger is only now starting to brief himself on the details. His strong first reaction is that the French are being far too rigid.

—They talked at length about the "repayment" issue, and agreed on its importance.

—Kiesinger said he wanted to be certain there would be enough "discipline" built in, to avoid misuse. (It might be useful to have a hard go at Emminger on the need to link discipline with quantity and decision-making rather than with the quality of the asset.)

—McCloy seemed pleased about the atmosphere of the talk. He found Kiesinger much more critical of deGaulle than in the past.

[Here follows discussion of the Near East.]

---

[1] Source: Johnson Library, Bator Papers, McCloy Trip, June 1967, Box 8. Secret. Drafted by Bator on June 22.

131.   Memorandum From the General Counsel, Department of Commerce (Giles) to Secretary of Commerce Trowbridge[1]

Washington, June 30, 1967.

SUBJECT

U.S. Travel Service—"Discover America, Inc."

I have reviewed the material in the attached file[2] and have the following comments and conclusions:

1) I don't understand John Black's assertion that Short's appointment by the President expired on December 31, 1965. This may be true with respect to the first so-called Ullman Resolution, but the President's appointment of Short, dated May 1, 1965, states that Short serves at the "pleasure" of the President. So far as we know, the President has *not* terminated his pleasure in this regard.

2) Actually, the President did not need the Ullman Resolution as a legal matter in order to encourage private industry to cooperate on the travel problem or in order to do the things done under that Resolution.

3) It is certainly clear that the U.S.T.S. act vests in the Secretary of Commerce the authority and responsibility to carry on a program of promoting foreign citizens to visit the United States. This does not mean, however, that the President of the United States cannot ask a private citizen (such as Short) to undertake a special effort, at no compensation, to encourage private industry's participation in promoting travel to the U.S. from abroad, as well as encouraging U.S. citizens to stay home and travel *within* the United States.

4) It seems to me that the problem is essentially *not* a legal one, but one of administrative policy. In other words, I do not see that the *legal* argument is really conclusive for either Short on the one hand, or for U.S.T.S. on the other. (This assumes of course that Short doesn't try to tell Commerce exactly how it will expend travel program money appropriated to this Department by Congress.)

5) Apparently, this is a controversy of some long standing, and I would suggest that you talk with the Vice President about Short's recent contacts with you and see if you cannot reach an appropriate understanding with him regarding Commerce relationship with Short. (This is not the same as asking the Vice President how Commerce should plan its

---

[1] Source: Washington National Records Center, RG 40, Secretary of Commerce Files: FRC 74 A 20, U.S. Travel Service, 1967–1968. No classification marking.

[2] The attached file includes Black's June 5 letter to Trowbridge (Document 127) and its attachments.

official responsibilities and how exactly it should expend its appropriations for the travel program.)

6) It would also be relevant to know what precise activities does Short propose to carry out which John Black disagrees with, and why? And what precise activities does John propose to carry out which Short disagrees with, and why? Is there a real difference of view on specific program *content*—not just a disagreement about who will do something and get the "credit"?

REG

---

132.   Current Economic Developments[1]

Issue No. 783   Washington, July 4, 1967.

[Here follow articles on unrelated subjects.]

PLANNING CONTINUES FOR CREATION OF NEW INTERNATIONAL LIQUIDITY

An outline of a contingency plan for the creation of new liquidity based on automatic drawing rights in the International Monetary Fund was worked out in general terms, but with a number of major points still unresolved at the fourth joint meeting of the Deputies of the Group of Ten and the IMF Executive Directors in Paris June 20–21. The plan will be considered by the Ministers of the Group of Ten in July in London, and hopefully the outstanding issues can be resolved at this level. Before then, the Ministers of the six EEC countries will meet to discuss some of the issues involved.

Our objective remains to achieve agreement at the annual meeting of the IMF in September in Rio on the structure and major provisions of an acceptable plan which will convincingly demonstrate that the world's need for reserves will be met by the timely creation of new reserves to supplement gold and US dollars. There remain, however, a number of issues to be resolved at the political level. The two most crucial are procedures for decision-making and reconstitution of the new asset.

Major Issues

The plan as it has evolved during the past year calls for creating new liquidity by means of special, automatic drawing rights linked to the

---

[1] Source: Washington National Records Center, RG 59, E/CBA/REP Files: FRC 72 A 6248, *Current Economic Developments*. Limited Official Use. The source text comprises pages 18–19 of the issue.

IMF. The idea is to have a contingency plan that could be called into action to meet possible future needs.

No major progress was made on the outstanding issues at the fourth joint meeting of the IMF Executive Directors and the Group of Ten Deputies. The major issues are: a) whether and the extent to which the resources, accounting, and administration of reserve creation should be separated from the IMF in its normal operations; b) acceptable provisions on holding and use of the new asset; c) the manner in which holdings of the asset should be reconstituted, i.e., repaid following use; d) decision-making; and e) EEC proposals to "reform" some aspects of the operations of the IMF, especially giving the EEC strong control.

US Position

Fundamentally, the US objective is that the new asset have the basic characteristics of money rather than be another form of international credit added to the credit forms already available which fails to give convincing assurance that the world's need for reserves will be met. The US position on the issues enumerated above is as follows: a) that reserve creation should preferably be undertaken by a separate affiliate of the IMF; b) that use of the asset should be permitted only when a country's other reserves are falling and that surplus countries should accept and hold the assets up to triple the amount of their allocations; c) that reconstitution should be required only in extreme cases of prolonged use which threaten the liquidity of the scheme; d) that decision-making procedures should avoid an EEC veto of reserve creation; and e) that any consideration of proposals for changing the present operations of the IMF should take place on their merits and not be linked in timing or otherwise to reserve creation. The US had introduced two alternative draft plans which spell out the US position on all the essential aspects of reserve creation.

In general, the US, Canada, Britain, and Japan want the drawing rights to be as liberal as possible so that they come close to a new form of international money. France, with varying degrees of support from Belgium, Holland, Italy, and Germany, wants the privileges to be no more than another kind of credit.

The proposal advanced last year by the US for creation of a new reserve unit is "semi-dead," Otmar Emminger of the German Bundesbank and Chairman of the Deputies of the Group of Ten, told a press conference after the Paris meeting. He also assessed the chance of reaching agreement among the major countries at "more than fifty percent."

[Here follow articles on unrelated subjects.]

133.   Memorandum for the Files[1]

Washington, July 10, 1967.

SUBJECT

Meeting of U.S. Delegation to the G–10 Ministers' Meeting—July 10, 1967 at 2:00 P.M.

PRESENT

Under Secretary Deming
Chairman Martin
Gov. Daane
Mr. R. Solomon
Mr. Willis

Secretary Fowler and Under Secretary Barr arrived later

Under Secretary Deming outlined the proposed schedule for Sunday, July 16, comprising luncheon for the Japanese, Swedish and Canadian Ministers, Governors and Deputies at our invitation, followed by bilateral discussions with other Ministers and Governors of the Ten from 3:00 P.M. to 7:00 P.M. on Sunday. The Secretary was to see Chancellor Callaghan in the morning and perhaps also for dinner. It was hoped that Chairman Martin would find time to see Governors Ansiaux, Blessing, Carli and Zijlstra sometime during the day.

Chairman Martin turned to substance, and said it was important to get clear what we are trying to do. He had become very much of a dove independently of Governor Daane and Mr. Solomon. It would be a disaster to have a collision now. We could have done so three months ago. Instead of coming out publicly for the IMF plan[2] on August 1, which he had favored last week, he now felt it desirable to support the IMF plan as a compromise at London.

Under Secretary Deming said we were not really far away from the IMF plan. Secretary Fowler wants to concentrate on decision-making and reconstitution. He wants to take up some of the points in the 1965 guidelines of the Reuss Committee.[3] He proposes a minimum amount of

---

[1] Source: Johnson Library, Bator Papers, Letters and Memoranda of Conversation, Box 9. Limited Official Use. Drafted by Willis on July 11 and approved by Deming. The signed original of this memorandum is Deming Group paper DG/67/211. (Washington National Records Center, RG 56, OASIA Files: FRC 75 A 101, Deming Group)

[2] Reference apparently is to the IMF plan, "An Outline of a Reserve Facility Based on Drawing Rights in the Fund," dated June 8, which was a revision of the IMF's May 29 proposals; for text of the two plans, see *The International Monetary Fund, 1966–1967*, vol. II, pp. 30–34 and 40–44.

[3] Apparent reference to Henry S. Reuss, Chairman of the Subcommittee on International Finance of the House Committee on Banking and Currency. The 1965 guidelines were contained in the subcommittee's report, *Guidelines for Improving the International Monetary System: Report of the Subcommittee on International Exchange and Payments of the International Exchange and Payments of the Joint Economic Committee, Congress of the United States* (Joint Committee Print of the Joint Economic Committee, Eighty-ninth Congress, First Session, transmitted August 30, 1965).

reserve creation during the first period that could be approved by a 75% vote, with 85% required to create reserves in the amount of more than a billion dollars a year. He might be prepared to go to an 80–85% version of this.

After the first activation, decisions would be on an 80% majority basis as in the present provision for enlarging Fund quotas. That is, the EEC should pay for a veto by increasing its quotas. Mr. Deming said the Fund Management would raise a number of arguments against this: (1) the statistics under the Bretton Woods formula do not raise the EEC to 20%, (2) the Fund could not hold back some other increases, and (3) the Canadians, Japanese and Indians would have to go up if the Italians went up. The idea of a minimum non-inflationary addition to reserves might be one billion a year or even less for 3 to 5 years.

Mr. Deming said the Secretary thought of his quota increase proposal as a counter proposal to the EEC suggestions for reform of the Fund.

On reconstitution, we would argue hard against reconstitution on our current lines, with any action to be taken on an ad hoc basis by the IMF after activation, but with no rules to define and clarify the general principle prior to experience under activation. A possible fallback was to defer negotiation of a protocol until after London or until after Rio.

If London failed to reach agreement in full, the alternatives were to leave some questions for later or have the U.S. introduce its own plan at Rio. He did not want to take the last course at this stage. The U.S. should hold a press conference after the meeting that would stress the U.S. position. Depending on the results of London, there might be more or less pointing of the finger at the EEC. If we were expecting to reach agreement on a plan, subject to further negotiation, the line would be softer. If it appeared we were not going to get anywhere, we might want to take a plan to the floor of a Rio session.

Chairman Martin objected to this latter course, and thought that the Secretary would be "clobbered" if he held such a press conference. Instead we should say that we are pleased with the recognition of the problem that has taken place and the progress made. Our position is vulnerable because the balance of payments is getting worse rather than improving and there are difficulties ahead in the gold market. We don't want to have a market upheaval blamed on our statements. Our tone with the press should be one of encouragement rather than that we are demanding something that we can't get. This is the line that the President is taking in general—to emphasize what is right rather than what is wrong. We should not be on the defensive but should try to take the view that the gold exchange standard can survive even with a shortage of gold.

Mr. Willis asked whether this approach would be expected to lead to continuing negotiation after Rio.

Chairman Martin said he would rather do this than precipitate a showdown. We have to meet our problems on an ad hoc basis with controls. Without peace in Vietnam, we may need these controls for a long time. We are not likely to have legislative restrictions on direct investment. We should do nothing to undermine the swap arrangements. He had been discouraged at the BIS meeting. He had gone down the line for a supplement to gold and found no disagreement. But there had been no support for our war in Vietnam. He feared that the breakdown in the negotiations would be what the French want. We should therefore come out with a hopeful attitude rather than forcing a collision. The French were winning the propaganda battle. Our line should be one of sweet reasonableness. He reiterated that he would propose to espouse the IMF plan now at the meeting instead of publicly on August 1. We should also make clear that we are not proposing reserve creation to solve our balance of payments problem and we are not trying to avoid drawing on the IMF or selling gold. We merely want a bona fide supplement to gold.

Under Secretary Deming pointed out that only on decision-making and reconstitution do we differ importantly with the IMF plan.

Secretary Fowler, who had arrived in time to hear Chairman Martin's reiteration of his position, outlined his own views. He wanted to develop his point of view along the following lines in both bilateral meetings and the Ministerial meeting itself.

Reserve creation is not an answer to our balance of payments problem and he would like to drive this home with arithmetic and charts. We thought the gold exchange standard served our purpose well, but a supplement will be needed. He would cite the guidelines in the Joint Economic Committee Report. The technicians have made very substantial progress. We have narrowed the issues down to one technical problem, that of reconstitution, and one political problem, that of decision-making. There is a third important element in the extraneous matter of reform of the IMF.

The United States wanted to put forward constructive proposals on the first two issues, hoping that some time between now and Rio agreement could be reached. The Secretary indicated that he would personally deal with the question of decision-making, and that Mr. Deming would handle reconstitution.

Concerning decision-making, we recognize that there may be concern as to the excessive amount of reserves, and that some kind of maximum is needed for Parliaments. The U.S. band proposal does not appear to attract support. At this point the Secretary would hope that Minister Schiller would have put forward a compromise proposal. If not, the United States would put it forward. This would call for a minimum of $1 to $1-1/2 billion a year of reserves to be created, with a case to support it. Such an amount would be non-inflationary and modest and would be authorized by a weighted vote of 75%. Amounts in excess of this would require an 85% vote during the first 5 years.

As a related part of this proposal, and an added starter in the discussion of reform of the Fund, there would be a proposal to change the structure of the IMF quotas to reflect the stronger position of the EEC. This would go far in dealing with the EEC concern with voting procedures in the Fund. This should be tabled along with the EEC proposals. We would hope that the first 5-year plan agreement would be announced simultaneously with the announcement that there was going to be consideration of the general working of the Fund.

The United States would then put forward the second part of its proposal relating to reconstitution. The general slant would be that we were really trying to move in their direction on these matters.

The purpose of the press conference would not be to declare war or to express defeat. It would be a sanitized statement of what we would say at the meeting so as not to be misrepresented in the press.

Chairman Martin thought this was all right. It should have a tone of commendation and approval, with perhaps a hint of disappointment. It should not be a demand or an ultimatum.

Mr. Willis suggested that both the Secretary's approach and Chairman Martin's suggested approach seemed likely to lead to further negotiations after Rio. He noted that the Kennedy Round reached a decision only because of a firm deadline.

Secretary Fowler said it was not time for an ultimatum now and there is room for further negotiations. He did not propose to burn any bridges on his right to take it to Rio but likewise did not wish to commit himself now to sponsor a proposal at Rio. He thought the meetings in London and Rio would be fairly decisive and we would either get results or not on a contingency plan. He did not want to let up on the pressure to get agreement at Rio. The only question was whether the tone was one of an ultimatum or hopeful expectation.

Mr. Willis expressed doubt that it would be possible to get agreement at Rio on a contingency plan on either of these two approaches.

Governor Daane recommended that we accept an 85% majority for decision-making and in return seek a favorable compromise on reconstitution. Secretary Fowler was not prepared to go so far as 85%.

Mr. Willis pointed out that the Europeans are also interested in the third question, the reform of the Fund, and questioned Governor Daane's hopes for a successful deal on the basis of 85% plus reconstitution.

Mr. Solomon saw dangers in the approach of a minimum amount, pointing out that Minister Debre would strongly resist the minimum and would say that this is not consistent with the idea of a contingency plan.

Governor Daane thought that the Six would probably not have any flexibility on anything except reconstitution. Mr. Willis pointed out that there were three stages in the operation—the Rio resolution, ratification, and activation. The Europeans might hold up the ratification stage if they were not satisfied on any of the three issues.

Under Secretary Deming said that the ratification problems might be a postponable issue. Under Secretary Barr thought it was best to proceed stage-by-stage, and to get agreement on a contingency plan even if it was not clear what further concessions might be necessary to get ratification. He did not want to see the Group of Ten let off the hook by a breakdown of negotiations.

Secretary Fowler said his objective was to put them in a position of having to turn down a reasonable proposal covering reconstitution and decision-making. He would not agree to 85% as a permanent majority procedure. He was not wedded to the initial 75% figure and would take 80% for the minimum vote in the first round.

George H. Willis

---

134.   Telegram From the Embassy in the United Kingdom to the Department of State[1]

London, July 18, 1967, 2240Z.

463. Dept pass Treasury and White House. White House for Bator. Treasury for Kane and Hunt.

18th July 1967

Communiqué of the Ministerial Meeting of the Group of Ten on July 17th and 18th in London.

1.   The Ministers and Central Bank Governors of the Ten countries participating in the General Arrangements to Borrow met in London on 17th and 18th July under the chairmanship of Mr. James Callaghan,

---

[1] Source: Department of State, Central Files, FN 10. Unclassified; Priority.

Chancellor of the Exchequer of the United Kingdom. Mr. Pierre-Paul Schweitzer, Managing Director of the International Monetary Fund, took part in the meeting, which was also attended by the Secretary-General of the Organization for Economic Co-operation and Development, the General Manager of the Bank for International Settlements, and the President of the National Bank of Switzerland.

2.   The Ministries and Governors had before them an outline of a contingency plan prepared after the recent fourth joint meeting in Paris of the Executive Directors of the International Monetary Fund and the Deputies of the Group of Ten.[2] The plan would establish new facilities, in the form of automatic drawing rights administered by the International Monetary Fund.

3.   The Ministers and Governors discussed major features of the plan and narrowed the remaining differences of view between them. They gave guidance to their Deputies to work out, in the coming weeks, proposals acceptable to all. It is expected that agreement will be reached on an outline plan to be embodied in a resolution of the forthcoming annual meeting of the Governors of the International Monetary Fund in Rio de Janeiro.

4.   The Ministers and Governors noted that the proposals to make certain changes in the rules and practices of the International Monetary Fund put forward by the E.E.C. countries are currently being examined in the International Monetary Fund.

5.   The Ministers and Governors took note of the other work done by their Deputies during the past year.

[Here follows the text of a statement by Secretary of the Treasury Fowler at the conclusion of this G–10 Ministerial Meeting in London.]

Bruce

---

[2] Reference is apparently to the draft outline prepared by the IMF staff following the fourth joint meeting of Executive Directors and Deputies of the Group of Ten held in Paris June 19–21. The outline served as a working document, which clearly identified the main unresolved questions for discussion and possible compromise. (*The International Monetary Fund, 1966–1971*, vol. I, pp. 153–155)

---

135. Editorial Note

On July 31, 1967, President Johnson signed into law the Interest Equalization Tax Extension Act of 1967 (P.L. 90–59; 81 Stat. 145). This legislation extended the term of this tax, first enacted on September 2, 1964 (P.L. 88–563; 78 Stat. 809), from July 31, 1967, to July 31, 1969. It also provided for a 1 percent increase in the tax on interest charged to foreign borrowers obtaining capital by selling securities to U.S. creditors, and gave the President discretionary authority to drop the tax or increase it to as much as 1.5 percent. The act also called for an increase in the tax by 1.5 percent from January 26, 1967, the day after President Johnson asked Congress for this legislation, until 1 month after enactment when it would revert to 1 percent unless the President ordered continuation of the existing rate or some other rate.

Regarding the President's proposal for this legislation, see Document 117. On August 28, 1967, President Johnson issued Executive Order 11368, which reduced the Interest Equalization Tax from 1.5 to 1.25 percent. For text, see Department of State *Bulletin*, September 25, 1967, pages 396–397.

---

136.   Current Economic Developments[1]

Issue No. 785   Washington, August 2, 1967.

DIFFERENCES REMAIN ON MONETARY REFORM
AFTER GROUP OF TEN MEETING

The Group of Ten Ministers made progress toward agreement on the creation of a new type of international monetary reserve but did not reach complete agreement, Secretary Fowler said after the meeting of the Ministers in London July 17–18.[2] He thought that the differences that remain on major points can be resolved so that a comprehensive outline of a contingency plan for supplementary reserve creation can be presented at the annual IMF meeting in Rio in September.

The Deputies to the Ministries are now meeting in an attempt to narrow the remaining differences. They are to report to the Ministers by mid-August on the status of their negotiations. If necessary, the Ministers will meet again on August 26.

---

[1] Source: Washington National Records Center, RG 59, E/CBA/REP Files: FRC 72 A 6248, *Current Economic Developments*. Limited Official Use. The source text comprises pages 1–4 of the issue.

[2] For the communiqué issued at the conclusion of this meeting, see Document 134.

Background

At US initiative serious negotiations to create reserves began in September 1965 in the Group of Ten and Executive Board of the IMF. The Group of Ten Ministers reached agreement on many essential points in July 1966.[3] Again at US initiative it was decided at the IMF annual meeting in September 1966 to broaden the negotiations to include representatives of all IMF members. As a result of this decision, the Group of Ten Deputies and the IMF Executive Directors have had series of joint meetings to reach agreement on a plan. At the fourth and last Joint Meeting in June 1967 the basic elements of a plan were set down but a number of major issues were left open for decision.

Plan Needed for Reserve Creation

A plan is needed for the creation, on a regular basis, of adequate amounts of a new reserve asset in order to supplement existing international reserves—gold and reserve currencies. Expansion of world trade and investment will be progressively hampered by restrictions unless the world's supply of reserve assets also grows. If one country's reserve gain must always be another country's loss there will be a cumulative use of measures to prevent losses of reserves through restrictions. Moreover, the shortage of reserves tends to raise the world level of interest rates through competitive monetary restraint and to stimulate gold and exchange speculation.

Over the long run, all countries need to see their reserves increase; none wishes to see them decline. However, gold entering into monetary stocks is insufficient and dollar reserves cannot expand as they have in the past. Reserve growth continued in 1965–66, although at a relatively slow pace, primarily because of the effects of temporary factors—largely based on credit arrangements which are reversible. This is not satisfactory for the long run as is increasingly recognized. That there is not enough gold to satisfy everyone's demands is very clear. Furthermore, the US reserve position is such that the flexibility with which dollar reserves has expanded in past is now limited. The global pressure for reserve growth has not been apparent in Europe because until recently the US has supplied reserves that have enabled European reserves to grow at a rate roughly equivalent to 2/3 the rate of growth in European trade. However, in this process the US has suffered deterioration in its own reserve position. For the future this is a global problem, not a US problem.

The need for created reserves may be felt sooner than had been earlier realized. Signs are accumulating that even European countries, though relatively well supplied with reserves, are reluctant to permit

---

[3] See footnote 4, Document 129.

their reserves to decline for any length of time and take steps to avoid any redistribution of their reserves. Moreover, growth of business activity and international trade appears to be a slowing down in many countries.

Reserve creation is needed to assure adequate long-run growth in global reserves. It is not designed to meet emergency situations, nor a kind of development assistance facility nor a scheme to help meet balance of payments problems of individual countries. Reserve creation will create a climate favorable to economic growth. By assuring adequate supply of global reserves, capital exporting countries will not face so much pressure to restrict aid or limit private capital outflow in order to increase their reserves from a very limited world supply.

In order to accomplish these objectives, it is necessary to have a money-like asset that will be regarded by monetary authorities as a supplement to gold and dollars and will be treated by them as reserves. Credit facilities which carry specific repayment obligations will not be so readily considered as reserves and will not meet the countries' desires to increase reserves. Nor will increased credit facilities be as effective in convincing the gold markets that dependence on gold to increase free world reserves has been broken.

Reserve creation is not an answer to the US balance of payments problem, and the fact that we still have this problem is not the reason we are pressing for a good plan by September. Reserve creation will best serve the US by providing a means whereby our reserve assets—now largely gold—can increase. Even if we were in a surplus position now, there is no assurance that our gold position would show much improvement, in view of global shortage of gold, large dollar reserves held by other countries, and the various facilities available for financing payments deficits. The addition of new assets to our reserves, therefore, would augment our gold stock—useful to the dollar both in times of US surplus as well as deficit.

Basic Elements of Reserve Creation

The new asset, which will take the form of drawing rights, would normally be created in a specific annual amount for a 5-year period, say $1 to $2 billion a year. It would be distributed to members in proportion to their IMF quotas and be held by and transferred only among monetary authorities. The asset would be gold value guaranteed and would be backed by members' obligations to accept the asset and to pay convertible currencies in return. This is a basic obligation which gives asset its value. This is the beginning of an international legal tender.

Countries needing to use new drawing rights—usually deficit countries—would be able to present them to other countries—usually surplus countries—to obtain from them the means used to support their currencies in the foreign exchange market—usually dollars or sterling.

This is how countries use gold. No conditions would be imposed on a country's economic policies as a prerequisite to use.

Because the asset is new and untried, it cannot at outset be unqualified legal tender. Three basic qualifications are under consideration:

a. In order to avoid the possibility of over-concentration of the asset in one country, a member need only accept, in addition to its cumulative distributions of the new asset, an amount equal to two times its distributions.

b. If there are no willing takers of the new asset, members can take advantage of rules requiring acceptance assuring, through guidance by Fund, an equitable distribution of the new asset among the countries in best position to take and hold it—usually surplus countries.

c. In the view of some countries, large and persistent users of the new asset may be asked to restore their holdings of the new asset. The US wishes to have this apply only in exceptional cases when overall liquidity of the scheme is threatened.

The successful operation of reserve creation depends upon a high degree of economic cooperation and understanding. It depends upon countries realizing that it is in their self interest to carry out their obligations to accept and hold the new asset. Careful attention must nevertheless be given in the agreement to problems which might arise in event a country fails to meet its obligations and to the details of provisions on withdrawal and liquidation. A basic agreed principle is that losses that might result in case of default will be borne by members in proportion to their share of distributions rather than in proportion to their holdings. This provision helps assure the security of the asset and an equitable share of any losses in the unlikely event of countries defaulting on fulfillment of their obligations.

Unresolved Issues

Agreement has not been reached on a number of issues of crucial importance to creation of an asset that would be meaningful international money. The most important areas of disagreement concern the formula for taking decisions to create the new asset and whether there should be a specific obligation to reconstitute any use of new asset within specified number of years.

The main division of opinion on almost all open issues is on whether the asset should be money-like or credit-like. After a series of unsuccessful maneuvers to block negotiations to create a new reserve asset, the French have taken the lead in a drive to make the new asset merely an extension of existing credit facilities in Fund and not a reserve asset. Thus, they have advocated that the resources be pooled in the IMF instead of separating them from IMF credit facilities in a special account or a new affiliate. They insist that stringent and specific provisions be imposed requiring repayment of use of the new asset within a few years—a characteristic of credit facilities. In another analogy to credit facilities, they wish to limit the amount of the new asset which a country must accept to an amount equal to its allocation instead of twice the allocations, and they would impose a specific precondition which would prevent activation of reserve creation until the United States no longer is in balance of payment deficit. If each of these issues were resolved as the French propose, the new asset might not be considered as a reserve asset, and to large extent we would have failed in our objective to create a supplement to gold and dollars and to convince the world banking, investing, and trading community that adequate reserve growth is assured.

On the question of decision-making, it is not so much French intransigence as a desire by European Community as a whole to have a larger say in the new reserve creation scheme than would be warranted by its present position in the IMF. The US with 20% of the IMF votes now has a veto over certain important decisions of Fund, such as to increase quotas. The European Community with 16% of the votes does not now have this power; but Six wish a veto over operations of the new reserve creation plan in view of their financial importance. They do not wish, however, to buy veto power by putting up additional resources in the IMF, but instead they want to raise the required majority for certain important decisions from the 80% now applicable in the Fund to 85% in the new plan.

As a practical matter, refusal of the European Community to participate in a reserve creation decision, in present circumstances, would mean that reserve creation would not be workable. On the other hand, it seems reasonable that if a country or a group of countries wants veto power the countries should be prepared to pay for it by increasing the quotas in IMF.

To give the plan specific meaning to the public and to Parliaments, we have proposed that agreement be reached at this time on the amount of reserve creation for the first 5-year period, set as a range up to $2 billion a year. The specific amount and when this period would begin would be decided at a later time. In this way, the public and Congress can know the extent of the US commitment. There is as yet no agreement on this provision.

A related issue which gives us serious concern is the desire of the European Community to amend the IMF Articles in such a way as to achieve a more dominant role in the regular operations of the IMF, through revisions of its procedures and particularly the voting procedures. An effort is being made by the European Community (EC) to tie any agreement on reserve creation to these changes in Fund, a procedure which could further delay or perhaps prevent agreement on reserve creation. Moreover, these changes are opposed not only by United States but by all other members of the Fund outside the European Community because they could effectively hamstring successful operations of the Fund as now conducted.

[Here follow articles on unrelated subjects.]

---

137. Memorandum From Secretary of the Treasury Fowler to President Johnson[1]

Washington, August 8, 1967.

SUBJECT

Balance of Payments

I.   Six-Month Results

We will announce second quarter balance of payments results next week. Together with first quarter results, they compare with 1966 as follows:

	Liquidity Deficit (000) (seasonally adjusted)		Official Settlements Deficit (000) (seasonally adjusted)	
	1967	1966	1967	1966
First Quarter	–$ 544	–$651	–$1,822	–$450
Second Quarter (Prel.)	– 514	– 122	– 833	– 175
Six-Month Total	–$1,058	–$773	–$2,655	–$625

These figures confirm the picture I described to you in my memorandum of March 24:[2]

"Overall, it looks at this point as if we will be doing very well to limit our liquidity deficit in 1967 to last year's $1.4 billion figure. On the official reserve transactions basis, last year's surplus will change to a large deficit this year . . ."

If anything, the results are somewhat worse than anticipated, for we received $1.1 billion of help in the form of "special transactions"—long-

---

[1] Source: Johnson Library, White House Central Files, Confidential File, FO 4–1, Balance of Payments (1967–1969). Confidential. A transmittal memorandum from Fowler to the President is not printed. At the bottom of that memorandum, the President wrote: "This is well done & greatly interests me. Lets spend some time in Cab. Com. on it. We just must do better. L."

[2] This memorandum reviews the administration's initiatives on the balance of payments front. (Ibid.)

term investments negotiated by the Treasury with foreign governments and international institutions—in the first six months of this year, compared with $600 million in the same period last year. Tab A shows where these inflows came from; Tab B contains a recent *Wall Street Journal* article on the subject.[3] The article takes the line that these transactions are nothing but statistical gimmicks.

What accounts for the deterioration in our basic payments position?

Using complete information for the first quarter and incomplete information for the second, I would attribute the disappointing showing to

—a lower than expected trade surplus ($4.2 billion annual rate in the first half versus our November, 1966, forecast of $4.9 billion for the year as a whole);

—a disappointing showing by our corporations under the voluntary program, both with respect to direct investment *outflows* and dividend, royalty, and fee *incomes;*

—a slightly higher than anticipated military deficit;

—miscellaneous adverse changes spread across a broad range of accounts (special remittances to Israel, for example, may have cost us $90 million in the second quarter).

Both the disappointing trade surplus and the level of corporate repatriations can be attributed, in part, to lower growth rates (and corporate profitability) in overseas markets—particularly in the U.K. and Germany. *Nevertheless, we simply must do better in these two areas—over both the short and long run—if we are ever to improve our overall performance.*

Our gold loss in the first half was small compared to previous years. The major reason: France, our biggest gold buyer, has been running a deficit; Germany, which has now formally agreed to buy no gold, has been the big EEC surplus country so far this year.

U.S. Gold Losses

	First Six Months 1967	First Six Months 1966
Loss to Domestic Industrial Users	− 62.4	− 75.7
Monetary Loss	− 2.8	−201.2
Total:	− 65.2	−276.9

II. Near Term Outlook

As I see it, we have a fighting chance to keep the deficit for the year close to $2 billion (on the liquidity basis) *if:*

—The trade surplus (which has dropped since April) again turns upward and averages out at $4.5–$4.6 billion for the year as a whole.

---

[3] None of the attachments is printed.

—Commerce exerts enough pressure on corporations to keep direct investment to the agreed target of $2.4 billion (the interagency forecasting group believes that in the absence of such pressure the figure could be as high as $2.9 billion).

—Treasury successfully negotiates "special transactions" of $300–$500 million in the second half—in addition to the $250 million we receive from the Bundesbank under the trilateral agreement.

—Military foreign exchange costs climb no higher than presently estimated ($2.7 billion for the year).

—The U.K. position is sufficiently strong to enable it to meet its year-end debt payment to us ($145 million) and to the IMF ($330 million) without spending any of the $600 million of long-term securities held here.

If these factors go against us in any significant degree, the liquidity deficit could easily move up into the $2.5–$3 billion range.

I believe that we will be able to keep our gold losses low relative to past years—whether the deficit is in the $2 billion or $3 billion range.[4] But the higher the deficit, the more criticism we are likely to encounter and the greater the risk of crisis—and continuing jitters in the London gold market.

Against this background, we must tread a careful path

—avoiding being forced into unnecessary and undesirable restrictionism (on trade, tourist, or capital account) and at the same time
—persuading our public at home and our critics abroad that we intend, purposefully and forcefully, to solve this problem through measures varying in nature and timing and requiring action on the part of the public and private sector and of foreign surplus nations as well.

I am in agreement with that part of the recent American Bankers Association's paper, "U.S. Gold Policy," which recommends "*general economic policies* designed to preserve stability in costs and prices in the domestic economy [your tax program is designed to accomplish this],[5] *selective reductions* in the foreign-exchange costs of Federal spending programs, and *selective measures* calculated to improve the net foreign exchange earnings of the private sector of the economy."

The question is just exactly what are these "*selective reductions*" and "*selective measures?*" The ABA promises to provide answers in a later paper—at the moment they do not have any.

---

[4] They will undoubtedly be higher, however, in the second half than in the first. [Footnote in the source text.]

[5] Brackets in the source text.

These are among the matters which the Cabinet Committee discussed at its last meeting on June 28[6] and which I would like to discuss with you at our meeting on August 10.

III. *Selective Reductions in the Foreign Exchange Costs of Federal Spending Programs*

There are two main areas of concern here: (1) the size of our net military deficit; and (2) the problem of AID-financed exports replacing commercial U.S. exports.

(1) *Net Military Deficit*

At the Cabinet Committee meeting, Secretary McNamara made it clear that the net military deficit could increase by at least $600 million next year (from $2.7 billion to $3.3 billion), taking into account short-falls in the German offset ($500 million) and increased costs in Vietnam ($100 million).

Clearly, no one can realistically expect our *gross* military expenditures to drop over the short term. But what we must make crystal clear to the world is that we intend to continue to make every possible effort to "off-set" or "neutralize" these expenditures. I think it particularly important that this be brought into focus during the coming Kiesinger visit and the Japanese Cabinet Committee visit in September.

Tab C provides background data on the military deficit with emphasis on Germany and Japan.

The Task Force which you established late last fall to examine ways of minimizing post-Vietnam military and aid expenditures in East Asia is attempting to see how we can avoid repeating the post-World War II and the post-Korean experiences. In both these cases, *we tended to underestimate the ability of the war-torn nations in question to recover and repay assistance.* The work of the group to date suggests that the foreign exchange cost of military expenditures and U.S. aid programs, which amounts now to $1.9 billion annually in East Asia ($1.4 billion in developing countries and $0.5 billion in Japan), will be substantial even after the fighting stops—in all probability no less than $1 billion annually—unless new approaches are conceived. This committee will submit a report to you this fall.

(2) *Relationship of AID to U.S. Exports*

Treasury heads an interagency task force which has been sending teams into the field to see whether:

---

[6] No formal record of this meeting has been found, but a memorandum from Secretary of Commerce Trowbridge to William H. Shaw and Lawrence C. McQuade, June 28, recounted discussion at the meeting regarding the Department of Commerce's request for expanded funding of its export promotion program. (Washington National Records Center, RG 40, Secretary of Commerce Files: FRC 74 A 20, Official Chron, June 1967, Trowbridge)

(a) Tied AID exports are replacing U.S. commercial exports;

(b) Sufficient attention is being given in our Missions to developing long range U.S. export markets consistent with AID development objectives;

(c) We are getting as much export "bang" for the AID "buck" as other countries.

Teams have visited Turkey, Chile, Peru, Colombia, and Costa Rica. A new mission will go to India and Pakistan later this month.

Preliminary findings indicate there is *some* substitution of AID-financed exports for commercial exports, and *there probably always will be.* But we can reduce this and improve our export performance to AID-recipient countries *without jeopardizing the program's basic objectives.* The gains will not be breath-taking and will not come about immediately but could eventually total $200–$300 million annually.

IV.   Selected Measures to Improve the Net Foreign Exchange Earnings of the Private Sector

In calendar 1968, the greatest single source of balance of payments improvement must come from the direct investment sector of the Commerce Voluntary Program. In my view we should aim for an improvement of at least $1 billion from the levels we had expected to reach under the 1967 program. This improvement would come from a combination of reduced outflows and increased repatriations. With respect to out-flows, we would expect *at the very minimum* a $500 million reduction from the $2.4 billion target figure we had in 1967.

To the extent that the 1967 program falls short of its goal, we would need a correspondingly greater improvement in 1968. But, the 1967 program should *not* fall short.

A number of people have stressed the need to strengthen this program—including Doug Dillon, Andre Meyer, and Bill Martin—for three basic reasons:

—Nothing will be so convincing to Europe that we mean business. And it could be salutary to European public opinion to see us slow down what Europeans regard as "buying up Europe" and might underline that such a slow down had real costs for Europe.

—No other program can provide as large and quick gains for our overall position, simply because the quantities involved are large.

—Other segments of the economy both public and private which have borne the brunt of the program so far would feel that there was more equity involved. Direct investment really has suffered little cut back so far.

I have met with Secretary Trowbridge a number of times to discuss this, and an inter-agency group is working with Assistant Secretary of Commerce Shaw to see how these savings can be obtained. It is clear that this will not be an easy assignment. It is sure to stir up the business community who will say that we are killing the goose that lays golden eggs. But, I believe a strong appeal to that business community could bring favorable results if the program is conceived and managed in a very hard-headed fashion. This is an issue we have to face up to. Tab D illustrates the nature of this exploration.

At the same time we call upon industry for real short-term sacrifices on the direct investment front, we should offer them an attractive and appealing long-term package of export assistance and incentives. Here is where we stand in this area:

—Secretary Trowbridge has already moved forward with a request for a $7.0 million supplemental appropriation for increased export promotion. His staff is analyzing the possible effects of spending substantially larger sums on export promotion over the longer run.

—Arthur Okun is heading up a group which will shortly make recommendations designed to improve *export financing* facilities.

—We are analyzing the impact of proposed EEC tax harmonization (and border tax adjustments) on our trade position.

—We have discussed a broad variety of tax and non-tax incentives with industry and believe the following, properly presented, can help our national export effort with minimal risk of retaliation:

—over-expensing of promotional outlays
—extension of the 7 percent investment credit to overseas *sales* facilities
—rebate of local excise and perhaps *property* taxes
—accelerated amortization privileges related explicitly to facilities for export production
—underwriting market surveys, in part or in whole.

This is a tricky, complex area, but I believe we are making progress toward a well-rounded group of export expansion measures which could be submitted to the Congress in 1968 in the form of an *Export Expansion Act.*

V.   *Timing of 1968 Program Announcements*

The Cabinet Committee believes that in order to minimize speculative outflows we should announce the 1968 balance of payments program no later than October. I have been wondering, and would like your guidance on, whether we should not include a balance of payments program announcement in *a gold cover message sent to Congress in mid-September.* Such a message would stress the determination of the United States

—to continue to sell gold at $35 per ounce;
—to bring its balance of payments into equilibrium;
—to work with other nations to produce a contingency plan at Rio which would provide a new form of liquidity to be used as and when needed by a growing Free World economy.

In connection with the balance of payments program, we could cite, *as short term measures:*

(1) The proposed 10 percent surcharge, designed to produce balanced economic growth without inflation in 1968.

(2) The recent strengthening of the Interest Equalization Tax.

(3) Substantial further tightening of the direct investment program in 1968.

(4) Moderate tightening of the Federal Reserve Program in 1968. (We would avoid the problem of increased out-flows in late 1967 in anticipation of tougher 1968 programs by making it clear that the new programs would take 1967 and 1968 performance, combined, into effect.)

We could cite, *as basic long-term measures:*

(1) A fiscal-monetary policy designed to ensure cost-price stability over the long run.

(2) A sustained effort to neutralize military expenditures both during and after the war. We would indicate that conversations with the Germans and Japanese were underway and post-war contingency planning in progress.

(3) An intensified effort to minimize substitution of AID-financed exports for commercial exports; we would summarize the findings of the inter-agency task force.

(4) A commitment to provide substantial budgetary support for export expansion in the fields of:

—promotion (Secretary Trowbridge's $7.0 million appropriation request would be described as a "new first step")
—finance
—tax and non-tax incentives.

(5) In connection with tax incentives, a commitment—in the post-Kennedy Round world—to re-examine GATT rules, to study proposed changes in European tax systems, and to negotiate, if necessary, tax "harmonization" for U.S. exporters. We would refer specifically to the proposed change in German border taxes (which German authorities themselves say amounts to a 2–3 percent export price cut and which, in effect, is a D mark devaluation of that amount) as a source of immediate and particular concern.

(6) Pledge new legislation to encourage foreign travel to the United States based on recommendations, to be submitted this fall, by the Travel Task Force.

We will not be in a position to announce specific numbers and details on each and every one of these programs by mid-September, but it seems to me that a disclosure of the general framework of our 1968 and longer-range program could help clear the air.

Henry H. Fowler

---

138. Memorandum From the President's Deputy Special Assistant for National Security Affairs (Bator) to President Johnson[1]

Washington, August 10, 1967.

Mr. President:

At your balance of payments meeting this morning (Fowler, Deming, Knowlton, Bator), Joe will raise two operational issues:

1. Should we use the Commerce Voluntary Program on *direct investment* to really squeeze Trowbridge's clients—for the first time? My own vote would be strongly in favor.

—Short of taxing tourists, or starting a trade war, or gutting your foreign policy, this is the only place where we can make a lot of money for the balance of payments. (I agree with Fowler that we should aim for an improvement in direct investment and repatriated earnings together of at least $1 billion in 1968 over the 1967 target. This should result in a net payments gain of some $600–$800 million.)

—Direct investment is about the only item which has not really been pinched so far. (The bankers, who have been squeezed, are especially resentful.)

—In getting the Europeans to cooperate in not buying gold, and accepting a U.S. deficit as not entirely illegitimate (we are not running an economy like Brazil), direct investment is our Achilles heel. They recognize the world-wide case for foreign aid, for military spending (even Vietnam) and for access to our capital markets. But many of them think that financing U.S. direct investment by means of a deficit is equivalent to buying up Europe with money borrowed from Europeans.

—The only *negative* argument is that the business community would not much like it. In the setting of Vietnam, however, I think it a

---

[1] Source: Johnson Library, National Security File, Subject File, Balance of Payments, Vol. IV, January 1967 [1 of 2], Box 3. No classification marking.

good bet that they will cooperate. They really don't have a leg to stand on. (You will not want to give us a final answer on this now. Trowbridge and Fowler and the rest of us will come back to you with concrete proposals soon.)

2. Should we build into the gold-cover message, in mid-September, a new balance of payments program, focussing on direct investment as above, and a few other longer-term items? Joe is for it. I myself have doubts, which are shared by Okun, Dewey Daane and others. Rather than spelling out the arguments on paper, I would suggest that you ask Joe and myself at the meeting about the possible disadvantages.

Francis M. Bator[2]

---

[2] Printed from a copy that bears this typed signature.

---

139. Memorandum From Secretary of the Treasury Fowler to President Johnson[1]

Washington, August 10, 1967.

SUBJECT

Our Balance of Payments Problems

In connection with our balance of payments problems, I believe it would be most desirable to have at least two informal off-the-record meetings with you and a very few others from the Administration. These meetings should be held in the very near future.

(1) We should have a meeting on the outlook with respect to our military costs in NATO and in the Far East. Essentially, it should be struc-

---

[1] Source: Johnson Library, White House Central Files, Confidential File, FO 4–1, Balance of Payments (1967–1969). Confidential. A handwritten note by Fowler on the source text reads: "Note: This was covered generally in our conference this morning." No record of this meeting has been found. Attached to the source text is a typed note dictated by the President to James R. Jones, dated August 10 at 11:30 p.m., which reads: "That's all right." Also attached is a covering memorandum for the record by Jones, August 12, indicating that the first meeting on military costs in NATO and the Far East was scheduled for August 12 at 5:30 p.m., and that Fowler had suggested that the second meeting on foreign exchange costs of direct investment programs not be scheduled until he got back to the White House.

tured on the Trilateral form, with Secretaries Rusk, McNamara, and myself as principals, and such deputies as would seem desirable. From the White House, I would assume Walt Rostow and Francis Bator would participate. Here, we need to explore the foreign exchange costs of our military deployments, ways and means to neutralize them, and lay out a program to accomplish that purpose.

(2) A meeting designed to discuss the foreign exchange costs of our direct investment program. As my memorandum to you indicates,[2] there is a great deal of work that has been done on this, but we need to get together to determine specifically what we should do now and for 1968. At that meeting, I would suggest Secretary Trowbridge and his principal advisor in this area, Assistant Secretary Shaw, Arthur Okun, myself, Fred Deming, and Win Knowlton. From the White House, I would think Francis Bator would attend.

Henry H. Fowler

---

[2] Presumably a reference to Document 137.

---

140.   Telegram From the Department of State to the Embassy in the United Kingdom[1]

Washington, August 24, 1967, 0345Z.

26200. For Griffin from Treasury. Following text of confidential letter from Secretary Fowler to Chancellor Callaghan. Request you arrange delivery soonest. Signed original being pouched.[2]

Begin text

Dear Jim:

I hope it will be possible for the two of us to meet before the Ministerial meeting at 10:00 a.m. on August 26, possibly at 8:30 or 9:00 in the morning. As you know, I will not be arriving in London until about 11:00

---

[1] Source: Department of State, Central Files, FN 10. Confidential; Priority; Limdis. Drafted by Willis on August 22 and approved by John F. L. Ghiardi (E/IMA).

[2] Not found. A similar message from Deming to Schoellhorn was transmitted in telegram 26201 to Bonn, August 24. (Ibid.)

p.m. on the evening of the 25th. It would be helpful to exchange views on the Ministerial meeting beforehand. However, there would probably not be time to go into any other matters on Saturday morning,[3] and I would be happy to have a further session with you at some time on Sunday on other subjects, if this would be convenient to you. In the meantime, you might be interested in the present state of our consideration of some of the major questions.

The Deputies have done yeoman work in trying to implement the package which you assigned them at our last meeting in London.[4] In addition to resolving a good number of the brackets in the Outline,[5] they made considerable progress in narrowing differences on the big issues. I understand that if the French representative had had more flexible instructions, it might have been possible to reach almost complete agreement on the Outline—with acceptance of the average net use formula as the centerpiece.

As it turned out in London, the major issues were left unresolved. Voting provisions, reconstitution, the right to purchase a country's own currency, the name of the asset, the magnitude of acceptance limits, and a satisfactory resolution for adoption by the Governors at Rio must all be considered by the Ministers this weekend.

One of the important accomplishments of the Deputies at the Paris meeting in July was to narrow and clarify the alternatives on reconstitution. Although there are five alternatives in the Emminger redraft of Chapter V, 4, the results of the Paris meeting—where agreement was almost achieved on the basis of Alternative A—would seem to justify concentration on Alternative A in our forthcoming discussions on reconstitution. In Paris Ossola indicated that the Italians would not want their harmonization proposal to stand in the way of the agreement on Alternative A. In large part this attitude seemed to reflect the fact that the harmonization principle was very difficult to define and apply practically. Whether or not this is the official Italian position, I cannot say. Governor Carli seems to be very closely attached to the harmonization principle.

You will recall that the first paragraph of Alternative A is really based on a French suggestion. In brackets, it contains also the elements of Minister Schiller's proposal of 75% over six years. At the same time, our version of Alternative A sub-paragraph (ii) would maintain the principle of harmonization as a general guide. (The Emminger formulation in paragraph (ii) A seems to us much too rigid. By emphasizing dispropor-

---

[3] August 26.

[4] Reference is to the London meeting July 17–18; see Document 134.

[5] Following a meeting in Paris July 27–28, the Deputies of the Group of Ten agreed on a version of an Outline, which has not been found, but is summarized in De Vries, *The International Monetary Fund, 1966–1971*, vol. I, pp. 157–158.

tionate *use*, without any qualification with respect to "over time", it would undesirably constrain the asset as a freely usable reserve.)

I would like you to know that, for our part, we could under no circumstances consider any operative combination of harmonization and average use such as is represented by the Emminger variant of Alternative A, paragraph (ii), or by Alternative C. Needless to say, the new French Alternative D is also outside the range of what is negotiable, since it combines the most stringent form of harmonization with average use.

All in all, our general view is that we could support Schiller's average use proposal of 75% over six years, supplemented by Fred Deming's language in paragraph (ii) of Alternative A. This seems to be the most reasonable of the formulae on the table. Of course, the 75% figure is an essential feature of the proposal.

On a different point, I would like to draw your attention to the fact that the right of a member to purchase balances of its own currency has been bracketed by the French. You will recall that the substance of this provision has been changed in an important respect since it was discussed at our July meeting. Previously it was provided that a country meeting the needs test could obtain balances of its currency held by another country if the latter country was eligible to receive the new drawing rights and was within its acceptance limits. Provided these conditions were met, a country could exercise this right without the consent of the country receiving the drawing rights. The provision has now been modified so that the right to obtain one's own currency from another country can be used only if the other country consents. Thus, for example, the U.S., if it meets the needs test, can obtain dollars held by another country if that country is eligible to receive special drawing rights, is within its acceptance limits, and agrees to take special drawing rights in return for dollars. We are fully in accord with this modification of the provision since it removes any possibility that it might be misconstrued to indicate that the U.S. was modifying its commitments to convert dollars into gold. Although this construction was completely unfounded even under the previous provision, the requirement of consent of the other country eliminates any possibility of misinterpretation.

Even as modified, this provision is of vital importance to the U.S. Under the regular rules of holding and use, in order to use 100 drawing rights we would have to obtain a basket of foreign currencies including, for example, 25 SDR in Deutsche Marks, 25 in Guilders, 25 in Lire and 25 in Sterling. However, all but one country contributing to this basket might be perfectly happy to be holding dollars. Thus, drawing down dollars from the other countries would be of no particular use to us. What we would like to be able to do is to use all 100 drawing rights with countries that want to exchange dollars provided they consent to accept drawing rights. Without this provision the drawing right scheme has a limited utility to us. Therefore, acceptance of this provision is a sine qua non to our agreement to new package proposals. I believe you share our interest in this provision, as your own needs might not always be covered efficiently by a straight package drawing.

Another important point that may come up is the resolution for Rio. A question may be raised as to whether it is advisable for the Ministers to take up the resolution which has not been discussed in advance by the Deputies, and on which discussion has begun in the Executive Board. As you know, I consider it essential that instructions be given at the Annual Meeting to authorize the task of drafting an amendment to the Articles to implement the provisions of the Outline. At the same time, I do not want to be placed in the position where agreement to the EEC proposals for changes in the present operations of the Fund, particularly in the voting majorities, becomes a condition to a report by the Executive Directors and an agreement by the Governors on an amendment implementing the Outline. As the French have indicated an interest in linking the two as part of the package, and the EEC have been meeting on their substantive proposals, the question may have to be faced in some way at London. There is no logical connection between these EEC proposals and the Outline. A linking of the two seems to me to be simply a case of placing a precondition on final action by the Board of Governors on the Outline.

From this point of view, the Fund Staff draft of the Rio resolution seems deficient. The implementation of the Outline and formulation of amendments to the Articles to allow the Fund to hold and use the new asset should be treated in one resolution and a second resolution, if desired by the EEC, should treat their proposals for changes in present operations of the Fund.

Since implementation of the Outline should be given priority, we should ask for proposed amendments establishing the plan and making other changes in the Articles in connection with the plan to be submitted to the Board of Governors not later than the end of February 1968. A separate report containing any agreed proposals on changes in the other operations of the Fund, such as those proposed by the EEC, could also be submitted in February or as soon as possible thereafter.

I hope that on Saturday morning we can have a quick review of reconstitution, the acceptance limits, the conversion right, and the resolution question, as well as other elements of the package. As you know, I feel very strongly that we cannot move on voting majorities unless we have a satisfactory solution of all the other problems that still remain open.

With best regards.

Sincerely, Henry H. Fowler

End Text.

Rusk

141. Editorial Note

At a meeting in London on August 26, 1967, the Finance Ministers and Central Bank Governors of the Group of Ten considered a revised Outline of a Contingency Plan for creating a new entity in the form of special drawing rights, which was intended to meet future needs for a supplement to existing reserve assets. A 32-page detailed "informal report" of the meeting, undated, prepared by George H. Willis, is in the Johnson Library, National Security File, Fried Papers, Group of Ten Ministerial Meeting, London, August 1967 (ERF), Box 1. Copies of Francis Bator's handwritten notes passed to Fowler during the meeting, together with Willis' report, provide a blow-by-blow account of the negotiations. In addition, Bator in August 1996 prepared "Notes" explaining his notes written at Lancaster House. All are ibid., Bator Papers, Box 5. At the conclusion of the meeting, the Ministers and Governors issued a communiqué announcing that they had agreed on a text of an Outline of a Contingency Plan. For text of the communiqué, see Department of State *Bulletin*, September 25, 1967, page 396. The Outline Plan agreed to at the London meeting on August 26 has not been found but is summarized in the communiqué and in De Vries, *The International Monetary Fund, 1966–1971*, volume I, page 158.

The Outline was then considered by the IMF Executive Directors, who were expected to endorse the Outline, or a revised version of it, for approval in a resolution at the forthcoming annual meeting of the International Monetary Fund in Rio de Janeiro.

President Johnson welcomed the return of the U.S. delegation, which had been chaired by Secretary of the Treasury Fowler, at the White House on August 28. For text of the remarks by the President commending the work of the delegation as well as a statement by Fowler on this occasion, see Department of State *Bulletin*, September 25, 1967, pages 392–393. On the following day, August 29, Fowler issued a lengthy statement to the press reviewing the incremental progress on the creation of a monetary reserve asset; text is ibid., pages 393–396. Much of the background information in Fowler's statement was made public earlier at the conclusion of the London Ministerial meeting on July 18 (see Document 134). Fowler's August 29 press statement was also transmitted in circular telegram 29397 to all diplomatic posts, August 30. (Department of State, Central Files, FN 10) Telegraphic communications regarding the preparations for and results of the August 26 London meeting are ibid. Miscellaneous press materials as well as a copy of an undated letter from Fowler to Canadian Finance Minister Mitchell Sharp thanking him for his key role in resolving a serious impasse during the monetary discussions at Lancaster House are in the Johnson Library, Bator Papers, International Monetary Matters, Box 10.

142.   Letter From French Finance and Economic Affairs Minister Debré to Secretary of the Treasury Fowler

Paris, September 7, 1967.

[Source: Johnson Library, Bator Papers, International Monetary Matters, Box 10. No classification marking. 4 pages of source text not declassified.]

143.   Memorandum From the Secretary of Commerce's Assistant (Simpich) to Secretary of Commerce Trowbridge[1]

Washington, September 8, 1967.

SUBJECT

Balance of Payments Advisory Committee

Here for the record and for your talks with Secretary Fowler are the positions taken yesterday by your Advisory Committee:

1.   The Committee will support a target figure for 1968 that is $300 million below the projected level of capital outflows for 1967, i.e., it will support a 1968 target figure of $1.3 billion—subject to the caveat that the recalcitrant companies can be brought $200 million closer to their target level.

2.   The Committee offered to form a small group to help persuade recalcitrant companies to cooperate. This offer was neither accepted nor rejected.

3.   The Committee asked for and was promised an opportunity to review the Administration's decision on the target figure before it is announced in order to determine whether the Committee will publicly support the decision.

4.   The Committee reiterated its position that LDC's should be treated as "program countries."

---

[1] Source: Washington National Records Center, RG 40, Executive Secretariat Files: FRC 74 A 30, Balance of Payments Background Material. Confidential.

5. The Committee raised again the proposal that credit should be given for investments in kind. You promised that you would have Bill Shaw look into this matter once again.

6. The Committee reiterated its view that the Administration cannot count on business support of the voluntary program much longer unless it also comes forward with a long range plan to supplement the "short term" voluntary program.

7. The Committee observed that if the target is below a figure it believes industry can meet, it would rather have a shot at controls. (Weinberg[2] probably dissents.)

FS

---

[2] Probably Sidney J. Weinberg, General Partner, Goldman Sachs & Company.

---

144. Letter From the President of General Electric Company (Borch) to Secretary of Commerce Trowbridge[1]

New York, September 14, 1967.

Dear Sandy:

To put it mildly, I was quite discouraged by the trend of events at the Balance of Payments Advisory Committee meeting last week,[2] to the point of asking myself whether it is any longer meaningful for such a group of businessmen to attempt to meaningfully advise the Administration on this very important subject.

There seem to be some in the Administration who profess to believe that if business would stop exporting dollars into direct foreign investments the balance-of-payments problem would be solved. This attitude reflects itself in a constant hammering to reduce this relatively minor element of the balance-of-payments deficit. It further overlooks what all the businessmen on the Advisory Committee keep repeating; namely, that

---

[1] Source: Washington National Records Center, RG 40, Executive Secretariat Files: FRC 74 A 30, Balance of Payments Background Material. No classification marking.
[2] See Document 143.

direct investments are a very significant element in maintaining or improving the US trade balance.

The voluntary program has served a major useful purpose; namely, in educating businessmen generally to the importance of the US balance-of-payments position to the health of our economy, and this has been reflected in results that some in the Administration said could not possibly happen. The record will show that the voluntary program has done an outstanding job by any measurement, and in my opinion this is because it was *initially* properly focused on the *overall* contribution that a business could make. This originally was the prime target, and properly so. In the last two years, emphasis has turned from the overall contribution to the matter of direct investments—in other words, from the "dog to the tail," as someone expressed it.

Now the year 1967 shows still further progress, both in terms of trade balance and direct investments to the program countries. The fact that direct investments to lesser developed countries has increased should surprise no one, since such investment has been encouraged by the Administration. Now to attempt to further reduce the target on program countries to offset the increase to lesser developed countries strikes me simply as game playing.

To the point that some companies are not cooperating, the fact that the program is voluntary would make this inevitable. This does not mean that the Administration cannot use person-to-person persuasion on this score, which has heretofore been lacking.

However, the main point is that business under the voluntary program has done an outstanding job, in the opinion of many of us, in serving the country in both its short- and long-term interests. The Administration, on the other hand, still seems to be unwilling to face up to the admittedly difficult political problems associated with the other more critical aspects of the balance-of-payments problem, among which foreign travel is often cited as an example, although many aspects of the import situation are much more important.

Overall, Sandy, it appears to me that businessmen have evidenced by their actions their understanding of the seriousness of this problem, both short- and long-term, and some of us are extremely discouraged that the efforts being made by business are not being matched in results by the public sector, which is where the deficit is created.

Thanks for taking the time to read this—it's more helpful to me to get it off my chest than it can possibly be to you!

Sincerely,

Fred

145. Memorandum From Secretary of the Treasury Fowler to President Johnson[1]

Washington, October 6, 1967.

SUBJECT

Report on the 22nd Annual International Monetary Fund and the International Bank for Reconstruction & Development Meeting in Rio de Janeiro, Brazil

The key decision taken at the Rio meeting was the adoption of the resolution approving the outline plan for a new international monetary asset—Special Drawing Rights in the Fund[2]—as originally agreed to in London by the Group of Ten.[3] The fundamental importance of this new undertaking was recognized both by industrial and developing countries, and the resolution was approved without dissent. The action taken by the Governors at Rio initiates the next stage—the preparation of the formal legal text by the IMF Board of Executive Directors for final legislative action by all member countries. The resolution directs the Executive Directors to proceed with their work on the basis of the outline "in order to meet the need, if and when it arises, for a supplement to existing reserve assets," and to submit their report to the Board of Governors as soon as possible but not later than March 31, 1968.

The resolution approved in Rio also provided for a parallel report by the Executive Directors on proposals for modification of the present IMF rules. This is an area where the clearest issue will shape up. While we go along with the parallel study of the present operations of the Fund, the study or the approval of the study's recommendations, if any, cannot be a pre-condition to action on the Special Drawing Rights facility. My statement on this point is shown in the attached copy of my IMF speech.[4] We will study new IMF reform proposals on their merits and I will consult with the Dillon Committee and members of Congress in the formulation of the U. S. position. We may have suggestions of our own. The fact that this parallel study is not a pre-condition to action on the SDR was clearly agreed to in London by the EEC countries. The Finance Minister of France took a different position, namely that "The parallel execution of

---

[1] Source: Johnson Library, National Security File, Fried Files, Chron, September 1, 1967–November 20, 1967 [2 of 2], Box 2. Limited Official Use. Attached to the source text is a memorandum from Rostow to the President, October 9, summarizing Fowler's memorandum.

[2] For text of the September 29 resolution on Special Drawing Rights, see *American Foreign Policy: Current Documents, 1967*, pp. 189–193.

[3] Regarding the London agreement, see Document 141.

[4] None of the attachments is printed. An excerpt from Fowler's September 26 speech at the meeting is printed in *American Foreign Policy: Current Documents, 1967*, pp. 186–189.

these two reforms is, I would recall, one of the conditions of the agreement of the French Government."[5] Only time and future negotiations will reveal to what extent France or any of the other Common Market countries will hold to this position.

One of the important pieces of unfinished business at the Rio meeting on the World Bank side was IDA replenishment. George Woods[6] and I made clear that there has not yet been a satisfactory response to the offer which you approved last March—to join with other developed countries in a very substantial increase in IDA under suitable balance-of-payments safeguards. There were a number of attempts, some inadvertent and some conscious, to imply that our balance-of-payments safeguards would subject IDA to tied procurement at the expense of the principle of international competitive bidding in the World Bank. I laid that to rest in my own statement and Mr. Woods did the same in his. In his concluding statement, Mr. Woods surfaced, for the first time officially, the size of the U.S. replenishment proposal. He also made it clear that the U.S. proposal was completely consistent with the operations of the Bank, including international competitive bidding. (Attached is an underscored copy of Mr. Woods' concluding remarks.) In an effort to reach agreement on the replenishment he also called for a ministerial meeting of donor countries in the near future.

In addition to our primary mission in Rio which took place in the plenary sessions, I had the senior members of the delegation lead in bilateral meetings with over 40 countries. About half of these were requests to go over matters of mutual concern between our two countries and about half were designed for political good will, including meetings with almost all the Latin American countries in regional grouping and individually in cases such as Brazil, Argentina, and Mexico. In most of these sessions the Congressional members of our delegation were invited to participate, acting in an observer role generally, and participating helpfully on a number of occasions. These bilaterals provided the Congressional delegation with very useful background on the Special Drawing Rights plan, which will be submitted for Congressional action in the next session. It also afforded them an opportunity to see first hand a wide-range of our international financial problems—ranging from balance of payments cooperation and international financial policy, to multilateral and bilateral assistance problems.

Under Secretary Rostow, in addition to his work on the delegation, handled the launching of the Convention for the Settlement of Investment Disputes—the World Bank facility to promote arbitration and conciliation by private investors in their disputes with governments. He also

---

[5] For an excerpt from Debré's September 26 address, see ibid., pp. 182–186.

[6] President of the International Bank for Reconstruction and Development.

participated actively in a series of bilaterals, especially with the Middle Eastern countries.

One potential disruptive feature at the plenary was the introduction by the French speaking African countries of a resolution dealing with the establishment of a mechanism for dealing with commodity price fluctuations. The proposal was handled by generalizing it and referring it to study by the IMF and the World Bank.

All in all the meeting was extremely gratifying, particularly the unanimous reception given by the non-Group of Ten to the Outline Plan for Special Drawing Rights. It was well understood and welcomed with enthusiasm by them. Only some of the less sophisticated expressed the hope that the SDR would be more generously allocated to the developing countries as an economic aid device. This was not a substantive issue, however, and even they wholeheartedly supported the proposal.

Henry H. Fowler

---

146.   Memorandum From the Secretary of Commerce's Assistant (Simpich) to Secretary of Commerce Trowbridge[1]

Washington, October 13, 1967.

SUBJECT

Balance of Payments Advisory Committee Meeting, October 9

Here, for future reference, is a summary of how we left matters at the October 9 BOP Advisory Committee Meeting:

1. The "target" is acceptable, subject to our promise to seek to squeeze $200 million from recalcitrant companies.

2. The responsibility for working on recalcitrants lies with the Department of Commerce, not the Advisory Committee.

3. The "goal" suggested to the Committee was rejected on the ground that it was largely attributable to what, in the Committee's view,

---

[1] Source: Washington National Records Center, RG 40, Executive Secretariat Files: FRC 74 A 30, Balance of Payments Background Material. No classification marking. A handwritten note on the source text reads: "Put with notebooks on BOP program."

was an overly sanguine estimate of exports for 1968. The Committee will agree to whatever goal we derive by polling the 50 or so largest exporters, determining an average anticipated percentage increase in exports, and using that average as the basis for our calculation of the goal.

4. There will be *no* "advisory group" on foreign borrowing.

5. Although credit will not be given for exports in kind, we will encourage such exports in our statements, letters, speeches, etc. and give informal recognition of efforts of this kind.

Fred

147. Memorandum From the President's Special Assistant (Rostow) to President Johnson[1]

Washington, October 19, 1967, 7:05 p.m.

SUBJECT

Contingency Support For Sterling

At Tab A is Joe Fowler's memo recommending an increase of $100 million in the funds he has available for market operations to support sterling.

What it comes down to is this.

Today's increase in the discount rate is part of the last ditch British effort to hold the sterling rate. As you know, they moved strongly last year to support the pound: they deflated their economy, cut down foreign commitments and borrowed heavily abroad.

The program worked well through the first quarter of this year. They were able to pay off more than $1 billion in debt. Then they ran into bad luck:

—disappointing exports, largely because of the recession on the continent;

---

[1] Source: Johnson Library, National Security File, Subject File, Monetary Crisis, November 1968, Cables and Memos, Vol. 1 [1 of 2], Box 22. Secret; Sensitive. A handwritten "L" at the top of the source text indicates that the President saw the memorandum. Rostow's handwritten note on the right margin, dated October 20, indicates that Fried, Fowler, and Ben Read had been notified.

—the Middle East crisis and the closure of the Canal;
—rising interest rates elsewhere while theirs were going down.

They began to lose reserves and had to draw heavily on their line of short term credits.

The increase in the bank rate is designed to draw funds back to London. The market's initial reaction was slightly disappointing because some expected a higher increase in the rate. But sterling is holding steady because of support operations.

Through selective and carefully timed actions, we have operated successfully in the market in the past to keep the rate from worsening on bad news or to strengthen it on good news. We do so at our own discretion but in cooperation with the British.

We now have $160 million available for this purpose. Fowler recommends that you authorize him to make $100 million more available out of the Exchange Stabilization Fund. This would give the necessary leeway to have a maximum impact on the market—either to continue defensive operations or to take advantage of favorable opportunities.

These funds are guaranteed against loss from devaluation. There is no balance of payments effect. If the funds are used, it would in effect amount to an increase in our lending to the U.K.

This is a contingency investment that could be used very effectively to support sterling. I believe Fowler's proposal makes sense. Deming, Okun, Daane and Fried who have gone into it carefully concur in the recommendation.

Your decision is needed as soon as possible so that our people in the exchange market will know how much ammunition they have and plan their operations accordingly from tomorrow on.

Walt

Approve[2]

No

See me

---

[2] This option is checked.

Attachment

Memorandum From Secretary of the Treasury Fowler to President Johnson[3]

Washington, October 19, 1967.

SUBJECT

Additional Assistance to the U. K. in Support of Sterling

1. The austerity program imposed by the British last year brought sterling out of its summer crisis and very considerable gains were made in restoring British reserves and repaying short-term credits. This favorable picture prevailed through the fourth quarter of last year and into April of 1967. The British predicted a sizable balance of payments surplus for the year.

A sharp reversal took place in May, following poor April trade figures, accentuated by the Mid-East crisis. The British reserves suffered from some movement of Mid-East funds accompanied by other speculative flight from sterling and more fundamentally due to closure of the Suez canal and related aspects of the Mid-East crisis. In addition, the hoped for resurgence in U. K. exports did not take place, due in large part to the stagnation in Germany and slow downs elsewhere, including the U. S. in the early part of the year. Finally, interest arbitrage relationships were turned against the British as interest rates in the United States rose.

As a result, the British again find themselves with reserves depleted and large debts on their short-term lines of credit.

Their reserves at the end of September stood at $2,733 million, down $425 million from a year earlier and short-term credits drawn at $2,072 million, up $250 million from a year earlier. This $2.1 billion of credits drawn is out of established short-term lines totaling $2,690 million leaving about $620 million remaining. Of the $2,690 million in credit lines, $1,750 million have been extended by the United States and the balance of $940 million by other, largely European, countries. The worsening of the short-term credit position has to a large extent been offset by reestablishment of medium-term facilities with the International Monetary Fund, but these latter are not as readily available and publicity surrounding an IMF drawing could be counterproductive.

At present the United States has two credit lines, one a swap line by the Federal Reserve amounting to $1,350 million of which $800 million is

---

[3] Secret; Limited Distribution.

drawn and a $400 million agreement shared $200 million by the Federal Reserve and $200 million by the Treasury Exchange Stabilization Fund.[4] Under this latter agreement the U.S. extends support by purchasing sterling generally in the market, subject to an exchange guarantee granted by the British. There is no fixed maturity at which the sterling will be resold to the Bank of England or the market. The Exchange Stabilization Fund also extends, on occasion, overnight assistance at month end.

2.   The drain on the British position in the past few months, after the Mid-East crisis settled down, seems to be largely related to the fact that interest rates elsewhere, particularly in the Euro-dollar market, are more attractive than rates on sterling investments when the cost of forward cover is taken into account. In addition, their trade figures have not been a cause of encouragement. Given the other problems of sterling, this drain is unsustainable. The increase today in the Bank of England rate of 1/2 percent is designed to reestablish the interest relationship which existed earlier. It may well prove to be not enough and another 1/2 percent increase could be around the corner.

In response to an inquiry by the Chancellor of the Exchequer, I have indicated the United States would not stand in the way of or retaliate to such a move. We could not, of course, make any promise as to the general trend of our own rates. The Bank of England had moved its rate down by 1-1/2 percent to 5-1/2 percent earlier this year (1/2 percent each in January, March and May). The United States reduced its rate by 1/2 percent in April.

3.   We wish to take advantage of what may be a favorable psychological moment to assist in a strengthening of the exchange rate for the pound sterling or at the least to lend sufficient support to avoid a worsening of the outlook. To this end we would propose to engage in market operations by buying guaranteed sterling under the aforementioned $400 million agreement of September 1965.

4.   With your approval, we agreed to extend the further $400 million assistance in September 1965. At that time we succeeded in obtaining additional pledges of assistance, known as the Basle agreement, from the European central banks. This is the present credit line of $690 million of which the British have now used $540 million.

A further credit package in the amount of $300 million, of which a group of foreign central banks would supply $275 million, is being currently discussed to assist the U.K. to make a repayment due to the International Monetary Fund this December. It is not sure as yet, however, whether this additional credit will materialize. Therefore additional assistance by the United States may not be matched by others.

---

[4] This agreement has not been further identified.

5. In connection with any current market operations, it would be helpful to have some more ammunition available now to reinforce their position. At present the Exchange Stabilization Fund has only $50 million left unused from its pledge of $200 million under the September 1965 agreement. The Federal Reserve has $110 million left but, as noted, already has undertaken assistance of $800 million under its swap line.

6. Following the weekend developments, I convened a meeting Tuesday morning[5] of the ad hoc group we normally call on to consider the U.K. problems and our role in dealing with them. It included, in addition to Treasury personnel, Mr. Fried of your staff, Chairman Martin and Governor Daane of the Federal Reserve Board, Mr. Okun of the Council of Economic Advisers, Assistant Secretary Solomon of the State Department, and Mr. Charles Coombs of the Federal Reserve Bank of New York, who acts as our agent in the market. We reviewed the overall U. K. situation, the various alternatives open, the risk of devaluation, and the situation in the gold market. After pooling our information and views, this ad hoc group referred a general proposal along the lines of this paper to the Interagency Steering Group operating under the Chairmanship of Under Secretary Deming of the Treasury. That group met on Wednesday and considered the problem at some length.

In light of the above, I recommend that you authorize me to increase the Exchange Stabilization portion of the September 1965 agreement by $100 million to $300 million. Sterling purchased under this authority would, of course, have to be subject to guarantee so that no exchange risk would be incurred. There would be no adverse balance of payments effect from the transaction.

Henry H. Fowler

---

[5] October 17.

148.   Department of Commerce Paper[1]

Washington, November 7, 1967.

STATUS OF PROPOSALS FOR THE 1968 BALANCE OF PAYMENTS
PROGRAM

1. *Commerce Voluntary Program*

Our package is approved.

2. *Federal Reserve Voluntary Program*

Secretary Fowler is scheduled to meet with Chairman Martin to
resolve the remaining difference of opinion regarding the placing of
Exim "associated loans" under the 109% ceiling. All other Agencies
oppose this Fed proposal. Such loans refer in particular to financings
undertaken by commercial banks for the export of jet aircraft. These are
made in conjunction with direct loans by the Eximbank for the same
transaction. In these instances, commercial banks take the early maturities without Exim guarantee.

Treasury has not yet given up hope that export financing, together
with LDC loans, can be excluded from the Fed ceiling altogether. While
such a drastically revamped Fed Program cannot be devised in time for
the mid-November announcement of the 1968 BoP Program, Treasury is
determined to keep up the pressure on the Fed to revamp its program.[2]

3. *Tax Incentives for Exports*

The following have been rejected, principally because of Treasury
and State opposition.

---

[1] Source: Washington National Records Center, RG 40, Executive Secretariat Files:
FRC 74 A 30, Balance of Payments Cabinet Committee. No classification marking. Drafted
by Gerald A. Pollack, Deputy Assistant Secretary of Commerce for Economic Affairs, and
Mark Feer, Deputy Assistant Secretary of Commerce for Financial Policy. Attached to the
source text is a November 7 note from William H. Shaw to Secretary Trowbridge, which
reads as follows:

"The attached report on the Status of Proposals for the 1968 Balance of Payments Program would seem to suggest—

"a. that final agreement on a complete program is not likely at the November 9 meeting, and

"b. that when such agreement is achieved, those points of the program intended to
increase exports will be relatively weak as compared with the initial hopes in this area."

No record of the November 9 meeting has been found.

[2] A handwritten note in the margin next to this paragraph reads: "Not issue today—
Study to be conducted on how to do it." The handwritten comments, here and elsewhere on
the source text, are presumably Shaw's.

(1) A credit against total income tax liability calculated as a flat percentage of export sales.

(2) A lower rate of corporate income tax for profits derived from exporting.

(3) A credit against income tax liability based on accelerated depreciation of plant and equipment used in the production of export goods.

(4) An investment tax credit applicable to plant and equipment used for the production of export goods.

(5) Exemption from income tax of remitted income of U.S. sales subsidiaries abroad.

(6) Rebate of property tax and indirect taxes for exported goods.

(7) Overexpensing for increases in export promotion expenditures.

Treasury is now considering administrative rulings to:

(1) clarify Section 482 regulations of the Code dealing with intercompany pricing

(2) establish alternative procedures under Section 863 for defining foreign-source income

(3) liberalize regulations concerning the amount of reserves for bad debts that banks may establish in connection with their financing of U.S. exports.

In addition, Treasury is now examining a series of technical, administrative and legislative changes to liberalize the scope of Export Trade Corporations.

No details on any of these matters have been provided. No agency is opposed at this general level. It is clear that any tax incentive which might become part of the final program will be very weak in relation to some of the proposals which were seriously considered at the outset.

4. BIC's Export Promotion Budget Supplemental

This supplemental for $7.1 million has survived several BOB reviews and still forms part of the overall Government supplemental request which we expect to be submitted to Congress in November.

5. "Joint Export Associations" for Export Expansion

The Executive Committee of the Balance of Payments Committee at its November 2 meeting[3] endorsed in principle this new form of export promotion which calls for cost sharing by Government and industry of certain designated export associated expenditures (advertising, participation in trade fairs, market research, overseas travel, cost of overseas sales offices, warehouses, etc.).

The Commerce Department would provide funds under contract to: (1) groups or firms, (2) trade and industry associations, and (3) export

---

[3] No record of this meeting has been found.

intermediaries. In order to avoid anti-trust complications, the Secretary of Commerce would be given the authority to issue charters to trade and industry associations or groups of firms that wished to form Joint Export Associations. Enabling legislation and appropriations would be needed for this new form of export promotion.

Many details remain to be worked out, including whether Commerce should enter into cost sharing contracts with individual export firms. No detailed budget estimates have been developed to date. Earlier studies indicated an expenditure level of $6 million in FY 1969.

This item is scheduled to be considered at the BoP Cabinet meeting of November 9.

6.   *Expanded Rediscount Facility at the Eximbank*

A meeting was held towards the end of October with Harold Linder.[4] Presented on this occasion was the proposal for a liberalized rediscount facility which was prepared by the Art Okun Committee on export financing and endorsed by the BoP Executive Committee. Larry McQuade who attended this meeting believes that Linder will go along with the suggestions after having "revamped" them somewhat in order to give them the "Linder imprint." The expanded facility calls for, among other things, rediscount loans of more than one year (present limitation) and for reduced lending rates.

7.   *Export Expansion Fund*

The concept of an Export Expansion Fund was endorsed in principle at the Cabinet level meeting of the BoP Committee on October 23.[5] State[6] and AID still have certain misgivings about the proposal and a meeting is scheduled between Treasury, State, Commerce and CEA for November 7.

Our current proposal calls for a Special Account to be set up at the Eximbank for National Interest Export Financing which would not exceed 5% ($675 million) of the Exim's requested lending authority of $13.5 billion. The Exim could have special P & L and balance sheet statements covering this Special Account. Loan or guarantees to be made with funds from this Special Account would need certification by a committee. This would be chaired by the Secretary of Commerce and would include the Secretaries of Treasury and State and the Chairman of the Eximbank.[7]

---

[4] Chairman and President of the Export-Import Bank of Washington.

[5] No record of this meeting has been found.

[6] A handwritten note in the margin, with a line drawn to this word, reads: "Worried about impact on AID budget."

[7] A handwritten note in the left margin next to this paragraph reads: "Slice of new lending authority—Special Comm. revisits & recommends—Can't force Ex-Im."

This proposal has not yet been presented to Linder and probably will not be until after the November 9 meeting of the Cabinet Committee. He is likely to resist it, as he wished to have appropriated funds for the Export Expansion Fund in lieu of a "set aside" of his existing lending authority.[8]

8.   *Reexamination of GATT rules* concerning the treatment of direct and indirect taxes, subsidies, and countervailing duties.

This proposal emerges as an alternative to a strong tax incentive for exports. All agencies agree that reexamination is desirable, but tactics remain to be worked out.

9.   *Tightening Gold Budget Procedures*

No specific proposals have yet been made. Indeed, the Budget Bureau, which is responsible for the Gold Budget, was not aware that Treasury planned any initiatives in this area before the agenda for the October 31 Executive Committee meeting was distributed.

---

[8] A handwritten note at the end of this paragraph reads: "New legislation? Review with Committee for Congress. Could do administratively—but criteria question is difficult."

---

149.   Memorandum From the President's Special Assistant (Rostow) to President Johnson[1]

Washington, November 11, 1967.

SUBJECT

Balance of Payments Program Announcement

Attached is Secretary Fowler's memo recommending a schedule of announcements and actions regarding the balance of payments.

The main immediate issue is the *announcement of 1968 guidelines for the Commerce and Federal Reserve voluntary programs* restraining foreign direct investments and bank credits. These should be announced as soon as possible so as to affect planning for next year by corporations and banks. Fowler proposes to do so at a press conference he would hold on

---

[1] Source: Johnson Library, National Security File, Subject File, Balance of Payments, Vol. IV, January 1967 [2 of 2], Box 3. Confidential.

Friday, November 17, with Trowbridge and Governor Robertson of the Fed. At the same time he will release the third quarter balance of payments figures—which will not make good reading.[2] I believe you should also announce earlier the same day, as Fowler suggests, appointment of the new Travel Task Force[3] so that Fowler at his press conference can refer to it as another action designed to help our balance of payments.

Fowler also proposes for possible release by December 1 *a special report on the Balance of Payments*—what we have been doing, where we are, and where we propose to go in dealing with the balance of payments.[4] Your Cabinet Committee briefly discussed and supported the general idea.

I believe the third recommendation—to *defer a message recommending elimination of the gold cover*—makes sense at this time. But we will have to look at this one carefully over the next two months in conjunction with developments in dealing with current pressures on sterling and with unsettled conditions in the gold market.

The fourth recommendation asks you *to defer a balance of payments message now* and submit it early next session. The message would be built on a good export expansion package—which is now being developed.

I concur in the four recommendations in Secretary Fowler's cover memo.

W. W. Rostow[5]

Attachment

Memorandum From Secretary of the Treasury Fowler to President Johnson[6]

Washington, November 9, 1967.

SUBJECT

Balance of Payments Program Announcement

This memorandum deals with the proposed schedule for handling our 1968 balance of payments program announcements.

---

[2] These figures were related at a press conference on November 16. A transcript of the press conference is ibid., Fowler Papers, International Balance of Payments: 1968 B of P Questions and Answers [2 of 2], Box 6. A summary analysis of these figures is in *Current Economic Developments*, Issue No. 793, November 21, 1967, pp. 14–16. (Washington National Records Center, RG 59, E/CBA/REP Files: FRC 72 A 6248, *Current Economic Developments*)

[3] See Document 153.

[4] No record has been found that this special report was released.

[5] Printed from a copy that bears this typed signature.

[6] Confidential.

It involves somewhat of a revision of the plans discussed at the time of my August 8 memorandum to you.[7]

In the light of intervening developments and current circumstances, to be discussed, I would recommend now that:

(1) There be an announcement on Friday, November 17, of the Commerce Department guidelines for 1968 as well as the new Federal Reserve Board guidelines in a joint press conference in which Secretary Trowbridge, Governor Robertson and I would participate. At the same time I am planning to announce the third quarter balance of payments figures. This is a quarterly release and I only have a one or two day leeway on the date. On September 21 you met with Secretary Trowbridge, Mr. Field and me and approved the Commerce Department program for 1968.[8] I do not believe we will find it necessary to involve you in any meeting on the Federal Reserve Board voluntary program which we expect to iron out finally at a Cabinet Committee meeting on Thursday, November 9.[9]

If you wish, there could be a simultaneous release on the day of the press conference announcing the voluntary programs and the new Travel Task Force.

Approve with simultaneous announcement of Travel Task Force

Approve without simultaneous announcement of Travel Task Force

Approve

Disapprove[10]

(2) As Chairman of the Cabinet Committee on Balance of Payments, I submit on December 1 for public release a rather lengthy, detailed report:

(a) reciting in some detail all that we have been doing and are doing to deal with our balance of payments problem, and
(b) describing in some detail the background and elements of a long-range program on which the Cabinet Committee has been working which would serve as a backdrop for a later Presidential Balance of Payments Message featuring concrete proposals on an export expansion program early in January.

---

[7] Document 137.

[8] No record of this meeting has been found.

[9] No record of this meeting has been found. The agenda for the meeting is in a memorandum from Knowlton to the Cabinet Committee on the Balance of Payments, November 8. (Washington National Records Center, RG 40, Executive Secretariat Files: FRC 74 A 30, Balance of Payments Cabinet Committee)

[10] None of these options is checked.

Approve

Disapprove

Approve as modified[11]

(3) That you defer sending a Message at this time recommending the elimination of the gold cover requirement.

Approve

Disapprove

Approve as modified[11]

(4) That instead of submitting a Balance of Payments Message this fall toward the end of this session, you submit it as a separate Message very early in the next session.

Approve

Disapprove

Approve as modified[11]

For your information in considering these recommendations, I am submitting an attached background memorandum.

Henry H. Fowler

Attachment[12]

BACKGROUND MEMORANDUM

At the time of my August 8 memorandum to you and our meeting on August 10,[13] we considered tentatively the presentation of a 1968 and long-range balance of payments program in a mid-September Message to the Congress requesting removal of the gold cover or the separate submission of a Balance of Payments Message later in this fall.

Subsequent events have caused a change in that procedure. These include the delay and deferment of action on the tax bill which is a center-

---

[11] None of these options is checked.

[12] Confidential.

[13] No formal record of this meeting has been found, but see Documents 137, 138, and 139.

piece for any meaningful balance of payments program in 1968 or the future, the emergence of an increasingly serious threat to the pound and a highly unsettled and precarious condition in the gold market, and the inability of the Cabinet Committee machinery to arrive in timely fashion on agreed recommendations for a truly meaningful and significant expansion of our balance of payments program.

Another consideration which I will relate to you orally also prompted me to defer requesting you to send forward a Message on eliminating the gold cover. It also underscores the desirability of a public report along the lines recommended.

Given these developments it seems wise to change our planned procedure to the pattern outlined in the cover memorandum. These are some of the elements of the background for the recommendations in the memorandum to which this is attached:

(1) Need to make voluntary program announcement no later than middle of November.

It is necessary to release publicly the guidelines for the Commerce Department voluntary program and the Federal Reserve Board voluntary program so that the elements of the private sector affected may crank the guidance into their forward planning for next year. It is desirable to have the Commerce Department guidelines out so that Secretary Trowbridge and his colleagues can begin a series of individual conferences with companies which appear to be out of line. Originally these figures have come out in the first and second week of December and I think this has been late. In fact, November 17—which is the date recommended in the memorandum to which this is attached—is a little later than the date I was originally hoping for.

(2) Balance of payments outlook.

In the first half of 1967 we were running along at a seasonally adjusted annual rate of about a $2 billion deficit. The third quarter has deteriorated and the prospects for the fourth quarter are no better. While in 1965 and 1966 we had liquidity deficits of $1.3 and $1.4 billion, we could double that level this year or end up with a deficit of around $2.6 billion despite the benefit from a sizeable amount of "Special Transactions" we have been able to negotiate on a temporary basis. It may be even worse, depending upon developments with respect to sterling and the impact these developments have on our own position. (In this regard, we *may* have some option as to whether to take a few hundred million dollars adverse effect of British actions in the fourth quarter of 1967 or in 1968. While it is our general feeling that it might be better to take it this year—and we can attribute it to the British—our thinking has been influenced by what we see as poor balance of payments prospects for 1968 in the $3 billion range.)

These large deficits—a return to the unacceptable levels of 1964 and 1965—underscore as nothing else could underscore the necessity of providing clear and positive stimulants to our industry, that is *to those elements which produce the surplus* which the Government must have to be able to achieve our international objectives in terms of the defense umbrella we provide, as well as the investment and economic assistance we provide.

These deficits also emphasize the crucial necessity in achieving any long-term equilibrium of neutralizing the foreign exchange costs of our military expenditures in NATO and the Far East to provide financial viability for the long term maintenance of our presence in those areas.

(3)   IMF review.

The International Monetary Fund sits down with the Government once a year to go over in considerable detail our economic and balance of payments policies and positions. These sessions are scheduled for November 27–30 this year and starting on the 28th or 29th they will focus primarily on our balance of payments posture and program. I would like very much to have the background elements for our program in the public domain by that time even though the implementing Message to Congress on the export expansion program is not before the Congress.

(4)   The special need for a positive export expansion program at the next session.

It has been my position for some time that the whole thrust of our long-term U.S. balance of payments program must concentrate on accentuating the positive; that is, encouraging additional exports as well as receipts from direct investments abroad, increased foreign travel in the United States and increased foreign investment in the United States, while containing excessive balance of payments outflow of both the private sector and the government alike.

You underscored this in your May 23 statement.[14] At that time you asked Secretary Trowbridge and the Cabinet Committee on Balance of Payments to undertake a far-reaching export study. On June 28, I held a meeting of the Cabinet Committee on Balance of Payments at which there were reviewed and approved in the broadest terms the thrust and major areas of the 1968 program.[15] Since that time we have been developing this in detail.

In the meantime, with the Kennedy Round behind us and the prospect for five years of periodic tariff reduction and with the increasing pressure of protectionism on the home front which could thwart the

---

[14] See footnote 2, Document 123.
[15] See footnote 6, Document 137.

advance of the Kennedy Round, it seems very much in our interest to describe now and advance early in the session a *positive* export expansion program.

The program elements we have developed include:

—*Non-tax incentives,* administered by the Commerce Department, focusing upon small and medium sized corporations, designed to assist them in selling overseas.

—Tax measures, including both administrative and legislative features, which would make exporting much more attractive. *This is the keystone of our program*—it would serve to create jobs at home and be the incentive for additional efforts in exporting.

—Financing designed to make export financing more attractive to the private community. We have a couple of administrative measures we can take as well as ones requiring legislative action. The Export-Import Bank figures very prominently in this area and the full cooperation of Mr. Linder will be necessary to achieve these objectives.

—*The GATT.* It is time for a positive and outward looking re-examination of those provisions of the GATT which are *trade restrictive* in their nature. These provisions may be trade restrictive in the sense of (1) what a country can do when it is in balance of payments deficits, and they may be trade restrictive; (2) in the area of non-tariff barrier practices; as well as (3) the permissible subsidies which act preferentially for one tax system (EEC, Japan, United Kingdom) and discriminate against a country using another tax system (U. S.).

A review of this type is totally in keeping with the 20th anniversary of GATT and falls in perfect stride with the post-Kennedy Round situation. *This would provide another occasion to demonstrate to the world at large and to our protectionists at home that we will use trade expansive and not trade restrictive measures and the rules of the game must be brought up to date to assure this.*

150.   Memorandum From Secretary of the Treasury Fowler to
        President Johnson[1]

Washington, November 12, 1967.

SUBJECT

Sterling Crisis

British Chancellor of the Exchequer Callaghan sent one of his principal aides, Sir Denis Rickett, along with a top official of the Bank of England, to see me yesterday on sterling.

*The message was that they were at the end of the line, unless they have
assurance of substantial long-term credit soon. They may be forced to devalue—
perhaps within a week.*

The British, as you well know, have come in for help before, but *they
have never previously indicated so clearly that, without help, they will be forced
to take the plunge.*

The austerity program imposed by the British last year brought sterling out of its summer crisis and very considerable gains were made in
restoring British reserves and repaying short-term credits. This favorable picture prevailed through the fourth quarter of last year and into
April of 1967. The British predicted a sizable balance of payments surplus for the year.

A sharp reversal took place in May, following poor April trade figures, accentuated by the Mid-East crisis. The British reserves suffered
from some movement of Mid-East funds, accompanied by other speculative flight from sterling and, more fundamentally, due to closure of the
Suez Canal and related aspects of the Mid-East crisis. In addition, the
hoped-for resurgence in U. K. exports did not take place, due, in large
part, to the stagnation in Germany and slow-downs elsewhere, including the U. S., in the early part of the year. Finally, interest arbitrage relationships were turned against the British, as interest rates in the United
States rose.

The fact is that they are now scraping the bottom of the barrel. They have
already used $2 billion in short-term credits, which mortgages nearly all
their total reserves. They have left only $600 to $800 million in short-term
credits, which could go in the attempt to defend the rate over the next few
weeks. The market could go heavily against them next week, when they
announce some very bad trade figures for October. Everyone expects
these figures to be bad because of the dock strike, but, even so, the impact
of the actual numbers is likely to be adverse.

---

[1] Source: Johnson Library, National Security File, NSC History, Gold Crisis, Nov.
'67–Mar. '68, Box 54. Secret.

If they have to conclude that devaluation is inevitable, they would rather act now, while they still have some cash and credit left to defend a new parity rate.

It might seem tempting to settle this perennial problem now and let sterling go. The arguments for this policy are:

—*If* the devaluation were modest (10–15 percent).

—*If* everybody cooperated (the Common Market, Japan, Canada, and Australia held—and few devalued).

—*If* Wilson were able to hold his foreign commitments—Germany and East of Suez.

—*If*, and this is the big if, Wilson can maintain his Government and the movement were not wasted because of internal British pressures.

Then it might be desirable to relieve sterling's long agony and try to get the U. K. economy on a more solid basis.

But the risks for us are just too great to take this gamble if we can find another alternative.

—While we believe the Common Market would hold, there is some evidence that France would try to follow the U. K.—in an effort to attack the dollar and try to force a gold price increase. Japan, Australia, and Canada probably could be held, although Japan, itself, would face great pressures.

But even if all this worked out:

—the dollar would come under attack;
—the gold market would come under very great pressure—and might explode;
—the world might not believe a "modest" devaluation would be adequate and pressure on sterling could continue.

The British would prefer to hold the rate, for political and economic reasons. To do so, they tell us they need a $3 billion package of long-term help. I believe they hoped for a multi-governmental loan at long-term, but we told them that such an approach was not feasible—at least now, with all governments having budget problems. Their other proposal was for a multi-governmental (U.S., Italy, Germany) agreement to hold guaranteed sterling. This avoids any fixed date of maturity. It would have no balance of payments or budgetary effect. They said that they had some favorable response from Germany on this proposal.

We suggest a package as follows:

—$1.4 billion IMF credit, which technically they can get by drawing their full line;
—$1 billion guaranteed sterling, *if Germany and Italy would take half;*
—perhaps some private bank credits.

Central bank governors met at Basle this weekend—their regular monthly meeting—and came up with a different approach. They believe it would be the best course to have the IMF give the U. K. a $3 billion standby commitment and announce it. This would do two things:

—announce to the world that the IMF thought the present parity was right;
—provide—on a standby basis—a lot of money to underwrite the present parity.

These are the negative factors:

—The U. K. would be drawing a lot more than its regular credit line. This can be done technically but may cause some problems. Neither Schweitzer nor the U. K. seem to favor this approach.

—This would require use of almost all GAB resources and would make it difficult for the U. S. to make a big IMF drawing if we need to.

—The operational and procedural matters will require five to six weeks to clear up before a firm announcement can be made.

Even with an IMF standby, there may be a short-term cash problem for the U.K., since the IMF package cannot be used until it is finally approved near the end of the year. It may be necessary for the U. K. to get some additional short-term credit soon, which could be liquidated when the IMF was drawn on. Should that need develop, I believe we should participate. This would involve no direct balance of payments or budget costs.

It is important to understand that even the IMF standby might not hold sterling. Our judgment is that it would give them a real chance for getting through the next two months, which are crucial for them, and gives some hope that they could hold on through 1968. *We believe this is an important factor.* And there is at least some prospect that, if they get through 1968, either they could hold longer or take the plunge under better circumstances.

If your schedule is manageable, I would like to go over this problem with you on Monday.[2] We need to get your reactions to possible approaches. The Federal Reserve Open Market Committee meets on Tuesday and would want to consider the guaranteed sterling question then. The situation is developing rapidly. Fred Deming will be talking to Rickett by phone at noon to get the current U. K. feeling. Schweitzer is coming to lunch with me and Bill Martin today.

It would be useful to have Bill Martin (or Dewey Daane), Gene Rostow, Deming, Okun, Fried, and Walt there.

Henry H. Fowler

---

[2] November 13.

151. Memorandum From the President's Special Assistant (Rostow) to President Johnson[1]

Washington, November 13, 1967.

SUBJECT

Sterling Crisis

I note you are seeing Joe Fowler at noon today.[2] He may have to give you some background on the sterling crisis on which we may need a decision from you later in the day. We do not yet have all the information to put the issues properly before you.

The British came in Saturday to tell Fowler they were near the end of the line. Without assurance of long-term credit they may have to devalue—perhaps within a week. Their line of short-term credit is down to $600 to $800 million. The announcement of poor trade figures on Tuesday could keep the pound under pressure.

I won't go into the pros and cons of letting the pound go. The main point is the risks for us are just too great to be worth the gamble—if it can be avoided through a good multilateral support operation. The European Central Bankers seem to be of the same mind.

It may be possible therefore to work out a support package through a large IMF stand-by credit, through a package of bilateral credits and swaps, or through a combination of both. There would be no budgetary or direct balance-of-payments costs for us in any action we might consider, and it would have to be multilateral or not at all.

It is our feeling, and it seems to be that of the Europeans, that this would be the last try at supporting sterling. But it would be well worth it, if it can be pulled off.

W. W. Rostow[3]

---

[1] Source: Johnson Library, National Security File, NSC History, Gold Crises, Nov. '67–Mar. '68, Box 54. Secret. Drafted by Edward R. Fried.

[2] The President met with Fowler to discuss balance-of-payment issues from 1:05 to 2:10 p.m. (Ibid., President's Daily Diary)

[3] Printed from a copy that bears this typed signature.

152.   Memorandum From the President's Special Assistant (Rostow) to President Johnson[1]

Washington, November 16, 1967.

Mr. President:

Fred Deming continues to report encouraging news from Paris on the sterling support operation.[2] There is a general consensus on the need for an impressive package. The impression one gets is that the central bankers went to the brink and didn't like what they saw.

The Group of Ten countries seem to be on board in support of a UK $1.4 billion IMF drawing or standby. We are looking into the possibilities of making it $2 billion.

Deming's German and Italian counterparts are optimistic about their governments going along with us on a multilateral support operation. We should know soon whether it is nailed down. We do not yet know terms and amounts or what other countries are going to do.

If both parts work out right, the package should be between $2.4 and $3 billion—and possibly more.

Deming also sounded out each of the Group of Ten countries on holding their rates should sterling be de-valued. It now looks as if they all would stand firm. The French representative said they would hold "until they were hurt".

The markets earlier this week were nervous and uncertain. But even with the announcement of the poor trade figures on Tuesday, the UK did not suffer serious exchange losses from support operations. The rumors of an additional support operation that broke in today's press strengthened the rate.

Walt

---

[1] Source: Johnson Library, National Security File, Subject File, Balance of Payments, Vol. IV, January 1967 [2 of 2], Box 3. Secret; Sensitive. A handwritten note on the source text reads: "Rec'd 11:45 a."

[2] For a British official's account of the sterling crisis, including reports of some of Deming's activities, see Alec Cairncross, *The Wilson Years*, pp. 243–249.

153.   Editorial Note

On November 16, 1967, the White House Press Office issued a statement by President Johnson, indicating his appointment of an Industry–Government Special Travel Task Force to recommend how the U.S. Government could best increase foreign travel to the United States and thus improve the nation's balance of payments. This statement also announced the President's appointment of Robert M. McKinney as working chairman of the new Task Force. McKinney had previously been Ambassador to Switzerland and had served on an earlier Balance of Payments Task Force.

Other members of the Task Force included leaders in the fields of travel, transportation, public relations, entertainment, publishing, and hotels. Government representatives on it were Anthony M. Solomon, Winthrop Knowlton, John W. Black, Donald G. Agger (Assistant Secretary for International Affairs, Department of Transportation), Andrew F. Brimmer (member of the Board of Governors of the Federal Reserve System), Charles S. Murphy (Chairman of the Civil Aeronautics Board), and Harry M. Shooshan (Deputy Under Secretary for Programs, Department of the Interior).

The statement also indicated that the Special Travel Task Force, which was to report to the President "no later than the early part of next summer," would supplement the already existing Cabinet Task Force on Travel, chaired by Vice President Humphrey.

In addition to preparing a program to meet the nation's balance-of-payment goals, the new Task Force was directed to "build into its program ways and means that will insure that more and more foreign visitors truly learn to know our country and our people," the results of which would "inevitably and beneficially broaden the areas of mutual understanding between the peoples of the world." The President also hoped the Task Force would recall his remarks of August 11, 1965, in which he encouraged Americans and foreigners alike to "travel to see more of the wonders and beauties of this vast and marvelous land of ours." (White House press release, November 16, 1967; Washington National Records Center, RG 40, Department of Commerce Files: FRC 74 A 20, U.S. Travel Service, 1967–1968)

Text of the President's remarks to the See U.S.A. Committee on August 11, 1965, is in *Public Papers of the Presidents of the United States: Lyndon B. Johnson, 1965,* pages 872–874.

President Johnson had earlier announced his intention to appoint such a Task Force in his Economic Message on January 26, 1967; see Document 114.

In a November 16 memorandum to Secretary of Commerce Trowbridge, attached to the White House press release, John W. Black noted that the White House made "several alterations in the last list of names which we saw on September 25" (the September 25 list has not been found), and he listed those approved, added, and dropped from the September 25 list. He also added some personal comments on the composition of the Task Force.

154.   Notes of Meeting[1]

Washington, November 18, 1967, 4:30 p.m.

NOTES ON THE PRESIDENT'S MEETING WITH THE LEADERSHIP

SUBJECT

Sterling Devaluation and the Need for Tax Increase—November 18, 4:30 to 7:00 P.M.

PRESENT

The President
Secretary Fowler
Chairman Martin
Under Secretary Barr
Under Secretary Deming
Budget Director Schultze
Walt Rostow
Joe Califano
Ernest Goldstein
Art Okun
Ed Fried

Senator Mansfield
Senator Long
Senator Anderson

Speaker McCormack
Representative Boggs
Representative Ullman

Secretary Fowler—Discussed actions to be taken in defense of the dollar during present crisis.[2]

—*The President's statement*—designed to remove any uncertainty regarding U.S. intention to stand firm.[3]

---

[1] Source: Johnson Library, National Security File, Fried Files, Chron, September 1, 1967–November 30, 1967 [1 of 2], Box 2. Confidential. Drafted by Fried on November 19 for Rostow.

[2] Callaghan announced the British devaluation of sterling on November 18; for text of his statement, see *American Foreign Policy: Current Documents, 1967*, pp. 194–195.

[3] For text of the President's November 18 statement, see *Public Papers of the Presidents of the United States: Lyndon B. Johnson, 1967*, pp. 1057–1058.

—*Financial diplomacy*—getting all other major countries to hold their rates with us and prevent a chain reaction.

—*Building confidence in the dollar* through demonstrating fiscal responsibility and other constructive measures to improve the balance-of-payments position. Read concluding portion of statement he made at November 16 press conference announcing programs to strengthen U.S. balance of payments.[4] Stressed that enactment of President's tax increase program at this Session of the Congress was the single most important and indispensable step the nation can take now to protect the dollar, safeguard the international monetary system, and stop the interest rate escalation that threatened our domestic and international position. The devaluation of the pound now brought the requirements for fiscal action and the tax increase into even sharper and more critical focus.

Chairman Martin—Stressed the great uncertainty that currently plagues the securities market and the cost it is exacting in higher interest rates. He cited recent examples: a Nova Scotia bond that required a 7-1/4% yield; postponement of the U.S. steel issue when financing was not obtainable at 6-3/8%; a Treasury 5-3/4% that sold below par.

Essential to stop and reverse the trend of accelerating deficits or inflation would get out of hand. Sterling devaluation complicated the situation and made it all the more important to restore a position of confidence—which required evidence of fiscal responsibility.

Under Secretary Deming—(The President said Deming had been sent to meetings in Paris during the week in an effort to mobilize a multilateral support operation to save the pound.)

Deming noted two points:

1. Situation in London was black; nobody wanted to see the pound go, but in the end they could not see any feasible alternative.

2. U.S. last year, in its financing operations, paid back $11 billion to the market in the second half of the year. This year, we would only be able to put back 2-1/2 billion—*even with a tax increase*. This tremendous swing from last year would greatly tighten credit conditions.

Under Secretary Barr—In the credit crunch, the big fellows would manage to meet their requirements but the smaller borrowers, the institutions, and housing will get squeezed and suffer.

Director Schultze—Discussed possible expenditure reductions totalling $4 billion:

—$1-3/4 billion Congress had already made or would make in the 14 appropriation bills (of which 12 already completed);
—$2-1/4 billion Administration could make in withholding expenditures if Congress prepared to stand the pressure.

---

[4] See footnote 2, Document 149.

The President—Prepared to cut actual expenditures by one dollar for each dollar of tax increase. Secretary Fowler had been ready to offer 4 different proposals to achieve this end to the Ways and Means Committee, but the Committee acted without giving him the opportunity to put these proposals before it.

We will rue the day if we fail to face up to these critical responsibilities. If we don't act now it will not be possible to undo the harm that will result. Every day's delay is costly.

He had had nine discussions with Chairman Mills.

He was trying to convince those members of the leadership he could—but the President cannot act for the Congress. He was prepared to accommodate his views to theirs and to this end advance proposals for a cut of $4 billion in expenditures.

Secretary Fowler—Senator Williams had written him a letter on November 7, which he has not yet answered.[5] The letter is essentially a campaign document designed to hurt the Democrats if it were answered under present circumstances. (Fowler read letter which made two central points.)

1. A tax increase bill has not been introduced in either House.

2. Uncertainty is causing financial disruption with serious consequences for the economy and our international position.

Senator Mansfield—Williams' argument is spurious. There is no indecision on the part of the Administration—it had constantly advanced its tax increase proposals.

Rep. Boggs—Normal to work from proposals. Was willing, ready, able and happy to introduce bill.

Speaker McCormack—Need for tax increase. In his view President not asking for big enough tax increase.

Secretary Fowler—Read his *proposed* answer to Senator Williams with stress on concluding portion outlining Administration's new proposal to break deadlock between spending and tax powers of the Congress.

Package would:

—reduce administrative budget deficit by $11 billion in Fiscal '68, and relieve credit market to this extent;
—increase income taxes of individuals by $3.9 billion;
—reduce actual expenditures (counting actions taken by Congress on appropriation bills) by about $4 billion;
—increase corporate tax receipts by $3.1 billion ($2.3 billion surtax—$.8 tax collection speedup).

Extending excise taxes could add $.3 billion.

---

[5] This letter has not been found.

Stressed again that expert opinion overwhelmingly supported need for tax increase. Same with major organizations—the Chamber of Commerce has now come around in support.

The President—He had reviewed the answer to Williams and the new proposal yesterday with Mills in light of the pending sterling devaluation and its serious potential consequences. He told Mills he wanted to review it with other members of the leadership. (He noted other members who had been invited to today's meeting, but were not available.) Mills had been unable to stay in Washington over the weekend.

The President summarized the situation. He said the President cannot impose reductions on the Congress. He is prepared to act and to share responsibility with the Congress if the Congress is prepared to accept its share. He does not want to cut expenditures, but each day of inaction brings increased costs and makes the situation worse. It will lead to some slippage in revenues and to automatic increases in expenditures (higher interest costs, more farm loans, etc.).

The Mills–Ford line is hard to break. Of course the public does not favor tax increases. Nobody likes them. But the leadership must accept its responsibilities or face far more serious difficulties. If reductions in appropriations are not adequate and there is no tax increase, then it will be necessary to impound expenditures—notably for highways, public works and other areas where the Congress will immediately feel repercussions. (He noted highway expenditures now were a billion dollars over any previous figure and were feeding inflation.)

But do we start or not? The President doesn't want to make the decision alone. Last year the leadership accepted the responsibility of impounding expenditures. If we have to make reductions they will be drastic and they will have to be made soon. This should be done with the full knowledge and approval of the leadership.

If we don't act soon, we will wreck the Republic. The President can't spend what the Congress does not appropriate. The Congress has now acted on appropriations, and now the President must act. He then reiterated the need for the proposed package of expenditure reductions and tax increases.

Rep. Ullman—Said he favors a tax increase, but a tax increase could not solve the situation alone. When Schultze testified before the Ways and Means there were ambiguities in expenditure reduction proposals.

The President—Cited instances where he had made clear the Administration was prepared to match tax increases and expenditure reductions dollar for dollar. He referred again to the Committee's unwillingness to hear Fowler's four alternative proposals to achieve this objective. He set the record straight on Schultze's testimony.

Rep. Ullman—Sterling devaluation made this a new ball game. There is no point in recriminations. Said he believed there would be widespread repercussions on Monday[6] throughout the economy. Repeated that he did not believe expenditure reductions had been adequately spelled out. But we should now try the new formula.

Secretary Fowler—Reviewed formula again, together with proposal for President to set up special group to go over programs and prospective expenditure cuts.

The President—Pointed to need for clearance from Government Operations Committee on $4 billion expenditure reductions.

Rep. Ullman—Important to try to put package together in next few days—before Thanksgiving. The sterling crisis should be a vehicle for getting it done.

The President—Asked for the views of the leadership on the proposal and on any alternatives they had to deal with the situation.

Senator Long—Asked Rep. Ullman whether the Committee would report favorably on the tax bill without Mills' support. Answer—probably not. Senator Long then said that Senator Talmadge doubted that the bill could be passed either in the House or the Senate. Said it would be even more difficult in the House, because the members had to run next year.

The President—Said any action taken would be unpopular but it would have to be done.

Rep. Ullman—The situation would be worse if we don't pass the tax bill. Unable to know the outcome beforehand.

Secretary Fowler—Said it is essential to report out the bill and put it in the glare of domestic and international publicity. Then vote it up or down so everyone would know where each stood.

Rep. Ullman—Said he would give every support he could.

The Speaker—Made following points:

1. No tax bill is popular.

2. We are faced with desperate situation and the Congress is on trial.

3. He had personally taken public position in favor of tax bill.

4. It should be possible to get bipartisan support and to begin through action by Mills and Mahon.

Senator Long—Reserved judgment on his own position but suggested following procedure to break impasse:

1. Sit down with as few people as possible.

2. Heart-to-heart talk between the President and Mills.

3. If the House sent the tax bill over, the Senate would take a look but he was not in favor of the expenditure reductions part of the package.

---

[6] November 20.

The President—Said this was not facing facts and pointed again to the consequences of sterling devaluation.

Senator Long—Repeated that it was important to get together with Mills, but said Mills could not lay down conditions on which he can't deliver.

Director Schultze—Pointed out that the tax increase bill provided for $7 billion during the remainder of this fiscal year, and $12 billion over the next fiscal year. It was essential to keep the latter in mind.

The President—Pointed out that the Defense budget for Fiscal '69 that had now been received came to $98 billion. If Congress did not act on a tax increase, then it would be necessary to start thinking not about a $4 billion expenditure cut, but about cuts of many billions of dollars.

Rep. Boggs—He had given thoughtful consideration to the possibilities of the bill. He pointed out that the Poverty Program had come out much better than anyone had guessed three weeks ago. His judgment is that if the Chairman supports the bill, it would be passed in the House.

Rep. Ullman—It was necessary to talk to Mills not only about the situation this year, but next year as well, and the consequences of a $98 billion Defense budget. Also said that Ways and Means cannot originate action on the bill where other Committees have jurisdiction. It's different when the President proposes the bill, and next year's situation is clearly critical. In his view, if the bill gets to the Floor, it will have bipartisan support, but Mills' approval is essential. Mills is critical of a tax increase and his speech on Monday is in that vein but the speech does not close the door on action on a tax bill.

The President—Asked when can we get the Committee to act.

Rep. Mahon—The House voted by continuing resolution to cut expenditures by $7 billion which was equivalent to a cut of $14 billion in appropriations. In his view, expenditure cuts were worse than a tax increase.

The way to get a tax increase was for the President to stick his neck out and cut expenditures by $4 billion—even without a tax bill. The cuts should include programs which he considers among his best programs, e.g., Federal Aid to Education.

Mahon would then try to get his Committee to endorse those specific cuts.

He recognized the risk—that the President would make cuts on his own and then end up without a tax bill.

Secretary Fowler—Reviewed the formula proposal for making cuts under which responsibility would in fact be shared. (Use of either of the following, whichever is lower: (a) a cut of 2% in personnel and 10% in program; or (b) the difference between the original appropriation request for each program and what Congress appropriated.)

The President—Stressed the need to work from the package proposal: the tax bill, the expenditure cuts (with the formula) and a review group. The need was to get the Committee to move now.

The consensus that emerged was to organize a meeting with the President Tuesday morning—which was the earliest it would be possible to get Chairman Mills back to Washington. Speaker McCormack and Secretary Fowler would try to get in touch with Mills. Others at the meeting might include the Speaker, Representative Mahon, Senator Mansfield and Senator Long.[7]

W.W. Rostow[8]

---

[7] No record of such a meeting has been found for November 21, but a meeting among the President, several of his senior advisers, and the bipartisan leadership of Congress (nine Senators and seven Representatives) was held on November 20. Senator Long and Representative Mills did not attend. (Notes on the President's Meeting with the Bipartisan Leadership, November 20, Johnson Library, National Security File, Fried Files, Chron, September 1, 1967–November 30, 1967 [1 of 2], Box 2)

[8] Printed from a copy that bears this typed signature.

---

155.   Telegram From the President's Special Assistant (Rostow) to President Johnson in Texas[1]

Washington, November 22, 1967, 1944Z.

CAP 67967. To the President from Walt Rostow. The gold market continues to be nervous as an aftermath of sterling devaluation. Rumors are circulating that the price of gold will not be held on the London market. These rumors have been fed by leaks out of Paris on the operation of the gold pool and French withdrawal from the pool (which actually took place in June).

We expected substantial gold losses after the devaluation. The gold pool lost $28 million Monday, $45 million Tuesday, and $104 million today. (We supply 60 percent, our European partners the other 40 percent.) Rumors were responsible for the sudden rise.

---

[1] Source: Johnson Library, National Security File, Subject File, Balance of Payments, Vol. V [2 of 2], Box 3. Secret. The telegram was received at the LBJ Ranch in Texas at 2:10 p.m. on November 22.

Bill Martin is going to call the other Governors of the Central Banks who are partners with us in the gold pool (Germany, Italy, the Netherlands, Belgium, U.K., and Switzerland), to support us in a statement today affirming business as usual.[2] If they won't, Bill Martin would issue a statement that U.S. intends to continue to support the market[3] and referring again to your statement of Saturday that the U.S. will buy and sell gold at $35 an ounce.[4]

We expect further heavy losses this week. An unequivocal statement of our position should calm things down. We will keep you advised.

---

[2] No such U.S. statement has been found.

[3] On November 30, the Federal Reserve System announced that it had increased its credit "swap" lines with foreign central banks by $1.75 billion to a total of $6.8 billion.

[4] See footnote 3, Document 154.

---

156.   Memorandum From the President's Special Assistant (Rostow) to President Johnson[1]

Washington, November 26, 1967.

Attached is a copy of the communiqué on the Frankfurt meeting on gold.[2] It has been released in Europe in time to be out before the opening of the London gold market.

It means in effect the adoption of our preferred alternative 1.[3] The London market will open with a strong multilateral commitment of support for the $35 price.

Although there is no indication of this in the statement, our partners wish to review the situation with us in a week if there is serious trouble.

---

[1] Source: Johnson Library, National Security File, Subject File, Balance of Payments, Vol. V [2 of 2], Box 3. Secret.

[2] Not printed; text is printed in *Annual Report of the Secretary of the Treasury on the State of the Finances for the Fiscal Year Ended June 30, 1968*, p. 349. Fowler sent 10 U.S. officials, including Deming, Okun, and Alfred Hayes, President of the New York Federal Reserve Board, to the Frankfurt meeting, which had been called to deal with the growing gold problem. (Telegram CAP 67999 from Rostow to Jim Jones, November 24; Johnson Library, National Security File, Subject File, Balance of Payments, Vol. V [2 of 2], Box 3)

[3] Not further identified.

In addition they are taking whatever steps they can, with the Swiss in the lead, to tighten up on credit available for gold speculation.

They will also operate with us in forward exchange markets to help protect the dollar against any speculative attacks.

The statement closes with an implied invitation to the French to join the party.

We are letting the statement speak for itself with no backgrounding.

Ed Fried[4]

---

[4] Fried signed for Rostow above Rostow's typed signature.

---

157.   Memorandum From Secretary of Commerce Trowbridge to Secretary of the Treasury Fowler[1]

Washington, December 15, 1967.

SUBJECT

Progress Report on Administration of the Voluntary Program

In the month since our joint press conference[2] and the announcement of the 1968 voluntary program, the following administrative steps have been taken or are currently being taken by the Department of Commerce:

1.   Personal letters outlining the program and restating its objectives have been sent to the Chief Executive Officers of nearly 750 companies. Each letter emphasized the seriousness of the balance of payments situation and the extreme importance we attach to their sustained cooperation with the voluntary program. Companies were again urged to look into the possibility of greater reliance on foreign borrowings. Further, mention was made of our intention to invite executives from selected companies to meet with us during the weeks immediately ahead to discuss their participation in the program and how this might be improved. Although these letters did not expressly call for any

---

[1] Source: Washington National Records Center, RG 40, Executive Secretariat Files: FRC 74 A 30, Treasury. Official Use Only.

[2] Reference presumably is to the press conference held by Fowler and Trowbridge on November 16 at which the balance-of-payments figures for the third quarter were also released; see footnote 2, Document 149.

acknowledgment, I have had a large and extremely encouraging response, which is still continuing. Virtually all of these assure me of their personal concern about the balance of payments and of their full support. Many have in addition specifically indicated that they were instructing their staffs to review corporate plans with a new urgency and have offered to discuss them with us.

2. As a second step, letters were sent during the latter part of November to the Chief Executive Officers of nineteen companies selected on the basis of several criteria—over-target, little if any foreign borrowing by parent or financing subsidiary, declining overall contributions, etc.—inviting them to meet with me on a specified date to discuss their position under the voluntary program.[3] Thus far in December, I have met with Sterling Drug Company, The Singer Company, W. R. Grace and Company, Control Data Corporation, and Amphenol Corporation. Yet to see this month are: American Smelting and Refining Company, Owens-Corning Fiberglas Corporation, Libbey-Owens-Ford Glass Company, Kellogg Company, Clevite Corporation, Xerox Corporation, Hewlett-Packard Company, and Sunray DX Oil Company. Occidental Petroleum Corporation, which has had extremely large outflows, was slated to come in today, but we have just received a wire indicating they could not appear. This will be rescheduled. In January, we are planning to meet with 18 or 20 companies in addition to five carried over from December (J. Ray McDermott, Polaroid, Ampex, Fairchild Camera and Instrument, and Barton Distilling). During December we also met with executives from General Mills at their own request, and will be doing the same with IBM in late January.

For our part, we have stressed the usual considerations, underscored the latest information we have on the current outlook for the balance of payments, pointed up any short-falls in their own performance, and at the same time thanked them for what they had done. While the company representatives in turn have cited various special circumstances to justify their actions, they have also shown themselves receptive to our suggestions on foreign borrowing, accelerated return of earnings, etc. The most encouraging aspect is that the majority have indicated before any urging from us that they were looking into ways whereby the impact of their investment transactions might be curbed, and were in the midst of negotiations.

For example, Control Data has negotiations underway to borrow in Europe between $15 million and $20 million. Singer is shifting the entire trading and financial arrangements of its British company and borrow-

---

[3] A schedule of meetings with company executives in December 1968, dated November 30, 1967, is attached to a note from Trowbridge to Fowler, December 1, 1967. (Johnson Library, Fowler Papers, International Balance of Payments: White Paper [5 of 7], Box 1)

ing in the London market between $8 million and $12 million which will improve its 1967 performance more than had been estimated at mid-year; Amphenol reported that it would have no major new investments in 1968 and had borrowing negotiations underway in England, Belgium, and Germany, involving a few million dollars. We have also been told by General Mills that they are willing to pay additional interest costs in order to support the government's objectives and will endeavor to finance long-term outside the United States.

Sterling devaluation apparently has caused some confusion and uncertainty, but no one has indicated they would not continue with their borrowing plans. Following each meeting I have written to the company summarizing the points made and again urging the utmost effort. We feel that these meetings have been most worthwhile and will pay off in subsequent decisions by the companies.

3. The Quarterly Worksheets covering the third quarter of 1967 have been coming in, and we now plan to issue a summary statement showing the results for release on Tuesday morning.[4] I am enclosing an advance draft copy[5] in which you will see that the data confirm our earlier expectations that overall contributions would exceed the original projections and that capital outflows would be less than last year. I have taken advantage of the release to include a reference to our meetings and to press for more intensive effort.

4. As a means of indicating the extreme importance of these matters and to answer certain criticisms, I have arranged to send with a brief transmittal note a copy of the President's latest address before the Business Council[6] to the Chief Executive Officers of all reporting firms.

5. Finally, while retaining February 15 as the filing date for the 1968 projections, Assistant Secretary Shaw in his memorandum which accompanies the new worksheets will be asking that all firms endeavor to return these forms to us by *not later* than February 15 and by February 1, if at all possible. By this method, we hope to identify earlier in the year firms whose projected performance falls short of what it should be and to invite them to discuss it with us.

By these means and others that may evolve we hope that the administration of the corporate voluntary program will contribute to additional improvement.

A.B. Trowbridge[7]

---

[4] December 19. The summary statement has not been found.

[5] Not found.

[6] For text of this December 6 speech, see *Public Papers of the Presidents of the United States: Lyndon B. Johnson, 1967*, Book II, pp. 1102–1104.

[7] Printed from a copy that bears this stamped signature.

158. Memorandum From the President's Special Assistant (Rostow) to President Johnson[1]

Washington, December 15, 1967, 4:20 p.m.

SUBJECT

Gold

The gold loss today ended up at $116 million—heavy, but much less than we feared.

Sterling was also under pressure. The UK put $100 million in the market to support the rate. Curiously enough, the franc had some small difficulties, apparently because of rumors.

Attached is the answer Bill Martin received from his approach to our gold pool partners. They have agreed to go along with us but expect us to bail them out of some of their gold losses. Each would make his own pitch to us if he finds it necessary. The UK is replying separately. Bill did a really impressive job.

We are working on a brief statement to clear with the Europeans and release tomorrow.[2] It should put a stop to the rumors and quiet things down a bit.

Walt

P.S. See also attached Fowler memo.[3] Good deed by Canadians.

W[4]

Attachment[5]

Washington, December 15, 1967.

Governor Hubert Ansiaux of Belgium phoned and talked to Mr. Martin at 10 a.m. He was calling from Paris, where Mr. Martin had reached him the evening of Thursday, December 14.

---

[1] Source: Johnson Library, National Security File, Subject File, Balance of Payments, Vol. IV, January 1967 [2 of 2], Box 3. Secret; Sensitive. The time is taken from another copy of the memorandum, which bears the typewritten initials "ERF" at the bottom left, indicating that Fried probably drafted it for Rostow's signature. (Ibid., NSC History, Gold Crises, Nov. '67–Mar. '68, Box 54) A handwritten note on the source text reads: "Rec'd 6:16 p."

[2] See Document 159.

[3] Fowler's December 15 memorandum to the President and a note from Fowler to the President, both attached, are not printed. The memorandum reported that Canadian Finance Minister Mitchell Sharp had called Fowler that afternoon to say that the Canadians were prepared to transfer $100 million in gold to the United States. The note added that Sharp "is in serious contention for the Prime Ministership of Canada."

[4] The postscript is handwritten.

[5] Secret; Sensitive.

In reply to the phone call of last night, Governor Ansiaux said:

1. I am speaking for myself, the Germans, the Italians, the Dutch, and the Swiss. These are our unanimous views.

2. Of course we are always ready to support you because we believe in the fundamentals of the policy of gold at $35 an ounce.

3. We wonder if you will find it possible to make your balance of payments program known as soon as possible—before the 10 days you mentioned—even if it is in very general terms.

4. We approve and strongly support your going to the IMF. Apart from the measures it shows the U.S. is ready to solve the problem.

5. We very much hope that the program will be really very fundamental and substantial; not just a stop-gap measure; something really affecting the root of the matter.

6. We wonder if it would not be better to close the London market for awhile until your program is known as it is open to speculators and is completely disorganized. The French cannot even deliver gold. However, we understand you may prefer to keep it open but this is up to the United States to decide; it represents not a condition but a reflection.

7. Having this in mind, we were strongly of the opinion until yesterday night, when you got in touch with all of us, to recommend that we should stop our intervention in the London market. But taking into account your request, the fact you have a program, the fact that public reaction to withdrawal from the London market would be bad, we are ready to stay in the market. You may say this is a common policy not only of the Fed and the U.S. Treasury but of all the European central banks concerned.

8. This does not mean that we will not ask for reimbursement in gold of any excessive accumulation of dollars which may be the result of our intervention. We will stay in the pool but on the other hand we cannot face a large depletion of our gold reserves. All of us agree on this in principle but it would be left for each central bank to work it out with the Federal Reserve.

9. We recommend that you issue a communiqué over the weekend indicating, if possible, the U.S. intentions on the balance of payments program, reaffirming our intent to maintain the $35 price of gold, and reaffirming no change in operations in the London gold market, and pointing out this is not only an American position but represents the unanimous views of the European central bankers, all of whom endorse

this position and are cooperating in the interest of maintaining stability in the international monetary system.[6]

---

[6] On December 18, Senator Mansfield telephoned President Johnson, and the two engaged in a wide-ranging conversation on foreign policy matters. Concerning the gold crisis, President Johnson complained of the desire of the French and Soviets "and all of our enemies" to get U.S. gold and bring the dollar down, and added that the U.S. Government was helping them by not having a tax bill and leaving the impression "with all the bankers and all the money people" that it was irresponsible and could not be believed. Mansfield interjected: "How can they blame you? It's Wilbur's fault." The President continued that there probably would be a tax bill now that Wilbur Mills was coming to recognize that "he's wrecking the damn world;" but gold reserves were down and there was danger that the dollar would be "busted like the pound was busted." More positively, he remarked that "the Germans will stay with us" as well as the British and Swiss. He said a bill to remove the gold cover was needed, although "everyone" hoped it could be put off until after the election. (Johnson Library, Recordings and Transcripts, Recording of Telephone Conversation between President Johnson and Senator Mansfield, December 18, 1967, 8:55 a.m., Tape F67.15, Side A, PNO 3)

---

159. Circular Telegram From the Department of State to All Posts[1]

Washington, December 16, 1967, 2220Z.

85849. Following statement issued December 16 by Secretary Fowler of the Treasury and William McChesney Martin, Chairman of Federal Reserve Board. "The United States stands firm in its determination to maintain the gold value of the dollar. The central banks of Belgium, Germany, Italy, the Netherlands, Switzerland, and the United Kingdom support this position and continue to participate fully with the United States in policies and practices in support of the price of gold at $35 an ounce. The operation of the London gold market will continue unchanged. The United States authorities and the European central banks concerned endorse this position unanimously and are cooperating in the interest of maintaining the stability of the international monetary system."

Rusk

---

[1] Source: Department of State, Central Files, FN 10. Unclassified. Drafted by F. Lisle Widman (Treasury) on December 16 and approved by Lawrence J. Kennon (E/OMA). The statement in the telegram is identical to a draft statement that had been worked on with the Europeans. This draft is attached to a memorandum from Rostow to the President, December 15, 9:20 p.m., in which Rostow noted that the Europeans were to give their final approval on the morning of December 16 and, if all went well, the statement would be released on the afternoon of December 16. (Ibid.)

160.   Memorandum From the President's Special Assistants (Rostow and Califano) to President Johnson[1]

Washington, December 18, 1967.

SUBJECT

Balance of Payments Program

At Tab A is Secretary Fowler's memo recommending an action program for the balance of payments.[2] It was completed today and is now being staffed out. Our objective is to get the Cabinet Committee recommendations to you within a week.

The following elements of the program have been worked out and are not likely to be controversial:

1. *Export expansion measures* through:

—improved financing facilities through the Ex-Im Bank. (This will require earmarking $500 million of Ex-Im's new authorization for an export expansion fund (which probably would have strong support in Congress) and a more liberal Ex-Im policy on rediscounting export paper. (Linder will object)

—a bigger export promotion program (with a gradual increase in the Commerce budget from $11 million this year to $50 million a year by 1973).

—setting up Joint Export Associations to help U.S. companies get into the export business. (No legislation)

2. *Reducing the foreign exchange cost of government programs* through:

—squeezing more offsets on military expenditures;

—new techniques for tying aid and making sure that it does not replace commercial exports.

3. *Promoting foreign investment in the United States.*

The controversial issues in Fowler's package are:

1. *Border tax adjustments.* This means calculating the amount of indirect taxes manufacturers pay and rebating it on exports and adding it as a levy on imports. The amount being discussed ranges from 2% to 4%. The ultimate trade effect would be significant if the other countries stood still for it. If they did not, we would be in a trade war. (Legislation required)

2. *Measures to reduce capital exports through* tightening the voluntary programs on direct investments and on bank credit. A lot can be done

---

[1] Source: Johnson Library, National Security File, Subject File, Balance of Payments, Vol. IV, January 1967 [2 of 2], Box 3. Secret; Sensitive.

[2] This 20-page memorandum is not printed.

here even without legislation, but it will be rough going with Trow-bridge's clients.

3. *Increase repatriation of earnings* through a temporary tax on earn-ings retained abroad where they exceed 25% of the total earned abroad. (Legislation required)

4. *Reduce the travel deficit* through a temporary tax on tourists to expire December 31, 1969. (Legislation required)

During the course of this week, we will set out for you how much we believe may be needed, how much each of these actions might bring in, the advantages and disadvantages of different mixes and what we may expect in the Congress.

Secretary Fowler is setting up small task forces for each of the major questions.

The Deming Group[3] will look at the program as a whole and seek to put it in numbers. Fowler will ask you whether you have any objections to his showing his memo to you to the Deming Group. They will need it to do a proper job of assessment and will handle it with care.

In line with your talk with Joe Califano, we will outline for you sepa-rately what could be accomplished through a program that did not require new legislation.

Ed Fried[4]
Joe Jr.

Mr. President:

Ed Fried and I will work on this while you are away. We will also develop a package of the maximum program we can have without legis-lative action.

Joe[5]

---

[3] In a telephone conversation with President Johnson on December 19, much of which was a procedural discussion of the next steps in the balance of-payments program, Fowler indicated that the members of this small committee, chaired by Deming, were Fried, Daane, Okun, Knowlton, and Solomon. He mentioned that Ambassador Roth would also participate in its meeting that morning at 10:30 a.m. President Johnson asked that Goldstein be added to the committee, and Fowler readily assented. (Johnson Library, Recordings and Transcripts, Recording of Telephone Conversation between President Johnson and Secretary Fowler, December 19, 1967, 9:17 a.m., Tape F67.15, Side B, PNO 1)

The Deming Group met in both the morning and the afternoon of December 19, and again on December 20, 22, and 23. George H. Willis' handwritten notes on these meetings (see footnote 3, Document 64) are in the Washington National Records Center, RG 56, Assistant Secretary for International Affairs, Deputy to the Assistant Secretary and Secre-tary of the International Monetary Group: FRC 83 A 26, Willis' Notes 66–69, notebook en-titled Deming Group, Dec. 1967.

[4] Fried signed for Rostow above Rostow's typed signature.

[5] The postscript is handwritten by Califano.

161.   Minutes of Meeting of the Cabinet Committee on Balance of Payments[1]

Washington, December 21, 1967, 4 p.m.

Secretary Fowler commenced the discussion and said this meeting was basically a reporting session although he would welcome comments. In general, the balance-of-payments figures for 1967 are *grim*. He emphasized the need of holding closely all information in this meeting and to impart it only on a "need-to-know" basis.

Historically, from 1958 to 1960 the United States was running an annual liquidity deficit of about $3.9 billion; from 1961 to 1964 this deficit was reduced to $2.5 billion; and in 1965 and 1966 it was reduced to about $1.3 billion in each of those years. The 1965 figures would have been even better had (1) the U.K. sterling problems not caused the liquidation of about $500 million in securities and (2) additional military costs of about $400 million due to the step-up in Vietnam. In 1967 we targeted a deficit in line with the results of the two prior years. However, by mid summer the annual rate deficit was $2 billion and by the time the year is over we will be in the $3 to $4 billion range.

Secretary Fowler said there are three factors presently at work which make our balance of payments planning an entirely new ballgame. The *first* is the size of the deficit we are running and the basic deterioration which can not be attributed to Vietnam. The *second* concerns the Special Drawing Rights arrangement which is being detailed in the International Monetary Fund and which should be ready for use, following ratification by the member countries, perhaps some time early in 1969. When this arrangement is operational it could supply through the deliberate creation of reserve assets the needs of the international monetary system. I look upon the SDRs as the light at the end of the tunnel. Before, when this Committee was considering the alternatives available, we were apprehensive about taking drastic measures which might serve to unsettle the position of other countries, recognizing that the substantial reduction of our deficit could cause disorder in other areas of the world financial system. The *third* development which makes it a new ball

---

[1] Source: Johnson Library, White House Central Files, Confidential File, FO 4–1, Balance of Payments (1967–1969). Confidential; Eyes Only. Drafted by John R. Petty. A list of 29 participants is not printed. The meeting was held at the Treasury Department. Four attachments, none printed, are as follows: A, "Possible Trade Account Action with Regard to Border Tax Adjustments, 12/21/67: Alternatives I and II; and Background Discussion;" B, "Table: Year-by-Year Record of Commerce Program, 708 Firms, 12/18/67;" C, "Table: Outflows to Less Developed Countries (708 Reporting Companies), 12/21/67; and D, "Tables: Reserve Increase of $100 Million or More in Past Three Years; Reserves of NATO Countries; and Reserves of Selected Countries, dated 12/21/67."

game is the devaluation of sterling which places the dollar in the front line and makes it essential that we right our imbalance.

We have been examining various additional alternatives these past several months and at our meeting on June 30,[2] we discussed many of the options available. This Committee has discussed this subject in the past as if we were passing a hot potato around the room waiting only for the whistle to blow to see whose hands were burned. Today, we have four to five hot potatoes to pass around the room.

Border Taxes

Ambassador Roth introduced his portion of the "package" which concerned trade. He argued that he is primarily concerned with the retaliation which the imposition of a U.S. border tax would probably involve, pointing out that our surplus makes us uniquely vulnerable. It is the *net* benefit which we must seek. He agreed that something must be done in order to show a complete package but he emphasized that other areas, especially capital flows, must be covered: if the restrictions in the area of capital flows are strong it is possible to go further in the area of trade.

Both the Dutch and Germans will increase their border taxes on January 1, 1968. The Dutch will go up 1–2 percent and the Germans, moving from their present cascade indirect tax system to the added-value system, will move from about 4 percent to about 10 percent. In considering what we might do in this area we must be mindful of the limitations of GATT. Can we put together our own border tax based upon our own tax structure that gives us something similar to the advantage the Europeans enjoy? Treasury has compiled the secondary indirect taxes in this country; a figure of 2–2.5 percent represents various state and local taxes, customs duties and some federal excise taxes. This figure is increased to 4.3 percent if property taxes are included. If these secondary indirect taxes were rebated on a product-by-product basis they could be considered legal under GATT. However, it is true that five European countries rebate these "hidden" taxes and compensate at the border on a basis somewhat closer to a national average basis than to a product-by-product basis.

Ambassador Roth pointed out that the basic question was not one of legal niceties but one of retaliation. We all agree that Canada, the U.S., Japan and maybe some EFTA countries would have to adjust with us. There are two basic proposals. The Treasury approach which would announce the legislation and seek discussions subsequently and the Roth approach which reverses the procedure.

(See Attachment A for the detailed alternatives presented by Ambassador Roth.)

The key issue is whether the Europeans will retaliate or not. The second approach is designed to reduce this possibility without sacrific-

---

[2] No record of this meeting has been found.

ing more than two or three weeks of time. Assistant Secretary Solomon pointed out that the proposal reduces the chances of retaliation, compared to the U.S. Treasury proposal. He indicated that it was necessary to consult with the nations which would probably follow our action; moreover, the request for a GATT waiver would make it difficult for the Common Market countries to retaliate.

Secretary Fowler emphasized the importance of our trade surplus and he referred to the President's May 23 directive to study ways to fire-up the producers of our countries to make them more active in export trade.[3] He emphasized that the keystone of equilibrium is a larger balance-of-trade surplus. As we have needed to restrict the private and public sector we can no longer neglect the trade account. We have scraped the bottom of the barrel on special transactions. He cited the Joint Economic Committee report which pointed out that the border taxes hurt our trade.[4] We must take action now that makes our export lazy producers export conscious. Treasury believes that there must be action now combined with serious efforts at negotiations. Moreover, the Treasury proposal would be prepared to exempt the less developed countries.

Ambassador Roth questioned whether the difference was really one of only 2.5% and 4%. If we are to make trade gains in the use of the border tax other countries must exercise restraint. Normally, in trade negotiations others would say, "What would you pay to achieve these trade gains?" Would you pay an injury clause in your countervailing duty law? Would you amend Section 22 of your Agricultural Assistance Act?

Under Secretary Rostow said that it was important for the President's statement to be firm and effective. The statement could say that legislation is being considered. He reminded the Committee of the recent OECD ministerial resolution that the balance-of-payments positions of member countries are "a matter of common concern".[5] The risk of retaliation is great and therefore pursuant to this resolution and through negotiations perhaps the risk of retaliation can be minimized. Concerned as he was with retaliation he seemed to be favoring Alternative Two.

Chairman Ackley pointed out that we needed retroactivity in announcing our border tax and it was also necessary to specify an exact rate to avoid anticipatory imports and a delay in exports waiting for the rebate. We must be mindful of the impact of the President's statement upon the exchange markets. If we get a big boost from the border tax

---

[3] The President expounded on this proposed study in his May 23 remarks upon presenting awards for excellence in developing export markets; see footnote 2, Document 123.

[4] This report has not been found.

[5] This resolution has not been further identified. The OECD communiqué, December 1, does not contain the quoted language but expressed the same concern. For text, see *American Foreign Policy: Current Documents, 1967*, pp. 316–318.

announcement will the props be knocked out of it when the retaliation starts?

Secretary Fowler referred to the visit today of an old friend who was familiar with the border tax area. Secretary Fowler read from Weir Brown's memorandum, dated December 21, on the border tax.

"The draft now under consideration in the Treasury is built on a good central principle. This central idea is that we could adopt a tax adjustment for imports and exports without introducing a new sales tax on domestic sales.

"My (Weir Brown) modifications to the present plan would be as follows:

"1. We should state that the U.S. has been aware that many of its major trading partners have for years made tax adjustments to their imports and exports. They have justified this essentially on the grounds that imported goods had not been subject to their domestic tax system and that exported products were to be consumed abroad.

"2. These countries are now in the process of making further increases in the levels of these border adjustments, having a still further impact on trade of other countries. The U.S. Government has questioned the wisdom of these increases, and in fact of the border adjustment system as a whole. We recognize, however, that Europeans have their own special reasons for their actions, including the objective of harmonization among the Six.

"3. The U.S. Government has now determined that—given the prevalence of border adjustments by certain other countries and given the need to correct its balance of payments deficit—it will adopt its own form of border adjustment. While it is impossible to identify exactly the tax component of prices for any country, our Government has determined that a suitable rate for us to adopt would be 8 per cent (or 6), and this figure would be used in calculating a rebate on exported goods and in applying a levy to imports.

"4. The foregoing border adjustment would be applied by the United States to imports coming from and exports going to all those countries *which themselves now practice a system of border adjustments.* (This would have the effect of excluding the applicability of the border adjustment from trade with Canada and Japan. I believe it would be possible also, by legal interpretation, to declare that the British purchase tax is not an across the board system and that the U.S. adjustment would not apply in the U.K. case.) Although many LDC's would automatically be covered by the foregoing provision, we could make a specific exemption for LDC's."

Governor Daane asked if the program would be adequate and convincing without the border tax? It seemed to him that we must go more in the direction of the Treasury alternative because we are concerned about the actions Germany and Holland are taking and, therefore, we are entitled to respond. Responding to a question from Under Secretary Nitze, Secretary Fowler said the program might achieve $1.5 billion improvement without the border tax and the border tax might contribute an additional $1.5 billion to perhaps $2-1/2 billion. Ambassador Roth said that he thought the State Department estimated net trade gain figure, after retaliation, might be in the $800 million range.

The Vice President commented that anything you can do under alternative number 2 you can do under alternative number 1. The basic issue is how do you best get into a negotiating position. No one can tell me the Germans are easy to negotiate with, they may be more stubborn than de Gaulle. Alternative number 2 says that there will be time enough; but in his judgment the time has gone by. They will not change their January 1 implementation date; nor will Congress wait. If you are going to be asking for a tax bill from Congress you have to offer them something like this. Why don't you admit that you are the world's biggest cowards? The Europeans are feeling their oats and we should show some of our muscles. It is time to treat a crisis like a crisis. We need a package and one without cosmetics. It must be firm; it must be creditable; and it must have muscle. We must also take administrative action. The Europeans do not think we have the guts to do it and let's be frank; the President cannot have Vietnam and the dollar crisis at the same time next summer! We need a program and we need to show that we mean it. The balance-of-payments position of the United States is worse than the public knows and we cannot have this creditability issue coming up again by us appearing to sweep something under the rug. Remember this, there are no votes in Germany. That is the Humphrey message for the day.

Ambassador Roth pointed out that alternative 2 did not involve long negotiations; just two weeks. Secretary Fowler said that it was time to move on and said that he would accept written comments to all items on the agenda by 4:00 p.m., Friday, December 22.

Government Expenditure

Secretary McNamara said he strongly supported the views of the Vice President; the border tax was the only substantive item in the entire package, practically nothing else is left. We cannot pull our troops out of Korea right now for political reasons even though we have 50% more than we need. We cannot pull our troops out of Western Europe right now because it would mean the disintegration of NATO. Again, this is a political decision because militarily we could do more with redeployment. Other reductions in expenditures are almost impossible. In effect, we have had a variable rate on the dollar for some time because we pay up to 50% additional cost to save foreign exchange. In the case of petroleum, we go as high as 120%. On offsets, we should try more but that might be mostly talk. We may get $500 million more in Germany and that may involve trilateral negotiation as well. We could repeat our statements about the obligations for Europeans to neutralize our military cost and this might get some help from Belgium and Italy—but this is more psychological than financial.

Under Secretary Deming said that he was not quite as pessimistic as Secretary McNamara. He pointed out that the gross NATO expenditures were only $30 million higher in 1967 than they were in 1966. In the Common Market countries U.S. military balance of payments costs were:

CY 1966	CY 1967	CY 1968
	(millions of dollars)	
–446	–213	–683

This latter figure includes $250 million from Germany invested in long-term bonds.

In 1968 we will be lucky to reduce the EEC area military balance of payments costs to the 1967 level. In the Far East we hope to get $300 to $500 million from Japan and, in Southeast Asia, while some funds may come, the prospect for improvement are not bright. Secretary Fowler at this point read a list of countries which, over the last three years, had increased their reserves $100 million or more. The realities of life call for a major diplomatic initiative. The Treasury can no longer go around the capitals with its hat in its hand.

Capital Movements

Secretary Trowbridge said he agreed with action in the trade field and probably alternative number 1.

With respect to the Commerce Voluntary Program he pointed out that there were many areas of agreement in the approach: it should be voluntary and the administration must be greatly stepped-up. It is essential to continue a voluntary program because this is the best way to get the support of the business community, support which is vital to the success of the VCP. The coverage should be expanded to the LDCs, targeting for the future the $900 million figure of reinvested earnings and direct investment outflow which we expect to be the level for 1967. This could sort of act as a *lid* but it would not involve any cut-back and 1967 itself will be a peak year. The administration of the program will involve *more frequent* and *more intensive* consultation, undertaken by a three-man review board. This board will discourage investment in unfriendly countries, reduce total outflows, gross plant and equipment expenditures, and discourage take-overs. In 1966 this figure was $427 million, which included the $182 million Texaco deal. (A 10% or more purchase is a "take-over" under these statistics.) This left a $245 million figure for take-overs in the Common Market, of a $400 million figure on a worldwide basis (net of Texaco). In addition, the balance of payments package includes a tax proposal which would eliminate the deferral on the unreasonable accumulation of liquid assets held abroad.

The difference or unresolved issue is the level of the target. What level can we reduce the program to and still keep the support of the businessmen? Secretary Trowbridge said he can see total reductions of $784 million from the 1967 projected actual of $2,766 million (of reinvested earnings and direct investment outflow of the programed countries). This involves a quarter reduction under that forecasted for 1967, leaving a combined new target of $1,908 million as opposed to the reduction of $800,000,000 the Treasury Department is proposing, or a 45% cut, down to $1,257 million. I think that the $800 million is attainable but it would be one hell of a sweat. This is a judgment; no one can say at what level things fall apart. The Vice President asked what part of the Corporate Program is mandatory—after all tourism will be mandatory. Secretary Trowbridge said nothing is mandatory. Secretary McNamara said he thought there would need to be legislation to make the program mandatory. Secretary Fowler said authority did exist.

Governor Robertson in commenting on the balance of payments problem said that the problem is even bigger than that presented. He said that we have reached the point where the voluntary approach is inadequate and either the Interest Equalization Tax had to be extended or new legislation obtained. Since the programs started the banks had $150 million in outflow, against the $7.5 billion direct investment outflow over the same period. A $600 million improvement in the direct investment goal is *in*adequate and the program should become mandatory. If the Commerce Department program would disapprove of take-overs, the Federal Reserve program would disapprove of take-overs. The Board unanimously recommends that the bank target for 1968 be reduced from 109% to 103% and this might provide an improvement of $500 million. The Fed program already prohibits the increase in non-export lending to developed countries. He would reduce the amount of the outstandings by not permitting roll-overs except, of course, for commitments already outstanding. This would include *all loans*, including short-term loans to developed countries in Continental Western Europe, except for export loans. With respect to non-bank financial institutions there is only a portfolio of about $1,800 million. Their holdings of liquid foreign assets would have to be reduced to zero, with no new credits to Western Europe, and a new form of individual consultation would be commenced.

Secretary Trowbridge in commenting on corporate flows pointed out that each year the remitted earnings far exceeded the direct investment outflow. He added that the banks are now at a 101% and he felt that the target should be reduced below the 103% recommended. Governor

Robertson said this would not leave enough money available to finance exports.

Under Secretary Rostow said he believed that the gravity of our balance of payments position required mandatory controls and, in this regard, through employing the IET retroactively, a promising system could be found. He pointed out that Tony Solomon almost persuaded him that a voluntary program would be as good as to extend the IET but he doubted that the target is enough. He wants something clean, perhaps a 50% improvement. Moreover, he very much opposed operating with a LDC ceiling, inasmuch as the only hope for growth in these countries is through private investment. We must achieve stiffer cuts for developed countries and exempt the LDCs. Moreover, perhaps we should have public reports from the review board from time to time.

Administrator Gaud pointed out that the AID Task Force would make recommendations to the President contrary to the proposed Commerce program. AID is trying to encourage more private investment in LDCs. He argued that 75–80% of all investments in LDCs represented exports from the United States. Moreover, the $900 million no doubt included oil and extra-active industries. If you had to go down this road perhaps the thing to do would be to exclude all agricultural products and anything associated with the War on Hunger.

Secretary Fowler read from his draft letter to the President, the paragraph pertaining to additionality. Next, he pointed out that the $900 million figure only included the Venezuelan and Nigerian oil countries. Finally, he asked, in an effort to create a balanced program can we afford to exclude LDCs under the present conditions? Can we afford to leave a "sky-is-the-limit" atmosphere? Secretary Trowbridge said that the base of 130% is well above the historical average. Administrator Gaud said it does not make any sense to use the meat axe approach, bearing in mind all the work we have been going through to get private investment in the fertilizer industry in India. Assistant Secretary Solomon said that perhaps we could rely upon the three man review board to see that the LDC exemption does not become a source of "significant leakage". The Vice President concurred with this idea. Secretary Fowler said that he hoped to get a reporting system which would keep us better informed on these flows. Secretary McNamara said that he strongly disagreed with Secretary Trowbridge's idea. The Vice President concurred.

Governor Brimmer raised the issue of the Export-Import Bank and its contribution to the balance of payments. He pointed out that in fiscal year 1965 the Export-Import Bank contributed $27 million; in the fiscal year 1966, it cost $100 million; and fiscal 1967, it cost the balance of payments $500 million: it may well exceed this figure in 1968. Moreover, we should have an increase in their interest rate. Assistant Secretary Solomon said that he strongly disagreed, in fact, he argued that we should go in the opposite direction and have a subsidized interest rate.

Assistant Secretary Knowlton outlined the tourist program. This included restraints up until December 31, 1969. The objective was to create a convincing program with major savings involving perhaps $500 million. A simple procedure was desired. The idea would be to favor the lesser developed countries, the Western Hemisphere and Canada.

There are several ideas out on the table:

(a) Per diem charge which would involve an advance deposit of $100–$150;
(b) Give a worldwide exemption for five days; or give a ten-day exemption to the Western Hemisphere and none at all to other places;
(c) Make the per diem tax more progressive;
(d) Exempt the first trip in five years;
(e) Create a 15–25% transportation excise tax.

A ticket tax would catch worldwide transportation and the per diem might apply just to Western Europe. The passport fee might be increased to $25 and Customs exemptions reduced.

The Vice President spoke and said that if we go the extreme and introduce a tax on tourism, you cannot get by with a Voluntary Program on direct investments. This balance of payments program must have equity and it must have balance. Certainly travel must be included and he pointed out this represented a major change of position for him. We should look at this Customs reduction down to $10, the tax on the tickets, and the passport fee.

The Vice President said, now, you can argue and quite forcefully, that the mandatory program on capital investment is both political suicide and bad economics; but at the same time you can place the freedom of movement of capital against the freedom of movement of people. He could get speaking engagements at all the women's clubs throughout the country arguing the importance of "getting-to-know" people better. In conclusion, he said, that he would be opposed to tourism unless there were provisions for mandatory action on direct investment.

In response to Under Secretary Rostow, Assistant Secretary Surrey said that what a mandatory control is aiming at is usually a certain level of outflow. The question then comes, what form best achieves that desirable level. When you consider the issue of corporate leverage and various returns on invested capital that vary from industry to industry, it is simply impossible to set a percentage to achieve a given volume of outflow. To do it practically, you must set an absolutely prohibitive tax, slowly working the percentage down until the desired level is achieved. But that does not make much sense. The IET system, therefore, is difficult and we ought to look more closely at the auction system. Secretary Fowler concurred and said that the IET on direct investments was a pigin-a-poke. It would simply not be able to achieve the task assigned to it. The Vice President pointed out that the public does not particularly like foreign direct investment. It means taking away investment from home and exporting jobs. The Vice President said that we must pay for national security just as we have to pay for health insurance. We also have what we call LDAs, that is, Lesser Developed Areas, right here at home. Secretary Trowbridge emphasized the importance of the private sector and the over-all contribution this element makes to the balance of payments. The Vice President agreed and said that this was a serious matter and emotion should be left out of the discussion. Ambassador Roth said that mandatory controls would permit you to get away from the border tax action.

John R. Petty

---

162. Telegram From the President's Special Assistant (Califano) to President Johnson in Thailand[1]

Washington, December 22, 1967, 1649Z.

CAP 671128. In line with your call yesterday,[2] I am meeting this afternoon with Dean Rusk, Charlie Schultze, Gardner Ackley, Joe Fowler, Sandy Trowbridge, Clark Clifford, Bill Roth, Ed Fried, Bill Martin, Bob McNamara and Ernie Goldstein.

Incidentally, Secretary McNamara has sent a memorandum to you indicating that he will be leaving tonight or tomorrow for Aspen, Colorado, for a vacation between Christmas and New Year's.[3]

At the meeting this afternoon, we will do our best to resolve the remaining issues.

The extent of agreement and disagreement is reflected in the following memorandum which Gardner Ackley prepared for you at my request.

---

[1] Source: Johnson Library, National Security File, Subject File, 1968 Balance of Payments Programs, Cables [2 of 2], Box 4. Secret. Drafted on December 22 and sent to the President who was then in Korat, Thailand. During December 19–24, the President visited Australia to attend the funeral of Australian Prime Minister Holt and then continued around the world, stopping in Thailand, Vietnam, Pakistan, the Vatican, Italy, and the Azores. (Johnson Library, President's Daily Diary)

[2] Not further identified.

[3] This memorandum has not been found.

The memorandum lays out the present balance of payments problem, the program that Fowler is proposing, the extent of disagreement in the government and some of the questions that you should consider in determining whether to go forward with it.

"Memorandum for the President

Subject: The U.S. balance of payments: facts, proposals, and issues

1. The over-all balance of payments has been in deficit (on liquidity basis) every year since 1950, with the one exception of 1957 (Suez). In the early years, this was a blessing to the world. Since about 1959, it has been a serious problem, the deficits in 1965–66 were considerably below earlier years:

    1960—$3.9 billion
    1961–64 average—2.5 billion
    1965—1.3 billion
    1966—1.4 billion

2. Through the first 3 quarters of 1967, the deficit widened to $1.7 billion ($2-1/4 billion at annual rate). Although our trade balance improved and U.S. direct investment was reduced, there were these adverse changes:

—Net military spending abroad, up more than $1/2 billion;
—Private remittances (mainly to Israel), up nearly $1/4 billion;
—Foreign security issues (especially to Israel and Canada), up more than $1/4 billion; and
—The tourist gap (mostly the effect of Expo '67), up about $400 million.

3. The 4th quarter, however, threatens to turn the year into a disaster. So far in this quarter, the outflow has been nearly $2 billion. The deficit for the full year may challenge 1960's unhappy record of $3.9 billion.

—The only major known special transaction was the $500 million liquidation of U.K. securities.

—By the process of elimination, speculative activity must be blamed for much of the 4th quarter trouble. The smart money has probably been moving out in fear either of devaluation or of new controls. We are now getting direct evidence of this (for example, from Chase Bank).

—Whatever 'special transactions' Joe Fowler has up his sleeve will help to dent the huge deficit for the current quarter.

—On the other hand, press stories hinting at the bad 4th quarter results and at a drastic new balance-of-payments program could stimulate the outflow in the final week of 1967.

4. Reasons for concern with the rising deficit include the following:

—A 'run' by private speculators here and abroad could quickly pour billions of dollars into the hands of foreign central banks.

—A renewal of speculation on a hike in the gold price could force us to part with up to $300 million of gold a week to support the price in the London market; this also puts dollars in the hands of the foreign central banks in the gold pool.

—As they get more dollars, foreign central banks will become more and more worried that they won't be able to convert them into gold, and may begin massive conversions while there's some left.

—The faster our gold stock declines, the more fearful the speculators will get and the more worried the central banks will become.

—Foreign central banks will ask a bigger and bigger voice in our domestic economic policies as their price for continuing to hold dollars and staying in the gold pool.

5.   It is important to move swiftly on our balance of payments decisions

—to remove speculative uncertainty about our plans, and
—to beat the publication of any hard figures on the size of the 4th quarter hemorrhage.

6.   Joe Fowler is firming up a program to announce before New Year's Day. In addition to a number of minor elements, it includes the following major items, the first 3 of which are particularly controversial:

—A 'border tax adjustment'—a tax of 2 percent (or more) on imports and an equal subsidy on exports. At 2 percent, this could be worth nearly a billion dollars a year when fully effective.

—A tourist tax of $6 a day on trips abroad other than to Canada, Mexico, or the Caribbean, possibly combined with a 15 percent excise on international airline fares. This could yield $1/2 billion a year.

—A major tightening of the commerce program on direct investment—still leaving it voluntary—designed to save over $1 billion and to insure greater cooperation through better administration.

—A set of offset negotiations to get other countries to bear a greater share of the foreign exchange costs of our troops abroad. With luck, we might pick up $200 million more than in 1967. Without new offset agreements, receipts would decline substantially.

—A tightening of the Fed voluntary programs for banks and financial institutions from the program already announced for 1968. This should be worth several hundred million.

7.   The border tax adjustment would add 2 percent (or more) to the cost of our imports and would rebate 2 percent of foreign sales to our exporters. It would be designed to make up for the cost of "hidden" excise taxes such as those on gasoline, freight, and telephones.

—A few other nations are doing this under GATT rules now, and many are doing things equally dubious under the rules.

—Fowler is particularly enthusiastic about this proposal because

—it will cost very little in revenues;
—in his judgment, it will sail through Congress and at the same time head off the quota drive;
—it shows toughness with the Europeans.

—The disadvantages and dangers are

—it is an obvious devaluation of the dollar in trade, despite our big export surplus;
—it looks like a move toward protectionism;
—it will surely be countered by Canada, Japan, the U.K., and perhaps others, either by similar action or by outright devaluation;
—if it provoked retaliation by continental Europe, we would lose all the potential trade gains, possibly trigger off a trade war, and stir up financial markets badly.

—Everyone agrees that we are being hurt under existing GATT practices. But some of your advisers (STR, State, and CEA) would prefer not to announce the action until we have a hard and quick (2 or 3 weeks) negotiation with the Europeans, either persuading them to reverse their own border tax practices or else to accept ours. This is intended to minimize the risk of retaliation (if we have to move), and to preserve our long-standing leadership in trade liberalization.

8.   The per diem tourist tax is obviously a hot potato. Some think it can be made more acceptable and more equitable by exempting trips by persons who haven't been abroad during the four prior years, and by making the per diem proportional to the traveler's income (e.g., 0.2 percent of his previous year's income tax for each day abroad), with a $6 minimum.

9.   Direct investment is the most glaring deficit account of the private economy, still exceeding $2-1/2 billion a year. It is also area that irritates the Europeans most. Commerce's voluntary program has helped some, mainly by encouraging more U.S. firms to raise money abroad to finance their foreign plants. But now we ought to slash this area far more drastically. Sandy Trowbridge feels he cannot promise the $1 billion Joe Fowler wants. Sandy thinks he can squeeze out $600 million and still hold the program together on a voluntary basis. We could slap on direct controls, but that would be messy at best and would be bitterly opposed by the business community. On the other hand, can we really have a compulsory program on tourists and trade, and still leave the capital program voluntary?

10. Fowler's basic strategy is 'the bigger the better.' He wants to show that we are taking promptly all action to deal with the balance of payments and to minimize the chance of a real explosion in international financial markets in 1968. The key issues raised by this strategy are:

—Will such a massive program look like an act of desperation and thus inflame the speculators?

—If the necessary legislation doesn't pass, won't we be in even worse shape than we are now?

—If we load the Ways and Means Committee with a bunch of other measures, does this improve or worsen the prospects for the income tax surcharge?

—Isn't removal of the gold cover an essential part of the program?

—We have been pounding away that the European surplus countries have an equal responsibility to help remedy the world imbalance. They have argued it's all our fault, and we have to correct it. This way, don't we admit we've been wrong, and let them off the hook? If we omit the tourist tax and the border tax adjustment (the things they will really scream about), aren't we in a better position to get them to help us to solve the problem cooperatively?

—Is all this worth doing just to preserve the gold-dollar link?

Signed, Gardner Ackley"

---

163. Telegram From the President's Special Assistant (Califano) to President Johnson[1]

Washington, December 23, 1967, 0234Z.

WH 70613. Ackley, Trowbridge, Boyd, Martin, Fried, Solomon, Gene Rostow, Fowler, Deming, Okun, Clark Clifford, Schultze, Rusk (for part of the meeting), Goldstein and I met today on the balance of payment program. The Vice President and Secretary McNamara had left town for Christmas, but they are in agreement. Except as indicated below all the above individuals are in agreement on the following program:

1. Import tax/export subsidy program (border tax).

—A 2 to 4 percent export subsidy, under which exporters would be given somewhere between 2 and 4 percent of the sales price of their

---

[1] Source: Johnson Library, National Security File, Subject File, Balance of Payments, Vol. IV [1 of 2], Box 3. Unclassified. Drafted on December 22 and sent to the President, who was probably aboard Air Force One en route from Vietnam to Pakistan. (Johnson Library, President's Daily Diary)

exports as a cash rebate and the same percentage would be applied as a tax on imports.

—The less-developed countries would be exempt from the import tax and there would be some sectoral differentials among product categories.

There is some disagreement on the precise percentage but that can be worked out. There is also some disagreement on the tactics:

Whether you should announce that you will be sending a bill with specific percentages forward when you announce a general balance of payment program next week (the Fowler view), or whether you should indicate that you intend to work out a program, which would include a border tax with the other countries (the Rusk view).

The issue revolves around the tone in any public announcement and Rusk, Rostow and Fowler believe they can straighten out the State–Treasury differences. Schultze, Martin and Trowbridge lean toward the Fowler view. Roth and Ackley lean toward the Rusk view. Rusk is concerned about an increase in imports due to anticipation of the tax and retaliatory actions if the tax is too specifically announced before it goes to Congress and before some negotiation and consultation with our allies. Fowler believes there will be some anticipatory imports in any case and a specific, firm announcement will assist negotiations with our allies.

As far as the percentage of import tax and export cash rebate is concerned, the trick is to pick the percentage which will get us the best net effect—to avoid or minimize retaliation.

2. A tourist package which would be the appropriate mix of a tourist tax, an international fare excise tax, a passport fee increase and a reduction in the duty free allowance. The precise nature of the mix is still being worked out, but it is likely to be something like this:

—A $6 per day tax on tourists for each day they are abroad, with exemptions for Mexico, Canada and Caribbean and probably with some kind of progressive add-on tax such as an additional .2 percent of income tax per day where that would exceed $6.
—an excise tax of between 15 and 33-1/3 percent of the fare on international travel.
—an increase in the passport fee from ten dollars to twenty-five dollars.
—a reduction in the value of goods a traveler can bring into the United States duty free from $100 to $10.

This program would probably raise about $500 million in revenues and reduce the balance of payments deficit by about $500 million. Everyone favors this. Ackley strongly believes it should have a progressive aspect. Boyd and McNamara would like to place as much burden on the excise tax as possible because they believe a tourist tax would be difficult.

3. Mandatory controls on capital investment abroad.

The objective would be to reduce the outflow from capital investment abroad by $1 billion. This would probably require mandatory controls.

Most favor this approach, with some variations. Fowler believes you should consider the option of saying you want corporations voluntarily to increase their contribution to a favorable balance of payments by $1 billion, but if they fail to do so, you will have a mandatory control program. All others who favor mandatory controls believe that such an announcement would be a futile gesture and you should go promptly to mandatory controls.

Trowbridge believes that if you go to mandatory controls, you must praise business for what they have done so far and put the need for mandatory controls in terms of the importance of being fair. Trowbridge believes mandatory controls are necessary if you want to pick up $1 billion. If you reduced the target to $600 million, Trowbridge would prefer a voluntary program.

Ackley and Okun raise questions about the serious implications of mandatory controls, and the scare impact of such controls.

Treasury and State lawyers believe that no legislative authority is needed and that you have authority under the Trading with the Enemy Act[2] to do this by executive order. Ramsey Clark was out of town, but I will have him check this as soon as he returns.

A group under Deming and Goldstein will begin work tonight to put together the detailed administrative arrangements for mandatory controls.

4. Tightening controls on overseas lending by U.S. banks.

The objective would be to decrease outflow by $500 million. Martin can do this administratively. While he said he could not commit his Board since they had voted on a lesser program, he indicated they would favor the necessary action to achieve the $500 million goal if the rest of the program were put forward.

5. An export expansion program involving increased appropriations to the Commerce Department for export promotion, the encouragement of export associations, and a soft loan window and guarantees by the Export-Import Bank. Some legislation will be needed on the Export-Import Bank portion of that program. The rest can be done administratively.

6. Mobilizing our gold reserves.

All those competent in this area recommend that this be done. Martin can act under his present authority, however, and as a result of my ear-

---

[2] Chapter 106, October 6, 1917 (40 Stat. 411); and subsequent amendments.

lier conversation with him, he has talked to some Congressmen on the Hill about it. He said that to his surprise, the Congressmen told him they would prefer to wait until Martin had to suspend the gold cover before taking any action to lift the gold cover.

Everyone agreed that lifting the gold cover will help abroad, but all also recognize that this could easily become a major political issue at home.

7.   Seek new tax legislation that would induce companies to bring back some of the earnings they keep abroad.

In brief, I think the program is in pretty good shape and all your advisers are in virtual agreement. The two issues involve the manner in which you handle the export cash rebate and import tax in an announcement and the manner in which a mandatory control program is worked out. Hopefully, these will be resolved by the time you return and we can have a unanimous view to present to you.

Fowler and I will meet with Wirtz tomorrow to try to work out a proposal for a moratorium on strikes that affect our balance of payments. Ackley, Trowbridge, Wirtz and I have been meeting on wage-price guidelines and still have no solution for you on this.

With respect to the total program, it is important to note that the pieces are interdependent in terms of interagency agreement. Everyone's ox is gored and they are all willing to take it if the other fellow will.

---

164.   Message From President Johnson to the President's Special Assistant (Califano)[1]

Undated.

Point two of the Ackley memo which begins "through the first three quarters of 1967, the deficit widened,"—which you transmitted and I received Saturday, December 23, 0230[2]—plus the first paragraph only of third point that follows, plus all the points in Paragraph Four should be outlined by you or Fowler to Mills over the telephone—repeat, on the

---

[1] Source: Johnson Library, National Security File, Subject File, Balance of Payments, Vol. V [2 of 2], Box 3. No classification marking. The source text bears no indication of how the message was transmitted.

[2] Document 162.

telephone, not in wire—and let him chew on this for the next day or two before I return. Every effort should be made to get Fowler, Ackley and company in complete agreement. This will be difficult, but you can handle tough assignments. See you Sunday.

---

165. Telegram From President Johnson to the President's Special Assistant (Califano)[1]

December 23, 1967, 1900Z.

These are views I should like to have Secretary Fowler and our Cabinet Committee seriously consider.[2]

Subject: The gold position and balance of payments

Confidence in world currencies demands a system which continues to have good support—particularly with regard to international systems.

The world supply and the world production of gold is insufficient to make the present system workable—particularly as the use of the dollar as a reserve currency is essential to create the required international liquidity to sustain world trade and growth—while, at the same time, our strength is required for so many extraneous situations: Vietnam, world wide defense, German installations, aid to underdeveloped countries, military aid abroad, etc. If all these or even some of them were eliminated, our monetary structure–balance of payments would be as strong

---

[1] Source: Johnson Library, National Security File, Subject File, 1968 Balance of Payments Programs, Cables [2 of 2], Box 4. Secret; Flash. The source text does not indicate the sending location, but the telegram was probably transmitted from Rome or the Vatican where the President visited the evening of December 23. (Johnson Library, President's Daily Diary)

[2] This introductory paragraph is identical to an undated typed note from President Johnson to Califano, which is attached to an undated paper prepared by Charles W. Engelhard, head of a precious metals company and friend of President Johnson. (Ibid., Subject File, Balance of Payments, Vol. V [2 of 2], Box 3) Except as indicated in footnotes below, the remainder of the telegram is a verbatim text of a December 21 memorandum by Engelhard.

Engelhard traveled with the President on his December 19–24 trip. This memorandum was one of at least six on the international financial crisis that Engelhard wrote for the President in late December 1967. All are ibid., except for the fifth, dated December 27 (transmitted in telegram CAP 671179 from Rostow to the President and Califano, December 27; ibid., National Security File, Subject File, Balance of Payments, Vol. IV [2 of 2], Box 3), and the sixth, December 30 (transmitted in telegram CAP 671258 from Bromley Smith to Rostow and Jim Jones, December 30; ibid., Vol. IV [1 of 2], Box 3)

as any nation. Dollars held by other countries would return. The risk of loss of gold would evaporate or, in fact, our gold stocks would increase. This would result in a disastrous withdrawal of the reserves which the other countries depend on to sustain their trade and development.

Point I. The point is that our role of world leadership in a political and military sense is the only reason for our current embarrassment in an economic sense on the one hand and on the other the correction of the economic embarrassment under present monetary systems will result in an untenable position economically for our allies.

Point II. The available gold resources must be maintained in the monetary systems and not dissipated by sale to speculators and loaders at prices which are riskless to the buyer. This will result in a 2-price structure but the argument that supports this is *world economic necessity*.[3] The current buyers of gold are not Americans scared of the dollar (they aren't allowed to anyhow) but people of many countries who have experienced inflation and are afraid of *their own* currencies which they exchange for dollars so that they can buy gold, as gold is only sold in terms of dollars by the London market which must have the dollars to replace it. In 1941–47–48 the International Monetary Fund took this position and the speculators had to pay premiums which substantially reduced the offtake. I recommend the following four [*three*] steps:

I.   On grounds of international economic necessity, state that if gold resources must be preserved for use in monetary systems and that pending establishment of a system under an international body, no further gold will be supplied by the supporting countries to the London market. I would *not even* supply at the official price to Arts and Industries who can easily obtain their requirements from newly mined or secondary sources just as they now do in other metals. As in the case of silver, let the consumer pay the free market price.

II.   Take the leadership in causing the International Monetary Fund or some suitable agency to establish a system of control which (1) prevents small countries from cheating through cut-off of replacement; (2) encourage with strong pressure those countries, i.e., South Africa, Canada, etc., who produce gold to deliver at least, say, one half into the monetary network. This will still provide more than enough for any legitimate use in art or industry.

III. Take steps to cause a prompt effect on our balance of payments particularly to strengthen our hand at the negotiating table in setting up a broader international system along the lines of the Rio[4] Conference so

---

[3] The italicized words here and below are underlined in Engelhard's memorandum but not in the source text.

[4] "Rio" in the source text corrects the words "Buenos Aires" in Englehard's memorandum.

that our clear leadership is maintained, because it is our leadership only which in the end will cause sufficient world confidence in the system to make it work. Many steps are possible, among them—

1. Encourage rather than penalize repatriation of capital gain and earnings from abroad—both corporate and individual. This should be same sort of specific moratorium not to go on forever so that it does not inadvertently encourage investment.[5]

2. Provide a more attractive tax result to foreigners investing here.

3. Prohibit the export of capital except under special license to any countries who do not support the U.S. economic [garble—structure by insisting][6] on 100 percent conversion of dollar credits into gold. Certainly it would not be unreasonable to expect a friendly country to be willing to hold dollars in the ratio of 3–4 to 1 to their gold withdrawals from U.S.

4. Develop an international monetary system which, while still having gold for support, broadens the base so that the available supply can support a much larger volume of currency, thereby providing international liquidity. This agency should also exert the controls on outside sales of gold if any or newly mined gold and on price or subsidy so as to remove any implication that the strength of the dollar or other currencies would also in any way be affected by the relatively low gold supply.

---

[5] The word "broader" precedes "investment" in Engelhard's memorandum.

[6] The words inserted here for the garbled text are from Engelhard's memorandum.

---

166. Telegram From President Johnson to the President's Special Assistant (Califano)[1]

December 23, 1967, 1900Z.

Apropos of the gold position memo transmitted earlier today, please have Committee carefully consider, evaluate, and be prepared to accept or give reasons why to the following comments on Gardner Ackley's memo with regard to Fowler proposal.[2]

---

[1] Source: Johnson Library, National Security File, Subject File, 1968 Balance of Payments Programs, Cables [2 of 2], Box 4. Secret; Flash. Regarding the transmission of this telegram, see footnote 1, Document 165.

[2] This introductory paragraph is the verbatim text of an undated typed note from President Johnson to Califano, which is attached to an undated paper prepared by Charles W. Engelhard. (Ibid., National Security File, Balance of Payments, Vol. IV, January 1967 [2 of 2], Box 3) The remainder of the telegram is identical to Engelhard's memorandum, which comments on Ackley's memorandum to the President, transmitted in Document 162.

Point 1—No comment except that if we had not suffered from continuing deficits, the rest of the world would have suffered for lack of international liquidity.

Point 2—The deficit for the first 3/4 of 1967 would not be alarming or cause any current problem because the reasons for the increase are reasonable and except for military, not primarily continuing.

Point 3—The fourth quarter is very serious. It is caused substantially by

1. The inept handling by the British of their devaluation which played unbelievably into the hands of speculators—smart money men and even amateurs.
2. Subsequent loss of gold to speculators and hoarders who saw the British devaluation as the opening wedge and under the present structure of the London gold[3] can buy gold at prices which carry no risk.
3. Subsequent uncertainties as to whether this source of gold would be shut off or restricted which still exist.

Much depends on what "special transactions" Fowler has in mind and how much they will help.

The 500 million liquidation of U.K. securities being a one time affair is explainable.

Point 4—If there is no cover (i.e., Fowler special transactions) or stop-gap foreign maneuevering particularly with continuing uncertainties and rumors stimulated by speculators and even respected European economists all the points in 4 are likely to occur unless we announce a strong and specific program. How strong must depend on how bad the fourth quarter deficit is.

Point 5—I agree entirely—that we must move quickly otherwise we risk a similar unnecessary further loss as happened to the British. In addition prompt action might even ease the fourth quarter loss.

Point 6—The Fowler program—

A. I don't like the "border tax adjustment" at all except as a bargaining point in GATT which is, of course, of no use for the present immediate requirement. It will stimulate speculators as a step toward devaluation. It will damage our international image in many areas. It hits at an area which is not the root of the problem. Under nbr 2 the balance of trade improved.

B. The tourist tax proposal is complicated—cumbersome—will obviously produce only limited results—advertises weakness to millions of people which in turn will probably increase the outflow by speculators—inhibits international good will which tourism builds—will encourage tourists to be more extravagant abroad—doubtful of Con-

[3] The word "market" appears after this word in the Englehard memorandum.

gressional passage—certain to be used by Republicans in an election year—*therefore damaging to the President.*[4]

The last three points I would endorse—

A. Offset negotiations and greater share of foreign exchange costs of troops abroad.

B. Bank and financial institution program.

C. Tightening of the Commerce program of direct investment and here is where I would put the bite depending on the extent of necessity—and for the duration of the Vietnam emergency or until the B of P is adjusted—

1. Permit foreign investment only under license, i.e., for special purposes or national interest—or undeveloped countries of specific foreign policy objectives—

This could be reversed to apply only to these countries which do not co-operate in an economic sense or who are unwilling to hold dollars in reasonable proportion to their gold withdrawals or to those with favorable balances who are unwilling to share world economic burdens equitably—

I would list the following advantages to this step—

1. Business has been well treated and is basically good.

2. Far fewer voters would be directly affected—less difficult in Congress and *better for President.*

3. Provides tremendous bargaining strength in international economic negotiations.

4. Money not sent abroad would be invested at home at least to some extent thereby increasing employment producing more tax revenue.

5. Can be readily adjusted administratively by granting more or less licenses as circumstances warrant.

6. Can be sufficiently substantial to convince skeptics promptly, thereby quickly discouraging speculators.

7. Would convince world we mean *business.*

The obvious disadvantage is business opposition. This could be substantially offset by providing tax concessions to business with overseas interest—for the emergency period—who repatriate capital and earnings at this time. This is one of my suggestions in the previous gold position memorandum.[5]

Point 7—The border tax adjustment—in addition to my own points as stated I agree entirely with the disadvantages listed:

1. Devaluation of dollar in trade despite export surplus,

2. Protectionism,

---

[4] The italicized words here and below are underlined in Engelhard's memorandum but not in the source text.

[5] Document 165.

3. Will be countered by others,
4. In the end retaliation by Europe might make U.S. worse off.

Point 8—Dislike of tourist tax covered above.

Point 9—Direct investment control covered above. The point made of encouraging U.S. firms to raise money abroad has limitations due to size of money markets.

Point 10—I agree with Secretary Fowler that strong measures must be taken. Half-hearted ones will only have the reverse effect—as per the British debacle and the present outflow of gold through the London market. This outflow should be stopped firmly and at once.

By taking strong action we will stengthen our hand in negotiating an international system along Rio lines which is absolutely essential.

---

167. Editorial Note

In the last week of December 1967, senior officials in the Johnson administration developed a set of proposals on balance of payments for a forthcoming major Presidential announcement. A December 26 memorandum from Califano to the President indicated the division of assignments for this effort (with names and/or agencies in parentheses), as follows: mandatory controls, including an Executive Order and proposed lists of a three-man board (Treasury leadership, with participation of Commerce, Justice, CEA, and Goldstein); negotiating team to leave promptly for foreign capitals with letters from the President to heads of state (State leadership with Treasury and Fried); Federal Reserve credit controls (Bill Martin); tax incentives (Fried, with Stan Ross and Treasury); and Congressional contacts (Fowler, Rusk, Trowbridge, and Barr, with a list of Senators and Representatives cleared by the White House). All these tasks were to be completed by the morning of December 28. (Johnson Library, National Security File, Subject File, Balance of Payments, Vol. IV, January 1967 [2 of 2], Box 3)

Barr's December 26 memorandum to Fowler on his conversations with Speaker John W. McCormack and Majority Leader Carl Albert on December 26, a December 27 memorandum from Trowbridge to Secretaries Fowler and Rusk of his telephone conversation with Senator Mike Mansfield, Bowman's December 28 memorandum for the files concerning his conversations with Representative Wilbur Mills and Senator Russell B. Long, and Fowler's December 28 memorandum for the files providing supplementary comment on the conversation with Mills are all ibid. A memorandum for the files of Fowler's conversation with Representative John Byrnes, a memorandum of his telephone conversation with Senator Everett Dirksen, and Barr's two memoranda to Fowler on his and Eugene Rostow's conversations with Senator George A. Smathers and Congressman Hale Boggs, all dated December 28, are ibid. Roth's report on the same conversations with Mills, Long, and Byrnes, and on his separate conversation with Senator Carl T. Curtis, attached to a December 29 memorandum from Walt Rostow to the President and Califano, is ibid.

Numerous briefing papers and miscellaneous memoranda prepared by administration principals in the last week of 1967, which reported on progress in the preparation of the proposals on a border tax, tourism, capital investment abroad, and other aspects of the balance-of-payments package, as well as drafts of the proposed Presidential message, Executive Order on mandatory controls for capital transfers abroad, and the Federal Reserve Program, are ibid.

On December 30, Secretaries Rusk, Fowler, and Trowbridge; Roth; Director of the Bureau of the Budget Charles L. Schultze; Rostow; and Califano agreed that the heads of foreign governments should be informed in advance of the President's upcoming announcement of the balance-of-payments program. Their strategy called for Secretary Rusk to arrange for U.S. Ambassadors to deliver a confidential letter on the balance-of-payments package from President Johnson to heads of government on December 31. Then, early on the following day, Katzenbach, Roth, and Deming would travel to Europe, Eugene Rostow and an aide would go to Japan, New Zealand, and Australia, and Solomon, Shaw, and Petty would visit Ottawa. They also agreed that the President's statement and the Executive Order would be released at 10:30 a.m. in San Antonio, Texas, on January 1, 1968, and that there would be follow-on briefings of the financial press, labor leaders, and commercial, banking, and manufacturing groups, and calls by State and Treasury people on about 100 Senators and Representatives. (Telegram CAP 671262 from Califano to the President, December 30; ibid.)

The President apparently approved this strategy, which was carried out as planned over the next few days. The transcript of a background press briefing by Califano in San Antonio on January 1 is in the Johnson Library, Fowler Papers, International Balance of Payments White Paper [5 of 7], Box 1. The transcript of a press briefing by Secretaries Rusk, Fowler, and Trowbridge, and others in Washington on the same afternoon is ibid., Fowler Papers, International Balance of Payments 1968, B of P Questions and Answers [2 of 2], Box 6.

For text of the President's December 31 letter to British Prime Minister Wilson, see Document 168. The telegraphic texts of similar letters sent to several other heads of government on December 31, along with

Embassy reports on the foreign leaders' reactions to the letters, dated December 31, 1967, and January 1, 1968, and memoranda of Solomon's conversations with Canadian Prime Minister Pearson and Canadian Acting Prime Minister Mitchell Sharp, December 31, are in Department of State, Central Files, FN 12 US.

Circular telegram 91714 to all posts, December 31, which detailed adjustments required by U.S. trading partners, including the need for multilateral cooperative action, adjustments in the relationship between deficits and surpluses, especially in EEC countries, and the potential for shifts in capital flows and in military expenditures, is ibid.

For text of Executive Order 11387, signed on January 1, on capital transfers abroad, see Department of State *Bulletin*, January 22, 1968, pages 114–115. Goldstein's memorandum for the files, October 4, 1968, attached to a note from Goldstein to the President, October 4, provides detailed background on the development of the foreign direct investments program as part of this balance-of-payments initiative. (Johnson Library, White House Central Files, Confidential File, FO 4–1 (1967–1969))

A revised text of the President's statement on balance of payments, following input from Secretaries Rusk, Fowler, Trowbridge, Wirtz, McNamara, Chairmen Ackley and Martin, and others, was sent in telegram CAP 80001 from Califano to the President, December 31. (Ibid., National Security File, Subject File, 1968 Balance of Payments Program, Cables [2of2], Box 4) Text of the President's January 1 message is printed in *Public Papers of the Presidents of the United States: Lyndon B. Johnson, 1968–69*, pages 8–13. A detailed summary of this balance-of-payments program is in *Current Economic Developments*, Issue No. 796, January 2, 1968, pages 1–6. (Washington National Records Center, RG 59, E/CBA/REP Files: FRC 72 A 6248, *Current Economic Developments*)

Katzenbach's meetings with European leaders are recounted in Documents 170–173. For Eugene Rostow's account of his conversations with Japanese leaders, see Document 169. For Katzenbach's and Rostow's summary reports of their trips, see Documents 174 and 175.

On January 1, 1968, it was also decided to send Ambassador Philip Trezise to visit the Scandinavian capitals and Vienna to explain the new balance-of-payments program to these governments. (Telegram 91844 to Copenhagen and six other European posts, January 1; Johnson Library, Fowler Papers, International Balance of Payments—Classified Material: 1968 Balance of Payments—Cables, Box 44)

Additional telegraphic reports on these foreign visits are in Department of State, Central Files, FN 12 US, FN 16 US, OECD 7, and ORG 7 U. Many of these reports were in turn transmitted in CAP telegrams to the President at the LBJ Ranch in Texas. Copies are in the Johnson Library, National Security File, Subject File, 1968 Balance of Payments Program,

Cables [2 of 2], Box 4. Numerous reports of foreign governments' and press reactions to the new balance-of-payments initiative are in Department of State, Central Files, FN 12 US. First foreign reactions are summarized in *Current Economic Developments*, Issue No. 797, January 16, 1968, pages 1–5. (Washington National Records Center, RG 59, E/CBA/REP Files: FRC 72 A 6248, *Current Economic Developments*) A Department of Commerce summary of foreign reactions is attached to a memorandum from McQuade to Trowbridge, January 11. (Ibid., RG 40, Executive Secretariat Files: FRC 74 A 31, A–B) A CIA Intelligence Memorandum, "Effect on Foreign Countries of US Balance-of-Payments Measures" (ER IM 68–16), February 5, 1968, is in the Johnson Library, National Security File, Subject File, Balance of Payments, Vol. V [2 of 2], Box 3.

Documentation on additional contacts with members of Congress on the balance-of-payments program in January 1968 is ibid., Fowler Papers, International Balance of Payments 1968: B of P Operations, Box 5; ibid., Fowler Papers, International Balance of Payments 1968: B of P Position, Box 6; ibid., Fowler Papers, International Balance of Payments 1968: B of Payments: Tourism, Box 7; and ibid., National Security File, NSC History, 1968 Balance of Payments Program [Tabs 19–34], Box 54.

A narrative history prepared by the National Security Council, entitled "The Balance of Payments Program of New Year's Day, 1968," covers the origins, development, and execution of the balance-of-payments program. (Ibid., National Security File, NSC History, 1968 Balance of Payments Program [Tabs 1–3], Box 54) An accompanying chronology, including attached key annotated documents, is ibid.

---

168.   Telegram From the Department of State to the Embassy in the United Kingdom[1]

Washington, December 31, 1967, 0859Z.

91707. For Ambassador. Please deliver Sunday, December 31 following letter to Prime Minister Wilson from President Johnson:[2]

"Dear Harold:

We are at the end of a difficult year, and both our countries have much unfinished business to carry forward. It is encouraging to recall

---

[1] Source: Department of State, Central Files, POL UK–US. Secret; Exdis; Flash. Drafted at the White House, cleared by Jeanne W. Davis (S/S) and Leddy (EUR), and approved by Enders (M).

[2] For background regarding this letter and similar ones from President Johnson to heads of government, see Document 167.

nonetheless that it has been a year in which our close consultations and collaboration have helped produce a number of memorable achievements—the maintenance of security arrangements in Europe, the agreement on the new reserve unit in the IMF, the completion of the Kennedy Round, to recall a few. We are not yet out of the woods in the Middle East, but we have certainly made progress, with the passage of your Resolution in the Security Council.[3]

We can take heart also from the success we have had through our joint efforts and through the cooperation of the other financial powers in meeting the critical problems of November and December and in restoring a sense of confidence and order to the world's financial system.

The speculative fever of these weeks has severely tested our methods of cooperating on economic problems; but, we have continued to work together effectively in a financial world suddenly beset by fear and disorder. We have, thus far, met and repelled a serious threat to the foundations of the international monetary system, which, in turn, could also have undone the accomplishments of the Kennedy Round and the unity of the system of international commerce.

Meanwhile, the agreements at London and Rio on a plan to supplement existing reserve assets are a further reason for solid satisfaction, as we look to the longer future.

In both of these achievements—the long-range improvement of our international monetary system and the recent defense of the existing system—James Callaghan at the Treasury and Leslie O'Brien at the Bank of England have played important and, indeed, vital roles. I know that they have contributed much to the recent efforts to preserve order in the gold and foreign exchange markets. I am reassured by our mutual determination to exert a constructive force in the world financial system. This, I know, reflects a clear common understanding of the importance of international monetary cooperation in creating that environment of safety and opportunity which is required for the continued growth and stability of our nations' economies.

As you know, we, as well as our trading partners, have been concerned about the balance of payments position of the United States. This concern has been increased by the events of recent weeks. As a result, I am announcing on January 1, 1968, a new and vastly strengthened program to reduce our deficit and guarantee the continued viability of the international monetary system.

In the program, I will press for the tax increase to restrain excessive demand in the United States and to reduce our budget deficit to manage-

---

[3] Reference presumably is to a British resolution, which became Resolution 242, adopted by the U.N. Security Council on November 22, 1967. For text, see *American Foreign Policy: Current Documents, 1967*, pp. 616–617.

able proportions. I hope that this bill will soon become law. This, in itself, should be a helpful factor in our balance of payments and should demonstrate to the world that we will keep our own economic house in order. And the Federal Reserve has already made clear its determination to use monetary policy to this end.

But much more needs to be done; and we propose to do much more. Our balance of payments actions are designed to improve both our current and our capital accounts.

These actions will be painful to the United States and, to some degree, to our international partners. They are designed to avoid as far as possible adverse effects on the developing areas of the world. We hope they will result more in the reduction of surpluses than in the shift or increase of deficits. And we have kept very much in mind the views of other countries and the international economic institutions.

In this effort we wish to proceed within the spirit and the letter of the recent Resolution of the OECD Ministerial Council that the adjustment of the American deficit and the European surplus is a matter of common concern, to be handled cooperatively. Surpluses in international payments are the mirror image of deficits. Thus, both surplus and deficit countries must strive to reach balance and act cooperatively to this end. This is no less true in the 1960's than it was in the late 1940's and '50's, when we carried the responsibilities of a surplus nation. This concept was definitively developed by our best economic and financial experts in a carefully prepared OECD Report on 'The Adjustment Process' in August 1966.[4]

Our deficits have been the net result of a current account surplus, including a trade surplus, inadequate to support foreign exchange costs of our external capital flows, foreign aid programs, and military expenditures for the common defense. During the period of the 'dollar gap,' these deficits helped redistribute the world's monetary reserves—the time has come, we all agree, to bring them to an end.

As we see the problem, we need to act to improve our current account, reduce capital outflows, and neutralize more fully our net foreign exchange expenditures in the common defense. Our new program is designed to move us strongly towards equilibrium. But full success will require the understanding and cooperation of our partners. It seems axiomatic to us, and basic to our view of the OECD Resolution, that those in strong reserve positions, or in surplus, should avoid actions that increase surpluses, should not take offsetting action to preserve their surpluses—indeed, that it will be necessary for them to take positive action to move toward balance. Otherwise, the only result will be to shift

---

[4] For a summary of this report, see *The New York Times*, August 15, 1966, p. 39.

the adjustment burden to those who can least bear it or to make it more difficult for us to achieve balance. In our judgment—and, I believe, in your judgment—it is important for the United States to move decisively toward balance with the least possible dislocation to the world's system of trade and finance. Our mutual security and collective well-being, which rest upon the continuing strength and unity of the international economic system, are at stake.

It is against these fundamental objectives, which I am sure are common objectives, that I hope you and your Government will judge our new and strengthened balance of payments program. I have asked Ambassador Bruce to call on you to explain our new program more fully. I have also asked Under Secretary Katzenbach to visit with you in London to review further both this program and the entire scope of our mutual cooperation. I trust you and your key ministers will support this program and, thereby, help preserve confidence in the system we have built so diligently together over the past twenty years. I am looking forward to seeing you in February.

Sincerely, Lyndon B. Johnson"

Mark letter "Secret" and request HMG make no public reference to fact or substance of this letter. Talking points on substance of program to be used by Ambassador contained in septel.[5]

Rusk

---

[5] Not further identified.

---

169.   **Telegram From the Embassy in Japan to the Department of State**[1]

Tokyo, January 3, 1968, 1145Z.

4400. Sato–Rostow meeting: from Rostow. Balance of payments program. In two and a half hour meeting today with Under Secretary Rostow, Ambassador Johnson and Barnett, fully reported by later septel,[2]

---

[1] Source: Department of State, Central Files, FN 12 US. Secret; Exdis. Repeated to Canberra.

[2] This telegram has not been found. A detailed, 15-page memorandum of this conversation as well as memoranda of conversations with other Japanese officials, January 2–4, are ibid., Conference Files: Lot 69 D 182, CF 270. Eugene Rostow's summary of conversations with Japanese officials on the border tax is in telegram 4427, January 4. (Ibid., Central Files, FN 16 US) For his summary of his talks with Sato and other Japanese officials, see Document 175.

Prime Minister Sato said that he now understood the background and context of President's balance of payments program, and expressed admiration and respect for the President's courage and candor in laying his cards on the table, and taking such firm and difficult decisions. The political meaning of the program in Sato's view is that the President refused to deal with the U.S. balance of payments problem by cutting security expenditures or aid, but absorbed the necessary adjustments purely on the economic side, and through tourism. That the President did not falter in his efforts for peace and security, Sato said, is "something we have to think about carefully." At Rostow's request, he later authorized Igimura, Secretary General of Cabinet, to tell the press this was his general view, and that Japan would cooperate with the United States in protecting the stability of the world monetary system.

Rostow's presentation put visit in context of regular consultations characteristic of present stage of Japanese–American relations, intended to facilitate not only exchanges of views, but harmonization of policy. President's approach dominated, Rostow said, by desire through international cooperation (1) to prevent reactions that could undo all that has been accomplished in Kennedy Round and Rio agreement, and (2) to find solutions that enlarge trade rather than restrict or contract it. Main burden of adjustment process, following principles of OECD resolution and debate, should fall on deficit and surplus countries, with as little dislocation as possible for countries like Britain, Japan, Australia and Canada, whose special concerns had been taken into account in preparation of President's program.

With respect to trade, Rostow stressed that trade should be regarded as significant element in balance of payments adjustment process: that we were anxious to proceed with post-Kennedy Round negotiations to reduce non-tarriff barriers, including import quotas and other quantitative restrictions; and were interested in revision of GATT rules to allow more flexibility in using trade policy to help deal with balance of payments problems, without being asked to choose between quotas or devaluation. Such procedures, however, like long run export promotion plans, would not permit us to use trade policy to help solve the balance of payments problem in 1968. For that purpose, our attention was directed to the problem of European border taxes, which had become an increasingly significant disadvantage to our trade, as they were to the trade of Japan.

It followed from the President's basic approach to the problem of trade policy that we strongly prefer to achieve the indispensable increase in the U.S. trade surplus through a reduction of other peoples' trade barriers (particularly those of Europe) rather than through an increase in our own. One goal of Katzenbach's mission to Europe was to discover whether it was reasonable to expect a reduction of European border taxes, or at least a suspension of recent increases. It would be helpful if Japan could back us in this effort. President would make his decision about possibility of U.S. legislation in the light of these discussions, and other factors. U.S. legislation, if it should be proposed, would be a border tax adjustment of the usual type, legal within GATT rules, and of modest proportions, probably within 2 percent–2.5 percent range, since indirect taxes play so small a part in U.S. tax system. If we did decide to proceed with such legislation, we hoped the Europeans would stand still. While we were sympathetic to Japan's balance of payments problems and prospects, our present view was that a border tax adjustment of such scope would not significantly affect Japanese trade, taking into account the range of export supportive devices, such as special depreciation allowances, Japan now had available to assist exports. We assumed that Japan would be studying the problem carefully, as the situation evolved. Rostow said "I hope you will authorize me to assure the President that you will take no steps in this field, and that while you will of course wish to consider the impact of these measures on Japan as the situation evolves in the weeks ahead, that impact should be discussed further if you desire it in the next meeting of our Joint Cabinet Subcommittee at Honolulu on January 25." To this question, Miki later gave assurances that the possible reaction of Japan to a possible decision on border tax would be taken up at the Honolulu meeting. He spoke of Sato's statement as an assurance of Japanese "cooperation."

In prolonged exchange of views, there was repeated Japanese stress on these themes: (1) strong support for the policy of solving trade aspect of balance of payments problem by trade expansion rather than by contraction; (2) shock at the thought that the United States as the "standard-bearer" of the world would engage in any practices of a protectionist character; (3) anxiety about possible success of protectionist movements within U.S.; (4) assurance of agreement with us on principle of multilateral-consortium–IMF control of Indonesian aid program; and (5) clear view that stability of dollar was indispensable to stability of world monetary and economic system. Tokyo is likely to take all the steps, good or bad, which we take.

Dept repeat for Katzenbach and other addressees as appropriate.

Johnson

170. Telegram From the President's Special Assistant (Rostow) to President Johnson, in Texas[1]

Washington, January 3, 1968, 1426Z.

CAP 80060. Herewith Nick's first contact with London. They are sympathetic but worried about the direct and indirect effects on the U.K.—direct via reduced U.S. direct investments; indirect, via higher European interest rates.[2]

1. Fred Deming, Bill Roth, David Bruce and I met for two hours this morning with Roy Jenkins and senior officials of British Treasury, Board of Trade, Foreign Office and Bank of England. I began my presentation by putting President's strong action on balance of payments in its broad political context. I stressed that President is faced with many pressures to reverse U.S. political and economic policies and that these pressures would certainly have been exacerbated by news of our worsening balance of payments. Failure to act would have increased the possibility that our recent successes in the Kennedy Round would be lost and would probably also have led to increased demands to reduce troops abroad with a subsequent effect on our security and the security of our allies. The President's decision to take these difficult actions was motivated by his keen desire to avoid this reversal of all that we have stood for in the postwar period. It is our hopes that the success of this program will enable us to avoid these consequences.

2. I also emphasized that the President feels very strongly that the longer term solution to the kind of problem we face in our balance of payments must be greater cooperation and a sense of responsibility, not just on the part of deficit countries, but more particularly by the surplus countries.

3. Throughout subsequent discussion, Jenkins and British officials stressed their sympathetic attitude and understanding for the problem we faced. They welcomed these measures as strengthening the dollar and therefore ultimately benefitting all trading nations. Jenkins recognized that such measures were bound to have unpleasant effects, even for those countries in a weaker balance of payments situation, but that this was certainly preferable to a return to protectionism. He welcomed the differentiation we were able to introduce into program in order to minimize effects on countries like the U.K. who have their own balance of payments difficulties, but he did not wish to hide from us the concern

---

[1] Source: Johnson Library, National Security File, Memos to the President, Walt Rostow, Vol. 56 [2 of 2], Box 26. Secret.

[2] Numbered paragraphs 1–6 below are taken verbatim from telegram 6778 from Bonn, January 2. (Department of State, Central Files, FN 12 US)

which Her Majesty's Government feels. The more they studied measures, the more pessimistic their assessments became of the effect on the U.K. He stressed that they had not yet reached any definitive conclusion, but wished to maintain the closest consultation with us as they went through their calculations.

4. Main substantive concern appears to be with effect of investment controls, where British calculation shows higher effect than our estimate of $150–$160 million in 1968. British thinking in terms of possibly as high as 100 million pounds, but Deming felt that this calculation on direct effect was too high. However, British are already beginning to think of indirect effects due to drying-up of available capital in Europe and consequent out-flows from London Eurodollar market. Effect on European interest rates also stressed.

5. Jenkins agreed U.K. would not reach firm conclusions until they have opportunity discuss again with us results of our talks on continent. Tentatively we plan return next Saturday[3] for talks with Harold Wilson.

6. Full report being sent by Embassy London.[4] Fessenden.

---

[3] January 6.
[4] Telegram 5143 from London, January 2. (Department of State, Central Files, ORG 7 U) A later report of discussions with British Treasury officials is in telegram 5269 from London, January 5. (Ibid., FN 12 US)

---

171.   Telegram From the President's Special Assistant (Rostow) to President Johnson, in Texas[1]

Washington, January 5, 1968, 1639Z.

CAP 80116. Herewith Nick and the Germans. On the whole, positive.[2]

1. We met Tuesday afternoon[3] with Foreign Minister and Vice Chancellor Willy Brandt in a large meeting attended by six of the German

---

[1] Source: Johnson Library, National Security File, Subject File, 1968 Balance of Payments Program, Memos and Miscellaneous [2 of 2], Box 4. Secret. The telegram was received at the LBJ Ranch Communications Center on January 5 at noon (CST).
[2] Numbered paragraphs 1–10 below are taken verbatim from telegram 6782 from Bonn, January 3. (Department of State, Central Files, FN 12 US)
[3] January 3.

Government. An obvious effort had been made to bring together this leading group of officials, some of whom had been on their holidays. The atmosphere was friendly and began with my presentation along the lines of the one I reported from London.[4] The two-hour meeting covered a series of detailed questions on specifics of the President's program. Most of the meeting was conducted by Lahr in highly methodical fashion moving through the program point by point. The questioning centered on possible effects of the U.S. investment actions which the German side clearly felt would tighten their capital market (although at one point Lahr seemed to be saying that very little American capital had come to Germany directly from us—a point refuted by facts). I welcomed their assurances that they were interested in promoting a high growth rate, which they considered to be a responsible position for a surplus country to take.

2.   On border taxes, the German side made an effort to disclaim that German actions have a serious trade effect, but listened attentively to my strong political arguments that regardless of whether and how much we can show trade effect to be, the fact of their rebates was a potential political issue in the U.S. which would enhance protectionist pressures. Bill Roth explained in detail that we wish to discuss in GATT and related this to the adjustment process.

3.   I would summarize the large initial meeting as revealing the Germans to be sympathetic to our goals of avoiding a resurgence of protectionism and of wishing to do all that is required to assure the continued presence of U.S. forces for the security of Europe. On offset, the Germans were interested in my mention of possible multilateral arrangements in the longer term, but agreed that we should concentrate on bilateral discussions to meet the immediate problems of the next several years.

4.   Following the large meeting, I asked Brandt for a more restricted session attended only by Fred Deming, Bill Roth, Russ Fessenden and me and on the German side by Brandt, Lahr, Harkort and Duckwitz.

5.   I explained to Brandt that, in political terms, two steps from the Germans are really essential to us.

(A) First, I stressed the prime importance which we attach to maintaining our commitments for the common defense. In this context I said, it is essential that we have full neutralization of the foreign exchange costs of our troops in Germany. I did not mention a specific figure, but spoke in terms of a two-year agreement that would cover us fully.

It was clear from what I said that we were not speaking only of continuance of this year's arrangements. I also made clear that we needed an understanding on this in the very near future.

---

[4] See Document 170.

(B) Second, I described the heavy protectionist pressures in the U.S. and our political need to have something which could forestall these pressures. I then referred to our consideration of new legislation which would give a 2 percent–2-1/2 percent tax rebate to American exporters as something positive which could enable the administration to contain protectionist pressure. What we needed, I stressed, was a German commitment to stand still if we put into effect such legislation. If German and other countries were to retaliate, obviously the whole effect would be lost. I added that in addition we need to have a full exploration in GATT of the whole question of inequalities in the tax field as far as international trade is concerned. The 2 percent–2-1/2 percent border adjustment plus re-examination of the GATT rules could provide a means for keeping protectionism under control.

6. I stressed that, in making these two requests of the German Government, I hoped consideration would be given to the politically courageous steps the President was taking in the balance of payments program, especially in an election year. I pointed out that the 10 percent tax increase, the stoppage of all direct investment to Western Europe and the tourist measures are all of them politically very difficult.

7. In his reply, Brandt said that serious and urgent consideration would be given to these request by the German Government. He commented sympathetically on the principle of the first in particular, and fully understood the significance of the second. He added that these matters would be considered at the next Cabinet meeting, January 10, after which the German Government would be in contact with the Embassy.

8. In a later conversation at the dinner which he gave for us, Brandt told me that the two requests which I had outlined to him in the private meeting presented "no real problem." Lahr, in somewhat more cautious terms, made similar comments to Fred and Russ Fessenden.

9. Brandt's toast at the dinner was unusually warm. He dwelt at some length on German appreciation and sympathy for President as he carries immense burdens of free world leadership. Brandt also spoke of high regard for you and asked that I send best wishes for the new year.

10. Full report being sent septel on large meeting.[5]

---

[5] Telegram 6792 from Bonn, January 3. (Department of State, Central Files, ORG 7 U)

172. Telegram From the President's Special Assistant (Rostow) to the President, in Texas[1]

Washington, January 6, 1968, 0044Z.

CAP 80132. Subject: Reactions to balance of payments program.

Market—quiet again yesterday and today.

Gold pool made no sales yesterday. Took in $4 million today.

Dollar and sterling quiet.

Official Reactions

1. Katzenbach Mission

A. Belgium—great concern over prospective cut in U.S. investment. Want to work out special arrangement with us. Non-committal on border tax but recognize problem. Accepted principle neutralizing U.S. military spending.[2]

B. European Community (President Jean Rey)—Commission reaction sympathetic and positive but made no commitments. Agreed Europeans suffer from surplus psychology. Fear moves toward protectionism in U.S. Rey is interested in more regular U.S.–European Community consultations and will probably raise this subject with you during his visit in February.[3]

C. Berlin problem—Germans worried effect investment moratorium on new U.S. investments in Berlin, which they believe necessary to keep up morale in city. (Berlin Mayor Schuetz coming here in February to promote U.S. investment in Berlin.)[4]

D. Netherlands—Dutch worried about discrimination in investment and tourism but attitude cooperative. Said we should make IMF drawing and discuss question outstanding U.S. dollar balances in IMF. Katzenbach believes Dutch will accept border tax if we can make GATT justification.[5]

E. Italy—Foreign Minister Fanfani in effect told Italian press that deficit and program linked to Vietnam. Nick Katzenbach in airport press

---

[1] Source: Johnson Library, National Security File, Subject File, 1968 Balance of Payments Program, Memos and Miscellaneous [2 of 2], Box 4. Secret. The telegram was received at the LBJ Ranch Communications Center on January 5 at 8:12 p.m. (CST).

[2] Reports of Katzenbach's meeting with Belgian leaders on January 4 are in telegram 3856 from Brussels, January 4, and telegram 3493 from Rome, January 4. (Both in Department of State, Central Files, ORG 7 U)

[3] Reports of Katzenbach's meetings with Rey and other EC Commissioners on January 3 and 4 are in telegram 3855 from Brussels, January 4, telegram 3861 from Brussels, January 5, and telegram 3499 from Rome, January 5. (All ibid.)

[4] No report on this issue has been found.

[5] Katzenbach's report of his meeting with Netherlands leaders on January 4 is in telegram 3500 from Rome, January 4. (Department of State, Central Files, ORG 7 U)

conference on leaving Rome rebutted Fanfani statement. Said U.S. would have balance of payments problem without Vietnam.[6]

2. Rostow Mission

A. Japan—Further reporting emphasizes concern others would follow border tax move by U.S. Japan has raised discount rate as defense measure against balance of payments pressures.[7]

B. Australia—Accepts need for U.S. action but expressed strongest concern yet received over serious consequences program could have on domestic economy. Requested special treatment insuring that capital inflow into Australia should not fall below 1966 levels, semi-annual Ministerial consultations, recognition that reserves should not fall below June 1966 level, exemption from 5 percent cut in lending by banks and financial institutions, expansion of EXIM arrangement enabling Australia to float loans in U.S. free from IET, and assurance that the U.S. trade policy will attempt avoid injure Australian exports. Said restrictions on capital flow could make it difficult for Australia to continue its efforts in aid and defense fields, including participation in Vietnam. Reacted negatively to U.S. consideration of border tax and indicated Australia likely emulate any such U.S. action.[8]

McEwen told press Australia supports program and said both countries consulting on problems posed for Australia.

3. Trezise Mission

A. Norway—Worried about cut in U.S. investment and effect of U.S. program on European interest rates. Want to be put in category of countries heavily dependent on U.S. capital. Said U.S. could count on Norwegian support and cooperation.[9]

European Press

Program continued to draw voluminous comment abroad. Many found U.S. measures justified in spite of "painful consequences". Press opinion was divided over whether measures would achieve the desired effect. These major themes emerged:

—U.S. was determined to defend the dollar and with it the international financial system.
—Measures might slow down world economic expansion.
—Action was in response to European criticism and pressure.
—Vietnam war was a main cause of the U.S. deficit.

---

[6] This statement has not been found. A summary of the Rome discussions on January 5 is in telegram 8727 from Paris, January 5. (Ibid.)

[7] See Document 169 and footnote 2 thereto.

[8] A memorandum of Eugene Rostow's meeting with Australian Prime Minister McEwen and other Australian officials, January 7, is in Department of State, Conference Files: Lot 69 D 182, CF 270.

[9] No other report on the Norwegian reaction has been found.

—Impact on the developing countries was uncertain.

—Those advocating reduced U.S. investment in European industry might soon be eating their words.

---

173. Telegram From the President's Special Assistant (Rostow) to President Johnson, in Texas[1]

Washington, January 6, 1968, 2056Z.

CAP 80157. Herewith Nick has a civilized talk with the French.[2]

1. Fred Deming, Bill Roth, and I met with Debre and some of his senior officials and then later I made courtesy call on Couve. I would describe atmosphere as one of friendly, if studied, understanding. I think this best typified by Couve's remark that having argued for us to take action, it would be difficult for French now to complain. Except for rather brief references to doctrinal differences, all the remarks and comments made by the French seemed positive and uncontentious.

2. Debre stressed one point several times—although he said he did not want to moralize. He said that measures will be accepted or rejected outside the United States in direct relation to the understanding of both govts and public opinion that the U.S. is also dealing effectively with its domestic economy. Both Couve and Debre emphasized the necessity of President getting his tax measures exactly as introduced, as well as the U.S. taking steps to control internal credit and stabilize prices and wages. They seemed to accept my point that outsiders should not wish U.S. deflation and Couve replied that, on contrary, French wish see stability in U.S. economy. The Embassy will report our conversations in detail but I think that the following points are worth noting here.

3. Debre stated position of French Govt that they accepted measures in principles and recognized the strong and determined efforts of the President in both the domestic and international areas. They put usual stress on responsibility of deficit countries to take action, but rather

---

[1] Source: Johnson Library, National Security File, Subject File, 1968 Balance of Payments Program, Memos and Miscellaneous [2 of 2], Box 4. Secret. The telegram was received at the LBJ Ranch Communications Center on January 6 at 4:25 p.m. (CST). A handwritten note at the top of the source text reads: "Jones told B. Smith."

[2] Numbered paragraphs 1–8 below are taken verbatim from telegram 5277 from London, January 6. (Department of State, Central Files, ORG 7 U) A much longer account of this meeting is in telegram 8738 from Paris, January 6. (Ibid.)

surprisingly indicated that surplus countries too had at least a secondary responsibility. They emphasized that overwhelming position of U.S. economy in world economy presents special problems and calls for U.S. to exercise special care.

4. Debre said on investment measures he was perplexed by discriminatory treatment. Particularly, he could not understand why oil countries had been included in Group B. He was careful to say that this discrimination could not be whole-heartedly, or for long accepted by the French Govt, but did not appear to reject measure for the time being. He questioned how U.S. could regulate foreign affiliates of American companies if the U.S. continued to wish them treated equally in countries such as France. I responded to these remarks by pointing out that any regulation is inherently discriminatory since situation differs from one country to another and one company to another. I stressed that we had acted responsibly in not wishing to put burden of our adjustment on less developed countries or those in weaker B/P position.

5. Debre expressed some concern that we might be about to start a credit war. He warned that this would lead to organized disorder. Both Fred and I attempted to reassure him on this and said we had no intention of beginning competition on export credit.

6. Debre's general conclusion was that he admired U.S. action. "France had hoped too long for this action to criticize it now." He recalled that the United States had led the world in eliminating exchange controls, liberalizing trade and freeing both capital and movements of people. He said the French recovery had taken its cue from this leadership as they reduced protection, supported the Kennedy Round, eliminated exchange control, and opened their doors to investment. The present French Govt had done more in the last few years than in the past 50 to eliminate French protectionism. He then went on to say that they could accept temporarily these measures but, aside from their doctrinal differences with the U.S., they would find it difficult to convince their public opinion unless the U.S. internal measures were perhaps stronger than those proposed. (I am not sure that he fully understood U.S. internal measures.) He also thought we should examine our investment measures to see whether they could be less discriminatory and possibly re-examine all our measures to make sure that they would have their desired effect and not be quite so inequitable. Couve also expressed approval for continuing exchange of views, particularly on effects of measures, in OECD economic policy discussions.

7. I think it was right for us to go to Paris and I think we now have a record from the French on which we can build. I have no doubt that they will use different arguments with their European colleagues and others. But it seems to me the correct position for us to take with France is one which emphasizes our determination to act responsibly and to take

account of our own strength and not jeopardize others who are in a weaker position.

8. Debre made a very strong statement at the beginning that he and the French Govt were "scandalized" by some of the things appearing in the foreign press. He said that these had completely misrepresented the actions and intentions of the French Govt. Fred observed that we too had been shocked by some of the things said in the press and that we could only assume that the French Govt had not inspired these things as we had not inspired the stories in our own press. Fred pointed to last night's "Le Monde" story which talked of a tax on gold. He said that he had denied that there was any consideration of a move of this nature but pointed to this story to indicate that it is very difficult, if not impossible, to control what the press says. Bruce.

---

174. **Report by the Under Secretary of State (Katzenbach), the Under Secretary of the Treasury for Monetary Affairs (Deming), and the Special Representative for Trade Negotiations (Roth) to President Johnson[1]**

Washington, January 7, 1968.

SUBJECT

Report on Our European Balance of Payments Trip

Introduction

This report contains the principal findings of our European trip. (We have also taken into account Phil Trezise's talks in Scandinavia and Luxembourg.) Our conclusions are based on the preliminary reactions of the people with whom we talked. Obviously, the President's B/P program cannot be easily or quickly comprehended, nor could the effects of the measures on individual countries be thoroughly analyzed in the short time between the announcement and our visits.

---

[1] Source: Johnson Library, National Security File, Subject File, Balance of Payments, Vol. V [2 of 2], Box 3. Secret. No drafting information appears on the source text. The text of this report was sent to the LBJ Ranch in telegram CAP 80173, January 7. (Ibid., 1968 Balance of Payments Programs, Memos and Miscellaneous [2 of 2], Box 4) Katzenbach also prepared a country-by-country summary of his European meetings, which was derived from his telegraphic messages. This summary was transmitted under cover of a letter from Katzenbach to Representative Mills, January 16. (Department of State, Central Files, ORG 7 U)

The purpose of our trip was to convey at the highest possible political level the rationale behind the program, and seek whatever cooperation was appropriate and possible. We put particular emphasis on the President's desire to maintain our commitments to European security and to a liberal trade policy. We emphasized that European leaders must not judge our measures on the basis of narrow technical considerations, but rather in terms of the high political stakes involved in maintaining a healthy and strong American economy.

As an over-all impression, we feel that the President's program is regarded as necessary and desirable. The central bankers approved in general of the total program and its parts—a domestic tax increase, reduction of expenditures and B/P measures. They seemed prepared to see their reserves fall somewhat and agreed that activation of the new special drawing rights in the IMF would have to come more quickly. The government people, while approving the strength of the total program, and specifically its domestic parts, were more critical about the B/P aspects—with the criticism varying from country to country.

We sought both understanding and, to the extent feasible, undertakings not to retaliate against our measures. Nobody, however, was prepared to give us a firm commitment until they had studied the program and weighed the possible consequences. We sought, therefore, to set a favorable political climate for the decisions they will have to make.

U.S. Domestic Policies

We were met with one common response—although with varying emphasis—everywhere we went, i.e., *a successful program depends on our ability to get additional taxes and to cut Government expenditures.* European reactions clearly will be strongly influenced—and tempered—if we can demonstrate that we can carry through tough measures to bring our own house in order. If we are to get European cooperation and understanding—and we *must* make the Hill understand this—we will have to move ahead on the domestic front.

Border Taxes

There was no immediate indication that a modest border tax—if it could be justified under the GATT—would face retaliation. There are, however, risks. The overwhelming size of our economy places a special responsibility on us for maintaining the health of the world economy. Thus, whether we like it or not, our conduct is judged by a set of standards substantially different than those applied to others. While European political leaders recognize and understand our domestic problems, what we do is likely to set the tone for the entire world trading community.

We must, therefore, weigh the domestic political and economic benefits of introducing a modest border tax against the reactions of others. One thing is certain—we must justify the border tax within existing GATT rules. If we keep the rate at something between 2–2-1/2% we can, we believe, stay generally, although not necessarily strictly, within the rules. Then the Europeans, who understand the political nature of our domestic problem, will probably be able to overcome the doubts of their technicians and, at least in the Common Market and in Switzerland, will be able to avoid counter measures. This is predicated on the assumption that our tax will be announced as a *temporary* measure pending further discussions in the GATT on the general questions of border taxes and of the B/P adjustment process. It also assumes that legislation can be controlled and that it will dampen rather than enlarge protectionists' fires.

In Bonn, Brussels and The Hague, we raised the possibility of a suspension of recent or contemplated actions in the tax field. While some effort might be made to explore compensating measures for the border tax effect of the new TVA tax system, the legislative problem is so great that we do not feel this is a realistic possibility in our time frame.

Harold Wilson clearly indicated that he could not suspend the British export rebate at a time when the United States was introducing a similar system.[2]

Both the Swiss[3] and the British made the point that the imposition of a border tax implies that a currency is overvalued and warned us that this might be a conclusion drawn in certain business and banking circles. None of the Common Market countries made this point.

Tourism

The uniform European reaction—although everyone agreed that the President could not ignore such a large element in our B/P deficit—is that any U.S. action to restrict tourism would hit unfairly at airlines and hotels and probably would not achieve the desired purpose. They were happy to learn we were not contemplating exchange controls. Again they will probably accept some modest limitations—particularly if they are part of a broader B/P program.

There is real substance to the European view that we should do much more to encourage tourism in the U.S. Greater emphasis, for example, on package tours, which give the middle income traveler a better idea exactly how much he will have to spend, would do a lot of good. We should also urgently examine the feasibility of persuading airlines to give lower preferential air fares to round trips originating in Europe.

---

[2] Katzenbach's report of his conversation with Wilson is in telegram 5279 from London, January 7. (Department of State, Central Files, ORG 7 U)

[3] Katzenbach's account of his conversation with Swiss Government officials and bankers on January 3 is in telegram 3831 from Brussels, January 3. (Johnson Library, National Security File, Subject File, 1968 Balance of Payments Programs, Cables [1 of 2], Box 4)

Two other suggestions are worth studying:

—If we decide to put a small tax on passports, impose a ticket tax or a head tax, we might earmark the income to promote foreign travel to the U.S. (this would do much to make the tax more politically acceptable at home);

—We should take a very hard look at ways to simplify or eliminate our tourist visa requirements.

Investment

There was almost uniform (if at times grudging) approval of our decision to control U.S. investment outflows, but several countries expressed concern. Belgium, in particular, was quite worried; Holland was concerned about its North Sea oil and gas; Italy by its problems in the south. The UK also had some worries but accepted the program as necessary. The Commerce Department should be prepared to exercise some flexibility in administering the program. Obviously we cannot grant so many exceptions that we fail to reach our target. But we should at least encourage American business overseas to attempt, as far as possible, to meet this highly political need as they make their investment decisions.

While in Paris we met with a group of American businessmen, who raised an issue that deserves Commerce's urgent attention. They pointed out that U.S. business has found it indispensable, when raising money in Europe, to offer a parent company guarantee. In some cases they have gone so far as to incorporate in Delaware simply to make their issues more appealing to European investors. These guarantees very rarely come into play, but their existence apparently is important.

We asked the businessmen to get their comments and suggestions about the particular effects of these measures into Washington quickly. It will be of the utmost importance to work closely with the business community in order to meet their legitimate concerns, while at the same time assuring that the program is not frustrated by their ingenuity.

Finally, we are all a bit concerned by Debre's remarks that he wondered how the U.S. could regulate American affiliates and still want them to receive equal treatment "in countries such as France" (see Secun 30).[4] He may well be preparing the ground for later GOF moves against U.S. affiliates in France—where and when it suits the French. But such action will be difficult technically to devise.

Export Expansion

All of us—and Phil Trezise on his swing through Scandinavia—reassured the Europeans that the President's proposed export expansion measures would not set off a credit race. It is important that we explain

---

[4] Another series indicator and number for telegram 5277 from London, January 6, sent to the President in Document 173.

publicly and repeatedly that we want to increase the efficiency of Ex-Im in the credit field—not to move toward a system of subsidized interest rates.

Neutralization of Military Expenditures Abroad

Every NATO partner we talked with was grateful for the President's determination not to play into the hands of those in the U.S. who want, for other reasons, to see substantial American troop cuts in Europe. For bargaining purposes (particularly in Bonn)—and despite the fact that we realized it would probably not be possible—we emphasized the need for *full* neutralization of our foreign exchange costs. The trilateral talks last year bought us some time, but it is important that we begin discussions with the FRG as soon as we can on arrangements for the next two years.

During each visit we mentioned the need for future multilateral arrangements. Everyone expressed interest, but recognized that we would probably have to proceed on a bilateral basis for the next two years. State and Treasury have already begun consideration of a multilateral system which we might propose in NATO; we will now make it a priority SIG agenda item.

The importance of the British problem must not be underestimated. If the U.K. fails to get a £100 million off-set agreement (or very close to it) and, as a result, cuts the BAOR, pressure for cuts of our own may well reach intolerable proportions. Harold Wilson made very clear that he would withdraw troops without the off-set.

Gold

Everywhere we went the question of the 25 percent gold cover was raised—not nervously, but with a question as to why we had not yet acted on it. We explained the Federal Reserve powers to suspend—a point already known to the central bankers—and said any legislative action would in any event have to await a propitious time.

Conclusions

At a time when both the U.S. and British Governments are trying to improve their payments positions by an aggregate figure of over $4 billion, we cannot ignore the possible cumulative effects of the measures taken by the two countries on our own economies and the economic fortunes of the world at large.

We must put our best economic brains to work on this problem—and soon. *We recommend* that the President appoint an advisory committee, or perhaps use the existing Dillon Committee (which includes people such as Walter Heller, Francis Bator, Bob Roosa and Kermit Gordon), to undertake an immediate examination of the measures we have taken or are likely to take. If these experts conclude that the US/UK program may cause serious economic problems, the U.S. should call for a conference—perhaps sponsored by the Economic Policy Committee of the OECD—to propose ways of ameliorating conditions arising from UK/US balance of payments measures. We must, for psychological reasons even more than technical ones, demonstrate our determination to create conditions for an expanding world economy—with deficit countries assuming their responsibilities, surplus countries playing their proper role, and both responsive to the needs to LDCs.

Also, as many of our European friends seem to recognize, the reduction or elimination of our deficit makes it even more important that we proceed as quickly as possible to approve and implement the special drawing rights mechanism. While this may be a modest step, it will have an important bearing on developing a sense of purpose and responsibility.

It is important that we continue to analyze the domestic and international consequences of various legislative proposals—particularly their net effect on the B/P.

How we handle ourselves in dealing with our partners abroad is almost as important as the measures themselves. It is extremely important that the USG speak with one voice, and that we handle our negotiations with the utmost skill. There will naturally be differences of view between the various Washington agencies concerned with specific aspects of the program, but the political stakes are high and we must find some way to settle our differences quickly and constructively.

We were heartened, but at the same time sobered, by the recognition abroad of the importance of US leadership and responsibility. Without exception, the people we talked to are aware of the tremendous burdens the President carries, and all (except France) spoke with admiration that forceful and positive action had been taken.

175. Memorandum From the Under Secretary of State for Political
Affairs (Rostow) to Secretary of State Rusk[1]

Washington, January 8, 1968.

SUBJECT

The Balance of Payments Program: Next Steps after the First Round of Talks

These observations were written on the plane coming back. They reflect reactions of the talks we had in Japan, Australia, and New Zealand, and to what we read of Nick Katzenbach's talks in Europe.

The first reactions to the announcement of our balance of payments program on January 1 have been constructive. The speculative pressure on the dollar through the gold pool has stopped, for the moment at least. The governments and central bankers, by and large, have said two things: (1) the American action was necessary, courageous, decisive, and useful, but (2) they are also worried about its possible impact not only on their own economies, but on the world economy as a whole. They are concerned about the prospect of an acute shortage of funds, credits, and reserves, causing higher interest rates; about the risks of an outbreak of protectionism, especially if we decide to move for border tax legislation; and about an atmosphere of uncertainty which could express itself in the postponement of investment decisions, and a rising tendency to sell securities and hold assets in liquid form. Such a tendency could break some of the weaker currencies, and even lead to a pell mell for liquidity, in the pattern of 1931.

Action by the United States has an entirely different psychological effect from that of any other country. If we take limited protective steps which other countries take as a matter of course men react altogether differently. The fact that we have undertaken a mandatory balance of payments program is in itself a shock. That we are considering a border tax adjustment as part of the program—effectively a devaluation pro tanto or an increase in tariffs—is a double shock, and a doubly disturbing one.

It is not yet clear whether the increase in confidence stemming from the announcement of the program outweighs the increase in anxiety, and whether the reduction in our own balance of payments deficit will work towards equilibrium or disequilibrium in the world economy as a whole.

---

[1] Source: Johnson Library, National Security File, Subject File, Balance of Payments, Vol. V [2 of 2], Box 3. Secret. The source text is a copy sent to Walt Rostow at the White House, whose handwritten notation on the source text directed Lois Nivens, a secretary at the White House, to provide a copy for Fried "for urgent comment & discussion." In a January 8 memorandum to Fowler, Sam Y. Cross and Robert G. Pelikan, two Treasury officials who accompanied Rostow, provided another report on this trip. (Johnson Library, Fowler Papers, International Balance of Payments—Classified Material: 1968 Balance of Payments—Cables, Box 44)

We shall need to move rapidly during the next few months if the opportunity implicit in the crisis is to be used effectively, and the several major risks of the situation avoided.

This memorandum attempts to deal with some of the substantive problems of the period immediately ahead, and with procedures to be considered in dealing with them.

I.   Managing the adjustment between the US deficit and the E.C. surplus.

For several years, we have advanced the thesis that the balance of payments relationship between the United States and Europe was a joint responsibility of the surplus and the deficit nations, to be handled cooperatively.

Actually, our thesis requires some qualifications. Both we and the Europeans have recently lost some reserves to the Less Developed Countries. The situation is no longer ours alone to control. And only Germany and Italy of the Community countries have significant current surpluses. What we are really thinking about is a move towards equilibrium which would involve (1) a cut in our deficit; (2) a reduction of current surpluses for Germany and Italy; and (3) a reduction of reserves on the part of France, Belgium and the Netherlands.

One key to the success of our present effort is whether Europe can provide the world economy with $1.5 billion in additional capital this year, to replace that amount in American credits and investments covered by our mandatory action. Last year, European sources increased the availability of capital to foreign borrowers by approximately 100% over 1966.

Will the increase continue, and if so, at what rate? Should international action be taken to help stimulate the response of supply to increasing demand, or should the process be left to the market? If international consultations are indicated to guide the adjustment process, through what procedure, and to what ends?

The magnitude and abruptness of the adjustments envisaged, and the nature of the political and economic risks if things go badly, make it essential to utilize existing (or new) procedures of consultation for the purpose of harmonizing policy with respect to the adjustment process as a whole, and to its several interrelated parts as well. In fact, I suggest that this cooperation be organized on a Crisis Management basis, both within our government and internationally, and handled for the next few months by a small, high level, international working party, in continuous session, probably in Washington.

Viewing the adjustment process in all its aspects, governments should act at the level of political responsibility to lay down certain agreed policy guidelines for their officials in the areas of trade, finance, and banking who will have day-to-day responsibility. The general object of these guidelines should be cooperation to achieve balance of payments equilibrium at high levels of employment and investment. This sentence should not be regarded as a cliché.

It should explicitly mean a willingness on the part of surplus countries to lose reserves if necessary, within a pattern of cooperative reserve surveillance, to sustain existing levels of investment at home and abroad, and correlatively to offset tendencies towards excessive credit restriction or liquidity in the coming months, due to severe competition for existing funds.

Secondly, this principle should mean cooperation to maintain existing parities, through the gold pool or otherwise. In this connection, the Solomon plan[2] should be discussed and negotiated.

Thirdly, it should mean a willingness to examine all problems that bear on the viability of the monetary system—issues relating to sterling, the availability of reserves during a period of contracting dollar supply, and so on.

I have put the issues relating to the impact of our balance of payments program on the monetary system first because they are primary. If the dislocations of this period start another round of monetary turbulence, the damage may be harder to contain, and more fundamental.

We should explore with Secretary Fowler and Chairman Martin how monetary cooperation of the types mentioned should be organized and handled. To launch the process, I suggest a carefully prepared meeting—conceivably of the Chequers type, or a Special Session of the OECD Ministerial Council—either before or after the meeting of Working Party 3 scheduled for January 22–23rd, and the Honolulu meeting of the same period.

II. The Issues of Trade Policy.

We have taken the view that flexibility in trade policy should be part of the armory with which governments handle the balance of payments adjustment process.

To this end, we have proposed a change in GATT rules to authorize such flexibility. This proposal must imply either movable tariff rates or balance of payments surcharges as an alternative to import quotas.

Point 6 of the President's Seven Point Program of January 1, 1968, is "Non-Tariff Barriers". Reaffirming that trade liberalization remains the basic policy of the United States, it calls for long range post-Kennedy Round negotiations to tackle non-tariff barriers in general. It calls also for discussions about the possibility of "prompt cooperative action among all the parties to minimize the disadvantages to our trade which arise

---

[2] Not further identified.

from differences among tax systems". Mr. Katzenbach explored the possibility of these discussions in Europe last week. One of our most urgent tasks, beyond cooperative surveillance of the workings of the monetary system, will be to appraise the results of these explorations—that is, the chances of success in quick negotiations to *reduce* border taxes, and perhaps other non-tariff barriers, as an alternative to American legislation to establish border tax adjustments of our own. On the trip another way to reach the same end—that is, the end of reducing the level of European tariffs or tariff equivalents—was suggested: that some of the chief surplus countries put their Kennedy Round tariff cuts into effect in advance of the agreed schedule. The feasibility of this idea is now being staffed out. If it seems promising, it could be examined in the same negotiating format.

From our talks in Japan, Australia and New Zealand there is no doubt that a decision by the President to propose border tax adjustments would cause profound and far-reaching concern. These governments would expect such a move on our part to trigger a world-wide series of protectionist steps, and they are convinced such a process would be nearly impossible to contain. They would strongly prefer prompt negotiations to reduce European border taxes (and perhaps some other non-tariff barriers) as an alternative to American border tax legislation. The Japanese specifically offered to make a contribution to such a process of reducing non-tariff barriers, if we chose that course rather than its alternative.

It is nearly certain—however irrational this thought may be in fact—that a border tax proposal on our part would be taken as signalling a profound change in the direction of trade policy.

I believe that the announcement of our program and the first reaction to it have given us some time. If we get the tax bill through soon, international opinion will be even calmer, and the risk of a new round of gold fever (absent trouble for sterling) will be correspondingly reduced.

I suggest that we use this period of time—a couple of months at most—to follow this course urgently—the course, that is, of prompt negotiations to *reduce* European border taxes and other non-tariff barriers, while we mark time on the decision to initiate border taxes.

Such a course would improve our chances for success in organizing monetary cooperation along the lines indicated in Part I.

176. Telegram From the Department of State to the Embassies in Germany, Belgium, France, Italy, and the Netherlands[1]

Washington, February 5, 1968, 0041Z.

109871. Subj: US Balance of Payments Program.

1. Please deliver following message at highest appropriate level governments and EC Commission on February 5:

US wishes to pursue consultations on Balance of Payments Program begun during mission of Undersecretary Katzenbach.[2] Our particular emphasis will be on trade.

Most of the major elements of the President's program are already in train. Proposed income tax surcharge is before the Congress. The programs to reduce direct investment and lending overseas are in effect. Today we are sending up to the Congress legislative proposals on travel. We have begun discussions of ways of neutralizing defense expenditures overseas. And we have already moved to reduce civilian expenditures of the government abroad.

We wish now to move ahead with remaining major portion of President's program: action to improve the trade account. Although action on non-trade accounts will produce a major reduction in the US deficit, there must also be action to improve the trade account if we are to avoid the dangerous consequences of continued large-scale deficits. As the President said in his January 1 message, we must improve our trade position by $500 million in 1968.

To this end, US is considering several alternative proposals. We wish to consult closely with our principal European trading partners.

Ambassador Philip Trezise will undertake these consultations for us and present to members of your government and your senior officials the elements of our thinking. We should be grateful if your government would receive him.

2. *For Bonn.* Letter from President to Chancellor concerning Trezise mission follows septel for presentation February 5.[3] We hope Trezise could make initial call on Germans no later than February 8. Trezise prepared to stay in Bonn as long as necessary to follow up.

---

[1] Source: Department of State, Central Files, FN 12 US. Confidential; Immediate. Drafted by Enders (M) on February 3; cleared by Solomon (E), Leddy (EUR), Henry L. Heymann (S/S), Deming, Roth, and Fried; and approved by Katzenbach. Sent to Brussels also for USEC and Paris also for OECD.

[2] Regarding Katzenbach's discussions with European leaders, see Documents 170–174.

[3] Document 178.

3. *For Paris, Rome, Brussels, The Hague.* Will be in touch with you on scheduling Trezise visit, which in any case would be no earlier than February 12.

4. *For Brussels (USEC).* Trezise mission intended to continue process of consultation started by Katzenbach and Rostow[4] and continued during Rey visit here.[5]

5. Essential to this mission that Trezise meet with responsible ministers at each stop.

6. Washington team accompanying Trezise will consist of John Rehm, Counsel to the Special Representative for Trade Negotiations; Lisle Widman, Director, Office of Industrial Nations, Treasury Department; Thomas O. Enders, Special Assistant to the Undersecretary for Political Affairs.

7. *For Trezise.* Terms of reference for your mission follow septel.[6]

Rusk

---

[4] In late January Eugene Rostow visited Europe and consulted with EC officials on January 29. A report of their discussion is in telegram 4349 from Brussels, January 29. (Department of State, Central Files, FN 12 US)

[5] For a memorandum of Rey's conversation with President Johnson in Washington on February 7, see *Foreign Relations, 1964–1968,* vol. XIII, pp. 662–664. Rey also met with other senior U.S. officials. A memorandum of Katzenbach's conversation with Rey on February 7 is in Department of State, Central Files, FN 12 US. A report summarizing a U.S.–EC combined meeting on the afternoon of February 7 and the morning of February 8 was transmitted in telegram 114351, February 13, to eight Western European posts. (Ibid.) A report of Fowler's meeting with Rey on February 8 was transmitted in telegram 113391, February 10, to the same posts. (Ibid., Central Files, EEC 7)

[6] Document 177.

177. Telegram From the Department of State to the Embassy in France[1]

Washington, February 5, 1968, 0043Z.

109872. CEDTO. Subj: Balance of Payments Mission.[2]

For Trezise. Framework in which you will be operating is laid out in following memorandum from Secretary Rusk dated January 30[3] which President has approved:

"1. The President has indicated his determination to improve our trade account. On the other hand, he does not wish to take any action that might undermine our basic trade policy or unravel the results of the Kennedy Round. He is deeply concerned that any action taken precipitately and unilaterally could begin a downward spiral which could restrict rather than expand world trade.

2. The Administration is still considering several alternatives:[4]

A. A 2 percent border tax adjustment on imports and exports based on State indirect taxes;

B. Asking the GATT for a waiver to permit a 2 percent border tax adjustment because of balance of payments reasons;

B Prime. A similar adjustment on the import side only of 2-1/2 percent. This might be done without legislation. Alternatively there is a possibility—although not a strong one—that the Europeans will offer expansionary action themselves in order to avoid restrictive measures by the U.S. This action could be: acceleration of the Kennedy Round, untying aid, reducing border tax adjustments, stepping up domestic economic growth, etc.

3. We propose to go to the Europeans late this week, explain our problem, and describe the trade measures we are now considering (Alternatives A, B and B Prime above). It is essential that we get a better reading than we presently have as to what extent they will stand still without retaliation if the US—and if other countries emulating the US—should go down any of these particular roads.

---

[1] Source: Department of State, Central Files, FN 12 US. Secret; Exdis; Immediate. Drafted by Enders on February 3; cleared by Solomon, Leddy, Henry L. Heymann, Deming, Roth, and Fried; and approved by Enders.

[2] Regarding this mission, see Document 176.

[3] No other text of this memorandum has been found.

[4] A task force composed of representatives of the Council of Economic Advisers, Commerce, State, Treasury, and the Office of the Special Trade Representative developed these three alternatives, which were summarized as alternatives A, B, and C (instead of B Prime) in a memorandum from Roth to Califano, January 12. (Johnson Library, Fowler Papers, International Balance of Payments—Classified Material: 1968 B/P Operations, Box 45)

Germany's attitude will be crucial. We propose to initiate our consultations there with a letter from the President to Kiesinger.[5]

4. Given the unpredictability of possible trade actions by others and the importance and delicacy of what we are trying to achieve, it is clearly in the US interest for the President and the responsible Congressional officials to have these readings before making a final decision on our next move. This move could be either a direct US action, or quite possibly negotiations to carry through on European expansionary action—if we thought that serious and substantial—or to lay a more manageable basis in the GATT for US legislative or executive action.

5. In light of the need for further urgent discussions, both bilaterally in Europe and in the GATT, we will not be prepared to discuss the specific alternative proposals with the Ways and Means Committee next Monday.[6] We would, however, keep in close contact with the Chairman as our negotiations and planning progress."

Procedure outlined above has been discussed with Chairman Mills, who is in agreement.

Rusk

---

[5] See Document 178.

[6] Fowler and Roth unveiled the administration's balance-of-payments legislative agenda in testimony before the House Ways and Means Committee on Monday and Tuesday, February 5–6. The hearings continued through March 1. See *Administration's Balance-of-Payments Proposals: Hearings Before the Committee on Ways and Means, House of Representatives, Ninetieth Congress, Second Session* (Washington: Government Printing Office, 1968), Parts 1–3.

---

178. Telegram From the Department of State to the Embassy in Germany[1]

Washington, February 5, 1968, 0046Z.

109873. Paris for Trezise. Please deliver following message from President Johnson to Chancellor Kiesinger at earliest appropriate time on Monday:[2]

---

[1] Source: Department of State, Central Files, ORG 7 U. Confidential; Exdis; Immediate. Drafted at the White House; cleared by Solomon, Leddy, Heymann, Deming, Roth, and Fried; and approved by Enders. Repeated to Paris for the Embassy and OECD.

[2] February 5.

"Dear Mr. Chancellor:

I thank you for the friendly reception accorded Under Secretary of State Katzenbach during his visit to Bonn early this year to explain our program for dealing with the U.S. balance of payments problem. The ready response of your Government to Mr. Katzenbach's presentation was most gratifying. Now we must move on to the phase of cooperative action.

I fully recognize, as I am sure you do, the serious political issues which face us all as the result of the U.S. balance of payments problem. Every aspect of our relationship—political, economic, commercial and especially security—could be affected by this situation. All our efforts to achieve a stable and prosperous world community will be in jeopardy if we have not the will to act together now—as we have done over the past twenty years.

You and I are old enough to remember how a lack of economic cooperation among the nations plunged us into the depression after 1929—with all its tragic consequences.

Therefore, these are matters of great concern.

I think we are in agreement that both deficit and surplus countries must take measures to restore international payments to equilibrium. These measures will be painful and politically difficult for all of us, but my government is determined to carry through with our program. The effectiveness of what we do—the course of action we follow—will be determined in large measure by the way in which our Atlantic colleagues—and especially Germany—react. With careful cooperation we can move forward to resolve this issue. We must preserve the political and economic gains we have achieved in the last two decades—and go on from there. This is our objective and we seek your cooperation.

It has become apparent to me as I have examined our balance of payments position that the United States—despite the efforts we are making to avoid excessive demand at home and to take action on capital account, tourism, the neutralization of military expenditures overseas and in other ways—cannot reach equilibrium without improving its trade account. I believe the consequences of continuing large-scale deficits are so dangerous that we must take action in this sector as in others.

To this end we are seriously considering a number of possible steps, including the introduction of border tax measures of our own or the use of measures available under GATT to countries with balance of payments problems.

It will, of course, be most desirable to find solutions which will result in trade expansion, rather than trade restrictions. I am sure you know that I—like others who believe in liberal trade principles—must deal with strong protectionist pressures.

We propose to consult closely with our European trading partners, of which Germany is of first importance. I have therefore asked Ambassador Philip Trezise to visit Bonn as my representative. I hope it would be possible for your Ministers and senior officials to receive him during the week of February 5.

Ambassador Trezise will convey our views on the need for trade adjustment and the possible alternative means of bringing it about. He will explain our urgent concern with the tax adjustments at the border of your country and other countries. He will present our views on the kinds of actions Germany and other European countries could take to contribute to a general expansion of world trade and income as we move toward balance of payments equilibrium and a stronger international monetary system.

I know that you agree with me on the importance of resolving our balance of payments problem in an environment of expansion.

I hope that the visit of Ambassador Trezise will help achieve that objective.

Lyndon B. Johnson"

Rusk

179.   Memorandum From the President's Special Assistant (Rostow) to President Johnson[1]

Washington, February 7, 1968.

SUBJECT

Report on Our Balance of Payments Negotiations with Japan

At T ab A is Secretary Fowler's memo giving you the results of our negotiations to get some balance of payments offsets for our military expenditures in Japan.[2] When Prime Minister Sato visited you in

---

[1] Source: Johnson Library, National Security File, Subject File, Balance of Payments, Vol. V [2 of 2], Box 3. Confidential. A handwritten notation next to the dateline on the source text reads: "Rec'd 12:28 p."

[2] Fowler's attached memorandum to the President, February 3, is not printed.

November[3] he said Japan would take cooperative actions that would have the effect of helping our balance of payments by $300 million in 1968, and if possible go up to $500 million.

In negotiations just completed by Treasury and State, Japan agreed to a package amounting to $350 million:

— increased purchases of time deposits in
   the U.S. .... $210 million;
— increased military purchases and direct
   investments in the U.S. combined .... $100 million;
— other .... $ 40 million
                                         $350 million

Japan also agreed to shift some of its borrowing from banks in the U.S. to the Eurodollar market.

We could not get the Japanese to take trade actions—such as removing some of their restrictions—but this is still under consideration. In any event, they will not move in this area until they know what we will do on the border taxes.

The Japanese asked us for assurances that we will continue our present policies on their $100 million IET exemption, on Export-Import loans, and on bank lending under the Federal Reserve program. Secretary Fowler plans to give them these assurances and, at the same time, tell their Finance Minister we want to meet with them again in the late spring to see if they can do more—particularly if their balance of payments position improves.

Fowler is disappointed over the Japanese offer and believes it shows that Japan has not yet accepted a clear responsibility to offset our military expenditures there.

My comments is that we are making progress and Fowler has a good series of consultations going. Japan had a balance of payments deficit of over $600 million in 1967 and they face a deficit of $400 million this year. This puts some limits on what they can do. We also have to remember that their reserves are low and they keep them almost entirely in dollars, not gold.

Walt

---

[3] Prime Minister Sato held discussions with President Johnson and other U.S. officials November 14–15, 1967. Extensive documentation on the talks is scheduled for publication in *Foreign Relations*, 1964–1968, volume XXIX.

180. Memorandum From Secretary of the Treasury Fowler to President Johnson[1]

Washington, February 7, 1968.

There is some belief in financial circles, particularly in the City of London, that a new international financial crisis may occur in March. This belief seems to be based on the following series of points:

(1) The present parity of sterling, $2.40, is not supportable without a very strong domestic economic program—significant budget cuts, higher taxes, and a continued strong wage/price policy.

(2) There is a significant body of opinion in the U.K. that sterling should have been devalued more than it was, or that it would have been better for sterling to "float," that is, not to have a fixed (e.g. $2.40) rate which can vary only between $2.38 and $2.42, but one that could vary much more widely.

(3) The new Chancellor of the Exchequer, Sir Roy Jenkins, is a very able man, but, according to some, he is not strong enough to carry through a tough austerity program or, according to others, has designs on Party leadership. Under either assumption, he would be expected to sponsor a less austere program than needed.

(4) Therefore, the British budget, to be announced as of March 19th, is not likely to be tough enough. And, to try to compensate for this, it is likely that the U.K. would announce a floating rate for the pound—perhaps from $2.30 to $2.50.

(5) This would not be acceptable to the rest of the world; there would be a wave of devaluations, and another international financial crisis.

I want to stress that this is all gossip, primarily coming out of the City of London. Each of the points noted above may contain some truth, but it is the chain of reasoning that produces the belief in a financial crisis.

We do not get any sense that this kind of belief is held widely in Continental Europe. Our representatives have not heard any gossip from the Continent on this question.

There is, of course, some doubt in the minds of the Continental Europeans as to whether the British program will be tough enough. Nevertheless, they do not seem to be looking for an early crisis.

The Europeans probably are convinced that the U.K. would not try to "float" the pound. They made quite evident to the U.K., at the time of devaluation, that there would be no help from Continental Europe if the

---

[1] Source: Johnson Library, National Security File, Country File, United Kingdom, 2/7–9/68, Visit of PM Wilson, Briefing Book, Box 216. Secret; Sensitive.

devaluation were too big or the pound "floated." The U.K. apparently gave some fairly hard assurances on this matter.

Furthermore, the exchange markets do not seem to be looking for an early crisis. Sterling is not as strong as we would like, but it has behaved fairly well and U.K. reserves have strengthened somewhat.

In sum, I think the probability of a March crisis is not all that great, but I think it well for you to have this background as you talk to the Prime Minister.[2] I do not think, however, you can go directly to this point with the Prime Minister. Furthermore, I doubt that he will be in a position to give you hard facts and numbers about the budget, because it is still being worked on.

Nevertheless, I hope that you could press him fairly hard on—(a) his candid appraisal of U.K. prospects; (b) his frank judgment as to how the devaluation has worked; and (c) what he can tell you about the British budget. It would be useful to get from him a hard personal appraisal about prospective measures and their ability to do the job.

Henry H. Fowler

---

[2] A summary record of Prime Minister Wilson's visit to Washington, February 7–9, is scheduled for publication in *Foreign Relations*, 1964–1968, volume XII.

---

181. Telegram From the Embassy in Germany to the Department of State[1]

Bonn, February 12, 1968, 1956Z.

8266. Department pass Treasury and Defense. Subject: Rostow–Deming–Trezise–Schiller talk.

1. Under Secretary Rostow, Under Secretary Deming, Ambassador Trezise, and DCM Fessenden met this morning with Economics Minister Schiller, Under Secretary Schoellhorn, and Assistant Secretary Schlecht.

2. Schiller stated that an increase in domestic demand in Germany was desirable and advised the Under Secretary, in his later meeting with

---

[1] Source: Department of State, Central Files, FN 12 US. Confidential; Priority. Repeated to Berlin for Ambassador McGhee.

the Chancellor, to make this argument as his own view of the situation.[2] Schiller said that it was necessary to run down the current account surplus. Schoellhorn also stressed this point but argued that the process, on the basis of December figures, is well underway. (*Comment:* The December figures may well have been so much affected by the value added tax as to be quite unrepresentative.)

3. Minister Schiller argued that U.S. protectionism is very dangerous. He said that Debre, with whom he had flown from New Delhi to Paris, had said that if the U.S. took restrictive measures on trade account, France would not ratify the Kennedy Round. Schiller added, "he shocked me." He then read a sentence from the President's economic report saying that protectionism is no answer to the U.S. balance of payments problem.

4. In commenting on the Debre conversation, Schiller said that he found him hardening on SDR's.

5. On unilateral Kennedy Round acceleration, which the Under Secretary mentioned as one specific thing which the EEC might do to be helpful, Schiller responded very positively. However, in this conversation we made no attempt to develop specifics of what Germans might do.

6. The final ten minutes was spent on offset. Schiller stressed the helpfulness of the Bundesbank in the gold pool operations and other monetary measures of recent months. He noted, however, that free reserves of dollars now only amounted to about DM 5 billion and claimed that offset on more than half that amount would be very difficult. Likewise, a two-year agreement would be difficult. He contended that multilateralism had doubtful merit in dealing with the offset problem.

7. During conversation, Schoellhorn said that Bundesbank was giving some thought to dividing up financial neutralization requirement. According to this proposal, Bundesbank would cover part of gap by bond purchases, while putting up remainder to government to cover by bond purchases of its own (presumably by appropriation). This is first we have heard of this notion and are unable to evaluate it.

8. *Comment:* As in New Delhi, Minister Schiller conveyed a sense of understanding of the U.S. balance of payments problem and program, and a desire that the FRG be helpful in regard thereto.

McGhee

---

[2] At this meeting, Chancellor Kiesinger said he would soon respond to the President's letter (see Document 178); and in response to Rostow's comment that "an expansionist policy in Germany was important if the [balance-of-payments] problem was to be solved," he indicated that he was "in the middle of the question with Schiller being very expansionist minded but others not." (Telegram 8265 from Bonn, February 12; Department of State, Central Files, FN 12 US)

182. Current Economic Developments[1]

Issue No. 800   Washington, February 27, 1968.

[Here follow articles on unrelated subjects.]

PRESIDENT'S TASK FORCE RECOMMENDS PROGRAM TO INCREASE TRAVEL TO US

The President's Industry–Government Special Task Force on Travel recommended to the President last week a seven point program to increase foreign travel to this country; thereby improving our balance-of-payments position.[2] The report also covers actions already initiated by the travel industry to reduce the cost of travel by foreigners to the US and actions to stimulate foreign travel to the US.

One outcome of the Task Force's endeavors was a meeting in New York February 20–23 of 21 airlines members of IATA engaged in transatlantic service to consider directional fares to encourage tourism to the US. The plan for a westbound family fare that emerged will be submitted to all IATA members for approval.

Point One—Actions to Lower the Cost of Travel to and within the US

The price of visiting the US must be attacked within each area of expenditure if potential tourist markets are to be tapped more effectively and profitably. Because of the urgency of action on costs, the Task Force concentrated on exploring with the travel industry the possibility of offering price reductions.

The response has been very good, with the following reductions already in effect:

—Up to 40 percent reduction of regular rates in certain hotels and motels.

—10 percent discount in the regular schedule of rates of the three largest car rental companies.

—25 percent discount for visitors on sightseeing bus tours of one-day's duration or less during 1968 and 1969.

Actions pending approval of regulatory bodies are:

—50 percent reduction in the regular cost of domestic airlines fares. (These will be the lowest available rates anywhere in the world.) Application was filed with the Civil Aeronautics Board for approval.

---

[1] Source: Washington National Records Center, RG 59, E/CBA/REP Files: FRC 72 A 6248, *Current Economic Developments*. Unclassified. The source text comprises pages 9–14 of the issue.

[2] Reference is to *Report to the President of the United States From the Industry–Government Special Task Force on Travel* (Washington: Government Printing Office, 1968), 48 pp., which was submitted to the President on February 19. Regarding the appointment of this committee, see Document 153.

—Lower family plan airline fares to the US on tickets purchased in Europe.

—Round-trip railway fares at approximately 75 percent of present one-way coach or first-class schedules. If the ICC does not object, new fares will become effective April 29.

—Reduced directional steamship fares to the US. The International Committee of Passenger Lines will seek approval at the Atlantic Passenger Steamship Conference meeting during the week of March 10.

—10 percent discount on charter coach rates for international travelers on trips involving 400 miles per day. If the ICC does not object, the new rates will become effective May 1.

—Significantly reduced prices for packaged tours from Europe to the US will be made immediately available by major US tour operators as soon as cost reductions become effective.

Recommendations on Lowering Costs

Results of temporary price reductions for foreign visitors should be evaluated by October 1, 1968 and extended if they have proven to be effective in improving the US balance of payments, the Task Force report continues.

After the proposed reduced transatlantic fares have been agreed upon within IATA, the USG should take steps to obtain agreement on similar reduced directional fares from other areas of the world.

The USG should continue discussions with US railroads concerning establishment of a "Eurail Pass" system for unlimited 60-day railway travel in the United States.

Federal, state, and local governments should be requested to waive admission charges for foreign visitors at publicly owned parks, museums, national monuments, beaches, camp grounds, lodges and on local transportation.

Air, bus and railway industries should develop special reduced combination fares allowing foreign visitors to cross the US in one direction by air and return by rail or bus.

The hotel-motel and car rental industries should develop more package programs offering foreign visitors vacations in the United States with unlimited mileage in rented cars and accommodations at a greatly reduced flat rate.

Car rental companies should be asked to increase the discount allowed foreign visitors subject to the waiving of airport fees charged on car rentals by foreigners.

All special price reductions available to foreigners only if purchased abroad should also be made available to foreign visitors if purchased within the US, subject to appropriate safeguards.

US international carriers, with the support of the CAB, should urge IATA to relax "group inclusive tour" and "charter" regulations for inbound traffic to: allow the airlines to carry one escort free of charge for every 15 paying passengers; create nonaffinity directional group and charter fares; and allow split-group charter flights.

The USG should take every appropriate opportunity, including bilateral negotiations, to encourage air fare proposals designed to increase traffic to the US.

The USG should seek to secure the necessary uplift rights in Europe and the Far East for charter flights to the United States by US air carrier.

Point Two—A Program to Promote Travel to the US

The Task Force recommended that a campaign mounted at once to convince millions of potential foreign travelers that America is an economical, manageable, and attractive tourist destination. The campaign should have two goals: 1) to convince potential visitors that during 1968 and 1969, they can visit the US at a cost they now finally can afford—possibly cheaper than ever again; and 2) to convince them that their travels will be easy, comfortable and pleasant.

Actions initiated include the following:

US flag transatlantic and domestic air carriers will spend $16.5 million outside the Western Hemisphere in 1968 to promote travel to the US, a $5.5 million increase over 1967.

Foreign flag air and sea carriers will take immediate steps to accelerate the development of European travel to the US.

US air carriers will bring more than 2,000 travel agents, tour operators, and travel editors to the US for familiarization tours in 1968.

Other US industries and news and entertainment media will significantly increase promotional efforts abroad to attract foreign visitors to the US.

Recommendations in the travel promotion category include the following:

The US Travel Service should issue to foreign visitors hospitality cards entitling holders to discounts on expenditures in this country.

US-based international corporations should be encouraged . . . to devise financial and professional incentives, including assistance with vacation arrangements for group and individual travel of foreign employees to the US in 1968 and 1969.

The Administration should appeal to the individual state governors to increase their promotional budgets and appropriately gear them toward attracting foreign tourists.

The US Travel Service should promote travel by foreign professional and "special activity" groups to the US, and assure that qualified travel agents are offering specific, attractive package tours for this purpose.

The National Park Service, Forest Service, and Bureau of Indian Affairs should prepare travel brochures and translate them into foreign languages so that they can be distributed worldwide.

The US Travel Service, air carriers, and travel organizations should publicize widely abroad the applicability of standby domestic fares to foreign youths.

All USG agencies, their employees and families, operating abroad should be directed, in cooperation with the US Travel Service, to encourage and facilitate the flow of foreign visitors to the US.

The travel industry and the US Travel Service should vigorously promote side trips or stopovers in the US by international visitors drawn to Mexico City by the 1968 Olympic games.

Ethnic groups in the US should mount letter campaigns to relatives and friends abroad informing them of the new economy and facility of travel to and in the US, inviting them to visit America in 1968–69.

Particular attention must be given to launching intensive promotion programs in Canada and Mexico to attract more visitors to the US.

Point Three—Recommendations on Removing Barriers

Existing immigration laws which authorize the Secretary of State and the Attorney General to waive the visa requirements for citizens of contiguous countries and adjacent islands should be implemented to the fullest.

US laws and regulations should be changed for business and leisure visitors. (Legislation which would grant the Secretary of State and Attorney General broad authority to waive visa requirements for business and pleasure visits of up to 90 days on the basis of reciprocity or for other reasons determined by the Secretary of State to be in the national interest was submitted by the President to the Congress on February 23.)[3]

Existing health, immigration, customs, and agricultural inspection functions at ports of entry should be consolidated to provide a one-stop entry procedure for foreign visitors.

Customs should adopt procedures for oral declarations by foreign visitors.

Special entry facilities should be provided for group visits.

The favorable treatment granted to Canada in regard to the proposed duty-free allowances, expenditure tax, and ticket tax should be withheld until Canada grants substantial reciprocity with regard to duty-free allowances granted by the US to its residents returning from Canada.

---

[3] Regarding this legislative initiative, see President Johnson's letter to the President of the Senate and Speaker of the House of Representatives, February 23, *Public Papers of the Presidents of the United States: Lyndon B. Johnson, 1968–69*, Book I, pp. 263–264. The proposed legislation was not enacted during 1968.

Preclearance procedures should be instituted at international terminals abroad whenever it is determined by industry and Government to be advantageous in facilitating the clearance of passengers entering the US. The reciprocal exchange of administration support between different governments inspection agencies should be explored.

The Department of Agriculture should undertake a substantially expanded educational program abroad to inform visitors of those agricultural products, imports of which is prohibited. Agriculture should also be directed to devise new procedures to expedite agricultural inspection.

The USG should press for acceptance by all OECD member governments of those provisions of the Code of Liberalization, without reservations or derogations, which call on all member countries to allow their citizens at least $700 of travel expenditure per trip.

USG agencies should make every effort to eliminate the necessity for visas for East Europeans attending international conferences in the US, so that the US can compete in the international convention market with nations that do not require visas.

To encourage the inclusion of US ports in cruise itineraries, Federal regulations should be amended to permit steamship operators to schedule cruises from abroad to include visits to two or more ports in the US.

Point Four—Changing Attitudes

The Task Force thought that much needs to be done to make the tourists' stay pleasant and stimulating. In the short run, this could best be accomplished by an intensive public service advertising campaign and by a special Presidential appeal. The campaign would be primarily directed toward the people with whom the foreign visitors may be expected to have the most contact: policemen, taxi drivers, air, rail and bus employees, hotel and motel staffs, government employees at all ports of entry and personnel at tourist attractions. However, for the campaign to be successful, every American should be prepared to render assistance to foreign visitors. Among the recommendations of the Task Force in this area are: a major public service campaign, under the Advertising Council, Inc. urging all Americans to be friendly and hospitable to foreign guests, US residents to invite foreign friends and relatives to be guests in their homes this summer; and a special orientation campaign addressed to business firms and organizations.

Point Five—Improving Services

Some fifteen recommendations of the Task Force pertain to improving services rendered foreign visitors in the US. These include such things as: a) a program to improve the foreign languages facilities at major US ports of entry, municipal reception centers; b) availability of low cost, short-term medical insurance for foreign visitors; c) a comprehensive guidebook of the US, translated into major languages; d) a national steering committee to organize volunteer hospitality groups throughout the country; e) programs to expand foreign exchange facilities to cover all international arrivals at international ports of entry; f) availability of automobile insurance at nominal cost; g) a wider variety of short courses during summer sessions of educational institutions that would be attractive to foreign students and teachers; and h) authorization by the CAB to US air carriers and foreign charter carriers to charter aircraft to foreign tour operators for tours destined for the US.

Point Six—Studying Markets

With the present jet fleets of the international air carriers and the sizable number of jumbo jets which will come on line by 1970, capacity will be available for a very substantial increase in foreign visitors. Market studies are urgently needed to take advantage of this available capacity and of the cost reductions that are already taking effect.

Recommendations include the following:

The US Travel Service should devote a portion of the budget increase recommended for urgent market research in Western Europe, Canada, and Mexico.

The US should seek the cooperation of other governments and segments of the private and travel industry in developing market data and in researching the potential markets for regional multi-country tours from Europe and the Far East to North America and the Caribbean area. Canada, Mexico, and the US have agreed to share the cost of a market survey in the Federal Republic of Germany.

Several suggestions are aimed at improving estimates of travel expenditure and receipts in the balance of international payments.

Point Seven—National Tourist Office

The Task Force recommended that a strong national tourist organization be created to coordinate and direct the entire US travel effort. Whatever the organization's structure, it should be responsible for: continued market research, a vastly stepped up, balanced tourism promotion program; cooperation with state and local organizations, banks, and Federal agencies concerned with or involved in the financing of transportation facilities; accommodations and special attractions; improving handling of foreign travelers; assisting in or sponsoring of training facilities for services needed at points visited by foreign tourists; and coordinating the widespread activities of the Federal government affecting international travel business. Initially the work of the proposed organization should be limited to travel by foreign visitors.

The Task Force recognized that it would take some months to set up the proposed travel organization and recommended that in the meantime the budget of the US Travel Service (USTS) be increased by $1.7 million over the $3 million already appropriated. Also, the function of the Travel Service should be expanded to permit it to launch an immediate promotion program abroad and to strengthen its existing operation. For fiscal year 1969, the Task Force recommended that the authorization for the US Travel Service be increased to $30 million. When the new travel development organization is launched, the USTS should be incorporated into it.

IATA Plan

Twenty-one airline members of the International Air Transport Association (IATA) engaged in transatlantic service met in New York February 20–23 and agreed upon a westbound family fare (to the US or Canada and return) which would permit dependents of a traveler to enjoy a 50% reduction in normal fares, either first class or economy class. If a traveler purchases an excursion fare ticket instead of first or economy class, his dependents may still travel at 50% of the economy class fares, which is approximately one-third less than the excursion fare price. Tickets must be purchased in Europe or the Middle East and the fare is good throughout the year. This action will now be circulated by mail to IATA members who have three weeks in which to respond.

[Here follow articles on unrelated subjects.]

---

183. Memorandum From the Director, Office of Industrial Nations, Department of the Treasury (Widman) to the Acting Assistant Secretary of the Treasury for International Affairs (Petty)[1]

Washington, February 28, 1968.

SUBJECT

Recent Meeting of the OECD Tourism Committee

I find that there is an extremely interesting story behind the report of the recent meeting of the OECD Tourism Committee[2]—one which should not be widely circulated but which I think you ought to know.

---

[1] Source: Johnson Library, Fowler Papers, International Balance of Payments—Classified Material: 1968 B/P Travel Expenditures Restraints [1 of 2], Box 46. Limited Official Use; No Other Distribution. An attached note from Douglass Hunt, Special Assistant to the Secretary of the Treasury, to Barr, April 8, mentions that Fowler wanted Barr to take up Widman's memorandum with Howard J. Samuels, Under Secretary of Commerce.
[2] No other written report of this meeting has been found.

The official representative of the United States at this Tourism Committee meeting was Mr. John Black of the U.S. Travel Service. He was the only person from Washington who attended the session. He was actually accompanied in the room by Jim Ammerman and John Ferriter of the Permanent Mission to the OECD.

One of the principal agenda items, and the only one of real interest to the Committee, was the scheduled discussion of the prospective U.S. measures to discourage foreign travel by U.S. residents. Apparently, in the middle of the afternoon session the Irish delegate presented specific language for the Committee report which was extremely critical of the proposed U.S. action. His proposal also contained language which accused the United States of not making a serious effort to promote foreign travel to the United States, citing as evidence the fact that the budget of the U.S. Travel Service was very low and that the Travel Service was closing some of its offices overseas.

Mr. Black did not oppose this language. He indicated that the United States would abstain on the Irish proposal and then announced to his colleagues that it was necessary for him to leave the meeting to catch a plane at about 4:00 for Geneva. He turned the U.S. chair over to Jim Ammerman and left the room.

Ammerman was appalled at the Irish proposal, which other members of the Committee were anxious to adopt. He refused to accept it. Finally, after long arguments failed, he reminded the Committee that it was a plenary session and operated on an unanimity rule. He was on very dangerous grounds because Black had announced that the United States would abstain. Nevertheless, he struggled with the language for quite some period of time and eventually managed to persuade the other delegates that the United States was making a serious effort to promote foreign travel to the United States and that it was not feasible for the United States to achieve the required balance of payments gains in the required period of time through this measure alone. He finally was able to get the language which was reported by cable, but, having in mind Black's earlier instructions, he did abstain on the final vote. This is an extraordinarily unusual situation.

The performance left the impression that Mr. Black was not in full sympathy with the proposal being advanced in the United States to restrain travel abroad and that he was more interested in getting the Committee to criticize the failure of the United States to increase the U.S.T.S. budget than in toning down the critical language about U.S. efforts to restrain travel abroad by Americans.

It may also be worth noting that when Black was asked why the United States proposed to discriminate in favor of the Western Hemisphere in its travel restraints, he explained that Western Hemisphere countries were willing to hold dollars whereas the others insisted on converting them into gold. It was this factor, he told the Committee, which caused the United States to draw the line between the Western Hemisphere and the rest of the world.

The Paris Mission did not feel that it was diplomatic to report what had happened in connection with this meeting and it would probably not be advisable to have the situation widely known. At the same time it does suggest that if the Treasury wishes to have its view on the question of travel restraint accurately and forcibly presented at any future meetings of the Committee, it would be inadvisable to have Mr. Black designated as the head of the U.S. Delegation. Under the circumstances, perhaps it would be better to take the line that, given the request to minimize unnecessary travel, no one from Washington should go to these meetings and then the matter could be left in the hands of the Mission where, provided the formal instructions were adequate, Messrs. Ammerman and Ferriter would forcefully present the approved position.[3]

---

[3] A second note attached to the source text from Barr to Fowler, May 20, reads: "Black resigned today—it is my understanding that he resigned by request. Frankly I thought that was going too far but Commerce evidently felt less of him than we."

---

184. Memorandum From the Assistant Secretary of Commerce for Domestic and International Business (McQuade) to the President's Special Assistant (Goldstein)[1]

Washington, February 29, 1968.

SUBJECT

5-Year Commerce Export Expansion Plan

I think you will want to read the attached staff paper which sets forth the conceptual basis for our 5-year export expansion plan. I am also sending a copy to Charlie Zwick and John Petty.

I have become increasingly worried that the Balance of Payments program announced by the President on January 1 is coming under attack, particularly the restrictive programs involving foreign invest-

---

[1] Source: Johnson Library, Office Files of Ernest Goldstein, Export Program–2, Box 7. No classification marking.

ment and travel, while the most positive feature of the program—export expansion—seems to be stalled. Legislation has not been sent up with respect to the new "Export Expansion Fund" for the Export–Import Bank, nor has the proposed improved rediscount facility of the Exim been explained to business or the public. Commerce's Joint Export Association plan has received favorable business comment but we necessarily must advertise it with some restraint since no funds have been made available for this program. Our supplemental budget request for Fiscal Year '68 contains half a million dollars for JEA's and the '69 budget estimate $2-1/2 million, but it is not possible even to refer to the funds in the supplemental publicly since the supplemental has not been submitted to Congress.

Congressman Rooney has tentatively scheduled our FY '69 budget hearing for the Bureau of International Commerce on March 22. If the supplemental budget is not submitted to Congress within the next few days I doubt that Mr. Rooney will be willing to take up the supplemental at the March 22 hearing. This is probably our only real opportunity to obtain additional funds in Fiscal Year '68 in sufficient time to be of practical value to us.

I wish you would do what you can to speed up action on these three items of immediate and direct importance to the export expansion program. I think prompt action is essential, particularly with the increasingly pessimistic comments being made in the press with respect to the declining trade account surplus developing so far this year.

Larry

Attachment

Paper Prepared by the Bureau of International Commerce, Department of Commerce[2]

Washington, February 28, 1968.

THE FIVE YEAR EXPORT EXPANSION
PROGRAM—CONCEPT AND SCOPE

I. General Plan

A.   *The General Premise*

The underlying premise of the 5-year export expansion plan is the need to make U.S. business export minded. In order to do this, we must a) understand more clearly the basic economic reasons why the United States continues to have the lowest ratio of exports to GNP of any major

---

[2] No classification marking.

industrialized Western (non-Communist) country; b) how to motivate American industry to alter its basic assessment of domestic marketing versus international marketing so as to induce an allocation of corporate resources to export; and c) to devise the tools, factual and analytical analyses, and other resources at the command of the Government (including appropriate and flexible types of export credit) to sustain a significant shift in business marketing plans toward exports. In essence, therefore, the approach of the 5-year strategic export plan is to help create the conditions which will induce and sustain an alteration in the composition of our GNP in the private sector.

Over the past decade or so U.S. exports have remained fairly constant at about 4% of GNP. If exports could be raised to 4.3% GNP, at current rates of GNP, this would amount to an addition of approximately $2.5 billion in exports above the trend line in export growth. If imports could be held to the secular trend line of growth, approximately 3.1% GNP over the past ten years, the net addition of $2.5 million in exports could provide the additional foreign exchange earnings necessary to bring us within striking distance of equilibrium in our international accounts. Assuming reasonable progress in other aspects of the Balance of Payments program (i.e., travel account, Government expenditures overseas, etc.), the projected improved trade surplus could presumably provide the necessary margin of increased foreign exchange earnings to "solve" the U.S. Balance of Payments problem.

B. Export Targets

  1. The Export Goal

The overall goal of the 5-year program (January 1, 1969–December 31, 1973) is to raise U.S. exports as a proportion of GNP from 4.0% to 4.3%. Specifically, at the current GNP level, this means about $2.5 billion in commercial exports above the trend line.

  2. Industry Targets

Export targets for the 5-year plan are to be set on an industry or sectoral basis. These targets will at first be developed on a fairly broad basis, possibly initially on a three digit SIC basis, and then refined and made more specific, ultimately perhaps on a six or seven digit SIC basis. The Department of Agriculture will be consulted and targets for the agricultural sector will be determined in conjunction with that Department. Similarly, targets will be established in the minerals area in conjunction with Interior (coal, for example). Official status for these goals will be established through the Cabinet Committee on Export Expansion or the Cabinet Committee on Balance of Payments.

The exports targets by major industry sector would be reviewed from time to time in relation to export performance. Progress in attainment of the overall export goal, as well as the major sectoral targets, would be reported to the President through the designated Cabinet Committee. The targets would be adjusted as necessary and presumably the necessary resources, e.g., Export–Import Bank credit, and other relevant resources, would also be considered.

II. Operational Plan

A.   Existing Commerce Trade Promotion Program

Export expansion efforts to date have been based on more or less unrelated but useful individual overseas promotional events, commercial information and economic analyses of foreign country developments and market potentials, and a fairly comprehensive system of foreign service reports on individual export opportunities and reports on individual foreign firms likely to be useful to American companies seeking export outlets. Much of the information on foreign firms has now been automated. Additionally, the American International Traders Index has been established on an automated basis and contains information on some 20,000 firms now engaged in exporting or definitely wishing to be so engaged. The state of the art permits selected electronic matching of foreign market opportunities, foreign firms appropriate as agents or export representatives of U.S. firms, and the U.S. firms at home interested or potentially interested in exploiting foreign markets through export. Lack of funds has limited a reasonable degree of utilization of the existing data.

Cost effectiveness analyses have indicated a high degree of pay-out for certain individual export promotional activities. For example, within 12 months of the particular show at a trade center or a trade fair, U.S. firms exhibiting at these events have reported and we have verified sales results approximately amounting to $15 for every $1 of Commerce budgeted expenditures. Since about half of the Commerce funds are spent in the United States, the Balance of Payments returns are in the order of 33 to 1. These results, based on present techniques and relatively modest promotional expenditures in support of particular individual trade promotion events overseas, have already established a limited basis for measuring the value of export results in relation to specific forms of export promotion. There is a presumption, as yet unproved, that a more systematic approach would produce greater results—by inducing more U.S. firms to participate in Commerce Department sponsored trade promotion activities and more importantly by inducing U.S. business firms to devote a larger portion of their marketing resources to overseas sales.

B.   The New Program: Integrated or Systematic Approach

The basic innovation to be introduced by the new export expansion program is the systematic or integrated approach based on a 5-year planning cycle. Corporate management plans marketing efforts at least 5 years ahead. To a degree still undetermined there is a presumption that major segments of U.S. industry do not plan export sales efforts with the precision and the necessary allocation of company resources as is done in the case of domestic marketing efforts. As a result, of course, the natural ease of selling in the United States market, the buoyancy and growth in the U.S. market, and similar factors tend over the 5-year company planning period, we think, to limit even further the allocation of company resources to the export markets even in those cases where companies have indeed included export markets in their 5-year overall marketing plan. Major companies, of course, plan for overseas marketing as a mix of export sales from the United States and investment in foreign plants (and sales in third country markets from foreign production). The requisite of success of the Commerce 5-year export expansion plan is the general introduction into corporate planning of the export marketing program as an integral and identifiable element in the total marketing and growth plan of the company.

How is this to be done? A variety of techniques and methods will be employed—but the unifying element will be a 5-year export target for an industry, yearly targets or 2-year targets as appropriate, and a schedule of export promotional events for the particular industry in the particular markets for which targets have been set. In other words, overall industry targets will be broken down as practicable, to identifiable foreign country targets for as narrow product groups as possible. In this way an industry generally and the Director of Marketing of a particular company can plan long-range foreign sales programs with full knowledge and reliance on supporting trade center, trade fair, trade mission and other overseas promotional events sponsored by the Department of Commerce. Additionally, research on overseas markets, analyses of changes in foreign markets, including changes in domestic production in those markets as well as changes in import shares being provided by particular foreign countries, will be provided.

New promotional techniques will be introduced as they are needed and in accordance with the nature of the markets to be served and the needs of the U.S. firms interested in exploiting these markets. For example, the Joint Export Association (JEA) will be used as a means of stimulating interest in and defraying part of the cost of entering new markets. Initially Commerce would let contracts with a group of firms forming the JEA for a 2-year period for a stated market objective. The export growth target for the JEA would be established in conjunction with the target. Progress would be assessed periodically toward the attainment of the target, and cost effectiveness analyses would determine whether contracts would be extended or terminated or modified. As experience is gained with the JEA program, it is contemplated that for certain markets, possibly in Latin America and other developing areas, contracts would be let for longer periods up to 5 years where the nature of the marketing problem necessitates longer term efforts. Initially, however, JEA efforts would be more heavily concentrated in product areas and country markets offering more immediate payout possibilities.

Implicit in the approach just outlined is a "commitment" by the Government to follow through on the necessary supporting efforts directed toward the elimination of unreasonable or unfair foreign barriers to the expansion of our trade. Our trade policy work, in conjunction with State Department and the Office of the President's Special Trade Representative (STR) will take this into account, both for shorter term and longer term trade expansion objectives.

Also implicit in this approach is a "commitment" by our Government to take the necessary steps with respect to domestic policy measures to place U.S. exports in a reasonably competitive position with foreign exporters. Controlling inflation is of central importance. But also the Government must do its part to provide competitive export credit facilities, improved transportation and other supporting services and facilities necessary to an economical and competitive export effort.

C.   *Stimulating Interest in Exports—The Task in the United States*

To accomplish the goal of a reallocation of resources from domestic to foreign marketing, by the small but crucial 3/10 of 1%, will require a major sustained promotional program throughout the United States. Mainly this program should address itself to trade associations or other groups of firms already in existence. The structure of trade associations in the United States generally limits the activities of such associations to information purposes. The trade associations can become a major vehicle for exploiting the concept of the export goal, the 5-year targets, and the 1 or 2-year specific promotional plans for particular industries and particular product lines. Association meetings can be used in a number of ways to stimulate interest and motivate American companies to meet or exceed the export targets. For example, after Commerce has set a target for Product X in Market Y, the industry will be informed of the target, the trend in U.S. exports of Product X to Market Y over a period of years, the degree of export penetration by foreign countries and share of the growth of that market, and domestic consumption in that market in relation to domestic production and imports. Additionally, each firm will be informed as to the proportion of the U.S. industry shipments going into export. In this way the individual company will know whether or not the company is exporting as much as the average firm in the industry. In addition, of course, each company will be able to judge the degree to which Japanese and Italian firms for example have been able to exceed the export growth rate for the U.S. industry as a whole or for their company in particular in relation to the particular market. The essence of the scheme, of course, is to provide enough information to stimulate the interest of the industry in exporting by providing foreign market analysis and growth trends and by providing the information which will permit the individual U.S. firm to judge whether or not its own export performance is commensurate with its competitors in U.S. industry, as well as that of foreign competitors for the particular market.

Obviously Department of Commerce promotional efforts will be framed for particular industries in relation to the nature of the foreign market potentials for that industry and the degree of difficulty in achieving those potentials. Analyses of domestic U.S. industry growth trends will be made so that the export target aspect can be related to trends in domestic growth and available or excess plant capacity in the United States.

Finally, the 5-year export plan will be directed and monitored by an export planning staff in Commerce. This staff will be guided by an advisory group of business executives, marketing specialists, and business economists. Ad hoc industry groups will be used in framing particular industry export targets and special industry promotional programs.

III. Measuring Results

It has not been proved, of course, that it is possible to achieve a real-location of resources by U.S. industry directed toward increased export effort. It is possible that structural factors in the U.S. economy make attainment of the goal impossible. We know that the two basic factors which determine the general level of U.S. exports, of course, are the buoyancy of foreign markets (particularly Western Europe, Canada and Japan) and the buoyancy of the domestic U.S. market. Excessive demand at home not only serves as a magnet to attract imports but also causes U.S. firms to neglect relatively unknown foreign markets in favor of known and proven domestic sales opportunities. Additionally, if as some U.S. businessmen assert, domestic sales are indeed more profitable generally than export sales, attainment of the export goal may indeed be impossible if we assume continued highly vigorous growth in the domestic economy.

A basic feature of the 5-year export planning effort provides for economic research and analysis to illuminate the structural factors affecting the long term U.S. position in world trade. The comparative studies of foreign economies and their export growth will also be made. Conclusions will be drawn as to what steps are necessary to assure an adequate degree of export growth for the U.S. relative to the export performance of other countries. Should it appear to be impossible to achieve the export goal by a wide margin, or if the import growth trend should be so great as to wash out on a net basis most of the positive gains in the trade account envisaged by the program, these conclusions will be brought to the attention of the Cabinet Committee on Balance of Payments and the President. The policy implications of such a conclusion are obviously very serious, particularly if our balance of payments deficit cannot be significantly moderated as a result of programs undertaken outside of the trade account.

The cautionary words in the paragraph above are necessary since available data do not demonstrate whether or not present conditions in the United States and the nature of international trade, which is highly competitive and in part subsidized by some national governments, indicate that the objective is attainable. It will be attained, presumably, only if the profit potential in export sales is at least commensurate with the return on capital and other company resources put to alternative uses. In the period 1960 through 1966 Italy has increased its exports as a proportion of GNP by 2.3 percentage points, from 10.8 to 13.1 percent; Germany by 1.5 percentage points, from 15.4 to 16.9 percent; and Japan by 0.5 percentage point, from 9.6 to 10.1 percent. The U.K. has been unable to increase its export ratio. Obviously structural factors within these countries help to provide clues to the success or failure of their export programs. In certain respects the problem facing the U.S. economy in achieving a reallocation of resources from domestic sales to export sales may be considerably more difficult and intractable than in many foreign countries.

Finally, whether or not the export goal can be achieved, it seems necessary and desirable that a major export expansion effort along lines described above be undertaken. Such an effort will make some impact in our trade account even if the goal itself may not be achieved. Since the problem is a long term problem of reallocation of industry resources, more than the 5-year period may be necessary to achieve the goal. In this respect structural changes may be taken into account. In any case the Commerce Department 5-year plan will be built around concepts of export targets which can be costed out in terms of budgetary expenditures. Cost effectiveness measurement techniques will be built in to the various export activities and will be useful tools in fashioning program objectives and related budgetary expenditures. The program mix, therefore, can be altered in future years to emphasize those activities which produce the best results for the budget dollar expended and in terms of balance of payments gains. A different system of cost effectiveness will have to be introduced to permit adequate judgment for export objectives in the developing countries since returns here will be of a longer term nature. Initially, however, program emphasis will be on the best return in the short-run and will concentrate most heavily on hard currency markets.

185. Editorial Note

Pressures on the Canadian dollar in the international financial markets prompted the Canadian Government on February 29, 1968, to draw $425 million from the International Monetary Fund to strengthen the reserves of the Bank of Canada. One week later it announced the availability of $900 million in standby credits, $500 million of which came from the Export-Import Bank.

Moreover, on March 8 the Johnson administration announced that Secretary Fowler and Canadian Finance Minister Mitchell Sharp had agreed to an exemption for Canada from the U.S. balance-of-payments measures affecting capital flows administered by the Department of Commerce and the Federal Reserve. This would enable Canadians to borrow in U.S. capital markets in order to finance Canada's current account deficit. In return, the Canadians promised to take steps to prevent Canada from becoming a "pass through" of U.S. funds elsewhere which would frustrate the U.S. balance-of-payments program. (*Current Economic Developments*, Issue No. 801, March 12, 1968, pages 4–6; Washington National Records Center, RG 59, E/CBA/REP Files: FRC 72 A 6248, *Current Economic Developments*)

In a March 12 letter to President Johnson, Canadian Prime Minister Lester Pearson expressed his pleasure at this arrangement. Referring to a March 1 discussion between Sharp and Fowler on the border tax problem, Pearson also wrote that he wanted to have "an international discussion of the issues involved and we have prepared some suggestions for an initiative on this subject." He hoped the two countries could "pursue these ideas and together contribute to a resolution of the serious difficulties which have arisen." (Department of State, Central Files, FN 12 US)

On March 27, President Johnson replied to Prime Minister Pearson that he shared his "view that the exemption, together with the measures Canada is taking, will benefit both our countries." He added that the GATT Council was meeting the same week to consider the creation of a working party to study the question of GATT rules on border tax adjustments, and his administration wanted "to cooperate with Canada in seeking an equitable solution of this important issue." (Ibid.)

186.   Letter From the Special Representative for Trade Negotiations (Roth) to Secretary of the Treasury Fowler[1]

Washington, March 8, 1968.

Dear Joe:

As you know, representatives of your Department, the State Department, and this Office have had two detailed and useful meetings over the past several weeks to explore those aspects of the tourism proposal which could create problems for us under the General Agreement on Tariffs and Trade (GATT).[2] Especially in view of the fact that the Ways and Means Committee began executive session on this proposal yesterday, I do want to give you our thoughts arising out of these meetings.

I regard the tourism proposal as an important part of the President's balance-of-payments program. I am also aware of the fact that your staff made a very genuine effort to render the proposal as fair as possible. Nevertheless, it does raise some fairly serious questions of consistency with our obligations under the GATT. The very fact that we all agree to the exemption for Canada, Mexico, and the Caribbean—which is not in accord with the most-favored-nation principle of the GATT—makes it all the more important to ensure that the rest of the proposal is consistent with the GATT. Otherwise, I am very apprehensive that any departure from our GATT obligations will provoke increased friction and ill-will at a time when we can least afford them and may be seized upon to justify retaliatory actions.

Setting aside the exemption for Canada, Mexico, and the Caribbean, the major GATT problem raised by the tourism proposal is the flat rate of duty of 25% on articles brought back by American tourists of a value between $10 and $500 and the flat rates of $2 and 25% on parcels sent by mail of a value to up to $10 and between $10 and $500, respectively. These flat rates would involve a breach of trade agreement rates with respect to a great number of imported products. This breach would be all the more serious since the flat rates would increase—and in many cases substantially—the rates of duty to which we agreed in the Kennedy Round and which began to become effective on January 1 of this year. There is some chance, however, that these flat rates would be tolerated by our trading partners if they were clearly temporary in nature.

But if it is your intention to make the flat rates permanent, then the returning tourists and recipients of the mail parcels must have an option

---

[1] Source: Department of State, Central Files, FT 7 GATT. Limited Official Use. The source text is Tab B to a memorandum from Solomon to Katzenbach, March 25. Regarding this memorandum and Tab A, see footnote 1, Document 192.

[2] No formal record of these two meetings has been found.

of paying the actual rates of duty provided for in the Tariff Schedules of the United States. So long as the option were reasonably available and its exercise did not involve an excessive delay or inconvenience, this would eliminate the GATT problem. Such an option is afforded by almost all the other countries which impose flat rates in similar circumstances. I recognize that the number of returning tourists and the quantity of mail parcels are large but, in light of the meetings held to date, I am not satisfied that the administrative problems cannot be overcome. Otherwise, we would be breaching trade agreement rates on millions of dollars worth of trade.

With respect to the level of the flat rate of 25%, I have one suggestion. I understand that as of January 1, 1968, the average rate for the products involved is slightly below 20% and as of January 1, 1969, will be about 18%. While it would not eliminate the GATT problem, it would be helpful if the flat rate could be pitched two or three points below the actual average—such as 15%. If this were done, it would be clear that we were not arbitrarily using a flat rate to increase the rates of duty on the goods concerned taken as a whole. Moreover, I understand that a number of other trading countries have a flat rate of 15% on the same kinds of articles.

I would appreciate it if you would let me know of your reaction to these ideas. They would not, in my judgment, impair the value of the proposal. At the same time, they would ensure, or at least substantially improve, its acceptability by our trading partners.

Sincerely yours,

Bill

---

187. Memorandum From the President's Special Assistant (Rostow) to President Johnson[1]

Washington, March 9, 1968, 4:45 p.m.

SUBJECT

The Gold Issue

Walter Heller gave me a rundown on last night's meeting of the Dillon Committee. (Sec. Fowler's Advisory Committee, consisting of: Dil-

---

[1] Source: Johnson Library, National Security File, Subject File, 1968 Balance of Payments Programs, Memos and Miscellaneous [1 of 2], Box 4. Secret. A handwritten notation next to the dateline on the source text reads: "Rec'd 4:46 p."

lon, Roosa, Heller, Kermit Gordon, David Rockefeller, Edward
Bernstein, Frazer Wilde, Andre Mayer, and Bator.) They met informally
in New York to go over the options on gold and the balance of payments
and will report to Sec. Fowler.

Their conclusions were:

1. The tax bill is a must. They agree on a strong public statement
(attached)[2] which they will release next week after going over it with
Fowler.

2. They are unanimously opposed to an increase in the price of gold
as a way of dealing with the present crisis.

3. Most would prefer to keep the present gold pool arrangement
going but they do not believe it will be possible to negotiate with the
Europeans the arrangements necessary (specifically, the gold certificate
proposal) to turn the market around and restore calm.

4. They, therefore, believe we will have to close the gold pool operation and let the market price go. They believe it is essential we do this in
cooperation with our gold pool partners and preferably at their request.

5. They were somewhat fuzzy on particular plans for getting non-
gold pool members to cooperate and suggest we perhaps can use the IMF
for this purpose. They believe we will have to act within 30 days and
must have a clear idea of where we want to go and how we plan to get
there.

Comment: As you can see, these views are not very different from our
own. After the meeting of the Central Bankers in Basel this week end, we
will have a better idea of what the Europeans are willing to do, what the
prospects are of keeping the gold market open and quiet, and what
would be the most orderly way of bringing about change. Deming
returns tonight, and Bill Martin on Monday.[3]

Fowler is working to get the gold cover bill on the floor of the Senate
on Tuesday. Passage of the bill should help quiet things down.[4]

Walt

---

[2] Not printed.

[3] March 11.

[4] In his Economic Report to Congress on February 1, President Johnson proposed legislation to remove entirely the gold cover requirement as 25 percent backing for outstanding Federal Reserve currency notes. See *Public Papers of the Presidents of the United States:
Lyndon B. Johnson, 1968–69,* Book I, pp. 136–137. The House of Representatives narrowly
passed this legislation on February 21, and the Senate also approved in a close vote on
March 14. President Johnson signed the legislation into law on March 18. (P.L. 90–269; 82
Stat. 50)

188. Memorandum From the President's Special Assistant (Rostow) to President Johnson[1]

Washington, March 12, 1968, 6:25 p.m.

Mr. President:

Here, as we understand it, is what Bill Martin found out and will report to you.

1. With respect to a change in the price of gold, the British and Dutch are inclined to flirt with this option. The Germans are wobbly. The Italians, Belgians and Swiss are strongly against.

2. He achieved agreement on the statement[2] and the willingness to back the gold pool with $500 million, with another $500 million contingent. (At the rate the market in London is going, this will only last a matter of days.)

3. The Europeans realize that we all may face soon some quite unpleasant choices; but they are not clear about what these choices are and what will be required of them if we are to hold the system together. They *are* prepared to close down the London gold market and let the free market price of gold float. What they have not thought through are the terms of the intimate collaboration which will be required to make that kind of system work—especially how to deal with the consequences of a two-price gold system.

4. In the light of this situation, Treasury, State, Federal Reserve, Council of Economic Advisers, and White House staff people have been driving all day, at Ed Fried's insistence, to get in shape an operational scenario of the kind that is attached.[3] The essential object of the scenario would be to get certain minimum essential commitments from the other members of the gold pool before the closing of the gold pool was announced. On this basis we could proceed in reasonable order to a monetary conference.

5. We do not yet know Joe Fowler's or Bill Martin's personal views of this particular scenario. But we will be presenting it to them either late this evening or tomorrow morning.

---

[1] Source: Johnson Library, National Security File, Subject File, Balance of Payments, Vol. V [2 of 2], Box 3. Secret; Sensitive. A typed note at the top of the source text reads: "7:00 p.m. meeting with Bill Martin." No record of this meeting has been found.

[2] Reference may be to the communiqué issued by the Bank for International Settlements in Basel on March 10, in which the central banks contributing to the London gold pool reaffirmed "their determination to continue their support to the pool, based on the fixed price of $35 per ounce of gold." For text, see *The New York Times*, March 11, 1968, p. 60.

[3] This untitled paper, not printed, appears to be an early draft of what became a longer and more elaborate paper attached as Tab A to Document 190.

6. It emerged from the Basel meeting that the U.S. tax bill and the austerity of the British budget of March 19 are absolutely critical factors. Joe Fowler and Bill Martin have been working Mills over hard on this point. They are also talking to the Republican Policy Committee this afternoon.

My own feeling is that the moment of truth is close upon us; and we shall have to convert some such scenario into action within the next few days.

Walt

---

189.   Memorandum From the President's Special Assistant (Rostow) to President Johnson[1]

Washington, March 14, 1968.

SUBJECT

Gold

Your senior advisers are agreed:

(1) We can't go on as is, hoping that something will turn up.

(2) We need a meeting of the gold pool countries this weekend in Washington.

(3) We want to negotiate the following package:

—Interim rules on gold.
—Measures to keep order in the financial markets.
—Acceleration of the SDR's.

(4) With the right kind of interim package, we could maintain our gold commitment to official holders.

(5) If we can't get this package, we would have to suspend gold convertibility for official dollar holders, at least temporarily, and call for an immediate emergency conference.

(6) This probably would mean a period of chaos in world financial markets, but it may be the only way to push the others into a sensible long-run arrangement which avoids a rise in the official price of gold. We are unanimously agreed that a rise in the price of gold is the worst outcome.

---

[1] Source: Johnson Library, White House Central Files, Confidential File, FI 9, Monetary Systems. Secret; Sensitive.

The decision you must make now is whether the London gold market should be closed at once.[2]

(a) *Arguments for closing:*

—Avoid losing perhaps $1 billion in gold tomorrow (we lost $372 million today).
—Such a gold loss would further shake the confidence of central banks and trigger their coming to us for gold.
—Makes it easier to arrange an emergency meeting of the gold pool countries this weekend.
—Evidence of U.S. decisiveness.

(b) *Arguments against closing:*

—Involves U.S. taking the lead in throwing in the towel.
—Closing the market will strengthen the hand of those who believe the official price of gold will be increased.
—May reduce the U.S. bargaining position with the Europeans.
—Gives us another fling at the Gold Certificate proposal.

Walt

---

[2] President Johnson agreed to the temporary closing of the London gold market on March 14. A statement by Secretary Fowler and Chairman Martin on the closing, March 14, affirmed the U.S. Government's commitment to continue to buy and sell gold in official transactions at $35 per ounce and indicated that they had "invited the central bank governors to consult with us on coordinated measures to ensure orderly conditions in the exchange markets and to support the present pattern of exchange rates based on the fixed price of $35 per ounce of gold." For text, see *Annual Report of the Secretary of the Treasury . . . , 1968*, p. 370.

---

190.   Memorandum From the President's Special Assistant (Rostow) to President Johnson[1]

Washington, March 14, 1968, 5:20 p.m.

Mr. President:

To give you a feeling for what lies ahead, I enclose two working documents:

—a scenario for negotiation with the Central Bankers of the Gold Pool (Tab A);[2] and

---

[1] Source: Johnson Library, National Security File, Subject File, Balance of Payments, Vol, V. [2 of 2], Box 3. Secret; Sensitive. A handwritten notation next to the dateline on the source text reads: "Rec'd 5:50 p."
[2] This undated strategy paper, drafted by Fried and entitled "Resolving the Gold Issue," is not printed.

—a draft communiqué indicating what we would like to be able to announce on Sunday night. (Tab B)[3]

On page 3 of the first document (para. 6) there is an outline of what might be in a Presidential statement on the occasion of the communiqué.

After we met with you, Joe talked to several of us about the attitude of the Hill with which he has been dealing, and the attitude among the Central Bankers.

He describes the attitude on the Hill as one of almost anarchistic willingness to pull down the temple around their ears on the grounds that our budgetary expenditures are out of control. He feels that the Europeans have the same kind of feeling and cannot understand that our Executive Branch and Congress are incapable of generating a tax-expenditure policy that would keep us in reasonable order.

He is almost in despair about being able to negotiate a package without some sign that a tax increase is at least over the horizon; and he is in despair about getting a tax increase unless there is some kind of commitment to expenditure limitation.

I know enough to know that I have no competence in figuring out how this nagging political problem can be solved. It obviously goes to the heart of our nation's capacity to carry its external commitments; maintain the world trade and monetary system; and avoid a serious domestic breakdown in our economy.

But I did want to report to you this further conversation.

Walt

---

[3] This undated paper is not printed.

---

191. Editorial Note

In their March 14, 1968, public statement, Secretaries Fowler and Martin invited the Central Bank Governors to consult on the gold problem (see footnote 2, Document 190). This initiative led to a meeting in Washington on March 16 and 17 of the Central Bank Governors of the seven nations active in the gold pool. The Managing Director of the International Monetary Fund and the General Manager of the Bank for International Settlements also attended these sessions.

Walt Rostow and Edward Fried sent several memoranda and tele-graphic reports to the President at the LBJ Ranch in Texas, March 15–17, on developments at this weekend meeting. Texts are in the Johnson Library, National Security File, Subject File, Balance of Payments, Vol. V [2 of 2], Box 3, and ibid., 1968 Balance of Payments Programs, Memos and Miscellaneous [1 of 2], Box 4. A "Position Paper for Gold Pool Negoti-ations, March 16–17," which contains no drafting information, is ibid., Bator Papers, Gold Crisis, March 13–16, FMB Washington Trip, Box 10.

On March 17 the Governors issued a communiqué supporting the U.S. Government's policy of continuing to buy and sell gold at $35 per ounce. The communiqué also noted the U.K. Government's determina-tion "to do all that is necessary" to end its balance-of-payments deficit, the intention of most European governments "to pursue monetary and fiscal policies that encourage domestic expansion consistent with eco-nomic stability," and the Governors' decision to increase the total of cred-its (including the IMF standby) available immediately to the United Kingdom to $4 billion.

The communiqué also stated:

"The Governors agreed to cooperate fully to maintain the existing parities as well as orderly conditions in their exchange markets in accordance with their obligations under the Articles of Agreement of the International Monetary Fund. The Governors believe that henceforth officially held gold should be used only to effect transfers among mone-tary authorities and, therefore, they decided no longer to supply gold to the London gold market or any other gold market. Moreover, as the exist-ing stock of monetary gold is sufficient in view of the prospective estab-lishment of the facility for Special Drawing Rights, they no longer feel it necessary to buy gold from the market. Finally, they agreed that hence-forth they will not sell gold to monetary authorities to replace gold sold in private markets." (*Annual Report of the Secretary of the Treasury . . . , 1968,* page 371)

The Governors' decision in effect led to two gold markets, one for official transactions only with the price fixed at $35 per ounce, and the second for private transactions with the price freely determined by sup-ply and demand.

Pierre-Paul Schweitzer, IMF Managing Director, also issued a per-sonal statement on March 17 endorsing the Governors' communiqué and urging the cooperation of other IMF members. Text is ibid., pages 371–372.

A full summary of the steps leading to the gold pool agreement as well as subsequent international reactions is in *Current Economic Develop-ments,* Issue No. 802, March 26, 1968, pages 1–6. (Washington National Records Center, RG 59, E/CBA/REP Files: FRC 72 A 6248, *Current Eco-nomic Developments*)

192. Letter From the Under Secretary of State (Katzenbach) to Secretary of the Treasury Fowler[1]

Washington, March 26, 1968.

Dear Joe:

I understand Bill Roth has written you on the GATT problems raised by our tourism proposals.[2] The Department of State shares this concern. We are convinced that some of these proposals—specifically, the mandatory flat rate on certain tourist and other noncommercial imports and the preferential treatment for Canada, Mexico and the Caribbean—will lead to a confrontation in the GATT.

We have already received representations of concern by a delegation representing the five Scandinavian countries and by the German Embassy.[3] If we persist in these proposals, we may seriously jeopardize our chances of receiving international cooperation in areas of major importance to the balance of payments, such as possible advance Kennedy Round implementation and directional air fares.

The mandatory flat rate customs proposal is, in our view, a clear violation of recently negotiated tariff concessions in the GATT. We would agree with Bill Roth that an option should be given to returning residents to pay the rates in the tariff schedules, in lieu of the proposed flat rate. We understand that the Bureau of Customs has objected on the grounds of the difficulty of administering such an option. This argument would not be convincing to GATT members in Europe, many of whom in fact offer similar options. (If the Bureau of Customs includes rates for common imports in its customs pamphlet and requires each returning resident to figure out his own option, the administrative problem could be largely eliminated.)

At the same time, we expect various nations to point out that a preferential treatment for Canada, Mexico and the Caribbean runs directly

---

[1] Source: Johnson Library, Fowler Papers, International Balance of Payments: 1968 B of P—Tourism, Box 7. No classification marking. Another copy of the letter indicates that it was drafted by Donald Herr (U.). A March 25 covering memorandum from Solomon to Katzenbach, attached to that copy, explained that the administration's tourism proposal raised several GATT problems that needed to be discussed with Fowler. Although Department of State and STR officials had met with Treasury people on these GATT problems, Fowler had rejected their proposals "(he has agreed to a small reduction in the level of the flat rate, which is not particularly helpful for our GATT problems)." Solomon worried that if Congress approved these measures as they then stood, "they would cause us GATT trade problems—far in excess of their significance in anticipated balance of payments gains—and could adversely affect European cooperation in other areas much more important to us." (Department of State, Central Files, FT 7 GATT)

[2] Document 186.

[3] These representations have not been found.

counter to our most-favored-nation obligations in the GATT and other commercial treaties. Our ability to mollify adverse reaction would be greatly enhanced if these provisions were made temporary, as is the case with the excise tax on travel.

I would much appreciate your further consideration of these proposals. I am afraid that adverse reactions to them by other countries could well outweigh the balance of payments benefits which might accrue. My staff will be happy to work with Treasury officials to obtain a mutually satisfactory resolution of these problems.

Sincerely,

Nicholas deB. Katzenbach

193. Editorial Note

On March 29 and 30, 1968, the Finance Ministers and Central Bank Governors of the Group of Ten convened in Stockholm. Secretary Fowler headed the U.S. delegation, which included Edward Fried. The major issue at this monetary conference was the nature of Special Drawing Rights (SDRs) as they had developed in recent discussions of draft amendments to the Articles of the International Monetary Fund. Regarding the IMF annual meeting in Rio de Janeiro, which on September 29, 1967, approved an "Outline of a Facility Based on Special Drawing Rights," see Document 145.

In a memorandum to President Johnson, March 27, Walt Rostow summarized the major issues at the upcoming conference. (Johnson Library, National Security File, Subject File, Balance of Payments, Vol. V [2 of 2], Box 3) Fried's report of the first day's meeting was transmitted in telegram [text not declassified] 8892 from Stockholm, March 29, and was forwarded to the President under cover of a March 30 memorandum from Rostow. (Ibid.) The text of Secretary Fowler's statement at the conference on March 30 was transmitted in telegram 1118 from Stockholm, March 30. (Department of State, Central Files, FN 10)

At the Stockholm meeting, French Finance Minister Michel Debré argued, among other things, that the draft amendments seemed to go well beyond the dictates of the Outline and would make SDRs more of a reserve account than a supplementary credit. Nevertheless, the conferees went ahead and agreed to proposed amendments to the Articles of the Agreement of the Fund, which included the creation of a facility based on Special Drawing Rights, for a later vote by the Governors. The French delegation reserved its position on this and other agreements at the meeting. The final communiqué reaffirmed the Ministers' and Governors' "determination to cooperate in the maintenance of exchange stability and orderly exchange arrangements in the world, based on the present official price of gold." For text of the communiqué, March 30, see *Annual Report of the Secretary of the Treasury . . . , 1968,* page 372.

George H. Willis, in a paper he drafted on April 1, advised members of the Deming Group on the "Agreement on Special Drawing Rights Reached by Ministers of the Group of Ten at Stockholm, March 30, 1968." (Deming Group paper DG/68/148; Washington National Records Center, RG 56, OASIA Files: FRC 75 A 101, Deming Group) For Rostow's April 2 memorandum to the President summarizing the conference, see Document 194. For additional details regarding this conference, see De Vries, *The International Monetary Fund, 1966–1971,* volume I, pages 170–172. Text of the proposed amendment to the Articles of Agreement is ibid., volume II, pages 52–94. A detailed summary of the Stockholm meeting is in *Current Economic Developments,* Issue No. 803, April 9, 1968, pages 1–3. (Washington National Records Center, RG 59, E/CBA/REP Files: FRC 72 A 6248, *Current Economic Developments*)

In a message to Congress, April 30, President Johnson requested approval of the amendment to the International Monetary Fund Agreement, which provided for the creation of new Special Drawing Rights. For text, see *Public Papers of the Presidents of the United States: Lyndon B. Johnson, 1968–69,* Book I, pages 545–549. Congress soon passed legislation approving this amendment, and President Johnson signed it on June 19. (P.L. 90–349; 82 Stat. 188) Meanwhile, on May 31, the Governors approved the proposed amendment, which entered into force on July 28, 1969.

194. Memorandum From the President's Special Assistant (Rostow) to President Johnson[1]

Washington, April 2, 1968.

SUBJECT

Stockholm Monetary Conference[2]

1. Stockholm completed another phase in the IMF Special Drawing Rights plan. It brings us closer to creation of "paper gold". The central issue was whether France would be able either to stall the proposal or change its basic character. Either outcome would have caused an international monetary crisis and a major drive to raise the official price of gold. Faced with this choice, the other European countries joined with us to settle the remaining questions and put the plan in shape for the ratification process.

2. There were few differences between the U.S. and France's European partners. The main reason for compromises was to help Germany, Italy, Belgium and the Netherlands take the political heat at home of dividing with the French on this fundamental issue. They had to be able to show that they were not knuckling under to the U.S. but were acting to protect world prosperity on an issue where France was unreasonable. This required a demonstration that they and the U.S. would go the last mile to meet French demands without prejudicing the plan or the quality of the SDR as a reserve asset.

3. We therefore agreed:

—on changes that amount, in effect, to a strict rather than a loose interpretation of the principles adopted at Rio;
—on making it easier for a country to opt out of the agreement after the decision is made to activate it;
—to give the EEC a veto on decisions for any future increases in IMF quotas and some related questions.

We were prepared beforehand to make most of these concessions in one form or another, in some instances, the compromises were more disturbing to France's Common Market partners than they were to us. Others we regretted making, because they reduced flexibility in the *future* development of the SDR. The provision giving the EEC a veto on some

---

[1] Source; Johnson Library, National Security File, Fried Files, Chron, March 1–April 30, 1968. Confidential. Drafted by Fried.

[2] Regarding this conference, see Document 193. Deputy to the Assistant Secretary of the Treasury for International Affairs George H. Willis was part of the U.S. Delegation to the Stockholm Ministerial, and his notes are another record of the meetings. (Washington National Records Center, RG 56, Assistant Secretary for International Affairs, Deputy to the Assistant Secretary and Secretary of the International Monetary Group: FRC 83 A 26, Willis' Notes 66–69, notebook entitled Ministers Mtg–Stockholm, March 20–30, 1968)

additional IMF decisions will give us some trouble on the Hill, but it is not a substantive issue.

4. The willingness of the Four to stand up against the French is a major political development. It demonstrates again that there are limits on how far de Gaulle can push them.

5. The French claimed that the system could not work because our economy had gotten out of hand and we were dumping unwanted dollars on the world. In joining with us, the Four showed they had confidence that we would bring our financial house in order and, specifically, that we would pass the tax bill. The tax bill has now become as much of a world issue as the controversy over the price of gold.

6. We are playing the Stockholm meeting not as a victory of the U.S. over France, but as a victory for the world monetary system and for reason in world financial affairs.

The French did not vote against the agreement, but abstained. They could decide to join when the final document is submitted. But this will be difficult for de Gaulle to do—particularly after France came out publicly for an increase in the price of gold.

The market reaction to Stockholm has been excellent. The price of gold in London is softening and the volume is small.

7. As a result of Stockholm, it should be possible to put the Special Drawing Rights proposal in final form within two weeks. It will then go to each of the Governors of the IMF for approval by a mail vote. This must be completed within thirty days. On this schedule, we should be able to put the proposal before the Congress for ratification by the end of May.[3]

8. The Stockholm agreement and the Washington Gold Pool decisions are building blocks in the development of a stronger monetary system. They have brought order to the financial markets and give us time to move on our fiscal and balance of payments programs. They also mean we must show results on these programs.

W. W. Rostow[4]

---

[3] In an April 17 memorandum, Assistant Secretary of State for Economic Affairs Solomon informed Under Secretary for Political Affairs Rostow that the Executive Directors of the IMF on April 16 had approved their report on the SDR facility and fund reform and that, along with its annexed resolution, the report would now be referred to the Governors of the Fund for their review and vote on the resolution. Solomon informed Rostow that Secretary Fowler, the U.S. Governor of the IMF, would need authorization from the National Advisory Council for his vote. A meeting of the NAC was scheduled for April 18, preceded by a meeting of the Dillon Committee (see footnote 4, Document 64) at which Fowler would review with the Advisory Committee the NAC Special Report and elicit the Committee's views on who might be non-governmental witnesses on the SDR/Fund Reform at Congressional hearings scheduled to begin May 1. Rostow concurred with Solomon's recommendation and recorded State's recommendation that the U.S. Governor vote affirmatively on the IMF Resolution. (National Archives and Records Administration, RG 59, Department of State Central Files: 1967–1969, Box 274, FN 10 IMF 4/1/69)

[4] Printed from a copy that bears this typed signature.

195. Telegram From the Department of State to the Embassy in
Japan[1]

Washington, April 4, 1968, 2243Z.

141958. 1. Please deliver following message from the President to
Prime Minister Sato as soon as possible.

"Dear Mr. Prime Minister:

I have read your thoughtful letter of March 25, 1968[2] and wish, first
of all, to express my appreciation for the renewed support you have
given to the goals of our balance of payments program announced on
January 1 of this year. The role that Japan is playing in support of this program is encouraging, particularly in view of the present balance of payments position in Japan. I am certain that I can continue to count on that
support in our common interest.

I also recognize the deep concerns you feel over the possibility of the
United States Government's taking measures such as border tax adjustments or an import surcharge. As I have frequently stated, the United
States Government has every intention of meeting its international
responsibilities in the promotion and expansion of world trade as well as
in all other areas. We are, however, faced with an extremely serious balance of payments deficit which must be reduced. Improvement in our
trade account is critical to the success of our balance of payments program. We would hope the improvement could be effected not only by the
internal measures to restrain inflation we are determined to take but also
by the early cooperative expansionary action of our major trading partners. In this connection, I particularly welcome the Japanese Government's readiness to accelerate its Kennedy Round cuts and its offer to
take other trade-freeing actions. It would be most heartening if a satisfactory solution could be found through cooperative international action. I
hope therefore that the Japanese Government will exert its maximum
influence toward finding an expansionary solution.

Sincerely, Lyndon B. Johnson"

2. White House does not plan to release and assumes Sato will treat
message as private correspondence.

Katzenbach

---

[1] Source: Department of State, Central Files, FN 12 US. Limited Official Use; Priority.
Drafted by P.K. Stahnke (EA/J) on April 4; cleared by Fried, Barnett (E), Malmgren (STR),
Ruth Gold (E), Thomas O. Enders (M), Richard L. Sneider (EA/J), and John R. Petty
(Treasury) all in draft; and approved by Francis J. Meehan (S/S).

[2] This letter has not been found, but its contents are briefly summarized in telegram
136790 to Tokyo, March 26. (Ibid., POL 7 JAPAN)

196.   Memorandum for the USTS File[1]

Washington, April 16, 1968.

SUBJECT

April 16 Meeting in the White House with the Under Secretary,[2] Ambassador McKinney, Mr. Goldstein, Mr. Pelikan,[3] Mr. Rommel,[4] and Mr. Dykman

Ambassador McKinney opened the meeting with the announcement that he plans to stay in Washington until he carries out the role given to the Industry–Government Special Task Force on Travel by the President in his statement of March 6, 1968.[5] He then outlined his reasons for developing legislation which will result in an independent semi-public U.S. Travel Office. These reasons can be summarized as follows:

1. He believes Congressman Rooney will not permit any agency of Commerce adequate resources to carry out a reasonable program.

2. He believes that an independent agency with dues paying industrial members would leverage Federal money (he spoke briefly about a budget of $50 million from the Federal Government and $7,500,000 from the private members).

3. He felt it would be easier to reorganize the management and to attract the requisite talent to an independent agency than to a unit of the Department of Commerce. This includes his belief that the independent agency could pay its chief much more than the salary of cabinet officer.

Ambassador McKinney went on to say that he plans to have a preliminary report in to the President by May 15 at which time he foresees Mr. Pelikan moving over to the Commerce Department as an Assistant Secretary to implement the new travel program.

Mr. Pelikan pointed out that the Treasury Department is already drawing up legislation for the independent travel bureau and that the

---

[1] Source: Washington National Records Center, RG 40, Department of Commerce Files: FRC 74 A 20, U.S. Travel Service, 1967–1968. No classification marking. Drafted by Jan T. Dykman, Executive Assistant to the Secretary of Commerce, on April 17.

[2] Howard J. Samuels.

[3] Robert G. Pelikan, Director, Office of International Economic Activities, Department of the Treasury, was also serving at this time as Executive Director of the President's Commission on Travel.

[4] Presumably Wilfred H. Rommel, Assistant Director for Legislative Reference, Bureau of the Budget.

[5] On March 6, President Johnson announced that he was putting McKinney in charge of the President's foreign visitor program, which would "coordinate the efforts of private industry and Government necessary to implement the recommendations of the commission on travel." For text of the President's statement, see *Public Papers of the Presidents of the United States: Lyndon B. Johnson, 1968–69*, Book I, pp. 349–350. Regarding the recommendations of the commission on travel, see footnote 2, Document 182.

commission has retained the services of various management consultant firms. One such firm is evaluating, through a PPBS system, the cost and benefits of various budgetary levels for the new travel organization and another firm is studying the travel offices of other nations in order to clearly outline the organizational options open to us in creating our own new travel agency. Mr. Pelikan did not have anything on paper at that time concerning the legal structure or a broad outline of the organization of his proposed semi-independent travel agency.

The Under Secretary indicated that Commerce was not anxious to divest itself of another agency, but we would certainly cooperate in whatever policy decision appeared to be best for the country without regard to our own parochial interest. He said that if it could be proven that Congressman Rooney would not permit adequate resources to the presently constituted U.S. Travel Service then it may be best for Ambassador McKinney to propose the independent agency idea to Secretary Smith. However, the Under Secretary made it clear that our posture at this time is:

1. To immediately submit an amendment to the U.S. Travel Act calling for an increase of authorized budgetary level from $4.7 million to $15 million.

2. To propose a supplemental for FY 69 of a budget for USTS somewhere in the neighborhood of seven to eight million dollars.

3. To continue developing a new program based on a seven to eight million budget which would be more market-oriented and could be put into effect immediately upon approval.

4. To study possible management reorganization of the USTS within the presently constituted agency. (There followed an off-the-record discussion of John Black.)

Mr. Goldstein pointed out that he felt the Department of Commerce and Ambassador McKinney's group should work more closely together. Everyone agreed. It was generally agreed that we would continue to work on two levels. Ambassador McKinney's group will continue to put together its plan for an independent agency with the $50 million budget and the Department of Commerce, relatively independent of the McKinney group, would continue with its activities as outlined by the Under Secretary (above). While these activities are going on, Ambassador McKinney and the Under Secretary would make every effort to work together in meetings with industry and other interested parties so that both groups are kept fully informed of what the other is doing and that a "solid front" would be shown to the world while the parties worked out their different programs. Between May 15 and May 30 Ambassador McKinney's proposal and ours will be in final form for presentation to Secretary Smith and the President. At that time, Mr. Goldstein opined, a

Presidential decision on which of the two proposals to endorse would probably be necessary.

There was a lengthy discussion concerning various budgetary matters in which we made it clear that Secretary Smith did not feel that a 50 or even fifteen million dollar budget could be justified. Everyone, except the Under Secretary and I, hotly disputed this. The Under Secretary mentioned that he also planned to hold a meeting next with marketing executives in the Travel Advisory Committee but agreed to cancel the meeting so that he and McKinney would not be meeting separately with industry groups. The Ambassador agreed to invite the Under Secretary to his meetings with industry thereby maintaining our "solid front" posture.

Jan

197. Current Economic Developments[1]

Issue No. 804   Washington, April 23, 1968.

DEVELOPMENTS IN IMPLEMENTING
BALANCE-OF-PAYMENTS PROGRAM

The President's balance-of-payments program announced on January 1 is leading to a variety of actions. Some of our major trading partners have come up with proposals for acceleration by them and/or deceleration by us of the Kennedy Round tariff cuts as a means of assisting our trade balance and helping to avert restrictive US trade legislation. The International Air Transport Association members have approved a reduced family fare for visitors coming to the US from Europe and the Middle East. A part of the travel package proposed by the Administration has been approved in the House. Other major developments pertain to our foreign investment regulations, the Eximbank, reduction of overseas personnel, and efforts to neutralize military costs overseas.

Kennedy Round Acceleration

As a means of averting restrictive trade measures as a part of the US balance-of-payments program, a number of countries have suggested

---

[1] Source: Washington National Records Center, RG 59, E/CBA/REP Files: FRC 72 A 6248, *Current Economic Developments*. Limited Official Use (Except Portion Marked Confidential). The source text comprises pages 1–7 of the issue.

differential cutting of Kennedy Round tariff concessions as a means of meeting the US problem. The suggestions vary in detail and structure. We have neither accepted nor rejected any offer. Since all of them are conditional upon similar action by many countries, no proposal actually exists until the offers have been coordinated. We have, however, attempted to gain improvement in the EC proposal for a one-year deceleration by the US combined with a one-year acceleration by the other major participants. We have also made clear that the strongly stated EC conditions requiring a unanimous finding by the EC Council, prior US passage of the American Selling Price legislation, and US abstention from any protectionist measures are unacceptable.

Last week GATT Director General Wyndham White called a meeting in Geneva of the EC, Japan, Canada, and the EFTA countries to discuss the divergence between the various KR deceleration/acceleration proposals that have been made. The declaration that came out of that meeting calls for one-year acceleration but improves the previous offers on deceleration so that we would get continued balance-of-payments advantages until 1973. If we do not pass the American Selling Price legislation and if we do pass protectionist legislation (presumably of a general nature), all countries would consider once again before the end of the year whether their offer to us on both acceleration and deceleration could still be maintained so that they would still take action on January 1, 1969. This latest proposal is now under consideration within the US Government and by the governments of the major GATT trading countries.

IATA Directional Fares

The members of the International Air Transport Association have agreed via a mail vote upon a directional family fare which would permit dependents of a traveler in Europe of the Middle East to enjoy approximately a 50 percent reduction in first class or economy fares on round-trip travel to the US. The new fares were filed with interested governments on April 11 and, subject to their approval, will become effective April 24. The new fares will entitle adult and adolescent family members in Europe and the Middle East to buy a round-trip ticket to the US, Canada, and Mexico for the price of a one-way ticket. When the head of a family buys a full fare, each member of his family who normally pays for a full fare will be entitled to a round-trip ticket at the price of the normal one-way fare. The family members may buy first or economy class tickets, regardless of the class in which the head of the family travels.

The new fares were initially agreed upon at a meeting in New York February 20 of 21 airline members of IATA engaged in transatlantic service. The meeting had been requested by Pan American Airways and Trans World Airways to consider proposals for directional fares to stimulate tourism to the US. When the proposal that evolved from that meeting was submitted to all IATA members it encountered some opposition from some of the Arab, British, Canadian, Mexican, and Colombian airlines. After concerted action by the Department, our Embassies concerned, and the IATA Secretariat, the opposing airlines were persuaded to abstain. As a price for Mexican abstention, Mexico, as well as Canada and the US, will benefit from the reduced fares.[2]

The USG was intensely interested in obtaining IATA agreement on the directional transatlantic family fares, despite the fact that the IATA proposal was more limited than we had initially hoped for. The new fares will, however, be a significant part of the overall effort to increase European tourism to the United States.

Travel Legislation

The House on April 4 passed a travel package by a large majority. In addition to extending the five percent domestic tax on air travel to international air tickets, the bill reduces tourist duty-free entry from $100 to $10 until October 1969, and gift parcel exemption from $10 to $1. It exempts Canada and Mexico from the reduction in customs duty exemptions, largely because of the administrative difficulty in dealing with the enormous number of border crossings. It also exempts certain US island possessions. The exemptions could give us some GATT problems against which our defense will be the seriousness of our balance-of-payments problem and the temporary nature of the discriminatory provisions.

The House Ways and Means Committee deferred action on the proposed travel expenditure tax proposed by the Administration "for further consideration along with measures related to improving our trade balance to which the President referred in his January 1 announcement." Specifically, the Committee decided to wait to see the extent to which factors swelling the deficit in the fourth quarter of 1967 proved to be temporary, "to consider the expenditures tax proposal in conjunction with efforts on the part of other countries to aid our balance of payments by accelerating tariff reductions . . . under . . . the Kennedy Round . . . and pending an opportunity to examine proposals for a tax on imports and/or rebate on exports . . . the so-called border tax adjustments." A desire to evaluate the effectiveness of directional fares and other measures to stimulate tourism to the US was given as an additional factor. Although the Committee's inaction on the expenditures tax is widely viewed as indicating that it will not be enacted, Chairman Mills indicated that this conclusion is not necessarily valid.

The Senate Finance Committee will take up the travel measures sometime after the Easter recess.

---

[2] Memoranda documenting progress on negotiations on directional air fares are in Department of State, Central Files, AV 10, and ibid., AV 10–2 IATA.

Visa Act Amendment

In February, President Johnson transmitted proposed legislation to the Congress calling for a lowering of visa barriers as a means of encouraging tourism to the US.[3] This was one of the recommendations of the President's Commission on Travel. In testifying in support of the pending legislation (H.R. 15651, the Non-Immigrant Visa Act of 1968), Under Secretary Katzenbach said that we have given substantial thought as to how this proposal would be implemented. He added, "We contemplate that the Secretary of State will designate, by public notice, the countries whose nationals may be admitted as 90-day visitors" without visas. The Under Secretary urged prompt enactment of the legislation.

Other Travel Measures

Progress is being made in implementation of the recommendations of the President's Commission on Travel (see page 1, February 13, 1968 issue).[4] Among these is an accelerated clearance program for air passengers arriving from abroad which is now being inaugurated at Kennedy Airport. Another is the issuance of Hospitality Cards permitting residents of foreign countries to take advantage of a wide variety of discounts on transportation, hotels, motels, car rentals, restaurants, etc., throughout the United States.[5] A card may be obtained by any resident, including American citizens, of a foreign country when he purchases a round-trip ticket to the US. Canadian and Mexican residents, however, are only eligible when they travel to the US by air, ship, or rail. Cards will be distributed by members of the travel industry, who will also have information on available discounts. Upon arrival in the US the traveler must have his card validated by an Immigration official at the port of entry. It will then be valid for 90 days.

US-Canada B/P Review

The semi-annual US-Canadian balance-of-payments review, which took place early this month, focused mainly on the recent exemption of Canada from the Commerce and Federal Reserve investment restraints and the Canadian undertaking to prevent the "pass-through" of US capi-

---

[3] See footnote 3, Document 182.

[4] "Developments of Travel and Other B/P Measures," *Current Economic Developments*, Issue No. 799, February 13, 1968, pp. 1–5. (Washington National Records Center, RG 59, E/CBA/REP Files: FRC 72 A 6248, *Current Economic Developments*)

[5] The 50% discount on domestic air fares is only available to residents outside the Western Hemisphere. [Footnote in the source text. The President's Commission on Travel issued a press release on April 11 announcing the implementation of the Hospitality Card. (Johnson Library, Fowler Papers, International Balance of Payments: 1968 B of P Travel Task Force [2 of [2], Box 9)]

tal to third countries.[6] Canadian action in this regard has been slowed by the cabinet change-over in that country. The Canadians have, however, taken interim steps to tighten controls on the chartered banks, the largest potential source of leaks. These controls are designed to prevent the banks from increasing their net position vis-à-vis third countries and also prevent the pass-back of deposits in the US and then use of this money in the New York call market, which, because of our balance-of-payments definition worsens our liquidity position without affecting their situation.

In the course of the b/p review, the US participants pressed the Canadians to liberalize the duty-free allowance on purchases by Canadian tourists returning from the US. This would relieve the present discrimination against the US and make more palatable the special status for Canada and Mexico in our pending tourism legislation. The Canadians promised to take another look at this question.

Foreign Investment Regulations

As the second quarter of the Foreign Direct Investment Program commenced, the Office of Foreign Direct Investment (OFDI) had received over 750 applications for special authorizations or exemptions. The OFDI had forwarded to American firms Base Period Report Form FDI–101 for completion by March 22, 1968. Due to the exemption of Canada from the FDIP and certain amendments in the instructions, the filing date for Amended Form FDI–101 was moved to April 5. When these forms have been received and processed, the Department of Commerce will be in a position to administer the program on the basis of more concrete information than is available at this time.

The OFDI intends to publish periodically general interpretive rules in order to clarify and implement the program. In addition, general authorizations or amendments to the regulations will be issued in proposed form, subject to revision and issuance in final format, after the public has been given the opportunity to furnish written comments or objections.

On January 23, 1968 General Authorization No. 1 relating to repayments of foreign borrowings and honoring guarantees of foreign affiliates of US companies was issued.[7] Subsequently, General Authorization No. 2 permitting direct investors in Schedule A and B countries to refrain from repatriation of earnings to the extent transfers of capital in equal

---

[6] This meeting was scheduled for April 11 (telegram 142478 to Ottawa, April 5; Department of State, Central Files, FN 12 US), but no record of the discussion has been found.

[7] Additional details on General Authorization No. 1 are in *Current Economic Developments*, Issue No. 798, January 30, 1968, pp. 16–17. (Washington National Records Center, RG 59, E/CBA/REP Files: FRC 72 A 6248, *Current Economic Developments*)

amounts would be generally authorized in that year and General Authorization No. 3, later rescinded, were issued on February 28. Miscellaneous technical Amendments and General Authorization No. 4 exempting Canada from the FDIP were published on March 12, 1968.

Under Executive Order 11387 the Secretary of State was authorized to advise the Secretary of Commerce with respect to matters under the FDIP involving foreign policy.[8] The Department has commenced a liaison function with the OFDI to transmit State/AID's views on projects which might affect our foreign political and/or economic relations with other countries and which should be taken into account in approving or denying applications for special authorizations or exemptions.

Foreign Investment Regulations and OECD Code

The b/p regulations governing foreign direct investment necessitated a derogation by the US to the OECD Code of Liberalization of Capital Movements. The Invisibles Committee considers the US justified in introducing its restrictions on capital operations on balance-of-payments grounds. Nevertheless, the majority of the Committee is of the opinion that the US measures are contrary to the letter of Article 7 (c) of the Code of Capital Movements (which specifies that any measures should be non-discriminatory) but that the probable effects of the measures will not run counter to the objectives of Article 7 (e) (to avoid unnecessary damage which bears especially on the financial or economic interests of another member). The report sets forth these views and is still under consideration within the OECD.

Eximbank

On March 13 the President signed into law S. 1155 which gives a new five-year mandate to the Eximbank and increases its lending authority to $13.5 billion.[9] As part of his b/p program, the President said he would ask Congress to earmark $500 million of the Eximbank authorization to: a) provide better export insurance, b) expand guarantees for export financing, and broaden the scope of government financing for exports. To this end, a proposed new law is pending in the Congress (S. 3218) which would authorize the Bank to facilitate, through loans, guarantees, and insurance, certain export transactions which, in the judgment of the Board of Directors of the Bank, do not meet the test of reasonable assurance of repayments as provided in the existing Eximbank legislation, but which in the judgment of the Board nevertheless deserve support. The principal emphasis of this program is expected to be export credit insurance and guarantees on export credits extended by private lenders. These are areas where the government-supported export credit facilities

---

[8] Regarding the executive order, see Document 167.
[9] P.L. 90–267; 82 Stat. 47.

of competing nations now provide broader coverage and more flexible terms than the current Eximbank–FCIA programs. The export expansion authority would also permit direct project loans on transactions that while still determined by commercial considerations, nonetheless fall marginally below the normal standards of the Export-Import Bank. It is envisaged that loans, guarantees, and insurance extended under the proposed authority would be considered according to commercial criteria and would not be used to supplement or augment foreign assistance programs authorized in other legislation.

To further stimulate exports, the Eximbank on April 1 announced changes in its Discount Loan Program. The changes will allow the Eximbank to lend against new export obligations at a preferential rate, to lend for the full term of export credit paper, and in some cases, to make outright purchases of export obligations owned by a bank.

Also pertinent to the b/p program is the fact that credits involving Eximbank participation continue to be exempt from the Federal Reserve voluntary guidelines on foreign lending.

End Limited Official Use—Begin Confidential

Neutralization of Military Costs Overseas

As part of the January 1 balance-of-payments program, the President directed Secretaries of State, Treasury and Defense to find ways of minimizing the foreign exchange cost of keeping US troops in Asia and elsewhere. Discussions of measures to deal with this problem are underway in Europe (Belgium, Denmark, UK, Germany, Netherlands) and Japan. We are planning to schedule talks with the Governments of China, Korea, Thailand, and Viet Nam and may consider an approach to the Philippines depending on an improvement in that country's reserve position. Our objective with the four Asian allies is to neutralize the b/p impact of US security expenditures. At present, we believe that the most practicable way these allies can help is by investment in special longer-term US Treasury securities. Therefore, the USG hopes to reach appropriate agreement with each of the four Asian nations to shift during CY 1968 further amounts of their reserves into such securities as follows:

China	$75–$100 million
Thailand	$150 million
Korea	$60 million
Viet Nam	$50–$100 million

These amounts would be in addition to what these countries presently hold of longer-term US investments which the USG expects they will maintain in semi-liquid form.

End Confidential—Begin Limited Official Use

Prepayment of Debt

As part of the President's program we are canvassing possibilities for payment of debts to the USG in advance of scheduled repayment dates. In addition, in some cases we have been able to arrange investment in non-convertible, non-marketable USG securities or certain obligations of USG agencies which result in an equivalent liquidity basis b/p improvement. Three techniques have been used to implement prepayments: a) appropriation of funds by Parliament which would be used to pay in full or in part the Government's debt to the US; b) Treasury borrowing domestically in order to raise the funds with which to pay off external obligations—in these cases there was merely a shifting in the composition of the Government's debts without any change in the total, and the role of Parliaments was limited; and c) Central Bank purchase of notes representing the long-term debt obligations of its government to the US. This last technique has been used for most repayments.

Overseas Personnel Reductions

The President on March 30 approved an initial reduction of 10 percent of USG employees serving overseas under Ambassadors as part of the b/p program.[10] Additional reductions will be made later this year.

Known as "operation BALPA," the overall plan for a reduction in US personnel overseas involves four steps, as directed by the President. The first step, already taken, provided for a 10–15 percent cutback (depending on the country-wide size of the mission) and met the President's April 1 deadline for a recommended reduction of at least 10 percent at overseas missions. Included in the cutback consideration were all Americans and foreign nationals presently employed by 21 Federal agencies and working under the jurisdiction of the Ambassadors in every country except Viet Nam. As a result of this initial action, full year savings in expenditures abroad beginning in 1970 is estimated at $20–22 million. In fiscal year 1969, the transitional year, these savings will amount to $12–15 million.

Of 22,757 US citizens now employed abroad, 2,770 and their families will no longer be stationed abroad when the reductions are completed. Of the 26,293 foreign nationals employed by American Embassies, 3,177 will be separated from employment to the maximum extent by attrition. Also, there are 2,800 Americans abroad who are contract employees; about 13 percent will be returned to this country.

---

[10] The President made a brief announcement of this reduction in U.S. personnel serving abroad at the outset of his news conference on March 30. For text, see *Public Papers of the Presidents of the United States: Lyndon B. Johnson, 1968–69,* Book I, p. 462.

Steps two and three of the President's directive, which call for special intensive reviews in selected countries with the aim of proposing additional substantial cutbacks, have been combined into one operation. The 28 countries selected for special intensive review are as follows: Guatemala, Honduras, Costa Rica, El Salvador, Nicaragua, Germany, Iran, Taiwan, Turkey, Ethiopia, the Philippines, India, Japan, the UK, Greece, Italy, France, Pakistan, Liberia, Spain, Colombia, Peru, Venezuela, Morocco, Argentina, Ecuador, Congo (Kinshasa), and Austria. The general objective in those countries will be to effect an overall personnel cut of 24 percent. The report on the special intensive review is to be submitted to the President by August 1.

Step four of the President's directive envisaged the initiation of special studies to reduce reporting requirements in the field and to restudy activities in functional areas with a view to reducing staff requirements. An interagency task force under the chairmanship of Ambassador Parsons has been established for this purpose. The task force, as part of its task is reviewing 388 suggestions for improvements in procedures and operations submitted by 60 posts. A notable achievement of the task force to date is a reduction by 10 percent in reporting requirements.

GATT WP on Border Taxes

The US persuaded the GATT Council to set up a working party to examine the GATT rules on border tax adjustments and their possible effects on international trade. The President called for such a review in his January b/p message. The compromise terms of reference are broad enough to meet our objectives for a thorough review of the rules and of current national practices with the possibility of linking the discussion to the b/p situation.

[Here follow articles on unrelated subjects.]

198.   Telegram From the President's Special Assistant (Rostow) to President Johnson, in Texas[1]

Washington, June 1, 1968, 1657Z.

CAP 81212. Following is Secretary Fowler's memorandum recommending an increase of $150 million in the authorization of the Exchange Stabilization Fund to buy guaranteed sterling.

Treasury purchase of additional guaranteed sterling would be part of a package to exchange some of the UK's short term debt for intermediate term credit. This would give the British necessary time for their balance of payments program to work. The Europeans are doing their share.

The British have drawn $1.8 billion of their $3 billion line of credit from the U.S. They have drawn $2.4 billion of their $2.8 billion line of credit from the Europeans.

They now propose to draw their standby credit of $1.4 billion from the International Monetary Fund. They will use $700 million to mop up short term credit from the U.S. and the other $700 million to mop up short term credit from the Europeans.

As part of this package, we would convert $400 million of their remaining short term debt to the Federal Reserve into guaranteed sterling—which has no maturity date. This could be done through the proposed increase of $150 million in the Treasury's authority to buy guaranteed sterling together with the existing authority the Treasury and the Federal Reserve now have to buy such sterling.

We would probably hold this sterling for about three years, but it could be cashed on demand if the UK position turned around more rapidly than we expect.

The package as a whole has two benefits for us:

—A U.S.-European-IMF funding of a major share of the UK short term debt is essential to avoid a sterling crisis. A sterling crisis now would be unjustified in view of the UK program.
—The $700 million the UK will pay us out of its drawing on the IMF will increase our reserve position in the Fund and will mop up some dollars held by other Central Banks.

This sterling is guaranteed against devaluation. Treasury purchases of such sterling have neither a balance of payments nor a budget effect.

Secretary Fowler discussed the general outline of the UK package with Chancellor Jenkins when Jenkins visited in Washington in April.[2]

---

[1] Source: Johnson Library, National Security File, Subject File, Balance of Payments, Vol. V [2 of 2], Box 3. Secret; Sensitive. The telegram was received at the LBJ Ranch Communications Center on June 1 at 12:50 p.m. (CDT). A handwritten notation on the source text reads: "6–2–68 Jones told Brom Smith."
[2] No record of this meeting has been found.

I believe the package makes sense. Deming's inter-agency group (Duesenberry, Tony Solomon, Daane, and Ed Fried) have gone into it carefully and concur in Secretary Fowler's recommendation.

MEMORANDUM FOR THE PRESIDENT[3]

Subject: Funding of British short-term credits

The U.K. program—sterling devaluation and austerity—has not yet had time to convince the world that it will work. Consequently, there has not yet been a reflow of funds into sterling that would enable the U.K. to repay her short-term liabilities to us or to the European central banks. In fact, the gold crisis, the French crisis, and general uncertainty in the world have led to sporadic losses of U.K. reserves and fairly extensive recourse to additional short-term credit.

It is our judgment—and that of European treasury and central bank authorities—that the U.K. program will work if given time. U.S. fiscal action is expected to improve general confidence and help sterling considerably. The problem—as we and the U.K. authorities see it at present—is to provide some time by "funding" some of the short-term credits and extending the remainder.

To accomplish this, the U.K. will draw its standby credit on the IMF of $1.4 billion and apply $700 million to repaying a like amount of short-term swap credit to the Federal Reserve. The remaining $700 million will repay short-term European central bank credits. Since the IMF drawing has a three to five year maturity, rather than the 3 to 6 month maturities of the swaps, this will automatically "fund" the short-term credits into intermediate-term credits. The presently outstanding credits to the U.K. by both U.S. and others are as listed on the attached table.[4]

Incidentally, to the extent we share in the IMF drawing, our own IMF position will improve. Present prospects are that our share will be $250 to $300 million.

The total U.K. drawings on the Fed swap line are now $1.2 billion, so the application of $700 million will still leave $500 million "unfunded." We are proposing to "fund" all but $100 million of this by taking on "guaranteed sterling"—sterling guaranteed against devaluation. We presently hold $260 million of such guaranteed sterling and would increase our holdings to $650 million. Of this $650, the Fed would hold $250 million, the Treasury $400 million.

Guaranteed sterling is really a demand credit in the sense that we can cash it in at any time. Nevertheless, we would not expect to do this— we would probably hold it for about three years. It is a perfectly good

---

[3] A copy of Fowler's memorandum to the President, June 1, is ibid.
[4] Attached to the copy of Fowler's memorandum, ibid.

asset—we could use portions of it, if we needed to and if its use would not put undue pressure on U.K. reserves.

To do this, we need your authority to increase the amount of sterling that the Exchange Stabilization Fund, under the September, 1965, credit arrangement with the U.K.,[5] may purchase from our present authority of $300 million to $450 million. I recommend that you authorize me to do so.

Henry H. Fowler

Approve:[6]

Disapprove:

---

[5] On September 10, 1965, the Bank of England announced that the Central Banks of the United States and nine other countries (not including France) had agreed to extend to it a package of additional financial aid to bolster the pound in exchange markets. For text of the statement, see *The New York Times*, September 11, 1965, pp. 1, 37.

[6] This option is checked.

---

199. Memorandum From Secretary of the Treasury Fowler to President Johnson[1]

Washington, June 6, 1968.

The present crisis in France offers both a threat and an opportunity.

—A threat to the international monetary system that could destroy it in its present form.

—An opportunity to make a major structural improvement in U.S.–Europe balance of payments and thereby strengthen the monetary system.

I. Background

The threat comes from two factors—possible *devaluation of the franc* and consequent *pressure on sterling*, which might cause the U.K. to float.

---

[1] Source: Johnson Library, National Security File, Subject File, Balance of Payments, Vol. V [1 of 2], Box 3. Secret. The source text is Tab A to a June 7 memorandum from Rostow to President Johnson. Rostow's memorandum indicates that a meeting between the President and his senior advisers on all these matters was scheduled for 6:30 p.m. the same evening. No record of this meeting has been found. The memorandum also summarizes Fowler's memorandum, endorses his recommendation for a meeting on the franc–sterling monetary crisis, and proposes that at the meeting the U.S. position on the offset talks with Germany should be reviewed. Another June 7 memorandum from Rostow to the President, which provides background information on the German offset talks, is ibid.

Even before the crisis, the franc was regarded as the weakest currency in the Common Market. French industry has not been in a strong competitive position. The French balance of payments was headed for deficit; the French economy was operating well below capacity. Whatever the settlement with the unions turns out to be, it will weaken the French cost/price position and make her less competitive. Her economy may expand faster than desirable, with inflationary results, and hurt her balance of payments position still further.

Barre, Vice President of the EEC Commission, is now visiting Washington. He is an extremely well informed and well qualified French observer. The Commission estimates that the prospective union settlements in France will add 23 percent to wages in 1968 and 1969, 10 percent to prices, and produce a $1 billion balance of payments deficit. Despite this, *Barre thinks France should not devalue.*

Schweitzer of the IMF thinks that such additions to costs and prices *will lead inevitably to a franc devaluation*—although he does not expect it until fall.

Mendes-France—a possible new government head in France—*is reported to favor devaluation quickly.*

Present French policy suggests no early devaluation—they have borrowed from the IMF and imposed exchange controls.

In sum—anything could happen. Quick follow-up of the big wage increases by devaluation would be unpopular politically in France—a new government could probably get away with such a step better than the present one. With respect to timing, the best that can be said now is that devaluation before the election is highly unlikely. A new government might take action early in July; the present government would be more likely to wait until fall.

France has large reserves and substantial international borrowing power. She could well afford to lose some of her reserves while she tried to work out of prospective cost increases. But fear of inflation and balance of payments deficits is almost pathological in France, and she might act quickly on the ground that "fundamental disequilibrium" was so certain, even if not yet proven, that there was no reason to wait.

Obviously, *the extent of possible devaluation can only be guessed at.* There is no real economic basis for such a guess. Any devaluation has to carry credibility. *Probably 10 percent* is as good a guess as can be made. Ordinarily, that would be classed as *mild devaluation.*

Mild devaluation of the franc *should not* cause so much substantive economic shock that it would *threaten the international monetary system.* *But the monetary system is in such fragile condition* that even a mild devaluation could bring about *massive fund movements*—into Germany and perhaps Italy, where revaluation might take place, or into Switzerland for safety. Almost certainly, it would have an *adverse effect on sterling,* which is still very weak. The U.K. reserves are short and are mortgaged to the hilt. Much pressure on sterling could force the *U.K. to float.* Should that happen, there would be *repercussions on the dollar* and, perhaps, *general monetary chaos*—with everyone trying to get out of currencies and into gold.

Whether the monetary system, in its present form, could survive this series of steps is problematical. The U.S. might well have to cut the gold convertibility link to the dollar and float itself. And that would destroy the present system and probably badly cripple world trade.

The opportunity comes from the possibility of revaluation of the Deutsche mark and perhaps other EEC currencies. Germany probably is in fundamental disequilibrium on the surplus side, and the other Common Market countries have currencies probably undervalued relative to the franc and certainly not overvalued relative to the dollar or sterling.

There is good reason to believe that the *Germans regard revaluation of the Deutsche mark as probable*—perhaps inevitable. Timing of such action is far from definite—most likely, it would be delayed until there was more calm in international monetary affairs. If the U.S. and U.K. balance of payments programs were showing good results and the gold frenzy was abated *by year-end*, the move might well take place then.

Until quite recently, it was regarded as highly unlikely that one EEC country would change its parity against the others. The EEC might move as a bloc, but only as a bloc. That doctrine no longer seems valid. French authorities were cautiously suggesting a Deutsche mark revaluation before the crisis. *There is no mechanical or technical reason why Germany could not move alone.*

Italy could be regarded as a revaluation candidate but does not so regard herself. Perhaps the strongest exponent of preserving all present parities is Carli.[2] The Italian surplus is shrinking, and the elections seem to forecast a further turn to the left in government and probable increases in government spending and in wages. Only four years ago, the lira was regarded as overvalued—Italy corrected its deficit by stringent policies. Among the EEC countries, Italy has seemed to be proceeding on the best economic course—good growth with reasonable price stability.

Holland and Belgium offer little economic reason for revaluation, but Holland is tied so closely to Germany by trade and other relations that she would probably have to move concurrently in time, but perhaps not as much in amount, with Germany, if the Deutsche mark were revalued.

Another possible candidate for revaluation is Switzerland. On its face, the Swiss franc is a strong currency. But the basic Swiss balance of payments position is not strong—the Swiss franc is strong because of the Swiss banking situation, which attracts money seeking safety.

---

[2] Guido Carli, Governor of the Bank of Italy.

II. Course of Action

  Your advisers recommend a three part course of action.

  A. *The most constructive action that could be taken is to get a realignment of rates in the EEC—ex-France—vis-à-vis the rest of the world.*

  The advantages are great—if the action can be carried through successfully. It could prevent a franc devaluation and it could settle the uncertainties about possible parity changes in Germany and Italy. This should help stabilize the whole monetary system. It would make a major contribution to the adjustment process by helping to eliminate the big EEC surpluses and reduce deficits in the U.S. and U.K.

  Proper timing and handling is an important factor in this approach. Any change in parity is a sensitive subject and generates fund movements. *We do not intend to run hard at this program right now.* The French elections are June 23 and 30; it is unlikely that there would be any devaluation before then—although, as noted below, we are planning contingently for such unlikely event. Passage of our own tax-expenditure package would put us in far stronger position to talk about EEC revaluation—and probably would produce a calmer atmosphere in the markets under which revaluation could take place. The Germans seem to be thinking seriously about some Deutsche mark action, but generally seem to think of its timing as late this year.

  Thus, we propose to do no more at this time than quiet but pointed conversations. We should start with the Germans—they are the key—and Rostow and Deming will be in Bonn this weekend to discuss the offset. This will provide an opportunity to lay the base for contingency planning with the Germans through conversations with the Chancellor, Schiller and Blessing.

  The key point we want to get across is that either franc devaluation, which forces sterling to float, or a sterling crisis, which forces a float and brings down the franc, could be fatal to the present system.

  We will not ourselves push the possibility of Deutsche mark revaluation at this time. Our objective is to get a serious conversation going with the Germans which will stress the German responsibility to maintain and strengthen the system and start the Germans thinking about their exchange rate. Sometime in late June or early July—depending on the situation at the time—we may want to press this course of action with more vigor. On the other hand, it may prove better to postpone the hard push until fall. We simply cannot be certain right now.

  B. We are *staffing out* the *economic and balance of payments consequences* of franc devaluation and EEC—ex-France—currency revaluation. Some work has already been done—we hope to complete it fairly quickly. This will give us a better basis to talk harder and in more practical terms.

C. We are developing immediately *contingency plans against* the pos-sibility—highly unlikely as it is—of a *quick and surprise franc devaluation* and/or sterling float.

Much of the work done here will be continuation of work already under way, which will be useful and perhaps necessary in any event:

—solution of the sterling balance problem;
—multilateral support for sterling as needed;
—central bank cooperation in neutralizing massive currency flows.

It would be useful to have a small meeting with you tomorrow (Friday) to brief you on our planning.

Henry H. Fowler

200.   Memorandum for the Record[1]

Washington, July 1, 1968, 6 p.m.

SUBJECT

   Meeting with The President—Sterling Balances Problem, July 1, 1968, 6:00 p.m.

(PARTICIPANTS

   Secretary Fowler, Deming, Chairman Martin, Vice Chairman Robertson, Gene Rostow, Okun, Fried)

At the President's request, Secretary Fowler outlined the problem:

—There were more than $10 billion in sterling balances. About $5 billion was held in official reserves by sterling area countries; $3 billion in private holdings in sterling area countries; and almost $2 billion in public and private holdings in non-sterling area countries.

—The sterling area countries were becoming increasingly uneasy about their official holdings. They had lost as a result of the November devaluation. Most of these countries preferred to move out of sterling reserves—in whole or in part—primarily because they were not confi-

---

[1] Source: Johnson Library, National Security File, Subject File, Balance of Payments, Vol. V [1 of 2], Box 3. Secret. Drafted by Fried on July 2.

dent that the new sterling rate would hold. Some were liquidating their holdings gradually.

—Liquidation of these sterling balances put additional pressure on the UK. The British redeemed the sterling for dollars which forced them to draw down their credit facilities. Thus, even if the British improve their current position, the move out of sterling balances could keep them in serious trouble and add uncertainty to the system as a whole.

—This action also put pressure on the dollar and the U.S. gold stock. Countries liquidating sterling shifted their reserves partly to gold which they got from the U.S. by asking for dollar conversion.

We needed to stop this process and remove the threat of sterling balance conversions as one step in our program to strengthen the international monetary system. The Central Bankers meeting at Basel, under the Bank for International Settlements (BIS) have been working on the problem for some time. They now had under consideration a British proposal which we had helped to shape and which we believe is feasible. The basic elements are:

—The British would offer an exchange guarantee to governments for most of the official sterling balances.

—The major industrial countries would provide a long-term credit of $2 billion for use as a "safety net". It would be drawn on only to the extent that the governments holding sterling reduce their balances—despite the British exchange value guarantee.

Our share would be a maximum of $700 million and possibly less—depending in part on whether the French were full participants. The remaining $1.3 billion would be taken up by the continental European countries, Canada and Japan. We could meet our obligations through the Exchange Stabilization Fund and through help provided, as necessary, by the Federal Reserve Board.

Under Secretary Deming added that the Basel group of Central Bankers were meeting this coming weekend (July 6–7) to take a position on the proposal. Vice Chairman Robertson would represent us. If the British got a green light, they would start sending their people on missions to the sterling area countries to outline the proposal and seek their cooperation. If all went well, the "safety net" would not only stabilize the sterling balances, but for the most part probably would not have to be used. This, in turn, would ease the pressure on our gold stock and on the system as a whole.

We have been pushing the British hard to move actively on this problem. Their decision to give an exchange value guarantee had been long in coming but they now recognize it is important to move fast.

Stabilizing the sterling balances would help to reduce the pressure on the system resulting from the troubles of the French franc and, at the same time, lessen the danger of a floating rate for sterling.

Gene Rostow said he supported our participation in the package. This would bring more confidence to the system. His main concern was whether the package was big enough to do the job.

He stated that he and Deming had discussed these matters with Blessing, Chairman of the German Central Bank, after the recent offset negotiations. Blessing had strongly supported action on the sterling balances and stressed that it should be done fast under the leadership and through the mechanism of the Central Bankers.

Chairman Martin said that action of this kind was essential to avoid a serious international monetary crisis. He recognized that the means of U.S. participation posed some problems. But he believed that if the President approved our participation the means could be managed through Treasury–Fed cooperation. The Fed and Treasury had cooperated in the past on previous sterling support operations and he believed his Open Market Committee would approve Fed participation in this package if it were clearly a U.S. Government position endorsed by the President. He urged the President to approve our participation and to authorize Governor Robertson to take the lead in supporting it at the Basel meeting over the coming weekend.

Governor Robertson said he saw no alternative to our supporting sterling through these means. If the sterling balance problem got out of hand the entire system would be in danger.

Fried said we had to recognize that the British were heavily mortgaged. They had accumulated a very large amount of debt and would need time to pay it off. On the other hand, their balance of payments program was a good one. Their measures were severe and over time their situation would improve.

The present proposal to stabilize sterling balances was a good one. Others were taking up far more of the contingent liability than was the U.S. If we did not act now we would be putting the international monetary system to serious risks, with consequences for our own economy.

Okun agreed that U.S. participation in this package was very much in our interest. We were buying time for the UK and for the international monetary system, and, at the same time, reducing the risks for our own economy.

The President asked whether the British were doing all they should be doing to bring their house in order. Secretary Fowler said the UK suffered from structural weaknesses—such as labor practices—that were going to take a long time to correct, but their program looked good. They had increased taxes and were trying to keep both wages and prices in line so as to cut domestic consumption and make room for increased exports.

Okun supported this judgment and added that the British measures had received the approval of the International Monetary Fund and had been discussed favorably in the working group in the OECD. British trade figures so far had been disappointing. It was taking longer for devaluation and the British program to work. But he believed that the results would eventually be seen.

The President said that unpleasant as the choices were he saw no alternative to going ahead in support of the program. He approved U.S. participation and our leadership in getting the support package into operation.

ERF

201.   Current Economic Developments[1]

Issue No. 810   Washington, July 16, 1968.

CREDIT ARRANGEMENT AND
IMPROVED TRADE FIGURES BOLSTER STERLING

The President of the Bank for International Settlements and representatives of twelve central banks reached tentative agreement at a July 7 meeting in Basel on a new 10-year, $2 billion credit for Britain for support of the pound.[2] The credit is to be used to offset fluctuations in the sterling balances held by sterling area countries. The object is to strengthen the position of sterling and thus of the international monetary system as a whole. The next step is for Britain to consult with the central banks of

---

[1] Source: Washington National Records Center, RG 59, E/CBA/REP Files: FRC 72 A 6248, *Current Economic Developments*. Confidential. The source text comprises page 1 of the issue.

[2] Regarding the President's decision to support this arrangement, see Document 200. Following the Basel meeting, Chancellor of the Exchequer Jenkins sent a message to Fowler on July 11. This message among other things expressed his "warm appreciation to you and your colleagues in Washington for the constructive and helpful attitude you have taken up about the new facility for sterling which has been discussed in Basel. The positive attitude which Governor Robertson gave to the proposals and the fact that he was able to do so with the full authority of the President, made, I am told, a considerable impression on the other Governors at the meeting." (Johnson Library, National Security File, Fried Files, Chron, May 2–July 31, 1968, Box 2)

sterling area countries, after which the arrangement is expected to be completed at the September meeting of the central bankers in Basel. Chancellor of the Exchequer Jenkins told House of Commons that the arrangement would not result in an increase of UK liabilities to foreigners, would not affect the need for achieving balance-of-payments surplus, and would not necessitate further deflationary measures.

Sterling rallied following the announcement of the Basel arrangement, and confidence was further bolstered by the considerably improved June trade figures. The visible trade deficit declined to £50 million, compared with a deficit of £86 million in May. Exports increased by £10 million to £508 million, imports declined by £39 million to £609 million (excluding US military aircraft). The cumulative trade deficit, excluding military aircraft, for the first half of 1968 totaled £418 million.

The monthly assessment by the British Treasury led off with a statement that consumer spending had fallen off sharply since the budget. Although imports eased in June, their level is still substantially higher than forecast in March. Exports have moved closer to the expectation at the time of the budget. The main effect up to now seems to have been on prices, with the major increases in volume yet to come. Exporters remain highly optimistic in their expectations for coming months, according to the Treasury assessment. The GNP rose about 1-1/2 percent in the first quarter.

The Chancellor of the Exchequer repeated in a statement to the House of Commons that it will take two years of "hard slog" to restore the economy to a sound footing. He refused to make any forecast of the date when balance-of-payments surplus would be achieved.

[Here follow articles on unrelated subjects.]

202.   Current Economic Developments[1]

Issue No. 811   Washington, July 30, 1968.

[Here follow articles on unrelated subjects.]

EXIMBANK GIVEN MORE LIBERAL EXPORT FINANCING
AUTHORITY

The President on July 8 signed into law a bill which breaks new ground in export financing by the Eximbank.[2] The law authorizes the Bank to use up to $500 million of its existing $13.5 billion commitment authority to support export transactions which carry a higher degree of risk than is permitted under the Bank's present statute. The President will establish an Export Expansion Advisory Committee to provide guidance to the Eximbank with regard to the use of this facility.[3]

Purpose of New Authority

The new legislation is a part of President Johnson's program designed to reduce the deficit in our balance of payments. In his January 1 b/p message the President said: "I shall . . . ask the Congress to earmark $500 million of the Export-Import Bank authorization to: provide better export insurance, expand guarantees for export financing, and broaden the scope of Government financing for exports." The President elaborated further in his letter to the Senate and House transmitting the bill requesting such authorization. He said that the requested $500 million allocation would support the determined efforts of the entire business community to expand exports, assist American firms which now sell only within the US to expand their markets and send their goods abroad, and make available to American firms export financing more competitive with that provided by other major trading nations and especially suited to developing new markets.

The legislation seeks to achieve these objectives by authorizing the Eximbank to support export transactions which give promise of helping our b/p and promoting the long-term commercial interests of the US, but which do not necessarily meet the Eximbank's statutory standard of

---

[1] Source: Washington National Records Center, RG 59, E/CBA/REP Files: FRC 72 A 6248, *Current Economic Developments*. Unclassified. The source text comprises page 18 of the issue.

[2] P.L. 90–390; 82 Stat. 296. The legislation was approved on July 7, not July 8.

[3] On July 31, President Johnson issued Executive Order 11420 (33 F.R. 10997), which established the Export Expansion Advisory Committee. For the President's statement the same day on the purposes of this committee, see *Public Papers of the Presidents of the United States: Lyndon B. Johnson, 1968–69*, Book II, pp. 853–854. Drafts of this executive order and the President's statement are in the Johnson Library, Office Files of Ernest Goldstein, Export Expansion Advisory Committee, Box 6.

"reasonable assurances of repayment." The law provides broader criteria for a limited volume of Eximbank guarantees, insurance, and credits. It does not entail any increase in the current $13.5 billion lending authority of the Bank.

Advisory Committee

To achieve the greatest benefit from the export financing plan, the President will establish an Export Expansion Advisory Committee, chaired by the Secretary of Commerce, to provide guidance to the Board of Directors of the Eximbank. The Committee will be established by an Executive Order which will indicate the Committee's membership and outline in broad terms the function of the Committee.

[Here follow articles on unrelated subjects.]

203.   Memorandum From Secretary of the Treasury Fowler to President Johnson[1]

Washington, September 10, 1968.

AGREEMENT ON STERLING CREDIT PACKAGE

At the BIS meeting in Basle on September 8, 1968, agreement was reached on the $2 billion credit package "safety net" for sterling balances. It was announced by the BIS on September 9 that the new arrangements will be brought into force immediately.

The Governor of the Bank of England reported on the results of the U.K.'s consultations with the sterling area countries. In these consultations, each of the 40-odd sterling countries was offered a dollar value guaranty on all but 10 percent of its official sterling reserves in exchange for an undertaking to hold substantially the same proportion of sterling in its total reserves as it does now. Each such agreement is legally binding for three years, with specific provision for two-year extension by mutual consent.

---

[1] Source: Johnson Library, National Security File, Subject File, Balance of Payments, Vol. V [1 of 2], Box 3. Confidential. Transmitted under cover of a September 10 memorandum from Rostow to the President, which summarized the memorandum and concluded: "The agreement is now in force. The market reaction was good."

The U.K. has completed negotiations on this basis with some thirty countries holding about 80 percent of official sterling balances. Final agreements with the remaining ones are expected very soon.

There was considerable discussion about the question of making up the $200 million French share, since the French Government in the light of present circumstances was unwilling to agree to participate. (France has lost almost $3 billion in reserves since the May riots.) Also, Belgium, Switzerland and Japan found it necessary to reduce their shares below the amounts envisioned last July. To offset these shortfalls and to increase the total, Germany, Italy, the three Scandinavian countries and the United States increased their shares and the BIS took a share. The U.S. share is just under one-third of the total.

The shares are as follows:

| | (Amount in millions of dollars) | |
| | *Original* | |
	Proposal	*Final*
Austria	$ 50	$ 50
Belgium	100	70
Canada	100	100
Denmark ⎫		
Norway ⎬	65	125
Sweden ⎭		
France	200	–
Germany	350	400
Italy	200	225
Japan	100	80
Netherlands	100	100
Switzerland	125	100
United States	550	650
BIS	–	80
Total	$ 1,940	$ 1,980

Note: Belgium and Japan will seek further governmental authorization to increase their shares by $10 million each to make the package an even $2 billion.

Under the agreement, the Bank of England will be entitled to draw some $600 million right away and probably will do so and use the proceeds to repay short-term credits provided in November 1967 and March of this year.

Henry H. Fowler

204. Memorandum From Secretary of the Treasury Fowler to President Johnson[1]

Washington, November 12, 1968.

SUBJECT

Balance of Payments Program for 1969—Early Announcement of the Foreign
Direct Investment Program

As you know I plan to be in Europe next week and two days of the following week for the NATO Ministerial meeting and bilateral consultations. These will have an important bearing on U.S. balance of payments for 1969 and ensuing years.

In considering the content and timing of the announcement of the balance of payments program for the coming year we have kept very much in mind the importance of these consultations. It has seemed very desirable to have an estimate of our military costs and the burden sharing we could expect from our NATO partners before recommending continuation of the Action Program you announced on January 1, 1968, with appropriate modifications. This timing has coincided with the equally important desire to protect the balance of payments and international monetary system from any buffeting in the political campaigns.

Shortly after my return from Europe I expect to present to you the over-all balance of payments program for 1969 recommended by the Cabinet Committee on the Balance of Payments. One item, however, the Foreign Direct Investment Program, should not wait until that time. The 3,000 or more business firms affected by that program are well along in their budgeting for this coming year. In view of this fact, as well as the mandatory nature of the program, it seems highly desirable to announce the Foreign Direct Investment Program as quickly as possible. The Cabinet Committee, including representatives of the White House, has reviewed the modified program proposed by Secretary Smith. The Committee unanimously recommends that you approve this program and its announcement on or about November 15. The announcement will make clear that it is only one feature of the continued Balance of Payments Program for 1969 and that the over-all program will be announced later.

We expect that the Commerce program in 1968 will achieve its goal of saving $1 billion in direct investment in comparison to 1967, notwithstanding the exemption of Canada granted in March. The program has not stifled the foreign activities of U.S. firms. Indeed, direct investment

---

[1] Source: Johnson Library, White House Central Files, Confidential File, FO 4–1, Balance of Payments (1968–1969). Confidential.

by U.S. firms in foreign countries will probably set an all-time record this year with continuing high levels of capital flows to the less developed countries despite the reduced outflow of funds from the U.S. and the Foreign Direct Investment Program.

The capital markets of Europe have proved much more vigorous than most observers expected. They have provided the capital needs of American business for direct investment abroad in place of capital outflows from the U.S. or increased reinvestment of foreign earnings. Nonetheless, the increased borrowings of the U.S firms have not reduced the ability of European firms or governments to meet their capital requirements on normal terms. There is a clear expectation that a similarly large supply of capital will be available in 1969 from these offshore sources.

In summary, Commerce proposes to continue the basic Foreign Direct Investment Program established under the Executive Order of January 1, 1968. This would still

—Seek maximum savings in direct investment flows to continental Western Europe;
—Permit high level of direct investment in less developed countries;
—Provide for ample amounts of direct investment in those countries that have been heavily dependent upon U.S. capital (e.g. United Kingdom, Australia and the oil producing regions); and
—Exempt Canada.

In addition, the proposed modifications of the Foreign Direct Investment Program in 1969 would

—Increase the foreign direct investment target from approximately $2,600 million to $2,850 million;
—Maintain the net savings of 1968 in the over-all balance of payments since the increase in the investment target would be offset by greater earnings remittances; and
—Use the increased leeway to provide additional flexibility for firms with limited or no foreign investment experience, relieve inequities for companies that received investment quotas unusually low in relation to direct investment earnings, remove potential blocks to the growth of inter-company exports by American firms to their foreign affiliates and reduce some unique problems for special industries which became apparent in 1968.

While the basic format of the 1969 program will remain the same as in 1968, there will be one major change bearing importantly upon 1969 and future years, should it be necessary to continue the program beyond 1969. The introduction of foreign earnings as the criterion for expanding the direct investment quota available to each company will introduce incentives benefitting both U.S. firms and the balance of payments. This concept will gradually free the program from the otherwise growing inequities inherent in a quota system based upon past amounts of investment.

In short, we will pass along to the incoming Administration a viable and much improved Foreign Direct Investment Program. Although the program was designed to be temporary it had been modified to minimize any adverse long-term effects. It has also been supplemented to facilitate an orderly transition to a more permanent system to restrain direct investment outflows should future circumstances so require.

Henry H. Fowler

Approve:[2]

Disapprove:

---

[2] This option is checked.

---

205. Memorandum From the President's Special Assistant (Rostow) to President Johnson[1]

Washington, November 15, 1968, 4:55 p.m.

Mr. President:

As the attached[2] indicates:

—the French franc is under heavy pressure;
—the British pound is under considerable, but less, pressure;
—money is flowing to Germany in a big way.

The heart of this is the requirement for a currency readjustment in Europe. Ideally, the pound and the franc should stay where they are; the German mark should be revalued upward—also the Italian lire and the Dutch guilder—to a lesser extent than the German mark.

We are lucky that Central Bankers were scheduled to meet in Basle tomorrow in any case; Joe Fowler, Fred Deming, and Ed Fried are in Europe and following this closely.

---

[1] Source: Johnson Library, National Security File, Subject File, Balance of Payments, Vol. V [1 of 2], Box 3. Secret.

[2] The attached memorandum from Joseph K. Newman (NSC Staff) to Rostow, November 15, not printed, summarizes that day's "extremely heavy" speculation in British, French, and German currencies.

The issue is complicated because Strauss, as Finance Minister, would probably resist on political grounds a response to this crisis simply in the form of an upward revaluation of the German mark. He might even resign on the issue and free himself for the next German election. Our people are working for an intelligent readjustment which would avoid any further devaluation of the pound and, if possible, any devaluation of the franc. They have a week end to work it out before the markets open on Monday.

Walt

---

206.   Telegram From the Embassy in Belgium to the White House[1]

Brussels, November 15, 1968, 2144Z.

3310. For Walt Rostow, White House Eyes Only. From Ed Fried. Subject: Fowler mission contingency plan discussions.

Quiet, limited and very careful discussions on possible parity moves have turned up the following:

UK—1. Strongly prefer no moves now and a period of stability until next spring. They fully recognize, however, the dangers in the current situation.

2. They believe France may move unilaterally but do not fear big devaluation (25 percent) which would bring down the house. Their major fear is unilateral modest French change (10 percent) without any simultaneous offsetting revaluation by Germans and Italians. This would cause great pressure on sterling.

3. They could and would stand still, if we would, for a modest French devaluation (up to 10 percent) if there were simultaneous German and Italian moves upward.

4. They believe a German move would trigger a French move—mainly because of speculative pressure but possibly because the French would use it as an excuse.

---

[1] Source: Johnson Library, National Security File, Subject File, Balance of Payments, Vol. V [1 of 2], Box 3. Secret; Sensitive; Eyes Only. Via [text not declassified] Channels. Attached to the source text is a memorandum from Walt Rostow to the President, November 15, 6:30 p.m., indicating that he wanted the President to have Fried's report in case he was interested in looking into it over the weekend.

5. They want any French or other moves—alone or in combination—to be taken multilaterally or to be approved multilaterally in a meeting of the Group of Ten called by the U.S. in Washington. They see the situation calling for a closing of the exchanges for a day or two. But multilateral agreement (along with the announcement of new credit lines) would demonstrate that this was the end of parity moves for the time being and therefore would quiet the markets and stop speculative movements. They hoped we would be able to get this message across to the Germans and the Italians.

France—At the close of their formal discussion, Minister Ortoli privately expressed interest and concern to Secretary Fowler as to what Secretary Fowler would say in Bonn regarding German revaluation.

In an unusually frank conversation at a private luncheon arranged at his request, Larre (French Treasury) outlined French position to Deming as follows:

(A) French did not want to devalue. Couve was absolutely firm on this; de Gaulle was also. There were too many political disabilities. Couve also believes there is no economic necessity for the French to devalue.

(B) If Germans moved up, Couve believed it would relieve pressure on the franc and was confident French could hold. The prevailing view in the French Treasury emphasized concern about money flows reacting on France after a German revaluation. Larre cited 1961 experience when the German-Dutch move had triggered inflows into those countries and Switzerland. Also, it was believed that a German move now might create stronger belief that a French move would be needed. Couve thought this was wrong.

(C) Larre's further view was that regardless as to which view is right, German revaluation talk was draining French reserves. There really was no hope for stability in the present situation. No action on the mark probably would mean action elsewhere. Deming took this to mean explicitly that the franc could not be held without a mark change.

(D) Larre hoped Secretary Fowler would not be neutral on this subject in Bonn, as Fowler had intimated to Ortoli.

(E) Larre said that under proper circumstances—international meeting; public announcement that there would be no other upward parity changes except mark, lira and maybe guilder; and an adequate credit package back-up—franc could and would hold.

(F) There was no real comment about lira during most of discussion—emphasis was on mark.

Netherlands—This subject was not discussed in any systematic way with the Dutch, but at one point in private conversations Van Lennep and

Zijlstra[2] said flatly they did not believe a German move would put pressure on the franc but that to the contrary if the Germans moved enough (e.g., 7 or 8 percent or more) it would help the French to hold.

Belgium—Ansiaux was most concerned about the pound and was worried that the British would again be forced to move and that this would give the French an excuse to move.

He believes the French will not move on their own because Couve is determined to hold the rate and is prepared to let reserves run down.

He believed a German revaluation would take some pressure off the French and would not be used by the French as an excuse to devalue themselves. He was not concerned about the possible destabilizing effects on markets of a unilateral German move—but his position on whether they should move was essentially neutral.

Deming expects to have discussion with Carli tomorrow in Rome.

Inform Bill Martin and Joe Barr and John Petty in Treasury.

---

[2] Emile van Lennep, Treasurer General, Netherlands Finance Ministry, and Jelle Zijlstra, Governor of the Netherlands Bank.

---

207.   Telegram From the White House to the Embassy in Italy[1]

Washington, November 17, 1968, 2258Z.

CAP 82761. For Secretary Henry Fowler via Ed Fried, literally eyes only, Rome, from Walt Rostow.

A. According to Bill Dale, the Fund representative at the BIS meeting this weekend in Basle reports that:

1. Governor Brunet of the Bank of France has concluded that in any likely set of circumstances France will not be able to hold its present exchange rate.

2. Governor Blessing of the Bundesbank continues to be opposed to any change in the DM rate.

---

[1] Source: Johnson Library, National Security File, Subject File, Monetary Crisis, November 1968, Cables and Memos, Vol. 1 [2 of 2], Box 22. Secret; Eyes Only; Via [text not declassified] Channels. A typed text of this telegram is attached to a memorandum from Walt Rostow to the President, November 17, 6 p.m.; ibid. Rostow's memorandum indicates that following a conference call with Fowler, Martin, Barr, Eugene Rostow, and Tony Solomon, it was agreed to send this message to Fowler.

3. A bilateral meeting takes place tomorrow between French and German Government and central bank officials.

4. An EEC meeting is set for Tuesday afternoon.[2]

5. IMF senior staff officials are going to Paris.

6. German IMF Executive Director Schleiminger[3] has informed the Fund management most recent figures show the maximum DM revaluation which could be considered as 6–2/3 percent (DM 3.75 per $1).

7. Southard, the Acting IMF Managing Director, has informed Schleiminger that the IMF management is taking the position that there is a strong case for revaluing the DM and that the management would be concerned about the implications for the international monetary structure of any other exchange rate change (French devaluation) without a DM revaluation.

B. In light of Brunet's alleged comment, call your attention to Paris 24001 (repeated to Rome)[4] with this passage:

"Larre said he understands U.S. has agreed not to put pressure on Germans to revalue 'for the time being.' However, U.S. 'needs to decide' in event of general European rate changes whether it wishes to adjust its rate accordingly, i.e., agree to raise gold price, or demonetize gold; Larre repeated oft-heard French thesis that France does not 'favor' increase in price of gold except in case that this only alternative to demonetization."

C. Herewith our substantive thoughts as of Sunday afternoon.

1. Would hope for revaluation by the Germans of not less than 10 percent. In absence of German move of that size, possibility of lira and guilder move negligible, and, therefore, likelihood a larger French move increased.

2. Presume that if this not feasible, you will explore with Germans what constructive move they intend to make through new credit and other measures to help maintain status quo.

3. If discussions between Germans and French and IMF on Monday and in the EEC on Tuesday are unsatisfactory, we feel you should seriously consider preparing for and taking leadership in convening G–Ten in Europe to arrive at a multilateral conclusion. Even if this effort should fail, we feel record of U.S. leadership and of maximum effort will be required in face of unpleasant eventualities that could arise.

---

[2] November 19.

[3] Guenther Schleiminger, German Executive Director of the IMF.

[4] Dated November 16. (Department of State, Central Files, FN 17 FR)

208. Telegram From the White House to the Embassy in Germany[1]

Washington, November 18, 1968, 1740Z.

CAP 82764. To Secretary Fowler from Walt Rostow. For delivery immed upon arrival.

The President wishes you, in his name, to contact Chancellor Kiesinger immediately and tell him:

We have unverified reports that the French may unilaterally act to devalue the franc so substantially as to upset the world monetary system. We cannot evaluate these reports.

These reports also state that the French would do this because the German Government is unwilling to revalue the mark upward.

We believe we must, as we have in the past, handle monetary problems on a multilateral and cooperative basis. We must do everything we can to avoid a unilateral French action of this kind.

We suggest, therefore, [unless?] Kiesinger's information is firmly to the contrary, that Kiesinger promptly contact President de Gaulle and urge no unilateral move until appropriate monetary authorities can convene and act on a multilateral basis.

---

[1] Source; Johnson Library, National Security File, Subject File, Monetary Crisis, November 1968, Cables and Memos, Vol. 1 [2 of 2], Box 22. Secret; Eyes Only; Via [text not declassified] Channel.

---

209. Message From the Embassy in Germany to the White House[1]

Bonn, November 18, 1968.

Mr. Fowler and group are here, including Amb Lodge.

Fowler speaking.

Met with Chancellor Kiesinger, Minister Schiller, Min Strauss and State Secretary Carstens and Vice Chancellor Brandt at around ten. Con-

---

[1] Source. Johnson Library, National Security File, Subject File, Monetary Crisis, November 1968, Cables and Memos, Vol. 1 [2 of 2], Box 22. No classification marking. Handwritten on the source text is "Telecon #1," although it appears to be a one-way telephonic message (without other transmission information). The source text bears no date or time of transmission, but the date and time of receipt in the White House Situation Room were November 18, 5:58 p.m. A summary of the rest of this conversation was transmitted in "Telecon 2" from Bonn to the White House, November 18. (Ibid.) A summary of a follow-on meeting between these U.S. and German representatives on November 19 was transmitted in "Bonn Telecon 13" to the White House, November 19. (Ibid.)

ference lasted hour and ten minutes. Kiesinger learning of the subject comments requested that others join us since they had been conferring on the same subject together and with Pres Blessing for preceding three to four hours. I opened by saying that the President wished me to deliver in his name a message to the Chancellor and thereafter quoted the message verbatim[2] adding some personal comments on the following points:

1. While we had departed from Wash DC last Friday feeling that a period of calm was desirable for all concerned events had overtaken the situation and it was not clear that we were facing a crisis which required a multilateral consideration and decision if the monetary system was to be preserved. I stated whereas a week or even a few days ago we had been neutral on the desirability of a German revaluation, at this time although feeling that it would fundamentally help the system over the long term we had now concluded that a German move was an indispensable part of a combination necessary to maintain the system.

2. That we were unequivocally opposed to any unilateral French action because it was not justified on the economics and would lead to a movement by the pound probably to float which would disrupt the system entirely. I stated that the U.S. was not in a mood or position to accept any further disadvantages unilaterally arrived at and that we would resist any such French action and urge that a multilateral approach to apply both carrots and sticks to bring about a rational result was the only course open. In particular I stated that the acceptance of a French unilateral move would drive us into a two world system and would be particularly dangerous at a time when a new administration was preparing to take over.

---

[2] See Document 208.

210. Telegram From President Johnson to Prime Minister Wilson[1]

Washington, November 19, 1968, 0230Z.

CAP 82769. I have instructed Fowler in my name to make recommendations to Kiesinger urging multilateral and cooperative solutions for present situation. He has done so with great vigor, and will stay in Europe to lead effort to persuade Germans to revalue and to prevent large unilateral French devaluation. German position strongly against revaluation at this time, proposing instead reducing border taxes on imports and lessening some export rebates. We do not believe this approach would work, or contain French devaluation to reasonable level.

Our tentative approach would be to work for something like 10 percent German revaluation and 5 percent French devaluation, with small corresponding moves by Italy and the Netherlands. To confirm this approach, we are considering G–10 meeting in Europe with Schweitzer present as soon as possible. We assume you will wish to cooperate fully in this approach and will not wish to move in any way pending the outcome of these efforts.

---

[1] Source: Johnson Library, National Security File, Subject File, Monetary Crisis, November 1968, Cables and Memos, Vol. 1 [2 of 2], Box 22. Secret. A copy of the telegram, identified as "Telecon 8," was sent from Walt Rostow to Fowler on November 19. (Ibid.) According to a memorandum from Rostow to President Johnson, November 18, 7:10 p.m., this message to Wilson "incorporates the approach that Joe, Bill Martin, Joe Barr, Gene Rostow, etc., agree is the right approach." A handwritten notation on Rostow's memorandum reads: "Approved, 9:25 p.m." (Ibid.)

---

211. Telegram From Prime Minister Wilson to President Johnson[1]

London, November 19, 1968, 1640BST.

[Source: Johnson Library, National Security File, Subject File, Monetary Crisis, November 1968, Cables and Memos, Vol. 1 [2 of 2], Box 22. Top Secret. 1 page of source text not declassified.]

212. Telegram From Prime Minister Wilson to President Johnson

London, November 19, 1968, 2330Z.

[Source: Johnson Library, National Security File, Subject File, Monetary Crisis, November 1968, Cables and Memos, Vol. 1 [2 of 2], Box 22, Top Secret. 1 page of source text not declassified.]

213. Telegram From the President's Special Assistant (Rostow) to President Johnson, in New York[1]

Washington, November 20, 1968, 0357Z.

CAP 82725.

Mr. President:

A second message came in from Wilson in your absence.[2]

The attached indicates how I handled it, after checking with Joe Barr.[3]

I also attached a formal copy of the message earlier received this evening from Wilson.[4]

Wilson is obviously pulling out all stops. If he can get the Germans to go above 4 percent on the basis of this pressure—fine.

But Wilson is wrong in treating the French problem as strictly secondary. If we can hold the French—or hold them to a modest devaluation plus big short-term loans—the pound can be protected; and I'm still not sure that's impossible because deGaulle has staked so much on a policy of "no devaluation," out of simple pride.

/s/ W.W. Rostow

---

[1] Source: Johnson Library, National Security File, Subject File, Monetary Crisis, November 1968, Cables and Memos, Vol. 1 [2 of 2], Box 22. Secret. Drafted on November 19. President Johnson was in New York on the evening of November 19 to address the National Urban League.

[2] Regarding Wilson's first message, see Document 211. In his memoirs, Prime Minister Wilson recounted in some detail his government's reactions to the Bonn monetary conference but nowhere mentions his messages to President Johnson about it. See Wilson, *The Labour Government, 1964–1970: A Personal Record* (London: Weidenfeld and Nicolson and Michael Joseph, 1971), pp. 582–585. For the perspective of a senior British Treasury official on the Bonn meetings, see Alec Cairncross, *The Wilson Years*, pp. 341–349, 356–357.

[3] Reference presumably is to Rostow's message to Fowler, the text of which appears below, after Rostow's message to the President.

[4] Not printed here, but see footnote 2 above.

The President is in New York at the moment; but I am forwarding to you this second message from Wilson indicating his line of attack.

Again I suggest you should take counsel with Jenkins and others and tell us what you think the optimum strategy for tomorrow's meeting should be.

Don't hesitate to get me to the office early to receive your messages, when you have had a chance to form a judgment and wish to check it here with highest authority.

Wilson's message follows.

[6 paragraphs of source text and 1 paragraph of text (1-1/2 pages) not declassified]

---

214.   Telegram From the Embassy in Germany to the White House[1]

Bonn, November 21, 1968, 0255Z.

Following is a summary of the discussion at the first G–10 plenary session.

The meeting began about 4:30 this afternoon with a long statement from Schiller extolling the virtues of the German tax package[2] and nailing down the proposition that the Deutschemark should not be revalued.

Secretary Fowler followed with the statement already transmitted.[3]

Roy Jenkins said that a 4 percent change on the trade balance was not equivalent to a 4 percent tariff change. It wouldn't cover the whole range of international transactions. It simply wasn't enough. It only eliminated one-third of the massive German trade surplus. We must come up with something more convincing. Proposed German action

---

[1] Source: Johnson Library, National Security File, Subject File, Monetary Crisis, November 1968, Cables and Memos, Vol. 1 [1 of 2], Box 22. Secret. The source text, identified as "Bonn Telecon Nbr 20," bears no additional information on the place of transmission, but the telegram was received in parts at the White House on November 20 beginning at 8:25 p.m. (Washington–Bonn Telecon Chronology of Events for November 20; ibid.)

[2] The Embassy's translation of the German Government's press release announcing the border tax measures and declaring that it would not revalue the mark is in telegram 19490 from Bonn, November 19. (Department of State, Central Files, FN 16 GER W)

[3] Text of Fowler's opening statement, November 20, was transmitted in Bonn Telecon No. 19, November 21. (Johnson Library, National Security File, Subject File, Monetary Crisis, November 1968, Cables and Memos, Vol. 1 [2 of 2], Box 22)

equivalent to 7-1/2 percent revaluation. There was an abortive discussion about what the bankers had done at Basle and it was agreed that they had done nothing.

Ortoli[4] then spoke. Said that the situation affects the whole monetary climate, which is very fragile. How can we effectively achieve a better system that in the long run, and he emphasized the long run, would be viable? First question to deal with is whether the technical measures of the Federal Republic will solve this problem. He agreed with Fowler and Jenkins that it wasn't adequate. He agreed that the Federal Republic had made a real effort, but there would still be a problem. He didn't want to set a rate for the Deutschemark in precise terms, but whatever rate it had should be realistic and credible (and by implication the present rate wasn't). He said that technical measures (the border tax) have two major drawbacks. It didn't cover the areas outside of trade and it was too short term. He thought it would invite speculation and that was a real risk. What needed to be done was readjustment in the whole level of international payments and we needed a durable solution with credible parities. This could apply to the Deutschemark and other currencies as well.

Colombo[5] spoke at some considerable length. His net conclusion was that the present system had to stand on a fixed parity basis and that parities should not be changed. This would require other measures for both creditor and debtor countries. The Schiller program should make a positive contribution to adjustment. Speculators act on the belief that currency parities will be changed. This doctrine must be refuted. There should be no parity changes. He said that Italy indeed had a surplus, but for reasons different from those of the German surplus. He was confident that the measures Italy was taking to expand its economy would soon eliminate their surplus and bring their accounts into equilibrium.

Witteveen[6] reacted to Colombo's presentation very strongly. He said that in a system of fixed parities when countries are in dis-equilibrium it was important to determine whether it was fundamental. If it wasn't fundamental, other measures could bring about proper adjustment, particularly demand management measures. If it was fundamental, such measures wouldn't work and parity changes were designed to cover such situations. This is what was envisaged at Bretton Woods.

The very large German surplus seemed to him to be fundamental. He congratulated the Germans on running a successful economic program, but their very success required a fundamental adjustment. He doubted that the German tax measures would be adequate and he also doubted that they were really consistent with the idea of tax neutrality.

---

[4] Francois-Xavier Ortoli, French Governor of the IBRD.
[5] Emilio Colombo, Italian Governor of the International Monetary Fund.
[6] Hendrikus Witteveen, Netherlands Finance Minister.

He saw some danger for the Common Market in using this as an adjust-ment factor. The program in his judgment was insufficient; therefore it would not make the necessary impression on the financial world. He also was concerned about it being temporary rather than it being a durable change. He asked, isn't something better possible? Finally, he asked about the Italian surplus. Would expansion of the domestic economy really cure that problem?

Schiller responded to the Dutch comment. He said he knew the TVA was meant to be neutral, but since it wasn't to go into full effect until 1970, Germany was free to adjust it in 1969. Also he viewed the German actions as being not for protection or for subsidy, and consequently they should not be regarded as bad adjustment policies. To the contrary, the German approach is to lower the obstacles to imports and raise the burden for exports.

Snoy of Belgium[7] was next. He said that if there is a fundamental dis-equilibrium, parity should be adjusted. He congratulated the Germans on the courage they were showing in the tax measure but he was some-what frightened about it. First he found some conflict with the principles of the Rome treaty. More importantly he doubted its credibility. He agreed with Witteveen on this point.

Stopper of Switzerland[8] followed. He said that he was only an observer; but because of Swiss financial role he felt he could speak. He thought it was wrong to change parity—apparently at any time—because it fed speculation. Germany had a surplus in 1961 and changed the parity then. Speculators automatically think it will change again. There is too much talk about this. We need to destroy speculative hopes of revaluation by stopping talk of revaluation. He argued that a DM revaluation would not stop speculation in other currencies.

Wickmann of Sweden[9] said that he would prefer a revaluation but the Germans had decided not to do this. The tax approach was inge-nious. What will come out of the meeting tonight should be a durable and concerted solution.

Benson of Canada[10] closed this round by noting that speculation is out of hand. He thought it could not be resolved without parity changes (by Germany and France). He was impressed with the imagination of the German measures but he doubted they were sufficient to bring equilib-rium. There must be changes in parities plus a credit package and ade-quate domestic measures to achieve long-term stability in both France and Germany.

---

[7] Baron Jean Snoy et d'Oppuers, Belgian Finance Minister.
[8] Edwin Stopper, President of the Swiss National Bank.
[9] Krister Wickmann, Swedish Finance Minister.
[10] Edgar J. Benson, Canadian Finance Minister.

Responding to the criticism, Schiller made these points. First, we must have a collective action abut all speakers mentioned only unilateral action by Germany. Second, he saw no reason in economic theory for the preference expressed for revaluation as against devaluation. Third, the German measures go to the bottom of correcting the German position since there is no surplus in the German basic balance but only in the trade accounts. Other items in the balance of payments are in equilibrium or deficit except for a short-term speculative capital inflow. He repeated his earlier points regarding the sacrifice to German traders resulting from cutting the trade surplus by one-third.

The German measure should be supplemented by measures in other countries that would directly affect the balance of payments; internal policies were not enough.

He invited Ortoli to call on other countries in a smaller meeting of the six with the Economic Commission representative (Barre) present.

On the credit package, he mentioned the German willingness to increase swap lines to $500 million or more and to extend the period of time of these credits for six months. Finally, he complained that the action proposed by the meeting would appear to be a punishment for a sound German policy.

Chancellor Jenkins intervened at this point and urged a decision closing all the markets on Thursday. After much discussion and differences of views among the Central Bank Governors, it was agreed that the Governors would meet separately to resolve this question.

Secretary Fowler and Chairman Martin agreed to handle the US market on Thursday and, if necessary, on Friday in the same way as it had been handled today.

Following the discussion of markets, Ortoli suggested a suspension of the plenary session, to resume later.

Secretary Fowler asked permission to make some further observations and break new ground. He wanted to clarify some misunderstanding. He said that we had not said or implied that the Federal Republic was bad or unwise and we welcome it as a step in the right direction. Our judgment is that it is not adequate to meet the situation. We have not said that action should be confined to Germany. The measures should be broader in scope. They would carry more conviction if accompanied by a change in the DM currency parity. We have not argued for other parity changes but would welcome them if they contribute to stability. We are not advocating solely unilateral action by Germany.

We believe there should be an adequate credit package and we are prepared to participate as we always have.

In response to Schiller's point on appreciation vs depreciation we have no theoretical doctrine of preference but are merely looking at the present situation in a practical manner and try to deal with it as it exists now. There is evidence of a fundamental German payments imbalance.

The German surplus has existed over a number of years in a sizable amount, and existed during a business cycle covering the years 1963 to 1967. The trade surplus is at the core of the problem. Germany has had trade surpluses in the years since 1961. The persistence of a small trade surplus in the year of peak demand such as 1965 shows that it is a structural surplus rather than cyclical.

The reason there is so much discussion of the role of Germany is because Germany is a strong country and is attracting large amounts of money. There is no desire to punish Germany. The Secretary indicated that we had been in the role of the strong country for many years and Germany is now also in that position.

The Germans are responding. We do not insist exclusively on a parity change but we point out that the Bretton Woods Agreements provide a standard procedure for a change in parity that is intended to be used when there is a structural imbalance. That is the question we confront.

Schiller did not undertake to reply and the meeting adjourned for supper. Schiller did indicate that he felt there was no proof that the structural disequilibrium of deficit countries can be solved by a single parity change.

The meeting as such never reconvened. Following supper the Common Market Ministers met among themselves for almost 2-1/2 hours and then there was a meeting solely of the Ministers of the 10, which lasted some one-half or three-quarters of an hour. In the intervening period, two or three interesting side conversations were held.

At supper Deming talked to Van Lennep, who said the Germans should revalue and that if another country, Italy, would revalue in a small amount, the Netherlands would follow. Van Lennep's figures were 10 for Germany and 5 each for Italy and the Netherlands. He suggested we talk to the Italians.

We had a long conversation with the Italians which began with Colombo, Carli and Ossola.[11] Colombo had to leave relatively soon for the Common Market Ministers meeting, but the conversation continued with Carli and Ossola. The Italians said that they simply could not revalue the lira on political grounds. Colombo himself said that it would be impossible to form a new Italian cabinet with a lira revaluation. He and Carli both said any new government would be inflationary and that the Italian surplus would disappear pretty fast. In addition, Carli repeated the arguments Colombo had used in the plenary session, that is that there should be no parity change, that other measures should be

---

[11] Rinaldo Ossola, Chairman of the Deputies of the Group of Ten.

used for adjustment. We finally convinced Carli that there were conditions of fundamental disequilibrium that logically required parity changes, but that did not convince him that Italy should move. Carli did suggest that Italy would be glad to participate in a credit package, and noted that it should be in two parts. One would involve a rechanneling of reserve losses from capital flight back to the central banks of the countries losing reserves. This would be completely separate from a conventional swap package for France, which he thought should be enlarged from the present $1.3 billion to at least $1-1/2 billion to $3 billion. He thought that we should take a bold approach to the granting of credits and convince speculators that capital flows between countries were no more destabilizing than capital flows within countries.

We raised the possibility of a border tax adjustment by Italy with Carli; Colombo had already left. Carli thought the present Italian Parliamentary situation precluded any such action for some time to come. Carli did think the German tax package was inadequate and thought it ought to be at least twice as big.

In a separate conversation with Emminger some time later, Emminger told Deming that he thought the German tax package could be enlarged to 5 percent, but that he saw no hope for a revaluation of the mark. Deming's impression is that Emminger favors revaluation, but regards it as politically impossible. Emminger's judgment is that a bigger border tax adjustment on the part of the Germans, a small, say 7 percent, devaluation of the franc, and an adequate credit package would restore confidence.

Van Lennep joined the conversation and stated again that the Netherlands was willing to revalue by a small amount if Germany and one other country would move. Emminger said that the German representatives at Basle had tried to get some other movements for support of their own feeling that the Deutschemark should be revalued, but had failed to get any support whatsoever.

Larre told Deming that he thought Fowler had made a very strong case in his presentation and that if the Germans would move some, plus the border tax adjustment, and perhaps there could be something done by Italy and Holland, that France would be in a reasonably comfortable position. He thought now, however, that the situation had gone so far that there would be some kind of devaluation in France, but that there was no reason for it to be more than 5 percent, if there were an adequate movement on the part of other countries.

In a conversation before dinner, Strauss told Fried and Deming that the British had called in the German Ambassador in London at 2 a.m. and had read him the Riot Act on the necessity for a German parity change. [6 lines of source text not declassified]

Late in the evening after the meeting of the Ministers of the 6 had ended, the Ministers of the 10, meeting by themselves, were in session for a half-hour or forty-five minutes. Colombo, President of the Common Market Ministers, made a formal report to the rest that there had been a meeting and the problem had been discussed at great length.

Schiller stated that it was a Common Market rule that any government contemplating a parity change should consult its Common Market partners before taking any action. Since Germany had no intention of changing its parity, it had seen no reason to consult its partners.

Schiller then asked pointedly whether any other Common Market countries needed to consult? There was no response. Schiller then said, what do we do now? Go home?

Jenkins said we needed to come to a convincing conclusion.

Fowler made a strong plea for continuation of the meeting, said there was nothing on the table so far but the German measures. Seven countries had said they were inadequate; two countries, Italy and Switzerland, opposed any parity change but had not commented on the adequacy of the parity measures. One country, Japan, had not spoken. He thought that the meeting needed to explore one aspect that hadn't been discussed in any explicit terms. That was credit arrangements. He intended to present in the morning some proposals for a wholly new type of arrangement, the rechanneling of reserve losses, and propose in addition to that, a new swap package for France. Finally, he thought there should be discussed tomorrow other substantive measures to deal with both structural and cyclical problems.

Schiller responded that the German measures had been announced. He had some doubts about credit measures as reflecting on the adequacy of the German measures and he wanted to know what deficit countries would do.

Jenkins stated that the United Kingdom had done a lot and Ortoli pointed to the French actions.

Schiller asked pointedly, twice, what would France do about its parity?

Ortoli responded that he could not give any answer until he knew what more the Germans would do, what other countries would do and what the credit package was. He had to judge the credibility of the total package.

Jenkins closed the meeting by strongly stating that the United Kingdom had no intention to change its parity. It was then decided that the meeting would reconvene at 10 in the morning in restricted session, three from each country, and reconvene in plenary session at 11 a.m.

215.   Telegram From the Embassy in Germany to the White House[1]

Bonn, November 21, 1968.

For Walt Rostow from Fried. Meeting is now at a very critical point. The Germans have been unwilling to budge from their offer of a 4 percent border tax adjustment and have ruled out any revaluation. Ortoli said this morning that if the Germans cannot do more the French would have to consider 15 percent. They would do less if the Germans do more. Our hope now is to get the French down to 10 percent or less with no other changes in parities. The British look as though they will hold firm and not move. But we need a credible package that will stop speculation.

Fowler proposed in the Ministers' meeting this morning that the German Government announce a best effort undertaking to seek approval for a border tax adjustment of 7-1/2 percent in place of 4 percent. We believe an improvement of the German offer along these lines coupled with the credit package we think we can get and the willingness of others to hold their parities could provide a reasonably successful outcome to the meeting.

Fowler would like to have a Presidential letter to Kiesinger along the attached lines to be used at his discretion in the next few hours. He is not at the moment confident that the impasse can be broken and will use the letter only if the prospects are there.

Draft letter follows.[2]

---

[1] Source: Johnson Library, National Security File, Subject File, Monetary Crisis, November 1968, Cables and Memos, Vol, 1 [2 of 2], Box 22. Secret; Sensitive. The source text, identified as "Bonn Telecon 21," bears no additional information on the place, date, or time of transmission, but the telegram was received at the White House on November 21, 10:34 a.m., as identified in the Washington–Bonn Telecon Chronology of Events for November 21. (Ibid.)

[2] The undated draft letter (Bonn Telecon 22) is ibid. The President cleared the letter with one suggested change, and added the following instruction: "He wants you to use your judgment as to whether or not this letter is used. But it is his judgment that you should not use it unless you feel there is a 'good possibility or even probability' that it would be decisive. He would wish to avoid engaging the President in an effort to move the Germans that failed." (Message from Rostow to Fowler (Washington Telecon 19), November 21; ibid.) No evidence has been found to indicate that the President's letter was actually delivered to Kiesinger.

216.   Telegram From the Embassy in Germany to the White House[1]

Bonn, November 21, 1968.

Following is summary of restricted meeting of Ministers and Governors of the Group of Ten, 10 a.m.–1:30 p.m., Nov 21, 1968.

Minister Schiller summarized the German position:

(1) German measures

A. Germany had proposed to reduce the border tax 4 percent on exports and imports. There was no chance that this figure would be changed.

B. A German regulation will pass the Cabinet this p.m. Short-term liquidity coming into German banks will be subject to a negative interest charge of 2-1/2–3 percent. This is an extraordinary measure under a 1961 German law. Minister Schiller said it was a dangerous law since it permits positive exchange controls but also negative controls.

(2) There should be an international credit arrangement of a special quality and quantity in addition to regular swap lines.

(3) Credibility of the package requires additional balance of payments measures by deficit countries.

The package is only good if all three points are covered with appropriate numbers. More progress will be made by discussing points 2 and 3. There is no point in saying the German measures under point 1 are not sufficient. The three elements are interdependent.

Secretary Fowler said he was attempting to find a pattern that would be both realistic and achievable. He proceeded with the talking points set forth in attachment A.[2]

Minister Schiller insisted that he was not empowered to do more than 4 percent for 15 months. Until March 1970 the parity was fixed and would be supported. He hoped that activation of SDRs, which he would support, would take place during this period and resolve the problem.

Minister Schiller continued that an overall alignment of all important parities is needed, but this cannot be done now even if the dollar is over valued in some U.S. opinion. Such a general alignment is not pos-

---

[1] Source: Johnson Library, National Security File, Subject File, Monetary Crisis, November 1968, Cables and Memos, Vol. 1 [2 of 2], Box 22. Secret. The source text, identified as "Bonn Telecon 24," bears no additional information on the place, date, or time of transmission, but the telegram was received at the White House on November 21, 2:53 p.m., as identified in a Washington–Bonn Telecon Chronology of Events for November 21. (Ibid.)

[2] Reference is presumably to an "outline of points," not attached, which Fowler used as the basis for his opening statement at this restricted session. (Bonn Telecon 23, November 21; ibid.)

sible politically and is dangerous. This is not a proposal now and may not be made in the future. The border tax adjustment cannot be extended beyond 15 months according to Common Market rules.

Minister Ortoli said he would comment on Secretary Fowler's statement and particularly point 3. To reach a solution we have to look at the whole thing. He shares Secretary Fowler's view that the German Government should do much more.

As to point 3, Secretary Fowler proposed a system of automatic compensation and this should be explored.

Minister Schiller and Secretary Fowler have raised the question of other currencies against which there is speculation. Secretary Fowler envisaged complementary measures if the franc were devalued. Such complementary measures would be important, but Ortoli said he would deal here only with French devaluation itself.

Minister Ortoli said he could propose a parity move to the French Government, but the French must know the whole package. The package must stop the speculation. With the German proposal as it stands, France would have to move on the order of 15 percent. If the Germans could extend their measures he could envisage a move slightly less than the one mentioned.

Minister Schiller called on Mr. Schweitzer for the expert opinion of the Fund on the French figure.

Mr. Schweitzer, before commenting on the French [figure] specifically, said he was frightened at the Schiller proposal for an overall parity review. This would be very destabilizing. At present only two currencies need to be changed—the D-mark and the French franc. He had nothing more to say about the D-mark. He could not say anything about the franc without further study. Speculative movements would continue. It seemed difficult to justify devaluation of 15 percent. As regards an IMF standby, such an agreement could be negotiated in traditional and conventional terms.

Minister Schiller interpreted Mr. Schweitzer's remarks as indicating that other parities were not out of line but Schweitzer refused to make a judgment on the 15 percent franc adjustment. Mr. Schweitzer said that we should have waited for the franc adjustment but cannot do so now. There is a necessity to do something but 15 percent was on the high side. Mr. Schweitzer said he had not commented on the D-mark because the Minister had said it was useless to do so. But he thought it was on the low side.

Chancellor Jenkins made these points: first, it would be unwise to move on general parity charges; this would cause speculation in every currency. Second, he supported Secretary Fowler's position on the inadequacy of the German measures, stating that the great weight of opinion is that it is not enough. He also endorsed Mr. Fowler's proposal

on the package. Third, the French devaluation should be lower than 15 percent which would place a heavy burden on the U.K. He would prefer a substantially greater German move and a substantially smaller French move.

In the strictest confidence Chancellor Jenkins said he hoped to present some further measures to help the United Kingdom's balance of payments. Just what these would be would depend upon the French action, and the United Kingdom improvement would move more slowly if the French move is as strong as 15 percent.

His comment on the credit package was that it will not work if we leave the meeting with the idea that it will need to be used. We cannot leave this meeting with instability. The only rechanneling of funds acceptable to the United Kingdom would be one that would not add to the already excessive short-term debt, but the United Kingdom would participate in technical discussions. He gave complete support to Secretary Fowler and Minister Ortoli.

Minister Schiller said the United Kingdom had explored a long-term loan in Germany to consolidate short-term credits. The government could not make such a loan, but was ready to mobilize commercial banks to do so. The United Kingdom rejected this. A long-term Canadian loan had been arranged this year at German initiative.

Minister Strauss made a long and very hard statement indicating German inflexibility on the rate. He denied that the Deutschemark rather than the French events of May was responsible for the present crisis. Rumors of revaluation have been fostered by interested persons. Germany has made a further contribution in the negative interest rate on foreign funds which is unpleasant and dirigiste. Germany would even go further and use tax relief for capital exports to the United States, but not retroactively. No other country has offered anything to solve the problem. The French 15 per cent is too high and should be carefully studied. Other countries cannot decide what Germany will do. The 1961 revaluation did not work. Measures must be taken by all countries to avoid realignment of parities. Germany has struggled against inflation and this should be a common goal. Germany had tried to eliminate the domestic recession, but domestic demand and foreign trade have not reacted as wished. Revaluation to 7-1/2 percent could be done without Parliamentary approval but would increase the budget deficit by DM 5 billion and break confidence internally between the government and Parliament, thus eliminating possibility of fiscal discipline in Germany. Both U.S. parties have indicated they will impose border taxes of 8 to 20 percent—a serious matter for Germany. Germany also carries the burden of military offset. The German basic balance has been equilibrium of deficit from 1962 to 1965 and thus Germany does not have a structural problem. The U.S. buys German companies at three to four times the price Europeans would pay. This makes it hard to understand U.S. balance of payments problems. Germany cannot go beyond what we have said. It is impossible. Please accept this.

At this point Schiller wanted to bring in the European Community representatives, but Ortoli and Witteveen objected. Finally Barre[3] alone was admitted.

Governor Carli made two points. He agreed that any discussion of a general realignment of parities was not necessary or desirable, and would be disastrous at present. The Italians survived a crisis in 1964 without devaluation. Parity changes should be made only in extraordinary circumstances. We should defeat the speculators. Secondly, he supported Secretary Fowler's proposal for rechanneling funds to support currencies under pressure and suggested that Ministers and Governors decide on a statement on this point. They should give a mandate to the BIS to offset these movements. Central banks should support it by depositing a portion of their reserves with the BIS.

Emminger discussed technical monetary arrangements. He had no authority to commit the Bundesbank, but probably special reserve requirements could be placed on foreign deposits. He would try to follow this up today and thought the requirement could be placed at a very high level.

Secondly, credit arrangements should be taken only in the context of an overall package endorsed and defended by the Group of 10. The Bundesbank on this basis would assume its full share of a $2 billion credit package though he could not make a formal commitment now.

Third, Emminger said the rechanneling proposal raised technical problems. It could not go beyond short-term arrangements having some quantitative limitation, but he hoped something could be done.

Governor Rasminsky (Canada)[4] asked what proportion of short-term capital inflow into Germany came to rest in the banking system. Would negative interest and reserve requirements really work? Emminger could not give precise answer for last two weeks, but said negative interest would apply not merely to inflow but to all foreign deposits, and would have very sizable effect. Reserve requirements would apply only to new capital inflow. There were other forms of liquidity that would escape these measures but banks get most of the influx.

Governor Ansiaux[5] asked these questions:

(1) Would new accumulation have 100 percent reserve requirement?
(2) Would banks or government receive the negative interest payments if the former banks would not refuse deposits?

---

[3] Raymond Barre, Vice President of the Commission of the European Community.
[4] Louis Rasminsky, Governor of the Bank of Canada.
[5] Hubert J. N. Ansiaux, Governor of the National Bank of Belgium.

(3) Does Carli assume all central banks would deposit with BIS or just those receiving funds? If decision on this point was accepted there should be no quantitative limit.

Emminger said it was very difficult to identify the direction of the inflow and the reserve losses due to speculation were also hard to identify. He proposed that the rechanneling suggestion be discussed in the central banks and in the BIS before putting anything in a communiqué. Governor Zijlstra agreed with Emminger and undertook to get the central bankers together to work at it today. Secretary Fowler endorsed Zijlstra's suggestion, remarking that the technicians needed the advice of the governors.

Baron Snoy (Belgium) said that Minister Schiller and Secretary Fowler had chosen the right road to reach agreement on a package deal. He had one comment. There was an overriding need for credibility, and all the elements in the package seemed to be short term in nature. We should say firmly that when a country like the Federal Republic of Germany is in structural difficulty it should follow expansionary policies and vice versa. Belgium was now in deficit and it was not proper for Belgium to contribute.

On the whole the ideas in the package deal seemed well chosen. The level of effort needs to be examined. He had been shocked by Minister Ortoli's statement.

Governor Stopper (Switzerland) said that since November 8 Switzerland had received no inflow of funds until yesterday. The amount yesterday was $50 million. The commercial banks had received funds but had merely transmitted them onward to Germany, with some to the U.S. Switzerland was studying the possibility of a rule for handling foreign deposits but paying no interest on them. This was a standby possibility only. Switzerland was ready to participate in a study of credit arrangements but had some technical questions.

217.   Telegram From the Embassy in Germany to the White House[1]

Bonn, undated.

Minister Witteveen (Netherlands) commented that Baron Snoy says we have made progress in the short run, but need more. He himself had doubts about the short-run solution. If the disequilibrium is structural, the German solution won't work well. Despite Strauss' comments it is obvious that there is a structural problem. If Germany has had more price stability than other countries, it should revalue. That is the policy to follow if Germany wants to preserve stability. This helps to do so and increases the welfare of Germans. It is not punishment but recompense. The tax measures may be technically nearly equivalent to revaluation but they are temporary. Schiller's proposed general realignment underlines the temporary character of the tax measures. The Netherlands was in fundamental disequilibrium in 1961, but is not now. With a minor German move and a large French move, there is no reason for the Netherlands to move at all.

Minister Schiller agreed the measures are temporary. Most international economists are against large and hurried parity changes. A revaluation or tax of 7-1/2 percent would mean a certain reduction of DM 9-1/2 billion out of a trade surplus of DM 16 billion. Public and private capital exports amount to DM 8.6 billion. If trade is cut too much, Germany can't export capital. For internal and external reasons Germany can't do more.

Concerning credit arrangements of $2 billion, Schiller said Germany would participate. If others do so, why do we need the French change of 15 percent?

Secretary Fowler, referring to Minister Strauss' statement, noted that the German trade surplus was comparable to a surplus of $25 billion in the United States. Everyone would consider this as too large, even allowing for the U.S. large external responsibilities. It wasn't unreasonable to expect Germany to do more than it has suggested.

Chancellor Jenkins urged that we look at the progress of the meeting in perspective. After 3-1/2 hours we are a long way from even a short-term solution. If we do not find this solution, many of our basic assumptions will be swept away. The French 15 percent may prove disruptive to the system. Secretary Fowler's credit proposals are constructive and can buttress, but cannot provide, a credible arrangement by themselves.

---

[1] Source: Johnson Library, National Security File, Subject File, Monetary Crisis, November 1968, Cables and Memos, Vol. 1 [2 of 2], Box 22. Confidential; Limdis. The source text, which bears no telecon number or information on the place, date, or time of transmission, appears to be a continuation of Bonn Telecon 24 (Document 216), although the classification is different.

Governor Ansiaux raised pertinent questions on the German banking proposals. He proposed a short adjournment to try to come closer together on a credible package. Germany must do more and France must do less, and the Central Banks must meet on the credit package.

Minister Schiller then proposed three separate meetings

(1) The Governors to meet on the credit package,
(2) The Deputies to meet on the general situation,
(3) The Common Market Ministers to meet on the French parity.

Minister Ortoli said credit arrangements are not a toy and should not be toyed with but they will buttress a credible arrangement. Secondly, the credit package seems weak. If we do not arrive at some understanding, we shall have to reconsider the $1.2 billion plus IMF, which adds up to $2 billion.

---

218.   Telegram From the Embassy in Germany to the White House[1]

Bonn, November 21, 1968.

Continuation of restricted meeting of Ministers of Group of 10. Summary of credit package.[2]

Zijlstra was called on to report on the credit arrangements. He stated that the new credit line is conditional and depends on a satisfactory solution to the main problems under discussion.

Schiller intervened to say that in substance the Governors worked out a standby credit of $2 billion in addition to the possibility of borrowing from the IMF. (Secretary Fowler had proposed $2 billion, including $750 million from the IMF.)

---

[1] Source: Johnson Library, National Security File, Subject File, Monetary Crisis, November 1968, Cables and Memos, Vol. 1 [1 of 2], Box 22. Secret. The source text, identified as "Bonn Telecon 25," bears no additional information on the place, date, or time of transmission, but the telegram was received at the White House on November 21, 4:55 p.m., as identified in the Washington–Bonn Telecon Chronology of Events for November 21. (Ibid.)
[2] For the record of the first parts of this restricted meeting, see Documents 216 and 217.

Zijlstra gave the following breakdown:

	$ (million)
Germany	625
United States	525
Scandinavia	100
Belgium	100
The Netherlands	100
Switzerland	100
Canada	100
Japan	50
Italy	200
BIS	100
United Kingdom	100
Total	2100

Zijlstra qualified the list, pointing out that everyone is not absolutely certain and it requires some clearance. But it is fairly sure there may be some reallocation among Germany, the United States and the BIS, as the United Kingdom wants to participate for $100 million, but the total would not be changed. In response to a question from Schiller as to the criteria for allocating the amounts, Zijlstra said this was a matter of judgment, taking into account recent developments as well as basic factors.

Rasminsky (Canada) pointed out that these commitments are dependent upon a satisfactory resolution of other questions. Unless the meeting is successful on these questions, he was doubtful that the communiqué should mention the credit line. The credit package was not firm until we have assured a successful outcome for the meeting as a whole. In response to Minister Schiller's inquiry, it was noted that these credit lines are in addition to those previously created but not used to date.

Minister Ortoli said this package makes it possible to make a more credible arrangement.

Franc Adjustment

Schiller said he had discussed the 15 percent devaluation figure with some members of his government, and they thought 15 percent was too much. Could that figure not be reduced?

Snoy (Belgium) said we risked too great a disparity in the parities of the Common Market.

Schiller thought this was a very important question that Ortoli must think about.

Witteveen agreed with Snoy and Schiller. He thought that 8 percent, or at the maximum 10 percent, would be compatible with a credit package of the size contemplated. The Swedish Minister joined in this view.

Schiller called on Mr. Schweitzer.

Schweitzer said that France would have to make a proposal which the IMF Board would consider. Personally, his feeling was that 15 percent was too much. The maximum should be 10 percent. But this is a decision for the Executive Board. Preliminary studies indicate that 10 percent is about right.

Schiller argued that the large credit package should be taken into account.

Schweitzer questioned whether there was a direct relationship between the credit package and the adjustment figure. The Fund looks at costs and prices and fundamental imbalance. They hope that credits will not be used except for psychological purposes. They think in more fundamental terms. The Fund would have the same view whether the credit package was $1 billion or $3 billion.

Emminger argued there is an important relationship between the credit package and the adjustment percentage. He understood that fundamental factors would not justify anything like 15 percent. That figure would have an element of safeguard against speculative pressures. But the credit facilities should deal with such pressures. Thus we should deal only with fundamental factors. Also the German trade measures should help and should be taken into account.

Fowler called attention also to the German banking measures.

Emminger said the German Central Bank Council would introduce a 100 percent reserve requirement on new foreign deposits as of November 15. That is, such deposits would have to be redeposited with the Bundesbank and would earn no interest. They were also preparing a measure to restrict certain short-term transactions of German residents or subject them to license.

Rasminsky asked whether the 2-1/2 percent penalty charge is impractical; and Emminger said the reserve requirement is a substitute for this proposal.

Schiller, however, said the negative interest rate was still under study in the government and might be preferable to licensing transactions. In response to further questions, Emminger said the 100 percent reserve requirement applies to the gross increase in foreign liabilities since November 15—not to the net increase. According to Emminger, this applies to any net increase over November 15 in the gross foreign liabilities of German banks.

Rasminsky suggested that it should apply to renewal of term deposits as well.

Returning to the 15 percent adjustment, Ferras (BIS)[3] argued that the important relationship was between German action and French action—not between the credit factors and the size of the adjustment.

---

[3] Gabriel G. Ferras, General Manager of the Bank for International Settlements.

Minister Schiller, however, persisted that it would be a major mistake to undertake a devaluation because of short-term capital flows when these could be covered by credit facilities. Such facilities should be allowed for in fixing the parity change.

Jenkins thought it was optimistic to expect that speculative forces would be swept away by a credit package. We have to stop the speculative forces and thus we need to do other things than the credit package. But Schiller insisted that the credits play a part.

Benson (Canada) stressed the need for a credible package in three parts:

1. The German part is too small and too temporary.
2. The French action is positive and credible, but 15 percent is too high. It should be less and is linked to the German action.
3. Credit is for the future and will be needed only if the German action is not credible.

Witteveen (Netherlands) said we need to see all parts of the package together. Probably the weakest part on the German side is the explicit temporary character of the action. He was glad to hear in the EC meeting that it could be prolonged. Thus, he appealed for a longer period, perhaps indeterminate in length.

Schiller argued that we don't know what conditions will exist in Europe a year from now.

Witteveen responded that he does not expect the German measures to be permanent, but they should not be made explicitly for 15 months. Keep them indefinite.

Schiller said the original plan was for 18 months, and this had been shortened to 15 months because of Parliamentary objections.

Ortoli said a parity is one thing and credits to defend it are something else. You cannot defend a parity which is wrong with short-term credits.

The meeting was suspended at 7PM at Ortoli's request. It reconvened at 9PM.

219.   Telegram From the Embassy in Germany to the White House[1]

Bonn, November 22, 1968.

For Walt Rostow. From: Fried.

Basic agreement reached 4:00 A.M. this morning on following package:

(1) 4 percent German border tax adjustment. In light of German program group publicly endorsed no change in DM parity.

(2) Agreement about any franc devaluation will not exceed 11 percent. Figure not announced yet and may not be made public until weekend.

(3) Standby Central Bank credit facility for franc of $2 billion. German share 600 million, U.S. share 500 million.

(4) No other parity changes.

Germans to the end refused to budge. Only problem then was to nail down French move and show clearly that it was made and negotiated in multilateral setting. Ortoli held out for 15 percent until last minute.

We believe important precedent established on border tax adjustment principle and on thorough airing of parity changes within group.

Our judgment is that markets will be calmed down by fact that Group of Ten reached agreement on the whole set of issues. Arrangements made for concerted Central Bank intervention on spot and forward exchange markets and on Euro-dollar market on a massive scale.

Also clear that German performance in publicly announcing position before meeting and refusing to budge gave Kiesinger government an impressive domestic victory. If package fails to calm down situation however, the domestic pluses will vanish and Germans will be on the spot internationally.

Communiqué draft completed but not yet approved. Text will follow on approval.[2]

---

[1] Source: Johnson Library, National Security File, Subject File, Monetary Crisis, November 1968, Cables and Memos, Vol. 1 [1 of 2], Box 22. Secret. The source text, identified as "Bonn Telecon 27," bears no additional information on the place, date, or time of transmission, but the telegram was received at the White House on November 22, 9:37 a.m., as identified in the Washington–Bonn Telecon Chronology of Events for November 22. (Ibid.) Attached to the source text is a memorandum from Rostow to President Johnson, November 22, 9:45 a.m., which notes that Rostow would be forwarding shortly "the stand-by credit package." This package would "not require formal Presidential approval, but I am sure you will wish to see exactly what is being negotiated."

[2] Transmitted in Bonn Telecon 29 to the White House, November 22. (Ibid.) Also printed in Department of State *Bulletin*, December 16, 1968, pp. 627–628.

220.   Paper by the President's Special Assistant (Rostow)[1]

Washington, November 22, 1968.

CREDIT PACKAGE

1. The G–10 meeting is arranging a $2 billion package for France:

—U.S. share is $500 million,
—German share is $600 million.

This is short-term money, about six months, intended to provide psychological support and to finance short-term speculative capital flows. Generally, under these circumstances and if the over-all program is effective, this type of credit is used little, if at all. The Federal Reserve will put up $300 million of the $500 million, and the Treasury, through the Exchange Stabilization Fund, will put up $200 million.

2. In addition, France will arrange a stand-by credit at the International Monetary Fund of $985 million, which is the full limit of funds available to it through that institution.

Through the mechanics of the IMF, and assuming they draw the full amount of $985 million with a good portion in U.S. dollars (as opposed to other currencies), this would mean that the full gold tranche position of the U.S. at the IMF will be re-established—which means that the United States will have virtually automatic credit of one billion two hundred ninety million dollars available to us from the Fund—a position we have not been in for about five years.

Walt

---

[1] Source: Johnson Library, National Security File, Subject File, Monetary Crisis, November 1968, Cables and Memos, Vol. 1 [1 of 2], Box 22. Secret. An attached memorandum from Rostow to President Johnson, November 22, 10:10 a.m., notes that the paper printed here outlines the credit package referred to in paragraph 3 of Fried's message (Document 219). The source text is apparently the retyped verbatim text of a telegraphic message sent by Fried to Rostow in a Bonn telecon, but this message has not been found.

221.   Memorandum for the Record[1]

Washington, November 23, 1968, 1 p.m.

Meeting with the President 1:00 p.m., November 23, 1968: Secretary Fowler's briefing on the International Monetary Crisis (Secretaries Fowler, Rusk, and Clifford, Under Secretary Deming, Federal Reserve Chairman Martin, Robert Murphy, Walt Rostow, Ed Fried, George Christian)

The President asked Secretary Fowler to report on his mission. He said that he would like then to explore the monetary and any other implications arising from the crisis. He welcomed Murphy to the meeting saying that he was happy he had agreed to help us and his country in the transition process.

Secretary Fowler said he would like to begin by outlining the position he had taken at the start of his mission two weeks earlier and how it had ended up. This is what he had told Chancellor Jenkins in London on November 10 when they discussed contingency plans in the event of a franc crisis:

—It was essential that any change in parities take place in a multilateral setting. The United States was not prepared to take any further disadvantages as a result of parity changes by others.

—The best thing now would be a period of calm. This would provide time: for the new U.S. Administration to get into place and to see how the U.S. program was working out; to see how the UK program worked out; and to see how the French program worked out.

—As we see it, the areas of possible change were the following:

(a) A revaluation of the D mark. This would have disadvantages as a stimulus to flight capital movements, such as occurred in 1961. But over the longer term it would clearly help the system with immediate advantages to the pound, the franc and the dollar. It could take place alone or accompanied by the revaluation of other strong currencies—notably the lira and the guilder.
(b) The devaluation of the franc.
(c) A combination of a DM revaluation and a franc devaluation.

---

[1] Source: Johnson Library, National Security File, Subject File, Monetary Crisis, November 1968, Cables and Memos, Vol. 1 [1 of 2], Box 22. Secret. Drafted by Fried on November 26. A transcript of a tape recording of this meeting, which provides additional detail and context, indicates that the meeting was held in the Cabinet Room of the White House. Unlike the memorandum printed here, the time of the meeting given on this transcript is 1:25 to 1:53 p.m. It begins at the outset of the meeting and concludes when the participants go to lunch. (Johnson Library, Transcripts of Meetings in the Cabinet Room) Notes of the same meeting, which were probably derived from the same tape recording and which cover only approximately the first half of the discussion, are labeled "President Johnson's Notes . . .," but more likely they were notes prepared for him. (Ibid.)

—A revaluation of the D mark would have clear net advantages and could take the pressure off the franc and the pound. If the size of the move was credible and it was decisively made, it should be viewed as a substitute for any franc devaluation. Nevertheless, we would not push for it now because another period of indecision and leaks in Germany would be destabilizing to the system.

—A unilateral French move had to be avoided. It is not justified on economic grounds and it could quickly lead to an impossible position for sterling and thus threaten to blow up the entire system. We are prepared to help France to work through her problems, but we are not prepared to accept a unilateral French devaluation.

—If the French say they are going to unilaterally devalue, we must insist that the Germans call a G–10 meeting immediately.

—If the Germans and the French work out a deal between themselves we would also insist that it be discussed multilaterally. Changes in rates are our affair as well as those of the specific countries involved.

Secretary Fowler went on to say that our position on a change in parities at the present time changed during the course of the NATO meetings.[2] Statements by German officials about the possibility of a mark revaluation created growing uncertainty in the markets and were a cause of very substantial French and British losses. By the weekend these losses were indicating the onset of a panic.

At the weekend the Central Bankers met in Basle. There was open discussion of a change in rates. The French representative said that the French would devalue by at least 15 percent. The Germans were talking about a mark revaluation. But in fact nothing happened after the weekend meeting and uncertainty grew.

Against this background, Secretary Fowler said that he greatly welcomed the President's instruction when he reached Bonn on the night of November 18 to meet with Chancellor Kiesinger and propose a multilateral discussion of the problem.[3] He felt that by that time such a meeting was essential to avoid the serious risk of a breakdown in the entire system.

Secretary Fowler said that he would not go over the developments during the meeting or the results of the meeting since these had been summarized fully in his reporting, and he knew the President had been fully briefed. He did want to point out one intervention he had made during the course of the meeting, when German Minister Schiller, as Chairman, complained that everyone said that they wanted multilateral

---

[2] The North Atlantic Council, attended by Foreign, Defense, and Finance Ministers, met in Brussels November 15–16.

[3] See Document 209.

decisions but in fact the only thing they seemed to want was a unilateral decision by Germany to revalue:

In reply Fowler had made the following points:[4]

—We had not said that the German proposal was bad but merely that it was inadequate.

—Nor did we believe that only the Germans should act. Others also should take measures that would help in this situation.

—We welcomed the German move both for its substance and for the innovation it marked in balance of payments adjustment practices. We would welcome it more if it were larger.

—We saw no reason for other parity changes but we would not resist one if it were moderate and if others agreed it were necessary.

—We welcomed border tax adjustments by other surplus countries.

—We were prepared to participate in any multilateral solution by participating fully in any credit package for countries under pressure.

Secretary Fowler listed our objectives as follows:

1. The meeting was called with our full support because we believed the decisions had to be multilateral.

2. We made clear that the U.S. was not prepared to suffer further disadvantages to its position as a result of devaluations of other countries. It is true that a country changing its parity had to get IMF approval, but this was a pro forma procedure. We made clear at this meeting that we would oppose a devaluation of a major currency if it was not considered in advance to be appropriate by the assembled group of major financial countries and if careful consideration was not given to offsetting actions by other countries.

3. We consistently made the point that the U.S. under the present rules cannot change its own parity. Therefore, we were not to be put in a constantly worsening position as a result of parity changes by others. We had to be parties to considerations of such changes. Fowler was confident that the other participants at the meeting were fully conscious of what we were trying to do. He read a note Minister Benson of Canada had written to him after the meeting in which Benson said that a precedent had now been clearly set and that he was sure that there never again would be a change in parity of a major currency without a meeting of this sort.

The President asked Secretary Fowler what he thought the French would do. Fowler said there were two general possibilities. First, a simple rate adjustment of something less than 11.11 percent. Second, no devaluation at all but presumably some trade measures. He said that the

---

[4] Fowler covered these issues in his response to Schiller at the first November 20 meeting; see Document 214.

French had given an absolute guarantee that they would not go above 11.11 percent but beyond that had left their options open.

As far as the effect of these changes on our own trade, Fowler said our estimates suggested that the disadvantages we might suffer from the UK import measures and possible French moves would probably be off-set by the trade advantages we would receive from the German action on border tax adjustments.

On the political side, he believed that considerable bitterness had developed during the meeting:

—The conflicting German announcements before the meeting had unsettled the markets and put pressure on the French franc.

—The French had acted badly in the tactics they used to put pressure on the Germans.

—The Wilson letter to Kiesinger had infuriated the Germans. Jenkins' strong words at the meeting created bitterness between the Germans and the British.

—On the whole he did not think that U.S.-German relations had been appreciably affected.

On the military side Fowler said that Strauss had strongly defended the German position and the need for large German trade surplus; among other reasons, because of the need to provide offsets for the $900 million of U.S. military expenditures in Germany.[5] Fowler somewhat banteringly had reminded Strauss of this point after the meeting and said that we would keep it in mind in our future negotiations.

At this point in the meeting with the President the news came that the French had decided they would not change the parity of the franc. After some brief comments, the President suggested that the Group continue the discussion at lunch.

The President asked again about the political implications of what has happened. It was the general view that the de Gaulle decision was in part politically motivated and a response to the hard-headed German tactics at Bonn.

The President then asked the economic implications of the French move. Rostow pointed out that it probably presaged trade measures as a substitute for a change in the rate and that we had given a great deal of thought to the possibility of using such measures as a way of helping countries get out of temporary balance of payments difficulties.

Fowler pointed out again that we had consistently taken the position that no change in the French rate was necessary on economic grounds and that if market expectations could be overcome this would

---

[5] See Document 216.

be the best solution both from the French and from our own point of view.

The President asked whether there was anything we should do at the present time. The general view was that we now had to wait on the specifics of the French measures and then take whatever actions were necessary in light of these measures.

The President asked Bill Martin whether he thought the French should have devalued. Martin said he thought they should have as long as it had gone this far. Fried said there was no reason why trade measures could not substitute for a rate move as long as the other countries showed they continued to back the French position. Deming and others pointed out that neither the credit package nor the German trade measures are dependent on the French devaluation. It was clear that the French had the option not to move at all. The only thing they guaranteed was that if they moved they would not move beyond 11 percent.

[Here follows discussion of the budget and the surtax.]

---

222. **Record of Meeting of the National Security Council**[1]

Washington, November 25, 1968.

NATIONAL SECURITY COUNCIL MEETING IN CABINET ROOM, MONDAY, NOVEMBER 25, 1968 WITH THE PRESIDENT, SEC-RETARY RUSK, J. R. WIGGINS, AMBASSADOR TO THE U.N. JOSEPH SISCO, ASSISTANT SECRETARY OF STATE, SEC-RETARY CLIFFORD, PAUL NITZE, SECRETARY FOWLER, DIRECTOR HELMS, GENERAL WHEELER, GEORGE CHRIS-TIAN, WALT ROSTOW, BROMLEY SMITH AND ED FRIED—12:06 P.M.

[Here follows a brief introductory discussion of two U.S. reconnais-sance planes that were shot down over Vietnam.]

---

[1] Source: Johnson Library, Transcripts of Meetings in the Cabinet Room. No classifi-cation marking. The source text, which is a transcript of a tape recording, bears no tran-scribing or drafting information. The file folder in which the source text was enclosed iden-tified the conclusion of the transcript as 1:18 p.m. Notes of the same meeting, which were probably derived from the same tape recording, cover Fowler's report on the monetary sit-uation in only a paragraph but provide extensive coverage of the discussion on Vietnam and the Middle East. Although labeled "President Johnson's Notes . . .," more likely they were notes prepared for him. (Ibid.) Draft minutes covering only the discussion of interna-tional financial matters at this NSC meeting, dated November 25, are ibid., National Secu-rity File, Fried Files, Chron, October 1–November 30, 1968, Box 3.

Fowler: The first place we always look to for answers on these things are the Departments. And I think, therefore, I will give you a quick report on what the market situation was as of 11 o'clock this morning which covers most of the trading day in Europe.

The exchange rate, movements and the flow of funds are very faithful because the money is going out of Germany and into France. And the French franc rate is up and the British pound rate is up and apparently this is the result of the real money flow rather than in marketing prevention.

The other significant thing from our point of view is that the dollar is strong and the gold market has remained very calm. Low rise, and high minor rise, in the morning from 30¢ the first fixing and a decline back to $40.10 in the afternoon. So the first market reactions are good.

As to the impact of the French measures, the details will not be announced until tomorrow, so we get impressions on these from our fellows in Paris the way they feel about these things.

The French exchange patrol measures that were issued last June, and then rescinded later, were fairly mild in form and not particularly effective, but the new regulations have all the markings of being very tough and very effective, as far as releasing money from France by Frenchmen—in other words, out of France.

Just one example. On tourism. Frenchmen can carry abroad $40.00 worth of French francs, and—in French bank notes—and $100.00 of foreign currency. They must carry evidence that they bought the currency from an authorized bank and it is a once in a year allowance.

People moving into France will have to—when you go in you will have to, if you are an ordinary tourist, register the amount of currency you are taking in, so that the effective currency rate is under control.

Characteristically, French exchange control regulations have been very effective in the past when they have been really tough enough, though I don't think we should underestimate the possibility that for a period of time they may be able to considerably arrest the flow.

The export tax percentage has not been made at all clear. DeGaulle simply said he would relieve corporations of "certain taxes that excessively weigh on their costs."[2] We have no details, but it seems to involve an increased tax rebate of some sort, like our investment credit on import–export taxes.

---

[2] After the brief announcement by the French Government on November 23 that it would not devalue the franc, on the following evening in a speech broadcast to the French nation, President de Gaulle outlined measures to restore stability to the French currency. An English translation of the speech is ibid., Subject File, Monetary Crisis, November 1968, Cables and Memos, Vol. 1 [1 of 2], Box 22.

On imports, nothing special expected. This could be a very effective way of quickly arresting the balance of payments problem, but there's no sign yet of a rigid issuance of import licenses. France has traditionally resisted import surcharges, that is, adding taxes to imports as being inflationary. And reducing the pressure of foreign competition.

We don't know what they are going to do in the wage-price field, although the General's message to the Nation clearly indicated a Hold the Line policy on wages and prices. Whether that would be by any further measures or not, or whether he's going to wait and see what's happening, we don't know.

I think insofar as the United States is concerned—impact on trade—it would be fair to say that what's happened in Germany, which is advantageous to us, will be adequate to prove to be a counterweight for anything that happens in Great Britain or anything that we see currently likely to happen in France. I would say it's a standoff and the benefits we receive from Germany would probably just about be offset by the French and the United Kingdom moves.

The overall impact of this that we should note is, of course, that now four of the major economies in the world—United States, United Kingdom, France, and to some extent Germany—are cutting back their growth and this will tend over a time to have some heavy impact on world trade.

Mr. President, I think the further implications for the Security Council would be largely in the political field. There has undoubtedly been a great impact as a result of this situation on Franco-German relationships and on German-United Kingdom relationships.

I think as far as the offset situation, instead of the reduction of their trade surplus being a minus, in view of the statements that Strauss and Schiller made during the course of the meeting, some of which have gotten into the press, it gives us a very firm position—that don't come around pleading now that because you did this you can diminish your offset and prolong it. One of the prime reasons that they put forward during the course of the meeting for not revaluing at 7-1/2 percent or greatly increasing these grave tax measures was that they needed to have adequate trade surplus in order to make good on a 900 billion dollar offset—the fact that this is something our successors should be made aware of.

President: What is the feeling between the Germans and the French?

Fowler: Considerable. [*8 lines of source text not declassified*]

There were—undoubtedly this pressure that was felt in the meeting of the Central Bank Governors at Bonn—and the Germans feel that the French put them in a very tough position.

In turn, the French, I think quite properly, feel that the Germans have not done as much as they could or should as partners in this operation. What they would have liked to have done is work out a straight Franco-

German deal—a package deal, and neither party—they were not able to work that out.

President: What conceivably could we be called upon to do extra? Put up more as far as France?

Fowler: No. The installment on the credit package. A French request for withdrawal (interrupted).

President: Four or five hundred million more?

Fowler: I don't think so.

President: Is there anything else that you can foresee that we ought to be planning?

Fowler: We, last night—yesterday, Mr. President, made an appraisal of the French measures, and what we could do in addition to help on this thing.

Bill Martin yesterday afternoon called the head of the German Central Bank, Blessing and _____ [3] the Head of the Mellon Central Bank, who's also Chairman of the Ball Group, and Stopper, the Head of the Swiss Bank, and asked them to do what they could do through their organizations to give objective press guidance on the French action of the sort that we are trying to give here. And also to speed up a settling program— that the Central Bank Governments were mandated to do with the BIS on a recycling of check flow—this wouldn't have any figures or any limit but the idea you see would be to make the gain completely useless. If one—let's say the Bank of France intervening in the market to protect the franc spent one hundred million and it went into Germany and that could be identified as speculative though the Germans would automatically put that back in the form of some credit arrangement to the Bank of France, so that there would be a kind of a circular flow of funds rather than a drain, an ever increasing drain, which would make the situation impossible.

In addition to those measures, Martin asked Blessing if there were any other measures that he thought the Germans could take to moderate capital outflow. Blessing and Martin have a very good relationship, and I am sure Blessing levelled with him when he said he couldn't think of another thing they could do.

He called the British Treasury and expressed the desirability of their making helpful noises. He talked to Douglas Allott. The number two man agreed and said they were trying to and would follow our lead on that. They seemed to have mixed emotions. They are very glad there was no franc devaluation, which was what they were deathly afraid of, certainly a major one.

---

[3] Presumably the tape recording was unclear at this point.

They are concerned over market reactions—probably feel better today after what has happened.

He talked also to Paul Schweitzer, the Director of the International Monetary Fund, who had developed that there was some case for devaluation, but felt that this move was a good move, a gracious move. He did not think the French would apply for a standby credit on the Fund at this time, but was less certain on this than he had been on Saturday afternoon. I think the IMF will make constructive comments, so the most, Mr. President, that we can do at this time, I think, is to try to keep this in an optimistic, favorable framework, this whole suggestion.

President: Is it fair to say that after reading DeGaulle's speech and after seeing the performance of the market and after talking to the bankers that Martin talked to and the contacts that you all have had, that you think that this is likely to be successful?

Fowler: I think I would say that.

President: And is it fair to assume that you do not anticipate any more serious calls for performance on our part?

Fowler: I hesitate to make a long-term projection on that. I think this thing could conceivably hold and stabilize the situation for months in advance. On the other hand—

President: Well, but I got the impression prior to reading the report[4] that before he even took this action, that he didn't feel that it was going to adversely affect us one way or the other.

Fowler: No, I don't think that—

President: And that there wasn't anything much that we needed to do.

Fowler: I don't think we're in it—

President: What I'm asking now is, should we pull in our belts, pull up our socks, take any additional steps, make any additional preparation? Look at any measures that we might have to take if we got into an emergency?

Fowler: No. I think that a—as I see it, the situation now, we have done all that we can do or that the minds of all the Ministers of Finance and the Central Bank Governors can conjure up. I think about all I would say on that is I think that over the next 60 or 90 days we ought to keep our situation extremely sound here at home, because the one sustaining element in the whole picture, psychologically, has been the strength of the dollar. Had we been rocking and rolling God knows what would have happened.

[Here follows discussion of Vietnam, several issues before the United Nations, the Middle East, and disarmament questions.]

---

[4] Not further identified.

223.   Message From the British Chancellor of the Exchequer (Jenkins) to Secretary of the Treasury Fowler[1]

London, undated.

I have been considering our position as regards reserves and short-term debt. As you know, a difficult position has been aggravated by the events of last month, and we shall have extremely heavy commitments to meet in the next year and more. Meanwhile the balance of payments, despite the severity of our policies, has not been improving as rapidly as we hoped. The new measures I introduced on 22 November[2] will, of course, make a considerable contribution, but the deficit for 1968 as a whole will be large. We expect a substantial surplus in the third quarter to be followed by a deficit in the fourth quarter.

In all the circumstances, I think it would be right for us this year once more to exercise our right, under the Agreement of 1957,[3] to defer payments of interest and repayments of capital under the post-war loans. As you know, the Agreement gave us the right, when we feel it necessary, in view of the present and prospective conditions of international exchange and the level of our gold and foreign exchange reserves, to defer these payments on seven occasions. So far this has been done three times, in 1957, 1964 and 1965. I feel, and I think you will agree, that the circumstances in which it was envisaged that we should exercise this right certainly exist at present.

The repayments, as you know, fall due at the end of December. I have not overlooked the fact that a deferment this year may add, in some degree, to your own difficulties by enlarging your balance of payments deficit. But I hope this will not cause you undue embarrassment, particularly since it should be possible to explain this part of the deficit as a special factor. The total sum involved, principal and interest together, is, I understand, $138.3 million.

I am sending a similar message to Mr. Benson in Ottawa saying that we would like similarly to defer the amounts due under the parallel Canadian line of credit.[4]

---

[1] Source: Johnson Library, Fowler Papers, International Countries: United Kingdom, 1968, Box 40. No classification marking. Attached to the source text is a December 9 letter from E. W. Maude, Economic Minister at the British Embassy in Washington, to Fowler, indicating that Jenkins had asked him to deliver the message to Fowler.

[2] Jenkins announced these measures in the House of Commons on November 22.

[3] Signed on March 6, 1957; 8 UST 2443.

[4] On December 20, 1968, Jenkins announced the deferment of British payments of principal and interest on postwar U.S. and Canadian loans.

224.   Editorial Note

In the final months of 1968, the Cabinet Committee on Balance of Payments began to develop a balance-of-payments program for 1969. Regarding these preparations, see Document 204.

When these preparations were completed, Secretary of the Treasury Fowler sent an explanatory memorandum to President Johnson, December 17, summarizing the recommended balance-of-payments program for 1969, which the Cabinet Committee on Balance of Payments had approved.

Attached to this memorandum was a 16-page letter from Fowler to President Johnson, December 17, which developed eight "underlying principles which your Cabinet Committee on Balance of Payments believes should govern the program in 1969." His letter also articulated the rationale behind these principles. To his letter, Fowler attached a short letter of approval of these recommendations from the President to Fowler, dated December 18, for the President's signature.

Also attached to Fowler's memorandum along with the two letters is a December 17 memorandum from Rostow to the President, which summarizes the two letters. A block for approval of the President's December 18 letter to Fowler at the end of Rostow's memorandum is checked. (Johnson Library, National Security File, Subject File, Balance of Payments, Vol. V [1 of 2], Box 3)

The exchange of the two letters was subsequently published in *Annual Report of the Secretary of the Treasury on the State of the Finances for the Fiscal Year Ended June 30, 1969* (Washington: Government Printing Office, 1970), pages 307–315.

Trade and Commercial Policy

225. Letter From Secretary of Commerce Hodges to Secretary of State Rusk[1]

Washington, January 15, 1964.

Dear Dean:

As you know, President Johnson has signed the attached Executive Order creating an interdepartmental, cabinet-level committee on export expansion, to be chaired by the Secretary of Commerce.[2]

On December 20, 1963, the President appointed Daniel L. Goldy (of Oregon) National Export Expansion Coordinator. Under the terms of the Executive Order, I have appointed Mr. Goldy to be Executive Director of the Committee.

This Interdepartmental Committee has been created to facilitate the coordination of the policies and programs of the Federal Government designed to expand the U.S. share of world markets. The problem of increasing U.S. exports has come to a sharp focus due to our persistently unfavorable balance of payments. In addition, every effort should be made to increase U.S. sales abroad so as to stimulate our domestic economy and to create additional jobs here at home. While the Department of Commerce has a primary responsibility for promoting the foreign commerce of the United States, other departments and agencies of government also have vital roles to play in this endeavor.

The Interdepartmental Committee and the National Export Expansion Coordinator will strive for maximum coordination of the policies and programs of the Federal Government in pursuit of our foreign trade objectives.

The White House Conference on Export Expansion, which was held on September 17 and 18, 1963 and attended by close to 300 leading businessmen resulted in a series of recommendations on export promotion.[3]

---

[1] Source: Department of State, Central Files, FT (EX) US. No classification marking. Similar letters were sent to the Departments of the Treasury, Defense, and Agriculture, Agency for International Development, Export-Import Bank, and Small Business Administration on January 15, and the following day to the Department of the Interior, whose head, Secretary Udall, had asked on January 10 to serve as a full member of the interdepartmental committee. (Washington National Records Center, RG 40, Secretary of Commerce Files: FRC 69 A 6828, Export Expansion Interagency Committee)

[2] A copy of Executive Order 11132, "Establishing the Interagency Committee on Export Expansion," December 12, 1963, is attached but not printed.

[3] The results of this conference were published in *Progress Report on Recommendations of the White House Conference on Export Expansion,* January 1964. (Washington National Records Center, RG 40, Records from the Office of Franklin D. Roosevelt, Jr., Under Secretary of Commerce, 1963–June 1965: FRC 68 A 5947, Export Expansion) For highlights of the report, see *Foreign Relations,* 1961–1963, vol. IX, pp. 616–618.

Many of these recommendations can be implemented by individual Departments. Others require joint action or coordination of Departmental policies. One of the functions of the Interdepartmental Committee, and a major responsibility of the National Export Expansion Coordinator, is to encourage and assist the relevant Departments and agencies to put into effect promptly as many of those recommendations as possible.

I will be calling a meeting soon and, meanwhile, I would appreciate it if you would have a member of your staff prepare a review of what your agency does or contemplates doing along export expansion lines so that the Coordinator and members of our Cabinet Committee may be kept informed.[4]

In the future, Mr. Goldy will make every effort to cooperate fully with you or whomever you designate concerning these important programs.

Sincerely yours,

Luther

---

[4] In a March 24 letter to Hodges, attached to the source text, Secretary Rusk reported that Robert Eakens, Department of State Coordinator for Commercial Activities, had been appointed the Department's representative to the interdepartmental committee. He also enclosed a 34-page paper, "A Review of the Export Expansion Program and the Department of State," March 10.

---

226. Memorandum From the Special Representative for Trade Negotiations (Herter) to Secretary of Agriculture Freeman and the Under Secretary of State (Ball)[1]

Washington, February 6, 1964.

I found our talk yesterday useful and will be looking forward to a further meeting next week.[2] It occurred to me, however, that it might be helpful to try to relate these discussions more closely to U.S. Government policy as presently approved. I say this, in part, because I feel that each of

---

[1] Source: Kennedy Library, Herter Papers, Agricultural Policy, 1/30/64–7/1/64, Box 5. Limited Official Use.

[2] No records of the Herter–Freeman–Ball talks of February 5 and the following week were found.

us in presenting our broad and general strategic concerns tended to over-simplify the issues.

Perhaps I was the first to do this in stating my opinion that the negotiations should be pursued with the utmost determination through whatever crises may arise and without fear that such determination might lead to the disruption of the Common Market. However, Under Secretary Ball made clear that the State Department was fully in accord with this position and was only concerned that our negotiating strategy and tactics be as little disruptive as possible. As he noted, the Common Market will not fall apart because of U.S. insistence on a fair and reasonable trade bargain. On the other hand, I would certainly agree that tactically we must use due diligence not to put ourselves into a position where we can be accused of attacking the Community as an institution or its just concerns. I believe this is the kind of trap Pisani was preparing for us and which Secretary Freeman, by refusing to be drawn into a public discussion, ably side-stepped.

Second, it seemed to me that the discussion of agriculture tended to center on market-sharing as a cure-all. I know this is not what Secretary Freeman had in mind, since his own speech in Houston carefully delineates at least three different types of agricultural trade, each needing separate solutions.[3] As the negotiations become more intense, however, it will become increasingly difficult but important to recognize the full range of agricultural interests and avoid over-simplification in seeking solutions.

In this light, I would be particularly concerned if the question of surplus disposal to under-developed countries became a major consideration in the commodity discussions, as the Community seems to suggest. Food aid, as such, is only a part of the complex problem of economic assistance to less developed countries, and should be treated in this context and not within the context of the GATT cereal negotiations. If food aid is allowed to become a central part of the agricultural negotiations, it will tend to de-emphasize the need of the EEC to supply disincentives to marginal production which is perhaps the only certain guarantee that access will, in effect, be maintained.

The agricultural phase of the trade negotiations is going to be difficult and complex. Probably no one formula can or should be adopted to apply to all segments of agriculture, whether it be a linear cut formula or a market-sharing concept. A flexible and pragmatic approach is required.

---

[3] Freeman's speech in Houston was not further identified. He commented on the memorandum printed here in a letter to Herter, February 11. (Kennedy Library, Herter Papers, Agricultural Policy, 1/30/64–7/1/64, Box 5)

It goes without saying that the forthcoming negotiations should try to improve upon the degree of agricultural trade liberalization achieved in past negotiations. We have acquired some valuable concessions in these negotiations. Mansholt's negotiating Plan No. 2 would seem intended to revoke all of these.[4] Likewise, a simple market-sharing formula applied across the board might produce the same effects.

We have considerably refined our initial position regarding the methods of including agriculture from what it was about a year ago at the first meeting of the GATT Working Party. At that time, we recognized there were three major categories of products: variable levy items, products subject to mixed forms of protection, and those for which fixed tariffs constituted the principal form of protection.

We indicated at the first Working Party meeting that our goal in agriculture was for fixed tariff items, application of the linear cut, and for other items, a comparable degree of liberalization.

This position has subsequently been modified along the following lines, the most recent occasion being the preparation for the Erhard visit:

1. Agricultural products for which fixed tariffs constitute the chief barriers to trade should be included to the maximum extent possible in the linear cut formula. This makes sense not only from a practical standpoint but also from the standpoint of our determination to keep agricultural products an integral part of the overall negotiations rather than being broken out entirely for separate treatment. For example, in tariff classifications processed products derived from agricultural primary materials are generally classed as agricultural products. There is no reason why processed agricultural products should not, generally speaking, be included in the linear cut along with other manufactured items. Indeed, there has been a large degree of success in doing this in most negotiations.

2. Where variable levies, deficiency payments or similar devices to protect domestic producers' incomes constitute the principal barriers to trade, our minimum objective is to negotiate access assurances comparable to those existing in a recent representative period.

We should try to attain this objective by negotiating limits on the trade restrictive effects of critical elements such as variable levies or deficiency payments, of national agricultural policies. To do this, we might have to consider the necessity of agreeing to limits on our own support prices, export subsidies, etc.

National agricultural policies and trade objectives might be reconciled by negotiating specific access targets or quotas underpinned by

---

[4] Sicco L. Mansholt, Vice President of the Commission of the European Economic Community's Plan No. 2.

commitments as to the level of producer prices, the amount of deficiency payments, etc. The GATT Ministers decided that with respect to cereals, meats, and dairy products, the negotiations should be carried out within the framework of commodity agreements. This is probably the most feasible means of negotiating limitations on national agricultural policies on a reciprocal basis.

It is important that quantitative access assurances be accompanied by as low prices as possible, since artificially high prices would encourage increases in production and agricultural surpluses that would make it difficult for a country to live up to quantitative access commitments.

The EEC is our main problem in the agricultural phase of the negotiations. It now looks certain that grain prices which are the control valve that basically determines the levels of protection on livestock products will be set at levels which will stimulate production in the Community at the expense of imports.

In summary, I do not see, for the time being, the need to alter our basic objectives set forth above for the agricultural phase of the negotiations. The matter of the strategy and tactics that will further the achievement of these objectives does require a great deal more coordinated attention and thought. I would hope this strategy could be one subject for our meeting next week.

Christian A. Herter[5]

---

[5] Printed from a copy that bears this typed signature.

227. Memorandum From Secretary of Agriculture Freeman to the President's Special Assistant for National Security Affairs (Bundy)[1]

Washington, February 14, 1964.

At a recent meeting you suggested that when conversations had been held between the Ambassador and the Secretary of Agriculture that you would like to be informed of agreements reached.

The following constitutes a recap of discussions held by the undersigned and Ambassador Blumenthal on February 14 which set down a procedure which I understand has been reviewed also with Governor Herter.

1. That an inquiring posture be adopted for the coming Agricultural Committee GATT meeting next week, probing thoroughly the Mansholt negotiating plan and other EEC proposals.

2. That following such examination and review on February 18, rather than reject the proposal out of hand our representatives will report back for review and instruction.

3. When Mansholt appears on March 5 and 6 he will be told firmly, if his plan is as we think it today, that it is unacceptable. Whereupon a counter proposal will be made which hopefully will break the current deadlock.

4. The counter proposal will provide that agriculture be recognized as presenting special problems and therefore not subject to the 50 percent rule which is being applied across the board to industrial commodities. Such a proposal will emphasize that our objective is global market sharing and real liberalization rather than quotas. It'll emphasize that liberalization is what the Kennedy round has been designed to accomplish. In the Ambassador's judgment this will put us in a strong position for the EEC must accept that objective or else be in a very poor light not only with the United States but all GATT countries.

As a part of this counter proposal to treat agriculture differently we will make it crystal clear that this will not preclude the kind of bargaining that might exchange an industrial concession for an agricultural one. In

---

[1] Source: Johnson Library, National Security File, Subject File, Trade—General, vol. I [1 of 2], Box 47. No classification marking. Bundy wrote on the source text: "Are these two guys in agreement?" In response to this query, Bromley Smith wrote Bundy a note, February 20, saying in part that "Freeman and Blumenthal are in agreement—State is also on board—on our current position and our strategy for the *immediate* future, i.e., for the next six weeks." Smith also noted that "Everyone agrees that many problems lie ahead" and mentioned some State concerns about Freeman's memorandum. (Ibid.) Notations on another copy of Freeman's memorandum indicate that Herter and Roth saw it. (Kennedy Library, Herter Papers, Agricultural Policy, 1/30/64–7/1/64, Box 5)

other words, cross bargaining will be a definite possibility even though agriculture will be approached procedurally on an item by item basis rather than with the application of the 50 percent cut across the board rule. We agreed that we must not get agriculture separated from industry in the sense that would preclude cross negotiations.

5. Assuming then that this new proposal liberalizing our position is acceptable we come to what will probably be the first crisis. Between the discussion and hoped for agreement with Mansholt and company early in March and the opening of the GATT negotiations formally in May we will proceed aggressively with preliminary discussions. These discussions will involve meetings of the Agricultural Committee of GATT to review on an ad hoc basis commodity by commodity possible agreements. Certainly the Cereals Committee will be meeting during this period. It will be our specific objective at such meetings to determine whether the Community is actually going to proceed in good faith to bargain and live up to the commitments we expect they will make to move towards liberalization. We will proceed in these discussions on a flexible basis, recognizing that liberalization may not be possible for a given commodity, but attainable in another and that our goal will be to maintain our trade and a fair competitive access to a growing market.

If during this period it is our judgment that the Community is not proceeding in good faith, but rather is conducting a systematic slowdown so that we will end up in the same position as agriculture found itself at the end of the Dillon round, to wit, everything else decided and agriculture still out on the limb, we will then refuse to proceed further in the negotiations. This will be a hard, tough judgment to make. I emphasize that fact at this time for it is one which has been faced in discussions now and which will need to be implemented at the time.

6. Finally, once negotiations have started there will no doubt be a number of other critical places but we ought to be able to determine before the negotiations formally open whether they really will bargain in good faith. If they are evasive in the pre-May Agricultural Committee meetings this will be the time to let them know we mean business.

This recap has been personally dictated from notes that I took during our consultation and embodies my interpretation of the conference this date with Ambassador Blumenthal. A copy has been sent to the Ambassador and to Governor Herter.

228.   Telegram From the Mission to the European Office of the United Nations to the Department of State[1]

Geneva, February 18, 1964, 1840Z.

Tagg 1826. For Governor Herter from Hodges. Agric meeting convened on schedule today. WW opened meeting by drawing attention to Ministerial decisions on agric as terms of ref for the group's work,[2] then invited dels to table proposals on how this shd be carried out. EEC (Rabot) gave one-hour presentation Mansholt II.[3] Nothing new provided but perhaps significant that he seemed place his presentation in the framework of sharing reflections which led community to choose support level of approach and was giving only initial thinking as to groundrules that might be followed if support level were adopted as the negotiating procedure. Before inviting discussion on Community's presentation, WW also emphasized that group shd consider Community proposal of focusing negots on level support only as working hypothesis. USDel supported this view and stated he had understood EEC was also putting forward their proposals on this basis; hence, no position either for or against the proposal need be implied by either the questions or answers that ensue. In the brief period remaining before adjournment, several dels then took up the line of questioning which will be continued at Wednesday's sessions.[4]

Tubby

---

[1] Source: Department of State, Central Files, AGR 3 GATT. Limited Official Use. Repeated to Brussels for USEC. Passed to the White House. A notation on the source reads: "No reply necessary."

[2] For text of the principles and procedures for conducting comprehensive trade negotiations adopted unanimously by the GATT Ministerial meeting of the Contracting Parties on May 21, 1963, see *American Foreign Policy: Current Documents, 1963*, pp. 1126–1129.

[3] Ecbus A–653 from Brussels, March 11, transmitted the EEC Commission's information memorandum summarizing Rabot's statement to the GATT Agriculture Committee concerning the Community's agricultural negotiating plan for the Kennedy Round. (Department of State, Central Files, AGR 1 EEC)

[4] Tagg 1830 from Geneva, February 21, reported the results of the Agriculture Committee meeting which concluded on Thursday, February 20, including an interpretation of the EEC's plan. (Ibid., AGR 3 GATT)

229. Editorial Note

On March 2, 1964, the White House announced that President Johnson had appointed 37 prominent citizens to a Public Advisory Committee on Trade Negotiations, which would advise Special Trade
Representative Herter in the upcoming Kennedy Round negotiations.
The announcement noted that Herter had said that the Committee
would be "a major channel for the exchange of advice and information
between my office and the American public. The Committee's contribution will add to the value of our increasingly frequent consultations with
individuals, companies and associations concerned with trade negotiations." (White House press release, March 2; Johnson Library, National
Security File, Subject File, Trade—General, vol. I [2 of 2], Box 47)

Bundy forwarded to Bill Moyers a copy of the White House press
release and a March 9 memorandum from Herter to President Johnson,
which suggested that the President make "some brief comments to this
important group on the occasion of their first meeting." In a March 18
memorandum to Moyers, attached to these materials, Bundy agreed that
"a brief, informal meeting with this group of fat cats seems to me a pious
idea and one which can do the President some good. A carefully balanced comment of about four sentences would be all he would need to
add to a personal handshake for each mogul." (Ibid.)

President Johnson received the Committee at the White House on
April 21. For text of his remarks on that occasion, see *Public Papers of the
Presidents of the United States: Lyndon B. Johnson, 1963–64*, Book I, pages
505–506.

---

230. Telegram From the Mission to the European Office of the
United Nations to the Department of State[1]

Geneva, March 20, 1964, noon.

Tagg 1897. For Governor Herter from Blumenthal. At meeting of
Agric Comte March 19, US spoke first giving reasons why Mansholt II

---

[1] Source: Department of State, Central Files, AGR 3 GATT. Limited Official Use.
Repeated to Bonn, Brussels for USEC, The Hague, Luxembourg for USEC, Paris for USRO,
Rome, London, Buenos Aires, Canberra, Ottawa, and Tokyo. Passed to the White House.

not acceptable approach as working hypothesis or even general basis for discussion. After noting some positive features, e.g. binding of levels of protection if reductions could be negotiated, suggested Comte proceed examine on pragmatic basis, bearing in mind directive of Mins and diversity of agriculture products, how agric products can be included in negots. Noted that in such an approach EEC, USA, and others free to advance any proposal deemed appropriate for treatment agric products. Objective to have broad agreement by May 1 on how agriculture is to be included.

Japan, UK, New Zealand, Canada, Denmark, Australia all made statements which included endorsement US approach. EEC (Rabot) agreed work could proceed on pragmatic basis.

Chairman directed discussion to procedures for getting on with job. Suggested setting up technical comte to examine and segregate agriculture products into major groups broadly grouping products on the basis of the nature of the product and the form of protection. It was then agreed this would be done using following guidelines:

1. Look at main trade flows.
2. Nature of product itself, e.g. raw material or processed.
3. Identify kind of protection employed by major trading countries.
4. Job to be done expeditiously and where impasse encountered report back promptly full comte.

(Products susceptible to commodity agreement treatment will be considered by special groups.)

Idea would be that after this sorting job done, full comte would address itself to policy question of how to treat product in question. Chairman also directed that agricultural non-tariff barriers should be included in scope of work of AgCom rather than NTB. First meeting technical comte scheduled Friday, March 20.

Tubby

231.   Memorandum From the Special Representative for Trade Negotiations (Herter) to President Johnson[1]

Washington, March 25, 1964.

You have asked for a report on what we can do about the problems discussed in the two memoranda given you by Messrs. Blough and McDonald on March 16 concerning the steel import situation.[2]

Dumping

The principal complaint of both memoranda is that the present antidumping law[3] is being administered improperly by both the Department of the Treasury and the Tariff Commission. In addition, Mr. Blough's memorandum contends that most steel imports into the United States are dumped. Accordingly, both memoranda recommend more stringent administration of the antidumping law.

There is no way to substantiate, or to dispute, a contention that most steel imports into the United States are dumped. However, the facts of the antidumping cases which have been litigated to date do not, in our opinion, show that dumping has played a significant part in the steel import picture. Moreover, it is our judgment that these cases have been fairly and conscientiously decided by both the Department of the Treasury and the Tariff Commission.

Nevertheless, a number of agencies are working together on a study of our antidumping law and procedures in general. This work has not yet been completed, but I expect that within the near future some affirmative steps will be taken.

The re-examination of our antidumping laws was initiated late last year in response to an earlier Blough-McDonald protest to President Kennedy, as well as a continuing wave of counter-protests from foreign governments claiming that the U.S. law was too harsh. Foreign governments have asked that antidumping laws be reviewed in the forthcoming Kennedy Round negotiations. One facet of this review has been an interagency study, under the direction of this Office, to evaluate the vari-

---

[1] Source: Kennedy Library, Herter Papers, Memoranda to the President, 9/19/63–10/15/65, Box 10. No classification marking. Drafted by Hudec and Auchincloss on March 25.

[2] These two memoranda, probably by Roger M. Blough, Chief Executive Officer of U.S. Steel Corporation, and David J. McDonald, President of the U.S. Workers of America (CIO), have not been found.

[3] Reference presumably is to the Antidumping Act of 1921, Title II of P.L. 67–10, approved May 27, 1961; 42 Stat. 9, 11–15; as amended by Title III of the Customs Simplification Act of 1954, P.L. 83–768, approved September 1, 1954; 68 Stat. 1138; and P.L. 630, approved August 14, 1958; 72 Stat. 583, 585.

ous complaints and thereby to develop a U.S. negotiating position on dumping. The Department of the Treasury, while participating in this study, has also been re-examining its own regulations.

Work on both projects is nearing a conclusion. Preliminary results indicate that a few improvements could be made in the Treasury regulations to meet some of the complaints on both sides. In addition, it is possible that some form of international agreement could be of benefit to the United States.

The Luxembourg Steel Pipe Case

A few words should be said about the recent case involving Luxembourg steel pipe, which Mr. Blough noted. This case was decided under a published Treasury regulation,[4] known to the litigants, which provides that sales prices in the country of origin will not be used for price comparison unless sales in the country of origin account for 25% of total sales. This rule plainly conforms to the law's purpose. One element of a dumping finding is a sale at less than the normal price for a product. Such sales are believed to be unfair because they permit a seller to use the leverage of profits made in one market in order to sell at an abnormally low price in another. In the Luxembourg case, 83% of the steel pipe was being sold at or below the United States price quoted in Mr. Blough's memorandum. A price covering 83% of production cannot realistically be regarded as abnormal. Nor is it possible to contend that the profits in the remaining 17% of the market could unfairly support the price in the other 83%.

Discrimination in "Levies"

The other problem raised in Mr. Blough's memorandum is the alleged disparity between "levies" on steel imports into the United States and "levies" on steel imports into other countries. I fear the memorandum is misleading. Import duties on steel are about the same in Europe as they are in this country—perhaps somewhat less. The European countries, however, have what amounts to a sales tax which is levied on all steel products, domestic and foreign. Mr. Blough has added these taxes in reporting the "levies" paid in Europe.

Although there is no apparent competitive disadvantage in the equal application of such sales taxes, this Office has undertaken a further study of this question in preparation for the coming negotiations.

Adjustment Assistance

Mr. McDonald's statement is concerned mainly with the Tariff Commission's decisions under the adjustment assistance provisions of the

---

[4] Not further identified.

Trade Expansion Act of 1962.[5] A few applications for adjustment assistance benefits for workers have been filed, but the Commission has not found any of these cases to qualify under the Act.

I have not reviewed these cases in detail, but my judgment is that none of these cases appears to qualify under the standards of the Act. One noteworthy point is that United States firms and workers have of course not yet experienced the effects of the broad tariff reductions envisaged under the Trade Expansion Act, for which the adjustment assistance provisions were primarily designed.

Christian A. Herter[6]

[5] P.L. 87–794, approved October 11, 1962; 76 Stat. 872.
[6] Printed from a copy that bears this typed signature.

232. Minutes of Meeting of the Cabinet Committee on Export Expansion[1]

Washington, April 7, 1964.

1. The meeting was opened by Secretary Hodges, Chairman of the Committee. He asked members for their opinions of how long the favorable surplus of some $7 billion (on an annual basis) of exports over imports, which we had experienced in the three months period, December–February, could be held.

Under Secretary Murphy indicated that one factor in the improvement was an increase in Agricultural exports. The Department of Agriculture expects agricultural exports to total about $6 billion for 1964, which would be substantially above the experience of recent years. He looked for an upward trend of agricultural exports in future years even

[1] Source: Washington National Records Center, RG 40, Secretary of Commerce Files: FRC 69 A 6828, Export Expansion-Interagency Committee. No classification marking. The source text bears no drafting information. The Chairman of the Committee, Secretary Hodges, presided at the meeting, which was held in the Fish Room of the White House. A list of the 25 attendees is not printed. The source text is attached to a May 12 memorandum from Acting Secretary of Commerce Roosevelt to the President's Special Assistant for Congressional Relations, Lawrence F. O'Brien, which reviews the status of the Committee.

without the benefits of the Kennedy round, although there may be some short-term contraction of recent high levels. A successful negotiation with improved terms of access would strengthen the upward trend.

Secretary Hodges then asked Assistant Secretary Holton to present his analysis of the recent improvement in exports in relation to imports. Dr. Holton stated that the spread of exports over imports in the December–February period was running at an annual rate of about $7 billion. While this is encouraging, Dr. Holton said it cannot be expected to continue since a good share of the increase in exports was a result of unusually large shipments of agricultural products. Moreover, unusually stable import volume which is an important factor in the $7 billion surplus is not expected to continue since the stimulus of the tax cut will no doubt increase the demand for imports.

On the optimistic side, however, Dr. Holton pointed out that when a 3-months moving average is used, the figures indicate a steady month-by-month gain in exports starting in the middle of 1963. This is closely related to the increase in industrial production which has occurred in Europe beginning in mid-1963.

2. Assistant Secretary Holton then presented charts which reflected the pattern of exports of the United States over the last ten years, indicating first of all the more rapid growth of exports to the industrialized areas of the world relative to the rest of the world. In 1963, the industrialized areas accounted for about $13.7 billion out of the $22.3 billion total. Looking at the industrialized markets alone, it is apparent that the sales to Western Europe have increased much more rapidly than have sales to Canada, although Canada increased its buying from the U.S. rather substantially in the last half of 1963. The exports to Japan in 1963 were running about 2-1/2 times as high as they were in 1953 and 1954, although they still only account for about $1.8 billion out of the $13.7 billion total exports to the industrialized countries.

About $3.5 billion of the $13.7 billion exports to the industrialized areas consists of agricultural commodities and this, as a share of total exports, has not changed significantly over the last decade. Looking at non-agricultural industrial materials exports to the industrialized areas, the growth has been relatively slow and exports of nonferrous metals and of steel mill products have actually declined very significantly over the last three years or so. The exports of machinery, however, have increased about 55 per cent, 1963 over 1959, and this is one of the more promising product groups on which the export expansion effort is concentrating.

The exports of consumer goods (excluding autos) to industrialized areas is still very small, only about $700 million out of the $13.7 billion. Exports of these consumer goods to Canada were falling off but showed improvement in the second half of 1963. The rate of increase of consumer goods exports to Western Europe has been quite promising. The rate of increase in the exports of consumer goods to Japan has been very great, but total consumer exports in 1963 to that country amounted to less than $40 million.

Merchandise exports are expected to rise from the $22.3 billion level achieved in 1963 to about $24.5 billion in 1964, an increase of about 10 per cent. This forecast is particularly sensitive to the rate of increase in industrial production in the industrialized countries of the world. Imports are expected to rise from the $17.2 billion level in 1963 to about $18.7 billion in 1964, an increase of 8 per cent. If this forecast should prove accurate, the trade balance would increase from $5.1 billion in 1963 to $5.8 billion in 1964.

3. Secretary Hodges then called on Assistant Secretary Behrman to report on the status of recommendations of the White House Conference on Export Expansion held September 1963.

Dr. Behrman said the White House Conference produced about 110 recommendations which have been grouped into three categories.

First, are general recommendations relating to increased productivity, maintenance of labor-management peace, reduced taxes, price/wage stability, foreign language teaching, greater interest by organized labor in export expansion, and the potentials for achieving full employment represented by the export expansion program. While no time limit has been set for achieving the general objectives, the Administration has had the tax cut enacted, is sponsoring industrial modernization conferences, and has announced language institute grants of $6.8 million for fiscal year 1965.

Second, are recommendations relating to increased export promotion. The Bureau of International Commerce opened a fifth U.S. trade center in Milan, Italy, in January 1964. A sixth is scheduled to open in Stockholm, Sweden, in early 1965. In addition, funds have been requested for two more trade centers. The number of commercial trade fairs and industry-organized/government-approved trade missions has been increased for 1964. New programs for mobile trade fairs and sample display centers will be under way soon. A target of 10,000 new exporters was recommended by the conference. The Commerce Department has identified over 5,000 nonexporting manufacturers and has contacted over 1,200 of them.

The Commerce Department has held four regional conferences with the commercial officers overseas in 1964; seven such conferences have been held since 1961. The 1964 conferences took place in Frankfurt, Germany; Beirut, Lebanon; Lagos, Nigeria; and Nairobi, Kenya.

AID and the FCIA have taken steps, as recommended by the White House Conference, to simplify the credit information required for insurance and investment guarantees. AID has also revised its procurement regulations.

The third category comprises basic policy recommendations such as tax incentives for exports, changes in anti-trust policies as they apply to exporters, elimination of discriminatory freight rate disparities, liberalization and expediting of export financing, etc. These recommendations call for fundamental policy decisions and constitute the major unfinished business of the White House Conference.

4. Administrator Bell led the discussion on AID policies as they affect long-term commercial interests of the U.S. This discussion was divided into three categories: (1) Administrator Bell indicated that he was prepared to consider criteria which would give priority in AID programming to projects with the greatest long-term export potential. He asked the assistance of the Commerce Department in developing appropriate criteria. A joint Commerce/AID working group will examine this question and attempt to come up with recommendations for submission to the AID Administrator. (2) Mr. Bell directed his attention to the AID policy of "last resort" financing. This policy, designed to assure that AID finances projects only when no other country or other source of credit is available, has had some unfortunate results. Other industrialized countries have moved in with offers of loans for prime commercial projects with interest rates higher than AID's but lower than Ex-Im is prepared to offer. They call these offers their contribution to the development assistance effort but it results in long-term commercial ties for their exporters to the exclusion of U.S. firms. Administrator Bell said the "last resort" policy of AID contributes to this problem and should be re-examined. To change the policy, however, would require prior clearance with Congress. He said that the Commerce Department paper on the subject[2] over-simplifies the legal problems involved in changing the policy. (3) Mr. Bell indicated that there is evidence that a "gap" exists in financing projects in LDCs, between the relatively hard terms of the Ex-Im Bank and the soft terms of AID. Secretary Dillon agreed that such a problem might exist, but that more work is needed to establish its dimensions. Mr. Bell stated that in his view, AID should not attempt to deal with this problem as this would require AID to continue in a country essentially for reasons of export expansion. Instead of AID, the Ex-Im Bank or other agencies of Government should do this job.

Mr. Linder said that credit availability is a secondary consideration to the main effort in the export expansion field which is to encourage more American manufacturers to enter the export market. He stated that Ex-Im, AID, and PL 480[3] now assist more than 20% of American exports.

---

[2] Not further identified.

[3] The Agricultural Trade Development and Assistance Act, approved July 10, 1954; 68 Stat. (pt. 1) 454.

Mr. Linder also said the evidence presented to date regarding the alleged gap in our financing arrangements does not indicate any serious problem. He pointed out that if we want the Europeans to share the burden of AID, we must let them finance their exports. It was agreed that the issues involved in export financing required further study.

5. The President arrived. After the swearing in of the National Export Expansion Coordinator, the President welcomed the Cabinet Committee emphasizing the importance he attaches to its deliberations and stating that he looks forward to receiving the Committee's recommendations. The text of the President's remarks is attached.[4]

6. Secretary Hodges asked Secretary Dillon if he would care to comment on the recent favorable developments in the export situation and our international balance of payments. Secretary Dillon said that we have programs well established now which should achieve the maximum in balance of payments savings as a result of government expenditures. Therefore, additional improvements in the balance of payments must come through the reductions in net capital flows and even more importantly, through increased exports. He indicated that while the first quarter of 1964 would show our international payments to be almost in balance, the figures for the entire year 1964 would likely reflect a deficit of about $2 billion. He emphasized that to offset the effects on our trade balance of the tax cut, greater effort would be needed to promote export expansion.

7. Deputy Assistant Secretary Kuss (DOD) presented a summary of the military export program. He reviewed: Defense expenditures abroad compared to receipts from military sales; the military sales history and potential, both short and long-term; sources of credit financing for military sales; and the major actions taken by the Executive Branch which resulted in the sharp rise in military exports during the FY 60–62 period. Military sales have increased from an average of approximately $380 million per year in the FY 51–60 period to slightly above $1.5 billion annually during FY–62 and 63 as a result of the initiative and emphasis of Secretary McNamara and Secretary Dillon.

To sustain the program at its high level, he said, requires

1) vigorous Executive Branch action to promote military sales;
2) an active program of Government and industry cooperation; and
3) continued availability of credit.

Secretary Rusk stated that while State supports the Defense military export promotion program, some countries and areas of the world, such as Latin America and Africa, require application of special policy consid-

---

[4] Not attached, but printed in *Public Papers of the Presidents of the United States: Lyndon B. Johnson, 1963–64*, Book I, pp. 444–446.

erations before we should encourage or promote the sale of military products.

Mr. Bell asked why Defense does not use lower interest rates, more in line with AID loans, when using their Military Assistance Program Credit Fund as a credit source. Mr. Kuss explained that

1) the rates of 4.5–5 percent were starting figures for negotiations and that actual sales negotiations may bring the rates down;
2) normal interest rates are now always detrimental to a sale. The most important aspects generally are—price, quality, availability and support capabilities—in which the U.S. is most competitive. And
3) the high interest policy can be used to discourage sales of military products to countries where political considerations weigh against the sale of such equipment.

8. Secretary Rusk asked the Committee to consider the role USIA can play in the export program. He suggested this subject be added to the agenda for the next meeting and that USIA be invited to participate. He also urged the Cabinet Committee to meet again at an early date to probe more deeply the policy issues which need consideration.

9. Secretary Udall reported briefly on the outlook for coal exports. He said we were now exporting at the rate of $500 million a year, but this performance could be improved substantially if certain obstacles could be overcome. Among the problems are rail and ocean freight rates and non-tariff barriers—particularly quotas—which have been raised against the importation of coal.

10. Secretary Hodges asked Mr. Goldy to outline the plans for organizing the Committee's work. Mr. Goldy said that with the concurrence of the full Committee, he would establish an Executive Committee at the Assistant Secretary level to develop facts and issues in depth for consideration when necessary by the principals of the Cabinet Committee. He said this would follow the pattern of the Balance of Payments Committee. He stated he intended also to establish interagency working groups as necessary to focus on specific problems such as those which were mentioned on the agenda. He said he would like to keep the arrangements as informal as possible so as to achieve maximum flexibility in getting on with the job. There was general concurrence in this approach to the Committee's organization.

11. The Chairman concluded the meeting, saying the next meeting would be scheduled as soon as the necessary staff work is completed.

233. Letter From the Special Representative for Trade Negotiations (Herter) to Secretary of State Rusk[1]

Washington, April 8, 1964.

Dear Dean:

We have reached the point in our preparations for the Kennedy Round of trade negotiations where we must begin formally the process of deciding which products the United States may have to except from the linear tariff reductions. I am writing to describe the procedures by which I think we might best undertake this task, which is so critical in terms both of the negotiations' success and of domestic sensitivity.

There are several general considerations about exceptions which I would also like to mention, since this subject will loom increasingly large in the months ahead. First, as you know, the GATT Ministers agreed last year that exceptions should be confined to "a bare minimum" and should be subject to international "confrontation and justification."[2] No numerical ceiling has been placed on countries' exception lists, but I feel that we must limit our exceptions to cases of clear and pressing necessity if this round of negotiations is to be successful. If we should submit a substantial list of exceptions, we cannot doubt that some countries would seize this opportunity to undermine the scope of the negotiations even further, placing the blame on us. As you know, the United States has played the leading role in bringing these negotiations about and moving them forward. It would be a severe blow to the negotiations themselves and to our prestige as a leader in trade liberalization if we were to undercut all we have said by tabling an extensive exceptions list.

Therefore, I think it is imperative that each agency, in suggesting items to be expected, should make every effort to keep its list very short and should prepare thorough written justifications for any products which they do recommend. These justifications must be persuasive and well documented, because they are essential to support our position in the "confrontation and justification" procedure.

The security problem regarding exceptions will inevitably be severe. We plan to limit documents on exceptions to the narrowest possible distribution, and I hope that in each agency the number of people

---

[1] Source: Department of State, Central Files, FT 13–2 US. Secret. Attached to the source text is a memorandum from Trezise to the Acting Secretary of State, April 16, indicating, among other things, that identical letters were sent to the Secretaries of Defense, Commerce, Agriculture, Labor, the Interior, and the Treasury. Also attached to the source text is a letter from Acting Secretary Ball to Herter, April 20, assuring him of the Department of State's "full cooperation in the preparation and handling of these lists."

[2] Reference is to the resolution adopted at the Ministerial meeting of the GATT Contracting Parties at Geneva, May 21, 1963; see footnote 2, Document 228.

who come into contact with exceptions lists can also be carefully restricted. One important point in this connection was made in the President's memorandum of December 20, 1963, to you on this subject: The exception lists will not be definitive until after the process of confrontation and justification, and no official of the Government should make or imply any commitments on specific products.[3] You can imagine the extreme difficulties that would be caused if our initial exceptions list were to become prematurely known, either to other countries or to domestic interests, especially in a period just prior to a Presidential election.

With these points in mind, I am establishing the following procedure to draw up our initial exceptions list:

1. The Trade Staff Committee (TSC) will begin consideration late this month of proposed exceptions, which your agency will be asked to submit, along with written justifications, in advance. The Chairman of the TSC will have available a single copy of the Tariff Commission's advice to the President, which he will make known to the TSC as each proposed exception is discussed.

2. After the TSC has acted, its recommendations will be submitted to this Office and considered by the Trade Executive Committee (TEC).

3. After consideration by the TEC, this Office will prepare its recommendations, of which you will be notified before they are transmitted to the President. The initial U.S. exceptions list will subsequently be subjected to international confrontation and justification, but final determination will always rest with the President.

I hope that we can begin work on this problem soon.

Best, as ever,

Chris

---

[3] The President's December 20 memorandum has not been found.

234. Memorandum From the Assistant General Counsel, Office of the Special Representative for Trade Negotiations (Hudec) to the Special Representative for Trade Negotiations (Herter)[1]

Washington, April 13, 1964.

SUBJECT

April 11 Meeting on Antidumping Policy

The participants were Secretary Dillon, Governor Herter, Under Secretary Ball, Mr. Hendrick,[2] Mr. Jacobson, and Mr. Hudec.

Governor Herter opened the meeting by presenting the STR memorandum to Secretary Dillon.[3] After reading the memorandum, Secretary Dillon replied by stating that Treasury believed that any delay in publishing these regulations would result in legislative action on antidumping. He referred to the fact that the House Office of Legislative Counsel had been asked to rush preparation of a new antidumping bill for Congressman Herlong[4] by the end of this month. In response to a question, he added that the Herlong request had been made "with Chairman Mills' blessing". He informed the meeting that there was a plan to take up the Herlong bill in Ways and Means just before the end-of-session matters—debt ceiling, etc. This information was accompanied by a lengthy reading and analysis of the sponsors of the Humphrey bill. Governor Herter and Mr. Jacobson related our information that Chairman Mills had no intention of having hearings on dumping this year. Secretary Dillon replied that this was not so, without elaborating further.

Governor Herter, Mr. Jacobson, and, later, Under Secretary Ball stated the case for international negotiations and the damage that publication of the regulations might do. Secretary Dillon replied that Treasury was not opposed to international negotiations on antidumping. He displayed general receptiveness to the whole idea.[5]

In his view, publication of the amendments would not "give away" anything in our bargaining posture. The regulations eliminating retroactive assessment were, he thought, minor matters. The biggest U.S.

---

[1] Source: Kennedy Library, Herter Papers, Antidumping, Box 5. Limited Official Use. Transmitted through Roth.

[2] James P. Hendrick, Deputy Assistant Secretary of the Treasury.

[3] Not further identified.

[4] A. Sydney Herlong, Jr., Democratic Representative from Florida.

[5] The Departments of Commerce, Labor, State, and the Treasury subsequently concurred with the recommendation by Herter to the President for negotiation of an international agreement on antidumping. (Memorandum from Herter to President Johnson, October 11, 1966; Johnson Library, National Security File, NSC Histories, Kennedy Round Crisis, April–June, Tabs 17–24, Box 52)

counter was the threat of worse legislation, which should be sufficient to persuade other governments not to go further than the U.S.

The others at the meeting disagreed with this appraisal. After some exchange of views on this point, Secretary Dillon developed what amounted to an alternative answer. He emphasized Mr. Hendrick's observation that the regulations might not come into effect for as much as 8 months after publication. He thought this delay could be used to minimize whatever bargaining "give-away" there was in the proposed regulations. The liberalizing changes in the regulations can be expected to come under heavy fire during the initial 60-day period for public comment. The U.S. could argue that such changes stood a chance of being withdrawn or nullified without the support of an international accord. He agreed to a period of consultations or negotiations that would follow this line. The others agreed that, with this kind of delay, there might be some room for negotiating.

The specific Treasury proposal was to publish the regulations on April 22. Ambassador Leddy would use the OECD meeting on April 21 to set up consultation sometime in the next 60 days. All agreed to this step.

Secretary Dillon disavowed any interest in the relative roles of OECD and GATT in the international discussions, stating that he would plead "nolo contendere" (?) in this matter. STR and State could work this one out to their own satisfaction. Everyone assumed that the first step would be OECD consultations, but their content and strategy were left open.

Governor Herter pressed Secretary Dillon on the matter of further interagency work to develop a negotiating position, noting that Treasury had heretofore dissented from the TSC Subcommittee report.[6] Secretary Dillon expressed some surprise at this fact.

Mr. Hendrick explained that Treasury saw nothing that could be gained, because antidumping policy is largely a matter of administrative discretion which cannot be controlled by international agreement. The Secretary noted that the possibility of this conclusion would always have to be kept in mind as a qualification, but went on to state that he was in agreement with the idea of negotiations, and he agreed to have Treasury participate actively in preparing a negotiating position for the coming negotiations.

---

[6] Not further identified.

235. Circular Telegram From the Department of State to Certain Posts[1]

Washington, April 22, 1964, 7:04 p.m.

1970. From Governor Herter. Subject: Kennedy Round Talks with Powell. Following are highlights of discussions on Kennedy Round held April 20 and 22, with U.K. group headed by Sir Richard Powell.

1. We made clear that we do not intend precipitate crisis at May 4 Geneva meeting. Ministers should take note of progress to date, urge further efforts during summer to settle rules. In speeches, we hoped ministers would express disappointment at slow pace. We suggested that in addition to confirming 50 percent rule, TNC report might confirm aspects of the disparities rule already agreed so as to prevent future backsliding. Powell agreed conference should be low key and resolution bland. He resisted idea of confirming partial disparities rule, for fear the EEC approach would thus become sanctified without our having got qualifications required to make it acceptable. We replied that any written endorsement of 2:1–10 rule must be made conditional on agreement on criteria. Issue was left in agreement to see what language on this point GATT Secretariat and TNC could come up with next week.

Throughout the talks, British expressed skepticism that acceptable disparities formula based on 2:1–10 rule would ever be achieved.[2]

2. On issue of timing of tabling offer-exceptions lists, we and British agreed we should for present hold to September 10 date of draft TNC report, keeping up pressure for early resolution of outstanding rules. We discussed possibility of holding another Ministerial Meeting before August to review progress on rules and re-examine timetable in that light, but left decision on this open pending developments at May 4 meeting.

3. On Rey's visit to London, Powell said that if EEC suggested bilateral discussions on disparities with U.K., British would not want to rebuff them. We had no objection provided such bilateral talks were

---

[1] Source: Department of State, Central Files, FT 13–2 US. Confidential. Drafted by Auchincloss (STR), cleared by Joseph A. Greenwald (E/OT), and approved by Roth. Sent to eight posts in Europe and to Tokyo.

[2] The European Economic Community developed the 2:1/10 disparities formula in late December 1963 and presented it to the GATT Tariff Plan Subcommittee in January 1964. The formula provided that a disparity exists where a high tariff country maintains a tariff twice that of another participant in negotiations and, except in semimanufactured products, where at least 10 percent ad valorem separates the two tariffs. In case of a disparity, the European Economic Community proposed that the high tariff country cut its tariff by 50 percent and the invoking country by 25 percent. (Tagg 1841 from Geneva, February 25, 1964; ibid.) No acceptable disparities formula was achieved.

aimed at clarifying a general rule. Both sides agreed that extenuated bilateral talks should be avoided.

4. On agriculture, we reported our feeling that to press for resolution any substantive issue before May 4 would be futile. TNC report should make clear the issues that divide us in agriculture, but leave it at that. Powell agreed with this approach. He believes best chance for agricultural settlement will come when negotiations on industrial products are near success, thus creating strong lure to those anxious for industrial concessions but aware they are unobtainable without concomitant agricultural liberalization. His tactic would therefore be to let industrial phase of negotiations precede agricultural by a few steps, though certainly not to let momentum of latter die. Nield of Agriculture Ministry added point that if industry got too far out in front of agriculture, there was a danger of split between agricultural exporting and importing nations which would lead to withdrawals on industrial side.

Nield was pessimistic on possibilities getting meaningful access deal from EEC; he believed French would be more adamant against this than Germans have been over grains prices.

Rusk

---

236.   Memorandum From the Special Representative for Trade Negotiations (Herter) to President Johnson[1]

Washington, April 29, 1964.

SUBJECT

Adoption of 50% Linear Rule in May 4 GATT Meeting

Recommendation:

I recommend that, in light of the information presented to you in this memorandum, you authorize me to accept on behalf of the United States a rule providing for a linear reduction in tariffs of 50%, subject to the significant qualifications described herein.

---

[1] Source: Johnson Library, National Security File, NSC Histories, Kennedy Round Crisis, Tab 1, Box 52. Confidential. Drafted by R. E. Hudec (STR) and John B. Rehm (STR). Herter sent this memorandum with a covering letter to McGeorge Bundy at the White House, requesting the President's decision before Herter's departure for Geneva on May 1. (Ibid.) Bundy told Herter that the President approved Herter's recommendation on April 30. (Memorandum for the files by Fay Steiner (STR), May 1; ibid., Tab 2, Box 52)

I have communicated the substance of this memorandum to the Departments of Commerce, Defense, Labor, and the Interior. They concur in the transmission of this recommendation.

Discussion:

On May 4, 1964, the Trade Negotiations Committee of the General Agreement on Tariffs and Trade (GATT) will meet in Geneva, at the ministerial level. The purpose of this meeting will be to take note of the progress which has been made to date in developing the rules to be applied in the trade negotiations and, wherever possible, to refine and elaborate some of the general principles agreed upon at last year's ministerial meeting.[2]

In particular, I believe it would be advantageous for the United States to be in a position to agree to a rule providing that the major participants would make a linear or across-the-board reduction of 50% in present tariffs. The meaning of a linear rule is that all dutiable imports are initially subject to the agreed tariff reduction of 50%, but each participant would reserve the right to except products from the list for reasons of overriding national interest. Due to the fact that the negotiating rules for agriculture have been set aside for separate consideration and have not yet been formulated, the commitment involved in adopting a 50% rule at this time would extend only to non-agricultural products.

The authority for the United States to make such 50% tariff reductions, subject to certain mandatory exceptions, is provided by the Trade Expansion Act of 1962. In the preparatory discussions to date, the United States has joined other governments in accepting a 50% linear reduction as the working hypothesis upon which we could formulate procedural rules for the coming negotiations. I am proposing that we agree to make this working hypothesis a rule for the negotiations.

I believe that the transformation of the working hypothesis into a rule would go far towards preserving the momentum of the negotiations and would, at the same time, establish as a firm proposition one of the most critical elements of these negotiations. It appears that the other important participating countries, including the EEC, United Kingdom, and Japan, will be prepared to do the same.

I should emphasize that the proposed 50% linear rule would be agreed to by the United States only on the basis of certain express conditions.

The first condition would entitle the United States to exclude from the general 50% tariff reduction whatever items we determine must be so reserved. At Geneva, the Trade Negotiations Committee will be asked to agree that exceptions to the linear rule should be kept to a bare minimum

---

[2] See footnote 2, Document 228.

and should be justified on the basis of overriding national interest. This formula has the advantage of putting some international pressure upon countries which might otherwise reserve a large number of items from a linear reduction of 50%. At the same time, it lays down no objective standards as to what constitutes a bare minimum and therefore does not commit the United States to any quantitatively defined number or value of exceptions. Under the Trade Expansion Act of 1962, we are required to reserve certain items, including those subject to national security and escape-clause actions. In addition, we will be free to reserve other items, although we hope such further exceptions would not exceed the principle of a bare minimum.

The second condition qualifying the linear rule would permit the United States to adjust the number of items which it would reserve in accordance with the principle of reciprocity. It has already been agreed that it shall be open to each country to request additional concessions or to modify its own offers where this is necessary to obtain a balance of advantages between it and the other participating countries. This principle constitutes as significant a condition to the linear rule as that concerning exceptions.

These two conditions serve a further purpose in making clear that the 50% linear rule would not predetermine which specific items in the United States Tariff Schedules will be subject to a tariff reduction of 50%.

Before the United States can accept even such a generalized and conditional rule, I believe the Trade Expansion Act of 1962 requires you to make a preliminary judgment about the probable economic impact of tariff reductions, based upon the advice of the Tariff Commission and upon other information received during the recent public hearings concerning the forthcoming trade negotiations. The requirement is not that you make any particular finding. Rather, it is merely that you be given sufficient information about the content of that advice and information so that you may form a preliminary judgment about probable economic effects, and that you make the decision whether to agree to the rule after considering that information.

I have now received, on your behalf, the advice rendered by the Tariff Commission on the basis of its public hearings and independent study.[3] I have also received the summary of the hearings of the Trade

---

[3] On October 22, 1963, the President submitted to the Tariff Commission a list of the articles that would be considered for concessions at the GATT Contracting Parties sixth round of tariff negotiations, and the Tariff Commission held public hearings December 21, 1963–March 27, 1964. It submitted its advice to the President regarding the probable economic effects of reductions in import duties on April 22, 1964. The advice was not made public. For further information, see U.S. Tariff Commission, *Operation of the Trade Agreements Program, 16th Report, July 1963–June 1964* (TC Publication 164, Washington, 1966), pp. 42–43.

Information Committee of this Office. My Office has made a preliminary survey of the Tariff Commission advice, as well as the information presented to this Office through the Trade Information Committee and other various sources.

I believe that this review has furnished us with sufficient information of a preliminary kind to serve as the basis for a decision to agree to the 50% linear rule described above. The Tariff Commission advice indicates a judgment that a 50% reduction in tariffs on a clear majority of negotiable non-agricultural items in the United States Tariff Schedules would not create serious economic consequences. That judgment is supported by the other information reviewed by this Office to date. Such a judgment necessarily takes into account the fact that virtually all tariff reductions are required by statute to be staged over a minimum of five years, the capacity of domestic industries to adapt to import competition, and the availability of adjustment assistance under the Trade Expansion Act of 1962.

Christian A. Herter[4]

---

[4] Printed from a copy that bears this typed signature.

---

237. Memorandum From the Special Representative for Trade Negotiations (Herter) to President Johnson[1]

Washington, June 2, 1964.

I recommend that you request the Tariff Commission to investigate the probable economic effect of reducing or terminating the present "escape-clause" action on stainless steel table flatware.

The escape-clause action, which amounts to a tariff 50 percent higher than the statutory rates on imports of stainless steel flatware in excess of 69 million units, dates from October 1959. Restrictions such as these are intended to afford temporary relief when tariff concessions cause injury to domestic industries.

---

[1] Source: Kennedy Library, Herter Papers, Chronological File, June 1964, Box 3. Confidential. Drafted by Auchincloss.

The Tariff Commission has submitted annual reports on the industry since the escape-clause action went into effect. The most recent of these was submitted on November 1, 1963 (and is attached).[2] It indicates that conditions in the domestic industry have been generally good in the 1962–1963 period and that imports have decreased to about half their volume prior to the escape clause action. In addition, past reports show a steady increase of domestic production and sales since the late 1950's. I attach a report of a Trade Staff Committee Subcommittee which sets out the economic situation in greater detail.[3]

The Tariff Commission report has been reviewed by the Trade Staff Committee and Trade Executive Committee, on which are represented the Departments of Agriculture, Commerce, Defense, the Interior, Labor, State, and the Treasury. All these agencies concur in my recommendation.

The authority for the recommended request to the Tariff Commission is contained in section 351(d)(2) of the Trade Expansion Act of 1962. I have attached a draft letter to the Chairman of the Commission and a draft White House press release which I feel should be issued if you concur in the recommended course of action.[4]

Christian A. Herter[5]

---

[2] Not attached. See U.S. Tariff Commission, *Stainless-Steel Table Flatware: Report to the President (No. TEA–IR–1–63) Under Section 351 (d) (1) of the Trade Expansion Act of 1962*, TC Publication 113, 1963.

[3] Not found.

[4] Neither has been found. At the request of the President, the investigation, which began June 24 and was completed April 14, 1965, was reported in U.S. Tariff Commission, *Stainless-Steel Table Flatware: Report to the President on Investigation No. TEA–IA–5 Under Section 351 (d) (2) of the Trade Expansion Act of 1962*, TC Publication 152, 1965.

[5] Printed from a copy that bears this typed signature.

238. Memorandum From Francis M. Bator of the National Security Council Staff to the President's Special Assistant for National Security Affairs (Bundy)[1]

Washington, June 8, 1964.

McG. B.

Kennedy Round and the Erhard Visit[2]

In the face of the dramatic German veto on grains prices last Tuesday,[3] if the President is noncommittal or reserved in his conversation with Erhard on the grains price/access issue—or, more broadly, on the importance of the Kennedy Round in Atlantic relations—the Germans are likely to conclude, if only for their own peace of mind, that the U.S. is content to let the negotiations stall. If so, there will be little or no chance that they will yield to Commission pressure and agree to a price before September—and, a fortiori, barring a minor miracle, before their elections. And without progress toward a "common agricultural policy"—the only item in the Kennedy Round package which is not distasteful to them—the French will certainly stonewall, especially since they will be able to blame the Germans. (Needless to say, even if the French were prepared to stick to the schedule on industrial questions, leaving agriculture out of it pro tem, we would not. Agriculture's notion that we can make progress on agricultural rules and access while the CAP is in limbo, while not technically impossible, is a mirage.)

To be sure, even a strong expression of Presidential concern may fail to budge the Germans, and the French may sabotage the negotiations in any case. All one can reasonably claim is that a Presidential intervention appears at this stage to be a necessary condition for progress—as indeed for a test of French intentions and good faith. (This last is not unimportant. In terms of our future options, it would be much better for the French to have played the villain rather than the Germans abetted by the U.S.)

The point of the above is not that we abandon agriculture. The President, after restating the case for the Kennedy Round in terms of Atlantic political relations, could point out that we want both a reasonably low common price *and* some access arrangement—that neither, taken by itself, will do.

---

[1] Source: Johnson Library, Bator Papers, Kennedy Round, 1964–1965 I, Box 12. No classification marking.

[2] Chancellor Erhard met with President Johnson and other U.S. officials in Washington on June 12 and 13.

[3] June 2.

It is important to keep in mind that last Tuesday evening's decision is widely regarded in Europe as having placed the entire negotiation in jeopardy. If we make no response and appear to acquiesce in drift, we shall be judged as party to the strangulation and will be in a poor position to take strong action to revive the negotiations after November.

Francis M. Bator[4]

---

[4] Printed from a copy that bears this typed signature.

---

239.   Summary of Discussion[1]

Washington, June 13, 1964.

Following is résumé of points made by Herter in discussion with Erhard June 13 in response to question: "Does the United States consider that a unified grains price decision in the EEC now is indispensable to the success of the Kennedy Round?":

1.   A unified grains price decision now is not indispensable as far as the United States is concerned. We believe that negotiations on industrial products, agricultural products other than grains, and even on grains, could be carried right up to the concluding stage in Geneva without a unified grains price decision, if the EEC negotiator were in a position to negotiate on these matters.

2.   In the view of the United States, the problem seems to lie therefore not in Geneva but in Brussels. It seems to have become an indispensable element in the internal bargaining situation with the EEC that the unified grains price decision be made now and that in the absence of such a decision the EEC representatives will be unable to enter into negotiations on virtually any matter in Geneva.

3.   Unless the capabilities of the EEC to negotiate on industrial products and on agricultural products including grains is restored in one

---

[1] Source: Kennedy Library, Herter Papers, Ludwig Erhard, 6/3/64–9/26/66, Box 8. No classification marking. The source text bears no drafting information. A longer record of this conversation, prepared by Hedges, was transmitted in a June 15 memorandum from Hedges to Roth. (Ibid.)

way or another, the timetable and even the final results of the Kennedy Round could be put in serious jeopardy. The preparations for the tabling of exceptions lists (which in the view of the United States must be done simultaneously for industry and agriculture) must be resumed at the latest by the end of the summer holidays if we are to meet the target date of November 16. In view of the already serious delays in the past, such further delays in the progress of the Kennedy Round would seriously endanger the negotiations. That would create a situation where the negotiations might well fail or at best be seriously impaired.

4. As far as the United States is concerned, the question of a unified grains price can in any case not be seen in isolation. While the United States wishes to see the lowest possible grains price in the Community, it is clear that any such price now being considered is so high as to require assurances for the maintenance of grain imports.

240.   Letter From Secretary of Commerce Hodges to Secretary of State Rusk[1]

Washington, June 16, 1964.

Dear Dean:

As I commented on signing the State–Commerce Agreement in November 1961,[2] if it did not work out, I would be back to discuss the matter. I told you last Friday night[3] that we should discuss our problem again.

The agreement has not been fully implemented for several reasons, including lack of funds from Congress and a change in view as to the desirability of the separate commercial career specialty provided for in

---

[1] Source: Washington National Records Center, RG 40, Secretary of Commerce Files: FRC 69 A 6828, State Department Agreements—1964. No classification marking. Drafted by Behrman and Wyman on June 15 and rewritten by Hodges.

[2] A copy of the memorandum of agreement between the Department of State and the Department of Commerce on International Commercial Activities, November 15, 1961, is ibid.

[3] June 12, presumably at a White House dinner for Erhard. (Johnson Library, Rusk Appointment Books)

the agreement. Neither conceptually nor in practice at the posts can the commercial functions be cleanly and clearly separated from economic functions. They are quite similar and I have checked them personally in a score of countries.

My view is supported by the reaction of practically all the officers who have attended the last four Commercial/Economic Officer Conferences where this subject was discussed. Senior officials of this Department who have recently been overseas make the same report. The similarity of functions is also attested by the job description on economic and commercial officers recently issued by the State Department.[4] In fact, many officers are performing both economic and commercial functions. We, therefore, proposed to Deputy Under Secretary Crockett in March *the creation of a unified economic/commercial career program* and requested the necessary participation by the Department of Commerce in the selection, assignment, and promotion of officers in this program.[5]

As I understand the objectives of the Foreign Service Act,[6] it was to unify the service overseas, while maintaining appropriate interest of the several departments. Above and beyond this, the Board of the Foreign Service was created to serve as a means by which you would receive recommendations incorporating the views of the other Agencies which were utilizing the Foreign Service as their overseas arm. We alone of the Agencies outside of State have a wide range of overseas interests; yet we rely wholly on the Foreign Service while many Departments with very specific interests have their own personnel overseas. For this reason we must work together to develop the strongest possible working relationship which meets our needs as well as yours.

Our March proposals for the economic/commercial set-up, which we thought had been favorably received, have been rejected this week, and we have been told, in effect, to be satisfied with the way that our interests will be handled by State. While we have had excellent cooperation from you and other top officers of State, there remains much to be desired. The inadequacies are mainly in the area of institutional arrangements and of attitude toward commercial work both on the part of Regional Bureaus in State and at posts overseas. I am greatly discouraged!

I think it necessary therefore that we sit down and discuss where we go from here in pursuing the objectives which we have agreed with the

---

[4] Not further identified.

[5] Reference is to a memorandum from Behrman to Crockett, March 6. (Washington National Records Center, RG 40, Secretary of Commerce Files: FRC 69 A 6828, State Department Agreements—1964)

[6] The Foreign Service Act of 1946, as amended; 22 USC 801.

President have a top priority in overseas activities. Let me know when it is convenient to you.

With best personal regards.

Sincerely yours,

Luther H. Hodges[7]

P.S. There is a long letter from Crockett dated June 6th raising certain objections,[8] many of which are not too pertinent. We will be glad if you wish to give you detailed comments on each point raised.

---

[7] Printed from a copy that indicates Hodges signed the original.
[8] Crockett's June 6 letter to Franklin D. Roosevelt, Jr., contains many handwritten marginal comments, presumably by Roosevelt. (Washington National Records Center, RG 40, Secretary of Commerce Files: FRC 69 A 6828, State Department Agreements—1964)

---

241. Letter From President Johnson to the Special Representative for Trade Negotiations (Herter)[1]

Washington, July 10, 1964.

Dear Governor Herter:

As you know, the Urban Mass Transportation Act,[2] which I have just signed into law, was amended to require that contractors employed with funds made available under the Act "shall use only such manufactured articles as have been manufactured in the United States." I regret that this objectionable provision was included in the Act. This provision goes well beyond the Buy American Act[3] and is incompatible with the trade policy we are pursuing under the Trade Expansion Act.

---

[1] Source: Johnson Library, National Security File, Subject File, Trade—General, vol. I [1 of 2], Box 47. No classification marking. This letter was requested in a July 9 memorandum from Acting Secretary of State Ball to President Johnson for use in discussions with other governments. (Ibid.) It was transmitted in Gatt 2015, July 16, to Geneva and eight other posts. This telegram also informed these posts that "Interested Washington embassies have been informed that Administration considers amendment incompatible with US trade policy and that it hopes it will be repealed in near future." (Ibid.)
[2] P.L. 88–365, approved July 9; 78 Stat. 302.
[3] Chapter 212, Title III, approved March 3, 1933; 47 Stat. 1520.

I hope that this provision will be repealed in the near future, and that similar provisions will not be adopted in the future. Furthermore, I hope it will be understood by all of our trading partners that the adoption of this provision does not reflect any change in the policies and purposes of this Administration.

Sincerely,

Lyndon B. Johnson

---

242. Telegram From the Mission to the European Office of the United Nations to the Department of State[1]

Geneva, July 14, 1964, 6 p.m.

Tagg 2167. For Governor Herter from Blumenthal. Reference: Tagg 2166.[2]

Statement by Blumenthal at July 13 TNC meeting:

Begin text.

Mr. Chairman:

My delegation fully concurs with the views you have expressed concerning the gravity of the situation which we face in our negotiations. My government is fully committed to the success of the KR. It is our firm objective to make maximum use of the tariff cutting authorities provided in the Trade Expansion Act of 1962. At the same time, it has been made clear by the President himself that we cannot conclude a negotiation that does not accomplish substantial liberalization in agricultural trade as well as in industrial products. To this end, we have repeatedly stated that there must be simultaneous progress in both the industrial and agricultural phase of the negotiations.

The lack of progress in agreeing on procedures and methods to be employed in the agricultural negotiations must be a matter of utmost concern to all of us. The US has tried to seek a compromise solution to this

---

[1] Source: Johnson Library, National Security File, Subject File, vol. I [1 of 2], Box 47. Limited Official Use; Priority. Repeated to Bonn, Brussels for USEC, The Hague, London, Luxembourg for USEC, Ottawa, Paris for USRO, Rome, Bern, Copenhagen, Oslo, Stockholm, and Tokyo. Passed to the White House on July 15.

[2] Dated July 14. (Department of State, Central Files, FT 7 GATT)

impasse. We repeatedly reviewed our position and have adjusted it to the negotiating realities. To this end, we have agreed that agricultural products be treated differently than industrial products and that a pragmatic approach be used. Essentially this means realistically negotiating concrete and substantial reductions in trade barriers, with the negotiations directed at the protective measures which an importer uses for a particular product or group of products. In the course of our deliberations, we have identified the following broad categories where different methods would apply:

1. Bulk commodities (notably grains, meat, and dairy products): It has been agreed that negotiations on these commodities will take place in special groups with the objective of negotiating global arrangements. These negotiations will deal with relevant internal policies as well as protection at the border. The US is willing to consider including an approach along lines of Montant de Soutien so far as the community is concerned as an element in negotiation of global arrangements, providing there are adequate provisions for assuring the maintenance and improvement of access to markets.

2. Products other than those in one above which are subject to variable levies[3] in community: For these products, the US is willing to consider an approach along the lines of the Montant de Soutien as long as negotiations are directed not to the mere binding of present support, but to the achievement of a significant degree of liberalization and hence increased opportunities for trade.

3. Commodities for which the importer maintains fixed tariffs: In the case of the EEC this would include products subject to the CXT. The major difficulty lies in this area because of the large export interests of world agricultural exporters including US in agricultural products protected by fixed tariffs. Neither the US nor apparently most other countries are willing to replace present methods of negotiating reductions in fixed tariffs with the Montant de Soutien approach. I do not wish to dwell on a full explanation of the reasons. We have previously stated them clearly. In simple terms, the reason is that the Montant de Soutien provides much greater freedom of action for increasing protection than does a fixed tariff. Moreover, substituting commitments relating to the Montant de Soutien, as now defined, for fixed tariffs would violate bindings

---

[3] Variable levies were "Charges applied to certain agricultural imports (cereals, poultry, eggs, pork) but varying or variable to adjust for differences between domestic prices in the importing EEC country and import prices. It is sometimes described as an equalization fee. Until 1970, there will be levies both for trade between Community partners and for imports from non-Community countries." (European Community Information Service, Basic Glossary of Terms for "Kennedy Round," January 1964; Kennedy Library, Herter Papers, Glossary, Box 9)

negotiated in the Dillon Round[4] and other previous negotiations, thereby creating problems of compensation which appear insurmountable and accomplishing the opposite of what a trade liberalizing program is intended to achieve.

4. Commodities on which an importing country maintains bound duty-free status: I take it that no further negotiating on such products is required in the KR.

To conclude: There is an urgent need for agreement on agricultural negotiating rules that will permit concrete and substantial reductions in trade barriers and the maintenance and improvement in access to markets. Such agreement must be reached in Geneva not later than the end of September so that countries can prepare their exceptions and offer lists in time to meet the November 16 deadline.

Tubby

---

[4] The tariff negotiations under GATT, concluded in 1962, were named after C. Douglas Dillon.

---

243. Telegram From the Mission to the European Office of the United Nations to the Department of State[1]

Geneva, July 14, 1964, 8 p.m.

Tagg 2169. For Governor Herter from Blumenthal. Following telegram sent action priority Brussels 15 July 12 repeated for your information:

"For McSweeney[2] from Blumenthal. Deliver 9 AM July 13.

Following is summary of points I made to Spaak. Suggest you transmit these to his office as agreed before his departure for Bonn. Unnecessary words ommitted.

1. The Kennedy Round is stalled on issue of negotiating rules for agricultural products. If present impasse is not broken and satisfactory progress in elaboration of rules to govern agricultural phase of negoti-

---

[1] Source: Department of State, Central Files, FT 13–2 US. Limited Official Use. Repeated to Bern, Bonn, Brussels for USEC, Copenhagen, The Hague, London, Luxembourg for USEC, Oslo, Paris for USRO, Rome, Stockholm, Vienna, and Tokyo. Passed to the White House on July 15.

[2] John M. McSweeney, Deputy Chief of Mission in Brussels.

ations is not made by end of September, success entire KR will be in jeopardy.

2.   Reasons for this impasse are two-fold: First, Community has insisted all agricultural products be dealt with in KR through so-called MDS (Montant de Soutien) approach. After thorough discussion and examination, MDS has been rejected as a universal approach for agricultural sector by US and virtually all other KR participants. This situation has been well known for some months.

Second, Community negotiators have equated questions of agreement on rules for agricultural products other than grains with grains problem within Community. Hence in absence of a Community grains price decision, there has been no progress on any KR agricultural negotiating rules. A Community grains price decision now seems likely to be considerably delayed.

3.   The urgency in resolving present impasse before October stems from agreement of all participants that KR shall include both industrial and agricultural products, and that exceptions lists shall be tabled November 16. The US will be unable to table its exceptions list on November 16 unless satisfactory progress in elaboration of agricultural negotiating rules is made sufficiently before November to permit agricultural phase of negotiations to proceed in step with industrial. Failure to table exceptions lists on November 16 would be a serious and possibly crippling blow to political will and momentum indispensable for a successful KR.

4.   In our efforts to resolve present impasse, following facts must be borne in mind:

(A) US cannot accept MDS as an across-the-board approach for agriculture whether or not Community reaches a grains price decision.

(B) The US recognizes importance of common grains price issue for Community and is aware that such a decision now could be helpful not only for Community but for KR. However, from point of view of negotiating situation in Geneva, it is not essential that common grains price be known now in order to permit agreement on ground rules and conduct of subsequent negotiations on all categories of agriculture products, including grains.

5.   To understand reasons for statements in paragraph (4) above, it is necessary to bear in mind following facts about agriculture trade and protection:

Agriculture trade can be grouped in four categories:

(A) Bulk commodities, notably grains, meat and dairy products: It has been agreed that negotiations on these commodities will take place in special groups with objective of negotiating global arrangements. These negotiations will deal with relevant internal policies as well as protection at border. The US is willing to consider including an approach along lines of MDS as an element in negotiation of global arrangements providing there are adequate provisions relating to maintenance and improvement of conditions of access. If negotiating rules along above lines can now be agreed upon, negotiation of most aspects of global arrangements can proceed without a Community common grains price. It is recognized, however, that final agreement on an arrangement for grains may require a common grains price. Such final agreement, however, cannot be expected before closing stages of KR which according to present indications should occur in late 1965.

(B) Commodities other than those in (A) above which are subject to variable levies in Community:

For these products, US and other countries are also willing to consider an approach along lines of MDS as long as negotiations are directed not to mere binding of present support, but to achievement of a significant degree of liberalization and hence increased opportunities for trade.

(C) Commodities on which importing country applies fixed tariffs:

The major difficulty lies in this area because of large export interests of world agricultural exporters including US in agricultural products protected by fixed tariffs. Neither US nor virtually any other country is willing to replace present method of negotiating reductions in fixed tariffs with MDS approach. While a full explanation is technical and complex, in simple terms reason is that MDS provides much greater freedom of action for increasing protection than does a fixed tariff. Moreover, substituting commitment relating to MDS as now defined for fixed tariff would violate tariff bindings negotiated in Dillon Round and other previous negotiations thereby creating problems of compensation which appear insurmountable.

(D) Commodities on which importing country maintains bound duty-free status: These products are not subject to negotiation.

6. In conclusion, there is an urgent need for a Community negotiating position which permits agreement on agricultural negotiating rules. Such agreement must be reached in Geneva not later than the end of September so that countries can prepare their exceptions and offers lists in time to meet November 16 deadline. US cannot move forward on industrial products unless negotiating rules for agricultural products have been defined. The Trade Expansion Act and history of its passage and its support in Congress quite apart from US trading interests and agreement of all GATT Ministers in May 1963 and 1964 make divorcing of agricultural and industrial trade impossible for US.

Minimum that is required in agreeing on ground rules is: (I) An understanding that for categories (A) and (B) in paragraph 5 above, application of MDS concept will involve liberalization creating increased trading opportunities for efficient producers. (II) The Community negotiators be provided sufficient flexibility to agree to modification of Montant de Soutien concept for category. (III) So that meaningful reduction and binding of fixed tariffs together with effective amelioration of other obstacles to trade can take place. (C) The Community undertake to negotiate seriously in agricultural sector, if necessary even in absence of a common grains price.

If these rules can be agreed upon, negotiations can start with offers on November 16 and proceed through 1965 with a view to concluding toward end of that year. Failure to agree on ground rules by late September could lead to a collapse of KR for reasons given in paragraph 3 above. Failure of KR under such circumstances would have ramifications extending well beyond realms of commercial policy.[3]

Tubby

---

[3] Spaak reiterated Blumenthal's points in his conversations in Bonn, and in consequence Spaak "now feels there is some reason for optimism as to German readiness negotiate cereals on price 'x' basis. He thinks we will see some movement on this soon." (Telegram 92 from Brussels, July 22; Department of State, Central Files, FT 13–2 US)

---

244. Telegram From the Department of State to the Mission to the European Communities[1]

Washington, July 21, 1964, 6:18 p.m.

Busec 50. For Fessenden from Herter. Request you deliver in person soonest following confidential letter to Hallstein. FYI. President has cleared text. End FYI.

Begin text.

Dear President Hallstein:

I am taking the liberty of writing to you personally about a matter of grave concern to my Government and to all of us, I think, who believe in the importance of the Kennedy Round.

At the present time, the negotiations appear to be in severe danger because of the continued failure to make progress in establishing nego-

---

[1] Source: Department of State, Central Files, FT 13–2 US. Confidential; Priority. Drafted by Auchincloss; cleared by Deane R. Hinton (EUR/RPE), Greenwald (E/OT), Hedges, A. Richard DeFelice (Agriculture), and Bator; and approved by Roth.

tiating rules for the various categories of agricultural products. If the negotiations are to go forward on schedule, substantial progress must be made on these rules and procedures well before November 16. The Executive Secretary of the GATT pointed out to the Trade Negotiations Committee on July 13 that unless we have made significant progress on agriculture by early autumn, it will be impossible to exchange offers and exceptions lists on November 16. Postponement would seriously risk the success of the entire negotiation.

In the past, your negotiators have taken the position that their mandate from the EEC Council will not permit them to move beyond the stand they have so far taken on agriculture in Geneva. I strongly hope that in facing the urgent test that now confronts us, your negotiators will be enabled to act more flexibly so as to permit a satisfactory solution to be reached.

For our part, let me reiterate, on behalf of President Johnson, our Government's firm commitment to spare no effort to bring the Kennedy Round to a successful conclusion.

Most sincerely yours, Christian A. Herter

End text.

In discussing details of situation and possible ways out you may draw on Blumenthal's statements to TNC (Tagg 2167 to Dept.) and to Spaak (Tagg 2169 to Dept.),[2] leaving copies if you wish.

Since letter might be used against us in some quarters, you should ask that it be treated most confidentially.

FYI. Virtually identical letter being sent Erhard.[3] End FYI.

Rusk

---

[2] Documents 242 and 243.

[3] In telegram 192 to Bonn, July 21. (Department of State, Central Files, FT 13–2 US)

245. Circular Telegram From the Department of State to Certain Posts[1]

Washington, August 3, 1964, 4:03 p.m.

202. Action addressees should inform government officials that U.S. believes, with end UNCTAD,[2] time seems appropriate make special effort stimulate interest of less developed countries in the practical advantages to their trade and development of active and full participation Kennedy Round. U.S. therefore intends to initiate bilateral discussions with selected LDC's to discuss importance and potentialities of their active participation in KR, the work of the GATT Trade Negotiation Committee (TNC) and Sub-Committee on LDC Participation and the nature of their possible contribution to trade liberalization in the negotiations.

Ambassador Blumenthal will initiate U.S. effort August 19 to September 2 by visiting Rio, Buenos Aires and Lima for high level discussions. Consideration being given to consulting with Pakistanis and Indians in Europe rather than through visits to Karachi and New Delhi.

To stimulate more African interest in GATT, also planning have U.S. Econ. Min. Geneva John Evans visit Cairo, Lagos and a French speaking African country at later date.

U.S. concern is that concentration of most LDC officials on far-reaching objectives at UNCTAD in past months diverted their attention from the more conventional but attainable trade benefits possible during KR. U.S. therefore wishes encourage as many LDC's as possible to participate in the negotiations and be active in LDC Sub-Committee. During UNCTAD, U.S. and other developed countries unable support many LDC proposals but repeatedly stressed genuine interest promoting LDC exports and U.S. pledged maximum effort KR achieve this objective. But this requires that LDC's participate and preferably pursue energetic course in both preparatory and negotiation stages.

U.S. wishes not only inform host governments of U.S. views and intention initiate bilateral discussions with these LDC's but also seek host governments instruct their missions in LDC capitals to encourage more active LDC participation in KR. In this respect U.S. recognizes that African countries present special problems. KR benefits for them less

[1] Source: Department of State, Central Files, FT 13–2 US. Limited Official Use. Drafted by Northrop Kirk (E/OT); cleared by Greenwald (E/OT), Joel W. Biller (EUR/RPE), Daniel J. James (NEA), Samuel Z. Westerfield (AF) (all in draft); and approved by Bernard Norwood (STR). Sent to 24 posts.
[2] For text of the Final Act adopted by UNCTAD in Geneva on June 16, see *American Foreign Policy: Current Documents, 1964*, pp. 149–170.

evident and will require greater coordination of effort by all developed countries. For our part U.S. is studying ways and means of developing constructive approach and would welcome cooperation in this effort.

Rusk

---

246.   Letter From Secretary of Commerce Hodges to President Johnson[1]

Washington, August 10, 1964.

Dear Mr. President:

Following your instructions to seek additional funds for the commercial specialist program of the Foreign Service, Secretary Rusk and I have personally appealed to the Senate Appropriations Committee for the addition of one million dollars to State's budget. The fact that State earlier claimed no increase in its personnel makes it desirable that you call Senator McClellan to indicate your approval of this change in State's budget. Deputy Under Secretary Crockett of State and Tom Wyman of my staff have detailed the request to the Senator this week, justifying the specific needs and the posts to which the new officers would be assigned.

For your use, the $1 million would permit assigning 37 new U.S. officers overseas in addition to the existing 149; 15 of the 37 officers would be assigned to posts where there are no commercial officers; we would also add 100 local and 8 U.S. clerical assistants. As you know, without these new officers our successful export drive simply cannot be sustained.

Respectfully yours,

Luther H. Hodges[2]

P.S. The Senate Subcommittee mark-up of the State Department appeal will start today.[3]

---

[1] Source: Washington National Records Center, RG 40, Secretary of Commerce Files: FRC 69 A 6828, White House, July–August. No classification marking. Drafted by Behrman and Wyman.

[2] Printed from a copy that indicates Hodges signed the original.

[3] On an August 6 transmittal memorandum from Wyman to Hodges, attached to the source text, Hodges wrote out the postscript, which in slightly amended form became the typed postscript to this letter.

247. Letter From Secretary of Commerce Hodges to Secretary of State Rusk[1]

Washington, August 21, 1964.

Dear Dean:

I had hoped that we would be able to continue our conversation on the State/Commerce agreement[2] at an early date, but unfortunately this seems not to have been possible for you. So that we can come to an early agreement on next steps. I think it best to set down the major problem areas, and I hope we can come to an early agreement.

1. *I feel very strongly that we should establish a single economic/commercial career,* such as we proposed in April.[3]

We have gone part of the way in achieving this through the method your people have proposed for handling promotions. I understand that four functional panels have been established, consisting of four members each, which will consider the promotion of both commercial and economic officers and that Commerce will have voting membership on these panels. The recommendations of these panels will be reviewed by the various Foreign Service Selection Boards consisting of seven members, and Commerce will have one voting member on each of these Boards.

But, this does not go far enough. We should make it clear that economic and commercial officers share the same career opportunities and are judged by similar precepts.

2. *We propose that all officers be designated as "economic/commercial" both on their records in the Department and at their posts.*

Despite the fact that the State/Commerce agreement of 1961 contemplated designations of Commercial Counselors and Commercial Ministers, only four Commercial Counselors have been designated; several embassies rejected suggestions that Counselors be named at their posts. In order to reflect the integration of these services and to raise career expectations to the appropriate levels, this single designation is necessary.

3. *Commerce should participate fully in the assignment of all "economic/commercial" officers overseas,* since their functions are so closely related and since we are deeply concerned over the priority assigned to our programs.

---

[1] Source: Washington National Records Center, RG 40, Secretary of Commerce Files: FRC 69 A 6828, State Department Agreements—1964. No classification marking.

[2] See footnote 2, Document 240.

[3] Hodges presumably meant March, not April; see footnote 5, Document 240.

Currently, we are involved only in assignments of commercial officers. In instances where there is disagreement between our respective
staffs, I think that senior officers of both Departments should review the
proposed assignments so as to reach agreement. In cases of serious disagreement over senior assignments, we would expect a review at Secretarial levels.

We propose *that the budget for the economic/commercial service be prepared jointly by State and Commerce,* that it be presented to Congress within
the State Department budget, and that supporting testimony be given by
Commerce officials as appropriate.

4. The State/Commerce agreement we signed in 1961 contemplated the Department of Commerce undertaking responsibility for
preparation of budget estimates and presentation to Congress. This was
never put into practice; rather, various compromise and delayed techniques were employed, as you know, and without success. You and I
took personal interest, but at a late stage.

5. *The Foreign Service Inspection Corps should give special consideration
to Commerce Department interests in their inspections.* In addition, joint
inspection of the economic/commercial service should be provided
where desired by the Department of Commerce.

There are other details, on other matters, which our staff can work
out and agree on, but the basic decision is to have you designate the economic and commercial as one service, and I hope you will agree to this
request.

Frankly, Dean, I'm disturbed as a taxpayer and as a member of the
President's "team" with you that we are frustrated down the line so often
on these matters. I feel this so strongly that I may recommend to the President that he instruct us to combine our economic staffs of State and Commerce here in Washington and make a substantial savings in money and
cut out unnecessary duplication.[4]

Looking forward to hearing from you soon, I am,

Sincerely yours,

Luther H. Hodges[5]

---

[4] Indicative of Hodges' frustration was his August 31 letter to Crockett, in which he
wrote that he was "most disturbed" at the misimpression Crockett had received that his
remarks before the Senate Appropriations Subcommittee "were critical of your handling of
the State/Commerce relationship and were directed at you personally." Hodges also noted
that the House of Representatives had denied their joint appeal for additional funds for
commercial attachés. (Washington National Records Center, RG 40, Secretary of Commerce Files: FRC 69 A 6828, State Department Agreements—1964)

[5] Printed from a copy that bears this typed signature.

248. **Memorandum From the Assistant Director for Legislative Reference, Bureau of the Budget (Hughes) to President Johnson**[1]

Washington, August 21, 1964.

SUBJECT

Enrolled Bill H.R. 1839—Free importation of certain wild animals and birds and imposition of quotas on the importation of certain meats

Sponsor—Rep. Teague (R) California

Last Day for Action

Purpose

To provide for the free importation of certain wild animals, and to provide for the imposition of quotas on fresh, chilled, or frozen meat of cattle, goats and sheep (except lambs).

Agency Recommendations

Bureau of the Budget—Approval

Department of Agriculture—No objection

Department of State—No objection

Department of Commerce—No objection

Office of Special Representative for Trade Negotiations—No objection (informally)

Department of the Treasury—No recommendation

Tariff Commission—No recommendation

Council of Economic Advisers—No recommendation (informally)

Discussion

Section 1 of this bill would permit the duty-free entry of wild animals and birds which would be imported for sale to any public zoo. Existing law permits such duty-free entry when the creatures are actually imported by a zoo but not when the zoo purchases them from an importer. By making the creatures duty-free in either case, this bill would permit zoos to escape the risks of transportation and death by purchasing the creatures duty-free from importers who can spread such risks over a larger volume of imports. Duty-free treatment would not be afforded to animals purchased by private or "roadside" zoos.

Section 2 of this bill establishes as Congressional policy an annual quota on fresh, chilled, or frozen beef, veal, goat meat, and mutton.

---

[1] Source: Johnson Library, National Security File, Subject File, Trade—General, vol. I [2 of 2], Box 47. No classification marking.

Annual imports of these items would be limited to 725.4 million pounds—the annual average of such imports for 1959 through 1963. This limit would be increased or decreased for any particular year in proportion to the change in domestic production.

When it is determined that imports will exceed by ten per cent the limits set by this policy, the President would be required to issue a proclamation which would keep imports from exceeding such limits. Under certain circumstances, however, the limitation would be removed when it is determined that anticipated imports will not exceed by ten per cent the limits set by Congressional policy.

The President would be authorized to suspend or increase any quota if he determines and proclaims that: (1) overriding economic or national security interests of the United States require such action; (2) the supply of meat will be inadequate to satisfy domestic demand at reasonable prices; or (3) trade agreements entered into after the date of the enactment of this bill insure that the Congressional policy will be carried out.

With regard to meat, this bill differs from the version that was passed by the Senate and strongly opposed by the Administration principally in that the types of meats covered are fewer, and certain discretionary authority to adjust or suspend quotas is permitted the President.

It may be noted that although the State Department and the Office of the Special Representative for Trade Negotiations do not recommend veto of this bill, they do indicate that they are opposed to it.[2]

Phillip S. Hughes

---

[2] A letter from G. Griffith Johnson to Kermit Gordon, August 21, noted that the Department of State had previously objected to the imposition of quotas on meat imports, but it believed that H.R. 1839 was "so drawn as to minimize the disadvantages inherent in such restrictive legislation." The letter concluded: "While the Department of State cannot support enactment of H.R. 1839, it does not wish to recommend that its enactment be opposed." (Ibid.) H.R. 1839 became P.L. 88–482, approved August 22, 1964; 78 Stat. 594.

249.   Memorandum From the Special Representative for Trade Negotiations (Herter) and the Under Secretary of State (Ball) to President Johnson[1]

Washington, August 25, 1964.

1.   In the last three months, the Administration has been forced into a number of protectionist moves: the Saylor Amendment,[2] the meat bill,[3] and the wool textile and shoe missions.[4]

2.   Pressure is now building in Congress behind a number of additional special interest, restrictive bills. (See attachments)[5]

3.   Enactment of these bills would:

—Materially injure our trading partners
—Invite retaliation against U.S. exports
—Undermine our bargaining position in the Kennedy Round
—Give the Administration a protectionist image

4.   The Administration's opposition to these bills has been made known—on a piecemeal basis—to the leadership and key committee figures. However, because they are minor and complicated bills, lobbying against each will only have limited effect. We believe they must be attacked as a package, through the congressional leadership.

5.   Accordingly, we suggest that at your Tuesday leadership meeting you emphasize your opposition to this legislation.[6] We believe that the best way to ensure death of these bills is through an appeal to the leadership to hold the line.

George Ball
Christian A. Herter[7]

---

[1] Source: Kennedy Library, Herter Papers, Memoranda to the President, 9/19/63–10/15/65, Box 10. No classification marking.

[2] This is the amendment to the Urban Mass Transportation Act summarized in the first sentence of Document 241.

[3] See Document 248.

[4] Documentation on the wool mission is printed in *Foreign Relations, 1964–1968*, volume IX. The shoe mission has not been identified.

[5] No attachments were found with the source text.

[6] No record of a meeting with the legislative leadership on this issue in 1964 has been found.

[7] Printed from a copy that indicates Ball and Herter signed the original.

250. **Message From Secretary of State Rusk and the Under Secretary of State (Ball) to President Johnson, in Texas[1]**

Washington, September 26, 1964.

We know that you are being pressed by John Pastore[2] and Ed Muskie[3] to give some hard assurances about the wool textile problem when you are in New England Monday.[4] We urge you very strongly, however, to avoid any commitments that might imply or subsequently involve legislation imposing mandatory quotas.

George Ball worked out some language today with Mike Feldman, Governor Herter and representatives of Commerce and Labor. We can live with this language but it represents the absolute maximum we can go without creating great difficulties for the future.

As you know, we have done more for the textile industry since 1961 than for any other industry. In order to counter the pressure for mandatory quotas George Ball successfully negotiated an unprecedented international agreement that has resulted in checking the rate of increase in imports of cotton textiles.[5] Obstructionist at first, the industry now enthusiastically supports this agreement, but we are going to have a rough time keeping it alive over the next few years since we have applied it in a very hard-nosed manner and created mounting resentment in other countries.

The situation in the wool textile industry is different from cotton. In the case of cotton, our imports come largely from the less developed countries. Wool textiles, however, come principally from the United Kingdom, Italy and Japan. Alec Home's government has made it clear to us that Britain is not going to agree to voluntary restraints on their wool textile exports to the United States any more than we would be prepared to accept voluntary restraints on our exports to them.

Our best hope is to try to work something out within the context of the Kennedy Round trade negotiations that will stabilize wool textile imports and this is what we all understand will be attempted. But we do not dare be too explicit in what we promise since no one can tell how things will work out.

---

[1] Source: Johnson Library, National Security File, Subject File, Trade—General, vol. 2 [2 of 2], Box 47. Limited Official Use. The message was actually addressed to the White House Message Center for transmission to the President. At the bottom of the source text are Ball's handwritten initials.

[2] Democratic Senator from Rhode Island.

[3] Democratic Senator from Maine.

[4] September 28.

[5] Reference is to the Long–Term Arrangement Regarding International Trade in Cotton Textiles signed in Geneva under GATT auspices by 19 countries in 1962. (13 UST 2672)

The textile industry knows that we have done our best to try to negotiate a voluntary arrangement for wool textiles. They themselves have been working at it in collaboration with us. They have learned the hard way that a voluntary arrangement is not feasible in the present climate. They are, therefore, bringing great pressure during the campaign period to try to get you to make some statement which they can construe as support for mandatory quota legislation. It seems altogether likely that they have timed a wave of woolen mill closings in the last month with this in mind. It seems hardly accidental that Bob Stevens chose to announce the closing of his mill in Lisbon Falls, Maine, on Thursday just in advance of your New England trip.

The wool textile industry is in a process of concentration and restructuring. Small family mills are being taken over by big companies and either closed or modernized. The most pressing problem for wool textiles is not imports but the competition of synthetics and other substitute fibres and the fact that large parts of the industry have been backward and asleep.

There is no doubt that imports have risen in relation to consumption in recent years but this year they are actually running at a rate 25 percent under last year.

We do not need to emphasize how unfortunate it would be if you said anything in New England that would be interpreted as approval for mandatory quotas for wool textile imports. We have worked strenuously for years to get rid of quota restrictions on industrial manufactures. Today there are hardly any such quotas left among the principal trading nations although some still treat Japan in a discriminatory fashion.

We ourselves have avoided quotas on industrial manufactures all during the post-war period in spite of enormous pressure. For you to show any sign of departing from this practice now would subject you to a flood of demands for similar treatment by practically every other industry—many of which have a better argument than wool textiles. In the course of the campaign you will be visiting thirty states and each has an industry that feels it has a strong case for quota protection.

Moreover, any indication of sympathy for quotas on your part would be a signal for similar action by other trading nations—to say nothing of the fact that the imposition of mandatory quotas on wool textiles would require the payment of compensation in the form of other trade concessions amounting to over $250 million.

So far in the campaign, you have not yet spoken on our world trading policy and whatever you say will be given great attention. The big metropolitan liberal newspapers have already expressed some concern over what they regarded as protectionist measures by the Kennedy Administration and the recent drive for beef import restrictions by Mike

Mansfield and other Democratic leaders has aroused their skepticism. Goldwater has now switched around. He is trying to establish himself as a liberal trader and has charged your administration with having "raised a host of new and inconsistent barriers to trade."

Other nations around the world are on the alert to see what you say on this issue. The woolen textile import problem is an old story and has become a test of American intentions in the whole trading field.

We are in real trouble in Japan as a result of the succession of restraints we have imposed on their trade over the past two or three years. We cannot afford again to make the same mistake with Japan that we made during the thirties. Italy also is, as you know, in a dangerous political phase—and actions by us to restrict their exports while their economy is so shaky would play into Communist hands.

We know Chris Herter is also greatly concerned about this problem because of its implications for the Kennedy Round.

---

251.   Telegram From the Mission to the European Office of the United Nations to the Department of State[1]

Geneva, October 10, 1964, 8 p.m.

Tagg 2355. For Herter from Blumenthal. References: Tagg 2354, 2356, 2357.[2] Following text tabled by US 7:00 p.m. October 9:

Begin text.

Rules for Negotiations on Agricultural Products

In accordance with the principles and procedures established by Ministers in May 1963[3] the negotiations regarding agricultural products shall be conducted as follows:

1.   *Bulk commodities: cereals, meats, dairy products, and sugar.*

Negotiations shall be directed toward the establishment of special arrangements for those specific products the inclusion of which is agreed to in the respective commodity groups. These negotiations shall cover those elements identified by each group as relevant to its negotiations.

---

[1] Source: Department of State, Central Files, FT 7 GATT. Limited Official Use; Priority. Repeated to Bonn, Brussels for USEC, The Hague, Luxembourg for USEC, Paris for USRO, Rome, and London. Passed to the White House for Herter on October 11.

[2] Tagg 2354 and 2356 are both dated October 10. (Ibid.) Tagg 2357 is Document 252.

[3] See footnote 2, Document 228.

The cereals and meats groups have already identified these elements, and an early meeting of the dairy products groups should be held for the same purpose. A group shall be established to study the most appropriate basis for negotiations regarding sugar.

2.   *Other products subject to special import regimes or special policy measures.*

A participating Contracting Party maintaining a form of protection or support other than a fixed tariff which adversely affects competitive conditions of trade in an agricultural product, shall make offers which substantially reduce such effects. In the case of variable levies the offers for reductions and binding may be in accordance with the techniques defined by the European Economic Community.

3.   *Fixed tariff items.*

Where fixed tariffs are used, separately or in combination with other measures of protection, the Contracting Party shall make substantial offers of reductions and bindings in such tariffs. In case of zero duties not already bound, the offers shall be to bind the zero duty.

If in addition to fixed tariffs a Contracting Party also maintains other measures for protection or support that adversely affect competitive conditions of trade in a particular product, it shall make offers which substantially reduce such effects.

4.   Any agricultural product not included in the negotiations in special commodity groups for which a Contracting Party is unable to make a significant offer in accordance with the above rules must appear on that country's exceptions list for agricultural products.

As in other phases of the negotiations exceptions shall be limited to items justified on the basis of overriding national interest.

5.   Nothing in these negotiating rules shall be construed so as to lead to the modification or withdrawal of existing concessions, or to bring about a situation less favorable to an exporting country than that existing as a consequence of previous negotiations. In accordance with the overall objective of the negotiations, offers with respect to products already subject to commitments under the General Agreement shall be directed towards the reduction of the level of protection thus bound.

6.   The negotiations regarding agricultural products including negotiations in special commodity groups shall proceed concurrently with other phases of the negotiations in the Kennedy Round, the objective being that the results in the agricultural phase shall be available to all participants in assessing the balance of advantages and disadvantages.

7.   Agricultural offers and exceptions shall be tabled on (blank) (date to be determined).

End text.

Tubby

252.   Telegram From the Mission to the European Office of the United Nations to the Department of State[1]

Geneva, October 10, 1964, 8 p.m.

Tagg 2357. For Herter from Blumenthal. Reference: A. Tagg 2354, B. Tagg 2355, C. Tagg 2356.[2] Reference telegrams B and C indicate why negotiations on agricultural rules have broken down. Following commentary discusses significance our differences with Commission. I have discussed matter with Governor Herter, he agrees posts may give copies US and Commission papers (reference telegrams B and C) to governments using following comments as appropriate. Papers in reference telegrams have no official standing, but indicate retreat of Commission from more promising line it had been taking prior to October 9.

If opportunity arrives posts may point out that governments can check with Wyndham White if they want view of third party.

Begin comment:

During three lengthy bilateral discussions between September 17 and October 2, US and EEC Commission discussed possible outlines of agricultural rules which might be agreeable to both sides and acceptable generally by other negotiating partners in Geneva. At end third bilateral discussions (October 2), both sides presented oral summary of points of general consensus reached to Wyndham White. Both sides at that point were of impression that large area of consensus in fact had been reached, and EEC Commission indicated that only major point still to be worked out involved treatment of fruits and vegetables. It should be noted that all bilateral discussions were oral—nothing had been reduced to paper. US paper (reference telegram B) represents best effort by US to represent fairly US understanding of points of agreement reached except that fruits and vegetable problem was not taken into account, and paper assumes agreement by EEC to treat fresh fruits and vegetables like other fixed tariff items.

After interval of one week during which EEC Commission representatives had returned to Brussels to consult on status of their bilateral talks with US, fourth and final bilateral meeting took place in presence Wyndham White on Friday October 9. EEC document (reference telegram C) tabled in later part this bilateral discussion gave clear indication substantial departure from points of general concensus reached in previous sessions.

---

[1] Source: Department of State, Central Files, FT 7 GATT. Limited Official Use; Priority. Repeated to Bonn, Brussels for USEC, The Hague, Luxembourg for USEC, Paris for USRO, Rome, and London. Passed to the White House for Herter on October 11.

[2] See Document 251 and footnote 2 thereto.

Parts I and III of EEC paper contain only substantive rules proposed in this paper for products other than bulk commodities. Read together with two footnotes to paragraph I, these provisions would mean that:

1. No offer would be required on a fixed tariff unless it is the only form of support maintained by any key country.

2. For products on which other measures of protection or support are maintained, either separately or in combination with a fixed tariff, no offer of any kind would be required. Rule simply states that these elements would be subject to negotiation.

3. Where a fixed tariff is not now bound, EEC language would clearly permit an offer along lines of MDS. Moreover, in subsequent discussion EEC strongly resisted suggestion by WW that introduction of variable levy on a bound item would require first that existing obligation be withdrawn through provisions of Article XXVIII.[3] It seems fair to assume, therefore, that language of EEC paper was intended to permit offers having effect of withdrawing an existing fixed tariff binding and replacing it with reference price and variable levy. Only exception being those cases where no key country has any form of support other than a fixed tariff.

As indicated, EEC paper makes no provision for an offer on non-tariff elements. It also makes no provision that those few offers that would be required for fixed tariff items represent offers to reduce level of protection.

Paragraph II of EEC paper deals with bulk products for which commodity groups have been established to negotiate commodity arrangements as well as sugar for which EEC had asked a group be established. This paragraph departs substantially from substance of earlier conversations. Instead of stating that groups would negotiate on those elements that have been identified by group in question, paper in effect provides those groups with new terms of reference fully covering elements which EEC had wished included in negotiations (internal prices and international price, which are essential to MDS approach) which avoiding stating that access would be element of negotiation. Instead paper states concept that negotiation of other elements would determine conditions of access.

During discussion of this paragraph, EEC representative at first resisted strongly an effort to replace this language by a reference to elements which had already been identified by groups in question. They finally agreed to this solution provided the same elements would apply to negotiations in the case of sugar. This was clearly unacceptable since

---

[3] Article XXVIII of the GATT permitted withdrawals or modifications of tariff concessions under specified circumstances.

no discussion has yet taken place re formation of such a group or its terms of reference. In previous discussions it had merely been stated that EEC would propose that a sugar group be formed and that US would be willing to agree with a view to seeing what might be done in case of sugar.

Finally, EEC made completely new proposal that a similar group be established on oilseeds. This had never been discussed before. Effect of such a proposal, if accepted, would have been to transfer to commodity group important category of US exports to EEC and to provide Community with opportunity to withdraw zero tariff binding US now enjoys on soybeans.

Final paragraph of EEC paper "IV. Procedures" would leave to an undetermined future date determination of what products fall into what categories.

End comment.

Tubby

---

253.   Letter From the Special Representative for Trade Negotiations (Herter) to Secretary of the Treasury Dillon[1]

Washington, October 26, 1964.

Dear Doug:

I am enclosing my preliminary recommendations to the President concerning those import items which I believe should be placed on the United States exceptions list, that is, reserved from a full 50% reduction in duties in the forthcoming trade negotiations.[2] In some cases, which are noted in my recommendations, I am proposing a reduction of less than 50%, and in all other cases, no reduction at all.

---

[1] Source: Kennedy Library, Herter Papers, White House Subject File, Withdrawn Documents, Box 15, Box 5. Secret. Drafted by John B. Rehm. The source text bears the handwritten note: "Identical letter to Dean Rusk (our copy to John Rehm)."

[2] Not found.

For the most part, I have accepted the recommendations of the Trade Executive Committee, which concluded its deliberations on the exceptions list last week. I have not accepted its recommendations with respect to the following items:

Hardwood Plywood (TSUS 240.14, ex 240.18, and ex 240.20)
Hardboard (TSUS 245.10 and 245.20)
Woven Silk Fabrics (TSUS 337.10 and 337.90)

At the end of my recommendations you will find a summary of the proposed exceptions and an identification of the countries whose trade with the United States would be primarily affected by such exceptions. In reviewing my preliminary recommendations, you may wish to refer to the documents which record the deliberations and decisions of the Trade Executive Committee and which have been sent to your Department's representative on that Committee.[3]

In order to facilitate our meeting on November 5th, I would ask that you notify me and the other members of the Trade Expansion Act Advisory Committee of any import items which you intend to raise for discussion at that meeting. This notification should, I believe, be accompanied by a brief written statement of justification.

As mentioned in my letter of October 16th,[4] I would be delighted to meet with you at any time before our meeting of November 5th, should you personally wish to discuss with me any aspect of my preliminary recommendations to the President.

Most sincerely yours,

Christian A. Herter[5]

---

[3] The documents are not further identified.
[4] Not printed. (Department of State, Central Files, FT 13–2 US)
[5] Printed from a copy that bears this typed signature.

254.   Memorandum of Conversation[1]

Washington, October 27, 1964, 4 p.m.

PARTICIPANTS

STR:
Honorable Christian A. Herter
Honorable William M. Roth
Mr. Kenneth Auchincloss

White House:
Honorable McGeorge Bundy
Mr. Francis Bator

State:
Honorable George W. Ball
Honorable G. Griffith Johnson

SUBJECT

Agricultural Rules for the Kennedy Round

Mr. Ball saw two problems confronting the U.S.: (1) how to handle the US–EEC discussions of agricultural rules in Geneva on Thursday,[2] and (2) what action to take on November 16.

He recommended that we make whatever deal on rules that we could on Thursday and then table our efforts on November 16. His arguments were:

1.   That the real negotiations on agriculture would not take place until January anyway. The outcome would not depend upon the semantic difference between words such as "substantial reduction" and "liberalization" in the rules, but upon hard bargaining on products.

2.   That the onus would then be clearly on the EEC for any postponement of the November 16 date. If no prior agreement on rules were reached, he thought it very likely that the French would use our insistence on rules to justify a refusal on their part to go forward on November 16 and would pin the blame on our rigidity.

3.   That we had to avoid a crisis this week.

Mr. Roth contended that it was necessary to reach final agreement on agricultural rules this week and doubted that this could be done anyway. In his view, the EEC would not be ready with its exceptions list by November 16 and consequently would not agree to any agricultural rules, because to do so would bring its unpreparedness on exceptions

---

[1] Source: Johnson Library, Bator Papers, Kennedy Round, 1964–1965 I, Box 12. Secret. The source text bears no drafting information. The meeting was held in Herter's office.

[2] October 29.

into the open. He suggested, as an alternative course of action to Mr. Ball's, that the United States announce next week that considerable progress on agricultural rules has been made but that there are still areas of disagreement. The United States would table its exceptions on November 16, but on the assumption that the effort to arrive at agreed rules would go on, looking forward to the opening of detailed negotiations in January.

Mr. Bundy felt that we might say that after November 16 we would press for certain objectives within whatever rules were agreed upon. But he shared Mr. Ball's view that the precise wording of the rules made little difference; he believed we would have a difficult time meeting our agricultural objectives solely within the context of the Kennedy Round. He was chiefly concerned about the very serious danger of the French using lack of agreement on rules to fix the blame for delay on the United States.

Gov. Herter pointed out that there seemed to be only two points of disagreement between ourselves and the EEC on rules:

1. Whether soybeans and soybean oil should be subject to a commodity agreement. Our interests here seemed protected by the EEC's agreement that nothing in the rules should be construed as permitting present bindings to be broken.

2. Whether on fixed tariff items the rules should call for "reductions" or "liberalization", the latter being the wording of the May 1963 and 1964 Ministerial Resolutions.[3] On this point the Governor felt that "liberalization" would be acceptable, especially since the EEC knows that we will insist on overall reciprocity.

One important question, he emphasized, is whether we should table both our agricultural and industrial offers or just our industrial. In any case, he maintained, we must have a time limit for the EEC's making agricultural offers, or else we will have a Dillon Round situation again.

In the Governor's conversation with Mr. Blumenthal the night before, Mr. Blumenthal had urged strongly that nothing be foreclosed until he returns this weekend. He also wanted to know by Thursday whether the U.S. could give anything on rules with respect to "oilseeds" and the "liberalization-reduction" issue, and whether we wanted to table agricultural offers November 16.

A State Department draft message to Mr. Blumenthal was then considered. At Governor Herter's suggestion, it was changed to call for Mr. Blumenthal to try to obtain agreement ad referendum at the Thursday meeting. Mr. Roth stressed that an instruction calling for him to reach an

---

[3] Regarding the May 1963 resolutions, see footnote 2, Document 228. For text of the rules for the Kennedy Round negotiations adopted by the GATT Trade Negotiations Committee Ministerial meeting on May 6, 1964, see *American Foreign Policy: Current Documents, 1964*, pp. 1210–1213.

agreement would be extremely unfortunate. He reiterated his feeling that the rules should be left open till after the end of the year, when hopefully they would no longer be enmeshed in internal EEC politics. Mr. Johnson thought it was most unlikely that the EEC rule would be broadened and that the crucial thing was getting offers on the table.

Mr. Ball pointed out the larger political implications of this issue: if the U.S. could be accused of taking an overly rigid stand on agricultural rules, we would be very badly off over the MLF and any new overtures that the Administration might want to make. If the November 16 date were postponed, he thought it would spell the end of the Kennedy Round, since it would get entangled with the GPU issue.

It was agreed to send out the cable, as amended, and request Mr. Blumenthal to give his reaction as soon as possible. Meanwhile Governor Herter would discuss the issue with Secretary Freeman.

The cable as sent was Gatt 2213.[4]

---

[4] To Geneva, October 27. (Department of State, Central Files, FT 13–2 US)

---

255.   Memorandum of Conversation[1]

Washington, October 28, 1964.

PARTICIPANTS

STR:
Honorable Christian A. Herter
Honorable William M. Roth
Mr. Kenneth Auchincloss

White House:
Honorable McGeorge Bundy
Mr. Francis Bator

State:
Honorable George W. Ball
Honorable G. Griffith Johnson

Agriculture:
Honorable Charles S. Murphy
Mr. Raymond Ioanes

---

[1] Source: Johnson Library, Bator Papers, Kennedy Round, 1964–1965 I, Box 12. Secret. The source text bears no drafting information. The meeting was held in Herter's office.

Agricultural Rules for the Kennedy Round

Under Secretary Murphy acknowledged that members of the Agriculture Department were not of one mind on the position drafted the day before for the treatment of agriculture in light of the failure of bilateral talks with the EEC. One problem, he said, was that our public claims that we would insist on tying agriculture into the Kennedy Round have assumed political importance domestically. Does yesterday's cable,[2] he asked, represent a radical change in our policy?

No, Mr. Bundy replied, we would continue to hold in good faith to our policy of pressing firmly for the inclusion of agriculture in the Kennedy Round.

Gov. Herter went over some of the arguments brought out in the conversation the night before. Mr. Bundy stressed the overriding importance of not having the KR appear to be delayed by U.S. stubbornness, which could have serious effects on our overall Atlantic policy. The French clearly want to block the KR, he believed, and will pin the blame on us if they can. Domestically, it would be unacceptable to "uncouple" industry from agriculture in the negotiations, and that appeared to be what Ambassador Blumenthal was suggesting in his telegram that morning.[3]

Under Secretary Murphy asked what really is meant by "rules" on agriculture? Under Secretary Ball felt that they were abstractions with little practical effect.

Gov. Herter noted that Amb. Blumenthal had asked what to do if the EEC representatives now should go back on even the basic points they had agreed to. Mr. Bator thought that with Wyndham White as a witness, we would have an airtight case for avoiding the blame for such a breakdown.

Under Secretary Murphy asked Gov. Herter whether he thought we would lose any ground by taking the stand proposed. The Governor felt that we had not lost any ground but had failed to gain some. What we had hoped was to get some agreement in advance that would to an extent prejudge the EEC's offers. This had now proved impossible. In view of the importance of holding to the Nov. 16 date, he thought that we should now move forward.

Mr. Bundy added that he could not see that this choice was contrary to our agricultural interests since the alternative was a strong risk of killing the KR. If that happened, it would create the most favorable situation

---

[2] See footnote 4, Document 254.
[3] Reference is to Tagg 2420 from Geneva, October 28. (Department of State, Central Files, FT 7 GATT)

for the EEC to take unilateral action to cut back imports of U.S. farm products. The only thing we have going for us in getting agricultural concessions, he contended, is our industrial offers.

Under Secretary Murphy asked what was the next step, if industrial exceptions were tabled on Nov. 16th. Gov Herter pointed out that if we begin the "confrontation and justification" on industrial products in January, we must make up our minds as to how far we'll go ahead without the inclusion of agriculture. In his judgment, agriculture should be brought in soon after that time, and everyone should be clear on this. He was convinced that the prospects for getting reasonable agricultural offers from the EEC would be much improved if the grains price issue could be patched up. However, he shared Mr. Murphy's worry about how firm the United States will be in fighting for agriculture in the negotiations. Mr. Bundy observed that we could not make the basic decision on the role of agriculture. Only the President could do so, when we are further along with the negotiations. Mr. Murphy asked whether this decision now will prejudice the Presidential decision later, and Mr. Bundy replied that it would not.

Under Secretary Murphy asked what we would do if the EEC agrees, and then fails, to table its agricultural offers early in 1965. Mr. Bundy thought that question was too hypothetical to be answered now.

Mr. Murphy said that he would concur in the message, with trepidation. Gov. Herter noted that if the EEC tried to retract any of the points on which it has already agreed, we would be "in a new ball game."

Mr. Ioanes asked when we should table our agricultural exceptions list—on Nov. 16th or at some later date. Under Secretary Ball recommended the latter. We would then have the advantage of holding back our agricultural list until the EEC is ready to present its. However, we should offer to exchange both lists on 16th if the EEC (as seemed highly unlikely) were prepared to do so. Gov. Herter felt that this issue, as well as the question of how to present our decision domestically, should be discussed with Amb. Blumenthal when he arrived that weekend.

256. Editorial Note

On October 29, 1964, the White House released Presidential Statement No. 8 on expanding world trade. This statement was one of a series of ten statements on economic issues that on October 25, 1964, the President announced would be issued over the new few days. For text of the October 25 announcement, see *Public Papers of the Presidents of the United States: Lyndon B. Johnson, 1963–64*, Book II, pages 1426–1427.

After mentioning that the policy of trade liberalization "has served this country well," Presidential Statement No. 8 referred to the Trade Expansion Act of 1962 and the Johnson administration's full commitment "to its vigorous implementation." The statement further noted that the current sixth round of the GATT negotiations "may be lengthy, complex, and at times difficult, but we are prudently confident of fruitful results." Although it conceded that "special import difficulties confronting certain sections of our economy may at times require remedial actions" and cited the administration's measures to meet the problems of meat producers and apparel manufacturers, it hoped that such actions would be "the exception rather than the rule." For text of this statement, see ibid., pages 1518–1519.

---

257. Letter From Secretary of the Treasury Dillon to the Special Representative for Trade Negotiations (Herter)[1]

Washington, October 30, 1964.

Dear Chris:

I am sending you herewith a copy of the proposed amendments to the Treasury regulations under the Antidumping Act,[2] which the Treasury expects to publish in the *Federal Register* on or about December 1.[3] I am also enclosing a memorandum setting forth and analyzing the changes in these proposed amendments[4] made in response to the comments submitted on the proposals as published in the *Federal Register* on April 23, 1964.[5] This may be useful to your staff in identifying these changes.

The Treasury Department has carefully analyzed the comments submitted by all parties, and has a number of changes in those areas where the objections seemed valid. The amendments have not, however, been changed to reflect some of the most basic complaints registered

---

[1] Source: Kennedy Library, Herter Papers, Treasury Department, 8/1/64–10/30/64, Box 15. No classification marking. Received in Herter's office on November 3.

[2] Regarding the Antidumping Act, see footnote 3, Document 231. The proposed amendments are not attached.

[3] Published on December 5, 1964. (29 *Federal Register* 16320)

[4] The memorandum has not been found.

[5] 29 *Federal Register* 5474.

both by the State Department and by foreign governments and importer groups, although the most careful consideration was given to their submissions. I am confident that as long as Treasury continues to administer the regulations fairly and impartially, particularly the part relating to confidential information, the fears expressed as to disastrous results will be proved groundless.

These amendments have been framed with a full awareness of the likelihood that in the Kennedy Round negotiations our Government will be faced with the charge that the new regulations are a protectionist move on the part of the United States. I do not feel that such a charge would be at all warranted. A number of important changes have been made favoring foreign interests and the importers which, incidentally, have been the subject of strenuous attack by domestic interests. The regulations as a whole are designed to improve administration of the Anti-dumping Act and reflect a careful effort to work out legitimate problems on both sides. If Treasury should be remiss in its obligation to improve these regulations, in my judgment the next session of Congress might well see the passage of restrictive legislation in this field which would be far more damaging to our international trading position than those parts of the proposed regulations which the foreign interests and importers now appear to find objectionable.

With best wishes,

Sincerely,

Douglas Dillon

---

258.   Letter From Secretary of Commerce Hodges to the Special Representative for Trade Negotiations (Herter)[1]

Washington, October 30, 1964.

Dear Governor:

The Department of Commerce, along with other agencies, in its careful work on exceptions, has recognized that the linear tariff cut should apply to as many products as possible. This position, however,

---

[1] Source: Kennedy Library, Herter Papers, White House Subject File, Withdrawn Documents, Box 2. Secret. The source text was attached to Herter's November 4 reply to Hodges.

has assumed that other countries would act accordingly and that countries' exceptions would not include broad categories of products that cannot be justified in the confrontation procedure.

It appears certain, however, that the European Coal and Steel Community (ECSC) is not going to reduce its duties on steel products below the 6 to 7 percent average level that prevailed prior to February of this year. The only undecided issue before the Community is how this result should be achieved—by a binding of these 6 to 7 percent average rates or by reductions to this level from the increased "temporary" rates made in February of this year (9 percent average) or by reductions from the preharmonized rates of 1958 (14 percent average). No matter how this issue is decided, the ECSC will make no effective tariff cuts on steel products.

If the ECSC does not cut its effective duties on steel products, we do not believe that the United States should cut its duties. A linear cut on steel tariffs by the United States would be impossible to defend on economic or political grounds unless other countries, particularly the ECSC, were to take comparable action.

Unless the exclusion by the ECSC of tariff cuts on steel products had economic justification, it would be a breach of the negotiating rules on exceptions. As compared with the United States, the ECSC has no economic grounds for excepting steel from tariff cuts. The United States is the world's largest importer of steel and has been a net importer, on a quantity basis since 1958 and, on a value basis, in 1959 and since 1961. United States imports of all steel products in 1963 totalled 5.5. million tons and are expected to exceed well over 6 million tons in 1964. Net United States imports in 1963 were at the record level of 3.3 million tons. The Community, on the other hand, is not only the world's largest exporter of steel, but is also a heavy net exporter. Community exports of all steel products totalled 12.5 million tons in 1963. Net exports totalled 8.6 million tons.

As compared with the Community and other steel producing countries, the United States is an open market for steel. United States tariffs on steel are either comparable to, or lower than, those of other industrial countries. Furthermore, the United States imposes no additional charges, such as border taxes on imports. These taxes run as high as 25 percent in European countries and are imposed on the c.i.f. duty-paid value of imports. Their cumulative effect greatly increases the landed cost of United States exports. In addition, the United States market is not restricted by "gentlemen's agreements", which appear to prevail among other countries' steel producers. These agreements further protect domestic markets to the detriment of our steel exports. Such factors are relevant to any consideration of tariff cuts, particularly because of the very similar cost structures of the steel industries in all producing countries.

I recommend very strongly and emphatically that the United States should not lower its duties on steel unless the Europeans make comparable cuts in its 6 to 7 percent rates. I am not, however, recommending that we put steel on our initial exceptions list but that we withdraw steel offers from the negotiations if and when it becomes clearly evident that the Europeans are not going to cut the rates that were in effect until February of this year.

Earlier this year the ECSC proposed a harmonization of steel tariffs among the major steel producing countries.[2] I understand that this proposal is being studied through a subcommittee of the Trade Staff Committee. I believe the question of harmonization should continue to be explored, for harmonization might turn out to be a desirable objective after the facts are known.

I would appreciate having my recommendation above considered at the November 5 meeting of the Trade Expansion Act Advisory Committee for the purpose of agreeing on a firm U.S. position for the treatment of steel in the trade negotiations. If you agree, I am enclosing copies of this letter for transmittal to other members of the Committee in advance of this meeting.[3]

Sincerely yours,

Luther H. Hodges

---

[2] Harmonized tariffs, levied by the European Coal and Steel Community on steel imports from non-member countries, "are set by each member country according to production costs at a level above the minimum rate (Benelux) and below the maximum rate (Italy). Steel tariffs thus differ from the EEC's CET [common external tariff] rates which are fixed on the basis of the arithmetical average of the national customs duties in force on January 1, 1957." (European Community Information Service, Basic Glossary of Terms for "Kennedy Round," January 1964; Kennedy Library, Herter Papers, Glossary, Box 9)

[3] In his November 4 reply (see footnote 1 above), Herter expressed "considerable sympathy" for Hodges' position but thought it "better not to try to settle this issue at the Advisory Committee meeting on November 5, which as you know will be devoted to the initial exceptions list that the United States will table on November 16." He expected that the proposal would be revived after the exceptions lists are tabled, if the ECSC does not offer "a reduction from the rates existing before February 1964."

259. Letter From the Secretary of Commerce's Deputy for Textile Programs (Love) to the Special Representative for Trade Negotiations (Herter)[1]

Washington, November 2, 1964.

Dear Ambassador Herter:

Following your letter of October 26 to Secretary Hodges[2] and our conversations last Friday,[3] Secretary Hodges asked me to recommend that you accept three changes in the recommendations made to you by the TEC on textile products to be placed on the exemptions list. The first of these concerns cotton textiles, the second concerns wool textile items which the TEC did not include in its recommendations, and the third concerns specific duties on wool textiles.

These changes in the TEC position are necessary for political reasons and for international bargaining. The textile industry and Congressional leaders were told that textiles would remain apart from the Kennedy Round. In addition, we should not discard any portion of those things we have to bargain as we will probably find them useful in accomplishing the Administration objectives of maintaining or achieving international arrangements.

1. *Cotton Textiles.* That cotton textile tariffs be negotiated only if the offering is made with the proviso that we have the right to restore duty reductions if there is a lapse in arrangements regarding international trade in cotton textiles. (Cotton textile trade available for negotiation is valued at $246 million.)

It will undoubtedly be an Administration objective to renew the Long Term Arrangement for Cotton Textiles. Preserving our right to restore duty reductions could be an important bargaining tool to accomplish this difficult objective.

It will of course be disappointing to the cotton textile industry when it learns, as it will eventually, that its duties are being reduced, but this action can be made saleable if it is understood that some international arrangement is a condition to the reductions.

As you know, the TEC agreed to inform other countries that an offering "takes into consideration the existence of satisfactory arrangements for the orderly marketing of cotton textiles". This was as far as it was possible to go and keep cotton textiles off the exceptions list. However, the

---

[1] Source: Johnson Library, National Security File, Subject File, Trade—General, vol. 2 [all], Box 47. Confidential.

[2] Not further identified, but the letter may be the one sent to Secretaries Dillon and Rusk; see Document 253.

[3] October 30.

TEC procedure would require us to pay compensation or accept retaliation if it became necessary to restore cotton textile duties because no international arrangements were continued. The procedure would also give away a possible bargaining tool for maintaining or renewing the present arrangement.

2. *Omitted Wool Textile Ad Valorem Duties.* That the ad valorem duties on certain wool textiles which the TEC recommended for the exceptions list ($161 million) be enlarged to include wool textiles which were omitted from the exceptions list ($7 million).

Out of a total $180 million wool textiles available for negotiation, $12 million of handwoven articles and rags are not recommended for the exceptions. There are $7 million of wool textiles which were not included on the exceptions list by the Trade Executive Committee, principally tufted wool floor coverings, tapestry and upholstery fabrics, and blankets, which should be on the list.

You know the difficulties already encountered in trying to meet the Administration commitment to try to negotiate an international wool textile agreement. Every bargaining tool we possess will be needed for this negotiation. It does not make sense to reduce any portion of our tariffs, thereby assisting the foreign exporters in whatever small way without helping to achieve our own objectives.

It is entirely possible that, because wool textiles are on our exceptions list an international arrangement can be negotiated as part of the Kennedy Round. The removal of some of the items from the exceptions list would weaken our position for making such a wool textile arrangement all inclusive, to prevent possible circumvention of the arrangement.

3. *Wool Textile Specific Duties.* That a compromise be made on the specific duties on wool products (on which TEC has recommended no exception), and that these duties be excepted beyond a reduction of 25 percent.

As you know, the specific duty on wool textiles was set to offset the duty on raw wool, because raw wool prices in the United States are set by the cost of the imported portion. This is not true of other fibers. Over the years increasing use of blends with man-made fibers and reused wool have increased the protection afforded by the specific duties beyond that for raw wool. Therefore, to reduce raw wool and wool textile duties equally, as the TEC recommended would reduce wool textile protection.

Items come in as wool textiles containing as much as 40 percent by value of other fibers (for instance cotton or man-made fibers). On this percentage the importer must pay the equivalent of the raw wool duty, though the foreign manufacturer does not have a corresponding raw material cost advantage. This element of the duty is protective.

However, there was an understanding in 1947 that wool textile specific duties and raw wool duties should be treated equally. Since then conditions of trade have changed and, especially, the compositions of wool fabrics have changed. The loss of protection from a cut in specific duties would not now be offset by lower raw material costs produced by an equal cut in wool fiber duties.[4] It is impossible to estimate accurately what the offset would be on an overall basis, but it is probably about half.

The TSC recommended that raw wool duty reductions be offered only if we could be released from the 1947 understanding. This is the ideal position from the point of view of putting us in the best bargaining position for an arrangement. This might be a possible alternate solution for meeting the Administration commitment to help the industry.

Unless an arrangement proves impossible to negotiate we could agree to a compromise between the TSC and TEC positions, that raw wool duty reductions be offered if the specific duty reductions can be made proportionately only half as large. This should, on the average, preserve the present bargaining position for an international agreement, yet treat exporting countries fairly.

The textile area is one that has special problems and political implications, and must therefore be given a treatment that is exceptional to the general policies and aims of the Administration in the Kennedy Round. For this reason, Secretary Hodges and I hope that these recommendations will be acceptable to you.

Sincerely,

James S. Love, Jr.

---

[4] At the end of a long, unsigned memorandum on the compensating duty for raw wool tariff, November 3, the following points were made concerning this sentence in Love's letter:

"1. On many products there is no bonus protection factor (all tops and most yarns).

"2. The AVE of the compensatory duty for the main body of trade averages about six percentage points. A cut of 50% would amount to three percentage points. Mr. Love suggests a cut of 25% only, amounting to 1-1/2 percentage points. Therefore, the most the "bonus protection" could be in his case would be 1-1/2 points, if all domestic production were blends. But that is impossible. Therefore, the bonus protection factor retained by his suggestion must be less than 1-1/2 percentage points, and probably of the order of 1/2 percentage point. That is miniscule protection compared to the negotiating price we would have to pay."

260.   Circular Telegram From the Department of State to Certain Posts[1]

Washington, November 2, 1964, 1:11 p.m.

800. From Herter. For Tuthill, Brussels. You should tell Rey tonight that the answer to his question is affirmative and that the U.S. intends to deposit its exception list November 16.[2]

In addition, you should emphasize that of course negotiations, to be successful, must ultimately move forward on both industrial and agricultural fronts. You should also emphasize that we are prepared to continue discussions on agriculture at any time. We would hope that in any case this can be done in time to open substantive discussions on both industry and agriculture in early 1965.

You should tell him that we are informing Wyndham White and other key governments of this intention tonight and tomorrow morning. Also show him following press release which we intend to issue here 9:00 AM Washington time and which you should release at 3:00 PM Brussels time November 3. Ask Rey to hold this information in strictest confidence until that time.

"The United States has notified the Executive Secretary of the GATT; the Commission of the European Economic Community; and its major trading partners that it is prepared to table its industrial exceptions list, together, with other key countries, in the GATT on November 16, the date earlier agreed to in GATT.

Discussions as to the treatment of agricultural products continue. It is expected that the substantive negotiations on both industrial and agricultural products will begin at an early date in 1965."

For Evans, Geneva.

Inform Wyndham White as above this evening.

For Other Posts.

Inform governments as above by 3:00 PM Brussels time November 3 if possible. Further guidance follows.[3]

Rusk

---

[1] Source: Department of State, Central Files, FT 13–2 US. Confidential; Immediate. Drafted by Auchincloss; cleared by Herter, G. Johnson (E), Hinton (EUR/RPE), Bator, R. McNeill (Commerce), and R. Ioanes (Agriculture); and approved by Roth. Sent to Brussels for USEC, Geneva for the Mission, Bonn, The Hague, Paris, Rome, Luxembourg, London, Tokyo, Bern, Stockholm, Copenhagen, Oslo, and Ottawa.

[2] Rey asked Tuthill that question in Brussels on October 30, as reported in Ecbus 440 from Brussels, October 30. (Ibid.)

[3] Circular telegram 801 to 14 posts, November 2, stated, among other things, that "Bonn and The Hague in particular should make point that present US action is intended in the first instance to facilitate completion of EEC exception list exercise for November 16 date." (Ibid.)

261. Telegram From the Mission to the European Communities to the Department of State[1]

Brussels, November 3, 1964, 4 p.m.

Ecbus 453. Ref: Dept circ 800 Nov 2.[2] Due to absence of Rey, I carried out instruction in reftel with Mansholt at 2345 Nov 2 and was able to confirm with Rey early this morning.

Both Mansholt and Rey welcomed US position and emphasized that Agric discussions must continue. Mansholt stated that even though substantive issues could not be resolved until "early in '65" nevertheless much preparatory work needs to be done. For example, he felt that work should be pushed in international commodity groups for grains, meats and dairy products. He mentioned this by way of illustration and reflected view that also in other areas agric work should continue.

Mansholt emphasized that he wanted this done for both technical and psychological reasons. As Washington is aware, Mansholt insists that agric must be effective part of Kennedy Round. He wishes progress to proceed along parallel lines for both agric and industry. He feels that in addition to technical reasons that it is psychologically essential that movement continue in field of agric.

I told Mansholt that I hoped he would also pay attention to size and content of Community exceptions list. If all of key countries deposit moderate sized lists then there will be in prospect a really significant Kennedy Round. If this in fact is prospect, one can anticipate continued interest and drive on part of industrialists (especially German) for a successful Kennedy Round. It will be evident that in order to obtain this objective that there will have to be a resolution of agric problems early next year. This might help them to use their efforts to see that there is settlement within Community before end of year which will allow Community to negotiate meaningfully in field of agric. Mansholt agreed, saying he would follow carefully exceptions list discussions, and recognized that for both purposes of industry and agric it is essential that lists be kept as small as possible.

I also discussed with Mansholt question as to whether with a renewal of discussions on agric rules it would be desirable to broaden participation, under Wyndham White's chairmanship, to include other important agric countries. Mansholt felt that this would probably be desirable not only as means of bringing in other countries who have important substantive interests but also in order to reduce public posture

---

[1] Source: Department of State, Central Files, FT 13–2 US. Confidential; Priority. Repeated to Bonn, The Hague, London, Luxembourg for the Embassy and USEC, Paris for the Embassy and USRO, Rome, and Geneva.

[2] Document 260.

of Community-US confrontation over next few weeks. Mansholt stressed that, while he was anxious to go ahead on technical discussion in next few weeks, Community of course will not be prepared to go to heart of pol issues in field of agric until early next year.

Rey's comments this morning were fully consistent with Mansholt's of last night. However, they were somewhat more specific regarding rules.

He stated that Committee III would meet Nov 4 after which there would be discussion amongst PermDels and later in Council of Mins meeting on Nov 9–11. He felt that Blumenthal and Rabot-Hijzen should probably meet again after Council of Mins meeting—presumably Nov 12 or 13. He felt that it probably would be desirable to have Agric Committee meet in order to bring in other interested countries. Rey also discussed question of written agric rules. Rey said that in his view, subject to what comes out of Committee III and Council of Mins next week, it would be desirable to renew attempts to obtain written agric rules. He reiterated that Commission does not withdraw any of tentative agreements reached during last two discussions in Geneva with Blumenthal. He hopes that after Nov 9–11 Council of Mins meeting, it will be possible to renew discussions starting from where we stood at end of meeting on Oct 29 and attempt to achieve a written understanding building on that base. I told Rey that, while I did not know what our specific suggestions would be, I was sure Washington would agree with his and Mansholt's objective of continuing to make progress on agric over next few weeks.

Tuthill

---

262.   **Memorandum From the Special Representative for Trade Negotiations (Herter) to President Johnson**[1]

Washington, November 9, 1964.

SUBJECT

Authority to Offer Tariff Concessions in the Kennedy Round

The purpose of this memorandum is to request that you authorize me, under the Trade Expansion Act of 1962 (TEA), to offer in the Kennedy Round tariff concessions within the limitations described below.

---

[1] Source: Johnson Library, National Security File, NSC Histories, Kennedy Round Crisis, April–June, Tabs 1–6, Box 52. Secret. Drafted by John B. Rehm on November 9. The date November 10, 1964, is handwritten on the approved line at the end of the source text.

All the legal requirements of the TEA pertaining to such offers have been satisfied. In particular, both the inter-agency Trade Information Committee established under this Office and the Tariff Commission have held hearings on the public list of articles issued by President Kennedy last fall.[2] The results of these hearings were made available to you last spring and have been carefully reviewed by this Office and the other agencies concerned with the trade agreements program, most recently at a Cabinet-level meeting of the Trade Expansion Act Advisory Committee.[3]

With respect to non-agricultural articles, we have announced our readiness to table offers on November 16, but only if other key participants, and especially the European Economic Community, are prepared to do the same.[4] Should they not do so, the United States offer of tariff concessions on these articles will not be disclosed to any participant in the Kennedy Round.

With respect to agricultural articles, we have been unable so far to reach international agreement on the basis on which offers of tariff concessions are to be made. Therefore, the offers to be tabled by the United States on November 16 will exclude agricultural articles. By approving this memorandum, however, you will authorize me to offer tariff concessions on agricultural articles at the appropriate time.

Any trade agreement which is negotiated on the basis of offers authorized by this memorandum and pursuant to the general negotiating authority already vested in me will be concluded subject to your final approval. During the negotiations, we may find it appropriate or necessary to hold back, reduce, or withdraw certain of these offers. On the other hand, it may become necessary for me to seek your authorization to offer additional concessions.

For your information, there is attached a detailed description of the background and important elements of the trade negotiations (Annex A).[5]

---

[2] The Trade Information Committee, consisting of a chairman (appointed by the Special Representative for Trade Negotiations from his office) and officials designated by the Secretaries of Agriculture, Commerce, Defense, Interior, Labor, State, and the Treasury, held concurrent but separate hearings from those of the Tariff Commission. For further information, see U.S. Tariff Commission, *Operation of the Trade Agreements Program, 16th Report, July 1963–June 1964* (TC Publication 164, Washington, 1966), p. 44.

[3] No record of this meeting has been found.

[4] See Document 260.

[5] Annex A, not printed, outlined agricultural, nonagricultural, and nontariff barrier negotiations, procedures, U.S. exceptions, the nonparticipants rule (exclusion from negotiation of products, such as petroleum, of nonparticipants), scope of recommended exceptions, special authorities under the Trade Expansion Act for the President in certain circumstances to reduce tariffs by 100 percent, and participation in the negotiations mainly of countries adhering to the linear rule of 50 percent reductions, namely the EEC, Japan, the United Kingdom, Austria, Denmark, Finland, Norway, Sweden, Switzerland, the United States, and possibly Portugal.

With the concurrence of the heads of the other agencies concerned, I now recommend that you authorize me, as your Special Representative for Trade Negotiations:

1. To offer under section 201 of the TEA a reduction of 50% in duties on all dutiable articles, with the following exceptions:

(a) Economic exceptions: Articles which should be partially or wholly reserved from a 50% reduction in duties in order to avoid the possibility of serious injury to domestic industries or the threat of impairing the national security (Annex A–1).[6]

(b) Mandatory exceptions: Articles on which the TEA prohibits the reduction or elimination of duties (Annex A–2).

(c) Technical exceptions: Articles on which a 50% reduction in duties cannot be made for one of a number of technical reasons: e.g., part of the TEA authority was used in the last round of trade negotiations (Annex A–3).

2. To offer the elimination of duties on the following articles:

(a) Articles with a duty of 5% or less which qualify for elimination of duty under section 202 of the TEA (Annex A–4).

(b) Agricultural articles which so qualify under section 212 of the TEA (Annex A–5).

(c) Tropical agricultural or forestry articles which so qualify under section 213 of the TEA (Annex A–6).

3. Where the reduction or elimination of duties is not proposed, to offer under section 201 of the TEA not to increase existing duties on dutiable articles or not to impose duties on articles now duty-free.[7]

Christian A. Herter[8]

---

[6] Annexes A–1 through A–6 have not been found.

[7] The tariff concessions which would become effective pursuant to a trade agreement concluded in the Kennedy Round would in no way affect the right of any industry, firm, or group of workers to seek escape-clause relief or other forms of adjustment assistance under the TEA. [Footnote in the source text.]

[8] Printed from a copy that bears this typed signature.

263.   Memorandum of Telephone Conversation[1]

Washington, November 11, 1964.

Governor Herter and McGeorge Bundy

Mr. Bundy telephoned Governor Herter and advised him that the President had signed the document November 10[2] for the U.S. exceptions to be submitted on November 16th.

The President had noted Secretary Hodges' appeal,[3] and was going to discuss it with him today. However, there was very little likelihood that the President would have any change of heart, and Mr. Bundy pointed out to the President that if he did, he would have to listen to everybody else on Thursday and Friday.

Mr. Bundy said that the document would not go into effect, however, until tonight, after the President had talked to Secretary Hodges. Mr. Bundy said he would be calling the ranch later today to confirm there was no change in the President's thinking, and that the signed document would be sent over to Governor Herter the first thing in the morning.

Governor Herter expressed his displeasure on Secretary Hodges' tactics with respect to the textile question. Mr. Bundy agreed, but added that in view of the overwhelming agreement at the Cabinet level TEAAC meeting to support Governor Herter and STR recommendations, that Secretary Hodges' arguments would not be persuasive. Governor Herter added it was a deliberate violation of the GATT commitment.

Governor Herter then turned to another subject; namely, the refusal of Mexico to draw up a trade agreement with us. Mr. Bundy said that Tom Mann was going to see the President tomorrow, and that perhaps Governor Herter would want to discuss this matter with him before he left for the Ranch. Governor Herter said he would.

Mr. Bundy then mentioned the clothespins, and said that the press release perhaps should be changed to say the President, on Governor Herter's recommendation, had approved it. Governor Herter agreed it would be a good idea. The President approved the clothespins document.[4]

---

[1] Source: Kennedy Library, Herter Papers, White House Subject File, Withdrawn Documents, Box 9, Exceptions Folder 1, Box 3. Secret. The source text bears Herter's handwritten initials.

[2] At this point, the source text bears the handwritten notation, "November 10." This reference may be to Herter's November 9 memorandum (Document 262), which may have been a draft of the final version sent to the President. No November 10 text has been found. For further information on President Johnson's decision, see Document 292.

[3] No formal appeal from Hodges to the President at this time has been found.

[4] Not found.

264.   Memorandum of Conversation[1]

Washington, November 13, 1964, 10:30 a.m.

PARTICIPANTS

Foreign Minister Halvard Lange
Ambassador Engen
Mr. Olaf Bucher-Johannesen

Governor Herter
Mr. Dallas Jones, Country Committee III
Mr. Eric Youngquist, EUR/BNA
Mr. Kenneth Auchincloss

The discussion centered on the many uncertainties involved in the current internal EEC debate on the Kennedy Round exception list and grains price unification. Mr. Lange was fearful that the EEC would claim a number of exceptions that would hit Norwegian trade and thus force Norway to withdraw some of its offers.

Governor Herter stressed the United States' concern that even if grains price unification is agreed within the EEC, the French will insist on a rigid application of the montant de soutien in the Kennedy Round. This would leave the United States with increased restrictions on 28 percent of its exports and would force it to make heavy withdrawals.

The Foreign Minister asked how long a delay the United States would accept before negotiations on agriculture began. The delay should certainly not be indefinite, Governor Herter replied. January or February of next year was about the limit. He pointed out that there has already been an adverse reaction among domestic farm groups to the United States decision to proceed with industrial exceptions lists on November 16th. The longer agricultural negotiations are delayed, the more hostile they will become.

The Governor made clear that the United States will put its exception list in Wyndham White's hands on November 16th but will ask him not to release it to others unless all key countries have also submitted their lists. Governor Herter added that the United States list was surprisingly short.

Governor Herter asked how Norway would be affected by the British import surcharge. Mr. Lange replied that Norway appeared to be the hardest hit of all the EFTA countries, particularly among industries that had just begun to develop British markets. Norway did not want to embarrass the UK, but it had to insist that the surcharges would really be temporary and would not have a permanent effect on British prices.

---

[1] Source: Kennedy Library, Herter Papers, Memoranda of Conversation, 7/25/63–4/21/66, Box 10. Limited Official Use. The source text bears no drafting information except the date November 16. The meeting was held in Herter's office.

265. Memorandum From the Agricultural Trade Representative, Office of the Special Representative for Trade Negotiations (Hedges) to the Special Representative for Trade Negotiations (Herter)[1]

Washington, November 19, 1964.

SUBJECT

U.S. attitude toward grain price unification

As you pointed out in the memorandum handed Erhard in June,[2] the problem of grain price unification cannot be seen in isolation.

The French appear to have made agreement on grain price unification indispensable to progress on agriculture in the Kennedy Round. Unless as a result the Community is willing to negotiate access arrangements for grains and reductions in trade barriers for other products, the grain price decision alone will not advance the Kennedy Round.

The wrong posture on our part could tend to freeze the Community in its present rigid position which prevents effective negotiation on agricultural products. We should therefore continue to emphasize the interconnection between grain prices and the decisions needed to advance agriculture in the Kennedy Round.

1. The grain price levels under consideration are so high as to stimulate Community grain production at the expense of imports. Some sort of access arrangements would be required, therefore, to assure continued grain imports by the Community, as you told Erhard in June.

2. *The Community position.* The Commission has repeatedly stated that price levels within the Community are the key to access to its market. Their negotiating proposal consists of an offer to bind (under the narrow conditions they prescribe) their level of domestic prices, product by product, after such prices have unilaterally been agreed upon among the member states. Mansholt recently said the Commission's negotiating mandate is predicated on price. It cannot be changed.

Unqualified U.S. support for grain price unification would likely be interpreted by the Commission as acceptance of their negotiating proposal and would encourage them to hold rigidly to their present position.

3. *Italian situation.* Unconditional U.S. support of grain price unification would make it all the more difficult to secure Italian cooperation in negotiating agricultural trade liberalization.

---

[1] Source: Kennedy Library, Herter Papers, Grain Negotiations, Box 9. No classification marking. The source text bears Herter's initials.

[2] Reference may be to Document 239, although no other evidence has been found to indicate that a copy of that document was given to Erhard.

Mansholt grain price proposals would raise Italian feed costs at least 40 per cent with disastrous effects on Italian production and consumption of livestock products. They are bitterly opposed to the levels proposed for feed grains. U.S. unconditional support would undermine the Italian position. We also have a strong interest in feed grain prices being set at levels substantially below what has been proposed by Mansholt.

The Italians already feel they are penalized by the Common Agricultural Policy. Italian agricultural exports are mostly horticultural. These were bound at fixed tariffs in the Dillon Round whereas the principal agricultural production of the other member countries enjoys the greater protection of variable levies. It is the Italians primarily who have already blocked the Community from showing any willingness to negotiate reductions in fixed tariffs. Indeed one of the results of the Community negotiating proposal would be to extend the variable levy system to the present fixed tariff items. If they are forced to again be penalized by higher feed grain prices, the Italians will oppose all the more firmly any liberalization in other sectors.

IH

266. **Letter From Secretary of the Treasury Dillon to Secretary of Commerce Hodges**[1]

Washington, December 4, 1964.

Dear Luther:

Your letter of December 2, 1964, asks where we stand on the Canadian auto parts question.[2]

In a meeting held in George Ball's office on Monday, November 23, which you were unable to attend, there was full agreement that countervailing duties should be imposed in early January if the problem arising from the Canadian rebate plan has not been solved before that time.[3]

---

[1] Source: Washington National Records Center, RG 40, Secretary of Commerce Files: FRC 69 A 6828, Treasury Department. No classification marking.

[2] Hodges' December 2 letter to Dillon is ibid.

[3] No other record of this November 23 meeting has been found.

Before taking such action, Treasury would, of course, advise the White House and the Departments of State and Commerce.

With best wishes,

Sincerely,

Douglas

---

267. Memorandum From the President's Special Assistant for National Security Affairs (Bundy) to President Johnson[1]

Washington, December 9, 1964.

SUBJECT

Wool Textiles

1. Pursuant to your instructions, I have reached an agreement with the Prime Minister on the way in which we will treat the wool textile matter.[2] It is agreed that we will both say on demand that you have raised the question with him, that you proposed a meeting of the representatives of the two governments to discuss a possible conference with Italy and Japan, and that the Prime Minister has agreed to consider this proposal. (It is not likely that the British will accept this particular way of going about it, which gives them great difficulties. I think they will agree, in sum, to continuing discussions among experts on both sides.)

2. In return, the Prime Minister asks to be able to say that he raised with you the problems created for British shipping by some of our rules and regulations. I agreed to this on the condition that your own position should be fully protected.

[1] Source: Johnson Library, National Security File, Subject File, Trade—General, vol. 2 [all], Box 47. No classification marking.
[2] Documentation on British Prime Minister Wilson's meetings with President Johnson and other U.S. officials in Washington, December 7–9, is scheduled for publication in *Foreign Relations*, 1964–1968, volume XII.

3. I am telling Mike Feldman that this mission has been accomplished and that we can expect in due course to hear back from the British.[3]

Mcg. B.[4]

---

[3] In a December 9 memorandum to Feldman, Bundy reported that in proposing to Wilson a U.S.–U.K. conference on wool textiles, "the President has carried out his undertaking to Senator Pastore." Bundy believed that the British would not agree to "the particular kind of conference with the particular terms of reference" suggested by the President, but at least "what the President said to Senator Pastore he would do he has done." (Johnson Library, National Security File, Subject File, Trade—General, vol. 2 [2 of 2], Box 47)

[4] Printed from a copy that bears these typed initials.

---

268. Memorandum From the President's Special Assistant for National Security Affairs (Bundy) and Francis M. Bator of the National Security Council Staff to President Johnson[1]

Washington, December 16, 1964.

SUBJECT

European Agricultural Deal

1. The six EEC (Common Market) countries agreed yesterday to establish a common market in grains, in 1967, with support prices fixed part way between the low French and high German prices, some 60% above world market prices. We don't yet know the details, but grain producers and experts in the Department of Agriculture are likely to come down hard against the decision as a serious threat to U.S. agricultural exports. We think this is natural; we also think they are likely to overstate their case.

2. The truth is that the 1965–1970 prospects for our grain sales to the Common Market (although not for our agricultural exports as a whole) have never been good. This new agreement simply confirms what was bound to happen in any case.

(1) Making five-year forecasts is an uncertain business, but a recent USDA exercise indicates that, with the newly agreed high support

---

[1] Source: Johnson Library, Bator Papers, Kennedy Round, 1964–1965 I, Box 12. Confidential.

prices, U.S. grain exports to the EEC may fall by 1970 by as much as $140 million, from $380 million in 1961/64 to some $240 million. Matched against total U.S. agricultural exports of $5.6 billion in 1963 the estimated loss is small. But it will hurt.

(2) Those who may blame the specifics of the new EEC policy will miss the point. The heart of the matter is:

a. the determination of individual European governments to protect their farmers' incomes largely through price supports, and

b. the technological revolution in European agriculture. Europe's farmers today are about where our farmers were a generation ago, but they are catching up fast. Even if common prices were set at the low, French end of the EEC spectrum—which would cause a revolution in Germany—our sales of grain to the EEC would still shrink by some $90 million by 1970 (a tentative estimate by the Economic Research Service of USDA).

(3) Our announced U.S. objective has been to maintain our recent percentage share in the EEC grain market. This target, set under pressure from Agriculture, has never been realistic. Given the support prices that are politically inevitable in Europe, it would require the Six to stockpile or give away, by 1970, some $325 million of imported grain each year. The central fact—which some of the agriculture people tend to ignore—is that we do not have the bargaining power to make the Common Market import $325 million of grain a year beyond its needs.

(4) With the politics of agriculture just as tough in Western Europe as here, our leverage on the grain price deal has been minimal. Agriculture has wanted us to say that we will not negotiate on industry in the Kennedy Round unless the internal agricultural arrangements of the EEC are favorable to U.S. agriculture. This threat simply wouldn't work vis-à-vis the French. They are protectionist across the board, and they have been in the driver's seat in Brussels. More generally, we do not have the cards to force Europe to keep its farmers poor on our behalf.

3. Moreover, there are some real and reasonable answers to U.S. agricultural worries.

(1) Before we finally strike a bargain in Geneva, across the entire front including industry, we shall have a fair chance to get some concessions on the way the Europeans run their grain scheme, so as to hold down their production and maximize their consumption. We will not throw in the towel. (On the other hand, we must not expect too much. The Six had a tough time striking *their* bargain, and they are not in a mood to tamper with the package.)

(2) More important: increased exports of other farm products, and of grain to non-EEC markets, will much more than offset the drop in sales of grain to the Community. It is expected that U.S. exports of farm products to our 14 largest commercial markets abroad, including the EEC,

will rise from $2.8 billion in 1961 to $3.4 billion in 1970. Even to the EEC, the *total* of our agricultural sales is expected to increase.

4. Apart from the economics, German agreement on a grain price represents a clear gain in terms of Atlantic politics. For over a year now, the Germans have been in the Common Market doghouse for failure to perform on their promises on agriculture.

The shoe is now on the other foot. The Germans are in a much better position:

(1) to stand up to French buffeting in cooperating with us on NATO matters, offset purchases, money arrangements, and the like;
(2) to take the lead within the Community in working for a large industrial tariff cut—in which they share with us a political as well as an economic interest, and to which the protectionist-minded French are distinctly cool. They may even be able to strengthen our hand a bit on the agricultural side.

We *cannot* be sure that the Germans will in fact stand up to the French. But we *can* be sure that before this agreement their bargaining position in Europe was hopeless.

5. Much of the above is bitter medicine for some of Orville Freeman's people. (Freeman has himself always tried to see both sides.) They may want Herter to dig in his heels and make unbargainable demands at Brussels. The danger in that is that we may paint ourselves into a corner and lose the chance for a really profitable deal on industry without making a nickel for agriculture.

If we are to stay loose, Herter will need a signal about not overplaying his hand in Geneva. I will give him such a signal on an interim basis, but before you set our final policy, you ought to hear from all sides. We'll arrange a meeting for January, if you're willing, and we'll get the arguments on both sides in order beforehand. Orville agrees to this procedure.

McG. B.
F. M. B.

Go ahead[2]

---

[2] This option is checked, and typed in under this line are the words: "(The President checked)".

269. Letter From Secretary of Commerce Hodges to President Johnson[1]

Washington, December 18, 1964.

Dear Mr. President:

As Secretary Dillon indicated in his December 9 memorandum to you on the balance of payments,[2] time did not permit a review of the final draft by the Cabinet Committee on Balance of Payments.[3] I would like to call your attention to certain supplementary points which I think are important.

First, as the memorandum states, our export performance in 1964 was very good indeed. For the full year 1964, merchandise exports are expected to be about $2.8 billion above 1963, and the merchandise trade surplus (exports minus imports) will be in the neighborhood of $6.2 billion, up $2.2 billion over 1963.

This good export performance is in large part a result of our export expansion program, I feel certain, and consequently we should continue to press ahead with a variety of measures which can make the export expansion effort even more effective.

(1) For example, although we have made some progress toward making our credit terms competitive with those of other countries, in many ways the policies of the Export-Import Bank still leave our exporters at a distinct disadvantage in world markets.

(2) We should give serious consideration to an export tax rebate system comparable to that used by European countries.

(3) We should consider the establishment of an export executives corps, which would enlist the skills of the private business community as a very useful adjunct to our commercial officers overseas.

Secretary Dillon's memorandum contains the forecast of a drop in our trade surplus next year based on a decline in the rate of increase in our exports and a more rapid increase in our imports. I believe that much can be done to offset the unfavorable impact that such possible results would have on our balance of payments problem by aggressively pursuing the opportunities that lie in the export expansion area. It is for this reason that I have written this letter to call your attention to certain of the measures which I think we should seriously explore in our efforts to keep our exports growing as rapidly as possible.

---

[1] Source: Washington National Records Center, RG 40, Secretary of Commerce Files: FRC 69 A 6828, Chronological Copies, September–December. No classification marking. Drafted by R. H. Holton on December 17 and rewritten by Hodges.

[2] Not found.

[3] Document 20.

I am sending a copy of this letter to Secretary Dillon.

Respectfully yours,

Luther H. Hodges[4]

---

[4] Printed from a copy that indicates Hodges signed the original.

---

270. Letter From the Special Representative for Trade Negotiations (Herter) to Jean Rey, Member of the Commission of the European Economic Community[1]

Washington, December 21, 1964.

Dear Mr. Rey:

May I offer my congratulations to you and your fellow commissioners on the swiftness with which the Community decided upon common grains prices at the Council meeting this month. Now that the important internal question regarding unified grain price has been settled, I trust that we are in a position to move forward with the agricultural phase of the Kennedy Round negotiations.

You will recall that I wrote President Hallstein on July 21 to express the hope that your negotiators would be enabled to act more flexibly in order to achieve a mutual agreement on the treatment of agriculture in the negotiations.[2] I was gratified by the statement in his reply to the effect

---

[1] Source: Kennedy Library, Herter Papers, Grain Negotiations, Box 9. Personal. The text of the letter was transmitted in circular telegram 1155, December 21, with Herter's instructions to Tuthill to deliver the letter to Commissioner Rey. (Department of State, Central Files, FT 13–2 US) In Ecbus 657 from Brussels, December 23, Tuthill reported that he delivered the letter that morning to Rey, who made some preliminary comments and added he would provide an "initial written reply" the same day and a more formal reply in January after discussing the letter with the other Commissioners. (Ibid.) Rey's initial reply was transmitted in Ecbus 664 from Brussels, December 23. (Ibid.) In early January Rey responded that the Commissioners would be happy to receive Herter at the end of January. They expressed "some surprise" at the contents of Herter's letter but wanted to continue discussions on grains between the two delegations in Geneva. (Ecbus 710 from Brussels, January 13; ibid.)

[2] See Document 244.

that the Commission agreed that no effort should be spared to bring about the success of the Kennedy Round.[3]

In past discussions it has become clear that more flexibility is required on the part of the EEC negotiators. We are particularly concerned about the montant de soutien formula, which neither the United States nor, as far as we know, any other GATT member accepts as a general negotiating formula. We continue to believe firmly that genuine trade liberalization in agriculture must be achieved in the Kennedy Round, and mere binding of a montant de soutien would not accomplish this purpose. Our negotiators have also indicated our readiness to include in the negotiations agricultural support measures wherever appropriate and justified.

Despite the lack of real progress in agreeing on negotiating rules for agriculture, the United States decided to table its industrial exceptions list on November 16 in the interest of maintaining progress in the Kennedy Round. This decision in no way represented a weakening of our resolve that the negotiations in the Kennedy Round must cover both industry and agriculture.

Thus, the urgent test which I mentioned in my letter to President Hallstein still confronts us. The agricultural deadlock must soon be broken if the Kennedy Round is to succeed. I remain hopeful that the Community will find ways for its negotiators to act more flexibly in order to permit the substantive phase of the negotiations in both industry and agriculture to proceed early in 1965. To this end, I suggest that the Community and all major negotiating partners should agree promptly to a date as early as possible in 1965 on which to table agricultural offers designed to achieve the objectives set forth by the GATT Ministers for agricultural negotiations in the Kennedy Round.

I plan to be in Brussels and Geneva in the latter part of January. I look forward to discussing with you personally at that time the procedures to be followed in agriculture.

Most sincerely yours,

Christian A. Herter[4]

---

[3] Ecbus 113 from Brussels, July 30, transmitted Hallstein's reply to Herter. (Department of State, Central Files, FT 13–2 US)

[4] Printed from a copy that bears this typed signature.

271.   Draft Circular Telegram From the Department of State to Certain Posts[1]

Washington, January 21, 1965.

SUBJECT
> Visit of Vice-Minister Ohsawa of the Japanese Ministry of Agriculture—Agriculture and the Kennedy Round

From Herter. The following were the main points that were made in discussions on the Kennedy Round with an interagency group on January 18, 1965.

The United States side:

1.   Reaffirmed strong interest in the Kennedy Round and the seriousness with which we view the agricultural side of the negotiations. About one-third of our exports to Japan are agricultural whereas only about 3 percent of Japan's exports to us fall into this category. Therefore unless there are reductions in agricultural restrictions, the imbalance between the U.S. and Japanese offers that already exists on the industrial side will be significantly widened.

2.   Reported the difficulties we had had with the EEC in trying to work our acceptable rules for the agricultural negotiations. The EEC is insisting on the montant de soutien approach; we have made clear that we cannot accept it as a general format for negotiations. Now Governor Herter was going to Geneva and would attend a meeting of the Agricultural Subcommittee devoted to devising procedures for getting the agricultural negotiations underway. He planned to suggest that by a given date—perhaps April 1—the participating countries should lay down their agricultural offers, without first having agreed on a set of rules.

In the period before that date, we would hope to have bilateral and multilateral meetings with our trading partners to try to see what hope there was of meaningful progress on agriculture. The move to offers, we felt, presents the best chance of clarifying the situation. If the present divergences with the EEC continued, the whole Kennedy Round could be seriously endangered.

The Japanese made no clear response to this proposal to proceed with offers. Ohsawa seemed hesitant to take a position, saying he felt he

---

[1] Source: Kennedy Library, Herter Papers, Chronological File, January 1965, Box 3. Limited Official Use. Drafted by Auchincloss (STR), cleared by Greenwald (E/OT), and approved by Hedges (STR). To be sent to Tokyo, Geneva, Brussels for the Embassy and USEC, London, Paris for the Embassy and USRO, Rome, Bonn, Luxembourg for the Embassy and USEC, and The Hague. The source text does not indicate if the circular telegram was sent.

must have some time to study the suggestion. He added that he would have an opportunity to discuss it with Ambassador Aoki in the near future.

The Japanese side:

1. Stressed that they wanted to avoid a situation in which rigid negotiating rules on agriculture compelled them to alter domestic policies. In particular, they were anxious not to be subject to montant de soutien bindings. They urged that there be a "pragmatic" approach, taking account of differences in countries' situations.

We recognized that, given the agreed objective of trade liberalization, the means to that end could vary according to the situation in particular countries. However, there should be, in our view, certain conditions, such as that existing bindings should be respected.

2. Described their internal agricultural problems at some length. Japan's rapid economic growth had imposed severe strain on its agricultural system. Farming was still marked by small plots and low productivity. Meanwhile the type of products consumed had changed rapidly. The Government had passed a Basic Agricultural Law to expand production, adjust to new consumption patterns, and preserve family farming. Even so, less than 10 percent of Japan's present farms are "economically viable." To expose Japanese agriculture at this delicate point in its development to competition with advanced farm economics would devastate Japan's farmers. Until the new program took effect, Japan could not afford to reduce its agricultural protection.

3. Estimated that even in the absence of the Kennedy Round, Japanese farm imports would rise to about $2 billion in 1968 compared to just over $1 billion in recent years. They felt that this increase indicated that in Japan there was already a satisfactory balance between internal support measures and trade liberalization.

4. On grains, expressed willingness to make an access commitment, if necessary, with a provision for review at the call of the exporters if a reasonable balance between imports and domestic production were impaired. They made clear that they were in a position to do this only because there was a natural tendency for their grains imports to increase.

We agreed with their estimate of a growing import market and admitted that we weren't as concerned about our trade with them as we were about our trade with the EEC. Any international agreement, we felt, would have to contain something more than an undertaking to consult. Though it needn't be exactly like the British Cereals Agreement,[2] we would expect it to have some such pattern.

5. On illegal trade restrictions, contended that it would not be fair to insist on revision of support systems just because they may be incon-

---

[2] Not further identified.

sistent with the GATT. They suggested that if it were possible to make an offer in the Kennedy Round to relax some of these restrictions, this would be desirable.

We agreed that this would be helpful, but it would not constitute an offer in the negotiating sense—that is, something for which compensation should be expected.

6.   As for offers that Japan might make, they simply said that if they proceeded according to last May's Ministerial statement,[3] they assumed this would be an acceptable offer.

In reply, we specified a few types of offers which we hoped Japan would be able to make:

a)   On poultry, for example, we recognized that even a binding of the present 20% tariff would be an important contribution towards the goal of acceptable conditions of access.

b)   On such items as soybeans, which bear a fixed 13% duty, we would hope that it would be in Japan's interest to reduce the tariff since domestic production is falling and the tariff is now at least partly a revenue device.

c)   On products subject to either levies or quotas, we described our beef quota law, based on a moving base period and providing for growth, as the sort of pattern which to our minds would provide "acceptable conditions of access."[4]

Attendance:

Japanese side:

Tohru Ohsawa, Vice Minister for Agriculture and Forestry
Osamu Morimoto, Counselor in the Ministry of Agri. and Forestry
Kiyoaki Kikuchi, Chief, U.S.-Canadian Section, Economic Affairs
Bureau, Ministry of Foreign Affairs
Akira Matsuura, Spec. Asst. in Ministry of Agri. and Forestry
Yoshio Ohkawara, Counselor
Akitake Futagoishi, Counselor for Agriculture
Hiromu Fukada, Second Secretary

United States side:

Governor Herter
Mr. Roth
Mr. Hedges
Mr. Hirabayashi
Mr. Hajda
Mr. Auchincloss
Mr. Ioanes
Mr. De Felice
Mr. Riley Kirby
Mr. Greenwald

---

[3] See footnote 3, Document 254.
[4] See Documents 248 and 249.

272. Memorandum From the Special Representative for Trade Negotiations (Herter) to President Johnson[1]

Washington, January 19, 1965.

SUBJECT

Agriculture in the Kennedy Round

We have reached a critical stage in the Kennedy Round. With the tabling of the industrial exceptions list by the principal trading countries on November 16, the industrial phase of the negotiations is actively under way. Agricultural products were not included. This has been interpreted by some as a weakening of our resolve that agriculture and industry must be closely linked and that the final package must result in significant liberalization of agricultural trade.

Unless steps are taken to get the agricultural phase of the negotiations under way promptly there is indeed a grave risk that the opportunity to achieve significant liberalization of agricultural trade will be seriously compromised. So far we have been unable to reach agreement with our largest agricultural customer, the EEC, on rules which offer reasonable prospects of liberalization of agricultural trade. Prior to November 16 it became apparent that further efforts to get the agricultural negotiations under way were futile until the EEC agreed upon unified grains prices. This decision has now been taken. On December 15 the Council agreed upon a schedule of grains prices to become effective July 1, 1967.

We must now determine if this decision has advanced the EEC's ability to negotiate meaningfully on agriculture. I am convinced that further efforts to get the EEC to agree on acceptable rules for agriculture would be unproductive. Most of our negotiating partners share this view. Rather I propose that we adopt a strategy that will test the EEC's willingness to make offers of agricultural trade liberalization.

To this end I propose to go to Geneva later this month and suggest that a date be set for the tabling of our agricultural offers consistent with the resolutions adopted by the GATT Ministers. We would seek a date that allowed us sufficient time for intensive exchanges with our negotiating partners. It would be my intention to make clear to our partners during the late January meeting that we would attach great importance to those talks and the resulting offers which are laid down.

---

[1] Source: Kennedy Library, Herter Papers, Memoranda to the President, August 11, 1964–August 8, 1966, Box 10. Confidential. The date was changed from January 15 to January 19.

These talks would also assist us in coming to a decision as to the extent we should use, in making our initial offers, the authority you have already given to me to offer a 50 per cent reduction in U.S. agricultural tariffs with a bare minimum of exceptions. In this connection I would plan to obtain your prior approval of the actual offers we lay down.

Since the EEC is our largest agricultural customer, what it is willing to do in the way of agricultural trade liberalization is crucial. So far EEC proposals for agricultural negotiations have consisted essentially of an offer to bind producer price supports for a specified period at the levels unilaterally set by the Community under its Common Agricultural Policy.

We, as well as most of the other major participants in the negotiations, have made clear that EEC offers on this basis would not meet the objectives established by the GATT Ministers. I would therefore intend again to indicate in Geneva that the proposals the Community has made to date would not constitute acceptable agricultural trade liberalization and that offers by the EEC solely or largely on this basis would have grave consequences for the Kennedy Round.

I am not prepared at this time to set forth the minimum degree of agricultural trade liberalization required of the EEC for us to obtain a meaningful agricultural bargain. Clearly, the negotiating proposals the EEC has advanced to date would not meet any minimum requirements and, unless supplemented by other measures, would even be of negative value.

We would face a crisis if, on the basis of the bilateral talks and the actual offers laid down, it were apparent that the EEC was unwilling to make the minimum degree of liberalization which we considered essential. The United States would have to decide whether to suspend the negotiations or to proceed with a negotiation limited to industrial products and the agricultural concessions which countries other than the EEC were willing to make. This latter alternative would have to be considered in light of relevant economic, legislative and political factors.

These issues need not be faced now, however. At the moment I am only asking your approval to proceed as indicated above in an effort to persuade the EEC and other major participants to negotiate significant reductions in agricultural trade barriers. On the basis of the results of these efforts I shall make appropriate further recommendations to you among the alternatives available to us. In the meantime the United States position would remain that the negotiations must provide for liberalization of agricultural trade.

Christian A. Herter[2]

---

[2] Printed from a copy that bears this typed signature.

273.   Letter From President Johnson to the Special Representative for Trade Negotiations (Herter)[1]

Washington, January 21, 1965.

Dear Governor Herter:

I approve the negotiating strategy proposed in your memorandum of January 19 to test the intentions of the EEC with respect to the liberalization of trade in agricultural products.[2]

As you know, I regard the Kennedy Round as of great importance and potential promise for our foreign economic relations and our own economic welfare. Both we and our trading partners would greatly benefit if together we could achieve the targets set forth in the Ministerial Resolution of May 1964.[3]

Your own strong leadership in this effort is adding another major chapter to your distinguished record of service to your country.

I look forward to having your further report, after you have completed your explorations.[4]

Sincerely,

Lyndon B. Johnson

---

[1] Source: Department of State, Central Files, FT 13–2 US. No classification marking. The source text is attached to a note from Bator to Ball, January 22, stating that the letter was a copy of one the President gave to Herter at their meeting on January 21, and that it was for internal use and would not be made public.

[2] Document 272.

[3] See footnote 3, Document 254.

[4] Following his meeting with President Johnson on January 21, Herter issued a statement that reads in part: "The President emphasized his deep interest in the successful outcome of the Kennedy Round as a means of promoting both our own economic welfare and the prosperity of our trading partners. He indicated the course of action he wishes me to follow and expressed the hope that it would lead to further progress in the negotiations." (Circular telegram 1312 to all posts, January 22; Department of State, Central Files, FT 13–2 US)

274. Editorial Note

On February 8, 1965, the United States and other Contracting Parties to the General Agreement on Tariffs and Trade (GATT) signed a protocol amending GATT to introduce a Part IV on trade and development. The signatories provided that a Part IV comprising three new articles would be inserted after Article XXXV. The agreement also added notes to Annex I of GATT. These additions set forth legal and contractual principles that were designed to facilitate progress of less-developed nations toward rising standards of living and sustained economic development through the growth of their export trade.

For text of a statement by John W. Evans, Chairman of the U.S. Delegation to GATT, on February 8, 1965, endorsing the Protocol, see Department of State *Bulletin,* March 8, 1965, pages 355–356.

Following acceptance by two-thirds of the Contracting Parties, Part IV entered into force de jure on June 27, 1966. For text, see 17 UST 1977; 572 UNTS 320.

A summary of these developments and a brief analysis of each article of Part IV is in *Current Economic Developments,* Issue No. 758, July 19, 1966, page 24. (Washington National Records Center, RG 59, E/CBA/REP Files: FRC 72 A 6248, *Current Economic Developments*)

---

275. Memorandum From the Deputy Special Representative for Trade Negotiations (Roth) to the President's Special Assistant for National Security Affairs (Bundy)[1]

Washington, February 9, 1965.

Secretary Freeman had breakfast with Mansholt this morning. He said he was quite sharp with him, indicating that there was a deep concern here over the delay in agricultural negotiations and in the rigid insistence of the Community on the montant de soutien formula.

He said there was real danger particularly in the grains that a price war could come about and that this would have serious consequences for

---

[1] Source: Kennedy Library, Herter Papers, McGeorge Bundy, Box 7. No classification marking. Drafted by Roth. The source text bears Herter's handwritten initials.

world agriculture. U.S. supports and farmer returns were going down, whereas the opposite trend was apparent within the Community.

He urged three things on Mansholt: (1) that he review the September date and attempt to establish an earlier one, (2) that grains negotiations begin immediately and that the Community proceed with their offers unequivocally, (3) that the tabling of agricultural offers in all sectors not be conditional on additional discussions between now and the date of tabling.

Freeman said he thought the talk was a good one and that an impression had been made on Mansholt.

William M. Roth[2]

---

[2] Printed from a copy that bears this typed signature.

---

276.   Memorandum of Conversation[1]

Washington, February 9, 1965.

Meeting between Vice President Humphrey and Mr. Sicco Mansholt, Vice President of the Common Market, at the Executive Office Building on February 9, 1965. Present were the Vice President; Mr. Mansholt; Ambassador Tuthill, United States Representative to the Common Market; Mr. Alfred Mozer, Chef de Cabinet to Mr. Mansholt; and Mr. John Rielly, foreign policy assistant to the Vice President.

Mr. Mansholt opened the discussion with a reference to his meeting earlier that day with Secretary Freeman.[2] He said he understood and is sympathetic to the many difficulties facing Secretary Freeman as the Secretary of Agriculture, and understood the pressures he was under vis-à-vis the Common Market countries. The Vice President suggested that it would be useful for Mr. Mansholt to read the President's message on

---

[1] Source: Kennedy Library, Herter Papers, Public Advisory Committee, January 6, 1965–November 1, 1965, Box 14. No classification marking. The source text bears no drafting information. Two March 4 letters from Vice President Humphrey to Herter are attached; one comments on his conversation with Mansholt: "I am not sure I got through to Mr. Mansholt but I laid it on pretty thick."

[2] See Document 275.

agriculture,[3] which gives a good indication of some of the problems confronting the U.S. Government in the field at present. He pointed out that the United States is the only country which has reduced acreage in recent years. American farmers consistently press the Administration to justify a reduction in acreage here when none takes place abroad. What we desire is not a further reduction in acreage but expanded markets.

Mr. Mansholt observed that the problem in Europe today is the same as that in the United States—that production is increasing beyond consumption. We now have the danger of surpluses accumulating in Europe just as they have in this country. The Vice President raised the question of whether the Europeans might be interested in giving some of their surplus food away, just as the U.S. does. Mr. Mansholt replied that the Europeans preferred to sell it, rather than to compete with the U.S. in dumping surplus food products around the world.

The Vice President said that it is difficult for Americans to understand how the Europeans can justify a policy of high grain price supports which may benefit the producer but certainly not the large mass of consumers. From the American point of view, the price is too high when the U.S. can sell it to the European countries cheaper than it can be grown at home. From the European point of view, Mr. Mansholt suggested, the price is too high when it encourages an increase in acreage. He added that Europeans are still importing cereals from the U.S. in large quantities, even though they could increase production further if they so desired.

Mr. Mansholt noted the parallel trends in Europe and the U.S., with labor from the farms drifting more and more to the cities and into industry. Whereas high prices have led to high acreage in the U.S., this has not necessarily been the case in Europe because they have prevented this through acreage controls. The justification of high prices for the consumer, according to Mr. Mansholt, lies in the obligation European governments feel to guarantee a fair income to farmers. This can be done only by maintaining a high support price.

The Vice President agreed that the farmers' interests must be looked after and that the farmer cannot be left purely to the mercy of fluctuating prices. However, our experience with support prices has indicated that over a long period of time they lead to great political difficulties. In the U.S. there is a great deal of political pressure building up from urban areas where people resent more and more the heavy burden of paying for high price supports. This of course has created stronger and stronger pressure to find markets abroad for American agricultural products.

---

[3] For text of President Johnson's Special Message to Congress on Agriculture on February 4, see *Public Papers of the Presidents of the United States: Lyndon B. Johnson, 1965*, Book I, pp. 139–148.

And this of course brings us to the Kennedy Round. We have reached agreement for the most part on the question of industrial products, but unless we can reach some similar agreement on the question of agricultural products, the Kennedy Round will flop. The U.S. Congress will never permit us to enter into any agreement that would permit Europe to sell its industrial products in the U.S. but effectively cut the American farmer out of the European market. Concessions must be mutual. Our European friends must realize this, and our State Department must realize this.[4] Given the prevailing sentiment in the American Congress, our Government will have no choice but to take stern measures unless Europe is willing to play fair on agriculture. The U.S. can, if necessary, subsidize sales abroad, undercutting competitors. We prefer, of course, not to do this.

Mr. Mansholt vigorously expressed the hope that both the U.S. and Europe could avoid selling subsidized products abroad. This would benefit neither Europe nor the U.S. He said he understood the political problems created for the government in this country, as most European governments were experiencing the same problems in regard to agriculture. A huge increase of U.S. exports to the Common Market countries is not possible, as European production is increasing. In regard to the surplus products which will be available for exports, he felt that it should be easy for the U.S. and Europe to agree on a common price. The underdeveloped countries which buy many of these agricultural products are also agricultural countries. They do not want to see prices for agricultural commodities forced down, as eventually it would hurt their own economics too.

The Vice President returned to the subject of U.S.-European trade, and emphasized once again that the Europeans could not continue to expect Americans to permit an increasing volume of imports of Volkswagens, machine tools, and china into this country, while holding agricultural exports to Europe at a stagnant level. The problem is likely to become more acute because when European farmers discover what they can produce with new fertilizers, their production will go way up, particularly if present high prices are maintained.[5]

Mansholt said that he appreciated the problem, but insisted that Americans should always remember that the U.S. continues to have a favorable balance of trade with Europe of over $3 billion. The Vice President acknowledged the favorable balance, and suggested the problem is not only economic but psychological. The feeling is strong in the U.S. that

---

[4] Following the comma and at the end of the sentence are handwritten brackets with the handwritten note, "omit," in the margin.

[5] Handwritten brackets appear at the beginning and end of this sentence, and handwritten notes in the margin read: "Omit" and "not good point."

Europe is becoming more protectionist. It is the feeling here that rather than increase trade in agricultural products which could afford a real benefit to the European consumer, many European countries will soon be repeating the U.S. experience. That is, they will soon have to build extensive warehouse facilities to take care of the surpluses as long as high price supports are maintained. If they proceed to do this and shut the U.S. out of the market, not only will they be causing grave economic problems but they will be undermining the internationalist policy of the last 25 years which has been based on the interdependence of Europe and the U.S. This is what disturbs the Congress. This is what disturbs the President of the US.

Mr. Mansholt said that he understood the basic problem: that of finding a type of agreement in the Kennedy Round which would maintain an acceptable level of support, but not exclude U.S. agricultural products. We want to do this in a way that will permit them to avoid state trading systems similar to those on the Soviet bloc. We want to arrive at an acceptable level of imports and exports. This, he insisted, must be negotiated product by product. The Vice President agreed that this was the problem, but pointed out that in solving this problem it was important not to build increasing protection into the solution. The solution must not have built into it the seeds of a rising wall of tariffs. If it has built into it an eventual reduction of tariffs—mutual reductions—then the U.S. and Europe can resolve their problems. At the present time it would appear to us in the U.S. that most Europeans are *not* thinking along these lines. Re-emphasizing this point again, he said that the over-all design, so far as there is one, leaves the impression of increasing protectionism. Unless we succeed in working out some formula that leads not to higher tariffs against agricultural products but to lower tariffs, the Kennedy Round will fail. The present trade act expires July 1, 1967. By that date, we must reach some understanding on both agricultural and industrial products. Otherwise the U.S. Congress will never extend the provisions of the present act.

Mr. Mansholt said he understood the Vice President's point of view, and insisted that Europeans are obliged to consider also the question of justice for the farm population. Solutions cannot be arrived at exclusively on the basis of international trade considerations. Farmers must be protected, all the more so because the younger population is tending to leave the farm, and this trend should not be accelerated. The Vice President agreed that the farmer should be protected in Europe just as he is in this country. At the same time, Europeans must understand why the U.S. is determined not to see European markets foreclosed to its agricultural products, just as the Europeans would be greatly disturbed if we were to attempt to foreclose our markets for French wines and German Volkswagens. This is a problem that pertains not only to the six countries of the

Common Market but to the U.S. and Europe as a whole. We must also consider our relations with the European Free Trade Association countries, and both we and the Common Market countries must bear in mind the question of relations between the Common Market and the Outer Seven.

The Vice President closed by noting that the problem of trade with Eastern European countries is becoming increasingly important. We have very little trade with these countries at the present time, but there is a general feeling in Congress that we should increase this trade. This is another problem, however. The important point is that the Europeans know that the point of view expounded by the Vice President today is a representative one in the Congress, that it is supported by all four principal leaders in the Congress today. All of these men share a disappointment in the Kennedy Round thus far and a grave concern that unless some progress is made in the agricultural sector in the near future, the prospects for success in the Kennedy Round as a whole are dim.

---

277. Airgram From the Mission to the European Office of the United Nations to the Department of State[1]

Tagg A–375   Geneva, February 21, 1965.

SUBJECT

    Confrontation of the EEC Exceptions Submission

REF

    Tagg A–368[2]

Exoff. For Governor Herter from US Delegation to Sixth Round of GATT Trade Negotiations.

---

[1] Source: Department of State, Central Files, FT 7 GATT. Confidential. Drafted by Winston Lord, cleared by Albert E. Pappano, and approved by James H. Lewis. Repeated to Paris, The Hague, Brussels for the Embassy and USEC, Rome, Bonn, and Luxembourg for the Embassy and USEC. A handwritten note under the subject line reads: "Report #3."

[2] Tagg A–368 from Geneva, February 16, reported on an examination of the EEC exceptions list by the linear participants in the sixth round of GATT trade negotiations and on the February 11 meeting of the heads of the principal delegations on the future conduct of the negotiations. (Ibid.)

I.   Summary Assessment

The multilateral confrontation of the European Economic Community's exceptions submission, the last of the linear participants' lists to be examined, took place from February 9 to February 12. Mr. Pierre Millet, Director General of the Internal Market Directorate of the EEC Commission, represented the Six throughout. Ambassador Blumenthal made the opening presentation for the United States,[3] and Minister Evans, Mr. Gates (STR) and Mr. Pappano (Country Team Chairman) did the questioning in the subsequent six sessions. Addressees have already received copies of the initial statements (the only major ones) of Mr. Millet and Ambassador Blumenthal.

As reported earlier (Tagg A–368), it was decided at the conclusion of this phase that an interval of at least the next month will be devoted to bilateral contacts between delegations to clarify questions and explore problem areas. The Chairman would reconvene multilateral meetings at an appropriate time thereafter.

The *entire confrontation phase* was cordial, often marked by humor, but a general tone of dissatisfaction with the EEC list was clearly established, primarily by the U.S. and the Scandinavians. While the *Community* was "noting" the various arguments of others, it never indicated it was convinced by any of them, nor that it planned to improve its offers.

The *questioning of the Community* was severe and penetrating in the *paper* and *pulp* and *metals* fields. It was generally gentle in the *textile* and *minor* chapters, and hurried in the *mechanical* sector due to lack of time. The confrontation on *chemicals* was restricted by the Community's refusal to discuss the two biggest chapters, 29 and 39.[4] Throughout the process Mr. Millet responded energetically to questions, whether on broad policies, sectors, or particular items, usually echoing the themes he introduced in his opening statement. Again and again he returned to his major points: the difficult integration process that many of the Community's industries are undergoing; their competitive disadvantages in such areas as technology, scale, financing, energy costs, and raw materials; the moderate protection of the CXT compared to other tariffs; the threat of low-priced imports; regional and social problems and adjustment difficulties; trade deficit with the U.S. in several sectors despite favorable global balance; and military and strategic considerations. Mr. Millet's performance was tactically skillful and often buttressed with specific facts and statistics. His defense was least effective in the metals field, and he would probably have been hard pressed in the mechanical sector if there had been sufficient time and stamina.

---

[3] Reference is to the February 9 opening statement by Blumenthal in the confrontation on EEC exceptions list; the text was transmitted as an enclosure to airgram A–368.

[4] Reference is to Chapters 29 and 39 of the Brussels Tariff Nomenclature.

The attitudes of the individual countries followed consistent patterns. The United States made the only substantive and forceful opening statement and did the most consistent questioning throughout the week. Comments were usually directed at sectors, although individual items were often used as illustrations. Statements or general comments were made on chemicals, paper and pulp, synthetic textiles, iron and steel, aluminum, and the mechanical sector. The United Kingdom was generally restrained in tone, often effective on specifics, and largely concerned with the impact of the EEC list on the smaller countries. It took the lead in asbestos, indicated a major interest in the mechanical sector, and supported others on chemicals, paper and pulp, ceramics, steel and aluminum. Japan did the main questioning on textiles, ceramics and some of the smaller chapters, and joined in the discussion of the mechanical sector. Switzerland was selectively forceful on chemicals, textiles, and machinery. The Scandinavians were sharply critical and extremely effective in paper and pulp and ferro-alloys, lent support in other sectors, and left the distinct impression that they would have to re-evaluate their own positions if the EEC could not improve its offers. Austria never mounted a general attack, only noting in each sector its own particular export items. Denmark hardly spoke at all, and then on specific commodities. Canada recorded its concern about paper and pulp and aluminum.

The *Community's position on the major ambiguities* in its submission was neither surprising nor encouraging: *Partial exceptions*. The depth of the cuts on these items is not known in general or particular, and cannot be estimated on even a few items because of delicate internal considerations. It is better to wait until a decision on the entire range of partial offers has been made, and this is difficult both procedurely and economically. The maneuvering room left by these uncertainties might be a useful tool for the negotiations.

Conditional chemical offers. As already stated, the Six will withdraw all offers in Chapters 29, 32 and 39 if the difficulties of the American Selling Price and Standard of Strength are not "suppressed." In the meantime, the EEC did not and will not subject to confrontation its exceptions in these Chapters (29 and 39). A U.S. challenge on the latter point went unanswered.

Conditional textile offers. The offers on cotton and cotton substitutes is conditional *both* on a meaningful extension of the LTA without serious modifications, *and* on the "correction" of tariff disparities in this sector between countries facing the same competitive situation.

Disparities. The only specific reference to this issue by Mr. Millet during the entire week was the above one on conditional textile offers. However, the theme of high U.S. and U.K. rates versus a moderate CXT was sounded in the opening statement and replayed as justification in sector after sector.

Base rates. No fixed rules for base rates and dates have been settled, and therefore each country is free to choose its own, subject to the comments and evaluation of its trading partners. In any event, it is premature to characterize others' offers related to this question (e.g. steel and petroleum) as exceptions when the issue is still open.

Sector reciprocity. The word "reciprocity" may be ill-chosen, for the Six do not insist on exact sectoral balances. The Community is referring to particularly sensitive sectors where it would be difficult for one linear country to make offers while other important partners except the same products. No other sectors besides the automotive and aircraft ones already cited could be identified at this time, although chemicals clearly present related problems.

Paper and Pulp discussions. The Community repeated only that it wished to consult with its major trading partners (Scandinavians) about their pricing policies on raw materials which favored their own processors at the expense of EEC industries. Mr. Millet could not be more specific, but imagined that the discussions would take place within the GATT framework.

Size of exceptions lists. This is not the time to begin comparisons of the various exceptions lists which might be inaccurate and hamper the negotiations. Certainly to use volume of trade as the only yardstick would be dangerous and biased. Other factors must be considered, including heights of duties, dispersion of rates, and hidden elements in certain lists such as exclusions and the invocation of certain GATT provisions.

Statistics. Trade coverage of the exceptions, especially on ex-outs, will be supplied by the Community and should clarify their impact.

[Here follows Part II, "Discussion Summarized by Sectors," which consists of 11 pages on the U.S. and other countries' positions on specific items.]

Tubby

278. Letter From the Special Representative for Trade Negotiations' Executive Assistant (Auchincloss) to the Special Representative for Trade Negotiations (Herter)[1]

Washington, March 8, 1965.

Dear Governor:

Naturally we are all hoping that you are feeling much better and will be back soon. Are there lady doctors to look after you in New York as there were in Geneva?[2]

Here is another short run-down on what has been going on:

1. *Agriculture:* At the EEC Council meeting last week, the 3-step schedule for the agriculture negotiations was approved in very short order. It calls for:

a) negotiations on grains to begin April 1.

b) a confrontation between all participating countries, starting April 1, on their policies on all other agricultural products with the objective of identifying the elements of support and protection which should enter into the negotiations.

c) presentation of concrete offers on other products on September 16. The Community offers, according to the Article 111 Committee report to the Council,[3] will be decided at the last Council session in July "in conformity with the mandate of December 1963. In deciding on Community offers, the Council will take account of the results of negotiations on cereals and of the confrontation of agricultural policies and of the status of work within the Community regarding the elaboration of the CAP."

Wyndham White has called a TNC meeting for next week, principally to settle the agricultural timetable. He plans to submit a short paper on these procedures for advance agreement this week by the UK, EEC, Japan, and U.S.

We have cabled Blumenthal asking for clarification of whether September 16 date clearly unconditional in view of the last sentence (above) in the 111 Committee report.[4] We also ask for clarification of the EEC's view of the April–September discussions on agricultural policies. In our opinion, these should amount to exchange of factual information and of views as to type of offers expected on specific products. We authorize him to approve, ad referendum, a paper which clearly makes the Sep-

---

[1] Source: Kennedy Library, Herter Papers, Kenneth Auchincloss, Box 5. No classification marking. Herter's initials appear on the source text.

[2] Herter was in the Presbyterian Hospital in New York.

[3] The report has not been further identified.

[4] Reference is to telegram 2615 to Geneva, March 5. (Department of State, Central Files, AGR 3 GATT)

tember 16 date unconditional, clearly requires specific offers on grains, and is as unambiguous as possible on April–September discussions, avoiding implication that purpose of the exercise is to agree on or identify elements to be encompassed by subsequent offers.

2. *Other Kennedy Round Issues:* Wyndham White also hopes at next week's TNC meeting to gain agreement on a rule for the participation of LDCs and others with which negotiations are not yet engaged. The progress of bilateral talks on the industrial exceptions lists and the future negotiating plans will also be taken up.

3. *Canada and LDC Country Teams:* Mike Blumenthal has asked that the Canadian and LDC teams now proceed to Geneva, and we are arranging to get them there during the next 4–5 weeks.

4. *Escape Clause Case on Watches:* The Tariff Commission's report was released Friday.[5] The Swiss reaction was that it contained both favorable and unfavorable elements, but they spoke of "entirely new atmosphere" in trade relations between our two countries if President does not decide to remove the escape clause action entirely. The TSC is beginning its review of the report.

5. *U.K. Grains Agreement:* Minister Peart has replied to the letter we sent in your name.[6] He expresses understanding of our position and recognition of the UK's obligations, but explains that it would be contrary to the terms of the Annual Farmers' Review to inform us of the steps they plan to take before the Review is over. We have replied with an Aide-Mémoire indicating that we appreciate that the British cannot give us *definitive* indications of these steps in advance, but we had hoped that they could meet with us to discuss their *preliminary* thinking on the 1965/66 standard quantities and guaranteed prices for cereals.

6. *Canadian Auto Parts Arrangement:* The only interagency issue left in drafting the Bill concerns subpoena power. John Rehm hopes that it can now be put in shape in quite short order.

7. *Public Advisory Committee Meeting:* At the meeting last Thursday, the Vice President gave an excellent and charming talk and Mr. Clayton made a strong statement on the agricultural negotiations (copy enclosed).

8. *Space:* We are grimly hanging on to our offices but have thrown the White House a sop by vacating 4 rooms down the hall.

---

[5] The Tariff Commission reported the probable economic effect on the domestic watchmaking industry of restoring trade-agreement concession rates of duty on watch movements as follows: (1) lower cost for imported watch movements; (2) lower watch prices; (3) assembly of watch movements in the Virgin Islands less attractive; (4) increased imports of watches with imported movements; (5) increased U.S. market share of watches with imported movements; and (6) increased imports by U.S. watchmakers. (Announcement of March 5 by Donn H. Bent, Secretary of the U.S. Tariff Commission; 30 *Federal Register* 3341)

[6] Not further identified.

Very best regards and warm hopes from us all that we will see you shortly.

Sincerely,

Ken

Enclosure[7]

STATEMENT PRESENTED AT THE MEETING OF THE PUBLIC ADVISORY COMMITTEE FOR TRADE NEGOTIATIONS

By Mr. W.L. Clayton
March 4, 1965

Agriculture is the main problem in our negotiations at Geneva.

Our agricultural exports to the European Economic Community have recently amounted to a little under $1,200,000,000 annually, or approximately an average of one third of our total exports to the EEC.

The representatives of all nations taking part in the Kennedy Round unanimously adopted at the GATT Ministerial Meeting in May, 1963, a resolution which—among other things—set forth the following principle:

"That a significant liberalization of world trade is desirable, and that, for this purpose, comprehensive trade negotiations . . . shall cover all classes of products . . . including agricultural . . . products . . . that the trade negotiations shall provide for acceptable conditions of access to world markets for agricultural products."

In the same resolution, the Ministers further directed the Trade Negotiations Committee to elaborate "the rules to govern, and the methods to be employed in, the creation of acceptable conditions of access to world markets for agricultural products in furtherance of significant development and expansion of world trade in such products."

In the view of the United States, these resolutions, adopted by the Ministers, adequately define the agricultural objective of the Kennedy Round.

Following the meeting of the GATT Ministers in May, 1963, an intensive effort was made to develop the rules and procedures for the agricultural phase of the negotiations. Two proposals were considered, one made by the USA, and the other made by the EEC. The U. S. proposal pro-

---

[7] No classification marking.

vided that agricultural products should be given treatment comparable to that of industrial products. The EEC proposal was a highly technical and involved plan relating to the freezing of the margin between domestic support prices and certain world reference prices. Among other objections, this would, if agreed to by the United States, have probably deprived the U. S. Congress of the power to legislate on farm prices.

In the Chase Manhattan Bank Circular No. 30, issued in June–July 1964, this paragraph appears:

"The United States has a one billion dollar stake in the Common Market's new agricultural policies. During recent years American farmers have been supplying the Common Market countries with such agricultural products as wheat and flour, feed grains, cotton, and tobacco. American farmers had expected a gradual expansion of this market along with Europe's growth in population and income. Instead, the Common Market now promotes a policy that stimulates Europe's high-cost agriculture and tends to reduce the import demand for low-cost, efficiently produced North American farm products."

On December 15, 1964, the Community's Council of Ministers agreed on the levels of grains prices within the Community, to go into effect July, 1967. The target wholesale prices have been set as follows:

Wheat—$2.89 per bushel
Corn—   2.30 per bushel, and
Barley— 1.99 per bushel.

These prices may be considered to be at the same point in the Community market system as wholesale grain prices in the United States in major markets, such as Kansas City and Chicago.

These prices will result in prices to domestic producers in the Community of $.80–.90 a bushel higher for wheat than the U. S. farmer receives and almost double the U. S. farm prices for corn.

Under the Community's grain regulation, a levy is to be paid on imports of grain to assure that the price of imported grain is at least as high as these target prices. If the U. S. or any other exporter is more efficient in grain production and offers grain at lower prices, it simply attracts a higher levy. Under these circumstances, the U. S. competitive position cannot be improved in the Community market.

This season, the U. S. export subsidy on wheat will average about $.25 a bushel. The Community at the same time has been paying an export subsidy of about $1.25 a bushel.

After the common agricultural grain policy is fully operative, these export subsidies will be financed from levies collected on our grain exports to the community.

The Community's price levels for grains, as stated above, are almost certain to stimulate production, at least in France, and thus reduce the exports of more efficient grain-producing countries.

Tariff concessions obtained by the U. S. in the Dillon Round would be jeopardized by the introduction of reference prices and the possibility of levies if offering prices fell below reference prices. This could impair existing bindings and would not meet the objective of trade liberalization, which can only be achieved by reducing trade barriers.

In view of the above I have told Mr. Herter if I were in his position I would say to the EEC at the proper time that if agriculture were not included in the negotiations in Geneva that there would be no negotiations.

I feel sure the American people would completely support this position.

Naturally this would have to be done with the approval of the President of the United States.

---

279. Letter From the Special Representative for Trade Negotiations' Executive Assistant (Auchincloss) to the Special Representative for Trade Negotiations (Herter)[1]

Washington, March 23, 1965.

Dear Governor:

I imagine this will be the last of my reports directed to you in New York. We are delighted to hear about your plans to go to Nassau and from now on I will send these summaries directly to the poolside in Lyford Key.[2]

Hallstein Visit—President Hallstein's trip went off very well. Bill Roth saw him last Wednesday and he was full of his usual convictions about the importance of the Kennedy Round's success. One thing that apparently is bothering him is recent talk about some accommodation between the British Labor Government and the EEC. This is revived discussion in Europe about an "interim arrangement" between the EEC and the EFTA, one form of which would call for the EEC to join EFTA. Hallstein feels strongly that any interim solution would probably be a barrier

---

[1] Source: Kennedy Library, Herter Papers, Kenneth Auchincloss, Box 5. No classification marking.

[2] A hotel in Nassau.

716 Foreign Relations, 1964–1968, Volume VIII

to the eventual entry of Great Britain and other EFTA countries into the EEC. It also could reduce the impetus of the Kennedy Round in European circles.

Work in Geneva—As I am sure you know by now the papers on the agricultural negotiations and on LDC participation were approved at the TNC meeting last Thursday.[3] This step forward generated quite a bit of favorable press coverage which generally took the line the Kennedy Round finally seems to be getting somewhere.

At the same meeting, the Scandinavian countries came forward with a proposal for the reduction or elimination of trade barriers on tropical products as soon as possible. This won general support from almost all delegations, but the EEC simply said that it would be prepared to discuss the suggestion at a later time.

A number of additional countries have now been admitted to "full participant" basis in the negotiations, Greece, Turkey and, in the near future, Israel which will announce the basis of its participation by April 15. Portugal said that it expects to table its offers on July 1st.

Budget Hearings—The House hearings on the 1966 Budget took place today and went very smoothly. Congressman Rooney was unaccountably absent and we got very mild and cordial treatment from the Subcommittee. Congressman Bow in the name of the entire Committee asked about your health and sent very best wishes to you.

Blumenthal Visit—Mike Blumenthal will be here next week and I expect that high on the list of subjects for discussion will be such problems as: How we handle the agricultural talks between May and September? What form our grains proposal should take and how the so-called sector studies on the industrial side will be handled. On the latter, we have been pushing forward under the leadership of Ted Gates to amass as much information as possible about the main foreign industries in a few key sectors. We have used our technical specialists a good deal and they have been most helpful.

I am enclosing an unclassified airgram from the Mission in Brussels[4] which gives some of the background for the agricultural decisions that face the EEC this Spring. Hallstein incidentally was quite pessimistic about the likelihood of the Germans agreeing to unification of dairy prices and perhaps some of the other regulations before their elections this autumn.

Warmest regards from all of us. I hope that Nassau turns out to be as delightful as it sounds.

Sincerely,[5]

---

[3] March 18.
[4] Not further identified.
[5] Printed from an unsigned copy.

280. Memorandum of Conversation[1]

Washington, March 29, 1965.

PARTICIPANTS

Honorable Jean Rey
Honorable Theodorus Hijzen

STR
Ambassador Roth
Ambassador Blumenthal
Mr. Hedges
Mr. Rehm
Mr. Norwood
Mr. Auchincloss

State
Ambassador Tuthill
Mr. Deane Hinton

After greeting Mr. Rey and passing on Governor Herter's best regards, Ambassador Roth raised the issue of having a permanent EEC staff located in Geneva. We recognize the problems covering Article 111 Committee activities in Brussels but now that the negotiations have become more active it is very difficult to operate without an EEC representative present with whom our delegation can communicate on a day to day basis. Rey said that the Community recognized the problem and knew that they would now have to have people at the staff level in Geneva on a permanent basis. However, given the nature of the problems with the member governments in Brussels, it was essential to have Hijzen available in Brussels whenever necessary. Hijzen himself added that he planned to be in Geneva at least three days a week from now on. One problem which the Commission now faces is to decide what sort of technical staff to station there. The Commission's personnel shortage would make it impossible to have duplicate staffs, one in Brussels and one in Geneva.

The discussion turned to agriculture and Rey suddenly became quite blunt. Did we really expect a major liberalization of agricultural trade in the Kennedy Round? he asked. He felt that we were really far more concerned that the EEC's agricultural policies not become more restrictive than they are at present. It is simply not realistic, he contended, to think that a broad liberalization is now possible. If it had been it

---

[1] Source: Kennedy Library, Herter Papers, Chronological File, April 1965. Limited Official Use. Drafted by Auchincloss on April 7, cleared by Hinton (EUR/RPE), and approved by Roth. An attached draft telegram, April 12, indicates that this memorandum of conversation was to be transmitted to eight diplomatic missions and to the Special Representative for Trade Negotiations.

could have been achieved in the Dillon Round. Certainly after the enormous difficulties of the EEC in fixing the common grains price, we could not expect a further lowering of the price in the Kennedy Round. On feed grains and fruits and vegetables, he understood that the United States has special problems and they will have to be dealt with. But he felt that the time had come for some frank talk between the EEC and the U.S. Delegations in order to make clear what our real interests were and what could be accomplished. He recognized that the EEC is not going to convince other countries to adopt the montant de soutien approach, so the EEC must make some adjustment of its position. But he felt that any adjustment would be impossible unless movement on the EEC side were matched by movement by its negotiating partners. Only then could the Six be persuaded to make some accommodation. In this context he had been most surprised at recent statements by Ambassador Blumenthal which appeared to reject the montant de soutien out of hand.

Ambassador Roth replied that the U.S. is indeed seeking liberalization of agricultural trade, in conformity with the Ministerial Resolution. Of course we have somewhat modified our position. We had first thought of liberalization carried out by tariff reductions just as would be done on the industrial side. Then, in Ambassador Blumenthal's proposal at the TNC meeting last summer, the U.S. had adopted a more flexible approach—more flexible in substance as well as in procedure. But this would not alter the fact that liberalization is still the goal.

As for our statements on the montant de soutien, what we reject is the effect of such a system; we do not believe that it would lead to trade liberalization. We are not, however, rejecting out of hand all elements of the proposal, as we have made clear by repeatedly stating our willingness to discuss our own internal agricultural policies and to make offers to place limitations upon them. Ambassador Blumenthal emphasized that we have made a great effort to meet the EEC's problems in our response to the montant de soutien proposal and stressed, along with Ambassador Roth, that we agreed with its key element: that internal policies should be considered in the negotiations. Obviously we are not in apposition to say that we are interested in concessions in some products but not in others. That would be politically impossible. But through the negotiations a fairly clear picture will emerge showing where our principal interests lie. He urged that the EEC not be too impatient to get this picture painted immediately. The next few months would bring this in the natural course of events.

Rey reiterated his view that the Kennedy Round would score a great success if, in the agricultural field present markets were maintained. Perhaps there has been a misunderstanding of the U.S. views on liberalization, Ambassador Roth suggested. He pointed to our meat liberalization as an example of what we view as provisions for reasonable access: the opportunity to maintain present trade levels and to share in normal expansion. Mr. Hedges added that one of our main problems with the CAP and the MDS is that in our judgment it would *not* maintain present trade levels, but would in fact be retrogressive, allowing for increased protection. In this sense the MDS is a rather self-serving formula since it would impose no obligation on countries maintaining a variable levy system (such as the EEC's) to bind their border protection or effectively bring internal policies into the negotiations. He also mentioned that when we agreed to have internal policies considered, this of course included programs for adjusting supplies to market outlets and that this issue must be dealt with in the negotiations when we consider internal policies.

Ambassador Blumenthal suggested it would be in the EEC's interest to use the Kennedy Round to keep the EEC common agricultural policy flexible.

Ambassador Roth mentioned President Hallstein's concern about rumors that the EEC and EFTA would draw closer together thus diminishing their interest in the Kennedy Round. The EFTA countries have stressed on a number of occasions their very great concern about the EEC exceptions list and so he hoped that the EEC would be prepared, when the time came, to review and modify its exceptions list. Rey said that that problem had not been very much discussed but he wondered what sort of bargaining we had in mind. Do we foresee a process of swapping items to be removed from the respective exceptions list much as was done in the Dillon Round? Ambassador Blumenthal said that his own view was that in the bilateral discussions now taking place the various delegations are making clear their real trade interests. He thought that the next phase of bargaining would not be very different from past negotiations. We do not yet know how the final balancing of offers will take place but we do not exclude tit-for-tat bargaining. Hijzen followed this up by commenting that whereas in the Dillon Round the negotiators had in general been faced with maximum offers with no chance for improvement, in this Round there were various possibilities for movement that could be worked out through discussion. He mentioned as an example that he was hopeful that the EEC could do something in the ceramics area.

Mr. Norwood pointed to the "over-riding national interest" rule for justification of exceptions. We feel that there have been considerable difficulties between the quality of the justifications and this is something that will have to be borne in mind as the negotiations move along.

281. Letter From the Special Representative for Trade Negotiations' Executive Assistant (Auchincloss) to the Special Representative for Trade Negotiations (Herter)[1]

Washington, April 7, 1965.

Dear Governor:

I hope Lyford Key has turned out well. My mother is very worried about this venture of hers into the art of cruise directing.

Mike Blumenthal was here for the past 10 days—he arrived just in time to be plunged into the hassle over the grains proposal that we will submit on April 26. One of the factors that has made interagency agreement difficult here is that our domestic farm program was sent up to the Hill only last Monday (copy enclosed)[2] and its provisions will of course affect the extent of the offers we can make on our internal policy. One millstone that we will have to carry internationally is that under the new legislation the "domestic certificate" price for wheat would be raised about 50 cents, bringing the overall return to the farmer to $2.50 a bushel. As it is taking shape our offer in CG will probably be to pledge not to raise our loan price ($1.25 a bushel) beyond some commonly agreed world reference price—perhaps $1.50. We would also offer to continue our acreage diversion plan to limit production. In return we would ask the EEC to bind the difference between the world reference price and its own internal support price and to undertake a program to limit its own cereals productions to that of a certain base period. There would also be provisions for storage of any excess production and for food aid disposals. If the EEC should not be willing to undertake a program to limit production we would then demand some form of access commitment, such as we obtained from the British. Similar requests would be made of the other importing countries. We are meeting with the other exporters tomorrow and the next day in order to compare notes and try to avoid clashes between ourselves when the CG negotiations begin.

On the industrial side Mike reports that our initial bilateral meetings with the EEC on exceptions have gone very well. The EEC representatives have been knowledgeable and the discussion has been frank. Mike thinks that we are moving naturally into the stage where each side makes clear its primary interests, thus laying the groundwork for actual bar-

---

[1] Source: Kennedy Library, Herter Papers, Kenneth Auchincloss, Box 5. No classification marking.

[2] Not enclosed, but the letter from the President transmitting to Congress the legislative proposals for farm commodity programs, Monday, April 5, is printed in *Public Papers of the Presidents of the United States: Lyndon B. Johnson, 1965*, Book I, pp. 383–386. The legislative proposals are in H. Doc. 137, 89th Cong.

gaining. The bargaining will probably not take place however until after the agriculture offers are laid down when everyone will have a full picture.

Rey was here, accompanied by Hijzen, for a short visit last week.[3] He seemed in an uncommonly blunt frame of mind. Surely, he said, United States does not expect real liberalization of EEC agricultural trade—what we really hope, he thought, was that EEC policies should not become more restrictive. We disillusioned him saying that we still held firmly to the Ministerial Resolution.[4] We felt that we had made some genuine concessions to the EEC point of view on agriculture. Rey admitted that the EEC was not going to get agreement on the montant de soutien and would have to modify its position. However, he believed, this would be possible only if other participants also changed their stand somewhat. He seemed anxious to have bilateral meetings between the EEC and the U.S. in the near future where we would talk frankly about what we really wanted and what was possible to get. We found ourselves in the unaccustomed position of urging Rey to be patient: we thought that a fairly clear picture of our respective interests would emerge fairly promptly from the May to September discussions on agriculture policies.

We are happy to report that the President has signed the Executive Order formally making this office a voting member of the interagency committees on textiles.[5]

Our review of the Tariff Commission's report on the watches escape clause case has begun. The industry is building most of its case for retention of the high duties upon a National Security argument. Consequently the President has asked OEP to undertake an investigation of the national security aspect of the watch industry and to report within 6 months.

Sincerely,

Kenneth Auchincloss[6]

---

[3] See Document 280.

[4] Regarding the GATT Ministerial resolutions, see footnote 3, Document 254.

[5] Executive Order 11214, April 7, is printed in 30 *Federal Register* 4527.

[6] Printed from a copy that bears this typed signature.

282. Letter From the Special Representative for Trade Negotiations' Executive Assistant (Auchincloss) to the Special Representative for Trade Negotiations (Herter)[1]

Washington, April 14, 1965.

Dear Governor:

I hope this will be my last report by letter and that you will be back next week. We all miss you, and I hope I'm not betraying any secrets by reporting that Cady had her hair done especially in preparation for her trip to see you today.

1. Cereals. Irwin has sent you a report on the exporters' meetings last week, so I won't try to elaborate.[2] As for the timing of the negotiations, the EEC Council takes up the Commission's cereals proposal again on May 13, and Hijzen says they will make this into a marathon session if necessary in order to reach agreement. We are urging them strongly to hold to the date of May 17 for the start of cereals negotiations, even though this means that countries will have little chance to study the various proposals by that time since they will not be laid on the table until sometime between May 13–17.

2. Adjustment Assistance. Senator Hartke has introduced a bill that would loosen somewhat the criteria that must be met for firms or workers to qualify for adjustment assistance under the Trade Expansion Act.[3] Instead of the tariff concession having to be the "major" cause of increased imports and "increased" imports the cause of serious injury, the bill would require only that the concession be "in whole or in part responsible" for the increased imports and that the increased imports be "the predominant factor" in causing injury. The criteria for escape clause relief would remain unchanged, so the bill would have the effect of making adjustment assistance easier to get than escape clause action. We are now discussing within the Office whether the Executive should support the bill. It really comes down to a question of whether the danger that the escape clause criteria might be loosened in the legislative process outweighs the danger that the trade legislation in general and the escape clause in particular would face heavy political sledding in 1967 if the adjustment assistance provisions remain completely inoperative.

---

[1] Source: Kennedy Library, Herter Papers, Kenneth Auchincloss, Box 5. No classification marking.

[2] The report of Irwin Hedges has not been further identified.

[3] Vance Hartke, Democratic Senator from Indiana, introduced S.1333, 89th Cong., on March 1 to amend the adjustment assistance provisions of the Trade Expansion Act of 1962 regarding determinations by the U.S. Tariff Commission of injury or threatened injury to firms or groups of workers. Congress did not act on this bill.

3. *Wyndham White Visit.* Wyndham White has tentative plans to come to Washington in the last week of this month. If the trip is confirmed, we will make arrangements for him to see a number of people in various agencies and in Congress.

4. *Canadian Auto Parts Bill.* Chairman Mills has just announced that he plans to take up the auto parts bill at the end of April.[4] After that will come the $50 duty-free exemption for tourists, and only then the Revised Tariff Schedules bill.[5] The much-battered RTS bill takes it on the chin again.

Very best regards,

Kenneth Auchincloss[6]

---

[4] Wilbur D. Mills, Democratic Representative from Arkansas and Chairman of the House Ways and Means Committee, presided at hearings held April 27–29 on the administration's bill (H.R. 9042, 89th Cong.) to implement the U.S.-Canadian executive agreement. This agreement, signed by President Johnson and Canadian Prime Minister Lester B. Pearson, at Johnson City, Texas, on January 16, 1965, called for removal of U.S. and Canadian tariffs on cars and car parts at the manufacturer's level (17 UST 1372). The bill authorizing the President to remove duties at the manufacturer's level on Canadian automobiles and parts for original equipment, the Automotive Products Trade Act of 1965, was enacted as P.L. 89–283, October 21, 1965; 79 Stat. 1016.

[5] Not further identified.

[6] Printed from a copy that bears this typed signature.

---

283. Letter From the Special Representative for Trade Negotiations' Executive Assistant (Auchincloss) to the Special Representative for Trade Negotiations (Herter)[1]

Washington, May 4, 1965.

Dear Governor:

The Wyndham White visit went very well, I think. He was sorry that he missed you, but he had meetings with the Vice President; Secretaries Freeman, Connor and Wirtz, and Mr. Bundy. The Dominican crisis interfered a bit with his meetings at State—both Mr. Ball and Mr. Mann were

---

[1] Source: Kennedy Library, Herter Papers, Kenneth Auchincloss, Box 5. No classification marking.

embroiled in Caribbean problems and so had to cancel their sessions with Wyndham White. But he did meet Mann at lunch and also had a number of useful talks with Tony Solomon, the new Assistant Secretary for Economic Affairs.

Perhaps the most interesting part of the trip was the interagency meetings when Wyndham White elaborated his thoughts on long-range trade policy problems—that is, beyond the Kennedy Round context. He is very much concerned that the rules of the GATT will become diluted by a host of special arrangements for the LDCs condoned or connived in by the developed countries. Preferences of course are one of his main worries. He feels it is important to hold to the most-favored-nation clause but not in a dogmatic fashion. If there are special circumstances in which a departure from MFN might be advantageous, and if all the countries that would be affected by it concur, he believes that MFN theology should not stand in the way. The main point, in his view, is to limit this special treatment to individual cases taken up on an ad hoc basis. What now appears to be happening, he warns, is that departures from MFN are being approved under the guise of free trade areas—EEC–Turkey, EEC–Nigeria, and the like. This will destroy the MFN clause if allowed to continue.

Wyndham White plans to meet with the "Big Four" (U.K., EEC, U.S. and Japan) this week to discuss next steps on the industrial side of the negotiations. He will try to get agreement on sectoral discussions to take place between now and the summer holidays. Certainly one motive behind this is the feeling that it is important to keep the negotiations in a multilateral framework. As you know, things have been proceeding mostly on a bilateral basis for some time, and there is a danger of separate deals being struck bilaterally that would limit the chances of broader multilateral cuts. The sector that he is most anxious to begin work on is textiles; he feels strongly that the cotton textile problem should be treated in the Kennedy Round context rather than entirely in the Long Term Arrangement.

I gather that Bill[2] has just talked to you about the latest chapter in the ASP saga and has also filled you in on our progress towards a grains proposal. I am enclosing the latest draft of the latter,[3] it will be the subject of a Trade Executive Committee meeting on Friday.[4]

I have also enclosed a floor plan for our new quarters at 1800 G Street. We approved this layout last week, and GSA estimates that it will take five to six weeks to outfit the space for us. So it looks as if we shall be

---

[2] Reference is to William M. Roth, Deputy Special Representative for Trade Negotiations.

[3] The enclosures to this letter have not been found.

[4] May 7.

moving in early June. I think we came out fairly well—we will have about 3,000 more sq. feet there than we do here.

Incidental intelligence: Congressman Curtis has gone to Geneva for a week.

Finally, I might mention that on that perennial question—definitive acceptance of the GATT—Wyndham White set out the arguments in favor of it at his lunch with our Congressional advisors, and the reaction was generally positive. We are hoping to get, through the intercession of Paul Kaplowitz,[5] a green light from Wilbur Mills and to proceed from there to try to get the White House's OK. On this issue, I imagine that the most we could really expect from Congress is absence of any negative reaction, and that is what we have so far received (except for some reservations on the part of Senator Byrd). So I hope that we will be able to push ahead.

Sincerely,

Kenneth Auchincloss[6]

---

[5] Chairman of the U.S. Trade Commission.
[6] Printed from a copy that bears this typed signature.

---

284.   Memorandum From the Deputy Assistant Secretary of State for European Affairs (Schaetzel) to the Deputy Director of the Office of Atlantic Political-Economic Affairs (Percival)[1]

Washington, July 7, 1965.

SUBJECT

Agriculture in the Kennedy Round

Ted Van Dyk[2] passed along to me on a personal basis the fact that the Vice President has become actively interested in the relationship of agriculture to the Kennedy Round. It apparently is the Vice President's tenta-

---

[1] Source: Department of State, Central Files, FT 7 GATT. Confidential.
[2] Office of the Vice President.

tive view that the way out of this dilemma is to find the answer to the present agricultural surplus situation in the rapidly growing needs of the less developed countries.

Van Dyk said there had been an initial discussion with Bill Roth and Humphrey would be meeting soon with Schnittker. Van Dyk promised that he would keep me informed and said that at some juncture we would be brought in. He hoped that Tom Enders[3] might give some thought to the question.

I said that before one became too enamored with the idea that this provided the answer to the problem one needed to realize that the first issue is how to share the somewhat inadequate commercial market on an equitable basis among the temperate zone agricultural producers. While the farmers might very well agree with the point Van Dyk made, namely that they are interested in the sale of their output rather than being too finicky about where the money comes from, one must face the hard fact that the noncommercial sales are financed by the Congress.

Van Dyk concluded on two points. One was that Humphrey realized that we had to reduce outlandish demands we were making earlier for the massive increase in our share of the commercial market. He also noted that Humphrey saw agriculture in the Kennedy Round as a means of putting some sense into the organization of American agriculture. He did not indicate just how this might be done.

---

[3] Office of Atlantic Political-Economic Affairs.

285. Record of Meeting[1]

Doc. 1617/Japan   Geneva, July 8, 1965.

UNITED STATES DELEGATION TO THE SIXTH ROUND
OF GATT TRADE NEGOTIATIONS
Geneva

Initial Detailed Meeting Concerning U.S. Exceptions List

TOPICS DISCUSSED

Separate prepared Japanese statements (attached) relating to: (a) their own
exceptions list and (b) the U.S. exceptions list

[Here follows a list of the six U.S. participants and the nine Japanese
participants. Martin Y. Hirabayashi headed the U.S. side; Takashi Oyamada, chief negotiator for Japan in the Kennedy Round, headed the Japanese side.]

U.S. Comments

We began the session by making a few additional concluding
remarks relating to the Japanese exceptions list. Referring to the statement which we made at the first meeting concerned with our examination of Japanese exceptions items (see minutes of first substantive
bilateral meeting),[2] we repeated our disappointment with the length of
the list and its impact on the U.S. We again expressed our disappointment at the non-tariff barriers imposed by Japan which affect U.S. trade
and strongly urged their removal. We can, in no case, consider as meaningful tariff reduction offers on items subject to illegal quantitative
restrictions.

While the phase of bilateral discussions just concluded provided an
opportunity for an additional exchange of information on exceptions
items, we still maintain our initial view that improvements in the Japanese offers could and should be made if the U.S. is to maintain its present
offers vis-à-vis Japan. In many instances we still remain unconvinced of
the overriding national interest which necessitates Japan's putting many
items on the exceptions list.

---

[1] Source: Department of State, Central Files, FT 7 GATT. Confidential. Drafted by
Edward M. Sacchet, Technical Secretary of the Japan Team of the Delegation, on July 16,
cleared by Martin Y. Hirabayashi, Chairman of the Japan Team, and approved by Helen L.
Brewster. The source text is enclosure 1 to Tagg A–493 from Geneva, July 22. As of December 26, the U.S. and Japanese Kennedy Round delegations held 38 bilateral meetings;
records of these meetings are ibid.

[2] Not found.

Japanese Comments

Mr. Oyamada stated that it is the feeling of his delegation that the U.S. has failed to appreciate the tremendous problems faced by Japan in participating in the Kennedy Round as a linear country, nor of the overriding national interest of Japan in excepting the items recently discussed in the bilaterals. He said that while there are four main reasons for excepting an item from a full tariff cut, two reasons were discussed repeatedly during the bilaterals, i.e., the need to improve industry structure, and the existence of small-scale industry. He said that these two reasons are the most important determinants of the Japanese exceptions list and therefore he wished to read a statement (see attachment A) relating to these justifications.[3]

In brief, the statement noted the heavy reliance of Japan on trade and the need to improve industry structure in order for Japanese industry to become more competitive. Fifty percent of Japan's exports are with LDC's which, in the field of light industry, are taking over many of Japan's markets. For this reason Japan wishes to shift emphasis from light industry to heavy and more sophisticated industry. In view of the rapid worldwide expansion of trade among industrial nations, Japan, in order to meet the demands of the future, must promote structural change of her domestic industry.

Citing statistics relating to national income in Japan and the technological level of industry, and noting disadvantages of Japanese industry with respect to level of productivity, ratio of borrowed to owned capital, the payment of high interest rates, and problems of a social and regional nature, Mr. Oyamada stated that it is the aim of the Japanese government to establish an industrial structure most suitable for economic growth and at the same time minimize economic and social dislocations within the economy.

The problem of small scale firms is particularly deep-rooted. Citing statistics relating to the number of firms involved and the large number of persons dependent upon these firms for employment, their low productivity and the social implications of subjecting these firms to a full tariff cut, Mr. Oyamada repeated that these firms could not survive a full linear cut. He said Japan cannot stress too much the over-riding national interest in protecting these small scale enterprises.

Commenting on the Japanese economy, he said that the short-run outlook is not bright and that, in fact, the Japanese economy is currently in the throes of a depression. At present the prevailing mood of business in Japan is one of pessimism.

---

[3] A note in place of Attachment A says that because of a delay by the Japanese Delegation in providing the U.S. Delegation with this text, it was to be forwarded at a later date. It has not been found.

U.S. Response

We pointed out that the U.S. is very much aware of the problems faced by Japan. In fact, the U.S. has many similar problems of its own. In spite of these problems, we are going ahead with significant offers in the Kennedy Round, and we feel that Japan's offer can be improved even though these problems exist. While not wishing to dwell at length on the various statistical data cited by the Japanese, since we had already done this at some length during the bilaterals, we hoped that Japan could improve its offers in the Kennedy Round since Japan itself had so much to gain from a substantial reduction of trade barriers.

Japanese Comments Relating to U.S. Exceptions

The Japanese representative made the attached statement (Attachment B) relating to U.S. exceptions.[4] Taking account of the huge value of U.S. Japanese bilateral trade, which amounted to $4.2 billion in 1964, he stated that it was incumbent on the two countries to make a model case of bilateral trade; nonetheless many problems exist. For example, the balance of trade for the past 10 years has been consistently in favor of the U.S. While Japan has sought to redress this balance, the burden of deficit has been exacerbated by U.S. trade barriers and "protectionist" trade policies which limit Japan's access to the U.S. market. It is Japan's hope that the U.S. will recognize Japan's circumstances and cooperate to redress this chronic trade imbalance. In addition to the NTB's which curb imports, discrepancies between U.S. foreign and domestic trade policies have embarrassed the trading partners of the U.S., including Japan. Moreover, tariff rates on certain items are so high that even a full linear cut would leave them still high and thus provide the U.S. with bargaining power in future tariff negotiations.

The U.S., he said, is now the world's leading industrial nation whose industrial structure is the most advanced in the world. Japan doubts that U.S. industry would be unable to absorb a full linear cut in many instances and, in general, is disappointed with the U.S. exceptions list. He said that in the opinion of the Japanese, the U.S. has not made sufficient effort to keep exceptions to a bare minimum and they hope that the offer will be improved.

With respect to NTB's which are applied on many items, Mr.Oyamada said that the existence of these NTB's nullify offers by the U.S. for tariff reductions. Unless drastic improvements are made, the value of tariff reductions will be discounted by Japan. Among the NTB's mentioned by the Japanese representative were: Customs valuation system

---

[4] Not printed. The Japanese representative's statement is summarized above.

(ASP), and section 402a of the U.S. Tariff antidumping legislation,[5] escape clause investigations, import restrictions such as Buy American and Mass Urban Transportation Acts,[6] various state administrative regulations, and voluntary export controls.

Mr. Oyamada said that it is the hope of the Government of Japan that the U.S. will improve its offers on tariff reductions and eliminate or substantially reduce existing NTB's. In addition, Article XXVIII renegotiations should be pursued along with Kennedy Round negotiations to achieve a solution to outstanding economic problems.

U.S. Response

Rather than comment at length on the various statements made by the Japanese representative, we reserved our more specific comments until the commodity discussions beginning on July 16.

---

[5] See footnote 3, Document 231.
[6] See footnotes 2 and 3, Document 241.

---

286.   Airgram From the Mission to the European Office of the United Nations to the Department of State[1]

Tagg A–489   Geneva, July 18, 1965.

SUBJECT

Report No. 19—U.S. Delegation to Sixth Round of GATT Trade Negotiations

1. Summary

On July 13, the Trade Negotiations Committee (TNC), in a final session before the summer recess, heard the Director General of the GATT review the status of negotiations and accepted the agreed portions of the report of the Tropical Products Group on procedures for negotiations on such products. During the week of July 12, a subcommittee of the TNC started the examination of developed countries' lists of exceptions of

---

[1] Source: Department of State, Central Files, FT 7 GATT. Confidential. Drafted by W. Kelly, Northrop H. Kirk, Guy A. Wiggins, and Courtenay P. Worthington, Jr., on July 15, and approved by Helen L. Brewster. Repeated to 51 diplomatic missions.

interest to the developing countries and completed its review of the lists of the United States and the United Kingdom. The first meeting of the sector group on steel was held on July 14. Bilateral negotiations with Canada were continued.

2.   Meeting of Trade Negotiations Committee

The Trade Negotiations Committee (TNC) was convened on July 13 for a final session before the summer recess in order a) to review the status of negotiations and preparations for resumption of work in September and b) to consider the report from the Tropical Products Group on procedures for negotiations on such products.

a.   Status of Negotiations

In reviewing the status of negotiations, the Chairman of the TNC, Mr. Wyndham White, referred to the extensive *bilateral discussions on industrial products* which had been taking place since the confrontation and justification exercise on industrial exceptions. These highly technical and time-consuming discussions have clarified a number of details concerning exceptions and offers. Mr. Wyndham White considered that the bilateral discussions had made significant progress in indicating where multilateral discussions are called for (sector discussions for some industrial products) and in defining negotiating desiderata regarding exceptions and offers.

With respect to *negotiations on agricultural products,* Mr. Wyndham White considered that a useful start had been made in the cereals negotiations, based on proposals tabled in May and subsequent discussions. He noted that technical discussions now underway should be continued in September with a view to an early resumption of general discussions aimed at developing a cereals arrangement. He also referred to the discussions recently concluded on the elements of protection to be negotiated and the scope of offers to be made on other agricultural products as a valuable prelude to the negotiations themselves. He said the present program calls for tabling offers on agricultural products other than grains on September 16 and the beginning of active negotiations thereafter.

Mr. Wyndham White noted that there would be a meeting on July 19 of the NTB Subcommittee's Group on Dumping. Otherwise, he commented, the *non-tariff barrier* work has either been deferred until a later stage in negotiations or was being conducted in connection with discussions on individual products.

Mr. Wyndham welcomed the fact that a number of *developing countries* were participating in the negotiations on the basis of agreed procedures. He noted that the examination of selected exceptions lists of interest to these countries had started. He noted also that *Poland* had made an offer, that some bilateral talks have taken place, and that multi-lateral discussions should be held in September.

With respect to the general progress of the negotiations, Mr. Wyndham White stated that negotiations were proceeding in general accordance with the anticipated timetable. He added that participants must seriously consider the question of timing and that negotiations should be fully engaged for all product areas and by all countries in the fall in the hope that negotiations could be brought to their final stage by early 1966.

There was no comment in the TNC on this review.

b. *Tropical Products*

Mr. Wyndham White noted that the Tropical Products Group in its report on procedures for negotiations on such products (TN.64/TP/3) had not reached agreement in all areas. He believed there was sufficient agreement on procedures that negotiations could get started. He urged that there be no further procedural discussions and the tropical products negotiations start on the basis of the agreed portions of the report of the Group. The TNC accepted this proposal and statement[2] that tropical products offers should be tabled on September 16, with each country free to determine its own basis for making offers, and with multilateral confrontation to follow the tabling of offers.

3. *LDC Examination of Linear Country Exceptions Lists*

a. *U.S Confrontation*

At the opening of the two week session of the TNC Subcommittee for examination of developed country exceptions of interest to less developed countries (LDC's), the U.S. list was examined in the first two sessions on July 12 and 13. Delegations of linear countries attending included the U.K., EEC, Japan, Sweden and some other EFTA countries part of the time. Non-linear countries included Argentina, Brazil, Canada, Chile, Ghana, India, Indonesia, Israel, Jamaica, Malta, Nigeria, Pakistan, Peru, Portugal, Rhodesia, Spain, UAR, Uruguay and Yugoslavia.

There was some open recognition (including that of Ambassador Lall of India) that the United States had tried to keep exceptions on items of interest to the LDC's to a minimum in the nonagricultural sector. The LDC's pressed, of course, in all cases for improvement in the U.S. offers. The LDC's did not query us on who is and is not an LDC, did not challenge our principle of excluding items because of the non-participation of principal suppliers in the negotiations, did not inject the long-term textile arrangement into the discussion and did not waste time in arguing over excepted items in which they have no trade interests.

As regards our economic exceptions, the LDC's, expectedly, expressed their greatest concern over U.S. exceptions on certain textiles

---

[2] Director General Wyndham White's July 13 statement was not found.

(especially Uruguay and Yugoslavia) and leather products (India, Spain and others); they argued that their interests in these and other products warranted U.S. reconsideration of excepted items. India said it wished to discuss bilaterally the possibility of U.S. ex-outs, and offers on various handmade articles.

The Peruvian representative pressed hard on the importance which Peru attaches to the need for U.S. liberalization on lead and zinc and was echoed by Yugoslavia. Our explanation of the reasons for these mandatory exceptions included reference to the recent Tariff Commission report[3] which attracted their interest. They will follow developments with interest and press for tariff reductions as well as the lifting of quotas. The UAR, Nigeria and Brazil, to a lesser extent, objected to the U.S. exclusion of crude petroleum. The comments of several LDC's made clear that U.S. explanations of mandatory exceptions based on the lack of legislative authority do not in their view relieve the United States from the commitments undertaken at the Ministerial meetings in 1963 and 1964 and in Part IV of the GATT[4] to keep exceptions on items important to LDC exports to a minimum. Several of them emphasized that the United States could and should rely more on adjustment assistance programs. We emphasized that the existence of adjustment assistance programs had already played a part in reducing our exceptions list but could not be expected to solve all of the problems.

The fact that the United States introduced an additional list of excepted items into the discussions on the second day did not bring forth critical comments. A short explanation that this was the result of further study of lists of interest submitted by participants was accepted and the fact that it related to items of interest to Israel, Yugoslavia and Spain was not disclosed at the request of the Israeli and Yugoslav delegations. The U.S. delegation offered to discuss these additional items later in the week if any delegations so desired. As yet no requests have been received.

Of the so-called borderline countries, Yugoslavia, Israel, Spain and Portugal participated in the meeting without challenge. Yugoslavia and Spain took an active part in the discussions but Israel went on record only once in regard to a minor technical point. Portugal spoke briefly only about items of interest to its overseas territories.

The LDC's welcomed the U.S. willingness to undertake bilateral discussions to clarify technical and statistical questions as well as to exchange further views on U.S. offers related to their specific trade interests. Bilateral meetings have already been held with representatives of Rhodesia, Malta, Peru, India, Israel, Yugoslavia and Chile.

---

[3] Not further identified.
[4] See Document 274.

b. *U.K. Confrontation*

The confrontation on the short U.K. exception list took only one session on July 14. The U.K. defense and justification was primarily based on: (1) the depressed status and process of reorganization in the industry involved; (2) the extensive degree of duty free treatment given to Commonwealth LDC's; and (3) the existence of disparities between U.K. rates of duty and the rates of other developed countries. The LDC comments were moderate in tone and the U.K. received some compliments on its general attitude towards LDC problems. The U.K. effort to shift the burden for improving its offers on to other developed countries (disparities) and on the Commonwealth countries including LDC's (preferences) was successful. India and Pakistan said that they wished to take a constructive and positive approach when they are asked to forego present advantages in the U.K. market but that they would require compensating advantages in other developed country markets.

4.   *Sector Discussion on Steel*

The first meeting of the sector group on steel was held on July 14. The United States, EEC, ECSC, U.K., Japan, Austria, and Sweden are the initial members of this group.

It was agreed that the group's work should cover "steel mill products," which includes BTN items in Chapter 73 of the EEC tariff schedules that are under the jurisdiction of both the ECSC and the EEC. Not all items in Chapter 73, however, are included. During the summer recess countries are to develop for "steel mill products" a concordance between their tariff schedules and the EEC tariff schedules. The group will reconvene on September 8 to develop a rough concordance among member countries' tariff schedules on the basis of the individual country concordances. A similar procedure will be followed with respect to ferroalloys.

There was general agreement that until a "map" of concordances is developed it is premature to discuss what road might be taken to achieve the group's objective of maximizing tariff reductions in the steel sector.

5.   *Negotiations with Canada*

The 25th and 26th United States and Canadian meetings marked the beginning of discussions on agricultural duties and agricultural nontariff barriers. The procedure is for the Canadians to review the U.S. tariff item-by-item and indicate those items on which they wish to have the rates reduced. The U.S. side, using a concordance, determines the corresponding Canadian tariff item. Where appropriate both sides examine the possibility of matching rates, as has been done on certain agricultural items in the past, or the U.S. side may indicate its interest in a reduction on the Canadian side.

The Canadians have included in their requests fifty percent reductions and in some cases elimination of the U.S. duty under either Section

202 (the five percent authority) or Section 212 (the authority to eliminate duties in excess of five percent on agricultural products under certain conditions) of the TEA.[5] The U.S. team has notified them that, while it is willing to listen to such requests, there can be no assurance that we will use the authority of the latter section.

In the course of these discussions the Canadians have reiterated their long-standing and oft-repeated plea for elimination of the U.S. quota on Canadian cheddar cheese. They have also complained about the refusal of the New York State Government to send milk inspectors to nearby Canadian dairy farms. This refusal precludes Canadian milk producers from selling over the border because they cannot meet the state's sanitary requirement that all milk marketed in New York bear an inspector's seal of approval.

As a follow-up to an earlier discussion, the Canadian Delegation also submitted a paper noting Canada's interest in the elimination of the manufacturing clause in the U.S. copyright law.[6] The bill revising this law which is now before Congress[7] retains a slightly modified version of this clause which has protected U.S. printers since 1891.

For the Ambassador:
Helen L. Brewster

---

[5] Reference is to the Trade Expansion Act of 1962, P.L. 87–794, approved October 11, 1962; 76 Stat. 872.

[6] The Canadian paper has not been found, but the reference is to the manufacturing clause in Section 3 of Chapter 565, approved March 3, 1891; 26 Stat. 1107; text as amended is codified in 17 USC 16.

[7] An omnibus copyright revision bill (S.1006; H.R. 4347, 89th Cong.), introduced February 4, 1965, to substantially revise copyright law, was not adopted by Congress because of conflicting views expressed by interested groups in hearings before House Judiciary Subcommittee No. 3 and the Senate Judiciary Patents, Trademarks, and Copyrights Subcommittee.

287.   Letter From the Special Representative for Trade Negotiations
(Herter) to the President's Special Assistant for National
Security Affairs (Bundy)[1]

Manchester, Massachusetts, July 20, 1965.

Dear Mac:

I should have written to you long ago to thank you not only for the
light reading which you and Mary sent me, but also for your kind tolerance of my long absence.

As of now, I am alive by miracle and ought to be as good as new by
early autumn. Fortunately, the whole so-called Kennedy Round has been
in the doldrums, so that I do not feel that my absence has been too important. However, as you know, my resignation is always in the President's
hands, so that if at any time he wished to fill the job with someone else, I
would quite understand.

It is becoming clearer every day that French agricultural policy and
the curious foibles of Le Grande Charles make it more and more doubtful
as to whether any meaningful Kennedy Round can be achieved prior to
the expiration of the Trade Expansion Act. This being the case, I hate to
see President Kennedy's name attached to an extraordinarily worthwhile effort which seemed to have petered out. It was Erhard who was
most insistent on Kennedy's name being maintained in connection with
the negotiations. Perhaps thinking about this matter should be postponed until after the general elections.

I have been talking to Bill Roth about the possibility of your wanting
a real blast taken against Le Grande Charles at some particular time. It
could, of course, be done with full justification from myself and my
office. Do keep this in mind. For the moment, I agree that we should be
greeting his efforts to dominate or destroy the Common Market with sad
silence.

Best, to you, as always, and hoping to catch a glimpse of you if you
can spare the time should you be coming up here some week-end.

As ever,

Christian A. Herter[2]

---

[1] Source: Kennedy Library, Herter Papers, McGeorge Bundy, Box 7. Personal and
Confidential.

[2] Printed from a copy that bears this typed signature.

288. Memorandum From Secretary of Agriculture Freeman to President Johnson[1]

Washington, August 9, 1965.

SUBJECT

Agriculture in the Kennedy Round

We face an early decision on whether the United States will make its offers to cut tariffs on agricultural products as scheduled on September 16 even though the European Economic Community will not do so. I have serious doubt that the EEC will be able to participate effectively in the agricultural negotiations in the two years left to complete the Kennedy Round.

Last fall it was decided against considerable agricultural resistance to table industrial offers but to withhold agricultural offers because the EEC was not ready. It was argued then that the EEC needed time to shape its agricultural system and that we should not press them to open agricultural negotiations. It is being argued with equal force today that it is imperative that the rest of us make our offers "in order to maintain the momentum of the industrial negotiations, despite the absence of the EEC." I find myself in the strange position of trying to understand why we should table now even though the EEC is not ready, when a year ago, we *could not* table until the EEC was ready.

You will recall that it was difficult to explain to farm groups why we went ahead in industry but not agriculture last fall. There will be similar resistance to tabling our offers now, particularly from those commodity interests here at home affected by our proposed tariff cuts.

The United States industrial offer now on the table is far better than the offers of the EEC and most other countries. To make offers now on all agricultural products would further overbalance that offer. Hence a procedure has been proposed to make limited offers on agricultural products if the other major countries do so, leaving out the items which could be of major benefit to the EEC, and making it clear that we are ready to withdraw our agricultural offers in whole or in part if necessary. This procedure, as outlined in detail in other memoranda,[2] does reduce the risks involved in making agricultural offers now, but I have grave doubts about the value to the United States of any such limited procedure. This tactic relies heavily on the possibility of our being able to withdraw agricultural offers if we do not achieve reciprocity. I fear that those advocating this seriously misjudge the difficulties of withdrawal.

---

[1] Source: Johnson Library, Bator Papers, Kennedy Round, 1964–1965 I, Box 12. No classification marking. Transmitted to President Johnson on August 10; see Document 290.

[2] See Document 289.

Offers stimulate counter-offers, and quickly become woven into the fabric of a negotiation, especially if they remain on the table until its close. Withdrawals then stimulate counter-withdrawals and start an unravelling process which could threaten the whole negotiation. The prospect of having the negotiation fall apart just as the Administration was preparing to seek renewal of Trade Agreements legislation would be a great deterrent to withdrawing our agricultural offers, no matter how weak the reciprocity situation.

It is not the only alternative open to us. There are in fact four distinct alternatives:

1. To suspend all negotiations—industry as well as agriculture—until the EEC is ready to participate in an effort to liberalize trade. This is the course of action which uses our maximum bargaining power. It is fully consistent with our previous statements, and with the legislative history of the Trade Expansion Act, which recognized the crucial role of the EEC in the negotiations.

2. Postpone agricultural offers until the EEC can participate—possibly early in 1966. This has the merit of not playing our cards in agriculture and sustains our position that no final bargain can be reached without significant liberalization in agriculture as well as industry.

3. Make limited and qualified offers as proposed by Governor Herter. In the form it has been proposed however, this has serious defects. To be reasonably acceptable to the U.S. farm community, the qualifications should be about as follows:

The U.S. agricultural offers would be subject to withdrawal in their entirety if the EEC failed to table offers early next year that would provide for meaningful liberalization of agricultural trade on a large proportion of the commodities now imported by the EEC. Offers by the EEC based on the montant de soutien would not be acceptable. These qualifications should be stated publicly at the time the offers are made, and should make it clear that in view of the fact that our position has consistently been that liberalization for agriculture must be an integral part of any final result of the Kennedy Round, such a withdrawal of agriculture offers would mean the end of the negotiations.

4. Withdraw agriculture completely from the negotiations now and stake our hopes for trade liberalization in agriculture on an extension of the Trade Expansion Act and the possibility that time will make the EEC more flexible.

I recommend alternative (2)—postponing agricultural offers while we wait to see whether the EEC can participate in the agricultural phase of the Kennedy Round. We can decide early in 1966 whether or not to go ahead on a limited basis as in (3) above if the EEC is again not ready. We would thus avoid the political hazards of making agricultural offers while the farm bill is before the Congress, while preserving the opportunity to move ahead later on agriculture. Agricultural interests in this country would probably support alternative (2) just as they would strongly support holding up the entire negotiations until the EEC is ready. I do not know of any major agricultural group that would support our going into an agricultural negotiation that does not include EEC.

Some argue that alternative (2) runs the risk of collapsing the entire negotiation; I know of no basis for this judgment. But I recall that it was being argued a year ago that the success of the entire negotiation depended on "*not* going ahead in agriculture", just as it is being argued today that everything depends on "going ahead in agriculture." I believe that if we go ahead without the EEC on September 16, the world will conclude that the U.S. is getting panicky and has decided to get the best deal it can before the Trade Act runs out on June 30, 1967, and will make the best deal possible in agriculture, even if the EEC makes no offer.

The domestic political danger of alternative (3) is that we cannot anticipate any clear benefits for U.S. agriculture, while at the same time some U.S. commodity interests will insist they will be adversely affected by proposed tariff cuts.

As in the past, then, so far as United States agriculture is concerned, any decision to table United States agricultural offers without a simultaneous tabling by the EEC must be justified on foreign policy grounds. The small benefit that United States agriculture might anticipate from a limited negotiation will not nearly offset the criticism we will receive as the result of failure to use the Kennedy Round to curb the growing protectionism in the EEC. This in turn would almost certainly cause grave difficulties in trying to extend the Trade Act.

---

289. Memorandum From the Special Representative for Trade Negotiations (Herter) to President Johnson[1]

Washington, August 9, 1965.

SUBJECT

Agriculture in the Kennedy Round

We have come to another critical point in the Kennedy Round negotiations. All the negotiating countries agreed some months ago that

---

[1] Source: Kennedy Library, Herter Papers, Chronological File, August 1965, Box 3. Confidential. Transmitted to President Johnson on August 10; see Document 290.

on September 16 they would exchange offers on agricultural products in order to achieve the Ministerial objective of significant liberalization of world trade for all classes of products, agricultural as well as industrial. Doubt has been cast on the observance of the September 16 tabling date because of the internal crisis which has paralyzed the EEC. The question facing us is whether we, along with other principal negotiating countries, should submit concrete and specific offers even if the EEC does not.

After full discussion with the interested departments and careful consideration of the pros and cons of various courses of action, I recommend that we announce promptly our intention to abide by the internationally agreed timetable and to table the agricultural offers of the United States in Geneva on September 16. This step would be taken in the expectation that other principal negotiating countries will also table concrete and specific offers on agriculture at the same time, even if the EEC does not. An essential part of my recommendation is that we approach the United Kingdom, other EFTA countries, Japan, Canada, Australia, and New Zealand at a high level, urging them to join us in the submission of agricultural offers. If it develops that the key countries other than the EEC do not agree to go along on September 16, we would then also withhold our agricultural offers.

Although there are some risks in following this course of action, I believe that it is the best approach for the following reasons:

1. The U.S. interest in the successful conclusion of the negotiations on both industry and agriculture requires that we take the lead in proceeding with the tabling of our offers and in urging other countries to do the same.

2. The alternative appears to be an indefinite postponement of the agricultural negotiations and the clear danger of the collapse of the entire Kennedy Round. This would put our national objectives—with respect to the expansion of trade, the less developed countries, and Europe—in jeopardy. Failure to move ahead would also let the initiative in the negotiations slip away to the EEC and the French.

3. While it is impossible to tell what, if any, effect the proposed action will have on the EEC, I believe it will maximize our chances of getting the EEC to modify its unacceptable approach and to make significant agricultural offers. With everyone going ahead without the EEC, there will be pressure on the Community, and a rallying point for those within the EEC who want to see the negotiations succeed.

4. The tabling of offers even without the EEC will permit useful negotiations on agriculture to begin (along with the cereals negotiations already under way with the EEC and others) and ensure that the industrial negotiations continue.

5. The position taken by the Administration both domestically and internationally is that agriculture as well as industry must be included in

the Kennedy Round. To postpone further the start of the agricultural negotiations would risk compromising this objective.

The disadvantages and risks in the course of the action I propose are related primarily to the reaction of the American farm community. They will undoubtedly be concerned about making offers to produce U.S. duties without simultaneously obtaining offers from the EEC inasmuch as lowering EEC agricultural protection is our primary target.

I intend to minimize those risks in the following ways:

1. In submitting our offers, we would include an introductory note (Tab A) which would make it crystal clear that the United States is tabling its offers on the assumption that it will receive reciprocal concessions in agriculture from its negotiating partners, or it will withdraw its offers to the extent deemed necessary, even if this means withdrawal of all offers. In addition, this headnote would reiterate the basic position that the United States must achieve overall reciprocity in the Kennedy Round.

2. Since the EEC will not be tabling significant offers on September 16, items of primary interest to the EEC countries will be withheld from the U.S. offer list until the EEC is ready to submit its offers.

3. Other politically sensitive items (e.g. beef) will be excluded from our offer list on the ground that they are covered by special commodity groups, are of primary concern to countries not participating in the negotiations, or are excepted for reasons of "overriding national interest."

It should be remembered that under the rules of the negotiations the offer lists are kept secret, although we can not of course be sure that some information about them will not leak.

For the dual purpose of explaining our action to the U.S. agricultural community and maximizing the pressure on other countries to join us in tabling offers on September 16, I would propose to issue a statement if you approve my recommendation. Such a draft statement is included at Tab B.[2]

These recommendations have the approval of the interested agencies, with the exception of the reservations expressed by Secretary Freeman in his separate memorandum to you.[3] If my recommendations meet with your approval we will, prior to September 16, submit to you the specific list of products we would offer for a tariff cut of 50 per cent, subject to the qualifications in our proposed introductory note. This list would be

---

[2] Not printed; the purport of the statement is stated above.

[3] Document 288.

drawn from the list of products on which you have already authorized a
50 per cent cut in approving the economic exceptions list last November.[4]

Christian A. Herter[5]

Tab A[6]

HEADNOTE TO ACCOMPANY AGRICULTURE OFFERS

1. The following United States offers on agricultural products are
made in accordance with the resolutions of the GATT Ministerial Meetings in 1963 and 1964, and in response to the TNC decision of March 18,
1965 to table concrete and specific offers, designed to achieve the objectives of the Ministers.

2. The United States is tabling these offers—

(a) in the expectation that other principal negotiating countries will
also table concrete and specific offers on agricultural products, and
(b) on the understanding that, if the other principal negotiating
countries are not willing to implement concrete and specific offers on
agricultural products which are of a trade coverage and of a degree of liberalization equal to that of the U. S. offers, the United States will withdraw such offers in whole or in part, to the extent it deems necessary.

3. The United States wishes to make it clear that it will implement
its agricultural and industrial offers only on the condition that it achieves
over-all reciprocity in the Kennedy Round. Further, the United States
reiterates its determination that the final bargain must include substantial liberalization of trade in agricultural as well as industrial products.

---

[4] See Documents 262 and 263.
[5] Printed from a copy that bears this typed signature.
[6] Confidential.

290. Memorandum From the President's Deputy Special Assistant for National Security Affairs (Bator) to President Johnson[1]

Washington, August 10, 1965.

SUBJECT

Agriculture in the Kennedy Round

We need instruction from you on an important Kennedy Round decision which might generate some political heat. The issue is whether we should:

1. Table our tariff offers on *agriculture* on schedule on September 16, even though the European Economic Community will not table. (Because DeGaulle has thrown a monkey-wrench in their machinery, the EEC will not be ready until January 1966 at the earliest.)

2. Postpone tabling until the EEC too is ready to go.

In a memo at Tab I, Chris Herter recommends that we *go ahead*, leaving out all items of interest to the EEC, and making clear in public that this is the beginning and not the end of the bargaining—that we will withdraw part or all of our offer unless the EEC comes through and we get a balanced bargain both in agriculture and overall.[2] Chris is strongly supported not only by Bill Roth and his Geneva negotiator, Mike Blumenthal (who is first rate), but also by Dean Rusk personally, as well as Ball and Mann and all the other departments except Agriculture.

Orville Freeman (at Tab II) recommends that we hold up until the Common Market is ready.[3] He is skeptical, as is everyone else, about their coming through on agriculture, and is worried about the political heat if we put even conditional offers on the table while the EEC sits on its hands.

The trouble with Orville's proposal is that it is likely to generate just as much political heat, while damaging our bargaining position. We would either have to bring the *industrial* negotiations, too, to a halt during the autumn, and risk having the Kennedy Round pronounced dead both here and in Europe. Or, if we push full steam ahead with industry, we will be charged with decoupling agriculture from industry, and throwing in the towel on agriculture without a real try.

No one is a very bullish about what the EEC will in the end offer on agriculture. However, by going forward now, we maximize the chance of

---

[1] Source: Johnson Library, Bator Papers, Kennedy Round, 1964–1965 I, Box 12. No classification marking.

[2] Document 289.

[3] Document 288.

getting worthwhile concessions for our farmers from the UK, Canada, and Japan—all important markets for us—and even of getting something useful from the EEC. Chris Herter and his people are right when they say that it is too early to quit, and to risk the collapse of the entire negotiation.

You might wish to hear the arguments in person. However, if you instruct us to go ahead without a meeting, Orville has made it quite clear that he will do his best to keep the agricultural community quiet. (My impression is that he and John Schnittker are much more open-minded about this than some of their staff.)

FMB

Organize meeting with Freeman, Rusk, Herter's man Blumenthal, the Vice President (?)[4]

Go ahead with Herter's proposal

Bundy speak to me

Ask the Vice President and Ellington to look at it[5]

---

[4] This option is checked, and the handwritten names "Ellington" and "McPherson" were added apparently by the President.

[5] This option is checked, and the President wrote: "This first. L." No record of these actions was found. The President did approve tabling the agricultural offers; see Document 292.

---

291.   Memorandum by John J. McCloy[1]

August 27, 1965.

Some time after President Johnson assumed office I was asked by him to examine into the possibilities of having the American automobile industry produce a car which would offset the drain on the U.S. balance of payments situation by the large sales of the Volkswagen in this country.

---

[1] Source: Washington National Records Center, RG 40, Secretary of Commerce Files: FRC 71 A 6617, White House, September–October. No classification marking. A covering letter from McCloy to Secretary of Commerce Connor, August 27, states, among other things, that he was sending this memorandum in accordance with their telephone conversation. The letter and the memorandum are attached to Document 294.

The President told me that he could not believe that we could not make as efficient and as economical a car as the Volkswagen once we set our minds to it. He said that he understood that if all the companies set about doing this there would be little money in it for anyone as the margins would be so small. He accordingly suggested that I explore the possibility of the leaders of our automobile industry getting together perhaps in a sort of composite corporation pooling their brains and resources to make such a car.

The President indicated that this was something which he did not wish to appear as pressing on the companies but he thought I might as a private citizen take a reading as to the possibilities for him. He said that for the moment at least I could ignore the anti-trust aspects for, though he had not approached the Attorney General on this matter, what he wanted was a judgment as to the practicability of such a project free of the legal considerations.

I talked separately with Fred Donnor, Henry Ford, and Lynn Townsend about it and, after putting the problem to each of them,[2] I asked them to give the matter more than cursory consideration since the inquiry made to me was a serious one and from a responsible government source.

Each of them came back to me in due course, I feel certain without consulting each other, and all were quite negative toward the idea.

The point was made that the margins were too small if all were in the field but, more importantly, they all resisted the thought of a joint effort almost as a matter of principle. They had difficulty envisaging a constructive cooperative effort in a commercial area; it ran against the grain of their competitive instincts and the entire basis on which our commercial system operated. This was not like making a tank for the Army during the war and, even in that case, there was great difficulty in joint efforts. Besides they said they could not envisage any sufficiently assuring pronouncement coming from the Department of Justice.

They said they had individually studied this problem of a small cheap Volkswagen-type car and periodically reviewed it. Thus far they had come to the conclusion that unless one company alone were in the field the thing would not work out on a profitable basis. At the same time each said if anyone entered the field the chances were that the others would have to follow along, if only from a point of prestige. This would bring them right back where they started from. In the case of General Motors they seemed to have made some serious researches in this field recently. After they had completed their costing and calculated the

---

[2] Frederic G. Donnor, Chairman of the Board, Chief Executive Officer, General Motors Corporation; Henry Ford II, Chairman, Ford Motor Company; and Lynn A. Townsend, President, Chief Operating and Administrative Officer, Chrysler Corporation.

duties they would run into on exports which would have to be part of their market, they had not been able to arrive at an affirmative conclusion as to its feasibility. Both Ford and General Motors were building small cars abroad which were competing with Volkswagens in Europe and they were worried about the possibility of some counter-action abroad if it was clear that the United States was entering into some extraordinary efforts to restrict the sales of Volkswagen here.

I have in the past talked with Bob McNamara about this matter and he told me that he had, when at Ford, given thought to the possibility of putting an American competitor to the Volkswagen on the market. He was somewhat doubtful about some of the negative arguments which were used at the Motor Company against this but that he had gone to Washington and lost track of it.

JJMcC[3]

---

[3] Printed from a copy that bears these typed initials.

---

292.   Memorandum From the Special Representative for Trade Negotiations (Herter) to President Johnson[1]

Washington, September 10, 1965, 2:15 p.m.

SUBJECT

Agricultural Offers in the Kennedy Round

On August 19 with your approval I announced that the United States would table its agricultural offers on September 16,[2] the date agreed upon by the GATT members, regardless of the action taken by the EEC, and would expect other major participants in the current round of

---

[1] Source: Johnson Library, White House Central Files, Confidential File, TA 1, Bator to President 8/4/66, Tab C. Secret. Another copy indicates that Irwin R. Hedges (STR) drafted the memorandum. (Kennedy Library, Herter Papers, White House Subject File, Box 4) A handwritten note at the top of the source text reads: "Mr. President: See page two for decision items." On the "Approved" line at the end of the memorandum appears the following handwritten note: "by the President—Sept. 13. McG. Bundy." An "Approved" line on a September 13 memorandum from Bundy to the President, summarizing Herter's memorandum, is checked. (Kennedy Library, Herter Papers, Agriculture and EEC, Box 5)

[2] The text of Herter's August 19 statement is printed in *American Foreign Policy: Current Documents, 1965*, pp. 1091–1092.

trade negotiations to do likewise. The conditions to be attached to the U.S. offers and the procedures to be followed in drawing up the list of offers were outlined in my memorandum to you of August 9.[3]

As indicated in that memorandum, we would withhold from our offers on September 16 (1) items already approved by you as exceptions to tariff cuts, (2) items imported principally from countries which have not indicated up to this time their intention to participate in the negotiations, (3) items for which negotiations will be conducted in commodity groups (major cereals and cereal by-products, and certain meats and dairy products), and (4) items imported principally from the European Economic Community.

On November 10, 1964, you authorized me to offer for tariff cuts all agricultural imports with the exception of a small list of products.[4] For most products the authorization was to make offers of cuts in duties of 50 percent in accordance with section 201 of the Trade Expansion Act of 1962. You also authorized me to offer for reductions to zero rate of duty all items eligible for such treatment in accordance with the provisions of sections 202 and 213 of the Trade Expansion Act. Section 202 of the TEA authorizes the President to reduce to zero the duty on products for which the present duty is equivalent to 5 percent or less. Section 213 authorizes the President to reduce to zero the duty on tropical products, provided the European Economic Community takes comparable measures for trade liberalization in the same products.

In accordance with the authority granted on November 10, 1964, therefore, I propose to:

1. Table offers of tariff cuts listed in Tab A on September 16.[5] Most of these offers would be for tariff cuts of 50 percent. On certain tropical products eligible for duty-free treatment under sections 202 and 213 of the TEA, the offer would be to cut duties to zero.

2. Table specific offers on products of primary interest to the European Economic Community as annotated in Tab B at such time as the EEC is ready to table its own concrete and specific offers in accordance with agreements already reached in Geneva.

3. Table offers on commodity group items (certain meats and dairy products, as annotated in Tab B)[6] at such time as may be appropriate.

---

[3] Document 289.

[4] See Documents 262 and 263.

[5] Tab A, "List of U.S. offers to be tabled on September 16, 1965," has not been found. The text may be the same as the list printed by GATT, "United States Offers on Agricultural Products," September 16, 1965, GATT 6–US Doc. 3. (Johnson Library, National Security File, NSC History, Kennedy Round Crisis, April–June 1967, Book 1, Tabs 7–16, Box 52)

[6] Tab B, "Master list of all U.S. agricultural imports with the negotiating status of each item indicated by an appropriate symbol," has not been found.

4. Table offers as may be appropriate in the course of the negotiations on items excluded from the September 16 list because imports are principally from countries which have not as yet indicated their intention to participate in the negotiations.

5. Table offers as may be appropriate in the course of the negotiations of duty reductions to zero on products other than tropical falling under sections 202 and 213.

I will of course consult with the Secretary of Agriculture and heads of other interested agencies before tabling any offers additional to those listed in Tab A.

Tab B is a master list of all U.S.agricultural imports with the negotiating status of each item indicated by an appropriate symbol.

These proposals are concurred in by all the interested agencies.

Your approval of this memorandum will constitute your authorization for me to proceed as indicated.

Christian A. Herter

---

293. Memorandum From Attorney General Katzenbach to President Johnson[1]

Washington, September 23, 1965.

RE

Economy Cars—Joint Venture

This is in response to your request for my views as to whether the major American automobile manufacturers may enter into a joint enterprise to produce an economy model car.[2] For the reasons set forth below, I

---

[1] Source: Washington National Records Center, RG 40, Secretary of Commerce Files: FRC 71 A 6617, White House, September–October. No classification marking. Katzenbach sent an earlier undated draft of this paper to Secretary of Commerce Connor with the comment, in a transmittal memorandum of September 20, that while he agreed with the conclusions in the paper, he thought it "too lengthy to transmit to the President." (Ibid.) Handwritten but unsigned instructions, presumably by Connor, on the transmittal memorandum to Connor directed his secretary to call Katzenbach's office to indicate that "the memo is well done. I see no need to prepare a shortened version for the Pres., but just put the conclusion and a few comments in a transmittal letter." Another handwritten note, dated September 22, indicates that these instructions were carried out.

[2] No formal request by the President on this subject has been found; see Document 291.

believe that such a joint venture would violate section 7 of the Clayton Act[3] and that the enactment of legislation immunizing the venture from section 7 would be undesirable.

I

Section 7 of the Clayton Act prohibits corporations from acquiring the stock or assets of other corporations if the acquisition may have the effect of substantially lessening competition in any line of commerce or may tend to create a monopoly. It is applicable where two or more corporations jointly form a new corporation and acquire stock in it.

I think it clear that under established criteria a joint venture of the type here envisaged would substantially lessen competition within the meaning of section 7.

In 1964, about 22% (or over 1,700,000 cars) of the production of major American automobile manufactures were compacts, the lower priced models of which include the Chevy II and Corvair (GM), Comet and Falcon (Ford), Dart and Valiant (Chrysler), and Rambler American (American). Over 1,380,000 lower-priced compacts were sold in 1964, or about 18% of total passenger car production. Although even lower-priced compacts are larger and more expensive than a Volkswagen-type economy car, for many prospective purchasers they represent an alternative to the economy car. It is clear that sales of economy type cars and sales of compacts, particularly the lower priced models, are sufficiently competitive that the success of one type affects the fortunes of the others.[4]

If American manufacturers enter into a joint venture for the production of an economy class car, they will have to make joint decisions on the price and output of the new car. In making such joint decisions, they necessarily must consider the price and output of the compact lines. The joint decisions on the new car necessarily affect sales of the compact lines, and price and output decisions as to compacts will affect sales of the economy cars. The inevitable consequence of this interrelationship and joint decision-making in the joint venture is that the manufacturers, when competing with one another in the compact line, will be unable to make independent price and output decisions. Competition will thus be adversely affected.

---

[3] Chapter 323, approved October 15, 1914; 38 Stat. 730. Section 7 is codified in 15 USC 18.

[4] The August 30, 1965, issue of *Automotive News*, p. 37, in an article captioned "Why No U.S. Answer to VW?" quotes Mr. Roche, president of GM, as saying that the Chevy II is "strongly competitive" with the economy type car; in the same article, a Chrysler official observes that an increase in the economy car market would be "more at the expense of our own present American cars than at the expense of foreign imports. . . ." [Footnote in the source text.]

Second, the formation of the joint enterprise would adversely affect competition in the present sale of economy-model cars. General Motors, Chrysler, and Ford presently import into the United States economy class cars—e.g., the Opel, the Simca, and the English Ford—which compete with one another and which would be squarely competitive with the economy car envisaged by the proposal. If, for example, General Motors and Chrysler were to participate in a joint venture to produce an economy car, their joint decisions as to price and output will necessarily substantially affect decisions they are required to make on the volume and price of imports of Opels and Simcas, with a resultant lessening of the independence of that decision-making and a lessening competition.

Third, formation of the joint venture would remove any possibility that the American manufacturers would come to compete with one another in the economy car field. Although the manufacturers claim that they do not intend to produce economy cars independently, the Supreme Court has indicated that it looks to objective economic criteria to determine whether a company is likely to enter a market. Such objective criteria of the likelihood of independent entry receives more credence than corporate disclaimers of intent. Recent antitrust experience bears out the wisdom of this. For example, Bethlehem Steel constructed its own plant in the Midwest after pleading, unsuccessfully, that merger with Youngstown was the only feasible means of entry to the Midwest.

In view of the great resources of the companies involved, their present activity in a closely related market, and probable market growth in demand for second cars, entry by one or more of the American automobile manufacturers in the economy car market is, despite the manufacturers disclaimer, not so improbable as to make a joint venture lawful. Moreover, it should be noted that it has been exceptionally difficult for new companies to enter and remain in the automobile industry. (The case of the Kaiser car is in point.) Any possibility that the economy car market may be entered by another American company, not now a major company in the automobile industry, will disappear in the face of a joint venture of the majors.

Nor do I believe that the joint venture can be justified by showing a business need for it. Business justifications for a joint venture which merit consideration may include the need to pool financial resources of otherwise small companies, the need for complementary technical contributions, or, in exceptional cases, the need for distribution of risks in a highly speculative undertaking such as an exploration venture subject to the vicissitudes of regulation by an unstable foreign government. Clearly the corporations here involved are not faced with inadequate financial resources nor want of technological ability. The companies may claim that they need this joint venture in order to share the risk of failure. But for the purposes of the antitrust laws, the risks here do not differ in kind from those surrounding the creation of any new business enterprise.

II

The basic objection to immunizing legislation is that if there is a market which merits cultivation, American automobile producers are capable of entering it individually. If, in fact, the market does not support their individual entry, the only purpose of the joint venture is to allocate the losses of a losing operation. If losses are so likely, new producers should not enter—through a joint venture or otherwise. If the market can be profitable, and the only deterrent to entry is fear of competition from other entering American producers, our entire antitrust history argues against special legislation to protect against such competition.

In addition, the immunizing legislation cannot eradicate the anticompetitive consequences described above. In an already heavily concentrated industry, the diminution of competition in the sale of compact cars may do economic damage which more than offsets any economic gains created by the joint venture.

Finally, I think that legislation approving such a joint venture will be regarded by other countries as an overt effort on the part of the Government of the United States to limit the success of foreign competition. It will be particularly prominent because it is at the cost of revision of a national antitrust policy which has been peculiarly identified with the United States. It will very likely invite retaliation with more injurious consequences in our economy than any benefits which might accrue from the venture. Of course, the limitation on foreign imports which this venture may impose is not without the immediate domestic cost—i.e., those Americans engaged in the distribution and servicing of foreign imports may experience hardships.

Nicholas deB Katzenbach[5]

---

[5] Printed from a copy that bears this stamped signature.

294.   Memorandum From Secretary of Commerce Connor to President Johnson[1]

Washington, September 29, 1965.

SUBJECT

Economy Automobiles

After discussions with Bob McNamara and Jack McCloy and later with Nick Katzenbach, and after reading and thinking about Nick's September 23 memo to you, and Jack McCloy's attached memo of August 25 [27][2] that he prepared at my request to summarize past activities, I suggest that we drop the subject.

Not only are the legal problems serious and apparently insurmountable, but from a competitive business point of view I'm convinced that sooner or later at least one U.S. manufacturer will enter this price range market when the economic climate is right, and I think this should be a free enterprise decision—my old friend Jack Bingham to the contrary notwithstanding.

John T. Connor[3]

---

[1] Source: Washington National Records Center, RG 40, Secretary of Commerce Files: FRC 71 A 6617, White House, September–October. No classification marking. An attached transmittal form to Trowbridge, September 29, reads: "The Secretary said today to ask you to give him a preliminary report based upon the work already done; and to tell you that no further work on this subject will be needed." A handwritten note on the transmittal form reads: "Trowbridge ready to report." No record of his report was found.

[2] Documents 293 and 291.

[3] Printed from a copy that bears this typed signature.

295.   Memorandum From the Acting Special Representative for Trade Negotiations (Roth) to President Johnson[1]

Washington, October 5, 1965, 10:12 a.m.

SUBJECT

Tariff Commission Study of American Selling Price System of Customs Valuation

Recommendation

For the reasons given below, I recommend that you sign the letter attached at Tab A requesting the Tariff Commission to make a special study of the system of customs valuation known as American selling price (ASP).[2]

Discussion

ASP System

Since the enactment of the Customs Simplification Act of 1956,[3] section 402 of the Tariff Act of 1930[4] has provided three alternative methods of customs valuation for purposes of computing ad valorem rates of duty on most imported products. The first and internationally-preferred method of valuation is known as "export value", or the wholesale price of the imported product offered in arm's-length transactions in the country of origin. If "export value" cannot be determined, the next method of valuation is "U.S. value", or the wholesale price of the imported product in the United States, less such elements as profit, duty, and transportation costs, in order to approximate "export value". If "U.S. value" cannot be determined, the final method of valuation is "constructed value", or an estimate of what "export value" would be based upon the costs of production in the country of origin.

The three normal methods of valuation under section 402 of the Tariff Act of 1930 do not apply as a matter of law to four groups of imported products: benzenoid chemicals, rubber-soled footwear (such as sneakers), canned clams, and woolen knit gloves.

---

[1] Source: Johnson Library, Bator Papers, Trade, Box 13. Limited Official Use. Another copy of the memorandum shows that it was drafted by John B. Rehm and cleared in draft by Robert L. McNeill (Commerce), James P. Hendrick (Treasury), and Joseph L. Greenwald (E/ITED). (Kennedy Library, Roth Papers, Chronological 7/1/65–12/31/65, Box 1) The source text was attached to Document 300.

[2] Attached to another copy of this memorandum. (Draft letter from President Johnson to Donn N. Bent (Secretary of the U.S. Tariff Commission), undated; Kennedy Library, Roth Papers, Chronological 7/1/65–12/31/65, Box 1) The required letter was ultimately sent by the Office of the Special Representative for Trade Negotiations; see Document 300.

[3] P.L. 84–92, approved August 2, 1956; 70 Stat. 943; see 19 USC 1401a.

[4] P.L. 71–361, approved June 17, 1930; 46 Stat. 590.

With respect to benzenoid chemicals, the law provides that any imported benzenoid chemical which is competitive with a similar domestic product shall be valued on the basis of the ASP, or wholesale price, of the domestic product. If the imported benzenoid chemical is not competitive, it is to be valued, first, on the basis of U.S. value and, if this cannot be determined, then export value or constructed value.

With respect to rubber-soled footwear, canned clams, and woolen knit gloves, the law provides that any such imported product which is similar to a domestic product shall be valued on the basis of the ASP of the domestic product. If the imported product is not similar to any domestic product, it is to be valued on the basis of the normal methods of valuation.

In accordance with the Customs Simplification Act of 1956, section 402 of the Tariff Act of 1930 largely superseded earlier valuation provisions and contains the current definitions not only of the three normal methods of valuation but also of ASP as it applies to most of the products falling into the four groups noted above. Certain of these, however, are included in the so-called "final list" of imported products established pursuant to the Customs Simplification Act of 1956. With respect to these products subject to the ASP system, section 402a of the Tariff Act of 1930 provides for the continued application of the old definitions of valuation, including ASP and U.S. value. Thus, depending upon the product, either the current or old definitions of ASP or U.S. value may apply.

It is to be noted that the application of ASP to imports of protective rubber footwear (such as rubbers and galoshes) will be abolished upon your approval of the Tariff Schedules Technical Amendments Act of 1965 (H.R. 7969),[5] which now awaits your signature.

Undesirability of ASP System

It is generally recognized in the U.S. Government that ASP is not a proper system of customs valuation for the following reasons.

First, the duty on an import subject to ASP is determined not by the value of that import but by the value of the competitive domestic product. As a result, the domestic manufacturer can adjust the protection afforded by the rate of duty by adjusting the price of his product.

Second, an exporter of an imported product potentially subject to ASP cannot know whether that product will be subject to ASP nor what the ASP will be until it has passed through customs. The resultant uncertainty concerning the basis of valuation which will be used to compute the final duty is one of the most undesirable aspects of the ASP system from the standpoint of foreign traders.

---

[5] Reference is to Section 57 of the Tariff Schedules Technical Amendments Act of 1965, P.L. 89–241, signed by the President on October 7, 1965; 79 Stat. 945.

Third, the use of ASP is inconsistent with the customs practice of all of our trading partners in the non-agricultural sector, and is inconsistent with Article VI of the General Agreement on Tariffs and Trade, which establishes internationally-accepted standards of customs valuation.

Fourth, the administration of the ASP system has proven to be very difficult and expensive, giving rise not only to serious legal problems but also to dissatisfaction on the part of importers, exporters, and domestic producers alike.

Fifth, it has long been subject to severe criticism by our trading partners and has made more difficult our commercial relations with such important countries as the U.K., the EEC countries, and Japan.

ASP System and Kennedy Round

The Kennedy Round has established as one of its major goals the liberalization or elimination of non-tariff barriers to trade. The other participants regard ASP as the most serious of U.S. non-tariff barriers and they are insistent that we take steps to change it. Indeed, the EEC has gone so far as to refuse to negotiate with respect to either tariff or non-tariff barriers in the entire chemical sector until we are willing to negotiate the modification or elimination of the ASP system. In addition, the U.K. has made maintenance of its present offers of tariff concessions with respect to chemical products conditional upon the modification of ASP.

Since ASP has become such a major issue in the Kennedy Round, it is our judgment that we must establish a basis for proposing a modification in the system itself. Our failure to do so would necessarily have a detrimental effect upon our negotiating posture and upon the whole Kennedy Round as well.

Elimination of ASP System

There are basically two ways to eliminate the ASP system. The first would be to abolish the use of ASP as a method of customs valuation and to leave the present ad valorem rates of duty where they are. We do not believe, however, that we can or should propose such an immediate and total elimination of the ASP system, primarily because it would constitute too abrupt a deprivation of protection long afforded certain segments of domestic industry.

The second way would be to abolish the ASP system but to maintain an approximately equivalent degree of protection. This would be done by taking all entries of imported products subject to ASP in a given year, such as 1964, and converting the ad valorem rates based upon ASP (or in the case of non-competitive benzenoid chemicals, U.S. value) to new ad valorem rates based upon the usual methods of customs valuation which will yield an approximately equivalent rate of duty, and hence about the same amount of protection. We consider this approach to the problem to be both sound and reasonable.

We are presently uncertain as to how the new ad valorem rates should be put into effect, that is, whether by legislation or by Presidential proclamation. While we are still studying this question, which is in part a legal one, we are inclined to favor the legislative approach. In either case, we would propose to continue to consult closely with key members of the Congress on this matter.

Tariff Commission Study

In order to formulate the conversion of rates, we believe that it would be appropriate as a first step to have an investigation carried out by the Tariff Commission, pursuant to a Presidential request. The Tariff Commission has indicated its willingness to undertake this task and to complete it by May 1, 1966, as indicated in the attached letter. Moreover, arrangements have already been made with the Bureau of Customs to develop the basic data upon which the Tariff Commission will formulate the conversion. It is our present view that the study, when finally submitted to you, should remain confidential and not be made public.

It should be emphasized that the Tariff Commission's study is a critical but only first step towards our ultimate goal of putting into effect a new set of rates for the products in question. After the results of the study are known and analyzed, we will propose a further course of action to you in the light of the negotiating situation prevailing in the Kennedy Round at the time.

Congressional Views

With respect to the Congress, we have had recent indications that key members of both the Senate Finance and House Ways and Means Committees would be agreeable to this course of action.

As noted above, the Congress had just passed the Tariff Schedules Technical Amendments Act of 1965, which provides a new rate of duty for imports of protective rubber footwear (such as rubbers and galoshes). In working out this new provision, the Congress consciously sought to arrive at a new rate which would afford an amount of tariff protection equivalent to that which had resulted from the application of ASP to imports to both natural and synthetic rubber footwear.

During Senate floor debate on the bill, it was made clear that Senators Long, Smathers, Douglas, Gore, Hartke, and Ribicoff were all generally opposed to the use of ASP as a method of customs valuation and supported the conversion of rates of duty based on ASP to new rates affording the same amount of protection.

In the Ways and Means Committee, Congressmen Curtis and King are known to favor this approach in abolishing the ASP system, and Chairman Mills has specifically expressed his support for having the Tariff Commission carry out the study proposed in the attached letter.

Industry Reaction

The only two significant sectors of domestic industry which can be expected to react to the proposed Tariff Commission study are the producers of benzenoid chemicals and of rubber-soled footwear. Both groups have long been protected by the ASP system and can be expected to resist strongly its elimination, even if an equivalent amount of protection is maintained. At the same time, they will have a full opportunity to express their views at the public hearing which the attached letter calls for.

Public Release of Letter

We believe that, upon its signature, the letter to the Tariff Commission should be made public. Such a release, however, is bound to provoke a number of questions, some of which cannot now be answered, including a question concerning the ultimate use to which the results of the study will be put.

We recommend that, if it is signed, the letter should be released with little or no elaboration. We shall at the same time prepare answers to the most predictable questions which may be raised, to be used on a background basis with the press.

Accordingly, with the concurrence of the Departments of Commerce, State, and the Treasury, the other agencies most directly concerned, I recommend that you sign the attached letter to the Tariff Commission.

William M. Roth

---

296. Memorandum From Secretary of Commerce Connor to President Johnson[1]

Washington, October 25, 1965.

SUBJECT

Weekly Briefing Report

Joint Mexico-U.S. Trade Committee Holds First Meeting

The Joint Mexico-U.S. Trade Committee, the first effort by both governments to create a permanent institution for the regular exchange of views on ways to promote mutually beneficial trade, met last week in Washington.

---

[1] Source: Washington National Records Center, RG 40, Secretary of Commerce Files: FRC 71 A 6617, White House Briefing Memoranda. No classification marking.

The discussions covered a wide variety of subjects affecting trade between Mexico and the United States, including the commercial policies of the two countries, impediments to the expansion of trade, export promotion activities, and the role of certain multi-national bodies in promoting international trade.

As a result of these discussions, the Department of Commerce now is preparing, as requested by the Mexican Delegation, documentation on problem cases arising from Mexico's restrictive import policy; trade data showing important losses arising from Mexican policies; and a list of suggested items to be admitted into Mexico on at least a token basis. The Department is also cooperating with the Mexican Government to develop export promotion techniques, including the exploration of U.S. market possibilities for certain Mexican exports.

Agreement was also reached on formal consultation procedures under which the United States and Mexico will each consult with the other on trade policy moves whenever possible before taking unilateral actions that would affect trade between the two countries.

[Here follow six items on unrelated subjects.]

John T. Connor[2]

---

[2] Printed from a copy that bears this typed signature.

---

297.   Memorandum of Conversation[1]

Washington, November 9, 1965.

PARTICIPANTS

Sir Richard Powell, Permanent Secretary, British Board of Trade
Mr. John E. Chadwick, Minister (Commercial) British Embassy
Mr. William Hughes, 2nd Secretary, British Board of Trade
Mr. Basil Engholm, Deputy Secretary, Ministry of Agriculture
Mr. Roy Denman, Assistant Secretary, British Board of Trade
Mr. Frederick Kearns, Assistant Secretary for the Ministry of Agriculture
Mr. Frederick Jackson, First Secretary (Commercial) British Embassy
Mr. John Eaton, Embassy Agricultural Attaché

---

[1] Source: Johnson Library, Roth Papers, Chronological, July 1–December 31, 1965, Box 1. Limited Official Use. The source text bears no drafting information except the date of December 22. The meeting was held in Herter's office.

STR
Governor Herter
Ambassador Roth
Mr. Norwood
Mr. Gates
Mr. Hedges
Mr. Malmgren
Mr. Simanis
Mr. Wilson

STR Geneva
Mr. Lewis

State
Mr. Greenwald
Mr. Hill
Mr. Hopp
Mr. Hinton
Mr. Enders

Labor
Mr. Weiss
Mr. Blackman
Mr. Schwenger

Treasury
Mr. Ryss

Commerce
Mr. Trowbridge
Mr. Garland
Mr. Fox
Mr. Nehmer
Mr. Strauss

Agriculture
Mr. Schnittker
Mr. Ioanes

EEC Crisis and Kennedy Round:

Governor Herter opened the discussion and requested Sir Richard Powell's views on the EEC crisis and its relevance to the Kennedy Round. Powell replied that the U.K. had received the impression from the French Embassy in London that the EEC crisis was serious but not insoluble. While it is not entirely clear what the French want, de Gaulle apparently does not intend to renegotiate the Rome Treaty. He will probably insist on a change in personnel at the Commission but not on formal abridgement of the Commission's powers. The issue of majority voting, in Powell's estimation, is not an essential one. Alluding to "power politics," he said that no issue would be forced by any group against the adamant opposition of one of its major members.

He emphasized that resolution of the crisis would be a time-consuming process and that the EEC would probably not be able to resume negotiations in the Kennedy Round before the Spring of 1966. Rather intensive work would then be necessary in the summer and fall to conclude the Kennedy Round according to the U.S. schedule. Powell said that, after his conversation with Under Secretary Ball,[2] he was aware of the difficulties the United States would encounter in obtaining an extension of the negotiating authority due to expire in the middle of 1967.

He doubted that technical discussions could be prolonged beyond the end of this year and believed that we could then expect a hiatus in Kennedy Round activity until the EEC returns. Nonetheless, we can also expect results from the Kennedy Round which will be substantial enough to justify the time and effort expended.

Powell concurred in Herter's observation that, if NATO deliberations become involved with trade, the timetable problems that would

---

[2] This conversation has not been further identified.

ensue in the Kennedy Round would be insurmountable. He added, however, that such an eventuality has never been suggested by the French in their discussions with the U.K.

Herter expressed basic agreement with Powell's comments but noted that the situation was so indefinite that it is impossible to predict when the EEC would return to the Kennedy Round. He remarked parenthetically that the Community's delegates are now empowered only to deliver rigid positions and it would be desirable if someone were given authority to negotiate.

In discussing the prospects for renewal of TEA negotiating authority, Herter pointed out that Congress has been growing more protectionist in the past few years and would not be so well disposed toward tariff cuts as it was when the Act was passed in 1962.

Ambassador Roth added that protectionist sentiment in Congress is abetted by delays in the negotiations. He thought it would be extremely difficult to obtain extension even if the Kennedy Round is close to a successful resolution. Still, if the timetable proceeds as Powell predicted, there was no reason why the negotiations could not be concluded before the deadline.

Roth continued that there had been several articles in the press which had erroneously reported that the United States was exploring alternatives to the Kennedy Round. He said that, if necessary, such alternatives could be devised quickly enough in the future but there is no point in considering the possibilities at this juncture. Powell responded that the U.K. also was not discussing alternatives. In fact it was difficult to conceive of tariff negotiations without the EEC; twenty-five percent of U.K. trade is with the EEC and the trend is upward. In answering a question from Roth, Powell said there has been no diminution of assurances by EFTA spokesmen that "bridge-building" with the EEC requires, first of all, a successful Kennedy Round.

EEC Exceptions List:

Denman, in response to a question from Roth, said that there was some chance that the EEC might improve its partial offers but, that it was unlikely that it will make offers on its exceptions. Germany will try to improve the package to avert extensive withdrawal of offers made by other participants. If there are significant withdrawals by others, we can expect the EEC to try to add to its exceptions.

Sectors:

Roth thought that it was time for considerable substantive work in sector meetings, all possibilities in bilaterals having been virtually exhausted. The United States, he continued, has been uneasy over decisions which might have been taken in paper and pulp discussions between the EEC and the Scandinavians. The British responded with an optimistic appraisal of paper and pulp. Powell discounted the possibility that there has been an EEC-Scandinavian agreement of detriment to third countries. He believed that the EEC simply did not want to have multilateral discussions until it had settled a number of problems bilaterally with the Scandinavians, who supply 80 percent of EEC imports in this sector. Hijzen has indicated he is now willing to start talks and is optimistic about prospects for agreement. The Scandinavians are also prepared to join in paper and pulp talks.

Turning to steel, Denman agreed with the U.S. view that a concordance could be of only limited value, resulting in simple harmonization of rates without any reduction. A more significant effort would be to try to get the EEC to reduce its present rates. It may be best, he said, to concentrate on a few specialties.

Roth noted that U.S. steel production is down to about 65 percent of capacity and that there is considerable unemployment in the industry. Powell countered that this might indicate structural overcapacity. The level of imports, Gates said, always rises when there is a threat of a strike and never returns completely to the previous level.

Adjustment assistance procedures, Roth explained, have not helped the workers in the United States. Congress will be asked next year to improve the law.

He then turned to the matter of ASP removal on benzenoid chemicals and outlined preparations now underway which will probably last about six months. A study is being conducted to determine actual prices. Often the prices quoted by foreign subsidiaries of U. S. firms have no meaning except for tax purposes. When Customs completes its collection of data on the difference between foreign invoice value and foreign export value, STR will ask the Tariff Commission to determine equivalent value for ASP. Subsequently, public hearings will be necessary. Ultimately, a decision will have to be made on whether further cuts will be offered in the Kennedy Round; but it is difficult to envisage a 50 percent cut in the face of expected industry objections. Since we shall probably have to ask Congress for authority to take any action on ASP, we shall also have to show that we have been offered reciprocal concessions in the non-tariff barrier field. Fox suggested that U.K. relaxation of the coal quota could be part of such a package.

In response to a statement by Powell on U.K. disappointment over the new tariff treatment replacing ASP on rubber footwear, Roth explained that we regarded it as unfortunate that Congress had established a higher rate on synthetic footwear; but, in the process, the rate on natural rubber items was set at a much lower rate then would have been possible by simple conversion of ASP. Jackson countered that U.K. footwear, being high priced, is now subject to higher rates in both categories.

Denman expanded the U.K. arguments against the projected U.S. scheme for action on benzenoid chemicals. He maintained that the U.K. chemical industry considered ASP rates to be prohibitive, in essence a device to permit protection of more than 100 percent. Simple conversion, even with an ensuing 50 percent cut, could hardly be considered adequate, he said. In his opinion, the EEC was even more opposed to ASP than the U.K. and might be prompted to exclude chemicals from the Kennedy Round entirely. Powell added that the end result could be an EEC–EFTA arrangement on chemicals similar to the U.S.-Canadian auto agreement.[3]

Fox, in reply, reiterated our need for reciprocity and pointed out that, until the outcries on ecretement materialized, cuts in high rates had always been regarded as more significant than cuts in low rates. He added that it would be difficult to get Congress to act if it became known that ASP conversion is regarded abroad as valueless. If there is to be no major reduction on chemicals in the Kennedy Round, he emphasized, it is important that we know early. Powell said that we would have to have another bilateral to review the U.S. resolution of the ASP problem when it is final.

Textiles:

Ambassador Roth noted that Wyndham White's package proposal on cotton textiles will be considered in the GATT on November 17 and 18. He said that we had disabused India's Ambassador Lall of his misconceptions regarding the LTA when Lall was in Washington recently. We had explained to him that, using the language of the LTA, it was still possible to move toward liberalization; practical problems could be solved in bilaterals. There is no rigidity on our part regarding liberalization, and we believe we could do more if the LTA is allowed to remain.

Mr. Nehmer remarked that U.S. imports of cotton textiles are at an all-time high—about 20 percent above last year in volume. He referred to textile trade figures which have appeared in the European press purporting to show that the EEC imports a larger share of its cotton textile needs than does the United States. One defect, however, in the EEC figures is that they do not separate out non-cotton apparel. It should also be noted that the EEC imports significant quantities from the bloc and consequently purchases proportionately less than the United States does from LDC's.

Powell said that the U.K.'s situation is a special one; it is necessary to allow for improvement in the structure of its domestic cotton industry. It also had difficult political problems with the Commonwealth over cotton imports. The U.K. had chosen to institute a global quota in order to

---

[3] See footnote 4, Document 282.

permit new suppliers among the LDC's to obtain part of the market. It would be willing to establish individual quotas instead, if the LDC's could decide among themselves on their respective share of the market.

Nehmer said that the proposals of the U.K. presented only limited possibilities for growth. The exporting countries don't look at problems as we do. If they are dissatisfied enough, there could be repercussions in the sector meetings. We will continue to point out that our imports have gone up considerably.

To Nehmer's comment that the U.K.'s policy may encourage U.S. wool producers to exert pressure for a similar arrangement Powell replied that he sees no parallel between cotton imports from LDC's and wool imports from DC's.

Non-Tariff Barriers

Sir Richard hoped that solutions to the U.S. non-tariff barrier problems of chief concern to Britain, i.e., dumping, ASP and wine gallon, could be pursued in the Kennedy Round. He was conscious of the domestic pressures in the United States in regard to these problems. Mr. Denman added that British requests in relation to these problems were clearly set out. He hoped there could be US–UK discussions on the anti-dumping question prior to the December meeting.

In regard to British barriers of concern to the United States, Sir Richard said that he could say nothing helpful on coal. In the face of more pit closings in politically sensitive areas, the government will not be able to make any move. On Northern Ireland imports, he doubted the possibility of liberalization, but the matter was under discussion.

He was not in a position yet formally to respond to the question of television programs. Decisions regarding the use of British vs. imported programs rested with the Independent Television Authority (ITA) and BBC. The government could not intervene. Although they recognized that an answer must be given to the American complaint, it would be improper for the government to put pressure on the ITA.

Mr. Greenwald pointed out that the new restrictions governing 8 to 9 p.m. weekday programs were directly discriminatory against United States programs. The British sell $10 million worth of TV programming to the United States while we sell only $3 million to Britain. The United States has no limitation on imported material. He urged that the British networks be given the right of free choice.

Mr. Fox voiced United States concern with the aspects of the National Plan which appeared to be forms of subsidization to encourage import substitution.

Sir Richard said that certain measures such as investment allowances were being discussed, but that they were not designed to be discriminatory against any particular import or source, but rather to stimulate efficiency in UK industry.

Concluding the NTB discussion, Mr. Roth urged that something be done on coal in the Belfast area. He warned that to get United States action on NTB's, particularly wine gallon, would require going to Congress with persuasive incentives in the form of concessions from other Kennedy Round participants. These would not necessarily be on the industrial side. On anti-dumping, we were preparing for the December meeting. We were facing grave problems on steel imports with some type of Congressional action certain in the spring. While realizing that the withholding of appraisals was the main problem for exporters, we wanted to have the whole dumping question explored in depth.

Sir Richard proposed bilateral talks prior to the December meeting, perhaps in London. Mr. Denman asked if we were prepared to accept the British proposal as the basis of the December discussion.

Mr. Roth responded that we wanted to focus on some of the underlying issues that the British proposal raised, and that we would discuss it in that context.

As a final matter, Mr. Roth raised the question of the U.S. request that a single UK tariff rate be applied on fruit cocktail. Sir Richard answered that Australian assent was needed and the Australians had not responded. He would personally prod them for an answer on his return.

Afternoon discussions opened on the subject of agriculture. Mr. Roth briefly reviewed U. S. reasons for deciding to table Kennedy Round agricultural offers on the scheduled September 16 date, and expressed appreciation that other participants agreed to do the same. Most of the offers were not as handsome as they should have been. We were disappointed in the U.K. offers. This was not the place to go into detail, as Geneva bilateral talks were set for late November, but we did not consider U.K. offers a rich package.

Turning to the US–UK grains agreement, Mr.Roth made it clear that the United States was unhappy with its experience under the arrangement. Imports the first year fell below the 3 year average foreseen in the agreement and our anticipated sharing in the growth of British consumption had not materialized. Future prospects for holding our own present share of the market appear dim. We understand that the United Kingdom is committed to increasing the level of standard quantities to reflect growth and also perhaps to maintaining price levels. The most obvious forms of remedial action are therefore precluded. Because our expectations had not been realized, we questioned the value of the agreement both as a bilateral arrangement and as the pattern for a multilateral grains agreement in the Kennedy Round.

Sir Richard responded first on the question of British Kennedy Round offers, saying that despite misgivings on the wisdom of tabling on September 16, they had agreed to follow the U.S. lead. In judging the value of the offer, it should be remembered that much had been withheld pending participation by the EEC. The British had been careful not to expose their hand. Secondly, the value of U.K. offers compared favorably with those of the United States. He valued total U.K. offers at $555 million and total U. S. at $500 million. A reason that offers to the United States were small was that none were tabled on products covered by Commonwealth preference because releases would be needed if rates were to be lowered. These items would be discussed in Geneva.

Mr. Roth mentioned the additional problem of the U.K. offers on products covered by illegal quantitative restrictions. The United States cannot take these offers into consideration. This was recognized by the British, who responded that the trade value for the United States of their offers would not be basically altered.

Under Secretary Schnittker had to leave the talks at this point. He commented that the idea of bringing domestic agricultural policies to the bargaining table was becoming a platitude. The United States had its eye on results and was looking forward hopefully to the December discussions on grains.

Mr. Engholm responded for the British on the grains agreement. The National Plan noted that a 4-3/4 million ton increase in cereals production was technically possible but it did not set such an increase as a goal. He also noted that while some increase in production could be expected, there would be an increase in consumption in response to the anticipated expansion in livestock production. Mr. Roth was correct in saying that there was a commitment on standard quantities. Levels would not be reduced but would be increased to reflect growth in consumption. There had been no commitment on prices, however. The United States had been aware before signing the bilateral of a White Paper which stated that standard quantity levels would have to provide for growth in demand.[4] This provision assured that domestic producers would not be penalized and was not inconsistent with the international arrangements.

He said the U.S. disappointment in the cereals agreement was understandable. However, the agreement had been in operation only fifteen months. The British had taken every reasonable step to make it work. The standard quantity levels were low in relation to the expected harvest. When the harvest was larger than expected the penalty provisions started to operate. At the suggestion of the United States at the first review, the British cut the guaranteed prices, which proved their good intentions. This act took political courage for a government in office only six months and facing a balance of payments crisis.

---

[4] This paper has not been identified.

The 1965 harvest would be larger than that of 1943, but there were signs that the rate of expansion was slowing. Imports were higher this year, although not up to the base level. Consumption was increasing at twice the expected rate. Remedial actions had not yet taken full effect, and imports from the United States would fall short of the base level this year. He hoped that by the time of the December talks, the British would have a good idea of the prospects for next year.

Mr. Engholm did not consider the results for the United States as unsatisfactory as they had been represented. Although total imports had fallen over the past two years, three countries last year had exceeded their average for the previous three years, and the United States might do the same this year. It was the minor suppliers that were most adversely affected by the import declines.

As to the Kennedy Round aspects, he said that the U.K. offer faithfully translates the principles of the agreement. He thought it unwise for the United States to discount the value of the agreement because of unexpected disappointments in the first fifteen months.

Mr. Roth pointed out that the agreement rested on two bases, the first that imports would hold their relative place in the U.K. market and, second, that mechanisms would work in a sufficiently flexible manner to make this possible. Because of the unexpected production increase, the mechanism went into action to cut prices the maximum 4%, however, at the same time the standard quantity levels were increased.

Mr. Engholm explained that the increase in the standard quantities made a greater than 5% price cut possible because the two were tied together.

In response to Mr. Roth's comment that the U.K. offer on grains was not as useful as had been hoped, Mr. Engholm said that in the Kennedy Round the British would go further if other countries were more forthcoming.

Mr. Ioanes stated that because its remedial features lack teeth, the United States cannot accept the arrangement as a model for a world grains agreement.

Mr. Engholm pointed out that the mechanisms had caused a reduction in subsidies to growers last year and would again this year. Price pressures had not, however, brought prices down to the minimum import level. Responding to Mr. Ioanes' request, he promised to provide figures to support his earlier contention that three exporters were ahead of their previous three-year average in shipments to the U.K. Imports are expected to increase this year, although not proportionate to the increase in production.

Mr. Ioanes pointed to this fact as the real issue. Exporters were not getting a fair proportion of growth because the remedial mechanism could not overcome the essential disadvantage of exporters caused by the inflated base figures.

Mr. Engholm responded that Britain had emphatically not agreed to U. S. imports getting a proportionate share of the growth. This was not in the agreement. They had only agreed to consider this as part of a multi-lateral agreement. He reiterated that it was too early to make an overall judgment of the value of the agreement.

Sir Richard concluded the discussion on the grains agreement, saying that a judgment of its first year of operation had to take into consideration the change in government, the severe balance of payments crisis and the severe pressure of imports. He did not think it practical to think the remedial mechanisms could be stiffened unless strong incentives were provided by the Kennedy Round.

298. Memorandum From the National Export Expansion Coordinator (Goldy) to Secretary of Commerce Connor[1]

Washington, November 10, 1965.

SUBJECT
   Analysis of Trade Account—1965

I.   Introduction and Summary

Exports during the first nine months of 1965 have been running at a seasonally adjusted annual rate of $25.7 billion. This is about the same as 1964's rate for the entire year of $25.6 billion, and about 3 percent higher than the seasonally adjusted annual rate for the first nine months of 1964.

Exports rose sharply during the final quarter of 1964 and, consequently, it may be that the 3 percent spread between the seasonally adjusted annual rates of 1965 over 1964 will diminish by the time the total year-end figures are available. We anticipate that the total performance for 1965 will be slightly larger than the total performance for 1964.

Imports on the other hand are currently running at a seasonally adjusted annual rate of approximately 12 percent above the seasonally

[1] Source: Kennedy Library, Herter Papers, Balance of Payments, July 18–November 10, 1965, Box 6. No classification marking.

adjusted annual rate for the same period in 1964. The final import figures at the end of the year are likely to be about $20.7 billion, representing an increase of approximately 11 percent. This increase compares with a 9 percent increase in imports in 1964 over 1963.

If, at year's end, 1965 exports have maintained their 3 percent spread over 1964 and our projections on imports are accurate, it will result in a trade surplus of $5.5 billion—a decline of almost $1.5 billion from the $6.9 billion surplus of 1964. If, however, the spread between 1965 and 1964 exports narrows in the fourth quarter, the surplus could be as low as $5.1 billion—a drop of approximately $1.8 million.

The more optimistic of these estimates is reflected in the attached Chart No. 1,[2] which depicts the trends in exports and imports since 1960 and projects the 1965 figures.

Whether or not the projections are accurate, it is clear that imports in 1965 have risen at a somewhat higher rate than in 1964, but exports, which rose 14 percent in 1964, have flattened out this year and will rise only slightly.

The $6.9 billion trade surplus of 1964 could have been maintained in 1965 notwithstanding the increase in imports this year had exports risen 7.5 percent, which compares with the 8.5 percent average annual rate of increase during the past three years.

The sharp decline in the U.S. trade surplus and the leveling off of the export curve raises some questions: Are U.S. exports merely reflecting the trends in worldwide imports in 1965? Notwithstanding the leveling off of exports, has the U. S. maintained its shares of the major import markets of the world, or has the U. S. been supplanted in some of these markets by increased exports from competitor nations? Which of the industries which contributed most significantly to the 14 percent increase in exports last year have lagged in exporting this year? Which of the geographic areas which contributed significantly to our export increases in 1964 account for the slowdown in exports in 1965? And, finally, what are the factors which may have produced the difference in export performance in 1965 as compared with 1964?

In seeking answers to these questions we have reviewed carefully all of the statistical data we could obtain. There are technical reasons why the data is inadequate. One of the more serious problems is that the U. S. trade classification system was changed in 1965, and, as a consequence, difficult corrections must be made for the 1964 data to be comparable. Moreover, certain statistical adjustments have been made in the figures for 1964 and 1965 which add to the difficulties in measuring changes from year to year. In addition, some information is available month by

---

[2] Not printed.

month, and some on a quarterly basis. Consequently, an analysis of the 1965 experience as contrasted with 1964 can be done more accurately when all of the data are available for 1965.

Notwithstanding the above limitations, we are setting forth herein such information as we have been able to glean so that the Cabinet Committee on Balance of Payments may be as fully informed as possible.

II.   U. S. Shares of World Markets

Most of the data on the shares on the world markets are available at this time only through June. Such data as we have shows that the U.S. share of free world exports to destinations other than the U.S. declined from 20 percent (January to June 1964) to 19 percent (January to June 1965).

If one looks at the manufactures segment of world exports, the decline in the U.S. percentage share for this same period was greater than for all commodities—from 24.3 percent in the first half of 1964 to 22.6 percent in the first half of 1965. Within the manufacturers category, the items in which the significant declines occurred were chemicals, 26.7 percent in the first half of 1964 to 24.2 percent in the first half of 1965, machinery and transportation equipment, 29.6 percent in the first half of 1964 to 28.7 percent in the first half of 1965. Within the machinery and transportation category, electrical apparatus declined from 26.4 percent in the first half of 1964 to 24.2 percent in the first half of 1965, and transportation equipment declined from 28.5 percent in the first half of 1964 to 27.7 percent in the first half of 1965, notwithstanding significant increases in aircraft exports. The decline in the transportation equipment category is believed to be due in large part to the relative decline in road vehicle exports.

The category of Other Manufactured Goods declined from 17.5 percent in the first half of 1964 to 15.3 percent in the first half of 1965, and within the category, metals declined from 15.3 percent in the first half of 1964 to 14.2 percent in the first half of 1965.

When one examines the latest available data on U.S. shares of imports into all foreign areas, one finds that our share has declined by 1 percentage point. Within the category, significant differences are noted in the change in U. S. shares of total imports by geographic area. The most significant declines in shares occurred in Japan where the U.S. share (January to August 1964) was 30.2 percent and had declined in the same months of 1965 to 28.8 percent. U. S. share of total imports into all developing countries declined from 29.4 percent (January to June 1964) to 28.4 percent during the first six months of 1965. With respect to 19 Latin American Republics, the U.S. share of total imports was 50.3 percent (January to June 1964) and the U.S. share is estimated to have declined to 48.6 percent during the first six months of 1965.

The United States has come close to holding its share of total imports into Western Europe, and this is true whether or not trade between the Common Market countries is excluded as being internal.

The United States has actually increased its share of the Canadian market, going from 69.6 percent of total imports (January through August 1964) to 70.5 percent during the first 8 months of 1965.

The conclusion to be derived from the foregoing figures is that the United States has not maintained its share of world trade during the first half of 1965, and that its exports have declined more than can be accounted for by worldwide export and import trends. A further indication of this is that Western Europe has increased its exports during the first half of 1965 to countries other than the U. S. by 10 percent, and Japan has increased its exports during that period by 36 percent.

III.   Changes in Export Performance by Industry

There is attached as Table I[3] a breakdown of U.S. exports by various major categories for the period 1960 through September 1965. This table reflects the values and percentage changes in exports that have occurred in each year and as between January–September 1965 and January–September 1964. Some of the more significant changes which have occurred are as follows: Agricultural exports during the first nine months of 1965 are off about 3 percent from 1964. This is reflected in Table I in the 4 percent decline that has occurred thus far this year in the Food and Live Animals category as contrasted with a 12 percent increase in 1964; the 9 percent decline in Beverages and Tobacco thus far in 1965 as contrasted with a 4 percent increase in 1964; the 4 percent drop in crude materials in 1965 as contrasted with the 19 percent increase in 1964; and a 28 percent increase in the Animal and Vegetable Oils and Fats section as contrasted with a 36 percent increase in 1964.

Another significant category is chemicals which increased 1 percent during the first 9 months of 1965 over the first nine months of 1964, but had increased 19 percent in 1964 over 1963.

Still another significant change in performance is in the Machinery and Transport Equipment category which has increased 7 percent in the first nine months of 1965 over 1964, but had increased 13 percent during 1964 over 1963. Within this category the most significant difference has been in the machinery component which has increased 6 percent during the first nine months of 1965 over 1964, but had increased 16 percent in 1964 over 1963.

It will be noted that the transport equipment category reflects a higher percentage increase in 1965 over 1964 than in 1964 over 1963. This reflects particularly the sizable increases in aircraft exports—29 percent

---

[3] Tables I and II are not printed.

during the first nine months of 1965 over the first nine months of 1964 as contrasted with a slight decline in 1964 over 1963. There has been, however, a significant change in the Road Motor Vehicle category which has increased only 4 percent during the first nine months of 1965 over 1964 as contrasted with a 12 percent increase in 1964 over 1963.

The broad category, "Other Manufactured Goods," which includes metals, paper, textiles, and most consumer goods, also shows a significant change in that exports have increased during the first nine months of 1965 over 1964 by 4 percent as contrasted with a 13 percent increase in 1964 over 1963.

While it is possible to refine further some of the above figures by using a more detailed classification, there are dangers in doing so because of the change in classification between 1965 and 1964, and the resulting noncomparability of some of the data.

IV. Changes in Export Performance by Major World Areas

Attached is Table II which sets forth U. S. exports to major world areas 1960 through August, 1965. This table reflects the export values and percentage changes year by year in broad geographic groupings. (The most recent detailed data with respect to imports from the U. S. into 50 of the major world markets and the U.S. share of those markets is contained in the World Market Report in the October 25 issue of *International Commerce.*)

An examination of Table II shows the following changes in export performance during the first eight months of 1965 as contrasted with the first eight months of 1964, and as compared with previous years: During the first eight months of 1965 exports to Western Europe were up by about one percent as compared with the same period of 1964, whereas in 1964 exports to this area increased by 11 percent over 1963. Similarly, exports to the American Republics declined in the first eight months of 1965 3 percent from 1964, whereas in 1964 exports increased 16 percent over 1963. Exports to Canada have increased 13 percent during the first eight months of 1965 over 1964, whereas they had increased 15 percent in 1964 over 1963. With respect to other developed countries (Japan, Australia, New Zealand, and South Africa), exports have increased 10 percent during the first eight months of 1965, whereas they had increased 20 percent in 1964 over 1963.

With respect to the Other Areas of the World grouping, exports neither increased nor declined in the first eight months of 1965 over 1964, whereas they increased 13 percent in 1964 over 1963.

V. Analysis of Export Performance

Although final figures for 1965 are not available, it can be concluded that the export performance of the United States in 1965 will be significantly less favorable to the trade account than was the performance in 1964. Many reasons have been offered to explain the difference. Among them are: The adverse effect on exports of the dock strike affecting our East and Gulf Coast ports in January and February; a slow-down in economic growth rates in certain countries of Western Europe and in Japan; reduced export earnings of certain less developed countries due to declines in world commodity prices and, hence, a reduced import capability; a reallocation of resources by U.S. companies to meet the demands of a booming domestic market; and the impact on exports of the inclusion of export credit within the foreign loan restraint program.

Undoubtedly, all of these factors have had some influence on U.S. exports in 1965. The economic slow-down in Japan and the reduced export earnings of the less developed countries could account for reduced exports from the United States but would not explain the reduction in U.S. shares of those markets.

Estimates have been made that the dock strike resulted in over-stating the 1964 trade balance by $160 million and understating the 1965 trade balance by approximately $170 million. If these estimates are correct, the dock strike could account for $330 million of the decline in our trade surplus comparing 1965 with 1964.

While comprehensive data are not available, there is some statistical evidence to demonstrate the likelihood that there has been a significant reallocation of resources by U.S. companies in favor of the domestic market as against the export markets in 1965. We have been told by company executives that this was being done. They indicated that generally sales in the domestic market were more profitable than sales in the export market, and consequently when their companies had to choose in allocating their resources, in most instances the domestic market was favored.

For example, in the non-electrical machinery category, U.S. exports increased during the first nine months of 1965 4 percent over the first nine months of 1964. During the comparable periods of 1964 there was an increase of 16 percent in exports over 1963. In the first nine months of 1964 there was a 9 percent increase in production in this industry whereas in the first nine months of 1965 there has been a 12 percent increase in production. Thus, in 1964, this industry increased its exports by a larger proportion than the total increase in production, and in 1965 it increased its exports by a substantially smaller percentage than its increase in production.

An even more dramatic example is that of machine tools. In 1964 exports of metal cutting tools increased more than 40 percent over 1963. This increase occurred at a time when employment was increasing by 11 percent. In the first nine months this year, exports of metal cutting tools have declined by 17 percent at a time when employment has increased by 10 percent.

Similarly, with respect to metal forming machine tools, exports in 1964 rose about 10 percent over 1963 while employment increased by 8 percent. During the first nine months of 1965 exports have declined by 15 percent while employment has continued to increase by 4 percent.

With respect to the iron and steel mill products category, exports increased in 1964 over 1963 by approximately 29 percent and its production increased by 15 percent. In the first nine months of 1965 exports have declined by 7 percent while overall production has risen by 21 percent.

With respect to automobiles, parts and accessories, exports increased 12 percent during the first nine months of 1964 over the comparable period of 1963 at a time when production was increasing by 1 percent and employment was increasing by 4 percent. During the first nine months of 1965 exports increased only 4 percent notwithstanding an increase of 6 percent in production and 12 percent in employment.

With respect to chemicals, exports increased 19 percent in the first nine months of 1964 over the comparable period of 1963 at a time when production was increasing 8 percent. During the first nine months of 1965, exports increased only 1 percent while production increased 6 percent.

In the case of plastics, exports in 1964 were approximately 25 percent above 1963 while employment increased 6 percent. During the first nine months of 1965, exports increased only 5 percent above 1964 while employment increased 11 percent.

Exports of fertilizers increased 60 percent in 1964 over 1963 with no increase in overall employment. During the first nine months of 1965, however, exports increased only 15 percent over the comparable 1964 period while employment was increasing 5 percent.

With respect to beverages and tobacco, exports increased 4 percent in 1964 over 1963 while employment rose by only 1 percent. Exports during the first nine months of 1965 declined by 9 percent as compared with the comparable period of 1964 while employment remained unchanged.

Exports of textiles other than clothing increased by 19 percent in 1964 over 1965 at a time when production was rising 5 percent. During the first nine months of 1965, exports declined by 8 percent at a time when production was rising by 9 percent.

A final example is in the telecommunications industry whose exports rose by 4 percent in 1964 over 1963 at a time when employment in the industry was declining by approximately 4 percent. During the first nine months of 1965, exports declined 17 percent at a time when employment was increasing 3 percent.

The banks have reported to us that there has been a significant tightening of export credit since the imposition of the 105 percent ceiling on foreign loans. The industries which are most dependent on export financing to maintain their competitive position in foreign markets are:

The capital goods industry; other machinery; transport equipment; farm equipment; telecommunications equipment; power equipment; and the engineering-construction industry.

It is interesting to note that most of these industries are included in the list above as among those whose export performance in 1965 has been significantly less favorable than in 1964, and who appear to be allocating more of their resources to the domestic market. In addition to the information already presented with respect to non-electrical machinery, machine tools, iron and steel mill products, automobiles, parts and accessories, and telecommunications, we have noted that the export of agricultural machinery and parts increased by approximately 30 percent in 1964 over 1963, but that during the first nine months of 1965 exports increased only 5 percent over 1964. The export of tractors and parts increased 35 percent in 1964 over 1963, but increased only 7 percent in the first nine months of 1965 over 1964. The export of textile and leather machinery increased approximately 21 percent in 1964 over 1963 but declined by 9 percent in the first nine months of 1965 as compared with 1964.

While these data are by no means conclusive, they do reflect the results we had anticipated based on the restrictions that have been placed on export financing.

---

299. Letter From the Special Representative for Trade Negotiations (Herter) to Secretary of the Treasury Fowler[1]

Washington, November 17, 1965.

Dear Joe:

I understand that your Department is nearing the point of making a final decision on whether to put into effect a new procedure concerning the customs valuation of imports of competitive rubber-soled footwear. Under this procedure, as we understand it, the Bureau of Customs would apply the lowest American selling price as the basis of customs valuation, instead of applying the highest American selling price, as is done at the present time.

---

[1] Source: Kennedy Library, Herter Papers, Chronological File, November 1965, Box 4. Limited Official Use. Drafted by John B. Rehm on November 17 and cleared by Theodore R. Gates (STR) and Bernard Norwood (STR) in draft.

Jim Hendrick was kind enough to suggest that the other interested agencies might wish to comment on the question whether the new procedure should be put into effect. For the reasons set out below, I would like to urge that the Department of the Treasury do so as soon as possible.

First, I believe that it would be particularly unfortunate, both in terms of our general trade relations with the foreign countries concerned and in terms of the Kennedy Round in particular, if the new procedure were not put into effect. This is so primarily because the procedure concerns the application of American selling price, a basis of valuation which other countries have long objected to and which they are especially determined to have modified in the Kennedy Round. For the Department of the Treasury to have announced its intention to put the new procedure into effect and then to fail to do so, would be immediately construed by the other countries as evidence of a protectionist mood of the United States and a weakening of its resolve to liberalize trade in the Kennedy Round. Moreover, such a failure would be especially aggravating to the other countries in light of the recent action of the Congress in tripling the rate of duty on imports of synthetic rubber footwear.[2] While this action was salutary in that the American selling price was removed from imports of natural rubber footwear, it did substantially increase the protection with respect to synthetic rubber footwear, which accounts for the great bulk of the trade, and will undoubtedly damage the trade of some of our major trading partners. Indeed, it has already created serious problems in our relations with both Japan and the United Kingdom.

Second, on the basis of our experience with the members of the House Ways and Means and Senate Finance Committees and in the light of our recent experience in the Congress with respect to synthetic rubber footwear, I do not believe that putting the new procedure into effect would lead to any serious Congressional repercussions. While the rubber footwear industry is admittedly vocal, at no time did it control even a substantial group in either the House Ways and Means or Senate Finance Committee. Indeed, in the latter Committee Senator Ribicoff's amendment to apply American selling price as a basis of customs valuation to synthetic rubber footwear was finally rejected. Moreover, on the floor of the Senate he had little support for his position, and his amendment was taken to conference primarily because he had raised a point of personal prestige. In the conference committee his amendment was very substantially modified. As we see it, whatever Congressional disadvantages there may be in putting the new procedure into effect are far outweighed by the disadvantages internationally in not doing so.

Third, I do not believe that a persuasive case can be made that putting the new procedure in effect would result in any harm to the

---

[2] This legislation has not been further identified.

domestic industry. It is our understanding that under the new procedure the rates of duty on imports of rubber footwear would be the equivalent of 70% to 80% ad valorem based upon normal methods of valuation. Such rates would far exceed the rates of duty ranging from 5% to 25% ad valorem which are applied to the entire range of footwear items other than rubber footwear. Moreover, on the basis of statements made to us by representatives of importers, I understand that whatever lower prices for imported products might be brought about under the new procedure have been in effect for the last year or more. Finally, while imports of rubber footwear are admittedly substantial, the domestic industry appears to have fared well in recent years, given the enormous increase in consumption of these products. Employment, production, and sales have all increased markedly in the last six or seven years.

Fourth, as you may know, in cooperation with the Bureau of Customs and the Tariff Commission, we are now attempting to establish a new set of rates of duty for benzenoid chemicals and rubber footwear, which, applied on the normal basis of valuation, would yield approximately the same amount of protection as is afforded by the present rates of duty based on American selling price. It has been pointed out that, if the new procedure is put into effect, the new rates of duty would be somewhat lower than what they would have been otherwise. While this is certainly true, we doubt that it argues very much either for or against putting the new procedure into effect. If the new procedure is put into effect, there may be some criticism of whatever new rates of duty are devised on the ground that they are too low. On the other hand, if the new procedure is not put into effect, importers, as well as consumers, would criticize the new rates on the ground that they are too high. Therefore, I do not believe that much can be made of the impact of either putting into effect or not putting into effect the new practice upon the acceptability of whatever new rates of duty we devise with respect to rubber footwear.

Fifth, I understand that, as a result of an investigation made by the Bureau of Customs of the application of American selling price to imports of rubber footwear, it was discovered that the highest American selling price was being used. This is directly contrary to the practice of applying what we understand to be the lowest American selling price to imports of competitive benzenoid chemicals, as well as canned clams and woolen gloves. Accordingly, as a matter of sound customs administration, there appears to be a strong reason for changing the present procedure. Moreover, if the present procedure is not changed, it might well lead to demands on the part of the influential chemical industry to apply the highest, rather than the lowest, American selling price in imports of competitive benzenoid chemicals. Needless to say, this would have a very serious impact upon our negotiating posture in the Kennedy

Round, where American selling price has proven to be such a provocative issue.

For these reasons, we seriously doubt that any arguments based either upon Congressional reaction or the condition of the domestic industry can justify not putting the new procedure into effect. On the contrary, we believe that the interests of sound customs administration and a liberal trade policy, including, in particular, the promotion of the Kennedy Round, argue strongly for putting the new procedure into effect as soon as possible.

Best, as ever,

Christian A. Herter[3]

---

[3] Printed from a copy that bears this typed signature.

---

300. Memorandum From the President's Deputy Special Assistant for National Security Affairs (Bator) to President Johnson[1]

Washington, December 7, 1965, 10:30 am.

SUBJECT

A Tariff Problem

We have a problem involving the so-called American Selling Price (ASP) system of calculating tariffs on chemical goods. A first step in solving it would be a Tariff Commission study. At Tab A, Chris Herter asks you to instruct the Commission to make a study.[2] I would recommend, instead, that you authorize Herter to make such a request to the Commission. Connor and Mann agree that we should ask for a study.

The Problem

As you know, tariffs are generally calculated on the basis of the price charged by the foreign exporter. However, on a few goods, mainly chem-

---

[1] Source: Johnson Library, Bator Papers, Trade, Box 13. No classification marking. The source text bears the handwritten notes: "Passed to Bator 12–10–65 3:00 p.m." and "This has been acted on."

[2] Presumably Document 295, which was signed by Roth not Herter.

icals, we are required by law to base the tariff on the U. S. *domestic* price of comparable products (the "American Selling Price", or ASP).

Such ASP valuation is not only an infernal nuisance, but is giving Herter's people all sorts of trouble in Geneva:

—It violates our obligations under GATT and gives the Europeans a negotiating club which they use with gusto.
—It subjects our importers, as well as foreign exporters, to uncertainty as to the amount of the tariff.
—It is costly and clumsy to administer.

The trick is to shift to a more defensible basis of valuation *without* reducing the amount of protection. Chris Herter's memo suggests that we follow the good precedent set by the Congress last summer on rubber overshoes. Essentially, we would shift the *base* for calculating the tariff from the high domestic price to the lower foreign price, but—to cancel out the effect—we would apply a higher tariff *rate* so as to leave unchanged the dollar amount of tariff actually paid.

Procedure

As a first step, and before you decide to go ahead with the necessary legislation, we need a careful Tariff Commission study to see how this would work. The Commission will be happy to go ahead if they receive a formal Administration request.

Congressional Attitudes

Bill Roth reports that Wilbur Mills is all for a study. Tom Curtis (with a Monsanto Plant in his district) has written Herter a strong letter in favor. (Copy at Tab B)[3] King and the other Ways and Means members are also friendly. This is primarily Ways and Means business, so Roth has not canvassed individual Senators on the precise question at issue. During last summer's rubber footwear debate, Long, Smathers, Hartke, Douglas, Gore, and Ribicoff argued for eliminating ASP.

Industry Reactions

I spoke to Jack Connor to get a personal reading from him on likely industry reactions. He does not think any of the big companies will make a fuss, with the possible exception of Allied Chemical. Some of the smaller companies will be unhappy. They are nervous about any change in the present comfortable status quo. Overall, Jack's view is that we are safe in going ahead.

---

[3] This letter from Thomas B. Curtis, Republican Representative from Missouri, to Roth, October 1, is not printed.

Recommendation

That you authorize Herter to ask the Commission to make a study. (A draft letter from Herter to the Commission is at Tab C.)[4] This would in no way force your hand. Once the study is in, you will have a free choice whether or not to do something about it.

FMB[5]

OK for Herter to request study[6]

Disapproved

Bundy speak to me

---

[4] Not attached, but regarding a similar letter requested by Roth, see footnote 2, Document 295.

[5] McGeorge Bundy initialed below Bator's initials.

[6] This option is checked.

---

301. Memorandum of Conversation[1]

Washington, December 15, 1965.

SUBJECT

> Kennedy Round discussions regarding antidumping

PARTICIPANTS

> *Treasury Department*
> Mr. Joseph Barr, Undersecretary
> Mr. W. True Davis, Assistant Secretary
> Mr. Merlyn Trued, Assistant Secretary for International Affairs
> Mr. Joseph Bowman, Assistant to the Secretary for Congressional Relations
> Mr. James Hendrick, Deputy Assistant Secretary
> Mr. Ralph Hirschstritt, Deputy to the Assistant Secretary for International Affairs
>
> *Office of the Special Representative for Trade Negotiations*
> Mr. William Roth, Deputy Special Representative
> Robert A. Burt, Assistant General Counsel

---

[1] Source: Kennedy Library, Herter Papers, Antidumping, Box 5. Limited Official Use. Drafted by Robert A. Burt on December 17. The source text bears Herter's handwritten initials.

Mr. Roth stated that at a meeting on December 10, Secretary Fowler, Undersecretary Barr, Ambassador Blumenthal and he had discussed the question of the Kennedy Round discussions regarding dumping laws, and that he suggested the meeting today as a result of that earlier meeting.[2]

Mr. Roth explained that he believed an international agreement regarding dumping could be in the U.S. interest, since other countries, particularly the EEC, were now indicating greater interest in dumping laws, and since pressures for restrictive use of those laws could develop if, at the conclusion of a successful Kennedy Round, traditional trade barriers were substantially reduced. Serious international negotiation on dumping would also help persuade the Ways and Means Committee, particularly Chairman Mills, to postpone any action on the restrictive amendments to our dumping law.[3]

Mr. Barr asked the history of previous international discussions on dumping. Mr. Hirschstritt responded that over the past few years, several meetings have been held at which U.S. practices have been criticized. Mr. Roth stated that in the past other countries have insisted that we unilaterally change our dumping law, but that we have persuaded the U.K. in particular that the best possibility for U.S. action is a multilateral agreement to which a number of countries would be bound. The U.K. decision to submit a draft international code is therefore a significant change from the past.

In responding to this draft code, Mr. Roth continued, we have felt that all issues should be open for negotiation and that our discussions should not be limited to justifying our present dumping law. We are aware, of course, of the difficulties in getting Congress to change our present law. But these difficulties are no reason to refuse to discuss possible changes internationally. We have taken the same position regarding international discussion of other non-tariff barriers, such as American Selling Price. We can decide whether to accept any changes in our law when we arrive at a final negotiated package. For example, other countries have criticized our withholding of appraisement practices, and want these changed; whether we can agree to this should depend on the final terms of a proposed international agreement. But the only acceptable negotiating position at this stage is freely to discuss all issues. In this connection, we wanted to submit a paper at the next Working Group meeting raising fundamental questions regarding dumping without suggesting to the U.K. that we were ignoring their Draft Code.

Mr. Hirschritt stated that he had some difficulty with our proposed paper, because he felt that some of the questions appeared to prejudice

---

[2] No record of this December 10 meeting has been found.

[3] Regarding the antidumping law, see footnote 3, Document 231.

the answers. Mr. Burt responded that we intended the questions to be wholly neutral, and that any apparent prejudgment was only a drafting problem.

Mr. Davis asked STR's view of the timing of the negotiations. Mr. Burt replied that we hoped other countries would respond positively to our suggestion regarding exploration of basic questions, and that, if such response was forthcoming, the next several meetings of the Working Group would be devoted to further exploration possibly on the basis of other countries' submissions in addition to ours. But there was a risk that the other countries would think we were merely stalling, and they might be reluctant to agree to such exploration. We must persuade them that we are serious.

Mr. Roth stated that we hoped at this meeting today to make sure that STR and the Treasury were on the same wave-length, and to reach mutual agreement that international discussions should be carried out as we proposed.

Mr. Barr stated that, in his view, Mr. Roth's position was reasonable, and he was sure that agreement could be reached on a paper such as Mr. Roth had in mind.

Mr. Hendrick asked why a paper raising questions about dumping shouldn't also include questions based on U.S. law. Mr. Roth replied that we didn't want our paper to appear as simply a justification for present U.S. law, but that we should certainly discuss U.S. law, as background to the fundamental questions we raise, at the Working Group meeting.

The question was then raised regarding the manner in which any change in U.S. law would be sent to Congress, whether by treaty or direct amendment. In the course of discussion, it was noted that the Ways and Means Committee and the Senate Finance Committee have more understanding of dumping questions than the Foreign Relations Committees, through which a treaty would go.

Mr. Barr asked whether White House clearance was necessary to submit the proposed paper and embark on these international discussions. Mr. Roth responded that STR had general White House approval to discuss internationally the entire area of non-tariff barriers. Further White House clearance was not necessary until we came close to an agreement.

Mr. Barr asked whether the U.S. paper would be made public. Mr. Roth responded that the paper would be a negotiating document restricted to GATT member governments, and that the record of confidentiality has been generally good. In addition, Mr. Roth stated, we don't give the texts of U.S. submissions to our Congressional delegates, but rather give them summaries of the status of negotiations in particular matters.

302.   Letter From Director-General of the General Agreement on Tariffs and Trade Wyndham White to Participating Governments in the Kennedy Round[1]

CGT/801   Geneva, January 3, 1966.

Sir,

In my capacity as Chairman of the Trade Negotiations Committee, I have the honour to submit herewith a report to participating governments on the present status of the negotiations.

The report sets out in some detail the main problems with which negotiators have been confronted. I have considered it my duty to draw the attention of governments to the decisions which must be taken in the near future in order to make possible a successful conclusion to the negotiations. The time-limits which I have indicated in the report are of particular significance in this connexion. I should also like to stress the necessity for all participants to have continuously present in Geneva negotiators with broad authority to negotiate in this crucial phase of the negotiations.

Accept, Sir, the assurance of my highest consideration.

E. Wyndham White

Attachment[2]

Geneva, January 3, 1966.

THE GATT TRADE NEGOTIATIONS

Report by the Director-General

Introduction

1.   In initiating the current trade negotiations the participants have embarked on two major ventures. The first is the launching of a negoti-

---

[1] Source: Kennedy Library, Herter Papers, GATT Trade Negotiations, April 2, 1964–January 3, 1966, Box 9. No classification marking. A covering letter is addressed to Herter and bears the handwritten note, "CAH saw."
[2] Confidential.

ation designed to secure a degree of liberalization of the present barriers to international trade which is both deeper and more comprehensive in coverage than has been secured in previous negotiations, covering all classes of products and dealing with non-tariff as well as tariff barriers. The second is a series of activities to meet the urgent trade and economic development problems of less-developed countries. Special responsibilities rest on the shoulders of the more highly developed countries which have in the Ministerial Resolutions on which the trade negotiations are based committed themselves specifically to making use of the negotiations to contribute in a substantial way to the solution of these problems.

2. After much delay, agreement on procedures designed to secure that the maximum possible offers were tabled by each participant was complete only in July 1965, when procedures for the tabling of offers on tropical products were adopted by the Trade Negotiations Committee.

3. All major negotiators are not, however, in a position at the present time to table offers in accordance with the agreed procedures. In some cases offers, where tabled, are not sufficiently precise to form the basis of actual negotiation. In other important areas progress has not been made because participants have been unwilling to move from their initial negotiating positions.

4. Hitherto the negotiating timetable has permitted a certain degree of flexibility. This is no longer the case. The negotiating authority delegated by the United States Congress to the President expires on 1 July 1967, and I am informed by the United States Administration that it is politically unrealistic to envisage the extension of these powers if the negotiations were then uncompleted. Allowing for the necessary legal and administrative formalities required to give effect to the results of the negotiations, this means therefore, that the negotiations must be completed in the early weeks of 1967. To make this possible it is essential that delegations with broader authority to negotiate are present continuously in Geneva and that negotiations on all fronts be actively engaged and continuously pursued as from March/April 1966.

5. This report focuses attention on the main problems at present confronting negotiators, and sets out the points on which specific decisions must be taken by March/April if the timetable outlined above is to be met.

Negotiations on Industrial Products

General

6. In May 1964 the Trade Negotiations Committee meeting at ministerial level noted that the rate of 50 per cent had been agreed as a working hypothesis for the determination of the general rate of linear reduction and that the confirmation of this hypothesis was linked with

the solution of other problems arising in the negotiations, for example, tariff disparities, agricultural problems, exceptions and non-tariff problems, and, in general, with the achievement of reciprocity.

7. Lists of exceptions from the linear reduction on industrial products were tabled on 16 November 1964. Precise initial offers have not yet, however, been tabled by certain participants for all industrial products on which they have indicated that they are prepared to negotiate. *These offers should be tabled by March/April.* The multilateral process of justification of exceptions lists is being followed by bilateral contacts between delegations. During these contacts negotiators have, for the most part, identified exactly what is on offer and where their trade interests are affected by the proposed exceptions.

8. During these bilateral contacts negotiators are also defining the desiderata which, if satisfied, would enable them to maintain their across-the-board offer of a 50 per cent reduction in duties. These contacts will enable negotiators to judge the extent to which their initial offers must be improved if their negotiating objectives are to be reached. It is already clear that participants having made linear offers with few or no exceptions will not maintain those offers unless the less comprehensive offers of other participants are substantially improved.

9. Although these bilateral contacts have been continuing for some months and while considerable progress has been made in some of these a large amount of work remains to be done before the principal negotiators can draw up the balance sheets which would form the basis of final negotiations. *It is essential, therefore, that this work should be carried as far as possible in the time available between now and the opening of the decisive phase of the negotiations in March/April.*

10. During the justification process and during subsequent bilateral contacts it has become clear that many specific problems exist for individual participants in cases where products of importance to their export trade are included in the exceptions lists of other participants.

11. To take an extreme case, one participant which has made an offer of a linear reduction in tariffs without exceptions finds that more than half of its industrial exports are included in the exceptions list presented by one of its major trading partners. If this situation is maintained the question arises to what extent that participant will be able to take part in the final phase of the negotiations.

12. Another factor which must be taken into account is the unresolved question of tariff disparities. The intention of a major participant to claim disparity treatment for certain items and to reduce its duties on these items by less than the rate of linear reduction has implications for the wider negotiations. To take once again an extreme case, a participant which has made a linear offer without exceptions estimates that two thirds of its exports of the items for which it is the principal supplier of

the participant in question may be affected by claims for disparity treatment. If these claims are made this participant has indicated that it would have to make compensatory withdrawals from its own offer. As is shown later, an important part of the disparity problem must be brought into the sector negotiations if progress is to be made. This problem also raises questions of reciprocity for individual participants.

13. Countries other than those participating on the basis of a linear reduction in duties have presented offers and are participating in the process of bilateral contact referred to above. *It is essential that these countries specify, where this has not already been done, the initial offers that they would make and that all the set countries become fully integrated into the negotiating process. The necessary technical work must be substantially completed before March/April.*

14. A problem of a rather special nature and importance arises from the acceptance of Poland as a full participant in the negotiations on the basis of an offer which takes into account the nature of its economic system. *If negotiations are to continue with Poland it is necessary that participants define their position with regard to this offer and to indicate by March/April the possibilities they see of negotiation with Poland.* In the negotiations an analogous problem arises in the case of Czechoslovakia.

Participation of less-developed countries

15. As pointed out in paragraph 1 of this report, all highly developed countries have gone on record as saying that the current trade negotiations provide an opportunity for them to contribute in a substantial way to the solution of the trade and development problems of the less-developed countries. Twenty-three countries have pledged their participation under the procedures drawn up for the less-developed countries and by now twelve of these have taken steps to become full participants to the negotiations.

16. A meeting has been held to examine exceptions from the linear reduction which the industrialized countries proposed to make on products of export interest to less-developed countries. This is being followed by bilateral talks between delegations. It has been demonstrated that a number of items of particular interest to less-developed countries have been excepted from the linear cut, and that there is therefore a gap between the declared intentions of industrialized countries and their performance in this area. *A number of ways limiting the impact of exceptions have been proposed, and to this end specific requests must be forthcoming from less-developed countries and the first phase of bilateral contacts completed by the end of February.*

17. It follows a fortiori that less-developed countries which have indicated their intention to take part in the negotiations but which have not yet taken steps to become full participants should do so without

delay so that they can make their negotiating requirements known in detail.

18. Assuming that the large amount of technical work which remains is carried out, it will also be necessary to take the political decisions, which would enable positive and far-reaching benefits in the present trade negotiations. *It is essential that these decisions be taken before the final phase of the negotiations opens in March/April.*

19. The statements of the offers which less-developed countries would make as their contribution to the objectives of the trade negotiations are for the most part general in nature and more precision is clearly necessary. Less-developed countries should therefore re-examine in detail the possibilities which are open to them. It would be of assistance to those countries if all participants were to make specific suggestions to them in this regard.

20. All countries taking part in the negotiations on the basis of the plan for the participation of the less-developed countries have indicated their readiness to study and negotiate measures designed to increase trade among themselves, but no specific offers or requests have yet been exchanged. Action in this important field must be accelerated if the negotiations in it are to be carried through to a successful conclusion. *Specific offers and requests should be exchanged by the beginning of February so that bilateral negotiations may start in March/April.*

Bilateral problems

21. It has become apparent that the negotiations on industrial products will, for the most part, best be carried forward bilaterally for the moment. The offers made have given rise to a large number of negotiating problems of a bilateral nature which should be dealt with in this way in the first instance, although clearly it will be necessary to assess the multilateral implications of the results of the bilateral negotiations.

22. Although it would be inappropriate to deal with bilateral problems on specific products in this report there are some cases where the products represent such a large percentage of the export trade of some participants, and in particular of relatively small countries, that the inclusion of individual products in exceptions lists presents a major negotiating problem for these countries. For example, it is of particular concern to one participant that most ferro-alloys have been totally excepted by one of its main trading partners. Another participant is concerned that watches have been included in the list of exceptions of one major country. It is of importance to this participant that the full 50 per cent reduction should be obtained on this product.

Sectoral problems

23. It became apparent that specific negotiating problems exist in certain important sectors and that some concerted effort should be made

in order to secure the maximum degree of trade liberalization in those sectors. These sectors are chemicals, pulp and paper, steel, cotton textiles and aluminum.

24. The following paragraphs outline these problems and indicate where action by governments is necessary during the next few months.

Chemicals

25. In the chemical sector action by the United States with respect to the American Selling Price system of valuation has become a key issue in that other major participants have stated that unless such action is taken they would not themselves be prepared to reduce their tariffs on a wide range of chemical items since effective reciprocity would not then, in this opinion, be available from the United States. Action on the American Selling Price system has been made a precondition of the opening of negotiations.

26. The Community has also excepted a fairly extensive range of chemical products from its linear offer on grounds of overriding national interest. The Community has indicated that it is prepared to offer duty reductions of less than the linear rate of reduction on the bulk of these items but precise offers have not yet been tabled because progress has not yet been made on the American Selling Price problem referred to above. The Community also claims that significant tariff disparities exist on other products in this sector and intend consequently to apply a reduction of less than the linear cut of these products.

27. The United Kingdom has also excepted virtually all plastics materials from the linear cut on grounds of overriding national interest, essentially because for these products differences in the tariffs between the major producers are extreme.

28. The United States is offering the linear reduction in duties on virtually all items in this sector. This would halve the effective rate of duty on all items to which the offer applies, including those covered by the American Selling Price system of valuation. This is the maximum which the United States Administration can offer under their existing authority as they interpret it. The United States initial negotiating position is that this offer is in itself more than equivalent compensation for the Community's present maximum offer, which is subject to exceptions and claims for disparity treatment.

29. The resulting stalemate in this sector is of concern to other exporters of chemical products, particularly because the possibility that major participants would not make the full tariff reduction in this sector creates a specifically European problem. This is of major concern since trade between the European countries is very important.

30. Other problems exist in this sector. Japan's offer in this field is subject to a considerable number of exceptions although to no other conditions. Canada has not yet made an offer in this sector.

31. It will be necessary to treat all aspects of the problem, including the American Selling Price system and disparities in tariff levels in one set of negotiations on the sector. Progress must be made in this sector, or chemicals will be withdrawn entirely from the scope of the negotiations. Negotiations must be fully engaged by March/April. What is required is, on the other hand, an assurance by the United States of its willingness to negotiate towards an acceptable solution of problems connected with the American Selling Price system and, on the other, an assurance from the European Economic Community that, having obtained this, they would enter unreservedly into comprehensive negotiations on the whole range of chemical products. *If the maximum result is to be achieved it will also be necessary for these participants to give renewed consideration to the rather complicated questions of reciprocity which arise.* In the nature of things, mathematically full reciprocity may not be attainable within the sector and, as in other sectors, an agreement might leave debits and credits to be balanced off in the final stage of the negotiations. In so far as a satisfactory solution to the problem of the American Selling Price system would be an important contribution to the negotiations on non-tariff barriers, it would probably be matched by action by other participants on other non-tariff barriers.

Pulp and paper

32. It has also been suggested that the negotiations on pulp and paper should take place in a multilateral group. Several problems exist in this sector. For instance Japan has put certain basic pulp and paper items on its list of exceptions. Negotiations have not yet been fully engaged in this sector, however, because the position of the European Economic Community is that their initial offers in this sector can be tabled only after they have reached agreement bilaterally on certain trading problems with the Scandinavian countries, their principal suppliers of the majority of these items.

33. Other exporters, which are the principal suppliers of the Community for certain important items in this sector, are concerned in particular that final arrangements may be worked out on a European basis which may be unacceptable to them.

34. The problem here is perhaps not that multilateral negotiations should be opened, but that it has not been possible for bilateral negotiations to be opened between all participants with a major interest in this area. While the problem has other facets it is principally one of timing. It is clearly desirable, here as elsewhere, that all major participants be kept informed of events taking place in bilateral negotiations. *Bearing in mind the timetable for the negotiations, it is essential that the initial negotiating posi-*

tions of all interested parties be defined in time to permit negotiations to be fully opened by March/April.

Steel

35. Discussions have already started in a multilateral group on iron and steel products. The negotiating problem in this sector stems in particular from the nature of the offer by the European Community and the reservation by the United Kingdom that before implementing its offer of a 50 per cent cut it would have to have regard to the outcome in the sector as a whole (a standpoint which, in practice, is shared by several other countries). The Community is offering the linear reduction without exception on steel items within the competence of the European Coal and Steel Community (which account for about 85 per cent of the Community's steel imports), but is proposing to apply this not to the duties actually applied by the six member States (which are themselves higher than the rates in the tariff, as a result of a temporary increase made at the beginning of 1964), but to the average of higher rates which existed prior to the creation of the ECSC.[3] The Community is offering to make only partial reductions on the majority of other steel items since it wishes to maintain the internal logic of its tariff in the sector. Precise initial offers have not yet, however, been made.

36. The Community have also indicated that, in view of the particular characteristics of production and trade in this sector, a measure of harmonization should be achieved in the present negotiations in the tariffs protecting the major steel producing and exporting countries.

37. The United States and Austria are offering the full 50 per cent cut without exception. Japan is offering the 50 per cent cut with few exceptions and has made an improvement in the anti-dumping policy of the United States a condition of its willingness to accept the objective of tariff harmonization in this sector.

38. The other participants with a major interest in this sector regard the offer at present made on ECSC products as an exception from the linear rule. If the Community's offer remains unchanged the United Kingdom will presumably not maintain its linear offer in this sector. While similar conditions are not explicitly attached to the offers of other major participants, it would then become difficult for them to maintain their offers.

39. These participants have also stressed that, if the Community wish to carry out their intention of introducing a common external tariff for ECSC products this should be done in the present negotiations, rather than as a separate exercise.

---

[3] The Community had stated that the arithmetical average of these higher rates is 14.4 per cent ad valorem, that the average of the rates in the tariff is 6.7 per cent and the average of the rates currently applied is of the order of 9 per cent. [Footnote in the source text.]

40. Work has been undertaken in connexion with the preparation of a concordance of the tariffs of participants with a major trade interest in this sector so that a picture may be obtained of the relative levels of the tariffs in these countries. This work will be completed during the next few weeks.

41. *If certain participants feel that the aim in this sector should be the harmonization of tariffs it is essential, however, that specific proposals with regard to the levels at which the tariffs of the participants concerned should be harmonized should be made soon enough to permit negotiations to start by March/ April.*

Cotton textiles

42. In the cotton textile sector the United Kingdom has stated that no reduction can be made in its tariff on cotton goods but has offered to reduce the existing mixed duties on goods containing cotton and man-made fibers to the basic rates for cotton goods. Before finally implementing this offer the United Kingdom would have to have regard to the outcome in the sector as a whole, but the offer is not conditional on the renewal of the Long-Term Arrangement Regarding Trade in Cotton Textiles. Canada has indicated that it is prepared to make offers on a large number of items in this sector but not its precise initial offers on these items. The offer is conditional in the sense that Canada "is prepared to reduce tariffs if other countries do so also".

43. The United States is offering the linear cut virtually without exceptions in this sector and is offering to negotiate on the application of the Long-Term Arrangement, on the understanding that the Long-Term Arrangement would be renewed in its present form for a further period. The European Economic Community has also tabled a list of conditional offers relating to thirty textile items, most of which are cotton textiles; they have indicated that any tariff reduction on these products is conditional on the extension of the Long-Term Arrangement or the adoption by the Contracting Parties of measures with the same effect as the Long-Term Arrangement. The Community have also excepted a number of textile items from the linear cut on grounds of overriding national interest and have tabled partial offers on these products.

44. The exporting countries wish to negotiate on tariffs and the improvement of access to their main export markets. Of these they regard access as much the most important.

45. I have concluded that, in order to permit negotiations to be opened in this sector, exporting countries should make known in as much detail as possible their desiderata with regard to tariffs, to quantitative restrictions imposed in accordance with the Long-Term Arrangement or otherwise and not to the administration of the Arrangement. Importing countries which have not specified the initial tariff offers

which they would be prepared to make should do so as soon as possible. Importing countries should then, in response to the requests submitted to them, where necessary reconsider their tariff offers and indicate the improvements which should be made in quantitative restrictions and the administration of the Arrangement. *These stages should be completed not later than the end of February.*

Aluminum

46. The European Economic Community and Japan have included aluminum and aluminum products as partial exceptions in their lists. The Community has not yet defined its initial offer.

47. This is an example similar to those referred to earlier where a product accounts for a large percentage of the export trade of certain participants for whom a successful outcome of negotiations on the product is of great importance. It is not possible to engage in negotiations until all initial offers are tabled. *Initial offers should therefore be tabled by March/ April.*

Non-tariff barriers

48. Participants have identified the particular non-tariff barriers on which they wish to negotiate. *In view of the overall negotiating timetable it is essential that all governments should specify their desiderata in this field and respond to requests already made so that negotiations can be taken up by March/ April.*

49. Discussions are being held on a draft code of general applicability amplifying Article VI of the General Agreement in a Group on Antidumping Policies. *It is essential that delegations should be given positive instructions on the proposal before the Group so that detailed discussions can take place in January.*

Fish

50. Different participants are applying different procedures to fish and fish products. Some countries treat fish in the industrial sector while others consider it should be dealt with under the procedure established for the agricultural part of the negotiations. In order that this important sector be properly dealt with in the negotiations it is essential that concrete and specific offers on fish and fish products be tabled by all participants not already having done so, designed to create acceptable conditions of access to world markets for these products. *In accordance with the overall timetable for the negotiations, such offers should be tabled not later than 30 April 1966.*

Negotiations on Agricultural Products

General

51. In the field of the agricultural negotiations after nearly two years of preparatory work, agreement was reached in March 1965 on a proce-

dure under which participating countries agreed to make specific offers on individual agricultural products designed to achieve the objectives set out by Ministers. I think it would be appropriate to examine the two terms of this agreement in turn.

52. With respect to the first point—specific offers on individual products—it is only on cereals that proposals were tabled last May in accordance with the timetable agreed upon. For all the other products—including meat and dairy products—on the other hand, for which it had been agreed that specific offers would be tabled on 16 September last, one of the major partners in the negotiations was not in a position to table offers for internal reasons. The result was that, in general, other participants decided to table only part of their offers, while in other sectors where the participation of the European Economic Community is recognized as being necessary the majority of participants purely and simply refrained from tabling offers.

53. This situation gives grounds for concern on more than one account. Indeed, it had always been agreed that agriculture constituted an essential part of the negotiations as a whole and that, particularly for a number of countries in which agriculture is the dominant activity, the negotiations as a whole were only of interest if they contributed to "the creation of acceptable conditions of access to world markets in agricultural products in furtherance of the significant development and expansion of world trade in such products."[4] Furthermore, the imbalance which is developing between the negotiations in the industrial sector and the difficulties in the agricultural sector threatens to affect the negotiations as a whole. This indeed, is one of the most disquieting features in the whole picture since, unless an acceptable settlement can be arrived at on agriculture concurrently with an agreement on industry, the negotiations will fail.

54. It is therefore absolutely essential in my view, in order to proceed effectively with the negotiations, that participating countries which have not or not fully tabled their offers on agricultural products should agree to do so in such a way that the negotiations can effectively commence well before the summer of 1966. *To this end it is indispensable that the offers be tabled on a fixed date which should not be later than 30 April 1966.*

55. In considering the offers, when tabled, it is understood that participating countries will inevitably keep in mind the overall balance of the ultimate result of the negotiations between offers and benefits in both the industrial and agricultural field. This brings me to the second point—offers designed to achieve the objectives set out by Ministers. A certain knowledge has been gained in the course of the discussions and of the

---

[4] The quotation is from the GATT Ministerial resolution of May 21, 1963, on principles and procedures; see footnote 2, Document 228.

preparatory work, of the various positions of the partners in the negotiations. It would, therefore, seem possible to identify certain areas, where progress is essential, and for which therefore, all delegations should have broader negotiating authority. These areas are identified below for the different sectors of the agricultural negotiations.

Group on Cereals

(a) Domestic policies and access

56. In the course of negotiations countries have expressed their willingness to negotiate on their domestic cereals policies or on certain commitments providing opportunities for access. However, partners in the negotiations are particularly concerned about the general tendency in nearly all countries of continuously increasing production. This may affect their commercial outlets to world markets and it will a priori make the possibility of achieving and maintaining acceptable conditions of access questionable. It would seem that a condition for a successful outcome of the negotiations would be that participating countries should be in a position to negotiate on a combination of undertakings, effective and acceptable to all parties concerned, with the ultimate objective of bringing some moderation in further production increases. Such undertakings might include the possibility of limiting support to a certain quantity of produce.

(b) International prices

57. Negotiations on an international price system applicable to wheat and coarse grains have not yet much advanced. An effective outcome of the negotiations would seem to be a price system including international minimum and maximum prices. These prices should be such as to provide a remunerative return to efficient producers. While the precise level of such prices is clearly a matter for detailed negotiation, participating countries should be prepared and should be in a position to enter into meaningful negotiations in this regard.

(c) Non-commercial disposals

58. This aspect of the negotiations has not yet received full attention of all delegations concerned. A co-ordinated organization of such disposals, complementary to normal commercial outlets, has been advocated by a number of countries as one of the corner-stones of an international arrangement on cereals. When resuming the negotiations delegations should be fully prepared to enter into more substantive negotiations in this regard.

59. *Directives on these various points would be needed prior to the next meeting of the Cereals Group which, in accordance with the overall timetable of the negotiations, should be held in the March/April period.*

Group on Meat/Group on Dairy Products

60. While the preparatory work in these Groups for the negotiations may be finalized by the end of April 1966, *it is essential that offers as laid down in the agreed procedure be tabled not later than 30 April 1966 by all participating countries concerned.* These offers should be so designed as to meet the objectives of the negotiations laid down by the Ministers and will indeed be appreciated against their ability to further a significant development and expansion in world trade. On the basis of the offers tabled, negotiations will then start without delay.

Other agricultural products

61. *It is essential that to the extent that participating countries have not yet already done so, concrete and specific offers be tabled as set out in the agreed procedure,* on individual products relating to all relevant elements of agricultural support or protection or to the total effect of these elements and designed to provide acceptable conditions of access to world markets as agreed by the Ministers. It is my understanding that an offer would only be considered a meaningful basis for the negotiations if it can be shown that it constituted an effective concession providing improved opportunities for access. It is also my understanding in cases where the tariff is presently bound the offer should in principle relate to the reduction of the tariff.

Tropical products

62. The offers will also relate to tropical products. In this connexion the Resolution of 6 May 1964 may be recalled according to which all participants are prepared to consider the possibility of taking such steps as are open to them to make cuts deeper than 50 per cent in, or to eliminate completely duties on products of special interest to less-developed countries.[5] *The possibility of coming to some joint action by all developed participating countries in this regard should be given serious consideration.* Such action might include the possibility of suspending duties on tropical products in advance of their being reduced or eliminated at the end of the negotiations.

---

[5] Reference is to the resolution adopted by the GATT Trade Negotiations Committee Ministerial meeting in Geneva on May 6, 1964; for text, see *American Foreign Policy: Current Documents, 1964,* pp. 1210–1213.

303. Airgram From the Mission to the European Office of the United Nations to the Department of State[1]

A–683   Geneva, January 6, 1966.

SUBJECT

ExOff—GATT Director General's Report of Kennedy Round[2]

REF

A. Tagg 3692;[3]
B. Depcirtels 1148, 1149;[4]
C. Tagg 3722 (not sent all posts)[5]
D. Depcirtels 1188, 1208[6]

For Governor Herter from Blumenthal.

1. Enclosed is a copy of the Kennedy Round report by Eric Wyndham White, Director General of the GATT. This document went forward January 4, 1966, addressed to the appropriate Ministers of the countries participating in the negotiations so as to assure high level governmental attention. The report surveys the status of each of the principal negotiating areas and highlights the current barriers to forward movement. Its objective is to point up the necessary decisions to be taken by all governments in the coming weeks so that substantive negotiations can be launched in the spring of 1966 and the Kennedy Round completed by the following winter (Refs A and B).

2. In general we believe the report is well drawn and should be a constructive element in the current process of focussing on negotiating obstacles and the action required of the European Economic Community and other negotiators by March/April 1966. Wyndham White held a series of information meetings with the major Kennedy Round participants (Ref A) before writing the report and we, as well as the EEC, Japan, and the United Kingdom, had brief opportunities to comment individually on the first draft. Although some of our (and presumably other countries') suggested amendments were incorporated in the final version, the paper remains strictly the responsibility of the Director General. Although the report is therefore correctly "neutral" in tone, we will have the opportunity, where necessary, to sharpen up points of particular

---

[1] Source: Department of State, Central Files, FT 7 GATT. Confidential; Air Priority. Drafted by Winston Lord (KR), and James H. Lewis (KR), and approved by Lewis. Received on January 10 and repeated to 18 diplomatic missions.

[2] Attachment to Document 302.

[3] Dated December 15. (Department of State, Central Files, FT 13–2 US)

[4] Both dated December 15, 1965. (Ibid.)

[5] Dated December 21, 1965. (Ibid., FT 4 GATT)

[6] Dated December 21 and 23, 1965, respectively. (Both ibid., FT 13–2 US)

interest in our Brussels meeting with the EEC Commission on January 11. For background and guidance in conversation with officials dealing with this subject, we offer the following observations on the document.

3. *General.* The report taken as a whole clearly indicates that responsibility for the present impasse rests to a large extent with the EEC, and that if the impasse is to be broken, the Kennedy Round successfully concluded, action is required by the EEC in the following major areas:

(a) Agricultural products including meat and dairy products—the EEC must make offers, and in doing so must go beyond mere bindings of montants de soutien.
(b) In the nonagricultural area, offers must be made by the EEC, or made complete, on: Chemicals, steel, pulp and paper, aluminum, other items where the EEC "partial" offer remains imprecise or unspecified, and fish.

There appears to be rather widespread misunderstanding of the fact that the EEC must move not only in agricultural but nonagricultural areas (e.g. see The Hague's 522 to Dept.).[7] Nonagricultural areas where no EEC offers have yet been made, or where so-called partial offers have not been made specific, or where unreasonable precondition has prevented EEC from negotiating (i.e. chemicals), account for a significant portion of EEC imports. (Further comment on specific problems is given below.)

4. *Specific Comments.* The following notes cover the major problem areas and are keyed to the numbered paragraphs of the report.

Offers—Para. 3. This paragraph primarily refers to the EEC's failure to table agricultural offers (except for an unspecific proposal on grains), to define many of its partial offers on industrial products and to show any flexibility in its initial positions with respect to industrial offers. Other countries, largely because of the inaction of the Community, tabled imprecise and/or incomplete agricultural offers this fall, and no participant has been willing to modify its basic opening Kennedy Round stances in view of the EEC paralysis.

EEC Representations in Geneva—Para. 4. The Community still does not have a permanent negotiating team in Geneva, and this has seriously impeded progress.

Technical Discussion of Offers—Para. 7 to 9. Our view is that the technical phase of the negotiations is largely concluded and that remaining technical work should be subsumed in active negotiations. What is immediately needed is the specification of offers and the filling of gaps, and then, at least exploration without commitment of possibilities for

---

[7] Dated January 4, 1966. (Department of State, Central Files, ECIN 3 EEC)

improvement. We do not wish the EEC or others to delay substantive negotiations by lingering in the technical stages (Ref C).

Balance Sheet—Para. 9. Precise comparisons and balancing attempts between participants is not desirable at this point in the linear negotiations. However, those EFTA countries with no exceptions and the United Kingdom and the United States with moderate lists would clearly consider the offers of the EEC and Japan as "less comprehensive."

Exceptions—Para. 11. This refers to the impact of the Community's industrial exceptions on Norway.

Disparities—Para. 12. We should have preferred to see this issue given less prominence in the report. Only the EEC has indicated an intention to invoke disparities, and this intention appears to be still firm. Switzerland is the country whose interests would be so severely sideswiped by EEC disparity invocations against the U.S./U.K., but other countries' exports would also be substantially affected unless adequate safeguards can be worked out. We are willing to leave the disparities issue open until the late stages of the negotiations, when we hope it may have been reduced to more manageable proportions as a result of discussions between EEC and third countries like Sweden and Switzerland.

Non-Linear Participants—Para. 13. This reference seems most applicable to Australia among the developed countries.

Poland—Para. 14. Poland's participation in the KR is related to its GATT status. Most countries, including the United States, have not taken precise positions concerning the Polish "offer," which is to increase by a certain percentage its purchases abroad under its state-trading system.

LDC's—Para. 17. Those participating LDC's who have not yet tabled offers or statements of contribution are Argentina (only proposals on cereals, meat, and dairy products), Ceylon, Cyprus, Ghana, Ivory Coast, Malta, Nicaragua, Niger, Pakistan, Portugal (non-European territories), Togo, and Uganda.

Para. 19. In addition to our own individual "suggestion papers," we know that Canada, Japan, Sweden, and the United Kingdom have suggested at least some KR contributions by the LDC's. In this connection the U.S. Delegation has held 45 meetings with LDC Delegations in Geneva to explain our offers and suggestions. We understand the EEC has not met with any LDC's.

Bilateral Problems—Para. 22. Norway is interested in ferro-alloys, Switzerland in watches. The EEC has excepted most ferro-alloys. The United States has most but not all watches on its mandatory exceptions list.

Sectoral Problems—Para. 23 et seq. In all these industrial major sectors, the negotiations are stalled to a greater or lesser degree by reason of the EEC position.

Chemicals—Para. 25. Although all countries in the informal sector group on chemicals have emphasized the importance of U.S. action on ASP, only the Community has stressed the reciprocity element to the extent this paragraph suggests and only the EEC has made ASP movement a precondition for opening negotiations. The EEC has not only important exceptions in chemicals but has refused even to discuss its partial chemical offers unless the U.S. indicates it will eliminate ASP. The United States, however, has no obligation to eliminate ASP, and considers that its full 50% linear offer virtually without exceptions is more than equivalent to the EEC offer. Nevertheless, the United States is willing to negotiate on ASP, and to consider eliminating it provided something sufficiently attractive can be obtained in return. Other countries are ready to negotiate on this basis but the EEC is not—it still insists that unless the United States unilaterally eliminates ASP *and* makes a 50% reduction on chemicals, the EEC will not offer even the limited concessions it has so far tabled, and even these will be subject to disparity invocations. The Director General's report clearly states in para. 31 what is required:

By the United States—an assurance that it is willing to negotiate toward an acceptable solution (we have already given such an assurance—see Tagg 3669[8]—and will reiterate it, referring also to Governor Herter's letter to the Tariff Commission on ASP (Ref. D).

By the EEC—a willingness to enter into negotiations. (This will require not only removal of the pre-condition about ASP, but a willingness to consider what contribution the EEC can make to a possible package in which the United States undertakes to do something about ASP.)

Chemical Disparities—Para. 26. The EEC, in an informal meeting December 7, appeared to recognize that it could not agree to a sector solution on chemicals and subsequently introduce chemical rate disparities in a broader context.

Sector Balancing—Para. 31. The warning against seeking precise intra-sector balances in chemicals applies equally to other areas of the negotiations (see General Comments below).

Pulp and Paper—Para. 33–34. There are several pulp and paper items, other than those for which we are *principal* suppliers, in which we and Canada have substantial interests, and our exports of pulp and paper to the Community amount to over $130 million. No EEC offers have yet been made on any of these items, on the excuse that arrangements must first be worked out with the Scandinavians. In this connection, we are just concerned about possible *final* European arrangements which may be unacceptable, but rather we would oppose any EEC-Scandinavian bilateral drawing of negotiating perimeters which might prove inhibit-

---

[8] Dated December 8, 1965. (Ibid., FT 7 EEC–US)

ing once we multilateralize the sector talks. We also have been informed by the Scandinavians that the EEC has made no specific proposals and apparently does not have any to make in the near future—therefore the outlook is for further indefinite delay.

Steel—Para. 41. The Communities, in a December 10 meeting, agreed to outline their ideas on harmonization in the steel sector in the latter half of January. We continue to have our doubts about harmonization in principle but we are willing to look to any proposal the EEC/ECSC makes and to see whether it results in any effective liberalization of trade. The important point is stated in para. 38—namely that we and others do not consider the ECSC offer to be a genuine linear offer because of the base rates used, and hence no progress can be made in the sector unless the Communities can discuss making *effective* reductions in rates.

Textiles—Para. 45. The United States and Japan have had several meetings along these lines and have reached bilateral agreement on how to carry forward cotton textile negotiations under Wyndham White's proposed package deal. The EEC has been asked by Japan to negotiate similarly, but it is clear that the EEC negotiator does not at present have any authority to discuss any "improvements" in QR's or the administration of the LTA.

Aluminum—Para. 46. As stated, the problem is that the EEC has not made any offer. This sector is of importance to Canada and Norway as well as the United States.

Fish—Para. 50. No EEC offers have been made in this important sector.

Agriculture—Para. 51 et seq. In general these are self-explanatory. There is recognition even by the EEC that there can be no progress until the EEC is in a position to make specific offers.

Para. 54. Wyndham White hopes the specific deadline will be useful in imparting a sense of urgency to the Member States of the Community.

Para. 56. We should have preferred some distinction between the situation regarding wheat and that of feed grains, where differentials would have to be negotiated, but the Director General believes this problem can be better dealt with in actual negotiations.

Para. 59. Because of the EEC failure to lay down meat and dairy proposals, most countries including the United States, have not tabled offers on these products. We are prepared to table our offers when the EEC does.

Para. 60. The lack of Community offers is of course the principal stumbling block here. We have held technical bilateral meetings on agriculture with several countries, but many partners' positions in this field remain incomplete and/or indefinite, pending action by the EEC. The last two sentences refer primarily to the present EEC position/intention of offering only to bind the MDS, even on products whose tariffs were previously bound.

Tropical Products—Para. 61. Sweden in particular has been urging joint action on tropical products, and the GATT Secretariat has compiled a list of all tropical products offers that have been submitted by developed countries. However, further progress in this field appears difficult without Community offers, *which have not yet been made.*

4. *General Comments.* There are a few other aspects of the report which should be noted. The U.S. *exclusions* policy has not been mentioned, but the Community on several occasions has stressed its objections to this approach and its intention to weigh such items as petroleum in the negotiating scales. One view that Wyndham White has repeatedly voiced, and with which we agree, is that precise *intra-sector balances* should not be sought. This point is mentioned in the chemicals section of the report, but it warrants further emphasis since it applies to all the special sectors and the negotiations in general. Countries must be willing to register debits and credits in individual areas and look for compensation within the total Kennedy Round package; otherwise, narrow, halting gestures will result in a series of sector deals leveled at the lowest common denominator. The reference to *disparities* is a reminder that all *ambiguities, conditions,* and *gimmicks* in countries' negotiating positions should be in the open by this spring. The Community's offers are the most murky—e.g., its unspecified partial reductions, its rather vague reciprocity demands in the automotive and aircraft fields, and its imprecise conditions for slicing cotton textile tariffs—but there are unknowns in other partners' initial positions as well. All relevant elements for a Kennedy Round package should be spelled out as substantive negotiations are joined in the coming months, in order to avoid last minute injections which might upset delicate deals and initiate unravelling.

5. The foregoing comments are intended solely to give addresses a more precise appreciation of the present status and major issues of the Kennedy Round negotiations, in conjunction with the Director General's account to the GATT Ministers. Detailed talks and bargaining, of course, must continue to be limited to Geneva.

For the Ambassador:
James J. Lewis
Counselor for Economic Affairs

304. Memorandum of Conversation Between U.S. and EEC Officials[1]

Brussels, January 11, 1966.

SUBJECT

    The Kennedy Round

[Here follows a list of 23 participants.]

Introduction

In opening the meeting, Commissioner Rey, after welcoming the American delegation, said that it was a good idea to have a meeting at that time for a number of reasons. The U.S. and the EEC were the principal partners in the Kennedy Round; the Wyndham White report had just been released;[2] time was short and it was a common goal of the U.S. and the Community to complete the Kennedy Round by the end of 1966; and also because the meeting would be helpful in the preparation of the Commission's report for the Council concerning the Kennedy Round. Rey expressed reasonable optimism regarding the present political situation in the Community. He doubted, however, that the Luxembourg meeting would solve everything. Rey felt that there was a common will among the Six, not just the Five, to develop the EEC, which meant also a common desire to deal successfully with the Kennedy Round.

Ambassador Roth responded that the U.S. realized the difficulty of discussions on the Kennedy Round at the time and that it had had some hesitation about proposing the meeting. However, in light of Wyndham White's report and since the Commission was preparing a report on the Kennedy Round, a meeting seemed opportune. Interest in the Kennedy Round was a perennial concern of both parties but Ambassador Roth assured the EEC representatives that the U.S. continued to have a paramount interest in the negotiations.

Strong U.S. interest in the Kennedy Round for both political and economic reasons had been stressed in the good discussions with Chancellor Erhard in December. In recent weeks the President had given more attention to problems of world trade, including taking liberal decisions on certain escape clause actions. It was also the President who had

---

[1] Source: Department of State, Central Files, FT 7 GATT. Limited Official Use. Drafted by Stanley D. Schiff (USEC) and David E. Biltchik (EC) on January 28. Transmitted as an enclosure to airgram Ecbus A–350 from the Mission to the European Communities, February 1. The airgram was received February 10 and repeated to 17 diplomatic missions. The meeting was held at the EEC Commission.

[2] Attachment to Document 302.

decided that the question of "American selling price" should be studied. The President has a strong interest in the Kennedy Round. The U.S. knew that the Commission's feelings concerning the Kennedy Round were also strong.

Kennedy Round Timetable

Ambassador Roth said the U.S. felt that 1966 was the critical period for the Kennedy Round. Within the first six months of 1966 we would all know whether there could be a successful Kennedy Round. It would be necessary that the negotiations in Geneva be resumed, with EEC participation, by spring, so that before the summer vacation period one could see a package beginning to emerge. This would allow the negotiations to be completed by the end of 1966 and an agreement signed in early 1967. The schedule now was so very tight that, if it were not kept, the U.S. doubted that the Kennedy Round could be successfully concluded.

Ambassador Roth continued that the question was often raised whether, if the present time schedule were not met, it would be possible to get an extension of the Trade Expansion Act (TEA) through Congress. The Administration believed, Ambassador Roth stated, there was no substance to such hope. First, the President is determined that Congress should adjourn its current session in July, 1966 in view of the fall elections. Thus, there would be no time to introduce a bill. Second, in 1967 there would be only six months left for such action by Congress. It could perhaps be done, the Ambassador observed, but the Administration was very concerned over the likelihood of the TEA's liberal authority being, in the case of Congressional extension, whittled down by protectionistic amendments. Each year protectionistic amendments were attached to many acts. Often such acts could be vetoed. In the case of an extension of the TEA, however, such veto could not be used. Therefore, the judgment of the Administration is to stick to the TEA and make full use of the existing liberal authority.

Ambassador Roth added that the U.S. had another concern. Commercial policy seldom stood still. If the Kennedy Round did not succeed, there was the danger of a more protectionistic attitude in the U.S. and probably also in Europe.

Ambassador Roth outlined what actions were necessary to meet the timetable: 1) The EEC had to be in a position to negotiate again. This involves a matter on which the U.S. cannot comment because it is an internal Community affair; 2) If the negotiations continued, there would be a need for the EEC to maintain in Geneva a permanent negotiating delegation at a senior level. We are aware of the EEC's problem and especially the one for Mr. Hijzen is having to negotiate in Geneva and Brussels; however, the presence of such a team was particularly necessary in the critical period which was hopefully ahead, when the negotiating situation would require decision-making on a day-to-day basis; and 3) We would also hope that the 111 Committee, under a new negotiating mandate would have flexible authority for taking day-to-day decisions. The U.S. had a large negotiating team in Geneva which could make certain decisions very quickly. Ambassador Blumenthal had wide authority in this respect.

Rey indicated that he would report to the Council the dangers of a further delay in the Kennedy Round, noting that the Commission fully shared this view, and in fact was basing all its efforts to keep within the time limits of the TEA. Unfortunately, Rey observed, it does not depend on the Commission alone. The Commission's present difficulty was in getting decisions from the Council of Ministers. Rey hoped the crisis would be solved in the spring, but observed that, of course, the Commission just did not know when the Six would resume functioning. The Commission would, in its report, inform the Council of the U.S. delegation's emphasis on the dangers involved in getting new legislation. He remarked that the TEA had been a remarkable achievement over protectionist opposition that no one could be sure of repeating.

Turning to the problem of permanent Community representation in Geneva, Rey said that the Commission was very near a solution, hopefully within the next few weeks. He added that there need not be any fear that the EEC would not be fully represented when it was able to resume in Geneva.

He noted that the 111 Committee was a matter for the Council. Council decisions concerning the mandate were closely linked with the solution of the crisis. But the question of finding means to accelerate the decision-making process was one the Council would have to resolve when it meets. Rey added that he believed the Council should meet as often as necessary, not just once a month, to cope with Kennedy Round issues, once the need arose. The Council will have to devise procedures to accomplish this.

Agriculture

Ambassador Roth commented that in Washington the decision to table agricultural offers on September 16 had posed many problems and has been very difficult. The two major reasons why the U.S. finally tabled were: 1) the necessity of maintaining the momentum of the negotiations; and, 2) because of a desire to emphasize U.S. concern that agriculture be as much a part of the Kennedy Round as industry. The U.S. felt that there had to be coordinated industrial and agricultural movement. Unfortunately, the Ambassador said, the agricultural negotiations were now out of step with those in industry, a fact which has caused considerable concern in American agricultural circles and in Washington. Most concern was over the question of timing: when would the EEC be ready to put its offers on the table? Would it be able to keep the early spring dates Wyndham White suggested? Ambassador Roth asked if the Community could make offers in steps, beginning perhaps with the CAP products where regulations were complete.

Ambassador Blumenthal observed that the U.S. had tabled its agricultural offers in September, 1965, leaving aside for the moment products of interest to the EEC, including dairy and meat. The U.S. considered these concrete and specific offers very good indeed and hoped that others would match them. The quality of the offers made by other countries in Geneva was mixed; some concrete and specific, others of a more general nature, but all offers had been affected by the uncertainty as to what the EEC would do. This was particularly true for countries which had important markets in the Community. Countries whose main export interests were meat and dairy products were, of course, particularly disappointed.

Thus, Ambassador Blumenthal continued, the big question remained: when would the EEC be ready to make its offers? At that time, the U.S. and others could complete their offers. The Ambassador asked for the Commissioners' views regarding the timing of Community offers. The U.S. fully concurred with Wyndham White that April was the latest period for resumption of the negotiations. The U.S. realized, of course, the internal difficulties of the EEC. But the U.S. was sure the Commission realized that the EEC could not wait for the completion of all CAP regulations before making offers.

Ambassador Blumenthal concluded by saying that this was, of course, not the time to discuss such issues as the MDS or a grain agreement. But he did feel it was necessary to point out that the U.S. could not afford the luxury of waiting for new offers of a general nature which then would involve more delay in being made more specific. The U.S. would look at offers in terms of increased trading opportunities they provided. Moreover, a MDS binding in place of a current fixed tariff binding would be unacceptable.

Commissioner Mansholt agreed with the need for keeping the agricultural and industrial negotiations in parallel. The Community also wished to do so. Unfortunately, however, the fact had to be faced that agriculture was not only lagging behind, but that the agricultural negotiations had come to a complete standstill. The Commission recognized that because of agriculture the Kennedy Round is endangered, and recognizes equally that this situation depends on the Community and its ability to get agriculture moving.

As to the timetable, Mansholt continued, it was very difficult to predict anything in such a clouded situation. The following week, at Luxembourg, would indicate the future. Hopefully the political crisis would be resolved in February or March.

After the political solution, he felt that the first thing which would have to be dealt with was agricultural policy—which meant a package of agricultural decisions. Mansholt thought the package would cover: a) the financing of the Common Agricultural Policy; b) price decisions on dairy products, meat, fats and oils, and rice; and c) certain other regulations. It would not be too difficult to obtain agreement on the financial regulation, he thought. The toughest problem was, however, agricultural prices. The Commission hoped to submit to the Council price proposals by mid-February, whether or not the crisis was solved. The Council might begin to deal with these problems in March or April, if it were assumed, optimistically, that the political crisis were resolved the end of February or early March. At any rate, the Council would have to take decisions of fundamental importance on the elements of the package. Only after these decisions had been taken would it be possible to obtain a concrete mandate for the Kennedy Round. Wyndham White's deadline of April 30, Mansholt observed, seemed too optimistic. It would be better not to expect a concrete mandate by April 30 for all agricultural products. After the solution of the crisis, the only real deadline which could not be changed was the expiration of the TEA. The Commission and the Council had to do their utmost to meet this deadline. For this purpose the Council would have to reorganize its working methods, including the scheduling of special Council meetings only for the purpose of preparing a negotiating mandate. Should the Kennedy Round be in full swing in the latter part of spring or in early summer, the Council would have to devote a great deal of attention to it, using more flexible working methods than in the past and also giving more flexibility to the Commission.

It would be very hard to get a mandate for staged agricultural offers, Mansholt continued. The Council could not agree on a negotiating mandate for only certain products if there were still no Common Agricultural Policy regulations for other products. This would create an imbalance in the gains and losses to be expected by the Member States, and no Member State was willing to give away its bargaining power. Thus, in his personal opinion, all offers had to come at the same time. However, this did not mean that all CAP regulations had to be decided, but it did mean that at least the regulations for fruits and vegetables, fats and oils and sugar had to be completed before offers could be made. Price decisions would be the greatest concern. However, a Common Agricultural Policy regulation for tobacco was not necessary to make offers on this product.

Mansholt summed up by repeating that everything depended on the Council. In settling the political issues of the present crisis, it would be difficult for at least two or three Member States not to accept a solution without the Kennedy Round being of part of it.[3] After the solution of the crisis, the Community would have to move very fast on the Common

---

[3] Clearly implied was a settlement of the purely political issues in Luxembourg and subsequent extraordinary sessions, followed by a package deal of which the Kennedy Round would be a part, in a later meeting of the Six in Brussels. [Footnote in the source text.]

Agricultural Policy and on the questions of the Kennedy Round. The deadline of April 30 was, however, premature.

Rey agreed with Mansholt that the Council would have to make decisions on tabling offers. He also conceived that the Kennedy Round brought both incentive and a pressure of time. The Ministers would have to make decisions. The Commission would have to tell them that time was pressing and decisions were necessary.

Ambassador Roth concurred in the hope that a specific Kennedy Round commitment would be part of such a deal.

Mansholt said he did not want to mention a date, but that the problem was time. Before the summer holidays there had to be a period of substantive negotiations. After the experience with September 16, however, he preferred to be cautious about mentioning a date. Mansholt hoped that the Community would be in a position to table by May or June.

Ambassador Blumenthal replied that the U.S. knew the political crisis had to be settled, but he wondered how all the agricultural regulations could be completed and offers made in time to permit negotiations before the summer vacation. Such pre-August negotiations were, of course, necessary to complete the Kennedy Round negotiations in time.

Turning to grains, the Ambassador indicated that all negotiating partners would have to re-examine their situation and positions. The EEC would have to make certain additional decisions on grains. Would it be able to make these decisions as something apart from the other decisions on offers?

Ambassador Blumenthal asked if, after the political crisis were settled, there were no chance that the Member States would face up to the necessity of getting started in cereals, non-CAP and completed CAP items and then, say, by June, get other offers on the table.

Mansholt replied that as for grains, he did not exclude the possibility of additional decisions being taken independently of the package, especially as grains had been treated in a different way. New Council decisions were needed so that the Community could continue, and the Commission would try to get these decisions.

As for the interdependence of the various decisions, it seemed very difficult, almost impossible, to Mansholt, to proceed when prices had not been decided. He had a feeling that price decisions would perhaps enable the Council to issue a Kennedy Round mandate—even if fats and oils regulations had not been completed. The difficulty was that in the past the Member States had refused to take price decisions without having regulations. An offer for sugar could not be made until the policy was decided. Mansholt observed he would not know what to propose to the Council as an offer if the policy had not been decided.

Mansholt's feeling was that as soon as the crisis was solved, agricultural decisions would be taken quickly. The Kennedy Round added pressure. The French had a political election not far off, which implied France would have some interest in getting the decisions.

Mansholt said he did not think August would be a holiday this year. If the EEC could make agricultural offers by the end of June, Mansholt thought there would still be time to conclude the Kennedy Round negotiations by the end of the year.

Ambassador Roth emphasized that it was most important to have offers on the table well before August in order to be able to discuss them in sufficient time.

Mansholt added that he did not think, insofar as the timetable was concerned, partial offers would do, but instead might produce a mess in the Council. The mandate was a process of give and take. Partial offers would take much more time.

Rey said he shared Mansholt's view that decisions would come quickly after the crisis was settled. He also wanted to clarify the point that Mansholt did not exclude the possibility, especially in grains, of partial decisions.

Industry

After Rey's brief opening remarks, Ambassador Roth began the afternoon discussions by drawing the Commission's attention to two recent Presidential decisions concerning the liberalization of earlier U.S. escape clause actions (stainless steel table flatware and clinical thermometers).[4] Ambassador Blumenthal followed with a review of the state of the industrial negotiations.

Completion of Offers

Ambassador Blumenthal agreed with Wyndham White that *full* offers had to be the starting point for the negotiations and with his appeal for *complete* initial offers as soon as possible. The U.S. had on November 16, 1964 made a complete and precise statement of its industrial offers and exceptions.

The Community's industrial offer was still not complete; still lacking were offers on partial exceptions in the sectors:

a) certain chemicals (BTN Chapters 29 and 39)
b) pulp and paper
c) iron and steel
d) aluminum
e) ceramics

---

[4] Not further identified.

The U.S. agreed with the Director General's judgment that completion of offers for those sectors was needed by March or early April so that negotiations could begin.

Bilaterals

Ambassador Blumenthal noted that Wyndham White urged early completion of the bilateral examination of the initial offers. The U.S. considered that technical work of this nature was essentially finished and that the substantive phase of the negotiations could not get underway until offers were completed and sector discussions begun.

Improvement of Offers

There had apparently been some misunderstanding of the U.S. position regarding improvement of offers. The U.S. did not insist that any participant take unilateral action to reduce its exceptions list. The U.S. would, however, be prepared to explore without commitment possibilities for improvements in offers if the EEC could participate in such exploration. It was important for negotiations to be able to indicate when improvements might be possible. Only in that way could the outlines of a final package begin to appear. Further bilateral exploration, however, was of limited value until present gaps in offers were filled in.

Disparities

Ambassador Blumenthal cautioned about the need to avoid misunderstandings on this issue. Since no rules had ever been agreed upon, the U.S. considered that each participant was free to deal with these cases as seemed appropriate. The U.S. was prepared to consider any such cases claimed by the Community on a case-by-case basis, as less-than-50 percent offers. We were quite happy to allow the EEC to choose the time when it would indicate its disparity claims, since we felt many potential disparities might be taken care of in the EEC's bilaterals with other countries and in the sector work.

Ambassador Blumenthal agreed with the Director General of GATT that the disparities issue would inevitably arise in various sector negotiations, and in each such case we would have to know what the disparity claims were. The U.S. hoped that few disparities would be invoked; we did not intend invoking any.

Sectors

The key to the industrial negotiations may lie in the sectors. Active negotiation in the five sector groups was, in the U.S. view, one of the major areas in which the Kennedy Round negotiations had to make progress. Even the completion of initial offers and further bilateral discussions were apt to be unproductive unless we could make real progress in the special sectors.

[Here follows discussion of chemicals, tariff disparities and concordances, iron and steel, cotton textiles, non-tariff barriers, and LDC and tropical products.]

---

305.   Memorandum From the Acting Special Representative for Trade Negotiations (Roth) to President Johnson[1]

Washington, February 4, 1966, 8 p.m.

SUBJECT

    Definite Acceptance of the GATT

For the reasons set out below, I recommend that you approve the definitive acceptance of the United States of the General Agreement on Tariffs and Trade (GATT).[2]

Since 1948, when the GATT entered into force, United States application of the GATT, like that of most of the other countries concerned, has been based upon a Protocol of Provisional Application. By that Protocol the United States, in addition to undertaking to give full effect of the most-favored-nation principle and to tariff concessions granted to other countries, agreed to apply the other general trade rules of the GATT to the fullest extent not inconsistent with domestic legislation existing on October 30, 1947. By this means, the United States was able to apply the GATT as an executive agreement pursuant to the President's constitutional powers and his authority under trade agreements legislation.

Article XXVI of the GATT establishes the formal procedures for the definitive acceptance of the GATT and provides, in particular, that the Agreement shall not definitively come into force until accepted by countries which account for 85% of the trade of the major countries of the free world. In 1955, all the members of the GATT adopted a resolution which

---

[1] Source: Johnson Library, Bator Papers, Kennedy Round, CAH, May 4, 1964 [1 of 2], Box 11. Limited Official Use. The source text is attached to a February 11 explanatory memorandum from Bator to President Johnson recommending approval. A note on another copy of Bator's memorandum reads: "Hold for staff mtg. Thursday [February 14]. McGB." (Ibid., National Security File, Name File, Bator Memos [2 of 2], Box 1)

[2] For text of the General Agreement on Tariffs and Trade, signed at Geneva on October 30, 1947, see 61 Stat. A3.

provides that definitive acceptance of the GATT pursuant to Article XXVI shall be valid even if accompanied by a formal reservation that the general trade rules of the GATT shall be applied to the fullest extent not inconsistent with domestic legislation which existed on October 30, 1947.[3] In other words, the members of the GATT agreed that any country choosing to accept definitively the GATT could do so with a reservation retaining the substance of the Protocol of Provisional Application.

Definitive acceptance of the GATT by the United States together with this permissible reservation, would involve the assumption of no greater legal obligation than the United States now has under the GATT. At the present time, there are two significant provisions of domestic legislation which were in existence on October 30, 1947, and which would be inconsistent with the GATT but for the Protocol of Provisional Application. They are section 303 of the Tariff Act of 1930,[4] which provides for the imposition of countervailing duties without a showing of serious injury, as required by Article VI of the GATT, and Schedule 4 of the Tariff Schedules of the United States[5] and section 336 of the Tariff Act of 1930, both of which provide for the use of American selling price as a basis of valuation for certain products, which is inconsistent with the provisions of Article VII of the GATT. By virtue of the reservation, definitive acceptance would not change the status of these domestic provisions under the GATT and could therefore be effected by Presidential, as opposed to Congressional, action.

On his last trip to the United States, Mr. Eric Wyndham White, Director-General of the GATT, again emphasized the desirability of having the United States definitively accept the GATT. In Wyndham White's judgment, definitive acceptance by the United States, though essentially a symbolic action, would be followed by similar action on the part of the other major members of the GATT, who are looking to the United States to take the lead in this matter. He feels that such a combined action would serve in a particularly effective way to emphasize the importance of the GATT and its trade rules. We fully share these views, and especially at the present time when efforts are being made by less-developed countries to establish an international trade organization which would rival or supplant the GATT.

We have discussed the definitive acceptance of the GATT with both Democratic and Republican members of the House Ways and Means and Senate Finance Committees. In the Ways and Means Committee we have

---

[3] For text of the revised GATT text resulting from a review of the Agreement conducted by the ninth session of the contracting parties in Geneva, October 28, 1954–March 7, 1955, see *American Foreign Policy: Basic Documents, 1950–1955,* vol. II, pp. 2953–3013; see also 8 UST 1767.

[4] Approved June 17, 1930. (P.L. 361; 46 Stat. 590)

[5] Not further identified.

encountered no objection, and Chairman Mills, in particular, has asked us to communicate to you his full support for this action.[6] In addition, Congressman King of California (D.) and Curtis of Missouri (R.) have indicated their approval. Because of the fact that this matter is less known in the Senate Finance Committee, it has been difficult to obtain a clear expression of views from the members to whom we have spoken, including Senators Talmadge, Ribicoff, Williams (of Delaware), and Carlson. However no clear objection to the proposal has been made.

Accordingly, with the concurrence of the Departments of Agriculture, Commerce, Defense, Interior, Labor, State, and the Treasury, and the Council of Economic Advisers, I recommend that you sign the attached document,[7] whereby the United States would definitively accept the GATT, subject to a reservation continuing the exception for inconsistent 1947 legislation contained in the Protocol of Provisional Application.

William M. Roth[8]

---

[6] No other record of Mills' communication has been found.
[7] Printed as Document 307.
[8] Printed from a copy that bears this typed signature.

---

306. Airgram From the Mission to the European Office of the United Nations to the Department of State[1]

Tagg A–727   Geneva, February 17, 1966.

SUBJECT

   Comments on EEC Commission's Report on KR

REF

   A. Tagg 3799,[2]
   B. Ecbus 646 to Dept.[3]

ExOff. For Governor Herter from Blumenthal.

---

[1] Source: Department of State, Central Files, FT 7 GATT. Confidential. Drafted by Winston Lord, Albert E. Pappano, cleared in draft by Blumenthal, J. Birkhead, W. Kelly, Ernest H. Preeg, and Courtenay P. Worthington, Jr. on February 14, and cleared by James H. Lewis. Received on February 19 and repeated to nine diplomatic missions.
[2] Dated February 4. (Ibid., EEC 3)
[3] Dated January 27. (Ibid.)

1. Since USEC is preparing a summary of the Commission's report (Ref. B), the present message is limited to comment on points of particular significance contained in the report. These points include indications of Community positions not known (or fully known) to us before, cases of incomplete statements of the negotiating situation, or of inaccurate presentation of U.S. positions. These comments are intended primarily for the background information of the addressee posts, to provide additional clarification of the principal KR issues in relation to the Community. [5 lines of source text not declassified]

2. As indicated in Ref. A, we consider the report generally well-designed and constructive in approach. Although on a number of points it omits important nuances or fails to make clear the interests or positions of other major participants, it succeeds for the most part in focusing attention on specific actions or decisions needed to enable Community negotiators to negotiate. Specific comments follow.

Disparities

3. This issue is raised first and frequently, and quite evidently looms large in Community thinking. While the lack of agreed rules is mentioned, the report glosses over this aspect of the problem and fails to mention the important fact that the "rules" that the Commission speaks of were rejected by other participants unless accompanied by additional rules to protect the interests of others. Also, no mention is made of the fact that presently only the Six intend to invoke disparity claims. We learn for the first time explicitly that the Community plans to claim "free exceptions" (i.e., uncounted for reciprocity purposes) on those disparity items which a high-rate country excepts from its linear offer. In effect, this proposal would mean that, since the U.S. has watches and wool textiles on its exceptions list, and since the EEC plans to claim disparities on these items, the EEC would be entitled to exclude them fully from its linear offer without having them counted as exceptions. In practical terms, it seems highly unlikely that the exporters of these products would accept this action by the Community. The Commission appears confident that talks with European countries (which clearly have made little progress) and technical criteria will sufficiently reduce the number of disparity cases to make the issue manageable with us and others. We plan to continue to make our views known and fully reserve our position, but to steer clear of theoretical arguments. Through use of the "European clause" and pragmatic handling in key sectors we hope to see the issue greatly reduced in the course of the negotiations, and our response will be determined by the significance of the disparities ultimately claimed by the Community in the light of the negotiating situation at that time. But potentially the EEC position means that the disparity problem may give rise to further serious US–EEC difficulties.

Exceptions

4. Partial offers and ex-outs are the two most interesting topics in this section. The Commission acknowledges that on 60% of the partial exception items the proposed depth of the tariff cut to be offered has not been revealed to third countries. The emphasis for selecting the degree of duty reduction on these partials is arithmetic, not economic, and rests on the same sliding scale formula that the Community proposed for disparities. This formula, which no one has accepted, works out to about 22% cut on all 2:1/10 disparity candidates, and the average reduction on partial offers revealed to date is 21%. This approach seems clearly inconsistent with the intent of the agreed formula contained in the GATT Ministers' directive for the negotiations (a bare minimum of exceptions to be justified on grounds of overriding national interest), which appears to refer to economic factors. The Community appears receptive to ex-out suggestions, but the report never raises the prospect of improving offers on entire exception items by removing them from the list or by increasing the partial reductions offered. The U.S. is preparing to make known a number of ex-out proposals covering identifiable items of particular interest, but the problems of the length of the EEC list and breadth of American export interests will not be solved through the ex-out method alone, and the Commission itself notes the technical limitations of this method.

Nontariff Barriers

5. There is a general readiness to discuss NTB's but no focus on the procedural problem of who will negotiate for the Six, the Member States still being individually responsible for this aspect of commercial policy under the Rome Treaty. Our views on *coal* and *road taxes* were set forth in July 1964 papers presented to the Multilateral Group on NTB's,[4] but the EEC has not been willing to schedule a bilateral meeting with us on nontariff obstacles. In this report our interest in road taxes is more than adequately reflected, while our complaints on coal (which cover state trading in France as well as the German tariff quota and licensing restrictions in the Netherlands and Belgium) and other barriers need more emphasis in Community consideration. We do not, as implied in the report, attach less importance to restrictions on coal than to road taxes. It should be borne in mind that when mention is made by the Community of such U.S. restrictions as the Wine-Gallon system and Buy American, there are a number of nontariff restrictions maintained by Member States of the Community that are of interest to us. Examples are government purchasing practices and the French prohibition against the advertising of whiskey.

---

[4] These papers have not been further identified.

Chemicals

6. We find this section somewhat confusing and ambiguous, but in its entirely not without hope. The U.S. position on ASP is at first (pages 20–21) fairly reflected, but then our willingness to negotiate on the system is clouded and questioned. There is much emphasis on the U.K. proposal, but only passing attention to what would be required of the Community (removal of its exceptions and disparities) in such an approach. An EEC quid-pro-quo for American movement on ASP is not discussed. Nevertheless, despite the steady theme that the U.S. position is restrictive and is stalling sector negotiations, the Commission urges that it be authorized to participate in discussions of an overall sector solution that would permit a softening of the American stance. We should continue to work for this development, in effect a dropping of the Community's "prealables" for negotiating in this field. We have stated that ASP is negotiable within the context of a chemicals sector package and overall KR reciprocity. Contrary to implications in the report, we have not precluded the possibility of elimination of ASP as a method of customs valuation, but have tried to make clear that our negotiating authority under the Trade Expansion Act limits us to a 50% reduction of the existing level of protection. We have said that the U.K. proposal can be discussed, although in its present form it is not sufficiently attractive to us, and have pointed out the reasons why it appears most unlikely that the U.S. could negotiate a greater-than-50% reduction in the protective incident of its chemical tariffs. The report suggests a belief by the Commission that our present position should be sufficient to permit the Council to authorize Community negotiators to begin exploring a possible package solution in the chemical sector. Additional missionary work, however, is needed to place the whole ASP question in proper perspective and to underline our willingness to bargain meaningfully, provided that others are also willing to make important contributions in the chemicals sector and elsewhere.

Pulp and Paper

7. Commission thinking in this sector is somewhat clarified. The prospect of a "European deal" seems dimmed because of the difficult demands for Scandinavian price data as a condition for agreement, and the emphasis appears to be a non-discriminatory consumption tax for paper products in order to support domestic pulp and newsprint production, reforestation and scientific research in the paper industry. The Commission offers to draw up specific proposals if the Council agrees in principle to this approach. Whether this latter device, coupled with lowering of tariffs, (eventual duty-free entry for pulp and a 50% cut for newsprint is mentioned) would help or hinder imports depends, of course, on the details. In any event, its compatibility with GATT articles will have to be closely studied. The report also reveals that on four basic tariff posi-

tions the existing mandate permits a maximum cut of only two percentage points (or about 13% reduction). These four items, which include *kraft paper and board,* cover roughly two-thirds of U.S. exports of all paper and board to the Community. *Kraft liner* is the only American interest cited, although U.S. *pulp* exports to the Six ($66 million in 1964 and rising rapidly) almost tripled our kraft trade. The document blurs the precise internal and/or external prerequisites for beginning talks with the U.S. and Canada, still looking to an accord with the Nordics in the "first months of 1966," but certainly moves us no closer to this objective.

Cotton Textiles

8.   We have no reason to believe that there has been a slackening of Community support for the extension of the LTA. However, the report reflects a greater uncertainty about the chances for renewal of the Arrangement than the facts seem to warrant, indicates serious Commission weighing of alternatives, and lays the uncertainty over the future of the LTA to US–LDC confrontation in the cotton textile issue. In our view the Wyndham White package approach for this sector, including LTA extension, has been tacitly accepted and the positions of the only holdouts, India and Pakistan, appear flexible. The report fails to make clear what actions (i.e., decisions authorizing the Commission to negotiate on Member States' quotas and on Community exceptions) are required by the Council in order to permit completion of the package deal.

Aluminum

9.   The report confirms that two alternatives that the Six have been rumored to be weighing on *unwrought aluminum:* a partial reduction from 9% to 7% with the removal of the present 5% tariff quotas (resort to Rome Treaty Article 25 still being applicable), or a maintenance of the 9% tariff and a binding of a Community tariff quota at 5%. We are examining these possibilities to determine which is less unpromising. Norway's interest in this sector is singled out, while the very substantial North American concerns are not reflected. The major problem underlying the sector remains the virtual certainty that offers of other interested participants on aluminum will not remain on the table in the absence of action by the Community to liberalize conditions of access to its aluminum market.

Minerals and Metals

10. The U.S. position on base rates for *petroleum* is fairly presented, but it is clear that the related subjects of exclusions and reciprocity (see below) will be of crucial importance to the US–EEC negotiations. Community preference for bilateral handling of *ferro-alloys* is confirmed, while the suggestion of studies of the economic situation of the ferro-alloy industries in various countries hints at some possible movement in

the present phalanx of total exceptions in this sector. The revelation that *ferro-silico-manganese* is slated for disparity treatment satisfies the curiosity of those who wondered why this ferro-alloy alone did not qualify for the Community's exceptions list. The situation for *iron and steel* is presented weakly and the ECSC base-rate position is termed legally defensible on the ground that the majority of the negotiating partners are using bound rates as base rates. (See Tagg 3792 for our comments on this topic.)[5] The action program refers only to EEC partial exceptions and not to the root problem of the ECSC "offers," which is the lack of ECSC offers to cut effective rates.

Mechanical

11. There is particular emphasis on ex-out possibilities and principal suppliers, while the huge U.S. (and U.K.) trade interest in this sector, which has been repeatedly stressed, does not emerge from the report. A Community reciprocity requirement in *agricultural machinery* is revealed for the first time and parallels its demand for reciprocity in the automotive and aircraft fields.

Agriculture

12. In our view the section of the report devoted to agriculture falls short in three respects. First, it concentrates on decisions relating to domestic policies and regulations, so that the focus of attention seems to be on the achievement of the CAP rather than on the formulation of KR agricultural offers. Second, it ignores the unacceptability of the MDS concept as a basis for negotiation which has been expressed by the U.S. and others at every occasion. Third, it seems to look forward to further discussion of *issues* rather than tabling of concrete and specific agricultural offers. What is really required in order to permit the Community to participate meaningfully in the negotiations on agricultural products are decisions authorizing offers that go beyond the mere binding of MDS margins and afford genuine prospects of increased trading opportunities.

Cereals

13. The report makes clear the need for a new mandate that would provide authority to negotiate international reference prices and differentials and to negotiate commitments for food aid in terms of a formula for sharing. Reference is made to the interests of U.S. and Australia in some form of *quantum* or other arrangement for limitation of production but otherwise the access problem is not dealt with. The Community's internal price is recognized as an element of the problem but there is no

---

[5] Dated January 31. (Department of State, Central Files, FT 7 EEC–US)

real discussion or analysis of its relation to international arrangements or KR offers.

Dairy Products, Meats, Sugar, Fats and Oils

14. The main conclusion for each of these groups of products is that the Community will not be able to negotiate effectively until the Council decisions on common internal prices have been made. In the case of *dairy products* there is no recommendation for any international measures to deal with surplus production, as proposed by New Zealand in the case of butter. For *meats,* while referring to the technical discussions to be carried on in Geneva beginning in March, the report appears to postpone consideration of the sort of international arrangement that might be proposed. In the case of *sugar,* the report notes that the Community has reserved the right to call for a sector group, (although in fact it has not called for one up to this point). While noting the need for a general international sugar arrangement and the interest of the LDC's in a reorganization of the world sugar market, the report cites the reluctance of most other countries (attributed mainly to problems of internal policy) to negotiate such an arrangement. The fact is that the emphasis on sugar by the EEC is directly related to internal problems of sugar policy. The U.S. view is that sugar is of relatively little importance as an item of negotiation in the KR since it is unrealistic to expect that interested countries will be prepared to agree in the KR context to do what they are not prepared to do in the context of the International Sugar Agreement.[6] Noting that most of the negotiating partners do not accept the idea of an international *fats and oils* arrangement and the fact that the United States has expressed outright opposition, (attributed to reluctance to bind internal policies and apprehension of less favorable conditions in foreign markets), the report urges such an agreement on grounds of LDC interest and calls for rapid decision on the organization of the Community's fats and oils market in order to be able to submit concrete proposals at Geneva. (The U.S. is in fact opposed to attempting to negotiate an international agreement on fats and oils, chiefly because we believe such an arrangement would worsen opportunities for trade and would be unworkable. The number and variety of fats, oils and oilseeds entering into world trade would require provisions and regulations of unmanageable complexity.)

Other Agricultural Products

15. The report divides these products between those related to products (e.g., grains) provided for in international arrangements (grain-based products such as pork and poultry) and others, many of which are provided for in Community regulations and market organizations (e.g.,

---

[6] Signed at London on December 1, 1958, and entered into force for the United States on October 5, 1959. (10 US 2189)

fruits and vegetables, processed products, etc.). The report points out also that for certain products, i.e., those for which all decisions have been made or those which are subject only to fixed duty protection, it would be possible to make offers immediately, while for others, offers must await decisions of the Council as to market organization, etc. That there has been no movement in the Commission's negotiating position is shown by a statement that the Community has held to the approach laid down by the Council in December 1963, i.e., the pursuit of undertakings as to the total effect of direct supports, and nothing more. This is merely another way of formulating the MDS binding as a basis for negotiations on these products. In any event, decisions relative to specific offers on these products are subordinated to the adoption of definitive Community regulations.

Tropical Products

16. The report merely urges that the Community's offers on tropical products be tabled as soon as possible, after appropriate consultations with the AOC's, but gives no indication of Commission thinking as to the scope or nature of such offers. One point of interest in relation to U.S. authority under TEA Section 213 is reference to the view, evidently expressed in the Tropical Products Group, that measures taken to reduce or eliminate barriers to trade in tropical products should not be conditioned upon similar action by other industrialized countries.

U.S. Exclusions and Reciprocity

17. In a section devoted to negotiating problems between the Community and particular countries, the report singles out, for the U.S., the question of reciprocity and the role that our exclusions might play in redressing the manifest imbalance between the two exceptions lists. Recalling that the U.S. delegation had many times characterized the EEC exceptions list as much longer than that of the United States, the report argues that U.S. "exclusions" (mainly petroleum and products) should properly be classed as exceptions, in which case the two exceptions list would be "parfaitement comparables." The launching of this argument at one of the bilateral negotiating sessions last summer gave rise to a spirited debate in which U.S. representatives reminded the EEC team that no participant in the KR negotiations has a significant trade interest in U.S. imports of petroleum—indeed the Community's interest is virtually nil—and asked the question (unanswered) what the Community would be willing to pay for a U.S. concession on petroleum if it were available. It is clear from the treatment of this issue in the report that the Commission will make a major effort to have our exclusions counted as exceptions in order to write off some $1.5 billion of EEC exceptions and thus hopefully to avoid withdrawals by the U.S. at the balancing stage of negotiations.

Conclusions

18. The concluding section of the report underlines three points, all of which are sound and constructive. *First,* referring to the Wyndham White report and to the meeting of Ambassadors Roth and Blumenthal with members of the Commission in Brussels on January 11, the Commission emphasizes the urgency of moving into the active phase of negotiations and commends the timing problem to the most serious attention of the Council. *Second,* while recognizing that all important decisions must be made by the Council, the Commission calls upon the 111 Committee to play a more active role in providing guidance for the EEC delegation in questions of less crucial or technical nature and states the Commission's intention to maintain close contact with the permreps of the Member States in matters pertaining to the KR negotiations. *Third,* the Commission calls upon the Council to schedule a special session, with participation of both ministers and technicians, for detailed examination of the Commission's report with a view to adopting the decisions required for "fruitful pursuit" of the Geneva negotiations.

For the Ambassador
James H. Lewis
Counselor for Economic Affairs

---

307. Acceptance of the General Agreement on Tariffs and Trade by the United States[1]

Washington, February 18, 1966.

ACCEPTANCE ON THE PART OF
THE UNITED STATES OF AMERICA

I, Lyndon B. Johnson, President of the United States of America, acting pursuant to the authority vested in me by the Constitution and the statutes of the United States of America, including section 350 of the Tariff Act of 1930, as amended, do hereby accept, on behalf of the United States of America, the General Agreement on Tariffs and Trade, dated at

---

[1] Source: Johnson Library, Bator Papers, Kennedy Round, CAH, May 4, 1964 [1 of 2], Box 11. No classification marking. The source text is attached to a February 18 note from Bator to Solomon, Greenwald, and Roth that reads: "The President approved the attached this morning. STR has the signed letter of acceptance."

Geneva on October 30, 1947, as amended, with the reservation that Part II thereof will continue to be applied to the fullest extent not inconsistent with Federal legislation which existed on October 30, 1947.

Done at Washington this 18th day of February, 1966.

Lyndon B. Johnson

---

308.   Report by the Chairman of the Trade Negotiations Committee (Wyndham White) to the 23d Session of the GATT Contracting Parties[1]

L/2624   Geneva, March 30, 1966.

TRADE NEGOTIATIONS COMMITTEE

Report by Chairman

It occurs to me as I begin to speak on this subject that we shall shortly be approaching the third anniversary of the launching of the trade negotiations, and as one surveys the state of progress which unfolds itself to our eyes, this indeed is a solemn thought.

In my last statement to the Contracting Parties on this subject I reported, perhaps with a certain professional optimism, that some progress had been made which I qualified as being perhaps slow and unspectacular, but nevertheless real.[2]

Unhappily, looking back over the period since making that report to the Contracting Parties it is somewhat difficult even to apply a similar degree of cautious professional optimism. In fact, as events proceeded towards the end of 1965 I became so preoccupied with, so disturbed at, the lack of progress in the negotiations that I felt it necessary to take the somewhat unusual step of drawing up a report on the state of the negotiations for consideration by responsible Ministers of governments participating in them.[3] In this report I drew attention to the limitations of time

---

[1] Source: Department of State, Central Files, FT 7 GATT. Unclassified. The source text is enclosure 1 to airgram Tagg A–776 from Geneva, April 7, which states that the report was released to the press. The airgram was repeated to 24 diplomatic missions.

[2] Not further identified.

[3] Attachment to Document 302.

which is still available to us to bring these negotiations to a successful conclusion, the difficult decisions which require to be made by governments to render this possible, and the very stringent programme of work which imposes itself now upon us.

In the preamble to that report I pointed out to governments that in initiating the current trade negotiations the participants had embarked upon two major ventures. First the launching of a negotiation designed to secure a degree of liberalization of the present barriers to international trade which is both deeper and more comprehensive in coverage than had been secured in previous negotiations, covering all classes of products and dealing with non-tariff as well as tariff barriers. The second, and at an equal level of importance, a series of activities to meet the urgent trade and economic development problems of less-developed countries. And I suggested that special responsibilities rested on the shoulders of the more highly developed countries which had, in ministerial resolutions on which the trade negotiations were based, committed themselves specifically to making use of the negotiations to contribute in a substantial way to the solution of these problems.

In all previous discussions I have counselled patience in considering the time-table. The operation in which we are engaged is a vast one. The stakes are very large. The consequences of both success and failure are extremely great and the time-table would naturally be somewhat proportionate to both the difficulties that such an ambitious negotiation involves and the magnitude of the issues involved.

But I felt at the end of 1965, and, naturally enough, feel even more greatly now that time is beginning to run out. It is true that in my report of 3 January I related this specifically to the expiration of the negotiating powers of the President of the United States under the Trade Expansion Act. We are told by the United States administration, and those of us who are familiar with the Washington scene I think have no difficulty in accepting this, that, in the context of uncompleted negotiations, the prospects of an extension of those negotiating powers must be regarded as non-existent. But I think it is perhaps wrong to think that time is running out only because of this factor. I think time is also running out only because there is a mounting degree of discouragement and disillusionment in other countries which have been preparing themselves for active negotiations over this extensive period. And I sense a growing scepticism, a growing doubt as to the credibility of this exercise, a growing difficulty for governments to maintain negotiating teams in the field, and of maintaining the interest of policy-making departments and Ministers, in an enterprise which appears to move with the velocity of a deeply submerged iceberg.

For all these reasons therefore it seemed to me then, and it seems to me even more so today, that unless governments can put themselves in a position whereby in a very short time in the future it will be possible to have delegations, with broad authority to negotiate, present continuously in Geneva and in a position to engage negotiations actively and continuously on all fronts, unless this happens we must begin to yield to a certain pessimism as to the possibilities of carrying this great enterprise forward to a successful conclusion. And, as I have said, the consequences of failure are hardly less impressive than the opportunities of success. It is, I think, no secret to anyone that in a number of important countries, a number of restrictive, protectionist, negative forces have been kept in check and control because governments have been able to point out in resisting such pressures that to yield to them would jeopardize their negotiating positions in the important trade negotiations proceeding in Geneva. I very much fear that if and when these inhibitions are lifted we may see a serious reversal of the trend of trade liberalization which has been such a profitable feature of the last decade both in terms of the international economy and in terms of national economy.

I think that I would therefore be failing in my duty to the Contracting Parties if I were to fail on this occasion to express a note of considerable and deep concern. Quite frankly, the condition which I described a few minutes ago of bringing the negotiations to a successful conclusion, seems to me, as I look at the scene now, far from being attained. It is true as I said before that some progress, perhaps even considerable progress, has been achieved in identifying the possible areas of agreement in relation to reduction of tariffs on industrial products. I am not, however, perhaps as deeply convinced as some others that even here the exploration of positions in bilateral discussions have really been carried to the point where the maximum possibilities of fruitful negotiation can be ascertained and be available by the autumn of this year.

If one looks at the vast and vital field of negotiations on agriculture the picture is frankly one inviting complete depression. It is true that as regards cereals there has been extensive discussion which has enabled us to identify the principal obstacles to an agreement on the Cereals Arrangement. In other important sectors in agricultural trade there has been a fruitful and instructive examination of existing material about the conditions of trade in these products. I refer particularly to dairy products and meat. But, except for some proposals made by some countries, there is no comprehensive set of offers on the table to form the basis for serious international negotiation, and we cannot see clearly at this time if and when such a situation will exist. As regards the rest of the whole range of agricultural products, whilst a number of countries have made some offers on some products, these are far from complete. Moreover, for reasons which are well-known, the prospect of getting practical concrete negotiating offers, even on the somewhat ambiguous negotiating rules which are the maximum which we have been able to agree on so far, seems at present impossible.

In the field of tropical products we are far from having any clear idea of the possibilities of obtaining a major advance in this field, which is of such great importance to so many of the developing countries and where one would have thought that it was not beyond ingenuity or the will of mankind to have found a more satisfactory basis for international trade, since this does not present a serious challenge to any vested interest in the industrial parts of the world.

I shall have an equally unpleasant task to present to the Contracting Parties in due course a report on conditions in the international trade in cotton textiles. I describe it as an unpleasant task. It is certainly one which I shall accomplish with little joy and not much satisfaction.

I apologise to the Contracting Parties for this somewhat gloomy statement. It is an aspect of my character to which I have not habituated the Contracting Parties in the course of the years, but I hope that perhaps if I depart on this occasion from my usual somewhat cheerful optimism the impact may be somewhat heightened on that account, rather than diminished. This then, Mr. Chairman, is the report which as Chairman of the Trade Negotiations Committee I feel bound to present to the Contracting Parties today.

In these circumstances it would be reasonable to anticipate that somebody would say: "What do you propose that we do about it?". I have put this question to myself and of course one of the obvious ideas that springs to mind is that, in view of the importance of this exercise, in view of the important political commitment to try and deal constructively with the urgent and economic and development problems of the less-developed countries which has been undertaken and in view of the fact that this enterprise is one which was launched by responsible Cabinet Ministers of the participating countries, the Contracting Parties should suggest the convening of these same Ministers to consider the present situation and to ascertain whether the possibilities still exist of activating the negotiations, of bringing about the necessary political decisions and of creating the conditions for success, or alternatively to draw the opposite conclusion. However, I have come to the conclusion that such a step at this time would not be fruitful and on the contrary might prove counter-productive at this time. It is clear, however, that if the present situation continues for very much longer, a period I would measure in terms of weeks rather than months, then this is a step to which we shall have to give careful consideration because this is clearly not the sort of enterprise which can be allowed to go by default. The decision to fail would be quite as important in another sense as a decision to succeed.

309.   Letter From the Special Representative for Trade Negotiations (Herter) to Secretary of the Treasury Fowler[1]

Washington, April 1, 1966.

Dear Joe:

Since our last meeting of the principals of the Cabinet Balance of Payments Committee, I have given the question of import restraints for balance-of-payments reasons much serious thought.

It is clear that we could design an import quota or surcharge system which would have a major direct impact on the level of imports. However, the attached memorandum shows that existing legislation does not make this possible and that new legislative authority would be required. I am doubtful such legislation could be enacted quickly, and you of course recognize the problem of speculation during the time in which legislation would be pending. I have attached a memorandum setting forth the nature and limitations of our domestic authority.

Whether we would benefit substantially from the imposition of import restraints now seems very doubtful to me, at least under present circumstances. I believe we must first of all accept the almost unanimous judgment of economists that the imposition of broad import restraints would have an inflationary impact on the domestic economy. We are already in a period in which we are running at full capacity and such a move would therefore prove counter-productive.

I have considered the possible implementation of import restraints under the GATT and should like to make the following general observations. Under the GATT, the United States could impose quotas because of balance-of-payments problems upon its own unilateral determination that the preconditions prescribed by the GATT do in fact exist. It would not need to obtain any prior finding or authorization from any country or international organization, but a finding by the IMF on the need for quotas would be ultimately required and would be binding, in the sense of defining our rights under the GATT, and the rights of others to retaliate. We would, in other words, have to demonstrate to the IMF that our balance-of-payments problems were of the requisite severity.

Under the GATT, the United States could not impose tariff surcharges because of balance-of-payments problems. If it did so, a GATT

---

[1] Source: Johnson Library, Bator Papers, Balance of Payments, 1966 [2 of 2], Box 15. Secret. An attached covering letter from Herter to Bator, April 5, states that "at the last meeting of the Cabinet Balance of Payments," Herter "suggested a review of the possibility of imposing import controls for balance of payments reasons." In the attached copy of his letter to Fowler, Herter was "giving my conclusions after further study of the subject." Herter was referring to the March 25 meeting; see Document 88.

country affected by the surcharges could bring an action under Article XXII and this could lead to retaliatory action against the United States. However, in theory at least, a waiver of the GATT could be sought.

Quotas could be limited to a selected list of imports without violating the GATT. Criteria which, for example, singled out "nonessential" or "luxury" products could provide a basis for selection. For domestic economic reasons it might be considered desirable to allow free access to raw materials and semi-finished products, so as to prevent bottlenecks at the early stages of manufacture. However, the curtailment of a broad list of "nonessential" or "luxury" imports alone would still provide domestic inflationary pressure.

I have also considered whether we might not select a product list which discriminated as among exporting countries, in order to focus the effects on those who give us most trouble in terms of gold flows. It is unlikely that this would help, since the GATT authority does not allow us to discriminate among suppliers without penalty of retaliation.

Import quotas or surcharges would probably trigger objections among many exporters to the U.S. who in turn might find ways to retaliate against our exports. It may, of course, be argued that foreign retaliation would be very limited if the import restraint action were seen to be a necessary condition for maintenance of the value of the dollar. If the dollar were under very heavy speculative attack, a drastic series of measures, including import controls, might be just what was required. But in situations short of an international crisis of dollar confidence, we should he hard put to gain general agreement among our trading partners that our situation was serious enough to warrant this type of action.

But, putting these problems aside, further reflection leads me to wonder whether the United States would gain any advantage from an improved trade account which resulted from the imposition of import restrictions. I recognize that one of our immediate objectives is to provide a stronger U.S. bargaining position for the negotiation of international monetary reform. But looking at this closely, I question whether our bargaining position would be much changed by the achievement of balance by means of direct controls on trade. For example, I noted in this regard the recent experience of the U.K. in its import surcharge consultations in Working Party III of the OECD, and elsewhere. The U.K. has been repeatedly informed by other nations that a return to equilibrium must be defined as a return to equilibrium without the surcharge.

Our long run basic objective is of course to maintain world confidence in the value of the dollar. I now question whether trade restraints would increase confidence in the dollar except under circumstances in which we were in real desperation, and unless coupled with stringent measures taken with respect to our domestic economy.

I must therefore conclude that the imposition of import quotas or surcharges involves many complications and appears more likely to boomerang than provide a useful aid in our present balance-of-payments difficulties.

Most sincerely yours,

Christian A. Herter[2]

Attachment[3]

DOMESTIC AUTHORITY TO IMPOSE QUOTAS AND SURCHARGES

The President has no existing authority unilaterally to impose quotas or surcharges on imports generally. Instead, he has the authority unilaterally to impose such import restrictions only on an article-by-article basis and upon a specific finding related to each article.

The broadest of these authorities are the national security provision and the escape clause. However, neither authority can be invoked without an investigation by either the Office of Emergency Planning or the Tariff Commission, which typically takes a number of months and becomes public knowledge, whether a public hearing is held or not. In addition, and more importantly, neither authority can be invoked with respect to any article unless a specific finding is made with respect to that article. In the case of the national security provision, the Director of OEP must find that a given article is being imported into the United States in such quantities or under such circumstances as to threaten or impair the national security. In the case of the escape clause, the Tariff Commission must find that tariff concessions have been the major cause of increased imports of a given article and such increased imports have caused or threatened serious injury to a particular domestic industry.

The necessity to impose import restrictions under either of these provisions with respect to particular articles and upon specific findings with respect to such articles would appear to prevent the President from moving rapidly to impose import restrictions upon a broad range of imports. In other words, the President has no existing authority to impose general import restrictions for balance-of-payments reasons.

---

[2] Printed from a copy that bears this typed signature.
[3] Secret.

310. Editorial Note

On May 3 and 4, 1966, the chemical sector group, one of the groups established to negotiate in the industrial area of GATT, held its first meetings. The United States, Switzerland, Japan, the United Kingdom, and the European Economic Community participated in these meetings at which they completed the tabling of their initial tariff offers in the chemical sector. It was understood that the participants would also discuss other matters, such as the American selling price (ASP), in parallel with the offers.

During these meetings, Deputy Representative Blumenthal made a detailed statement of the U.S. position on chemicals, including the American selling price. He advanced a working hypothesis that might eliminate the ASP valuation system for the United States in return for concessions from the others. He also noted that any such agreement by the United States would require legislation. A report of the meeting was transmitted in airgram Tagg A–840 from Geneva, May 14. (Department of State, Central Files, FT 7 GATT)

This airgram also summarized meetings of the sector group on steel beginning on May 5, the group on antidumping policies on May 10 and 11, and negotiations and renegotiations with various countries on the U.S. revised tariff schedules in late April and early May.

311. Telegram From the Embassy in Belgium to the Department of State[1]

Brussels, July 1, 1966, 1306Z.

009. Busec. Subj: RTS negotiations.

1. Following is French text of letter which Commission delivered to Mission last night:

2. "Brussels, June 30, 1966 to the Director General.

3. "Representatives of the United States and the European Economic Community have conducted negotiations pursuant to Article

---

[1] Source: Department of State, Central Files, FT 13–2. Unclassified; Priority; Official Translation. Repeated to Geneva. A note at the end of the source text states that the foreign language text was received July 1, lists its distribution, and states that the official translation was given normal distribution on July 5.

XXVIII for the purpose of establishing codified list of concessions No. XX, in accordance with the United States revised tariff. The two delegations call attention, on the one hand, to the fact that their negotiations have not yet ended and, on the other, to the fact that the decisions of the Contracting Parties dated July 20, 1963, June 25, 1964, June 30, 1964, and December 1, 1965,[2] by virtue of which the customs duties, as provided for in the United States revised tariff, were put into force before the completion of the procedures indicated in Article XXVIII of the General Agreement, will cease to be valid on June 30, 1966.

4.   "In view of the desire of the United States and the Community to terminate the negotiations and the desire of the United States Government to put into force, as soon as possible, Codified List No. XX, based on the United States revised tariff, the two delegations have agreed as follows:

5.   "(1) It being understood that the negotiations will be continued, the representative of the Community signifies his agreement that, during the period prior to January 1, 1967, the concessions appearing in the annexed list[3] shall be substituted for the concessions in present list XX in which the Community or member states have negotiation rights under Article XXVIII.

6.   "(2) The United States representative signifies his agreement to the continuation of the negotiations and, subject to the condition of acceptance by the President of the United States, to substitution of the United States concessions indicated in the annex for the concessions in present list XX.

7.   "(3) The two delegations agree that the reciprocal rights and obligations of their respective authorities under the General Agreement will be maintained under the same conditions as if the validity of the decisions of the Contracting Parties referred to above had been extended from June 30, 1966 to January 1, 1967. Consequently, the substitution of the United States concessions contained in the annexed list for the concessions in present list No. XX does not prejudge final agreement between the United States and the Community with respect to the items still under discussion.

8.   "The two delegations request that a copy of the communication be sent to all the Contracting Parties.

9.   "Accept, Mr. Director General, the assurances of my high consideration."

10. Signed Hijzen. *End.*[4]

---

[2] None of the decisions on these dates has been further identified.
[3] The annexed list is not included in the telegram and has not been found.
[4] The telegram is unsigned.

312.   Airgram From the Mission to the European Office of the United Nations to the Department of State[1]

Tagg A–906   Geneva, July 10, 1966.

SUBJECT

    RTS Negotiations with Japan

REF

    Tagg 4171[2]

From Blumenthal. Shown as enclosure 1 is a draft text of a letter to be signed by representatives of the Delegations of the United States and Japan to indicate that a settlement has been reached with respect to (1) the claim for compensation by the United States for an increase in duty on magnesia clinker of seawater origin and (2) the claim for compensation by Japan for an increase in duty on trucks exported to the United States.

The draft text was shown to and tentatively accepted by the Japanese Delegation on July 7, 1966, as correctly reflecting the substance of the understandings with respect to the above claims. The U.S. Delegation has made clear to the Japanese Delegation that the draft text is subject to potential amendments and changes by Washington.[3]

No reference is made in the proposed letter to the question of either the amount of net impairment arising from these claims or the two Governments' continuing reservation of positions concerning the legal status of the claims. Recognizing that the United States did not accept Japan's claim for compensation for the increase in U.S. duty on trucks on the basis of "substantial supplier rights" the U.S. Delegation suggested including a sentence which might read as follows: "The settlement of these issues is without prejudice to the positions taken by each Delegation in the 1964 RTS discussions." This suggestion was not considered acceptable by the Japanese Delegation, and hence, was dropped from the enclosed text.

---

    [1] Source: Department of State, Central Files, FT 7 GATT. Limited Official Use. Drafted by Martin Y. Hirabayashi on July 7, cleared by Helen L. Brewster (KR), and approved by James H. Lewis. Repeated to Tokyo.
    [2] Dated June 30. (Ibid., FT 13–2 US)
    [3] Airgram A–34 to Geneva, August 5, stated, among other things, that the letter attached to this airgram was acceptable provided that the phrase "constitute a package which" was omitted from paragraph A. (Ibid.; FT 7 GATT)

The Delegation requests Washington reactions to the enclosed text together with such amendments as may be necessary to meet United States requirements.

Tubby

Enclosure[4]

Draft text of letter relating to RTS negotiations with Japan:

Dear Mr. Ambassador:

The Delegation of the United States wishes to refer to two issues which have been outstanding between our Governments relating to (1) the claim for compensation by the United States for tariff action by Japan affecting imports of magnesia clinker of seawater origin and (2) the claim for compensation by Japan for tariff action by the United States affecting imports of trucks valued at more than $1,000, which are referred to in the "Agreed Minute of Discussions between the Delegation of the United States and the Delegation of Japan", signed in Geneva on December 16, 1964.[5] With respect to these issues, the following are our understandings:

A. In negotiations under GATT Article XXVIII for the establishment of a consolidated Schedule XX in terms of the revised Tariff Schedules of the United States which were concluded on June 28, 1966, the Delegation of the United States and the Delegation of Japan agreed that the new concessions in the consolidated Schedule XX constitute a "package" which takes into consideration the respective claims on magnesia clinker of seawater origin imported by Japan, and on trucks valued at more than $1,000 imported by the United States.

B. The above claims therefore shall be considered settled upon implementation of the new concessions in the consolidated Schedule XX.

Your confirmation of the above understandings on behalf of the Delegations of Japan would be appreciated.

Sincerely yours,

W. Michael Blumenthal[6]

---

[4] Limited Official use.
[5] Not further identified.
[6] Printed from a copy that bears this typed signature.

313   Final Report by the United States[1]

Undated.

UNITED STATES TARIFF CLASSIFICATION

Final Report by the United States on the Negotiations under Article XXVIII on the Revised Tariff Schedules of the United States

The United States has reached the agreement envisaged by Article XXVIII with all thirty-five contracting parties which had negotiating rights under that article in relation to the application of rate increases involved in the revised Tariff Schedules of the United States and the eventual certification of a consolidated Schedule XX in terms of such revised tariff. This is, therefore, the final report in accordance with the Decision of June 30, 1965.[2]

It will be recalled that the United States Government informed the Contracting Parties on 14 March 1966 (L/2592)[3] that interim agreements had been signed with twenty-five contracting parties. Since the submission of the progress report of 14 March 1966, negotiations have been completed and agreements signed with Japan,[4] South Africa and the United Kingdom.[5] The settlements with Japan and the United Kingdom were similar to the agreement with Canada in that the United States made compensatory rate reductions.[6]

---

[1] Source: Department of State, Central Files, FT 13–2 US. No classification marking. The source text is attached to circular airgram CA–251 to Geneva, July 11, which requests the Mission to transmit the report to the GATT Secretariat in accordance with the GATT Contracting Parties' Decision on June 30, 1965, that the United States submit status reports to the GATT Contracting Parties. CA–251 was also sent to Brussels for USEC, to Bern, and to Stockholm.

[2] The decision of June 30, 1965, extended the waiver granted under GATT Article XXV, paragraph 5 to June 30, 1966; text in General Agreement on Tariffs and Trade, *Basic Instruments and Selected Documents, Fourteenth Supplement* (Geneva, July 1966), p. 43.

[3] Not found.

[4] "Following repeated requests from the Japanese for offers of deeper cuts on items contained in the proposed compensation package, the U.S. Delegation obtained sufficiently broadened negotiating authority to permit a conclusion of the negotiations" on June 28. The GATT Secretariat was informed of the successful conclusion of these U.S.–Japan talks on June 30. (Tagg A–909, July 10; Department of State, Central Files, FT 7 GATT)

[5] Negotiations with South Africa and the United Kingdom have not been further identified.

[6] Not further identified.

With respect to the two remaining negotiations, with Sweden and the European Economic Community, joint letters have been submitted to the Secretariat[7] providing for, subject to the continuation of negotiations, the substitution during the period prior to January 1, 1967 of United States concessions in terms of the new Tariff Schedules of the United States for concessions in the existing Schedule XX in which the EEC or its member states and Sweden have negotiating rights under Article XXVIII.

The United States will prepare as soon as possible a consolidated Schedule XX for review by the Contracting Parties.

A list of the countries with which agreements have been concluded is attached.

Attachment[8]

Agreements Concluded by the United States with:
Australia
Austria
Brazil
Canada
Ceylon
Chile
Denmark
Dominican Republic
European Economic Community
Finland
Greece
Haiti
India
Indonesia
Israel
Japan
New Zealand
Nicaragua
Norway

---

[7] The U.S. and EEC joint notification to the GATT Secretariat was signed on June 30; an identical joint letter was signed by the United States and Swedish delegations. (Tagg A–909 from Geneva, July 10; Department of State, Central Files, FT 7 GATT)

[8] No classification marking.

Pakistan
Peru
Portugal
Rhodesia
South Africa
Spain
Sweden
Switzerland
Turkey
United Kingdom
Uruguay

314. Current Economic Developments[1]

Issue No. 758   Washington, July 19, 1966.

[Here follow articles on unrelated subjects.]

PARTICIPANTS IN KENNEDY ROUND HOPEFUL
OF SUCCESSFUL CONCLUSION BY EARLY 1967

A tone of prudent optimism with regard to the Kennedy Round dominated the recent meeting of the GATT Trade Negotiations Committee. The general feeling of the participants was that it will be possible to complete successful negotiations on time, and everyone pledged the necessary political will and hard work. All the participants, including the EEC, welcomed the GATT Director's schedule which calls for the period of intensive negotiations to begin immediately after the August recess and for the negotiations to be concluded in the early part of 1967. Essential to this schedule, however, is the tabling of the EEC agricultural offers by the end of July.

The ability of the EEC to table its agricultural offers is dependent on a series of decisions on regulations and prices for certain agricultural commodities, and the EEC Agricultural Ministers were unable to agree on the latter at their meeting July 13–14. They will continue their delib-

---

[1] Source: Washington National Records Center, RG 59, E/CBA/REP Files: FRC 72 A 6248, *Current Economic Developments*. Limited Official Use. The source text comprises pages 5–7 of the issue.

834 Foreign Relations, 1964–1968, Volume VIII

erations July 21—just before the Foreign Ministers' meeting.[2] EEC Vice-President Mansholt remains moderately optimistic that agreement can be reached on the agricultural regulations and prices and on the KR agricultural offers before the August recess.

TNC Meeting

The Trade Negotiations Committee met in Geneva July 8 to discuss progress in the Kennedy Round negotiations, a general timetable looking toward conclusion early in 1967, and more specific plans for the summer months.[3]

GATT Executive Director Wyndham White gave a mixed verdict on the progress of the negotiations, referring to his January report[4] outlining the steps necessary to bring the negotiations to a successful conclusion in the early part of 1967. He said that most of the outstanding industrial offers have now been tabled. This, inter alia, has created the possibility of activating negotiations in such sectors as pulp and paper, chemicals, aluminum, and steel. The negotiations on these products have been, or will shortly be, actively engaged. Countries other than those participating on the basis of a linear reduction have largely specified their non-linear offers. Little progress has been made, however, with regard to the special offer made by Poland and to the negotiating proposals for Czechoslovakia.

On textiles, a pragmatic basis has been established for continuing discussions on a bilateral basis without awaiting the outcome of the pending discussion of the fate of the GATT Long Term Agreement on Cotton Textiles. The result of the discussion of the latter, however, will have important repercussions on the scope of the tariff reduction in the course of the present negotiations.

The major lacuna, Wyndham White said, is the absence of comprehensive offers on agricultural products. The April 30 deadline was missed. He expressed confidence that such offers can now be expected by the end of July at the latest and said that this is the last possible date if we are to achieve our objective. Such a move would make it possible to engage in intensive and continuous negotiations on agricultural products from the beginning of September. In one important agricultural sector—cereals—an earlier start can be made. All the principally interested countries have tabled proposals on the various elements which have been defined as relevant to the negotiation of a cereals arrangement. Dis-

---

[2] For an excerpt from Hallstein's optimistic statement on July 24, see *American Foreign Policy: Current Documents, 1966,* pp. 387–388.

[3] A summary of Herter and Roth's informal conversations with the U.S. and other delegations and the full TNC meeting on July 8 is in Tagg A–932 from Geneva, July 24. (Department of State, Central Files, FT 7 GATT)

[4] Attachment to Document 302.

cussion on cereals will, therefore, be resumed later this month. (We have proposed that the major exporters meet here just before the Cereals Group meeting.)

All the offers on tropical products have been tabled. A representative group of interested governments is now reviewing these offers.

Wyndham White has defined as the second major objective of the KR "a series of activities to meet the urgent trade and economic development problems of the less-developed countries," and at the TNC he urged the developed countries to give more concrete form to the desiderata of the less-developed countries. He outlined the desiderata as: a) the elimination from exception lists of products of special interest in the LDCs; b) reduction of duties on these products beyond the 50 percent which is the general working hypothesis; c) accelerated application of the reduction agreed upon for these products by exempting them from the phasing which is proposed for the tariff reductions in general; d) an effort to maximize reduction of tariff and non-tariff barriers on tropical products; and e) for some countries, consideration of the problem of compensation for the loss of preferences consequent upon reduction in MFN rates of duty.

Wyndham White suggested that the period of intensive negotiation, beginning immediately after a brief August recess, should be directed toward building up a position of maximum negotiating opportunities which would provide the basis on which the participating governments can, by the middle of November, reach an assessment against which they can reconsider their initial negotiating position. The fruits of these assessments and reconsiderations would then be shared with the other negotiators so that by the end of November governments would be in a position to consider against a comprehensive background the negotiating instructions with which to equip negotiators for the final bargaining stage, which Wyndham White envisages as starting in mid-January and hopefully leading to an over-all and positive settlement in the following weeks.

Constant themes voiced at the TNC meeting were the crucial importance of the agricultural negotiations and the negotiations with the LDCs, both of which are lagging. The LDCs expressed impatience and unhappiness with the results of the Kennedy Round to date, recalling the initial promise of the Kennedy Round and the repeated assurance of industrialized countries in international forums. The EFTA countries without industrial exceptions cited the need for flexibility in timing the modification of offers, i.e., withdrawals. They and others hoped that emphasis in the autumn would be on improvement in offers and on positive balancing.

Our delegate stressed the importance of completing the offers, especially agricultural, by the end of July and our readiness to do so. He stressed that the Kennedy Round cannot succeed without complete inclusion of agriculture. He welcomed the tight but realistic schedule. He hoped for closest possible approximation of 50 percent cuts on the tariffs on industrial products. He reaffirmed our commitment to help the LDCs and noted our efforts in this area. (The US is now considering additional offers for LDCs.) He said that we look for further progress in the discussions of non-tariff barriers but emphasized the importance of reciprocity in this difficult period.

[Here follow articles on unrelated subjects.]

315. Memorandum From Secretary of Agriculture Freeman to President Johnson[1]

Washington, August 1, 1966.

SUBJECT

Kennedy Round Negotiations—Tabling Offers, Agriculture Department exception

I take this occasion to call to the President's attention a decision which apparently has been made subject to final Presidential approval to table U.S. agricultural offers of interest to the EEC in the Kennedy Round negotiations regardless of the fact that the EEC will not make any real offers. The Department of Agriculture has expressed its reservations to this procedure and has recommended that instead of tabling our generous offers, we table an offer roughly commensurate with what the EEC will offer.

Basically, this is a question of strategy. The strategy has been reviewed in detail with the Herter Office and the State Department who carry the negotiating responsibility. The Trade Expansion Act Advisory Committee has also considered it. Other Departments, including Commerce and Interior, expressed certain reservations at the proposed strategy. Nonetheless, the decision has been made to go forward, subject to the President's final approval, by the Herter Office. Because this is a strategy question, I am prepared to acquiesce in the course of action recommended. I have not asked for a meeting with the President. I did want him, however, to be apprised of my reservations.

---

[1] Source: Johnson Library, Bator Papers, Kennedy Round (GATT) (May 4, 1964) [1 of 2], Box 11. No classification marking.

Agriculture's reservation in this matter is based on the following facts:

1. The United States agricultural offer to the EEC is a very generous one, encompassing a 50 percent cut in tariff on some $315 million of U. S. agricultural imports in 1965. The items covered include some that are very sensitive politically, such as tobacco. At the same time we are being called on to make offers on dairy and meat products, specifically beef. (An offer to cut the duty on canned pork was tabled last September.) If it should become known that such offers are being considered, particularly in the absence of anything even remotely commensurate by the EEC, there would be swift and serious political repercussions in the United States, and there is every reason to expect that they will become known through the EEC.

2. *The EEC will make no meaningful offer.* From advance information we have, it seems likely that their offer, rather than representing progress, would result in a more protectionist rather than more liberal trade position. It is argued that we have made progress in the negotiation because the EEC has on some few items abandoned its completely unrealistic Montant de Soutien position, which would have only frozen high EEC support levels and which would not have liberalized trade. Initially the EEC insisted this system cover all products. The fact that the EEC will now offer shallow duty cuts on a few items does not represent any real progress in my judgment. Their offers, overall, still do not constitute a basis for negotiating anything but increased protection in the EEC market. It appears that all the EEC is trying to do is legalize internationally its notorious variable levy and gate price system, which relegates third countries to a residual supplier position. The EEC has just finished setting its internal agricultural support prices. The EEC internal price levels on many products are now at least half again as high as the United States price levels, and considerably higher than was previously the case. Such an uneconomic high level of internal pricing can have only one effect. It will certainly increase domestic production within the EEC. With the application of the notorious variable fee system which protects the most inefficient internal producer from any outside competition, it will limit trade possibilities. Moreover, the process of setting these prices is difficult, time-consuming and both economically and politically hazardous. This being the case, it is impossible to conceive the EEC Ministers will now turn around and reverse these decisions.

3. *This latest tabling of offers increases the necessity for withdrawals.* This offer comes on top of an already imbalanced industrial offer and a seriously imbalanced U.S. agricultural offer to countries other than the EEC, which was tabled a year ago. Thus we are widening the offers gap and increasing sharply the degree to which U.S. withdrawals will have to be made.

4. *We do not believe that full withdrawal of these imbalanced offers will be feasible.* It is argued that if the EEC and others do not improve their offers, we can at the end of the negotiations withdraw as many of ours as necessary. But once an offer is laid on the table for each country to see, it becomes very difficult to withdraw that offer. For example, our offer on tobacco, involving $100 million worth of trade, is a generous one. Greece and Turkey will find it very attractive. If at the end of the negotiation we try to withdraw it, they will protest strongly. Yet there is a strong likelihood that we would want to withdraw it. The EEC will not even tell us until November whether it will make an offer on tobacco.

There are many other similar examples.

The United States has repeatedly told the less developed countries who complain bitterly about the lack of preferential access to our markets for their raw materials, that rather than seeking the establishment of bilateral quotas and such systems, they should put their confidence in the Kennedy Round and in world-trade agreements. We have told them that they will come out much better through international trade liberalization. If we table offers they find very attractive, and then proceed to withdraw them because we are unable to reach any commensurate arrangement with our commercial equals, these countries will react bitterly. The positions taken and the arguments made which we have had great difficulty meeting at the UNCTAD will come swiftly to the front, aided and abetted by such withdrawals on our part at the Kennedy Round.

Further there will be a great temptation to hold U.S. agricultural offers on the table for the benefit of other agricultural exporters like Australia and New Zealand. This temptation will be sharpened by the fact that other agricultural exporting nations will argue strongly and with some merit that they, as substantial importers of U.S. industrial items, are entitled to this improved access to our market for their agriculture. Withdrawals of U.S. offers from these countries, and even from the EEC, could start a chain reaction of withdrawals which could threaten the unravelling of the whole trade negotiation.

It would, therefore, seem much sounder strategy on our part now only to match the EEC offers, to indicate to the EEC privately but clearly that we are prepared to go a long way if they indicate their willingness to change, and to hold that position rather than exposing our whole hand first.

Orville L. Freeman

316. Memorandum From the Acting Special Representative for
      Trade Negotiations (Roth) to President Johnson[1]

Washington, August 2, 1966, 2:45 p.m.

SUBJECT

   Kennedy Round Agricultural Offers

Summary

   On Saturday, August 6, 1966, the European Economic Community
will table in Geneva its agricultural offers in the Kennedy Round. This
Office now intends unless otherwise instructed to follow the general
negotiating strategy approved by you in September of last year, i.e., to
put forward our agricultural offers of principal interest to the Community that we had previously withheld. In addition, we propose to table
initial offers in the meat and dairy sectors.[2]

Discussion

   You will recall last September you authorized Governor Herter to
table agricultural offers in the Kennedy Round.[3] Items of primary interest to the European Economic Community were to be withheld until the
Community was ready to reciprocate.

   Ten days ago the six EEC member countries reached agreement on a
common agricultural policy for most of the major products. They also
agreed to table their agricultural offers. This memorandum, therefore,
proposes that we now table the U.S. offers of principal interest to the EEC
as well as offers in the meat and dairy sectors. This procedure has the
strong support of Under Secretary Ball and the reluctant acquiescence of
Secretary Freeman.[4] In addition, the Vice President is in agreement with
the proposal, subject, of course, to whatever withdrawals are ultimately
necessary to establish reciprocity.

   The Community's new agricultural policy is based, for many products, on very high support prices and tightly protected markets, and the
EEC offers related to these policies are consequently expected to be
entirely inadequate. Should they not be substantially improved, and it
would be unrealistic to expect very much improvement, it will be necessary for the U.S. to make extensive withdrawals of its own agricultural

---

   [1] Source: Johnson Library, Bator Papers, Kennedy Round, (GATT) (May 4, 1964) [1 of
2], Box 11. Secret.
   [2] A handwritten note in the margin next to this paragraph reads: "Approved by the
President August 4, 1966. F. M. Bator."
   [3] See Documents 290 and 292.
   [4] See Documents 288 and 289.

offers. Nevertheless, we are convinced that a strategy of generous U.S. initial offers creates the most effective pressure possible on the EEC to improve its offers.

The overall strategy in the Kennedy Round—both in industry and in agriculture, has been to make a strong opening bid. Given the internal politics of the six nations of the Community, this continues to appear to be the most effective way of achieving the maximum result in the negotiations.

Position of the Department of Agriculture

At the request of Secretary Freeman, a meeting of the Trade Expansion Act Advisory Committee was held last Friday.[5] Subsequently, he addressed a memorandum to you (copy of which is attached) indicating that although he questioned the wisdom of the decision, he regarded it as a tactical question and was prepared to acquiesce in the basic strategy decided upon in the meeting with you last August. Nevertheless, he has serious doubts about this strategy in three principal areas:

1. Domestic political repercussions: *Should it become known that the United States had tabled an offer of considerably greater magnitude than that of the Community, the political repercussions would be serious.*

We do not believe that details of the negotiations, which are secret, will become fully known for some time. The industry offers which now have been on the table for a year and a half are still, on the whole, very much a secret—both from industry and from Congress. Further, in one of the two most sensitive categories, dairy products, the proposed U. S. offer, as approved by the Department of Agriculture, is merely an expression of willingness to examine issues such as market access, the use of export aids by high-cost producers, and disposal of dairy products in non-commercial channels. In the meat sector, the other sensitive category, the central aim of the U. S. is to create acceptable conditions of access for meat exporters in other markets than our own, principally in the EEC and Japan. We, ourselves, would only be willing to undertake commitments to maintain access to our market for beef, veal and mutton, along the lines of our present meat import quota legislation. In other words, the U. S. would be offering no more than the present law in beef already permits. No tariff reduction is offered at this time.

2. Reciprocity: *Secretary Freeman doubts that the U. S. will be in a position to make sufficient withdrawals of offers to achieve reciprocity.*

Governor Herter has made very clear to the Secretary, to Congress, and to the European Community that full reciprocity must be achieved under our legislative mandate. He is absolutely committed to this and is fully supported in his determination by George Ball. Neither foreign

---

[5] No record of this July 29 meeting has been found.

policy considerations, nor problems of the less-developed countries will, of themselves, require less than full reciprocity with the EEC and the other developed countries.

The headnote accompanying the U. S. agricultural offers tabled last September 16 stated that:

The United States is tabling these offers:
(a) in the expectation that other principal negotiating countries will also table concrete and specific offers on agricultural products, and
(b) on the understanding that, if the other principal negotiating countries are not willing to implement concrete and specific offers on agricultural products which are of a trade coverage and of a degree of liberalization equal to that of the United States offers, the United States will withdraw such offers in whole or in part, to the extent it deems necessary.

These conditions will, of course, also apply to the additional offers of interest to the EEC which we now propose to table.

3. Strategy: *Secretary Freeman questions the basic U.S. negotiating strategy of beginning with full offers.*

This strategy, as approved by you, remains the most effective method of eliciting full offers from our negotiating partners. Experience in previous negotiations clearly indicates that the opposite tactic of beginning with low offers and negotiating upwards tends to lessen the total scope of substance of the negotiations. In addition, to change this strategy at this time would indicate to the Community and to the other agricultural exporters that the U. S. did not now feel that the agricultural part of the negotiations was as important as the industrial. It would lessen rather than enlarge the hope of achieving the continuing access to the European market that Secretary Freeman desires.

William M. Roth

Attachment[6]

U.S. OFFER SUBMITTED TO THE GATT MEATS GROUP

1. The central aim of the U. S. offer is to create acceptable conditions of access to its market for meat exporters. It goes without saying that the U. S. offer could only be implemented as a part of an arrangement under

---

[6] Secret.

which other major meat importers likewise undertake commitments that provide acceptable conditions of access to their markets.

2. *Product coverage.* Beef, veal, mutton (fresh, frozen, chilled).

3. The United States would be prepared within the context of the Kennedy Round, and subject to the conditions set forth in paragraph 1 above, to undertake commitments respecting the meats concerned to permit imports to share in the United States' market, and to share in any growth in that market, as follows: The annual aggregate quantity which will be admitted will not be less than the average quantity imported during the period 1959–1963 adjusted by the same percentage that domestic production of these articles has increased or decreased in comparison with the average annual production during the base period 1959–1963.

4. The United States has no fixed ideas as to the form of a meat arrangement. On the basis of the discussion held to date by the GATT Meats Group, it appears likely that an international meat arrangement might take the form of an agreement on a statement of general principles supplemented by bilateral agreements registered with the GATT between principal importing countries and their major supplies. The Meats Group has identified certain elements that should be taken into consideration in the negotiations. These elements are listed in Annex A to TN 64/17, the report of the Group to the TNC.[7] The United States is prepared to participate in the further examination of these elements by the Meats Group.

Attachment[8]

U. S. OFFER SUBMITTED TO THE GATT DAIRY GROUP

1. *Product coverage.* Butter, the principal types of cheese, non-fat dried milk.

2. The discussions in the Dairy Group have not yet progressed to the point where there have emerged the outlines of arrangements which would carry out the Ministerial Directive of improved access to markets in furtherance of the development and expansion of trade. The United States is, however, prepared to continue to participate in the work of the Dairy Group with the view to carrying out the Ministerial Directive.

3. The issues which the United States would consider as appropriate to be considered by the Dairy Group would include access to mar-

---

[7] Not found.
[8] Secret.

kets, the use of export aids by high cost producers, and disposal of dairy products in non-commercial channels. It is the U. S. view that export aids and non-commercial disposals should not be used to disrupt normal commercial markets of efficient dairy exporting countries. It is prepared to cooperate in the examination of measures or commitments which could be undertaken by all countries to avoid this occurring.

317. Memorandum From the President's Deputy Special Assistant for National Security Affairs (Bator) to President Johnson[1]

Washington, August 2, 1966.

SUBJECT

Another Tactical Decision on the Kennedy Round

We face another tactical decision on agriculture in the Kennedy Round, and I am afraid we need your instructions by Thursday or Friday.[2] I apologize for the short notice, but the situation in Geneva has moved very quickly. (Actually, you made this decision last September. But last evening Orville Freeman decided that he wants to flag for you once again his doubts about the approved strategy[3]—so I feel you should have another shot at the problem.)

The Situation

You will recall that last September you approved (1) immediate tariff offers on agricultural products of only secondary interest to the Common Market; and (2) later offers on products of major interest to the Six "at such time as the EEC is ready to table. . . ." (At that time, the EEC was not yet ready to table *any* offers on agriculture. Orville argued that *we*

---

[1] Source: Johnson Library, Bator Papers, Kennedy Round (GATT) (May 4, 1964) [1 of 2], Box 11. Confidential. Attached to the source text are copies of notes from Bator to Ball and Solomon, and to Roth, both dated August 2, saying he would inform them of the President's decision as soon as he heard it. Also attached is a note from Bator to the President, August 3, indicating, among other things, that he had set up "your Kennedy Round mtg" for August 4 at 6 p.m. Also attached is a memorandum from Bator to the President, August 4, setting forth the agenda and three options for decision at the meeting: making full 50 percent initial offers on agricultural items, matching "the EEC's very poor offers," or a compromise (medium) offer of 25 percent cuts. Bator favored the first option.

[2] August 4 and 5.

[3] See Document 315.

should not table anything until the EEC was ready. The rest of us, including the Vice President, voted the other way.)

The Six are now ready. Saturday is the tabling date. We know in advance that their offers will be quite poor.

The Issue

Should we (1) go through with the original strategy of 50% initial offers on the agricultural items we withheld in September; or (2) make much more limited offers, matching the EEC? (It is understood that we would not offer tariff cuts on beef, poultry and a few other sensitive items in either case.)

The Line-Up

At Tab A, Bill Roth, speaking also for Governor Herter and his negotiator Mike Blumenthal, argues for tabling full offers, subject to later withdrawal as necessary to achieve a balanced bargain.[4] Roth's recommendation is strongly and personally supported by the Vice President, Secretary Rusk and George Ball. (Acting on your instruction of September that we bring the Vice President into this, I checked with him personally.)

At Tab B, Orville indicates that he is prepared to go along with the Herter strategy, but would much prefer a much smaller offer designed just to match the EEC.[5] (At Tab C is the paper outlining the Herter strategy which you approved last September.)[6]

The Arguments

Everybody agrees that

—we should maximize pressure on the Common Market and our other customers (UK, Canada, Japan, etc.) to improve their offers on agriculture;
—we will make it clear to all concerned that our initial offers are conditional, and that we will tailor our *final* list to assure a fair bargain.

Herter and company argue that the best way of putting pressure on the EEC is to stay with the September strategy. They have no illusions that it will be easy to move the Six. But they think it is worth a hard try. And they are clear that, in the end, they will have to make whatever withdrawals are necessary to achieve balance.

Freeman recognizes that "this is a question of strategy" and "is prepared to acquiesce". And he has explicitly decided not to ask for a meeting with you. He is, however, (1) skeptical that even an aggressive

---

[4] Document 316.
[5] Document 315.
[6] Document 292.

strategy will cause the EEC to move; (2) worried that, in the crunch, we will lack the fortitude to make the necessary withdrawals; and (3) nervous that our efforts might leak and we will face some political flack from his clients.

My vote is with Herter. The trouble with Orville's strategy is that it will badly damage our bargaining position in Geneva, and, if the offers leak, it is likely to generate just as much political heat. Judged in the light of our aggressive strategy thus far, a small U. S. offer now will be taken as a signal that we have given up on agriculture in the Kennedy Round. We will be charged at home and abroad with throwing in the towel before the opening bell. (In fact, the chances of a leak specific enough to cause trouble are small. We have had industrial offers on the table for two years with no publicity problem. And despite Agriculture's anxieties, we have had no trouble with our September agricultural offers either. Moreover, if there is a leak, we have a good answer; we are following an aggressive strategy to get maximum access for our farmers in foreign markets; we will withdraw wherever there is no adequate response from the others.)

After all the offers are on the table, and after we have bargained item by item for all we are worth, we will know what is the best obtainable bargain in agriculture and overall. It will then be up to Herter and the rest of us to advise you whether such a bargain is better or worse than no bargain at all. And it will be up to the President to decide. Herter, Roth, et al are right that it is too early to quit now.

FMB

Follow through on the Herter strategy as approved last September

Want to hear Freeman argue his case—set up meeting Wednesday or Thursday with Herter/Roth, Rusk, Ball, Vice President[7]

Speak to me

---

[7] This option is checked. No record of the August 4 meeting at 6 p.m. has been found. (Johnson Library, President's Daily Diary)

318.   Memorandum From the Under Secretary of State (Ball) to President Johnson[1]

Washington, August 15, 1966.

SUBJECT

Trade Policy—A Proposed Strategy for the United States

During the past several months, Secretary Rusk and I have become increasingly aware of the need to develop a new trade policy strategy for the United States after the Kennedy Round. You may recall that during your meeting with State Department Assistant Secretaries on May 31,[2] Tony Solomon mentioned a possible U.S. initiative in this area.

Our ideas have now become a bit clearer and I want to acquaint you with the direction of our thinking. Enclosed is a copy of a memorandum Secretary Rusk proposes to send to Governor Herter, Secretary Connor, and Secretary Wirtz outlining our views as to the need for a new trade policy strategy and a possible way of meeting these needs. We are requesting the support and assistance of these key agencies in developing these ideas further so that an inter-agency proposal (in which Agriculture, Interior and Treasury would subsequently participate) can be submitted to you.

Speculation about possible changes in U.S. trade policy could, I know, be a sensitive issue domestically. It could also have repercussions in the Kennedy Round negotiations which must remain our principal focus in the trade field over the coming months. However, I believe that by restricting inter-agency consideration of this matter to a very small group at the Assistant Secretary level, potentially embarrassing leaks can be prevented.

Although it is not likely that we will be seeking major new trade legislation in the next year, it is necessary that we begin now to develop a policy. What we propose is to refine a strategy which, with your approval, could be tested with Congressional leaders. You would then be in a position, if this seemed desirable, to use this as one element of a positive U.S. program to help ensure a successful meeting of the Inter-American system.

George W. Ball

---

[1] Source: Johnson Library, National Security File, Subject File, Vol. I [2 of 2], Box 47. Confidential. A memorandum from Anthony M. Solomon (E) to Ball, August 12, recommended that he sign this memorandum. (Ibid., Solomon Papers, Chronological File, August 1966, Box 13)

[2] No record of this meeting has been found.

Enclosure[3]

MEMORANDUM FOR

Governor Herter
Secretary Connor
Secretary Wirtz

SUBJECT

Trade Policy—A Proposed Strategy for the United States

I am deeply concerned that the world trading community appears to be drifting into regional blocs and discriminatory arrangements which, unchecked, would have serious political and economic consequences for the United States.

We need a new trade policy strategy following the Kennedy Round to check this drift. A sound strategy for the United States must, I believe, take account of:

—The likelihood of increased discrimination against our exports as more countries in Western Europe associate themselves with the European Economic Community and form the largest market in the world with free trade among themselves and barriers against the United States and other outsiders.

—The further proliferation of special trade arrangements which discriminate among poor countries, against Latin America, and against the United States.

—The persistent appeal of the poor nations for preferred treatment for their exports. The countries of Southeast Asia as well as Africa and elsewhere will judge the sincerity of our interest in their progress by what we are prepared to do in the field of trade as well as aid.

—The willingness of other industrialized countries to respond to this appeal which leaves the United States virtually isolated, a position which carries with it significant political costs.

United States political and economic interests require us to take the initiative and try to guide developments in a manner likely to advance our own national interests. We cannot let matters drift, leaving it to other nations to continue to work out ad hoc arrangements which adversely affect our interests.

This memorandum sets forth a possible way of meeting these challenges. I commend it to your personal attention and invite your support

---

[3] Confidential. Another copy indicates that this memorandum was cleared in substance with Walter J. Stoessel, Jr. (EUR), Allen D. Gordon (ARA/LA), Joseph Palmer II (AF), Rodger P. Davies (NEA), Samuel D. Berger (FE), Joseph J. Sisco (IO), and Douglas MacArthur II (H). (Johnson Library, Solomon Papers, Chronological Files–August 1966, Box 13) For evidence that the proposed memorandum was sent to the President, see Document 330.

and assistance in developing it further so that an inter-agency proposal can be submitted to the President.

If our prognosis of a link between the EEC and most other Western European nations proves correct, the resulting continental trade wall against us would jeopardize our export position. We could, like Joshua, trumpet against such a wall and perhaps it would crumble. But prudence dictates that we arm ourselves with other tools. The only realistic way, in my view, is to move to the maximum extent possible toward free trade among all industrialized countries. This would be the first element in the proposed new trade strategy and would be in line with the authority to eliminate duties contained in the Trade Expansion Act but which could not be used because the United Kingdom did not join the EEC.

Appropriate legislation would be needed to enable us to enter into negotiations after the Kennedy Round. One approach would be to seek authority to negotiate the mutual reduction and possible elimination of trade barriers staged over an extended period, perhaps ten or fifteen years. An alternative would be to seek authority for another round of negotiations to reduce duties by a specific percentage as a further step toward our ultimate goal.

The second element of the proposed strategy would be to offer the poor countries of the world a "head start" in such a move toward ultimate free trade. The benefits of tariff reductions would be given to them immediately while reductions among industrialized countries are phased over a longer period. This would have a number of advantages for us:

—It would improve our position vis-à-vis the developing countries.

—It would, to the extent the developing countries support this approach, make it politically more difficult for other industrialized countries to resist the longer-term move to reduce barriers among themselves.

—It would result in the phasing out of existing trade preferences which discriminate among developing countries, Latin America in particular.

—It would strengthen our ability to insist on the elimination of preferences enjoyed by the European industrialized countries in the markets of some poor countries which discriminate against United States exports.

—It would probably increase the trade earnings of the poor countries and assist in their economic development; they need trade as well as aid.

There is the problem, of course, of possible injury to U.S. industry and labor arising from increased imports from low-wage countries. This may require additional safe-guards and expanded adjustment assistance. Particularly sensitive items might be excluded entirely. In other cases, quantitative limitation on the amounts which could enter from developing countries at reduced rates might be appropriate.

No formal action should be taken which might divert attention from the Kennedy Round (which has to be substantially wrapped up by February–March 1967). We would not seek new authority until the basis for negotiations has been worked out with our trading partners. This process might take a year—from mid-1967 to mid-1968. In this event, the new program could be included in the 1969 State of the Union message. If the pre-negotiations moved faster and the traditional bias against trade legislation in an election year were overcome, the bill might be sent up in early 1968. In any case, for July 1967 (when the Kennedy Round is concluded), we would propose a simple one or two year extension of the period during which the existing authority under the Trade Expansion Act could be used.

These targets for submission of new legislation may seem far off, but we need to elaborate an inter-agency proposal so that we are in a position to:

—Initiate consultations with Congressional leaders;
—Refer to the direction of our thinking at the prospective meeting of Presidents of the Inter-American system toward the end of this year; and
—Present a proposal in some detail at the Second United Nations Conference on Trade and Development in the summer or fall of 1967.

I believe the trade policy strategy outlined above is in the best interests of the United States because:

—It offers the possibility of dealing realistically with the major commercial policy problem we face in the coming years, namely the strong likelihood of increased discrimination against our exports to Western Europe as these nations enter into various forms of associations with the Common Market;
—It is responsive to the appeal of more than 100 poor nations for a special boost for their exports;
—It would involve only a temporary departure from the basic objective of non-discrimination in world trade but simultaneously will enable us to obtain elimination of the invidious forms of discrimination which exist at present;
—It would include adequate safeguards against injury to American producers and labor; and
—It would help retain the historic US position of leadership in the trade policy field.

I would appreciate your designating a senior officer to meet with Assistant Secretary Solomon to develop further the proposed strategy so that an inter-agency proposal can be sent to the President within the reasonably near future. If the President agrees with this general approach, Congressional sentiment could then be tested.

Because of the sensitivity of this whole subject, I would appreciate your holding this memorandum closely within your respective agencies.

319.   Memorandum From the Acting Special Representative for Trade Negotiations (Roth) to President Johnson[1]

Washington, August 19, 1966.

SUBJECT

New Trade Legislation

Summary

1.   The negotiating authority of the Trade Expansion Act of 1962 runs out on June 30, 1967. Assuming that a moderately successful Kennedy Round has been concluded by that time, legislative authority to take care of continuing routine tariff matters would be required in 1967. There may also be certain agreements reached on an ad referendum basis in the Kennedy Round (i.e., dumping, American selling price, and possibly grains) that will need Congressional approval next year.

2.   *We do not, however, recommend a major trade bill in 1967,* since the Congress probably would not be willing to move so quickly after completion of the Kennedy Round. Rather, we should begin developing a longer range and more comprehensive trade program that would bridge over the following election year and be submitted in 1969.

3.   In preparing such a major effort, it will be necessary to study the changed conditions of world trade since 1962. The growing pressures of the less-developed countries, the development of regional trading blocs, and the growth of U. S. investment abroad, all have had their impact on the current posture of trade. Consultations both domestically and abroad and close cooperation with Congress would be essential in the preparation of a new program.

4.   The development of such a program could be handled either by a citizens', Randall-type commission, or internally, through this Office. The latter course is probably easier to control, particularly as the channels for consulting with both industry and the Congress already exist.

Recommendations[2]

1.   If agreement is reached in the Kennedy Round on matters requiring additional Congressional authority (dumping, American selling price, and possibly grains) that such legislation be submitted in the late spring of 1967.

---

[1] Source: Johnson Library, National Security File, Subject File, Trade—General, Vol. I [2 of 2], Box 47. Confidential. An attached undated discussion memorandum is not printed.

[2] There is no indication whether President Johnson approved or disapproved these recommendations.

2. That legislation to replace the expiring Trade Expansion Act (June 30, 1967) should be limited to an interim two to three year authorization designed only to take care of routine tariff adjustments. This bill would include the new adjustment assistance provision agreed upon by the Executive branch this year, and should be submitted in March or April.

3. That the possibility of resubmitting an East-West trade bill be reevaluated after further discussions with Chairman Mills in November.

4. That you authorize this Office to explore with your staff and the other agencies concerned, procedures leading to the development of major trade legislation for 1969. This new effort, which would include a proposal to give serious consideration of the granting of general preferences to the less-developed countries, could be announced by you in the spring of 1967.

William M. Roth

---

320. Statement by the Deputy Special Representative for Trade Negotiations (Blumenthal)[1]

Geneva, September 14, 1966.

UNITED STATES OPENING STATEMENT ON AGRICULTURAL OFFERS IN GATT KENNEDY ROUND, GENEVA

Committee on Agriculture

Mr. Chairman, I would like to say some general words about the offer on agricultural products presented by the United States. I shall be brief since we fully agree that the work that now has to be done is of a negotiating nature and involves individual and specific negotiations on the different commodities which these countries have placed on the table in terms of offers.

---

[1] Source: Department of State, Central Files, FT 7 GATT. Confidential. The source text is enclosure 1 to Tagg A–56 from Geneva, September 25. The date of the statement is taken from this airgram. Five tables, which further defined the U.S. offer, were additional enclosures. They are not printed.

May I say at the beginning that my delegation is, of course, gratified that we have finally reached that stage where we can begin this process and where the actual negotiations can start. It is no secret that this is a stage of the negotiations that we have long and anxiously awaited. As we see it, the next stage is to bring our agricultural negotiations, as quickly as possible, at least to the same point in which our industrial negotiations have progressed. Towards the end of the year we must be in a position to make the kind of over-all assessment that will be necessary in order to judge the adjustments required to achieve balance in the Kennedy Round.

I should like now to refer to a few figures in order to illustrate what the United States has done.

Total United States agricultural imports in the year 1964 amounted to $4.1 billion. Out of that $4.1 billion, $2.1 billion, or slightly more than half, already entered the United States free of duty in 1964. In virtually all cases, except one, for all major items these zero duties are bound. So, of course, there is no further offer on these. Let me just say that that large group of over $2 billion worth of commodities already entering free of duty into the United States are heavily concentrated in the tropical products area. The single largest item is coffee, with $1.2 billion; and such other commodities as rubber, cocoa beans, bananas, certain types of wool, and tea make up the rest.

Some of the countries represented around this table have an interest in these products, but as far as the others are concerned, I take it that there is no particular problem with those since they already come in free of duty.

Out of the remaining $1.9 billion in items which are dutiable and available for concessions, there are some commodities which are going to be discussed in the Cereals, Meats and Dairy Groups. They amount to $331 million of imports. I shall not be commenting on the offers on those commodities here since I understand that we will be dealing very shortly with the offers that have been placed on the table in the Dairy Group. The same thing applies to the Meat Group, and, of course, in cereals we are already engaged in our negotiations.

There is another group of items, comprising $61 million, on which we have not made offers. These are commodities for which, quite frankly, we have economic exceptions. They are commodities where, on the basis of a very careful judgment, we feel that it is not possible to offer concessions. That $61 million, of course, represents a very, very small proportion of the over-all volume of imports into the United States. These items, moreover, come in a very high proportion from countries which are not participants in the negotiations.

The largest single item, involving $21 million, is in tobaccos, of which the principal suppliers are the Dominican Republic, Colombia, and Brazil. There are some other items, such as mushrooms, which come, primarily, from China and, to the small extent of about $1 million, from the European Economic Community. There are three or four other items in this group of exceptions. These are frozen strawberries, dates, figs and fig paste, pepper and lemon juices. Cotton is also included. The United States holds very large stocks of cotton and is the only world producer in that position. Liberalization is therefore not possible.

That leaves us, Mr. Chairman, with another category of $740 million of items on which we are not making offers. These are in commodities which, to a very large extent, are supplied to us by countries who are not participating in this negotiation. The largest part of that $756 [$740?] million represents sugar ($458 million). In the case of sugar, the United States reserves a very sizeable portion of its protected internal market at the same premium prices to foreign suppliers as it guarantees to domestic producers. It is well known that we—as well as many other major consuming countries—have a rather clear sugar import program and sugar policy, under which we allocate quotas. These quotas are valuable and constitute considerable sources of income for many exporting countries.

We have, of course, made no further offer in this area, because the Sugar Act and the sugar policy that we follow is a matter of separate determination. All of the countries who supply to us are constantly in touch with us on those matters.

The main items in the group of $740 million, which are supplied primarily by non-participants, are the following:

Coconut oil—which comes from the Philippines, not participating in this negotiation.
Copra—totally coming from the Philippines, not in this negotiation.
Coconut meat—Philippines, not in this negotiation.

There are certain items, such as non-edible molasses, which account for $34 million, and which very heavily come from countries not in this negotiation. One other important item, fresh tomatoes, is in its totality supplied to the United States by Mexico, another country not participating in this negotiation.

This brings us to the United States offers being examined this week. These cover about $750 million worth of items where the U.S. offer is of real relevance; and it is these $750 million worth of imports to which I wish to address myself at this time.

Our offer is a very simple one. For these imports, after considerable deliberation and soul-searching, and in spite of some difficulty and pressures which, I am sure, will be readily understood around this table, and in spite of the fact that this is a difficult undertaking for us, we have placed a full 50 percent offer on the table. In fact, for all items, other than those covered in the special commodity groups, for which countries represented around this table have a principal export interest to the United

States, we are offering to cut our tariff by 50 percent. This is significant because in virtually all of these cases there is no other import protection, no other protective device, in existence in the United States. So that an offer to cut these tariffs by 50 percent represents, in fact, an offer to reduce the total import protection by that amount, and these offers are therefore not impaired or nullified in any way.

Let me very quickly run through some of the major items which we have offered for a 50 percent cut in this group.

The largest single item is canned pork ($106 million). We have offered a full 50 percent cut. The major suppliers are Denmark, the EEC and Poland. It is clear that this is a precise offer on an item in which these countries have a major export interest to the United States. This item is now unbound.

The second item is wool ($101 million), supplied to us by Australia, the largest single supplier, South Africa and New Zealand. This, too, is a full 50 percent cut.

The next item is tobacco ($83 million), supplied by Turkey, Greece and Yugoslavia, for a full 50 percent cut.

The next item is wine ($61 million), supplied largely by the EEC, which exports $50 million to the United States. We have no other protective device. We have offered a full 50 percent cut in the duty.

The next item is cashew nuts ($33 million), supplied to us by India and Mozambique. That is also on the table for a 50 percent reduction. Certain beef and veal products supplied by Argentina, Uruguay and Brazil are all subject to full 50 percent offers.

There are many more, Mr. Chairman, up to a total of just about all the commodities of export interest to the countries around this table; and for all of these we have placed the 50 percent offer on the table.

We are now anxious to move at the earliest possible date to individual discussions with our various negotiating partners on these offers, to listen to their comments and to answer any questions that they may have. We believe that our offer is by its very nature a simple one, easily understood; but we are, of course, prepared to deal with any questions or comments which may arise and to negotiate seriously on these commodities. And, Mr. Chairman, we want to discuss the offers of other countries with them, as well as the offers which they have not made. I do not propose to make any particular comments at this time as regards the individual offers that have been placed on the table by other countries. It is clear that we have many questions, comments and suggestions with regard to these offers; but again, by their very nature, we think that what is required is the sort of thing that you suggested a moment ago, Mr. Chairman: real negotiation on each of the specific problems and commodities involved, either bilaterally or perhaps in groups of three or four countries which have a particular interest, as the case may be. I do wish to say, however, that, looked at globally, the sum total of the offers in agriculture placed on the table by other countries, if examined by us in the light of commodities in which we have an export interest, gives us considerable cause for concern. Last year, after multilateral discussions in this Committee, we presented to the fourteen countries who are our most important agricultural export markets, requests for 50 percent reductions in their tariffs on about $1.2 billion of our exports. If we look at the offers made by others on the totality of these items, we find that there are offers for a 50 percent cut on $267 million of that U.S. $1.2 billion, in other words less than 25 percent. That is a misleading figure, moreover, because virtually three-quarters of that $267 million on which we have offers for 50 percent cuts is accounted for by one offer on one commodity from one country and is a rather special case. If you subtract that item from the total, we have really only about $50 or $60 million worth of offers of interest to us and which are offered for a 50 percent cut. On the rest, about a billion dollars in which we have an export interest, the offers are more modest or there are no offers at all. That is obviously no secret to anyone who has looked at these offers. In many cases they are considerably more modest and in some cases the offers are of a nature which, it appears to us, is indeed of really very questionable value. We look forward to exploring the offers of other countries with them in our individual discussions and to exploring the possibility of improving them. We sincerely hope that it may be possible to do so, because it is clear that if it were to prove not possible to do so the implications for the entire United States offer in agriculture and industry as well could be serious. It is clear that our offer for 50 percent cuts in agriculture and elsewhere will have to be reviewed very seriously in the light of what improvements we are able to negotiate—or cannot negotiate—through the discussions we are having here. With that comment, Mr. Chairman, I would like to conclude my opening remarks and say again that we are ready with a full team to go into detailed negotiation on a case-by-case basis without delay.

321. Memorandum of Conversation[1]

Washington, September 20, 1966, 3 p.m.

PARTICIPANTS

Fruit Growers—(See Enclosure 1)[2]

STR—
Christian A. Herter, Special Representative
Bernard Norwood, Chairman, Trade Staff Committee
Joseph G. Simanis, Assistant to the Chairman, Trade Staff Committee

SUBJECT

U.S. Fruit Export Problems: Kennedy Round and Country Problems

Mr. Falk,[3] speaking for the Council, outlined the attitude of the fruit exporters regarding U.S. trade and the Kennedy Round. He said that they wished to obtain fair access to export markets. In this connection, they had supported passage of the Trade Expansion Act. He said that U.S. fruit producers were gratified by the removal of some barriers to sales of U.S. fruit that had resulted from GATT Article XXIII consultations with France. (This comment was repeated several times during the meeting by other members of the group.) Falk said that the EEC agricultural offer seemed, from the information that had been made public, to be extremely poor and was perhaps a step in the direction of greater protectionism rather than a move toward liberalization.

Governor Herter expressed his continuing sympathy for the problems of the fruit growers and canners. He agreed that the EEC's agricultural offer was not encouraging and, noting particularly the extension of reference prices to a new range of products, was regressive in some respects. Lack of provision in the CAP for production controls, he added, detracted further from the offer. We had informed the EEC, he said, that their offer, if not a trading position from which they were willing to retreat, was valueless.

In commenting on a statement by Falk that "no agreement was better than a poor agreement," he said that an agreement could be considered poor if it were extremely limited but that it seemed to him to be wise in such a case to accept the agreement as long as adequate reciprocity was

---

[1] Source: Department of State, Central Files, FT 7 GATT. Unclassified. Drafted by Joseph G. Simanis (STR) and Bernard Norwood (STR) on September 26 and approved by Herter. The meeting was held in the Office of the Special Representative for Trade Negotiations. The source text is an attachment to CA–2653 to Brussels (USEC) and five other posts, October 5.

[2] The list of 23 representatives of fruit growers is not printed.

[3] Ernest Falk, Northwest Horticultural Council, Yakima, Washington.

involved. In this connection, he noted that the American Farm Bureau had recommended immediate withdrawal of all U.S. offers of interest to the EEC until they improved their agricultural offers. As a matter of timing and tactics, Governor Herter disagreed. If the EEC does not eventually offer adequate concessions, withdrawals would be made; but for the time being, we should allow what we have tabled to remain as our offer.

Falk agreed that reciprocity was the crucial factor. He pointed out that the Fruit Exporters' Council had prepared a statement to be presented to a group of Senators which included a recommendation similar to the cited proposal of the American Farm Bureau. However, in order not to create difficulties for the United States in the negotiations, he suggested that a change might be made in the Council's wording. Governor Herter agreed that a few changes in the wording could make it acceptable. (Immediately after the meeting, the Council approved changes in the last paragraph of the statement so that it would recommend withdrawal of U.S. offers, but not necessarily "immediately," and "unless" rather than "until" the EEC improved its offers. See Enclosure 2.)

Further reference to the Council's meeting with a group of Senators scheduled for the following day was made in a statement read by Mr. Elliott.[4] After cataloguing the import restrictions encountered by U.S. fruit exporters in Latin America, he proposed that a Senate body be requested to hold hearings on these trade barriers.

In response to Governor Herter's questions regarding the basic objective to be sought by the Council in its discussions with the Senators, Falk said that they would emphasize the importance of reciprocity and would urge Congressional support for the views expressed by the Governor. Falk suggested to his associates that the Council give further consideration to how such a request for hearings should be presented in the light of Governor Herter's comment that Congressional hearings, if conducted in the next few weeks, would interfere with efforts of his limited staff to bring the Kennedy Round to a successful conclusion. The hearings, it turned out, were envisaged by the Council as a means of putting pressure on the Executive branch, particularly the State Department, to abandon its policy of favoring regional arrangements.

It was generally acknowledged that the positions of the Council and of the Executive branch were in accord insofar as Kennedy Round objectives were concerned and that the Council was intervening—helpfully, it intended—into the area of negotiating tactics, which Governor Herter believed had to be left to his discretion.

---

[4] Frank Elliott, California Canners and Growers, San Francisco, California. The statement has not been found.

Mr. Miller[5] asked clarification of our policy toward Mexico to which we extend MFN treatment despite numerous restrictions in places on entry of our products. Norwood described the representations that the U.S. Government often makes to the Mexicans concerning arbitrary and harmful trade actions. He also stated that we had been prepared to negotiate a new bilateral trade agreement to replace the one which Mexico denounced about 15 years ago and to negotiate with Mexico in the Kennedy Round with a view to its becoming a GATT member. We wish to avoid retaliatory action which might evoke counter-measurers. Mexico, he observed, constitutes a growing market despite difficulties raised for the United States in exporting some products. U.S. imports from Mexico, contrary to Mr. Miller's understanding, are not completely unrestricted, cotton textiles being an area in which the United States has considered quotas to be warranted. U.S. withdrawal of MFN treatment would invite several possible forms of retaliation by Mexico, possibly including Mexican export control materials vital to our economy.

Governor Herter added that, in our trade negotiations, we do not generally offer concessions on items which are supplied primarily by countries that are not members of GATT.

Mr. Reter[6] referred to problems in gaining access to the Venezuelan market for U.S. apples. Norwood replied that this problem has been discussed with the Venezuelans and that we had achieved a modest, but transitory benefit, in getting an understanding on apple quotas for the current year. He observed that the Venezuelans are able to counter our complaints by citing our restrictions on petroleum imports, which cover trade many times that represented by fruit.

Governor Herter commented that our trade relations with the less-developed countries are complicated by a growing feeling in the poorer parts of the world that the world's wealth should be more equitably distributed. The arguments presented are similar to those which were raised a century ago in our country against the tremendous gap between the mass of the poor and the great wealth concentrated in the hands of a few.

In closing, spokesmen for the Council expressed their continued support for the manner in which trade negotiations are being conducted.

---

[5] Henry W. Miller, Consolidated Orchard Company, Paw Paw, West Virginia.

[6] Ray R. Reter, Northwest Horticultural Council, Medford, Oregon.

Enclosure[7]

U.S. NATIONAL FRUIT EXPORT COUNCIL

Statement of Position

The U. S. National Fruit Export Council, representing non-price-supported perennial fruit crops and their products, has from its inception supported the principle of reciprocal trade agreement negotiations and specifically the Trade Expansion Act of 1962. Since the passage of that Act we have supported the U.S. hopes and efforts for achieving meaningful trade negotiations with balanced and reciprocal concessions.

The U. S. position in the initial stages of preparing for negotiations under the Trade Expansion Act was that it "would not take part" in the exchange of exceptions lists for nonagricultural products unless there had first been some agreement on how agricultural products were to be handled.

In November, 1964, the U.S. policy position was modified when the U.S. agreed to table offers on industrial products separately from agricultural products.

That action was followed by a modified policy statement that the United States would not "conclude" any agreement that did not provide for acceptable conditions of access for U. S. agricultural exports into foreign markets.[8]

In 1964 the United States had advised the EEC that its proposal to negotiate support levels was not acceptable. That proposal was the essential element of the EEC's reference price and compensatory levy system of agricultural protectionism.

It is now clear from published reports from Europe that the EEC agricultural offers do not provide a basis for meaningful negotiations for trade liberalization. In fact, they embody and perpetuate the restrictions on agricultural imports which the United States had already rejected as a basis for negotiations.

Governor Herter has stated (before the Subcommittee on Foreign Economic Policy of the House Committee on Foreign Affairs, on August 10, 1966):

"In regard to agriculture the United States has made it clear that its offers have been put forward in the expectation that the other major par-

---

[7] No classification marking.
[8] Not further identified.

ticipants will make comparable concessions, and has warned that if this proves not to be the case these offers will be withdrawn or modified to the extent it deems necessary. It has also warned that both its agricultural and industrial offers will be withdrawn to the extent required to achieve reciprocity in the over-all negotiations."[9]

The statement from Governor Herter's Office recognizes that reductions in U.S. industrial tariffs are the purchase price with which the U. S. will buy improved conditions of access for U. S. agricultural exports. This has been the U. S. position since the start of the Kennedy Round, and its soundness is based on the importance of U. S. agricultural exports to the domestic economic well-being of the U.S. and the contribution of agricultural exports to the U. S. balance of payments. It would be unthinkable for the U. S. to lower its tariffs on industrial products from the EEC without achieving its objectives with respect to agricultural trade liberalization. To do so would preclude hopes for future improvement in conditions of access for U.S. agricultural exports or even for the maintenance of our present level of agricultural exports.

In line with previous U.S. Government policy statements, we insist that the EEC reference price and variable levy system, if implemented, is incompatible with trade liberalization.

Notwithstanding the steadfast support that the U. S. National Fruit Export Council has given the U.S. efforts at trade liberalization, we can come to no other conclusion but that no trade agreement at all is better than a bad trade agreement.

In view of the course of events which is outlined herein, it is the conclusion of the U.S. National Fruit Export Council that the United States should immediately withdraw all offers, industrial and agricultural, on articles of interest to the EEC until the EEC submits agricultural offers that represent trade liberalization, rather than protection.

Adopted by the U. S. National Fruit Export Council September 20, 1966, at its annual meeting in Washington, D.C.

---

[9] The quotation is from an undated background paper that Herter submitted to the subcommittee at the outset of his testimony on August 10. (*The Foreign Policy Aspects of the Kennedy Round: Hearings Before the Subcommittee on Foreign Economic Policy of the Committee on Foreign Affairs, House of Representatives, Eighty-ninth Congress, Second Session* (Washington, 1966), pp. 25–26)

322. Telegram From the Mission to the European Office of the United Nations to the Department of State[1]

Geneva, September 23, 1966, 1711Z.

1118. GATT. For Governor Herter from Blumenthal. BUSEC. Ref: Geneva 1103.[2]

Subject: Opening of US–EEC bilateral discussion of KR agricultural offers, September 23.[3]

1. After brief discussion procedures for remainder of series, first meeting devoted to exchange general preliminary reactions each other's offers and indications general emphasis each plans give in forthcoming meetings.

2. U.S. opening statement said we would seek clarification and improvement of present EEC offer on specific, case-by-case basis, using criterion of expanded trade opportunities. Emphasized willingness approach with open minds and examine all means achieving real trade liberalization. Recognized Community's achievement in tabling offers and difficulties involved, but stressed disappointment with present offers, as we understand them, and concern that expanded trade opportunities which they would produce seem extremely modest and in some cases nonexistent. Concluded that if improvements not possible, consequences for maintenance present US offer in both agricultural and industrial areas could be serious. Hoped that bilaterals would put both parties in position to assess what each needed and what each needed to do to make negotiation success.

3. EEC (Rabot) agreed that real trade liberalization goal of negotiation, and that US–EEC bilaterals of extreme importance for negotiations as a whole. EEC would discuss all its offers and examine gaps in constructive manner. After noting EEC interest in relatively unimportant list US exceptions affecting EEC exports, EEC expressed disappointment that US offers limited to tariff reduction. Said it would wish explain value of comprehensive character its own offers and discuss internal US policies affecting trade opportunities which not included in present US offer. In EEC view, inclusion in negotiation of all elements support and protec-

---

[1] Source: Department of State, Central Files, FT 7 GATT. Limited Official Use. Repeated to Bonn, Brussels, The Hague, Luxembourg, Paris, and Rome and passed to the White House.

[2] Dated September 22. (Ibid.)

[3] Tagg A–81 from Geneva, October 13, which provided a detailed account of this first bilateral meeting with the EEC on agricultural offers, offered this general conclusion: "the tone of the meeting was good; both sides professed a willingness to discuss their offers and the points at issue between them in a specific and comprehensive manner." (Ibid., FT 7 GATT)

tion of a necessity if real trade liberalization to be achieved. Reserved right to request bilateral discussion of products now reserved for group treatment including cereals and dairy, and to require multilateral discussion of commodities which in EEC view might require such treatment. Said primary EEC emphasis would be on present and future condition of world markets in addition to expansion of export interest.

4. Tone of meeting frank and constructive. Both sides agreed no publicity desirable and that press and public have no part to play in present discussions.

5. Detailed examination will begin with bilateral meeting scheduled for September 30.

6. US opening statement follows by airgram.

Brodie

---

323.   Editorial Note

The second through the sixth U.S.–EEC bilateral meetings on agricultural offers in the Kennedy Round at Geneva, September 30–October 14, 1966, were devoted to discussions of offers on a case-by-case basis. For text of Blumenthal's opening statement at the first of these meetings on September 14, see Document 320. In the second through the fourth meetings, which examined EEC offers on fruits and vegetables, the United States requested deeper tariff cuts; asked for discussions with third countries on the EEC reference price system (protection to maintain the price received by domestic producers); and strongly opposed the variable levy on the added-sugar content of canned fruits and juices. The fifth and sixth meetings concerned among other things the EEC offer on rice, which, the United States claimed, increased protection. Regarding manufactured tobacco, the two sides agreed to treat the Kennedy Round and Article XXIV:6 negotiations in parallel fashion. (Article XXIV:6 refers to that part of the General Agreement on Tariffs and Trade that provides for compensation to a GATT Contracting Party by a customs union which raises tariffs to a nonparticipant in the customs union above those existing before formation of the customs union, while taking into account tariff reductions to the members of the customs union; see 4 Bevans 721.) The United States expressed its interest in a substantial reduction of protection of manufactured tobacco. (Tagg A–82, October 13, Tagg A–83 and Tagg A–88, October 15, Tagg A–114, October 30, and Tagg A–132, November 8, from Geneva; Department of State, Central Files, FT 7 GATT)

324. Letter From Thirteen Senators to President Johnson[1]

Washington, October 3, 1966.

Dear Mr. President:

We are writing you to express our concern about the current status of the GATT negotiations as they relate to U.S. agriculture. We are especially concerned by reports in the European press that the EEC is attempting to incorporate support levels, reference prices, and compensatory levies for agricultural products into the GATT tariff structure. These measures are restrictive of trade; they are protectionist in essence, not trade liberalization.

The U. S. National Fruit Export Council has forcefully called this situation to our attention in the attached statement of the Council's position.[2] Also attached are data compiled by the Foreign Agricultural Service (1960–1965) showing the importance to the United States of fruit and vegetable exports to the EEC countries totalling about $91 million in 1965.[3] The export market is an integral and essential part of the industry's market. All sales of such products currently are for dollars, thereby contributing materially to the U.S. balance of payments position.

We have been gratified by the repeated assurances from your office and from Governor Herter during the course of these negotiations that the United States would not enter into any agreement which does not provide satisfactory conditions of access for U. S. farm products to these traditional markets. However, we are frankly concerned over reports that "overriding political considerations" may be put forward as justification for entering into an agreement which would damage the legitimate economic interests of the United States.

We believe the proposals of the EEC are in direct conflict with the philosophy of the Trade Expansion Act, and particularly section 252, wherein our opposition to "non-tariff trade restrictions", "variable import fees" and other "unjustifiable foreign import restrictions" is clearly stated. The EEC proposals represent "policies unjustifiably restricting United States commerce."

We urge that the United States remain steadfast in its adherence to the publicly announced policy that we must achieve reciprocity in these negotiations which must include access for United States agricultural products to foreign markets on an equitable basis as stated in section 252(a)(3) of the Act.

---

[1] Source: Department of State, Central Files, FT 7 GATT. Unclassified. The letter is an enclosure to CA–2992 to 22 diplomatic missions, October 17, which informed the posts they could use "the letter informally to illustrate the scope of United States domestic pressures to assure continued access to Community markets."

[2] See Document 321.

[3] Not printed.

The purpose and principle of the Trade Expansion Act must not be sacrificed to achieve an unmeaningful agreement which will not ". . . maintain and enlarge foreign markets for the products of United States agriculture, industry, mining and commerce;".

With kind regards, we remain,

Yours truly,

George D. Aiken[4]
Wayne Morse
Thomas H. Kuchel
Jennings Randolph
Milton R. Young
George Smathers
Spessard L. Holland
George Murphy
Warren G. Magnuson
Leverett Saltonstall
Daniel K. Inouye
Maurine B. Neuberger
Robert C. Byrd

---

[4] Printed from a copy that bears these typed signatures.

---

325. Circular Airgram From the Department of State to Certain Posts[1]

CA–2863   Washington, October 12, 1966, 2:18 p.m.

SUBJECT

Statements US Farm Groups—Kennedy Round

REF

Deptel 62827, Oct. 10, 1966;[2] CA–2653, Oct. 5, 1966[3]

---

[1] Source: Department of State, Central Files, FT 7 GATT. Limited Official Use. Drafted by James Johnson (EUR/RPE) on October 11; cleared by Leonard U. Wilson (STR), Julius L. Katz (E/OT), Thomas W. Fina (EUR/RPE); and approved by Deane R. Hinton (EUR/RPE). Sent to 22 diplomatic missions.

[2] Telegram 62827 to 19 diplomatic missions, October 10, transmitted the text of the press release by the Office of the Special Representative for Trade Negotiations responding to farm organizations' proposals to withdraw U.S. Kennedy Round agricultural offers unless EEC offers were substantially improved. (Ibid., FT 13 2 US)

[3] See footnote 1, Document 321.

Statement of the three US farm groups referred to in the referenced telegram and, where pertinent, STR replies thereto are enclosed in single copies for all addressee posts.[4]

To date, three national agricultural bodies—The National Council of Farmer Cooperatives, the American Farm Bureau Federation and the US National Fruit Export Council—have demanded complete withdrawal of American offers from the Kennedy Round negotiations (for text of Fruit Council Statement see CA–2653). Three farm groups—The National Grange (no statement available), the National Farmers Union and the National Livestock Feeders Association) have suggested that the time has arrived either for withdrawal of US agricultural offers or reassessment of the direction in which the talks are headed. Great Plains Wheat, Western Wheat Associates, and the National Association of Wheat Growers have focused on the KR cereals negotiations urging assured access to EEC markets and that industrial and agricultural sectors be negotiated jointly.

As suggested in the reftel, posts should use statements informally to illustrate the buildup of domestic pressures urging US withdrawal from the Kennedy Round should the EEC fail to improve significantly its agricultural offers as appropriate. The measured replies of Governor Herter should also be drawn upon.

Rusk

---

4 The five enclosures, none printed, are as follows: 1) letter from B. H. Jones (National Livestock Feeders Association), September 26, and Herter's reply, October 4; 2) letter from Charles B. Shuman (American Farm Bureau Federation) to Herter, September 14, and Herter's reply, September 27; 3) letter from Kenneth D. Naden (National Council of Farmer Cooperatives) to Herter, September 29, and Herter's reply, October 4; 4) letter from James G. Patton (National Farmers Union) to Herter, October 5; and 5) statement by three wheat associations, September 9.

326.   Telegram From the Mission to the European Office of the United Nations to the Department of State[1]

Geneva, December 5, 1966, 1736Z.

1777. GATT—For Governor Herter from Blumenthal. BUSEC–CEDTO. Subject: Assembly of Kennedy Round offers—U.S. and EEC. Ref: Geneva 1758.[2]

1. We met Dec. 1 with EEC del., chaired by Hijzen and including Rabot, Schlosser Braun and Malve, to explain U.S. assessment and transmit bilateral list priority requests for improved offers. Member states observers present also.

2. We noted assessment showed overall imbalance present offers in favor other countries and imbalance with EEC. On industrial side, we pointed out that by any standard of comparison, EEC offers fall short of U.S. offers and that EEC exceptions bear heavily on sectors of greatest U.S. interest. Re agriculture, situation even more critical and room for improved EEC offers even greater.

3. In describing requests and possible modifications, U.S. noted that trade coverage of modifications much smaller than trade coverage of requests to allow EEC flexibility in improving offers and because of unknowns in crucial sectors. Emphasized that moment not yet come make withdrawals and that no offer being pulled back: lists indicated improvements needed, and modifications U.S. might have to have if improvements not forthcoming

4. Noting that our assessment omitted consideration of disparities, we restated position that in absence of agreed rule we would examine any disparity claims on case-by-case basis to see if disparity element significant in trade terms. Noting also that in introduction to list of U.S. exceptions of Community export interest received Nov. 30, EEC claimed right to "free exceptions" on CXT items corresponding to disparities excepted by other countries, we said we do not accept argument, and would take any such "free exception" claims into account in assessing balance.

5. Hijzen made following comments on points raised in our assessments:

A. Re conditional offers, said requirement of reciprocity in automotive sector attached to EEC offers satisfied by offers of U.S. and UK but others would have to match.

---

[1] Source: Department of State, Central Files, FT 7 GATT. Confidential. Repeated to Bonn, Brussels, The Hague, Luxembourg, Paris, and Rome and passed to the White House.

[2] Telegram 1758 from Geneva, December 2 (misdated November 2). (Ibid.)

B. Re disparities, admitted no agreed rule; said EEC going on basis of 2:1/10 formula;[3] regretted slow pace concordance work has prevented EEC submission of definite list of disparity items but hoped submit list soon; reaffirmed EEC thesis that Community entitled free exceptions on products in disparity which excepted by others.

C. Re statistical basis of assessment, deprecated use of figures and said solution of problems presented by trade negotiation of this importance depends on appreciation qualitative rather than quantitative elements.

D. Re balance, said preliminary EEC assessment shows U.S. and EEC close to bilateral balance and stated that in EEC view withdrawals by U.S. would be indefensible. (Note that he did not say EEC offers equal to or better than U.S.).

6. Copies our talking paper on bilateral assessment being pouched addressee posts.[4]

Tubby

---

[3] See footnote 2, Document 235.
[4] Not found.

---

327. Letter From Secretary of Commerce Connor to President Johnson[1]

Washington, December 5, 1966.

Dear Mr. President:

The Special Representative for Trade Negotiations is recommending that you terminate the escape clause action on watch movements. Pursuant to section 351(c)(1)(A) of the Trade Expansion Act of 1962, I have been requested to furnish you with advice as to whether such a termination would be in the national interest. Accordingly, I wish to concur with the recommendations of the Special Representative to terminate the escape clause action, and I further believe that this would be in the national interest.

---

[1] Source: Kennedy Library, Herter Papers, Memoranda to the President, August 11, 1964–August 8, 1966, Box 10. Confidential.

The recommendation is the result of an investigation instituted by the Tariff Commission in accordance with section 351(d)(2) of the Trade Expansion Act. The Tariff Commission was to report on the probable economic effect on the industry concerned at the reduction or termination of the increase in duties which was imposed on watch movements in 1954. The report, submitted by the Tariff Commission on March 5, 1965,[2] was studied by a special interagency task force created under the Office of the Special Representative for Trade Negotiations and was reviewed by the Office of the Special Representative.

I believe the following factors are significant to the determination as to whether the termination of this escape clause action would be in the national interest.

The probable effect of the recommended action of our national security was of serious concern to me. In this regard, at the request of the Office of Emergency Planning, the Department of Commerce conducted an extensive survey on the capacity of the domestic watch industry to produce goods for civilian and military uses in time of national emergency. The results of this survey were reported to the Office of Emergency Planning and were reviewed by that Office and by the Department of Defense. On the basis of their review and the current and planned activities of the Department of Defense, I am assured that the possible idling of productive facilities due to a further shift to imports by domestic watch manufacturers does not pose a significant problem and that increased imports of watch movements do not now or in the future threaten to impair the national security.

From the economic standpoint, it appears that termination of the escape clause rates of duty would not have a serious adverse effect on the domestic producers. The domestic industry producing watch movements is composed of two segments: a pin-lever segment and a jeweled-lever segment.

The U.S. Time Corporation is the only producer of pin-lever wrist watch movements in this country. The firm has successfully developed the market for inexpensive, quality watches and has become the sole domestic producer of pin-lever wrist watches. Through extensive advertising and aggressive sales promotion, the company has achieved a strong hold on the market for its Timex brand. It has enjoyed a good record of consistently rising sales and excellent earnings.

The Bulova, Hamilton, and Elgin watch companies constitute the jeweled-lever segment of the industry. During the period of escape clause protection, these firms have not increased their production of jeweled-lever movements. On the contrary, they have shifted to increased

---

[2] See footnote 5, Document 278.

imports of 17 jewel movements, principally in the men's sizes and have concentrated their domestic production on the more profitable lines, notably women's watches and electric-powered watches. All three firms now import far more than they produce in the United States, and their rate of profit from imports exceeds that from their domestic production.

During the period of escape clause protection, these firms have been unable to increase their domestic production of jeweled-lever movements. They have adjusted to import competition principally by increasing their overseas investments. Bulova, for example, is the largest single manufacturer of watches in Switzerland.

While domestic output of jeweled-lever movements has remained fairly stable in recent years, the U.S. market has been expanding. Despite the escape clause rates, imports of watch movements have increased over the past twelve years. Since 1958, the domestic producers themselves have accounted for most of the increase in imports of jeweled-lever movements.

It is extremely unlikely that further continuance of the escape clause action would enable the jeweled-lever segment of the industry to increase domestic output to pre-1954 levels.

The companies have asserted that if the escape clause rates were terminated they would be compelled to abandon their domestic watch manufacturing facilities and shift entirely to imports from foreign plants. In the event that the companies do resort to such action, they could suffer short-run capital losses and a number of production workers in their watch manufacturing establishments could be laid off. According to statements of officials of the companies, however, the long-run profitability of the companies likely would be improved. Furthermore, under the present level of economic activity in the affected areas, reemployment prospects appear good for the workers who may become unemployed.

Given the strong competitive position of the pin-lever producer and the fact that domestic jeweled-lever production already is concentrated in movements other than those subject to escape clause protection, it does not appear at all clear to me that all domestic production of watch movements would be discontinued if the rates of duty were rolled back.

The escape clause action in 1954 resulted in negotiation of compensatory concessions with Switzerland, the principal supplying country. In this regard, your acceptance of the recommendation will enable us to withdraw the compensatory concessions or to negotiate equivalent concessions for the benefit of U.S. exports. Acceptance of the recommendation would enable the Swiss to maintain current offers in the Kennedy Round of interest to United States exporters. The Swiss on many occasions have indicated that without termination of the escape clause action on watch movements, it would be necessary to withdraw substantial tariff reduction offers of direct interest to this country.

At the time relief was granted to the domestic industry it was understood that the escape clause action was temporary and would be terminated when conditions warranted. A rollback in these rates, which have been in existence longer than any other escape clause measure, would remove a long-standing irritant in our otherwise excellent relations with Switzerland.

Based on the above facts together with the findings and data submitted by the Special Representative it is my opinion that the national interest would best be served by termination of the escape clause action on watch movements. Accordingly, I concur with the recommendation for termination of the escape clause rates of duty and restoration of the 1936 trade agreement rates.

Respectfully yours,

John T. Connor

328.   Telgram From the Mission to the European Office of the United Nations to the Department of State[1]

Geneva, December 19, 1966, 1807Z.

1893. GATT—For Governor Herter from Blumenthal. Subject: Exoff—Assessment of US and Japanese KR offers. Ref: Geneva 1752.[2]

1. On December 19 we met with Ambassador Aoki who had just returned to Geneva from Tokyo following consultations on KR matters with Prime Minister Sato, members of new Cabinet and industrial leaders. Said he was without instructions but wished to provide impressions concerning GOJ views of assessment of bilateral offers:

---

[1] Source: Department of State, Central Files, FT 7 GATT. Confidential. Repeated to Tokyo and passed to the White House for Herter.

[2] Telegram 1752 from Geneva summarized Blumenthal's negative assessment of Japan's Kennedy Round offers, which "fall considerably short of matching US offers" at their November 29 meeting, and the response of the Japanese delegate. It also noted that Japan submitted its assessment of Kennedy Round offers to the GATT Secretariat on November 30, including specific requests of the United States. (Ibid.)

A. Prime Minister expressed view KR is reaching "eleventh hour" and Japan should endeavor to arrive at fair agreement which takes full cognizance of problems and views of each participant.

B. Ministry of Agriculture is unable understand why US has not made an assessment of Japanese offer on cereals agreement; moreover, in light poor EEC agricultural offer it is difficult for Japan to maintain present agricultural offers. Aoki said he urged his Minister to keep offer on table until the end and latter agreed to study.

C. Ministry of International Trade is very much disturbed by fact "modification list" in US assessment paper to GATT Nov. 30[3] affects Japanese industrial products to greater extent than products of interest to EEC; also, the large amount of trade affecting Japan can only mean "US is taking orthodox approach in assessing offers and is not buying Japanese view that zero binding offers are of value." For textile Bureau of MITI, inclusion in modification list of large amount of commodities under jurisdiction this Bureau has given rise to difficulties, particularly since Japan has endeavored in past to cooperate on textile matters.

D. Aoki expressed view that if US is unable to move on NTB's (Section 402A of Tariff Act) and should withdraw offers on steel (on which US has reserved its position), the Japanese Government would be forced to make modifications in its offers. Aoki reiterated several times that impact of US modification list against Japan was too great and asked the US delegation to study other approaches in assessing offers. In this connection, he thought Japanese offer was comparable to that tabled by US depending on assumptions used.

2. We made following comments:

A. US delegation did not use any one method of assessment, contrary to Aoki view we used only "orthodox method of assessment:" every measure shows Japanese offer does not match US offer. This is true even if credit were given to Japan's zero binding offers which in many cases are of dubious trade value. We would welcome opportunity to discuss in greater detail our bilateral offers to establish fact there is an imbalance.

B. Concerning proposed grains agreement, the US would be prepared ascribe appropriate negotiating credit. This was left out of US assessment of Nov. 30 because of indefiniteness final outcome, particularly on questions such as price and food aid.

C. Concerning the impact of US modification list on Japan as against the EEC, consideration should be given to three points: 1) EEC industrial offer is relatively better than that tabled by Japan; 2) listed agricultural items affect the EEC more than Japan; and 3) US reservations on

---

[3] Not found.

chemicals, aluminum and steel should be considered as part of our modification list.

D. We urged that Japan not use EEC's poor offer on agricultural products as an excuse for not improving Japan's agricultural offers.

E. In conclusion we agreed to study any assessment calculations the Japanese may have to support view there is not an imbalance in offers to degree suggested in US assessment paper.

Mace

---

329.   Memorandum From the President's Deputy Special Assistant for National Security Affairs (Bator) to President Johnson[1]

Washington, January 3, 1967, 3:45 p.m.

SUBJECT

Replacement for Governor Herter

Negotiations in Geneva will be reaching a climax during the next two or three months. It seems to me important to avoid any appearance of a vacuum in the Herter office during the hard bargaining to come.[2] I think it is important that you make clear who will be in charge.

The choices are:

1. Elevate Governor Herter's deputy, William Roth, who now has the title of Deputy Special Representative (with the rank of Ambassador).

2. Let Roth *act* as Special Representative, but without your appointing him. (The TEA empowers the Deputy to act in these circumstances.)

3. Appoint someone else to succeed Herter.

As you know, I have kept a close eye on the Kennedy Round during the past 3 years, and have come to know well the people, and the workings of the Herter staff. This experience leads me strongly to recommend choice No. 1: appointment of Bill Roth as your Special Representative.

---

[1] Source: Johnson Library, National Security File, Name File, Bator Memos [2 of 2], Box 1. The source text bears the handwritten notation, "Eyes Only—Mr. Rostow."

[2] Herter died December 30, 1966.

During the past year and a half—ever since the Governor's health deteriorated—Bill has been the effective day-to-day chief of the organization. He has done a superb job, both in managing the organization and in handling relations with the business community and the Congress. He has good and close relations with Wilbur Mills and others on the Hill who have shown an interest in the negotiations.

Appointing someone from the outside—just six months before the windup of the negotiations—could be damaging in terms of the continued effectiveness of a good, tightly knit organization. It would be difficult for an outsider to acquire the intimate knowledge of the details of the negotiations which will be needed during the February–March period in Geneva. In any case, I know of no one who would be competent to take on this job on short notice who could give you the political protection with protectionist Republicans you got from Herter.

Appointing Bill—rather than letting him serve as acting Special Representative—would *not* limit your choice beyond the end of the Kennedy Round in June. Bill is determined to get out of the trade negotiation business, and would not be prepared to stay in the Herter job beyond June. There are strong pressures on him to leave Government—personal business as well as the University of California, where he is a key member of the Board of Regents. (I think he might stay in Washington if an attractive offer were available outside of the trade field. He has clearly had enough of chicken wars, hassles over safety-pin duties, etc.)

I think it is very important that we move on this quickly, and give a clear signal of Presidential support for Roth, his organization, and the U.S. team in Geneva. I am confident that Rusk, Connor and Freeman would support the promotion of Roth. If you wish, I can check. I did not want to restrict your choices by telephoning around before a signal from you.

Francis M. Bator[3]

---

[3] Printed from a copy that bears this typed signature.

330.   Memorandum From Secretary of State Rusk to President Johnson[1]

Washington, February 11, 1967.

SUBJECT

A New Trade Policy for the United States

Recommendation

Last August George Ball sent you a memorandum outlining a new trade strategy designed to reverse current trends not in the United States interest and to maintain our leadership in free world trade policy in the post-Kennedy Round era.[2] In accordance with your instruction, a small group led by Tony Solomon has examined these ideas further within the Executive Branch. We have consulted with Secretary Connor (and Acting Secretary Trowbridge) and with senior officers of Agriculture, Labor and Treasury. Ambassador Roth and Francis Bator also have taken part in the discussions. The result: unanimous agreement both on the need for a new United States trade policy and on the broad outlines of the policy itself.

We do not envisage a request for major new trade legislation before 1969. It is important, however, to consult informally with key Members of Congress now if we are to adopt a positive posture at several important international meetings over the next 12 months, including your meeting with the other Presidents of the Inter-American system. We must know soon whether the new policy direction—described below—can command the support of the Congress. If it does, the new policy should be taken up as the first order of business of a blue-ribbon public committee which Ambassador Roth will recommend be established to assist him in developing recommendations for trade legislation after the Trade Expansion Act expires on June 30.

You could then announce at the Latin American meeting in April that a major re-examination of our trade policy is under way with a view to improving the trade position of developing countries in ways that will further the historic United States objective of liberalizing world trade. This statement would be warmly welcomed by the Latin Americans and would, Linc Gordon feels, be a critically important contribution to a successful summit meeting. A careful statement along these lines would not arouse serious protectionist opposition, since only a general approach would be outlined at that time. Recently, Congressional leaders as

---

[1] Source: Johnson Library, National Security File, Name File, Bator Memos, Box 1–2. Confidential; Exdis. Another copy indicates that this memorandum was drafted in the Office of International Trade on February 9. (Ibid., Bator Papers, Post Kennedy Round and Trade Policy Study, June 1967, Box 13)

[2] Document 318.

diverse in their trade views as Senators Dirksen and Fulbright have comments on the unresponsiveness of the United States Government to the problem of the poor countries' declining share in world trade.

I recommend, therefore, that you approve informal soundings with key Congressional leaders.

Approve Congressional Consultations

Disapprove[3]

Discussion

The Need for a New United States Trade Policy

For the next few months our primary effort must be devoted to a successful conclusion of the Kennedy Round trade negotiations. At the same time, however, we must address ourselves to future United States policy—to new problems which have arisen and to old problems which have acquired new dimensions. To meet these and to maintain our leadership in the field of trade policy, we must take into account:

—the vital importance of maintaining our own export surplus;
—the strong likelihood that the European Economic Community will be enlarged over the coming years, forming the largest market in the world with free trade among its members, but retaining substantial barriers against the United States and other outsiders;
—the danger of further proliferation of special trade arrangements which discriminate:

—among developing countries,
—against Latin America, and
—against the United States;

—and, above all, the passionate and persistent appeal of the developing nations of the world for preferred tariff treatment for their exports. At the present time, the willingness of other industrialized countries to respond to the appeal leaves the United States virtually isolated in its opposition to preferences. For this we are paying significant political costs.

The challenge presented by these developments coincides with our need to obtain new trade legislation. After the Trade Expansion Act expires at the end of June, we will need a period of reflection and discussion with our trading partners. Thus, a simple extension of the Act for two years seems appropriate. But to exercise leadership and attract international support for a policy designed to meet these new circumstances, we need a new and flexible Congressional mandate.

Basic Elements of a New Trade Policy

1. To meet the objective of keeping open our commercial markets in developed countries, we propose:

---

[3] Neither option is checked.

—That we seek legislation in 1969 which will enable us to urge the Europeans and other industrialized countries to join in a policy of progressive reduction and, where possible, elimination of trade barriers. Where agreements can be reached on specific products or groups of products, tariffs might be phased out over a period of five to twenty years.

2. To meet the twin problems of growing discrimination among poor countries and their appeal for tariff treatment more in keeping with their competitive abilities, we propose:

—That the legislation enable us to offer the poor countries of the world a "head start" in the movement toward tariff disarmament among the advanced countries. The benefits of tariff reductions would be given to poor countries in advance of reductions among industrialized countries which would be phased over a longer period.

3. To meet the growing problem of regional bloc discrimination against United States exports, we propose:

—That this approach be conditioned on agreement by the advanced countries to give up the preferential treatment they enjoy in the markets of associated developing countries.

4. To meet the problem of possible injury to United States industry and labor arising from increased imports from low-wage countries, we propose:

—That the adjustment assistance provision be improved.

—That there be an additional escape clause applicable to the special tariff treatment for the developing countries. Should difficulties arise, the advance cut might have to be withdrawn or, alternatively, a tariff quota might be established.

Dean Rusk

331. Memorandum From the Acting Special Representative for Trade Negotiations (Roth) to President Johnson[1]

Washington, February 13, 1967, 10 a.m.

SUBJECT

Supplemental Authority to Offer Tariff Concessions in the Kennedy Round

Request for Negotiating Authority

This memorandum requests that you authorize me, under the Trade Expansion Act of 1962 (TEA), to offer in the Kennedy Round the tariff concessions specified herein as supplements to those previously offered with your approval. All legal requirements of the TEA for such offers have been met.

Offering these concessions will: (1) dispel the legal cloud which was cast over a substantial portion of our previous offers by tariff legislation enacted after those offers were made; (2) improve our negotiating prospects by responding to other delegations' requests for U. S. concessions previously withheld with your concurrence; and (3) permit us to offer, for the benefit of developing countries, the elimination of duties on tropical hardwoods without staging.

Any trade agreement which is negotiated on the basis of offers for which I now seek your authorization will be concluded subject to your final approval. During the negotiation, we may find it appropriate or necessary to hold back, reduce, or withdraw certain of these offers. On the other hand, it may again become necessary for me to seek your authorization to offer specific additional concessions in return for foreign concessions of particular importance to U. S. exporters.

Discussion:

(1) *Confirmation of Previous Offers*—Changes in tariff rates and tariff classifications made by the Tariff Schedules Technical Amendments Act (TAA),[2] which corrected "errors and inadvertencies" in the Tariff Schedules of the United States (TSUS), and by a few other acts cast a legal cloud over a substantial portion of the articles that you authorized us to offer for concessions in the Kennedy Round, and that we had in most cases actually offered. On August 16, 1966, you issued a list of the articles affected by such legislation, and thus initiated the steps required by the

---

[1] Source: Johnson Library, National Security File, Subject File, Trade Negotiations, Kennedy Round, "Potatoes," [2 of 2], Box 47. Confidential.

[2] The Tariff Schedules Technical Amendments Act of 1965, P.L. 89–241 (79 Stat. 933) signed by President Johnson on October 7, 1965, corrected oversights and errors in the Tariff Classification Act of 1962 (P.L. 87–456; 76 Stat. 72).

TEA for reconsideration of such articles for trade agreement concessions. The Trade Information Committee (TIC) and the Tariff Commission held hearings to receive information and views on these products. The advice of the Tariff Commission and the summaries of the TIC hearings have been made available to you in accordance with section 224 of the TEA and, together with other material, have been carefully reviewed by this Office and other agencies concerned with the trade agreements program.

(2) *New Offers on Articles Previously Withheld*—On November 10, 1964, you authorized Governor Herter to offer concessions on most articles in the TSUS and agreed to withhold certain dutiable articles from offers of tariff concessions. In the course of the Kennedy Round negotiations, other delegations have urged us to make offers on certain of these excepted articles, and our delegation advises that our negotiating prospects could be enhanced by responding to some of these requests. We have accordingly re-examined the situation with respect to articles withheld and have concluded that, in a limited number of cases, it would not be consistent with the standards and purposes of the TEA to offer concessions in the Kennedy Round in such cases.

(3) *New Offers on Tropical Hardwoods*—On November 10, 1964, you authorized Governor Herter to offer the elimination of duties on certain tropical hardwoods under section 202 of the TEA, which permits the elimination, in five annual stages, of the duty on any product dutiable at 5 percent or less. An offer on these tropical hardwoods under section 202 has already been made in the Kennedy Round.

Section 213 of the TEA, which authorizes the elimination of duties applicable to certain tropical agricultural and forestry products, is not subject to the staging requirement. In order to maximize our negotiating position with respect to the less-developed countries, we required the Tariff Commission to determine those tropical hardwoods which satisfy the requirements of section 213.

On February 18, 1965, you issued a public list of the tropical hardwoods with respect to which the elimination of duties under section 213 was to be considered. The TIC and the Tariff Commission provided an opportunity to interested parties to appear at public hearings or submit written statements concerning the public list.

The advice of the Tariff Commission concerning the tropical hardwoods has been made available to you in accordance with section 224 of the TEA. Since no views of any kind were presented to the TIC, there is no summary of hearings to submit pursuant to section 224.

Recommendation:

With the concurrence of the other agencies concerned, I recommend that you authorize me, as your Acting Special Representative for Trade Negotiations:

1. With respect to articles listed in the public notice of August 16, 1966 (Annex 1A),[3] to make the following offers in substitution for or confirmation of offers previously made in the Kennedy Round:

A. To offer, under TEA section 201, the full 50 percent reduction in duties on all dutiable articles so listed except those specified in Annex 1B.
B. To offer the elimination of duties on articles which so qualify under TEA sections 202 or 212.
C. Where the reduction or elimination of duties is not proposed, to offer under TEA section 201 not to increase existing duties on dutiable articles on such list and not impose duties on articles now duty-free.

2. With respect to certain other articles, previously withheld from offer with your concurrence, to offer, under TEA section 201, duty reductions as specified in Annex 2 to augment offers previously made in the Kennedy Round.

3. With respect to the tropical hardwoods listed in the public notice of February 18, 1965 (Annex 3A) to offer the elimination of duties under TEA section 213.

William M. Roth

[3] The annexes are as follows:
Annex 1, "Confirmation of Previous Offices: A. Public Notice of August 16, 1966; B. List of Exceptions to Offers to Reduce Duties by 50 Percent; C. Tariff Commission Advice, November 1966; D. Summary of TIC Hearings;" Annex 2, "New Offers on Articles Previously Withheld;" Annex 3, "New Offers of Tropical Hardwoods: A. Public Notice of February 18, 1965; B. Tariff Commission Advice, May 1965." None is printed.

---

332. Memorandum From the Acting Special Representative for Trade Negotiations (Roth) to President Johnson[1]

Washington, February 15, 1967, 4:30 p.m.

SUBJECT
American Selling Price System of Customs Valuation

Recommendation

For the reasons given below, I recommend that you authorize me, as the Acting Special Representative for Trade Negotiations, to offer in the

[1] Source: Johnson Library, White House Central Files, Confidential File, TA, Bator to President, 2/21/67, Tab A. Confidential.

Kennedy Round of trade negotiations the elimination of all the present ad valorem rates of duty subject to the American selling price (ASP) system of customs valuation and the substitution of those new ad valorem rates of duty based on normal methods of customs valuation which are set out in the last column of the table attached at Tab A.[2] This offer would apply to the four categories of products now subject to ASP—benzenoid chemicals, rubber-soled footwear, canned clams, and wool-knit gloves.

Such an offer would be subject to the following basic conditions: (1) any agreement involving such an elimination of the ASP system must be entirely separate from the overall Kennedy Round agreement; (2) such an agreement must contain reciprocal benefits for the United States, including concessions on tariffs and, if at all possible, non-tariff barriers; and (3) such an agreement will be subject to your express approval before signature and, if signed, will require enactment by the Congress of implementing legislation before it can enter into force.

The Departments of Agriculture, Commerce, Defense, Interior, Labor, State, and Treasury all concur in this recommendation.

Statement of Reasons

1. *Undesirability of ASP.* ASP—whatever its original justification—is, in our judgment, not a legitimate system of customs valuation. It subjects an exporter to a two-fold uncertainty. He does not know at the time of exportation whether his product will be subject to duty according to its own value or according to the value of a domestic competing product. In addition, if his product is found to be dutiable on the latter basis, he does not know what the price of the domestic product will be and hence what amount of duty he must pay—a duty which is usually very high and often prohibitive. The ASP system has long been criticized by other countries and would be illegal under the General Agreement on Tariffs and Trade (GATT) but for an exception for certain legislation in existence at the time the GATT was negotiated. It is especially damaging to our liberal trade position since it has considerable similarity to the variable levy system which the EEC has imposed on a number of agricultural imports and to which we have made strenuous objections over the last several years.

2. *Need to Make Offer on ASP in Kennedy Round.* As we enter the critical phase of the Kennedy Round, one issue dominates the industrial sector of the negotiations—ASP as it relates to benzenoid chemicals. The Europeans, and especially the EEC, U.K., and Switzerland, regard ASP as a serious obstacle to their exports of benzenoid chemicals to the United States, as well as a symbol of American protectionism. As a result, these countries have made the elimination of the ASP system an express condition of any reduction in their tariffs on most of our chemical

---

[2] Not found.

exports, as well as an implied condition of liberalizing trade generally throughout the industrial sector. Failure to offer the elimination of ASP would, in our judgment, seriously jeopardize the entire Kennedy Round and could be used as a pretext for placing the blame for its collapse on the United States.

3. *Nature of Proposed Offer on ASP.* The proposed offer is designed to eliminate the ASP system and yet retain adequate tariff protection for the benzenoid chemical industry and the other industries which benefit from that system. Drawing upon the advice and data furnished by the Tariff Commission after extensive hearings, as well as our own sources of information, we have made an intensive inquiry into the economic conditions of the industries concerned and the probable impact of eliminating the ASP system. In the case of the benzenoid chemical industry, viewed in its entirety as well as in terms of its basic subdivisions, we have concluded that the proposed ad valorem components of the duties, which range from 4% to 40%, should give both the large and small firms sufficient tariff protection to avoid any serious dislocation. With respect to the rubber footwear industry, we believe that the high rate of 47-1/2% which we are proposing should permit that industry to cope with imports from Japan and several other Far Eastern countries. In the case of canned clams and wool-knit gloves, we are proposing that the same amount of duty protection now afforded to the domestic industries under the ASP system be continued under the new rates.

4. *Congressional Views on Elimination of ASP.* The ASP issue is not only critical to the successful conclusion of the Kennedy Round, it is also the trickiest political issue we face in the negotiations.

Committee Views on ASP

In the House Ways and Means Committee, there appears to be no general support for the ASP system and a willingness to consider an agreement eliminating ASP on its merits. This was confirmed with Chairman Mills on February 13. Moreover, conversations with most of the senior Democratic and Republican members indicate either outright approval of, or at least no objection to, the manner in which we would propose to eliminate ASP. This is true, in particular, of King, Byrnes, and Curtis.

In the Senate Finance Committee, there seems to be no strong feelings that the ASP system should be retained for its own sake. During Senate consideration in 1965 of a bill to eliminate ASP on protective rubber footwear,[3] Smathers, Hartke, and Ribicoff stated that they were opposed to the ASP system. Moreover, Smathers said that he believed that Long, Gore, and Carlson were also against ASP.

---

[3] See footnote 5, Document 295.

However, there is considerable opposition in the Finance Committee to the signature of a trade agreement ad referendum to the Congress. The opposition stems largely from the fear that such an agreement would present the Committee and the Senate with a fait accompli. Last year, the Finance Committee reported out and the Senate passed (with only a handful of Senators on the floor) S. Con. Res. 100.[4] This resolution, which died in the House, expressed the sense of the Congress that no agreement should be concluded in the Kennedy Round which could not be implemented pursuant to the TEA. We believe we can allay this fear by continuing to make clear in the Congress and in Geneva that any ASP agreement must be totally unrelated to the Kennedy Round agreement.

Among the interested members in both Committees—and the Congress as a whole—there is a widespread concern that elimination of the ASP system might result in serious economic dislocation. It is our impression that most of these Congressmen are not necessarily wedded to ASP but will insist that sufficient tariff protection be maintained—as we think our proposals will do.

Congressional Support for Rubber Footwear

About 40 members of Congress from 12 states have written letters generally urging the retention of ASP on rubber footwear. Twenty-one are from the four New England states—Connecticut, Maine, Massachusetts, and Rhode Island—which together have the greatest interest in rubber footwear.

The leader of the New England bloc, as well as the rubber-footwear association, is Ribicoff. On the basis of a conversation with him on February 9, we believe that he might agree to the elimination of ASP and the substitution of a fairly high rate.

In the Finance Committee, only Hartke, Talmadge, and Dirksen, in addition to Ribicoff, have expressed concern over the elimination of ASP on rubber footwear. We are reasonably sure, however, that if we can reach agreement with Ribicoff, the rest of the Finance Committee will come along.

Congressional Support for Benzenoid Chemicals

About 140 members of Congress from 12 states have written letters generally opposing the elimination of ASP on benzenoid chemicals. The benzenoid chemical industry is significant in 10 of these states—Alabama, Illinois, New Jersey, New York, North Carolina, Ohio, Pennsylvania, South Carolina, Texas, and West Virginia.

In many of these states, however, a substantial number of workers are engaged in the production of non-controversial chemicals or chemi-

---

[4] Reference is to S. Con. Res. 100, 89th Cong., introduced by Senator Russell B. Long on June 28, 1966.

cals like low-value intermediates which are the least vulnerable to import competition. This is true, for example, of Illinois, North Carolina, Pennsylvania, Texas, and West Virginia. Moreover, we have reason to believe that many of the Senators and Congressmen who have signed letters are prepared to consider an ASP agreement on its merits. For example, Congressman Rodino, dean of the New Jersey Delegation, told us this was his position in a conversation on January 31, although New Jersey is the leading producer of benzenoid chemicals.

Most Senators on the Finance Committee have some benzenoid chemical production in their states, but in only two states—Georgia and Illinois—is there any portion of production at all involved in the controversial areas. This may explain why only Talmadge and Dirksen have written letters opposing the elimination of ASP, although when we saw Dirksen this afternoon and raised ASP, he did not seem concerned. Dirksen has no more than 1300 intermediate and dye workers in Illinois, and Talmadge about 200 dye and other benzenoid chemical workers in his state. Just today, in a conversation with Joe Bowman of Treasury, Long indicated he was not committed to ASP. However, because of large chemical firms in Louisiana which may have an interest in ASP in other states, Long may not be easy to bring around, and we intend to meet with him early next week.

Conclusions

This discussion leads me to the following conclusions:

1.   We must make an offer on ASP in the Kennedy Round. Otherwise, there is a serious risk that the negotiations will collapse.

2.   Any separate ASP agreement we negotiate must contain important export concessions for the chemical industry, which exports over $2 billion worth a year. This should make it harder for the benzenoid chemical segment to oppose the agreement.

3.   The ASP agreement must also contain reductions in European non-tariff barriers that are of interest to other American industries. This would help bring into play interests outside the chemical area.

4.   Such an ASP agreement—if it contains substantial benefits for American industry—would not, we believe, encounter serious problems in the Ways and Means Committee or the House.

5.   There would still remain a difficult problem in the Senate but not an unsurmountable one, depending principally on Long's position. If the rubber footwear industry is largely taken care of, this would leave only the benzenoid chemical industry, whose strength in terms of consistent interest in the Finance Committee is not great.

6.   We would make it quite clear to the Europeans that in offering to take a negotiated agreement back to the Congress, we are not guarantee-

ing that the Congress will approve it. The *offer* to do so, however, is an essential ingredient to a successful conclusion of the negotiations.

There is attached at Tab B a background memorandum which deals with all the principal aspects of the ASP issue.[5]

William M. Roth

---

[5] Not found.

---

333. Memorandum From the President's Deputy Special Assistant for National Security Affairs (Bator) to President Johnson[1]

Washington, March 8, 1967, 5 p.m.

SUBJECT

Trade Policy

At Tab A, Secretary Rusk sketches a post-Kennedy Round trade policy—assuming that things turn out well in Geneva.[2] The work was done by a small committee consisting of Bill Roth, Tony Solomon, Sandy Trowbridge and myself. It has been approved by Rusk, Connor (before he left) and the appropriate Assistant Secretaries of Agriculture, Labor and Treasury.

The basic recommended strategy is that we *not* go for major trade legislation until 1969. Rather, we would:

—*Seek a simple two-year extension of the TEA* (now scheduled to expire in June). This would not give us much new tariff-cutting authority, but it would allow us to do the necessary housekeeping and keep the trade agreements program alive.

—*Establish a blue-ribbon public committee to help Roth (and his successor) develop recommendations for the next big trade bill,* to be proposed in 1969.

Neither of these steps requires immediate Presidential action (you have already tentatively approved the TEA extension). But it would be most useful at the Latin American Summit and elsewhere if we could mention some of the policy ideas we would propose to take up with the

---

[1] Source: Johnson Library, National Security File, Name File, Bator Memoranda, Box 1–2. Confidential.

[2] Document 330.

blue-ribbon committee. It makes no sense to talk in public about these ideas, however, until we have some notion of how they would be greeted on the Hill.

Therefore, *Rusk recommends that you authorize quiet soundings with key people on the Hill* about the steps summarized below. If we could get positive reactions, you would have a sweetner at Punta Del Este, and we would be less vulnerable to the barrage of complaints we now get from the less-developed countries about trade policy. If the Congress reacted badly, we would know to move slowly.

New Policy Directions

The major initiatives recommended are as follows:

—Major new trade legislation in 1969 authorizing us to propose phased reduction and elimination of all trade barriers throughout the industrialized world. (Full elimination would take a long time—perhaps 10–15 years.)

—A "head start" advanced cut for poor countries. (We would keep an escape clause in case of serious damage to domestic producers.)

—Insistence, as a condition of the elimination of trade barriers, that some rich countries give up the regional preferential treatment they now receive from their former colonies, etc.

—More liberal adjustment assistance for domestic industry affected by changes in import patterns.

These steps are designated to head off the present trend toward special trade arrangements which exclude us and threaten future U.S. exports. They would provide a liberal trade alternative which makes more economic and political sense for all nations. They would also include special benefits for the poor countries who feel that current trade arrangements are designed only to keep them poor.

You may want a fuller discussion of this strategy before authorizing talks on the Hill. If so, I could spell out the proposals for you in more detail, and/or set up a small meeting of the relevant people. In either case, we need to move as soon as possible if you are to have this in your pocket for the Summit. (At Tab B is a sample of the points you might make at Punta Del Este if we can be ready by then.)[3]

FMB

Tell Rusk and Roth to go ahead with quiet talks on the Hill[4]

Set up meeting

Speak to me

---

[3] Not printed.

[4] This option is checked, and the handwritten notation "fully with large representative number—L" was written next to it by President Johnson.

334.   Memorandum From the Acting Special Representative for Trade Negotiations (Roth) to the President's Deputy Special Assistant for National Security Affairs (Bator)[1]

Washington, March 13, 1967.

SUBJECT

Kennedy Round: Supplemental U.S. Offers

Summary

This memorandum (a) supplements my memorandum to the President of February 13[2] by commenting on probable Congressional interest in the supplemental Kennedy Round offers that I have asked the President to approve and (b) amends that memorandum by deleting a request concerning one commodity category.

February 13 Memorandum

In response to the request that Ed Hamilton made of Bernie Norwood earlier this month, we have reviewed the articles for which, in my February 13 memorandum, I requested the President's authority to offer concessions at Geneva.

You will recall that that memorandum requested authority: (a) to reaffirm well over 100 existing offers for which our negotiating authority became "clouded" because of the enactment of legislation correcting or otherwise amending the TSUS; (b) to offer a few minor improvements in offers by "exing-out" subitems that previously had been excepted; and (c) to offer duty eliminations without staging (under section 213 authority) on certain tropical hardwood to improve the existing offer of duty eliminations subject to staging (under section 202).

One reason for early Presidential action on the request is to permit us rapidly at Geneva to exchange with other delegations a "positive" list of current offers. The delegation is planning to do this during the current week—incorporating the supplemental offers if they are approved in time. This exchange is an important element in our pushing other lethargic participants.

Congressional Interest

Of the items covered in my request, our review of files indicates that there would be significant Congressional interest in only a handful of cases. I shall comment on these.

---

[1] Source: Johnson Library, National Security File, Subject File, Trade Negotiations, Kennedy Round, "Potatoes," Box 47. Confidential. An attached memorandum from Bator to President Johnson, March 22, stated among other things that Roth's "recommendation was supported by all relevant agencies." Bator recommended that Johnson approve it. The "approve" line on Bator's memorandum is checked.

[2] Document 331.

TSUS 182.70—Wild Rice

Congressional interest seems to have been confined to ex-Senator Hubert Humphrey. Wild rice is grown in Minnesota by Indians. They like it so much that they eat all of it and do not market it. Our proposal does not call for a duty reduction, but only for a binding of the existing tariff treatment.

TSUS 609.40, –.41, –.43—Round Wire

The only expression of Congressional interest seems to have been Mr. Chenoweth (R., Colo.). He is no longer in the Congress.

TSUS 700.51, – .52, – .53—Protective Rubber Footwear

Congress removed the requirement for ASP valuation, subdivided the item into three categories, and established a separate rate for each subitem. The only item of significant interest is rubber boots and galoshes. Although Senator Ribicoff wanted a rather high rate of duty for this item, a rate of 37-1/2% was established. Wilbur Mills knocked the rate down to that level from a rate that emerged from previous discussions. We are seeking authority for only a "partial" (that is, less than 50%) reduction on this item to a level of 30% ad valorem.

TSUS 745.40—Button Blanks

Reductions have been opposed by Dow (D., N.Y.); Schmidhauser (D., Iowa); Hungate (D., Mo.); and Duncan (R., Tenn.). We had not offered concessions on this item in November 1964 because we wanted to await legislation which would close a loophole that led to the importation of virtually finished buttons under a low tariff rate for button blanks. This loophole has been closed. We are offering buttons for a full reduction and should offer button blanks also for a full reduction in order to maintain the existing relationship between the rate of duty on the finished product and the lower rate of duty on the intermediate product. With the loophole closed, we doubt there would be any serious opposition to the proposed rate reduction.

TSUS 745.65, –.68—Snap Fasteners

In connection with the issuance of the August 1966 public notice,[3] we heard from Senators Ribicoff (D. Conn.); Talmadge (D., Ga.); Pell (D., R.I.); and Congressmen McCormack (D., Mass.); Fogarty (D., R.I.) and Curtis (R., Mo.). In connection with the 1963 public notice,[4] we heard from Senator Hartke (D., Ind.). Our judgment—which reflected a complete absence of requests for exception in our interagency deliberations—was that there would be no adverse effect on the domestic industry as a whole although some small producers might be affected. Incidentally, when we were considering whether to recommend ter-

---

[3] 31 *Federal Register* 10949, August 16, 1966.
[4] 28 *Federal Register* 11251, October 21, 1963.

mination of the safety pin escape-clause case, we received some Congressional representations against the decrease—in particular from some of the Connecticut delegation on behalf of the highly diversified and healthy Scovill Manufacturing Company. Scovill is also an important producer of snap fasteners. The elimination of the escape-clause duty seems to have had no adverse effect on the economy of Connecticut or on Scovill. Indeed, the company is doing markedly better than ever.

Modification of February 13 Memorandum

Among the items for which, in my February 13 memorandum, I sought authority for a full reduction was brooms (750.26 through –.32). Because of a negotiating decision, we are withdrawing fully our original 50% reduction offer on this item. Accordingly, we do not believe it useful to request authority for reduction and propose expressly excepting this item from the general authorization requested in my February 13 memorandum. To accomplish this change in my request, I attach some revised pages to Annex 1B that is a part of the memorandum.[5] Please (a) substitute the attached pages (each of which for easy identification) is marked with an "r" at the lower left corner of the page for page 2 of the original text and (b) renumber the old page 3 as the new page 4.

---

[5] Not printed.

---

335. Memorandum From the President's Deputy Special Assistant for National Security Affairs (Bator) to President Johnson[1]

Washington, April 18, 1967, 10:30 a.m.

SUBJECT

Management of Last Minute Strategy in the Kennedy Round

As you know, we will be facing the crunch in the trade negotiations during the next 2–3 weeks. Bill Roth himself will be in Geneva leading the negotiations. The problem is to provide appropriate backstopping in

---

[1] Source: Johnson Library, National Security File, Subject File, Trade Negotiations, Kennedy Round, "Potatoes," Box 47. Secret; Sensitive.

Washington, and to assure that you have an open shot at the really critical decisions.

The existing Cabinet Committee for the Kennedy Round is large and unwieldy, and leaks like a sieve. (It involves a large group of staff aides.) To protect your options, I would suggest the following alternative (which has the approval of Secretary Rusk and Bill Roth—I thought it unwise to check with anyone else, pending your approval):

—a very small command group, operating from the building on the strictest need-to-know basis, consisting of Gene Rostow (Tony Solomon), John Schnittker, Sandy Trowbridge and myself. We would maintain open communications with Roth and take responsibility for spelling out the critical choices for your decision. Gene and Schnittker, in turn, would be responsible for keeping Rusk and Freeman informed.

I apologize for making this sound like a battle plan. However, not only five years of work, but your entire trade policy is at stake. Only this kind of handpicked top-level group, under direct Presidential discipline, can both keep on top of a fast moving situation involving enormous amounts of technical detail, and make certain that your options will be protected.

During the next three weeks, I will probably have to ask for your time—perhaps twice. I will do my best to economize on meetings with you, but I am afraid that no one but the President will be able to make the final crucial decisions.

On balance, my own judgment at the moment is that we have a 2-to-1 chance of making a good bargain—one which will be good economics, good international politics, and, overall, even good domestic politics. But we will need cool nerves and fine negotiating judgment to pull it off.

Francis

OK[2]

No

Speak to me

---

[2] This option is checked.

336.   **Memorandum From the President's Deputy Special Assistant for National Security Affairs (Bator) to the Executive Secretary of the National Security Council (Smith)**[1]

Washington, April 19, 1967.

Brom:

The President has ordered me to set up a small and secret command group operating from the White House to manage last minute Kennedy Round strategy. The group will consist of Eugene Rostow, John Schnittker, Alexander Trowbridge and myself.

By instruction of the President, all communications on this subject will be distributed on a strictly need-to-know basis. State has set up a separate communications link to be used by the group. The slug will be "Limdis–Potatoes". Distribution within the State Department (made by the Secretariat) will be limited to the Secretary, the Under Secretary and Gene Rostow. Five copies will be sent to the White House Situation Room. One of these is for Walt, for personal information; the other four should be sent to me. I will manage further distribution from here.

Many thanks.

Francis M. Bator[2]

---

[1] Source: Johnson Library, Bator Papers, Kennedy Round, March–April 1967, Box 12. Secret; Sensitive.

[2] Printed from a copy that bears this typed signature.

---

3 37.   **Telegram From the Mission to the European Office of the United Nations to the Department of State**[1]

Geneva, April 20, 1967, 1546Z.

3299. For Bator from Roth deliver 12:00 noon.

1. This will be first general report on negotiating situation and should not be discussed outside your small group. It is impossible to

---

[1] Source: Department of State, Central Files, FT 13–2 US. Limited Official Use; Immediate; Limdis–Potatoes. Passed to the White House.

send detailed balancing figures at this time because negotiating situation is too fluid and there are too many imponderables. As this thing moves along we will attempt to keep you informed but you must bear in mind our time pressure here.

2. As general cable yesterday indicated,[2] we agreed in Steering Committee that positive offers would be tabled Monday[3] or, if negotiations were going well, perhaps somewhat later in week. It is question whether Community would join this exercise. Our main strategy is to use tabling of positive offers as a club to force Community into meaningful negotiations.

While tabling of positive offers is in any case necessary before end of Kennedy Round threat to do so in next few days is however a weapon which, once used, could have a decidedly negative impact on the negotiations because it could mean a settlement after the inevitable unravelling process at the lowest common denominator. Therefore, in our private negotiations, particularly with the Community, we will be doing everything possible to work out agreements on individual parts of the Kennedy Round before the positive offers are tabled. EEC has been told for instance that the present US–EEC imbalance of approximately $300 million would be increased by another $300 million if chemicals have to come out of the negotiations. This indicates kinds of problems that would arise in tabling positive offer before we have reached agreement in basic areas, in this instance of decoupage.

3. Yesterday, I met privately with Rey while Hijzen and Blumenthal were trying to agree on improved offers in next room. After they were finished we met together. Hijzen and Rey were shocked we did not accept disparity list they had tabled and Rey made very strong speech about it. I expressed shock at small agricultural improvement they have made and then made statement that this in effect indicated agriculture not being included in negotiations in meaningful way. Our position was quite clear that, unless this was done, we could not conclude Kennedy Round. Rey was rather defensive and said that of course if we wished to take responsibility for scuttling Kennedy Round that was our business. After this exchange we agreed to meet again today. It is my feeling that if further progress is not made today, that I will want to make a similar statement in multilateral steering committee tomorrow. It is now necessary to build up crisis atmosphere if we are to make progress.

---

[2] Telegram 3292 from Geneva, April 19. (Ibid.)

[3] April 24.

4. Meanwhile, I have come to conclusion that only way in which negotiations can be successfully concluded is to put together a package including all problem areas and at right time and in right manner, surface it. This would include a new approach to the grains situation that John[4] knows about and can discuss privately with you; secondly, a chemical package including decoupage; third, meaningful non-group agricultural offers and certain machinery offers from the EEC; and, fourth, on our part, acceptance of a good proportion of the disparity items indicated by the Community. My thinking on latter point is that even if we get most of what we want from EEC there will still be some imbalances. We could use this imbalance to accept a good portion of their disparity list without hurting our interests. I have asked a small group here to work privately on this question. I would come back and discuss proposal in Washington at the appropriate time. As we are working on these problems on a day-to-day basis I hope you will appreciate that anything I have said here must be kept entirely to yourselves and that circumstances here could shift quite rapidly. We will, in no way, in anything we do, commit ourselves in such a manner that the President's options are narrowed or either agriculture or industry is disadvantaged. I hope our friends in Brussels and EUR will appreciate the fact that, unless we go through certain crises here, there is absolutely no chance in my view of saving the Kennedy Round. Therefore, they must be patient as we try to work through these problems in as careful and sensitive way as possible.

Tubby

---

[4] Reference possibly is to Under Secretary of Agriculture John A. Schnittker.

---

338.   **Telegram From the Department of State to the European Office of the United Nations[1]**

Washington, April 21, 1967, 12:36 a.m.

179528. Ref: Geneva 3299.[2]

1. Wish to share with you results of two-hour conversations with group on basis your very helpful cable. Following comments are simply

---

[1] Source: Johnson Library, National Security File, Subject File, Trade Negotiations, Kennedy Round, "Potatoes," Box 47. Secret; Immediate; Limdis. Drafted by Enders (M) and Rehm (STR); cleared by Trowbridge (Commerce), Schnittker (Agriculture), Solomon (E), Roger Morris (S/S–S), and in substance by Eugene Rostow; and approved by Bator.

[2] Document 337.

exploratory and for your consideration in the light of your best estimate of the negotiating situation.

2. If we understand correctly your four-part package, U.S. would maintain substance of pre-November offer—as modified by pullback in steel, cotton textiles and synthetics and necessary adjustments to agriculture—and accept good portion of EEC disparities claims. In return we would need: (a) more food aid and higher grain prices, and SSR if we can get a useful number, (b) something solid from EEC in non-group agriculture along with better EEC machinery offers, and (c) satisfactory decoupage.

3. We share your view on how to handle disparities issue. Our export interest in most of these items is not great. Both hold-back on formal acceptance of any disparities list and size of list we finally do accept give us some leverage. However in light 1963 ministerial resolution EEC believes it has disparities coming to it anyway, and our final acceptance not—at least as seen from here—likely to buy very much.

4. Understand you will be pressing hard on grains, non-group agriculture, and decoupage: the US items in four-part package. Our own reading of domestic political situation is that the greatest need in agriculture is movement on non-group items (fruits and vegetables, poultry parts, tobacco) combined with a somewhat bigger food aid package and higher wheat prices. Based on cables from Geneva and Bonn it would appear too early to discuss grains arrangement without access. Would be grateful for your judgment of best SSRs obtainable in context on other objectives.

5. Questions we have been asking ourselves is whether chemicals decoupage—while clearly desirable—need be sine qua non and whether at some point we should not seriously consider trading it off for satisfaction of other US objectives, particularly in agriculture. Additional EEC concessions could not of course be conditional on elimination of ASP, but only on abandonment decoupage.

Basic question is whether for purposes of balance—at least as far as US concerned—chemical sector could be treated as self-contained. Obviously this would give Congress clear shot at ASP decision.

Answer appears to depend essentially on two factors: (a) how close could we come to balancing remainder of KR including agriculture if all chemicals set aside; clearly this is a function of what we could buy by giving up decoupage; (b) what are our chances of getting a decoupage whose KR slice would make significant contribution towards balance?

Our instinct is that it would be politically easier for President to confront a divided if unhappy chemical industry than an angry farm bloc. This does not mean that we would be disposed to take a long risk with Senate Finance Committee and confront them with fait accompli. It does mean that in our view Congress would be less concerned with exact statistics of KR minus all chemicals if basic TEA goals in agriculture as well as industry are met. Key judgment of course is what statistical result would meet TEA goals. We must not end up in situation where ASP action would appear necessary to balance otherwise defective KR. However, this does not mean that exact quantitative matching is necessarily required.

Would much appreciate your judgment of (a) what balance might look like on basis of your four point package if all chemicals treated separately; will cable for your comment our own estimate on basis imperfect data available here; (b) what we might be able to buy from EEC and how if we acquiesced in putting all chemicals into separate package; and (c) what are chances that KR slice of chemicals decoupage would in fact contribute significantly to balancing KR.

6. Agree wholly with your assessment of use of positive list as bargaining tactic before it is formally tabled and of danger that it could hurt US by irreversible fixing KR at lower level once list is tabled. Although we are not entirely clear on timing as you see it, we assume you would not wish in any case table list before results of April 24 EEC Council are known. Further question is how far US would attempt convey informally to EEC contents of four-part package prior to formal tabling of positive list. Assume you share our feeling that formal tabling of positive list is move of such importance that President would wish to have opportunity to go over whole KR picture and his options before we act. Given Adenauer funeral[3] he would not be able to focus on negotiations before Thursday or Friday next week.[4] This would not of course prevent you from showing US positive list to Rey on informal basis beforehand.

Rusk

---

[3] Funeral services for Konrad Adenauer, who died on April 19, were held at Bonn and Cologne on April 25.

[4] April 27–28.

339. Telegram From the Mission to the European Office of the United Nations to the Department of State[1]

Geneva, April 24, 1967, 1801Z.

3356. Roth to Bator.

1. At your discretion you may also wish to discuss some aspects of the following cable with Wirtz. Weaver of course is in on discussions here.

2. The full cables of last week undoubtedly have given you a feel as to the present state of play. Key questions now are how much the Community will move in non-group agriculture; what sort of a grains agreement we can put together, and whether the outline of the decoupage-chemicals package Rey has given faint signals he can accept can be negotiated beginning this week and will contain numbers that make sense or not. Hanging over all is the question of time.

3. Wyndham White still does not feel that member countries have any real sense of urgency of some of these problems. Yet, Mike[2] and I do [not] feel that any additional appeals to capitals at this point make any sense as our Embassies have discussed these problems ad nauseam.

4. Therefore, our strategy will be as follows: Tuesday,[3] intensive bilateral meetings with Community to see what Rey has brought back from Brussels. These will continue until Wednesday when there will be a Steering Committee meeting. By Thursday we, and most likely British, will then be ready to surface positive offers. Whether these will be formally tabled or given to Rey on a more informal basis will depend on degree of progress we have made and on tactics best suited to situation as of Thursday. These offers will be ad referendum and therefore will not commit any of us irrevocably. We intend to put the offer together in following manner:

The positive offer will basically be our original exceptions list converted into a positive list with a single multilateral addendum. This addendum will consist of our withdrawals. The withdrawals will be in three parts, i.e., a basic minimum list; secondly, a larger list; and, thirdly, a still larger list. These three sets of withdrawals will in turn be related to three sets of assumptions.

A. The first set of assumptions relate to the maximum package and, conversely to the smallest number of withdrawals, i.e., some agricultural items, man made fibers and an amended steel offer. It would involve, for instance, full US offers on aluminum to meet a 6 percent cut in the Community tariff, a meaningful grains agreement, EEC acceptance of all our key agricultural requests, a satisfactory decoupage package plus all our requested improvements in industry from all participants. We, in turn, would do the most we can on requests made to us. It would also include acceptance of a large part of Community's disparities request which amounts only to $100 million (U.S. trade) on a weighted trade coverage basis. ("50 percent equivalent" offers.)

B.   In second package, an additional group of withdrawals would be added to the above if maximum assumptions were not met. In it, we would assume no EEC or U.S. tariff cut on aluminum, that only industrial offers presently on table were possible and that we would accept a lesser figure in disparities, etc. We would still in the minimum package as in the maximum our basic non-group agricultural items from Community. [*sic*]

C.   Finally, in a third package, additional withdrawals would be added to above on assumption that chemicals were taken substantially out of the negotiation.

5.   The strategy here is to put a positive offer on the table that is realistic. We, the British, and Wyndham White all agree that this is only way that issues can be clarified before Council of Ministers meet next week. On other hand I would be concerned from a negotiating point of view if we table a positive offer that was expressed only in terms of what was already on the table. Therefore even the two smaller packages assume as a necessary minimum our basic agricultural requests to EEC. In addition it is important by using the technique of minimum and maximum packages to indicate the flexibility that is available for U.S. if the other countries can join with us in pushing toward a wider result. This also avoids the impression that the blame for no Kennedy Round or a mini Kennedy Round is placed at doorstep of U.S. I think, too, this approach would help Rey in his discussions with the Community and avoid any unpleasant surprises at last moment since the positive offer step is one that has to be gone through before the end of Kennedy Round in any case. I would expect to show this document to Rey and discuss it with him before it was officially tabled on Thursday.

6.   Even the minimum packages, i.e., package #2 and #3, contain our full demands in agriculture. This is necessary if we are going to continue to press the Community for adequate movement in this area. It could be possible, however, that we might come to Wednesday and find that so little progress has been made with the Community in agriculture and with all the countries concerned in grains that even such a minimum package was unrealistic. Tentatively, I would then think we should still table our positive offer alternatives indicating that minimum requirements of the second or third package must be met but saying that as there

is apparently no movement, I believe further discussion would not be productive and am therefore requesting a full Ministerial meeting after the Council of Ministries meeting next week.

7. I am not sure what agency problems may come up in putting these packages together this week. On the whole I think there is general agreement with the approach and with what should go in. I think on the whole we are working well as a team.

8. If this goes according to schedule, Mike and I will probably both come back Thursday night or Friday for discussions over weekend and into next Monday. I would hope we could have at least one discussion with the President at that time.

Tubby

---

340. Telegram From the President's Deputy Special Assistant for National Security Affairs (Bator) to the President's Special Assistant (Rostow), in Bonn[1]

Washington, April 24, 1967, 1808Z.

CAP 67324. From Bator to Rostow for the President. Subject: What we want from the Germans, Part II:[2] Kennedy Round.

After making clear to Kiesinger[3] that both Kennedy Round and liquidity negotiations represent major political events, and failure of either could lead to serious difficulties in US-European relations, you may wish to emphasize, with respect to Kennedy Round that:

1. We are really down to the wire. Essential that Germans push EEC partners into speeding up decision process, and giving EEC negotiators flexible enough mandate to permit striking of final bargains in Geneva. Must have initial understanding on shape of overall package by end of next week (May 6). Critical EEC Ministers meeting next Tuesday, May 2.

---

[1] Source: Johnson Library, National Security File, Subject File, Trade Negotiations, Kennedy Round, "Potatoes," [2 of 2], Box 47. Secret; Eyes Only. Rostow was with President Johnson in Bonn April 23–26 to attend the funeral of Konrad Adenauer, April 25.

[2] Part I was transmitted in CAP 67323 from Bator to Rostow, April 24. (Ibid.)

[3] President Johnson conferred with other heads of state and government in Bonn including West German Chancellor Kiesinger.

2. In agriculture, we need movement by EEC on two fronts:

(A) On grains, they should come up with combination of more food aid and access rule which will assure us growing commercial market. Critical relationship is between food aid commitment and percentage of EEC consumption reserved from non-EEC producers. (FYI. With present three million ton food aid proposed, EEC should reserve 13 percent of EEC markets for imports. So far, they have only offered three million tons and 10 percent. If EEC would agree to overall food aid program of five million tons, reservation of 12.5 percent for imports would be good enough. You may not wish at this stage to spell out these numbers but only to point out that they must go up both in food aid pledge and share of markets reserved for imports.)

(B) Single most important move needed in agriculture (since EEC has made some progress in grains) is significant reduction on items protected largely by tariffs, where EEC has made only nominal offers. Improvement by EEC on tobacco, turkeys, offals, fruits and vegetables per U.S. list advanced to EEC in March absolutely essential. U.S. must be able to show results in agriculture apart from grains.

(C) You might also say that you have instructed your negotiators to look carefully at EEC agricultural demands from U.S., including question of feed grain prices, to see what more we might offer.

3. The most important part of the industrial negotiation is an agreement in the chemical sector. Major reductions in chemicals on both sides, including our converting from American selling price, would probably result in a $300 million benefit surplus in our favor. Most of this necessary to right current overall imbalance between U.S. and EEC offers. We are willing to propose elimination of ASP to our Congress (you agreed to this in meeting with Roth), but politics are such that Congressional agreement much more likely if ASP package presented separately. (Problem with one package is Finance Committee resistance to gun-at-the-head proposal on ASP with entire Kennedy Round at stake.)

The two packages would yield respectively, (1) a Kennedy Round chemical tariff reduction which will contribute to overall Kennedy Round balance; and (2) a post-Kennedy Round legislative package negotiated now which would eliminate ASP in exchange for a significant additional EEC quid quo pro in chemicals. This second package must stand on its own.

4. Above has been fully cleared with Kennedy Round "command group" (Gene Rostow, Solomon, Schnittker, Rehm for Roth. Trowbridge out of town.).

341. Telegram From the Mission to the European Office of the United Nations to the Department of State[1]

Geneva, April 25, 1967, 2040Z.

3374. Roth to Bator.

1. We met this morning with Rey and Hijzen and explained our three list approach. Also said we would show them the lists before they are officially distributed. As indicated para. 3 Geneva 3356,[2] WW and the British feel strongly that Rey must have specific withdrawal lists in order to make governments focus on real situation at the Council meeting next Tuesday.[3] Rey himself has made (and repeated it again today) the point to us several times that by the end of the week he must know where we stand in each of our major areas of mutual concern.

2. At meeting today Rey welcomed way in which we planned to indicate our necessary withdrawals under different assumptions. He particularly appreciated fact that our presentation made clear what changes were being proposed in original U.S. offers and fact that our three package approach would allow EEC to see clearly range of possibilities (presumably so they could make intelligent choices). Our approach had added advantage of showing relationships between specific offers on both sides, i.e. what were consequences of EEC movement or lack of movement in a particular sector.

3. This favorable reaction was in sharp contrast to Rey's negative attitude toward British list which is in form of entirely new offer unrelated to previous offer—in other words, it is impossible to tell from British list what is being withdrawn without much difficult technical analysis. Rey also concerned that British positive offer list will probably be based only on what is not presently offered by EEC (not clear what assumptions UK will make about others).

4. This morning's meeting made a small breakthrough on chemicals. For first time Rey agreed to discuss overall package and decoupage concurrently. This is, of course, only on a hypothetical basis and I wouldn't want to make too much of it. We are having a technical chemicals meeting tomorrow on this basis and we may then get a better feel for possibilities in this sector with the EEC.

5. Re your 181484,[4] you correctly surmise that each package differed on the industrial side but was static in agriculture. The reason for

[1] Source: Johnson Library, National Security File, Subject File, Trade Negotiations, Kennedy Round, "Potatoes," Box 47. Confidential; Limdis–Potatoes; Flash. Passed to the White House.
[2] Document 339.
[3] May 2.
[4] Dated April 25. (Department of State, Central Files, FT 13–2)

this is that we have already retreated from our original non-group agricultural request to a hard-core list of some seventeen items. We do not expect to get all these but unless we get a sufficient number of them, it will create a very difficult political decision for the President in that he will be unable to say that agriculture had been included in a meaningful way by the EEC.

From a Congressional point of view, we need not only a grains agreement but something of value in each of the agricultural product groups, i.e. citrus, canned fruits, meats, etc. produced in the various states. Therefore, the minimum package we are suggesting goes considerably beyond the present token non-group agricultural offers of the EEC. To ask for even more in the maximum package is unrealistic. We would expect to negotiate something less in non-group agricultural than presently appears in the minimum package. You may call this a hard line but we are convinced it is the only possible line at this point. We intend to make it more attractive to the Community by tying certain possible industrial offers into the agriculture items. I do not agree that the abandonment of two package approach in chemicals would buy us anything significant in the agricultural section and, as you know, would open an almost unbridgeable gap in industry.

6.   The question of ASP is, of course, by far the most difficult in the negotiation. In my view, the one package approach raised two insurmountable obstacles in the negotiations. First, the Swiss and the British would probably have to withdraw other non-chemical industrial offers and put them in the second package because we and the Community would have withdrawn all chemicals offers in the KR and they could not rely on Congressional action to restore the balance. On our side, we would be going back on a commitment both the Governor and I gave the Congress, i.e., we would not put them in the position that unless Congress approves conversion of ASP, the KR would not be reciprocally balanced for the U.S. Let me say, however, I have no personal problem about being on a cut-off limb but I think this would substantially hurt the President's relationship with Congress. As you well know, many members of the Senate Finance Committee and some in Ways and Means have strongly objected to the Executive branch facing them with faits accompli. To put the burden of achieving a balance in the KR on the Congress will give them no real option and further exacerbate this situation.

7.   Secondly, and perhaps even more important taking the chemical section out of the KR and putting it into a separate package would upset our balance with the EEC, the UK and Japan by almost a half-billion dollars, as our chemical exports are that much greater than our imports. In effect, the third package we will be presenting on Thursday will indicate for everybody exactly what the one package approach would mean. In

other words, the balance problem is the same whether we take chemicals out of the KR and put it in a separate package or merely take it out period.

Tubby

---

342. Telegram From the President's Deputy Special Assistant for National Security Affairs (Bator) to the Special Representative for Trade Negotiations (Roth)[1]

Washington, April 26, 1967, 0055Z.

CAP 67348. Personal for Roth from Bator. Subject: Tactics on Positive List.

Recognize that your sense of tactical situation superior to any in Washington, but want to share with you my worries concerning tactics outlined in your message of yesterday.[2]

Basic question in my mind is utility of formal tabling of Alternative C: mini-package without chemicals. Understand your desire to shock your counterparts into realization that non-decoupage will result in birth of anemic mouse. Wonder, however, whether at political level in Brussels mini-package will appear not as threat but rather as opportunity for those who would prefer small bargain. Result could be EEC seizing on mini-package in industry with relief and turning energies to scaling down US demands in agriculture. By tabling mini-package as a formal alternative, we might appear to have handed EEC silver-platter opportunity to duck out of serious try for big package.

Alternative might be to table only larger Packages A and B, but to show mini-package to Rey as part of informal presentation. This might apply the threat to those susceptible—Rey and the Commission—without offering an attractive way out to those who prefer a small Kennedy Round and/or high chemical tariffs.

Again, defer to your judgement on this problem, but thought it might be of some value to you to know my concerns.

---

[1] Source: Johnson Library, Bator Papers, Chron Box 5. Secret; Eyes Only; Limdis; Potatoes.

[2] Document 339.

Your cable 3374[3] just arrived. What is risk that our British friends are about to spoil the party? Is there any way you and we might try to dissuade them? Would hope you might be able to take a crack at Richard Powell. Let us know if we can be of help on this end or in London.

Pending your return to Washington, prepared to cease fire on decoupage. Bring rifle, leave shotgun.

More seriously, please also come bearing latest statistics. We cannot go to President for decisions without them. Good luck.

---

[3] Document 341.

---

343.   Telegram From the Mission to the European Office of the United Nations to the Department of State[1]

Geneva, April 26, 1967, 1749Z.

3388. Roth to Bator.

1. Full report on this morning's Steering Committee meeting on its way,[2] Delegation returned from discussions in mood of deep pessimism.

Absolutely no sign of progress to date in any areas of U.S. interest. For example, this morning before the Steering Committee meeting Rabot met with us on grains and rejected our offer to bind loan rate on feed grains as a substitute for minimum price. He also reversed his position of several days ago that a grains agreement could be put together without the inclusion of feed grains. We have not surfaced our ultimate position in this area.

2. Rey in his main presentation at Steering Group gave a much clearer statement than even before that US should not expect any meaningful concessions in agriculture. He expressed particular concern over US indication that industrial offers might have to be withdrawn if agriculture offers not forthcoming and has refused to take seriously our position that the KR must include agriculture if it is to succeed at all.

---

[1] Source: Department of State, Central Files, FT 13–2 US. Confidential; Immediate; Limdis–Potatoes. Passed to the White House.

[2] Telegram 3390 from Geneva, April 26, reported on the April 26 GATT Steering Group meeting. (Ibid.)

3. In the Steering Group and privately with Rey, I have made it crystal clear that, in addition to movement in the industrial sector (particularly on chemicals), we must have something on grains and non-group agriculture. Otherwise there is no deal. We will continue to press hard for enough concessions from the Community to enable us to face inevitable Congressional criticism with a reasonable case. However, I believe the President will shortly be faced with having to choose between a KR with no offers of substance in non-group agriculture (and perhaps even no grains agreement) or no KR agreement at all.

4. We now intend to table the packages on Friday PM after prior discussions with Community and other delegations. I have duly noted concern about package number 3, and although I believe you have a point, feel we must probably go ahead with third package. However, I will keep you abreast of thinking as it develops.

5. At the next Steering Group meeting on Friday PM,[3] I intend to take up Wyndham White's suggestion that a full Ministerial meeting be tentatively scheduled, perhaps for May 6th. Today and tomorrow I will consult with other key delegations to line up support for this idea. I feel strongly that if no real progress is evident as a result of May 2 EEC Council meeting, time will have run out. At that point, I think our only hope is a full Ministerial meeting. Such meetings always carry risks but it seems to me that we cannot afford to let the KR go down the drain or deescalate into a mini-package without a political confrontation.

For obvious reasons, Rey will resist the participation of member state Ministers and HMG will have a special problem if they follow through on their apparent intention to make the formal EEC application announcement around May 8 (there may not even be a BOT President at the time). The reactions on Friday will determine our immediate tactics re a formalization of the Ministerial meeting request. Also, we will want Washington instructions to Ambassadors at the right time.

6. As of now Blumenthal and I will return Saturday morning and I would appreciate having a dinner meeting with the "command group" Sunday at my house. Suggest Rehm notify my wife and also that Leddy be invited. If at all possible Blumenthal, Bator and I should see the President on Monday. If the President then feels a restricted Cabinet meeting is necessary or desirable, that can be arranged Tuesday. We will return Tuesday night for Wednesday meeting.

7. Although our eyes are somewhat glassy and spirits low, nerves are in quite adequate shape. Food excellent and weather has improved.

Tubby

---

[3] April 28.

344.   Memorandum From the President's Deputy Special Assistant for National Security Affairs (Bator) to President Johnson[1]

Washington, April 28, 1967.

SUBJECT

Scheduling Kennedy Round Decisions

Roth and Blumenthal will be back from Geneva from this Sunday night until Tuesday afternoon. I think it important for Bill and Mike and myself to give you a *short briefing on where we stand, next Monday afternoon or, better, early Tuesday. This would not be a decision session.* During the *last* part of next week, or early the following, we will have to put to you what may be very tough decisions—and I think you will find it useful to have a few days to turn over the problem in your mind. Also, I will need to have your thinking about procedure, especially on consulting on the Hill.

Situation Report

The crucial Common Market Ministerial Meeting will be next Tuesday. Bill and Mike (who has been our negotiator in Geneva, and is first-rate) will be going back to Geneva to get the results on Wednesday/Thursday. These will face us with some major decisions. (I will probably ask for *decision* meetings with you for *late* next week, or early the following.)

It is too early to forecast where the EEC will come out. But I am afraid they might well stonewall on two critical issues: (1) tariff reductions on non-grain agriculture (fruits, vegetables, tobacco, etc.); (2) a two-part arrangement in chemicals, to permit us to deal with the American Selling Price problem (ASP) separately from the rest of the Kennedy Round. If they do stonewall, we will probably want to escalate to a Foreign Ministers Meeting in Geneva early in the week of May 8.

In the end, if there is really no give, the basic choice will be:

(1) Settle with what little we can get in non-grain agriculture from the EEC, plus a good industrial bargain. (We would have a reasonable grains agreement and fairly valuable agricultural offers from *other* than the EEC.)

(2) Pull agriculture out of the negotiations completely, and strike an industrial bargain—despite what we have said about insisting on agriculture as well as industry, and despite the legislative history.

(3) Let the Kennedy Round die with no bargain whatever.

---

[1] Source: Johnson Library, National Security File, Subject File, Trade Negotiations, Kennedy Round, "Potatoes," [2 of 2], Box 47. Secret; Strictly Eyes Only.

I will not here waste your time spelling out the pros and cons. There is still a chance that the choices will be more palatable. We will know better next week.

Procedure

Orville Freeman may call you to urge a larger cabinet session on Monday/Tuesday. I would strongly vote *against* this as premature. I think it important that Roth–Blumenthal have a chance to give you a quiet and full report. Roth is genuinely committed to your interests — he is truly Presidential, and your quarterback. In briefing you, he should not be inhibited by Orville arguing the Agriculture case—especially since if we have Agriculture we would have to have Commerce and Labor too, and there would be a serious problem of leaks. (By now I have done all my homework on this, so you will have an independent judgment.)

The time for hearing the views of your other advisers with special concerns will come when we face *decisions*—after we have the news from the EEC, and after I have given you a meticulous presentation of the elements of the problem. If Orville calls in about this, you might wish to say that you do *not* plan to make any decisions on Monday/Tuesday and, at the right time, will give him a full chance to speak his piece. (Incidentally, I am sure that in the clutch Orville personally will be eminently reasonable, despite enormous pressure from his bureaucrats. John Schnittker has been playing a most constructive role in our little command group, which has been working very well.)

Francis

1. Have Marvin set up an appointment with Roth, Blumenthal and Bator on Monday afternoon, or early Tuesday morning. (If possible, Tuesday morning would be better. Roth–Blumenthal will fill me in on Geneva after they get here Sunday night, and I can do a paper for night reading on Monday.)[2]

2. Speak to me

---

[2] This option is checked, and a handwritten note by the President's personal secretary reads: "phoned Bator that Pres. checked #1 and that memo was being given to M[arvin] W[atson] 4–28–67 5:40 p.m."

345.   Memorandum From the Special Representative for Trade Negotiations (Roth) to President Johnson[1]

Washington, May 1, 1967.

We are presently in the final, critical stage of the Kennedy Round. Chances are better than ever that an agreement can be achieved. However, there are still major unsolved problems that at least raise the possibility of failure.

The most important negotiating problems we face at this time are:

1.   Grains

We have been pushing for a grains agreement with a *minimum price of $1.70–1.75;* an access commitment with certain automatic safeguards; and a food aid contribution of at least six million tons of which the U.S. would take 40 percent. Although the Canadians and Australians have been increasingly rigid on price, I believe it is possible to finally agree on something between $1.70 and $1.75.

On *food aid* the Community has tentatively said they would consider a three million ton program and the British would accept their share. We think it is possible to get the Community to somewhere between four and six million tons which would mean a contribution of one million tons from them. The Japanese may also agree to a small program, but only at the very end of the negotiations.

The major sticking point between the U.S. and the EEC is their demand for a minimum price range on feed grains. The only answer we can presently see to this impasse is the possibility of dropping our demand for access and, in effect, having only a wheat agreement involving food aid and price. Our consultations on the Hill and with the trade would indicate that politically a complex access arrangement would be difficult to sell under any circumstances and that we might be better off with merely the two elements of price and food aid. Further Congressional consultations on this will be necessary.

Schnittker will be joining us in Geneva this week for a final attempt at putting an agreement together. Meanwhile, it could be that Pearson or Holt[2] might appeal to you to press for a higher price range, but anything higher than $1.75 is unrealistic.

---

[1] Source: Johnson Library, National Security File, Subject File, Trade Negotiations, Kennedy Round, "Potatoes," Box 47. Confidential. The source text is attached to Document 346.

[2] Lester Pearson, Prime Minister of Canada, and Harold Holt, Prime Minister of Australia.

2. Non-group Agriculture

Over the last two weeks we have gone much further than ever before in saying that we could not complete the Kennedy Round without some adequate offers from the EEC in the various areas of agriculture, i.e., canned fruit, offals, tobacco, tallow, etc. The Community negotiators have slowly reacted to this pressure by offering very small reductions in a number of hard core items. As of now, we have in excess of $200 million in trade offered which has a trade value of between $90 and $95 million. This is not enough, but we think by continuing pressure we can improve this somewhat.

Offers from non-EEC countries amount to approximately $400 million in agriculture.

3. Industry

There are a number of areas still to be negotiated out in industry, but I do not see any major problems in this area. We have pulled back our offers substantially in man-made fibers, and reduced the proposed cut in the new Long-Term Cotton Arrangement tariff from 50 percent to approximately 20 percent. Steel offers also have been reduced by almost 80 percent.

4. Chemicals

Perhaps the single most difficult problem other than grains lies in the chemical sector. Here we face the problem of *American Selling Price* which I discussed with you several weeks ago. We are maintaining that it will be necessary to bring back a separate package to the U.S. Congress and that it should include benefits both for the chemical industry and non-tariff barriers of interest to other segments of U.S. industry. The Europeans would prefer to put *the whole chemical sector* in the ad referendum package, but because our chemical exports are greater than imports this would create an additional imbalance in the Kennedy Round of almost a half billion dollars. We would then be in a position of saying to the Congress: "Unless you agree to the ASP conversion the U.S. will not have received a balanced deal in the Kennedy Round". We have consistently told Congress this would not happen, but rather that the Kennedy Round would be fully reciprocal. The package that we brought back to them on ASP would, in effect, stand on its own feet.

5. Reciprocity

Last week we submitted to the other participants two offers: One a maximum package and the other a minimum package, each one having what we believe to be a sufficient degree of reciprocity. It is our hope to negotiate something in between these two extreme approaches.

Although we cannot achieve exact reciprocity with each country— especially Japan—*overall* we would expect to have a balanced package.

Of a necessity, industry would pay for some of the benefits achieved for agriculture, but the payment should be kept within reasonable limits. The less-developed countries, of course, are not required to reciprocate in full what we are offering them and therefore there would be an imbalance in that area.

Schedule

The EEC negotiators have been resisting any terminal date for the negotiations. They have agreed to several, but have never been able to keep them. This is partly a result of their own internal difficulties in reaching common negotiating positions, but partly their belief that by pushing the U.S. against its deadline their negotiating position is improved.

We meet again in Geneva on Thursday and I would expect to say that we were still looking forward to the conclusion of the negotiations by Tuesday, May 9th. I would also like to add that after consultations in Washington I am able to report that Secretary Rusk would be available for a Ministerial meeting on that date if it were found necessary. A number of the other participants, including Japan, Canada, Australia and perhaps the Nordics may also indicate their desire for a final meeting at a Ministerial level. The Community, on the other hand, even if they finally agreed, would push for a later date. It would then be possible for us to allow a few more days and still keep to our timetable.

William M. Roth

---

346.   **Memorandum From the President's Deputy Special Assistant for National Security Affairs (Bator) to President Johnson**[1]

Washington, May 1, 1967, 10:15 p.m.

SUBJECT

Meeting Tomorrow on Kennedy Round (Bill Roth, Mike Blumenthal, Bator—11:30 a.m., Tuesday, May 2)[2]

---

[1] Source: Johnson Library, National Security File, Subject File, Trade Negotiations, Kennedy Round, "Potatoes," [2 of 2], Box 47. Confidential. The source text bears the handwritten notation "Mr. Rostow" in the upper right corner of the first page, presumably indicating this was his copy. It also bears numerous handwritten notations possibly by him.
[2] The President met with Roth, Blumenthal, and Bator on May 2 at 11:47 a.m. (ibid., President's Daily Diary), but no record of this meeting has been found.

Attached is a briefing paper from Bill Roth.[3] He and Blumenthal will be prepared to give you a full rundown on each issue as well as a general picture of the road ahead. All we will need from you is a general approval of our proposed tactics (summarized in #3 below). If you are pressed for time, the essentials are as follows:

1. *Status Report.* Roth and Blumenthal have conducted an effective campaign in the last week to convince the EEC we are near the end of our rope. They *may* be beginning to believe us. Their Ministers meet today and tomorrow; there is a *small* chance of significant movement on the key items—chemicals, grains, and agricultural tariffs. More likely, however, they will throw us a small bone or two and try to ignore our deadline. (Roth has said the negotiation must end by next week if we are to sign before the TEA runs out on June 30.)

2. *Major Issues.* Most of the elements of a reasonably successful Kennedy Round are present, but we are in deadlock—largely with the EEC—on two major fronts.

—*Grains.* Things are moving well on the food aid part of a grains agreement. We will have trouble with Canada and Australia on a minimum wheat support price, but Roth thinks this is manageable. We cannot, however, agree to the EEC demand for a support price for feed grains. The only way out is probably to drop our demand for a guaranteed percentage share of the EEC market ("access") in return for elimination of feed grains from the agreement. (This will take work on the Hill; Schnittker has already begun.)

—*Agricultural tariffs.* The EEC has been giving us progress on our "must" items in bits and pieces. We will probably get a tolerable deal in the end.

—*Chemicals.* We are still playing "chicken" with the Community on American Selling Price (ASP). They insist on putting the whole chemical sector into a single package which our Congress would vote up or down. We maintain we must separate out ASP items and reciprocal chemical concessions by the EEC into a *second* package which would stand on its own feet and could be presented to Congress separately. Roth is now convinced that the EEC will come around on this, but it could be the stopper in the whole Kennedy Round bottle. You will want to question him closely on the Congressional and other costs of conceding this point— and on what we could buy if we did.

3. *Tactics/Timing.* Assuming the current meeting of EEC Ministers doesn't produce significant movement, your Kennedy Round "command group"—including Roth and Blumenthal—recommends that Roth return to Geneva and announce that he is under instructions to

---

[3] Document 345.

leave for good on the evening of Tuesday, May 9. (Confronting the EEC with the limit is the only way to get them to face the tough political decisions necessary for a successful bargain.) Bill would say that if there were no agreement by May 9, the U.S. would consider the Kennedy Round a failure. He would add, however, that we are ready to join in a final meeting of Foreign Ministers the week of May 8–12 if other countries so desire—though we would be happy to strike a bargain before that if possible. We think there would be a groundswell for such a ministerial meeting, and that it would give us a pretty good chance of bringing the negotiations to a successful close.

Francis

---

347. **Memorandum From the Special Representative for Trade Negotiations (Roth) to President Johnson**[1]

Washington, May 2, 1967, 11:10 a.m.

SUBJECT

Supplemental Authority to Offer Tariff Concessions in the Kennedy Round

Request for Negotiating Authority

In order to improve our ability to obtain concessions from certain countries in the Kennedy Round, I request that you authorize me, under the Trade Expansion Act of 1962 (TEA), to offer certain new tariff concessions. Although we consider that our present offers to the countries to which I should like to make improved offers are already more valuable than their present offers to us, the modest new offers which I am recommending should help us to get those countries to make the important adjustments necessary to bring their offers into balance with ours.

Discussion

The contemplated new U.S. offers, set forth in Tab A,[2] are intended principally to benefit Italy. Italy has already been hit harder than most

---

[1] Source: Johnson Library, Bator Papers, Kennedy Round, March–April 1967, Box 12. Confidential. The source text was transmitted to President Johnson under cover of a May 4 memorandum from Bator, in which Bator strongly recommended the President grant Roth the authority to make further tariff offers involving glassware, gloves, and certain noncompetitive woolens. (Ibid., May–June 1967, Box 12)

[2] None of the tabs was found with the source text.

other major participants by our having withheld a number of industrial and agricultural offers. By improving our offers of benefit to Italy, we should encourage the Italian Government to be more agreeable to concessions that would increase our exports to Italy and to urge the other European Economic Community (EEC) member states to take a more liberal position on EEC offers to the United States. We are particularly interested in getting new agricultural offers from the EEC. The contemplated new U.S. offers would also help us in our negotiations with Sweden, the United Kingdom, Canada, and Japan.

Glassware—TSUS 546.35 and 546.45–.57: To benefit Italy and Sweden, I request authority to offer a reduction of approximately 20 percent in the duty on "bubble glass" and to make an overall improvement— involving a partial withdrawal of existing offers but a more than offsetting new offer on other glassware items, including ashtrays, tableware, and perfume bottles.

The new U.S. tariff rates for these glassware articles would provide a very small reduction in duties on items that compete with those produced in West Virginia and other Appalachian areas. Because the glassware industry in this region has been beset by economic difficulties, we believe that the tariff protection which it presently enjoys should be substantially maintained. The principal item for which we would be maintaining protection is found in a low-price bracket of certain "other" glassware; the rate of duty of 50 percent ad valorem would be maintained.

In order to simplify customs administration, the number of different rates of duty that apply to the sector would be reduced by the new proposal.

In explanation of the proposal set forth fully in Tab A, the substance of the glassware proposal is contained in the simplified table under Tab B1.

Gloves—TSUS 705.40–.78: To strengthen our negotiating position with Italy, and consequently with the EEC, I request authority to improve our present offer on certain women's and men's leather gloves and, in so doing, to simplify customs administration by establishing new tariff classifications that would reduce the number of tariff rates applicable in this sector.

Because the U.S. leather glove industry, concentrated in Gloversville, New York, has been regarded as competitively weak, early in our negotiations we withheld fully offers on certain items and made very small offers on other items. The proposed offer would result in a reduction in tariffs of approximately 18 percent, setting aside a small measure of adjustment resulting from the revision of the classifications according to price categories.

Taking account of factors of competition and of customs administration, the proposed offers would entail a reduction in the number of tariff rates among the related items and a revision of the price brackets. In place of the present complex rate structure, the new offers would provide for two rates for men's gloves ($5 per dozen pairs for gloves valued not over $20 per dozen pairs, 25 percent ad valorem for those over $20 per dozen pairs) and four rates for women's gloves (specific rates in two low-price brackets and ad valorem rates in two high-price brackets).

Subject to formal confirmation by the Tariff Commission, we propose the conversion of some tariff rates that are involved in the proposal, that is, changing some dollars-per-dozen-pairs duties in percentages of value duties in some cases and the reverse in other cases. The particular conversions of rates are noted in Tab B2.

Woolens—TSUS 372.30, 372.40, 372.45, 374.50, ex 380.60, 382.48, ex 382.57: To benefit Italy and the United Kingdom, I request authority to offer modest reductions in the tariffs on such woolen items as mufflers, hosiery, cashmere sweaters, and infants' outerwear.

These items, which will be of considerable interest to these two countries, have been carefully chosen and are among the woolen imports to which the domestic industry is least sensitive. It is therefore believed that the negotiating advantage of offering concessions on these items outweighs any political disadvantages of doing so.

Dicyandiamide—TSUS ex 425.40 and Limestone (imported for the manufacturers of cement—TSUS ex 513.34: The Bureau of the Budget will shortly recommend that you approve enrolled bill H.R. 286. This bill would permit the President, under the authority of the TEA, permanently to eliminate the duty on dicyandiamide and limestone pursuant to a trade agreement, without having to satisfy the usual prenegotiation and staging requirements of the TEA.

Subject to your approval of this bill, I request authority to offer the permanent elimination of duty on these two items. They are both of interest to the Canadians, and we have determined that we can expect reciprocal concessions from the Canadians. As a result of Congressional consideration of this bill, we are satisfied that there is no domestic opposition to the duty-free treatment for these items.

Titanium—TSUS 629.15: To respond to the Japanese request I request authority to make a small offer on titanium, so that the rate on unwrought titanium (TSUS 629.15) would be reduced by 10 percent to match the existing rate of 18 percent ad valorem on wrought titanium (TSUS 629.20).

To the extent that there is a national security need to maintain protection on titanium in either or both forms, that protection would be at least as effective as at present by bringing the rate of duty on the unwrought material down to the level of the rate of the processed product.

After receiving from the Office of Emergency Planning (OEP) its view that a tariff concession would be undesirable on national security grounds, we decided to make no offer on either unwrought or wrought titanium. We recently asked OEP to review the situation and have obtained its concurrence to the 10 percent reduction in the rate of the unwrought product.

The present rate relationship is perverse since the protection for the processed material is less than the burden imposed on the material used in that processing.

Congressional Aspect: Of the articles dealt with in this memorandum, only the glassware, gloves, and woolen items appear to present any political problems.

We believe that, although there is considerable Congressional concern about textile imports, concessions on the few woolen items should not be troublesome, because they do not, for the most part, compete with domestic production. The gloves and glassware, on the other hand, are politically sensitive, since imports are increasing steadily and since the domestic articles are made in Gloversville, New York, and Appalachia, respectively, which are both depressed areas. Accordingly, while it appears that imports will rise steadily whether tariff concessions are granted or not, Congressional criticism can be expected.

Legal Authority: All the applicable prenegotiation requirements of the TEA for making these offers have been met. The tariff concessions on the items in question would be made under the authority of section 201 of the TEA, and all, with the exception of dicyandiamide and limestone, would be subject to the requirement in the TEA that concessions be put into effect in five annual stages.

Any trade agreement which is negotiated on the basis of the offers for which I now seek your authorization will be concluded subject to your final approval.

Recommendation

With the concurrence of other agencies concerned, I recommend that you authorize me, as your Special Representative for Trade Negotiations, to offer the concessions listed in Tab A in addition to concessions on these articles that you have previously authorized be offered.

William M. Roth

348.   Editorial Note

A disagreement arose among U.S. officials over U.S. offers at Geneva on the tariff on canned hams. As of May 5, 1967, the United States had offered to cut the present duty of 4.5 percent by 50 percent, and to bind the duty at that level; that is, not to raise the duty without compensating foreign suppliers. In a May 5 memorandum to the President, Francis Bator indicated that Secretary Freeman wanted to withdraw both offers, whereas "Roth, Blumenthal, Rusk, Katzenbach, Solomon and the rest of us" believed that the United States could "afford to withdraw the offer to *cut* the present tariff, but we must not withdraw the offer to *bind* the tariff," because an adverse reaction by the Nordic countries in support of Denmark's interest in a lower tariff could throw agricultural tariff negotiations into disarray. Bator believed that the Vice President favored "the compromise: bind but don't cut." (Johnson Library, National Security File, Subject File, Trade Negotiations, Kennedy Round, "Potatoes" [2 of 2], Box 47)

Following a May 6 meeting with Secretary Freeman, Katzenbach, Roth, Blumenthal, Bator, and Solomon, Vice President Humphrey pointed out that the President had to decide the issue, as Freeman opposed talks on canned hams, while "all the others feel canned hams imports present no problems," since "there is no effective lobby on this commodity such as on beef." Humphrey suggested binding the present tariff. (Memorandum from Jim Jones to the President, May 6; ibid.) Bator, the Geneva negotiators, and the Vice President recommended that the President approve the suggested compromise. (Memorandum from Jim Jones to the President, May 8; ibid.) In telegram 190533 to Geneva, May 9, Bator reported that the "President had decided that you may maintain offer binding on canned hams, but not duty cut." (Ibid.)

349.   Telegram From the Mission to the European Office of the United Nations to the Department of State [1]

Geneva, May 9, 1967, 1210Z.

3557. BUSEC. LUXCO. GATT for Bator from Roth for STR. Subj: KR Steering Group meeting morning May 9.

1. Steering Group met 9 AM May 9 in wake-like atmosphere hear report of failure of US and EEC to reach agreement.

2. Roth explained US and EEC had carried on extensive bilaterals on theory if impasse on major issues between them broken, rest of negotiations would have fallen into place. Reported that both EEC and US had tried to reach compromise but this had not proved possible. While there are not many issues, those which exist are difficult, e.g., decoupage on chemicals and improvement in non-group agricultural offers. On grains US had suggested "revolutionary" idea of giving up request for access and confining grains arrangement to agreement on price and food aid. This based on assumption that effective access and continuity of access commitments from the UK and EEC not obtainable. US, of course, still interested in meaningful access commitments if obtainable. New approach made in effort to break through on grains but EEC apparently had problems with it.

3. Re future procedure, Roth said US would be available all day and night if necessary for bilaterals and multilaterals. He emphasized importance of our having ad referendum agreement by this evening or tomorrow morning on major issues; failure to do so would put us in impossible position in view of our timing problem. He also suggested Steering Group meet at end of day to review situation.

4. Rey said he wanted to refrain from making detailed comments on previous evening's discussion because he didn't want to spoil chances of agreement which he still thought possible. He stated that Community had accepted WW compromise proposal on chemicals whereas US had not been able to. With respect to US grains proposal, he said proposal had come at 3 o'clock in the morning, and the Community needed time to think about it before being able to respond.

5. He suggested WW schedule resumption of bilateral meeting to determine where matters stand. Rey said he had to leave at 6 PM in order to be able to report to the Commission tomorrow morning and to EEC

---

[1] Source: Department of State, Central Files, FT 13–2 US. Confidential; Flash. Received at 9:11 a.m. Repeated to Bern, Bonn, Brussels, Copenhangen, The Hague, Helsinki, London, Luxembourg, Oslo, Ottawa, Paris, Rome, Stockholm, Tokyo, and Vienna, and passed to the White House and USIA.

Perm Reps and Council on Wednesday and Thursday[2] and would return to Geneva Thursday night. He pointed out that in any event it would not have been possible to solve steel problem by this evening since UK was going to Cabinet for more authority. He thought that after consultations with governments, delegations might return with fresh ideas. He thought that three to four more days of negotiations were reasonable and suggested in meantime that we aim at finishing the negotiations by Sunday or Monday.

6.   Roth replied that unless the main outlines of the US–EEC package had been agreed by tonight or tomorrow morning he saw no possibility of continuing on Thursday or Friday.

7.   Swiss urged WW to use his vast authority and propose an overall package for delegations to refer back to capitals. Nordics referring to Roth's insistence on ad referendum US–EEC agreement by tonight, asked whether Rey could delay his departure and/or US timetable couldn't be stretched. Roth explained US didn't expect have detailed agreement by this evening, but if major issues unresolved would be impossible to conclude negotiations in time. He urged using rest of day as fruitfully as possible and reviewing situation at end of day.[3]

8.   Canadians said would be a pity for other countries to be prisoners of US and EEC because of their schedules. Swiss supported this idea and said that if Rey considered consultations with Ministers desirable, this possibility should not be eliminated. Steering Group convened again for 5 o'clock this afternoon. Grains meeting convened at 10 am to hear explanation of new US proposal. At end of meeting Japanese circulated new request on steel to us.

Tubby

---

[2] May 10 and 11.

[3] Apparently in response to the impasse with the EEC reported in this telegram, Bator cabled back to Roth "our firm view" that "we must avoid breaking off negotiations" in the face of Rey's requirements. "The President must not be in a position of risking failure of 5 year effort to make good on an arbitrary deadline when EEC can point to some movement and when Rey can legitimately claim need for personal consultation with his ministers." Bator added that Secretary Rusk wanted Roth to check with him and the President before any break off. (Telegram 190345 to Geneva, May 9, 11:24 a.m.; Department of State, Central File, FT 13–2 US) In telegram 3573 from Geneva, May 9, Roth responded that "happily I had not pulled the plug" on the talks and that the EEC and U.S. negotiators had agreed to a statement by Wyndham White that all parties accepted the final concluding date of Sunday, May 14. (Ibid.)

350. Telegram From the Mission to the European Office of the United Nations to the Department of State[1]

Geneva, May 10, 1967, 1607Z.

3597. GATT for Freeman from Schnittker. Ref: Geneva 3538.[2] Subject: Steering Committee meeting, end of day, Tuesday May 9.

1. Meeting scheduled close KR marathon ended with proposal by WW to not consider KR dead but give countries, especially EEC and UK, opportunity consult Ministers as requested and return Geneva Thursday[3] night for continuous talks beginning Friday morning ending Sunday night May 14.[4] Predictably this would mean about dawn Monday May 15. In a sense, this consistent with US agreed deadline per Washington consultations last week which set weekend as absolute finish KR. It does not, however, include possible Ministerial within deadline. I continue to believe Ministerial probably essential, especially as leverage during final three days and as means of ending KR successfully or unsuccessfully. Roth tells me possibility Ministerial still open.

2. In final mission consultations here just prior last Steering Group meeting which set new deadline I argued strongly Sunday deadline be met, including possible Ministerial to be held Sunday if needed after two days of talks following EEC and UK consultations. Very important in my view stick to dates once set and keep pressure on all negotiators, especially Rey who rejects idea of Ministerial but who has finally accepted Sunday night as ending date for negotiations. Also need pressure on countries where we have bilateral problems, like Canada and Japan on grains.

3. Re grains, US advanced new position on access 3 A.M. Tuesday, May 9, after five-hour deadlock meeting on chemicals and non-group agriculture. Community expressed shock we would do this so late in negotiations. We repeated had concluded no meaningful access possible and no point in negotiating for worthless concession. Community showed softness on food aid commitment after our access move, but my judgment this not serious. Our move on access should terminate further discussion of need for coarse grain price range but EEC may press this again. In case that discussion resumed, want your advice soonest whether US binding of minimum loan rate one dollar per bushel corn,

---

[1] Source: Department of State, Central Files, FT 13–2 US. Confidential; Immediate; Limdis. Passed to the White House and USIA.
[2] Telegram 3538 from Geneva, May 8. (Ibid., SCI 30–3 WMO) Reference may be to telegram 3588 from Geneva, May 10. (Ibid., Eyes Only Reels)
[3] May 11.
[4] See footnote 3, Document 349.

average farm location, for next three years politically plus or minus at home. Unless we can buy something very valuable for this, assume this of negative value. My concern is that farmers who today have $1.05 loan rate will not be overjoyed if we say we will not cut them below one dollar for next three years. Hence I conclude should not consider this, but would value Washington advice.

4. Re food aid, have advanced three-year formula 4.5, 5.0, 5.5 million tons over three-year agreement with country division as proposed earlier. Some objection food aid no longer relevant grains agreement if access not included. US and Canada met this point sharply. Doubt this major problem.

5. During next two days will continue detailed talks bilaterally to set stage for final grain settlement, assuming chemicals etc. settled. Key questions will be: (1) to get Canada down from $1.75–1.77 for US ordinary at Gulf and UK and Japan up from $1.70 and solve difficult price differential questions at same time; (2) make sure our need for "loose" interpretation and role of minimum indicator prices is accepted; (3) attempt minimize possibility last minute fight by Australians regarding basing point system; (4) lay groundwork for retention negotiating rights under standstill agreements with EEC and insure that other partners, i.e., UK and Japan, accept fact that grains agreement will not impair existing duty concessions on grain.

6. By now you have seen Geneva 3538 [3588?] reporting the complete deadlock with EEC on non-group agriculture. They remain principal problem in this area although there are some problems with others.

7. I am concerned about the fuzzy nature of these EEC negotiations. We will have a struggle with them. In next meeting they may not improve, and may even withdraw some or all of their offers in response to our balancing offer given them Monday night. In that case, struggle would be over getting more EEC offers put on table while holding line to keep US offer list from becoming unbalanced in their favor.

8. The background here is that the US had put revised offer on table to EEC at $150 million value in expectation of EEC improvement to $200 million. This would have required an improvement by EEC from $23 million already tabled to $200 million. Before deadlock EEC had offered on ad referendum basis improvement to roughly $100 million. On basis this situation US indicated to EEC that it would have to reduce value its offer to roughly $75 million. It was this US attempt to improve EEC offers to $220 million by reducing US offer in accordance with 4:3 ratio which resulted in deadlock.

9. Questions will be (1) can KR be completed "with substantial agricultural settlement" if EEC offer remains at $100 million, and (2) if EEC improves value of offer will US be able to maintain the indicated 4:3 ratio? I foresee great pressure from EEC to have US put offers on 4:4 ratio

or more despite fact we have repeatedly said 4:3 ratio in favor US appropriate balance, and in spite fact 2:1 ratio justifiable considering US export trade position, possible offer both sides, depth of cut, and other possible negotiating measurements.

10. I consider ham withdrawal still open question,[5] especially in view of EEC situation. If EEC offers not substantially improved, I would continue recommend hams be withdrawn. I recognize Ambassador Roth has full authority this item.

Tubby

---

[5] See Document 348.

---

351. Memorandum From the President's Deputy Special Assistant for National Security Affairs (Bator) to President Johnson[1]

Washington, May 10, 1967, 11:30 p.m.

SUBJECT

Your meeting tomorrow on the Kennedy Round (11:15 AM): Vice President; Rusk, Eugene Rostow, Solomon; Freeman; Wirtz; Trowbridge; John Rehm (for Bill Roth); Bator

Where We Stand

It now appears that the negotiations will end Sunday night[2]—win or lose. The Common Market is having its final ministerial meeting today and tomorrow. We expect to get final instructions to Bill Roth by tomorrow afternoon, our time.

We can now see the outlines of what is possible in terms of a final bargain. Essentially, they are as follows:

World-Wide Balance. In very rough terms, the U.S. will probably:

—be on about even terms with the EEC and the other continental Europeans, with large tariff cuts all around;

---

[1] Source: Johnson Library, National Security File, Subject File, Trade Negotiations, Kennedy Round, "Potatoes" [2 of 2], Box 47. Confidential. Rusk's copy of this memorandum bears the handwritten note: "Eyes Only for Sec Rusk (thru Mr. Read)" and bears Rusk's handwritten initials.

[2] May 14.

—give more than we get from Japan (the Japanese sell us so much more than we sell them in industry that arithmetic balance is practically impossible);

—give more than we get from the UK;

—with luck, be only slightly behind with the Canadians—after some very hard bargaining;

—vis–à–vis the rich countries *as a whole*, be in appreciable deficit in industry (Japan, UK, Canada), but in considerable surplus in agriculture (counting the grains agreement);

—vis–à–vis the less-developed countries (which all the rich countries have agreed to exempt from reciprocity) we will have offered concessions on some $80 million worth of temperate "competitive" imports and $260 million of non-competitive tropical products.

The calculations on which the above is based are pretty arbitrary. They are based on the value of imports covered by a particular tariff concession, counted at full value for a 50% tariff cut, half-value for 25%, etc. On this basis, our total balance with the advanced countries will be some $600 million in the red. However, in my view, this reflects a strong conservative bias in the method of estimation. Though I cannot be sure, I think that the final numbers on which the *public* debate will focus will be more favorable to us.

In any case, in terms of the real economic effect on our exports and imports, any such number is terribly misleading. At worst, for example, a $600 million imbalance would only mean that in five years—after the tariff cuts are fully in effect—our total annual export surplus might be reduced by some $25 million on a total now running between $4–7 billion. Nevertheless, there will be a public relations problem, and we shall have to use some skills and good sense in constructing our case.

Key Issues

1. *Chemicals.* As you know, we have pressed the EEC to accept a two-package approach to the American Selling Price (ASP) problem. They have finally agreed to two packages. They propose that in the *first* package (which would be part of the Kennedy Round itself) we would cut tariffs on all chemicals by 50% and the EEC would cut by 20%. This would give us "balance" in terms of trade coverage because our chemical exports to the EEC are three times as large as our chemical imports.

In the *second* package, which would stand on its own feet and require legislation, we would eliminate ASP and cut chemical tariffs further—to a 20% ceiling, with some exceptions for dyes and certain drugs. In return, the Community would cut *their* chemical tariffs by an additional 30%.

In combination, the two packages would be a good bargain for us. However, the apparent disparity in the *first* package between our cut of 50% and the Community cut of 20% *will* cause some trouble on the Hill. Roth will try very hard to narrow the spread to 25 or even 20 percentage points. *But we should give Bill guidance tomorrow on whether failure to get EEC to move by Sunday night is serious enough political business to force us to scuttle the negotiations.* (I myself certainly do *not* think so, but you will want to get the views of the others around the table.)[3]

2. *Non-Grain Agriculture.* After three years of stonewalling, the EEC has finally offered benefits valued at about $100 million (an average tariff cut of about 12%). This corresponds to cuts on our side of about the same size. (Freeman may offer a complicated argument for further withdrawals on our part; the rest of us believe this would involve a serious risk of a general unravelling.)

The question you should address tomorrow is whether a bargain of this size is enough to avoid a major political war with the farm community. (It is relevant here that the agricultural benefits we stand to receive from others than the EEC are substantial.)

The Congress

We should decide tomorrow how and when to bring key people on the Hill into the picture. We should probably include the leadership, Bill Roth's Congressional advisers (Senators Smathers, Talmadge, Ribicoff, Williams (Del.) and Carlson; Congressmen King and Curtis), and other leading people on Ways and Means and Finance. You may want to chair a meeting on Friday or Saturday, with the Vice President, Rusk et al. to back you up. Alternatively, you may prefer to have us speak to a very few key individuals now, and to leave the general consultations for later when we have a more precise package to sell. (In any case, it will be almost impossible to make any *major* changes in the bargain at this stage without risking the whole negotiation.)

Because of the history of ASP (the rubber footwear war, etc.), we should expect a fair amount of heat on chemicals even if we get the EEC to move somewhat more in our direction. In my judgment, we have enough ammunition to counteract it. But you will want to go over this ground carefully tomorrow with the Vice President and Trowbridge.

Apart from the general problem of agriculture, textiles will be the other hot issue. The details of our present textile offers are at Tab B.[4] We are presenting a very small target on cotton and wool. However, on manmade fibers, our offer—while small and defensible—will trigger some flack. I telegraphed Roth this morning to hold back everything on manmades that can be withdrawn without pulling the house down.[5] In fact, however, I don't expect that he will be able to take much off the table

---

[3] An attached paper, Tab A, entitled "Chemicals," provides additional details on the negotiations on this subject.

[4] Not printed.

[5] Telegram 191229 to Geneva, May 10. (Department of State, Central Files, FT 13–2 US)

without risking wholesale unravelling. My own view is that we can also manage this issue—the industry is now crying wolf, but they simply do not have a case that they are in serious trouble. As you know, however, they have a lot of friends on the Hill.

Procedure

Tomorrow morning I will give you an agenda for the meeting with some key questions you may want to ask. I don't think any of your advisers will recommend that we scuttle the negotiations on any of the above issues. Orville Freeman may be worried about the non-grain package and the relatively toothless grains agreement. He may advise that we insist upon a ministerial meeting in Geneva to exert maximum political leverage on the EEC and others and to make a show to the home folks. The Secretary of State and Bill Roth believe—and I very much agree—that a ministerial would be a mistake except perhaps as a very last resort. It would give the French an excellent opportunity to subvert the negotiation and it might well result in disintegration of all we have hammered out over the last four years. I don't know how Wirtz and Trowbridge will vote if this issue comes up, but I doubt that either will be very strongly in favor of a meeting.

Recommendation

In summary, my vote is that we push as hard as we can between now and Sunday but that, in the end, we initial the bargain Sunday night even if the more pessimistic assumptions about the EEC position prove out.

In economic terms, failure of the Kennedy Round could lead to the kind of commercial warfare in which we, as a trade surplus nation, have a great deal to lose.

The central point here is not primarily the level of tariffs. Rather, it is holding to a reasonable set of trade rules without which international trade would become jungle warfare, commodity by commodity, and country by country. I think that the failure of the Kennedy Round would risk just that kind of deterioration into spiraling protectionism, with parliaments holding the whip hand (e.g., the present sugar situation).

The direct political implications of Kennedy Round failure would, in my judgment, be even more serious. It would encourage strong forces now at work to make the EEC into an isolationist, anti-US bloc, while, at the same time, further alienating the poor countries. None of the above issues are worth these risks. Nor would they give us a plausible public basis for blowing up the negotiations.

But this is one man's view, and I am not the one who will have to face most of the music.

Francis

352. Memorandum of Telephone Conversation[1]

May 11, 1967.

PARTICIPANTS

Ambassador William M. Roth
Honorable Francis M. Bator

Bator began by reporting that the meeting with the President went well. The President had been fully briefed and went into the issues in considerable detail during the 90-minute discussion. At the end of the meeting the President asked all the participants whether they were in favor of initialing the agreement by Sunday night[2] on the basis of the offers presently on the table. All voted yes. However, Bator emphasized that the President had not given his final decision. Nevertheless, Bator was confident that it would be affirmative and that he would be receiving it some time tomorrow or Saturday.

Subject to receiving the President's final okay, Bator said that Roth could in the final analysis settle on the present basis, assuming that there was no further deterioration in the offers of the other countries. In particular, Roth could finally agree to 50/20 in the first ASP package if all efforts to move the EEC up fail. Moreover, Roth could go as low as 28% on dyes if something valuable could be bought in return. Roth said he appreciated this, but that he was going to try to do better than 50/20 and that he would not go to 28% on dyes unless be could get something very valuable in return.

Bator stressed that perhaps the key element in the affirmative vote at the Presidential meeting was the fact that we were just about in balance overall with the EEC. He therefore stressed how important it was that there be no slippage in the next three days. Roth said he understood this very well but pointed out that we would have to accept some disparities which might create a final imbalance of about 100 million. Bator asked whether such a figure included the grains arrangement and Roth said it did not because, unlike the U.K., the EEC exported as well as imported grains and therefore the Delegation had not been giving a value to the grains arrangement in our balance with the EEC.

Bator urged Roth to push very hard to try to reduce the imbalance with the U.K., Japan, Canada, and the so-called borderline countries, pointing out that imbalance with the U.K., for example, was quite large.

---

[1] Source: Johnson Library, Bator Papers, Kennedy Round, May–June 1967, Box 12. Secret; Eyes Only. Drafted by Rehm on May 12 and approved by Bator. Ambassador Roth was in Geneva; Bator was in Washington.

[2] May 14.

Roth said that they would make a serious attempt to do so, but he could not see much give. He said that he was surprised that the imbalance with the U.K. was that great, and Bator said that he would immediately send out a cable setting out the two tables we had worked up in the last several days, and which were used at the meeting with the President.[3] The first showed our balance with the EEC, and the other the balance with all the major participants. Roth said that would be useful.

With respect to the U.K. in particular, Roth said that they had been completely unhelpful recently and that he was going to make a very strong attempt to get them to improve their offers. Bator asked whether there was anything we could do in Washington about this. Roth explained that he was expecting to receive tomorrow morning a reply to a personal note he had sent to Sir Richard Powell.[4] He thought it best to wait until he got the reply and then he would be in touch with us some time tomorrow. We could then decide what steps might be taken to make a very high political approach on this matter.

Bator stressed that the most serious domestic political problem facing us during the negotiations concerned textiles, and, in particular, man-made fibers. He therefore urged Roth to do everything he could to reduce our man-made offers without pulling down the house. Roth said he understood the problem completely and that he would have his people look at all offers on man-made fibers in this light.

Bator said that the groundwork was being laid for extensive Congressional consultations and a general press campaign following the completion of the negotiations on Sunday. Roth thought that was fine.

Bator asked Roth if he had any news with respect to the EEC Council meeting in Brussels other than that which had been reported over the ticker. Roth said that he did not and we would have to wait until he saw Rey before he knew just what the Council had done.

In conclusion Bator said that the scrambler had worked well and they should try and talk again tomorrow some time early in the afternoon Washington time, and Roth agreed.

---

[3] Reference is to telegram 192864 to Geneva, May 11, 9:26 p.m. (Department of State, Central Files, FT 13–2 US)

[4] Roth's note to Sir Richard has not been found.

353. Memorandum From the President's Deputy Special Assistant for National Security Affairs (Bator) to President Johnson[1]

Washington, May 11, 1967, 4:45 p.m.

SUBJECT

Procedure for Kennedy Round Wrap-up

As I understand your instructions, we will proceed as follows:

1. Except for some quiet backgrounding at Hot Springs by Rusk, Trowbridge, Solomon, et al., we will keep generally quiet until after the deadline on Sunday night. I believe all of your advisers are agreed that the risk of weakening Roth's negotiating hand is too great for us to blanket the town with the proposition that we have a good balanced bargain.

Yes
No
Speak to me[2]

2. *Congressional Consultation.* It is the Vice President's view that a joint meeting with the Leadership, and key people from Finance, Ways and Means, Foreign Relations, and Agriculture would involve too many people—that we need intimate meetings, not a large party. His suggestion would be that we take it in three bites:

i. A meeting with Roth's Congressional delegates, who have a statutory mandate to follow this negotiation. If your schedule permits, we might set this up for sometime Monday. It would involve: Senators Smathers, Talmadge, Ribicoff, Williams (Del.), and Carlson, and Messrs. King and Curtis.

Yes
No
Speak to me

ii. A Leadership breakfast Tuesday morning, with Wilbur Mills added. (I suspect that Mills will be the real swing man in the House; you might want to have a telephone conversation with him first. Dirksen is likely to be the principal antagonist.)

Yes
No
Speak to me

---

[1] Source: Johnson Library, National Security File, Subject File, Trade Negotiations, Kennedy Round, "Potatoes," [1 of 2], Box 47. Confidential. An attached undated note from Bator to the President reads: "The original of this went to you yesterday afternoon. Since you may have missed it in night reading, I attach a copy. I need your instruction on some of the items as soon as possible."

[2] None of the options in this memorandum was checked.

iii. A meeting, later on Tuesday, with key people on Finance, Ways and Means, Foreign Relations, Foreign Affairs, and the two Agriculture Committees. A proposed list is at Tab A.[3]

Yes

No

Speak to me

The *alternative* would be to have a *large* group, throwing all these people together, at breakfast on Tuesday. A possible list is at Tab B.[4]

Yes

No

Speak to me

After your Congressional consultations, the rest of us will fan out and get to work on the Hill generally.

3. You will want to decide after the Congressional sessions, whether there should be any other White House meetings involving you (with editors, etc.). I will try to get Dillon, McCloy, Andre Mayer, Henry Ford, etc., to make the right sort of speeches in the next several weeks, and, in general, to get the right government people to call the right outsiders in the business community.

4. After the Congressional sessions, we will blanket the town and the newspapers with our story. Over the weekend, we will work out an agreed line for everyone to follow. (I have already told Sandy Trowbridge to keep away from any foolishness about $1 billion. As an economist, I will concede to no one on what these numbers do and do not mean. When the returns are in, we will work hard to put together the right sort of numerical defense in depth. But you should know, in terms of bread-and-butter economics—and quite apart from *international* politics—this bargain really is a good deal for the United States.)

5. I'll ask the Vice President to help Orville organize the campaign with the agricultural community.

6. Throughout, we will have to cope with the fact that we will not fully know the *precise* details until close to the end of June.

7. As soon as I finish this memo, I will do a one-page talking paper for your use (gently and in round-about terms until Monday, and more aggressively thereafter).[5]

---

[3] Not printed. A handwritten note with a bracket around subparagraphs i–iii in the left margin of the text reads: "Alternative I."

[4] Not printed. A handwritten note with a bracket around this paragraph reads: "Alternative II."

[5] Reference is to a memorandum from Bator to the President, May 11, 5:15 p.m. (Johnson Library, Bator Papers, Kennedy Round, May–June 1967, Box 12) On the source text, a handwritten bracketed note in the left margin next to paragraph 7 reads: "In last night's reading."

8. At Tab C is Ed Hamilton's record of the teller vote this morning.[6]

9. *Final Decision.* I will be suspended on the other end of the telephone waiting for your final decision. By Friday night my feet will begin to leave the ground.

Francis

---

[6] Not printed. Reference is to Hamilton's memorandum for the record, May 11, 1:30 p.m. (Johnson Library, National Security File, Subject File, Trade Negotiations, Kennedy Round, "Potatoes" [1 of 2], Box 47)

---

354. Memorandum for the Record[1]

Washington, May 13, 1967.

SUBJECT

Kennedy Round Situation Report, May 13, 1967

I have had an emergency call for help from Bill Roth via the British. Apparently they are stonewalling a number of critical issues. Bill is worried that this might start a general unravelling with the risk that the entire house of cards will crumble.[2]

We have gone to London on every channel and hit them with all we have, short of personal Presidential intervention with Harold Wilson.

Dean Rusk called George Brown[3] on the telephone. They missed each other, but got George's private secretary before leaving for Hot Springs.[4] Later Gene Rostow talked to Brown and explained the problem.[5]

---

[1] Source: Johnson Library, Bator Papers, Kennedy Round, May–June 1967, Box 12. Confidential.

[2] Roth transmitted this pessimistic report in telegram 3652 from Geneva, May 13. (Department of State, Central Files, FT 13–2 US)

[3] British Foreign Secretary.

[4] A memorandum of Secretary Rusk's telephone conversation with Macklehose, Brown's private secretary, May 13, 1:55 p.m., is in the Johnson Library, Bator Papers, Kennedy Round, May–June 1967, Box 12.

[5] Reported in telegram 194050 to London, May 13. (Department of State, Central Files, FT 13–2 US) Brown replied in a message to Secretary Rusk on May 13: "Following your message to me I have been in touch with Powell in Geneva. If I may say so, there has I think been some misunderstanding over our position, and some of the points which are giving you concern do not seem to accord with the facts as reported to us. I can assure you that we are determined to do all in our power to help to bring matters to a conclusion which is fair all round, and we are certainly not going to let things down. Powell is in the closest touch with us, and will remain similarly close touch with Roth, Rey and Wyndham White." (Ibid.)

—David Bruce is going in to see the Prime Minister right now.

—Both Gene and I have talked to Michael Stewart here (Pat Dean is unavailable).

—I called Harold Wilson's private secretary, Michael Palaser on the direct line. Michael is an old friend and I laid it hard on the line that this is political business of the highest sort, and should receive immediate attention from his boss. I said that the President has been personally involved in managing our Kennedy Round over the past few days, and considers the successful outcome of the negotiations a matter of greatest concern.

Francis M. Bator[6]

---

[6] Printed from a copy that bears this typed signature.

---

355. Telegram From the Mission to the European Office of the United Nations to the Department of State[1]

Geneva, May 15, 1967, 0338Z.

3663. For Bator from Roth.

1. This will be a brief report before going to bed.

2. As of 3:30, Japanese bilaterals still going on in Mission and grains discussions endlessly bickering in Bocage over basing points. Everything else on grains except Japanese food aid settled.

3. After impossible bilateral with Rey and Hijzen at 10:00 and subsequent Rey discussion with Wyndham White, it was apparent that no further movement in key chemical section was available. Mike and I had several talks with Wyndham White and persuaded him not to stop the clock as this would merely allow the negotiators to go to bed.

4. Finally, we decided that the only way to break the impasse was to give Wyndham White a compromise decoupage package and then to persuade him to issue it as his own suggestion.

5. We therefore made the following proposal:

For chemical products in BTN Chapters 28–39

---

[1] Source: Department of State, Central Files, FT 13–2 US. Confidential; Flash; Limdis–Potatoes. Received on May 15 at 12:13 a.m. and passed to the White House.

A. Firm KR commitment

1. EEC cuts 20 percent generally. 30 percent on rates 25 percent ave and over. 35 percent on Swiss annex items.
2. UK cuts 20 percent generally. 30 percent on rates 25 percent ave and over.
3. US cuts 50 percent generally. 20 percent on rates 8 percent ave and under.
4. Japan, Switzerland, and all others commit full offer in KR.

B. Conditional package

1. EEC, UK, and Switzerland make additional commitment on NTB or other appropriate concession.
2. US converts ASP and lowers rates where indicated to general level of 20 percent.
3. EEC and UK make remaining cuts to 50 percent overall reductions; UK cuts 33-1/3 percent rates to 12-1/2 percent.

6. The approximate consequence of the above formula is a U.S. overall cut of somewhere between 42 and 43 percent against a combined EEC–Japan–UK cut of somewhere between 25 and 30 percent. Given the confusion of the formula and a certain European logic the figures do not come out too badly. Obviously the Community will in the first instance reject it, but at least we will now have a Secretariat recommendation that is acceptable to us.

7. We now plan to call a meeting of the heads of delegations of the EEC, UK, Japan, and U.S. for 11 o'clock tomorrow. We have a little more time left, but not very much as this situation can begin to unravel very quickly.

8. Don't worry, we will not let this unravelling happen, but we must push as far as possible in an effort to avoid putting the President in a most difficult domestic situation.

9. We are still in deep negotiations with the Japanese and bickering with the British. I am sure our problems with the latter can be solved, and ultimately the Japanese must come along if all other pieces fall together.

Goodnight Potatoes.

Tubby

356. Telegram From the Embassy in Japan to the Department of State[1]

Tokyo, May 15, 1967, 0435Z.

8224. Subject: Kennedy Round. Ref: State 194134.[2]

1. Following telecon with Secretary early this morning and receipt of reftel, I immediately telephoned Foreign Vice Minister Ushiba (who is GOJ expert on these matters) and told him that unless he could assure me that GOJ delegation in Geneva had accepted cereals agreement I desired, under instructions from Washington, immediately to see Prime Minister or Foreign Minister. Ushiba said that he would call Geneva to determine facts of situation and immediately get in touch with me. During several subsequent telephone conversations with him, there appearing to be confusion on what the facts of the situation actually were, I called Ambassador Roth who informed me that GOJ delegation had not accepted the principle of food aid within the KR.

2. Accordingly I saw FonMin Miki at 10 A.M. just prior to our scheduled SCC meeting and gave him an oral statement substantively drawn from text reftel (Ushiba and Tsurumi were also present). I stressed the highest level concern with Japan's role at this crucial point in the KR. I urged a reconsideration of the Japanese position and pointed to the relatively small amount of aid involved. Miki said he appreciated the importance and significance of my representations. The amount of money involved is not the question, he said, but rather the issue for the GOJ is how to implement a food aid arrangement within the cereals agreement. Ushiba said the GOJ accepts the principle of food aid and questioned what was meant by food aid being part of KR. Having accepted this principle the Japanese del is working out with WW the language of a reservation on how to implement. The actual negotiating situation at Geneva is not clear with a different situation minute to minute. Ushiba indicated that the issues could be resolved if Japan could implement the arrangement with provision of, for example, fertilizer. I pointed to the two aspects of the cereals agreement—food aid and trade interest for US; if the GOJ contemplated resolving the matter with a reservation as suggested by Ushiba we would not, I said, find it attractive at all. Tsurumi

[1] Source: Department of State, Central Files, FT 13–2 US. Secret; Immediate; Limdis–Potatoes. Received on May 15 at 1:27 a.m. and repeated Flash to Geneva, and passed to the White House.

[2] Telegram 194134, May 14, asked that telegram 3661 from Geneva be repeated to Tokyo. (Ibid.) Telegram 3661 from Geneva, May 14, recommended that because of the stubbornness of the Japanese negotiator, Kiichi Miyazawa, Director-General, Economic Planning Agency, the President should send a message to Prime Minister Sato urging Japan's contribution to food aid. (Department of State, Eyes Only Reels)

interrupted and argued hotly that when we withdrew our demand for access to obtain our trade interest through food aid Japan was set upon unfairly. Miki concluded the discussion by saying that the FonOff would get in touch with Miyazawa immediately and inform him of our representations (and the Secretary's personal intervention) and ask him how things stand at Geneva. If Miyazawa feels he needs additional instructions and asks for them Miki said he would send them.

3. We urge USDel press Miyazawa to point where he will be obliged to seek further instructions.

Johnson

---

357. Telegram From the Mission to the European Office of the United Nations to the Department of State[1]

Geneva, May 15, 1967, 1559Z.

3668. GATT—For STR and Bator from Roth. This will be the last roundup until later tonight.

1. We have just settled with the UK and we are in final stages with Japanese. I hope to clear the latter up this afternoon.

2. The grains negotiation has been a most trying and difficult one, partly because of the Canadians, but especially because of the Australians who have been quite impossible. Negotiations have been going on intensively and without stopping for several days and nights under the general leadership of Schnittker and Hedges. Hedges is absolutely exhausted but has done a fine job and everything appears to be just about buttoned up except the question of Japanese food aid. I hope to crack this one in the late hours tonight.

3. At a meeting this morning at the Bocage with the four principals, Eric[2] gave out our chemical proposal (reftel Geneva 3663)[3] as his own suggestion as part of overall package. He said he was not recommending package as it entailed hard political decisions for all governments, but that he saw no other way at this point to save KR. Main areas he outlined were chemicals, nongroup agriculture and steel.

---

[1] Source: Department of State, Central Files, FT 13–2 US. Secret; Flash; Limdis–Potatoes. Received on May 15 at 12:39 p.m. and passed to the White House.

[2] Eric Wyndham White.

[3] Document 355.

4. I asked whether his recommendations for nongroup agricultural package between US and EEC was on basis of exact reciprocity and he indicated to us later that US should attempt to come as close as possible to absolute reciprocity.

5. In steel, Powell accepted his suggestion to cut specifics by 20 percent. This in effect allows both the Community and ourselves to maintain our offers, so steel is now solved.

6. Both Rey and I, however, said that we would have to consult our authorities as the proposals went far beyond our mandates (in his case he will talk to the 111 Committee and perhaps some Ministers).

7. I have spoken on this package only to the senior advisers from Washington and have said that I do not want anybody else on the staff, no matter how senior, to know about the proposal. I also said that I had authority from the President to settle on the basis of the proposed package if we could work it out. We are now in the process of putting together an overall EEC package, which would fall within the perimeter of WW's proposal.

8. Our basic strategy here is to try to get approximately $100 million in agricultural offers from the Community and to almost reciprocate in terms of US offers. If pressed on chemicals, I believe that we could make a lesser cut on the lowest 7 percent of our tariff items rather than 8 percent as this would not make a substantial difference in the average cut.

9. This maneuver with WW last night has shifted the burden of accepting the Director General's suggestions from the US to the Community. Undoubtedly, when we meet again at 5:00 P.M. this afternoon, Rey will attempt to chisel, although it would probably be difficult politically to turn the whole package down although this is of course a possibility. I would intend, in our EEC package, to be as forthcoming as possible. It will be in general balanced with the exception of certain disparities which we have said we would allow.

10. I remain very proud of the way the total team is functioning under exhausting and difficult circumstances, and can only hope for the best tonight.

Tubby

358. Telegram From the Department of State to the Mission of the European Office of the United Nations[1]

Washington, May 15, 1967, 7:03 p.m.

194633. Personal from the President for Ambassador Roth. Francis has just reported to me that we have a Kennedy Round bargain. I want you to know what a first-rate job you, Mike and your team have done, and how much I appreciate it. Congratulations. I look forward to your report.

Rusk

---

[1] Source: Department of State, Eyes Only Reels. Secret; Flash; Limdis/Potatoes. Text received from the White House, and approved by Roger Morris (S/S–S).

---

359. Telegram From the Mission in Geneva to the White House[1]

Geneva, May 16, 1967, 1902Z.

3694. GATT for the President from Roth.

1. Mr. President. Mike and I deeply appreciated your cable[2] on the agreement we reached yesterday in the Kennedy Round. This successful outcome was due, in large part, to the fine spirit displayed by our agency representatives in Geneva. Under Secretary Schnittker, Ambassador Trezise, Weaver of Labor, Greenwald of State, McNeill of Commerce, Shooshan of Interior, Ryss of Treasury, among others, took important negotiating assignments in the final difficult weeks. They worked with the Geneva delegation as a single and effective team. Mike as you know is a tremendous negotiator and performed brilliantly. Equally impor-

---

[1] Source: Johnson Library, Bator Papers, Chron, Box 5. Confidential; Exdis. A handwritten note on the source text reads: "This was sent directly to the Pres. when it came off the wire. LSE[agleburger]".

[2] Document 358.

tant, however, was the great backstopping of Francis and his control group in Washington.[3] Again, we are deeply appreciative.

2. Basically, I feel we have achieved a reciprocal bargain that can be fully and honestly defended in the coming months as being in the overall interest of American industry, labor and agriculture. Thank you very much for your confidence and support.

Tubby

---

[3] In telegram 3697 from Geneva, May 16, Roth sent the following message to Bator: "Now that the frenzy is over and only disagreeable details remain to be put together, Mike and I would like to express our deep thanks to you for holding the Washington end together while we were wildly circling in Geneva. I frankly don't know how we could have pulled this off in the last final weeks without the kind of home-front support that you gave us. We are both deeply grateful." (Johnson Library, Bator Papers, Chron, Box 5)

---

360. Memorandum From the President's Deputy Special Assistant for National Security Affairs (Bator) to President Johnson[1]

Washington, May 15, 1967, midnight.

SUBJECT

Talking Points on Kennedy Round for Leadership Breakfast (Tuesday, May 16, 1967)[2]

I want to talk with you briefly this morning about the Kennedy Round. As you know, our negotiators came up with a package late last night—after several days of round-the-clock bargaining.

In 1962, under your leadership, the 87th Congress took the most creative step in the history of international trade. The Trade Expansion Act

---

[1] Source: Johnson Library, Bator Papers, Chron, Box 5. No classification marking. A May 15 note from Bator to the President, 11:45 p.m., attached to the source text, reads: "The attached Talking Points were designed for a larger breakfast involving the full bipartisan Leadership, Cabinet Officers, etc. However, you might wish to glance at it and use some of the Points anyway."

[2] According to the President's Daily Diary, this meeting took place in the second floor dining room of the White House on May 16, from about 8:30 to 10:20 a.m. It was attended by the President, Vice President Humphrey, Senators Mansfield, Byrd, and Long, Speaker McCormack, Congressmen Albert, Boggs, and Mills, Postmaster General O'Brien, Harold Saunders, Mike Manatos, Bator, and Califano. Bator briefed those present on the Kennedy Round beginning at 9:15 a.m. A footnote following Mills' name reads: "Cong. Mills was invited at Francis Bator's suggestion—The President tried to call him and thank him last night re Kennedy Round legislation and could not reach him. Bator says, 'Mills played a key role in the birth of the Trade Expansion Act, and he will be a key figure in the chemicals legislation we will need.'" (Ibid., President's Daily Diary)

authorized the President to lead the Free World into a new era of economic partnership. It authorized him to cut our tariffs in half wherever we could get our partners to give us equal benefits in return. I can assure you that, before Bill Roth initialed this bargain, I went over the package item by item, offer by offer—together with the Vice President and my senior advisers in trade matters. I became convinced—as were all my advisers—that the overall bargain is a good one for the United States and a good one for the world.

In terms of the purposes of the TEA:

—it *will* stimulate economic growth at home;
—it *will* strengthen economic relations with the rest of the world;
—it *will* maintain our economic strength and vitality in the cause of freedom.

I cannot yet go into detail—much work remains to be done—but let me give you a few highlights:

In industry, with a few exceptions, we are talking about an average tariff cut of more than 30%—by far the largest ever negotiated. We will be giving our industrial plant, the largest and most efficient in the world, access to markets several times the size of our own.

In agriculture, the package includes a revolutionary Grains Agreement, and substantial tariff concessions on a wide variety of farm products. The Grains Agreement will guarantee a high international trading price for our wheat exports. And, for the first time, it will require other rich nations to join us in providing food aid to the poor countries. It will also leave room for more U.S. wheat in the commercial markets of the world.

We have had some very hard bargaining. Some will say we should have done better. Others will say that we shouldn't have done this at all.

However, it was my judgment when I agreed to let Bill Roth go ahead yesterday that—in the end—the Kennedy Round will be judged a great achievement:

—We will, in one move, have done more to promote the free and efficient exchange of goods in the Free World than any Administration, or any Congress has ever been able to do.

—Beyond the specific benefits of the tariff cuts, this package will go far to guarantee the kind of economic world most profitable to us. We export nearly $30 billion in goods and services every year—more by several billion than we import. We have an enormous stake in maintaining orderly rules of world trade. Each of the last eight Administrations tried to strengthen and liberalize those rules. We can do more now for this cause than they have done in 35 years of effort.

And we must all keep in mind the alternative. Movement toward liberal trade is a steep climb up a slippery slope. If you don't more forward, you slip back. And if you slip far, you tumble—into an economic cold war where nobody trusts anybody and everybody stagnates. We could have jungle warfare in short order if we can't maintain the momentum we have so painfully built up since 1934.

This is a matter of international politics as well as economics. We all recognize that this is a time of stress and redirection for the Atlantic Community. We can emerge stronger and more mature. Or we could dissolve into rival islands. Many things will go into determining the outcome. But it is clear that this negotiation was an important test. And it is clear that, during the past few weeks, we and our friends have passed it with flying colors.

So, in thinking about the Geneva results, I urge each of you to try to see it from my chair for a moment. Imagine yourself as trustee for 200 million people, and the most effective Alliance constructed. These are the real issues at stake.

I spent many, many days and hours studying the situation, and consulting with my advisers. Although we don't have all the final details yet, I am confident that we have a solution here which:

—makes economic sense;
—moves us a giant step toward the economic world most profitable to us, the economic world which provides the best basis for the political arrangements which have kept the general peace and promoted prosperity for 20 years.

Francis M. Bator[3]

---

[3] Printed from a copy that bears this typed signature.

---

361.   **Memorandum From the Under Secretary of State for Political Affairs' Special Assistant (Enders) to Secretary of State Rusk**[1]

Washington, May 16, 1967.

SUBJECT

Kennedy Round Briefing at the Capitol, Room S–126, 9:30 A.M. and 10:30 A.M.

As you know, Bill Roth has brought off a handsome deal in Geneva. Its basic structure is:

—Concessions on $7-1/2 to $8 billion of US exports and the same volume of US imports.

---

[1] Source: Department of State, Central Files, FT 13–2 US. Confidential. The source text bears Rusk's initials.

—Average cuts of 33–35% in industry.

—Important concessions in agriculture.

—Strict bilateral balance with the EEC; slightly short of balance with the British; a net plus with the Nordics; short with Japan; a very significant—in some ways brilliant—deal with Canada; overall balance with the rich countries even in terms of our most conservative numbers.

—4-1/2 million tons of food aid; a major breakthrough in feeding the hungry. (Japan is still not clearly in—or out, for that matter).

—A good deal on chemicals in the Kennedy Round, unprejudiced by the ASP package to be put to Congress.

One caveat: not only is there a vast amount of mopping up to do in Geneva, but legally we won't have a deal until the President (and other governments) sign off. There is no need to emphasize the distinction, but it has to be kept in mind.

Tab A gives the specifics of the package, as far as we now know them.[2] Tab B is the Vice President's revised talking points.[3] Tab C is a draft Presidential Statement now in the White House mill.[4]

We gave you yesterday some talking points on the political meanings of the negotiation.[5] In the end our bargaining partners—the EEC, Canada, and the Nordics in particular, Britain also—went far to meet our demands. Apparently Jean Rey for the EEC performed exceptionally well, and in the end got strong backing from the member states, France included.

Bill Roth stresses the need to recognize these efforts publicly and build an atmosphere of good feeling around them. You may wish to speak to this point also on the Hill.

TOE

Tab A[6]

Washington, May 16, 1967.

GENERAL RESULTS OF THE KENNEDY ROUND

While a great many details are still to be worked out, the general outline of the Kennedy Round agreement is clear. It consists of the elements discussed below.

---

[2] Freeman and Trowbridge will be speaking from the same piece of paper. [Footnote in the source text.]

[3] Not printed.

[4] Not printed. For the May 16 statement by President Johnson on the general agreement reached in the Kennedy Round negotiations at Geneva, see *Public Papers of the Presidents of the United States: Lyndon B. Johnson, 1967*, Book I, p. 540.

[5] See Document 360.

[6] Confidential.

Overall Balance

In overall trade terms and taking both industry and agriculture, the tariff cuts made by the U.S. are in balance with those of the other industrialized countries. The United States is giving tariff cuts on about $7-1/2–$8 billion of industrial and agricultural imports and is obtaining tariff concessions on about the same amount of U.S. exports.

In industry, the U. S. and the other countries have agreed on cuts averaging between 33–35%. In agriculture, the average cut is less but the United States has obtained important concessions covering a substantial volume of trade.

Country-by-Country Balance

With the EEC, the U.S. is roughly in balance on a trade coverage basis in the industrial sector. In the agricultural sector, the balance is somewhat in our favor, with the EEC giving the U.S. concessions averaging about 15%, with a significant range of products covered.

With the U.K., we are somewhat short of balance overall; with the other EFTA countries the balance is in our favor.

With Japan, the overall results are satisfactory although complete balance on a trade coverage basis is not possible. This is largely due to the fact that 44% of our exports to Japan are already duty-free.

With Canada, we have a significant bargain involving substantial cuts on $1.3–1.4 billion on trade on each side. Almost half of our concessions involve eliminating duties of less than 5%, while most of Canada's reductions are on duties of 25% or more.

With the so-called "borderline countries"—such as Australia, New Zealand, Spain, Portugal, and Israel—negotiations even in broad terms are still continuing. We will probably have some imbalance with these countries, principally because they benefit as secondary suppliers from U.S. tariff reductions granted to the major participants.

Grains Agreement

The Grains Agreement establishes a minimum price for ordinary wheat at $1.73 a bushel (23¢ above the minimum now in the International Wheat Agreement) and a maximum of $2.13—or a range of 40¢. However, the prevailing world price for ordinary wheat is now above $1.73 and is expected to stay above that level for the next three years.

The agreement calls for a food-aid package of 4.5 million tons of grains each year for three years. The U.S. will contribute 42%, the EEC 23%, Canada 9%, and Australia, the U.K. and Japan each 5%. 4.5 million tons is the equivalent of $350 million a year—ten times the value of the annual FAO program. Importing countries will contribute 2 million tons per year ($150 million) which will help make room for U.S. commercial exports.

The grains agreement lasts for three years. It does not affect in any way our rights under the so-called "Standstill Agreement" with the EEC, nor our right to the zero binding given by the U.K.

Non-Grain Agricultural Products

Returns in this sector are quite incomplete.

With the EEC, the balance is slightly in our favor in the non-grains sector. In this sector, we are giving concessions to the EEC on such items as canned hams and Turkish-type tobacco—but not fresh or frozen meats, dairy products, or wines. In return, we are getting concessions on such items as tobacco, canned vegetables, and such meat products as tallow, offals, and canned poultry.

In our non-grain negotiations with countries other than the EEC, we are acquiring valuable concessions, as on fresh fruits and vegetables from Canada, and on fish products from Canada and Japan.

Chemicals

In the first package, which will be part of the overall agreement of tariff concessions, the U.S. will make tariff cuts averaging about 42%. The EEC, U.K., and Japan will make cuts which combined average 25%–30%. On this basis we have a balance in our favor in the chemical sector.

In the second package, the U.S. agrees to seek legislation eliminating ASP and establishing new duties for chemicals at 20%, except for certain drugs at 25% and dyes at 30%. In return, the EEC, U.K., and Japan will make further cuts of 20%–25%. The second package will therefore stand on its own feet.

In addition, conditional upon elimination of ASP, the EEC will modify its discriminatory road taxes and the U.K. will make a 20% reduction in the Commonwealth preference on tobacco.

Rubber Footwear

The U.S. has agreed to eliminate ASP on rubber footwear but to substitute a new compound duty of 20% plus 25¢ per pound, with the proviso that the combined duty shall not be less than 58%.

Textiles

With respect to cotton textiles, the extension of the Long-Term Agreement has been agreed to. Moreover, the U.S. has agreed to cuts of no more than 20%.

Almost all woolen textiles have been excepted from negotiation. However, a part of the wool textile duties depends upon the U.S. duty on raw wool, which has been the subject of negotiations. It now appears unlikely that Australia will grant concessions significant enough to justify our cutting the raw wool duty. Without such a cut, there will be no cut whatever.

With respect to man-made textiles, the average tariff cut by the United States will be 13 per cent, or, if we include the products of the chemical industry, about 20%. A large share of these products were totally excluded from the negotiations.

Steel

The U.S., EEC and U.K. have agreed on a general harmonization of duties with the U.S. making cuts of less than 10% on the average. This will bring our steel duties to about 6%. Japan is making substantially greater cuts.

Aluminum

On unwrought or ingot aluminum, the EEC has agreed to bind a duty of 9% and enlarge a tariff quota with a duty of 5%. Accordingly, the U.S. is making a token cut in its duty on ingot.

On wrought aluminum, negotiations are continuing.

Significant U. S. Exceptions

The U.S. excluded the following from the negotiations:

Most dairy products
Most meats
Most wines
Many fresh fruits and vegetables
Most cigars
Most petroleum products
Most wool and many man-made textiles
Most footwear and gloves
Most glass items
Watch movements
Lead and zinc
Carpets

Anti-Dumping Code

The major negotiating countries, including the U.S., EEC, U.K., Japan, Canada and most EFTA countries, have reached agreement on an anti-dumping code. This code will make the anti-dumping practices of the big trading nations uniform. The code will provide major benefits for U.S. exporters, including provisions for open hearings in foreign countries, and the introduction by Canada of an injury test in dumping cases.

The EEC has been in the process of setting up a general dumping regulation for member countries, and this could have been adverse if not nailed down by the new code. On the downside, anti-dumping procedures will be speeded up once action has been deemed necessary.

The dumping code will not require new legislation, since it is consistent with present U. S. law.

362. Report on the Congressional Briefings[1]

Washington, undated.

CONGRESSIONAL BRIEFINGS ON
KENNEDY ROUND—MAY 16, 1967

On Tuesday morning, May 16, 1967, the Vice President, together with Secretaries Rusk and Freeman, Acting Secretary Trowbridge, Under Secretary Reynolds,[2] and others briefed 23 Senators and Congressmen (see list attached).[3] The briefing was based largely on the paper entitled "General Results of the Kennedy Round" and dated May 16, 1967.[4]

Overall, the 9:30 and 10:30 meeting went well. As is indicated by the summary which follows, some of the members of Congress expressed concern with respect to certain categories of products and certain domestic industries. On the whole, however, no attempt was made to dispute the conclusion of the Vice President that the general agreement reached in Geneva seemed to be a balanced one and in the interest of the United States. At the same time, however, it was clear that many were reserving judgment until they were able to scrutinize the details of the agreement.

There follows a detailed summary of the significant exchanges which took place between members of Congress and representatives of the Executive Branch.

Overall Balance

Apparently for the record, Pastore asked whether we had lost our shirt in our anxiety to bring the Kennedy Round to a successful conclusion. The Vice President replied with an emphatic "No".

Industry and Agriculture

Pastore asked whether we had obtained concessions on our agricultural exports at the expense of granting concessions on industrial imports. Secretary Rusk pointed out that with respect to the EEC, for example, we were in balance in both sectors, thus suggesting that we did not have to buy benefits for agriculture with concessions on industrial products. Mr. Bator added that, in overall terms, each sector was generally in balance.

---

[1] Source: Johnson Library, Bator Papers, Kennedy Round—Congressional Briefings, Box 13. Limited Official Use. The source text bears no drafting information. The briefings were held at the Capitol.

[2] James J. Reynolds, Under Secretary of Labor.

[3] Not printed.

[4] Tab A to Document 361.

Market Disruption

Pastore asked whether any country is qualifying its tariff concessions by a proviso permitting duties to be increased or quotas imposed if imports cause market disruption. The answer was given that the General Agreement on Tariffs and Trade permits a country to take an escape-clause action if imports are causing injury to an industry. Pastore noted that this would require an industry to file a petition with the Tariff Commission and asked whether an economic entity smaller than an industry could petition for relief from imports. This question was left hanging as the discussion returned to other matters.

Justification of Agreement

Ford, as well as others, stressed the need for a full statement of the reasons why the agreement was concluded. In particular, he wanted information telling why he had granted concessions in sectors which seemed to be vulnerable to imports. He thought it was important that we provide our justification as soon as possible. The Vice President and others made the point several times during the meetings that it will take another month or so to work out all the details of the negotiation, but that material would be supplied to interested members of Congress as soon as possible.

American Selling Price

The issue of ASP, as it pertains to both chemicals and rubber-soled footwear, provoked perhaps the most discussion. The Vice President and others stressed that the second package, which would require Congressional action to eliminate ASP, was completely separate from the Kennedy Round agreement and stood on its own two feet. There seemed to be general acceptance of this, with the notable exception of Ribicoff. He noted that the second package includes EEC and U.K. concessions with respect to road taxes and the margin of preference on tobacco, respectively. He argued that this would stimulate industries outside the chemical sector to urge the enactment of the necessary legislation and that this would put a gun to the head of the Congress. In reply, the Vice President and others stressed that the President had insisted upon a separate package, that the Vice President has been emphatic about this during his European trip, and that the Congress was completely free to accept or reject the ASP agreement. It was also pointed out that the Congress had expected that if we took action on one of our non-tariff barriers we would obtain concessions with respect to other countries' non-tariff barriers.

The Vice President stressed that both the first and second packages, viewed separately, were balanced deals and that, taken together, they were very much in the interest of the chemical industry. Williams (Del.) did not disagree but pointed out that the industry might be sufficiently satisfied with the concessions granted by the other countries in the first package that it would not press hard for the second package.

With respect to rubber-soled footwear, Adair asked whether the new compound duty provided the same tariff protection as the present rate of duty based upon ASP. When an affirmative answer was given, Pastore asked why, if that were so, we should bother to eliminate ASP on rubber-soled footwear. At this point, Curtis explained that the ASP system was objected to in large part because it left a foreign exporter uncertain as to what the final value would be on the basis of which he would pay duty.

Textiles

The Vice President reviewed the status of cotton textiles, woolen textiles, and man-made fibers. Pastore asked what the reaction of the textile industry was. Under Secretary Reynolds reported that the industry seemed to feel that their concerns were taken into account and that, while no tariff cuts would have been preferred, overall the final agreement on textiles was acceptable.

Cotton asked whether our granting tariff concessions on textiles in any way prejudices our ability to seek international agreements imposing quotas on textiles. The Vice President replied that nothing in the Kennedy Round agreement would preclude us from trying to negotiate such agreements. Pastore then asked whether the fact that we did not grant any concessions on woolen textiles would prejudice our ability to negotiate an international agreement regulating trade in such textiles. The Vice President answered no, but the impression seemed to be left that in those cases where we were granting concessions—particularly on man-made fibers—we weakened our case for quotas.

Grains

After the Vice President outlined two basic elements of the International Grains Agreement, Carlson said that his present position was one of "reserved acceptance". He pointed out that, with respect to prices, the agreement was nothing more than an extension of the International Wheat Agreement (IWA),[5] but without Russian participation. Moreover, he regarded the food-aid component as only a small step forward. Finally, he noted that the new minimum represents an increase of only 23¢ above the present floor established in the IWA, although he granted that the minimum of $1.73 was a good figure. Carlson stressed that we had a lot of work to do to sell this agreement in Congress.

---

[5] Entered into force on July 16, 1962. (13 UST 1571; 444 UNTS 3)

Shoes

Cotton asked whether the agreement concerning shoes and textiles would return to the Congress—presumably for its approval or its disapproval. When the answer was no, he said that that was what he was afraid of. At a later point, Cotton asked whether the jobs of the workers making shoes in this country had been left secure by the Kennedy Round agreement. The Vice President answered that, as a general matter, shoes had been excluded from the negotiations, but he undertook to provide the details for Cotton.

Dairy Products

Aiken asked whether tariff concessions were granted on dairy products and whether the quotas established under section 22 of the Agricultural Adjustment Act of 1937[6] had been changed. The answer was "No", and during the two meetings the Vice President emphasized that for the most part both meats and dairy products had been excluded from the negotiations, with the major exception of canned hams.

Role of STR

During the discussion of ASP, Ribicoff returned to a favorite theme of his, which is that, contrary to the intent of the Congress, STR has not provided that dominant voice in the Executive Branch on matters of trade policy and tends to be dominated by the Department of State. He gave as examples the U.S.-Canadian auto agreement, which he said was a State Department measure, and the change by the Department of the Treasury in the guidelines concerning the determination of ASP with respect to rubber-soled footwear. Secretary Rusk replied that he had never given Governor Herter or Ambassador Roth an instruction and that the negotiations had been handled by STR, as was envisaged by the Trade Expansion Act. In addition, Mr. Bator emphasized that, especially in the closing days of the negotiations, it was the President who had been responsible for giving directions to Ambassador Roth.

---

[6] P.L. 137, approved June 3, 1937; 50 Stat. 246. Section 22 relating to imports reenacted the same section in the Agricultural Adjustment Act of 1933.

363. Memorandum From Acting Secretary of Commerce Trowbridge to President Johnson[1]

Washington, June 7, 1967.

SUBJECT

U.S. Tariff on Raw Wool

You requested my recommendation on Prime Minister Holt's request to you the we reduce the tariff on raw wool.[2]

I recommend against acceding to Australia's request without the United States receiving something in return from Australia. During the Kennedy Round negotiations we consistently maintained that we would be willing to cut the raw wool duty if Australia would reduce its restrictions on American tobacco and make worthwhile concessions on industrial products. Australia has refused and presumably the Prime Minister is asking us to cut the raw wool duty unilaterally without Australia taking any reciprocal action. This would be inconsistent with the basic concept of the Kennedy Round which all major participants have recognized as an economic exercise aimed at achieving balance in tariff reductions among nations.

There is no doubt that domestic wool growers would be unhappy if the raw wool duties were reduced. If they were reduced, however, without the United States receiving some equivalent commercial gain, I believe that the dissatisfaction could become a substantial problem, particularly when we will be seeking the support of agricultural interests for the new grains agreement.

Whatever tariff cuts are made on raw wool, a commensurate reduction must be made in the specific tariffs on wool textiles and products. Here too, we could justify such reductions to the wool textile industry, but not in the absence of reciprocal action by Australia.

I would urge, therefore, that in reply to the Australian Prime Minister, we indicate our continued willingness to reduce the duty on raw wool providing Australia is willing to grant meaningful reciprocal trade benefits to the United States.[3]

A.S. Trowbridge

---

[1] Source: Johnson Library, National Security File, Subject File, Trade—General, vol. 2, Box 47. No classification marking.

[2] This request has not been found.

[3] No reply has been found.

364.   Airgram From the Mission to the European Office of the United Nations to the Department of State[1]

Tagg A–471

Geneva, June 18, 1967.

SUBJECT

ExOff—Exchange of Letters Concerning Japan's Proposed Measures on Selected QR Items

REF

Gatt A–9, June 8, 1967[2]

For Roth from Lewis. On June 9, Mr. Rehm and Mr. Hirabayashi again met with the Japanese Kennedy Round Delegation (Ohtaka) to exchange views on the most appropriate method of handling in GATT Japan's measures intended to ease present import quota controls on selected commodities. We urged, as had been done during previous meetings, that Japan send a letter to the GATT Secretariat informing it of these measures. If that were done, Japan would have on record a clear indication of its efforts to move in the direction of complete elimination of import quota controls on these items. The United States would receive a copy of that communication. If desired, we could send an appropriate letter to the Japanese Delegation commenting on Japan's commitments with respect thereto.

Mr. Ohtaka reiterated the Japanese Delegation's position that Japan wished to exchange letters bilaterally rather than follow the U.S. Delegation's suggestion. He said the Japanese Delegation had already agreed with our negotiating partners (U.K., Canada, and the EEC) to exchange bilateral letters on the QR items. Presentationally, the Japanese Government would have difficulty explaining to the Diet why letters were exchanged with all countries, except the United States. Moreover, certain quota liberalization measures of interest to the United States would not be of direct interest to other negotiating partners. The Japanese Delegation therefore urged strongly that the U.S. Delegation consider a bilateral exchange on the QR items of interest to the U.S.

We repeated the provisions of the Trade Expansion Act which prevent the United States Government from giving Japan negotiating credit for measures relating to QR items which are contrary to Japan's obligations to GATT. Following a lengthy exchange on this problem, the Japanese expressed full understanding of the U.S. position.

---

[1] Source: Department of State, Central Files, FT 7 GATT. Limited Official Use. Drafted by Martin Y. Hirabayashi (KR) on June 15; cleared by Rehm (KR), Brewster (KR), J. Birkhead (KR); and approved by Lewis (U.S. Mission, Geneva). Repeated to Tokyo.

[2] Gatt A–9 to Geneva, June 9, discussed prospects for the liberalization of quota restrictions on agricultural products as part of the Kennedy Round. (Ibid.)

Attachments 1 and 2 show the verbatim text of the proposed exchange of letters on Japan's measures relating to QR items.[3] The Japanese Delegation has sent a message to Tokyo requesting approval of the proposed language.

The Delegation believes that the language in the proposed U.S. letter fully protects the U.S. position that Japan's QR's are illegal in GATT and that they should be eliminated. We request, therefore, Washington approval of the proposed exchange of letters and the language contained therein.

Tubby

---

[3] Not printed.

---

365. Telegram From the Department of State to the Embassy in Japan[1]

Washington, June 19, 1967, 9:05 p.m.

212730. GATT. Refs: A) Geneva 4261;[2] B) Tokyo 8962;[3] C) Tokyo 8885.[4] Please deliver following letter from President to Prime Minister Sato immediately, with request that Japan lift its reservation on food aid.

"Dear Mr. Prime Minister:

Some months ago your Government and mine joined with other nations to meet the threat of famine in India. Together we were able to avoid disaster. The Government of Japan played a most positive and enlightened role in this historic effort.

---

[1] Source: Johnson Library, Bator Papers, Kennedy Round, May–June 1967, Box 12. Confidential; Immediate. The text of letter, drafted by Hedges, was received from the White House. The telegram was cleared by Hamilton (White House) (in draft), Katz (E/OT), Enders (M), and Sherrod McCall (S/S–S). Repeated to Geneva for the Mission.

[2] Telegram 4261 from Geneva, June 16, provided a summary of a meeting between the heads of cereals delegations and Wyndham White on June 16. (Department of State, Central Files, AGR 15)

[3] Telegram 8962 from Tokyo, June 17, described a meeting between the Embassy's Economics Minister and Tsurumi, Director of Economic Affairs in the Japanese Foreign Office, on the food aid question. (Ibid., FT 13–2 US)

[4] Telegram 8885 from Tokyo, June 13, requested guidance for making the most persuasive case to Miki on food aid. (Ibid., AGR 15)

Now, as you know, our representatives in Geneva are working on a grains agreement that would provide a more dependable mechanism for meeting the urgent food needs of the developing countries while they are taking the steps necessary to increase their own production. Not only would this agreement represent a long step toward the goal of providing reliable and substantial aid to countries in need of food, but it is for the United States an indispensable element in the balance of the entire negotiation.

I understand that Japan alone among the major participants in the negotiations has yet to pledge its quota in grain or cash equivalent. The failure of Japan to contribute to the program could, I fear, cause other countries to reconsider their position, and place the entire agreement in jeopardy. Moreover, it is now clear that none of the major parties accepted or will accept the proposed Japanese reservation.

The time is now very short for the further consideration which it was agreed would be given the question of Japanese participation when the Kennedy Round agreements were concluded in mid-May. I very much hope that your Government will find it possible to reconsider its position as a matter of urgency. I believe that a strong and active Japanese role is essential to a successful Kennedy Round and to an equitable and effective program to meet the urgent needs of the developing nations.

Accept, Mr. Prime Minister, my warmest personal good wishes. Sincerely, Lyndon B. Johnson"

Discussion

At meeting of major participants Geneva June 16 all those present including EEC, UK, Canada, Nordic Countries, Director-General of GATT, as well as US, said the Japanese reservation had not been accepted either tacitly or explicitly. In light of the position other major participants took at this meeting regarding Japanese reservation on food aid, it appears that entire Kennedy Round is jeopardized by Japanese reservation (ref. A). While alternative proposed in State 202165[5] would be acceptable to US we have no assurance it would be acceptable to other participants. Since time is very short and Japanese decision needed if possible for Wyndham White meeting in Geneva Tuesday, suggest you urge Japanese to meet their quota either in grain or cash equivalent ($14

---

[5] Telegram 202165 to Tokyo, May 25, summarized Japan's stated reservation on food aid in the agreement and its rejection of a proposed U.S. amendment in the Geneva talks, and urged Ambassador Johnson to make another personal appeal to Miki to reconsider Japan's position. The first U.S. preference continued to be for Japan to contribute cash or grain in the full amount of its quota, which on the basis of 5 per cent of 4.5 million metric tons would be 225 thousand metric tons or about $14 million. Alternatively, it believed that other countries could be persuaded to accept the Japanese offer with the proposed U.S. amendment. (Ibid., FT 13–2 US)

million). Japanese benefits from overall Kennedy Round fully justify such move.

We could not accept Japanese access offer as substitute for food aid commitment and doubt that other major participants would.

Background info requested ref. C transmitted by separate cable.

Rusk

366. Telegram From the Embassy in Japan to the Department of State[1]

Tokyo, June 20, 1967, 1115Z.

9027. GATT. Refs: A. State 212564;[2] B. State 212730.[3]

1. Immediately upon receipt reftel B, I asked for appointment with Prime Minister who received me at 4:30 this afternoon. Miyazaki of Fon-Off was also present.

2. In presenting President's letter to Prime Minister I tried to emphasize gravity of situation by saying this was the most serious problem that had arisen since I arrived here and fact President has personally written to Prime Minister on subject emphasized gravity with which President viewed question.

3. I also handed Prime Minister talking paper[4] based on material in reftel A.

4. After reading letter, Prime Minister said this was most serious problem that had arisen in relations between two countries since he became Prime Minister; that he and all those concerned in GOJ had honestly thought that principle of Japanese reservation on food aid, which GOJ had made consistently clear throughout Geneva negotiations, had been accepted by all delegations—only possible question being formula-

---

[1] Source: Department of State, Central Files, FT 13–2 US. Confidential; Immediate. Repeated to Geneva for the Mission and passed to the White House and USIA.

[2] Telegram 212564 to Tokyo, June 13, discussed the rationale for inclusion of food aid in a grains arrangement. (Ibid., AGR 15)

[3] Document 365.

[4] Not found.

tion of terms of reservation. (In later conversation with Vice FonMin Ushiba he said that fact that several days after Wyndham White announced agreement on all essential points Blumenthal made approach to Aoki for modification of Japanese statement of intent was further indication to them that USG had accepted principle of Japanese reservation.)

5. Prime Minister said that new instructions had been carried by Tsurumi to Geneva which he hoped would resolve problem. However when I pressed him, he was not willing to say that instructions would fully meet position taken in President's letter. He said, "We have to face the fact that we differ on what has happened and on what should be done." I said I agreed and wanted to emphasize the problem faced by the President, particularly noting statement in President's letter that food aid was "an indispensable element in the balance of the entire negotiation."

6. Prime Minister said that he felt it best for locus of negotiations to continue to be in Geneva; that he would ask Vice FonMin Ushiba to immediately telephone Tsurumi in Geneva to discuss his instructions in light of President's letter and my call on Prime Minister. After about forty minutes of discussion he asked that I immediately go to see Ushiba, which I did.

7. I gave Ushiba copies of President's letter and talking paper, and in long discussion emphasized gravity of situation and points made in President's letter and in talking paper.

8. Ushiba emphasized "consistent position" Japan has taken on food aid throughout the negotiations and the honest understanding of representatives of all GOJ Ministries present at Geneva that principle of Japanese reservation had been accepted, also the problem within the GOJ and the Diet of now reversing position on a matter of such important principle. He said he honestly doubted whether GOJ could obtain approval of Diet for an agreement incorporating our position on food aid, "Thus it is essential that we find a compromise."

9. He indicated that GOJ was willing to: (1) modify the language on the statement of intent as suggested by Blumenthal, overcoming the problem of GOJ "insuring" what recipient countries would do; (2) reiterate Japanese assurance on access; (3) agree to sale of commodities for local currency to be used for grant aid economic development; and (4) provide assurance on "additionality". He also said that some of Japan's commodity assistance could be in the form of food. He went on to say, however, that Japanese Government must reserve on the principle of cash or grain assistance.

10. I said that this clearly did not meet the position taken in President's letter and we were therefore confronted with a most serious situation. However, as we did not seem to be getting anywhere tonight we

agreed that we would each await reports from tonight's meeting in Geneva and be in touch in the morning.

11. During course our discussion on balance of advantages, Ushiba said that at one point in negotiations in Geneva U.S. side offered to improve its industrial concessions to bring Japan into the food-aid program; however, Japan rejected this because GOJ is opposed to principle of having food aid incorporated as part of KR package.

Johnson

---

367. Memorandum From the Special Representative for Trade Negotiations (Roth) to President Johnson[1]

Washington, June 26, 1967, 7:15 p.m.

SUBJECT

Approval of Multilateral Kennedy Round Agreements

This memorandum requests that you authorize signature, on behalf of the United States, of the multilateral trade agreements described herein, which have been negotiated in the Sixth (or Kennedy) Round of Trade Negotiations.

The principal free world trading nations have succeeded in negotiating a balanced and mutually beneficial reduction of trade barriers opening vast new commercial opportunities for all the free world community. Concessions made by the other major participants (the European Economic Community, the United Kingdom and other countries in the European Free Trade Area, Japan, and Canada) compare favorably with those of the United States. In terms of trade coverage, the concessions of all these countries cover $6.5 billion of their dutiable imports of United States products in 1964 and $879 million of their duty-free imports of such products. The concessions being made by the United States cover $6.5 billion of dutiable 1964 imports from the above countries and $223 million of duty-free imports from them.

---

[1] Source: Johnson Library, Bator Papers, Kennedy Round Windup, Box 13. Confidential. Drafted by Brewster (STR), Norwood (STR), and S.G. Kallis (STR), concurred in by Rehm.

Tariff Concessions—General

The tariff concessions agreed upon are substantial, even though short of the initial goal of the United States and some of the other major participants for a "linear", that is, across-the-board, reduction in their duties by 50 percent, with a minimum of exceptions. (Trade data are in Annex A, a list of participants in Annex B, and country summaries in Annex C.)[2]

The agreement we have reached with the other major participants is balanced as between our tariff concessions and theirs. To less-developed countries, on the other hand, we have given more in terms of tariff concessions then we have received from them. This result is consistent with the rules that the United States and other major participants accepted for the negotiations. The lowering of barriers by the United States and other countries to exports of the less-developed countries will increase their foreign exchange earnings, thereby strengthening their economies and providing better markets for exports of the developed countries, including the United States.

Agricultural Concessions

In our negotiations on agriculture, we obtained concessions that are significant in terms of aiding U.S. exports and that compare favorably with the concessions the United States is granting for imports of foreign agricultural products. The results of the negotiations, while smaller for agriculture than originally contemplated, are in the interests of U.S. agriculture as well as the economy as a whole. I believe this conclusion is warranted even though we were not able to get agriculture fully included in the negotiations, as we had hoped at the outset of the negotiations, but found it necessary to settle for a more limited coverage of agricultural concessions, particularly insofar as the EEC was concerned. (See Annex A, part 2, for table summarizing trade coverage of the agricultural concessions exchanged.)

Memorandum of Agreement on Cereals

The essentials of a World Grains Agreement were agreed to during the trade conference and incorporated in a Memorandum of Agreement. A further negotiation will be carried out over the coming weeks to complete the arrangement. The benefits expected from the contemplated grains arrangement are difficult to quantify or to equate with tariff reductions. However, the arrangement should benefit the United States by providing reasonably effective assurance of an increased price range for exports of United States wheat and by securing increased commitments from some foreign countries to a food aid program that will assist

---

[2] None of the annexes is printed.

hungry nations and help to relieve the occasional depressing effects of
surpluses on world grains prices. (Annex C briefly describes the
arrangement.)

Industrial Concessions

Concessions which the United States is making and obtaining in the
industrial sector are in approximate balance. United States exporters of a
wide range of products will benefit from reduced duties in all of our
major markets. Some commodity sectors—chemicals, steel mill products, cotton textiles, aluminum, and paper and pulp—were to a large
extent negotiated multilaterally as self-balancing "packages." This sector approach was utilized because these commodity groups presented
particularly difficult problems for several participants. By using this
negotiating procedure, we were able to obtain better results than would
otherwise have been possible. (Results of the five sector negotiations are
described in Annex E.)

Exceptions from Negotiations

At the outset of the negotiations, the United States excepted from its
offers the products, both industrial and agricultural, which were considered by this Office and the agencies that are responsible for advising it to
be most sensitive economically. As the negotiations progressed, the
United States added some items to its offers and withdrew others. Its
withdrawals were determined both by negotiating considerations and
by the relative economic sensitivity of the products. (A list of selected
products on which the United States is making no concession or is making less than a 50-percent tariff reduction is contained in Annex F.)

Accession

During the course of the negotiations, several countries negotiated
for the purpose of acceding to the General Agreement. Korea and Yugoslavia completed all necessary steps and acceded before the Kennedy
Round was completed. Of the remaining countries, the United States
reached agreement on exchanges of tariff concessions with Argentina,
Iceland and Ireland. In lieu of a schedule of tariff concessions, Poland is
undertaking a commitment to maintain purchases from foreign sources
at not less than stipulated levels.

Non-tariff Barriers

As a result of multilateral negotiations, agreement was reached on
an antidumping code to reinforce the provisions of GATT Article VI with
agreed practices and procedures to be followed by the major trading
countries. American exporters will benefit from this agreement, which
removes uncertainties now hampering our commerce with various
countries.

A multilateral agreement was also negotiated envisaging elimination of the American selling price system of customs valuation. In return for the elimination of this system, which will require Congressional action, other countries have agreed to give us additional tariff concessions, to modify certain automobile road tax systems, and to reduce a British excise preference for Commonwealth tobacco.

A few actions on other non-tariff barriers were agreed in bilateral negotiations. (See Annex G.)

Additional Authority Requested

Because of last minute technical problems or negotiating situations, we found it desirable to make a few minor modifications, subject to your approval, in offers that you had previously authorized. The improved offers for which your approval is now requested are explained in Annex H.

Legal Aspects

The agreements for which your approval is now sought were negotiated within the basic authorization you have already granted to the Special Representative for Trade Negotiations. With regard to the principal agreement relating to tariff concessions, all legal requirements of the Trade Expansion Act pertaining to each of our offers of tariff concessions have been satisfied. Our concessions are set forth in detail in a schedule which is attached.

These requirements included: issuance of public notice of intention to negotiate, the holding of public hearings by the Tariff Commission and the Trade Information Committee, and the consideration of the advice of the Commission and of Executive agencies.

The concessions under the principal agreement are within the authorities of the TEA; notably, section 201 for reductions not exceeding 50 percent of, or binding of, existing rates; section 202 for elimination of duties which are five percent or less; section 213 for elimination of duties on tropical products; and section 254 for rounding of rates. All concessions under TEA authority will be staged over not more than five annual stages in accordance with the requirements of section 253. In accordance with the exception permitted by that section, the elimination of duties on certain tropical products will become effective at one time.

It is intended that the first stage of the United States tariff concessions will come into effect on January 1, 1968 by a proclamation to be submitted at a later date for your signature. The concessions of some other countries are expected to start coming into force on that date or, with some compensatory acceleration, on July 1, 1968.

The agreements on American selling price, on cereals, and on anti-dumping, have been negotiated pursuant to the President's Constitutional authority concerning international agreements. Of these agreements, only one will require Congressional action—legislation to implement the agreement to eliminate ASP.

Request

I request your approval to have the United States, under the authority of the Trade Expansion Act and your Constitutional authority, enter into the multilateral trade agreements negotiated within the framework of the Kennedy Round. If you approve, either Ambassador W. Michael Blumenthal, Ambassador Roger W. Tubby or I will sign the following instruments:[3]

1. Final Act authenticating the results of the 1964–67 GATT Trade Conference,[4]

2. Geneva (1967) Protocol to the GATT (to which will be annexed the schedules of tariff concessions of the participants),[5]

3. American selling price agreement,[6]

4. Memorandum of Agreement on basic elements for the negotiation of a World Grains Arrangement,[7]

5. Antidumping agreement (Agreement on implementation of Article VI of the GATT).[8]

William M. Roth

---

[3] The President approved on June 28; see Document 366.

[4] Text is in *General Agreement on Tariffs and Trade: Basic Instruments and Selected Documents, Fifteenth Supplement* (Geneva, 1968), pp. 4–5.

[5] Ibid., pp. 5–8.

[6] Ibid., pp. 8–18

[7] Ibid., pp. 18–24.

[8] Ibid., pp. 24–35.

368.   Memorandum From the Special Representative for Trade Negotiations (Roth) to President Johnson[1]

Washington, June 28, 1967, 6 p.m.

SUBJECT

Three Bilateral Agreements Concluded in Kennedy Round

This memorandum requests that you authorize signature, on behalf of the United States, of three significant bilateral trade agreements which have been negotiated in the Sixth (or Kennedy) Round of Trade Negotiations.

Bilateral ASP Agreement with Japan

We have negotiated a bilateral agreement with Japan under which the United States undertakes to seek from the Congress the elimination of the American selling price (ASP) system of customs valuation concerning certain canned clams and wool-knit gloves. In return, Japan will give us a tariff concession on abrasive paper.

In particular, if the ASP system is eliminated, the new rates based upon normal methods of valuation would be for canned clams 8.5. cents per net pound if not over 40 cents per pound, and 14 per cent ad valorem if over 40 cents per pound, and for wool-knit gloves 30 cents per pound plus 26 per cent ad valorem.

The text of the proposed agreement is attached at Tab A.[2]

Bilateral Cereals Agreement with United Kingdom

There is presently in force a bilateral agreement between the United States and the United Kingdom concerning U.S. exports of cereals to the United Kingdom. Among other things, this agreement establishes a system of minimum import prices to be applied by the United Kingdom to such exports under certain conditions.

In mid-July, the United States and most of the other parties to the International Wheat Agreement will begin the negotiation of a new World Grains Arrangement, which will deal not only with minimum and maximum world prices for grains but also a food aid program. The proposed agreement would ensure that, in implementing the world grains arrangement, the United Kingdom will abide by its present minimum import price system, which is quite tolerable from our point of view, and not substitute a more protectionist system.

The text of the proposed agreement is attached at Tab B.

---

[1] Source: Johnson Library, Bator Papers, Kennedy Round Windup, Box 13. Confidential.

[2] None of tabs is printed.

Bilateral Agreement with EEC on "Standstill Rights"

At the conclusion of the Dillon Round early in 1962, we concluded two bilateral agreements with the EEC whereby we maintained our rights under the General Agreement on Tariffs and Trade to try to negotiate terms of adequate access to the EEC for quality wheat and other grains and, failing that, to obtain compensatory tariff concessions from the EEC on other products or to make retaliatory withdrawals of concessions granted to the EEC.

The EEC has requested that, during the three-year duration of the new World Grains Arrangement, we agree to refrain from exercising our rights under these agreements. In return, we have asked that the EEC affirm that its system of variable levies for imports of grains continue to be applied on a most-favored-nation basis.

The text of the proposed agreement is attached at Tab C.

Authority for Bilateral Agreements

These three bilateral agreements for which your approval is now sought have been negotiated, and may be concluded, pursuant to the President's Constitutional authority concerning international agreements. Of these agreements only one will require Congressional action—legislation to implement the bilateral agreement to eliminate ASP.

Request

I request your approval to have the United States, under the authority of your Constitutional powers, enter into the three bilateral trade agreements negotiated within the framework of the Kennedy Round. If you approve, either Ambassador W. Michael Blumenthal, Ambassador Roger W. Tubby, or I will sign in Geneva the bilateral ASP Agreement with Japan and the bilateral Agreement on Standstill Rights with the EEC, and Ambassador Bruce or his designee will sign in London the bilateral grains agreement with the United Kingdom.[3]

William M. Roth[4]

---

[3] The President approved on June 28; see Document 369.

[4] Printed from a copy that bears this typed signature.

369. Memorandum From the President's Deputy Special Representative for National Security Affairs (Bator) to President Johnson[1]

Washington, June 28, 1967, 7 p.m.

SUBJECT

Final Authorization to Sign the Kennedy Round Bargain

At Tabs A and B,[2] Bill Roth formally notifies you that—if you approve—the final Kennedy Round will be signed in Geneva (and London) at 5:00 A.M. our time on Friday, June 30. You know the general outlines of the bargain. There has been minor jockeying around the edges in the past two weeks, but the deal remains essentially unchanged. It is balanced over-all and with the EEC, and it contains a healthy agriculture component.

Mike Blumenthal would do the actual signing for us in Geneva, and David Bruce the UK grains bilateral in London. They need no further legal authority, beyond your OK. I recommend you authorize us to tell them to go ahead.

Press Treatment

Roth will be at George Christian's Thursday[3] briefing to describe the Geneva procedure and to answer questions. Over the next few weeks, Roth plans a series of press sessions on specific commodity areas. We will check out that schedule with you next week before going ahead.

In addition, I think it would be useful to have a small ceremony *after the Congressional recess,* at which the President would present copies of the final Kennedy Round report to members of the Congress and public advisory committees established by the TEA.[4] We can try to pretty-up the reports so that they will be reasonably attractive mementos of the most important single tariff negotiation in history.

---

[1] Source: Johnson Library, Bator Papers, Kennedy Round, May–June 1967, Box 12. No classification marking.

[2] Neither tab is printed.

[3] June 29.

[4] See Office of the Special Representative for Trade Negotiations, *General Agreement on Tariffs and Trade Conference, Geneva, Switzerland, Report on United States Negotiations,* 2 vols. (Washington, 1967–1968).

Remaining Odds and Ends

Like all major negotiations, this one will involve some pulling and hauling on minor points up until the last minute. (We will come back to you if any *major* issue should arise. I don't expect any.)

B

O.K. to go ahead[5]

Speak to me

---

[5] This option line is handwritten above the typed line "Approve Roth memos." The option is checked and initialed by the President. Telegram 218689 to Geneva, June 29, informed Blumenthal that the President had authorized signature of seven Kennedy Round instruments: (1) Final Act, (2) Geneva (1967) Protocol, (3) multilateral ASP agreement, (4) Memorandum of Understanding on cereals, (5) Antidumping Code, (6) bilateral ASP agreement with Japan, and (7) bilateral agreement with EEC on standstill rights. (Department of State, Central Files, FT 13–2 US)

---

370 . Telegram From the President's Deputy Special Assistant for National Security Affairs (Bator) to President Johnson, in Texas[1]

Washington, June 30, 1967, 1757Z.

CAP 67614. Subject: Textiles and the Kennedy Round.

You may receive inquiries from the Hill about the final Kennedy Round arrangements on cotton textiles. Some textile interests are worried that we have not protected ourselves. I won't bother you with the technical details, but the gist of the settlement is as follows:

1. The U.S., the European Economic Community and Japan have each attached reservations to the Kennedy Round agreement providing for a "snap-back" of the cuts in cotton textile tariffs if the Long-Term Arrangement (LTA) is not renewed again three years from now. In other words, for each of us the Kennedy Round tariff cuts on cotton textiles are tied to the duration of the Long-Term Arrangement.

---

[1] Source: Johnson Library, Bator Papers, Kennedy Round Windup, Box 13. Confidential. Sent through Walt Rostow. The President was at the LBJ Ranch.

2. Thus, we are fully protected as the other major parties against any failure of LTA negotiations in 1970.

3. The present three-year renewal of the LTA[2] is a direct consequence of the cuts in U.S. cotton textile tariffs negotiated in the Kennedy Round. Without these cuts, there would be no LTA now. This would be the worst of all possible worlds for the industry.

I will be glad to give you more details at any time.

As you know from the ticker, the bargain was signed early this morning our time. We are hard at work on the Hill.

---

[2] Reference is to the Protocol Extending the Arrangement Regarding Trade in Cotton Textiles of 1 October 1962, done at Geneva May 1, 1967, and entered into force October 1, 1967; 18 UST 1337.

---

371.   Memorandum From the Special Representative for Trade Negotiations (Roth) to President Johnson[1]

Washington, October 9, 1967.

SUBJECT

Disposition of Four Remaining Escape-Clause Actions

Recommendation

I recommend that the four remaining escape-clause actions—involving temporary increases in duties for the protection of domestic industries—be handled as follows:

1. By permitting the actions concerning cotton typewriter-ribbon cloth, stainless-steel flatware, and carpets to expire by operation of law at the close of October 11, 1967. This requires no action on your part.

2. By extending the action on sheet glass for a little over two years until January 1, 1970. This will require your signature of the proclamation attached at Tab C–4.[2]

---

[1] Source: Johnson Library, National Security File, Fried Files, Carpets—Escape Clause Action, Box 1. Confidential.

[2] None of the 17 tabs was found with the source text.

My recommendations concerning cotton typewriter-ribbon cloth, stainless-steel flatware, and sheet glass are concurred in by the Departments of Agriculture, Commerce, Defense, Interior, Labor, State, and the Treasury.

My recommendation on carpets is opposed by the Departments of Agriculture, Commerce, Defense, Interior, and Labor and is supported by the Department of State, with the Department of the Treasury abstaining.

This recommendation on carpets has been the most difficult one to make, since it basically involves a political judgment. Over 20 of the legislative or administrative assistants of the 51 Senators who signed a joint letter to you urging an extension of this escape-clause action have been contacted. For the reasons set out in this memorandum, I believe this round-robin letter does not reflect a serious concern on the part of most of the Senators who signed it.

In short, the carpet campaign has been a clever one, but does not seem to have as much power as might appear. My recommendation therefore is based on three factors:

1. Extension of this escape-clause action would not placate the textile interest in the least. In spite of their noisy support, they have a very marginal interest in the Wilton and velvet carpet industry.

2. Indeed, extension might only indicate that the Administration is on the run and thereby offset some of the advantage gained by your action in asking the Tariff Commission to review textile imports. We are beginning to organize a campaign against the growing protectionism on the Hill. There is increasing public awareness of the seriousness of the situation as indicated last week by editorials in the *New York Times*, *The Washington Post*, and the *Wall Street Journal* (Tab E). Extension of a higher duty—unsupported by economic facts—would only be seen as a weakening of the Administration's determination to fight for its historical bipartisan trade policy.

3. Extension of the escape-clause actions on both carpets and sheet glass would have a decidedly negative impact in Europe and would add to the growing protectionism there which especially threatens our agricultural exports. From a domestic, economic point of view, it is of much greater importance to extend the action on sheet glass.

Discussion

The four escape-clause actions have been thoroughly reviewed by the Tariff Commission and by this Office, working with the other agencies concerned. Moreover, they have been discussed at a meeting of the Trade Executive Committee, where the agencies are represented at the Assistant Secretary level.

Cotton Typewriter-Ribbon Cloth

It is quite clear that the expiration of the escape-clause action on cotton typewriter-ribbon cloth will not affect the sole domestic producer. Indeed, expiration of the escape-clause action would have a healthy effect by bringing back some degree of competition.

At the same time, there appears to be little likelihood that the European firms could regain any substantial part of the domestic market, primarily due to the fact that they do not have the capacity and are not as efficient as the U.S. firm. The Japanese producers could be a threat, on the other hand, but imports from that country could be controlled under the Long-Term Cotton Textile Arrangement.

All the agencies support these conclusions, but the Department of Commerce recommends that the U.S. firm be informed that, if imports should increase substantially, steps would be taken to restrict them. Unless you object, the Department of Commerce will proceed to do so if you decide to permit this escape-clause action to expire.

Attached at Tabs A–1 and A–2 are the report of the Tariff Commission on cotton typewriter-ribbon cloth and the letters of advice from the Secretaries of Commerce and Labor. At Tab A–3 is a brief memorandum giving our reasons why a confidential affidavit suggesting considerable export potential on the part of European firms should be disregarded.

To our knowledge, Congressional interest in this escape-clause action is limited to two Congressmen. Dorn (S.C.) has written in support of an extension because the sole U.S. producer is located in his district. Irwin (Conn.), on the other hand, has urged expiration, because he has in his district a firm which has had difficulty obtaining the cloth domestically.

Stainless-Steel Flatware

In January of 1966, you modified the tariff quota on stainless-steel flatware so as to increase the size of the quota and to reduce the rate on over-quota shipments. This was done because a number of firms in this industry had succeeded in improving their competitive position.

It has become even clearer since then that to extend this escape-clause action would provide excessive protection for the major U.S. producers, which account for about two-thirds of domestic production. It is true that there are several small firms, operating with obsolescent plants, which might be seriously injured by the expiration of the escape-clause action. However, the Department of Labor has provided data showing that these few firms are located in areas where the workers could obtain other employment without difficulty.

Attached at Tabs B–1 and B–2 are the report of the Tariff Commission on stainless-steel flatware and the letters of advice from the Secretaries of Commerce and Labor.

We know of only six letters from members of Congress urging an extension of the escape-clause action on stainless-steel flatware. They include Dodd (Conn.) and Brooke (Mass.) and four Congressmen from Connecticut, New York, and New Jersey. In addition, Burke (Mass.), Conable (N.Y.), and Pirnie (N.Y.) have introduced a bill to extend this action. At Tab B–3 is attached a full list of the members of Congress who have written the White House or this Office on this matter.

Sheet Glass

Last January, you terminated the escape-clause duties on the light-weight and heavy-weight kinds of sheet glass and reduced the escape-clause duties on the medium-weight glass. This was done essentially to protect the one small firm in the industry, which otherwise consists of three large and efficient companies. The small firm—Fourco—has two plants in Clarksburg, West Virginia. If imports had forced the firm to cur-tail or cease production, it was clear that about 900 workers in the heart of Appalachia would have had little or no chance of alternative employ-ment.

This situation has not changed, and all the agencies therefore felt that there was no justification for permitting the escape-clause action to expire. Nevertheless, since under the best of circumstances Fourco will probably continue to be a marginal firm, it was concluded that a full four-year extension as permitted by the Trade Expansion Act would not be in order. The extension in the proclamation attached at Tab C–4 therefore continues the escape-clause action until January 1, 1970. Immediately before that time, it should be clearer what the ultimate fate of Fourco will be and what, if anything, should be done to assist it and its employees.

In recommending an extension, we have taken into account the con-siderable interest which Randolph and Byrd of West Virginia and Edmundson of Oklahoma, in particular, have had in this matter.

Attached at Tabs C–1 and C–2 are the report of the Tariff Commis-sion on sheet glass and the letters of advice from the Secretaries of Com-merce and Labor. At Tab C–3 is the letter from the Department of Justice approving the proclamation and Tab C–4 is the proclamation itself for your signature.

Congressional support for an extension of the escape-clause action has apparently been moderate, with letters from Lausche (Ohio), Monro-ney and Harris (Okla.), Scott (Pa.), and Baker (Tenn.), and six Congress-men. At Tab C–5 is a full list of the members of Congress who, to our knowledge, have written the White House or this Office on this matter.

Carpets

In our view, there is no economic justification for extending the escape-clause action on woven Wilton and velvet carpets. Since June of

1962, when it was first imposed, both imports and domestic production have fallen steadily. So-called tufted carpets have taken over more and more of the floor-covering market from the woven carpets. They now account for more than 85% of that market and are expected to increase their share.

Meanwhile, over this five-year period the domestic Wilton and velvet carpet industry has on the whole made significant economic adjustments. Two-thirds of the producers now make tufted as well as woven Wilton and velvet carpets, and one-half produce more tufted than woven.

Imports now occupy no more than 2.5% of the market and there is no indication that the expiration of the escape-clause action would bring about a substantial increase in imports. Import prices have risen sharply while the average unit value of domestic Wilton and velvet carpets has decreased. Moreover, imports appear for the most part to occupy a residual market for higher-priced specialty products.

The other agencies generally admitted that the economic case for extension was not a strong one, although the Departments of Commerce and Labor expressed concern over the workers in a small number of firms which have been doing poorly even during the lifetime of the escape-clause action.

Attached at Tabs D–1 and D–2 are the report of the Tariff Commission on carpets and the letters of advice from the Secretaries of Commerce and Labor recommending an extension.

The major concern which has led most of the other agencies to favor an extension is political. Accordingly, it is important to determine the true strength of Congressional feeling on this matter.

To our knowledge, about 16 Congressmen, from Massachusetts, Connecticut, Indiana, Nebraska, New York, Pennsylvania, New Jersey, North and South Carolina, and Georgia, have written the White House or this Office urging an extension. These include Conte and Philbin (Mass.), Cunningham (Neb.), Stratton (N.Y.), Thompson (N.J.), Green and Schweiker (Pa.), Kornegay (N.C.), Dorn (S.C.), and Landrum (Ga.).

More significantly, 51 Senators have jointly signed a letter to you urging the extension of this escape-clause action. Over the last several days, contacts have been made with the legislative or administrative assistants of almost half of these Senators. In the light of these contacts, it is our impression that most of the Senators signed the letter rather perfunctorily.

Of the 51 Senators, 33 have no Wilton and velvet carpet plants in their States. The offices of over 20 of these Senators were contacted. They all have indicated that, in fact, the Senators have little or no concern about the disposition of this escape-clause action. Some signed because they were told that the issue of increasing textile imports was somehow involved (Carlson (Kansas), McCarthy (Minn.), Harris (Okla.), Baker (Tenn.)). Others signed because of the wool growers in their States, who apparently related the Wilton and velvet carpet case to the well-being of the overall carpet industry (Allott (Colorado), Mundt (S.D.), Bennett (Utah), McGee (Wyo.)). Some signed because others signed (Holland (Fla.), Curtis (Neb.), Pell (R.I.)). Still others had forgotten they had signed (Metcalf (Mont.), Young (Ohio)), or their assistants had no real explanation as to why they had signed (Kuychel (Calf.), Murphy (Calif.), Fong (Hawaii), Miller (Iowa), Bible (Nev.), Montoya (N.M.)).

While we cannot be certain, these reports do suggest that most of the Senators who signed but who do not have plants in their States did so because it was politically convenient.

The 10 Senators who signed and who do have constituents dependent upon the Wilton and velvet carpet industry represent 11 states. Of these, five have prospering and even thriving Wilton and velvet carpet firms—Connecticut (Dodd and Ribicoff), Virginia (Byrd and Spong), North Carolina (Ervin and Jordan), South Carolina (Thurmond and Hollings), and Georgia (Russell and Talmadge). It would appear that most of these signed because of their concern about the overall textile industry. Of the group, only Talmadge wrote a personal letter to you.

This leaves 8 Senators who signed from five states—Maine (Smith and Muskie), New Hampshire (Cotton), Massachusetts (Kennedy and Brooke), New Jersey (Case), and Pennsylvania (Clark and Scott)—where there are small firms who are in a difficult condition, typically with old plants and a small work force. Yet not even one of these Senators has, to our knowledge, done anything more than sign the joint letter in expressing his concern. Indeed, Case's office has indicated that he signed not out of conviction but simply because the textile union in his state had been badgering him.

In short, I believe that the joint letter should be substantially discounted in determining how the escape-clause action on carpets should be handled and that, for the other reasons which I have given, this action should be allowed to expire.

Attached at Tab D–3 is a full list of the members of Congress who, to our knowledge, have written the White House or this Office on this matter.

At Tab D–4 is a letter from the Department of Justice approving the proclamation and at Tab D–5 is the proclamation itself for your signature, should you decide to extend the escape-clause action on carpets. Consistent with the recommendations of the Secretaries of Commerce and Labor, it provides an extension of a little more than two years until January 1, 1970.

In their letters of advice, both the Secretaries of Commerce and Labor recommend, in addition to an extension, the creation of a task force to develop a program which would enable the firms and workers most directly concerned to work out their problems. I fully support this recommendation.

However, I do not agree with the Secretary of Commerce that the task force should consist of representatives of management, labor, and Government. I believe that it should be wholly governmental. Experience has shown, in my judgment, that a task force made up of representatives of the interested agencies would be more flexible and effective in taking into consideration all the interests involved.

William M. Roth[3]

---

[3] Printed from a copy that bears this typed signature.

---

372. Memorandum From Secretary of State Rusk to President Johnson[1]

Washington, October 10, 1967.

SUBJECT

Trade Policy—Protectionist Threats and Countermeasures

Recommendation:

To help bolster the forces attempting to throw the current trade protectionist movement off balance, I recommend you authorize me to join other Cabinet members before the Senate Finance Committee October 18–20.[2] In an interagency meeting on October 2, chaired by Bill Roth, it was recommended that the Secretaries of State, Commerce, Agriculture, Labor and Interior should testify, along with Roth and Gardner Ackley. I propose to speak out very strongly against a retreat to protectionism both on foreign policy and economic grounds.[3]

---

[1] Source: Johnson Library, National Security File, Subject File, Trade—General, vol. I [2 of 2], Box 47. Confidential.

[2] For texts of the statements by Secretaries Rusk, Udall, Freeman, and Trowbridge, and Roth on October 18, and a letter from Secretary Fowler to Senator Russell B. Long, Chairman of the Committee, October 18, see Department of State *Bulletin,* November 13, 1967, pp. 634–652.

[3] There is no indication whether the President approved or disapproved the recommendation.

Discussion:

There are some encouraging recent signs that the protectionist forces in America may have overreached themselves or at least made a tactical error in pressing simultaneously for trade restrictions covering such major and diverse sectors of the economy as textiles, steel, meat, dairy products, petroleum, lead and zinc. Other protectionist ploys such as the Dent "fair labor standards" bill and restrictionist riders to the Defense Appropriations and Foreign Aid bills have also served to draw more public attention than usual to the threat to our traditional trade policy.

Your own action last week in calling for a Tariff Commission investigation of the economic condition of our textiles and apparel industries has already done a great deal to help slow down precipitate Congressional action in this important sector.[4] I trust your attention has already been drawn to the Sunday[5] *New York Times* editorial which begins, "President Johnson once again demonstrated that he does not panic in the face of pressures exerted by an arrogant protectionist lobby."

I strongly feel, however, that your Cabinet officers should not sit back and let you take the heat of the protectionist pressures and see if you can turn the tide by your own actions. There are steps we can take to initiate a major campaign to wake up the sleeping majority of American economic and political interests whose fortunes are in jeopardy if the more highly-organized minority of protectionist forces have the field to themselves.

An excellent opportunity is open to us in the public hearings Senator Long and the Senate Finance Committee will hold on trade policy October 18–20. I propose to join my Cabinet colleagues in appearing at these hearings.

There is also a need for Cabinet-level and other senior officials to speak out over the coming months in support of a liberal trade policy. I did so myself on September 15.[6] Bill Roth made an excellent speech on this in Detroit last week.[7] Nick Katzenbach will address the National Foreign Trade Council later this month.[8] Failure to speak out would be misunderstood throughout the country; it would tend to undermine the Kennedy Round which is one of the major accomplishments of your Administration.

---

[4] For text of the President's October 4 statement, see *Public Papers of the Presidents of the United States: Lyndon B. Johnson, 1967*, Book II, p. 891.

[5] October 8.

[6] Reference may be to the Secretary Rusk's remarks at a press conference on September 15, after taking part in the meetings of the Joint U.S.-Japan Committee on Trade and Economic Affairs; see Department of State *Bulletin*, October 9, 1967, pp. 455–459.

[7] On October 5; for text, see ibid., October 30, 1967, pp. 574–578.

[8] For text of Katzenbach's speech to the National Foreign Trade Council in New York on October 30, see ibid., November 20, 1967, pp. 686–689.

But more than speeches will be needed to throw the present protectionist movement off balance. We will have to urge leading American exporters, importers, financiers and shippers to be more visible and more vocal.

The need for a major campaign of this kind is, I believe, very real. Quantitatively, the combination of current protectionist pressures pose a threat to our trade policy of an entirely different order of magnitude than we have had to face for many years. US import restrictions on steel and all forms of textiles, for example, would affect close to $3 billion, or about 11% of our total imports last year.

If meat, lead and zinc, and a number of other trade interests pressing for protection are added, the figures would, of course, be much higher. By way of comparison, a rough estimate of the trade significance of all US escape clause actions since the end of World War II is less than $1/2 billion.

The combination of textile and steel pressures for trade restrictions, organized labor's disenchantment, and Congressional receptivity to pressure groups in an election-year adds up to an ominous conjuncture. It is made even more dangerous by the following factors:

—the certainty of retaliation by our major trading partners;
—the undermining of the good faith and credit of the U. S. abroad;
—the strengthening of anti-American sentiment in Europe;
—the unsatisfied trade needs of the developing countries would suffer another blow if trade restrictions break out among the industrialized countries; our efforts to develop a constructive approach to generalized trade preferences for developing countries would have to be abandoned for a number of years.

There is, I am convinced, still a reservoir of support in America for the trade policy we have pursued for so many years and with such demonstrably favorable results for our own economy. With your approval, I propose to launch an effort to reach that untapped reservoir. A strong Administration position will, I believe, win support from the majority of the press, business community and virtually all the academic community.

The ultimate objective is to convince the Congress that in voting to reverse our traditional trade policy in order to placate one or more disaffected sectors, they run the political risk of incurring much greater domestic political disapproval from the larger number of American interests whose well-being rests on liberal trade. We also have to remind the Congress of the contribution of liberal trade policies to our own domestic prosperity.

Dean Rusk

373. Editorial Note

The Contracting Parties to the General Agreement on Tariffs and Trade held their 24th session in Geneva, November 9–24, 1967, to review the work of the Kennedy Round and to develop a future program of work. In view of the recent conclusion of the Kennedy Round, they noted that "no new major initiatives for a multilateral and comprehensive move forward" in liberalization of world trade "could reasonably be expected in the near future." They instituted a Committee on Trade in Industrial Products, instructed the Secretariat to analyze the tariff situation after the Kennedy Round concessions went into effect and to draw up an inventory of nontariff barriers to trade, and agreed to establish an agricultural committee to examine problems in that sector. The Contracting Parties also arrived at numerous conclusions supporting an increase in the trade of developing countries. The Report of the U.S. Delegation was submitted to the Secretary of State by Henry Brodie, Chairman; for text, see *American Foreign Policy: Current Documents, 1967*, pages 1130–1133.

In the final communiqué, the Contracting Parties stated that the major problems remaining included barriers to trade in industrial products after implementation of Kennedy Round concessions, problems of trade in agricultural products, and the trading problems of the developing countries. (Typescript of the Report of the U.S. Delegation; Department of State, Central Files, FT 4 GATT)

374. Editorial Note

President Johnson transmitted the multilateral trade agreement concluding the Kennedy Round of trade negotiations with a special message to Congress on November 27, 1967. He stated that the standards governing the U.S. negotiators, namely reciprocity in trade concessions and safeguarding domestic industries vulnerable to trade competition, had been achieved. He outlined the major features of the basic agreement to "illustrate its depth and potential benefits." He referred to the *Report on United States Negotiations*, which each member of Congress had already received, summarizing the concessions granted by other countries and the results of special multilateral negotiations in the Kennedy Round and listing the concessions granted by the United States. He said an additional report would soon be transmitted showing the tariff concessions each of the major Kennedy Round participants granted on the principal commodity groups in the negotiations. He stated that he would shortly issue a proclamation making the U.S. tariff reductions effective beginning January 1, 1968 (see Document 375).

He would seek the advice and consent of the Senate to U.S. participation in the World Grains Arrangement, an international agreement "reached in Rome as a consequence of the understanding on grains negotiated in the Kennedy Round." (The International Grains Arrangement 1967: Wheat Trade Convention and Food Aid Convention was signed by John A. Schnittker on November 8, 1967, and entered into force July 1, 1968; 19 UST 5501) Finally, he stated that he would submit a trade bill to Congress to give effect to the American Selling Price agreement reached in the Kennedy Round, to revise the Adjustment Assistance Program for firms and workers, and to authorize efforts "to make further progress in promoting world trade."

The full text of President Johnson's message is printed in *American Foreign Policy: Current Documents, 1967*, pages 1133–1135. Five volumes entitled *General Agreement on Tariffs and Trade—Legal Instruments Embodying the Results of the 1964–1967 Trade Conference* are printed as House Document 184 (90th Congress, 2d session).

---

375. Editorial Note

On December 16, 1967, President Johnson signed Proclamation No. 3822, entitled "'Proclamation To Carry Out Geneva (1967) Protocol to the General Agreement on Tariffs and Trade and Other Agreements." It reads in part as follows:

"(1) Subject to the applicable provisions of the General Agreement, the Geneva (1967) Protocol, and other agreements supplemental to the General Agreement, the modification or continuance of existing duties or other import restrictions and the continuance of existing duty-free or excise treatment, provided for in Schedule XX (Geneva—1967), shall be effective on and after January 1, 1968, as provided for therein; and

"(2) To this end and to give effect to related parts of other agreements, the Tariff Schedules of the United States are modified, effective on and after January 1, 1968, as provided for in Annexes II and III to this proclamation." (82 Stat. 1455)

Upon signing the proclamation in the Cabinet Room at the White House, President Johnson said, among other things, that U.S. tariffs would drop on January 1 in the first of five annual reductions, lowering prices to consumers and costs to manufacturers. He hoped that equivalent lowering of tariffs by U.S. trading partners would result in greater American export sales. Negotiators at Geneva had driven a "hard bargain," but he believed it was a "fair bargain" from which "all will gain." For full text of his remarks, see *Public Papers of the Presidents of the United States: Lyndon B. Johnson, 1967*, Book II, pages 1148–1150.

On President Johnson's signing the proclamation, the Geneva (1967) Protocol to the GATT entered into force for the United States on January 1, 1968. The text of the Protocol is in *General Agreement on Tariffs and Trade: Basic Instruments and Selected Documents, Fifteenth Supplement* (Geneva, 1968), pages 5–8.

376. **Memorandum From the Assistant Secretary of Commerce for Domestic and International Business (McQuade) to Secretary of Commerce Trowbridge**[1]

Washington, December 27, 1967.

SUBJECT

Japanese Automobile Talks

As reported in the press (see attached article from the *Washington Post* of December 17),[2] the Japanese gave little ground at the first round of U.S.-Japan discussions on more favorable access to the Japanese market for the American automobile industry. However, it is the consensus, of both the American industry and government participants, that the talks served a useful purpose. The Japanese side was left no doubt as to how seriously the United States views the formidable barriers to both sales and the manufacture or assembly of American automobiles in Japan. An immediate favorable response to the U.S. representations was in any case

---

[1] Source: Washington National Records Center, RG 40, Secretary of Commerce Files: FRC 74–30, McQuade, Larry (August–December). Official Use Only. An attached covering note, December 27, indicates that the memorandum was prepared by Eugene J. Kaplan on December 20, and cleared by A. Andrews, Acting Director, Bureau of International Commerce, Mark C. Feer, Deputy Assistant Secretary of Commerce for International Financial Policy, and by McQuade.

[2] Not printed.

out of the question because of the political considerations involved. It is possible, however, that some action, most likely the removal of QR's on engines, chassis, and the other auto parts still under quantitative restrictions, may be taken early next year.

Progress will be slower on the other items in the bill of particulars presented by the American delegation. Unlike the elimination of residual QR's which can be done administratively, reductions in commodity and road taxes require parliamentary action, and the politics of cutting excise taxes in particular, levied as they are on "luxury" items, pose special problems. Nevertheless, this is one area where the support of the Japanese auto industry is likely to be forthcoming, and this may help. Further cuts in the Japanese tariff on automobiles so soon after the Kennedy Round do not appear practical either. The nub of the automobile problem, which is Japan's policy on foreign investment, is not likely to be resolved in the near future for the automobile or any other industry.

Given the prospect of little change in Japanese foreign investment policy, the elimination of residual QR's on auto parts is of some interest to the U.S. industry. Their preference, although not precisely stated, would be to establish wholly-owned manufacturing plants in Japan. The Japanese industry and government are greatly concerned that this will be done by takeovers of existing Japanese firms by each of the American big three manufacturers. The possibility of assembling in Japan automobiles produced by their European satellites through a joint venture, or even a licensing arrangement (as in Korea, for example) therefore has some appeal for the American industry. U.S. producers, nevertheless, can be expected to continue their efforts to attain their ultimate goal of manufacture in Japan through a wholly-owned subsidiary as part of their integrated international operations.

It is important also to note, in this connection, that what has not been reported in the press is in the role played by representatives of the American automobile industry in these proceedings. Their principal spokesman, Mr. Joseph Frank of the Ford Motor Company, eloquently, but in low key, made it known that the American auto industry would continue to support a liberal U.S. trade policy, but this position requires "sophisticated understanding" and the industry finds it increasingly difficult to accept these restrictions in view of the rising and formidable competition of Japanese cars and trucks in all markets, including the United States. The implications of this statement were not lost upon the Japanese Government observers present. The Japanese industry representative, for their part, recognized the dependence of their industry, and of all Japanese industry, on American technology. It is expected that the dialogue between the two industries will continue, and it is hoped that the American industry will make the continued sharing of their technology conditional on further progress on the elimination of barriers to their access to sales and operations in Japan.

It is important that the momentum generated by these talks be maintained, and it is likely that this topic will again be reviewed at the U.S.-Japan Sub-Cabinet level talks which will be held in Honolulu at the end of January.

The industry representatives, Gene Kaplan reports, were pleased that this Department was represented at the automobile talks. The Far Eastern Division will continue, together with the other components of the Department concerned with these matters, to follow up further developments on this problem.

Lawrence C. McQuade

---

377. Editorial Note

On May 28, 1968, President Johnson submitted the Trade Expansion Act of 1968 to Congress with a message explaining the bill's provisions and outlining the administration's foreign trade policy. The bill would:

extend the President's authority to make tariff adjustments through June 30, 1970, authority which had expired June 30, 1967;
eliminate the American Selling Price valuation system to give effect to the supplementary agreement negotiated at Geneva which would lower foreign tariffs on American chemicals and reduce certain nontariff barriers—road taxes and tariff preferences—on American automobiles and tobacco;
authorize appropriations for the American share of expenses of the General Agreement on Tariffs and Trade;
broaden eligibility for assistance to businessmen and workers facing serious problems as a result of increased imports; and,
extend similar provisions for assistance in the Automotive Trade Act of 1965 (P.L. 89–283, approved October 21, 1965; 79 Stat. 1016) for 3 years to June 30, 1971.

President Johnson also cautioned against passage of trade restrictive bills then before Congress covering about $7 billion of American imports. He urged passage of an anti-inflation tax bill he had recommended to prevent price increases which would result in decreased exports and increased imports. He also called for elimination of nontariff barriers, citing the example of the American Selling Price valuation system, and referring to American efforts in the General Agreement on Tariffs and Trade in this regard. In order to develop a long-range policy to guide American trade expansion through the 1970s, he said that he had asked the Special Representative for Trade Negotiations to prepare a study on future requirements. For text of his message, see *Public Papers of the Presidents of the United States: Lyndon B. Johnson, 1968–69,* Book I, pages 648–652.

The House Ways and Means Committee held hearings for 18 days in June and July 1968 on trade policy including the proposed Trade Expansion Act of 1968 (H.R. 17551, 90th Congress), but took no further action on it. (*Foreign Trade and Tariff Proposals: Hearings Before the Committee on Ways and Means, House of Representatives, Ninetieth Congress, Second Session, on Tariff and Trade Proposals,* Parts 1–11 (Washington, 1968–1969) The administration, however, did succeed in beating back the protectionist drive in Congress as protectionist measures either failed of adoption or were contained by compromise. The Revenue and Expenditure Control Act of 1968, referred to as the income tax surcharge, was approved June 28; P.L. 90–364; 82 Stat. 251.

On January 15, 1969, the President announced that William M. Roth, Special Representative for Trade Negotiations, had submitted a report entitled, "Future United States Foreign Trade Policy: Report to the President Submitted by the Special Representative for Trade Negotiations." The report, which was prepared with the collaboration of the Public Advisory Committee on Trade Policy established on August 30, 1968, by Executive Order 11425 (33 *Federal Register* 12363; 3 CFR 133), is summarized in *Weekly Compilation of Presidential Documents,* volume 5, page 92.

Index

Banks—*Continued*
Dollar term loans by foreign branches
of, 261–262
Foreign agency, 155–156
Barnet, Sylvan M., Jr., 372
Barnett, Robert W., 484, 545*n*
Barr, Joseph W., 184*n*, 244, 248, 296, 388,
392, 440–441, 478–479, 521*n*, 576,
580*n*, 779–881
Barre, Raymond, 560, 585, 593
Bartley, Ammon O., 51*n*
Barton Distilling Co., 449
Barzel, Rainer, 140
Base closings, 65
Basle Agreement, 422
Bator, Francis M., 74*n*, 75*n*, 98*n*, 124*n*,
133*n*, 172*n*, 174*n*, 284*n*, 289*n*, 299*n*,
306*n*, 319*n*, 368*n*, 384*n*, 651*n*, 680*n*,
701*n*, 809*n*, 819*n*, 824*n*, 839*n*, 892*n*
Agency for International
Development, 295
Agricultural exports, 207
American selling price (ASP) system,
777–779
Balance-of-payments programs,
102–104, 199–201, 271, 278,
282–283, 291–292, 318, 330–333,
499
Cabinet Committee on the Balance of
Payments, 184, 196, 198, 209, 226,
245, 255
Direct U.S. investment abroad, 222,
309, 334, 406–408
Gold cover requirement, elimination
of, 534
International liquidity, 170–171, 377,
380–383
Kennedy Round, 897–898, 903,
959–960
Agriculture, 642–643, 668, 670–671,
690–692, 914
Bilateral talks, 915, 916*n*
Concluding phase of, 919–928, 931,
934–936, 941, 958–959
Positive lists, 899, 901–902
Submission of offers in, 743–744,
843–845, 886
U.S. strategies for, 888–890,
904–905, 908–910
Military expenditures, 185, 205, 408
Monetary conference, Chequers,
January *1967*, 334
Reserve assets,-international, 348–350,
374–375, 392, 412

Bator, Francis M.—*Continued*
Special Trade Representative,
appointment of, 872–873
Sterling crisis, 178–179
Trade policies of the U.S., 884–885
Travel abroad by U.S. citizens, 221,
264, 266–267, 311, 325, 332
Voluntary Cooperation Program,
192–193, 218, 225–226, 230,
235–238, 250
Bauxite, 254, 281
Behrman, Jack N., 627–628, 643*n*, 644*n*
Belgium (*see also Belgian and Belgium
subheadings under other subjects*), 43,
45*n*, 71, 114, 252, 288, 450, 491, 498,
502, , 506 561, 570, 576, 813
Bell, David E., 237*n*, 279*n*
Agency for International
Development:
Aid tying in, 254
Delaying of aid until *1966*, 212
Program for *1966*, 228, 230, 236
Spending targets, 216–217, 251, 271,
295
Balance-of-payments programs, 3, 77,
104, 216–217
Cabinet Committee on the Balance of
Payments, 6, 56*n*, 184–186, 226,
255
Cabinet Committee on Export
Expansion, 9*n*
Military exports, 630
P.L. *480* agreements, 186
Task Force on Foreign Economic
Policy report, 63
Taxation on travel abroad by U.S.
citizens, 264–267
U.S. exports to Latin America, 183
Benelux, 676*n*
Bennett, Wallace F., 965
Benson, Edgar J., 584, 599, 604, 611
Bent, Donn H., 712*n*, 753*n*
Benzenoid chemicals. *See under*
Industrial products *under* Kennedy
Round.
Berger, Samuel D., 847*n*
Bergsten, C. Fred, 120*n*
Berlin, 35, 37, 491
Bernstein, Edward M., 174*n*, 182*n*, 534
Bethlehem Steel, 750
Bible, Alan, 965
Biller, Joel W., 653*n*
Biltchik, David E., 801*n*
Bingham, Jack, 752